Lecture Notes in Computer Science 10701

Commenced Publication in 1973
Founding and Former Series Editors:
Gerhard Goos, Juris Hartmanis, and Jan van Leeuwen

More information about this series at http://www.springer.com/series/7410

Joseph K. Liu · Pierangela Samarati (Eds.)

Information Security Practice and Experience

13th International Conference, ISPEC 2017
Melbourne, VIC, Australia, December 13–15, 2017
Proceedings

 Springer

Editors
Joseph K. Liu
Monash University
Clayton, VIC
Australia

Pierangela Samarati
University of Milan
Milan
Italy

ISSN 0302-9743   ISSN 1611-3349 (electronic)
Lecture Notes in Computer Science
ISBN 978-3-319-72358-7   ISBN 978-3-319-72359-4 (eBook)
https://doi.org/10.1007/978-3-319-72359-4

Library of Congress Control Number: 2017960876

LNCS Sublibrary: SL4 – Security and Cryptology

Printed on acid-free paper

This Springer imprint is published by Springer Nature
The registered company is Springer International Publishing AG
The registered company address is: Gewerbestrasse 11, 6330 Cham, Switzerland

Preface

This volume contains the papers presented at ISPEC 2017: the 13th International Conference on Information Security Practice and Experience held during December 13–15, 2017 in Melbourne, Australia.

In response to the call for papers, 105 submissions were received. Submissions were evaluated on the basis of their significance, novelty, and technical quality, with an average of three reviews per paper. Based on the review and the Program Committee discussions, 34 full and 14 short papers were accepted. The program also includes nine papers from the SocialSec (3rd International Symposium on Security and Privacy in Social Networks and Big Data) Track.

We would like to express our thanks to all Program Committee members. Without their hard effort in reviewing papers in such a short time, the conference would not have been successful. We would also like to thank our general co-chairs, Prof. Robert Deng, Prof. Yang Xiang, and Prof. Wanlei Zhou, and our publicity chair, Dr. Yu Wang. They all devoted a large amount of time for the preparation of this conference.

Finally we would like to thank our sponsor, Huawei, for their continuing support of this conference!

December 2017

Joseph K. Liu
Pierangela Samarati

Organization

Program Committee

Man Ho Au	Hong Kong Polytechnic University, Hong Kong, SAR China
Joonsang Baek	University of Wollongong, Australia
Zubair Baig	Edith Cowan University, Australia
Carlo Blundo	Università degli Studi di Salerno, Italy
Colin Boyd	Norwegian University of Science and Technology, Norway
Alvaro Cardenas	University of Texas at Dallas, USA
Aniello Castiglione	University of Salerno, Italy
Jinjun Chen	University of Technology Sydney, Australia
Liqun Chen	University of Surrey, UK
Xiaofeng Chen	Xidian University, China
Raymond Choo	University of Texas at San Antonio, USA
Sabrina De Capitani di Vimercati	Università degli Studi di Milano, Italy
Sara Foresti	Università degli Studi di Milano, Italy
Angelo Genovese	Università degli Studi di Milano, Italy
Dieter Gollmann	Hamburg University of Technology, Germany
Stefanos Gritzalis	University of the Aegean, Greece
Andreas Holzer	University of Toronto, Canada
Xinyi Huang	Fujian Normal University, China
Mitsugu Iwamoto	University of Electro-Communications, Japan
Julian Jang-Jaccard	Massey University, New Zealand
Sokratis Katsikas	Norwegian University of Science and Technology, Norway
Ryan Ko	University of Waikato, New Zealand
Noboru Kunihiro	The University of Tokyo, Japan
Miroslaw Kutylowski	Wroclaw University of Technology, Poland
Junzuo Lai	Jinan University, China
Costas Lambrinoudakis	University of Piraeus, Greece
Albert Levi	Sabanci University, Turkey
Li Li	University of Luxembourg, Luxembourg
Ming Li	University of Arizona, USA
Kaitai Liang	Manchester Metropolitan University, UK
Joseph Liu	Monash University, Australia
Shengli Liu	Shanghai Jiao Tong University, China
Zhe Liu	University of Luxembourg, Luxembourg
Giovanni Livraga	Università degli Studi di Milano, Italy

Takashima, Katsuyuki
Takayasu, Atsushi
Tian, Haibo
Tsiatsikas, Zisis
Tzouramanis, Theodoros
Wang, Qin
Wang, Yujue
Wang, Yunling
Wang, Zheng
Watanabe, Yohei
Yang, Xu

Yu, Zuoxia
Yuan, Xingliang
Zhang, Lei
Zhang, Ning
Zhang, Wentao
Zhang, Xiao
Zhang, Xiaoyu
Zheng, Haibin
Zhu, Fei
Zhu, Youwen
Zuo, Cong

Contents

Signature

Authentication

Cloud Security

Network Security

Cyber-Physical Security

Blockchain

An Adaptive Gas Cost Mechanism for Ethereum to Defend Against Under-Priced DoS Attacks

Ting Chen[1,2], Xiaoqi Li[2], Ying Wang[1], Jiachi Chen[2], Zihao Li[1],
Xiapu Luo[2(✉)], Man Ho Au[2], and Xiaosong Zhang[1]

[1] Cyber Security Research Center,
University of Electronic Science and Technology of China,
Chengdu 611731, China
{brokendragon,johnsonzxs}@uestc.edu.cn, 769836805@qq.com,
gforiq@qq.com
[2] Department of Computing, Hong Kong Polytechnic University,
Kowloon, Hong Kong
lee1843@gmail.com, chenjiachi317@gmail.com,
{csxluo,csallen}@comp.polyu.edu.hk

Abstract. The gas mechanism in Ethereum charges the execution of every operation to ensure that smart contracts running in EVM (Ethereum Virtual Machine) will be eventually terminated. Failing to properly set the gas costs of EVM operations allows attackers to launch DoS attacks on Ethereum. Although Ethereum recently adjusted the gas costs of EVM operations to defend against known DoS attacks, it remains unknown whether the new setting is proper and how to configure it to defend against unknown DoS attacks. In this paper, we make the *first* step to address this challenging issue by first proposing an emulation-based framework to automatically measure the resource consumptions of EVM operations. The results reveal that Ethereum's new setting is still not proper. Moreover, we obtain an insight that there may always exist exploitable under-priced operations if the cost is fixed. Hence, we propose a novel gas cost mechanism, which dynamically adjusts the costs of EVM operations according to the number of executions, to thwart DoS attacks. This method punishes the operations that are executed much more frequently than before and lead to high gas costs. To make our solution flexible and secure and avoid frequent update of Ethereum client, we design a special smart contract that collaborates with the updated EVM for dynamic parameter adjustment. Experimental results demonstrate that our method can effectively thwart both known and unknown DoS attacks with flexible parameter settings. Moreover, our method only introduces negligible additional gas consumption for benign users.

1 Introduction

Being the second largest blockchain [8], Ethereum distinguishes itself by its Turing-complete execution environment (i.e., EVM) [19] that can run various applications through smart contracts. Besides transferring money, transactions

© Springer International Publishing AG 2017
J. K. Liu and P. Samarati (Eds.): ISPEC 2017, LNCS 10701, pp. 3–24, 2017.
https://doi.org/10.1007/978-3-319-72359-4_1

in Ethereum are also involved in deploying and invoking smart contracts. To ensure that the execution of smart contracts will be terminated eventually, Ethereum charges *gas* (i.e., execution fee) from transaction senders, and lets it be part of the rewards to miners for executing smart contracts. In particular, gas serves as a protection mechanism against resources abusing in case executing certain smart contracts consumes lots of computing resources. The money paid for executing an EVM operation (e.g., addition, multiplication, reading the balance of an account) is the multiplication of the *gas price* with the *gas cost* of that operation, where the gas price indicates the value of one unit of gas and the gas cost of an EVM operation stands for the units of gas required to execute the operation. The gas cost is determined by the EVM in Ethereum client, and the gas price can be set by transaction senders. Every transaction has a *gas limit*, dubbed TGL (Transaction Gas Limit), so that the execution of a smart contract will trigger an *out-of-gas* exception if the execution requires more gas than the TGL. Ethereum attempts to associate EVM operations' gas costs proportionally to the computing resources needed to execute them [19], because a proper setting of gas costs can give miners proper awards and thwart DoS attackers who aim at wasting a large amount of resources.

However, it is non-trivial to properly set the gas cost of each operation because it requires a deep understanding of EVM internals, an accurate measurement of resource consumptions by EVM operations, and the awareness of the market price for different types of computing resources (e.g., CPU, memory, etc.). Failing to select suitable gas costs for EVM operations gives attackers opportunities to launch DoS attacks on Ethereum at low cost by exploiting under-priced operations. An operation is regarded as under-priced if its gas cost is lower than what it should be. Actually, two DoS attacks exploiting such operations were discovered in 2016, which repeatedly execute two under-priced operations, namely EXTCODESIZE [7] and SUICIDE [6], thus resulting in slow transaction processing, wasted hard drive space, and long synchronization time. More seriously, the confidence of users in Ethereum will be shaken, and consequently the market price of Ethereum will be impacted [21]. Since each Ethereum node should maintain the complete copy of blockchain and replay all transactions in history for synchronization, such DoS attacks happened in history will also impact the newly enrolled nodes. Although Ethereum adjusted the gas costs of operations to defend against such known attacks [6,7], it remains unknown whether or not the new setting is resistant to unknown attacks and how to properly configure the gas costs of operations to mitigate DoS attacks.

In this paper, we make the *first* step to address this challenging issue by first proposing an emulation-based framework (in Sect. 4) to automatically measure the consumptions of computing resources of EVM operations. The framework consists of the interpretation handler for each EVM operation, the related data structures and diverse simulated environments in an attempt to explore all program paths of those handlers. The experimental result reveals that the latest setting in Ethereum is still not proper although it can mitigate the known DoS attacks. From this investigation, we obtain the insight that there may always exist exploitable under-priced operations if the operation costs are fixed, because the factors influencing the costs of EVM operations keep changing.

Therefore, we propose a novel adaptive gas cost mechanism (in Sect. 5), which will dynamically adjust the costs of EVM operations according to the number of executions, to defend against known and unknown DoS attacks. This mechanism punishes the operations leading to abnormal high gas costs if they are executed much more frequently than before. Consequently, the exponentially increased gas costs will impede the attackers without unlimited money from conducting effective DoS attacks. Our experiments in a private blockchain show that the new mechanism can effectively thwart both known and unknown DoS attacks and introduce negligible additional gas consumption to benign users.

Moreover, by exploiting Ethereum's unique feature, we realize our mechanism through a novel approach in order to make it secure and flexible in terms of parameter adjustment. More precisely, we develop a specific smart contract and provide a patch to EVM. After patching the EVM, the developers of Ethereum can adjust the parameters by sending transactions to that smart contract, and then the updated EVM can fetch the parameters periodically by reading the storage of that smart contract. Our new approach leverages the underlying blockchain technique to make the parameters auditable and untamperable. Moreover, our approach has good deployability because it only needs updating the EVM once.

In summary, we make the following major contributions:

(1) We propose the first emulation-based measurement framework, which can automatically estimate the resource consumptions of EVM operations, to assess whether or not the gas costs in Ethereum are properly configured (Sect. 4).
(2) We propose a novel adaptive gas cost mechanism, which dynamically adjusts operation costs according to their execution times, to defend against known and unknown DoS attacks with negligible impacts on benign users.
(3) We design a new approach to realize our gas cost mechanism by exploiting Ethereum's smart contract and its underlying bloackchain technique. This approach makes our mechanism secure, flexible, easy to be deployed.
(4) We conduct experiments in a private blockchain to evaluate our mechanism. The results show that it can effectively thwart both known and unknown DoS attacks and introduce negligible additional gas consumption to benign users. Moreover, the parameters can be dynamically adjusted by authorized users.

The remainder of this paper is organized as follows. Section 2 introduces background knowledge. Section 3 presents our analysis of two real DoS attacks on Ethereum. Section 4 details the measurement framework. We describe the adaptive gas cost mechanism and its implementation in Sect. 5 and Sect. 6, respectively. The experiment results are introduced in Sect. 7. After summarizing related studies in Sect. 8, we conclude the paper in Sect. 9.

2   Background

This section introduces some background knowledge of Ethereum. Besides providing a cryptocurrency (i.e., Ether), Ethereum supports deploying and running smart contracts. There are two types of accounts in Ethereum, including external owned accounts (EOA) and smart contracts. The major difference between them is that only smart contracts contain executable bytecode [1]. Ethereum uses the underlying P2P overlay to deliver transactions among Ethereum nodes. A *transaction* refers to the signed data package that stores a message to be sent from an EOA to another account on the blockchain [1]. A block is a data structure to store zero or more transactions. Each node runs an Ethereum client that obeys Ethereum protocol [24]. The consensus in Ethereum is achieved by using a modified version of GHOST protocol [19], and as the result of the consensus, every node maintains the same copy of the blockchain. In particular, a newly joined node should download all blocks (i.e., synchronization) and then run all historical transactions to reach the same state as the other nodes.

Ethereum can be considered as a state machine where a state is a snapshot of the blockchain (e.g., the balances of all accounts, the value of a variable in a smart contract) and a transaction results in a state transfer. If the target of a transaction is a smart contract, the smart contract will be executed in EVM. Since EVM is usually embedded in the Ethereum client, the execution of smart contracts consumes the computing resources (e.g., CPU, disk, network) of each node. Consequently, a DoS attack will impact all nodes because each of them should execute all historical transactions. To prevent abusing computing resources, Ethereum leverages gas to charge execution fee from transaction senders. The amount of gas consumption is determined by the executed EVM operations, and different operations may have different gas costs [24]. In Sect. 3, we use real attacks to explain how attackers exploit the improper setting of gas cost to launch DoS attacks at low expense.

3   Analyzing Real DoS Attacks on Ethereum

This section dissects two real DoS attacks exploiting under-priced operations.

3.1   EXTCODESIZE Attack

Approach: The attacker sends lots of transactions to invoke a deployed smart contract involving many EXTCODESIZE operations, which gets the size of an account's code [24]. Such attack forces EXTCODESIZE to be executed roughly 50,000 times per block [7].

Symptom: Clients spend a very long time to process those blocks that contain the transactions sent from the attacker, and hence the throughput of Ethereum for processing transactions is decreased.

Cause: EXTCODESIZE has a very low gas cost (i.e., 20 in go-ethereum V 1.3.5), but it involves expensive operation (i.e., reading information from the disk). Hence, the execution of a great number of EXTCODESIZE results in busy I/O and slow transaction processing speed.

Countermeasure: New Ethereum (e.g., go-ethereum V 1.6) increases the gas cost of EXTCODESIZE to 700 [5] (in the source file gas_table.go). Consequently, the transaction senders have to pay 35 (= 700/20) times more money when using go-ethereum V 1.6. 700 gas is equal to about 0.000014 Ether (many senders set the gas price to 0.00000002 Ether at August, 2017), whose value is about 0.0042 USD (1 Ether can be exchanged into about 300 USD at August 13th, 2017 [11]). Although a single operation does not cost much, the accumulative gas consumption is considerable, because each transaction incurs the execution of many operations and there are more than 45 million transactions from the launch of Ethereum to August 13th, 2017 [2].

3.2 SUICIDE Attack

Approach: The attacker creates lots of smart contracts with a loop in their constructors. In the loop, the SUICIDE operation is executed. According to Ethereum's protocol, SUICIDE is used to remove the executed smart contract from the blockchain and send the remaining Ether to the designated account [24]. For each generated smart contract, the transaction for creating it triggers its constructor, and hence lots of SUICIDE whose target accounts do not exist, will be executed. Note that a nonexistent account does not need to be stored in the Ethereum state tree [6], which represents the state of the blockchain.

Symptom: About 19 million accounts were created by the attack, which consume considerable disk space, and thus the synchronization and transaction processing are slowed down.

Cause: If the target account does not exist, a SUICIDE operation will turn it into existent, which will be stored in the Ethereum state tree [6]. However, the gas cost of SUICIDE is zero. Therefore, an attacker creates a huge number of accounts by executing SUICIDE repeatedly at very low cost.

Countermeasure: New Ethereum increases the gas cost of SUICIDE to 5,000 and additional 25,000 if it creates a new account [5] (in the source file gas_table.go). Moreover, new clients can delete the zombie accounts created by the attack.

3.3 Remarks

From the above analysis, we learn that to exploit the under-priced operations for launching DoS attacks, the attacker has to first find or prepare a smart contract containing the under-priced operations, and then cause such operations to be executed lots of times by sending transactions to the smart contract. Moreover, since the gas cost for sending a transaction is high (e.g., at least 21,000 in go-ethereum V 1.6), the attacker usually lets each transaction trigger multiple executions of the under-priced operations. To defend against such DoS attacks, we should either properly set the costs of EVM operations (i.e., remove under-priced operations) or force the attacker to pay a lot of money for executing the under-priced operations many times.

In Sect. 4, we propose a novel emulation-based measurement framework to assess whether or not the latest gas cost setting is proper. Unfortunately, we find that the latest setting still has exploitable under-priced operations, and it is difficult, if not impossible, to eliminate all under-priced operations if the operation costs are fixed, because the factors influencing the cost of each EVM operation keep changing. Therefore, we explore an alternative approach by proposing a novel adaptive gas cost mechanism in Sect. 5.

4   Emulation-Based Measurement Framework

Although Ethereum has changed the gas costs of some under-priced operations to defend against the known DoS attacks [6,7], little is known whether or not the latest gas cost setting is immune to DoS attacks exploiting under-priced operations. To address this issue, the resource consumption of each EVM operation should be measured. However, it is non-trivial to measure the computing resources consumed by a single EVM operation because the execution of a smart contract involves not only many EVM operations but also various utility functions for supporting the execution.

To tackle this problem, we propose a novel emulation-based measurement framework. More precisely, by exploiting EVM's architecture, we extract the interpretation handler for each operation (e.g., the *opAdd()* function is responsible for executing the addition operation), the related data structures (e.g., stack, memory, storage) from the EVM implementation, and prepare an emulated environment, which consists of the *Go* compiler, runtime libraries (e.g., the *bigInt* library to handle large integers) and the state of the blockchain (e.g., the balance of an account), for executing the operation. Then, we run the interpretation handler in the emulated environment millions of times, because a single run is too short to conduct the measurement, and record the execution time. Note that the current implementation of our framework can automatically measure the CPU consumption in terms of the execution time, and we will support the measurement of other resources in future work.

There is a challenge in preparing the emulated environment. In particular, since a handler may have various execution paths with different resource consumption, we need to explore all execution paths for measuring the handler's resource consumption. The example in Fig. 1 shows that the handler for executing SUICIDE consists of an expensive path (Line 15, *CreateStateObject()* allocates disk space to store accounts) if the target account is nonexistent since it will become existent after executing SUICIDE and a cheap path (Line 16)

```
1   func opSuicide(contract *Contract, stack *stack, ...){
2       balance := env.Db().GetBalance(contract)
3       env.Db().AddBalance(stack.pop(), balance)
4       env.Db().Delete(contract)
5   }
6   func (self *StateDB) AddBalance(addr common.Address, amount *big.Int) {
7       stateObject := self.GetOrNewStateObject(addr)
8       if stateObject != nil {
9           stateObject.AddBalance(amount)
10      }
11  }
12  func (self *StateDB) GetOrNewStateObject(addr common.Address) *StateObject {
13      stateObject := self.GetStateObject(addr)
14      if stateObject == nil || stateObject.deleted {
15          stateObject = self.CreateStateObject(addr) //a heavy path
16      }//else..., a cheap path
17      return stateObject
18  }
```

Fig. 1. An expensive path and a cheap path of *opSuicide*

if the target is existent. To address this challenge, we run the handler millions of times, providing with different inputs and proper runtime environment. If the operation manipulates the stack/memory/storage, we synthesize the stack/memory/storage with random length and generates random numbers as their items. If the operation needs the information from EVM (e.g., block number, gas price, gas limit) or the smart contract (e.g., code length, input to the contract, the address of the contract), we prepare an EVM/smart contract object with randomly generated fields. If the operation needs to interact with another account, we take into account the following three situations. First, if the target account is nonexistent, no special preparation is needed. Second, if the target account is an EOA, we generate one using the command provided by Etheruem's client. Third, if the target account is a smart contract, we develop and deploy one in the private chain, whose code is a RETURN since we measure the resources consumed by the invocation, rather than the execution of the invoked smart contract.

We classify all EVM operations into five categories in terms of the data structures on which they operate. The operations in the first category do not manipulate any data structures (e.g., JUMPDEST). The operations in the second category handle the stack (e.g., ADD). The operations in the third category get access to the specific fields related to blockchain (e.g., ORIGIN). The fourth category of operations manipulates the memory (e.g., MSTORE). The operations in the fifth category manipulate the storage (e.g., SLOAD). Note that in Ethereum *memory* is an infinitely expandable byte-array that resets after computation ends, while *storage* is a long-term key/value store that persists for the long term [19].

Figure 2 (the y-axis is on a log scale) presents the CPU consumptions of some EVM operations running 50 million times from all the five categories. Experiments are conducted on a desktop equipped with an Intel i3-4160 CPU and 8 GB memory. The number on top of each box is the operation's gas cost according to Ethereum's yellow paper [24]. All measurements repeat 100 times. JUMPDEST is the destination of a jump (e.g., JUMP, JUMPI) operation, which belongs to the first category. ADD, SUB, MUL, DIV, SDIV, MOD, SMOD, ADDMOD, MULMOD are arithmetic operations. NOT and XOR are bitwise operations. ISZERO and LT are comparison operations. These operations belong the second category. ORIGIN is the representative of the third category which reads a field of the block's head. MSTORE and SHA3 belong to the fourth category. MSTORE writes a word to memory while SHA3 can operate multiple items in memory. In particular, SHA3 hashes the data in memory and its gas cost is the summation of basic gas (i.e., 30) with the gas for operating memory. The more memory it reads, the more gas it requires. EXP is a special arithmetic operation whose gas cost is the summation of basic gas (i.e., 10) with the remaining part which is determined by the bit length of the exponent. In other words, the gas cost of EXP becomes high if it has a large exponent. Figure 2 shows that EXP costs considerable CPU resources. SLOAD loads an item from the storage.

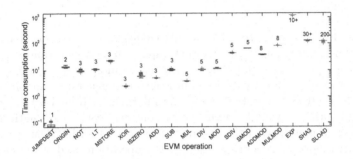

Fig. 2. Time consumptions of EVM operations

The results show that the latest gas costs are not proportional to the consumptions of CPU resources. For example, DIV (division) has the same gas cost of SDIV (signed division), but the execution time needed by DIV is about 23% (10.4 s/45 s) of that needed by SDIV. We find the reason by investigating the source code of handlers for DIV and SDIV, which is listed in Fig. 3. Figure 3 lists the source code (from go-ethereum V 1.6) of division (function *opDiv()*, Line 10) and signed division (function *opSdiv()*, Line 26), respectively, whose gas costs are equivalent. For the ease of presentation, we simplify the source code. We can see that the functions *opDiv()* and *opSdiv()* consist of stack operations (e.g., *stack.pop()*) and math computations (e.g. *x.And()*) provided by the *bigInt* library. Further experiments reveal that math computations (in red color) take up most of the execution time. We also find that the execution of a division operation needs 4 math computations (i.e., 1 *Div*, 1 *And*, 1 *Sub* and 1 *Exp*) at most whereas the execution of a signed division needs 11 (i.e., 3 *Sub*, 3 *Exp*, 2 *Abs*, 1 *Mul*, 1 *Div* and 1 *And*) at most. Hence, SDIV is more resource-consuming than DIV. Consequently, some operations (e.g., EXP, SHA3, as shown in Fig. 2) may be under-priced and thus could be exploited by DoS attacks.

```
 1  func BigPow(a, b int64) {            18  tt255 = BigPow(2, 255)
 2      r := big.NewInt(a)               19  func S256(x *big.Int) {
 3      return r.Exp(r, big.NewInt(b), nil)  20      if x.Cmp(tt255) < 0 {
 4  }                                     21          return x
 5  tt256 = BigPow(2, 256)               22      } else {
 6  tt256m1 = new(big.Int).Sub(tt256, big.NewInt(1))  23          return new(big.Int).Sub(x, tt256)
 7  func U256(x *big.Int){               24      }
 8      return x.And(x, tt256m1)         25  }
 9  }                                    26  func opSdiv(stack *Stack) {
10  func opDiv(stack *Stack){            27      x, y := math.S256(stack.pop()), math.S256(stack.pop())
11      x, y := stack.pop(), stack.pop()  28      if y.Sign() == 0 {
12      if y.Sign() != 0 {               29          stack.push(new(big.Int))
13          stack.push(math.U256(x.Div(x, y)))  30      } else {
14      } else {                         31          if evm.interpreter.intPool.get().Mul(x, y).Sign() < 0 {
15          stack.push(new(big.Int))     32              n.SetInt64(-1)
16      }                                33          } else {
17  }                                    34              n.SetInt64(1)
                                         35          }
                                         36          res := x.Div(x.Abs(x), y.Abs(y))
                                         37          res.Mul(res, n)
                                         38          stack.push(math.U256(res))
                                         39      }
                                         40  }
```

Fig. 3. EVM source code for executing DIV and SDIV (Color figure online)

5   Adaptive Gas Cost Mechanism

The investigation in Sect. 4 shows that it is not easy to properly assign gas costs to EVM operations. Hence, we propose a novel adaptive gas cost mechanism for defending against DoS attacks.

5.1   Threat Model

We assume that the attacker can discover under-priced operations (if any) and then launch the attack by invoking either existing smart contracts or new smart contracts crafted by the attacker. Moreover, the attacker is rational and does not have unlimited money for launching attacks. In this case, she will give up the attack if her money cannot force the under-priced operations to be executed for lots of times. Moreover, she will not send a transaction that can execute the under-priced operations only a few times because sending a transaction is not cheap (i.e., gas cost is 21,000). Last but not least, normal users will not accept a gas cost mechanism that charges much money from them.

5.2   Adaptive Adjustment of Gas Costs

Exploiting the observation in Sect. 3.3 that a successful DoS attack has to trigger lots of executions of under-priced operations, we propose a new mechanism that increases the gas cost of an operation dynamically if it has been executed much more frequently than before. More precisely, we collect the execution traces (i.e., a sequence of executed operations) of normal transactions, and model the execution frequency of each EVM operation. Then, for every new transaction, we set a basic gas cost for each operation by default, and count the number of executions of each operation. If the number of an operation is larger than a threshold, its gas cost will be increased. The advantage of our mechanism is that it does *not* need to know which operations are under-priced. Instead, it punishes the over-frequent EVM operation through the increased gas cost. Hence, it can defend against known and unknown DoS attacks.

We define a threshold μ_i for the operation i as shown in Eq. (1). The operation i that has been executed for more than μ_i in *one* transaction is regarded as over-frequent, and its gas cost will be increased. ave_i and std_i stand for the average and the standard deviation of the number of executing operation i, respectively. Section 6.1 details how to compute them. $base\_count$ is an integer used to prevent increasing the gas cost of an infrequently-executed operation too fast. m is a parameter for adjusting the threshold.

$$\mu_i = max\{base\_count, ave_i + m \times std_i\} \tag{1}$$

The gas cost of an EVM operation is dynamically adjusted according to Eq. (2), where $count_i$ is the number of executions of operation i, $base\_gas_i$ is the default gas cost of i. We uses an exponential function to punish over-frequent operations with accelerating increments in gas costs. Its base (i.e. $\alpha > 1$) determines the speed of increasing the gas cost. We let the exponent as $\frac{count_i}{\mu_i} - 1$ that includes μ_i for taking into account the operation's normal frequency. Since our mechanism will assign an operation a very high gas cost if it has been executed much more times in a transaction than before, it deters an attacker from executing an under-priced operation many times by one transaction. Moreover, our mechanism avoids charging much more gas from benign senders by setting proper parameters. We evaluate the effects of various parameters in Sect. 7.3. gas_i is restored to $base\_gas_i$ for a new transaction, and hence the attacker cannot affect the initial operation costs of benign transactions. Figure 4 shows the curves of Eq. (2) with various parameters, indicating that μ_i and α can affect the point from where to increase gas cost and the speed to increase gas cost, respectively. We have several observations. First, μ_i determines the point from where gas_i should be increased. Moreover, α determines the increasing speed of gas_i. Typically, gas_i should be increased with the increase of execution number $count_i$, and hence α should be larger than 1.

$$gas_i = \begin{cases} base\_gas_i, & if\ count_i \leq \mu_i \\ base\_gas_i + \alpha^{\frac{count_i}{\mu_i} - 1}, & if\ count_i > \mu_i \end{cases} \tag{2}$$

Section 5.3 will describe the way to adjust the parameters in Eqs. (1) and (2), and we will try other functions (e.g., linear, polynomial) in Eq. (2) in future work.

5.3 Dynamic Parameter Configuration

Since Ethereum and its smart contracts evolve over time, the parameters should be changed accordingly. Therefore, we need an approach for dynamic parameter configuration. This approach should meet the following requirements. First, the parameter configuration should be auditable by any users of Ethereum. Second, the parameter configuration should be secure so that attackers cannot modify the parameters. Third, the approach should not need to frequently update Ethereum client due to the risk of hard fork.

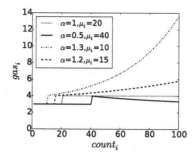

Fig. 4. Curves of Eq. (2), $base\_gas_i = 3$

Exploiting Ethereum's unique feature, we propose a novel approach for realizing dynamic parameter configuration by developing a specific smart contract and providing a patch to EVM. The developers of Ethereum can adjust the parameters by sending transactions carrying new parameters to that smart contract. They can adjust a variable, *block number*, in the smart contract, which is used to determine when the new setting takes effect. Then, the patched EVM can fetch the parameters periodically by reading the storage of that smart contract. The period (measured by blocks) of querying new parameters should be shorter than the difference between the variable, block number, in the smart contract and the block number when setting the new parameters so that all clients can get the newest setting before the block when the setting takes effect.

Our new approach leverages the underlying blockchain technique to make the parameters auditable and untamperable. Note that no one can change the setting of gas costs by just subverting her EVM. Moreover, the smart contract for updating parameters cannot be tampered by attackers who do not have more than 50% computing power because the contract itself will be validated in the process of consensus. The change of parameters will be auditable because all transactions are publicly available in the blockchain. Last but not least the Ethereum client (i.e., its EVM) should only be updated once for adopting our new gas cost mechanism. After that, they do not need to be updated again for using the new parameters.

6 Implementation

The implementation of our new mechanism consists of four parts (Fig. 5). The first part collects execution traces of smart contracts and computes ave_i and std_i. Part 2 is the smart contract storing the parameters that can be updated by Ethereum developers. Part 3 and 4 describe the patch to EVM, including how to fetch new parameters and how to apply them, respectively.

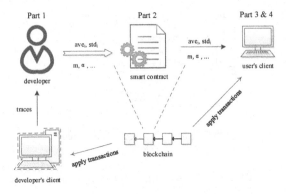

Fig. 5. Overview of our implementation.

6.1 Computing ave_i and std_i

To compute ave_i and std_i, we first leverage EVM's built-in tracing ability to record all execution traces. We define a sliding window, and use all traces within that window for computing ave_i and std_i. Figure 6 shows ave_i and std_i of PUSH1 with different window sizes (i.e., 100, 1,000 and 10,000) in the first 16,000 execution traces since the launch of Ethereum. We assume that these traces were triggered by benign transactions since no known attacks were discovered in them. Please note that PUSH1 is the most frequent operation, which pushes one byte on stack.

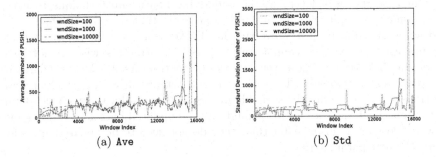

(a) Ave   (b) Std

Fig. 6. Average number and standard deviation of the executions of PUSH1. (Color figure online)

The x-axis gives the window index and for example, a point (x, y) on the red line of Fig. 6(a) indicates that ave_i of PUSH1 of the traces within the window $[x + 1, x + 10,000]$ is y. We can see that the ave_i of PUSH1 increases as time goes on, indicating that smart contracts become more complicated than before. Second, as we expected, the larger the window is, the more stable ave_i and std_i will be. Moreover, it is difficult for an attacker to tamper ave_i and std_i by filling the large window with crafted transactions. Our approach allows developers to adjust the window size.

6.2   Smart Contract

We implement a smart contract (as shown in Fig. 7) to store parameters which allows the contract's creator to update parameters through executing transactions, and then we deploy it on our private blockchain. For ease of presentation, we omit the details of updating ave_i and std_i of each operation i, which is the same as the updating the other parameters (e.g., m). Line 2 declares several global variables which store in the storage. *address* (Line 3) is a built-in variable type of Ethereum which can only be used for storing account address. N is the time interval of two consecutive queries, and *delta* is a small number that we consider all clients can get the new setting in the time period of $N + delta$ (Line 13). The function *AdaptiveGas()* is the construct function that will be executed during the creation of the smart contract. Please note that the arguments of *AdaptiveGas()* are also given in the transaction for contract creation.

```
1   contract AdaptiveGas {
2      uint base_count, m, alpha, blk_num, N, delta;
3      address creator; //owner
4      function AdaptiveGas(uint init_base_count, uint init_m, uint init_alpha,
            uint init_blk_num, uint default_N, uint default_delta){
5         base_count = init_base_count; m = init_m;
6         alpha = init_alpha; blk_num = init_blk_num;
7         N = default_N; delta = default_delta;
8         creator = msg.sender; //set contract owner
9      }
10     function UpdateSetting(uint new_base_count, uint new_m,
            uint new_alpha, uint new_blk_num){
11        require(msg.sender == creator); //authentication
12        if (new_blk_num < block.number + N + delta)
13           new_blk_num = block.number + N + delta;
14        base_count = new_base_count; m = new_m;
15        alpha = new_alpha; blk_num = new_blk_num;
16     }
17 }
```

Fig. 7. The smart contract for updating the setting of parameters

Besides setting the default parameters in *AdaptiveGas()* (Lines 5–7), we record the contract owner (Line 8), ensuring that only the owner can change parameters setting (Line 11). The function *UpdateSetting()* accepts the new setting of parameters from transaction senders. Lines 12, 13 ensure that the time period $(N + delta)$ is enough for all clients to check the update. Please note that *msg.sender* and *block.number* are two built-in properties of Ethereum that get the address of transaction sender and the number of block which contains the transaction, respectively. Please note that the transaction fees for sending the transactions to adjust paramters are negligible for Ethereum official society because a single transaction does not cost much (always less than 1 USD [2]) and parameters do not need to adjust very frequently.

6.3   Querying New Parameters

Figure 8 shows the code snippet (simplified for presentation) for an EVM to get the new setting of parameters. Since each Ethereum node keeps a complete copy of blockchain, their EVMs can get the values of all storage variables given the address of the smart contract by accessing the local copy of blockchain. It is more efficient than an intuitive approach that fetches the new parameters by sending a transaction to the smart contract, because the latter will add transactions to the blockchain periodically and cause additional fee for sending transactions. Our approach can avoid these issues. Line 1 specifies the address (i.e., $ac43...$) of the contract, which is known because the contract is developed and deployed by us. Then, Lines 2–5 obtain individual parameters by directly accessing (i.e., invoking the internal function $evm.StateDB.GetState()$ of EVM) the storage of the contract. The integers 0, 1, etc. give the locations of parameters stored in the storage. Finally, those parameters are used for computing gas costs.

```
1   var contract = common.HexToAddress("ac43...")
2   base_count = evm.StateDB.GetState(contract, 0)
3   m = evm.StateDB.GetState(contract, 1)
4   alpha = evm.StateDB.GetState(contract, 2)
5   blk_num = evm.StateDB.GetState(contract, 3)
```

Fig. 8. Modifications of EVM to obtain new parameters.

6.4   Applying New Parameters

We modify go-ethereum V 1.3.5 to realize our mechanism because it has several known under-priced operations, and we compare the original V 1.3.5 with the patched one in Sect. 7.1. When Ethereum starts, we load the setting of parameters (e.g., ave_i, std_i, m, α) in the entry function (i.e., the $main()$ function in \cmd\geth\main.go). Please note that the default gas cost of each operation (i.e., $base\_gas_i$) is the same as that in go-ethereum V 1.3.5. We replace the code in the function $CalculateGasAndSize()$ in \core\vm\vm.go, which is responsible for computing the gas consumption of individual operation, with our code to calculate gas cost and increase the execution number of the EVM operation by one. In other words, Eqs. (1) and (2) are implemented in $CalculateGasAndSize()$. The number of executions will be reset before the execution of each transaction, which is implemented in the function $ApplyTransaction()$ in \core\state_processor.go. To reduce the runtime overhead, we cache the gas costs of operations, which have already been computed, in main memory.

7   Evaluation

This section answers the following questions through experiments.

RQ1: Can our mechanism thwart known and unknown DoS attacks effectively?
RQ2: How much additional gas will be charged from benign users by our mechanism?
RQ3: What are the effects of parameters?

All experiments are conducted in a private Ethereum blockchain on a desktop equipped with an Intel Xeon E312 processor and 8 GB memory. Our private blockchain has one miner and is isolated with the public Ethereum blockchain and other testing blockchains. We create an account to hold the rewards from mining. We guarantee that the account has enough money to send transactions by setting a low mining difficulty. Every block also has a gas limit, dubbed BGL (Block Gas Limit), which restricts the size of a block (i.e., the number of transactions contained in the block). The BGL is set as 4 million, which is comparable with that in the public chain at present. We let the TGL be equal to the BGL, in order to see how many under-priced operations can be executed by a single transaction using the original gas cost mechanism and our mechanism, respectively. The parameters $base\_count$, m and α in Eqs. (1) and (2) are set to 5, 3 and 2 by default, respectively. We evaluate our mechanism under different settings in Sect. 7.3.

7.1 Experiments with DoS Attacks

We simulate the two real attacks [6,7] in our private blockchain. To launch the EXTCODESIZE attack, we develop a smart contract with a public function $extAttack()$ that can be called by our account. $extAttack()$ has a loop where we use inline assembly to execute EXTCODESIZE directly. The SUICIDE attack is launched in a more intricate way since a smart contract will be removed (i.e., cannot get accessed) by executing SUICIDE. The SUICIDE attack exploits the feature of Ethereum: a smart contract will not be removed before the completion of the transaction that triggers the SUICIDE operation. Consequently, we create a smart contract whose constructor invokes SUICIDE in a loop. When creating the contract, the corresponding transaction executes SUICIDE repeatedly. We also use the built-in tracing ability of EVM to record the execution traces of smart contracts as well as the gas consumption of each operation.

The experimental results reveal that the two attacks execute 92,494 and 11,335 times of EXTCODESIZE and SUICIDE, respectively, in one transaction using the original (i.e., go-ethereum V 1.3.5) gas cost mechanism. By contrast, the two attacks only execute 99 and 81 times of EXTCODESIZE and SUICIDE, respectively, with the same cost (i.e., 4 million gas) after our mechanism is applied. Figure 10(a) (y-axis is on a log scale) and Fig. 10(b) shows the gas cost of each operation in descending order after the attacks when our mechanism used. Note that these two figures do not include all operations due to the page limit. We can see that the gas costs of the two under-priced operations become very expensive (i.e., 457,119 and 37,640 respectively) after attacks. We also find some other expensive operations (e.g., CALLDATALOAD, CALL) because they are also in the loop, resulting in over-frequent executions than before. Figure 9 demonstrates that the execution frequencies of different operations vary. Moreover, the two under-priced operations (i.e., EXTCODESIZE and SUCIDE) exploited by real attacks are rarely executed by benign users.

To evaluate our approach against unknown DoS attacks, we synthesize three attacks by executing three under-priced operations (i.e., EXTCODECOPY, SLOAD

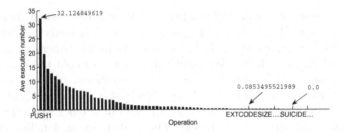

Fig. 9. Average execution number of every EVM operation, 10,000 benign transactions collected from 07:40:00 AM, April 28, 2017 to 01:58:56 PM, April 28, 2017

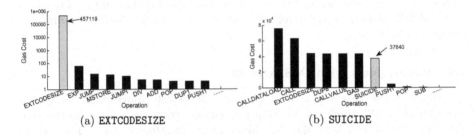

Fig. 10. Gas of each operation after attacking

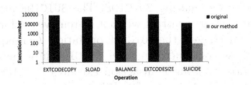

Fig. 11. Execution numbers of under-priced operations

and `BALANCE`) in a loop, respectively, which are similar to the `EXTCODESIZE` attack. Note that go-ethereum V 1.3.5 will be affected by the DoS attacks exploiting these operations whereas the latest version of Ethereum has increased their gas costs. Figure 11 demonstrates that our method reduces the number of executions of under-priced operations by several orders of magnitude. Therefore, the answer to RQ1 is:

Our gas cost mechanism can effectively thwart known and unknown DoS attacks.

7.2 Experiments with Normal Transactions

To evaluate how much additional gas will be charged from normal users by our mechanism, we first randomly select 10 smart contracts and then replay their transactions in the original go-ethereum V 1.3.5 and the updated go-ethereum

V 1.3.5 with our gas cost mechanism, respectively. 84 transactions in total are replayed, and 15 transactions (2 to one contract and the other 13 to another contract) out of them incur additional gas by our mechanism. The total gas consumed by 84 transactions under the original gas cost setting is 2,441,340, and the total additional gas incurred by our mechanism is 444. Therefore, the percentage of additional gas charged from benign users is about 0.018%.

As a case study, we detail the experiment with one smart contract. More precisely, the smart contract is deployed at 0x61F9d1cE56aC1623FeD4e949 D7D420251fef0896. We compile the source and deploy the smart contract in the private blockchain. There are 37 transactions to that smart contract in total until April 29, 2017. We do not replay the transaction for contract creation since it does not trigger the execution of any public functions provided by the smart contract, nor the 4 transactions with internal transactions because our private blockchain is isolated from other accounts. Note that an internal transaction is not a real transaction and will not be stored in the blockchain. Instead, it is made by calling (via CALL, CALLCODE, DELEGATECALL etc.) an account from a smart contract. We also skip the transaction running out of gas, and hence we replay 31 ($37 - 1 - 4 - 1$) transactions.

The results show that 18 out of 31 transactions consume the same amount of gas under our mechanism and the original mechanism. The total increment in gas consumption of the other 13 transactions incurred by our mechanism is 130, and the largest increment in gas consumption of one transaction is 10. Please note that the total gas consumption of the 31 transactions under original mechanism is 1,357,654. That is, the increment in gas consumption due to our mechanism is negligible (i.e., 0.01%). Hence, the answer to RQ2 is:

> Our gas cost mechanism charges negligible additional gas from benign users.

7.3   Different Parameter Settings

We evaluate our mechanism under three different settings as listed in Table 1. For example, "3(5/1.2)" means that in setting 3, m and α are set to 5 and 1.2, respectively. Please note that the setting 2 is the default setting. Table 1 also presents the execution numbers of under-priced operations and the highest gas costs of them. For example, "48/1,026,690" in row 2, column 2 indicates EXTCODECOPY executes 48 times under setting 1 and the gas cost of the 48th EXTCODECOPY is 1,026,690. Please note that the gas cost of an operation keeps increasing if its execution number exceeds μ_i (Eq. (2)).

The experimental results demonstrate that our approach is sensitive to DoS attacks by setting a small m and a large α. The setting 1 detects attacks quicker (i.e., the execution numbers of under-priced operations are the lowest) than the other two settings. For example, the EXTCODESIZE attack executes 48 EXTCODESIZE, and its gas cost reaches 1,026,187 under the setting 1 whereas the attack executes 328 EXTCODESIZE and the gas cost of EXTCODESIZE reaches 131,049 under the setting 3. The results are as expected since the threshold μ_i depends on m and α determines the speed of increasing gas costs.

Table 1. Execution numbers (before/) and the highest gas costs (after/) of under-priced operations under different settings

Setting	BALANCE	EXTCODECOPY	EXTCODESIZE	SLOAD	SUICIDE
1(1/5)	48/1,026,387	48/1,026,690	48/1,026,687	48/1,026,187	22/237
2(3/2)	99/456,819	99/457,122	99/457,119	99/456,619	81/37,640
3(5/1.2)	329/135,590	328/131,052	328/131,049	329/135,390	289/31,440

One may feel strange that SUICIDE presents different trend with the other attacks under different settings. For example, the gas cost of SUICIDE under the setting 2 is larger than that under the other two settings, whereas the gas costs of the other four under-priced operations under the setting 1 reach the largest value. The reason is that SUICIDE is not the most expensive operation during attack (as shown in Fig. 10(b)), and thus the execution number of SUICIDE is influenced by the gas consumption of other expensive operations. Figure 12 shows the increment in gas consumption of applying 31 transactions to the smart contract at 0x61F9d1cE56aC1623FeD4e949D7D420251fef0896 under three different settings. The x-axis specifies transactions in short, e.g., *3d1b* is the first two bytes of a transaction hash which is 32 bytes in length. The results reveal that a setting that is more sensitive to DoS attacks may charge more execution fee from benign users.

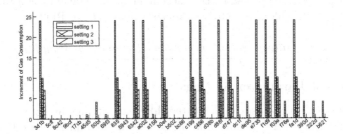

Fig. 12. Additional gas consumption of 31 transactions under three different settings

We also evaluate whether our mechanism can defend against DoS attacks exploiting the five under-priced operations under the default setting with different window sizes. We compute ave_i and std_i of each operation i for different windows sizes, including 100, 500, 1,000, 5,000 and 10,000. We use the first 16,000 transactions since the launch of Ethereum for experiments, which do not include attacks. The attacks exploiting the five under-priced operations are conducted in our private chain for this experiment.

Figure 13 presents the execution numbers of SLOAD with different window sizes (the experiments of other four under-priced operations produce similar results). It shows that our method is effective using the parameters computed

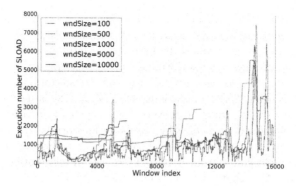

Fig. 13. Execution numbers of `SLOAD` with different window sizes

from all window sizes because the under-priced operation executes more than the threshold μ_i at any window sizes and hence its gas cost increases during attacks. More precisely, the original gas cost method allows `SLOAD` to execute nearly 100,000 times (Fig. 11) whereas our method reduces this number significantly.

We assume all transaction in the windows for computing parameters are benign. Attackers may want to place crafted transactions into the windows to affect the process of computing ave_i and std_i for the sake of evading the detection. To make our approach more robust, we suggest analysts to set a relatively large window size (e.g., 10,000) that consists of many transactions. In another words, a large window size raises the difficulty for attackers to fill the window with crafted transactions and tamper parameters. Besides, after detecting an attacking transaction, we can filter out the attacking transactions in the windows by matching the transaction senders, attached data (specifying which function to call and providing augments) of transactions, the execution traces of contracts etc.

Hence, the answer to RQ3 is:

> *The experimental result show that DoS attacks can be detected quickly and negligible additional gas is introduced to benign users under different parameter settings. Our mechanism allows developers to easily adjust parameters with the evolving of Ethereum.*

8   Related Work

DoS attacks have posed a severe threat to the Internet [17,25] and various systems [10,14] and services [23]. Although DoS attacks on Ethereum have been reported, there lacks of a systematic study on the attacks and the defense mechanisms. To the best of our knowledge, this paper presents the first work on defending against under-priced DoS attacks on Ethereum.

BLOCKBENCH [12] is an evaluation framework for measuring the throughput, latency, scalability and fault-tolerance of private blockchains. Yasaweerasinghelage et al. propose to predict the latency of blockchain-based applications using architectural performance modeling and simulation tools [26]. However, they [12,26] do not investigate the consumptions of computing resources for executing EVM operations. OYENTE [18] is a symbolic executor for smart contracts which discovers four types of security vulnerabilities. GASPER [9], based on OYENTE, finds under-optimized smart contracts automatically that cost more gas than necessary. A recent survey [3] reports that smart contracts suffer from several kinds of vulnerabilities. One kind is *gasless send*, indicating that a transaction sender may not consider the situation that sending Ether to another account is possible to fail due to the out-of-gas exception. Sergey et al. reveal that smart contracts will suffer from similar problems that often occur in transitional concurrent programs [22]. However, they [3,9,18,22] do not consider DoS attacks to Ethereum, which exploit under-priced EVM operations.

Verification is used for verifying the runtime safety and functional correctness of smart contracts. Bhargavan et al. propose to translate a smart contract into F*, a functional language before formal analysis [4]. Similarly, Pettersson and Edström suggest developing smart contracts in Idris, a functional language, and using type system to capture errors at compile time [20]. Hirai formally defines EVM in Lem, an intermediate language similar to a functional language, facilitating further analysis and generation of smart contracts [13]. However, they neither verify nor detect DoS attacks due to under-priced operations [4,13,20]. Hawk is a smart contract system protecting transactional privacy [16]. Town Crier [27] aims at providing trustworthy data to smart contracts since they need data out from the blockchain. Juels et al. report that smart contracts can be used to commit crimes, such as privacy leakage, theft of cryptographic keys [15]. However, they [15,16,27] do not discuss the threats resulting from Ethereum DoS attacks.

9   Conclusion

We investigate the gas cost setting in Ethereum because it could be exploited to launch DoS attacks. By proposing an emulation-based framework to automatically measure the resource consumptions of EVM operations, we find that Ethereum does not assign proper gas costs to operations and it is difficult to properly assign fixed gas costs to operations for defending against known and unknown DoS attacks. Therefore, we propose a DoS-resistant gas cost mechanism, which dynamically adjusts the costs of operations according to the number of executions. Our approach is flexible and secure, and we design a special smart contract that collaborates with the customized EVM to avoid frequently updating Ethereum client. Experimental results show that our method effectively thwarts known and unknown DoS attacks, and introduces negligible additional gas to benign users.

Acknowledgment. This work was supported in part by the National Natural Science Foundation of China, No. 61402080, No. 61572115, No. 61502086, No. 61572109, China Postdoctoral Science Foundation founded project, No. 2014M562307, and Shenzhen City Science and Technology R&D Fund (No. JCYJ20150630115257892).

References

1. Ethereum homestead documentation (2017). https://goo.gl/V6PmCg
2. Etherscan - transactions (2017). https://etherscan.io/txs
3. Atzei, N., Bartoletti, M., Cimoli, T.: A survey of attacks on Ethereum smart contracts (SoK). In: Proceedings of the POST (2017)
4. Bhargavan, K., Delignat-Lavaud, A., Fournet, C., Gollamudi, A., Gonthier, G., Kobeissi, N., Rastogi, A., Sibut-Pinote, T., Swamy, N., Zanélla-Beguelin, S.: Formal verification of smart contracts: short paper. In: Workshop, PLAS (2016)
5. Buterin, V.: Eip150: long-term gas cost changes for IO-heavy operations to mitigate transaction spam attacks (2016). https://goo.gl/8gwNCL
6. Buterin, V.: A state clearing faq (2016). https://goo.gl/x5QRrd
7. Buterin, V.: Transaction spam attack: next steps (2016). https://goo.gl/uKi9Ug
8. Carter, J.: Bitcoin vs distributed ledger vs ethereum vs blockchain (2016). https://goo.gl/3EQVdJ
9. Chen, T., Li, X., Luo, X., Zhang, X.: Under-optimized smart contracts devour your money. In: Proceedings of the SANER (2017)
10. Chen, T., Li, X., Luo, X., Zhang, X.: System-level attacks against android by exploiting asynchronous programming. Softw. Qual. J. 1–26 (2017). https://doi.org/10.1007/s11219-017-9374-6
11. CoinGecko: Ethereum/us dollar price chart (2017). https://goo.gl/pezZAn
12. Dinh, T., Wang, J., Chen, G., Liu, R., Ooi, B., Tan, K.: Blockbench: a framework for analyzing private blockchains. In: Conference on SIGMOD/PODS (2017)
13. Hirai, Y.: Defining the ethereum virtual machine for interactive theorem provers. In: Proceedings of the WTSC (2017)
14. Jiang, M., Wang, C., Luo, X., Miu, M., Chen, T.: Characterizing the impacts of application layer DDoS attacks. In: Proceedings of the IEEE ICWS (2017)
15. Juels, A., Kosba, A., Shi, E.: The ring of Gyges: investigating the future of criminal smart contracts. In: Proceedings of the CCS (2016)
16. Kosba, A., Miller, A., Shi, E., Wen, Z., Papamanthou, C.: Hawk: the blockchain model of cryptography and privacy-preserving smart contracts. In: Proceedings of the S&P (2016)
17. Luo, X., Chang, R.: Optimizing the pulsing denial-of-service attacks. In: Proceedings of the DSN (2005)
18. Luu, L., Chu, D.H., Olickel, H., Saxena, P., Hobor, A.: Making smart contracts smarter. In: Proceedings of the CCS (2016)
19. Maltsev, P.: White paper: a next-generation smart contract and decentralized application platform (2017). https://goo.gl/6Y8ivs
20. Pettersson, J., Edström, R.: Safer smart contracts through type-driven development. Master's thesis, Chalmers University Of Technology And University Of Gothenburg (2016)
21. Rocky: Ethereum faces another dos attack (2016). https://goo.gl/sAUjJ7
22. Sergey, I., Hobor, A.: A concurrent perspective on smart contracts. In: Proceedings of the WTSC (2017)

23. Tang, Y., Luo, X., Hui, Q., Chang, R.: Modeling the vulnerability of feedback-control based internet services to low-rate dos attacks. IEEE Trans. Inf. Forensics Secur. **9**(3), 339–353 (2014)
24. Wood, G.: Ethereum: a secure decentralised generalised transaction ledger, EIP-150 revision (2016). http://gavwood.com/paper.pdf
25. Xue, L., Luo, X., Chan, E., Zhan, X.: Towards detecting target link flooding attack. In: Proceedings of the USENIX LISA (2014)
26. Yasaweerasinghelage, R., Staples, M., Weber, I.: Predicting latency of blockchain-based systems using architectural modelling and simulation. In: Conference on ICSA (2017)
27. Zhang, F., Cecchetti, E., Croman, K., Juels, A., Shi, E.: Town crier: an authenticated data feed for smart contracts. In: Proceedings of the CCS (2016)

A User-Friendly Centrally Banked Cryptocurrency

Xuan Han[1,2,3], Yamin Liu[1,2(✉)], and Haixia Xu[1,2]

[1] State Key Laboratory of Information Security,
Institute of Information Engineering, Chinese Academy of Sciences, Beijing, China
{hanxuan,liuyamin,xuhaixia}@iie.ac.cn
[2] Data Assurance and Communication Security Research Center,
Chinese Academy of Sciences, Beijing, China
[3] School of Cyber Security, University of Chinese Academy of Sciences,
Beijing, China

Abstract. In the absence of the trusted third party, the cryptocurrencies headed by Bitcoin realized the consistency of the distributed ledger successfully. However, Bitcoin, based on proof of work, has serious waste of computational resources, poor scalability and bad monetary policy. Compared with Bitcoin, RSCoin utilizes two-phase commit to construct a scalable centrally banked cryptocurrency frame, avoiding the waste of computational resources caused by proof of work. But it does not consider the communication cost of users. We present a user-friendly centrally banked cryptocurrency, UFCBCoin, based on RSCoin. We take advantage of a representative mechanism that the user entrusts a representative to send messages, to reduce half of the communication cost of the user. We also prove that UFCBCoin is secure theoretically in the synchronous network communication model we defined, and introduce an evaluation mechanism to enhance security.

Keywords: Cryptocurrency · RSCoin · Scalability
Evaluation mechanism

1 Introduction

Since Bitcoin has been proposed in [1] in October 2008 and implemented in January 2009, it has spread throughout the world. The anonymity and decentralization it offers attracts more and more researchers, business and even governments. As of March 2017, almost 16 million Bitcoins are in circulation [2], whose exchange rate is more than 2000 US dollars [3]. Moreover, alternative cryptocurrencies derived from Bitcoin such as Litecoin and ETH have been already in circulation as a form of payment.

Bitcoin, as the representative of decentralized cryptocurrencies, has gained great success. However, it is exposed to some problems in the following aspects.

First, Bitcoin is faced with poor scalability [4]. The size of blocks is limited and cannot be infinitely increased. Each transaction is confirmed when it is

© Springer International Publishing AG 2017
J. K. Liu and P. Samarati (Eds.): ISPEC 2017, LNCS 10701, pp. 25–42, 2017.
https://doi.org/10.1007/978-3-319-72359-4_2

included in the blockchain with several blocks behind it, while a new block is generated by miners after finding a mathematical puzzle solution on average 10 min [5]. Due to the block structure and delayed confirmation, it can only handle 3.3–7 transactions per second. In comparison, VISA [6] had reported to deal with 2000 transactions per second at least in 2016. Thus improving scalability is a major challenge for Bitcoin to deal with fast payments [7].

Second, Bitcoin causes serious waste of computational resources by utilizing proof of work. The mining process relies on a huge amount of computational power to find a meaningless number to solve the proof-of-work puzzle [5]. The resource needed for generating a new block is positive correlated to the difficulty target of puzzle. In the process of generating a new block, a mass of electricity fritters away.

Additionally, the intrinsic value and sustainability of Bitcoin is questioned in the centralized society. Because of the elimination of the trusted central bank, the exchange rate of Bitcoin is out of control, undulating dramatically from less than 1 US dollar to more than 3000 US dollars. Furthermore, the total gross of Bitcoin, 21 million, may cause deflation and other economic issues. It is an open question that how Bitcoin keeps progressing when miners cannot get reward any more [8], apart from the transaction fee.

Against these problems, RSCoin [10], a centrally banked cryptocurrency framework was published in 2016, allowing any central bank to deploy monetary currency on it. The central bank makes the monetary policy and authorizes mintettes to maintain the blockchain. Besides, RSCoin replaces proof of work with two-phase commit to avoid the waste of computational resources. The central bank divides all the miners into shards, also known as mintettes, to validate and confirm transactions. The users just submit their transactions to a certain shard of mintettes and gets the valid signatures from the corresponding shard. If the user gets enough valid signatures in both two phases, the transaction will be deemed to be confirmed. It is more scalable than Bitcoin because the users do not need to wait 60 min to confirm transactions. However, from the view of users, it is not efficient and scalable enough for the reason that the amount of transaction messages those the user sends and receives is the same with the mintettes for every transaction. High communication cost for users is a barrier for RSCoin to be implemented in lightweight devices, e.g. mobile phone. Our study focuses on reducing the user's traffic in centrally banked cryptocurrencies.

Our Contributions. We present UFCBCoin, a user-friendly centrally banked cryptocurrency, inspired by RSCoin. We consider the communication cost of the user as a measure of performance of centrally banked cryptocurrencies. In more detail, our contributions are as follows.

Firstly, we present a representative mechanism and describe a user-friendly centrally banked cryptocurrency based on it. In UFCBCoin, the user randomly selects a representative to post transactions to other corresponding mintettes on behalf of itself. By this way, the user's traffic is transferred to the representative mintette it selected.

Secondly, we redefine the security of cryptocurrencies and require that a cryptocurrency system is secure only if every valid transaction can be confirmed by the system and every confirmed transaction is valid. We also prove that our scheme is secure under the assumption that the majority of every shard is honest in the synchronous network communication model.

Thirdly, we compare RSCoin and UFCBCoin in the aspect of user's communication cost. For simplification, we assume that each transaction has only one input and one output. The analysis results show that the communication cost of the user in our scheme, including all transactions that the user sends and receives, is nearly halved compared to RSCoin in the best case. In other cases, UFCBCoin is also more efficient than RSCoin.

Finally, we provide a new evaluation mechanism without additional messages. In order to restrict malicious behaviour, we propose a more concise evaluation mechanism than RSCoin. We define the degree for evaluating the mintettes behaviour. The degree of a mintette is determined by the number of valid signatures it created, and the malicious mintette with the lowest degree will be punished by the central bank.

Related Work. Many researches have focused on solving the problem of scalability and computational resource waste of cryptocurrencies based on blockchain. Alternative cryptocurrencies based on Bitcoin take efforts to find methods to replace proof of work. Litecoin, published in 2011, uses scrypt [9] instead of SHA256 as the proof-of-work algorithm to achieve nearly 2.5 min to generate a block. PPcoin, published in 2012, reduces the cost of block generation by utilizing both proof-of-stake and proof-of-work algorithms [12]. Proof of stake avoids wasting resources by changing computational puzzles into virtual mining. Proof of space [13] is another method to replace proof of work. Removing a lot of computation, these schemes do shorten the time of the block generation. However, the mining processes based on scrypt or proof of space depend on the size of memory or space, resulting in another demand of memory. The simple proof of stake may cause the security and fairness problems due to the inappropriate stakes. In these schemes in which the balance is chosen as the stake, the adversary with high balance can allocate the balance reasonably or bribe others to control the system [14]. When time is considered as the stake [12], the adversaries can keep some old transactions not being spent to destroy the security.

Others try to modify proof of work into a more efficient and resource-friendly mechanism. Bitcoin-NG [15] utilizes proof of work to select a leader. The leader validates and records all transactions until the next leader appears by solving the proof-of-work puzzle. In this way, the transactions those users submit can always be confirmed in a short time. But it can not avoid the simultaneous creation of two or more leaders. It can bring about forks. Byzcoin [16] combines the Byzantine agreement with proof of work. After selecting leaders by proof of work, the leaders implement the Byzantine agreement to agree on a set of transaction. It also causes disagreement in the leader selection phase, and its security relies on a lower fault tolerance. Elastico [17] tries to find a reasonable grouping method to improve the efficiency of transaction confirmation. All nodes are grouped randomly by proof of work. Only in the particular group, they can validate and record transactions. Despite the savings of resources, the restriction on adversarial computing power gets stricter. In all the discussion above, they do not reckon the communication cost of users because they submit transactions in the form of broadcast. We consider users' communication cost as an important measurement criteria.

Organization of the Paper. The remaining part of the paper is organized as follows. In Sect. 2 we introduce the background of our study, including the basics of Bitcoin and RSCoin. In Sect. 3 we present the notation and threat model in which we formally describe the adversarial attack goal and the definition of security. In Sect. 4 we elaborate our system in detail focusing on the interaction among the central bank, mintettes and users. In Sect. 5 we provide a comprehensive proof of security and comparison with RSCoin in the respect of users communication traffic. In Sect. 6, we propose an evaluation mechanism to ensure the security and other improvements on the system. Finally, we conclude our construction briefly in Sect. 7 and list the main algorithms of UFCBCoin in the Appendix.

2 Background

We start by describing the basics of Bitcoin and RSCoin briefly, mainly introducing the whole process of the transaction confirmation in these systems. Our introduction only focuses on the terms of scalability. Readers can learn more details from the original Bitcoin paper [1] and RSCoin paper [10].

2.1 Bitcoin

Bitcoin [1] is the most successful decentralized cryptocurrency until now, published in October 2008 and implemented in January 2009. It is a peer-to-peer electronic payment scheme, accepted by 100,000 merchants and vendors until February 2015.

In the Bitcoin system, the users transfer money through the transactions among their addresses. The transaction is formed by the payers' signatures on the key items, including the origins of money, the transaction value, the recipients' addresses and the transaction fee. The origin of money is the previous transaction that the user received but not spent yet. The one who owns the recipients private key can spend the corresponding Bitcoin. When a transaction has been created, the user broadcasts it to all nodes in the network. Every node validates all transaction it receives and transmits the valid one. Among the nodes, there are many special nodes called miners, responsible for recording the legal transactions. They record valid transactions on the block. In order to achieve consistency on the transaction records, the miners compete to find a solution of a mathematical puzzle. For simplicity, the fastest one can add its new block to the blockchain, a data structure storing the transaction set in chronological order. A transaction is finally confirmed, when it is in the blockchain included in several blocks.

From the user's point of view, Bitcoin is struggling between the strengths and weaknesses. Due to the form of transaction, users do not need to interact with miners or other nodes. For one trade, each user simply sends a transaction message and then waits for the transaction confirmation. Unfortunately, considering the security and consistency of the system, the performance and scalability of the system is poor. The transaction confirmation delay reaches approximately 60 min as a result of broadcasting latency and the proof-of-work mining mechanism. Apart from this, every new block is created with a lot of energy consumption. Some opponents of Bitcoin worry about the stability of the system when the mining reward gradually diminishes.

2.2 RSCoin

RSCoin [10], a centrally banked cryptocurrency, was released in 2016. Taking it into account that Bitcoin's poor scalability, high resource consumption and worrisome monetary policy, RSCoin presents a centralized cryptocurrency framework which is applicable to multiple cryptocurrencies.

Unlike maintaining only one complete blockchain by all nodes in Bitcoin, RSCoin is separated into two parts, the generation of the monetary supply and the maintenance of the transaction ledger. The central bank is a trusted third party, responsible for money supply and recording the transaction but not transaction collection and verification. The central bank authorizes the mintettes to manage the stage of transaction collection, verification and confirmation. All mintettes are divided into shards. Every shard is in charge of a set of transactions. Meanwhile, the validation and confirmation of the same transaction is handled by the different shards. They use a two-phase commit method, composed of the vote collection phase and the commitment phase. The blockchain in RSCoin is seemed to resemble a distributed database with undeniable property.

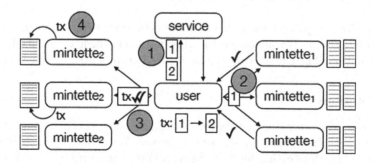

Fig. 1. Two-Phase commit in RSCoin [10]

For simplification, we describe the process of two-phase commit in detail, taking Bitcoin as an example running on RSCoin. The data structure of transaction is the same with Bitcoin, where $tx := (tx_{prev}, addr_A, addr_B, v, \sigma_A)$ means that user A transfers vBTC to user B which the money originates from the transaction tx_{prev} that user A received before, and $addr_A$ and $addr_B$ donate respectively the address of A and B, and v is the transaction value. As described in Fig. 1 from [10], the user first learns which shards should be used to validate and confirm its transaction. Then it enters into the vote collection phase. The user sends tx to every member of the corresponding shard. After receiving tx, every mintette validates tx_{prev} independently. If tx_{prev} has not appeared as an input before, the mintette returns its signature on tx. Otherwise, return $\perp$. Every valid signature is considered as a vote on the transaction. If A receives more than half number of the votes, it deems tx_{prev} is legal. Then, it turns into the commitment phase. The user sends tx with the set of valid signatures from previous shard to every member of the corresponding shard. After receiving tx and a set of signatures, each mintette validates all the signatures independently. If valid signatures are more than half, it records tx in its own lower-level blockchain and returns its signature on it. Otherwise, it abandons tx and returns $\perp$. Here, blockchain is utilized as a distributed ledger [11]. In this method, the set of transactions in lower-level blockchains maintained by different shards are different. The central bank ultimately incorporates all lower-level blockchains in the main blockchain, called high-level blockchain.

In comparison with Bitcoin, RSCoin eliminates unnecessary electricity consumption and decreases the transaction confirmation delay in the way that the mintettes manage the ledger authorized by the central bank. In the terms of the whole system, RSCoin certainly improves the scalability. From the view of users, however, its scalability is hardly ideal in the fact that the communication cost of the user is as much as the whole mintettes. For users, the communication cost is too high to transfer a transaction so that it is hard for RSCoin to be deployed on the lightweight devices such as the smart phone.

3   Notations and Threat Model

In this section, we present the related notations in order to facilitate the description of the system. We introduce the threat model which is modified on the RSCoin and redefine the security requirement of cryptocurrency schemes.

3.1   Notations

We introduce the notations first. In the system, the main cryptographic building blocks are hash functions and signature schemes. We denote by $H(\cdot)$ the hash function and by (SigKeyGen, Sig.Sign, Sig.Verify) the signature scheme. There are three different roles in the system, the central bank, mintettes and users. We denote the central bank as CB. The set of mintettes is represented as M. All mintettes are divided into x shards on average in which every shard is composed of q members, with $q = 2k + 1$, where $k \in N$. $m_{i,j}$ denotes the mintette which is the jth member in shard i, where $i,j \in N$, $i \leqslant x$ and $j \leqslant q$. Every mintette $m_{i,j}$ is certificated by CB with key pairs $(pk_{i,j}, sk_{i,j})$. The user is identified by (pk, sk). Every user can create its address through calculating $addr = H(pk)$. In addition, every user has two types of operations called query message and commit message.

We use the data structure of Bitcoin transaction in the system represented by $(TX_{prev}, ADDR_{in}, ADDR, V_{out}, \{\sigma\})$ supporting multiple input and output addresses. For simplicity, there is only one input address and one output address for each transaction. The transaction is denoted by $(tx_{prev}, addr_A, addr_B, v, \sigma_A)$, as described in the previous section.

In the system, the central bank and every shard maintain different blockchains with different functionalities. In a nutshell, the blockchain maintained by the central bank is composed of the blockchains of shards. This blockchain is the higher-level blockchain, denoted HLBC. Similarly, the blockchain held by each mintette is the lower-level blockchain, denoted $LLBC_{i,j}$. Every mintette holds three lists for the transaction validation. L_{utxo} and L_{stxo} contain all unspent transactions and all received transactions which the mintette is responsible for. Another one contains all valid transaction waiting to be recorded to the blockchain, denoted by L_{tx}. In each epoch, every mintette generates a new block. Meanwhile, the central bank generates a new block by processing all blocks from mintettes in a period. For describing the system, we take the round as the minimum unit of time. For each user, it can only submit one query message in a round. In round n, the user selects a mintette as its representative for two types of messages, denoted $r_{n,query}$ and $r_{n,commit}$.

3.2   Threat Model

We describe our system in the synchronous network communication model. In our system, we do not study the blockchain formation in detail, but the interaction among the three roles to maintain the ledger. We assume that the central bank is trusted and the majority of mintettes is honest in each shard. In other words, there are k malicious mintettes at most in every shard. We refer to our model as the (q, k) −bounded model. However, in our system, a valid transaction can be confirmed by more than half mintettes even if there is no central bank.

The adversarial model in our system is adaptive. We give a brief description of the adversaries' attack goals and behaviours. Because of multiple roles in the system, the goals of adversaries are slightly different.

– If a user is malicious, its goal is to submit an illegal transaction and make it valid, including double spending attack. The ability of a malicious user is as follows.

1. It can submit two transactions with the same transaction origin simultaneously or change the order of its own transactions.
2. It can take control of a part of mintettes less than the half of every shard and even conclude with the representative.
3. It is incapable of producing valid signatures from the honest parties.

– If a mintette is malicious, its goal mainly includes two parts, confirming an illegal transaction and rejecting a valid transaction. The ability of a malicious mintette is as follows.
   1. It can collude with others only limited by quantity, whose amount is less than half in each shard. It can also conspire with the users.
   2. It can respond or ignore the messages received from the honest users or mintettes, and even send some illegal messages.
   3. If an adversarial representative mintette, which a user chosen, intends to refuse the transaction submission, it will not send the transaction to other mintettes for validation in consideration of his own communication cost.
   4. The same as the adversarial users is that they cannot forge signatures from the honest users or mintettes.

3.3   Security

In comparison with no double spending or double spending detection, we define system security from a positive perspective. The definition of security we proposed is universally applicable in both cryptocurrencies and distributed ledgers, regardless of whether there is a trusted third part in the system.

Definition 1. *A cryptocurrency system is secure only if every valid transaction can be confirmed by the system and every confirmed transaction is valid.*

Taking into account different constructions of the systems, the definition of valid and confirmed transaction may vary. In our system, a transaction is valid only if the input transaction has not appeared as the input of any valid transaction in more than half corresponding lower-level blockchains. A transaction is confirmed in our system means that it is recorded in more than half corresponding lower-level blockchains.

The security definition we proposed above is stronger than no double spending. The security a system can reached is restricted. We call the system reaches the bounded security when it is secure under some assumption. In our system, we refer it as (q, k) −bounded security that the system is secure in our (q, k) −bounded model.

4   Construction of UFCBCoin

In this section, we present a user-friendly centrally banked cryptocurrency scheme. We intuitively explain the basic process of the scheme. The main algorithms of UFCBCoin is presented in the Appendix. From the view of the lower-level blockchains, the entire process of the scheme can be divided into two parts, the validation phase and the confirmation phase. In the validation phase, the mintettes only verify the transactions that users submit without logging them in their lower-level blockchains. In contrast, the mintettes in the confirmation phase are only responsible for recording the valid transactions. We propose the representative mechanism in each phase which can reduce the communication cost of users. The basic algorithms of UFCBCoin is presented in the Appendix (Fig. 2).

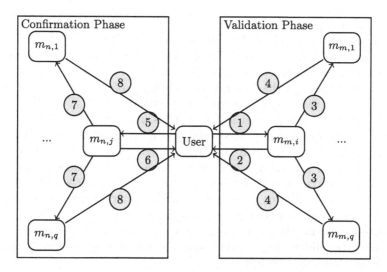

Fig. 2. The frame of UFCBCoin

- In the validation phase, a user requests to verify the input of the transaction is legal or not.
  1. The user finds the corresponding shard of mintettes and selects a representative mintette randomly through $H(tx_{prev})$. The user sends a query message with the transaction tx to the representative mintette.
  2. Upon receiving a query message and tx, the representative mintette does as follows.
     - It first determines whether the transaction is verified by itself. If it is true, then it validates that the input of the transaction has not been any other transactions input before and the value of tx_{prev} is no less than the value of tx. If tx_{prev} is valid, the representative mintette returns its signature on tx.
     - Then it removes tx_{prev} from L_{utxo} and records it in L_{stxo}. Otherwise, it returns $\perp$ and sends the query message with tx to the remaining.
     - Finally it sends other corresponding mintettes with the query message and tx.
  3. Upon receiving the query message and tx, every mintette validates tx_{prev} in the same way with the representative mintette except relaying messages.
  4. In the process of the validation phase, each signature the user received can be considered as the evidence of the related mintette, wherein the legal signature can be viewed as a vote on the legal transaction.
- If the user receives more than half signatures than the shard size, then it turns into confirmation phase.
  1. The user finds the corresponding shard of mintettes for confirmation and selects a representative mintette from the shard in the same way with the

validation phase. It collects all signatures associated with tx, and sends a commit message including all signatures and tx.

2. Upon receiving a commit message with tx and a set of signatures, the representative mintette does as follows.
   - It judges that the transaction is in charge of itself or not. If it is true, then it verifies the signatures respectively.
   - If the total legal signatures on tx is more than half the size of the shard, tx will be deemed valid by the representative mintette. Then it returns its signature on tx and sends the commit message and tx to other related mintettes in the same shard. Besides, it adds tx to its own L_{tx} waiting for recording in the next lower-level block.
   - If not, it returns $\bot$ and sends the commit message and tx to the remaining mintettes in the same shard.
3. Upon receiving the commit message with tx and a set of signatures, every mintette validates tx_{prev} in the same way with the representative mintette except relaying messages.
4. In the end of this stage, if the user has a reception of majority signatures from confirmation mintettes, it can ensure that the transaction will be recorded in more than half lower-level blockchain. It is meaning that the transaction that it submitted is confirmed.

5   Analysis of Security and Scalability

We now proceed to analyze the system from two aspects of security and scalability. We show that our system achieves security in the (q, k) −bounded model. We theoretically analyze the scalability of our system and compare with the RSCoin.

5.1   Security

We show that our system is secure in the (q, k) −bounded model. Recall that in this model all mintettes are randomly divided into m shards in which each shard is composed of q mintettes. The majority of mintettes is honest in each shard while at most k mintettes are malicious where $k = \lfloor \frac{q}{2} \rfloor$.

In our informal definition, the security of cryptocurrencies should satisfy the following two properties:

- **Validation.** Any transaction confirmed is valid.
- **Confirmation.** Any valid transaction will be confirmed in a reasonable period of time.

Because of different roles and different attack goals, we analyze security in a variety of cases.

- From the user's point of view, a malicious user aims to submit an illegal transaction and to make it valid. In the worst case, the adversarial user colludes k

mintettes respectively in two corresponding shards, one of which is in charge of the validation and the other is in charge of the confirmation. Moreover, the user can control the representative mintettes helping it to implement the attacks. In the validation phase, for every query the user submits, it can receive k signatures at most, not exceeding half in number. Even though the user submits the transaction with k signatures into the confirmation phase, the majority of the related mintettes do not record the invalid transaction into their own lower-level blockchains. The malicious user can not get half of votes on both the validation and confirmation phases. Eventually, this kind of attack cannot succeed.

- From the mintette's point of view, a malicious mintette can destroy the security in two ways that confirming the invalid transactions or rejecting the valid transactions.

  1. Considering that the malicious mintette aims to confirm an invalid transaction, it is the same with the case of the malicious users. The mintette cannot conspire with more than $k - 1$ mintettes in every corresponding shard to get over half valid signatures of the invalid transaction. The system is secure under this circumstance.

  2. Considering that the malicious mintette aims to reject a valid transaction, the security of the system is analyzed as follows.

     - We first focus on the validation phase. Assume that the user is lucky to select an honest mintette as the validation representative in the first round. It can give an honest response and forward information. Although the malicious mintette may not return a valid signature, the user will still receive at least $k + 1$ valid signatures.

     - If the user chooses a malicious representative, the representative returns $\bot$ to it. Then the user will select another representative to submit transaction once more. In the worst case, the user may select k consecutive malicious representatives until the $k + 1$th selection is honest. The probability of this extreme case is quite small. There is a theoretical analysis of probability in the next part. Eventually, the user can get half valid signatures on the transaction and turn to the confirmation phase.

     - The analysis of security in the confirmation is similar with the validation phase. Overall, in the worst case, the user can still gain success through $k + 1$ selection in each of two phase.

5.2   Scalability

Compared with the RSCoin, we exactly reduce the transaction communication cost of users by the representative mechanism. Meanwhile, the overall communication cost of the system and the throughput of the mintettes rise slightly. In this part, we compare the communication and computational cost between two systems.

Recall the model first. The threat models of two systems are generally consistent. Assume that there are only one input address and one output address in every transaction. All mintettes are divided into x shards on average and each shard is composed of q members, where $q = 2k + 1$, $k \in N$. The process of the two phases is so similar that we can only analyze the transaction communication cost of the validation phase. Suppose that T transactions should be processed per second.

In RSCoin, a user submits a transaction to q corresponding mintettes and waits for q response messages. Obviously, the total amount of communication messages handled by the system is $2q$ per transaction. The total communication messages the user processed are $2q$ per transaction, including q query messages and q received messages. The amount of messages the related mintettes handled is the same. The transaction communication cost of the system is $4qT$ per second.

In our scheme, because of the introduction of the representative mechanism, the scalability analysis of the system is relatively complicated. Whether the representative the user chosen is honest or not has a direct impact on the communication volume of the system. Here we assume that the user does not select an honest representative until the ith round, where $i \in N^+$, $i \le k + 1$. $\Pr(i)$ denotes the probability that the user does not select an honest representative until the ith round:

$$\Pr(i) = \frac{A_k^{i-1} \cdot (k+1)}{A_{2k+1}^i} \tag{1}$$

Now we analyze the communication costs of different roles in different situations. In the best case, the user is so lucky that it selects an honest mintette in the first round. It creates one query message and receives at most q signature messages from the shard of validation mintettes, totally $q + 1$ transactions for the user in this stage. For the representative, it receives a query message, returns a signature and sends the query message to other $q - 1$ mintettes. For the ordinary mintettes, each of them receives a query from the representative and sends its own signatures to the user. All mintettes in the related shard send and receive $3q - 1$ messages totally. Above all, the transaction communication cost of our scheme is $4qT$ per second, identically with the RSCoin.

In other cases, the user may find an honest representative first in the ith round. For the previous $i - 1$ failed selections, the user sends only one query message and gets one $\bot$ response in each round. For each malicious mintette, it does not forward the target messages considering its communication costs. The user deals with $2i - 2$ transaction messages in the first $i - 1$ rounds. Meanwhile, the first $i - 1$ malicious mintettes hold a communication volume of $2i - 2$ transaction messages. The communication volume of the system in the ith round is consistent with the best case. Consequently, the transaction communication costs of the system, user, and the whole mintettes are $4q + 4i - 4$, $q + 2i - 1$ and $3q + 2i - 3$ respectively, equal to $8k + 4i$, $2k + 2i$ and $6k + 2i$. In the worst case, the user may try $k + 1$ times to submit its transaction. The user sends and receives $4k + 2$ messages and all mintettes send and receive $8k + 2$ transactions in total. Therefore, the communication volume of the system is $12k + 4$ messages per transaction. Above all, assuming that k is too large, the average of the communication volume of the system is

$$\sum_{i=1}^{k+1} Pr\left(i\right) \cdot \left(8k + 4i\right) < \frac{16\left(k+1\right)^2}{2k+1}. \tag{2}$$

The average of the communication volume of the user is

$$\sum_{i=1}^{k+1} Pr\left(i\right) \cdot \left(2k + 2i\right) < \frac{4\left(k+1\right)\left(k+2\right)}{2k+1}. \tag{3}$$

The average of the communication volume of the mintettes is

$$\sum_{i=1}^{k+1} Pr\left(i\right) \cdot \left(6k + 2i\right) < \frac{4\left(k+1\right)\left(3k+2\right)}{2k+1}. \tag{4}$$

Table 1 illustrates the comparison between RSCoin and UFCBCoin in terms of the communication volume for one transaction. When k is quite large, in general, the whole communication volume of our scheme is nearly equal to the RSCoin. The amount of the transactions a user handles for one transaction in our scheme is nearly half of that in RSCoin. The amount of the transactions the mintettes handle for one transaction in our scheme is nearly one and half of that in RSCoin.

Table 1. Comparison of communication cost between RSCoin and UFCBCoin in general

k	User		Mintettes		Total	
	RSCoin	UFCBCoin	RSCoin	UFCBCoin	RSCoin	UFCBCoin
0	2	2	2	2	4	4
1	6	4.67	6	8.67	12	13.33
2	10	7	10	15	20	22
3	14	9.2	14	21.2	28	30.4
4	18	11.33	18	27.33	36	38.67
5	22	13.43	22	33.43	44	46.86
6	26	15.5	26	39.5	52	55

However in practice, the amount of mintettes in a system is limited. The number of mitettes in one shard affects the system communication cost. Table 2 illustrates the comparison of communication volume between RSCoin and our scheme in the average case when k is from 1 to 13. Observing that when k gradually increases, the total communication volumes of two systems are almost the same, while the communication volume of user in our scheme is approximately half of RSCoin. Our scheme is superior to RSCoin in the view of users with a not-too-large shard.

6   Evaluation Mechanism and Improvements

Our scheme is inspired by the RSCoin. However, the form of shards places restrictions on the security of the system. When the number of shards increases, the system achieves security hardly when less than half of total mintettes is malicious. In this section, we propose a new evaluation to guarantee the mintettes' behaviours. We also offer some aspects that can be improved on the basis of UFCBCoin.

6.1   Evaluation Mechanism

Without adding new data structures, the evaluation mechanism can be implemented directly in our scheme. In fact, a valid signature for a transaction is the proof of the honest behaviour of the mintette. In the end of a period, every mintette submits its lower-block to the central bank, together with the set of signatures of the transactions included in the new lower-block. The valid signatures can be used to evaluated the mintette's behaviour by the central bank.

In the confirmation phase, upon receiving a transaction and a set of signatures of it, the mintette (no matter it is the representative or not) judges whether the number of valid signatures is over a half firstly. If the transaction it refers is valid, it invokes the evaluation mechanism. Every mintette has a degree in other mintettes lower-blocks with its valid signatures as witness. $degree_{n,j}(pk_{m,i})$ denotes the amount of valid signatures that mintette $m_{n,j}$ received from the mintette whose public key is $pk_{m,i}$. In the end of a period, every mintette submits all $degree_{n,j}(pk_{m,i})$ to the central bank. As the central bank receives all lower-blocks and degrees, it counts the legal transactions and all degrees. Because the degree is decided by all others, the central bank counts the degree for the validation phase as follows.

$$degree'(pk_{m,i}) = \frac{\sum_{n \in [x] \setminus \{m\}} \sum_{j \in [q]} degree_{n,j}(pk_{m,i})}{x \cdot q}. \tag{5}$$

But $degree'$ is calculated from the valid signatures from the validation phase. For the confirmation phase, ones degree is rated by the central bank based on the amount of final legal transactions that its submits, denoted by $degree''(pk_{m,i})$. Therefore, the actual degree that the mintette gets is

$$degree(pk_{m,i}) = degree'(pk_{m,i}) + degree''(pk_{m,i}). \tag{6}$$

At the start of next period, the central bank rearranges the mintettes and punishes the mintettes whose degrees are too low. By this way, the risk of malicious behavior of adversaries is increased.

6.2   Improvements

Representative Selection. In the basis of UFCBCoin, the users select the representatives randomly in different phases, by $\mathsf{H}(tx_{prev})$ and $\mathsf{H}(tx)$. After the introduction of the evaluation mechanism, the user can select the representative in corresponding shard according to the degree the mintette gained. It is reasonable that the mintette with higher degree is likely to be honest. In this way, the mintette with the highest degree is the only representative of this shard in the current period. We can consider it as the leader during this period. Assume that the majority of each shard is honest. If there is a valid transaction which can not be confirmed finally, the related representative must be punished by the central bank.

We can also adopt the proof-of-stake mechanism to select the representative. At the start of the period, every mintette can compute a hash function with its degree as the input to verify that the output is in a certain range or not. When the mintette solves the proof-of-stake problem, it broadcasts its public key with the proof of solving the proof-of-stake problem. If no one in a shard can pass the proof of stake mechanism, the central bank will modify the proof-of-stake problem and the corresponding mintettes will try again.

Incentivizing Mechanism. The miners are incentivized by the transaction fee and the mining rewards in Bitcoin. But the limited total number of Bitcoin and the transaction fee cause the problems of stability and fairness. In UFCBCoin, the central bank can not only punish the adversaries, but also can incentivize the honest. There are two kinds of incentives. For the short-term honesty, the central bank can increase the honest mintettes' degrees by the evaluation mechanism. In the case of representative selection by solving proof-of-stake problem, these mintettes have higher probabilities to be chosen. For the long-term honesty, the central bank can reward some money to the honest, which the money comes from the adversaries by punishing their malicious behaviours.

7   Conclusion

In this paper, based on RSCoin, we present a user-friendly centrally banked cryptocurrency scheme firstly considers the communication costs from the view of users. We utilize a representative mechanism to assist the users to communicate with the mintettes the central bank has authorized. We also demonstrate the security of our scheme and give a complete theoretical analysis of the scalability and efficiency. By the representative mechanism we proposed, we decrease communication costs of the users to the half of RSCoin. We finally propose a new evaluation mechanism to enhance the security of our scheme.

Acknowledgement. The authors would like to thank anonymous reviewers for their helpful comments and suggestions. This work is supported by the National Key R&D Program of China (2017YFB0802502) and the National Natural Science Foundation of China (No.61379140 and No. 61502480).

Appendix

In this appendix, we provide the main algorithms of UFCBCoin. Algorithm 1 is run by a user to submit and validate a transaction, including the representative selection. Algorithm 2 is run by the mintettes to validate or confirm a transaction. Algorithm 3 is used to check the transaction has been spent or not.

Algorithm 1. Submitting and validating a transaction run by user A

Input: A transaction $tx\,(tx_{prev}, addr_A, addr_B, v, \sigma_A)$ that user A created before; TIMEOUT is the maximum time for each phase, and t and t' are timers. owners (tx) is used to find the shard of mintettes who are charge of tx.

1: $bundle \leftarrow \phi$;
2: $M \leftarrow$ owners (tx_{prev});
3: $m_i \in_R M$;
4: Send tx to m_i;
5: **On receiving a signature σ on tx from M;**
6: **if** $(tx_{prev} \mapsto (pk_m, \sigma)) \notin bundle$ AND $t <$ TIMEOUT **then**
　　　$bundle \leftarrow bundle \cup \{tx_{prev}x \mapsto (pk_m, \sigma)\}$;
7: **end if**
8: $M' \leftarrow$ owners (tx);
9: $m'_j \in_R M'$;
10: Send $(tx, bundle)$ to m'_j;
11: **On receiving a signature σ' on tx from M';**
12: **if** $(tx_{prev}x \mapsto (pk_{m'}, \sigma')) \notin bundle'$ AND $t' <$ TIMEOUT **then**
　　　$bundle' \leftarrow bundle' \cup \{tx \mapsto (pk_{m'}, \sigma')\}$;
13: **end if**
14: **if** $|bundle'| \geq \frac{q}{2}$ **then**
　　　return True;
15: **else**
　　　return False;
16: **end if**

Algorithm 2. CheckNotSpend, run by a mintette

Input: A transaction $tx\,(tx_{prev}, addr_A, addr_B, v, \sigma_A)$ and a mintette identifier m;
1: **if** $m \notin$ owners (tx_{prev}) **then**
　　return $\perp$;
2: **else**
3:　　**if** $tx \in \mathsf{L}_{m,utxo}$ OR $(tx_{prev} \mapsto tx) \in \mathsf{L}_{m,stxo}$ **then**
　　　　$\mathsf{L}_{m,utxo} \leftarrow \mathsf{L}_{m,utxo} \setminus \{tx_{prev}\}$;
　　　　$\mathsf{L}_{m,stxo} \leftarrow \mathsf{L}_{m,stxo} \cup \{(tx_{prev} \mapsto tx)\}$;
　　　　return $(pk_m, \mathsf{Sig.Sign}\,(pk_m, tx))$;
4:　　**else**
　　　　return $\perp$;
5:　　**end if**
6: **end if**

Algorithm 3. Validating and confirming a transaction run by a mintette m

---

1: **On receiving a transaction** $tx\left(tx_{prev}, addr_A, addr_B, v, \sigma_A\right)$ **from user A;**
2: $M \leftarrow$ owners (tx_{prev});
3: **if** $m \in M$ **then**
    $(pk_m, \sigma_m) \leftarrow$ CheckNotDoubleSpend (tx_{prev}, m);
4: **end if**
5: Send (pk_m, σ_m) to user A;
6: Send $tx\left(tx_{prev}, addr_A, addr_B, v, \sigma_A\right)$ to all others $m' \in M$;
7: **On receiving a transaction** $tx\left(tx_{prev}, addr_A, addr_B, v, \sigma_A\right)$ **from a mintette;**
8: $M \leftarrow owners\left(tx_{prev}\right)$;
9: $count = 0$;
10: **if** $m \in M$ **then**
    $(pk_m, \sigma_m) \leftarrow$ CheckNotDoubleSpend (tx_{prev}, m);
11: **end if**
12: Send $tx\left(tx_{prev}, addr_A, addr_B, v, \sigma_A\right)$ to all others in M;
13: **On receiving** $(tx, bundle)$ **from user A;**
14: $M' \leftarrow$ owners (tx);
15: **if** $m \in M'$ **then**
16:     **for all** $(pk, \sigma) \in bundle$ **do**
17:         $b \leftarrow$ Sig.Verify (pk, tx, σ);
18:         $count = count + b$;
19:     **end for**
20: **end if**
21: **if** $count > \frac{q}{2}$ **then**
    $\mathsf{L}_{utxo} \leftarrow \mathsf{L}_{utxo} \cup \{tx\}$;
    $\mathsf{L}_{tx} \leftarrow \mathsf{L}_{tx} \cup \{tx\}$;
    Send $(pk_m, \text{Sig.Sign}\,(pk_m, tx))$ to user A;
    Send $tx\left(tx_{prev}, addr_A, addr_B, v, \sigma_A\right)$ to all others in M';
22: **else**
    Send $\bot$ to user A;
    Send $tx\left(tx_{prev}, addr_A, addr_B, v, \sigma_A\right)$ to all others in M';
23: **end if**
24: **On receiving** $(tx, bundle)$ **from a mintette;**
25: $M' \leftarrow owners\,(tx)$;
26: $count' = 0$;
27: **if** $m \in M'$ **then**
28:     **for all** $(pk, \sigma) \in bundle$ **do**
29:         $b \leftarrow$ Sig.Verify (pk, tx, σ);
30:         $count' = count' + b$;
31:     **end for**
32: **end if**
33: **if** $count' > \frac{q}{2}$ **then**
    $\mathsf{L}_{utxo} \leftarrow \mathsf{L}_{utxo} \cup \{tx\}$;
    $\mathsf{L}_{tx} \leftarrow \mathsf{L}_{tx} \cup \{tx\}$;
    Send $(pk_m, \text{Sig.Sign}\,(pk_m, tx))$ to user A;
34: **else**
    Send $\bot$ to user A;
35: **end if**

References

1. Nakamoto, S.: Bitcoin: A Peer-to-Peer Electronic Cash System (2008). bitcoin.org/bitcoin.pdf
2. Bitcoin Block Explorer (2016). https://blockchain.info/
3. Wikipedia. Economics of Bitcoin (2016). https://en.wikipedia.org/wiki/Economics_of_bitcoin
4. Barber, S., Boyen, X., Shi, E., Uzun, E.: Bitter to Better — How to Make Bitcoin a Better Currency. In: Keromytis, A.D. (ed.) FC 2012. LNCS, vol. 7397, pp. 399–414. Springer, Heidelberg (2012). https://doi.org/10.1007/978-3-642-32946-3_29
5. Bonneau, J., Mille, A., Clark, J., Narayanan, A., Kroll, J.A., Felten, E.W.: SoK: research perspectives and challenges for Bitcoin and cryptocurrencies. In: S&P, pp. 104–121 (2015)
6. Visa: Visas transactions per second (2016). https://usa.visa.com/content_library/modal/benefits-accepting-visa.html
7. Karame, G., Androulaki, E., Capkun, S.: Double-spending fast payments in Bitcoin. In: CCS, pp. 906–917 (2012)
8. Carlsten, M., Kalodner, H.A., Weinberg, S.M., Narayanan, A.: On the instability of Bitcoin without the block reward. In: CCS, pp. 154–167 (2016)
9. Haferkorn, M., Quintana Diaz, J.M.: Seasonality and interconnectivity within cryptocurrencies - an analysis on the basis of Bitcoin, Litecoin and Namecoin. In: Lugmayr, A. (ed.) FinanceCom 2014. LNBIP, vol. 217, pp. 106–120. Springer, Cham (2015). https://doi.org/10.1007/978-3-319-28151-3_8
10. Danezis, G., Meiklejohn, S.: Centrally banked cryptocurrencies. In: NDSS (2015)
11. Brühl, V.: Bitcoins, blockchain and distributed ledgers. In: Wirtschaftsdienst, pp. 135–142 (2017)
12. King, S., Nadal, S.: PPcoin: Peer-to-Peer Crypto-Currency with Proof-of-Stake (2012). http://peerco.in/assets/paper/peercoin-paper.pdf
13. Ateniese, G., Bonacina, I., Faonio, A., Galesi, N.: Proofs of space: When space is of the essence. In: Abdalla, M., De Prisco, R. (eds.) SCN 2014. LNCS, vol. 8642, pp. 538–557. Springer, Cham (2014). https://doi.org/10.1007/978-3-319-10879-7_31
14. Gilad, Y., Hemo, R., Micali, S., Vlachos, G., Zeldovich, N.: Algorand: scaling Byzantine agreements for cryptocurrencies (2017). https://eprint.iacr.org/2017/454.pdf
15. Eyal, I., Efe Gencer, A., Sirer, E.G., Renesse, R.V.: Bitcoin-NG: a scalable blockchain protocol. In: NSDI, pp. 45–59 (2016)
16. Kogias, E.K., Jovanovic, P., Khoffi, N.G.I., Gasser, L., Ford, B.: Enhancing Bitcoin security and performance with strong consistency via collective signing. In: USENIX Security Symposium, pp. 279–296 (2016)
17. Luu, L., Narayanan, V., Zheng, C., Baweja, K., Gilbert, S., Saxena, P.: A secure sharding protocol for open blockchains. In: CCS, pp. 17–30 (2016)

Contract Coin: Toward Practical Contract Signing on Blockchain

Haibo Tian[✉], Jiejie He, and Liqing Fu

Guangdong Key Laboratory of Information Security,
School of Data and Computer Science, Sun Yat-Sen University,
Guangzhou 510275, Guangdong, People's Republic of China
tianhb@mail.sysu.edu.cn

Abstract. We envision a scenario where contract signers put their portable document format (PDF) contract into a blockchain application that outputs a signed contract, while blockchain nodes don't know the contract content, contract signers' identities and contract signatures. Comparing to current centralized online contract signing services, blockchain applications could avoid single point of failure, internal attacks and data loss. More importantly, the application also provides fairness and privacy properties. By fairness, we mean that contract signers obtain a signed contract simultaneously, or obtain nothing, or some signer obtains a singed contract at the cost of paying contract coins. By privacy, we mean that contract contents, signatures, and signers' identities are hidden from blockchain nodes. At last, we support RSA signatures whose verification is embedded in most PDF readers, which makes the whole solution practical.

Keywords: Contract signing · Fairness · Privacy · Blockchain · Practice

1 Introduction

Blockchain is roughly a growable list of linked data blocks distributed in many dynamic nodes. A list of linked data blocks are nothing to amazing since researchers found the similarities of the blockchain data structure to a basic data structure linked list and to a basic hash function structure Merkle-Damgard construction. However, a blockchain could grow longer and the data in the longest chain are consistent with a high probability among many dynamic nodes. This requires a practical consensus mechanism, which could be viewed as the soul of a blockchain. Bitcoin provides the proof of work as a practical consensus mechanism. With a good incentive for minters, Bitcoin blockchain records almost consistent Bitcoin transactions among globally dynamic nodes for about eight years.

Bitcoin is a witness of the possible success of blockchain techniques. Many alternative coins appeared after Bitcoin. From the website "coinmarketcap", we could find more than 1000 kinds of coins. The top one is certainly Bitcoin. The second is Ethereum, which redefines part of the consistent data in a

© Springer International Publishing AG 2017
J. K. Liu and P. Samarati (Eds.): ISPEC 2017, LNCS 10701, pp. 43–61, 2017.
https://doi.org/10.1007/978-3-319-72359-4_3

blockchain as Turing machine states and supports a Turing complete scripts. Programs on the Turing machine are called as smart contracts, which are executed consistently in many nodes. The third is Ripple, which is designed as a basic coin for a global financial balancing network. Ripple has get supported by more than 20 banks. Generally, some alternative coins are designed with new features for general usage, some are designed for special application scenarios.

Following the approach, we propose a contract coin for business companies to sign commercial contract easily. We observe that the conditions for electronic contracts are mature:

- Digital signatures are widely accepted as Law evidences. From the wiki item "electronic signatures and law", we could find worldwide legislation status concerning the effect and validity of electronic signatures. Here the electronic signatures include cryptographic digital signatures. United States, European Union, China, Japan etc. have legislations about electronic signatures.
- Certificate Authorities (CAs) are widely available. Although there is no a globally trusted CA, there are many national or regional CAs. These CAs could provide certificates for commercial companies in the same nation or region to sign contracts.
- Portable document format (PDF) file is widely used. PDF is a file format used to present documents in a manner independent of application software, hardware, and operating systems. Especially, PDF/A is an ISO-standardized version of the PDF specialized for use in the archiving and long-term preservation of electronic documents. This makes PDF a practical choice for contract signing.

However, practical online services to produce a signed contract are not well developed.

- Trustable online contract signing services (CSSs) are rare. An online CSS should grantee the fairness in a contract signing process. That is, if party A sends a signed contract to party B, a CSS should make sure that party A could receive party B's signed contract back within an expected time period. The best practice is to employ an offline trustable third party (TTP) to solve possible disputes. However, why should contract signers trust a CSS to be fair? Employees in a CSS may be corrupted to help one party of contract signers to get return.
- Proposed online CSS solutions usually consider no privacy. Blockchain based CSSs could solve the internal attack problem and could be trustable. However, data on a blockchain are typically open to all. If we don't consider the privacy property, everybody could know the identities of signers and contract signatures. Note that, as a commercial contract, the identities in a contract could make people think a lot about their collaboration and affects their stock prices. And the contract signatures may be used to guess some valuable information about a contract since most commercial contracts are uniform. A valid signature may help an attacker to guess some sensitive information about the contract. The attacker also has a chance to rebuild a valid signed contract with the contract signatures.

Currently, Liu et al. [26] proposed a fair exchange smart contract to help an offline TTP to be stateless without privacy. Wan et al. [39] proposed distributed timestamp servers as witnesses and storage servers of contracts without privacy. Tian et al. [22] gave a blockchain CSS with privacy. However, they only support a pairing based signature [43] that is not default in PDF [2].

Our contract coin system fills the gap to give a practical blockchain CSS. Basically, we propose a new RSA blinded verifiable encrypted signature (RSA-BVES) scheme to exchange RSA signatures on blockchain. Since RSA signatures are supported by PDF/A specification, the exchanged signature could really be filled into a PDF contract file to form a signed contract. The contract signing procedure needs the underlying blockchain system to support a signature verification algorithm **RSA-BVESVer** in the RSA-BVES scheme which makes it different to Bitcoin.

We notice the hard fork of Bitcoin to BTC and BCC recently, and believe that it is difficult to incorporate our special script opcode into the Bitcoin system. And the transaction fee of the Bitcoin system is a little high. Ethereum platform could support our system theoretically. However, Ethereum platform does not support some cryptographic operations. If these operations are embedded in a smart contract, the smart contract will be fat and will cost a lot of gas similar to that in [33]. Additionally, as the cost of supporting more script commands, smart contracts may exist subtle program flaws and need to be checked carefully [30]. These considerations make us finally choose to propose a new coin specially for our application. We believe our application serves as a positive application of cryptographic currencies since we only use them as deposits to sign PDF contracts used in our real life, which is against the cases in [27].

1.1 Related Works

Contract Signing. At present, there are many proposals on contract signing. According to their degree of dependence on a TTP, we give a very brief classification survey.

The first category includes no TTP protocols. Blum [12] gave a protocol to exchange RSA secret factors based on Rabin encryption scheme. Contract signers first claim "A contract is valid if and only if the signer knows the RSA secret factors related to the RSA modules in the contract". The signers then fairly exchange their RSA secret factors to produce a contract. Even [16], Goldreich [21], Okamoto and Ohta [32], Stini and Mauve [37] also gave similar protocols.

The second category includes protocols with online TTPs. Deng et al. [14] proposed a fair authenticated email protocol in which a TTP transmits each email and the corresponding email receipt. Franklin et al. [17] also employed a TTP to ensure the fairness of each transaction. Alawi et al. [3] required a TTP to record every contract to be signed.

The final category needs an offline TTP. Ben-Or et al. [10] introduced the method of using an offline TTP to solve a premature stop problem. The problem is that if one party stops a protocol too early, the other party has to wait indefinitely. A TTP could act as an arbiter, allow the party who has to wait indefinitely to apply for arbitration. Asokan et al. [6] used a TTP to recover encrypted signatures when disputes occur between signers. Garay et al. [18], Ateniese [7], Wang [40] also used TTPs in a similar way. Huang et al. [24] employed a TTP to produce a ring signature when there is a dispute.

Blockchain. Dwork and Naor [15] proposed a method for dealing with spam, which required an email sender to compute some moderately expensive function of the message. This work is taken as an early-stage example of the "proof-of-work" consensus mechanism. Back [1], Vishnumurthy [38] developed the mechanism in different fields. Nakamoto [31] proposed to use the mechanism in a pure cash system, resulting in the Bitcoin system. Since then, there have been many alternative coins similar to the Bitcoin system, including Litecoin, Primecoin [35], Namecoin [29] and so on. Wood [41] gave a yellow paper to describe the basic mechanism of the Ethereum. As an innovative platform, the Ethereum enables developers to quickly design a new coin system. The blockchain is a common underlying technique of all these digital currencies and the Ethereum.

Protocols on the Blockchain. Barber et al. [8] gave a fair exchange protocol to construct a bitcoin transaction mixer. Andrychowicz et al. [4] gave a simultaneous timed commitment protocol that could be used to construct a two party fair computation protocol. Kiayias et al. [28] introduced a general fair multiparty secure computation protocol. Zhao [44] presented a secret ballot protocol based on the blockchain. While there are many other blockchain protocols, we focus on possible contract signing protocols below.

Wan [39] proposed a fair contract signing protocol that could be implemented on blockchain. In their paper, contract signers Alice and Bob first negotiate a contract signing deadline, and then claim in the contract that the contract is valid only if both parties sign the contract before the deadline. Next Alice signs the contract with the deadline, and sends the signature to Bob. And then Bob signs the contract with the deadline and Alice's signature, and sends everything about the contract to their timestamp servers (Blockchain nodes). Finally, the timestamp server verifies their signatures, checks the deadline, and generates a timestamp on their contract. The fairness property is a little weak since within the deadline, Bob get Alice's signed contract while Alice gets nothing. The timestamp servers know the signers' identities and everything of their contract.

Liu et al. [26] proposed a smart contract to build a stateless TTP of a fair exchange protocol. Basically, Alice sends Bob a verifiable encrypted item and its expectation of Bob's item. Bob responds its verifiable encrypted item to Alice. Alice then sends the plain item to Bob and Bob sends back its plain item to Alice. If Bob does not respond to Alice after Alice's first message, Alice may invoke an "abort" function in their smart contract. If Alice does not sends its plain item, Bob could ask a TTP to resolve. The TTP decrypts Alice's encrypted item, returns it to Bob, and invokes an "resolve" function in their smart contract to record Bob's plain item in the blockchain, where Alice could get Bob's plain item from a possible later "abort" invocation. The fairness of the proposal is the same as that of [6]. It is better if there is no TTP involved at all.

Tian et al. [22] proposed a privacy preserving fair contract signing protocol on blockchain. In their proposal, Alice and Bob produce a joint commitment Bitcoin transaction where the output script includes a new script opcode *BV* to verify a bilinear equation. Then Alice and Bob produce an open transaction including their BVES signatures to finish their protocol. They first coin the name of BVES and give a bilinear based BVES scheme. We here propose a RSA-BVES scheme which could be used in PDF files directly.

1.2 Contributions

We propose a contract coin system based on which contract signers could produce signed PDF contracts:

- Contract coin: We introduce two time functions used as output script opcodes, which could exactly specify what operation is expected in which time period. We also define a verification opcode to execute the **RSA-BVESVer** algorithm, which is used to verify RSA-BVES signatures. Except these modifications and some parameters, we currently do not need to modify other aspects of the Bitcoin system.
- RSA-BVES scheme: Basically, we turn the RSA version of verifiable encrypted signature (VES) in [7] into a RSA-BVES scheme. Roughly, in the RSA version of VES, there is a signer, a verifier and a TTP. In a RSA-BVES scheme, the signer keeps unchanged, the verifier acts as a blockchain node, and the TTP is a normal signature extractor. We add some steps for the extractor and signer to get an agreement about the signing contents, public keys and a freshly shared secret. The secret is used to hide messages to be signed.
- Fair PDF based contract signing (FPCS) protocol: It is roughly an application of the RSA-BVES scheme on the blockchain. A small exception is that we use a temporal key pair to sign a contract. Contract signers hold a chain of certificates so that they know whether a temporal key is the expected one. However, blockchain nodes could only get a temporal public key and have no chance to link that key pair to an identity. So the signers' identities are hidden from the blockchain nodes. Only the contract signers could link a transaction on the blockchain to a real signed PDF file, which could be viewed as a tamper resistant evidence of the contract signing process when necessary.

1.3 Organizations

The next section describes some concepts and symbols of Bitcoin system. Section 3 is the RSA-BVES scheme and proofs. Section 4 is the contract coin and the FPCS protocol with security and performance analysis. The last section concludes the paper.

2   Bitcoin

The Bitcoin system contains a chain of blocks. A block contains a header and some Bitcoin transactions. Each transaction has an identity which is the hash value of the entire transaction. All identities of the transactions in a block form the leaves of a Merkle tree. The root of the Merkle tree is in a field in the block header. So the transactions are bound together with a block header. Another field in the block header is the hash value of the previous block header. This field makes the blocks a chain. New blocks are generated under the proof of work consensus mechanism. Minters compute hash values of header candidates to generate and broadcast a new block. When most minters verify and accept the new block, it is added to the chain, and the transactions in the new block are confirmed once.

2.1   Basic Assumptions of Bitcoin System

There are some common assumptions about the Bitcoin system [5, 28].

1. Assume that the parties are connected by an insecure channel.
2. Assume that each party can access the current contents of the Bitcoin blockchain.
3. Assume that each party can post transactions on the Bitcoin blockchain within a maximum delay max_D.
4. The confirmed transactions on the blockchain are tamper resistant.

The assumptions 2 and 3 state that each party could connect to the Bitcoin blockchain. These assumptions are not true if the observations of Heilman et al. [23] and Gervais et al. [20] could not be fixed. Their attacks could lead to double spending, which breaks the baseline of any electronic cash system. We believe the Bitcoin system will take advices in [19, 20, 23, 25] to defend against such attacks. So as long as the Bitcoin system is usable, the assumptions 2 and 3 hold.

2.2   Bitcoin Transactions

A Bitcoin transaction has some inputs and outputs. We follow the work in [5] to express a transaction in a box. In Fig. 1, we give two transactions T^A and T^B. The producer of the transactions is expressed as A and B. They are actually two public keys. If an input of T^B contains the $TxID$ of T^A and an output index of T^A, the input of T^B should be connected to the output of T^A. The connection is represented as a line with an arrow in Fig. 1. T^B is usually called as the redeeming transaction of T^A.

The input of T^B contains the input script (is) that matches the output script (os) of T^A. Roughly, the input script of T^B contains a signature Sig_B and the public key B. The signature message of T^B contains the output script of T^A and all of the contents of T^B except the input script. This signature message is denoted by $[T^B]$. Sometimes, one need to express the content of a transaction excluding its input script, which is called as a simplified transaction [44]. It is not equivalent to the signature message of a transaction that includes some information of its connected transaction. The output script of T^A contains a hash value of the public key B and a signature verification opcode. To connect the T^B to T^A, minters match the hash value in the output script of T^A to the hash value of the public key in the input script of T^B, and verify the signature in the input script of T^B. The connection requirement of T^A is denoted by $os(body, \delta_B)$. That is, the output script requires a signature message and a signature to form verification conditions. Here the verification condition is mainly to verify a signature, which is denoted by $ver_B(body, \delta_B)$. An output of a transaction also includes a value representing Bitcoins. The symbol C and δ_C in Fig. 1 denote the public key of any user C and their signature.

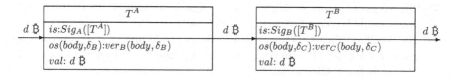

Fig. 1. Two connected transactions.

The Bitcoin system includes many other aspects such as chain forking, mining, networking and so on. These contents are not closely related to the contract signing protocol and are omitted here.

3 The RSA-BVES Scheme

Tian et al. [22] coined the name BVES since the verifiers in a BVES scheme knows nothing about the message to be signed. Their scheme relies on a special bilinear signature scheme [42, 43]. We here give the RSA version.

3.1 Construction

We design a RSA-BVES scheme based on the full domain hash (FDH) RSA [9] scheme and a VES scheme in [7]. A RSA-BVES scheme consists of three players, a signer Alice, a signature extractor Bob, and a verifier Minter. With the help of the Minter, Bob gets a signature from Alice on a message m known by Alice and Bob. The scheme consists seven algorithms. Three of them are the **KeyGen, Sign,** and **Verify** algorithms which rewrites the FDH RSA scheme [9]. A **PreSignAgree** algorithm builds a special label l for the message to be signed for Alice and Bob. The signature corresponding to the label l is produced by the **RSA-BVESSign** algorithm. Minter executes the **RSA-BVESVer** algorithm to verify the signature for the label. Bob uses the **Ext** to extract a normal signature from Alice.

- **KeyGen:** On input 1^k, it picks a pair of random distinct $(k/2)$-bit safe primes and multiplies them to produce a modulus N. It also picks, at random, an encryption exponent $e \in \mathbb{Z}^*_{\phi(N)}$ and computes the corresponding decryption exponent d so that $ed = 1 \bmod \phi(N)$. The public verifying key is (N, e) and the private signing key is (N, d). There is a full domain hash function $H : \{0,1\}^* \to \mathbb{Z}^*_N$.

- **Sign:** On inputs a message m and the signing key (N, d), it computes a signature

$$\delta = H(m)^d \bmod N.$$

- **Verify:** On inputs a message signature pair (m, δ) and the verifying key (N, e), it checks whether

$$\delta^e = H(m) \bmod N.$$

- **PreSignAgree:** Suppose Alice wants to sign a message m for Bob.
  1. Alice sends her certificate of (N, e) to Bob.
  2. Bob verifies Alice's certificate and selects randomly $g_1 \in \mathbb{Z}^*_N$ and a k-bit integer $x_B \in \{0,1\}^k$. He computes $g = g_1^2 \bmod N$ and $y_B = g^{x_B} \bmod N$. He sends back Alice g, y_B.
  3. Alice selects randomly a k-bit integer $x_A \in \{0,1\}^k$ and an integer $r \in \{0,1\}^k$. She computes $s = y_B^{x_A} \bmod N$, $y_A = g^{x_A} \bmod N$, $y_r = g^r \bmod N$ and $m_b = s^e H(m) \bmod N$. Alice sets $l = (N, e, g, y_B, y_A, y_r, m_b)$ and sends (y_A, y_r, m_b) to Bob.
  4. Bob computes $s' = y_A^{x_B} \bmod N$, and verifies whether $m_b = s'^e H(m) \bmod N$. If all validations are good, Bob sets $l' = (N, e, g, y_B, y_A, y_r, m_b)$.

- **RSA-BVESSign:** On inputs l, d and r, Alice randomly selects $t \in \{0,1\}^k$, computes $\delta_b = m_b^{2d} y_B^r \bmod N$, $y_e = y_B^e \bmod N$, $y_{er} = y_e^r \bmod N$, $y_t = g^t \bmod N$, $y_{et} = y_e^t \bmod N$, $c = H(m_b, y_{er}, y_r, y_e, g, y_{et}, y_t)$, and $z = t - rc$. She sets $\delta_B = (\delta_b, c, z)$ as the RSA-BVES signature.

- **RSA-BVESVer:** On inputs l' and δ_B, Minter computes $w_{er} = \delta_b^e m_b^{-2} \bmod N$, $y_e' = y_B^e \bmod N$, $w_{et} = y_e'^z w_{er}^c \bmod N$, and computes $c' = H(m_b, w_{er}, y_r, y_e', g, w_{et}, w_t)$. If $c = c'$, Minter returns true.

- **Ext:** On inputs δ_b, y_r, s' and x_B, Bob computes $\delta_{squ} = \delta_b (y_r^{x_B})^{-1} s'^{-2} \bmod N$, and gets a normal signature $H(m)^d$ from δ_{squ} by the Euclidean algorithm. That is, suppose $2\alpha + e\beta = 1$, then $H(m)^d = \delta_{squ}^\alpha H(m)^\beta \bmod N$ where α and β are two integers.

3.2   Security Model

The security model is based on the VES security model in [13] where an adversary has a signing oracle. In the unforgeability game, we remove an arbitration oracle that provides normal signatures. The reason is that our adversary in the unforgeability game may be Bob. That is, our adversary could extract normal signatures by itself with private keys.

Unforgeability. The unforgeability property is defined in a game played by a simulator and an adversary. The adversary has to forge a selected message. The unforgeability game is defined as follows:

- **Init:** The simulator gives the adversary a public key as a signature verification key. The adversary selects a message m^* as the target, and selects a key pair to extract a normal signature from a RSA-BVES signature. The simulator interacts with the adversary to produce a label l^*.
- **SignQueries:** The adversary adaptively requests at most q_s messages $\{m_1, \ldots, m_{q_s}\}$. The simulator responds to the ith query with a valid RSA-BVES signature and a label (l_i, δ_{Bi}) where $i \in \{1, \ldots, q_s\}$.
- **Output:** The adversary should output a valid RSA-BVES signature δ_B^* to the label l^*, and wins the game.

The advantage of the adversary is directly defined as the probability that the adversary wins the game. A RSA-BVES scheme is unforgeable if the adversary's advantage is negligible.

Opacity. The opacity property is defined in a game played by a challenger and an attacker. The attacker has to extract a normal signature from a RSA-BVES signature after it is fully trained.

The opacity game is defined as follows:

- **Init:** The challenger gives the attacker a public key as a signature verification key.
- **SignQueries:** The adversary adaptively requests at most q_s messages $\{m_1, \ldots, m_{q_s}\}$. The simulator responds to the i-th query with a valid RSA-BVES signature δ_{Bi} with a label l_i where $i \in \{1, \ldots, q_s\}$.
- **ExtQueries:** The adversary adaptively requests at most q_b RSA-BVES signatures and labels $\{(\delta_{B1}, l_1), \ldots, (\delta_{Bq_b}, l_{q_b})\}$. The simulator responds to the i-th query with a normal signature δ_i where $i \in \{1, \ldots, q_b\}$.
- **Output:** To win the game, the adversary should output a valid normal signature δ^* for a RSA-BVES signature (l^*, δ_B^*) that has never been requested.

The advantage of the adversary is directly defined as the probability that the adversary wins. A RSA-BVES scheme has the opacity property if the adversary's advantage is negligible.

3.3 Unforgeability Proof

Claim. If the FDH RSA scheme [9] is unforgeable under the chosen message attack, the RSA-BVES scheme is unforgeable according to the unforgeability definition.

Proof. Suppose a simulator Sim. The simulator tries to break the FDH RSA that is known secure under the chosen message attack. The strategy of Sim is to run a RSA-BVES adversary Adv against the unforgeability property. Sim and Adv play as follows:

- Sim takes as input a public key (N, e) of a FDH RSA scheme. Sim then sends (N, e) to Adv as a **PreSignAgree** message.
- Adv receives (N, e), computes (g, y_B) as Bob, and replies Sim (g, y_B) as another **PreSignAgree** message.
- Adv selects a message as m^* and sends it to Sim.
- Sim computes (y_A^*, y_r^*, m_b^*) as Alice in the step 3 of the **PreSignAgree** algorithm and sets $l^* = (N, e, g, y_B, y_A^*, y_r^*, m_b^*)$. Sim returns l^* to Adv.
- Adv then asks Sim to sign messages $m_i \neq m^*$, $1 \leq i \leq q_s$.
- For each signing request m_i, Sim computes (s, y_A, y_r, m_b) as Alice in the step 3 of the **PreSignAgree** algorithm. Sim takes m_i as a chosen message, asks the FDH RSA to produce a signature $\delta_i = H(m)^d \bmod N$. Sim then computes $\delta_{squ} = \delta_i^2 \bmod N$, $\delta_b = s^2 \delta_{squ} y_B^r$. Sim then computes (c, z) as the **RSA-BVESSign** algorithm. Finally, Sim sets $l_i = (N, e, g, y_B, y_A, y_r, m_b)$ and $\delta_{B_i} = (\delta_b, c, z)$, and returns (l_i, δ_{B_i}) to Adv.
- When the adversary produces a forged RSA-BVES signature δ_B^* matching to the label l^*, Sim verifies the RSA-BVES by the **RSA-BVESVer** algorithm. If it is a valid RSA-BVES signature, Sim computes $(\delta^*)^2 = \delta_b^*(y_B^r)^{-1}(s^*)^{-2} \bmod N$ and get δ^* by the Euclidean algorithm.

The simulation is sound since Sim feeds Adv with qualified RSA-BVES signatures. So Adv is expected to produce a valid δ_B^* corresponding to l^*. Sim could extract δ^* from δ_B^* as an output of the chosen message attack game. The advantage of Sim is the same as that of Adv except a negligible probability. Since the FDH RSA is secure under the chosen message attack, the RSA-BVES scheme is also secure according to the unforgeability definition here.

3.4   Opacity

Claim. If an ElGamal encryption scheme under a decisional generalized Diffie-Hellman assumption [11, 36] is sematic secure, the RSA-BVES scheme has the opacity property.

Proof. Suppose a challenger Cha. The challenger tries to break the sematic security of an ElGamal encryption scheme with public parameters (N, g, y_B). The strategy of Cha is to run a RSA-BVES scheme attacker Tac against the opacity property. Cha and Tac play as follows.

- Cha selects e to form a public key (N, e) and sends it to Tac as a **PreSignAgree** message.
- Tac then asks Cha to sign messages m_i, $1 \leq i \leq q_s$.
- Cha has no private signing key. So Cha maintains a random oracle $\mathcal{H}$ to set $\delta_i^e \bmod N = H(m_i)$ for a randomly selected δ_i. Cha randomly selects $i^* \in q_s$. If $i \neq i^*$, Cha computes $(s_i, g_i, y_{Bi}, y_{Ai}, y_{ri}, m_{bi})$ as Alice and Bob in the **PreSignAgree** algorithm. It computes $\delta_{bi} = s_i^2 \delta_i^2 y_{Bi}^{r_i}$, and computes (c_i, z_i) as the **RSA-BVESSign** algorithm. Next, Cha sets $l_i = (N, e, g_i, y_{Bi}, y_{Ai}, y_{ri}, m_{bi})$ and $\delta_{B_i} = (\delta_{bi}, c_i, z_i)$, and returns (l_i, δ_{B_i})

to Tac. If $i = i^*$, Cha sets g, y_B as public parameters of the ElGamal encryption scheme. Cha computes y_{Ai^*} and s_{i^*} as the **RSA-BVESSign** algorithm. It then computes $m_0 = s_{i^*}^2 \delta_{i^*}^2$, randomly selects $m_1 \in QR(N)$. Cha then asks the ElGamal encryption scheme (m_0, m_1) to obtain an encryption of $m_b \in \{m_0, m_1\}$ as $(\delta_{bi^*}, y_{ri^*})$. Without r_{i^*}, Tac randomly selects $c^* \in \mathbb{Z}_N^*$ and $z^* \in \{0,1\}^{2k}$, and sets c^* as the random oracle output of a query $(m_{bi^*}, w_{eri^*}, y_{ri^*}, y'_{ei^*}, w_{eti^*}, w_{ti^*})$ where the computations are according to the **RSA-BVESVer** algorithm. Tac then sets l_{i^*} and δ_{Bi^*}, and sends Tac (l_{i^*}, δ_{Bi^*}).

- Tac could ask Cha to extract a normal signature from (l_j, δ_{B_j}), $1 \leq j \leq q_b$.
- For each extraction queries, Cha simply computes $H(m)$ from m_{bj} in l_j and returns the selected δ_j to Tac.
- When Tac produces a normal signature δ_{j^*}, Tac wins if $(l_{j^*}, \delta_{B_j^*})$ has not been extracted.

The simulation of Cha is not perfect since δ_{bi^*} may be not qualified. Suppose Tac has a probability ϵ_1 to distinguish the bad simulation and stops when Tac feels the simulation is wrong. Then Cha could guess $b = 1$ to win the sematic security game of the ElGamal encryption scheme. However, if Tac could not distinguish a bad simulation, it should always produce a qualified output with an advantage ϵ_2. If $j^* = i^*$, Cha could judge m_b and win the sematic security game. The probability of $j^* = i^*$ is $1/q_s$ since Tac knows nothing about i^*.

So if Tac could extract a normal signature from public labels and RSA-BVES signatures with an advantage ϵ_2 or could distinguish a bad simulation with an advantage ϵ_1, Cha could wins the sematic security game of the ElGamal encryption scheme with an advantage $\epsilon_1 + (1 - \epsilon_1)\epsilon_2/q_s$. The ElGamal encryption under a decisional generalized Diffie-Hellman assumption [11,36] could be proven sematic secure similar to a standard ElGamal encryption scheme under a standard decisional Diffie-Hellman assumption. So the advantage of Tac should be negligible.

4 Contract Coin and FPCS Protocol

4.1 Contract Coin

We add some new script opcodes to the Bitcoin system. We coin the name contract coin and use the symbol Ȼ to denote contract coins.

- $BF(t)$ opcode: It specifies a time period. The beginning time point is the height or time when the transaction is recorded. The ending time is the beginning time plus t blocks or seconds. If the current time is in the time period, the $BF(t)$ function returns true. Otherwise, the $BF(t)$ function returns false.
- $AT(t)$ opcode: It is similar to the BIP 65 proposal of Bitcoin [34]. It specifies a time point after which the function returns true. The beginning time point of $AT(t)$ is just the ending time of $BF(t)$.

- $BV(l, \delta)$ opcode: We redefine the BV opcode in [22]. It is now parameterized as a label l and a signature δ. It runs the **RSA-BVESVer** algorithm and returns the result of the algorithm.
- Parameter modifications: The contract coin system modifies the block size, block producing time and so on of Bitcoin system for a well accommodation of contract signing applications.

All these modifications make our system different to Bitcoin. The value of the contract coin could be determined by the market. As it has value, it could be used as deposit in the following contract signing protocol.

4.2   FPCS Protocol

Suppose two contract signers party A and party B. Party A and party B should find a common CA as their identity trust root. Party A has a pair of long term key (pk_A, sk_A) and pk_A is in a certificate $Cert_A$ issued by the common CA. Party B similarly has a key pair (pk_B, sk_B) and pk_B is in a certificate $Cert_B$. Now Party A and Party B want to sign a PDF contract file C. The contract has an agreed value about $d\ ¢$.

The goals of the protocol are as follows:

- If party A and party B exchange the contract's signatures, no one will lose contract coins.
- If party A and party B do not exchange anything, no one will lose contract coins.
- If only one party obtains a signature on the contract, the party should lose $d\ ¢$.
- Minters could not infer the contract to be signed and the identities of contract signers.

The details of the protocol are as follows. Figure 2 shows all the transactions in the protocol.

- **BeforeBlockChain Phase:**
  1. Party A produces a temporal RSA key pair (N_A, e_A, d_A). Party A then uses sk_A to sign the temporal public key (N_A, e_A) to produce a temporal certificate TC_A. Now Party A sends $Cert_A$ and TC_A to party B.
  2. On receiving $Cert_A$ and TC_A, party B verifies that the $Cert_A$ is trustable, and the signature in TC_A is valid. If the verifications are passed, party B produces a temporal certificate TC_B including a temporal public key (N_B, e_B) similar to party A. And party B produces (g_A, y_{AB}) as specified in the step 2 of the **PreSignAgree**, and sends $Cert_B, TC_B, (g_A, y_{AB})$ to party A.
  3. On receiving $Cert_B, TC_B, (g_A, y_{AB})$, party A verifies $Cert_B$ and TC_B similar to party B. If the verifications are passed, party A produces (g_B, y_{BA}) as specified in the step 2 of the **PreSignAgree**. And then party A

computes s_A, y_{AA}, y_{Ar} and m_{Ab} as specified in the step 3 of the **PreSignAgree**. Then, party A sends (g_B, y_{BA}), y_{AA}, y_{Ar}, m_b to party B. Party A sets $l_A = (N_A, e_A, g_A, y_{AB}, y_{AA}, y_{Ar})$.

4. On receiving (g_B, y_{BA}), y_{AA}, y_{Ar} and m_b, party B verifies m_{Ab} as specified in the step 4 of the **PreSignAgree**. If the verification passed, party B sets $l'_A = (N_A, e_A, g_A, y_{AB}, y_{AA}, y_{Ar})$. Party B then computes s_B, y_{BB}, y_{Br}, m_{Bb} as specified in the step 3 of the **PreSignAgree**. Then party B sends y_{BB}, y_{Br}, m_{Bb} to party A. Party B sets $l_B = (N_B, e_B, g_B, y_{BA}, y_{BB}, y_{Br})$.

5. On receiving y_{BB}, y_{Br}, m_{Bb}, party A verifies m_{Bb} as specified in the step 4 of the **PreSignAgree**. If the verification passed, party A sets

$$l'_B = (N_B, e_B, g_B, y_{BA}, y_{BB}, y_{Br}).$$

- **BlockChain Phase:**
  1. **Joint Commit Transaction:** Party A finds an unspent transaction T^A with d Ȼ. Party A sends the $TxID$ of T^A to party B. Party B finds an unspent transaction T^B with the same d Ȼ. And party B sends the $TxID$ of T^B to party A. Now Party A could produce a partially joint commit transaction $Commit$ as follows:
  (a) The input script includes the signature of Party A.
  (b) Party A specifies two outputs:
     - The first output script requires $body$, δ_A, δ_B and δ_{AB} as inputs. The boolean condition requires that either within time t there is a valid signature δ_A from party A and the $BV(l_A, \delta_{AB})$ algorithm returns true, or beyond time t, there is a valid signature δ_B from party B. The first output has a value d Ȼ.
     - The second output script similarly requires $body$, δ_A, δ_B and δ_{BB} as inputs. The boolean condition requires that either within time t there is a valid signature δ_B from party B and the $BV(l'_B, \delta_{BB})$ algorithm returns true, or beyond time t, there is a valid signature δ_A from party A. The second output has the same d Ȼ value.
  Party A then sends the partially joint commit transaction to Party B. Party B checks the two outputs. It checks the output values and output scripts. Note that Party B has l'_A and l_B, knows transaction identities of T^A and T^B. Party B checks that the signature of Party A could possibly redeem T^A. If all checks passed, party B adds its own signature to the input scripts field. And Party B broadcasts the joint commit transaction $Commit$ to the contract blockchain.
  2. **Open Transaction:** If the $Commit$ transaction appears on the blockchain on time, party A produces a RSA-BVES signature δ_{AB} as specified by the **RSA-BVESSign** algorithm. Party A produces a transaction $Open^A$ as follows:

(a) The input script includes the signature of Party A and the RSA-BVES signature δ_{AB}.
(b) Party A specifies an output with d Ȼ. The output script only requires *body* and a signature from party A. The boolean condition requires that the signature from party A should be valid.

Party A then broadcasts its $Open^A$ transaction.

Similarly, after party B finds that the *Commit* transaction appears on the contract blockchain on time, party B produces a RSA-BVES signature δ_{BB} as specified by the **RSA-BVESSign** algorithm. And then party B produces and broadcasts a $Open^B$ transaction as party A.

Contract signers may stop the contract signing procedure if the expected *Commit* transaction does not appear after an expected time period. To do so, one party may simply redeem their deposit and stops. For example, party A waits for half an hour, but the *Commit* transaction does not appear. Party A then redeem T^A and quits the contract signing procedure.

3. **Claim Transaction:** If the $Open^A$ transaction appears on the contract blockchain on time and the $Open^B$ transaction does not appear even when the $AF(t)$ function returns $True$, party A produces a $Claim^A$ transaction as follows:
   (a) The input script includes the signature of Party A.
   (b) Party A specifies an output with d Ȼ. The output script only requires *body* and a signature from party A. The boolean condition requires that the signature from party A should be valid.

   Party A then broadcasts the transaction to get the deposit of party B.
   Similarly, party B could get the deposit of party A if the $Open^A$ transaction does not appear on the contract blockchain on time.

- **AfterBlockChain Phase:**
  1. If the $Open^B$ transaction appears on the contract blockchain on time, party A could extract a RSA signature from (l_B, δ_{BB}) in the scripts of *Commit* and $Open^B$ transactions. Party A runs the **Ext** algorithm with inputs δ_{Bb} in δ_{BB}, y_{Br} in l_B, s'_B and x_{BA} of y_{BA}. It is expected to produce a valid RSA signature with respect to (N_B, e_B).
     Similarly, party B could produce a normal RSA signature with respect to (N_A, e_A).
  2. Party A now could put the RSA signature with respect to (N_B, e_B), and the temporal certificate TC_B, and the certificate $Cert_B$ as a whole evidence list of Bob's signature on the contract $\mathcal{C}$. Party A puts these evidences into the PDF format contract to form a signed contract of party B.
     Similarly, party B could produce a signed contract of party A.

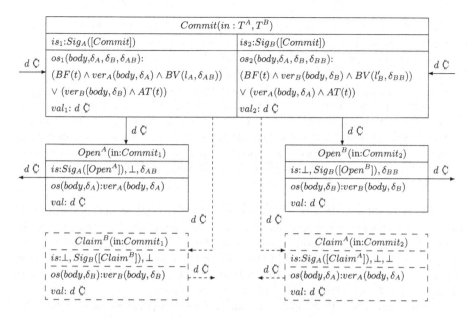

Fig. 2. A fair PDF contract signing (FPCS) protocol

4.3 Security Analysis

Claim. The FPCS protocol is fair for party A and party B, and keeps contract signatures and signers' identities private to blockchain nodes.

Proof. Party A and party B in the "before blockchain" phase establish common labels. Party A has l_A and l'_B. Party B has l'_A and l_B. According to the steps in the "before blockchain" phase, $l_A = l'_A$ and $l'_B = l_B$.

Then at the "blockchain phase", party A produces a partial *Commit* transaction. The output script in the *Commit* transaction specifies t, l_A and l'_B. Party B could verify that l_A and l'_B are the same as l'_A and l_B. Party B could also check the time parameter t for a quality evaluation. That is, t is not too big or small. If party B satisfies the three parameters, party B checks the signature of party A and the linkage to T^A. If all verifications pass, party B believes that party A provides a good transaction. Party B should sign the transaction and broadcast it out. If party B stops too long time, party A could redeem T^A to falsify the partial *Commit* transaction. There is no premature stop problem here. If party B signs and broadcasts the *Commit* transaction, party A and party B redeem their T^A and T^B simultaneously. And the time counter for this transaction begins.

Note that we assume party A and party B could access blockchain contents. After the *Commit* transaction is included in a block, party A and party B have the following choices:

- Within time t, party A and party B produce their $Open^A$ and $Open^B$ transactions, and these transactions are included in a block. This is the expected case.

Party A and party B could extract normal signatures from the $Open^B$ and $Open^A$ transactions, and could get their deposit back.

- Within time t, party A and party B broadcast nothing. After time t, party A gets the deposit of party B and party B gets the deposit of party A. Since the deposit of both parties are the same, no one losses contract coins.
- Within time t, one party, say B, broadcasts its $Open^B$ transaction. Then after time t, party A has no chance to get the deposit back, and party B could get the deposit of party A as a compensation. So party A get a signed contract of party B at the cost of losing the deposit. Note that we require that the deposit should have a similar value as the contract to be signed. So the compensation should satisfy party B.

Minters could get RSA-BVES signatures (l_A, δ_{AB}), (l'_B, δ_{BB}). According to the opacity property, no minters could extract a normal signature from them. So the contract signature is hidden. The public keys (N_A, e_A) in l_A and (N_B, e_B) in l'_B are temporal keys selected in the "before blockchain" phase. Except party A and party B, no one knows the linkage of these keys to contract signers' identities. So the contract signers' identities are hidden.

In summary, the FPCS protocol could achieve the design goals of fairness and privacy.

Remark 1. A small detail is about the communication channel of party A and B in the "before blockchain" phase. Since certificates are transmitted in that phase, if the communication channel is not secure, an attacker may link temporal keys on the blockchain to real signers' identities. So we suggest a secure channel for party A and party B.

4.4   Performance Analysis

We use the symbol t_{comm} to denote the time to transmit a message, the symbol t_{me} to denote the modular exponentiation time. We assume one modular exponentiation to sign a temporal certificate. Suppose party A and party B begins the FPCS protocol at time t_0. Then the "before blockchain" phase mainly needs two rounds of communication time $4t_{comm}$ and eighteen modular exponentiations $18t_{me}$. At time about $t_0 + 4t_{comm} + 18t_{me}$, party A begins the blockchain phase. Party A signs the partial *Commit* transaction and sends it to party B. So at the time about $t_0 + 5t_{comm} + 19t_{me}$, party B receives the partial *Commit* transaction. Party A signs it and broadcasts it to the blockchain nodes at the time about $t_0 + 5t_{comm} + 20t_{me}$. Since we suppose the maximal delay of a transaction is max_D. At the time $t_1 \le t_0 + 5t_{comm} + 20t_{me} + max_D$, the *Commit* transaction should appear on the blockchain. Then before the time $t_1 + t - max_D$, party A and party B should broadcast their $Open^A$ and $Open^B$ transactions. Before the time $t_1 + t$, $Open^A$ and $Open^B$ should appear on the blockchain. Roughly, before the time $t_1 + t + 3t_{me}$, party A and party B could get a signed contract. In summary, the maximal contract signing time is $5t_{comm} + 20t_{me} + max_D + t$ where $t > max_D$.

The communication cost of party A is three times unicast and one time broadcast. Party B needs two times unicast and two times broadcast. The computation cost of party A or party B is mainly about 19 modular exponentiations.

5 Conclusion

We give new script functions and name the modified Bitcoin system as contract coins. On the contract coin system, we build a fair PDF based contract signing protocol that could hide contract signatures and signers' identities. The core of the contract signing protocol is a RSA-BVES scheme that could transmit a RSA signature in a verifiable encryption fashion without the leakage of the message to be signed. Next, we shall adjust parameters to evaluate the overhead and network latency in a real contract coin system.

Acknowledgment. This work is supported by the National Key R&D Program of China (2017YFB0802503), Natural Science Foundation of China (61672550), Natural Science Foundation of Guangdong Province, China (2015A030313133), and Fundamental Research Funds for the Central Universities (No. 17lgjc45). We are grateful to the fruitful discussion with Prof. Qianhong Wu about contract signers' anonymity.

References

1. Adam, B.: Hashcash - amortizable publicly auditable cost-functions. http://www.hashcash.org/papers/amortizable.pdf. Accessed 4 Aug 2017
2. Adobe: Digital signatures in a PDF. http://120.198.244.57:9999/www.adobe.com/devnet-docs/acrobatetk/tools/DigSig/Acrobat_DigitalSignatures_in_PDF.pdf. Accessed 4 Aug 2017
3. Al-Saggaf, A.A., Ghouti, L.: Efficient abuse-free fair contract-signing protocol based on an ordinary crisp commitment scheme. IET Inf. Secur. **9**(1), 50–58 (2015)
4. Andrychowicz, M., Dziembowski, S., Malinowski, D., Mazurek, L.: Fair Two-party computations via bitcoin deposits. In: Böhme, R., Brenner, M., Moore, T., Smith, M. (eds.) FC 2014. LNCS, vol. 8438, pp. 105–121. Springer, Heidelberg (2014). https://doi.org/10.1007/978-3-662-44774-1_8
5. Andrychowicz, M., Dziembowski, S., Malinowski, D., Mazurek, L.: Secure multi-party computations on bitcoin. In: 2014 IEEE Symposium on Security and Privacy, pp. 443–458, May 2014
6. Asokan, N., Shoup, V., Waidner, M.: Optimistic fair exchange of digital signatures. IEEE J. Sel. Areas Commun. **18**(4), 593–610 (2000)
7. Ateniese, G.: Verifiable encryption of digital signatures and applications. ACM Trans. Inf. Syst. Secur. **7**(1), 1–20 (2004)
8. Barber, S., Boyen, X., Shi, E., Uzun, E.: Bitter to better — how to make bitcoin a better currency. In: Keromytis, A.D. (ed.) FC 2012. LNCS, vol. 7397, pp. 399–414. Springer, Heidelberg (2012). https://doi.org/10.1007/978-3-642-32946-3_29
9. Bellare, M., Rogaway, P.: The exact security of digital signatures-how to sign with RSA and Rabin. In: Maurer, U. (ed.) EUROCRYPT 1996. LNCS, vol. 1070, pp. 399–416. Springer, Heidelberg (1996). https://doi.org/10.1007/3-540-68339-9_34
10. Ben-Or, M., Goldreich, O., Micali, S., Rivest, R.L.: A fair protocol for signing contracts. IEEE Trans. Inf. Theor. **36**(1), 40–46 (1990)

11. Biham, E., Boneh, D., Reingold, O.: Breaking generalized Diffie-Hellman modulo a composite is no easier than factoring. Inf. Process. Lett. **70**(2), 83–87 (1999)
12. Blum, M.: How to exchange (secret) keys. In: Proceedings of the Fifteenth Annual ACM Symposium on Theory of Computing, pp. 440–447. ACM (1983)
13. Boneh, D., Gentry, C., Lynn, B., Shacham, H.: Aggregate and verifiably encrypted signatures from bilinear maps. In: Biham, E. (ed.) EUROCRYPT 2003. LNCS, vol. 2656, pp. 416–432. Springer, Heidelberg (2003). https://doi.org/10.1007/3-540-39200-9_26
14. Deng, R.H., Gong, L., Lazar, A.A., Wang, W.: Practical protocols for certified electronic mail. J. Netw. Syst. Manag. **4**(3), 279–297 (1996)
15. Dwork, C., Naor, M.: Pricing via processing or combatting junk mail. In: Brickell, E.F. (ed.) CRYPTO 1992. LNCS, vol. 740, pp. 139–147. Springer, Heidelberg (1993). https://doi.org/10.1007/3-540-48071-4_10
16. Even, S.: A protocol for signing contracts. SIGACT News **15**(1), 34–39 (1983)
17. Franklin, M.K., Reiter, M.K.: Fair exchange with a semi-trusted third party (extended abstract). In: Proceedings of the 4th ACM Conference on Computer and Communications Security, pp. 1–5. ACM (1997)
18. Garay, J.A., Jakobsson, M., MacKenzie, P.: Abuse-free optimistic contract signing. In: Wiener, M. (ed.) CRYPTO 1999. LNCS, vol. 1666, pp. 449–466. Springer, Heidelberg (1999). https://doi.org/10.1007/3-540-48405-1_29
19. Germanus, D., Ismail, H., Suri, N.: PASS: an address space slicing framework for P2P eclipse attack mitigation. In: 2015 IEEE 34th Symposium on Reliable Distributed Systems (SRDS), pp. 74–83, September 2015
20. Gervais, A., Ritzdorf, H., Karame, G.O., Capkun, S.: Tampering with the delivery of blocks and transactions in bitcoin. In: Proceedings of the 2015 ACM SIGSAC Conference on Computer and Communications Security (CCS 2015), pp. 692–705. ACM (2015)
21. Goldreich, O.: A simple protocol for signing contracts. In: Chaum, D. (ed.) Advances in Cryptology, pp. 133–136. Springer, Boston (1984). https://doi.org/10.1007/978-1-4684-4730-9_11
22. Haibo, T., Jiejie, H., Liqing, F.: A privacy preserving fair contract signing protocol based on block chains. J. Cryptol. Res. **4**(2), 187–198 (2017)
23. Heilman, E., Kendler, A., Zohar, A., Goldberg, S.: Eclipse attacks on bitcoin's peer-to-peer network. In: Proceedings of the 24th USENIX Conference on Security Symposium (SEC 2015), pp. 129–144. USENIX Association, Berkeley (2015)
24. Huang, Q., Yang, G., Wong, D.S., Susilo, W.: Efficient optimistic fair exchange secure in the multi-user setting and chosen-key model without random oracles. In: Malkin, T. (ed.) CT-RSA 2008. LNCS, vol. 4964, pp. 106–120. Springer, Heidelberg (2008). https://doi.org/10.1007/978-3-540-79263-5_7
25. Ismail, H., Germanus, D., Suri, N.: Detecting and mitigating P2P eclipse attacks. In: 2015 IEEE 21st International Conference on Parallel and Distributed Systems (ICPADS), pp. 224–231, December 2015
26. Jian, L., Wenting, L., Karame, G.O., Asokan, N.: Towards fairness of cryptocurrency payments (2016)
27. Juels, A., Kosba, A., Shi, E.: The Ring of Gyges: investigating the future of criminal smart contracts. In: Proceedings of the 2016 ACM SIGSAC Conference on Computer and Communications Security, CCS 2016, pp. 283–295. ACM, New York (2016)

28. Kiayias, A., Zhou, H.-S., Zikas, V.: Fair and Robust multi-party computation using a global transaction ledger. In: Fischlin, M., Coron, J.-S. (eds.) EUROCRYPT 2016. LNCS, vol. 9666, pp. 705–734. Springer, Heidelberg (2016). https://doi.org/10.1007/978-3-662-49896-5_25
29. Loibl, A.: Namecoin (2014)
30. Luu, L., Chu, D.-H., Olickel, H., Saxena, P., Hobor, A.: Making smart contracts smarter. In: Proceedings of the 2016 ACM SIGSAC Conference on Computer and Communications Security, CCS 2016, pp. 254–269. ACM, New York (2016)
31. Nakamoto, S.: Bitcoin: a peer-to-peer electronic cash system (2008)
32. Okamoto, T., Ohta, K.: How to simultaneously exchange secrets by general assumptions. In: Proceedings of the 2nd ACM Conference on Computer and Communications Security, pp. 184–192. ACM (1994)
33. McCorry, S.S.P., Hao, F.: A smart contract for boardroom voting with maximum voter privacy. In: Financial Cryptography and Data Security 2017, pp. 1–18 (2017)
34. Peter, T.: Op_checklocktimeverify. https://github.com/bitcoin/bips/blob/master/bip-0065.mediawiki. Accessed 4 Apr 2017
35. Sprankel, S.: Technical basis of digital currencies (2013)
36. Steiner, M., Tsudik, G., Waidner, M.: Diffie-Hellman key distribution extended to group communication. In: Proceedings of the 3rd ACM Conference on Computer and Communications Security, CCS 1996, pp. 31–37. ACM, New York (1996)
37. Stini, M., Mauve, M.: Enabling fair offline trading. In: Proceedings of the 2009 International Conference on Wireless Communications and Mobile Computing: Connecting the World Wirelessly, pp. 973–978. ACM (2009)
38. Vishnumurthy, V., Chandrakumar, S., Ch, S., Sirer, E.G.: KARMA: A secure economic framework for peer-to-peer resource sharing (2003)
39. Wan, Z., Deng, R.H., Lee, D.: Electronic contract signing without using trusted third party. In: Qiu, M., Xu, S., Yung, M., Zhang, H. (eds.) Network and System Security. LNCS, vol. 9408, pp. 386–394. Springer, Cham (2015). https://doi.org/10.1007/978-3-319-25645-0_27
40. Wang, G.: An abuse-free fair contract-signing protocol based on the RSA signature. IEEE Trans. Inf. Forensics Secur. 5(1), 158–168 (2010)
41. Wood, D.G.: Ethereum: a secure decentralised g generalised transaction ledger homestead (2014)
42. Zhang, F., Safavi-Naini, R., Susilo, W.: Efficient verifiably encrypted signature and partially blind signature from bilinear pairings. In: Johansson, T., Maitra, S. (eds.) INDOCRYPT 2003. LNCS, vol. 2904, pp. 191–204. Springer, Heidelberg (2003). https://doi.org/10.1007/978-3-540-24582-7_14
43. Zhang, F., Safavi-Naini, R., Susilo, W.: An efficient signature scheme from bilinear pairings and its applications. In: Bao, F., Deng, R., Zhou, J. (eds.) PKC 2004. LNCS, vol. 2947, pp. 277–290. Springer, Heidelberg (2004). https://doi.org/10.1007/978-3-540-24632-9_20
44. Zhao, Z., Chan, T.-H.H.: How to vote privately using bitcoin. In: Qing, S., Okamoto, E., Kim, K., Liu, D. (eds.) ICICS 2015. LNCS, vol. 9543, pp. 82–96. Springer, Cham (2016). https://doi.org/10.1007/978-3-319-29814-6_8

TTP-free Fair Exchange of Digital Signatures with Bitcoin

Wentao Zhang[1,2], Qianhong Wu[1(✉)], Bo Qin[3,4], Tianxu Han[1],
Yanting Zhang[1], Xiaofeng Chen[5], and Na Li[1]

[1] School of Electronics and Information Engineering,
Beihang University, Beijing, China
yifan.zhang0601@gmail.com, {qianhong.wu,wsttx,yantingzhang}@buaa.edu.cn
[2] State Key Laboratory of Cryptology, P. O. Box 5159, Beijing 100878, China
[3] Key Laboratory of Data Engineering and Knowledge Engineering,
Ministry of Education, School of Information, Renmin University of China,
Beijing, China
bo.qin@ruc.edu.cn
[4] State Key Laboratory of Information Security, Institute of Information
Engineering, Chinese Academy of Sciences, Beijing 100093, China
[5] State Key Laboratory of Integrated Service Networks,
Xidian University, Xi'an 710071, China
xfchen@xidian.edu.cn

Abstract. Based on the decentralized Bitcoin network, this paper proposes a novel TTP-free fair exchange scheme with monetary penalization for exchange of digital signatures, and presents its corresponding construction with ECDSA-based signature scheme deployed in the Bitcoin. The scheme has following features: (1) *Fairness*, meaning that the honest party will be compensated with predefined deposit if the other party misbehaves in the *execution phase* of exchange; (2) *TTP-freeness*, meaning that the scheme does notengage any TTP throughout the execution of the scheme; (3) *Asynchronism*, meaning that digital signatures of two parties do not need to be released simultaneously; (4) *Pseudonymity*, meaning that there is no intuitive difference between transactions designed in the scheme and ordinary ones, and Bitcoin users may own pseudonyms through one-time address. Of independent interest, we propose a new primitive called committed key generation that converts committed message into public/private key paring, specifically, an ECDSA key pair used in the Bitcoin in our construction, with non-interactive zero-knowledge proof. This tool allows us to bind a committed file with a transaction in Bitcoin. With this approach, the proposed TTP-free scheme can be applied to a wide range of scenarios, as long as the signatures represent some items of value such as contract and electronic check.

Keywords: TTP-free · Fair exchange · Digital signatures · Bitcoin
Asynchronism · Pseudonym

© Springer International Publishing AG 2017
J. K. Liu and P. Samarati (Eds.): ISPEC 2017, LNCS 10701, pp. 62–81, 2017.
https://doi.org/10.1007/978-3-319-72359-4_4

1 Introduction

As the basis of E-commerce, fair exchange over Internet has increasingly important significance in the modern society. Broadly speaking, two potentially distrusted parties, say Alice ($\mathcal{A}$ for short) and Bob ($\mathcal{B}$ for short) want to exchange digital items in a fair manner, which means that by the very end of the exchange, either each participant gets prospective item, or neither participant does. Digital items here could be regarded as its owner's signature in most cases, thus, it's of great significance to focus on the fair exchange of digital signatures on the Internet.

The gradual release protocol was the first paradigm proposed to resolve fair exchange problems, which only needs two parties to be engaged in. Even et al. [17] raised the corresponding protocol of contract signing in 1985. Afterwards, Okamoto [23] put forward specific exchange protocol. In the exchange each party releases the its secret bit by bit, meaning that either party has a slight advantage of one bit over the other in every round. Besides, it also takes many information interactions between parties. After that, online TTP (third trusted party) was first involved to propose a new purchase protocol by Cox et al. [13], improving fairness to some extent. And Gollman et al. [28] raised relative non-repudiation scheme in 1996. However, the TTP has to stay online during the whole exchange process, or even simply relaying the message to parties, which makes it of great difficulty to keep transmission channel reliable. Based on this consideration, Bao et al. [5] and Asokan et al. [4] put forward a more efficient fair exchange protocol with offline TTP, which includes the TTP to guarantee fairness only in the event of disputes. Without participation of TTP in most cases, it decreases the cost of time and money in some way. In 2004, Chen et al. [12] gave a contract signing protocol without TTP, namely concurrent signature, to solve fair exchange of signature in the random oracle model. It has gradually become a new hotspot due to no participation of TTP and fairness guarantee.

In summary, fair exchange problem has been studied for over three decades due to its extensive applications and inherent characteristics. However, either the gradual release protocol or fair protocol with online (or offline) TTP cannot guarantee complete fairness while circumventing the reliance on the TTP. Although Chen has proposed the concurrent signature scheme to solve the problem, it seems hard to witness its wide range of application at present.

Bitcoin is a peer-to-peer digital network proposed by Satoshi [22] at 2008. it's widely agreed that Bitcoin is the first practical decentralized digital payment system, which substitutes the trusted bank in the way that all electronic transactions are visible to any network nodes (see Miers et al. [21] for more details). Bitcoin use one-time ECDSA signature to endorse bitcoin transfer and achieve pseudonym based on elliptic curves which has shown a powerful tool in cryptography [27]. More importantly, the employment of this cryptographic scheme makes it rather secure than some traditional payment paradigms. Apart from simple transactions, it supports creating complex transactions by setting certain conditions for redemption of the output of transactions, with its original script language. Later, Barber and Boyen [6] raised some proposals in 2012 to optimize Bitcoin, making it a better e-cash payment system. Also, that Bitcoin system is energy-consuming and not environment sustainable [11], and some work has been proposed to address this problem with proof of stake (PoS) [25]. However, these proposals need more time to be recognized. Although other analogous digital currency system (e.g., Zerocash [7], Litecoin, and Dash) has been presented since then, Bitcoin is still believed to be the most well-developed, robust and widespread e-cash system.

1.1   Our Contribution

As a decentralized digital system, Bitcoin has inspired many new ideas to resolve some traditional cryptographic problems. Since Bitcoin deploys the ECDSA signature scheme[1] to keep its transactions working accurately, we focus our attention on achieving the exchange of digital signatures with Bitcoin. And, we here design a novel primitive called committed key generation denoted as $\mathcal{F}_{MK}$, with which we can convert any committed messages m into an ECDSA key pair (sk^m, pk^m) embedded in the Bitcoin transactions, thereby translating the release of digital signatures into the broadcast of corresponding transactions. By combining the primitive with Bitcoin transactions, we propose a new TTP-free fair exchange scheme with monetary penalization for digital signature exchange and demonstrate the concrete construction meanwhile.

Based on Bitcoin, the exchange can be implemented without any TTP. The construction consists of two phases: *preparation phase* and *execution phase*. In the first phase, each party computes the key pair with respect to its message content by calls of the committed key generation $\mathcal{F}_{MK}$, and pays a deposit of its digital signature via Bitcoin. Here, the deposit is some bitcoins of value higher than that of the signature itself to achieve strong misbehavior penalization. During the *execution phase*, the honest party that releases the valid digital signature by signing Bitcoin transaction timely can successfully redeem the deposit. However, the misbehaving party that does not release valid signature timely will be penalized by losing the deposit. In other words, we guarantee the fairness of the participants through the penalization mechanism that the honest party will be compensated whenever the adversary misbehaves.

By means of address pseudonym, Bitcoin provides the users with privacy to some extent. And the transactions deployed here is designed masterly, which makes two parties may release valid signature asynchronously. Through appropriate extension, the scheme can also be extended to multi-party fair exchange of digital signatures and other Bitcoin-like environments, thereby may having a wide range of application scenarios.

---

[1] The security parameter λ equals a 128-bit number viewed as discrete logarithm security level.

1.2   Related Work

To solve fair exchange problems, the gradual release protocol was first proposed in [17,23]. However, either party has a slight advantage of one bit over the other in every round of the interactions. Later protocols with TTP [4,5,13,28] involved the third party while guaranteeing fairness, giving raise to some inefficiency in other ways. Chen's work [12], namely concurrent signature also seems few applications to practical scenarios in spite of abandoning any TTP in the exchange. To the best of our knowledge, fair exchange protocol with offline TTP [4,5] is the most well-developed protocol to resolve fair exchange problems.

Besides, Jayasinghe *et al.* [18] constructed an anonymous optimistic fair exchange protocol based on Bitcoin. However, Bitcoin not only occupies some kind of trade anonymity, but provides a decentralized secure environment for interactions between the stakeholders. A scheme of secure multi-party computations on Bitcoin was introduced in 2013 by Andrychowicz *et al.* [1,2], who also put forward a fair two-party computation construction afterwards. However, the two-party computation construction was infeasible then. Concurrently, Bentov *et al.* [8] gave a functional overview of Bitcoin system to design fair protocols in 2014, including secure multi-party computing, multi-gambling, and fair exchange.

Either these work only gives a functional design to achieve fair exchange with Bitcoin, without defining concrete implementation, or relative constructions were infeasible then. Different to [1] about signature exchange, we focus on taking the ECDSA-based signature deployed in Bitcoin as the digital signature scheme, thereby constructing such a specific and practical scheme for digital signature exchange between two parties. Moreover, the committed key generation primitive $\mathcal{F}_{MK}$ we proposed here may own some potential to other contexts.

1.3   Paper Organization

The rest of the paper is organized as follows. In Sect. 2, we present some preliminaries employed in our fair exchange scheme of digital signatures. In Sect. 3, we introduce our basic scheme with system model and new tools. In Sect. 4, we then give a concrete construction about contract signing in the random oracle model. Section 5 discusses the security of the construction in terms of completeness and fairness, and analyzes the performance of the novel primitive committed key generation. In Sect. 6, we involve its possible variants, and future work. In Sect. 7, we make a conclusion about our scheme in short.

2   Preliminaries

Before introducing the system model, we briefly review some cryptographic building blocks deployed in the fair exchange scheme.

2.1   Collision-Resistant Hash Function

With regard to message m to be signed, we simplify it by viewing its digest as a random oracle. To make it more practical, we instead employ a collision-resistant one-way hash function $H : \{0,1\}^* \rightarrow \{0,1\}^L$ where L stands for the length of the digest satisfying the following properties:

1. For any $m \in \{0,1\}^*$, it's easy to compute hash value $h = H(m) \in \{0,1\}^L$;
2. Given h, it's hard to find any message m such that $h = H(m)$;
3. Given m, it's hard to find another message m' such that $H(m) = H(m')$;
4. It's hard to find two messages m, m' such that $H(m) = H(m')$.

Note that we discuss properties in the sense of polynomial time. Dang [16] has provided some secure hash functions, of which SHA-256 is deployed in the Bitcoin system.

2.2   Non-interactive Zero-Knowledge Proof

Assume that there is one player $\mathcal{A}$ who informs player $\mathcal{B}$ that he possesses some secret information s, zero-knowledge proof of knowledge is a method by which $\mathcal{A}$, say prover, can prove to $\mathcal{B}$, say verifier, that the statement $\mathcal{A}$ possesses the secret information s is true, without disclosing any information apart from the statement itself. Non-interactive zero-knowledge proof of knowledge (NIZK) is one of that which may help the prover convince the verifier with only one information tuple. We refer the reader to [10, 26]. Besides, we assume that the zero-knowledge proof system here is a special *honest verifier non-interactive zero-knowledge proof of knowledge* (HVNIZK for short), i.e. the proof system release nothing extra information to the honest verifier, but it does notown security against a cheating verifier. Cramer and Bitansky discussed these concepts in [9, 14] respectively.

Informally, given a language $\mathcal{L}$, a general NIZK system consists of a triple of polynomial algorithms (KeyGen, Prove, Verify) as follows:

- KeyGen(1^λ) $\rightarrow$ (PK, VK). Taking as input a security parameter λ, the *key generator* KeyGen probabilistically samples a *proving key* PK and a corresponding *verification key* VK. The algorithm can be run during an offline phase by the verifier or someone verifier trusts. Both keys are claimed as public parameters to prove/verify membership in $\mathcal{L}$.
- Prove(PK, x, w) $\rightarrow \pi$. Taking as input x and PK, the *prover* Prove produces a proof π for the statement $x \in \mathcal{L}$ given a witness w.
- Verify(VK, x, π) $\rightarrow b$. Taking as input x, proof π, and VK, the *verifier* Verify outputs $b = 1$ if he is convinced that $x \in \mathcal{L}$.

An NIZK system satisfies the following properties.

Completeness: For every security parameter λ, $x \in \mathcal{L}$, and $w \in R_\mathcal{L}(x)$, the prover can convince the honest verifier with overwhelming probability.

In other words, algorithm Verify outputs $b = 1$ with probability $1 - negl(\lambda)$ in the experiment:

$$(\text{PK}, \text{VK}) \rightarrow \text{KeyGen}(1^{\lambda}); \pi \rightarrow \text{Prove}(\text{PK}, x, w); b \rightarrow \text{Verify}(\text{VK}, x, \pi)$$

where $negl()$ is a polynomial-time function.

Soundness: If the prover does notknow the witness, he can only convince the honest verifier with negligible probability. Namely, for every $ploy(\lambda)$-size adversary $\mathcal{A}^{\star}$, there is a $ploy(\lambda)$-size extractor $\mathcal{E}^{\star}$ such that $\text{Verify}(\text{VK}, x, \pi) = 1$ and $w \notin R_{\mathcal{L}}(x)$ with probability $negl(\lambda)$ in the following experiment:

$$(\text{PK}, \text{VK}) \rightarrow \text{KeyGen}(1^{\lambda}); (x, \pi) \rightarrow \mathcal{A}^{\star}(\text{PK}, \text{VK}); w \rightarrow \mathcal{E}^{\star}(\text{PK}, \text{VK})$$

Zero-knowledge: The proof π gives no information apart from the validity of it. Namely, there is no computational difference between verifier convinces himself and prover convinces the verifier with the same x, π. We refer readers to [7] for more details.

2.3 Bitcoin Transaction

We assume the reader is familiar with the basic knowledge of Bitcoin. Here, we review some details related to our scheme about the Bitcoin transaction. In Bitcoin system, a transaction tx is a transfer of bitcoins, which can include multiple inputs and outputs. More precisely, the inputs of tx are specified by a list $[(h_1, \alpha_1, \sigma_1), \ldots, (h_m, \alpha_m, \sigma_m)]$, where each h_i stands for the hash of some previous transaction tx_{h_i}, α_i is the index of some output in transaction tx_{h_i}, and σ_i called *ScriptSig* is the input script satisfying the *ScriptPubKey* of the α_i-th output in transaction tx_{h_i}. The outputs of tx are presented as a list $[(\mu_1, w_1), \ldots, (\mu_n, w_n)]$, where each μ_j reveals the exact value of the j-th output and w_j defines the condition for how the j-th output of tx can be redeemed. Both the *ScriptSig* and *ScriptPubKey* are described using a non-Turing-complete stack-based script language, which can be used to set the conditions for redemption of corresponding transaction. Besides, any difference between the values of the inputs and that of the outputs is considered to be a transaction fee for the miners who includes it into a Bitcoin block with PoW [22] first.

Unlike other currency system, transactions in Bitcoin are not encrypted, thereby visible to the whole Bitcoin network. It keeps anonymity of the traders by means of one-to-many mapping between the identity and addresses, which is usually the hash of the corresponding public key pk.

2.4 Basic Propositions

RSA Problem. The RSA problem is stated as follows [15]. Given a randomly generated RSA modulus N of unknown factorization, a ciphertext C, a random $e \in Z_N^{\star}$, find $m \in Z_N^{\star}$ such that $c = m^e \mod N$. Note that here N is a large semiprime (i.e., $N = p \cdot q$ for two large prime numbers p, q).

Proposition 1 (RSA Assumption). *The RSA problem is intractable in polynomial time so long as $(e, \varphi(N)) = 1$ holds.*

ECDL Problem. The Elliptic Curve Discrete Logarithm Problem (ECDLP) states as follows [19]. Given an elliptic curve E defined over a finite field $\mathbb{F}_p$, a point $P \in E(\mathbb{F}_p)$ and a point $Q = lP$ where $0 \leq l \leq n - 1$, determine the parameter l.

Proposition 2 (ECDSA Assumption). *The ECDLP is intractable in polynomial time.*

3   System Model and New Tools

Assume that there are two parties, named $\mathcal{A}$ and $\mathcal{B}$, who do nottrust each other, and yet agree on the value of each other's digital signature of some messages (e.g. the context of some contracts). The fair exchange problem is that either party wants obtains the other's digital signature while revealing his, however, neither party wants to reveal his signature first with the risk of the other disappearing after learning his signature.

3.1   The Exchange Model

Based on the decentralized Bitcoin system, we employ the Bitcoin transactions to realize the fair exchange of digital signature without any TTP. And by the digital signature here, we mean the ECDSA-based signature deployed in Bitcoin. The keys used to generate and verify the digital signature are generated based on the secp256k1 elliptic curve E_{BT}.

The digital signature is presented as a triple of algorithms (Sig = K_{sig}, S_{sig}, V_{sig}). For lack of space we do notgive more details, which is described in [19]. For simplicity, we denote $sig^m = S_{sig}(m, sk)$ as the digital signature signed on message m under corresponding private key sk. And $V_{sig}(sig^m, m, pk) \rightarrow$ true holds for any valid signatures and corresponding parameters.

We denote $\prod$ as the basic scheme for the fair exchange problem, which is also the abstract expression of the concrete construction in Sect. 4. It consists of a tuple of polynomial-time primitives denoted as $(\mathcal{F}_{MK}, \mathcal{F}_{BT})$. Functionality $\mathcal{F}_{MK}$ stands for the committed key generation, which converts the message m into a valid ECDSA key pair (sk^m, pk^m) in Bitcoin. Functionality $\mathcal{F}_{BT}$ stands for the transaction model construction, which constructs a complex exchange model with Bitcoin transactions.

Based on these two primitives, the execution of the scheme consists of two phases described as follows.

- In *preparation phase*, each party first performs offline computations with primitive $\mathcal{F}_{MK}$ in random oracle to acquire necessary parameters. After that, they transfer information through the communication channel to construct the transaction model with $\mathcal{F}_{BT}$. Here, we assume that the channel is resilient [3], meaning that a message transferred here may be delayed by an attacker with arbitrary but finite amount of time, and it will eventually be delivered.

– In *execution phase*, each party reveals his valid signature by signing and broadcasting the corresponding transaction. Here we use the security model defined in [1,2]. However, with the deployment of Segregated Witness, the non-malleability of Bitcoin transactions is solved right now. Similarly, we denote $\max_d$ as the max delay between sending a transaction and including it in a block. Besides, we simply assume that the transaction fee paid to the miners are zero and leave it to latter section to discuss.

By monetary penalization, we mean that each party has to pay some deposit (denoted as z BTC) in the *preparation phase*, and it's guaranteed that he can redeem the deposit so long as he complies with the scheme until the very end of the *execution phase*. Moreover, whoever misbehaves during the *execution phase* will lose his deposit that will be given to the other party instead. Note that the deposit evaluates more than the value of its signature, and it's not that difficult for two parties to reach agreement. More importantly, we set the time T of the *execution phase* to force players to release valid signature timely.

Behavior of Honest Party. As we stated before, each party is involved in signature generation and interaction with the other. By honest party, we mean the player who first generates signature on agreed message under valid private key, and broadcasts corresponding Bitcoin transaction with signature embedded within T time. Here, time T is set longer than the time required for a Bitcoin transaction to be confirmed $\max_d$ described below.

Behavior of Malicious Party. Analogous to the definition above, the malicious party is defined as the player who either does notbroadcast its valid signature on corresponding message in T time, or tries cheating counterpart with a signature on another message m' to obtain counterpart's valid signature.

3.2 New Tools

With the intractability assumptions stated before, we give the formal definition of the two primitives $\mathcal{F}_{\mathrm{MK}}$, $\mathcal{F}_{\mathrm{BT}}$ below.

Functionality $\mathcal{F}_{\mathrm{MK}}$ takes as inputs message m and outputs a valid ECDSA key pair (sk^m, pk^m). It's described as follows.

$$\mathcal{F}_{\mathrm{MK}}(m) \rightarrow (sk^m, pk^m)$$

The private key sk^m stay secret along the whole exchange, and the public key pk^m is used to generate a Bitcoin address to redeem the deposit. We stress that the key pair (sk^m, pk^m) generated from message is not related with the key pair (sk, pk) employed to sign and verify the signature on transaction including hash of pk^m. In later section we give the concrete construction and take advantage of HVNIZK system to prove the consistency between pk^m and message m.

Functionality $\mathcal{F}_{BT}$ takes as inputs public key pk^m, pk, deposit z BTC and other parameters necessary for Bitcoin transactions, then outputs a concrete exchange model consist of some Bitcoin transactions. It's described as follows.

$$\mathcal{F}_{BT}(pk^m, pk, z, *params) \to *tx$$

It is skillful that the primitive sets the hash value of the public key pk^m as the payment address of corresponding transaction so that the deposit is directed to the public key address. Consequently, the player can redeem the deposit so long as he provides a valid signature of the transaction and broadcast it[2]. We would like to stress that we use the BIP of Segregated Witness [20] in the construction.

3.3 Security Definition

We define the security in terms of *completeness* and *fairness*.

Completeness of the TTP-free scheme $\prod = (\mathcal{F}_{MK}, \mathcal{F}_{BT})$ requires that each party will acquire the desired valid signature and redeem his deposit by the very end of the exchange guaranteeing that each party is honest. Under the security model stated above, we formalize an *incompleteness game* called **IN-COMP** as follows. Assume that there is an adversary $\mathcal{E}$ who can delay the information transferred between two honest players $\mathcal{A}, \mathcal{B}$ by arbitrary but finite amount of time and delay the transactions broadcast by time at most max_d. When the game ends, the adversary $\mathcal{E}$ wins if he succeeds in making the honest player lose his deposit whether he releases his valid signature timely or not.

Definition 1 (Completeness). *A TTP-free fair exchange scheme $\prod$ is complete if no polynomial-time adversary $\mathcal{A}^\star$ wins in the **IN-COMP** with more than negligible probability.*

Asokan *et al.* [3] introduced the fairness property formally. In the economic sense, fairness of the TTP-free scheme with the monetary penalization $\prod = (\mathcal{F}_{MK}, \mathcal{F}_{BT})$ requires that any misbehaving player will be penalized by loss of deposit that can be redeemed by the other party. Since the deposit of z BTC is worth much more than the value of signature itself, the honest party then benefits more than the valid signature. Under the security model stated above, we formalize an *unfairness game* called **UN-FAIR** as follows. Assume that there is an adversary $A^\star$ who tries to learn the counterpart's valid signature without releasing his valid signature. When the game ends, the adversary $\mathcal{A}^\star$ wins if he succeeds in acquiring desired signature without loss of deposit while not releasing his valid signature.

Definition 2 (Fairness). *A TTP-free fair exchange scheme $\prod$ is fair if no polynomial-time adversary $\mathcal{A}^\star$ wins in the **UN-FAIR** with more than negligible probability.*

---

[2] Due to the fact that the player is aware of the private key sk^m corresponding to the public key, it obtains the ownership of the deposit again.

4   Concrete Construction

The language deployed in Bitcoin only supports the signature generation and verification of the raw transaction itself. Considering this, we design the primitive $\mathcal{F}_{MK}$ to convert the message m into a valid ECDSA key pair (sk^m, pk^m) in Bitcoin, and then construct a complex Bitcoin transaction model with $\mathcal{F}_{BT}$ for the concrete fair exchange of signatures. Note that the hash value of relevant public key pk^m is embedded into the $ScriptPubKey$ of some transaction, therefore the player's signature of the transaction is equivalent to the signature of the contract text. And each party can reveal the digital signature by broadcasting corresponding transaction in time T. The honest party who releases a valid signature in time T may successfully redeem the deposit and be compensated with counterpart's deposit whenever the other misbehaves.

4.1   A Concrete Committed Key Generation Scheme

We design the committed key generation denoted as $\mathcal{F}_{MK}$ to convert the message into a valid key pair (sk^m, pk^m) according to the secp256k1 curve E_{BT} in Bitcoin. Here, the private key sk^m is only known to the generator for redemption of the deposit, and the public key pk^m is used to generate a Bitcoin transaction containing signature in $ScriptSig$.

There maybe many possible implementations, we here only give one feasible construction. Without loss of generality, we introduce the committed key generation in $\mathcal{A}$'s perspective as follows. We denote λ as the security parameter.

Step 1. $\mathcal{A}$ randomly choose a RSA modulus N_A with $N_A = \tilde{p}_A \cdot \tilde{q}_A$ holds. Here $N_A, \tilde{p}_A, \tilde{q}_A$ are numbers satisfying the RSA assumption.

Step 2. $\mathcal{A}$ randomly samples $r_A \in \{0,1\}^\lambda$, and compute $c_A = H(m_A \| r_A)$ as the digest of message m_A.

Step 3. Let $sk_A^m = (c_A{}^{\frac{1}{3}} \mod N_A) \mod q$ where q is the order of basic point G in curve E_{BT}. If $sk_A^m \neq 0$, $\mathcal{A}$ chooses $(sk_A^m, pk_A^m) = (sk_A^m, sk_A^m \cdot G)$; otherwise $\mathcal{A}$ returns to the previous step.

With each of $\tilde{p}_A, \tilde{q}_A$ mutually prime to the other, it concludes that $\varphi(N_A) = (\tilde{p}_A - 1)(\tilde{q}_A - 1)$ holds. Here, tuple $(m_A, r_A, c_A, N_A, q, G, pk_A^m)$ is available as public parameters to $\mathcal{B}$, while $(sk_A^m, \tilde{p}_A, \tilde{q}_A)$ is only known to $\mathcal{A}$ itself.

We achieve the conversion from message m_i to public key pk_i^m with these steps for $\forall i \in \{\mathcal{A}, \mathcal{B}\}$. However, to sign on the transaction including the public key pk_i^m above instead of signing on message m_i, each party must prove that pk_i^m is indeed generated by message m_i without disclosing private key sk_i^m.

Theorem 1. *The public key pk_i^m claimed to be generated by message m_i is publicly verifiable with HVNIZK system.*

From Theorem 1, we mean that the public key of $(pk_i^m, sk_i^m) \leftarrow \mathcal{F}_{MK}(m)$ is publicly verifiable with NIZK system if the verifier is honest. Here, $pk_i^m = sk_i^m \cdot G$ holds and the NIZK proof only reveals the validity of public key. In this way, either party is accountable for its behavior in this round of interaction. For lack of space, we will give the related proof in the extended version of this paper.

4.2   Concrete Fair Exchange of Signatures

Differently from the fair two-party computation due to Andrychowicz *et al.* [1], our construction of the Bitcoin transaction model does notrely on the *Simultaneous Commitment*. Broadly speaking, the exchange process works as follows. In the *preparation phase*, each party acquire the key pair (sk_i^m, pk_i^m) by calls of $\mathcal{F}_{MK}$, then pays z BTC as deposit to create a *Funding Transaction* tx^F. Meanwhile, each party takes as input relevant parameters including pk_i^m to create the *Refunding Transaction* tx^R, and *Timeout Refunding Transaction* tx^T. In the *execution phase*, each party can release valid digital signature by broadcasting *Refunding Transaction* within time T. Either party complying with the scheme above can redeem his deposit z BTC as the payment address of *Refunding Transaction* is generated from pk_i^m. Either party not broadcasting *Refunding Transaction* timely is considered as misbehaving party, whose deposit is gained by the counterpart through broadcasting *Timeout Refunding Transaction* after time T.

Concrete Exchange Model. In Bitcoin, each transaction tx has a unique identifier, namely, $txid$ (transaction identification). Generally, $txid$ is calculated by hashing the raw transaction, therefore, it is infeasible to acquire $txid$ before signing the transaction. Hence it's also infeasible to generate a new transaction tx_{new} consuming output of previous transaction tx_{prev} before tx_{prev} is signed. However, this problem has been solved with the application of Segregated Witness, which suggests the Bitcoin to compute the $txid$ without input script $ScriptSig$. Consequently, we may generate a sub-transaction tx_{new} allocating the output of parent transaction tx_{prev} before tx_{prev} is signed. Once parent transaction tx_{prev} is included in the Bitcoin block chain, the sub-transaction tx_{new} can also be broadcast immediately. Indeed, our work is heavily inspired by Poon and Dryja [24], who proposed a Lightning Network for building new offline micropayment schemes to improve the transaction processing capacity of Bitcoin. Likewise, we construct a Bitcoin transaction model for digital signature exchange in Fig. 1. We would like to stress that the transaction model achieving fairness is not unique, and we leave other possibilities in future work.

The *In Script* indicates the *ScriptSig* to make transaction valid, and the *Out Script* sets the condition for redemption of the output with *ScriptPubKey*. For instance, the first output of tx^F can be redeemed either by tx_A^R with $\mathcal{A}$ providing the signature sig_A^M and sig_B^1 within time T, or by tx_B^T with $\mathcal{B}$ providing signature sig_B^2 after time T. (sk_i^m, pk_i^m) where $i \in \{\mathcal{A}, \mathcal{B}\}$ is the key pair generated from message m_i. The signature sig_i^m is generated by signing on transaction including pk_i^m under private key sk_i, therefore sig_i^m is equivalent to the signature on contract m_i under private key sk_i. And the signature sig_i^* is generated by signing on any transaction under private key sk_i^m. Here, the signature sig_i^j where $i \in \{\mathcal{A}, \mathcal{B}\}, j \in \{1, 2, 3\}$ is generated by signing on relevant transaction under other different private key sk_i^j.

Here we deploy the 2-of-2 multisig to deter each party from creating false transactions, which can be implemented with the Pay-To-Script-Hash (*P2SH*) script

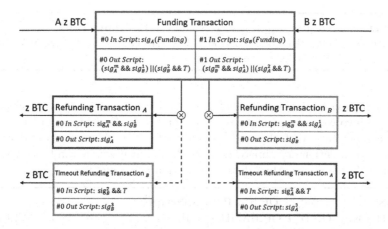

Fig. 1. *Funding Transaction* is generated by both parties to pay z BTC, where z BTC needs to be larger than the value of digital signatures in bitcoins. Only one of the *Refunding Transaction* tx_A^R and *Timeout Refunding Transaction* tx_B^T can be confirmed, and likewise, tx_B^R and tx_A^T. Only after transactions tx^R and tx^T are ready *Funding Transaction* tx^F can be broadcast.

and opcode *OP_CHECKMULTISIG*. Also we set the time limit T for transaction tx_i^R with the parameter *nsequence* and opcode *OP_CHECKSQUENCEVERIFY*.

Funding Transaction tx^F is generated by $\mathcal{A}$ and $\mathcal{B}$ together, with inputs of $2z$ BTC and outputs of $2z$ BTC. Look at $\mathcal{A}$'s perspective, he has to broadcast *Refunding Transaction* tx_A^R within time T to redeem the output of tx^F; otherwise, $\mathcal{B}$ can broadcast the *Timeout Refunding Transaction* tx_B^T after time T to gain $\mathcal{A}$'s deposit. The *ScriptPubKey* of first output is designed as follows.

ScriptPubKey: OP_HASH160 $<$ HASH160(**RedeemScript^F**) $>$ OP_EQUAL
RedeemScript^F: OP_IF
$\qquad\qquad\qquad$ OP_2 $<$ pk$_B^1$ $>$ $<$ pk$_A$ $>$ OP_2 OP_CHECKMULTISIG
$\qquad\qquad$ OP_ELSE
$\qquad\qquad\qquad$ $<$ T time $>$ OP_CHECKSQUENCEVERIFY OP_DROP
$\qquad\qquad\qquad$ $<$ pk$_B^2$ $>$ OP_CHECKSIG
$\qquad\qquad$ OP_ENDIF

Refunding Transaction tx^R is generated by each party with output of z BTC. It involves two valid signatures in the *In Script*. Look at $\mathcal{A}$'s perspective, the *ScriptPubKey* contains the hash value of pk_A^m, hence the signature on raw transaction is equivalent to that on contract text m_A under private key sk_A. After getting $\mathcal{B}$'s signature, he may provide valid signature and broadcast tx_A^R to Bitcoin network within T time. In this way, $\mathcal{A}$ redeems the deposit cause only he knows sk_A^m corresponding to pk_A^m. It's designed as follows in terms of $\mathcal{A}$.

ScriptSig: OP_0 $< \mathrm{sig}_B^1 > < \mathrm{sig}_A^m >$ OP_1 $< \mathbf{RedeemScript^F} >$
ScriptPubKey: OP_DUP OP_HASH160 $<$ HASH160$(\mathrm{pk}_A^m) >$ OP_EQUALVERIFY
        OP_CHECKSIG

Timeout Refunding Transaction tx^T is generated by each party with output of z BTC. It involves one signature and time limit T in the *In Script*. Either party can be compensated with the other's deposit whenever his counterpart does not-broadcast transaction tx_i^R timely. Look at $\mathcal{A}$'s perspective, he can broadcast tx_A^T after time T if $\mathcal{B}$ does notbroadcast transaction tx_B^R timely.

ScriptSig: $< \mathrm{sig}_A^2 >$ OP_0 $< \mathbf{RedeemScript^F} >$
ScriptPubKey: OP_DUP OP_HASH160 $<$ HASH160$(\mathrm{pk}_A^3) >$ OP_EQUALVERIFY
        OP_CHECKSIG

Concrete Exchange Process. Now we describe the exchange process in two phases: *preparation phase, execution phase.*

Preparation Phase. In this phase, each party first achieves the conversion from message m_i to public key pk_i^m, then pays z BTC as deposit to construct the exchange model above. Assume $\mathcal{A}$ is organizer, it follows these steps.

Step 1. each party computes the ECDSA key pair (sk_i^m, pk_i^m) by calls of $\mathcal{F}_{\mathrm{MK}}$ and reaches agreement on the deposit denoted as z BTC.
Step 2. $\mathcal{A}$ offers information of z BTC deposit, denoted as (h_A, α_A), and the *RedeemScript*$_A^F$ of transaction tx^F's first output, then he sends them to $\mathcal{B}$.
Step 3. $\mathcal{B}$ checks whether these parameters are reasonable. If so, he offers tuple (h_B, α_B) and *RedeemScript*$_B^F$, generates transaction tx^F without *In Script*, tx_B^T with his signature sig_B^2, tx_B^R without signature, and sends (h_B, α_B), *RedeemScript*$_B^F$, tx^F, tx_B^R to $\mathcal{A}$; otherwise, he aborts the interaction.
Step 4. $\mathcal{A}$ checks whether these parameters and transactions are reasonable. If so, he signs transaction tx_B^R, generates transaction tx_A^T with his signature sig_A^2, tx_A^R without signature, and sends sig_A^1, tx_A^R to $\mathcal{B}$.
Step 5. $\mathcal{B}$ checks whether tx_A^R is reasonable. If so, he offers the sig_B^1 to $\mathcal{A}$.
Step 6. $\mathcal{A}$ signs transaction tx^F and sends the signature to $\mathcal{B}$.
Step 7. $\mathcal{B}$ signs transaction tx^F and broadcasts it to the Bitcoin network.

Either $\mathcal{A}$ or $\mathcal{B}$ can always force a timely and fair termination because of whatever reason in this phase. Note that public signature sig_i^1 can be detected with corresponding public key pk_i^1 if it's invalid. More importantly, every step here is harmless for each party. Therefore, two parties will execute the above steps in most cases.

Execution Phase. It takes some time for the *Funding Transaction* to be confirmed by the Bitcoin network. In this phase, each party wanting to redeem his deposit has to broadcast corresponding *Refunding Transaction* tx_i^R within time T. Assume $\mathcal{A}$ is organizer, it follows these steps.

Step 1. Before time T runs out, $\mathcal{A}$ may sign on transaction tx_A^R under sk_A, and broadcast it to the Bitcoin network.

Step 2. If tx_A^R isn't broadcast after time T, $\mathcal{B}$ may broadcast *Timeout Refunding Transaction* tx_B^T to gain $\mathcal{A}$'s deposit of z BTC.

Complying with the agreement, $\mathcal{A}$ can consume the output of *Refunding Transaction* tx_A^R whenever he wants since only $\mathcal{A}$ is aware of private key sk_A^m corresponding to pk_A^m. If $\mathcal{A}$ misbehaves, he will suffer deposit loss of z BTC which is much larger than the value of its digital signature in bitcoins and the counterpart is compensated with this deposit.

As the channel of offline interactions described in Sect. 3.1 is resilient, it's hard to estimate the time of *preparation phase*. However, it takes at most T time to carry out the *execution phase*. The concrete value of T may change over different occasions, however, it reasonable that time T is longer than the max network delay max_d between sending a transaction and including it in a block.

5   Construction Analysis

In this Section, we first discuss the security in terms of fairness and completeness, then we give a brief performance analysis of the construction described above.

5.1   Security

Here, we discuss the security of the concrete construction of the TTP-free fair exchange scheme in terms of completeness and fairness.

Completeness. The completeness requires that each player will acquire the desired valid signature by the very end of the exchange guaranteeing both players are honest. We formalize an *incompleteness game* called **IN-COMP** where an adversary $\mathcal{E}$ can only delay the information transmission by arbitrary but finite amount of time in the *preparation phase* and the propagation of Bitcoin transactions by at most max_d time in *execution phase*. Then we discuss the probability of $\mathcal{E}$ winning in the game in polynomial time.

Theorem 2. *The construction of scheme* $\prod = (\mathcal{F}_{\mathrm{MK}}, \mathcal{F}_{\mathrm{BT}})$ *is complete in polynomial time.*

Proof. If both players are honest, then each player can inform the other necessary parameters after offline computations in spite of some delay. Thus, two players can successfully construct the transaction model with correct pk^m embedded into the *Refunding Transactions* tx^R. In *execution phase*, each player can broadcast the tx_i^R containing the valid signature of pk_i^m timely since time limit T is set to be larger than the max delay time max_d. In consequence, each player acquires the other's valid signature and redeem the deposit so long as tx_i^R is included in a Bitcoin block. Note that we combine the digital signature with transaction *ScriptSig* so that it's difficult for others to figure out the transaction with digital signature. As the adversary $\mathcal{E}$ cannot succeed in breaking the information transmission, he may win this game with no more than negligible probability. In other words, the construction of scheme $\prod$ is complete in polynomial time.

Fairness. Assume that there is an adversary $A^\star$ who tries to learn the counterpart's valid signature without releasing his valid signature. The fairness requires that $\mathcal{A}$ can succeed in acquiring desired signature without loss of deposit even not releasing his valid signature with no more than negligible probability. We have defined a *unfairness game* called **UN-FAIR** to simulate the situation and evaluate probability of $\mathcal{A}^\star$ winning in the game in Sect. 3.3.

Theorem 3. *The construction of scheme* $\prod = (\mathcal{F}_{\text{MK}}, \mathcal{F}_{\text{BT}})$ *owns fairness in polynomial time.*

Proof. By fairness, we mean the fairness achieved by monetary penalization when either player misbehaves during *execution phase*. Note that either player not complying with the agreement makes no influence on the fairness as the other party can terminate subsequent interactions unilaterally. We discuss three situations where adversary $\mathcal{A}^\star$ may try to cheat as follows.

- $\mathcal{A}^\star$ *informs* $\mathcal{B}$ *with incorrect* pk_A^m. We give the accountability of each player generating public key pk_i^m from message m_i with NIZK proof system in Sect. 4.1. Based on Theorem 1, there is no doubt that $\mathcal{A}^\star$ can be detected for cheating in publishing a public key not generating form m_A. It owns fairness as $\mathcal{B}$ can terminate the exchange without any loss right away.
- $\mathcal{A}^\star$ *informs* $\mathcal{B}$ *with incorrect* tx_A^R. As stated before, *Refunding Transaction* tx_i^R requires 2-of-2 multisig to be confirmed by the Bitcoin network. Thus, $\mathcal{B}$ can refuse to sign on transaction tx_A^R in *preparation phase* if tx_A^R conflicts with the correct pk_A^m received before and abort the exchange, which still does notaffect the fairness of the scheme.
- $\mathcal{A}^\star$ *does notbroadcast valid* tx_A^R *within* T *time.* Assume that $\mathcal{B}$ broadcasts the valid tx_B^R independently, thereby redeeming his deposit. The *Refunding Transaction* tx_A^R won't be confirmed whether $\mathcal{A}^\star$ does notbroadcast tx_A^R within T time or the tx_A^R contains invalid signature. Thus, $\mathcal{B}$ can also gain the deposit of $\mathcal{A}^\star$ by broadcasting transaction tx_B^T after T time. As z BTC of deposit owns more than the signature, the scheme owns fairness by compensating $\mathcal{B}$ and penalizing $\mathcal{A}^\star$ simultaneously with more valuable bitcoins than signature.

By the discussion above, it concludes that the construction of scheme $\prod$ indeed owns fairness in polynomial time.

5.2   Performance

We introduce an instantiation of the TTP-free fair exchange scheme for digital signatures with Bitcoin in Sect. 4. Compared the traditional paradigms with TTP, there are two innovations about our scheme. First, we design a primitive $\mathcal{F}_{\mathrm{MK}}$ converting any message into a valid ECDSA key pair, which also can be extended into other contexts. Then, we design an exchange model with monetary penalization by Bitcoin transactions. Here we discuss the performance of two parts more seriously.

Key Pair Generation. To construct primitive $\mathcal{F}_{\mathrm{MK}}$, we involve the numerical computations and the HVNIZK proof system, resulting in two distinct choices for security parameter λ. However, the key pair generation only involves the former. Assume that The RSA modulus N is a semiprime of n-bit. Thus the offline generation involves a hash operation of SHA256, a multiplication of n-bit, a modular exponentiation of n-digit number and n-bit exponent, and a multiplication in elliptic curve group $E_{BT}(\mathbb{F}_p)$. We then program to achieve the generation in pure Python 3.x and conduct several experiments with different platforms, parameter sizes of RSA modulus N and message m.

Here, modulus N is of five sizes: 1024 bits, 1536 bits, 2048 bits, 2560 bits, 3072 bits[3] and message m is of five sizes: 1 KB, 10 KB, 100 KB, 1 MB, 10 MB. We conduct the experiment both on a laptop and a mobile phone to demonstrate its efficiency. The laptop running 64-bit Ubuntu System is equipped with an Intel i5-7300 HQ (2.50 GHz quad-core) processor with 8 GB of RAM, and the mobile phone running Android 5.0 is equipped with a Hisilicon Kirin 935 processor with 3G of RAM. Each number stands for the average time of 100 loops. The results are shown in Fig. 2.

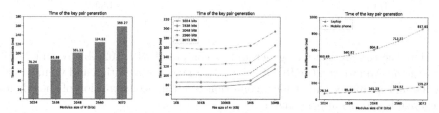

(a) Time cost with 1KB m under different sizes of N on laptop

(b) Time cost trend under different sizes of N and m on laptop

(c) Time cost with 1KB m and 1024-bit N on different platforms

Fig. 2. $\mathcal{F}_{\mathrm{MK}}$ performance under different conditions

Obviously, it costs no more than 200 ms on the laptop even with 3072-bit N and 10 MB m, and the generation can be completed within 1 s on the

---

[3] Viewed as discrete logarithm security level, modulus N of 3072 bits equals to security parameter $\lambda = 128$ bits.

mobile phone. In reality, it will be 30 times faster if the code is programmed with C language. Given the results above, it concludes that the key pair generation offers relatively high efficiency.

Exchange with Transactions. In the Bitcoin transaction model, we involve a *Funding Transaction*, two *Refunding Transaction*, and two *Timeout Refunding Transaction*. However, $\mathcal{A}$ and $\mathcal{B}$ may broadcast corresponding transaction with asynchronous clock in the *execution phase*. We denote max_d as the max delay between sending a transaction and including it in a block. And the time limit is set to T ($T > max_d$) for the *Refunding Transaction* to be confirmed. Considering this, it concludes that the total time for the Bitcoin transactions confirmation is $T + max_d$ in the ideal environment.

Assume that the whole network delay is zero and $\mathcal{A}$, $\mathcal{B}$ execute the exchange procedure with no delay, we then estimate the time consumption of the whole exchange in Table 1.

Table 1. Time consumption of whole exchange under ideal condition

Phase	Behavior of $\mathcal{A}, \mathcal{B}$	Time (ms)
Preparation phase	Each party generate a key pair	76.24
	$\mathcal{A}$ Signs on transaction tx_B^R	36.95
	$\mathcal{A}$ Signs on transaction tx^F	36.95
	$\mathcal{B}$ Signs on transaction tx^F	36.95
	Transaction tx^F is validated	73.54
Execution phase	Each party signs on tx_i^R	36.95
	Transaction tx_i^R is validated	73.54
Total		408.07

Here the time of key pair generation is computed with 1024-bit N and 1 KB message m. And we run the RCDSA-based signatures generation and verification on the laptop above. Under ideal condition, the time consumption of the whole exchange is 400 ms approximately.

6 Extensions

6.1 Non-zero Transaction Fees

In Sect. 4, we design the exchange model with Bitcoin transactions assuming that the transaction fee is zero. However, it's out of the fact in both main network and testnet network. We would like to stress that it does not affect the fairness property of our scheme. We can solve this problem simply by modifying the value of each output. And the scheme still owns fairness as each party will pays the same fee to the miners.

6.2 Multi-party Fair Exchange

With the application of Segregated Witness, we can extend the scheme to multi-party fair exchange of digital signatures. Assume that there are three parties every of which wants to exchange its valuable signature for others'. To implement this, we just need modify the exchange model moderately with every party still paying the identical deposit to the *Funding Transaction* tx^F that has three outputs respectively. Each output can be redeemed either by the *Refunding Transaction* with a 3-of-3 valid multisig, or by the *Timeout Refunding Transaction* with a 2-of-3 multisig. And every deposit is equally divided into two parts in the latter situation. Still, the scheme possesses fairness by designing the model suitably.

6.3 Future Work

We proposed a TTP-free fair scheme for digital signature exchange with Bitcoin in this paper, which is feasible under the application of the Segregated Witness. Based on this, we will focus on the following two improvements in later work.

- The scheme is only applicative to the two-party situation now. By extending the transaction model, we will give the multi-party fair exchange scheme with full description and concrete construction.
- We convert the message into a public key and embed it into corresponding transaction in this scheme. There may also exist other possibilities for the transaction model. We will try to design other schemes with more efficiency.

7 Conclusion

We have proposed a novel TTP-free scheme with Bitcoin to resolve fair exchange problem of digital signatures. It achieves fairness through penalization mechanism with Bitcoin transactions. The security is guaranteed by the intractability assumptions of some difficult problems in polynomial time. Furthermore, the primitive $\mathcal{F}_{MK}$ we described here is capable of converting any message into a valid ECDSA key pair, and it may also show application in other contexts. Due to its feasibility with Bitcoin and property of TTP-free, the scheme may occupy a wide range of scenarios in the E-commerce nowadays.

Acknowledgment. Qianhong Wu is the corresponding author. This paper is supported by the National Key Research and Development Program of China through project 2017YFB0802505, the Natural Science Foundation of China through projects 61772538, 61672083, 61370190, 61572382, 61532021, 61472429 and 61402029, and by the National Cryptography Development Fund through project MMJJ20170106.

References

1. Andrychowicz, M., Dziembowski, S., Malinowski, D., Mazurek, L.: Fair two-party computations via bitcoin deposits. In: Böhme, R., Brenner, M., Moore, T., Smith, M. (eds.) FC 2014. LNCS, vol. 8438, pp. 105–121. Springer, Heidelberg (2014). https://doi.org/10.1007/978-3-662-44774-1_8
2. Andrychowicz, M., Dziembowski, S., Malinowski, D., Mazurek, L.: Secure multi-party computations on bitcoin. In: 2014 IEEE Symposium on Security and Privacy, pp. 443–458. IEEE Computer Society (2014)
3. Asokan, N., Shoup, V., Waidner, M.: Asynchronous protocols for optimistic fair exchange. In: 1998 IEEE Symposium on Security and Privacy, pp. 86–99 (1998)
4. Asokan, N., Shoup, V., Waidner, M.: Optimistic fair exchange of digital signatures. IEEE J. Sel. Areas Commun. 18(4), 593–610 (2000)
5. Bao, F., Deng, R.H., Mao, W.: Efficient and practical fair exchange protocols with off-line TTP. In: 1998 IEEE Symposium on Security and Privacy, pp. 77–85. IEEE Computer Society (1998)
6. Barber, S., Boyen, X., Shi, E., Uzun, E.: Bitter to better — how to make bitcoin a better currency. In: Keromytis, A.D. (ed.) FC 2012. LNCS, vol. 7397, pp. 399–414. Springer, Heidelberg (2012). https://doi.org/10.1007/978-3-642-32946-3_29
7. Ben-Sasson, E., Chiesa, A., Garman, C., Green, M., Miers, I., Tromer, E., Virza, M.: Zerocash: decentralized anonymous payments from bitcoin. In: 2014 IEEE Symposium on Security and Privacy, pp. 459–474 (2014)
8. Bentov, I., Kumaresan, R.: How to use bitcoin to design fair protocols. In: Garay, J.A., Gennaro, R. (eds.) CRYPTO 2014. LNCS, vol. 8617, pp. 421–439. Springer, Heidelberg (2014). https://doi.org/10.1007/978-3-662-44381-1_24
9. Bitansky, N., Chiesa, A., Ishai, Y., Paneth, O., Ostrovsky, R.: Succinct non-interactive arguments via linear interactive proofs. In: Sahai, A. (ed.) TCC 2013. LNCS, vol. 7785, pp. 315–333. Springer, Heidelberg (2013). https://doi.org/10.1007/978-3-642-36594-2_18
10. Blum, M., Feldman, P., Micali, S.: Non-interactive zero-knowledge and its applications (extended abstract). In: Proceedings of the 20th Annual ACM Symposium on Theory of Computing, pp. 103–112. ACM (1988)
11. Castiglione, A., Santis, A.D., Castiglione, A., Palmieri, F., Fiore, U.: An energy-aware framework for reliable and secure end-to-end ubiquitous data communications. In: 2013 5th International Conference on Intelligent Networking and Collaborative Systems, Xi'an City, Shaanxi Province, China, 9–11 September 2013, pp. 157–165 (2013)
12. Chen, L., Kudla, C., Paterson, K.G.: Concurrent signatures. In: Cachin, C., Camenisch, J.L. (eds.) EUROCRYPT 2004. LNCS, vol. 3027, pp. 287–305. Springer, Heidelberg (2004). https://doi.org/10.1007/978-3-540-24676-3_18
13. Cox, B.: Netbill security and transaction protocol. In: First USENIX Workshop on Electronic Commerce, New York, USA, 11–12 July 1995. USENIX Association (1995)
14. Cramer, R., Damgård, I., Schoenmakers, B.: Proofs of partial knowledge and simplified design of witness hiding protocols. In: Desmedt, Y.G. (ed.) CRYPTO 1994. LNCS, vol. 839, pp. 174–187. Springer, Heidelberg (1994). https://doi.org/10.1007/3-540-48658-5_19
15. Cramer, R., Shoup, V.: Signature schemes based on the strong RSA assumption. ACM Trans. Inf. Syst. Secur. 3(3), 161–185 (2000)

16. Dang, Q.H.: Secure hash standard. National Institute of Standards and Technology, Gaithersburg, MD, Technical report, August 2015
17. Even, S., Goldreich, O., Lempel, A.: A randomized protocol for signing contracts. Commun. ACM **28**(6), 637–647 (1985)
18. Jayasinghe, D., Markantonakis, K., Mayes, K.: Optimistic fair-exchange with anonymity for bitcoin users. In: ICEBE 2014, pp. 44–51. IEEE Computer Society (2014)
19. Johnson, D., Menezes, A., Vanstone, S.A.: The elliptic curve digital signature algorithm (ECDSA). Int. J. Inf. Sec. **1**(1), 36–63 (2001)
20. Lombrozo, E., Wuille, J.L.P.: Segregated witness (consensus layer). https://github.com/bitcoin/bips/blob/master/bip-0141.mediawiki
21. Miers, I., Garman, C., Green, M., Rubin, A.D.: Zerocoin: anonymous distributed e-cash from bitcoin. In: 2013 IEEE Symposium on Security and Privacy, pp. 397–411 (2013)
22. Nakamoto, S.: Bitcoin: a peer-to-peer electronic cash system (2008). https://bitcoin.org/bitcoin.pdf
23. Okamoto, T., Ohta, K.: How to simultaneously exchange secrets by general assumptions. In: CCS 1994, pp. 184–192. ACM (1994)
24. Poon, J., Dryja, T.: The bitcoin lightning network: scalable off-chain instant payments (2015)
25. Qin, B., Chen, L.C.H., Wu, Q.H., Zhang, Y.F., Zhong, L., Zheng, H.B.: Bitcoin and digital fiat currency. J. Crypt. Res. **4**(2), 176–186 (2017)
26. Rackoff, C., Simon, D.R.: Non-interactive zero-knowledge proof of knowledge and chosen ciphertext attack. In: Feigenbaum, J. (ed.) CRYPTO 1991. LNCS, vol. 576, pp. 433–444. Springer, Heidelberg (1992). https://doi.org/10.1007/3-540-46766-1_35
27. Sun, Y., Wu, Q., Qin, B., Wang, Y., Liu, J.: Batch blind signatures on elliptic curves. In: Lopez, J., Wu, Y. (eds.) ISPEC 2015. LNCS, vol. 9065, pp. 192–206. Springer, Cham (2015). https://doi.org/10.1007/978-3-319-17533-1_14
28. Zhou, J., Gollmann, D.: A fair non-repudiation protocol. In: 1996 IEEE Symposium on Security and Privacy, pp. 55–61. IEEE Computer Society (1996)

Asymmetric Encryption

The KDM-CCA Security of REACT

Jinyong Chang[1,2], Honglong Dai[2], and Maozhi Xu[2(✉)]

[1] School of Information and Control Engineering, Xi'an University of Architecture
and Technology, Xi'an, Shannxi, People's Republic of China
[2] School of Mathematics, Peking University, Beijing, People's Republic of China
{changjinyong,daihonglong}@pku.edu.cn, mzxu@math.pku.edu.cn

Abstract. In CT-RSA 2001, Okamoto and Pointcheval proposed a
general conversion: Rapid enhanced-security asymmetric cryptosystem
transform (REACT, for short), which achieves the CCA security in the
random oracle from very weak building blocks and is (almost) optimal
in terms of computational overload.

In this paper, we consider the key-dependent message (KDM) security
of REACT and prove that it can be KDM-CCA secure under exactly the
same assumptions on its building blocks as those used by Okamoto and
Pointcheval. When presenting our proof, we mainly adopt the deferred-
analysis technique proposed in [25] and the random-oracle-splitting technique which has been used in [17,23] according to the roles of the random
oracles in different phases.

Keywords: Key-dependent message (KDM)
Chosen ciphertext attack (CCA) · REACT · Random oracle

1 Introduction

Secure encryption is the most basic task in cryptography, and significant works
have gone into defining and attaining it. Many commonly accepted definitions,
such as chosen-plaintext attack (CPA) security and chosen-ciphertext attack
(CCA) security, assume that the plaintext messages don't depend on the secret
keys. However, in the last few years, it was observed that, in many situations,
such as anonymous credential system [12], BitLocker disk encryption utility (used
in Windows Vista) [7], fully homomorphic encryption [20], the event that the
plaintext messages do depend on the secret keys may occur or even be desirable.
In [6], Black et al. formally call them key-dependent message (KDM) security.
In fact, around the same time, Camenisch and Lysyanskaya [12] introduced the
notion circular security, which can be seen as a special case of KDM security,
when they were designing the anonymous credential system.

It seems that KDM security does not follow from standard security [13,14],
and there are also indications that KDM security (at least in its most general
form) can not be obtained using standard techniques [22]. Therefore, KDM security has received much attention in many setting, including the public-key [7],

© Springer International Publishing AG 2017
J. K. Liu and P. Samarati (Eds.): ISPEC 2017, LNCS 10701, pp. 85–101, 2017.
https://doi.org/10.1007/978-3-319-72359-4_5

secret-key [8], and identity-based [15] settings. In this paper, we mainly focus on the public-key encryption (PKE) setting.

In the standard model, the definition of KDM security is often accompanied by a function family Φ, which consists of functions of secret keys, since the existing work indicates that it is almost impossible to construct an encryption scheme satisfying the KDM security for any family [22]. Therefore, in 2008, Boneh et al. gave the first KDM-CPA secure PKE scheme under the decisional Diffie-Hellman (DDH) assumption, in which the KDM security is relative to the family of affine functions (affine-KDM, for short). Later, affine-KDM secure encryption schemes are constructed based on other assumptions, including quadratic residuosity (QR) [9], decisional composite residuosity (DCR) [9], learning with errors (LWE) [2] etc. In recent years, some non-affine-KDM secure schemes are also be introduced, such as [1,4,10]. However, all of them are limited in the KDM-CPA case. How to construct KDM-CCA secure schemes seems to be much harder and the related works are rare. In this direction, Camenisch et al. showed that a variation of the Naor-Yang paradigm allows one to combine any KDM-CPA secure scheme and any regular CCA secure encryption scheme, together with a non-interactive zero knowledge (NIZK) proof, to obtain a KDM-CCA secure encryption scheme [11]. In recent work [21], Han et al. constructed an efficient KDM-CCA secure PKE for polynomial functions based on DDH and DCR assumptions (free of NIZK and pairing) with the help of authenticated encryption with auxiliary-input (AIAE).

In the random oracle model, the situations seem to be better and almost all the designed schemes can be KDM-CCA secure with respect to any (length-regular) function families. In particular, in 2008, Backes et al. proved that the famous OAEP (see [5]) is KDM-CCA secure if the underlying trapdoor permutation is partial domain one-way [3]. In 2014, Davies and Stam studied the KDM security of hybrid encryption. Concretely, they proved that if a key derivation function (KDF) is used between key encapsulation mechanism (KEM) and data encapsulation mechanism (DEM), and this KDF is modelled as a random oracle, then the one-wayness (OW) of KEM and the indistinguishability (IND) of DEM will be sufficient for the KDM-CCA security of the resulting hybrid scheme [17]. In the recent work [23], Kitagawa et al. considered the KDM-CCA security of the two conversions introduced in [18,19], which are denoted by *FO-I* and *FO-II*, respectively. As a result, they obtained that, in general, the scheme *FO-I* is not KDM-CCA secure while *FO-II* satisfies KDM-CCA security under exactly the same assumptions on the building blocks.

Our Contribution. In this paper, we consider the KDM-CCA security of the famous scheme: REACT (i.e. Rapid Enhanced-security Asymmetric Cryptosystem Transform), which is proposed by Okamoto and Pointcheval in [24] and has been proven to be CCA secure in the random oracle model.

In REACT, one can obtain the CCA security from very weak building blocks: An asymmetric encryption scheme with one-way plaintext-check attack (OW-PCA, for short) security and an indistinguishable symmetric scheme, together with two hash functions. The encryption algorithm of this conversion works as follows.

$$c_1 \leftarrow Enc^{asym}(pk, r),\ c_2 \leftarrow Enc^{sym}(G(r), m),\ c_3 = H(r, m, c_1, c_2),$$

where r is random, G and H are two hash functions. Here, we remark that REACT does not belong to the standard hybrid encryption model [16], which consists of two separated parts: KEM and DEM, as well as the intermediate transition part: KDF. The reason lies in that the authentication part c_3 needs to choose "KEM-part" c_1 as its input. Morever, when giving the security proof, both of the hash functions G and H are modeled as the random oracles. Therefore, this is different from that of [17], in which they consider the KDM-CCA security of the standard hybrid encryption model and only the KDF is modeled as the random oracle.

As the main result of this paper, we prove that the conversion REACT achieves the KDM-CCA security based on exactly the same assumptions on the building blocks.

Organizations of the Paper. In Sect. 2, we introduce some basic notations and definitions of the building blocks. In Sect. 3, we first recall the original conversion of REACT and then prove its KDM-CCA security in detail. Conclusions can be found in Sect. 4.

2   Preliminaries

In this section, we review some useful notations and definitions.

Notations. If $\mathcal{M}$ is a set, then $|M|$ denotes the number of elements in it and $m \xleftarrow{\$} \mathcal{M}$ denotes the operation of picking an element m uniformly at random from $\mathcal{M}$. For two strings x and y, $x||y$ denotes the concatenation of x and y. $[\ell]$ means the set of integers $\{1, \cdots, \ell\}$. We denote by λ a security parameter and by 1^λ the unary form of λ. For notational clarity, we usually omit it as an explicit parameter. PPT denotes probabilistic polynomial time. Let $z \leftarrow A(x, y, \cdots)$ denote the operation of running an algorithm A with inputs $(x, y, \cdots)$ and output z. We say a function $negl(\lambda)$ is *negligible* (in λ) if for $\lambda > k_0$ and $k_0 \in \mathbb{Z}$, $negl(\lambda) < \lambda^{-c}$ for any constant $c > 0$.

2.1   PKE Scheme and OW-PCA Security [24]

A public key encryption (PKE) scheme Σ consists of the following algorithms:

- *GenP.* Input: A security parameter 1^λ. Output: A pair of public-secret keys (pk, sk).
- *EncP.* Input: The public key pk and a plaintext $m \in \mathcal{M}$. Output: A ciphertext c.
- *DecP.* Input: The secret key sk and a ciphertext c. Output: A plaintext m or a symbol $\perp$, which denotes that this ciphertext is invalid.

The correctness requires that, for any $(pk, sk) \leftarrow GenP(1^\lambda)$, $m \leftarrow \mathcal{M}$, it holds that

$$DecP(sk, EncP(pk, m)) = m.$$

The OW-PCA security of Σ is defined by the following experiment between a challenger and an adversary $\mathcal{A}$.

OW-PCA-Experiment:

- **Initialization.** The challenger runs $(pk, sk) \leftarrow GenP(1^\lambda)$ and gives pk to $\mathcal{A}$.
- **Query and Challenge Phase.** $\mathcal{A}$ is allowed to adaptively query (m, c) to the Plaintext-Checking Oracle (played by the challenger), which returns 1 if c is a ciphertext of m and returns 0 if it is not. Then the challenger chooses $m^* \xleftarrow{\$} \mathcal{M}$ and runs $c^* \leftarrow EncP(pk, m^*)$. Give c^* to $\mathcal{A}$.
- **Guess.** $\mathcal{A}$ outputs a message m as the guess of m^*.

We call $\mathcal{A}$ wins the experiment if $m = m^*$. Denote by $Adv_{\mathcal{A}, \Sigma}^{\text{OW-PCA}}(1^\lambda)$ the probability that $\mathcal{A}$ wins the experiment. If for any PPT adversary $\mathcal{A}$, $Adv_{\mathcal{A}, \Sigma}^{\text{OW-PCA}}(1^\lambda)$ is negligible, then Σ is called OW-PCA secure.

2.2   Secret Key Scheme and IND Security [24]

A secret key scheme Π consists of the following two algorithms:

- *EncS.* Input: A random secret key $k \in \mathcal{K}$ and a message $m \in \mathcal{M}$. Output: A ciphertext c (of m).
- *DecS.* Input: A secret key $k \in \mathcal{K}$ and a ciphertext c. Output: A message m or a symbol $\perp$, which means that the ciphertext c is invalid.

The correctness requires that, for all $k \in \mathcal{K}$, $m \in \mathcal{M}$, it holds that

$$DecS(k, EncS(k, m)) = m.$$

The IND security of Π is defined by the following experiment between a challenger and an adversary $\mathcal{A}$.

IND-Experiment:

- **Initialization.** The challenger chooses $k \xleftarrow{\$} \mathcal{K}$, and a bit $b \xleftarrow{\$} \{0, 1\}$.
- **Challenge Phase.** $\mathcal{A}$ submits two messages m_0 and m_1 (in $\mathcal{M}$). Then the challenger runs $c^* \leftarrow EncS(k, m_b)$ and returns it to $\mathcal{A}$.
- **Guess.** $\mathcal{A}$ outputs a bit $b' \in \{0, 1\}$ as a guess of b.

Let

$$Adv_{\mathcal{A}, \Pi}^{\text{IND}} := \left| \Pr[b = b'] - \frac{1}{2} \right|$$

be the advantage of $\mathcal{A}$ winning the IND experiment. If for any PPT adversary $\mathcal{A}$, its advantage is negligible, then Π is called IND secure.

2.3   KDM-CCA Security

In this subsection, we present the stronger security of PKE scheme: KDM-CCA security. In particular, let $\Gamma = (Gen, Enc, Dec)$ be a PKE scheme. We define the following KDM-CCA-experiment played by a challenger $\mathcal{CH}$ and an adversary $\mathcal{A}$.

KDM-CCA-Experiment:

- **Initialization.** First, $\mathcal{CH}$ chooses $b \xleftarrow{\$} \{0,1\}$ and runs ℓ times $Gen(1^\lambda)$ and obtains the key-pairs

$$(pk_1, sk_1), \cdots, (pk_\ell, sk_\ell).$$

Give $(pk_1, \cdots, pk_\ell)$ to $\mathcal{A}$. Then, initialize an empty list L_{kdm}, which will be used to store the pairs that $\mathcal{A}$ obtains through KDM encryption query.
- **Queries.** The adversary $\mathcal{A}$ is allowed to *adaptively* make the following queries.
  - **KDM Encryption Queries.** When $\mathcal{A}$ submits (j, f), where $j \in [\ell]$ and f is a function, $\mathcal{CH}$ returns $c^* \leftarrow Enc(pk_j, f(sk_1, \cdots, sk_\ell))$ if $b = 1$ or $c^* \leftarrow Enc(pk_j, 0^{|f(\cdot)|})$ if $b = 0$. Add (j, c^*) into L_{kdm}.
  - **Decryption Queries.** When $\mathcal{A}$ submits (j, c), $\mathcal{CH}$ first checks if $(j, c) \in L_{kdm}$. If it is, then return $\perp$. Otherwise, run $m \leftarrow Dec(sk_j, c)$ and return m to $\mathcal{A}$.
- **Guess.** $\mathcal{A}$ outputs a bit $b' \in \{0,1\}$.

Define

$$Adv_{A,\Gamma}^{\text{KDM-CCA}}(1^\lambda) := \left| \Pr[b = b'] - \frac{1}{2} \right|,$$

which is called the advantage of $\mathcal{A}$ winning the KDM-CCA experiment. If for any PPT adversary, its advantage is negligible, then we call the PKE scheme Γ is KDM-CCA secure.

Remark. In [6], when Black et al. first giving the definition of KDM security, they assumed the functions that the adversary $\mathcal{A}$ queries in the KDM experiment are *length-regular*. Specifically, we call a function f (of secret keys $sk_1, \cdots, sk_\ell$) is length-regular if the length of $f(sk_1, \cdots, sk_\ell)$ is independent of the value of $sk_1, \cdots, sk_\ell$. Therefore, we can determine $0^{|f(sk_1, \cdots, sk_\ell)|}$ only from f and does not need $sk_1 \cdots, sk_\ell$. In this paper, we also assume the functions $\mathcal{A}$ queries are length-regular.

In addition, when proving the KDM security of PKE schemes in the random oracle model, the adversary $\mathcal{A}$ is allowed to make queries to the random oracle (i.e. hash queries). Hence, it is also natural to permit the KDM function f ($\mathcal{A}$ queries) to access to the random oracle, which can be denoted by $f^H(sk_1, \cdots, sk_\ell)$, for some random oracle H.

3   REACT and Its KDM-CCA Security

3.1   REACT

First, we recall the classical transform REACT proposed by Okamoto and Pointcheval in [24]. Concretely, let $\Sigma = (GenP, EncP, DecP)$ be a PKE scheme and $\Pi = (EncS, DecS)$ a secret key scheme. Let G and H be two hash functions which output k_1-bit and k_2-bit strings, respectively. Then the REACT scheme $\mathsf{REACT} = (Gen, Enc, Dec)$ can be constructed as follows.

- $Gen(1^\lambda)$: Run $(pk, sk) \leftarrow GenP(1^\lambda)$ and output (pk, sk).
- $Enc(pk, m)$: Choose $r \xleftarrow{\$} \{0, 1\}^{\ell_1}$ and run

$$c_1 \leftarrow EncP(pk, r).$$

Then compute

$$c_2 \leftarrow EncS(K, m),$$

where $K := G(r)$, and the checking part

$$c_3 \leftarrow H(r, m, c_1, c_2).$$

Finally, output the ciphertext (of m) $c := (c_1, c_2, c_3)$.
- $Dec(sk, c)$: First, parse c as $c_1 || c_2 || c_3$. Run

$$r \leftarrow DecP(sk, c_1),$$

and compute

$$m \leftarrow DecS(G(r), c_2).$$

Then, check if

$$c_3 = H(r, m, c_1, c_2).$$

If it is, output the message m. Otherwise, output the "reject" symbol $\bot$.

3.2 The KDM-CCA Security of REACT

In this subsection, we describe and prove the KDM-CCA security of the above scheme REACT. Concretely, we have

Theorem 1. *If the schemes Σ and Π are OW-PCA and IND secure, respectively, and the hash functions G, H are two random oracles, then the scheme REACT is KDM-CCA secure.*

Proof. Let $\mathcal{A}$ be a PPT adversary who attacks on the scheme REACT, and makes at most q_e KDM encryption queries, q_d decryption queries, q_G G-hash queries and q_H H-hash queires. Now, the theorem can be proved via the following games. (Denote by Win_i the adversary $\mathcal{A}$ wins in the i-th game.)

Game$_0$: This is the original KDM-CCA experiment on the scheme REACT *in the random oracle model,* played between a challenger $\mathcal{CH}$ and the adversary $\mathcal{A}$. In particular,

- **Initialization.** First, $\mathcal{CH}$ chooses $b \xleftarrow{\$} \{0, 1\}$ and runs ℓ times $Gen(1^\lambda)$ and obtains the key-pairs

$$(pk_1, sk_1), \cdots, (pk_\ell, sk_\ell).$$

Give $(pk_1, \cdots, pk_\ell)$ to $\mathcal{A}$. Then, initialize three empty lists L_{kdm}, L_G, and L_H, which will be respectively used to store $\mathcal{A}$'s KDM encryption queries, G-hash queries, and H-hash queries.

– **Queries.** The adversary $\mathcal{A}$ is allowed to *adaptively* make the following queries.
  - **Hash Queries.**
    * G-Hash Queries. When r is submitted to G oracle, $\mathcal{CH}$ checks if it has been queried in L_G. If it is, return the corresponding value. Otherwise, choose and return $K \xleftarrow{\$} \{0,1\}^{k_1}$. Then add (r, K) into L_G.
    * H-Hash Queries. Same as the G-hash queries except that the input of H is the form (r, m, c_1, c_2) and the output is k_2 bits.
  - **KDM Encryption Queries.** When $\mathcal{A}$ submits (j, f), where $j \in [\ell]$ and f is a (length-regular) function, $\mathcal{CH}$ returns $c^* \leftarrow Enc(pk_j, f(sk_1, \cdots, sk_\ell))$ if $b = 1$ or $c^* \leftarrow Enc(pk_j, 0^{|f(\cdot)|})$ if $b = 0$. Add (j, c^*) into L_{kdm}.
  - **Decryption Queries.** When $\mathcal{A}$ submits (j, c), $\mathcal{CH}$ first checks if $(j, c) \in L_{kdm}$. If it is, then return $\perp$. Otherwise, run $m \leftarrow Dec(sk_j, c)$ and return m to $\mathcal{A}$.
– **Guess.** $\mathcal{A}$ outputs a bit $b' \in \{0, 1\}$.

Naturally, it holds that

$$Adv_{\mathcal{A}, \text{REACT}}^{\text{KDM-CCA}}(1^\lambda) = \left| \Pr[b = b'] - \frac{1}{2} \right| = \left| \Pr[Win_0] - \frac{1}{2} \right|. \tag{1}$$

Game$_1$: This game is identical to the above game except that the two random oracles G and H are "subdivided" into G, G^*, GG^* and H, H^*, HH^*, respectively, according to the type of queries made by $\mathcal{A}$. Here, we also use the random-oracle-splitting technique, which has been widely used in [17,23]. In particular, we have known that the random oracles G and H are queried at the following four cases:

– **Case 1.** $\mathcal{A}$ makes a direct hash query;
– **Case 2.** When $\mathcal{A}$ makes a KDM query, the challenger needs to compute the hash values to generate the key K of DEM-part and the checking part c_3^*;
– **Case 3.** When $\mathcal{A}$ makes a KDM query (j, f), the function f has access to the random oracles;
– **Case 4.** When $\mathcal{A}$ makes a decryption query, the challenger needs to compute the hash values to respond to it.

The random oracles in Case 1 are still denoted by G and H. The random oracles in Case 2 are now denoted by G^* and H^*. The other cases (i.e. Case 3 and Case 4) are denoted by GG^* and HH^*. The oracles G, H, G^* and H^* respectively maintain the query/answer pairs lists L_G, L_H, L_{G^*}, and L_{H^*}, and are implemented by lazy sampling. Moreover, G and G^* are synchronized. That is, both of them refer not only to their own list but also to the list of the other one. H and H^* are also synchronized. The remainder ones GG^* and HH^* are implemented still by lazy sampling. But both of them do not have their own list. When needing to sample a fresh (random) value, GG^* adds it into the list L_G and HH^* adds it into the list L_H. In addition, GG^* runs by referring to both lists L_G and L_{G^*}, and HH^* runs by referring to both lists L_H and L_{H^*}.

For clarity, we describe in Table 1 how the challenger answers to $\mathcal{A}$'s KDM query, decryption query and how the six random oracles work.

Table 1. The challenger's responses to $\mathcal{A}$'s KDM query, decryption query and the modes of random oracles in Game$_1$.

KDM-Query (j, f):	Decryption-Query $(j, c) \notin L_{kdm}$:
$m_1 \leftarrow f^{GG^*, HH^*}(sk_1, \cdots, sk_\ell)$	Parse c as $c_1 \| c_2 \| c_3$
$m_0 \leftarrow 0^{\|f(\cdot)\|}$	$r \leftarrow DecP(sk_j, c_1)$
$r \xleftarrow{\$} \{0,1\}^{\ell_1}$	$m \leftarrow DecS(GG^*(r), c_2)$
$c_1^* \leftarrow EncP(pk_j, r)$	Check if $c_3 = HH^*(r, m, c_1, c_2)$
$c_2^* \leftarrow EncS(G^*(r), m_b)$	If it is, output m
$c_3^* \leftarrow H^*(r, m_b, c_1^*, c_2^*)$	Else, output $\bot$
add $(j, (c_1^*, c_2^*, c_3^*))$ to L_{kdm}	
Output $c^* = (c_1^*, c_2^*, c_3^*)$	
$G(r) : (= GG^*(r))$	$H(r, m, c_1, c_2) : (= HH^*(r, m, c_1, c_2))$
If $(r, K) \in L_G \cup L_{G^*}$	If $((r, m, c_1, c_2), c_3) \in L_H \cup L_{H^*}$
return K	return c_3
Else	Else
$K \xleftarrow{\$} \{0,1\}^{k_1}$	$c_3 \xleftarrow{\$} \{0,1\}^{k_2}$
add (r, K) to L_G	add $((r, m, c_1, c_2), c_3)$ to L_H
return K	return c_3
$G^*(r) :$	$H^*(r, m, c_1, c_2) :$
If $(r, K) \in L_G \cup L_{G^*}$	If $((r, m, c_1, c_2), c_3) \in L_H \cup L_{H^*}$
return K	return c_3
Else	Else
$K \xleftarrow{\$} \{0,1\}^{k_1}$	$c_3 \xleftarrow{\$} \{0,1\}^{k_2}$
add (r, K) to L_{G^*}	add $((r, m, c_1, c_2), c_3)$ to L_{H^*}
return K	return c_3

Since the difference between Game$_0$ and Game$_1$ is only conceptual, we have

$$\Pr[Win_0] = \Pr[Win_1]. \tag{2}$$

Game$_2$: This game is identical to Game$_1$ except for the following behaviors of the random oracles G^* and H^*. Concretely, for G^*, it does not refer to the list L_G. Moreover, when given an input r, it randomly chooses a value $K \in \{0,1\}^{k_1}$ and adds (r, K) to the list L_{G^*}, even if there exists some query/response pair(s) $(r, K_1) \in L_{G^*}$. Hence, in the list L_{G^*}, it is possible that there exist multiple responses for the same input r. However, when the random oracles G and GG^* referring to the list L_{G^*}, they only adopt the first entry that was added in L_{G^*}. The random oracles H^*, H and HH^* run analogously to G^*, G and GG^*, respectively. The pseudocodes of G^* and H^* can be found in Table 2.

Denote by Col the event that there exists an entry of the form $(r, \cdot) \in L_G \cup L_{G^*}$ or the form $((r, \cdot, \cdot, \cdot), \cdot) \in L_H$ when the challenger chooses $r \xleftarrow{\$} \{0,1\}^{\ell_1}$ to answer $\mathcal{A}$'s KDM query.[1]

---

[1] Note that $(r, \cdot) \in L_{G^*}$ if and only if $((r, \cdot, \cdot, \cdot), \cdot) \in L_{H^*}$.

Table 2. The pseudocodes of G^* and H^* in Game$_2$.

$G^*(r)$:	$H^*(r, m, c_1, c_2)$:
$K \xleftarrow{\$} \{0,1\}^{k_1}$	$c_3 \xleftarrow{\$} \{0,1\}^{k_2}$
add (r, K) to L_{G^*}	add $((r, m, c_1, c_2), c_3)$ to L_{H^*}
return K	return c_3

Table 3. The pseudocodes of G and H in Game$_3$.

$G(r)$:	$H(r, m, c_1, c_2)$:
If $(r, K) \in L_G$	If $((r, m, c_1, c_2), c_3) \in L_H$
return K	return c_3
Else	Else
$K \xleftarrow{\$} \{0,1\}^{k_1}$	$c_3 \xleftarrow{\$} \{0,1\}^{k_2}$
add (r, K) to L_G	add $((r, m, c_1, c_2), c_3)$ to L_H
return K	return c_3

Obviously, Game$_1$ and Game$_2$ are identical if Col does not occur. Hence, we have

$$|\Pr[Win_1] - \Pr[Win_2]| \leq \Pr[Col]. \tag{3}$$

We can easily know that, for each KDM query, a random $r \in \{0,1\}^{\ell_1}$ causes the event Col occurs with probability at most $\frac{2q_e + 2q_d + q_G + q_H}{2^{\ell_1}}$. Hence, for the total q_e KDM queries,

$$\Pr[Col] \leq \frac{q_e(2q_e + 2q_d + q_G + q_H)}{2^{\ell_1}},$$

which is negligible.

Game$_3$: This game is identical to Game$_2$ except that G does not refer to the list L_{G^*} and H does not refer to the list L_{H^*}. The concrete pseudocodes of them can be found in Table 3. However, we remark that the other random oracles GG^* and HH^* still refer to the lists $L_G \cup L_{G^*}$ and $L_H \cup L_{H^*}$, respectively.

In this and subsequent games, we denote by BHQ_i the event that, in Game$_i$, when the adversary $\mathcal{A}$ queries r to G-oracle or (r, m, c_1, c_2) to H-oracle, there exists an entry $(r, \cdot) \in L_{G^*}$.

We can easily know that, if BHQ_3 does not occur, then Game$_2$ and Game$_3$ are identical. Therefore, we have

$$|\Pr[Win_2] - \Pr[Win_3]| \leq \Pr[BHQ_3]. \tag{4}$$

In order to bound the value $\Pr[BHQ_3]$, we need to adopt the deferred analysis technique [25]. Hence, we continue to introduce the following game(s).

Game$_4$: This game is identical to Game$_3$ except that the challenger answers $\mathcal{A}$'s decryption queries by querying the lists of random oracles instead of using the

Table 4. The concrete description of challenger's answering decryption queries in Game$_4$.

Decryption-Query $(j, c) \notin L_{kdm}$:
  Parse c as $c_1 || c_2 || c_3$
  If $\exists ((r, m, c_1, c_2), c_3) \in L_H \cup L_{H^*}$
    Compute $K \leftarrow GG^*(r)$
    Check if $c_2 = EncS(K, m)$
    If it is,
      Submit $(j, (r, c_1))$ to Plaintext-Checking Oracle
      If the response is 1
        Output m
      Else, output $\perp$.
    Else, output $\perp$.
  Else, output $\perp$

---

secret keys. The concrete description of answering the decryption queries can be found in Table 4.

Denote by BDQ the event that the query $(j, c) = (j, (c_1, c_2, c_3))$ (from $\mathcal{A}$) is a correct ciphertext (i.e. c_1 is a legal ciphertext of some message r under the public key pk_j, c_2 is the encryption of some plaintext m under the key $GG^*(r)$, and it holds that $c_3 = HH^*(r, m, c_1, c_2)$) but the query (r, m, c_1, c_2) has not been asked to HH^* (i.e. $((r, m, c_1, c_2), c_3) \notin L_H \cup L_{H^*}$).

We note that the two games Game$_3$ and Game$_4$ are identical unless BDQ occurs. Therefore, we have

$$|\Pr[BHQ_3] - \Pr[BHQ_4]| \leq \Pr[BDQ], \tag{5}$$

and

$$|\Pr[Win_3] - \Pr[Win_4]| \leq \Pr[BDQ]. \tag{6}$$

However, the value $\Pr[BDQ]$ is negligible. The reason lies in that, if the adversary $\mathcal{A}$ does not query (r, m, c_1, c_2) to HH^*, then he can correctly guess the value $HH^*(r, m, c_1, c_2)$ only with probability $1/2^{k_2}$. That is,

$$\Pr[BDQ] \leq \frac{1}{2^{k_2}}. \tag{7}$$

Game$_5$: This game is identical to Game$_4$ except that the challenger answers the decryption queries with the manner described in Table 5.

Here, we define BDQ' as the event that the decryption query $(j, c) = (j, c_1 || c_2 || c_3) \notin L_{kdm}$ (from $\mathcal{A}$) satisfies one of the following two conditions:

- **Condition 1.** There exist $((r, m, c_1, c_2), c_3) \in L_H$, $(r, K) \in L_{G^*}$, and

$$r \leftarrow DecP(sk_j, c_1), \quad m \leftarrow DecS(K, c_2). \tag{8}$$

Table 5. The manner of challenger's answering decryption queries in $Game_5$.

```
Decryption-Query (j, c) ∉ L_kdm:
  Parse c as c₁||c₂||c₃
  If ∃ ((r, m, c₁, c₂), c₃) ∈ L_H
    Compute K ← G(r)
    Check if c₂ = EncS(K, m)
    If it is,
      Submit (j, (r, c₁)) to Plaintext-Checking Oracle
      If the response is 1
        Output m
      Else, output ⊥.
    Else, output ⊥.
  Else, output ⊥
```

– **Condition 2.** There exist $((r, m, c_1, c_2), c_3) \in L_{H^*}$, $(r, K) \in L_{G^*}$, and (8) holds.

In order to analyze the differences of $Game_4$ and $Game_5$, we still need to use the deferred analysis technique. Hence, in this and the subsequent games, we denote by BDQ_i' the event BDQ' occurs in $Game_i$. Obviously, if BDQ_5' (or BDQ_4') does not occurs, then the two games are identical. Therefore, we have

$$|\Pr[Win_4] - \Pr[Win_5]| \leq \Pr[BDQ_5'] \leq |\Pr[BDQ_5'] - \Pr[BDQ_6']| + \Pr[BDQ_6']. \quad (9)$$

$$|\Pr[BHQ_4] - \Pr[BHQ_5]| \leq \Pr[BDQ_5'] \leq |\Pr[BDQ_5'] - \Pr[BDQ_6']| + \Pr[BDQ_6']. \quad (10)$$

Game₆: This game is identical to $Game_5$ except that the challenger ignores the challenge bit b and always encrypts the message $0^{|f(\cdot)|}$ when answering $\mathcal{A}$'s KDM encryption queries.

Note that, in $Game_6$, the challenger always responds to the KDM queries (j, f) by returning an ciphertext of $0^{|f(\cdot)|}$ regardless of the challenge bit b. That is, the choice of b and the behavior of $\mathcal{A}$ (in $Game_6$) are independent. Thus, it holds that

$$\left|\Pr[Win_6] - \frac{1}{2}\right| = 0. \quad (11)$$

Combining with the (in)equalities (1-11), and the following Lemmas 1 and 2, we know that the scheme REACT is KDM-CCA secure in the random oracle if Σ and Π are OW-PCA and IND secure, respectively.

∎ **(Theorem 1)**

Lemma 1. *If the secret key scheme Π is IND secure, then*

$$|\Pr[Win_5] - \Pr[Win_6]| = negl(\lambda), \quad (12)$$

$$|\Pr[BHQ_5] - \Pr[BHQ_6]| = negl(\lambda), \quad (13)$$

and

$$|\Pr[BDQ_5'] - \Pr[BDQ_6']| = negl(\lambda). \tag{14}$$

Proof of Lemma 1. For lack of space, we only prove the Eq. (12) by using hybrid argument. The other ones (i.e. (13) and (14)) are similar and hence omitted, which can be found in the full version of this paper.

Now, we first introduce $q_e + 1$ games $\text{Game}_{5,0}, \cdots, \text{Game}_{5,q_e}$, where $\text{Game}_{5,0}$ equals to the game Game_5, and other ones are defined as follows. For $1 \le t \le q_e$,

Game$_{5,t}$: This game is identical to the game $\text{Game}_{5,t-1}$ except that the challenger returns the ciphertext of $0^{|f(\cdot)|}$ when $\mathcal{A}$ makes the τ-th KDM query, where $q_e - t < \tau \le q_e$.

Obviously, Game_{5,q_e} is just the game Game_6. If we can prove that, in the two adjacent games, the difference of the probabilities for $\mathcal{A}$ winning is negligible, then (12) follows. Now, we prove it holds for any two adjacent games $\text{Game}_{5,t-1}$ and $\text{Game}_{5,t}$. In particular, we construct an adversary $\mathcal{B}_t$, attacking on the IND security of Π, by using $\mathcal{A}$ as a subroutine.

- **Initialization.** $\mathcal{B}_t$ generates $(pk_i, sk_i) \leftarrow GenP(1^\lambda)$, for $1 \le i \le \ell$, chooses $b \xleftarrow{\$} \{0,1\}$, and sets

$$L_{kdm} = L_G = L_{G^*} = L_H = L_{H^*} = \emptyset.$$

Return $(pk_1, \cdots, pk_\ell)$ to $\mathcal{A}$.
- **Queries.** $\mathcal{A}$ is allowed to adaptively make the following queries.
  - Hash Queries. When $\mathcal{A}$ queries r to G-oracle, $\mathcal{B}_t$ checks if there exists an entry $(r, K) \in L_G$. If it is, return K to $\mathcal{A}$. Else, choose $K \xleftarrow{\$} \{0,1\}^{k_1}$, return it to $\mathcal{A}$, and add (r, K) to L_G. When $\mathcal{A}$ queries (r, m, c_1, c_2) to H-oracle, $\mathcal{B}_t$ checks if there exists an entry $((r, m, c_1, c_2), c_3) \in L_H$. If it is, return c_3 to $\mathcal{A}$. Else, choose $c_3 \xleftarrow{\$} \{0,1\}^{k_2}$, return it to $\mathcal{A}$, and add $((r, m, c_1, c_2), c_3)$ to L_H.
  - KDM Queries. For the τ-th KDM query (j, f), $\mathcal{B}_t$ responds to it as follows.
    * For $1 \le \tau < t$, set $m_1 = f^{GG^*, HH^*}(sk_1, \cdots, sk_\ell)$ and $m_0 = 0^{|f(\cdot)|}$. Choose $r \xleftarrow{\$} \{0,1\}^{\ell_1}, K \xleftarrow{\$} \{0,1\}^{k_1}, c_3^* \xleftarrow{\$} \{0,1\}^{k_2}$, and run

$$c_1^* \leftarrow EncP(pk_j, r), \ c_2^* \leftarrow EncS(K, m_b).$$

Add $(j, (c_1^*, c_2^*, c_3^*)), (r, K)$, and $((r, m_b, c_1^*, c_2^*), c_3^*)$ to L_{kdm}, L_{G^*} and L_{H^*}, respectively. Maintain the lists L_G and L_H according to $\mathcal{A}$'s queries. Finally, return (c_1^*, c_2^*, c_3^*) to $\mathcal{A}$.
    * For $\tau = t$, still set $m_1 = f^{GG^*, HH^*}(sk_1, \cdots, sk_\ell)$ and $m_0 = 0^{|f(\cdot)|}$. Submit them to its own encryption oracle and obtain the response c_2^*. Then choose $r \xleftarrow{\$} \{0,1\}^{\ell_1}$ and run $c_1^* \leftarrow EncP(pk_j, r)$. Also choose $c_3^* \xleftarrow{\$} \{0,1\}^{k_2}$. Return (c_1^*, c_2^*, c_3^*) to $\mathcal{A}$. Finally, add $(r, \perp)$ and $((r, \perp, c_1^*, c_2^*), c_3^*)$ to L_{G^*} and L_{H^*}, respectively. That is, $\mathcal{B}_t$ simulates the random value $G^*(r)$ of r with its challenger's secret key, which he does not know.

∗ For $t < \tau \leq q_e$, choose $r \xleftarrow{\$} \{0,1\}^{\ell_1}, K \xleftarrow{\$} \{0,1\}^{k_1}, c_3^* \xleftarrow{\$} \{0,1\}^{k_2}$, and run

$$c_1^* \leftarrow EncP(pk_j, r), \ c_2^* \leftarrow EncS(K, 0^{|f(\cdot)|}).$$

Add $(j, (c_1^*, c_2^*, c_3^*)), (r, K)$, and $((r, 0^{|f(\cdot)|}, c_1^*, c_2^*), c_3^*)$ to L_{kdm}, L_{G^*} and L_{H^*}, respectively.

- Decryption Queries. For the decryption query $(j, c) \notin L_{kdm}$, $\mathcal{B}_t$ first parses c as $c_1 \| c_2 \| c_3$. Then look for all the pairs (r, m) such that the query (r, m, c_1, c_2) has been asked to H with the answer c_3. For any of these pairs, $\mathcal{B}_t$ computes $K = G(r)$ (using his simulation of G-oracle), checks if $c_2 = EncS(K, m)$ and $r = DecP(sk_j, c_1)$. In the positive case, $\mathcal{B}_t$ outputs m. Otherwise, output $\bot$.

- **Guess.** Finally, when $\mathcal{A}$ outputs a bit b, $\mathcal{B}_t$ also outputs it.

This ends the description of $\mathcal{B}_t$, from which we know that, if $\mathcal{B}_t$'s challenger responds with the encryption of m_1 (resp. m_0), then he simulates the game $\text{Game}_{5,t-1}$ (resp. $\text{Game}_{5,t}$) for $\mathcal{A}$. Therefore, we have

$$|\Pr[Win_{5,t-1}] - \Pr[Win_{5,t}]| \leq Adv_{\mathcal{B}_t, \Pi}^{\text{IND}}(1^\lambda).$$

Since the secret key scheme Π is IND secure, $Adv_{\mathcal{B}_t, \Pi}^{\text{IND}}(1^\lambda)$ is negligible. Hence, (12) follows.

■ **(Lemma 1)**

Lemma 2. *If the public key scheme Σ is OW-PCA secure, then*

$$\Pr[BHQ_6] = negl(\lambda), \tag{15}$$

and

$$\Pr[BDQ_6'] = negl(\lambda). \tag{16}$$

Proof of Lemma 2. We first prove the Eq. (15). In particular, we construct an adversary $\mathcal{B}$ attacking on the OW-PCA security of Σ by using $\mathcal{A}$ as a subroutine.

- **Initialization.** Given a public key pk^* and his challenge ciphertext c_1^{**}, $\mathcal{B}$ first chooses $s \xleftarrow{\$} [\ell]$, sets $pk_s = pk^*$, and runs $(pk_i, sk_i) \leftarrow GenP(1^\lambda)$ for $i = 1, \cdots, s-1, s+1, \cdots, \ell$. Then choose $t \xleftarrow{\$} [q_e]$, and initialize

$$L_{kdm} = L_G = L_{G^*} = L_H = L_{H^*} = L_{ans} = \emptyset.$$

Return $pk_1, \cdots, pk_\ell$ to $\mathcal{A}$.
- **Queries.** $\mathcal{A}$ is allowed to adaptively make the following queries.
  - Hash Queries. When $\mathcal{A}$ queries r to G-oracle, $\mathcal{B}$ checks if there exists an entry $(r, K) \in L_G$. If it is, return K to $\mathcal{A}$. Else, choose $K \xleftarrow{\$} \{0,1\}^{k_1}$, return it to $\mathcal{A}$. Add (r, K) to L_G and r to L_{ans}. When $\mathcal{A}$ queries (r, m, c_1, c_2) to H-oracle, $\mathcal{B}$ checks if there exists an entry $((r, m, c_1, c_2), c_3) \in L_H$. If it is, return c_3 to $\mathcal{A}$. Else, choose $c_3 \xleftarrow{\$} \{0,1\}^{k_2}$, return it to $\mathcal{A}$. Add $((r, m, c_1, c_2), c_3)$ to L_H and r to L_{ans}.

- KDM Queries. For the i-th KDM query (j, f), $\mathcal{B}$ first chooses $K \xleftarrow{\$}$ $\{0,1\}^{k_1}$, and $c_3^* \xleftarrow{\$} \{0,1\}^{k_2}$. Run $c_2^* \leftarrow EncS(K, 0^{|f(\cdot)|})$. Then check if $i = t$.
  * If it is not, then he continues to choose $r \xleftarrow{\$} \{0,1\}^{\ell_1}$, and run $c_1^* \leftarrow EncP(pk_j, r)$. Add (r, K) to L_{G^*} and $((r, 0^{|f(\cdot)|}, c_1^*, c_2^*), c_3^*)$ to L_{H^*}.
  * Else, he continues to check if $j = s$. If it is not, he stops the simulation and output $\perp$. Else, set $c_1^* = c_1^{**}$, add $(\perp, K)$ to L_{G^*} and $((\perp, 0^{|f(\cdot)|}, c_1^*, c_2^*), c_3^*)$ to L_{H^*}.
  Add $(j, (c_1^*, c_2^*, c_3^*))$ to L_{kdm} and return $c^* = (c_1^*, c_2^*, c_3^*)$ to $\mathcal{A}$.
- Decryption Queries. For the decryption query $(j, c) \notin L_{kdm}$, $\mathcal{B}$ first parses c as $c_1 || c_2 || c_3$ and looks for all the pairs (r, m) such that the query (r, m, c_1, c_2) has been asked to H with the answer c_3. For any of these pairs, $\mathcal{B}$ then computes $K = G(r)$ (using his simulation of G-oracle), checks if $c_2 = EncS(K, m)$, and $r = DecP(sk_j, c_1)$ using the Plaintext-Checking Oracle if $j \neq s$ and sk_s if $j = s$. In the positive case, $\mathcal{B}$ outputs m. Otherwise, output $\perp$.
- **Guess.** When $\mathcal{A}$ outputs a bit $b \in \{0,1\}$, $\mathcal{B}$ randomly chooses the τ-th element r in L_{ans} and outputs it.

This ends the description of $\mathcal{B}$.

If $\mathcal{B}$ does not stop the simulation, then he perfectly simulates the game Game_6 for $\mathcal{A}$. We note that s, t, and τ are chosen uniformly and the choice of them is information-theoretically hidden to $\mathcal{A}$ if $\mathcal{B}$ does not abort. Therefore, all of them are independent of $\mathcal{A}$ (in the case that $\mathcal{B}$ does not abort).

When $\mathcal{A}$ queries r to G-oracle or (r, m, c_1, c_2) to H-oracle, $\mathcal{B}$ adds it to L_{ans}. If BHQ_6 occurs, then there exists an entry $(r, \cdot)$ in L_{G^*}. That is, for some item $r \in L_{ans}$, it is used to answer $\mathcal{A}$'s some KDM query.

Therefore, if BHQ_6 just occurs in the t-th KDM query (j, f) and $\mathcal{B}$ does not abort the simulation (i.e. $j = s$), then $\mathcal{A}$ has queried the "plaintext" r^* of c_1^{**} to G-oracle or H-oracle. Since t, s are independent of $\mathcal{A}$'s view, the event BHQ_6 occurs in the t-th KDM query occurs with probability $1/q_e$ and the other event $j = s$ occurs with probability $1/\ell$. At the final phase, since $\mathcal{B}$ randomly chooses the "answer" in L_{ans}, he can correctly obtain r^* at least with probability $1/|L_{ans}|$. Putting all the facts together, we have

$$\Pr[BHQ_6] \leq q_e \cdot \ell \cdot |L_{ans}| \cdot Adv_{\mathcal{B}, \Sigma}^{OW\text{-}PCA}(1^\lambda),$$

which is negligible. That is, the Eq. (15) holds.

Next, we consider the Eq. (16). Recall that BDQ_6' means that, in Game_6, the decryption query $(j, c_1 || c_2 || c_3) \notin L_{kdm}$ (from $\mathcal{A}$) satisfies one of the following two conditions:

- **Condition 1.** There exist $((r, m, c_1, c_2), c_3) \in L_H$, $(r, K) \in L_{G^*}$, and

$$r \leftarrow DecP(sk_j, c_1), \quad m \leftarrow DecS(K, c_2). \tag{17}$$

- **Condition 2.** There exist $((r, m, c_1, c_2), c_3) \in L_{H^*}$, $(r, K) \in L_{G^*}$, and (17) holds.

Now, we first bound the probability of Condition 2. According to the description of Condition 2, we know that there exists some entry $(j^*, c_1^* \| c_2^* \| c_3^*) \in L_{kdm}$ satisfying

$$r = r^*, \ m = m^*, \ c_1 = c_1^*, \ c_2 = c_2^*, \ \text{and} \ c_3 = c_3^*,$$

where

$$r^* = DecP(sk_{j^*}, c_1^*), \ m^* = DecS(G^*(r^*), c_2^*).$$

Hence, it naturally holds that $j \neq j^*$. In addition, from (17), we know that $r \leftarrow DecP(sk_j, c_1)$, which yields

$$DecP(sk_j, c_1^*) = DecP(sk_{j^*}, c_1^*) \tag{18}$$

when combined with $r = r^*, c_1 = c_1^*$. However, the probability that (18) occurs is at most negligible, since the OW-PCA security of Σ guarantees that the common ciphertext c_1^* is decrypted to the same plaintext $r(= r^*)$ under independent secret keys sk_j, sk_{j^*} with at most negligible probability.

Therefore, the decryption query $(j, c_1 \| c_2 \| c_3) \notin L_{kdm}$ satisfies Condition 2 with at most negligible probability $negl(1^\lambda)$.

As a result, we only need to consider the event BDQ_6' when Condition 1 holds, which can still be reduced to the OW-PCA security of Σ. Concretely, we construct another adversary $\mathcal{B}'$ attacking on the OW-PCA security of Σ by using $\mathcal{A}$ as a subroutine. In fact, $\mathcal{B}'$ runs in exactly the same way as $\mathcal{B}$ except that, when answering $\mathcal{A}$'s hash queries, he only adds r to L_{ans}, where r is the first element of some entry (r, m, c_1, c_2) queried to H-oracle.

If the event BDQ_6' satisfying Condition 1 occurs, then there exists $((r^*, m, c_1, c_2), c_3) \in L_H$, where r^* is some randomness used to answer $\mathcal{A}$'s i_0-th KDM query (j_0, f). We note that only when $\mathcal{A}$ makes a H-oracle query, an entry is added to L_H. Hence, $((r^*, m, c_1, c_2), c_3) \in L_H$ means that the adversary $\mathcal{A}$ has queried (r^*, m, c_1, c_2) to H-oracle. From the construction of $\mathcal{B}'$, we know that this r^* is included in L_{ans}.

Therefore, if $i_0 = t$ and $\mathcal{B}'$ does not abort the simulation (i.e. $j_0 = s$), then $\mathcal{B}'$ just embeds his own challenge ciphertext c^{**} in the t-th KDM ciphertext (for $\mathcal{A}$) and this r^* is just the decryption of c^{**}. By randomly choosing element from L_{ans}, $\mathcal{B}'$ can find r^* with probability $1/|L_{ans}|$. On the other hand, s, t are also randomly chosen by $\mathcal{B}'$, and the choice of them is information-theoretically hidden to $\mathcal{A}$. Hence, the probabilities of $i_0 = t$ and $j_0 = s$ equal to $1/q_e$ and $1/\ell$, respectively.

Putting all the facts together, we know that

$$\Pr[BDQ_6'] = \Pr[BDQ_6' \text{ when Condition 1 holds}] + \Pr[BDQ_6' \text{ when Condition 2 holds}]$$

$$\leq q_e \cdot \ell \cdot |L_{ans}| \cdot Adv_{\mathcal{B}', \Sigma}^{\text{OW-PCA}}(1^\lambda) + negl(1^\lambda),$$

which is still negligible. That is, the Eq. (16) holds.

$$\blacksquare \text{ (Lemma 2)}$$

4 Conclusion

In this paper, we prove the KDM-CCA security of the REACT scheme, which has been proven to be CCA secure in the random oracle if the asymmetric encryption part is OW-PCA secure, the symmetric encryption part is IND secure and both the hash functions G and H are modeled as random oracles. Our result illustrates that it can naturally "obtain" KDM security based on exactly the same assumptions on its building blocks as those used in original REACT.

Acknowledgements. We are grateful to the anonymous reviewers for their helpful comments and suggestions. This research is supported by the National Natural Science Foundation of China (No. 61602061; No. 61672059; No. 61272499; No. 61472016; No.61472414; No.61402471) and China Postdoctoral Science Foundation (Grant No. 2017M610021).

References

1. Applebaum, B.: Key-dependent message security: generic amplification and completeness. In: Paterson, K.G. (ed.) EUROCRYPT 2011. LNCS, vol. 6632, pp. 527–546. Springer, Heidelberg (2011). https://doi.org/10.1007/978-3-642-20465-4_29
2. Applebaum, B., Cash, D., Peikert, C., Sahai, A.: Fast cryptographic primitives and circular-secure encryption based on hard learning problems. In: Halevi, S. (ed.) CRYPTO 2009. LNCS, vol. 5677, pp. 595–618. Springer, Heidelberg (2009). https://doi.org/10.1007/978-3-642-03356-8_35
3. Backes, M., Dürmuth, M., Unruh, D.: OAEP is secure under key-dependent messages. In: Pieprzyk, J. (ed.) ASIACRYPT 2008. LNCS, vol. 5350, pp. 506–523. Springer, Heidelberg (2008). https://doi.org/10.1007/978-3-540-89255-7_31
4. Barak, B., Haitner, I., Hofheinz, D., Ishai, Y.: Bounded key-dependent message security. In: Gilbert, H. (ed.) EUROCRYPT 2010. LNCS, vol. 6110, pp. 423–444. Springer, Heidelberg (2010). https://doi.org/10.1007/978-3-642-13190-5_22
5. Bellare, M., Rogaway, P.: Optimal asymmetric encryption. In: De Santis, A. (ed.) EUROCRYPT 1994. LNCS, vol. 950, pp. 92–111. Springer, Heidelberg (1995). https://doi.org/10.1007/BFb0053428
6. Black, J., Rogaway, P., Shrimpton, T.: Encryption-scheme security in the presence of key-dependent messages. In: Nyberg, K., Heys, H. (eds.) SAC 2002. LNCS, vol. 2595, pp. 62–75. Springer, Heidelberg (2003). https://doi.org/10.1007/3-540-36492-7_6
7. Boneh, D., Halevi, S., Hamburg, M., Ostrovsky, R.: Circular-secure encryption from decision diffie-hellman. In: Wagner, D. (ed.) CRYPTO 2008. LNCS, vol. 5157, pp. 108–125. Springer, Heidelberg (2008). https://doi.org/10.1007/978-3-540-85174-5_7
8. Böhl, F., Davies, G.T., Hofheinz, D.: Encryption schemes secure under related-key and key-dependent message attacks. In: Krawczyk, H. (ed.) PKC 2014. LNCS, vol. 8383, pp. 483–500. Springer, Heidelberg (2014). https://doi.org/10.1007/978-3-642-54631-0_28
9. Brakerski, Z., Goldwasser, S.: Circular and leakage resilient public-key encryption under subgroup indistinguishability. In: Rabin, T. (ed.) CRYPTO 2010. LNCS, vol. 6223, pp. 1–20. Springer, Heidelberg (2010). https://doi.org/10.1007/978-3-642-14623-7_1

10. Brakerski, Z., Goldwasser, S., Kalai, Y.T.: Black-box circular-secure encryption beyond affine functions. In: Ishai, Y. (ed.) TCC 2011. LNCS, vol. 6597, pp. 201–218. Springer, Heidelberg (2011). https://doi.org/10.1007/978-3-642-19571-6_13

11. Camenisch, J., Chandran, N., Shoup, V.: A public key encryption scheme secure against key dependent chosen plaintext and adaptive chosen ciphertext attacks. In: Joux, A. (ed.) EUROCRYPT 2009. LNCS, vol. 5479, pp. 351–368. Springer, Heidelberg (2009). https://doi.org/10.1007/978-3-642-01001-9_20

12. Camenisch, J., Lysyanskaya, A.: An efficient system for non-transferable anonymous credentials with optional anonymity revocation. In: Pfitzmann, B. (ed.) EUROCRYPT 2001. LNCS, vol. 2045, pp. 93–118. Springer, Heidelberg (2001). https://doi.org/10.1007/3-540-44987-6_7

13. Cash, D., Green, M., Hohenberger, S.: New definitions and separations for circular security. In: Fischlin, M., Buchmann, J., Manulis, M. (eds.) PKC 2012. LNCS, vol. 7293, pp. 540–557. Springer, Heidelberg (2012). https://doi.org/10.1007/978-3-642-30057-8_32

14. Chang, J., Dai, H., Xu, M., Xue, R.: Separations in circular security for arbitrary length key cycles, revisited. Secur. Commun. Netw. 9(18), 5392–5400 (2016)

15. Chen, Y., Zhang, J., Deng, Y., Chang, J.: KDM security for identity-based encryption: construction and separations. IACR Cryptology ePrint Archive 2016: 1020

16. Cramer, R., Shoup, V.: Universal hash proofs and a paradigm for adaptive chosen ciphertext secure public-key encryption. In: Knudsen, L.R. (ed.) EUROCRYPT 2002. LNCS, vol. 2332, pp. 45–64. Springer, Heidelberg (2002). https://doi.org/10.1007/3-540-46035-7_4

17. Davies, G.T., Stam, M.: KDM security in the hybrid framework. In: Benaloh, J. (ed.) CT-RSA 2014. LNCS, vol. 8366, pp. 461–480. Springer, Cham (2014). https://doi.org/10.1007/978-3-319-04852-9_24

18. Fujisaki, E., Okamoto, T.: How to enhance the security of public-key encryption at minimum cost. In: Imai, H., Zheng, Y. (eds.) PKC 1999. LNCS, vol. 1560, pp. 53–68. Springer, Heidelberg (1999). https://doi.org/10.1007/3-540-49162-7_5

19. Fujisaki, E., Okamoto, T.: Secure integration of asymmetric and symmetric encryption schemes. In: Wiener, M. (ed.) CRYPTO 1999. LNCS, vol. 1666, pp. 537–554. Springer, Heidelberg (1999). https://doi.org/10.1007/3-540-48405-1_34

20. Gentry, C.: A full homomorphic encryption scheme. PHD thesis, Standford University (2009). crypto.standford.edu/craig

21. Han, S., Liu, S., Lyu, L.: Efficient KDM-CCA secure public-key encryption for polynomial functions. In: Cheon, J.H., Takagi, T. (eds.) ASIACRYPT 2016. LNCS, vol. 10032, pp. 307–338. Springer, Heidelberg (2016). https://doi.org/10.1007/978-3-662-53890-6_11

22. Haitner, I., Holenstein, T.: On the (Im)possibility of key dependent encryption. In: Reingold, O. (ed.) TCC 2009. LNCS, vol. 5444, pp. 202–219. Springer, Heidelberg (2009). https://doi.org/10.1007/978-3-642-00457-5_13

23. Kitagawa, F., Matsuda, T., Hanaoka, G., Tanaka, K.: On the key dependent message security of the fujisaki-okamoto constructions. In: Cheng, C.-M., Chung, K.-M., Persiano, G., Yang, B.-Y. (eds.) PKC 2016. LNCS, vol. 9614, pp. 99–129. Springer, Heidelberg (2016). https://doi.org/10.1007/978-3-662-49384-7_5

24. Okamoto, T., Pointcheval, D.: REACT: rapid enhanced-security asymmetric cryptosystem transform. In: Naccache, D. (ed.) CT-RSA 2001. LNCS, vol. 2020, pp. 159–174. Springer, Heidelberg (2000). https://doi.org/10.1007/3-540-45353-9_13

25. Shoup, V.: Sequences of games: a tool for taming complexity in security proofs. IACR Cryptology ePrint Archive 2004: 332

Privacy-Preserving Extraction of HOG Features Based on Integer Vector Homomorphic Encryption

Haomiao Yang[1]([✉]), Yunfan Huang[1]([✉]), Yong Yu[2], Mingxuan Yao[1], and Xiaosong Zhang[1]

[1] School of Computer Science and Engineering, Center for Cyber Security, University of Electronic Science and Technology of China, Chengdu, China
haomyang@uestc.edu.cn, huangyf0714@163.com, mingxuanyao@hotmail.com, s_x_zhang@163.com
[2] Shaanxi Normal University, Xi'an, China
yuyong@snnu.edu.cn

Abstract. Along with the growing popularity of social networks, the number of multimedia image grows explosively. For the resource constrained owners, dealing with tremendous number of images on their own is a challenging job. Therefore, there is a general trend to outsource the heavy image processing (e.g., feature extraction) to the cloud. Abundant contents in images may expose the owner's sensitive information (e.g., face, location and event), and outsourcing the image data to the untrusted cloud directly has raised privacy concerns of public. In this work, we explore the outsourcing of the famous feature extraction algorithm-Histogram of Oriented Gradients (HOG) to the public cloud with privacy protection. In our proposed scheme, the image owner encrypts the original images by using the Vector Homomorphic Encryption (VHE) that encrypt vector directly and is much suitable for image processing. Then the image owner sends the encrypted images to the cloud which elaborately applies the *linear transformation* of VHE to the realization of the improved HOG algorithm in ciphertext domain. The security analysis based on the hardness of Learning with Error (LWE) Problem verifies that the extraction of HOG features is privacy-preserving in our scheme without leaking privacy contents to any other parties. We implement pedestrian detection by using the extracted HOG features to validate the efficiency and effectiveness of our proposed scheme, and the result shows that our solution can extract the HOG features correctly in ciphertext domain and approximate the original HOG in plaintext domain. Compared with existing solution, our scheme has less time and communication cost of HOG feature extraction.

Keywords: Privacy-preserving · HOG · Homomorphic encryption

© Springer International Publishing AG 2017
J. K. Liu and P. Samarati (Eds.): ISPEC 2017, LNCS 10701, pp. 102–117, 2017.
https://doi.org/10.1007/978-3-319-72359-4_6

1 Introduction

With the arrival of the era of Big Data, the number and manner of image generation are increased considerably, which stimulates a lot of image applications, e.g., pedestrian detection, machine vision. Especially, along with the popularity of multimedia social network, the number of user-contributed images is sharply increased. According to the statistics, a number of images users upload to the social network servers only through Facebook has reached 500 million every day, making it difficult to deal with massive image in storage, sharing and search etc. In order to eliminate the influence of random factors of original images such as noise information, lack of pixels etc., and to get more efficient results in these image applications, it is essential to extract features from the original images, which means extracting information is of strong robustness to express the attributes of the images. The research of image feature extraction is of great significance in processing and analyzing massive image data, and it is the base of the applications of massive images.

Because of the powerful storage and computing in the cloud, more and more social server providers choose to provide image service based on the cloud server, such as Amazon Cloud Drive, Apple iCloud, Flicker and Google etc. However, the original images always contain users' sensitive information, e.g., personal identity, home address, and even financial conditions. And the cloud is not such believable as people imagine, existing the leakage of users' privacy information intentionally or unintentionally. In 2013, the report of PRISM [6] revealed privacy invasion to user-contributed data. In this event, the security authority has access to the social network servers owning to IT giants' permission. As a result, the security authority can inspect all the image data stored in cloud server, and it cause the public's concern about their own privacy.

Therefore, the privacy in image feature extraction with large-scale magnitude is an urgent problem that eagerly to be solved. When the cloud is not as reliable and trustworthy as people think, some other cloud security methods has been proposed, such as, data anonymization, secure multi-party computation (SMC) [9]. However, those methods are not very suitable and practical to deal with large-scale images under privacy protection. For example, multiple interactions between image owners and the queries in SMC lead to high communication cost. The other way to protect the privacy of image is image encryption. Traditional encryption schemes (e.g. DES, AES) change the original image data format in the encryption process, which will hinder further feather extraction and applications. Compared with those scheme, Homomorphic Encryption (HE) can handle the ciphertext before decryption, and there is a great possibility that HE can become a good solution to guarantee the privacy and security of images. After using of the homomorphic encryption, image data has converted from plaintext to ciphertext. By utilizing homomorphism, the ciphertext of images are computed and processed under the protection of privacy, and then the results as equivalent as the plaintext results can be obtained.

In previous researches, Hsu et al. [7] studied privacy-preserving SIFT algorithm under ciphertext domain through Paillier HE [11]. But this solution either has a large overhead in computation or has security weaknesses as discussed in [14]. In [13], Qin et al. proposed an alternative solution on the basis of order-preserving encryption (OPE) [1] and random permutation to ensure confidentiality and privacy. From [17], the authors Wang et al. set out to find a better solution to privacy problems through garbled circuits [8] and homomorphic encryption scheme, and they respectively proposed two schemes with different security levels. Although there are obvious improvements in both privacy and efficiency, the proposed schemes are lackof comprehensive analysis and evaluation as previous schemes. As a following work, Q. Wang et al. carried out a research on the HOG algorithm [16] in ciphertext domain with somewhat homomorphic encryption, but it need the support of SIMD [15] to perform well.

In this paper, we provide a feasible solution to extract image feature by using HOG algorithm, meanwhile users privacy is well protected. The main ideas are as follows: The image owners encrypt their own image data by homomorphic encryption based integer vector and upload the ciphertext to the cloud, the cloud gains the image data in ciphertext domain and then carries out extraction algorithm—Histogram of Oriented Gradient (HOG), as s result, the cloud finally gets the HOG feature vectors in encrypted domain. In practice, the features of HOG are widely used in object detection, especially in pedestrian detection. In the whole process, the most time-consuming work is the generation of image features, and the main challenge is how to protect the untrusted cloud against the sensitive information of the images, meanwhile, the extracted feature can be effective and valid in object detection. In response to this challenge, we proposed a novel and original scheme that combines HOG feature extraction and integer-vector-based homomorphic encryption [18], which can achieve secure and efficient HOG feature extraction of the encrypted images.

Compared with the previous work [7,13,16,17], the contribution of this paper mainly includes three aspects:

1. We explore the privacy-preserving Extraction of the HOG features by utilizing the vector homomorphic encryption (VHE) that is more efficient than existing homomorphic scheme. Especially, the HOG extraction algorithm in our scheme has been improved to better adapt the homomorphic operations in ciphertext domain. And in our proposed system model, the cloud can know nothing but the ciphertext of images when it conducts the outsource computation of our HOG feature extraction, which ensure the privacy of image owners.
2. We have carried out a lot of experiments to verify the correctness of our solution with a large number of images in INRIA Database. And by the comparison with existing work, our scheme shows apparent efficiency and safety advantages.
3. We conduct the pedestrian detection in the Support Vector Machine (SVM) algorithm with extracted HOG descriptors from our scheme, the results of detection indicate that our solution can extract the HOG features correctly in ciphertext domain and approximate well the original HOG in plaintext domain.

The organization of the remaining paper is illustrated as follows: The system and threat models are proposed detailedly in Sect. 2. The integer vector homomorphic encryption(VHE) and the original HOG algorithm are depicted as preliminaries in Sect. 3. Section 4 presents our privacy-preserving HOG algorithm in ciphertext domain. Then we conduct implementations and analyze the whole scheme in multiple aspects in Sect. 5. At last, Sect. 6 gives some conclusions.

2   System Model and Design Goals

In this part, we design the system model according to the practical requirements in the HOG feature extraction of encrypted images, in addition, we construct our threat model. On one hand, the image owners has large-scale multimedia image data, but they have little ability to handle the data by theirselves due to resource constraints. When the image owners want to do the object detection jobs, they may have a tendency to delegate the heavy work of feature extraction to the cloud so that they can be free from the burden of image storage and heavy computations. On the other hand, original multimedia data contains sensitive information of the owners, outsourcing the data directly to the untrusted cloud leads to owners' privacy leaking. To solve this problem, we consider our system model is mainly composed of two entities: the image owners O and the cloud C as shown in Fig. 1.

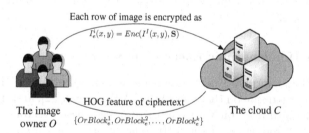

Each row of image is encrypted as
$$I_e^i(x,y) = Enc(I^I(x,y), \mathbf{S})$$

The image owner O

HOG feature of ciphertext
$$\{OrBlock_e^1, OrBlock_e^2, \ldots, OrBlock_e^k\}$$

The cloud C

Fig. 1. System model

In this model, the image owners O encrypt original images using vector-based homomorphic encryption, and upload the ciphertext to the cloud C. After receiving the ciphertext, the cloud C will carry out the improved HOG algorithm in ciphertext domain. All the computations of the algorithm are conducted by the cloud, and because of the encryption, the owners' privacy information is well protected from the cloud, i.e. the cloud can get nothing about the image contents through the process.

Under the design of this system model, we set a hypothesis that the cloud is not absolutely honest. In fact, the cloud will honestly execute the HOG algorithm and return the results of feature vectors in ciphertext to the image owners O, but it is curious about the image contents, and infer the sensitive information from the encrypted images and all the data it can get in computational process. Therefore, we must ensure the cloud can infer nothing about the image contents from the encrypted images so that the owners' privacy is guaranteed.

We consider the challenge how to outsource computing process of the HOG descriptor to the cloud without leaking the original image information, the final purpose of our system is that the system model must ensure image owners' privacy through the whole process under this threat. The overall design goal of our system is as follows:

- Correctness: The HOG features extracted by the improved HOG algorithm have the same attribute as those extracted by the original HOG algorithm, which can performs well in the pedestrian detection.
- Security: By the usage of vector homomorphic encryption scheme, the real contents of images can not be revealed to the cloud or other parties to protect the image owner's privacy.
- Efficiency: Compared with existing work, ensure time and communication cost of our scheme have obvious advantages.

3   Preliminaries

To make this paper better understanding, before elaborating our scheme, it is essential to give some preliminaries, including the integer vector homomorphic encryption and the overview of the original Histogram of Oriented Gradient (HOG) algorithm.

3.1   Vector Homomorphic Encryption Scheme

The Vector Homomorphic Encryption scheme that we utilize in the system is designed as an expansion on the basis of the PVW scheme [12], and the encrypted objects are changed from bit-wise vectors to integer-based vectors.

Before the introduction of the VHE scheme, we give some basic notations in advance to lead a easy understanding as below Table 1. Note that the lower-case bold and capital bold characters represent vectors and matrices respectively (e.g., $\mathbf{v}$ is a column vector and $\mathbf{A}$ is a matrix):

Key Generation: Under a security parameter λ, select some appropriate integers $l, w, m, n, p, q \in Z$ as parameters in VHE. Construct the secret key $\mathbf{S} = [\mathbf{I}, \mathbf{T}] \in Z_q^{m \times n}$, where $\mathbf{I}$ is an identity matrix.

Encryption Operation: Given the secret key $\mathbf{S} \in Z_q^{m \times n}$, so the $\mathbf{x} \in Z_p^m$, $\mathbf{c} \in Z_q^n$, $\mathbf{S}$ can satisfies:

$$\mathbf{Sc} = \omega \mathbf{x} + \mathbf{e} \tag{1}$$

For keeping the error term small later, it's necessary to assume that $|\mathbf{S}| << \omega$ when applying operations in ciphertext domain.

Table 1. Notations

Notation	Meaning
λ	A security parameter in VHE
l	The length parameter in VHE
p, q	Two large prime integers in VHE and $q \gg p$
m, n	Two integers as length parameters in VHE and $n > m$
χ	The probability distribution
ω	A large integer as a parameter in VHE
$\mathbf{e}$	An error vector with elements smaller than $\omega/2$ in χ
Z_p	A finite field with alphabet size p
$a \in Z_p^m$	An integer vector a with length m in the finite field Z_p
$\|v\|$	$Max_i\{\| v_i \|\}$, for a vector $v \in \mathbb{Z}^n$
$\|M\|$	$Max_i\{\| M_{ij} \|\}$, for a matrix $M \in \mathbb{Z}^{n \times m}$
$\lceil a \rfloor_q$	The nearest integer to a with the modulus q
$\lceil \mathbf{a} \rfloor_q$	Round each a_i to the nearest integer with modulus q

Decryption Operation: As for the decryption, it's straightforward:

$$\mathbf{x} = \lceil \frac{\mathbf{Sc}}{\omega} \rfloor_q \tag{2}$$

Addition: For arbitrary plaintexts $\mathbf{x}_1, \mathbf{x}_2$ and their corresponding ciphertexts $\mathbf{c}_1, \mathbf{c}_2$ that are encrypted with the same secret key $\mathbf{S}$, then

$$\mathbf{S}(\mathbf{c}_1 + \mathbf{c}_2) = \omega(\mathbf{x}_1 + \mathbf{x}_2) + (\mathbf{e}_1 + \mathbf{e}_2) \tag{3}$$

Let $\mathbf{c}' = \mathbf{c}_1 + \mathbf{c}_2$, $\mathbf{x}' = \mathbf{x}_1 + \mathbf{x}_2$, and we can observe that

$$\mathbf{Sc}' = \omega\mathbf{x}' + (\mathbf{e}_1 + \mathbf{e}_2) \tag{4}$$

Linear Transformation: Given a plaintext $\mathbf{x}$ and its corresponding ciphertext $\mathbf{c}$ with the secret key $\mathbf{S}$, the linear transformation $\mathbf{Gx}$ can be computed that

$$(\mathbf{GS})\mathbf{c} = \omega\mathbf{Gx} + \mathbf{Ge} \tag{5}$$

with an arbitrary matrix $\mathbf{G} \in Z^{m' \times n}$. Therefore, we can treat $\mathbf{c}$ as the encryption of $\mathbf{Gx}$ with the secret key $\mathbf{GS}$.

When several ciphertexts need to be computed, it's essential to keep their secret keys to be the same. Key switching technique makes it possible to convert a secret key to another chosen secret key and maintain to encrypt the original integer vectors. Based on the relinearization technique introduced by Brakerski et al. in [3] and matrices switching method in [2], the key-switching technique in VHE achieves this conversion.

Key Switching Technique: Suppose the initial secretkey-ciphertext pair $\{\mathbf{S}, \mathbf{c}\}$ and a new secretkey-ciphertext pair $\{\mathbf{S}', \mathbf{c}'\}$ with predefined $\mathbf{S}' = [\mathbf{I}, \mathbf{T}]$, which can satisfy

$$\mathbf{S}'\mathbf{c}' = \mathbf{S}\mathbf{c} \tag{6}$$

Select a length parameter l satisfies $|\mathbf{c}| < 2^l$ and convert each element c_i of the ciphertext c to l-bit binary form $b_i = [b_{i(l-1)}, \cdots, b_{i1}, b_{i0}]^T$, and the ciphertext can be expressed as:

$$\mathbf{c}^* = [b_1{}^T, \cdots, b_n{}^T]^T. \tag{7}$$

Then construct $S^* \in Z^{m \times nl}$ by converting each element S_{ij} in S to a vector $[S_{ij}, S_{ij} \cdot 2, \cdots, S_{ij} \cdot 2^{l-1}]$, which can absolutely satisfy $\mathbf{S}\mathbf{c} = \mathbf{S}^*\mathbf{c}^*$.

Key switching matrix $\mathbf{M}$ can be generated through the transformation as:

$$\mathbf{M} = \begin{bmatrix} \mathbf{S}^* - \mathbf{T}\mathbf{A} + \mathbf{E} \\ \mathbf{A} \end{bmatrix} \tag{8}$$

where $\mathbf{A}$ is a random matrix and $\mathbf{E}$ is a noise matrix with $|\mathbf{E}|$ is small enough. Then the new ciphertext $\mathbf{c}'$ is computed as $\mathbf{c}' = \mathbf{M}\mathbf{c}^*$.

3.2 Histogram of Oriented Gradients (HOG) Algorithm

For a fixed-size image (e.g., 128×64 pixels in human detection), the detail extraction of HOG features is descripted as the following steps [4].

Image Preprocessing: The raw images are usually color images containing a lot of color information, however, because the focus of HOG descriptor is on gradients rather than the color of pixels, it is necessary to reduce this redundant information by graying the raw images. Besides, for adjusting the contrast of the images and decreasing the effects of local shadows and illumination changes, the grayscale images are standardized in color space by using Gamma Correction as the following formula:

$$\mathbf{I}(x, y) = \mathbf{I}(x, y)^\gamma$$

where the value of γ can be $1/2$.

Orientation histogram building: For each pixel $\mathbf{I}(x, y)$ in the image $\mathbf{I}$, let $Diff_x = \mathbf{I}(x+1, y) - \mathbf{I}(x-1, y)$ and $Diff_y = \mathbf{I}(x, y+1) - \mathbf{I}(x, y-1)$ represent the horizontal and vertical gradients of the pixel. Then the gradient magnitude $m(x, y)$ and the orientation $\theta(x, y)$ can be computed as $m(x, y) = \sqrt{Diff_x^2 + Diff_y^2}$ and $\theta(x, y) = tan^{-1} \frac{Diff_y}{Diff_x}$.

In an image $\mathbf{I}$, a *cell* is defined as a local square region with a certain predefined size, such as 8×8 pixels, and then 4 adjacent cells are defined as a *block* that contains 16×16 pixels. Within a cell, the gradient orientation is divided into 9 bins equably among the angle space $0°–180°$ (unsigned gradient), and the bin that a pixel belongs to can be decided by its orientation. In each pixel, consider the gradient magnitude as a weighted vote, the orientation histogram of a cell can be built by accumulating the bins of all pixels. Finally, concatenate the four orientation histograms of cells orderly, the orientation histogram of a block is obtained.

Block normalization: Obviously, the formed orientation histogram of each block contains a 4×9 dimensional feature vector. Suppose $\mathbf{v}$ be the unnormalized block descriptor vector, then its $\sigma - norm$ is defined as $||\mathbf{v}||_\sigma$, where σ can be $1, 2$. The normalization procedure of each block descriptor vector with $L_2 - norm$ is executed as $\mathbf{v} \leftarrow \frac{\mathbf{v}}{\sqrt{||\mathbf{v}||_2^2 + \epsilon}}$, where ϵ is a minimal constant. The process of normalization further weakens the interference of light to the images.

HOG descriptor generation: Concatenate the normalized block descriptor from left to right and top to bottom by the step of 8 pixels in the fixed-size image, the final HOG descriptor is generated (e.g., in a 128×64 pixels image, a 3780-dimensional feature vector is enmerged).

4 Privacy-Preserving Extraction of HOG

In this section, the privacy-preserving extraction of HOG is proposed between the image owners and the untrusted cloud. The final purpose is stated detailedly as follows. Firstly, the original image contents must be protected from any other parties except the image owner to ensure the security of our scheme. Secondly, after improvement and simplification, the HOG algorithm should have as much similar extraction results as the original HOG algorithm, which can keep the effectiveness. Finally, the image owner is always considered as resource constrained, so the computation cost on owner side must reduced significantly and the computational burden on the cloud side must be acceptable and practical to guarantee the efficiency of the HOG algorithm.

In the previous studies, [7,16] have done the similar research on exploring privacy-preserving outsourcing of HOG algorithm with SHE and HE cryptosystem respectively. Different from that scheme, we build our system by using the VHE (Vector Homomorphic Encryption) scheme as described above. The key point in our scheme is that the fully combination of image data format and vector-based encryption leads to much higher efficiency under privacy protection.

4.1 Image Encryption

For the protection of image owners' privacy, the encryption of the original image data is an essential process before uploading to the cloud. Assume that, the image data has been preprocessed, including graying and Gamma Correction. The owner generates a secretkey $\mathbf{S}$ to encrypt preprocessed images. We regard the image $\mathbf{I}$ as a matrix $\mathbf{I}(x, y)$ with the size of $n \times m$, and take each row of this image matrix as an integer vector to be encrypted. In the support of the Vector Homomorphic Encryption scheme, the encryption of each row vector can be expressed as

$$\mathbf{I}_e^i(x, y) = Enc(\mathbf{I}^i(x, y), \mathbf{S}),$$

which means the ciphertext of the i_{th} row pixels of image $\mathbf{I}$. After encryption, the ciphertext vector group of the image $\mathbf{I}$ is generated:

$$\{\mathbf{I}_e^1(x,y), \mathbf{I}_e^2(x,y), ..., \mathbf{I}_e^n(x,y)\}.$$

4.2 Computing Gradient Magnitude

Because of the limited computing operations that the VHE supports, some complex operation in the original HOG algorithm must be simplified. So we eliminate some steps and reduce the amount of the original orientation directions from nine to four ones (i.e., $0°, 45°, 90°, 135°$), which represent 4 bins for each orientation descriptor in a cell. The detail computing method is expressed in the plaintext form as below:

$$Diff_{0°} = \mathbf{I}(x+1,y) - \mathbf{I}(x-1,y),$$
$$Diff_{45°} = \mathbf{I}(x-1,y-1) - \mathbf{I}(x+1,y+1),$$
$$Diff_{90°} = \mathbf{I}(x,y+1) - \mathbf{I}(x,y-1),$$
$$Diff_{135°} = \mathbf{I}(x+1,y-1) - \mathbf{I}(x-1,y+1).$$

In the ciphertext domain, we utilize the *Linear Transformation* in the VHE to achieve these gradients computation over the encrypted image vector. Define some certain transformation matrices to shift the vector correspondingly, and then carry out different homomorphic operations to get the gradient of different orientation. Especially, considering the image edge, we add the last pixel value to the original pixel value when shifting, in other words, the pixel value at the right edge is set to the original value when the vector moves left, and the pixel value at the left edge is set to the original value when the vector moves right.

Thus, the gradient magnitude along $0°$ direction of the i_{th} row is computed as following steps. First, define two shifting linear transformation matrices, left-shifting matrix $\mathbf{G}_L$ and right-shifting matrix $\mathbf{G}_R$, which can lead the plaintext vector to move a single position left and right respectively. Second, according to the *Linear Transformation*, computing a new secret key $\mathbf{G}_L\mathbf{S}$ can obtain a relative pair of plaintext-ciphertext $\{\mathbf{G}_L\mathbf{I}^i(x,y), \mathbf{I}_e^i(x,y)\}$. To support the direct homomorphic operation later, we use key-switching to keep the same secretkey $\mathbf{S}$. So in the procedure of changing $\mathbf{G}_L\mathbf{S}$ to $\mathbf{S}$, we can get the key-switching matrix $\mathbf{M}_L$, and the left-shifting plaintext vector $\mathbf{I}^i(x+1,y) = \mathbf{G}_L\mathbf{I}^i(x,y)$ can correspond to the following ciphertext vector under the secret key $\mathbf{S}$:

$$\mathbf{I}_e^i(x+1,y) = \mathbf{M}_L\mathbf{I}_e^i(x,y).$$

The right-shifting plaintext vector $\mathbf{I}^i(x-1,y) = \mathbf{G}_R\mathbf{I}^i(x,y)$ and the relative ciphertext vector can be computed analogously,

$$\mathbf{I}_e^i(x-1,y) = \mathbf{M}_R\mathbf{I}_e^i(x,y).$$

Finally, under the same secret key $\mathbf{S}$, the orientation gradient magnitude of the i_{th} row ciphertext vector is derived as:

$$Diff_{0°}^i = \mathbf{I}_e^i(x+1,y) - \mathbf{I}_e^i(x-1,y). \tag{9}$$

Therefore, the gradient magnitude along the other three directions can be obtained as:

$$Diff^i_{45°} = \mathbf{I}^i_e(x-1, y-1) - \mathbf{I}^i_e(x+1, y+1) \qquad (10)$$

where $\mathbf{I}^i_e(x-1, y-1) = \mathbf{M}_R \mathbf{I}^{i-1}_e(x,y)$ and $\mathbf{I}^i_e(x+1, y+1) = \mathbf{M}_L \mathbf{I}^{i+1}_e(x,y)$.

$$Diff^i_{90°} = \mathbf{I}^i_e(x, y+1) - \mathbf{I}^i_e(x, y-1) \qquad (11)$$

where $\mathbf{I}^i_e(x, y+1) = \mathbf{I}^{i+1}_e(x,y)$ and $\mathbf{I}^i_e(x, y-1) = \mathbf{I}^{i-1}_e(x,y)$.

$$Diff^i_{135°} = \mathbf{I}^i_e(x+1, y-1) - \mathbf{I}^i_e(x-1, y+1) \qquad (12)$$

where $\mathbf{I}^i_e(x+1, y-1) = \mathbf{M}_L \mathbf{I}^{i-1}_e(x,y)$ and $\mathbf{I}^i_e(x-1, y+1) = \mathbf{M}_R \mathbf{I}^{i+1}_e(x,y)$.

4.3   HOG Descriptor Generation

On the owner's side, it predefines several linear transformation matrices $\mathbf{G}$ and compute the relevant key-switching matrices $\mathbf{M}$. After a few round of communications, the cloud get a series of key-switching matrices from the owners. Then the cloud can conduct linear transformation and key switching to generate HOG descriptor based on those matrices.

Given that a *cell* contains 8×8 pixels. The feature vector of a cell is formed by accumulating the gradient magnitude of four orientations among all the 8×8 pixels. Let $\mathbf{G}_H$ be the transformation matrix to add every 8-pixel gradient in a ciphertext vector horizontally. Take the accumulation of the direction $0°$ in a cell for example, translate the secret key $\mathbf{G}_H \mathbf{S}$ to $\mathbf{S}$ by key-switching method and get the key-switching matrix $\mathbf{M}_H$. Then compute the new ciphertext $\mathbf{M}_H Diff^i_{0°}$ to represent the sum gradient of every 8-pixel in each ciphertext vector row. Finally, adding 8 consecutive rows of gradient ciphertext leads to the accumulation of the direction $0°$ in a cell as following:

$$Or0^j_e = \mathbf{M}_H(Diff^i_{0°} + ... + Diff^{i+7}_{0°}).$$

Similarly, the accumulation of the other three directions in a cell are computed, i.e., $Or45^j_e, Or90^j_e, Or135^j_e$.

Define four transformation matrices $\mathbf{G}_0, \mathbf{G}_{45}, \mathbf{G}_{90}, \mathbf{G}_{135}$ to shift the sum orientation of four directions in cells, and let the four matrices $\mathbf{M}_0, \mathbf{M}_{45}, \mathbf{M}_{90}, \mathbf{M}_{135}$ to be the corresponding key-switching matrices when transformating secret key. Every row of cell descriptor can be derived by

$$OrCell^j_e = \mathbf{M}_0 Or0^j_e + \mathbf{M}_{45} Or45^j_e + \mathbf{M}_{90} Or90^j_e + \mathbf{M}_{135} Or135^j_e$$

A *block* contains 2×2 cells, so the block descriptor of each row can be obtained by two adjacent rows of cell descriptor in the ciphertext domain. In the cell descriptors of two rows, we cascade the block descriptor by the order of zigzag with the step of a cell. By the usage of two transformation matrices $\mathbf{G}_u, \mathbf{G}_d$ and corresponding key-switching matrices $\mathbf{M}_u, \mathbf{M}_d$, the block descriptor of each row in ciphertext is derived as:

$$OrBlock^k_e = \mathbf{M}_u OrCell^j_e + \mathbf{M}_d OrCell^{j+1}_e.$$

Because the limit of division operation in ciphertext domain, the block normalizations are carried out by the image owners O. Thus, the final HOG descriptor can be described by block descriptors of all rows:

$$HOG = Dec\{(OrBlock_e^1, OrBlock_e^2, ...OrBlock_e^k), \mathbf{S}\}.$$

4.4 Descriptor Descryption

Once the cloud C has completed the process of HOG descriptor extraction in encrypted domain, it sends the results in ciphertext to the image owners O. Next, the owners O will descript the HOG descriptor with the secret key $\mathbf{S}$, and perform normalization operations on each block descriptor by using $L_2 - norm$ algorithm. Ultimately, the owners O get the actual HOG deacryptors.

5   System Analysis and Evaluation

In this part, we complete the simulation on the C++ environment to prove the feasibility and practicality of our scheme, combining the MATLAB with its image processing functions. We show the experimental results based on hundreds of pedestrian images in INRIA Database, in which we choose 1000 sample images with and without humans respectively. According to the experimental results, We first present the correctness evaluation to prove that our proposed solution is feasible and practical. Then the security analysis shows that our system can be practical in protecting the owners' privacy. Finally, we evaluate the efficiency, which proves the better performance of our scheme.

5.1 Correctness Evaluation

For pedestrian detection, we conduct the SVM algorithm to detect whether there are humans in an image. In the training stage, we use 1000 HOG features extracted by the original HOG and our improved HOG under privacy respectively, which contains 500 negative samples and 500 positive samples. In the testing stage, the same number of image samples are detected. Through many experiments, we choose two types of kernel functions in SVM algorithm with a comprehensive consideration of various factors.

First, we can contrast the *Undetected Rate* and the *Wrong-Detection Rate* under different kernel functions in Table 2. Though our improved HOG performs a little bit inferior than the original HOG in the undetected rate, our solution shows a better results in terms of wrong detection rate under the two functions. In practice, the effect of detection is dependent on these two rates, meaning that our HOG is acceptable and practical.

To further evaluate the detection results, we measure the SVM detector by precision and accuracy as follows:

$$precision = \frac{TruePositive}{TruePositive + FalsePositive},$$

Table 2. Average detection error rate

	Kernel function	The original HOG	The improved HOG
Undetected rate	'Quadratic'	0.068	0.308
Wrong detection rate		0.292	0.122
Undetected rate	'rbf', 'rbf_sigma' = 100	0.066	0.252
Wrong detection rate		0.264	0.188

$$accuracy = \frac{TruePositive + TrueNegtive}{TotalSamples}.$$

An image sample is detected as true positive if it matches the ground truth annotation with less than 50% overlap errors according to the PASCAL criteria [5]. The construction of the *precision* between our HOG features detection and the original HOG feature detection in different kernel functions is shown as follows Table 3. Not surprisingly, both our improved HOG and the original HOG perform very well in precision and accuracy, indicating that our solution is consistent with the original HOG. This result is a better proof that our solution can extract the HOG features correctly in ciphertext domain and approximate the original HOG in plaintext domain.

Table 3. Precision and accuracy

	Kernel function	The original HOG	The improved HOG
Precision	'Quadratic'	0.7614	0.808
Accuracy		0.82	0.785
Precision	'rbf', 'rbf_sigma' = 100	0.7796	0.7991
Accuracy		0.835	0.78

5.2 Security Analysis

As described in our model, the cloud can get nothing but the ciphertext image to preserve the privacy of the image owners. The security of our homomorphic encryption scheme VHE plays an important role in the security of our solution, which can be reduced to the speculated difficulty of an mathematical problem named "Learning with Error" [2]. Next we illustrate our scheme is secure by using VHE as follows.

Definition 1: Learning with Error (LWE) Problem. Given polynomial multiple samples of $(\mathbf{a}_i, b_i) \in Z_q^m \times Z_q$ satisfy

$$b_i = \mathbf{v}^T \mathbf{a}_i + \varepsilon_i \tag{13}$$

where error term $\varepsilon_i \in Z_q$ is generated from a certain probability distribution χ. and there is almost no chance to get the vector $\mathbf{v} \in Z_q^m$ with non-ignored possibility.

Theorem 1: If the problem of *Learning with Error* (LWE) is difficult, there is of little possibility to retrieve $\mathbf{S}'$ from $\mathbf{S}'\mathbf{M} = \mathbf{S}^* + \mathbf{E}$, given $\mathbf{M}$ and $\mathbf{S}^*$ is available.

Obviously, we can reduce this problem to LWE to prove the safety of our encryption scheme. Suppose there is a solver to the $\mathbf{S}'\mathbf{M} = \mathbf{S}^* + \mathbf{E}$, and we take each of the elements in the matrices to be the element of Z_q with a large prime integer $q >> max\{|\mathbf{S}'|, |\mathbf{M}|, |\mathbf{S}^*|, |\mathbf{E}|\}$. Take this special circumstance into account, i.e., given $\mathbf{S}' = (\mathbf{s}')^T$ is a n-dimensional row vector, meanwhile $\mathbf{S}^* = \mathbf{s}^*$ and $\mathbf{E} = \mathbf{e}$ are both row vectors in the same dimension n. Next the transformation of our problem can be stated that m_i and s^* are available in

$$(\mathbf{s}')^T m_i = \mathbf{s}^* + \mathbf{e},$$

i.e., there are n samples of $(m_i, s_i{}^*)$ in

$$\mathbf{s}_i{}^* = (\mathbf{s}')^T m_i - e_i.$$

Then we can use the solver to solve the above equation for s', which is equivalent to solving $b_i = \mathbf{v}^T \mathbf{a}_i + \varepsilon_i$ for $\mathbf{v}$.

Therefore, if the problem of LWE is hard, solving $\mathbf{S}'\mathbf{M} = \mathbf{S}^* + \mathbf{E}$ is also hard. In other words, given the LWE problem is hard to conjecture, it is also impractical to retrieve the new secret key $\mathbf{S}'$ on the premise of the key-switching matrix $\mathbf{M}$ under known. Thus any other adversaries who intercept the communication between the image owners and the cloud can not recover the secret key $\mathbf{S}$ and the plaintext image.

5.3   Efficiency Evaluation

In the simulation implementation, we consider every row of an image as a plain-text to be encrypted. Because the same secret key $\mathbf{S}$ is used to encrypt each plaintext vector, we compute the key-switching matrix $\mathbf{M}$ in advance, and then conduct encryption operations, i.e., $\mathbf{M}(w\mathbf{x})$ based on $\mathbf{M}$, which can be time-saving on the image owner's side. In comparison with the HE scheme - the Paillier cryptosystem [10] in [7], in which the parameter setting is within a 1024-bit modulus under the comprehensive consideration, although the time cost of our scheme increases nearly linearly with the change in image size, its quantity is still within a reasonable scope. As shown in Fig. 2, and the comparison results are shown in Fig. 3. Obviously, due to the vector based encryption in VHE, our scheme performs excellent advantages than the pailliar cryptosystem in time cost. Especially, the images in our dataset are preprocessed in fixed size (i.e., 128 * 64 pixels), which can be encrypted in less than 1 s.

In the cloud, the main operation of HOG algorithm in ciphertext domain is *linear transformation*, therefore the cloud only need to compute the $\mathbf{M}\mathbf{c}^*$ to

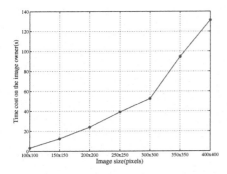
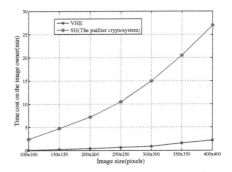

Fig. 2. Encryption Time Cost on VHE with different image sizes

Fig. 3. Comparison of Time Cost with different image sizes

get the new ciphertext, where the **M** is the key-switching matrix corresponding to the linear transformation **G**. Due to the strong computing capability of the cloud, the time cost is largely shortened when it conducts the cipher computing steps. With different sizes of image, the changing tendency of time cost in the cloud is shown as follows Fig. 4.

Also, we evaluate the communication cost between the image owner and the cloud in the outsourcing HOG extraction. In Fig. 5, although the communication costs also increase when image sizes grow, all of those cost are acceptable in practice. In the whole process of our scheme, merely the occurrence of the computation of key-switching matrices **M**, the communication would be made between the image owners and the cloud. So the interaction times can be controlled as a constant, which has important significance. In order to better reflect the efficiency advantage in our solution, we still compare the communication costs of the VHE used in our scheme with the HE scheme - the Paillier cryptosystem. The comparison results are shown in Fig. 6, and we can observe that the VHE scheme outperforms the HE scheme in the time and communication

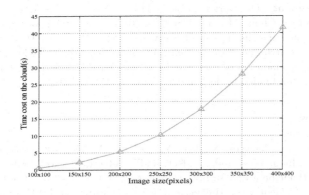

Fig. 4. Time Cost on cloud with different image sizes

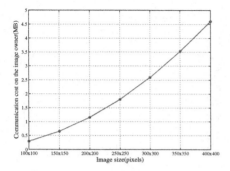

Fig. 5. Communication Cost on VHE with different image sizes

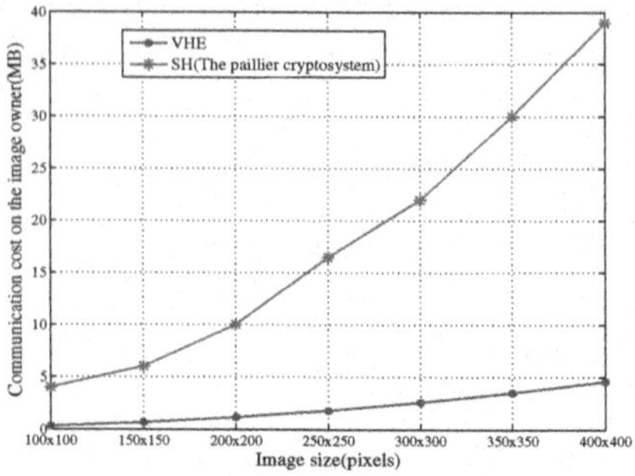

Fig. 6. Comparison of communication Cost with different image sizes

costs. Therefore, in terms of efficiency, our scheme has great improvement owing to the use of the VHE scheme.

6   Conclusion

In this paper, we first simplify the original HOG algorithm to adapt our encryption scheme-VHE. Then we conduct the extraction operations of the improved HOG in the ciphertext domain, which outsource most heavy computation to the cloud to release the burden of the image owners. In this proposed model, the original contents of images are well protected against the cloud and any other party by using of VHE, so the privacy preservation of image owner has been achieved. Finally, we analyze the security and effectiveness of the system to show that our proposed scheme is feasible and practical. Besides, to verify these analysis, we carry out a lot of experiments by comparing the improved HOG and the original HOG, and the results of experiments indicate that our solution is well consistent with and approximate the original HOG solution.

Acknowledgement. This work is supported by the National Key Research and Development Program of China (2017YFB0802003, 2017YFB0802004) National Cryptography Development Fund during the 13th Five-year Plan Period (MMJJ20170216), the Fundamental Research Funds for the Central Universities (GK201702004), the National Natural Science Foundation of China under Grants U1633114 and China Postdoctoral Science Foundation funded project under Grant 2014M562309.

References

1. Boldyreva, A., Chenette, N., Lee, Y., O'Neill, A.: Order-preserving symmetric encryption. In: Joux, A. (ed.) EUROCRYPT 2009. LNCS, vol. 5479, pp. 224–241. Springer, Heidelberg (2009). https://doi.org/10.1007/978-3-642-01001-9_13
2. Brakerski, Z., Gentry, C., Halevi, S.: Packed ciphertexts in LWE-based homomorphic encryption. In: Kurosawa, K., Hanaoka, G. (eds.) PKC 2013. LNCS, vol. 7778, pp. 1–13. Springer, Heidelberg (2013). https://doi.org/10.1007/978-3-642-36362-7_1

3. Brakerski, Z., Vaikuntanathan, V.: Efficient fully homomorphic encryption from (standard) LWE. SIAM J. Comput. **43**(2), 831–871 (2014)
4. Dalal, N., Triggs, B.: Histograms of oriented gradients for human detection. In: IEEE Computer Society Conference on Computer Vision and Pattern Recognition (CVPR 2005), vol. 1, pp. 886–893. IEEE (2005)
5. Everingham, M., Zisserman, A., Williams, C.K., Van Gool, L.: The pascal visual object classes challenge 2006 (voc2006) results (2006)
6. Greenwald, G., MacAskill, E.: NSA prism program taps in to user data of Apple, Google and others. Guardian **7**(6), 1–43 (2013)
7. Hsu, C.Y., Lu, C.S., Pei, S.C.: Image feature extraction in encrypted domain with privacy-preserving SIFT. IEEE Trans. Image Process. **21**(11), 4593–4607 (2012)
8. Huang, Y., Evans, D., Katz, J., Malka, L.: Faster secure two-party computation using garbled circuits. In: USENIX Security Symposium, vol. 201 (2011)
9. Lindell, Y., Pinkas, B.: A proof of security of yaos protocol for two-party computation. J. Cryptol. **22**(2), 161–188 (2009)
10. Paillier, P.: Public-key cryptosystems based on composite degree residuosity classes. In: Stern, J. (ed.) EUROCRYPT 1999. LNCS, vol. 1592, pp. 223–238. Springer, Heidelberg (1999). https://doi.org/10.1007/3-540-48910-X_16
11. Paillier, P., Pointcheval, D.: Efficient public-key cryptosystems provably secure against active adversaries. In: Lam, K.-Y., Okamoto, E., Xing, C. (eds.) ASIACRYPT 1999. LNCS, vol. 1716, pp. 165–179. Springer, Heidelberg (1999). https://doi.org/10.1007/978-3-540-48000-6_14
12. Peikert, C., Vaikuntanathan, V., Waters, B.: A framework for efficient and composable oblivious transfer. In: Wagner, D. (ed.) CRYPTO 2008. LNCS, vol. 5157, pp. 554–571. Springer, Heidelberg (2008). https://doi.org/10.1007/978-3-540-85174-5_31
13. Qin, Z., Yan, J., Ren, K., Chen, C.W., Wang, C.: Towards efficient privacy-preserving image feature extraction in cloud computing. In: Proceedings of the 22nd ACM International Conference on Multimedia, pp. 497–506. ACM (2014)
14. Schneider, M., Schneider, T.: Notes on non-interactive secure comparison in image feature extraction in the encrypted domain with privacy-preserving SIFT. In: Proceedings of the 2nd ACM Workshop on Information Hiding and Multimedia Security, pp. 135–140. ACM (2014)
15. Smart, N.P., Vercauteren, F.: Fully homomorphic SIMD operations. Des. Codes Crypt. **71**, 57–81 (2014)
16. Wang, Q., Wang, J., Hu, S., Zou, Q., Ren, K.: Sechog: privacy-preserving outsourcing computation of histogram of oriented gradients in the cloud. In: Proceedings of the 11th ACM on Asia Conference on Computer and Communications Security, pp. 257–268. ACM (2016)
17. Wang, S., Nassar, M., Atallah, M., Malluhi, Q.: Secure and private outsourcing of shape-based feature extraction. In: Qing, S., Zhou, J., Liu, D. (eds.) ICICS 2013. LNCS, vol. 8233, pp. 90–99. Springer, Cham (2013). https://doi.org/10.1007/978-3-319-02726-5_7
18. Zhou, H., Wornell, G.: Efficient homomorphic encryption on integer vectors and its applications. In: Information Theory and Applications Workshop (ITA 2014), pp. 1–9. IEEE (2014)

Hierarchical Conditional Proxy Re-Encryption: A New Insight of Fine-Grained Secure Data Sharing

Kai He[1], Xueqiao Liu[2], Huaqiang Yuan[1(✉)], Wenhong Wei[1], and Kaitai Liang[3]

[1] School of Computer and Network Security, Dongguan University of Technology,
Guangdong 523808, China
kaihe1214@163.com, hyuan66@163.com, weiwh@dgut.edu.cn
[2] School of Computing and Information Technology, University of Wollongong,
Wollongong, NSW 2512, Australia
xl691@uowmail.edu.au
[3] Department of Computer Science, University of Surrey, Guildford, UK
ktliang88@gmail.com

Abstract. Outsource local data to remote cloud has become prevalence for Internet users to date. While being unable to "handle" (outsourced) data at hand, Internet users may concern about the confidentiality of data but also further operations over remote data. This paper deals with the case where a secure data sharing mechanism is needed when data is encrypted and stored in remote cloud. Proxy re-encryption (PRE) is a promising cryptographic tool for secure data sharing. It allows a "honest-but-curious" third party (e.g., cloud server), which we call "proxy", to convert all ciphertexts encrypted for a delegator into those intended for a delegatee. The delegatee can further gain access to the plaintexts with private key, while the proxy learns nothing about the underlying plaintexts. Being regarded as a general extension of PRE, conditional PRE supports a fine-grained level of data sharing. In particular, condition is embedded into ciphertext that offers a chance for the delegator to generate conditional re-encryption key to control with which ciphertexts he wants to share. In this paper, for the first time, we introduce a new notion, called "hierarchical conditional" PRE. The new notion allows re-encryption rights to be "re-delegated" for "low-level" encrypted data. We propose the seminal scheme satisfying the notion in the context of identity-based encryption and further, prove it secure against chosen-ciphertext security.

Keywords: Hierarchical conditional proxy re-encryption
Fine-grained data sharing · Identity-based encryption
Chosen-ciphertext security

1 Introduction

To date cloud computing has been regarded as a successful and prevalent business model for many real-world applications due to its long-list features, such

© Springer International Publishing AG 2017
J. K. Liu and P. Samarati (Eds.): ISPEC 2017, LNCS 10701, pp. 118–135, 2017.
https://doi.org/10.1007/978-3-319-72359-4_7

as considerable storage and computing power. Internet users have been "encouraged" to outsource their data to cloud in order to save the cost of local data maintenance and management but also to enjoy various cloud-based data services. To prevent their sensitive data from being compromised by cloud server, Internet users may choose to encrypt the data before outsourcing. However, the encryption may limit "out-of-physical" sharing. For example, a user $\mathcal{A}$ may share his data with another user, say $\mathcal{B}$. Assume the data of $\mathcal{A}$ is stored in a cloud server. A naive way for the sharing is to let $\mathcal{A}$ first download his encrypted data locally and decrypt it, then re-encrypt the data for $\mathcal{B}$. The solution, however, may require $\mathcal{A}$ to be on-line and meanwhile, bear all the workloads of decryption-and-re-encryption. To offload the workloads to the server, one may choose to allow the server to execute the decrypt-then-re-encrypt task. But this will compromise the confidentiality of the data.

Proxy re-encryption (PRE), which is a useful cryptographic primitive, has been introduced to tackle the above dilemma. By using PRE, $\mathcal{A}$ does not need to download, decrypt and re-encrypt the data. Instead, he is only required to generate a re-encrypted key, which supports ciphertext conversion, so that a semi-trust (i.e. honest-but-curious) cloud server (i.e. proxy) can use the re-encryption key to transform the ciphertext of $\mathcal{A}$ for $\mathcal{B}$. Even if the proxy obtains the re-encryption key, it cannot gain access to the underlying data. Since its introduction, PRE has been widely applied in many real-world applications, such as digital rights management systems [35], secure distributed files systems [1,9] and email forwarding systems [2].

In a traditional PRE mechanism, using a re-encryption key from $\mathcal{A}$ to $\mathcal{B}$, the proxy may transform all ciphertexts of $\mathcal{A}$ into those intended for $\mathcal{B}$. This "all-or-nothing" data sharing mode may not scale well in practice. What if some data is extremely sensitive to $\mathcal{A}$ so that he does not want it to be shared with others, even including $\mathcal{B}$? A fine-grained PRE may be desirable in this case. In 2009, Weng et al. [41] introduced the notion of conditional PRE (CPRE), in which the proxy who has a re-encryption key with a special condition can only convert the ciphertext of a delegator (e.g., $\mathcal{A}$) with the same special condition for a delegatee (e.g., $\mathcal{B}$). Due to its innate feature, CPRE, however, limits the data sharing in the sense that one re-encryption key only corresponds to the sharing of one ciphertext. This one-to-one sharing mode brings inconvenience for delegator. Specifically, if $\mathcal{A}$ plans to share 10,000 encrypted files (which are embedded with distinct conditions) with $\mathcal{B}$, he has to generate the same amount of re-encryption keys.

To address the above limitation, we introduce a new notion, which we call "hierarchical conditional" PRE (HCPRE). The new notion allows re-encryption rights to be "re-delegated" to lower level of encrypted data. It brings convenience and flexibility for delegator in the sense that a delegator may only need to generate a re-encryption key for high level data and further, the key can be "reformed" for the lower level data shoring. Below we use cloud data sharing as an example to illustrate the basic idea behind the notion to motivate our work.

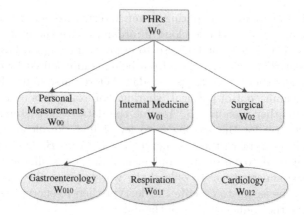

Fig. 1. Hierarchical conditional access structure

Assume outsourced data is under a specific data structure for some purposes, e.g., efficient retrieval. $\mathcal{A}$ first forms his data in a hierarchical structure as shown in Fig. 1, in which a data is tagged with a hierarchical condition set, for example, the data (related to) *Respiration* is with a condition set $W = \{W_0, W_{01}, W_{011}\}$. $\mathcal{A}$ further encrypts the data together with the corresponding hierarchical condition set before outsourcing to a cloud serer. Assume $\mathcal{B}$ is a Physician, who is allowed to access all of the *Internal Medicine* data of $\mathcal{A}$. To share the data with $\mathcal{B}$, $\mathcal{A}$ may generate a re-encryption key $RK_{\{W_0, W_{01}\}|A \to B}$, which is embedded with hierarchical conditions $\{W_0, W_{01}\}$, and sends it to the semi-trust cloud server. When $\mathcal{B}$ requests to access the *Internal Medicine* data, including *Gastroenterology*, *Respiration* and *Cardiology*, the proxy uses the re-encryption key $RK_{\{W_0, W_{01}\}|A \to B}$, which is for the conditions $\{W_0, W_{01}\}$, to "delegate" a new re-encryption key $RK_{\{W_0, W_{01}, W_{01i}\}_{i \in \{0,1,2\}}|A \to B}$ for the "lower-level" hierarchical conditions $\{W_0, W_{01}, W_{01i}\}_{i \in \{0,1,2\}}$. The proxy further uses the resulting key $RK_{\{W_0, W_{01}, W_{01i}\}_{i \in \{0,1,2\}}|A \to B}$ to convert the encrypted data for $\mathcal{B}$, so that $\mathcal{B}$ may use his private key to access the *Internal Medicine* data of $\mathcal{A}$. In particular, if $\mathcal{A}$ decides to share all of his data to $\mathcal{B}$, he only needs to generate a "root" re-encryption key for condition W_0 from $\mathcal{A}$ to $\mathcal{B}$; while $\mathcal{A}$ chooses to share one leaf data to $\mathcal{B}$, he generates a re-encryption key for one of the conditions $\{W_0, W_{01}, W_{01i}\}$ corresponding to the leaf of the structure.

1.1   Related Work

In 1998, Blaze et al. [2] constructed the first bidirectional PRE scheme. In 2005, Ateniese et al. [9] proposed the first unidirectional PRE scheme. Both of the schemes are secure only against chosen-plaintext attacks (CPA). In 2007, Canetti et al. [3] designed a bidirectional PRE scheme with chosen-ciphertext security. In 2008, Libert et al. [24] introduced a re-playable chosen ciphertext secure (RCCA) unidirectional PRE scheme. Since then, various PRE schemes have been proposed in the literature (e.g., [7,11,25,29,34,37,40]).

PRE can be extended in the context of identity-based encryption. In 2007, Green and Ateniese [10] proposed the first identity-based proxy re-encryption (IBPRE) scheme, which is CCA secure in the random oracle model, where hash functions are assumed to be fully random. Chu and Tzeng [6] constructed a CCA secure IBPRE scheme in the standard model. After that, many identity-based proxy re-encryption (IBPRE) schemes have been proposed, such as [6,10,18,20, 28,30,31,33,38].

However, among all of the aforementioned schemes, the semi-trust proxy can use a given re-encryption key to transform all the ciphertexts of a delegator into those of a delegatee. But in reality, the delegator does not want to transform all of his data for the delegatee. Therefore, type-based PRE [36] and conditional PRE (CPRE) [41,42] were proposed, in which the proxy can only fulfill ciphertext conversion "conditionally". Later, Liang et al. [16,19] proposed two IBCPRE schemes with CCA secure in the standard model. However, He et al. [12] presented the security analysis to show that their schemes only achieve CPA security. In 2016, He et al. [13] proposed an efficient identity-based conditional proxy re-encryption (IBCPRE) scheme with CCA secure in the random oracle model.

PRE can be extended in the attribute-based setting. Attribute-based proxy re-encryption (ABPRE) can effectively increase the flexibility of data sharing. In 2009, Liang et al. [23] first defined the notion of ciphertext-policy ABPRE (CP-ABPRE), where each ciphertext is labeled with a set of descriptive conditions and each re-encryption key is associated with an access tree that specifies which type of ciphertexts the proxy can re-encrypt, and they presented a concrete scheme supporting AND gates with positive and negative attributes. After that, several CP-ABPRE schemes (e.g., [27]) with more expressive access policy were proposed. In 2011, Fang et al. [8] proposed a key-policy ABPRE (KP-ABPRE) scheme in the random oracle model, whereby ciphertext encrypted with conditions W can be re-encrypted by the proxy using the CPRE key under the access structure $\mathcal{T}$ if and only if $\mathcal{T}(W) = 1$. More recent ABPRE systems can be seen in [15,17,21,22].

In 2016, Lee et al. [14] proposed a searchable hierarchical CPRE (HCPRE) scheme for cloud storage services, and cloud service provider is able to generate a hierarchical key, but the re-encryption key generation algorithm also requires the private keys of the delegator and delegatee.

So far, the proxy re-encryption scheme [13] is the only one which is conditional and chosen-ciphertext secure scheme in the identity-based setting. Therefore, based on the scheme [13], we propose a HCPRE scheme with more scalability and flexibility in controlling data sharing and which is in identity-based setting and further achieves CCA security. Note that secure access control have also been proposed in the literature for fine-grained data sharing (e.g., [4,5,32]).

We here compare our scheme with other related PRE schemes, namely CPRE, IB-PRE and AB-PRE, in terms of computation, communication, features as well as security in the following tables. We state that AB-PRE allows proxy to convert a group of ciphertext satisfying attribute description embedded into re-encryption key. This is somewhat similar to our scheme. But the distinct feature of our scheme is that we can support re-encryption key re-delegation in a secure and scalable way. Let C_e, C_p, C_S and C_E be the computational cost of an exponentiation, a bilinear pairing, a signature and a symmetric encryption, respectively. u is the total number of attributes used in system, w is the number of conditions in the ciphertext and d is the size of an access formula. $|G_1|$ and $|G_T|$ denote the bit-length of an element in $\mathbb{G}_1$ and $\mathbb{G}_T$, respectively. $|Sym|$ and $|Sign|$ denote the bit-length of a symmetric encryption and a signature, respectively.

From Table 1, it can be seen that our scheme achieves constant pairing cost in all metrics, much like others, except for the re-encryption phase. We state that this will not bring heavy computational burden to system user because this phase is handled by cloud server. Since our scheme supports flexible condition control, the number of condition used in ciphertext and sharing/re-encryption is based on the preference of user. If a user chooses to use only one condition (i.e. $w = 1$), our scheme also achieves constant computational cost in all metrics.

Table 2 shows the communication cost comparison. Much like the analysis mentioned previously, our scheme would achieve constant communication cost while $w = 1$. We note that $w = 1$ may indicate that a delegator delegates the decryption rights of a "root" data to a delegatee.

Table 1. Computation cost comparison

Schemes	Enc	Re-Enc	Dec$_1$	Dec$_2$	Rekey
[16]	$8C_e + C_p + C_S$	$6C_e + 7C_p$	$5C_e + 6C_p$	$5C_e + 6C_p$	$16C_e$
[41]	$4C_e + 2C_p$	$8C_p$	$2C_e + 2C_p$	$C_e + C_p$	$2C_e$
[10]	$4C_e + C_p + C_S$	$2C_e$	$2C_e + 3C_p$	$2C_e + 10C_p$	$4C_e + C_p + C_S$
[26]	$3C_e + C_p$	$4C_p$	$2C_p$	$2C_p$	$4C_e$
[23]	$(2 + u)C_p$	$(1 + u)C_p$	$(1 + u)C_p$	$2C_p$	$(2u + 1)C_e$
Ours	$(2 + w)C_e + C_p$	$(3 + w)C_p$	$C_e + 2C_p$	$2C_e + 2C_p$	$(2w + 1)C_e + C_p$

Table 2. Communication complexity comparison

Schemes	RKey	Original ciphertext	Re-encryption ciphertext
[16]	$6|G_1|$	$3|G_1| + |G_T| + |Sign|$	$3|G_1| + |G_T| + |Sign|$
[41]	$2|G_1|$	$4|G_1|$	$2|G_1| + |G_T|$
[10]	$3|G_1| + |G_T| + |Sign|$	$9|G_1| + 2|G_T| + 2|Sign|$	$5|G_1| + |G_T| + |Sign|$
[26]	$2|G_1|$	$3|G_1| + |G_T|$	$2|G_1| + |G_T|$
[23]	$(3 + 3u)|G_1| + |G_T|$	$(2 + u)|G_1| + |G_T|$	$(3 + u)|G_1| + (4 + u)|G_T|$
Ours	$(3 + w)|G_1| + |G_T|$	$(3 + w)|G_1| + |G_T|$	$3|G_1| + 2|G_T|$

Table 3. Feature and security comparison

Schemes	Conditional sharing RKey number	Complexity	Security	Adaptivity	RKey re-delegation
[16]	$O(d)$	ℓ-wBDHI*	CCA	×	×
[41]	$O(d)$	3-QBDH	CCA	√	×
[10]	$O(d)$	DBDH	CPA	√	×
[26]	$O(d)$	DBDH	CPA	×	×
[23]	$O(1)$	ADBDH	CPA	×	×
Ours	$O(1)$	DBDH	CCA	√	√

The comparison of feature and security is shown in Table 3. We can see that our scheme is the first and only achieving all features. Like [23], our scheme only needs constant number of re-encryption key while the others need the number of $O(d)$. It also achieves adaptively CCA security under well-study complexity assumption, DBDH. A re-encryption key in our scheme can be further re-delegated by proxy (for re-encryption key recycle purpose) without jeopardizing security.

1.2 Contributions

The contributions of this paper are described as follows.

- Taking into account structured data, we introduce the new notion, hierarchical conditional PRE. The new notion allows a proxy to "re-formed" a given re-encryption key, so that the resulting key can be used to re-encrypt "lower-level" encrypted data. In other words, a re-encryption key in our notion may be "recycled".
- We concretely explore the notion in the context of identity-based encryption, and further define the corresponding system and security notion. We present a concrete construction satisfying the notion, which is the first of its type. Specifically, the construction is inspired by [13].
- The premise of our construction is quite similar to the hierarchical identity-based secret key re-delegation technique. A semi-trust proxy is allowed to delegate an "upper level" re-encryption key generation to lower-level "conditions". Therefore, a delegator can control which specific data blocks located in the structure can be accessed by others without generating a huge amount of re-encryption key.
- Our scheme is proved secure against chosen-ciphertext attacks in the random oracle model.

1.3 Organization

The rest of this paper is organized as follows. Some necessary preliminaries, system definition and security notion are given in Sect. 2. The concrete construction is introduced in Sect. 3 and the security analysis are described in Sect. 4. The conclusion is presented in Sect. 5.

2   Preliminaries

2.1   Bilinear Map

Two multiplicative cyclic groups $\mathbb{G}$ and $\mathbb{G}_T$ whose orders are prime p and a bilinear map $e : \mathbb{G} \times \mathbb{G} \rightarrow \mathbb{G}_T$ has following three properties:

- Bilinearity: $e(u^a, v^b) = e(u, v)^{ab}$ given $u, v \in \mathbb{G}$ and $a, b \in \mathbb{Z}_p$.
- Non-degeneracy: $e(g, g) \rightarrow \mathbb{G}$ given a generator g of $\mathbb{G}$.
- Computability: There exists a probabilistic algorithm to compute $e(u, v)$ given $u, v \in \mathbb{G}$.

2.2   Decisional Bilinear Diffie-Hellman (DBDH) Assumption

The definition of DBDH assumption [39] in a bilinear group $(p, \mathbb{G}, \mathbb{G}_T, e)$ is given as follows: A challenger takes as input (g, g^a, g^b, g^c, Z) for the unknown $a, b, c \leftarrow_R \mathbb{Z}_p$. A probabilistic polynomial time (PPT) adversary needs to decide whether $Z = e(g, g)^{abc}$ or Z is a random chosen from $\mathbb{G}_T$. The advantage of the PPT adversary $\mathcal{A}$ solving the DBDH assumption is defined like this:

$$Adv_{\mathcal{A}}^{\text{DBDH}} = |\Pr[\mathcal{A}(g, g^a, g^b, g^c, e(g, g)^{abc}) = 1] - \Pr[\mathcal{A}(g, g^a, g^b, g^c, Z) = 1]|.$$

If the advantage is negligible, it means that the DBDH assumption holds.

2.3   Identity-Based Hierarchical Conditional Proxy Re-encryption (IBHCPRE)

We here define the algorithms and security notion for IBHCPRE. An IBHCPRE scheme includes the following algorithms:

- Setup(1^λ): Intake a security parameter 1^λ, output a public parameter $params$ and a master secret key msk.
- Extract(msk, ID): Intake the master secret key msk and an identity ID, output a private key sk_{ID}.
- Enc($params, ID_i, W_n, m$): Intake the public parameter $params$, an identity ID_i, a condition vector $W_n = \{w_1, w_2, \cdots, w_n\}$ of depth n and a plaintext $m \in \mathcal{M}$, output an initial ciphertext $CT_{(ID_i, W_n)}$.
- ReKeyGen(sk_{ID_i}, ID_j, W_n): Intake a private key sk_{ID_i}, an identity ID_j, and a condition vector $W_n = \{w_1, w_2, \cdots, w_n\}$ of depth n, output a re-encryption key $rk_{W_n|ID_i \rightarrow ID_j}$ from ID_i to ID_j associated with the condition vector W_n.
- HCReKeyGen($rk_{W_n|ID_i \rightarrow ID_j}, W_{n+1}$): Intake a re-encryption key $rk_{W_n|ID_i \rightarrow ID_j}$ for the parent condition $W_n = \{w_1, \cdots, w_n\}$ of depth n and a condition vector $W_{n+1} = \{W_n, w_{n+1}\}$ of depth $n+1$, output the re-encryption key $rk_{W_{n+1}|ID_i \rightarrow ID_j}$ from ID_i to ID_j for condition $W_{n+1} = \{w_1, \cdots, w_n, w_{n+1}\}$.

- ReEnc($rk_{W_n|ID_i \to ID_j}, CT_{(ID_i, W_n)}$): Intake a re-encryption key $rk_{W_n|ID_i \to ID_j}$ and an initial ciphertext $CT_{(ID_i, W_n)}$, output a transformed ciphertext $CT_{(ID_j, W_n)}$.
- Dec2($sk_{ID_i}, CT_{(ID_i, W_n)}$): Intake a private key sk_{ID_i} and an initial ciphertext $CT_{(ID_i, W_n)}$, output a plaintext m or an invalid symbol $\perp$.
- Dec1($sk_{ID_j}, CT_{(ID_j, W_n)}$): Intake a private key sk_{ID_j} and a transformed ciphertext $CT_{(ID_j, W_n)}$, output a plaintext m or an invalid symbol $\perp$.

Correctness: For any $m \in \mathcal{M}$, sk_{ID_i} and sk_{ID_j} are generated from Extract algorithm, it holds that $\mathsf{Dec2}(sk_{ID_i}, CT_{(ID_i, W_n)}) = M$ and $\mathsf{Dec1}(sk_{ID_j}, \mathsf{ReEnc}(\mathsf{ReKeyGen}(sk_{ID_i}, ID_j, W_n), CT_{(ID_i, W_n)}) = M$.

Next, we give the security definition for IBHCPRE in the sense of indistinguishability under chosen-ciphertext attacks (IND-CCA), which is described by the following game between a challenger $\mathcal{C}$ and an adversary $\mathcal{A}$. Adversary $\mathcal{A}$ is able to obtain a series of queries. In spite of this, an adversary $\mathcal{A}$ cannot distinguish which message is encrypted from the challenge ciphertext.

- Setup: Challenger $\mathcal{C}$ runs $(params, msk) \leftarrow \mathsf{Setup}(1^\lambda)$, it sends $params$ to $\mathcal{A}$ and keeps msk itself.
- Phase 1: Adversary $\mathcal{A}$ adaptively issues a polynomial number of queries:
  - *Extraction query* $\langle ID_i \rangle$: Challenger $\mathcal{C}$ runs $\mathsf{Extract}(msk, ID_i)$ to obtain a private key sk_{ID_i} and returns it to adversary $\mathcal{A}$.
  - *Re-encryption key query* $\langle ID_i, ID_j, W_n \rangle$: Challenger $\mathcal{C}$ first gets the private key $sk_{ID_i} \leftarrow \mathsf{Extract}(msk, ID_i)$ and runs $rk_{W_n|ID_i \to ID_j} \leftarrow \mathsf{ReKeyGen}(sk_{ID_i}, ID_j, W_n)$, and then it returns $rk_{W_n|ID_i \to ID_j}$ to adversary $\mathcal{A}$.
  - *Hierarchical condition re-encryption key query* $\langle rk_{W_n|ID_i \to ID_j}, W_{n+1} \rangle$: Challenger $\mathcal{C}$ gets the re-encryption key for parent condition vector W_n of depth n and runs $rk_{W_{n+1}|ID_i \to ID_j} \leftarrow \mathsf{HCReKeyGen}(rk_{W_n|ID_i \to ID_j}, W_{n+1})$.
  - *Re-encryption query* $\langle ID_i, ID_j, CT_{(ID_i, W_n)} \rangle$: Challenger $\mathcal{C}$ first gets the re-encryption key $rk_{W_n|ID_i \to ID_j} \leftarrow \mathsf{ReKeyGen}(sk_{ID_i}, ID_j, W_n)$ and runs $CT_{(ID_j, W_n)} \leftarrow \mathsf{ReEnc}(rk_{W_n|ID_i \to ID_j}, CT_{(ID_i, W_n)})$, and then it returns $CT_{(ID_j, W_n)}$ to adversary $\mathcal{A}$.
  - *Decryption query* $\langle ID, CT_{(ID, W_n)} \rangle$: Challenger $\mathcal{C}$ first gets the private key $sk_{ID} \leftarrow \mathsf{Extract}(msk, ID)$ and runs the decryption algorithm and returns the result $\mathsf{Dec1}(sk_{ID}, CT_{(ID, W_n)})$ or $\mathsf{Dec2}(sk_{ID}, CT_{(ID, W_n)})$ to adversary $\mathcal{A}$.
- Challenge: Adversary $\mathcal{A}$ outputs a target identity ID^* and condition W_n^* as well as two distinct plaintexts $m_0, m_1 \in \mathcal{M}$. Challenger $\mathcal{C}$ picks $\beta \in_R \{0, 1\}$ and returns $CT^*_{(ID^*, W_n^*)} = \mathsf{Enc}(params, ID^*, W_n^*, m_\beta)$ to adversary $\mathcal{A}$.
- Phase 2: Adversary $\mathcal{A}$ keeps on issuing all queries as in Phase 1, challenger $\mathcal{C}$ responds the queries as in Phase 1. But the difference is that Phase 2 needs to satisfy the following conditions:
  - Adversary $\mathcal{A}$ cannot issue *Extraction query* on ID^*.
  - Adversary $\mathcal{A}$ cannot issue *Decryption query* on neither $\langle ID^*, CT^*_{(ID^*, W_n^*)} \rangle$ nor $\langle ID_j, \mathsf{ReEnc}(rk_{W_n^*|ID^* \to ID_j}, CT^*_{(ID^*, W_n^*)}) \rangle$.

- If adversary $\mathcal{A}$ gets sk_{ID_j} on ID_j, it cannot issue *Re-encryption query* on $\langle ID^*, ID_j, CT^*_{(ID^*, W_n^*)} \rangle$ and *Re-encryption key query* on $\langle ID^*, ID_j, W_k^* \rangle$, where $W_k^* = \{w_1, \cdots, w_k\}$ and $k \in [1, n]$.
- Guess: Adversary $\mathcal{A}$ makes a guess $\beta' \in \{0, 1\}$ and wins the game if $\beta' = \beta$.

We define adversary $\mathcal{A}$'s advantage in the above game as

$$Adv_{\mathcal{A}}^{\text{IND-IBHCPRE-CCA}} = |\Pr[\beta' = \beta] - 1/2|.$$

Definition 1 *(IND-IBHCPRE-CCA Security). We say that an IBHCPRE scheme is IND-CCA secure, if for any PPT adversary $\mathcal{A}$, the advantage in the above security game is negligible, that is $Adv_{\mathcal{A}}^{\text{IND-IBHCPRE-CCA}} \leq \epsilon$.*

3   Construction

- Setup(1^λ): Given a security parameter 1^λ, first output a bilinear group $(p, \mathbb{G}, \mathbb{G}_T, e)$, and then choose a generator $g \in_R \mathbb{G}$, $\alpha \in_R \mathbb{Z}_p$ and compute $g_1 = g^\alpha$. Finally, choose six hash functions H_1, H_2, H_3, H_4, H_5 and H_6, where $H_1 : \{0,1\}^* \to \mathbb{G}$, $H_2 : \mathbb{G}_T \times \mathcal{M} \to \mathbb{Z}_p$, $H_3 : \mathbb{G}_T \to \mathcal{M}$, $H_4 : \{0,1\}^* \times \mathbb{G} \times \mathbb{G}_T \times \mathcal{M} \times \mathbb{G}^n \to \mathbb{G}$, $H_5 : \{0,1\}^* \to \mathbb{G}$ and $H_6 : \mathcal{M} \to \mathbb{G}$, where $\mathcal{M}$ is the massage space. The public parameter is

$$PPs = ((p, \mathbb{G}, \mathbb{G}_T, e), g, g_1, H_1, H_2, H_3, H_4, H_5, H_6)$$

and the master secret key is $msk = \alpha$.
- Extract(msk, ID): Given the master secret key msk and an identity ID, it computes $Q_{ID} = H_1(ID)$ and sets the private key as

$$sk_{ID} = Q_{ID}^\alpha.$$

- Enc($PPs, ID_i, W_n = \{w_1, \cdots, w_n\}, M$): Given the public parameter PPs, an identity ID_i, a condition vector $W_n = \{w_1, \cdots, w_n\}$ and a message $M \in \mathcal{M}$, pick $\delta \in_R \mathbb{G}_T$ and set $r = H_2(\delta \| M)$,

$$
\begin{aligned}
A &= g^r \\
B &= \delta \cdot e(g_1, H_1(ID_i))^r \\
C &= H_3(\delta) \oplus M \\
D_1 &= H_5(ID_i \| w_1)^r \\
D_2 &= H_5(ID_i \| w_1 \| w_2)^r \\
&\cdots \\
D_n &= H_5(ID_i \| w_1 \| \cdots \| w_n)^r \\
S &= H_4(ID_i \| A \| B \| C \| D_1 \| \cdots \| D_n)^r
\end{aligned}
$$

Then output an initial ciphertext

$$CT_{(ID_i, W_n)} = (A, B, C, D_1, \cdots, D_n, S, W_n).$$

- ReKeyGen($sk_{ID_i}, ID_j, W_n' = \{w_1', \cdots, w_n'\}$): Given the private key sk_{ID_i}, an identity ID_j and a condition vector W_n', first pick $\theta \in_R \mathcal{M}$, $\delta' \in_R \mathbb{G}_T$ and set $r' = H_2(\delta'||\theta)$ and pick $s_1, \cdots, s_n \in_R \mathbb{Z}_p^n$

$$rk_1 = g^{r'}$$
$$rk_2 = \delta' \cdot e(g_1, H_1(ID_j))^{r'}$$
$$rk_3 = H_3(\delta') \oplus \theta$$
$$RK_1 = sk_{ID_i} \cdot H_5(ID_i||w_1')^{s_1} \cdots H_5(ID_i||w_1'||\cdots||w_n')^{s_n} \cdot H_6(\theta)$$
$$RK_2^1 = g^{s_1}$$
$$\cdots$$
$$RK_2^n = g^{s_n}$$

Finally, output the re-encryption key

$$rk_{W_n'|ID_i \to ID_j} = (rk_1, rk_2, rk_3, RK_1, RK_2^1, \cdots, RK_2^n).$$

- HCReKeyGen($rk_{W_n'|ID_i \to ID_j}, W_{n+1}'$): Give the re-encryption key $rk_{W_n'|ID_i \to ID_j}$ for a parent condition vector $W_n' = \{w_1', \cdots, w_n'\}$, compute a hierarchical conditional re-encryption key $rk_{W_{n+1}'|ID_i \to ID_j}$ for a condition vector $W_{n+1}' = \{w_1', \cdots, w_n', w_{n+1}'\}$ as follows: Choose $r'', s_1', s_2', \cdots, s_n', s_{n+1}' \in_R \mathbb{Z}_p$ and compute

$$rk_1' = rk_1 \cdot g^{r''}$$
$$rk_2' = rk_2 \cdot e(g_1, H_1(ID_j))^{r''}$$
$$rk_3' = rk_3$$
$$RK_1' = RK_1 \cdot H_5(ID_i||w_1'||\cdots||w_{n+1}')^{s_{n+1}'} \cdot H_5(ID_i||w_1')^{s_1'} \cdots$$
$$\qquad H_5(ID_i||w_1'||\cdots||w_n')^{s_n'}$$
$$RK_2'^1 = RK_2^1 \cdot g^{s_1'}$$
$$\cdots$$
$$RK_2'^n = RK_2^n \cdot g^{s_n'}$$
$$RK_2'^{n+1} = g^{s_{n+1}'}$$

Finally, output the re-encryption key

$$rk_{W_{n+1}'|ID_i \to ID_j} = (rk_1', rk_2', rk_3', RK_1', RK_2'^1, \cdots, RK_2'^{n+1})$$

which is a valid re-encryption key, as the distribution of the re-encryption key is the same as the distribution of keys generated by ReKeyGen.

- ReEnc($rk_{W_n|ID_i \to ID_j}, CT_{(ID_i, W_n)}$): Given a re-encryption key $rk_{W_n|ID_i \to ID_j}$ and an initial ciphertext $CT_{(ID_i, W_n)}$, check whether

$$e(SD_1 \cdots D_n, g) =$$
$$e(H_4(ID_i||A||B||C||D_1||\cdots||D_n)H_5(ID_i||w_1)\cdots H_5(ID_i||w_1||\cdots||w_n), A).$$

If not, output $\perp$; otherwise compute

$$B' = B \cdot \frac{e(D_1, RK_2^1) \cdots e(D_n, RK_2^n)}{e(A, RK_1)} = \delta/e(A, H_6(\theta)).$$

Then output the transformed ciphertext

$$CT_{(ID_j, W_n)} = (A, B', C, rk_1, rk_2, rk_3).$$

- $Dec_2(sk_{ID_i}, CT_{(ID_i, W_n)})$: Given the private key sk_{ID_i} and the initial ciphertext $CT_{(ID_i, W_n)}$, first check whether

$$e(SD_1 \cdots D_n, g) =$$
$$e(H_4(ID_i||A||B||C||D_1|| \cdots ||D_n)H_5(ID_i||w_1) \cdots H_5(ID_i||w_1|| \cdots ||w_n), A).$$

If not, output $\perp$; otherwise, compute

$$\delta = B/e(A, sk_{ID_i})$$
$$M = H_3(\delta) \oplus C.$$

Then check whether
$$A = g^{H_2(\delta||M)}.$$

If not, output $\perp$; otherwise output M.
- $Dec_1(sk_{ID_j}, CT_{(ID_j, W_n)})$: Given the private key sk_{ID_j} and the transformed ciphertext $CT_{(ID_j, W_n)}$, first compute

$$\delta' = rk_2/e(rk_1, sk_{ID_j})$$
$$\theta = H_3(\delta') \oplus rk_3.$$

Then it checks whether
$$rk_1 = g^{H_2(\delta'||\theta)}.$$

If not, output $\perp$; else compute

$$\delta = B' \cdot e(A, H_6(\theta))$$
$$M = H_3(\delta) \oplus C.$$

Finally, check whether
$$A = g^{H_2(\delta||M)}.$$

If not, output $\perp$; otherwise output M.

4   Security Analysis

In the following, we prove that our construction is IND-IBHCPRE-CCA secure in the random oracle model.

Theorem 1. *Suppose that the DBDH assumption holds in a bilinear group* (p, G, G_T, e), *then the above IBHCPRE scheme is IND-CCA secure in the random oracle model.*

Concretely, if adversary $\mathcal{A}$ with a non-negligible advantage against the above IBHCPRE scheme, then there exists a challenger $\mathcal{C}$ to solve the DBDH assumption with a non-negligible advantage.

Proof. Suppose that adversary $\mathcal{A}$ has a non-negligible advantage to attack the above IBHCPRE scheme. We can build a PPT challenger $\mathcal{C}$ that makes use of adversary $\mathcal{A}$ to solve the DBDH problem. Challenger $\mathcal{C}$ is given a DBDH instance (g, g^a, g^b, g^c, Z) with unknown $a, b, c \in \mathbb{Z}_p$, challenger $\mathcal{C}$'s goal is to decide $Z = e(g, g)^{abc}$ or Z is a random value. Challenger $\mathcal{C}$ works by interacting with $\mathcal{A}$ in the above security game as follows:

- Setup: Adversary $\mathcal{A}$ is given the public parameter $params = ((p, G, G_T, e), g, g_1, H_1, H_2, H_3, H_4, H_5, H_6)$ where $g_1 = g^a$ and $H_1, H_2, H_3, H_3, H_4, H_5, H_6$ are random oracles managed by challenger $\mathcal{C}$. The master secret key a is unknown to challenger $\mathcal{C}$.
- Phase 1: Adversary $\mathcal{A}$ adaptively asks the following queries:
  - *Hash Oracle Queries.* Adversary $\mathcal{A}$ freely queries H_i with $i \in \{1, 2, 3, 4, 5, 6\}$. Challenger $\mathcal{C}$ maintains six hash tables H_i-list with $i \in \{1, 2, 3, 4, 5, 6\}$. At the beginning, all of the tables are empty. Challenger $\mathcal{C}$ replies the queries as follows:
    $Hash_1$ Query (ID_j):
    If ID_j is on the H_1-list in the form of $\langle ID_j, Q_j, q_j, \varpi_j \rangle$, challenger $\mathcal{C}$ returns the predefined value Q_j; otherwise, it chooses $q_j \in_R \mathbb{Z}_p$ and generates a random $\varpi_j \in \{0, 1\}$, if $\varpi_j = 0$, challenger $\mathcal{C}$ computes $Q_j = g^{q_j}$; else it computes $Q_j = g^{bq_j}$ and adds $\langle ID_j, Q_j, q_j, \varpi_j \rangle$ into the H_1-list, and then it returns Q_j.
    $Hash_2$ Query $(\delta || M)$:
    If $\langle \delta || M \rangle$ is on the H_2-list in the form of $\langle \delta || M, r, g^r \rangle$, return r; otherwise, challenger $\mathcal{C}$ selects $r \in_R Z_p^*$ and adds $\langle \delta || M, r, g^r \rangle$ into the H_2-list, then it returns r.
    $Hash_3$ Query $(\delta \in G_T)$:
    If δ is on the H_3-list in the form of $\langle \delta, X \rangle$, challenger $\mathcal{C}$ returns X; otherwise, it chooses $X \in_R \mathcal{M}$ and adds $\langle \delta, X \rangle$ into the H_3-list, then it returns X.
    $Hash_4$ Query $(ID_j || A || B || C || D_1 || \cdots || D_n)$:
    If $\langle ID_j || A || B || C || D_1 || \cdots || D_n \rangle$ is on the H_4-list in the form of $\langle ID_j || A || B || C || D_1 || \cdots || D_n, T_j, t_j \rangle$, challenger $\mathcal{C}$ returns the value T_j; otherwise, it chooses $t_j \in_R \mathbb{Z}_p$, computes $T_j = g^{t_j}$ and adds $\langle ID_j || A || B || C || D_1 || \cdots || D_n, T_j, t_j \rangle$ into the H_4-list, and then $\mathcal{C}$ returns T_j.
    $Hash_5$ Query $(ID_j, W_n = \{w_1, \cdots, w_k\})$:
    1. If $k = 1$, that is while $\langle ID_j, w_1 \rangle$ is on the H_5-list in the form of $\langle ID_j || w_1, \widehat{Q_1}, \widehat{q_1}, \widehat{\varpi_1} \rangle$, challenger $\mathcal{C}$ returns the value $\widehat{Q_1}$; otherwise, it picks $\widehat{q_1} \in_R \mathbb{Z}_p$ and $\widehat{\varpi_1} \in_R \{0, 1\}$. If $\widehat{\varpi_1} = 0$, it computes $Q_1 = g^{\widehat{q_1}}$;

else it computes $Q_1 = g^{b\hat{q_1}}$. It adds $\langle ID_j || w_1, \widehat{Q_1}, \hat{q_1}, \widehat{\varpi_1} \rangle$ into the H_5-list and responds with $\widehat{Q_1}$.

2. If $k \neq 1$, that is while $\langle ID_j, w_1, \cdots, w_k \rangle$ is on the H_5-list in the form of $\langle ID_j || w_1 || \cdots || w_k, \widehat{Q_k}, \hat{q_k} \rangle$, challenger $\mathcal{C}$ returns the value $\widehat{Q_k}$; otherwise, it picks $\hat{q_k} \in_R \mathbb{Z}_p$ and computes $Q_k = g^{\hat{q_k}}$. It adds $\langle ID_j || w_1 || \cdots || w_k, \widehat{Q_k}, \hat{q_k} \rangle$ into the H_5-list and then responds with $\widehat{Q_k}$.

$Hash_6$ Query $(\theta \in \mathcal{M})$:
If θ is on the H_6-list in the form of $\langle \theta, Y \rangle$, challenger $\mathcal{C}$ returns the value Y; otherwise, it chooses $Y \in_R \mathbb{G}$ and adds $\langle \theta, Y \rangle$ into the H_6-list, and then challenger $\mathcal{C}$ returns Y.

- *Extraction query* (ID_j): Challenger $\mathcal{C}$ recovers the tuple $\langle ID_j, Q_j, q_j, \varpi_j \rangle$ from the H_1-list. If $\varpi_j = 1$, challenger $\mathcal{C}$ outputs $\bot$ and aborts; otherwise, challenger $\mathcal{C}$ returns $sk_{ID_j} = g_1^{q_j}$ to adversary $\mathcal{A}$. (Note that $sk_{ID_j} = g_1^{q_j} = g^{aq_j} = Q_j^a = H_1(ID_j)^{\alpha}$, so that this is a proper private key for the identity ID_j).

- *Re-encryption key query* (ID_i, ID_j, W_n): Challenger $\mathcal{C}$ first picks $\delta' \in_R \mathbb{G}_T$, $\theta \in_R \mathcal{M}$ and recovers $\langle ID_i, Q_i, q_i, \varpi_i \rangle$ and $\langle ID_j, Q_j, q_j, \varpi_j \rangle$ from the H_1-list and $\langle \delta' || \theta, r', g^{r'} \rangle$ from the H_2-list, $\langle \delta', X \rangle$ from the H_3-list, $\langle ID_i || w_1, \widehat{Q_1}, \hat{q_1}, \widehat{\varpi_1} \rangle$ and $\langle ID_i || w_1 || \cdots || w_n, \widehat{Q_n}, \hat{q_n} \rangle$ from the H_5-list and $\langle \theta, Y \rangle$ from the H_6-list. Lets $rk_1 = g^{r'}$, $rk_2 = \delta' \cdot e(g_1, Q_j)^{r'}$, $rk_3 = X \oplus \theta$. Then challenger $\mathcal{C}$ constructs $RK_1, RK_2^1, RK_2^2, \cdots, RK_2^n$ as follows:

  1. If $\varpi_i = 0$, challenger $\mathcal{C}$ picks $s_1, \cdots, s_n \in_R \mathbb{Z}_p$ and lets $RK_1 = g_1^{q_i} \cdot \widehat{Q_1}^{s_1} \cdots \widehat{Q_n}^{s_n} \cdot Y$, $RK_2^1 = g^{s_1}, \cdots, RK_2^n = g^{s_n}$.

  2. If $\varpi_i = 1$ and $\widehat{\varpi_1} = 1$: challenger $\mathcal{C}$ picks $s', s_2, \cdots, s_n \in_R \mathbb{Z}_p$ and sets $RK_1 = g^{b\hat{q_i}s'} \widehat{Q_2}^{s_2} \cdots \widehat{Q_n}^{s_n} \cdot Y$, $RK_2^1 = g_1^{-q_i/\hat{q_1}} g^{s'}$, $RK_2^2 = g^{s_2}, \cdots, RK_2^n = g^{s_n}$, where $s_1 = -aq_i/\hat{q_1} + s'$.

  3. If $\varpi_i = 1$ and $\widehat{\varpi_1} = 0$: challenger $\mathcal{C}$ outputs $\bot$ and aborts.

  Finally, challenger $\mathcal{C}$ returns the re-encryption key $rk_{w|ID_i \to ID_j} = (rk_1, rk_2, rk_3, RK_1, RK_2^1, \cdots, RK_2^n)$ to adversary $\mathcal{A}$.

- *Hierarchical condition Re-encryption key query* $\langle rk_{W_n|ID_i \to ID_j}, W_{n+1} \rangle$: Challenger $\mathcal{C}$ first gets the re-encryption key $rk_{W_n|ID_i \to ID_j}$ for a condition $W_n = \{w_1, \cdots, w_n\}$, it first chooses $r', s_1, s_2, \cdots, s_n, s_{n+1} \in_R \mathbb{Z}_p$ and computes $rk_1' = rk_1 \cdot g^{r'}$, $rk_2' = rk_2 \cdot e(g_1, H_1(ID_j))^{r'}$, $rk_3' = rk_3$, $RK_1' = RK_1 \cdot H_5(ID_i || w_1 || \cdots || w_{n+1})^{s_{n+1}} \cdot H_5(ID_i || w_1)^{s_1} \cdots H_5(ID_i || w_1 || \cdots || w_n)^{s_n} \cdot H_6(\theta)$, $RK_2'^1 = RK_2^1 \cdot g^{s_1}, \cdots, RK_2'^n = RK_2^n \cdot g^{s_n}, RK_2'^{n+1} = g^{s_{n+1}}$. Challenger $\mathcal{C}$ returns the hierarchical conditional re-encryption key $rk_{W_{n+1}|ID_i \to ID_j}$ for the conditional $W_{n+1} = \{w_1, \cdots, w_n, w_{n+1}\}$ to adversary $\mathcal{A}$.

- *Re-encryption query* $(ID_i, ID_j, CT_{(ID_i, W_n)})$: Their exists the following two cases to generate the re-encrypted ciphertext:

  1. If $\varpi_i = 1$ and $\widehat{\varpi_1} = 0$, challenger $\mathcal{C}$ first parses the ciphertext $CT_{(ID_i, W_n)}$ as $(A, B, C, D_1, \cdots, D_n, S, W_n)$ and checks whether $e(SD_1 \cdots D_n, g) = e(H_4(ID_i || A || B || C || D_1 || \cdots || D_n) H_5(ID_i || w_1) \cdots H_5(ID_i || w_1 || \cdots || w_n), A)$. If not, it returns $\bot$; otherwise, challenger $\mathcal{C}$ checks whether there exists a tuple $\langle \delta || M, r, g^r \rangle$ from the

H_2-list such that $A = g^r$. If no, it returns $\perp$; otherwise, $\mathcal{C}$ recovers the tuple $\langle ID_j, Q_j, q_j, \varpi_j \rangle$ from the H_1-list and then it picks $\theta \in_R \mathcal{M}$, $\delta' \in_R \mathbb{G}_T$, $\mathcal{C}$ recovers the tuple $\langle \delta', X \rangle$ from the H_3-list and sets $r' = H_2(\delta'||\theta), rk_1 = g^{r'}, rk_2 = \delta' \cdot e(g_1, Q_j)^{r'}$, $rk_3 = X \oplus \theta$. Next, $\mathcal{C}$ recovers the tuple $\langle \theta, Y \rangle$ from the H_6-list and sets $B' = \delta/e(A, Y)$. Finally, $\mathcal{C}$ outputs the transformed ciphertext $CT_{(ID_j, W_n)} = (A, B', C, rk_1, rk_2, rk_3)$ to adversary $\mathcal{A}$.

2. Otherwise, challenger $\mathcal{C}$ first queries the re-encryption key to get $rk_{W_n|ID_i \to ID_j}$, and then it runs ReEnc $(rk_{W_n|ID_i \to ID_j}, CT_{(ID_i, W_n)})$ algorithm to obtain the transformed ciphertext $CT_{(ID_j, W_n)}$. Finally challenger $\mathcal{C}$ returns the transformed ciphertext $CT_{(ID_j, W_n)}$ to adversary $\mathcal{A}$.

- *Decryption* query$(ID, CT_{(ID, W_n)})$: Challenger $\mathcal{C}$ checks whether $CT_{(ID, W_n)}$ is an initial or a transformed ciphertext.
  1. For an initial ciphertext, challenger $\mathcal{C}$ first extracts $CT_{(ID, W_n)}$ as $(A, B, C, D_1, \cdots, D_n, S, W_n)$. Then it recovers a tuple $\langle ID, Q, q, \varpi \rangle$ from the H_1-list. If $\varpi = 0$ (meaning $sk_{ID} = g_1^q$), challenger $\mathcal{C}$ decrypts the ciphertext $CT_{(ID, W_n)}$ using sk_{ID}; otherwise, challenger $\mathcal{C}$ first checks whether $e(SD_1 \cdots D_n, g) = e(H_4(ID_i||A||B||C|| D_1|| \cdots ||D_n)H_5(ID_i||w_1) \cdots H_5(ID_i||w_1|| \cdots ||w_n), A)$ holds. If no, it returns $\perp$; else challenger $\mathcal{C}$ searches the tuple $\langle \delta||M, r, g^r \rangle$ from the H_2-list such that $A = g^r$. If it cannot find such tuple, it returns $\perp$; else it searches whether there exists a tuple $\langle \delta, X \rangle$ from the H_3-list such that $M \oplus X = C$, a tuple $\langle ID||w_1, \widehat{Q_1}, \widehat{q_1}, \widehat{\varpi_1} \rangle$ and some tuples $\{\langle ID||w_1|| \cdots ||w_k, \widehat{Q_k}, \widehat{q_k} \rangle\}_{1 \le k \le n}$ from the H_5-list and a tuple $\langle ID||A||B||C||D_1|| \cdots ||D_n, T, t \rangle$ from the H_4-list, such that $\widehat{Q_1}^r = D_1, \cdots, \widehat{Q_k}^r = D_k$ and $T^r = S$. If not, it returns $\perp$; otherwise, challenger $\mathcal{C}$ returns $M = C \oplus X$ to adversary $\mathcal{A}$.
  2. For a transformed ciphertext, challenger $\mathcal{C}$ first parses $CT_{(ID, W_n)}$ as $(A, B', C, rk_1, rk_2, rk_3)$. Then challenger $\mathcal{C}$ recovers tuple $\langle ID, Q, q, \varpi \rangle$ from the H_1-list. If $\varpi = 0$ (meaning $sk_{ID} = g_1^q$), challenger $\mathcal{C}$ decrypts the ciphertext $CT_{(ID, W_n)}$ using sk_{ID}; otherwise, challenger $\mathcal{C}$ searches whether there exists a tuple $\langle \delta'||\theta, r', g^{r'} \rangle$ from the H_2-list such that $rk_1 = g^{r'}$. If not, it returns $\perp$; else searches whether there exists a tuple $\langle \delta', X \rangle$ from the H_3-list and a tuple $\langle ID, Q, q, 1 \rangle$ from the H_1-list such that $\theta \oplus X = C$ and $\delta' \cdot e(g_1, Q)^{r'} = rk_2$. If not, it returns $\perp$; otherwise, challenger $\mathcal{C}$ recovers $\langle \theta, Y \rangle$ from the H_6-list, and it computes $\delta = B' \cdot e(A, Y)$ and $M = H_3(\delta) \oplus C$. Finally, challenger $\mathcal{C}$ returns M to adversary $\mathcal{A}$.

- Challenge: Adversary $\mathcal{A}$ outputs an identity ID^*, a condition W_n^* of depth n and two different plaintexts $M_0, M_1 \in \mathcal{M}$. Challenger $\mathcal{C}$ recovers the tuple $\langle ID^*, Q^*, q^*, \varpi^* \rangle$ from the H_1-list, a tuple $\langle ID^*||w_1^*, \widehat{Q^*}, \widehat{q^*}, \widehat{\varpi^*} \rangle$ and several tuples $\{\langle ID^*||w_1^*|| \cdots ||w_k^*, \widehat{Q_k^*}, \widehat{q_k^*} \rangle\}_{1 \le k \le n}$ from the H_5-list. If $\varpi^* = 0$ or $\widehat{\varpi^*} = 1$, challenger $\mathcal{C}$ outputs $\perp$ and aborts; else challenger $\mathcal{C}$ first picks $\beta \in_R \{0, 1\}$, $\delta^* \in_R \mathbb{G}_T$, $X^* \in_R \{0, 1\}^n$, and then it inserts the tuple $\langle \delta^*, X^* \rangle$ into the

H_3-list and the tuple $\langle \delta^*, M_\beta, \cdot, g^c \rangle$ into the H_2-list. Next challenger $\mathcal{C}$ sets $A^* = g^c$, $B^* = \delta^* \cdot T^{q^*}$, $C^* = X^* \oplus M_\beta$, $D_1^* = g^{\widehat{cq^*}}, \cdots, D_n^* = g^{\widehat{cq_n^*}}$ and selects $t^* \in_R \mathbb{Z}_p$, and then it inserts the tuple $\langle ID^* || A^* || B^* || C^* || D_1^* || \cdots || D_n^*, g^{t^*}, t^* \rangle$ into the H_4-list, and sets $S^* = g^{ct^*}$. Finally, challenger $\mathcal{C}$ sends the challenge ciphertext $CT^*_{(ID^*, W_n^*)} = (A^*, B^*, C^*, D_1^*, \cdots, D_n^*, S^*)$ to adversary $\mathcal{A}$.

- Phase 2: Adversary $\mathcal{A}$ continues to adaptively issue queries as in Phase 1. But it needs to satisfy the conditions which are described in the above security model.
- Guess: Adversary $\mathcal{A}$ outputs a guess $\beta' \in \{0, 1\}$.

5   Conclusion

In this paper, we propose an identity-based hierarchical conditional proxy re-encryption scheme, which is the first of its type. The new scheme allows delegator to achieve more flexibly encrypted data sharing. The scheme is proved secure against chosen-ciphertext attacks in the random oracle model. Via comparison, we show the flexibility and scalability of our scheme. This paper leaves some interesting open problems, for example, how could we prove the security in the standard model, and how to reduce the re-encryption key size to constant.

Acknowledgment. This work was supported by National Science Foundation of China (No. 61572131), Guangdong Provincial Science and Technology Plan Projects (No. 2016A010101034) and Project of Internation as well as Hongkong, Macao & Taiwan Science and Technology Cooperation Innovation Platform in Universities in Guangdong Province (No. 2015KGJHZ027).

References

1. Ateniese, G., Kevin, F., Green, M., Hohenberger, S.: Improved proxy re-encryption schemes with applications to secure distributed storage. ACM Trans. Inf. Syst. Secur. **9**(1), 1–30 (2006)
2. Blaze, M., Bleumer, G., Strauss, M.: Divertible protocols and atomic proxy cryptography. In: Nyberg, K. (ed.) EUROCRYPT 1998. LNCS, vol. 1403, pp. 127–144. Springer, Heidelberg (1998). https://doi.org/10.1007/BFb0054122
3. Canetti, R., Hohenberger, S.: Chosen-ciphertext secure proxy re-encryption. In: Proceedings of the 2007 ACM Conference on Computer and Communications Security (CCS 2007), Alexandria, Virginia, USA, 28–31 October 2007, pp. 185–194 (2007)
4. Castiglione, A., De Santis, A., Masucci, B., Palmieri, F., Castiglione, A., Huang, X.: Cryptographic hierarchical access control for dynamic structures. IEEE Trans. Inf. Forensics Secur. **11**(10), 2349–2364 (2016)
5. Castiglione, A., De Santis, A., Masucci, B., Palmieri, F., Castiglione, A., Li, J., Huang, X.: Hierarchical and shared access control. IEEE Trans. Inf. Forensics Secur. **11**(4), 850–865 (2016)
6. Chu, C.-K., Tzeng, W.-G.: Identity-based proxy re-encryption without random oracles. In: Garay, J.A., Lenstra, A.K., Mambo, M., Peralta, R. (eds.) ISC 2007. LNCS, vol. 4779, pp. 189–202. Springer, Heidelberg (2007). https://doi.org/10.1007/978-3-540-75496-1_13

7. Deng, R.H., Weng, J., Liu, S., Chen, K.: Chosen-ciphertext secure proxy re-encryption without pairings. In: Franklin, M.K., Hui, L.C.K., Wong, D.S. (eds.) CANS 2008. LNCS, vol. 5339, pp. 1–17. Springer, Heidelberg (2008). https://doi.org/10.1007/978-3-540-89641-8_1

8. Fang, L., Susilo, W., Ge, C., Wang, J.: Interactive conditional proxy re-encryption with fine grain policy. J. Syst. Softw. **84**(12), 2293–2302 (2011)

9. Giuseppe, A., Kevin., Matthew, G., Susan, H.: Improved proxy re-encryption schemes with applications to secure distributed storage. In: Proceedings of the Network and Distributed System Security Symposium (NDSS 2005), San Diego, California, USA (2005)

10. Green, M., Ateniese, G.: Identity-based proxy re-encryption. In: Katz, J., Yung, M. (eds.) ACNS 2007. LNCS, vol. 4521, pp. 288–306. Springer, Heidelberg (2007). https://doi.org/10.1007/978-3-540-72738-5_19

11. Hanaoka, G., Kawai, Y., Kunihiro, N., Matsuda, T., Weng, J., Zhang, R., Zhao, Y.: Generic construction of chosen ciphertext secure proxy re-encryption. In: Dunkelman, O. (ed.) CT-RSA 2012. LNCS, vol. 7178, pp. 349–364. Springer, Heidelberg (2012). https://doi.org/10.1007/978-3-642-27954-6_22

12. He, K., Weng, J., Deng, R.H., Liu, J.K.: On the security of two identity-based conditional proxy re-encryption schemes. Theor. Comput. Sci. **652**, 18–27 (2016)

13. He, K., Weng, J., Liu, J.K., Zhou, W., Liu, J.-N.: Efficient fine-grained access control for secure personal health records in cloud computing. In: Chen, J., Piuri, V., Su, C., Yung, M. (eds.) NSS 2016. LNCS, vol. 9955, pp. 65–79. Springer, Cham (2016). https://doi.org/10.1007/978-3-319-46298-1_5

14. Lee, C.-C., Li, C.-T., Chen, C.-L., Chiu, S.-T.: A searchable hierarchical conditional proxy re-encryption scheme for cloud storage services. ITC **45**(3), 289–299 (2016)

15. Liang, K., Au, M.H., Liu, J.K., Susilo, W., Wong, D.S., Yang, G., Yu, Y., Yang, A.: A secure and efficient ciphertext-policy attribute-based proxy re-encryption for cloud data sharing. Future Gener. Comput. Syst. **52**, 95–108 (2015)

16. Liang, K., Chu, C.-K., Tan, X., Wong, D.S., Tang, C., Zhou, J.: Chosen-ciphertext secure multi-hop identity-based conditional proxy re-encryption with constant-size ciphertexts. Theor. Comput. Sci. **539**, 87–105 (2014)

17. Liang, K., Fang, L., Wong, D.S., Susilo, W.: A ciphertext-policy attribute-based proxy re-encryption scheme for data sharing in public clouds. Concurr. Comput. Pract. Exp. **27**(8), 2004–2027 (2015)

18. Liang, K., Liu, J.K., Wong, D.S., Susilo, W.: An efficient cloud-based revocable identity-based proxy re-encryption scheme for public clouds data sharing. In: Kutyłowski, M., Vaidya, J. (eds.) ESORICS 2014. LNCS, vol. 8712, pp. 257–272. Springer, Cham (2014). https://doi.org/10.1007/978-3-319-11203-9_15

19. Liang, K., Liu, Z., Tan, X., Wong, D.S., Tang, C.: A CCA-secure identity-based conditional proxy re-encryption without random oracles. In: Kwon, T., Lee, M.-K., Kwon, D. (eds.) ICISC 2012. LNCS, vol. 7839, pp. 231–246. Springer, Heidelberg (2013). https://doi.org/10.1007/978-3-642-37682-5_17

20. Liang, K., Su, C., Chen, J., Liu, J.K.: Efficient multi-function data sharing and searching mechanism for cloud-based encrypted data. In: Chen, X., Wang, X., Huang, X. (eds.) Proceedings of the 11th ACM on Asia Conference on Computer and Communications Security (AsiaCCS 2016), Xi'an, China, May 30 - June 3, 2016, pp. 83–94. ACM (2016)

21. Liang, K., Susilo, W.: Searchable attribute-based mechanism with efficient data sharing for secure cloud storage. IEEE Trans. Inf. Forensics Secur. **10**(9), 1981–1992 (2015)

22. Liang, K., Susilo, W., Liu, J.K.: Privacy-preserving ciphertext multi-sharing control for big data storage. IEEE Trans. Inf. Forensics Secur. **10**(8), 1578–1589 (2015)
23. Liang, X., Cao, Z., Lin, H., Shao, J.: Attribute based proxy re-encryption with delegating capabilities. In: Proceedings of the 2009 ACM Symposium on Information, Computer and Communications Security (ASIACCS 2009), Sydney, Australia, 10–12 March 2009, pp. 276–286 (2009)
24. Libert, B., Vergnaud, D.: Unidirectional chosen-ciphertext secure proxy re-encryption. In: Cramer, R. (ed.) PKC 2008. LNCS, vol. 4939, pp. 360–379. Springer, Heidelberg (2008). https://doi.org/10.1007/978-3-540-78440-1_21
25. Libert, B., Vergnaud, D.: Unidirectional chosen-ciphertext secure proxy re-encryption. IEEE Trans. Inf. Theory **57**(3), 1786–1802 (2011)
26. Wang, L., Wang, L., Mambo, M., Okamoto, E.: New identity-based proxy re-encryption schemes to prevent collusion attacks. In: Joye, M., Miyaji, A., Otsuka, A. (eds.) Pairing 2010. LNCS, vol. 6487, pp. 327–346. Springer, Heidelberg (2010). https://doi.org/10.1007/978-3-642-17455-1_21
27. Lin, S., Zhang, R., Wang, M.: Verifiable attribute-based proxy re-encryption for secure public cloud data sharing. Secur. Commun. Netw. **9**(12), 1748–1758 (2016)
28. Luo, S., Shen, Q., Chen, Z.: Fully secure unidirectional identity-based proxy re-encryption. In: Kim, H. (ed.) ICISC 2011. LNCS, vol. 7259, pp. 109–126. Springer, Heidelberg (2012). https://doi.org/10.1007/978-3-642-31912-9_8
29. Matsuda, T., Nishimaki, R., Tanaka, K.: CCA proxy re-encryption without bilinear maps in the standard model. In: Nguyen, P.Q., Pointcheval, D. (eds.) PKC 2010. LNCS, vol. 6056, pp. 261–278. Springer, Heidelberg (2010). https://doi.org/10.1007/978-3-642-13013-7_16
30. Matsuo, T.: Proxy re-encryption systems for identity-based encryption. In: Takagi, T., Okamoto, T., Okamoto, E., Okamoto, T. (eds.) Pairing 2007. LNCS, vol. 4575, pp. 247–267. Springer, Heidelberg (2007). https://doi.org/10.1007/978-3-540-73489-5_13
31. Mizuno, T., Doi, H.: Secure and efficient IBE-PKE proxy re-encryption. IEICE Trans. **94–A**(1), 36–44 (2011)
32. Nabeel, M., Bertino, E.: Privacy preserving delegated access control in public clouds. IEEE Trans. Knowl. Data Eng. **26**(9), 2268–2280 (2014)
33. Shao, J., Cao, Z.: Multi-use unidirectional identity-based proxy re-encryption from hierarchical identity-based encryption. Inf. Sci. **206**, 83–95 (2012)
34. Shao, J., Rongxing, L., Lin, X., Liang, K.: Secure bidirectional proxy re-encryption for cryptographic cloud storage. Pervasive Mobile Comput. **28**, 113–121 (2016)
35. Smith, T.: DVD jon: Buy DRM-less tracks from Apple iTunes, January 2005. http://www.theregister.co.uk/2005/03/18/itunespymusique
36. Tang, Q.: Type-based proxy re-encryption and its construction. In: Chowdhury, D.R., Rijmen, V., Das, A. (eds.) INDOCRYPT 2008. LNCS, vol. 5365, pp. 130–144. Springer, Heidelberg (2008). https://doi.org/10.1007/978-3-540-89754-5_11
37. Isshiki, T., Nguyen, M.H., Tanaka, K.: Proxy re-encryption in a stronger security model extended from CT-RSA2012. In: Dawson, E. (ed.) CT-RSA 2013. LNCS, vol. 7779, pp. 277–292. Springer, Heidelberg (2013). https://doi.org/10.1007/978-3-642-36095-4_18
38. Wang, L., Wang, L., Mambo, M., Okamoto, E.: Identity-based proxy cryptosystems with revocability and hierarchical confidentialities. IEICE Trans. **95–A**(1), 70–88 (2012)
39. Waters, B.: Efficient identity-based encryption without random oracles. In: Cramer, R. (ed.) EUROCRYPT 2005. LNCS, vol. 3494, pp. 114–127. Springer, Heidelberg (2005). https://doi.org/10.1007/11426639_7

40. Weng, J., Chen, M.-R., Yang, Y., Deng, R.H., Chen, K., Bao, F.: CCA-secure uni-directional proxy re-encryption in the adaptive corruption model without random oracles. Sci. China Inf. Sci. **53**(3), 593–606 (2010)
41. Weng, J., Deng, R.H., Ding, X., Chu, C.-K., Lai, J.: Conditional proxy re-encryption secure against chosen-ciphertext attack. In: Proceedings of the 2009 ACM Symposium on Information, Computer and Communications Security (ASI-ACCS 2009), Sydney, Australia, 10–12 March 2009, pp. 322–332 (2009)
42. Weng, J., Yang, Y., Tang, Q., Deng, R.H., Bao, F.: Efficient conditional proxy re-encryption with chosen-ciphertext security. In: Samarati, P., Yung, M., Martinelli, F., Ardagna, C.A. (eds.) ISC 2009. LNCS, vol. 5735, pp. 151–166. Springer, Heidelberg (2009). https://doi.org/10.1007/978-3-642-04474-8_13

New Proof for BKP IBE Scheme and Improvement in the MIMC Setting

Song Luo[1], Lu Yan[2(✉)], Jian Weng[3], and Zheng Yang[1]

[1] School of Computer Science and Engineering, Chongqing University of Technology, Chongqing, China
songluo16@gmail.com, yangzheng@cqut.edu.cn
[2] School of Science, Chongqing University of Technology, Chongqing, China
yanlu@cqut.edu.cn
[3] College of Information Science and Technology, Jinan University, Guangzhou, China
cryptweng@gmail.com

Abstract. In CRYPTO 2014, Blazy et al. [2] proposed a new and efficient identity-based encryption scheme (denoted by BKP) with almost tight security in the prime order setting. However, their scheme is transformed from affine message authentication code and cannot give a standard proof in the IBE setting. Furthermore, it is not proven secure in the multi-instance, multi-ciphertext (MIMC, or multi-challenge) setting. Based on Blazy et al.'s work, we propose a generalized almost tightly secure IBE scheme from BKP IBE scheme and give a new proof in the standard security model under the Matrix Diffie-Hellman (MDDH) assumption. Based on the generalized IBE scheme, we propose a new almost tightly secure IBE scheme in the MIMC setting. Compared with a recent IBE scheme proposed by Gong et al. in the MIMC setting, our scheme is more efficient under the decisional linear (DLIN, or 2-LIN) assumption in the symmetric bilinear groups.

Keywords: Identity-based encryption · Tight security · Multi-challenge security

1 Introduction

The concept of Identity-Based Encryption (IBE) was proposed by Shamir [17] in 1984 to simplify the public-key infrastructure. In an IBE system, any arbitrary strings can form users' public keys, such as e-mail addresses, IP addresses or other meaningful strings. Anyone can encrypt messages for any identity, and only the owner of the corresponding identity can decrypt the messages. However, no concrete construction of IBE was given by Shamir until Boneh and Franklin [4] proposed the first practical IBE system based on bilinear groups. At the same year, Cocks [7] proposed another but less efficient IBE system using quadratic

© Springer International Publishing AG 2017
J. K. Liu and P. Samarati (Eds.): ISPEC 2017, LNCS 10701, pp. 136–155, 2017.
https://doi.org/10.1007/978-3-319-72359-4_8

residues. Following Boneh and Franklin's work, many new IBE schemes are proposed considering several features such as security model, strength of complexity assumption, or public key size [3, 9, 18, 19].

In order to gain confidence for the security of the scheme, we always reduce the security of an IBE scheme to the hardness of a computational problem. Namely, we assume an adversary $\mathcal{A}$ who breaks the scheme and then show another adversary $\mathcal{B}$ who solves the (assumed) hard problem using $\mathcal{A}$. Such a reduction should be as tight as possible, in the sense that $\mathcal{B}$'s success probability is as large as $\mathcal{A}$.

Recently, Chen and Wee [6] proposed the first almost tightly secure IBE scheme in the standard model under the k-LIN assumption. Here almost tight means the security loss can be bounded by a polynomial in security parameter. To achieve almost tight security, Chen and Wee combined the proof idea underlying Naor-Reingold PRF [16] and the dual system methodology [19]. Following Chen and Wee's method, Blazy et al. [2] proposed a more efficient IBE scheme (denoted by BKP) which is transformed from an almost tightly secure affine message authentication code (MAC). Unfortunately, since their scheme is transformed from affine MAC, their IBE cannot provide a standard proof in the IBE setting. Furthermore, BKP IBE is not proven secure in the multi-instance, multi-ciphertext (MIMC, or multi-challenge) setting.

Inspired by Blazy et al.'s work, we naturally consider the following two questions:

- Can BKP IBE scheme be proven secure in the standard IBE setting?
- Can BKP IBE scheme be extended to the MIMC setting?

1.1   Our Result

In this paper, we focus on the construction and proof technique of almost tightly secure IBE schemes. We begin with Blazy et al.'s IBE construction, try to prove its security in the standard IBE setting and obtain the following results.

- We propose a generalized almost tightly secure IBE scheme (denoted by Φ_{ibe}) from BKP IBE scheme and give a new proof in the standard IBE security model under the MDDH assumption.
- Like BKP IBE, we also prove the weak anonymity of Φ_{ibe}. We show that anonymity can be proven by adding a restriction in key generation that the same randomness should be used for the same identity.
- Based on Φ_{ibe}, we propose a new almost tightly secure IBE scheme in the MIMC setting (denoted by Φ_{mimc}). Compared with a state-of-the-art IBE scheme proposed by Gong et al. [11] in the MIMC setting (denoted by $GDCC_{mimc}$), our scheme is more efficient than $GDCC_{mimc}$ in storage and decryption under the DLIN assumption in the symmetric bilinear groups.

We give a brief comparison for Φ_{mimc} with $GDCC_{mimc}$ in Table 1. We consider group number of master public key (MPK), secret key (SK), ciphertext (CT), the number of pairing in decryption (Pairing) and tightness in both schemes. In the following table, n is the binary length of an identity. Furthermore, both schemes are limited to the symmetric bilinear groups which means $\mathbb{G} := \mathbb{G}_1 = \mathbb{G}_2$ and $\mathsf{XDLIN} = \mathsf{DLIN}$.

Table 1. Brief comparison

Scheme	MPK	SK	CT	Pairing	Security	Tightness
GDCC$_{\mathsf{mimc}}$ [11]	$(8n+12)\lvert\mathbb{G}\rvert + 2\lvert\mathbb{G}_T\rvert$	$8\lvert\mathbb{G}\rvert$	$8\lvert\mathbb{G}\rvert + \lvert\mathbb{G}_T\rvert$	8	DLIN	$\mathcal{O}(n)$
Φ_{mimc}	$(8n+8)\lvert\mathbb{G}\rvert + 2\lvert\mathbb{G}_T\rvert$	$6\lvert\mathbb{G}\rvert$	$6\lvert\mathbb{G}\rvert + \lvert\mathbb{G}_T\rvert$	6	DLIN	$\mathcal{O}(n)$

1.2 Our Technique

Our core idea is trying to prove BKP IBE in the IBE setting using Chen and Wee's original technique. Fortunately, when we compared Chen and Wee's almost tightly secure IBE in the composite-order setting and Blazy et al.'s almost tightly secure IBE, we found there exists a direct map between these two schemes. The hardness comes from how to use the Matrix Diffie-Hellman (MDDH) assumption to simulate Chen and Wee's composite assumption. We use an equivalent MDDH assumption (see Definition 3) to overcome this problem.

1.3 Related Work

Chen and Wee [6] proposed the first almost tightly secure IBE by using a bit-based partitioning strategy which in turn draws from an argument of Naor and Reingold [16]. Their IBE scheme has constant ciphertext size but linear public parameters. Blazy et al. generalized this method and proposed a transformation from an almost tightly secure affine MAC to an almost tightly secure IBE. However, in Chen and Wee's proof, they should guess the i-th bit of the challenge identity which makes their technique cannot be extended to the MIMC setting. Hofheinz et al. [14] solved the problem and proposed the first almost tightly secure IBE in the MIMC setting by composite-order bilinear groups. In the prime-order setting for the MIMC security, Attrapadung et al. [1], Gong et al. [10,11] proposed new almost tightly secure IBE schemes with different properties. Quite recently, Chen et al. [5] proposed a new almost tightly secure IBE scheme in composite-order groups, but surprisingly with constant-size public parameters.

Recently, Hofheinz [12,13] proposed a series of novel techniques called algebraic partitioning and adaptive partitioning based on Chen and Wee's technique, which achieved constant-size parameters and better efficiency for public key encryptions with chosen-ciphertext security and signatures. However it is not clear how to apply these techniques to IBE.

Independent Work. An independent work by Gong et al. [11] extended BKP IBE to the MIMC setting. Their start point is also BKP IBE and they achieved a new IBE in the MIMC setting, but their proof is within the general framework of nested dual system groups while we focus on direct proof and concrete constructions of almost tightly secure IBE schemes.

1.4   Organization

The paper is organized as follows. We give necessary background information and definition of security in Sect. 2. Section 3 shows a generalized IBE scheme from BKP IBE scheme, while Sect. 4 shows how to modify the generalized scheme to achieve anonymity. In Sect. 5 we show a specified IBE scheme from the generalized IBE scheme is also secure in the MIMC setting.

2   Preliminaries

Notation. For $n \in \mathbb{N}$, let $[n]$ denote the set $\{1, \ldots, n\}$. If $\mathbf{x} \in \mathcal{B}^n$, then $|\mathbf{x}|$ denotes the length n of the vector. Further, we use the notation $x \leftarrow_{\mathrm{R}} S$ to express that x is chosen from the finite set S uniformly at random. A function $f : \mathbb{N} \to \mathbb{R}_{\geq 0}$ is said to be negligible, if for all $c > 0$, there exists N such that $f(n) < 1/n^c$ for all $n > N$. We denote by $\mathsf{negl}(n)$ a negligible function. If $\mathbf{A} \in \mathbb{Z}_q^{\ell \times k}$ is a matrix with $\ell > k$, then $\overline{\mathbf{A}} \in \mathbb{Z}_q^{k \times k}$ denotes the upper square matrix of $\mathbf{A}$ and then $\underline{\mathbf{A}} \in \mathbb{Z}_q^{(\ell-k) \times k}$ denotes the remaining $\ell - k$ rows of A. With $\mathsf{span}(\mathbf{A}) := \{\mathbf{Ar}|\mathbf{r} \in \mathbb{Z}_q^k\} \subset \mathbb{Z}_q^\ell$, we denote the column span of $\mathbf{A}$. We will use $\mathbf{E}$ and $\mathbf{0}$ to denote the identity matrix and the zero matrix, respectively. We will omit a matrix's size when its size is clear from the context; if necessary, we may give out its size in the subscript.

2.1   Bilinear Groups

Let GGen be a probabilistic polynomial time (PPT) algorithm called a bilinear group generator that takes as input a security parameter 1^λ and outputs a tuple $\mathcal{G} := (q, \mathbb{G}_1, \mathbb{G}_2, \mathbb{G}_T, g_1, g_2, e)$ where q is a λ-bit prime, $\mathbb{G}_1$, $\mathbb{G}_2$ and $\mathbb{G}_T$ are multiplicative cyclic groups of order q, g_1 and g_2 are generators of $\mathbb{G}_1$ and $\mathbb{G}_2$, respectively, and $e : \mathbb{G}_1 \times \mathbb{G}_2 \to \mathbb{G}_T$ is an efficiently computable map (or "pairing") satisfying the following properties:

- (Bilinear) $\forall a, b \in \mathbb{Z}_q$, $e(g_1^a, g_2^b) = e(g_1, g_2)^{ab}$.
- (Non-degenerate) $e(g_1, g_2)$ has order q in $\mathbb{G}_T$, i.e., $e(g_1, g_2)$ is a generator of $\mathbb{G}_T$.

We assume that the group action in $\mathbb{G}_1, \mathbb{G}_2$ and $\mathbb{G}_T$ as well as the bilinear map e are all polynomial time computable in λ. For simplicity, we define $g_T := e(g_1, g_2)$.

We use implicit representation of group elements as introduced in [8]. For $s \in \{1, 2, T\}$ and $a \in \mathbb{Z}_q$, define $[a]_s = g_s^a \in \mathbb{G}_s$ as the implicit representation of

a in $\mathbb{G}_s$. More generally, for a matrix $\mathbf{A} = (a_{ij}) \in \mathbb{Z}_q^{n \times m}$ we define $[\mathbf{A}]_s$ as the implicit representation of $\mathbf{A}$ in $\mathbb{G}_s$:

$$[\mathbf{A}]_s := \begin{pmatrix} g_s^{a_{11}} & \cdots & g_s^{a_{1m}} \\ \cdots & \cdots & \cdots \\ g_s^{a_{n1}} & \cdots & g_s^{a_{nm}} \end{pmatrix} \in \mathbb{G}_s^{n \times m}$$

We will always use this implicit notation of elements in $\mathbb{G}_s$, i.e., we let $[a]_s \in \mathbb{G}_s$ be an element in $\mathbb{G}_s$. Note that from $[a]_s \in \mathbb{G}_s$ it is generally hard to compute the value a (discrete logarithm problem in $\mathbb{G}_s$). Further, from $[b]_T \in \mathbb{G}_T$ it is hard to compute the value $[b]_1 \in \mathbb{G}_1$ and $[b]_2 \in \mathbb{G}_2$ (pairing inversion problem). Obviously, given $[a]_s, [b]_s \in \mathbb{G}_s$ and a scalar $x \in \mathbb{Z}_q$, one can efficiently compute $[a + b]_s$ and $[ax]_s$. Further, given $[a]_1, [b]_2$ one can efficiently compute $[ab]_T$ using the pairing e. For two matrices $\mathbf{A}, \mathbf{B}$ with matching dimensions define $e([\mathbf{A}]_1, [\mathbf{B}]_2) := [\mathbf{A}^\top \mathbf{B}]_T \in \mathbb{G}_T$.

2.2 Matrix Diffie-Hellman Assumption

We recall the definition of the Matrix Diffie-Hellman (MDDH) assumption [8] and get some related results.

Definition 1 (Matrix Distribution). *Let $\ell, k \in \mathbb{N}$ with $\ell > k$. We call $\mathcal{D}_{\ell,k}$ a matrix distribution if it outputs matrices in $\mathbb{Z}_q^{\ell \times k}$ of full rank k in polynomial time. We write $\mathcal{D}_k := \mathcal{D}_{k+1,k}$.*

Without loss of generality, we assume the first k rows of $\mathbf{A} \leftarrow_R \mathcal{D}_{\ell,k}$ form an invertible matrix. The $\mathcal{D}_{\ell,k}$-Matrix Diffie-Hellman problem is to distinguish the two distributions $([\mathbf{A}]_s, [\mathbf{Aw}]_s)$ and $([\mathbf{A}]_s, [\mathbf{u}]_s)$ where $\mathbf{A} \leftarrow_R \mathcal{D}_{\ell,k}$, $\mathbf{w} \leftarrow_R \mathbb{Z}_q^k$, $\mathbf{u} \leftarrow_R \mathbb{Z}_q^\ell$ and $s \in \{1, 2, T\}$.

Definition 2 ($\mathcal{D}_{\ell,k}$-Matrix Diffie-Hellman Assumption $\mathcal{D}_{\ell,k} - MDDH$). *Let $\mathcal{D}_{\ell,k}$ be a matrix distribution and $s \in \{1, 2, T\}$. We say that the $\mathcal{D}_{\ell,k}$-Matrix Diffie-Hellman ($\mathcal{D}_{\ell,k}$-MDDH) Assumption holds relative to GGen in group $\mathbb{G}_s$ if for all PPT adversaries $\mathcal{A}$, $\mathbf{Adv}_{\mathcal{D}_{\ell,k},\mathsf{GGen},\mathbb{G}_s}^{\mathrm{MDDH}}(\mathcal{A}) :=$*

$$|\Pr[\mathcal{A}(\mathcal{G}, [\mathbf{A}]_s, [\mathbf{Aw}]_s) = 1] - \Pr[\mathcal{A}(\mathcal{G}, [\mathbf{A}]_s, [\mathbf{u}]_s) = 1]| = \mathsf{negl}(\lambda),$$

where the probability is taken over $\mathcal{G} \leftarrow_R \mathsf{GGen}(1^\lambda)$, $\mathbf{A} \leftarrow_R \mathcal{D}_{\ell,k}$, $\mathbf{w} \leftarrow_R \mathbb{Z}_q^k$ and $\mathbf{u} \leftarrow_R \mathbb{Z}_q^\ell$.

For each $\ell > k \geq 1$, [8] specifies distributions $\mathcal{L}_k, \mathcal{SC}_k$ (and others) over $\mathbb{Z}_q^{(k+1) \times k}$, $\mathcal{U}_{\ell,k}$ over $\mathbb{Z}_q^{\ell \times k}$ such that the corresponding $\mathcal{D}_{\ell,k}$-MDDH assumptions are generically secure in bilinear groups and form a hierarchy of increasingly weaker assumptions. $\mathcal{L}_k$-MDDH is the well known k-Linear assumption k-LIN with 1-LIN = DDH and 2-LIN = DLIN.

$$\mathcal{L}_k : \mathbf{A} = \begin{pmatrix} a_1 & 0 & 0 & \cdots & 0 \\ 0 & a_2 & 0 & \cdots & 0 \\ 0 & 0 & a_3 & \cdots & 0 \\ & & & \ddots & \\ 0 & 0 & 0 & \cdots & a_k \\ a_{k+1} & a_{k+1} & a_{k+1} & \cdots & a_{k+1} \end{pmatrix}, \mathcal{U}_{\ell,k} : \mathbf{A} = \begin{pmatrix} a_{1,1} & \cdots & a_{1,k} \\ \vdots & \ddots & \vdots \\ a_{\ell,1} & \cdots & a_{\ell,k} \end{pmatrix},$$

where $a_i, a_{i,j} \leftarrow_{\mathrm{R}} \mathbb{Z}_q$.

Let $Q > 1$. For $\mathbf{W} \leftarrow_{\mathrm{R}} \mathbb{Z}_q^{k \times Q}$, $\mathbf{U} \leftarrow_{\mathrm{R}} \mathbb{Z}_q^{\ell \times Q}$ and $s \in \{1, 2, T\}$, we consider the Q-fold $\mathcal{D}_{\ell,k}$-MDDH assumption which consists in distinguishing the distributions $([\mathbf{A}]_s, [\mathbf{AW}]_s)$ from $([\mathbf{A}]_s, [\mathbf{U}]_s)$. That is, a challenge for the Q-fold $\mathcal{D}_{\ell,k}$-MDDH assumption consists of Q independent challenges of the $\mathcal{D}_{\ell,k}$-MDDH assumption (with the same $\mathbf{A}$ but different randomness $\mathbf{w}$). In [8] it is shown that the $\mathcal{D}_{\ell,k}$-Matrix Diffie-Hellman assumption has the random self-reduction property, i.e., the two problems are equivalent, where (for $Q \geq \ell - k$) the reduction loses a factor $\ell - k$ and a negligible constant $1/(q-1)$. The following lemma is implied by the random self-reduction property, but we get a slightly tighter version for the special case of $\mathcal{D}_{\ell,k} := \mathcal{D}_k$.

Lemma 1 (Random Self-Reduction of $\mathcal{D}_k$-MDDH). *Let $s \in \{1, 2, T\}$. For any PPT adversary $\mathcal{A}$, there exists an adversary $\mathcal{B}$ such that* $\mathbf{Time}(\mathcal{B}) \approx \mathbf{Time}(\mathcal{A}) + Q \cdot \mathrm{poly}(\lambda)$ *with* $\mathrm{poly}(\lambda)$ *is independent of* $\mathbf{Time}(\mathcal{A})$, *and*

$$\mathbf{Adv}_{\mathcal{D}_k, \mathrm{GGen}, \mathbb{G}_s}^{Q\text{-MDDH}}(\mathcal{A}) = \mathbf{Adv}_{\mathcal{D}_k, \mathrm{GGen}, \mathbb{G}_s}^{\mathrm{MDDH}}(\mathcal{B})$$

where $\mathbf{Adv}_{\mathcal{D}_k, \mathrm{GGen}, \mathbb{G}_s}^{Q\text{-MDDH}}(\mathcal{A}) := |\Pr[\mathcal{A}(\mathcal{G}, [\mathbf{A}]_s, [\mathbf{AW}]_s) = 1] - \Pr[\mathcal{A}(\mathcal{G}, [\mathbf{A}]_s, [\mathbf{U}]_s) = 1]|$ *and the probability is taken over* $\mathcal{G} \leftarrow_{\mathrm{R}} \mathrm{GGen}(1^\lambda)$, $\mathbf{A} \leftarrow_{\mathrm{R}} \mathcal{D}_k$, $\mathbf{W} \leftarrow_{\mathrm{R}} \mathbb{Z}_q^{k \times Q}$ *and* $\mathbf{U} \leftarrow_{\mathrm{R}} \mathbb{Z}_q^{(k+1) \times Q}$.

Proof. To prove it, we show that there exists an efficient transformation of any instance $([\mathbf{A}]_s, [\mathbf{z}]_s)$ of the $\mathcal{D}_k$-MDDH problem into another instance $([\mathbf{A}]_s, [\mathbf{Z}]_s)$ of the Q-fold problem, and vice versa.

Given $([\mathbf{A}]_s, [\mathbf{z}]_s)$, we pick $\mathbf{R} \leftarrow_{\mathrm{R}} \mathbb{Z}_q^{k \times Q}$, $\mathbf{r} \leftarrow_{\mathrm{R}} \mathbb{Z}_q^Q$ and compute $\mathbf{Z} = \mathbf{AR} + \mathbf{zr}^\top$. If $\mathbf{z} = \mathbf{Aw}$ then $\mathbf{Z} = \mathbf{AW}$ for $\mathbf{W} = \mathbf{R} + \mathbf{wr}^\top$, which is uniformly distributed in $\mathbb{Z}_q^{k \times Q}$; if $\mathbf{z}$ is uniform, note that $\mathrm{rank}(\mathbf{A}) = k$, so $\mathrm{rank}(\mathbf{A}|\mathbf{z}) = k + 1$ then $\mathbf{Z} = (\mathbf{A}, \mathbf{z}) \begin{pmatrix} \mathbf{R} \\ \mathbf{r}^\top \end{pmatrix}$ is uniformly distributed in $\mathbb{Z}_q^{(k+1) \times Q}$.

Given $([\mathbf{A}]_s, [\mathbf{Z}]_s)$, we pick $\mathbf{r} \leftarrow_{\mathrm{R}} \mathbb{Z}_q^k$, $\mathbf{t} \leftarrow_{\mathrm{R}} \mathbb{Z}_q^Q$ and compute $\mathbf{z} = \mathbf{Ar} + \mathbf{Zt}$. If $\mathbf{Z} = \mathbf{AW}$ then $\mathbf{z} = \mathbf{Aw}$ for $\mathbf{w} = \mathbf{r} + \mathbf{Wt}$, which is uniformly distributed in $\mathbb{Z}_q^k$; if $\mathbf{Z}$ is uniform, then $\mathbf{z}$ is uniformly distributed in $\mathbb{Z}_q^{k+1}$.

The lemma follows readily. $\square$

Note that $\mathbf{Aw} = \begin{pmatrix} \overline{\mathbf{A}} \\ \underline{\mathbf{A}} \end{pmatrix} \mathbf{w} = \begin{pmatrix} \overline{\mathbf{A}}\mathbf{w} \\ \underline{\mathbf{A}}\mathbf{w} \end{pmatrix}$. Let $\mathbf{t} = \overline{\mathbf{A}}\mathbf{w}$, then $\mathbf{w} = \overline{\mathbf{A}}^{-1}\mathbf{t}$, we can get an equivalent definition of the $\mathcal{D}_{\ell,k}$-Matrix Diffie-Hellman assumption.

Definition 3 ($\mathcal{D}_{\ell,k}$-Matrix Diffie-Hellman Assumption $\mathcal{D}_{\ell,k}$-MDDH). *Let $\mathcal{D}_{\ell,k}$ be a matrix distribution and $s \in \{1, 2, T\}$. We say that the $\mathcal{D}_{\ell,k}$-Matrix Diffie-Hellman ($\mathcal{D}_{\ell,k}$-MDDH) Assumption holds relative to GGen in group $\mathbb{G}_s$ if for all PPT adversaries $\mathcal{A}$, $\mathbf{Adv}^{MDDH}_{\mathcal{D}_{\ell,k}, GGen, \mathbb{G}_s}(\mathcal{A}) :=$*

$$|\Pr[\mathcal{A}(\mathcal{G}, [\mathbf{A}]_s, [\mathbf{t}]_s, [\mathbf{A}\overline{\mathbf{A}}^{-1}\mathbf{t}]_s) = 1] - \Pr[\mathcal{A}(\mathcal{G}, [\mathbf{A}]_s, [\mathbf{t}]_s, [\mathbf{u}]_s) = 1]| = \mathsf{negl}(\lambda),$$

where the probability is taken over $\mathcal{G} \leftarrow_R GGen(1^\lambda)$, $\mathbf{A} \leftarrow_R \mathcal{D}_{\ell,k}$, $\mathbf{t} \leftarrow_R \mathbb{Z}_q^k$ and $\mathbf{u} \leftarrow_R \mathbb{Z}_q^{\ell-k}$.

By this definition we could establish a many-tuple lemma which is implied by the random self-reduction property of the $\mathcal{D}_k$-MDDH assumption. When $\mathcal{D}_k = \mathcal{L}_k$, it is the many-tuple lemma of k-LIN shown in [15, 16].

Lemma 2 (Many-Tuple Lemma of $\mathcal{D}_k$-MDDH). *Let $\mathbf{A} \leftarrow_R \mathcal{D}_k$. For $s \in \{1, 2, T\}$, there exists an efficient algorithm that on input 1^Q and*

$$[\mathbf{A}]_s, \; [\mathbf{t}]_s, \; [\mathbf{A}\overline{\mathbf{A}}^{-1}\mathbf{t} + z]_s$$

we can generate Q tuples of the form $([\mathbf{t}_j]_s, \; [T_j]_s)$ where

$$T_j = \begin{cases} \mathbf{A}\overline{\mathbf{A}}^{-1}\mathbf{t}_j & \text{if } z = 0 \\ \mathbf{A}\overline{\mathbf{A}}^{-1}\mathbf{t}_j + z_j & \text{if } z \neq 0 \end{cases}$$

and $\mathbf{t}_j \leftarrow_R \mathbb{Z}_q^k$, $z_j \leftarrow_R \mathbb{Z}_q$ for each j from 1 to Q.

Proof. The algorithm works exactly like the transformation of a $\mathcal{D}_k$-MDDH instance $([\mathbf{A}]_s, [\mathbf{z}]_s)$ into a Q-fold $\mathcal{D}_k$-MDDH instance $([\mathbf{A}]_s, [\mathbf{Z}]_s)$ where $\mathbf{z} = \begin{pmatrix} \mathbf{t} \\ \mathbf{A}\overline{\mathbf{A}}^{-1}\mathbf{t} + z \end{pmatrix}$ and the j-th column of $\mathbf{Z}$ is $\begin{pmatrix} \mathbf{t}_j \\ T_j \end{pmatrix}$, as shown in the proof of Lemma 1. $\square$

Let $s \in \{1, 2\}$. Note that in the $\mathcal{D}_{\ell,k}$-MDDH assumption, we are provided only $[\mathbf{A}]_s$ while $[\mathbf{A}]_{3-s}$ is not provided. We state the external decisional linear assumption in $\mathbb{G}_s$ as follows, which considers the analogous elements in $\mathbb{G}_{3-s}$ for the decisional linear assumption.

Definition 4 (External Decisional Linear Assumption XDLIN). *Let $s \in \{1, 2\}$. We say that the External Decisional Linear (XDLIN) Assumption holds relative to GGen in group $\mathbb{G}_s$ if for all PPT adversaries $\mathcal{A}$,*

$$\mathbf{Adv}^{XDLIN}_{GGen, \mathbb{G}_s}(\mathcal{A}) := |\Pr[\mathcal{A}(\mathbb{D}, [a_3(s_1 + s_2)]_s) = 1] - \Pr[\mathcal{A}(\mathbb{D}, [z]_s) = 1]| = \mathsf{negl}(\lambda),$$

where

$$\mathbb{D} := \left(\mathcal{G}, \begin{matrix} [a_1]_1, [a_2]_1, [a_3]_1, [a_1 s_1]_1, [a_2 s_2]_1 \\ [a_1]_2, [a_2]_2, [a_3]_2, [a_1 s_1]_2, [a_2 s_2]_2 \end{matrix} \right)$$

and the probability is taken over $\mathcal{G} \leftarrow_R GGen(1^\lambda)$ and $a_1, a_2, a_3, s_1, s_2, z \leftarrow_R \mathbb{Z}_q$.

2.3   Identity-Based Encryption

An identity-based encryption scheme consists of the following five algorithms:
Par, Setup, KeyGen, Encrypt, and Decrypt.

$Par(1^\lambda, n) \rightarrow (pp, sp)$. This algorithm takes as input a security parameter 1^λ and
the length of identity n, outputs a public parameter pp and a secret parameter
sp. The public parameter also implies a message space $\mathcal{M}$, a key space $\mathcal{K}$ and
an identity space $\mathcal{ID}$.

$Setup(pp, sp) \rightarrow (mpk, msk)$. This algorithm takes as input a public parameter
pp and a secret parameter sp, outputs a master public key mpk and a master
secret key msk.

$KeyGen(mpk, msk, ID) \rightarrow sk_{ID}$. This algorithm takes as input the master public
key mpk, the master secret key msk and an identity ID and outputs a private
key sk_{ID} associated with ID.

$Encrypt(mpk, ID, M) \rightarrow CT$. This algorithm takes as input the master public key
mpk, an identity ID and a message M, and outputs a ciphertext CT.

$Decrypt(sk_{ID}, CT) \rightarrow M$. This algorithm takes as input a private key sk_{ID} and the
ciphertext CT. If the ciphertext is an encryption to ID, then the algorithm
outputs the original message M.

In our scheme, the identity $ID = (x_1, \ldots, x_n)$ is a binary vector from $\mathbb{Z}_2^n$. To
avoid the birthday attack, we always set $n = \mathcal{O}(\lambda)$.

Security Model. We define the (chosen-plaintext) security for an IBE scheme
$\Phi = $ (Par, Setup, KeyGen, Encrypt, Decrypt) in the single-challenge, single-
instance setting according to the following game.

Setup. The challenger $\mathcal{B}$ gets $(pp, sp) \leftarrow_R Par(1^\lambda, n)$ and creates $(mpk, msk) \leftarrow_R$
Setup(pp, sp) and gives mpk to the adversary $\mathcal{A}$.

Phase 1. $\mathcal{A}$ submits an identity $ID \in \mathcal{ID}$. $\mathcal{B}$ creates a private key sk_{ID} and gives
it to $\mathcal{A}$.

Challenge. $\mathcal{A}$ submits a challenge identity $ID^* \in \mathcal{ID}$ and a message $M_0 \in$
$\mathcal{M}$ to $\mathcal{B}$ with the restriction that each identity $ID \neq ID^*$. Then $\mathcal{B}$ chooses
$M_1 \leftarrow_R \mathcal{M}$, flips a random coin $\beta \in \{0, 1\}$, creates the ciphertext $CT^* =$
$Encrypt(mpk, ID^*, M_\beta)$ and passes CT^* to $\mathcal{A}$.

Phase 2. Phase 1 is repeated with the restriction that any queried identity
$ID \neq ID^*$.

Guess. $\mathcal{A}$ outputs its guess β' of β.

The advantage of $\mathcal{A}$ in this game is defined as $\mathbf{Adv}_{\Phi, \lambda, n}^{ind\text{-}cpa}(\mathcal{A}) = |\Pr[\beta' = \beta] - \frac{1}{2}|$.

Definition 5. *An IBE scheme Φ is fully (or adaptively) secure if $\mathbf{Adv}_{\Phi, \lambda, n}^{ind\text{-}cpa}(\mathcal{A})$
is negligible for any valid PPT adversary $\mathcal{A}$.*

Anonymity. We also consider anonymity for identity-based encryption. To
define anonymity for an IBE scheme Φ, we change the form of **Challenge** phase
in the above game as follows.

Challenge. $\mathcal{A}$ submits a challenge identity ID_0^* and a message $\mathsf{M}_0 \in \mathcal{M}$ to $\mathcal{B}$ with the restriction that ID_0^* is not queried . Then $\mathcal{B}$ chooses $\mathsf{ID}_1^* \leftarrow_{\mathrm{R}} \mathcal{ID}$ and $\mathsf{M}_1 \leftarrow_{\mathrm{R}} \mathcal{M}$, flips a random coin β and creates the ciphertext $\mathsf{CT}^* = \mathsf{Encrypt}(\mathsf{mpk}, \mathsf{ID}_\beta^*, \mathsf{M}_\beta)$, and passes CT^* to $\mathcal{A}$.

The advantage of $\mathcal{A}$ in this game is defined as $\mathbf{Adv}_{\Phi,\lambda,n}^{\mathrm{anon}}(\mathcal{A}) = |\Pr[\beta' = \beta] - \frac{1}{2}|$.

Definition 6. *An IBE scheme Φ is anonymous if $\mathbf{Adv}_{\Phi,\lambda,n}^{\mathrm{anon}}(\mathcal{A})$ is negligible for any valid PPT adversary $\mathcal{A}$.*

3   Generalized IBE from BKP with Almost Tight Security

Let $\ell, k_1, k_2 \in \mathbb{N}$ with $\ell > k_1$ and $\ell > k_2$. We call the generalized IBE scheme $\Phi_{\mathsf{ibe}}(\mathcal{D}_{\ell,k_1}, k_2)$, or Φ_{ibe} for short.

3.1   Construction

$\mathsf{Par}(1^\lambda, n) \to \mathsf{pp}, \mathsf{sp}$. Given the security parameter λ and the binary length of identity n, the algorithm first gets $\mathcal{G} = [q, \mathbb{G}_1, \mathbb{G}_2, \mathbb{G}_T, g_1, g_2, e] \leftarrow \mathsf{GGen}(1^\lambda)$. Then it chooses $\mathbf{A} \leftarrow_{\mathrm{R}} \mathcal{D}_{\ell,k_1}$ and $\mathbf{U}_1, \ldots, \mathbf{U}_{2n} \leftarrow_{\mathrm{R}} \mathcal{U}_{\ell,k_2}$. It sets the master public parameter as

$$\mathsf{pp} := \left(\mathcal{G}, [\mathbf{A}]_1, [\mathbf{U}_1^\top \mathbf{A}]_1, \ldots, [\mathbf{U}_{2n}^\top \mathbf{A}]_1 \right).$$

The master secret parameter is

$$\mathsf{sp} := (\mathbf{U}_1, \ldots, \mathbf{U}_{2n}).$$

$\mathsf{Setup}(\mathsf{pp}, \mathsf{sp}) \to \mathsf{mpk}, \mathsf{msk}$. The setup algorithm chooses $\boldsymbol{\alpha} \leftarrow_{\mathrm{R}} \mathbb{Z}_q^\ell$ and sets the master public key as

$$\mathsf{mpk} := \left(\mathsf{pp}, [\boldsymbol{\alpha}^\top \mathbf{A}]_T \right).$$

The master secret key is

$$\mathsf{msk} := (\mathsf{sp}, \boldsymbol{\alpha}).$$

$\mathsf{KeyGen}(\mathsf{mpk}, \mathsf{msk}, \mathsf{ID}) \to \mathsf{sk}_{\mathsf{ID}}$. On input an identity $\mathsf{ID} = (x_1, \ldots, x_n) \in \mathbb{Z}_2^n$, the key generation algorithm chooses $\mathbf{t} \leftarrow_{\mathrm{R}} \mathbb{Z}_q^{k_2}$ and computes $\mathbf{k} = \boldsymbol{\alpha} + (\sum_{i=1}^n \mathbf{U}_{2i-x_i})\mathbf{t}$.
The private key is created as $\mathsf{sk}_{\mathsf{ID}} := ([\mathbf{k}]_2, [\mathbf{t}]_2)$.

$\mathsf{Encrypt}(\mathsf{mpk}, \mathsf{ID}, \mathsf{M}) \to \mathsf{CT}$. The message space $\mathcal{M}$ is $\mathbb{G}_T$. On input a message $\mathsf{M} \in \mathcal{M}$, an identity $\mathsf{ID} = (x_1, \ldots, x_n) \in \mathbb{Z}_2^n$, the encryption algorithm chooses $\mathbf{s} \leftarrow_{\mathrm{R}} \mathbb{Z}_q^{k_1}$ and computes

$$\mathsf{C} = \mathsf{M} \cdot [\boldsymbol{\alpha}^\top \mathbf{A}\mathbf{s}]_T, \quad \mathbf{c}_1 = \mathbf{A}\mathbf{s}, \quad \mathbf{c}_2 = \sum_{i=1}^n \mathbf{U}_{2i-x_i}^\top \mathbf{A}\mathbf{s}.$$

The ciphertext is created as $\mathsf{CT} := (\mathsf{C}, [\mathbf{c}_1]_1, [\mathbf{c}_2]_1)$.

Decrypt($\mathsf{sk_{ID}}, \mathsf{CT}) \to \mathsf{M}$. The decryption algorithm takes in a private key $\mathsf{sk_{ID}}$ for $\mathsf{ID} = (x_1, \ldots, x_n)$ and a ciphertext $\mathsf{CT} = (\mathsf{C}, [\mathbf{c}_1]_1, [\mathbf{c}_2]_1)$ encrypted to ID. The decryption algorithm computes

$$B := \frac{e([\mathbf{c}_1]_1, [\mathbf{k}]_2)}{e([\mathbf{c}_2]_1, [\mathbf{t}]_2)}.$$

Then the message is computed as $\mathsf{M} = \mathsf{C}/\mathsf{B}$.

Correctness

$$B = \frac{e([\mathbf{As}]_1, \ [\boldsymbol{\alpha} + (\sum_{i=1}^n \mathbf{U}_{2i-x_i})\mathbf{t}]_2)}{e([\sum_{i=1}^n \mathbf{U}_{2i-x_i}^\top \mathbf{As}]_1, \ [\mathbf{t}]_2)} = [\boldsymbol{\alpha}^\top \mathbf{As}]_T.$$

Note. Let $k_1 = k_2 = k$ and $\ell = k + 1$, then $\Phi_{\mathsf{ibe}}(\mathcal{D}_k, k)$ is BKP IBE.

3.2 Security

Our IBE scheme has the following security result.

Theorem 1. *Under the $\mathcal{D}_{\ell, k_1}$-MDDH assumption in $\mathbb{G}_1$ and the $\mathcal{D}_{k_2}$-MDDH assumption in $\mathbb{G}_2$, $\Phi_{\mathsf{ibe}}(\mathcal{D}_{\ell, k_1}, k_2)$ is fully, almost tightly secure. More precisely, if the binary length of identity is n, for any adversary $\mathcal{A}$ that makes at most Q key queries against the IBE scheme, there exist adversaries $\mathcal{B}_1$ and $\mathcal{B}_2$ such that*

$$\mathbf{Adv}_{\Phi_{\mathsf{ibe}}, \lambda, n}^{\mathsf{ind\text{-}cpa}}(\mathcal{A}) \leq \mathbf{Adv}_{\mathcal{D}_{\ell, k_1}, \mathsf{GGen}, \mathbb{G}_1}^{\mathsf{MDDH}}(\mathcal{B}_1) + 2n \cdot \mathbf{Adv}_{\mathcal{D}_{k_2}, \mathsf{GGen}, \mathbb{G}_2}^{\mathsf{MDDH}}(\mathcal{B}_2),$$

and

$$\max\{\mathbf{Time}(\mathcal{B}_1), \ \mathbf{Time}(\mathcal{B}_2)\} \approx \mathbf{Time}(\mathcal{A}) + Q \cdot \mathsf{poly}(\lambda, n),$$

where $\mathsf{poly}(\lambda, n)$ is independent of $\mathbf{Time}(\mathcal{A})$.

Proof. To prove Theorem 1, we need to define some auxiliary structures. These will not be used in the real construction, but they will be used in our proof.

For each i from 0 to n we use RF_i to denote a random function from $\{0,1\}^i$ to $\mathbb{Z}_q$ where $\{0,1\}^0$ denotes the singleton set containing just the empty string ε. Next, let $\mathsf{ID}_{|i}$ denote the i-bit prefix of ID, i.e., $\mathsf{ID}_{|i} := (x_1, \ldots, x_i)$.

Let $\mathbf{A}$ be the matrix chosen by the Par algorithm, we choose $\mathbf{a} \leftarrow_{\mathrm{R}} \ker(\mathbf{A}) \backslash \{\mathbf{0}\}$ and define the auxiliary structures as follows.

Pseudo-normal ciphertext
Given an identity $\mathsf{ID} = (x_1, \ldots, x_n)$ and a message M, we choose $\mathbf{r} \leftarrow_{\mathrm{R}} \mathbb{Z}_q^\ell$ and create the pseudo-normal ciphertext as

$$\mathsf{M} \cdot [\boldsymbol{\alpha}^\top \mathbf{r}]_T, \ [\mathbf{r}]_1, \ [\sum_{i=1}^n \mathbf{U}_{2i-x_i}^\top \mathbf{r}]_1.$$

Semi-functional ciphertext of type i, **for** $i = 0, 1, \ldots, n$

Given an identity $\mathsf{ID} = (x_1, \ldots, x_n)$ and a message M, we choose $\mathbf{r} \leftarrow_{\mathrm{R}} \mathbb{Z}_q^\ell$ and create the semi-functional ciphertext of type i as

$$\mathsf{M} \cdot [\boldsymbol{\alpha}^\top \mathbf{r} + \mathsf{RF}_i(\mathsf{ID}_{|i}) \cdot \mathbf{a}^\top \mathbf{r}]_T, \ [\mathbf{r}]_1, \ [\sum_{j=1}^n \mathbf{U}_{2j-x_j}^\top \mathbf{r}]_1.$$

Semi-functional key of type i, **for** $i = 0, 1, \ldots, n$

Given an identity $\mathsf{ID} = (x_1, \ldots, x_n)$, we choose $\mathbf{t} \leftarrow_{\mathrm{R}} \mathbb{Z}_q^{k_2}$ and create the semi-functional key of type i as

$$[\boldsymbol{\alpha} + \mathsf{RF}_i(\mathsf{ID}_{|i}) \cdot \mathbf{a} + (\sum_{j=1}^n \mathbf{U}_{2j-x_j})\mathbf{t}]_2, \ [\mathbf{t}]_2.$$

We prove Theorem 1 via a hybrid argument over a series of games based on normal ciphertext and key and the above structures. These related games are defined as follows.

Game 0: This is the chosen-plaintext security game for IBE defined previously in which the challenge ciphertext and all private keys are normal.

Game 1: This is like **Game 0** except that the challenge ciphertext is pseudo-normal.

Game 2.i, $0 \leq i \leq n$**:** This is like **Game 1** except that the challenge ciphertext and all private keys are semi-functional of type i.

Game 3: This is like **Game 2.n** except that the challenge ciphertext is a semi-functional encryption of a random message in $\mathbb{G}_T$.

For simplicity, we write $\mathbf{Adv}_{xx}(\mathcal{A})$ to denote the advantage of $\mathcal{A}$ in **Game xx**. Obviously, $\mathbf{Adv}_0(\mathcal{A}) = \mathbf{Adv}_{\Phi_{\mathsf{ibe}}, \lambda, n}^{\mathsf{ind\text{-}cpa}}(\mathcal{A})$. Observe that we have $\mathbf{Adv}_3(\mathcal{A}) = 0$ since the view of $\mathcal{A}$ is independent from the value of β in **Game 3**. In the following lemmas, we will show these games are indistinguishable.

Lemma 3. *If the binary length of identity is* n*, for any adversary* $\mathcal{A}$ *that makes at most* Q *key queries, there exists an adversary* $\mathcal{B}_1$ *such that* $|\mathbf{Adv}_0(\mathcal{A}) - \mathbf{Adv}_1(\mathcal{A})| \leq \mathbf{Adv}_{\mathcal{D}_{\ell, k_1}, \mathsf{GGen}, \mathbb{G}_1}^{\mathsf{MDDH}}(\mathcal{B}_1)$ *and* $\mathbf{Time}(\mathcal{B}_1) \approx \mathbf{Time}(\mathcal{A}) + Q \cdot \mathsf{poly}(\lambda, n)$.

Proof. **Game 0** and **Game 1** only differ in the distribution of $\mathbf{r}$ in the challenge ciphertext, namely, $\mathbf{r} \in \mathsf{span}(\mathbf{A})$ or uniform. From that, we obtain a straightforward reduction to the $\mathcal{D}_{\ell, k_1}$-MDDH assumption. $\square$

Lemma 4. *For any adversary* $\mathcal{A}$, $\mathbf{Adv}_1(\mathcal{A}) = \mathbf{Adv}_{2.0}(\mathcal{A})$.

Proof. Observe that $\boldsymbol{\alpha}$ and $\boldsymbol{\alpha} + \mathsf{RF}_0(\varepsilon) \cdot \mathbf{a}$ are identically distributed, so in **Game 2.0** we syntactically replace $\boldsymbol{\alpha}$ with $\boldsymbol{\alpha} + \mathsf{RF}_0(\varepsilon) \cdot \mathbf{a}$. The resulting distribution is identically distributed to that in **Game 1** except we use $[(\boldsymbol{\alpha} + \mathsf{RF}_0(\varepsilon) \cdot \mathbf{a})^\top \mathbf{A}]_T$ instead of $[\boldsymbol{\alpha}^\top \mathbf{A}]_T$. Note that $\mathbf{a} \in \ker(\mathbf{A})$, then $(\boldsymbol{\alpha} + \mathsf{RF}_0(\varepsilon) \cdot \mathbf{a})^\top \mathbf{A} = \boldsymbol{\alpha}^\top \mathbf{A}$, the master public key mpk remains unchanged. So **Game 1** and **Game 2.0** are identically distributed. $\square$

Lemma 5. *If the binary length of identity is n, for each i from 1 to n, for any adversary $\mathcal{A}$ that makes at most Q key queries, there exists an adversary $\mathcal{B}_2$ such that $|\mathbf{Adv}_{2.i-1}(\mathcal{A}) - \mathbf{Adv}_{2.i}(\mathcal{A})| \leq 2\mathbf{Adv}_{\mathcal{D}_{k_2},\text{GGen},\mathbb{G}_2}^{\text{MDDH}}(\mathcal{B}_2)$ and $\mathbf{Time}(\mathcal{B}_2) \approx \mathbf{Time}(\mathcal{A}) + Q \cdot \mathsf{poly}(\lambda, n)$, where $\mathsf{poly}(\lambda, n)$ is independent of $\mathbf{Time}(\mathcal{A})$.*

Proof. We construct an adversary $\mathcal{B}_2$ who attacks the $\mathcal{D}_{k_2}$-MDDH problem in $\mathbb{G}_2$ from an adversary $\mathcal{A}$ who distinguishes the games. At the beginning of the game, $\mathcal{B}_2$ is given a $\mathcal{D}_{k_2}$-MDDH challenge $([\mathbf{B}]_2, [\mathbf{t}]_2, [T]_2) \in \mathbb{G}_2^{(k_2+1)\times k_2} \times \mathbb{G}_2^{k_2} \times \mathbb{G}_2$, $\mathcal{B}_2$ needs to decide whether T is either $\underline{\mathbf{B}}\overline{\mathbf{B}}^{-1}\mathbf{t}$ or uniform. From Lemma 2, $\mathcal{B}_2$ can generate Q tuples $([\mathbf{t}_j]_2, [T_j]_2)$, $j = 1, \ldots, Q$.

For simplicity, We let ID_j denote the j-th value of ID, i.e., if $\mathsf{ID} = (x_1, \ldots, x_j, \ldots, x_n)$ then $\mathsf{ID}_j := x_j$. With additional input $i \in [n]$, $\mathcal{B}_2$ first picks a random value $b \in \{0,1\}$ which is a guess for ID_i^* at the challenge phase, then proceeds as follows.

Setup. $\mathcal{B}_2$ chooses $\mathbf{A} \leftarrow_R \mathcal{D}_{\ell,k_1}$, $\boldsymbol{\alpha} \leftarrow_R \mathbb{Z}_q^\ell$, $\widetilde{\mathbf{U}}_1, \ldots, \widetilde{\mathbf{U}}_{2n} \leftarrow_R \mathbb{Z}_q^{\ell \times k_2}$, $\mathbf{a} \leftarrow_R \ker(\mathbf{A}) \setminus \{\mathbf{0}\}$, and computes $\mathbf{U}_j, j = 1, \ldots, 2n$ as follows.

$$\mathbf{U}_j = \begin{cases} \widetilde{\mathbf{U}}_j & j \in [2n] \setminus \{2i - 1 + b\} \\ \widetilde{\mathbf{U}}_j + \mathbf{a} \cdot \underline{\mathbf{B}}\overline{\mathbf{B}}^{-1} & j = 2i - 1 + b \end{cases}$$

Note that $\mathbf{a} \in \ker(\mathbf{A})$, so $\mathbf{a}^\top\mathbf{A} = \mathbf{0}$ and $(\widetilde{\mathbf{U}}_j + \mathbf{a} \cdot \underline{\mathbf{B}}\overline{\mathbf{B}}^{-1})^\top\mathbf{A} = \widetilde{\mathbf{U}}_j^\top\mathbf{A} + (\underline{\mathbf{B}}\overline{\mathbf{B}}^{-1})^\top \cdot \mathbf{a}^\top\mathbf{A} = \widetilde{\mathbf{U}}_j^\top\mathbf{A}$. Hence all $[\mathbf{U}_j^\top\mathbf{A}]_1$ and $[\boldsymbol{\alpha}^\top\mathbf{A}]_T$ can be easily computed since we know $\mathbf{A}$, $\widetilde{\mathbf{U}}_j$ and $\boldsymbol{\alpha}$. Finally $\mathcal{B}_2$ publishes the master public key mpk to $\mathcal{A}$.

$\mathcal{B}_2$ picks an injective function $\mathsf{IF}_i : \{0,1\}^i \to \{1, \ldots, Q\}$. $\mathcal{B}_2$ also picks a random function $\mathsf{RF}_{i-1} : \{0,1\}^{i-1} \to \mathbb{Z}_q$ and implicitly sets $\mathsf{RF}_i(\mathsf{ID}_{|i}) = \mathsf{RF}_{i-1}(\mathsf{ID}_{|i-1})$ for $\mathsf{ID}_i = b$. The other case $\mathsf{ID}_i = 1 - b$ will be defined later.

Key Queries. On input a secrete key query for ID, we consider two cases: –
Case 1: $\mathsf{ID}_i = b$. Note that $\mathsf{RF}_i(\mathsf{ID}_{|i}) = \mathsf{RF}_{i-1}(\mathsf{ID}_{|i-1})$, so $\mathcal{B}_2$ chooses $\mathbf{t}' \leftarrow_R \mathbb{Z}_q^{k_2}$ and outputs the semi-functional key as

$$[\boldsymbol{\alpha} + \mathsf{RF}_{i-1}(\mathsf{ID}_{|i-1}) \cdot \mathbf{a} + (\sum_{j=1}^n \mathbf{U}_{2j-\mathsf{ID}_j})\overline{\mathbf{B}}\mathbf{t}']_2, [\overline{\mathbf{B}}\mathbf{t}']_2.$$

Here we implicitly set $\mathbf{t} = \overline{\mathbf{B}}\mathbf{t}'$. Since $\overline{\mathbf{B}}$ is invertible, $\mathbf{t}$ is also uniform in $\mathbb{Z}_q^{k_2}$. Note that when $\mathbf{U}_j = \widetilde{\mathbf{U}}_j$, we can easily compute $\mathbf{U}_j\mathbf{t} = \widetilde{\mathbf{U}}_j\overline{\mathbf{B}}\mathbf{t}'$, while when $\mathbf{U}_j = \widetilde{\mathbf{U}}_j + \mathbf{a} \cdot \underline{\mathbf{B}}\overline{\mathbf{B}}^{-1}$, $\mathbf{U}_j\mathbf{t} = \widetilde{\mathbf{U}}_j\overline{\mathbf{B}}\mathbf{t}' + \mathbf{a} \cdot \underline{\mathbf{B}}\mathbf{t}'$, so all components in the semi-functional key can be computed.
– Case 2: $\mathsf{ID}_i = 1 - b$. Let $c = \mathsf{IF}_i(\mathsf{ID})$, $\mathcal{B}_2$ chooses $\mathbf{t}' \leftarrow_R \mathbb{Z}_q^{k_2}$ and outputs the semi-functional key as

$$[\boldsymbol{\alpha} + \mathsf{RF}_{i-1}(\mathsf{ID}_{|i-1}) \cdot \mathbf{a} + (\sum_{j\in[n]\setminus\{2i-\mathsf{ID}_i\}} \mathbf{U}_{2j-\mathsf{ID}_j} + \widetilde{\mathbf{U}}_{2i-\mathsf{ID}_i})\mathbf{x} + \mathbf{a} \cdot \underline{\mathbf{B}}\mathbf{t}' + T_c \cdot \mathbf{a}]_2,$$

$$[\overline{\mathbf{B}}\mathbf{t}' + \mathbf{t}_c]_2.$$

Here $\mathbf{x} = \overline{\mathbf{B}}\mathbf{t}' + \mathbf{t}_c$ and we implicitly set $\mathbf{t} = \overline{\mathbf{B}}\mathbf{t}' + \mathbf{t}_c$. Note that $T_c = \underline{\mathbf{B}}\overline{\mathbf{B}}^{-1}\mathbf{t}_c + z_c$, if $z_c = 0$ then this is a semi-functional key of type $i-1$; else if z_c is uniform, then this is a semi-functional key of type i where we implicitly set $\mathsf{RF}_i(\mathsf{ID}_{|i}) = \mathsf{RF}_{i-1}(\mathsf{ID}_{|i-1}) + z_c$. Furthermore, when z_c is uniform, $\mathsf{RF}_i(\mathsf{ID}_{|i-1}\|0)$ and $\mathsf{RF}_i(\mathsf{ID}_{|i-1}\|1)$ are independent and both uniformly random.

Challenge Ciphertext. $\mathcal{B}_2$ receives a challenge identity ID^* and a messages M_0. If $\mathsf{ID}_i^* \neq b$, $\mathcal{B}_2$ will output a random bit and halt. Assume $\mathcal{B}_2$ correctly guesses b such that $\mathsf{ID}_i^* = b$ (which happens with probability $1/2$), it chooses $\mathbf{r} \leftarrow_{\mathrm{R}} \mathbb{Z}_q^\ell$, $\mathsf{M}_1 \leftarrow_{\mathrm{R}} \mathcal{M}$, picks a bit $\beta \leftarrow_{\mathrm{R}} \{0,1\}$ and outputs the challenge ciphertext as $\mathsf{M}_\beta \cdot [\boldsymbol{\alpha}^\top \mathbf{r} + \mathsf{RF}_{i-1}(\mathsf{ID}^*_{|i-1}) \cdot \mathbf{a}^\top \mathbf{r}]_T$, $[\mathbf{r}]_1$, $[\sum_{j=1}^n \mathbf{U}_{2j-\mathsf{ID}_j^*}^\top \mathbf{r}]_1$. By the definition of RF_i and by $\mathsf{ID}_i^* = b$ we have $\mathsf{RF}_i(\mathsf{ID}^*_{|i}) = \mathsf{RF}_{i-1}(\mathsf{ID}^*_{|i-1})$, which implies this challenge ciphertext is identitcally distributed in **Game 2.i-1** and **Game 2.i**.

Guess. When $\mathcal{A}$ outputs β', $\mathcal{B}_2$ outputs 1 if $\beta' = \beta$ and 0 otherwise.

Analysis. If $T = \underline{\mathbf{B}}\overline{\mathbf{B}}^{-1}\mathbf{t}$, we have $T_j = \underline{\mathbf{B}}\overline{\mathbf{B}}^{-1}\mathbf{t}_j$ for $j = 1, \ldots, Q$, the output is identical to that in **Game 2.i-1**; else if T is uniform, all T_j are uniform, the output is identical to that in **Game 2.i**. Hence, we have

$$\mathbf{Adv}^{\mathsf{MDDH}}_{\mathcal{D}_{k_2},\mathsf{GGen},\mathbb{G}_2}(\mathcal{B}_2) = \left| \Pr[\mathsf{ID}_i^* = 1 - b] \cdot 0 + \Pr[\mathsf{ID}_i^* = b] \right.$$

$$\left. \cdot (\Pr[\mathcal{A} \text{ outputs } \beta' = \beta \text{ in } \mathbf{Game\ 2.i\text{-}1}] - \Pr[\mathcal{A} \text{ outputs } \beta' = \beta \text{ in } \mathbf{Game\ 2.i}]) \right|$$

$$= \tfrac{1}{2} \cdot \left| \Pr[\mathcal{A} \text{ outputs } \beta' = \beta \text{ in } \mathbf{Game\ 2.i\text{-}1}] - \Pr[\mathcal{A} \text{ outputs } \beta' = \beta \text{ in } \mathbf{Game\ 2.i}] \right|$$

$$\geq \tfrac{1}{2} \cdot \left| \mathbf{Adv}_{2.i-1}(\mathcal{A}) - \mathbf{Adv}_{2.i}(\mathcal{A}) \right|.$$

We then have $\left| \mathbf{Adv}_{2.i-1}(\mathcal{A}) - \mathbf{Adv}_{2.i}(\mathcal{A}) \right| \leq 2\mathbf{Adv}^{\mathsf{MDDH}}_{\mathcal{D}_{k_2},\mathsf{GGen},\mathbb{G}_2}(\mathcal{B}_2)$. $\square$

Lemma 6. *For any adversary $\mathcal{A}$, if the binary length of identity is n, then*

$$\mathbf{Adv}_{2.n}(\mathcal{A}) = \mathbf{Adv}_3(\mathcal{A}).$$

Proof. In **Game 2.n**, the message is masked by $[\boldsymbol{\alpha}^\top \mathbf{r} + \mathsf{RF}_n(\mathsf{ID}^*) \cdot \mathbf{a}^\top \mathbf{r}]_T$. Note that $\mathsf{RF}_n(\mathsf{ID}^*)$ is uniformly distributed over $\mathbb{Z}_q$ and all of the secret key queries reveal no information about $\mathsf{RF}_n(\mathsf{ID}^*)$. So $[\boldsymbol{\alpha}^\top \mathbf{r} + \mathsf{RF}_n(\mathsf{ID}^*) \cdot \mathbf{a}^\top \mathbf{r}]_T$ is hence uniformly random, which implies that the challenge ciphertext is identically distributed to a semi-functional encryption of a random message in $\mathbb{G}_T$, as in **Game 3**. $\square$

Taking Lemmas 3, 4, 5 and 6 together, we complete the proof of Theorem 1. $\square$

4   Anonymity

Note that the original BKP IBE is anonymous. However, the anonymity of BKP IBE is weaker than standard anonymity which was first pointed out by Attrapadung et al. In BKP IBE, anonymity is proven under the restriction that all secret keys for the same identity must be created using the same randomness.

In this section, we show that Φ_{ibe} can be also proven weak anonymity with the same restriction, i.e., the key generation algorithm **KeyGen** always use the same randomness t for the same ID. This restriction can be easily accomplished by using a PRF or an internal log. We have the following result for Φ_{ibe}'s anonymity.

Theorem 2. *Under the $\mathcal{D}_{\ell,k_1}$-MDDH assumption in $\mathbb{G}_1$ and the $\mathcal{D}_{k_2}$-MDDH assumption in $\mathbb{G}_2$, Φ_{ibe} is almost tightly anonymous. More precisely, if the binary length of identity is n, for any adversary $\mathcal{A}$ that makes at most Q key queries against the IBE scheme, there exist adversaries $\mathcal{B}_1$ and $\mathcal{B}_2$ such that*

$$\mathbf{Adv}^{\mathsf{anon}}_{\Phi_{\mathsf{ibe}},\lambda,n}(\mathcal{A}) \leq (1+k_2)\mathbf{Adv}^{\mathsf{MDDH}}_{\mathcal{D}_{\ell,k_1},\mathsf{GGen},\mathbb{G}_1}(\mathcal{B}_1) + 2n \cdot \mathbf{Adv}^{\mathsf{MDDH}}_{\mathcal{D}_{k_2},\mathsf{GGen},\mathbb{G}_2}(\mathcal{B}_2),$$

and

$$\max\{\mathbf{Time}(\mathcal{B}_1),\ \mathbf{Time}(\mathcal{B}_2)\} \approx \mathbf{Time}(\mathcal{A}) + Q \cdot \mathsf{poly}(\lambda,n),$$

where $\mathsf{poly}(\lambda,n)$ is independent of $\mathbf{Time}(\mathcal{A})$.

Proof Sketch. We define pseudo-normal, semi-functional ciphertexts and semi-functional keys as in Theorem 1. Furthermore, to prove anonymity, we define pseudo-random and random ciphertexts as follows.

Pseudo-normal ciphertext
On input an identity $\mathsf{ID} = (x_1,\ldots,x_n)$ and a message M, the algorithm chooses $\mathbf{r} \leftarrow_{\mathrm{R}} \mathbb{Z}_q^\ell$ and creates the pseudo-normal ciphertext as

$$\mathsf{M} \cdot [\boldsymbol{\alpha}^\top \mathbf{r}]_T,\ [\mathbf{r}]_1,\ [\sum_{i=1}^n \mathbf{U}_{2i-x_i}^\top \mathbf{r}]_1.$$

Semi-functional ciphertext of type i, for $i = 0,1,\ldots,n$
Given an identity $\mathsf{ID} = (x_1,\ldots,x_n)$ and a message M, we choose $\mathbf{r} \leftarrow_{\mathrm{R}} \mathbb{Z}_q^\ell$ and create the semi-functional ciphertext of type i as

$$\mathsf{M} \cdot [\boldsymbol{\alpha}^\top \mathbf{r} + \mathsf{RF}_i(\mathsf{ID}_{|i}) \cdot \mathbf{a}^\top \mathbf{r}]_T,\ [\mathbf{r}]_1,\ [\sum_{j=1}^n \mathbf{U}_{2j-x_j}^\top \mathbf{r}]_1.$$

Pseudo-random ciphertext of type i, for $i = 0,1,\ldots,k_2$
Given an identity $\mathsf{ID} = (x_1,\ldots,x_n)$ and a message M, we choose $\mathsf{R} \leftarrow_{\mathrm{R}} \mathbb{G}_T$, $\mathbf{r} \leftarrow_{\mathrm{R}} \mathbb{Z}_q^\ell$, $y_1,\ldots,y_i \leftarrow_{\mathrm{R}} \mathbb{Z}_q$ and create the pseudo-normal ciphertext of type i as

$$\mathsf{R},\ [\mathbf{r}]_1,\ [\sum_{j=1}^n \mathbf{U}_{2j-x_j}^\top \mathbf{r} + y_1\mathbf{e}_1 + \cdots + y_i\mathbf{e}_i]_1.$$

Here we denote the pseudo-random ciphertext of type 0 by

$$\mathsf{R},\ [\mathbf{r}]_1,\ [\sum_{j=1}^n \mathbf{U}_{2j-x_j}^\top \mathbf{r}]_1.$$

Random ciphertext

Given an identity $\mathsf{ID} = (x_1, \ldots, x_n)$ and a message M, we choose $\mathsf{R} \leftarrow_\mathrm{R} \mathbb{G}_T$, $\mathbf{r} \leftarrow_\mathrm{R} \mathbb{Z}_q^\ell$, $\mathbf{u} \leftarrow_\mathrm{R} \mathbb{Z}_q^{k_2}$ and create the random ciphertext as

$$\mathsf{R}, \ [\mathbf{r}]_1, \ [\mathbf{u}]_1.$$

Semi-functional key of type i, for $i = 0, 1, \ldots, n$

Given an identity $\mathsf{ID} = (x_1, \ldots, x_n)$, we choose $\mathbf{t} \leftarrow_\mathrm{R} \mathbb{Z}_q^{k_2}$ and create the semi-functional key of type i as

$$[\boldsymbol{\alpha} + \mathsf{RF}_i(\mathsf{ID}_{|i}) \cdot \mathbf{a} + (\sum_{j=1}^{n} \mathbf{U}_{2j-x_j})\mathbf{t}]_2, \ [\mathbf{t}]_2.$$

We prove Theorem 2 via a hybrid argument over a series of games based on normal ciphertext and key and the above structures. These related games are defined as follows.

Game 0: This is the real security game for anonymity.

Game 1: This is like **Game 0** except that the challenge ciphertext is pseudo-normal.

Game 2.i, $0 \le i \le n$: This is like **Game 1** except that the challenge ciphertext and all private keys are semi-functional of type i.

Game 3.i, $0 \le i \le k_2$: This is like **Game 2.n** except that except that the challenge ciphertext is pseudo-random of type i.

Game 4: This is like **Game 3.k_2** except that the challenge ciphertext is random.

For simplicity, we write $\mathbf{Adv}_{\mathrm{xx}}(\mathcal{A})$ to denote the advantage of $\mathcal{A}$ in **Game xx**. Obviously, $\mathbf{Adv}_0(\mathcal{A}) = \mathbf{Adv}^{\mathrm{anon}}_{\Phi_{\mathrm{anon}}, \lambda, n}(\mathcal{A})$. We remark that the challenge ciphertext in **Game 4** leaks no information about the identity and the message since it is composed of random group elements. Hence, $\mathbf{Adv}_4(\mathcal{A}) = 0$. We will show these games are indistinguishable via a series of lemmas. Concrete proof is put in full version of this paper for space consideration.

5   Extending to the MIMC Setting

In this section we consider whether Φ_{ibe} can be proven secure in the MIMC setting. Surprisingly, we found Φ_{ibe} with a specified parameter can be proven secure in the MIMC setting. For convenience, security definitions for IBE in the MIMC setting are provided in Appendix A.

Let $\Phi_{\mathrm{mimc}} := \Phi_{\mathrm{ibe}}(\mathcal{U}_{4,2}, 2)$. We can show that Φ_{mimc} is *weakly* secure in the MIMC setting. However, with an additional assumption (the BDDH assumption), we can prove that Φ_{mimc} is fully secure in the MIMC setting.

Theorem 3. *Under the DLIN assumption in $\mathbb{G}_1$, the XDLIN assumption in $\mathbb{G}_1$ and the DLIN assumption in $\mathbb{G}_2$, Φ_{mimc} is weakly secure in the multi-instance,* *multi-ciphertext setting. More precisely, if the binary length of identity is n, for any adversary $\mathcal{A}$ that makes at most Q_k key reveal queries and at most Q_c challenge queries for pairwise distinct challenge identity against at most μ instances, there exist adversaries $\mathcal{B}_1$, $\mathcal{B}_2$ and $\mathcal{B}_3$ such that*

$$\mathbf{Adv}^{\text{ind-cpa}}_{\Phi_{\text{mimc}},\lambda,n}(\mathcal{A},\mu,Q_k,Q_c,1) \leq$$
$$\mathbf{Adv}^{\text{DLIN}}_{\text{GGen},\mathbb{G}_1}(\mathcal{B}_1) + 4n \cdot \mathbf{Adv}^{\text{XDLIN}}_{\text{GGen},\mathbb{G}_1}(\mathcal{B}_2) + n \cdot \mathbf{Adv}^{\text{DLIN}}_{\text{GGen},\mathbb{G}_2}(\mathcal{B}_3),$$

and

$$\max\{\mathbf{Time}(\mathcal{B}_1),\ \mathbf{Time}(\mathcal{B}_2),\ \mathbf{Time}(\mathcal{B}_3)\} \approx \mathbf{Time}(\mathcal{A}) + \mu(Q_k + Q_c) \cdot \text{poly}(\lambda, n),$$

where $\text{poly}(\lambda, n)$ is independent of $\mathbf{Time}(\mathcal{A})$.

Proof Sketch. The overall structure of the proof is similar to [14] but slightly different. We first define some auxiliary structures of ciphertexts and private keys as follows. In the following, we will pick random functions $\widehat{\mathsf{RF}}_i : \{0,1,\perp\}^i \to \mathbb{Z}_q$, $\widetilde{\mathsf{RF}}_i : \{0,1\}^i \to \mathbb{Z}_q$ for $i = 0, 1, \ldots, n$ where $\{0,1\}^0$ denotes the singleton set containing just the empty string ε. Furthermore, we use $\mathsf{ID}_{|i}$ to denote the i-bit prefix of ID.

Let $\mathbf{A}$ be the matrix chosen by the Par algorithm, we expand $\mathbf{A}$ to an invertible matrix $\mathbf{D} = (\mathbf{A}, \widehat{\mathbf{d}}, \widetilde{\mathbf{d}}) \in \mathbb{GL}_4(\mathbb{Z}_q)$. We compute $\mathbf{D}^* = (\mathbf{D}^\top)^{-1} = (\mathbf{d}_1^*, \mathbf{d}_2^*, \widehat{\mathbf{a}}, \widetilde{\mathbf{a}})$. Note that $\mathbf{D}^\top \mathbf{D}^* = \mathbf{E}$, so we have $\widehat{\mathbf{a}}, \widetilde{\mathbf{a}} \in \ker(\mathbf{A})$. Furthermore, we have $\widehat{\mathbf{a}}^\top \widehat{\mathbf{d}} = \widetilde{\mathbf{a}}^\top \widetilde{\mathbf{d}} = 1$ and $\widehat{\mathbf{a}}^\top \widetilde{\mathbf{d}} = \widetilde{\mathbf{a}}^\top \widehat{\mathbf{d}} = 0$. We define the auxiliary structures as follows.

Pseudo-normal ciphertext
Given an identity $\mathsf{ID} = (x_1, \ldots, x_n)$ and a message M, we choose $\mathbf{s} \leftarrow_R \mathbb{Z}_q^2$, $\hat{s} \leftarrow_R \mathbb{Z}_q$ and create the pseudo-normal ciphertext as

$$\mathsf{M} \cdot [\boldsymbol{\alpha}^\top(\mathbf{As} + \hat{s}\widehat{\mathbf{d}})]_T,\ [\mathbf{As} + \hat{s}\widehat{\mathbf{d}}]_1,\ [\sum_{i=1}^n \mathbf{U}_{2i-x_i}^\top (\mathbf{As} + \hat{s}\widehat{\mathbf{d}})]_1.$$

Semi-functional ciphertext of type $(\wedge, i)$ and $(\sim, i)$, for $i = 0, 1, \ldots, n$
Given an identity $\mathsf{ID} = (x_1, \ldots, x_n)$ and a message M, we choose $\mathbf{s} \leftarrow_R \mathbb{Z}_q^2$, $\hat{s} \leftarrow_R \mathbb{Z}_q$ and create the semi-functional ciphertext of type $(\wedge, i)$ as

$$\mathsf{M} \cdot [\boldsymbol{\alpha}^\top \mathbf{As} + \widehat{\mathsf{RF}}_i(\mathsf{ID}_{|i}) \cdot \hat{s}]_T,\ [\mathbf{As} + \hat{s}\widehat{\mathbf{d}}]_1,\ [\sum_{j=1}^n \mathbf{U}_{2j-x_j}^\top (\mathbf{As} + \hat{s}\widehat{\mathbf{d}})]_1.$$

We choose $\mathbf{s} \leftarrow_R \mathbb{Z}_q^2$, $\tilde{s} \leftarrow_R \mathbb{Z}_q$ and create the semi-functional ciphertext of type $(\sim, i)$ as

$$\mathsf{M} \cdot [\boldsymbol{\alpha}^\top \mathbf{As} + \widetilde{\mathsf{RF}}_i(\mathsf{ID}_{|i}) \cdot \tilde{s}]_T,\ [\mathbf{As} + \tilde{s}\widehat{\mathbf{d}}]_1,\ [\sum_{j=1}^n \mathbf{U}_{2j-x_j}^\top (\mathbf{As} + \tilde{s}\widehat{\mathbf{d}})]_1.$$

Semi-functional ciphertext of type i, for $i = 0, 1, \ldots, n$

Given an identity $\mathsf{ID} = (x_1, \ldots, x_n)$ and a message M, we choose $\mathbf{s} \leftarrow_{\mathrm{R}} \mathbb{Z}_q^2$, $\hat{s}, \tilde{s} \leftarrow_{\mathrm{R}} \mathbb{Z}_q$ and create the semi-functional ciphertext of type i as

$$\mathsf{M} \cdot [\boldsymbol{\alpha}^\top \mathbf{As} + \widehat{\mathsf{RF}}_i(\mathsf{ID}_{|i}) \cdot \hat{s} + \widetilde{\mathsf{RF}}_i(\mathsf{ID}_{|i}) \cdot \tilde{s}]_T, \ [\mathbf{As} + \hat{s}\widehat{\mathbf{d}} + \tilde{s}\widetilde{\mathbf{d}}]_1, \ [\sum_{j=1}^n \mathbf{U}_{2j-x_j}^\top (\mathbf{As} + \hat{s}\widehat{\mathbf{d}} + \tilde{s}\widetilde{\mathbf{d}})]_1.$$

Semi-functional key of type i, for $i = 0, 1, \ldots, n$

Given an identity $\mathsf{ID} = (x_1, \ldots, x_n)$, we choose $\mathbf{t} \leftarrow_{\mathrm{R}} \mathbb{Z}_q^2$ and create the semi-functional key of type i as

$$[\boldsymbol{\alpha} + \widehat{\mathsf{RF}}_i(\mathsf{ID}_{|i}) \cdot \widehat{\mathbf{a}} + \widetilde{\mathsf{RF}}_i(\mathsf{ID}_{|i}) \cdot \widetilde{\mathbf{a}} + (\sum_{j=1}^n \mathbf{U}_{2j-x_j})\mathbf{t}]_2, \ [\mathbf{t}]_2.$$

Next, we define a sequence of games to establish the security of the IBE scheme. We write $\mathbf{Adv_{xx}}(\mathcal{A})$ to denote the advantage of $\mathcal{A}$ in **Game xx** for simplicity.

Game 0: This is the $(\mu, Q_k, Q_c, 1)$-security game for IBE.

Game 1: This is like **Game 0** except that the challenge ciphertext is pseudo-normal.

Game 2.i.0, $i \in [n+1]$: This is like **Game 1** except that all the challenge ciphertexts are are semi-functional of type $(\wedge, i-1)$ and all secret keys are semi-functional of type $i-1$.

Game 2.i.1, $i \in [n]$: This is like **Game 2.i.0** except that
  – all challenge ciphertexts for identities whose i-th bit is 1 are semi-functional of type $i-1$.

Game 2.i.2, $i \in [n]$: This is like **Game 2.i.1** except that
  – all challenge ciphertexts for identities whose i-th bit is 1 are semi-functional of type $(\sim, i-1)$.

Game 2.i.3, $i \in [n]$: This is like **Game 2.i.2** except that
  – all secret keys are semi-functional of type i;
  – all challenge ciphertexts for identities whose i-th bit is 0 are semi-functional of type $(\wedge, i)$;
  – all challenge ciphertexts for identities whose i-th bit is 1 are semi-functional of type $(\sim, i)$.

Game 2.i.4, $i \in [n]$: This is like **Game 2.i.3** except that
  – all challenge ciphertexts for identities whose i-th bit is 1 are semi-functional of type i.

Game 2.i.5, $i \in [n]$: This is like **Game 2.i.4** except that
  – all challenge ciphertexts for identities whose i-th bit is 1 are semi-functional of type $(\wedge, i)$.

Game 3: This is like **Game 2.n + 1.0** except that all challenge ciphertexts are for random messages.

Obviously, $\mathbf{Adv}_0(\mathcal{A}) = \mathbf{Adv}_{\Phi_{\mathrm{mimc}}, \lambda, n}^{\mathrm{ind\text{-}cpa}}(\mathcal{A}, \mu, Q_k, Q_c, 1)$. Observe that we have $\mathbf{Adv}_3(\mathcal{A}) = 0$ since the view of $\mathcal{A}$ is independent from the value of β in **Game 3**. We will show these games are indistinguishable via a series of lemmas. Concrete proof is put in full version of this paper for space consideration.

Acknowledgments. We thank all anonymous reviewers of ISPEC 2017 for their helpful comments. This work was supported by Natural Science Foundation of Chongqing City (Grant No. cstc2013jcyjA40019), National Natural Science Foundation of China (Grant No. 11547148), Research Program of Chongqing Municipal Education Commission (Grant Nos. KJ1600932, KJ1500918), and Research Project of Humanities and Social Sciences of Ministry of Education of China (Grant No. 15YJC790061).

A   IBE in the MIMC Setting

Security Model. We define (μ, Q_k, Q_c, Q_r)-security for an IBE $\Phi = ($Par, Setup, KeyGen, Encrypt, Decrypt$)$ in the MIMC setting according to the following game.

> **Setup.** The challenger $\mathcal{B}$ gets $($pp, sp$) \leftarrow_{\mathrm{R}}$ Par$(1^\lambda, n)$ and creates $($mpk$^{(j)}$, msk$^{(j)}) \leftarrow_{\mathrm{R}}$ Setup$($pp, sp$)$ for $j \in [\mu]$ and gives $\{$mpk$^{(j)}\}_{j \in [\mu]}$ to the adversary $\mathcal{A}$. The challenger flips a random coin $\beta \in \{0, 1\}$ whose value is fixed throughout the game.
> Finally the challenger initializes $\mathcal{Q}_k$ and $\mathcal{Q}_c$ as two empty sets.
> **Query.** The adversary $\mathcal{A}$ can adaptively make the following two types of queries in an arbitrary order.
> - **Key Query.** $\mathcal{A}$ submits an index $j \in [\mu]$ and an identity ID $\in \mathcal{ID}$. The challenger creates a private key sk$_{\mathsf{ID}} \leftarrow_{\mathrm{R}}$ KeyGen$($mpk$^{(j)}$, msk$^{(j)}$, ID$)$ and gives the adversary the private key. Finally the challenger updates $\mathcal{Q}_k := \mathcal{Q}_k \cup \{(j, \mathsf{ID})\}$.
> - **Challenge Query.** $\mathcal{A}$ submits an index $j^* \in [\mu]$, a challenge identity ID$^* \in \mathcal{ID}$ and a message M$_0 \in \mathcal{M}$ to $\mathcal{B}$. $\mathcal{B}$ chooses M$_1 \leftarrow_{\mathrm{R}} \mathcal{M}$, creates the ciphertext CT$^* =$ Encrypt$($mpk$^{(j^*)}$, ID*, M$_\beta)$ and passes CT* to $\mathcal{A}$. Finally the challenger updates $\mathcal{Q}_c := \mathcal{Q}_c \cup \{(j^*, \mathsf{ID}^*)\}$.
> **Guess.** $\mathcal{A}$ outputs its guess β' of β.

We say that the adversary $\mathcal{A}$ is valid if and only if (1) $\mathcal{Q}_k \cap \mathcal{Q}_c = \emptyset$, i.e., for each $(j, \mathsf{ID}) \in \mathcal{Q}_k$, for all $(j^*, \mathsf{ID}^*) \in \mathcal{Q}_c$, if $j = j^*$, ID $\neq$ ID*; (2) $\mathcal{A}$ has made at most Q_k key reveal queries, i.e., $|\mathcal{Q}_k| \leq Q_k$; (3) $\mathcal{A}$ has made at most Q_c challenge queries for every scheme instance and identity, i.e., $|\mathcal{Q}_c| \leq Q_c$; (4) for each $(j^*, \mathsf{ID}^*) \in \mathcal{Q}_c$, $\mathcal{A}$ has made at most Q_r challenge queries.

The advantage of $\mathcal{A}$ in this game is defined as $\mathbf{Adv}_{\Phi, \lambda, n}^{\mathsf{ind\text{-}cpa}}(\mathcal{A}, \mu, Q_k, Q_c, Q_r) = |\Pr[\beta' = \beta] - \frac{1}{2}|$.

Definition 7. *An IBE scheme Φ is (μ, Q_k, Q_c, Q_r)-secure if $\mathbf{Adv}_{\Phi, \lambda, n}^{\mathsf{ind\text{-}cpa}}(\mathcal{A}, \mu, Q_k, Q_c, Q_r)$ is negligible for any valid PPT adversary $\mathcal{A}$.*

Weak Security. We consider a weak adversary in the above game who cannot request challenge ciphertexts for the same scheme instance and identity twice, i.e., $Q_r = 1$. An IBE scheme is weakly secure if and only if $\mathbf{Adv}_{\Phi, \lambda, n}^{\mathsf{ind\text{-}cpa}}(\mathcal{A}, \mu, Q_k, Q_c, 1)$ is negligible for all weak PPT adversaries.

References

1. Attrapadung, N., Hanaoka, G., Yamada, S.: A framework for identity-based encryption with almost tight security. In: Iwata, T., Cheon, J.H. (eds.) ASIACRYPT 2015. LNCS, vol. 9452, pp. 521–549. Springer, Heidelberg (2015). https://doi.org/10.1007/978-3-662-48797-6_22

2. Blazy, O., Kiltz, E., Pan, J.: (Hierarchical) identity-based encryption from affine message authentication. In: Garay, J.A., Gennaro, R. (eds.) CRYPTO 2014. LNCS, vol. 8616, pp. 408–425. Springer, Heidelberg (2014). https://doi.org/10.1007/978-3-662-44371-2_23

3. Boneh, D., Boyen, X.: Efficient selective-ID secure identity-based encryption without random oracles. In: Cachin, C., Camenisch, J.L. (eds.) EUROCRYPT 2004. LNCS, vol. 3027, pp. 223–238. Springer, Heidelberg (2004). https://doi.org/10.1007/978-3-540-24676-3_14

4. Boneh, D., Franklin, M.: Identity-based encryption from the Weil Pairing. In: Kilian, J. (ed.) CRYPTO 2001. LNCS, vol. 2139, pp. 213–229. Springer, Heidelberg (2001). https://doi.org/10.1007/3-540-44647-8_13

5. Chen, J., Gong, J., Weng, J.: Tightly secure IBE under constant-size master public key. In: Fehr, S. (ed.) PKC 2017. LNCS, vol. 10174, pp. 207–231. Springer, Heidelberg (2017). https://doi.org/10.1007/978-3-662-54365-8_9

6. Chen, J., Wee, H.: Fully, (Almost) tightly secure IBE and dual system groups. In: Canetti, R., Garay, J.A. (eds.) CRYPTO 2013. LNCS, vol. 8043, pp. 435–460. Springer, Heidelberg (2013). https://doi.org/10.1007/978-3-642-40084-1_25

7. Cocks, C.: An identity based encryption scheme based on quadratic residues. In: Honary, B. (ed.) Cryptography and Coding 2001. LNCS, vol. 2260, pp. 360–363. Springer, Heidelberg (2001). https://doi.org/10.1007/3-540-45325-3_32

8. Escala, A., Herold, G., Kiltz, E., Ràfols, C., Villar, J.: An algebraic framework for Diffie-Hellman assumptions. In: Canetti, R., Garay, J.A. (eds.) CRYPTO 2013. LNCS, vol. 8043, pp. 129–147. Springer, Heidelberg (2013). https://doi.org/10.1007/978-3-642-40084-1_8

9. Gentry, C.: Practical identity-based encryption without random oracles. In: Vaudenay, S. (ed.) EUROCRYPT 2006. LNCS, vol. 4004, pp. 445–464. Springer, Heidelberg (2006). https://doi.org/10.1007/11761679_27

10. Gong, J., Chen, J., Dong, X., Cao, Z., Tang, S.: Extended nested dual system groups, revisited. In: Cheng, C.-M., Chung, K.-M., Persiano, G., Yang, B.-Y. (eds.) PKC 2016. LNCS, vol. 9614, pp. 133–163. Springer, Heidelberg (2016). https://doi.org/10.1007/978-3-662-49384-7_6

11. Gong, J., Dong, X., Chen, J., Cao, Z.: Efficient IBE with tight reduction to standard assumption in the multi-challenge setting. In: Cheon, J.H., Takagi, T. (eds.) ASIACRYPT 2016. LNCS, vol. 10032, pp. 624–654. Springer, Heidelberg (2016). https://doi.org/10.1007/978-3-662-53890-6_21

12. Hofheinz, D.: Algebraic partitioning: fully compact and (almost) tightly secure cryptography. In: Kushilevitz, E., Malkin, T. (eds.) TCC 2016. LNCS, vol. 9562, pp. 251–281. Springer, Heidelberg (2016). https://doi.org/10.1007/978-3-662-49096-9_11

13. Hofheinz, D.: Adaptive partitioning. In: Coron, J.-S., Nielsen, J.B. (eds.) EUROCRYPT 2017. LNCS, vol. 10212, pp. 489–518. Springer, Cham (2017). https://doi.org/10.1007/978-3-319-56617-7_17

14. Hofheinz, D., Koch, J., Striecks, C.: Identity-based encryption with (Almost) tight security in the multi-instance, multi-ciphertext setting. In: Katz, J. (ed.) PKC 2015. LNCS, vol. 9020, pp. 799–822. Springer, Heidelberg (2015). https://doi.org/10.1007/978-3-662-46447-2_36

15. Lewko, A.B., Waters, B.: Efficient pseudorandom functions from the decisional linear assumption and weaker variants. In: Al-Shaer, E., Jha, S., Keromytis, A.D. (eds.) Proceedings of the 2009 ACM Conference on Computer and Communications Security, CCS 2009, Chicago, Illinois, USA, 9–13 November 2009, pp. 112–120. ACM (2009). http://doi.acm.org/10.1145/1653662.1653677

16. Naor, M., Reingold, O.: Number-theoretic constructions of efficient pseudo-random functions. J. ACM **51**(2), 231–262 (2004). http://doi.acm.org/10.1145/972639.972643

17. Shamir, A.: Identity-based cryptosystems and signature schemes. In: Blakley, G.R., Chaum, D. (eds.) CRYPTO 1984. LNCS, vol. 196, pp. 47–53. Springer, Heidelberg (1985). https://doi.org/10.1007/3-540-39568-7_5

18. Waters, B.: Efficient Identity-based encryption without random oracles. In: Cramer, R. (ed.) EUROCRYPT 2005. LNCS, vol. 3494, pp. 114–127. Springer, Heidelberg (2005). https://doi.org/10.1007/11426639_7

19. Waters, B.: Dual system encryption: realizing fully secure IBE and HIBE under simple assumptions. In: Halevi, S. (ed.) CRYPTO 2009. LNCS, vol. 5677, pp. 619–636. Springer, Heidelberg (2009). https://doi.org/10.1007/978-3-642-03356-8_36

A Secure Variant of the SRP Encryption Scheme with Shorter Private Key

Bo Lv, Zhiniang Peng, and Shaohua Tang$^{(\boxtimes)}$

School of Computer Science and Engineering,
South China University of Technology, Guangzhou, China
shtang@IEEE.org, csshtang@scut.edu.cn

Abstract. The study of multivariate encryption algorithm is an important topic of multivariate public key cryptography research. However, quite few secure and practical multivariate encryption algorithms have been found up to now. The SRP encryption scheme is a multivariate encryption scheme that combines Square, Rainbow and the Plus method technique, which is of high efficiency and resistant to existing known attacks against multivariate schemes. In this paper, an improved SRP scheme with shorter private key and higher decryption efficiency is proposed. We introduce rotation relations into parts of the private key, which enables us to reduce the private key size by about 61%. And the decryption speed is 2.1 times faster than that of the original SRP. In terms of theory and experiment, we analyze the security of the improved SRP for several attacks against SRP. The results show that our modifications do not weaken the security of the original schemes.

Keywords: Multivariate public key algorithm · SRP encryption
Quantum-safe public key cryptography · Shorter private key

1 Introduction

Multivariate public key cryptography is one of the promising candidates for quantum-safe public key cryptography. And its security depends on the difficulty of solving a set of multivariate polynomial equations over a finite field. Multivariate schemes have fast computational speed and take fewer computational resources, so it is very suitable for resource-limited environments such as wireless sensor network environment.

There exist many multivariate encryption and signature schemes such as MI [13], HFE [16], PMI+[2], ABC [22], ZHFE [19], SRP [26], UOV [12], QUARTZ [17], Rainbow [3], STS [24], RGB [20], Gui [18] and so on. However, most schemes are compromised by a variety of attacks, such as Direct attack [5–7], Differential attack [10,21], Rank attack [1,8,9,25], Linearization Equation attack [15] and so on. At present, practical multivariate signature schemes mainly include UOV, Rainbow, Gui, etc., while the secure and practical multivariate encryption

J. K. Liu and P. Samarati (Eds.): ISPEC 2017, LNCS 10701, pp. 156–167, 2017.
https://doi.org/10.1007/978-3-319-72359-4_9

scheme is quite rare. Therefore, the study of multivariate encryption scheme is a key point of multivariate public key cryptography research.

In 2015, Yasuda et al. [26] proposed a multivariate encryption scheme which combines Square and Rainbow. The scheme is highly efficient and can resist all existing attacks. In 2016, Duong et al. [4] proposed a method that insert circular series into the public key matrix to reduce the size of the public key and improve the speed of encryption.

In this paper, the rotation method is applied to the private key to reduce the size of the private key by making the rotation relation appearing among the different polynomials of the central map. At the same time, this relationship benefits us in getting some better structure in the process of decryption, thus improving the speed of decryption. By using our construction it can reduce the size of the private key by about 61%. Furthermore, the special structure obtained in the process of decryption allows us to speed up the decryption process of the scheme by up to 68%. Through security analysis, our improvements will not affect the security of the original scheme.

The rest of this paper is arranged as follows. Section 2 concisely introduces scheme theory of SRP encryption scheme. Section 3 describes the construction of our improved SRP and the influence of the improved method on SRP, including the efficiency of decryption, the probability of decryption success and the size of the private key. The impact of the improved method on the original scheme is analyzed from the security aspect in Sect. 4. In Sect. 5, the improved scheme and the original scheme are compared with the key size and the performance of decryption. And Sect. 6 draws conclusions.

2 Preliminaries

We describe the basic theory of the encryption and decryption of SRP [26] in this section. The SRP encryption scheme combines Square and Rainbow. So the decryption of SRP is efficient.

2.1 Notations for SRP

Let $K = GF(q)$ be a finite field of odd characteristic and cardinality $q(q \equiv 3 \ mod \ 4)$, E be an extension of degree d over K, and ϕ be an isomorphism between the field E and the vector space K^d. Let $o_1, ..., o_h, r, s$ and l be non-negative integers, and $n = d + o_1 + ... + o_h - l$, $n' = d + o_1 + ... + o_h$, $m = d + o_1 + ... + o_h + hr + s$. The number of equations is m and number of variables is n.

The central map $F : K^{n'} \rightarrow K^m$ of SRP is the concatenation of three maps F_S, F_R and F_P . These maps are defined as follows.

The Square part $F_S : K^{n'} \rightarrow K^d$ is defined by:

$$F_S : K^{d+o_1+...+o_h} \xrightarrow{projection} K^d \xrightarrow{\phi^{-1}} E \xrightarrow{X \mapsto X^2} E \xrightarrow{\phi} K^d.$$

The Rainbow part $F_R : K^{n'} \rightarrow K^{d+o_1+\ldots+o_h+hr}$ is constructed as follows. Let h be the number of layers in Rainbow. For each layer $k = 1, \ldots, h$, let $v_k = d + o_1 + \ldots + o_{k-1}$, $V_k = \{1, 2, \ldots, v_k\}$, $O_k = \{v_k + 1, \ldots, v_k + o_k\}$. The kth layer consists of $o_k + r$ polynomials which are chosen by the multivariate quadratic polynomials of the form

$$f_R{}^k(x_1, \ldots, x_{n'}) = \sum_{i \in O_k, j \in V_k} \alpha_{ij} x_i x_j + \sum_{i,j \in V_k, i<j} \beta_{ij} x_i x_j + \sum_{i \in O_k \cup V_k} \gamma_i x_i + \eta,$$

where $\alpha_{ij}, \beta_{ij}, \gamma_i, \eta$ are randomly chosen in K.

The Plus part $F_P : K^{n'} \rightarrow K^s$ consist of randomly chosen s multivariate quadratic polynomials of the form

$$f_P(x_1, \ldots, x_{n'}) = \sum_{1 \le i \le j \le n'} \alpha_{ij} x_i x_j + \sum_{1 \le i \le n'} \beta_i x_i + \gamma (\alpha_{ij}, \beta_i, \gamma \in K),$$

The central map $F = F_S \| F_R \| F_P$. Randomly chooses an affine embedding $T : K^n \rightarrow K^{n'}$ of full rank and an invertible affine map $S : K^m \rightarrow K^m$. The public key is given by $P = S \circ F \circ T : F^n \rightarrow F^m$ and the private key includes of S, F and T.

2.2 SRP Encryption

For a given message $M \in K^n$, the ciphertext C corresponding to M is obtained by the polynomial evaluation

$$C = P(M) \in K^m.$$

2.3 SRP Decryption

For a ciphertext $C \in K^m$, the decryption is executed as follows.

Step 1. Compute $Y = (y_1, \ldots, y_m) = S^{-1}(C)$ and $X = \phi^{-1}(y_1, \ldots, y_d)$.
Step 2. Compute $R = \pm X^{(q^d+1)/4}$ and $D_0 = \phi(R)$.
Step 3. For $k = 1$ to h do:
(3-1) For $Y_k = (y_{t_k+1}, \ldots, y_{t_k+o_k+r})$, where $t_k = v_k + (k-1)r$, substitute D_{k-1} into $f_R{}^k$ to get a system of linear equations with respect to $X_k = (x_{v_k+1}, \ldots, x_{v_k+o_k})$,

$$f_R{}^k(D_{k-1}, X_k) = Y_k.$$

(3–2) Solve the system using Gauss Elimination and denote the solution by D'_k. Let $D_k = D_{k-1} \| D'_k$.
Step 4. Compute $M' = T^{-1}(D_h)$, which is the corresponding plaintext.

3   Our Improved Scheme

In [4], Duong et al. proposed a method to reduce the public key size of SRP by applying the idea of circulation. Inspired by this idea, we propose a method to reduce the size of the private key and improve the speed of decryption.

During the SRP decryption process, the inverse process of the central map is divided into two parts, Square part and Rainbow part, while the private key only needs to store the OV polynomials coefficients of the Rainbow. Therefore, we aim to reduce the size of the private key. In the inverse process of Rainbow, we need to plug in the Vinegar variables layer by layer, and thus calculate Oil variables of the corresponding layer, namely solving $Lx = u$, in which L is a coefficient matrix of size $(o_k + r) * o_k$ obtained by substituting Vinegar variables into the OV polynomials. The Rainbow part of SRP has an extra r OV equations per layer compared to the original Rainbow scheme. Because the Vinegar variable of the scheme is not selected randomly, it increase the number of equations to reduce the probability of degeneration. Here, we introduce rotation relations into parts of the private key so that L becomes a Toeplitz matrix. We define a $(o_k + r) * o_k$ Toeplitz matrix L take the form:

$$
L = \begin{bmatrix}
l_1 & l_2 & \cdots & l_{o_k-1} & l_{o_k} \\
l_{o_k+1} & l_1 & \cdots & l_{o_k-2} & l_{o_k-1} \\
\vdots & \vdots & \ddots & \vdots & \vdots \\
l_{2o_k-1} & l_{2o_k-2} & \cdots & l_{o_k+1} & l_1 \\
l_{2o_k} & l_{2o_k-1} & \cdots & l_{o_k+2} & l_{o_k+1} \\
\vdots & \vdots & \ddots & \vdots & \vdots \\
l_{2o_k+r-1} & l_{2o_k+r-2} & \cdots & l_{o_k+r+1} & l_{o_k+r}
\end{bmatrix}
\tag{1}
$$

3.1   Construction

First, for each central polynomial, its coefficient matrix is represented by M, as is shown in Fig. 1. Among them, VV denotes the coefficients of Vinegar-Vinegar cross-terms and VO denotes Oil-Vinegar quadratic cross-terms coefficients. V stands for the coefficients of the linear term of Vinegar variables and O stands for the coefficients of the linear term of Oil variables, C denote the constant term. The white area stands for zero elements.

To suit L for the above form, for each layer of Rainbow, we construct the central map as follows.

(i) For the kth layer, we randomly select the first central Oil-Vinegar equation. In other words, all non-zero elements of M_{k1} are randomly selected. Shown as the follows:

$$VV_1^k = (\mathbf{vv}_1^k, \mathbf{vv}_2^k, \cdots, \mathbf{vv}_{v_k}^k),$$

$$VO_1^k = (\mathbf{vo}_1^k, \mathbf{vo}_2^k, \cdots, \mathbf{vo}_{o_k}^k),$$

$$V_1^k = (\alpha_1^k, \alpha_2^k, \cdots, \alpha_{v_k}^k)^T,$$

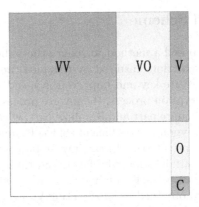

Fig. 1. Coefficient matrix of central polynomial

$$O_1^k = (\beta_1^k, \beta_2^k, \cdots, \beta_{o_k}^k)^T,$$

$$C_1^k = c_1^k.$$

(ii) For the next $o_k + r - 1$ Oil-Vinegar polynomials, we first arbitrarily choose VV_i^k, V_i^k and $C_i^k (i = 2, \cdots, o_k + r - 1)$, then, we let

$$VO_2^k = (\mathbf{vo}_{o_k+1}^k, \mathbf{vo}_1^k, \cdots, \mathbf{vo}_{o_k-1}^k)$$
$$VO_3^k = (\mathbf{vo}_{o_k+2}^k, \mathbf{vo}_{o_k+1}^k, \mathbf{vo}_1^k, \cdots, \mathbf{vo}_{o_k-2}^k)$$
$$\vdots$$
$$VO_{o_k}^k = (\mathbf{vo}_{2o_k-1}^k, \mathbf{vo}_{2o_k-2}^k, \cdots, \mathbf{vo}_{o_k+1}^k, \mathbf{vo}_1^k)$$
$$VO_{o_k+1}^k = (\mathbf{vo}_{2o_k}^k, \mathbf{vo}_{2o_k-1}^k, \cdots, \mathbf{vo}_{o_k+1}^k)$$
$$\vdots$$
$$VO_{o_k+r}^k = (\mathbf{vo}_{2o_k+r-1}^k, \mathbf{vo}_{2o_k+r-2}^k, \cdots, \mathbf{vo}_{o_k+r}^k).$$

and

$$O_2^k = (\beta_{o_k+1}^k, \beta_1^k, \cdots, \beta_{o_k-1}^k)^T$$
$$O_3^k = (\beta_{o_k+2}^k, \beta_{o_k+1}^k, \beta_1^k, \cdots, \beta_{o_k-2}^k)^T$$
$$\vdots$$
$$O_{o_k}^k = (\beta_{2o_k-1}^k, \beta_{2o_k-2}^k, \cdots, \beta_{o_k+1}^k, \beta_1^k)^T$$
$$O_{o_k+1}^k = (\beta_{2o_k}^k, \beta_{2o_k-1}^k, \cdots, \beta_{o_k+1}^k)^T$$
$$\vdots$$
$$O_{o_k+r}^k = (\beta_{2o_k+r-1}^k, \beta_{2o_k+r-2}^k, \cdots, \beta_{o_k+r}^k)^T.$$

Where $\mathbf{vo}_{o_k+i}^k$ and $\beta_{o_k+i}^k$ $(i = 1, 2, \cdots, o_k + r - 1)$ are random selected.

3.2 Inverting the Central Map

In the process of decryption, take the inverse of the Square part as the Vinegar variable of the first layer, and substitute it into the central polynomials, and solve the linear system. The calculation result and the Vinegar variable of the layer together are substituted into the central polynomials of the next layer as the Vinegar variable of the next layer, and thus continuing the same process until the calculation result of the last layer is generated. If the Vinegar variable of the kth layer is $\mathbf{v} = (v_1, \cdots, v_{v_k})$, we plug it into the central polynomial and a linear equation system of $o_k + r$ linear equations in o_k variable can be got.

$$\underbrace{\mathbf{v}^T \cdot VV_i^k \cdot \mathbf{v} + \mathbf{v}^T \cdot V_i^k + C_i^k}_{\text{constant}} + \underbrace{\mathbf{v}^T \cdot VO_i^k \cdot \mathbf{o} + O_i^k \cdot \mathbf{o}}_{\text{linear in } \mathbf{o}} = y_{t_k+i} (i = 1, \cdots, o_k + r).$$

Let

$$e_{t_k+i} = y_{t_k+i} - (\mathbf{v}^T \cdot VV_i^k \cdot \mathbf{v} + \mathbf{v}^T \cdot V_i^k + C_i^k),$$

We have

$$\underbrace{\begin{bmatrix} \mathbf{v}^T \cdot VO_1^k + O_1^k \\ \mathbf{v}^T \cdot VO_2^k + O_2^k \\ \vdots \\ \mathbf{v}^T \cdot VO_{o_k}^k + O_{o_k}^k \\ \mathbf{v}^T \cdot VO_{o_k+1}^k + O_{o_k+1}^k \\ \vdots \\ \mathbf{v}^T \cdot VO_{o_k+r}^k + O_{o_k+r}^k \end{bmatrix}}_{L} \begin{bmatrix} x_{t_k+1} \\ x_{t_k+2} \\ \vdots \\ x_{t_k+o_k} \end{bmatrix} = \begin{bmatrix} e_{t_k+1} \\ e_{t_k+2} \\ \vdots \\ e_{t_k+o_k} \\ e_{t_k+o_k+1} \\ \vdots \\ e_{t_k+o_k+r} \end{bmatrix}.$$

and L is a $(o_k + r) * o_k$ Toeplitz matrix:

$$\begin{bmatrix} V^T \cdot \mathbf{vo}_1^k + \beta_1^k & V^T \cdot \mathbf{vo}_2^k + \beta_2^k & \cdots & V^T \cdot \mathbf{vo}_{o_k}^k + \beta_{o_k}^k \\ V^T \cdot \mathbf{vo}_{o_k+1}^k + \beta_{o_k+1}^k & V^T \cdot \mathbf{vo}_1^k + \beta_1^k & \cdots & V^T \cdot \mathbf{vo}_{o_k-1}^k + \beta_{o_k-1}^k \\ \vdots & \vdots & \ddots & \vdots \\ V^T \cdot \mathbf{vo}_{2o_k-1}^k + \beta_{2o_k-1}^k & V^T \cdot \mathbf{vo}_{2o_k-2}^k + \beta_{2o_k-2}^k & \cdots & V^T \cdot \mathbf{vo}_1^k + \beta_1^k \\ V^T \cdot \mathbf{vo}_{2o_k}^k + \beta_{2o_k}^k & V^T \cdot \mathbf{vo}_{2o_k-1}^k + \beta_{2o_k-1}^k & \cdots & V^T \cdot \mathbf{vo}_{o_k+1}^k + \beta_{o_k+1}^k \\ \vdots & \vdots & \ddots & \vdots \\ V^T \cdot \mathbf{vo}_{2o_k+r-1}^k + \beta_{2o_k+r-1}^k & V^T \cdot \mathbf{vo}_{2o_k+r-2}^k + \beta_{2o_k+r-2}^k & \cdots & V^T \cdot \mathbf{vo}_{o_k+r}^k + \beta_{o_k+r}^k \end{bmatrix}$$

The matrix L that is constructed at this point is exactly what we want.

Computing L: It can be seen from the structure of L that we have to compute only $2o_k + r - 1$ elements of L. The rest of L are generated by shift operations. Consequently, large amount of time and cost could be saved.

Solving the linear equation system: In general, solution for x can be calculated by Gaussian elimination. By our construction, we only need to solve a Toeplitz system which would be easier. There are many methods which can be used to solve a Toeplitz systems [11, 14, 27]. Therefore, we can obtain the solution in $O(n^2)$ time.

3.3   Probability of Decryption Success

In order to get the unique correct plaintext in the decryption process of SRP, the inverse result of the central map is hoped to be unique. Given that any ciphertext is generated from a certain plaintext, it can be concluded that $Lx = u$ has at least one solution. For such a solvable linear equation system of $o_k + r$ equations in o_k variables, to make it have a unique solution, the rank of matrix L must be o_k. In the case of random selection of L, the probability that the rank is o_k is $(1 - q^{-o_k-r})(1 - q^{-o_k-r+1} \cdots (1 - q^{-r-1}))$. Based on the three sets of security parameters given by [26], the probability of full rank of a random matrix of size $(o_k + r) * o_k$ and a Toeplitz matrix of size $(o_k + r) * o_k$ are tested respectively. The results of our test are averaged over 10^5 set test results. The probability of full rank of different types of matrices is displayed in Table 1. As is presented, under the three sets of parameters, the probability of the full rank is very close to 1.

Table 1. The probability of full rank of different types of matrices

$(K, d, h, \{o_1, \cdots\}, r, s, l)$	Security level	Random matrix $((o_1 + r) * o_1)$	Toeplitz matrix $((o_1 + r) * o_1)$
$(GF(31), 33, 1, \{32\}, 16, 5, 16)$	80-bit	1.0000	1.0000
$(GF(31), 47, 1, \{47\}, 22, 5, 22)$	112-bit	1.0000	1.0000
$(GF(31), 71, 1, \{71\}, 32, 5, 32)$	160-bit	1.0000	1.0000

3.4   Key Sizes of Our Improved SRP

Compared with the original SRP scheme, our improved scheme only needs to store the following items for each layer of the Rainbow Part: $VV_i^k(i = 1, \cdots, o_k + r)$, $V_i^k(i = 1, \cdots, o_k + r)$, $C_i^k(i = 1, \cdots, o_k + r)$, $\mathbf{vo}_i^k(i = 1, \cdots, 2o_k + r - 1)$, $\beta_i^k(i = 1, \cdots, 2o_k + r - 1)$. Therefore,

The size of the private key of our improved scheme is :

$$m \cdot (m+1) + (n+l) \cdot (n+1) + \sum_{k=1}^{h} ((r + o_k) \cdot (\frac{v_k \cdot (v_k + 1)}{2} + v_k + 1) + (v_k + 1) \cdot (2o_k + r - 1))$$

field elements.

The size of the public key of our improved scheme is: $m \cdot \frac{(n+1)\cdot(n+2)}{2}$ field elements.

4   Security Analysis

In order to study the impact of the proposed method on the security of the original SRP scheme, existing mainstream attacks are applied to carry out the security analysis from the theoretical and experimental aspects.

4.1   Direct Attack

The basic principle of direct attack is to compute the plaintext by directly solving the equation system obtained by the ciphertext and the public key. This is also the most intuitive way. The direct attack algorithm includes F4/F5 algorithm, XL algorithm, Zhuang-Zi algorithm and so on. Currently, the most effective direct attack method is F4/F5 algorithm. Therefore, we carried out a number of experiments using the Magma implementation of F4. The results of our experiments against the original SRP scheme and our improved scheme are displayed in Table 2.

Table 2. Timing results of the direct attack using Magma

q, d, o, r, s, l	m, n	Random system	The original SRP	Our improved SRP
31, 11, 10, 6, 5, 6	32, 15	0.839 s	0.841 s	0.843 s
31, 11, 10, 6, 5, 4	32, 17	37.765 s	37.127 s	37.127 s
31, 11, 10, 6, 5, 3	32, 18	105.864 s	104.742 s	104.826 s
31, 11, 11, 6, 5, 6	33, 16	2.333 s	2.385 s	2.391 s
31, 13, 10, 6, 5, 6	34, 17	27.238 s	27.318 s	27.312 s

4.2   Linearization Equation Attack

The linearization equation attack was first applied to break MI. Its basic idea is to obtain the potential linear relationship between the input and the output of the public key polynomial by analyzing the special structure of the central map, as is shown below:

$$\sum_{i=1}^{n}\sum_{j=1}^{m} a_{ij}x_iy_j + \sum_{i=1}^{n} b_ix_i + \sum_{j=1}^{m} c_jy_j + d.$$

where, $Y = \{y_1, ..., y_m\}$ is comprised of m polynomials on $k[x_1, ..., x_n]$. This linear relationship is derived from that the central map also suits the linear relationship similar to the above form. In fact, the linear affine will not change the linear relation of this form in the process of constructing a public key. The coefficients in the linear relationship can be solved as long as the attacker has obtained enough plaintext-ciphertext pairs in advance. For SRP or improved SRP, the Rainbow part and the Plus part of central map are immune to this attack. We generate enough plaintext-ciphertext pairs and substitute them into the equations for solving. Experimental results show that there exists no linear relationship between the plaintext and ciphertext. Actually, there is no special relationship between the input variable and the output variable of the central map of our improved SRP, which means linear relationship or higher order linear equations is inexistent. Therefore, it can resist the linearization equation attack and the high order linearization equation attack.

4.3   Differential Attack

Given the public key P, the difference equation is defined as follows:

$$DP(A, X) = P(X + A) - P(X) - P(A) + P(0).$$

Differential attack can be used to find the invariant space of the simple Square scheme to recover the key of simple Square. However, the singature schemes UOV and Rainbow can resist against the differential attack. The SPR scheme introduces the central map F_R, F_P, therefore, differential attack is not feasible for SRP or improved SRP scheme.

4.4   MinRank Attack

MinRank attack transforms the security analysis of the scheme into the problem of MinRank, which is a very effective attack for multivarite public key cryptography. The principle of MinRank attack is to find a linear combination of the coefficient matrix corresponding to the public key polynomial, so that the rank of the obtained matrix is less than or equal to r. A partial key is restored by obtaining such a linear combination. By construction, we have rank $(f_s^i) \leq d$, rank $(f_r^{i,k}) \leq V_{k+1}$, rank $(f_p^i) \leq n'$ for the overall structure of SRP. Therefore, the MinRank attack against SRP is to look for a combination of the public key polynomials having a rank of at most d. Thomae and Wolf [23] adapt the method of [1] to analyze the complexity of MinRank attack against Double-Layer Square, which is also used in our scheme. For a random but fixed Sw, the probability that it lies in the kernel of a linear combination of $f_s^i (i = 1, .., d)$ is greater than $1/q$. Because T is a not a $n' \times n'$ square matrix but a $n' \times n$ matrix, so we will obtain q^l parasitic solutions. Therefore, the complexity of MinRank attack against SRP is approximately $O(d * q^{l+1} * m^3)$. It can be seen that the improved SRP does not affect the rank of $f_s^i (i = 1, .., d)$. As a result, the complexity of the MinRank attack is not reduced. So we conclude that the complexity of MinRank attack against the improved SRP is $O(d * q^{l+1} * m^3)$.

5   Experiments

To demonstrate the efficiency of our improved SRP, our improved scheme and the original scheme are compared with the key size and the performance of decryption. We implemented the three sets of secure parameters proposed in [4] with Sage, and performed 125 times for each set of parameters. The results of the experiment are given in Table 3. It can be seen from the table that the improved scheme has a significant improvement in performance. Under the 128-bit security level, the private key of our improved scheme can reduce by 61%, and the decryption speed is 2.1 times faster than that of the original scheme.

Table 3. Comparison between our improved SRP and the original SRP

q, d, o, r, s, l		31, 33, 32, 16, 5, 16	31, 47, 47, 22, 5, 22	31, 71, 71, 32, 5, 32
m, n		86,49	121,72	179,110
Security level		80-bit	112-bit	160-bit
The original SRP	Public Key Size (KB)	68.5	204.3	695.4
	Private Key Size (KB)	57.2	161.5	528.3
	Encryption (ms)	0.84	1.26	2.39
	Decryption (ms)	3.69	7.25	13.45
Our improved SRP	Public Key Size (KB)	68.5	204.3	695.4
	Private Key Size (KB)	26.2	67.6	206.9
	Encryption (ms)	0.85	1.25	2.38
	Decryption (ms)	1.91	3.86	4.35

6   Conclusion

In this paper, we propose a SRP variant with shorter private key and higher decryption efficiency. The improved scheme can reduce the size of the private key by 61% and the speed of decryption is 2.1 times faster than the original scheme. Such improvements can make the SRP encryption scheme more applicable to resource-limited environments. We analyzed the improved scheme from the security perspective, and the results show that the improved scheme does not reduce the security of the scheme.

Acknowledgment. This work was supported by the National Natural Science Foundation of China (Nos. 61632013, U1135004 and 61170080), 973 Program (No. 2014CB360501), Guangdong Provincial Natural Science Foundation (No. 2014A030308006), and Guangdong Provincial Project of Science and Technology (no. 2016B090920081).

References

1. Billet, O., Gilbert, H.: Cryptanalysis of rainbow. In: De Prisco, R., Yung, M. (eds.) SCN 2006. LNCS, vol. 4116, pp. 336–347. Springer, Heidelberg (2006). https://doi.org/10.1007/11832072_23
2. Ding, J., Gower, J.E.: Inoculating multivariate schemes against differential attacks. In: Yung, M., Dodis, Y., Kiayias, A., Malkin, T. (eds.) PKC 2006. LNCS, vol. 3958, pp. 290–301. Springer, Heidelberg (2006). https://doi.org/10.1007/11745853_19
3. Ding, J., Schmidt, D.: Rainbow, a new multivariable polynomial signature scheme. In: Ioannidis, J., Keromytis, A., Yung, M. (eds.) ACNS 2005. LNCS, vol. 3531, pp. 164–175. Springer, Heidelberg (2005). https://doi.org/10.1007/11496137_12
4. Duong, D.H., Petzoldt, A., Takagi, T.: Reducing the key size of the SRP encryption scheme. In: Liu, J.K., Steinfeld, R. (eds.) ACISP 2016. LNCS, vol. 9723, pp. 427–434. Springer, Cham (2016). https://doi.org/10.1007/978-3-319-40367-0_27

5. Eder, C., Faugére, J.C.: A survey on signature-based algorithms for computing Gröbner bases. J. Symb. Comput. **80**, 719–784 (2017)
6. Faugère, J.C.: A new efficient algorithm for computing Gröbner bases (F4). J. Pure Appl. Algebra **139**(1), 61–88 (1999)
7. Faugère, J.C.: A new efficient algorithm for computing Gröbner bases without reduction to zero (F5). In: ACM ISSAC 2002, pp. 75–83 (2002)
8. Faugère, J.C., Din, M.S.E., Spaenlehauer, P.J.: On the complexity of the generalized MinRank problem. J. Symb. Comput. **55**, 30–58 (2013)
9. Faugère, J.-C., Levy-dit-Vehel, F., Perret, L.: Cryptanalysis of MinRank. In: Wagner, D. (ed.) CRYPTO 2008. LNCS, vol. 5157, pp. 280–296. Springer, Heidelberg (2008). https://doi.org/10.1007/978-3-540-85174-5_16
10. Fouque, P.-A., Granboulan, L., Stern, J.: Differential cryptanalysis for multivariate schemes. In: Cramer, R. (ed.) EUROCRYPT 2005. LNCS, vol. 3494, pp. 341–353. Springer, Heidelberg (2005). https://doi.org/10.1007/11426639_20
11. Gover, M.J.C., Barnett, S.: Inversion of certain extensions of Toeplitz matrices. J. Math. Anal. Appl. **100**(2), 339–353 (1984)
12. Kipnis, A., Patarin, J., Goubin, L.: Unbalanced oil and vinegar signature schemes. In: Stern, J. (ed.) EUROCRYPT 1999. LNCS, vol. 1592, pp. 206–222. Springer, Heidelberg (1999). https://doi.org/10.1007/3-540-48910-X_15
13. Matsumoto, T., Imai, H.: Public quadratic polynomial-tuples for efficient signature-verification and message-encryption. In: Barstow, D., et al. (eds.) EUROCRYPT 1988. LNCS, vol. 330, pp. 419–453. Springer, Heidelberg (1988). https://doi.org/10.1007/3-540-45961-8_39
14. Ng, M.K., Rost, K., Wen, Y.W.: On inversion of Toeplitz matrices. Linear Algebra Appl. **348**(1), 145–151 (2002)
15. Patarin, J.: Cryptanalysis of the Matsumoto and Imai public key scheme of Eurocrypt'88. In: Coppersmith, D. (ed.) CRYPTO 1995. LNCS, vol. 963, pp. 248–261. Springer, Heidelberg (1995). https://doi.org/10.1007/3-540-44750-4_20
16. Patarin, J.: Hidden Fields Equations (HFE) and Isomorphisms of Polynomials (IP): two new families of asymmetric algorithms. In: Maurer, U. (ed.) EUROCRYPT 1996. LNCS, vol. 1070, pp. 33–48. Springer, Heidelberg (1996). https://doi.org/10.1007/3-540-68339-9_4
17. Patarin, J., Courtois, N., Goubin, L.: QUARTZ, 128-bit long digital signatures. In: Naccache, D. (ed.) CT-RSA 2001. LNCS, vol. 2020, pp. 282–297. Springer, Heidelberg (2001). https://doi.org/10.1007/3-540-45353-9_21
18. Petzoldt, A., Chen, M.-S., Yang, B.-Y., Tao, C., Ding, J.: Design principles for HFEv- based multivariate signature schemes. In: Iwata, T., Cheon, J.H. (eds.) ASIACRYPT 2015. LNCS, vol. 9452, pp. 311–334. Springer, Heidelberg (2015). https://doi.org/10.1007/978-3-662-48797-6_14
19. Porras, J., Baena, J., Ding, J.: ZHFE, a new multivariate public key encryption scheme. In: Mosca, M. (ed.) PQCrypto 2014. LNCS, vol. 8772, pp. 229–245. Springer, Cham (2014). https://doi.org/10.1007/978-3-319-11659-4_14
20. Shen, W., Tang, S.: RGB, a mixed multivariate signature scheme. Comput. J. **59**(4), 439–451 (2015)
21. Smith-Tone, D.: On the differential security of multivariate public key cryptosystems. In: Yang, B.-Y. (ed.) PQCrypto 2011. LNCS, vol. 7071, pp. 130–142. Springer, Heidelberg (2011). https://doi.org/10.1007/978-3-642-25405-5_9
22. Tao, C., Diene, A., Tang, S., Ding, J.: Simple matrix scheme for encryption. In: Gaborit, P. (ed.) PQCrypto 2013. LNCS, vol. 7932, pp. 231–242. Springer, Heidelberg (2013). https://doi.org/10.1007/978-3-642-38616-9_16

23. Thomae, E., Wolf, C.: Roots of square: cryptanalysis of double-layer square and square+. In: Yang, B.-Y. (ed.) PQCrypto 2011. LNCS, vol. 7071, pp. 83–97. Springer, Heidelberg (2011). https://doi.org/10.1007/978-3-642-25405-5_6
24. Wolf, C., An, B., Preneel, B.: On the security of stepwise triangular systems. Des. Codes Crypt. **40**(3), 285–302 (2006)
25. Yang, B.-Y., Chen, J.-M.: Building secure Tame-like multivariate public-key cryptosystems: the new TTS. In: Boyd, C., González Nieto, J.M. (eds.) ACISP 2005. LNCS, vol. 3574, pp. 518–531. Springer, Heidelberg (2005). https://doi.org/10.1007/11506157_43
26. Yasuda, T., Sakurai, K.: A multivariate encryption scheme with rainbow. In: Qing, S., Okamoto, E., Kim, K., Liu, D. (eds.) ICICS 2015. LNCS, vol. 9543, pp. 236–251. Springer, Cham (2016). https://doi.org/10.1007/978-3-319-29814-6_19
27. Zohar, S.: Toeplitz matrix inversion: the algoritm of W. F. Trench. J. ACM **16**(4), 592–601 (1969)

Key Bit-Dependent Attack on Protected PKC Using a Single Trace

Bo-Yeon Sim and Dong-Guk Han[⊠]

Kookmin University, 77 Jeongneung-ro, Seongbuk-Gu, Seoul 02707, South Korea
{qjdusls,christa}@kookmin.ac.kr

Abstract. Public key cryptosystems are typically based on scalar multiplication or modular exponentiation algorithms where the key is unknown to an attacker. Such algorithms are vulnerable to side-channel attacks, and various countermeasures have been proposed. However, no combination of countermeasures is effective against single trace attacks. Hence, template and collision attacks have been the focus of research. However, such attacks require complicated pre-processing to eliminate noise. In this paper, we present a single trace attack based on the power consumption properties of the key bit check phase. The proposed attack does not require sophisticated pre-processing. We apply the attack to hardware and software implementations. In hardware implementation, we target the Montgomery-López-Dahab ladder algorithm and determine that private key bits can be extracted at a 100% success rate. In software implementation, we target the key bit check functions of mbedTLS and OpenSSL, and observe that private key bits can be recovered at 96.13% and 96.25% success rates, respectively. Moreover, if we use leakage associated with referred register addresses, the success rate is 100% in both cases. We propose two countermeasures to eliminate these vulnerabilities. Experimental results show that the proposed countermeasures can address these vulnerabilities effectively.

Keywords: Side-channel analysis · Public key cryptosystems · Single trace attack · Simple power analysis · Clustering

1 Introduction

Physical vulnerabilities that occur when algorithms are performed on an embedded system, i.e., side-channel attack (SCA), were discovered by Paul Kocher in 1996 [17]. Subsequently, various attacks against public key cryptosystems (PKCs) have been studied. In particular, diverse power and electromagnetic analysis, which are differentiated into simple power analysis (SPA), differential power analysis (DPA), template attack (TA), and collision attack (CA), have also been studied [3,5,6,9–12,18,23–28]. Various algorithms that are resistant to SPA and DPA have been suggested [2,4,15,16,20,21]; consequently, TA and CA focus on single trace attacks. Thus, sophisticated methods to obtain traces with high signal-to-noise ratio (SNR) are required.

© Springer International Publishing AG 2017
J. K. Liu and P. Samarati (Eds.): ISPEC 2017, LNCS 10701, pp. 168–185, 2017.
https://doi.org/10.1007/978-3-319-72359-4_10

Previously proposed attacks were primarily based on patterns of data dependent branches, statistical characteristics according to intermediate values, or the interrelationships between data. However, such attacks did not consider using the private key bit check phase. Private key bits are directly loaded during the check phase, and no countermeasures have been considered to protect this phase. If vulnerabilities are revealed, private keys can be exposed even if previously proposed SCA countermeasures are applied. Thus, investigating leakage associated with the key bit check phase to determine whether it is sufficient to recover private keys is required. The contributions of this paper are summarized as follows.

Our Contributions. In this paper, we categorize the power consumption properties of the key bit check phase and show that attacks based on these properties are practical. The proposed attack requires a single trace and does not require any knowledge about the input values; thus, it can defeat any combination of existing countermeasures. Moreover, pre-processing to reduce noise is not required. Two platforms, i.e., hardware and software, are targeted, and we can extract private keys by applying SPA and a k-means clustering algorithm. In hardware implementation, we target the Montgomery-López-Dahab ladder algorithm and determine that it is possible to extract private key bits at a 100% success rate. In software implementation, we target the mbedTLS and OpenSSL key bit check functions. Here, private key bits can be recovered at 96.13% and 96.25% success rates, respectively. Moreover, if we use leakage associated with referenced register addresses, the success rate is 100% in both cases. We propose two types of countermeasures and demonstrate experimentally that they can be applied effectively.

The remainder of this paper is organized as follows. In Sect. 2, we briefly describe SCA on PKCs and define our attack target. In Sect. 3, we summarize the power consumption properties of the attack target. Experimental results are given in Sect. 4. Potential countermeasures are discussed in Sect. 5, and conclusions are presented in Sect. 6.

2 Preliminaries

2.1 Conventional SCA on PKCs

SPA exploits the patterns of data-dependent conditional branches from a single power trace [18]. For example, binary scalar multiplication can be broken by distinguishing differences between doubling and addition operations. In other words, an n-bit private key k can be recovered because the algorithm behaves irregularly according to the key bit k_i. Similarly, binary modular exponentiation can be broken by distinguishing squaring and multiplication.

To make algorithms behave regular, various countermeasures have been proposed. The algorithms presented in Fig. 1 are representative examples [15, 16, 21]. However, these SPA-resistant algorithms can be defeated due to DPA [18]. Specifically, since power consumption can be correlated to manipulated data values, an adversary can obtain the private key k by analyzing the power consumption measurements from multiple cryptographic operations. Thus, countermeasures that apply a randomization method to eliminate the association between intermediate data and power consumption have been proposed [2,4,20].

These countermeasures are effective against SPA and DPA; thus, sophisticated attacks, such as TA [10,24] and CA [11,23,25], that can recover private keys from a single trace are receiving increasing attention. A TA is a type of profiling attack that combines statistical modeling and power analysis. A CA is a type of higher-order DPA based on the interrelationships between data. Given the focus on TA and CA, research to obtain traces with high SNR has been actively pursued. Decapsulation and localization [10,11,23,25], multi-probe [11], principle component analysis (PCA) [25] have been used for attacks. However, there are environmental constraints that make practical application of such methods difficult. Decapsulation requires physically modifying the target devices, and numerous electromagnetic or power consumption traces are required to build templates.

An interesting single trace attack on scalar multiplication has been reported previously [22]. This approach appears to be associated with the experimental results of our software implementation. However, this is a TA, and can be applied to a conditional move (or conditional XOR swap) instruction based on secret dependent memory accesses. Furthermore, use of this instruction depends on the microcontroller.

2.2   Key Bit Check Phase

Scalar multiplication and modular exponentiation are a fundamental calculations in numerous PKCs. They are consisted of iterative operations determined by the value of the private key bit k_i [15,16,19,21]. For example, in the algorithms shown in Fig. 1, the referring registers are determined by the k_i value.

Left to Right	Right to Left
Input : $P = (x, y)$ a point on **EC**, an n-bit key $k = (k_{n-1}, \cdots, k_0)_2$ **Output :** $Q = kP$	**Input :** $P = (x, y)$ a point on **EC**, an n-bit key $k = (k_{n-1}, \cdots, k_0)_2$ **Output :** $Q = kP$
1: $R_0 \leftarrow \infty$, $R_1 \leftarrow P$ 2: **for** $i = n - 1$ down to 0 **do** 3: $\quad R_{1-k_i} \leftarrow R_{k_i} + R_{1-k_i}$ 4: $\quad R_{k_i} \leftarrow 2R_{k_i}$ 5: **end for** 6: **Return** R_0	1: $R_0 \leftarrow \infty$, $R_1 \leftarrow P$, $R_2 \leftarrow P$ 2: **for** $i = 0$ up to $n - 1$ **do** 3: $\quad R_{1-k_i} \leftarrow R_{1-k_i} + R_2$ 4: $\quad R_2 \leftarrow R_0 + R_1$ 5: **end for** 6: **Return** R_0

Fig. 1. Examples of regular algorithms for scalar multiplication

Therefore, at the beginning of each loop, there generally exists a phase that checks the k_i value, i.e., the key bit value is extracted from an n-bit key string $k = (k_{n-1}, k_{n-2}, \cdots, k_0)_2$ and stored in a k_i variable. We refer to this step as the key bit check phase, which has two common characteristics, i.e., private key bits k_i are extracted at the beginning of each loop and referring register addresses are determined by the k_i value. In this paper, we take note of two common characteristics of these regular algorithms.

3 Key Bit-Dependent Attack

This section describes the properties of the key bit check phase and how protected PKCs can be attacked using a single trace.

3.1 Key Bit-Dependent Properties

Scalar multiplication and modular exponentiation consist of iterative operations associated with the private key bit k_i value (Fig. 1). Accordingly, at the beginning of each iteration, the key bit value is extracted from an n-bit key string $k = (k_{n-1}, k_{n-2}, \cdots, k_0)_2$ and stored in a k_i variable. Thus, power consumption is related to the k_i value. Currently, there are two common power models, i.e., hamming distance (HD) and hamming weight (HW) models. The HD model is commonly used in hardware implementation, while the HW model is employed in software implementation. Thus, we can summarize power consumption properties as follows.

Property 1. In hardware implementation, power consumption in the key bit check phase is associated with the HD between k_{i+1} and k_i ($0 \leq i < n - 1$). In other words, if $k_{i+1} = k_i$, power consumption related to $k_{i+1} \oplus k_i = 0$ occurs. Otherwise, power consumption is associated with $k_{i+1} \oplus k_i = 1$.

Property 2. In software implementation, power consumption in the key bit check phase is associated with the HW of k_i ($0 \leq i \leq n-1$), i.e., if $k_i = 0$, power consumption related to 0 occurs. Otherwise, power consumption is associated with 1.

Power consumption differs when leakage is zero or one, i.e. $Pw(0) \neq Pw(1)$; therefore, by exploiting Properties 1 and 2, we can classify power consumption traces into two groups. Once the traces are classified, the private key can be recovered based on the properties. We define a study based on these properties as **Case study 1** (Fig. 4(a)).

3.2 Key Bit-Dependent Properties of Regular Algorithms

To cope with SPA, the algorithms in Fig. 1 are configured to repeatedly perform regular operations regardless of the k_i value. Therefore, steps 3 and 4 are composed identically. However, the referred register addresses differ according to the k_i value, and these affect power consumption. In particular, in hardware implementation, registers to be accessed and the k_i value are determined simultaneously, i.e., the operations are executed in parallel. Hence, power consumption when checking the k_i value is also affected by the HD between the register addresses used in two consecutive loops. In software implementations, the operations are performed sequentially. Thus, differing from hardware implementations, these two types of information do not affect power consumption simultaneously. In what follows, additional power consumption properties are described. The register address is symbolized as $RegAddr$.

Property 3. In hardware implementation, power consumption in the key bit check phase is affected by the HD between k_{i+1} and k_i ($0 \leq i < n-1$) and the HD between the register addresses determined by k_{i+1} and k_i ($0 \leq i < n-1$). In other words, if $k_{i+1} = k_i$, power consumption related to $k_{i+1} \oplus k_i = 0$ and $RegAddr_{k_{i+1}} \oplus RegAddr_{k_i} = 0$ occurs. Otherwise, power consumption is associated with $k_{i+1} \oplus k_i = 1$ and $RegAddr_{k_{i+1}} \oplus RegAddr_{k_i} \neq 0$.

Property 4. In software implementation, power consumption is affected by the HW of k_i ($0 \leq i < n-1$) and the HW of register addresses determined by k_i ($0 \leq i < n-1$), i.e., if $k_i = 0$, power consumption related to 0 and $RegAddr_0$ occurs. Otherwise, power consumption is associated with 1 and $RegAddr_1$. Note that in general $RegAddr_0$ is not equal to $RegAddr_1$. Thus we can assume that the power consumption depending on the $RegAddr_0$ is different from that on the $RegAddr_1$.

By exploiting Properties 3 and 4, we can classify power consumption traces into groups G_1 and G_2. Power consumption associated with G_1 occurs when leakage is zero and the remainder occurs when leakage is non-zero. Once the traces are classified, the private key can be recovered based on these properties. We define a study based on these properties as **Case study 2** (Fig. 4(b)).

3.3   Key Bit-Dependent Attack Framework

In this paper, we consider implementations based on regular algorithms protected by intermediate data randomization. Therefore, we assume that an attacker must attack a single trace rather than use numerous traces. In addition, we suppose that the attacker can identify the iterative structure in the trace. The attack framework is composed of four steps.

Step 1. Pre-processing: First, a trace is divided into sub-traces corresponding to each iteration. We describe trace T as a series of n sub-traces (Fig. 2) as

$$T = \{O_{n-1} \mid\mid O_{n-2} \mid\mid \cdots \mid\mid O_0\}$$

because the loop performs a total of n iterations (Fig. 1). Therefore, we align sub-traces after dividing the trace into n sub-traces.

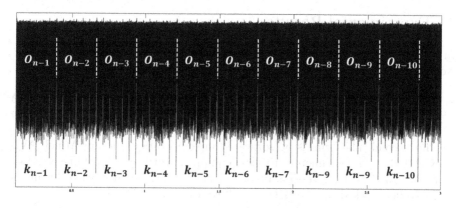

Fig. 2. Power consumption trace of 10 iterations (cf. Fig. 1(left))

Step 2. Choose Points of Interest (PoIs): If we can use the same device as the target, it is easy to find PoIs. First, record a power trace using known input, and then calculate the sum of squared pairwise t-differences (SOST) [8] of the sub-traces classified according to the property described in Sects. 3.1 and 3.2. Then, select points with high SOST values as the PoIs. SOST is calculated as follows:

$$SOST = \left(\frac{m_{G_1} - m_{G_2}}{\sqrt{\frac{\sigma^2_{G_1}}{n_{G_1}} + \frac{\sigma^2_{G_2}}{n_{G_2}}}} \right)^2 \tag{1}$$

where m denotes the mean, σ is standard deviation, and n is the number of elements. If we cannot use the same device, we must know how the target algorithm is implemented. Besides, we need to identify the key bit check phase position through SPA. Then, we can select points where the target operation is performed as PoIs. In general, PoIs are positioned near the beginning of each sub-trace O_i ($0 \leq i \leq n - 1$) because k_i must be determined prior to each loop operation. Note that p_i represents PoI of each sub-trace O_i.

Step 3. Classification into Two Groups: Apply SPA or a clustering algorithm (e.g. k-means, fuzzy k-means [7] or EM algorithm [1]) to divide p_i ($0 \leq i \leq n - 1$) into two groups G_1 and G_2. Consequently, p_i in G_1 indicates that leakage is zero, while that in G_2 indicate that leakage is non-zero.

Step 4. Extract Private Key Bit: Since the most significant bit is always 1, set $k_{n-1} = 1$ and recover the respective bit k_i ($0 \leq i \leq n - 2$) according to the power model. With the HD model, if p_i is included in G_1, k_i has the same value as k_{i+1}; otherwise, the value of k_i differs. With the HW model, if p_i is included in the group that includes p_{n-1}, $k_i = 1$; otherwise, $k_i = 0$.

4   Experimental Results

In this section, we present the experimental results of a key bit-dependent attack. Note that we use two platforms to demonstrate the feasibility of the attack.

1. The first platform is a VHDL implementation on a SASEBO-GII FPGA board. We measure power consumption at a sampling rate of 2.5 GS/s. Power consumption is recorded using an FPGA clocked at 24 MHz.
2. The second platform is a software implementation on an Atmel AVR XEMEGA 128D4 microcontroller equipped with a ChipWhisperer-Lite (CW1173) Two-Part Version. Power consumption is recorded using the microcontroller clocked at 29.5 MHz and CLKGEN × 4 via DCM.

4.1   Key Bit-Dependent Attack on Hardware Implementation

We focus on 224-bit scalar multiplication over elliptic curves. Specifically, we discuss an attack on the Montgomery-López-Dahab ladder algorithm [19] protected by scalar randomization [4]. Hence, we assume that an attacker is obliged to attack a single trace. The attack is executed as follows.

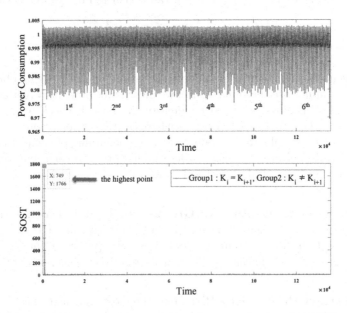

Fig. 3. Hardware implementation: one of the sub-traces (top) and SOST between two sub-trace groups (bottom)

Step 1. Pre-processing: Because the loop of the target algorithm performs except for the most significant bit (Algorithm 1, steps 4 to 13; Appendix A) a trace T is made up of $n - 1$ sub-traces for an n-bit scalar. Thus, we align after uniformly dividing the trace T into $n - 1$ sub-traces O_i ($0 \leq i \leq n - 2$). Figure 3(top) shows one of the sub-traces captured from the first platform. Each sub-trace consists of six finite field multiplications.

Step 2. Choose Points of Interest: The target algorithm performs the key bit check operation on the second clock of each sub-trace. Accordingly, we choose points of the second clock of the sub-traces as PoIs. The SOST value is the greatest before starting the first multiplication, as shown in Fig. 3(bottom), when we classify sub-traces into two groups according to Property 1 (or 3) described in Sects. 3.1 and 3.2. This point is located on the second clock of the sub-traces that perform the key bit check operation.

```
1: assign  Ki = regK[REGSIZE - 1];

2: assign  Out1 = regA;
3: assign  Out2 = regB;

4: always @(posedge CLK or negedge RSTn) begin
5:     if (state == `STATE_SHFTK)
6:         regK <= {regK[REGSIZE - 2:0], 1'b0};
7: end
```

```
1: assign  Ki        = regK[REGSIZE-1];

2: assign  Out1      = (Ki) ? regA : regB;
3: assign  Out2      = (Ki) ? regB : regA;

4: always @(posedge CLK or negedge RSTn) begin
5:     if (state == `STATE_SHFTK)
6:         regK <= {regK[REGSIZE - 2:0], 1'b0};
7: end
```

(a) Hardware case study 1   (b) Hardware case study 2

Fig. 4. The key bit check phase (Hardware Implementation)

Step 3 & 4. Classification into Two Groups and Extracting Private Key Bit: Figure 4(b) shows some parts of the hardware implementation of the target algorithm, and we determine that this satisfies Property 3. Consequently, we can classify p_i ($0 \leq i \leq n - 2$) into two groups based on this property. Since there is no regular algorithm that satisfies only Property 1, we modify the implementation as Fig. 4(a) to identify the amount of leakage of Property 1. Note that we do not consider side-channel atomicity algorithms. Here, the registers are fixed, so there is no HD leakage between the register addresses used in two consecutive loops. The experimental results are shown in Fig. 5. There is no need for additional processes, such as decapsulation and localization, to obtain trace with high SNR.

(a) Two distributions overlap as shown Fig. 5(a), and it is impossible to perfectly classify two groups through SPA. Hence, we apply a k-means clustering algorithm [7] to classify p_i ($0 \leq i \leq n - 2$) into two groups. The success rate reaches 95.5% (i.e. 12 errors). This is sufficiently small. As a result, a brute-force attack may still be feasible to recover the entire key. (b) We can clearly distinguish two groups through SPA. The classification success rate is 100%, and we

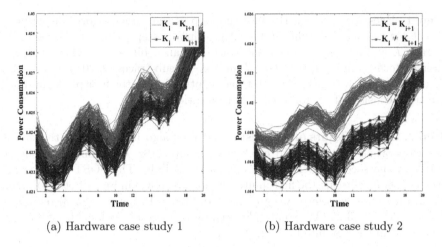

(a) Hardware case study 1   (b) Hardware case study 2

Fig. 5. Classification according to hamming distance between k_i and k_{i+1}

can recover the entire key. This provides evidence to support that changing a register operation according to private key bits leaks more significant information than changing the key bits. The attack is repeated over 100 power consumption traces.

4.2   Key Bit-Dependent Attack on Software Implementation

In this section, we present experimental results based on Properties 2 and 4. It is impossible to capture a whole scalar multiplication trace from the second platform; thus we use the modified algorithm shown in Fig. 7, which is based on the functions in Fig. 6.

Figure 6 shows the private key bit check function of the mbedTLS (polarSSL), which is the most widely used embedded transmission security TLS/SSL public

```
1: int mbedtls_mpi_get_bit(const mbedtls_mpi *X, size_t pos)
2: {
3:     if (X->n * biL <= pos)
4:         return(0);
5:
6:     return((X->p[pos / biL] >> (pos % biL)) & 0x01);
7: }
```

Fig. 6. The key bit check function of mbedTLS (Software Implementation)

```
1: key_bit = mbedtls_mpi_get_bit(&key, i);
2: BN_MUL(&C, &A[key_bit], &B);
```

Fig. 7. Trace acquisition range

encryption library. Figure 14 shows the function that determines the private key bit in OpenSSL. The key bit check functions are called each time at the beginning of the loop to extract the k_i value from an n-bit key string $k = (k_{n-1}, k_{n-2}, \cdots, k_0)_2$. The experimental results for an openSSL key bit (Fig. 14) are described in Appendix B.

Step 1. Pre-processing: We align after uniformly dividing the trace into sub-traces. Figure 8(top) shows one of the sub-traces.

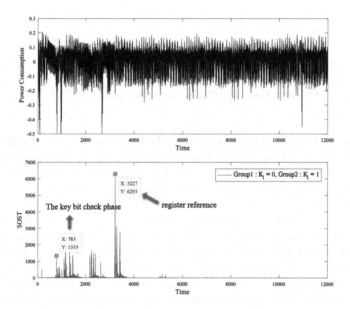

Fig. 8. Software implementation (mbedTLS): one of sub-traces (top) and SOST between two groups of sub-traces (bottom)

Step 2. Choose Points of Interest: The first target position comes immediately after the & 0x01 operation is performed, as shown in Figs. 6 (step 6) and 14 (step 9). The position where the register is referenced according to k_i is the second target. With our second platform, there is an operation to the register LOAD when performing a long integer operation. Thus we select these positions as the second target. We classify the sub-traces into two groups according to Property 2 (or 4) described in Sects. 3.1 and 3.2, and calculate the SOST value. Similar to the results described in Sect. 4.1, a high SOST value occurs when the key bit check function is performed, see Fig. 8. The other point is that HW leakage of the referred register address occurs later because the operations are performed sequentially in the software implementations. Here, we select a section containing a high SOST value as PoIs.

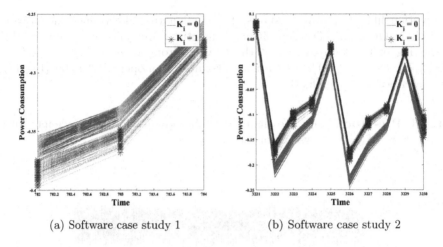

(a) Software case study 1   (b) Software case study 2

Fig. 9. Classification according to hamming weight of k_i (mbedTLS)

Step 3 & 4. Classification into Two Groups and Extracting Private Key Bit: The points where the key bit check function is called comprise the first PoIs, and this satisfies Property 2. The points where HW leakage of the referenced register address occurs comprise the second PoIs; thus, we can validate Property 4.

(a) The first target position comes immediately after the & $0x01$ operation is performed. As shown in Fig. 9(a), the distribution of power consumption overlaps; so, we classify two sets using a k-means algorithm. Consequently, there are misclassified bits, and the success rate is approximately 96.13%. The number of error bits is sufficiently small; thus, a brute-force attack may still be feasible to recover the entire key. (b) The second target position is where the register is referenced according to k_i, i.e., the operation to the register LOAD when performing a long integer operation. It is possible to distinguish two groups through SPA. Here, the classification success rate is 100%, and we can recover the entire key. This shows that referenced register address according to the private key bits has greater effect than the key bits, similar to the results in Sect. 4.1. The attack is repeated over 1000 power consumption traces.

Remark. With the OpenSSL key bit check function, the success rates are 96.25% and 100%, refer to Appendix B for more details.

5 Countermeasures

Thus far, we have shown the key bit-dependent attack using a single trace and that we can recover the entire private key. Here, we discuss countermeasures against the proposed attack.

First, we propose the initialization of k_i to a random value before the key bit check operation is performed, as Fig. 10. Note that it is possible to eliminate

```
 1: assign  Out1 = regA;                                    1: assign  Out1 = (Ki) ? regA : regB;
 2: assign  Out2 = regB;                                    2: assign  Out2 = (Ki) ? regB : regA;
 3:                                                         3:
 4: always @(posedge CLK or negedge RSTn) begin            4: always @(posedge CLK or negedge RSTn) begin
 5:     if (state == `STATE_SHFTK)                          5:     if (state == `STATE_SHFTK)
 6:         regK <= {regK[REGSIZE - 2:0], 1'b0};            6:         regK <= {regK[REGSIZE - 2:0], 1'b0};
 7: end                                                     7: end
 8:                                                         8:
 9: always @(posedge CLK or negedge RSTn) begin            9: always @(posedge CLK or negedge RSTn) begin
10:     `STATE_SHFTK : state <= `STATE_K_SHIFT_REG;        10:     `STATE_SHFTK : state <= `STATE_K_SHIFT_REG;
11:     `STATE_K_SHIFT_REG : begin                         11:     `STATE_K_SHIFT_REG : begin
12:         Ki <= regK[REGSIZE-1];                         12:         Ki <= regK[REGSIZE-1];
13:         state <= `STATE_OP;                            13:         state <= `STATE_OP;
14:     end                                                14:     end
15:     `STATE_OP : if(finish) state <= `STATE_RK_REG;     15:     `STATE_OP : if(finish) state <= `STATE_RK_REG;
16:     `STATE_RK_REG : begin                              16:     `STATE_RK_REG : begin
17:         Ki <= radom_value;                             17:         Ki <= radom_value;
18:         state <= `STATE_SHFTK;                         18:         state <= `STATE_SHFTK;
19:     end                                                19:     end
20: end                                                    20: end
```

(a) Hardware case study 1   (b) Hardware case study 2

Fig. 10. Countermeasure: Initialized by random bit

leakage of Properties 1 and 3. According to the experimental results, we confirm that the success rate is approximately 50%, which is similar to randomly guessing the key bits with a probability of 1/2, see Fig. 11.

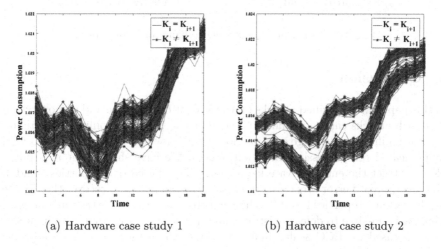

(a) Hardware case study 1   (b) Hardware case study 2

Fig. 11. Classification according to hamming distance between k_i and k_{i+1}

Second, we suggest bit masking as a countermeasure to eliminate leakage of Properties 2 and 4, as Fig. 12. This is a type of address-bit randomization [13,14]. Here, an important difference is that masking must be performed before loop operation begins. The experimental results show that this can eliminate HW leakage according to the secret value, see Fig. 13. Similar to the previous results, the success rate is approximately 50%, which is similar to randomly guessing the key bits with a probability of 1/2.

```
1: mk = key ^ (key << 1) ^ r;

2: key_bit = BN_is_bit_set(&mk, i);
3: BN_MUL(&C, &A[key_bit], &B);
```

Fig. 12. Countermeasure: Masking with random bit

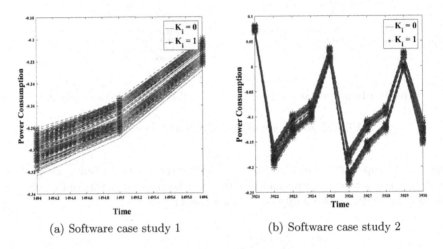

(a) Software case study 1   (b) Software case study 2

Fig. 13. Classification according to hamming weight of k_i

6   Conclusion

In this paper, we described attacks on the key bit check phase and demonstrated that such attacks can be applied to a single trace without profiling. This represents a significant advantage over previous attacks, which have typically required sophisticated pre-processing and multi-traces. We have shown that it is possible to extract the entire private key through SPA based on Properties 3 and 4. Moreover, even if error bits exist, the attacks are sufficient to recover the private key based on Properties 1 and 2. This leads to a very strong attack model, with which it is possible to defeat existing countermeasures. Note that, although this paper focused on ECC scalar multiplications, our attacks are also applicable to RSA modular exponentiation algorithms. Accordingly, we proposed possible countermeasures and confirmed that the attacks were not applicable.

However, we did not consider attacks on various encoding methods, such as k-ary, sliding window, and NAF. Thus, many open problems remain, and these pose interesting challenges. We plan to address such challenges in future.

Acknowledgments. This work was supported by Institute for Information & communications Technology Promotion(IITP) grant funded by the Korea government(MSIT) (No.20170005200011001, Development of SCR-Friendly Symmetric Key Cryptosystem and Its Application Modes)

A   Target Algorithm 1

The loop steps 4 to 13 of Algorithm 1 perform except for the most significant bit. Since steps 7 to 9 (step 10 to 11) consist of six finite field multiplications, and each loop consists of six multiplication patterns.

Algorithm 1. ECC Scalar Multiplication: Montgomery-López-Dahab Ladder

---

Input : $P = (x, y)$ a point on elliptic curve E, an n-bit scalar $k = (k_{n-1}, \cdots, k_0)_2$
Output : $Q = kP$

1: **if** $k = 0$ *or* $x = 0$ **then** output $(0, 0)$ and stop
2: **end if**
3: $X_1 \leftarrow x$, $Z_1 \leftarrow 1$, $X_2 \leftarrow x^2 + b$, $Z_2 \leftarrow x^2$
4: **for** $i := n - 2$ down to 0 **do**
5:     $Z_3 \leftarrow (X_1 Z_2 + X_2 Z_1)^2$
6:     **if** $k_i = 1$ **then**
7:         $X_1 \leftarrow x Z_3 + (X_1 Z_2)(X_2 Z_1)$, $Z_1 \leftarrow Z_3$
8:         $X_2 \leftarrow X_2^4 + b Z_2^4$, $Z_2 \leftarrow X_2^2 Z_2^2$
9:     **else**
10:         $X_2 \leftarrow x Z_3 + (X_1 Z_2)(X_2 Z_1)$, $Z_2 \leftarrow Z_3$
11:         $X_1 \leftarrow X_1^4 + b Z_1^4$, $Z_1 \leftarrow X_1^2 Z_1^2$
12:     **end if**
13: **end for**
14: $A \leftarrow Z_1 Z_2$, $B \leftarrow x Z_2$, $C \leftarrow (xA)^{-1}$
15: $D \leftarrow \left((x^2 + y) A + (B + X_2)(x Z_1 + X_1) \right) C$
16: $x_0 \leftarrow B X_1 C$, $y_0 \leftarrow (x + x_0) + y$
17: **Return** $kP = (x_0, y_0)$

B   OpenSSL Key Bit Check Function Experimental Results

The points where the key bit check function is called comprise the first PoIs, which satisfied Property 2. The points where HW leakage of the referred register address occurs comprise the second PoIs; thus, we can validate Property 4. (a) As shown in Fig. 17(a), the distribution of power consumption overlaps; so we classify into two sets using a k-means algorithm. Consequently, there are bits misclassified, the success rate is approximately 96.25%. Since the number of error bits is sufficiently small, a brute-force attack may still be feasible to recover the entire key. (b) It is possible to distinguish two groups through SPA. Here, the classification success rate is 100%, and we can recover the entire key. This shows that referenced register address according to private key bits has greater effect than the key bits, which is similar to the results in Sect. 4.1. The attack was repeated over 1000 power consumption traces.

```
 1 : int BN_is_bit_set(const BIGNUM *a, int n)
 2 : {
 3 :     int i, j;
 4 :
 5 :     bn_check_top(a);
 6 :     if (n < 0) return 0;
 7 :     i = n / BN_BITS2; j = n % BN_BITS2;
 8 :     if (a->top <= i) return 0;
 9 :     return (int)(((a->d[i]) >> j) & ((BN_ULONG)1));
10 : }
```

Fig. 14. The key bit check fucntion of OpenSSL (Software Implementation)

```
 1 : key_bit = BN_is_bit_set(&key, i);
 2 : BN_MUL(&C, &A[key_bit], &B);
```

Fig. 15. Trace acquisition range

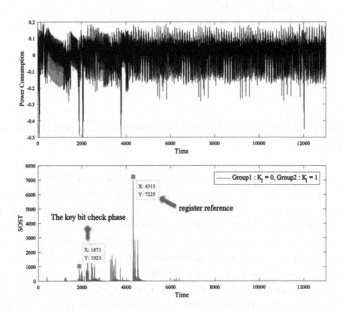

Fig. 16. Software implementation (OpenSSL): one of sub-traces (top) and SOST between two groups of sub-traces (bottom)

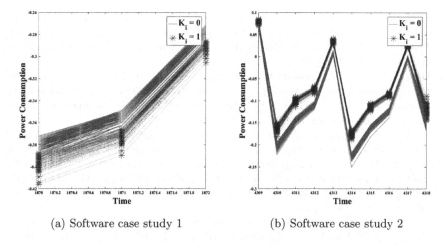

(a) Software case study 1   (b) Software case study 2

Fig. 17. Classification according to hamming weight of k_i (openSSL)

References

1. Bishop, C.M.: Pattern Recognition and Machine Learning. Information Science and Statistics. Springer, New York (2007)
2. Ciet, M., Joye, M.: (Virtually) free randomization techniques for elliptic curve cryptography. In: Qing, S., Gollmann, D., Zhou, J. (eds.) ICICS 2003. LNCS, vol. 2836, pp. 348–359. Springer, Heidelberg (2003). https://doi.org/10.1007/978-3-540-39927-8_32
3. Clavier, C., Feix, B., Gagnerot, G., Roussellet, M., Verneuil, V.: Horizontal correlation analysis on exponentiation. In: Soriano, M., Qing, S., López, J. (eds.) ICICS 2010. LNCS, vol. 6476, pp. 46–61. Springer, Heidelberg (2010). https://doi.org/10.1007/978-3-642-17650-0_5
4. Coron, J.-S.: Resistance against differential power analysis for elliptic curve cryptosystems. In: Koç, Ç.K., Paar, C. (eds.) CHES 1999. LNCS, vol. 1717, pp. 292–302. Springer, Heidelberg (1999). https://doi.org/10.1007/3-540-48059-5_25
5. Diop, I., Liardet, P.Y., Maurine, P.: Collision based attacks in practice. In: DSD 2015, pp. 367–374 (2015)
6. Diop, I., Carbone, M., Ordas, S., Linge, Y., Liardet, P.Y., Maurine, P.: Collision for estimating SCA measurement quality and related applications. In: Homma, N., Medwed, M. (eds.) CARDIS 2015. LNCS, vol. 9514, pp. 143–157. Springer, Cham (2016). https://doi.org/10.1007/978-3-319-31271-2_9
7. Duda, R.O., Hart, P.E., Stork, D.G.: Pattern Classification, 2nd edn. Wiley Interscience, New York (2001)
8. Gierlichs, B., Lemke-Rust, K., Paar, C.: Templates vs. stochastic methods. In: Goubin, L., Matsui, M. (eds.) CHES 2006. LNCS, vol. 4249, pp. 15–29. Springer, Heidelberg (2006). https://doi.org/10.1007/11894063_2
9. Hanley, N., Kim, H.S., Tunstall, M.: Exploiting collisions in addition chain-based exponentiation algorithms using a single trace. In: Nyberg, K. (ed.) CT-RSA 2015. LNCS, vol. 9048, pp. 431–448. Springer, Cham (2015). https://doi.org/10.1007/978-3-319-16715-2_23

10. Heyszl, J., Mangard, S., Heinz, B., Stumpf, F., Sigl, G.: Localized electromagnetic analysis of cryptographic implementations. In: Dunkelman, O. (ed.) CT-RSA 2012. LNCS, vol. 7178, pp. 231–244. Springer, Heidelberg (2012). https://doi.org/10.1007/978-3-642-27954-6_15

11. Heyszl, J., Ibing, A., Mangard, S., De Santis, F., Sigl, G.: Clustering algorithms for non-profiled single-execution attacks on exponentiations. In: Francillon, A., Rohatgi, P. (eds.) CARDIS 2013. LNCS, vol. 8419, pp. 79–93. Springer, Cham (2014). https://doi.org/10.1007/978-3-319-08302-5_6

12. Homma, N., Miyamoto, A., Aoki, T., Satoh, A.: Comparative power analysis of modular exponentiation algorithms. IEEE Trans. Comput. **59**(6), 795–807 (2010)

13. Itoh, K., Izu, T., Takenaka, M.: A practical countermeasure against address-bit differential power analysis. In: Walter, C.D., Koç, Ç.K., Paar, C. (eds.) CHES 2003. LNCS, vol. 2779, pp. 382–396. Springer, Heidelberg (2003). https://doi.org/10.1007/978-3-540-45238-6_30

14. Izumi, M., Ikegami, J., Sakiyama, K., Ohta, K.: Improved countermeasure against address-bit DPA for ECC scalar multiplication. In: DATE 2010, pp. 981–984. IEEE (2010)

15. Joye, M., Yen, S.-M.: The montgomery powering ladder. In: Kaliski, B.S., Koç, K., Paar, C. (eds.) CHES 2002. LNCS, vol. 2523, pp. 291–302. Springer, Heidelberg (2003). https://doi.org/10.1007/3-540-36400-5_22

16. Joye, M.: Highly regular right-to-left algorithms for scalar multiplication. In: Paillier, P., Verbauwhede, I. (eds.) CHES 2007. LNCS, vol. 4727, pp. 135–147. Springer, Heidelberg (2007). https://doi.org/10.1007/978-3-540-74735-2_10

17. Kocher, P.C.: Timing attacks on implementations of Diffie-Hellman, RSA, DSS, and other systems. In: Koblitz, N. (ed.) CRYPTO 1996. LNCS, vol. 1109, pp. 104–113. Springer, Heidelberg (1996). https://doi.org/10.1007/3-540-68697-5_9

18. Kocher, P., Jaffe, J., Jun, B.: Differential power analysis. In: Wiener, M. (ed.) CRYPTO 1999. LNCS, vol. 1666, pp. 388–397. Springer, Heidelberg (1999). https://doi.org/10.1007/3-540-48405-1_25

19. López, J., Dahab, R.: Fast multiplication on elliptic curves over $GF(2^m)$ without precomputation. In: Koç, Ç.K., Paar, C. (eds.) CHES 1999. LNCS, vol. 1717, pp. 316–327. Springer, Heidelberg (1999). https://doi.org/10.1007/3-540-48059-5_27

20. May, D., Muller, H.L., Smart, N.P.: Random register renaming to foil DPA. In: Koç, Ç.K., Naccache, D., Paar, C. (eds.) CHES 2001. LNCS, vol. 2162, pp. 28–38. Springer, Heidelberg (2001). https://doi.org/10.1007/3-540-44709-1_4

21. Montgomery, P.: Speeding the pollard and elliptic curve methods of factorization. Math. Comput. **48**(177), 243–264 (1987)

22. Nascimento, E., Chmielewski, L., Oswald, D., Schwabe, P.: Attacking embedded ECC implmentations through cmov side channels. In: Avanzi, R., Heys, H. (eds.) Selected Areas in Cryptography SAC 2016. Lecture Notes in Computer Science, vol. 10532, pp. 99–119. Springer, Cham (2016)

23. Perin, G., Imbert, L., Torres, L., Maurine, P.: Attacking randomized exponentiations using unsupervised learning. In: Prouff, E. (ed.) COSADE 2014. LNCS, vol. 8622, pp. 144–160. Springer, Cham (2014). https://doi.org/10.1007/978-3-319-10175-0_11

24. Perin, G., Chmielewski, Ł.: A semi-parametric approach for side-channel attacks on protected RSA implementations. In: Homma, N., Medwed, M. (eds.) CARDIS 2015. LNCS, vol. 9514, pp. 34–53. Springer, Cham (2016). https://doi.org/10.1007/978-3-319-31271-2_3

25. Specht, R., Heyszl, J., Kleinsteuber, M., Sigl, G.: Improving non-profiled attacks on exponentiations based on clustering and extracting leakage from multi-channel high-resolution EM measurements. In: Mangard, S., Poschmann, A.Y. (eds.) COSADE 2014. LNCS, vol. 9064, pp. 3–19. Springer, Cham (2015). https://doi.org/10.1007/978-3-319-21476-4_1
26. Sugawara, T., Suzuki, D., Saeki, M.: Internal collision attack on RSA under closed EM measurement. In: SCIS (2014)
27. Sugawara, T., Suzuki, D., Saeki, M.: Two operands of multipliers in side-channel attack. In: Mangard, S., Poschmann, A.Y. (eds.) COSADE 2014. LNCS, vol. 9064, pp. 64–78. Springer, Cham (2015). https://doi.org/10.1007/978-3-319-21476-4_5
28. Walter, C.D.: Sliding windows succumbs to Big Mac attack. In: Koç, Ç.K., Naccache, D., Paar, C. (eds.) CHES 2001. LNCS, vol. 2162, pp. 286–299. Springer, Heidelberg (2001). https://doi.org/10.1007/3-540-44709-1_24

Group-Based Source-Destination Verifiable Encryption with Blacklist Checking

Zhongyuan Yao$^{(\boxtimes)}$, Yi Mu, and Guomin Yang

School of Computing and Information Technology, Institute of Cybersecurity
and Cryptology, University of Wollongong, Keiraville, Wollongong 2522, Australia
zy454@uowmail.edu.au

Abstract. We consider user conditional privacy preservation in the context of public key encryption. Unlike the full privacy preservation, our conditional one ensures that the message sender's as well as the intended receiver's privacy are well preserved while their legitimation can still be verified; besides, the actual sender of an encrypted message can only be identified by the intended receiver. Furthermore, considering the practical scenario where the communication channels between some senders and receivers are controlled with a blacklist (BL), we address the issue how a message sender proves the legitimation of the communication channel with its intended communicator according to the BL. Previous works only partially solve the former problem and there exists no solution addressing the two aforementioned problems simultaneously. In this paper, we present an encryption scheme which keeps not only the transmitted message confidential but also the user's conditional privacy preserved. Besides, given the BL, our scheme also empowers the message sender the capability to give a proof of the legitimation of the communication channel with its communication partner without leaking their identities. In other words, only message senders form unblocked communication channels are able to produce such a proof. We provide the security models for our scheme and prove its security under the random oracle model.

Keywords: Public key encryption · Blacklist checking
Conditional privacy preservation · Source-destination verifiability

1 Introduction

Background. The security concerns of the public key encryption are mainly on the secrecy of the encrypted data. Some well studied security models, such as indistinguishably and non-malleability [8,13,20], are examples catering for different security requirements of the encrypted data. However, since encryption schemes are deployed in various hostile environments, the user privacy preservation problem should also be considered seriously since the attackers may be more interested in the exact parties participated in the communication.

© Springer International Publishing AG 2017
J. K. Liu and P. Samarati (Eds.): ISPEC 2017, LNCS 10701, pp. 186–203, 2017.
https://doi.org/10.1007/978-3-319-72359-4_11

In fact, the user privacy preservation problems have been the subject of formal studies in cryptographic literature, for example, the primitives ring signature [21] and group signature [6] are popular tools protecting a message sender's privacy while still keeping the user authenticated. In the area of public key encryption (PKE), since the sender privacy preservation is considered to be an inherent property, literature related to user privacy preservation are mainly about key-privacy [4], or anonymity, which are security notions for receiver privacy preservation. In this paper, we are particularly interested in the user conditional privacy preservation property in PKE, which is different from the conventional one. The conditional privacy preservation notion keeps not only the privacy of the message sender as well as its communicator well preserved but also their legitimation publicly verifiable; besides, it also requires that, given a ciphertext, its actual sender can only be discovered by its intended receiver.

Apart from that, we take one step further by considering a more complex but practical scenario (e.g., in e-mail or other network communication systems), where an authority (or gateway) is able to forbid communications between specific message senders and receivers by blocking their communication channels, and those blocked channels are published as a blacklist by the authority. Under such condition, the message sender should be empowered with the capability to prove the legitimation of the communication channel between itself and its communicator; meanwhile, message senders from the blacklist should never be able to forge such a proof. In addition, the proof should not leak any privacy-related information of either the message sender or its communication partner.

There exists a primitive which solves our former problem partially. An example is the ring signcryption [16] which keeps the transmitted message confidential and the legitimation of the message sender publicly verifiable, but it cannot maintain the privacy preservation property of the message receiver. To the best of our knowledge, there is no solution tackling the two aforementioned problem at the same time properly.

Our Contribution. In this paper, we first present a group-based source-destination verifiable encryption scheme with blacklist checking. Our solution utilizes the zero-knowledge proof of membership and also zero-knowledge of inequality technique to handle the two previously mentioned problems, respectively.

Considering the security requirements of our scheme, we define four security models, which capture the message confidentiality, the sender and receiver privacy preservation, and the soundness of the legitimation proof. We then give security proofs under our predefined models with the help of the random oracle.

Related Work. Among all the existed primitives, the most promising one related to our problems is the ring signcryption, which was first proposed by Huang et al. [16]. As it inherits properties from both the ring signature [21] and public key encryption, this primitive provides anonymity, authenticity of the sender along with the message confidentiality. Following the work in [9], this primitive also considers protecting the receiver's privacy in the multi-recipient setting. Although some ring signcryption schemes have been proven to be insecure, this primitive remains to be a potential candidate when dealing with problems about maintaining message confidentiality and user privacy simultaneously. However, because of the inherent property of the ring-based construction, this primitive always considers the complete anonymous of the message sender rather than the user conditional privacy preservation.

The user conditional privacy preservation is a more practical and attractive research problem comparing to the complete privacy preservation. Many existing works have considered it. The work in [18] addresses the issue about anonymous authentication of messages with traceability between the on-board-units (OBUs) and roadside units (RSUs) in vehicular ad hoc networks (VANETs), this conditional privacy preservation protocol relies on the authority to trace the origin of the authenticated messages. Another similar authentication with conditional privacy example can be found in [15], where it considers not only user conditional privacy but forward user revocation in wireless networks. The work in [10] uses pseudonym techniques to construct conditional privacy preservation methods and to protect the privacy of users in the NFC electronic payment environment.

The receiver privacy preservation, or key-privacy, problem was first formalized by Bellare et al. in [4] and later extended in [1], according to their paper, the receiver's privacy means that an eavesdropper, even in possession of a given ciphertext and a list of public keys, can not tell which specific key is the one used to generate the given ciphertext. This is the reason why they call this property key-privacy or anonymity. The paper defines practical security models about the key-privacy. Although some classical encryption schemes, such as the El Gamal scheme [12] and the Cramer-Shoup scheme [7], have already provided such key-privacy property, encryption schemes with careless construction, such as the broadcast encryption [11], still cannot hold this requirement. In [19], Mohassel discusses the key-privacy problem in hybrid encryption scenario, it shows that the combination of an anonymous key encapsulation mechanism (KEM) and an anonymous data encapsulation mechanism (DEM) cannot make the resulted hybrid encryption still anonymous unless the KEM is also weakly robust [2]. After considering the relation between the robustness and collision-freeness [2] properties of the KEM, this paper finally gives non-keyed transformation to transfer a collision-free PKE into a robust PKE. Key-privacy requirement is always considered in multi-receiver settings where multiple intended receivers are conventionally included in the generated ciphertext for the benefit that they can be easily identified by the message receiver. The work [14,22] discuss key-privacy in multi-receiver encryption scheme and use extended receiver sets including users who are not the intended receivers to hide the real receiver set. The anonymous broadcast encryption in [3] is the first work considering receiver's privacy in broadcast encryption schemes, in that paper, a broadcast encryption scheme is constructed achieving anonymity and IND-CCA security against static adversaries from a key-private, IND-CCA secure PKE scheme, however, the technique in [3] is only analyzed in Random Oracle Model. Later, Libert et al. in [17] proposed an anonymous broadcast encryption scheme with adaptive security in the Standard Model.

Paper Organization. The rest of our paper is organized as follows: Sect. 2 presents some notations and preliminaries. In Sect. 3, we give the formal definition of our group-based source-destination verifiable encryption scheme with blacklist checking and also define four security models in this section for the purpose of proving the security of our scheme. Our concrete construction of the scheme is presented in detail in Sect. 4. In Sect. 5, we prove the security of our scheme under the previously defined models respectively. In Sect. 6, we give the conclusion of our paper.

2   Notations and Preliminaries

Notations. We give notations which are used through the whole paper. Let 1^k be a binary string with length k while k is also called the security parameter. Let $\{r_i\}$ denote a set while r_i is one of its elements. When $\mathcal{PK}$ represents a set, then $|\mathcal{PK}|$ denotes the number of elements in this set, however, if a is an integer, then $|a|$ denotes the length of the binary representation of that integer. Let $\mathbb{G}$ be a multiplicative group of prime order q, then $x \xleftarrow{\text{R}} G$ means the element x is randomly chosen from $\mathbb{G}$, while $X \in \mathbb{G}^l$ denotes that X is a tuple with l elements while each of them is chosen from $\mathbb{G}$. We use $\wedge$ to represent "AND" logic and $\vee$ to represent "OR" logic.

Decisional Diffie–Hellman Assumption (DDH). Let $\mathbb{G}_1$ be a multiplicative group of large prime order q with generator g. The DDH assumption for $\mathbb{G}_1$ holds if for any probabilistic polynomial time (PPT) adversary $\mathcal{A}$, the following probability is negligibly close to $\frac{1}{2}$.

$$\Pr[a, b \leftarrow \mathbb{Z}_p; C_0 = g^{ab}; C_1 \leftarrow \mathbb{G}_1; d \leftarrow \{0, 1\} : \mathcal{A}(g^a, g^b, C_d) = d]$$

Discrete Log Problem (DLP). The DLP in $\mathbb{G}_1$ is defined as follows: given a generator g of $\mathbb{G}_1$, a random element $C \in \mathbb{G}_1$ as input, output a $x \in \mathbb{Z}_p$ such that $g^x = C$. The DLP assumption holds in $\mathbb{G}_1$ if for any PPT adversary $\mathcal{A}$, the following probability is negligible.

$$\Pr[C \leftarrow \mathbb{G}_1; g^x = C : \mathcal{A}(g, C) = x]$$

3   Definitions and Security Models

3.1   Definition of the GSVEBC

There are three parties, the message sender, verifier and receiver respectively, involved in a group-based source-destination verifiable encryption scheme with blacklist checking (GSVEBC). In this scheme, the authority can publicly publish a set of sender receiver pairs as the blacklist denoted by BL, and each item of the BL is a block rule to forbid the communication between the sender and receiver specified in that item. The message sender creates and sends encrypted messages called GSVEBC ciphertexts to the receiver. It is the verifier which verifies whether a given GSVEBC ciphertext comes from a given legitimated sender set and goes to a given legitimated receiver set without knowing the exact sender and receiver of that ciphertext. Besides, according to the blacklist BL, the verifier can also check whether the communication channel between the sender and receiver of a given GSVEBC ciphertext is blocked without learning any privacy information about them. The intended receiver of a GSVEBC ciphertext is the only party who recovers the original message as well the actual sender of that ciphertext. We give a definition of our GSVEBC scheme as follows;

Definition 1 (GSVEBC). *A group-based source-destination verifiable encryption scheme with blacklist checking (GSVEBC) scheme consists of the following polynomial time algorithms.*

- Setup(1^k): *Taking 1^k as input, this algorithm outputs the public parameter pp. For the ease of description, we assume the BL is included in pp, and each time when BL is changed by the authority, the pp should be changed accordingly.*
- KeyGen(pp): *For each user, this algorithm, on input pp, outputs a public key pair (pk, sk). In order to make the notation more clear, let (pk_s, sk_s) denote a sender's key pair and (pk_r, sk_r) be a receiver's key pair.*
- Enc(pp, m, sk_s, pk_r, $\mathcal{PK}_S$, $\mathcal{PK}_R$): *This PPT algorithm can be executed by every message sender. Given a message m, the public parameter pp, two users' public key sets $\mathcal{PK}_S$, $\mathcal{PK}_R$, the message sender's private key sk_s and the receiver's public key pk_r, this algorithm outputs a GSVEBC ciphertext C.*
- Ver(pp, C): *The verification algorithm is deterministic. Taking pp and a given GSVEBC ciphertext C as inputs, that algorithm would first check whether the ciphertext comes from a given legitimated sender set and is sent to a given legitimated receiver set. Note that the given legitimated sender and receiver set should be included in the ciphertext C. After that, this algorithm can also check whether the communication between the sender and receiver of that given ciphertext C is permitted according to the blacklist BL included in pp. This algorithm returns a symbol of true if and only if all the above checks are successfully complete, otherwise, it returns a symbol of false. For privacy consideration, this algorithm is executed without the knowledge of the exact sender and receiver of the ciphertext C.*
- Dec(pp, C, sk_r): *The decryption algorithm Dec is deterministic and executed by the intended receiver. When a receiver gets C, he would first execute the previous verification algorithm Ver, if Ver returns a symbol of false, he just drops this message. Otherwise, the receiver executes Dec, which takes pp, C and the receiver's private key sk_R as inputs, and recovers the original message m as well the actual sender of C.*

Definition 2 (Security Model towards Message Confidentiality). *Setting the security parameter as k, then given our scheme GSVEBC = (Setup, Key-Gen, Enc, Ver, Dec), a polynomial $n(\cdot)$, a PPT (polynomial probabilistic time) adversary $\mathcal{A}$ and a simulator $\mathcal{S}$, we consider the following game between a simulator $\mathcal{S}$ and an adversary $\mathcal{A}$ capturing the message confidentiality property of our scheme:*

- *Setup phase: At the setup phase, the* Setup *algorithm of the scheme, which takes* 1^k *as input, is first run by* S *to produce the system parameter pp. Given a polynomial* $n(\cdot)$, S *runs* KeyGen, *with pp as input,* $n(k)$ *times. After all executions are properly finished,* S *gets a public key set* $\mathcal{PK}$, *a private key set* $\mathcal{SK}$, *where* $|\mathcal{PK}| = |\mathcal{SK}| = n(k)$. *The adversary* $\mathcal{A}$ *is given pp and* $\mathcal{PK}$.
- *Corruption phase: In order to enable* $\mathcal{A}$ *to do encryption itself,* $\mathcal{A}$ *is permitted to corrupt users with public keys from the set* $\mathcal{PK}$. *Namely,* $\mathcal{A}$ *can get the secret key of a user after submitting the corresponding public key to* S *as the query message in this phase. Let* $\mathcal{UPK}$ *denote the collection of all uncorrupted users.*
- *Decryption phase 1:* $\mathcal{A}$ *can also ask decryption queries adaptively to* S. *That is, when* $\mathcal{A}$ *provides* S *a valid ciphertext,* S *needs to return the corresponding plaintext of that ciphertext to* $\mathcal{A}$.
- *Challenge phase:* $\mathcal{A}$ *chooses two messages* m_0, m_1 *from* $\mathcal{M}$, *two public keys* pk_s, pk_r *from* $\mathcal{UPK}$ *as the sender and receiver's public key respectively, two subsets* $\mathcal{PK}_S, \mathcal{PK}_R$ *from* $\mathcal{UPK}$ *such that* $pk_s \in \mathcal{PK}_S, pk_r \in \mathcal{PK}_R, |\mathcal{PK}_S| \geq 2, |\mathcal{PK}_R| \geq 2$, *and then sends them to the simulator. Upon receiving those information,* S *randomly chooses a bit b from* $\{0, 1\}$ *and encrypts* m_b *using the encryption algorithm of our scheme, which takes* $m_b, sk_s, pk_r, \mathcal{PK}_S, \mathcal{PK}_R$ *and pp as inputs. After that, the generated ciphertext is given to* $\mathcal{A}$ *as the challenge ciphertext.*
- *Decryption phase 2: After receiving the challenge ciphertext,* $\mathcal{A}$ *can still query the decryption oracle adaptively with the only restriction that the queried ciphertext must be different from the challenge one.*
- *Guess phase: At the end of the game,* $\mathcal{A}$ *outputs the guess* b' *from* $\{0, 1\}$ *about b. If* $b' = b$, *then* $\mathcal{A}$ *succeeds in the game, otherwise* $\mathcal{A}$ *fails.*

Remark: $\mathcal{A}$ is allowed to ask hash queries under the random oracle model. According to the defined model, let $\mathsf{Adv}^{\mathcal{A}}_{\mathsf{IND\text{-}CCA}}$ denote the probability that $\mathcal{A}$ wins the above game over random guess, then $\mathsf{Adv}^{\mathcal{A}}_{\mathsf{IND\text{-}CCA}} = \left| \Pr\left[b' = b\right] - \frac{1}{2} \right|$.

Definition 3 (Security Model towards Sender Privacy Preservation).
Setting the security parameter as k, then given our scheme GSVEBC = (Setup, KeyGen, Enc, Ver, Dec), *a polynomial* $n(\cdot)$, *a PPT (polynomial probabilistic time) adversary* $\mathcal{A}$ *and a simulator* S, *let's consider the following game, which captures the sender privacy property, played by* $\mathcal{A}$ *and* S:

- *Setup phase: At the setup phase, the* Setup *algorithm of the scheme, which takes* 1^k *as input, is first run by* S *to produce the system public parameter pp. Given a polynomial* $n(\cdot)$, *the simulator runs* KeyGen, *with pp as input,* $n(k)$ *times. After all executions are properly finished,* S *gets a public key set* $\mathcal{PK}$, *a private key set* $\mathcal{SK}$, *where* $|\mathcal{PK}| = |\mathcal{SK}| = n(k)$. *The adversary* $\mathcal{A}$ *is given pp and* $\mathcal{PK}$.
- *Corruption phase: In order to enable* $\mathcal{A}$ *to do encryption itself,* $\mathcal{A}$ *is permitted to corrupt users with public keys from the set* $\mathcal{PK}$. *Namely,* $\mathcal{A}$ *can get the secret key of a user after submitting the corresponding public key to* S *as the query message in this phase. Let* $\mathcal{UPK}$ *denote the collection of all uncorrupted users.*

- *Sender extraction phase 1: When $\mathcal{A}$ makes such kind of query, he submits a ciphertext to $\mathcal{S}$, then he gets the public key of the original encryptor of that ciphertext from $\mathcal{S}$ when it is valid, otherwise, he gets nothing.*
- *Challenge phase: $\mathcal{A}$ chooses one message m from $\mathcal{M}$, pk_r from $\mathcal{UPK}$ as the receiver's public key and two subsets $\mathcal{PK}_S, \mathcal{PK}_R$ from $\mathcal{UPK}$ such that $pk_r \in \mathcal{PK}_R, |\mathcal{PK}_S| \geq 2, |\mathcal{PK}_R| \geq 2$, then sends them to $\mathcal{S}$. $\mathcal{S}$ randomly chooses a public key pk_s from the chosen subset $\mathcal{PK}_S$, and encrypts m by taking pk_s, $sk_s, pk_r, \mathcal{PK}_S, \mathcal{PK}_R$ and pp as inputs. The corresponding ciphertext is given to $\mathcal{A}$ as challenge ciphertext.*
- *Sender extraction phase 2: After receiving the challenge ciphertext, $\mathcal{A}$ can still ask sender extraction queries with the only constraint that the queried ciphertext must not be identical to the challenge one. The simulator behaves the same as in the sender extraction phase 1 in this phase.*
- *Guess phase: At the end of the game, $\mathcal{A}$ outputs his guess pk'_s about the public key of the actual sender of the challenge ciphertext from the chosen subset $\mathcal{PK}_S$. If $pk'_s = pk_s$, then $\mathcal{A}$ succeeds in the game, otherwise $\mathcal{A}$ fails.*

Remark: Under the random oracle model, $\mathcal{A}$ is allowed to ask hash queries. According to the defined model, let $\text{Adv}^{\mathcal{A}}_{\text{Sender-Anonymity}}$ denote the probability that $\mathcal{A}$ wins the above game over random guess, then $\text{Adv}^{\mathcal{A}}_{\text{Sender-Anonymity}} = \left| \Pr\left[pk'_s = pk_s \right] - \frac{1}{|\mathcal{PK}_S|} \right|$, where $|\mathcal{PK}_S|$ represents the size of the subset $\mathcal{PK}_S$.

Definition 4 (Security Model towards Receiver Privacy Preservation).
Setting the security parameter as k, then given our scheme GSVEBC = (Setup, KeyGen, Enc, Ver, Dec), a polynomial $n(\cdot)$, a PPT (polynomial probabilistic time) adversary $\mathcal{A}$ and a PPT simulator $\mathcal{S}$, let's consider the following game, which captures the receiver privacy property, played by $\mathcal{A}$ and $\mathcal{S}$:

- *Setup phase: At the setup phase, the Setup algorithm of the scheme, which takes 1^k as input, is first run by $\mathcal{S}$ to produce the public parameter pp. Given a polynomial $n(\cdot)$, the simulator runs KeyGen, with pp as input, $n(k)$ times. After all executions are properly finished, $\mathcal{S}$ gets a public key set $\mathcal{PK}$, a private key set $\mathcal{SK}$, where $|\mathcal{PK}| = |\mathcal{SK}| = n(k)$. The adversary $\mathcal{A}$ is given pp and $\mathcal{PK}$.*
- *Corruption phase: In order to enable $\mathcal{A}$ to do encryption itself, $\mathcal{A}$ is permitted to corrupt users with public keys from the set $\mathcal{PK}$. Namely, $\mathcal{A}$ can get the secret key of a user after submitting the corresponding public key to $\mathcal{S}$ as the query message in this phase. Let $\mathcal{UPK}$ denote the collection of all uncorrupted users.*
- *Receiver extraction phase 1: In this phase, when $\mathcal{A}$ submits a ciphertext to $\mathcal{S}$, $\mathcal{S}$ needs to send back the public key of the actual receiver of that ciphertext to $\mathcal{A}$ as response when it is valid. Otherwise, $\mathcal{A}$ gets nothing.*
- *Challenge Phase: In the phase, $\mathcal{A}$ randomly chooses a message m from $\mathcal{M}$, pk_s from $\mathcal{UPK}$ as the sender's public key, two public key pk_0, pk_1 and two public key sets $\mathcal{PK}_S$, $\mathcal{PK}_R$ from $\mathcal{UPK}$ such that $pk_s \in \mathcal{PK}_S, pk_0, pk_1 \in \mathcal{PK}_R, |\mathcal{PK}_S| \geq 2, |\mathcal{PK}_R| \geq 2$. $\mathcal{A}$ then sends those information to $\mathcal{S}$. $\mathcal{S}$ randomly chooses $pk_c \in \{pk_0, pk_1\}$ as the receiver's public key and encrypts message m using algorithm Enc, which takes $m, sk_s, pk_s, pk_c, \mathcal{PK}_S, \mathcal{PK}_R$ and pp*

as inputs. S sends the generated ciphertext as response and challenge cipher-text to A.

- **Receiver extraction phase 2:** *After the challenge phase, A can still ask S to extract the public key of the receiver of a valid ciphertext for him adaptively, the only restriction is that A cannot use the challenge ciphertext as a queried message in this phase.*
- **Guess phase:** *At the end of the game, A would make a guess c' about the public key pk_c of the receiver of the challenge ciphertext from the subset $\mathcal{PK}_R$. If $c' = c$, then A succeeds in the game, otherwise A fails.*

Remark: A is allowed to ask hash queries under the random oracle model. According to the defined model, let $\mathsf{Adv}^{\mathcal{A}}_{\text{Receiver-Anonymity}}$ denote the probability that A wins the above game over random guess, then $\mathsf{Adv}^{\mathcal{A}}_{\text{Receiver-Anonymity}} = \left| \Pr\left[c = c' \right] - \frac{1}{2} \right|$.

Definition 5 (Security Model towards Soundness of Legitimation Proof). *Setting the security parameter as k, then given our scheme GSVEBC = (Setup, KeyGen, Enc, Ver, Dec), a polynomial $n(\cdot)$, a PPT (polynomial prob-abilistic time) adversary A and a PPT simulator S, let's consider the following game, which captures the user impersonation resistance property, played by A and S:*

- **Setup phase:** *At the setup phase, the Setup algorithm of the scheme, which takes 1^k as input, is first run by S to produce the public parameter pp, here the blacklist BL is also generated by S and included in pp. Given a polyno-mial $n(\cdot)$, the simulator runs KeyGen, with pp as input, $n(k)$ times. After all executions are properly finished, S gets a public key set $\mathcal{PK}$, a private key set $\mathcal{SK}$, where $|\mathcal{PK}| = |\mathcal{SK}| = n(k)$. The adversary A is given pp and $\mathcal{PK}$.*
- **Corruption phase:** *In order to enable A to do encryption itself, A is permitted to corrupt users with public keys from the set $\mathcal{PK}$. Namely, A can get the secret key of a user after submitting the corresponding public key to S as the query message in this phase. Let $\mathcal{UPK}$ denote the collection of all uncorrupted users.*
- **Decryption phase:** *A can also ask decryption queries adaptively to S. That is, when A provides S a valid ciphertext, S needs to return the corresponding plaintext of that ciphertext to A.*
- **Forge phase:** *In this phase, A chooses a message $m \in \mathcal{M}$, one sender-receiver pair g^{S_i}, g^{R_j} from BL randomly as the message sender and intended receiver's public key respectively, two user sets $\mathcal{PK}_S, \mathcal{PK}_R \in \mathcal{UPK}$ as its corresponding message sender and receiver set. After that, A tries to produce a valid cipher-text CT. A sends $(m, g^{S_i}, g^{R_j}, \mathcal{PK}_S, \mathcal{PK}_R, CT)$ to S. S outputs 1 if and only if $\mathsf{Dec}(R_j, CT) = (g^{S_i}, m) \bigwedge \mathsf{Ver}(pp, CT) = 1$. Otherwise, S outputs 0.*

Remark: A is allowed to ask hash queries under the random oracle model. According to the defined model, let $\mathsf{Adv}^{\mathcal{A}}_{\text{Soundness}}$ denote the probability that A wins the above game, then $\mathsf{Adv}^{\mathcal{A}}_{\text{Soundness}} = \left| \Pr[\mathsf{Dec}(R_j, CT) = (g^{S_i}, m) \bigwedge \mathsf{Ver}(pp, CT) = 1] \right|$.

4   Our Concrete Construction

For the ease of description, we first give a group-based source-destination verifiable encryption scheme without blacklist checking capability, then we extend this scheme to the one with full functionalities.

4.1   A Simple Construction Without Blacklist Checking

Setting the security parameter as k, our scheme works as follows;

- Setup(1^k): On input 1^k, it produces a cyclic group $\mathbb{G}$ of large prime order q with generator g, where $\mathbb{G}$ is a subgroup of $\mathbb{Z}_p^*$ and $q|p-1$. This algorithm also outputs a description of the message space $\mathcal{M} = \{0,1\}^q$ and a ciphertext space $\mathcal{C}$. $\mathbb{G}, q, g, \mathcal{M}, \mathcal{C}$ are considered as the system parameter pp and default inputs to all the following algorithms. pp also includes three collision resistance hash functions: $H_1 : \{0,1\}^q \times \mathbb{G}^3 \to \mathbb{Z}_q, H_2 : \mathbb{G} \to \{0,1\}^q, H_3 : \{0,1\}^* \to \mathbb{Z}_q$.
- KeyGen($\cdot$): For one user, U_i for example, he randomly chooses $x_i \in \mathbb{Z}_q$ as his private key and computes $y_i = g^{x_i} \in \mathbb{G}$ as his corresponding public key. Assuming the public key set $\mathcal{PK} = \{\ldots, y_i, \ldots\}$ contains all users' public key and is also published publicly.
- Enc($m, sk_s, pk_r, \mathcal{PK}_S, \mathcal{PK}_R$): When a sender, U_i, wants to send a message to a receiver, U_j, for the purpose of illustrating our scheme more clear, let S_i, R_i denote the sender U_i and receiver U_j's secret key sk_s, sk_r respectively, accordingly, the sender and receiver's public key should be $pk_s = g^{S_i}$ and $pk_r = g^{R_j}$. Given a message $m \in \mathcal{M}$, the sender encrypts m as follows;

$$r_1 \xleftarrow{R} \mathbb{Z}_q, C_1 = g^{r_1}, C_2 = g^{S_i r_1}, C_3 = g^{R_j r_1},$$
$$r_2 = H_1(m, g^{S_i}, g^{R_j}, g^{S_i R_j r_1}),$$
$$C_4 = g^{S_i r_2}, C_5 = g^{S_i} g^{S_i R_j r_2}, C_6 = m \oplus H_2(g^{S_i R_j \cdot (r_1 + r_2)}).$$

After that, the sender chooses a subgroup $\mathcal{PK}_S \subset \mathcal{PK}$, which includes the sender's public key g^{S_i}, and then proves its legitimation in that group. Here, we utilize the zero-knowledge proof technique to deal with the group membership issue. That is, the sender needs to give a proof like:

$$pf(S_i : \log_g g^{S_i} = \log_{C_1} C_2 = \log_{g^{r_1}} (g^{S_i})^{r_1} \wedge g^{S_i} \in \mathcal{PK}_S).$$

To do such a proof, the sender does as follows;

- For each public key $g^{x_l} \in \mathcal{PK}_S$ except g^{S_i}, the sender chooses challenge and response c_l, z_l randomly from $\mathbb{Z}_q$ respectively, then it computes two commitments

$$\alpha_l = g^{z_l}(g^{x_l})^{c_l}, \beta_l = (C_1)^{z_l}(C_2)^{c_l}.$$

- For the sender's own pubic key g^{S_i}, it chooses $w_i \in \mathbb{Z}_q$ and sets the commitments as

$$\alpha_i = g^{w_i}, \beta_i = (C_1)^{w_i}.$$

Let $\{\alpha\}$ denote commitments set $\{\dots\alpha_l\dots\alpha_i\dots\}$ and $\{\beta\}$ commitments set $\{\dots\beta_l\dots\beta_i\dots\}$, where $|\alpha| = |\beta| = |\mathcal{PK}_S|$. The sender computes its challenge and response as:

$$h = H_3(\{\alpha\}, \{\beta\}, C_1, C_2, C_3, C_4, C_5, C_6),$$

$$c_i = h - \sum_{g^{x_l} \in \mathcal{PK}_S} c_l, z_i = w_i - c_i S_i.$$

- The sender sets the challenges set as $\{c\} = \{\dots c_i \dots c_l \dots\}$ the responses set as $\{z\} = \{\dots z_i \dots z_l \dots\}$, and value this two sets $\{c\}, \{z\}$ as the proof value.

The sender needs still to prove to the verifier that the generated ciphertext is sent to a legitimated receiver. To do this, the sender chooses a receiver subset $\mathcal{PK}_R \subset \mathcal{PK}$, which includes the receiver's public key, and gives a proof like:

$$pf(r_1 : \log_g C_1 = \log_{g^{R_j}} C_3 \wedge g^{R_j} \in \mathcal{PK}_R),$$

the sender generates the proof as follows;

- For each public key $g^{x_t} \in \mathcal{PK}_R$ except the intended receiver's public key g^{R_j}, the sender chooses challenge and response $\widehat{c}_t, \widehat{z}_t$ randomly from $\mathbb{Z}_q$ respectively, then it computes the commitments

$$\widehat{\alpha}_t = g^{\widehat{z}_t}(C_1)^{\widehat{c}_t}, \widehat{\beta}_t = (g^{x_t})^{\widehat{z}_t}(C_3)^{\widehat{c}_t}.$$

- For the intended receiver's pubic key g^{R_j}, it chooses $\widehat{w}_j \in \mathbb{Z}_q$ and sets the commitments as

$$\widehat{\alpha}_j = g^{\widehat{w}_j}, \widehat{\beta}_j = (g^{R_j})^{\widehat{w}_j}.$$

Let $\widehat{\{\alpha\}}$ denote commitments set $\{\dots\widehat{\alpha}_t\dots\widehat{\alpha}_j\dots\}$ and $\widehat{\{\beta\}}$ $\{\dots\widehat{\beta}_t\dots\widehat{\beta}_j\dots\}$ respectively, where $|\widehat{\{\alpha\}}| = |\widehat{\{\beta\}}| = |\mathcal{PK}_R|$. The sender computes its challenge and response as:

$$\widehat{h} = H_3(\widehat{\{\alpha\}}, \widehat{\{\beta\}}, C_1, C_2, C_3, C_4, C_5, C_6),$$

$$\widehat{c}_j = \widehat{h} - \sum_{g^{x_t} \in \mathcal{PK}_R} \widehat{c}_t, \widehat{z}_j = \widehat{w}_j - \widehat{c}_j r_1$$

- The sender sets the challenges set as $\widehat{\{c\}} = \{\dots\widehat{c}_j\dots\widehat{c}_t\dots\}$ the responses set as $\widehat{\{z\}} = \{\dots\widehat{z}_j\dots\widehat{z}_t\dots\}$, and value this two sets $\widehat{\{c\}}, \widehat{\{z\}}$ as the proof value.

After the two proofs are generated, the final ciphertext should be $CT = (C_1, C_2, C_3, C_4, C_5, C_6, \mathcal{PK}_S, \{c\}, \{z\}, \mathcal{PK}_R, \widehat{\{c\}}, \widehat{\{z\}})$.

- $\mathsf{Ver}(CT)$: Every user can act as the verifier. Upon receiving a given ciphertext like the above format $CT = (C_1, C_2, C_3, C_4, C_5, C_6, \mathcal{PK}_S, \{c\}, \{z\}, \mathcal{PK}_R, \widehat{\{c\}}, \widehat{\{z\}})$, a verifier does the following steps to verify the validity of the ciphertext:

- For the ciphertext components $(C_1, C_2, C_3, C_4, C_5, C_6, \mathcal{PK}_S, \{c\}, \{z\})$, the verifier recomputes

$$\alpha'_l = g^{z_l}(g^{x_l})^{c_l}, \beta'_l = (C_1)^{z_l}(C_2)^{c_l} \text{ for each } g^{x_l} \in \mathcal{PK}_S$$

and gets two sets $\{\alpha'\} = \{\ldots \alpha'_l \ldots\}, \{\beta'\} = \{\ldots \beta'_l \ldots\}$, then it checks whether the equation

$$H_3(\{\alpha'\}, \{\beta'\}, C_1, C_2, C_3, C_4, C_5, C_6) = \sum_{c_l \in \{c\}} c_l$$

holds. If no, it returns a symbol of false and drops this ciphertext, otherwise it continues to the next step.

- For the ciphertext components $(C_1, C_2, C_3, C_4, C_5, C_6, \mathcal{PK}_R, \widehat{\{c\}}, \widehat{\{z\}})$, the verifier further computes

$$\widehat{\alpha'}_t = g^{\widehat{z}_t}(C_1)^{\widehat{c}_t}, \widehat{\beta'}_t = (g^{x_t})^{\widehat{z}_t}(C_3)^{\widehat{c}_t} \text{ for each } g^{x_t} \in \mathcal{PK}_R.$$

Then it gets two sets $\widehat{\{\alpha'\}} = \{\ldots \widehat{\alpha'}_t \ldots \widehat{\alpha'}_j \ldots\}, \widehat{\{\beta'\}} = \{\ldots \widehat{\beta'}_t \ldots \widehat{\beta'}_j \ldots\}$. The verifier finally checks whether the equation

$$H_3(\widehat{\{\alpha'\}}, \widehat{\{\beta'\}}, C_1, C_2, C_3, C_4, C_5, C_6) = \sum_{\widehat{c}_t \in \widehat{\{c\}}} \widehat{c}_t$$

holds. If no, the verifier returns a symbol of false and drops this ciphertext, otherwise it returns a symbol of true and then relays this ciphertext to the receiver set.

- Dec(CT, R_x): This decryption algorithm are executed by all the possible receivers of a given ciphertext. When given a copy of the ciphertext $CT = (C_1, C_2, C_3, C_4, C_5, C_6, \mathcal{PK}_S, \{c\}, \{z\}, \mathcal{PK}_R, \widehat{\{c\}}, \widehat{\{z\}})$, all possible receivers in set $\mathcal{PK}_R$ do as following:
  - They would first execute the verification algorithm Ver of our scheme as a subroutine. If Ver returns false, they drop CT and return a symbol of failure, otherwise they continue to the next step.
  - Each user U_x in $\mathcal{PK}_R$ uses its secret key R_x to check whether equation $C_1^{R_x} = C_3$ holds. If not, it drops CT and returns a symbol of failure, otherwise, this user goes to the next step.
  - For each of the users whose secret key satisfying the above equation, it first gets the possible public key, which is denoted by $g^{s'}$, of the original sender of the given CT by computing

$$g^{s'} = \frac{C_5}{C_4^{R_x}},$$

then it recover the encrypted message, denoted by m', as

$$m' = C_6 \oplus H_2((C_2 C_4)^{R_x}).$$

After getting $g^{s'}$ and m', it would check whether the equation

$$C_4 = g^{s' H_1(m', g^{s'}, g^{R_x}, C_2{}^{R_x})}$$

holds, if yes, this user outputs $g^{s'}$ as the public key of the actual message sender and m' as the original message. Otherwise, this user drops CT and returns a symbol of failure.

4.2   Our Concrete Construction with Blacklist Checking

Basing on the former scheme, We give another construction to empower our scheme with blacklist checking capability. Here, for simplicity, we assume the blacklist BL is publicly produced by the system authority. It contains numbers of block rule and each of which can be expressed as $< pk_s, pk_r >$, where the former is one specific sender's and the other is one specific receiver's public key respectively, such block rule is used to disable the communication from one message sender to one receiver. Our scheme assures that a verifier can check whether a given ciphertext should be rejected according to the BL.

By applying the technique of zero-knowledge proof of inequality of two discrete logarithms, which was proposed in [5], we find a way to extend our original scheme to a scheme with blacklist checking, which only add a set of proof values to the original one. Because those two schemes are pretty similar, we only give explicit description of the most different part between them.

Our public key encryption scheme with source-destination verifiability and block rules checking consists of the following polynomial time algorithms.

- Setup(1^k): This algorithm is similar to the previous scheme except that the public parameter pp should include the blacklist BL. Notice that pp is also considered as default input to all the following algorithms.
- KeyGen($\cdot$): This algorithm is also identical to the aforementioned one.
- Enc($m, sk_s, pk_r, \mathcal{PK}_S, \mathcal{PK}_R$): Apart from the encryption process of the encryption scheme of the previous scheme, here the sender also needs to generate a proof to convince the verifier that the generated ciphertext should not be blocked according to the blacklist. Assuming there is a blacklist in pp like follows;

$< . , . >$
$< g^S, g^R >$
$< . , . >$

Assuming there is one message sender with identity g^{S_i}, one ciphertext

$$CT = (C_1, C_2, C_3, C_4, C_5, C_6, \mathcal{PK}_S, \{c\}, \{z\}, \mathcal{PK}_R, \{\widehat{c}\}, \{\widehat{z}\})$$

which is generated by that sender and sent to a receiver with identity g^{R_j}, for each block rule, $< g^S, g^R >$ for example, in the blacklist, the message sender needs to prove that CT does not come form a user with identity g^S or goes to a user with identity g^R. That is, according to our scheme, the message sender should produce a proof like

$$pf((S_i \vee r_1) : \log_{C_1} C_2 \neq \log_g g^S \vee \log_g C_1 \neq \log_{g^R} C_3)$$

for this rule.

According to the technique given in [5], the message sender produces such a proof pf for that ciphertext basing on the following different conditions of CT;

- When $\log_{C_1} C_2 = \log_g g^S$ and $\log_g C_1 \neq \log_{g^R} C_3$, that is $g^{S_i} = g^S$ and $g^{R_j} \neq g^R$:

  * For the case $g^{S_i} = g^S$, the message sender needs to simulate a proof like
    $$pf((\gamma = S_i \cdot \delta, \delta) : St_0 = g^\gamma/(g^S)^\delta \neq 1 \vee St_1 = (g^{r_1})^\gamma/(g^{S_i r_1})^\delta = 1),$$
    where $\delta \in_R \mathbb{Z}_q$.

    That is, the message sender first chooses two statements $St_0 \in \mathbb{G}$ and $St_1 = 1 \in \mathbb{G}$, a challenge $CH \in \mathbb{Z}_q$ and two responses $e_0, e_1 \in \mathbb{Z}_q$ respectively, and sets the two commitments

    $$COM_0 = St_0{}^{CH}(g)^{e_0}/(g^S)^{e_1},$$
    $$COM_1 = St_1{}^{CH}(g^{r_1})^{e_0}/(g^{S_i r_1})^{e_1}$$

  * For the case $g^{R_j} \neq g^R$, the message sender gives a real proof like
    $$pf((\widehat{\gamma} = r_1 \cdot \widehat{\delta}, \widehat{\delta}) : \widehat{St_0} = (g^R)^{\widehat{\gamma}}/(g^{R_j r_1})^{\widehat{\delta}} \neq 1 \vee \widehat{St_1} = (g)^{\widehat{\gamma}}/(g^{r_1})^{\widehat{\delta}} = 1),$$
    where $\widehat{\delta} \in_R \mathbb{Z}_q$.

    That is, the message sender first chooses two elements $\widehat{w_0}, \widehat{w_1} \in \mathbb{Z}_q$ and computes the two commitments

    $$\widehat{COM_0} = (g^R)^{\widehat{w_0}}/(g^{R_j r_1})^{\widehat{w_1}}, \widehat{COM_1} = (g)^{\widehat{w_0}}/(g^{r_1})^{\widehat{w_1}}.$$

    The sender then computes a hash value

    $$X = H_3(COM_0, COM_1, \widehat{COM_0}, \widehat{COM_1})$$

    and sets the challenge of this proof as $\widehat{CH} = X - CH$, the two responses should be

    $$\widehat{e_0} = \widehat{w_0} - \widehat{CH} \cdot \widehat{\gamma}, \widehat{e_1} = \widehat{w_1} - \widehat{CH} \cdot \widehat{\delta}$$

    respectively.

  * After all the required values are properly computed, let pf denote the proof values for that block rule, then

    $$pf = (St_0, St_1, CH, e_0, e_1, \widehat{St_0}, \widehat{St_1}, \widehat{CH}, \widehat{e_0}, \widehat{e_1}).$$

- If $\log_{C_1} C_2 \neq \log_g g^S$ and $\log_g C_1 = \log_{g^R} C_3$, that is $g^{S_i} \neq g^S$ and $g^{R_j} = g^R$:

* For the case $g^{R_j} = g^R$, the message sender needs to simulate a proof like
$$pf(\widehat{\gamma} = r_1 \cdot \widehat{\delta}, \widehat{\delta}) : \widehat{St_0} = (g^R)^{\widehat{\gamma}}/(g^{R_j r_1})^{\widehat{\delta}} \neq 1 \vee \widehat{St_1} = (g)^{\widehat{\gamma}}/(g^{r_1})^{\widehat{\delta}} = 1),$$
where $\widehat{\delta} \in_R \mathbb{Z}_q$.

That is, the message sender chooses two statements $\widehat{St_0} \in \mathbb{G}$ and $\widehat{St_1} = 1 \in \mathbb{G}$, a challenge $\widehat{CH} \in \mathbb{Z}_q$ and two responses $\widehat{e_0}, \widehat{e_1} \in \mathbb{Z}_q$ respectively, and sets the two commitments

$$\widehat{COM_0} = \widehat{St_0}^{\widehat{CH}} (g^R)^{\widehat{e_0}}/(g^{R_j r_1})^{\widehat{e_1}},$$
$$\widehat{COM_1} = \widehat{St_1}^{\widehat{CH}} (g)^{\widehat{e_0}}/(g^{r_1})^{\widehat{e_1}}.$$

* For the case $g^{S_i} \neq g^S$, the message sender gives a real proof like $pf((\gamma = S_i \cdot \delta, \delta) : St_0 = (g)^{\gamma}/(g^S)^{\delta} \neq 1 \vee St_1 = (g^{r_1})^{\gamma}/(g^{S_i r_1})^{\delta} = 1)$, where $\delta \in_R \mathbb{Z}_q$.

That is, the message sender first chooses two elements $w_0, w_1 \in \mathbb{Z}_q$ and computes the two commitments

$$COM_0 = (g)^{w_0}/(g^S)^{w_1}, COM_1 = (g^{r_1})^{w_0}/(g^{S_i r_1})^{w_1}.$$

The sender then computes a hash value

$$X = H_3(COM_0, COM_1, \widehat{COM_0}, \widehat{COM_1})$$

and sets the challenge of this proof as $CH = X - \widehat{CH}$, the two responses should be

$$e_0 = w_0 - CH \cdot \gamma, \ e_1 = w_1 - CH \cdot \delta$$

respectively.
* After all the required values are properly computed, let pf denote the proof values for that block rule, then

$$pf = (St_0, St_1, CH, e_0, e_1, \widehat{St_0}, \widehat{St_1}, \widehat{CH}, \widehat{e_0}, \widehat{e_1})$$

- If $\log_{C_1} C_2 \neq \log_g g^S$ and $\log_g C_1 \neq \log_{g^R} C_3$, that is $g^{S_i} \neq g^S$ and $g^{R_j} \neq g^R$:
  * For the case $g^{S_i} \neq g^S$, the message sender gives a real proof like $pf((\gamma = S_i \cdot \delta, \delta) : St_0 = (g)^{\gamma}/(g^S)^{\delta} \neq 1 \vee St_1 = (g^{r_1})^{\gamma}/(g^{S_i r_1})^{\delta} = 1)$, where $\delta \in_R \mathbb{Z}_q$.

  That is, the message sender first chooses two elements $w_0, w_1 \in \mathbb{Z}_q$ and computes the two commitments

  $$COM_0 = (g)^{w_0}/(g^S)^{w_1}, \ COM_1 = (g^{r_1})^{w_0}/(g^{S_i r_1})^{w_1}.$$

  The sender then chooses a challenge of this proof $CH \in \mathbb{Z}_q$, the two responses should be

  $$e_0 = w_0 - CH \cdot \gamma, \ e_1 = w_1 - CH \cdot \delta$$

  respectively.

* For the case $g^{R_j} \neq g^R$, The message sender gives a real proof like
$$pf((\widehat{\gamma} = r_1 \cdot \widehat{\delta}, \widehat{\delta}) : \widehat{St_0} = (g^R)^{\widehat{\gamma}}/(g^{R_j r_1})^{\widehat{\delta}} \neq 1 \vee \widehat{St_1} = (g)^{\widehat{\gamma}}/(g^{r_1})^{\widehat{\delta}} = 1),$$
$\widehat{\delta} \in_R \mathbb{Z}_q$.
That is, the message sender first chooses two elements $\widehat{w_0}, \widehat{w_1} \in \mathbb{Z}_q$ and computes the two commitments

$$\widehat{COM_0} = (g^R)^{\widehat{w_0}}/(g^{R_j r_1})^{\widehat{w_1}}, \widehat{COM_1} = (g)^{\widehat{w_0}}/(g^{r_1})^{\widehat{w_1}}.$$

The sender then computes a hash value

$$X = H_3(COM_0, COM_1, \widehat{COM_0}, \widehat{COM_1})$$

and sets the challenge of this proof as $\widehat{CH} = X - CH$, the two responses should be

$$\widehat{e_0} = \widehat{w_0} - \widehat{CH} \cdot \widehat{\gamma}, \ \widehat{e_1} = \widehat{w_1} - \widehat{CH} \cdot \widehat{\delta}$$

respectively.
* After all the required values are properly computed, let pf denote the proof values for that block rule, then

$$pf = (St_0, St_1, CH, e_0, e_1, \widehat{St_0}, \widehat{St_1}, \widehat{CH}, \widehat{e_0}, \widehat{e_1}).$$

Assuming there are n rules in BL, the message sender needs to generate n proofs accordingly. Let $\{pf\}$ denote all those proofs, then the full ciphertext CT should be $(C_1, C_2, C_3, C_4, C_5, C_6, \mathcal{PK}_S, \{c\}, \{z\}, \mathcal{PK}_R, \widehat{\{c\}}, \widehat{\{z\}}, \{pf\})$.

- Ver(CT): During the execution of this algorithm, a verifier would first do the same as what in the verification algorithm of the previous scheme. Besides, to check the block rules in BL, for each proof $(St_0, St_1, CH, e_0, e_1, \widehat{St_0}, \widehat{St_1}, \widehat{CH}, \widehat{e_0}, \widehat{e_1})$ in $\{pf\}$ and its corresponding rule $< g^S, g^R >$, the verifier computes

$$COM'_0 = St_0{}^{CH}(g)^{e_0}/(g^S)^{e_1}, COM'_1 = St_1{}^{CH}(g^{r_1})^{e_0}/(g^{S_i r_1})^{e_1},$$
$$\widehat{COM}'_0 = \widehat{St_0}^{\widehat{CH}}(g^R)^{\widehat{e_0}}/(g^{R_j r_1})^{\widehat{e_1}}, \widehat{COM}'_1 = \widehat{St_1}^{\widehat{CH}}(g)^{\widehat{e_0}}/(g^{r_1})^{\widehat{e_1}})$$

and then checks whether the equation

$$CH + \widehat{CH} = H_3(COM'_0 + COM'_1 + \widehat{COM}'_0 + \widehat{COM}'_1)$$

holds. If yes, the verifier turns to the next proof in the list $\{pf\}$, otherwise it drops this ciphertext. The verifier would relay the ciphertext if all the proofs in $\{pf\}$ and rules in BL are successfully checked.
- Dec(CT, R_j): This algorithm shares no difference from that in the previous scheme.

5 Security Proofs

Theorem 1. *Our scheme maintains message confidentiality under the previously defined message confidentiality model assuming the DDH problem is hard in $\mathbb{G}$ when hash functions H_1, H_2, H_3 are modeled as random oracles. Concretely, if there is an adversary $\mathcal{A}$ which can break our scheme with non-negligible probability ϵ, supposing $\mathcal{A}$ makes at most $q_{H_1}, q_{H_2}, q_{H_3}$ queries to the H_1, H_2, H_3 hash oracles respectively, and q_D queries to the decryption oracle, then we can construct another algorithm $\mathcal{B}$ that solves the DDH problem in $\mathbb{G}$ with advantage at least $\frac{1}{n^2}(1 - \frac{q_D}{2^k})\epsilon$, where k is the security parameter and n is a constant.*

Theorem 2. *Our proposed scheme holds sender privacy under the previously defined model assuming the DDH problem is hard in $\mathbb{G}$ where hash functions H_1, H_2, H_3 are modeled as random oracles. Concretely, if there exists such an adversary $\mathcal{A}$ which can break our scheme with non-negligible probability ϵ, supposing $\mathcal{A}$ makes at most $q_{H_1}, q_{H_2}, q_{H_3}$ queries to the H_1, H_2, H_3 hash oracles respectively, and q_{se} sender extraction queries, then we can construct another algorithm that solves the DDH problem in $\mathbb{G}$ with probability at least $\frac{1}{n}(1 - \frac{q_{se}}{2^k})\epsilon$.*

Theorem 3. *Our scheme holds receiver privacy under the predefined security model assuming the DDH problem is hard in $\mathbb{G}$ when hash functions H_1, H_2, H_3 are modeled as random oracles. That is, if there is an adversary $\mathcal{A}$ which can break our scheme with non-negligible probability ϵ, assuming $\mathcal{A}$ asks $q_{H_1}, q_{H_2}, q_{H_3}$ queries to H_1, H_2, H_3 respectively and q_{re} receiver extraction queries during the game, then we can construct another algorithm $\mathcal{B}$ which breaks the DDH problem with probability at least $\frac{1}{2} \cdot \epsilon - \frac{1}{2^{k-1}}$, where k is the security parameter.*

Because of the page limitation, here we only give the theorem. People can find the formal proof in the full version of this paper.

6 Conclusion

We considered the user conditional privacy preservation problem. With the blacklist scenario, we explained how a message sender proves the legitimation of the communication channel with its communication partner. To solve the aforementioned two problems, we proposed a group-based source-destination verifiable encryption scheme with blacklist checking. In order to discuss the security of our scheme, we further defined three security models to capture the message confidentiality, sender privacy preservation and receiver privacy preservation accordingly, and then gave three formal proofs under the predefined models with the help of the random oracle.

References

1. Abdalla, M., Bellare, M., Catalano, D., Kiltz, E., Kohno, T., Lange, T., Malone-Lee, J., Neven, G., Paillier, P., Shi, H.: Searchable encryption revisited: consistency properties, relation to anonymous IBE, and extensions. J. Cryptol. **21**(3), 350–391 (2008)
2. Abdalla, M., Bellare, M., Neven, G.: Robust encryption. In: Micciancio, D. (ed.) TCC 2010. LNCS, vol. 5978, pp. 480–497. Springer, Heidelberg (2010). https://doi.org/10.1007/978-3-642-11799-2_28
3. Barth, A., Boneh, D., Waters, B.: Privacy in encrypted content distribution using private broadcast encryption. In: Di Crescenzo, G., Rubin, A. (eds.) FC 2006. LNCS, vol. 4107, pp. 52–64. Springer, Heidelberg (2006). https://doi.org/10.1007/11889663_4
4. Bellare, M., Boldyreva, A., Desai, A., Pointcheval, D.: Key-privacy in public-key encryption. In: Boyd, C. (ed.) ASIACRYPT 2001. LNCS, vol. 2248, pp. 566–582. Springer, Heidelberg (2001). https://doi.org/10.1007/3-540-45682-1_33
5. Camenisch, J., Shoup, V.: Practical verifiable encryption and decryption of discrete logarithms. In: Boneh, D. (ed.) CRYPTO 2003. LNCS, vol. 2729, pp. 126–144. Springer, Heidelberg (2003). https://doi.org/10.1007/978-3-540-45146-4_8
6. Chaum, D., van Heyst, E.: Group signatures. In: Davies, D.W. (ed.) EUROCRYPT 1991. LNCS, vol. 547, pp. 257–265. Springer, Heidelberg (1991). https://doi.org/10.1007/3-540-46416-6_22
7. Cramer, R., Shoup, V.: A practical public key cryptosystem provably secure against adaptive chosen ciphertext attack. In: Krawczyk, H. (ed.) CRYPTO 1998. LNCS, vol. 1462, pp. 13–25. Springer, Heidelberg (1998). https://doi.org/10.1007/BFb0055717
8. Dolev, D., Dwork, C., Naor, M.: Non-malleable cryptography (extended abstract). In: Proceedings of the 23rd Annual ACM Symposium on Theory of Computing, New Orleans, Louisiana, USA, 5–8 May 1991, pp. 542–552 (1991)
9. Duan, S., Cao, Z.: Efficient and provably secure multi-receiver identity-based signcryption. In: Batten, L.M., Safavi-Naini, R. (eds.) ACISP 2006. LNCS, vol. 4058, pp. 195–206. Springer, Heidelberg (2006). https://doi.org/10.1007/11780656_17
10. Eun, H., Lee, H., Oh, H.: Conditional privacy preserving security protocol for NFC applications. IEEE Trans. Consum. Electron. **59**(1), 153–160 (2013)
11. Gafni, E., Staddon, J., Yin, Y.L.: Efficient methods for integrating traceability and broadcast encryption. In: Wiener, M. (ed.) CRYPTO 1999. LNCS, vol. 1666, pp. 372–387. Springer, Heidelberg (1999). https://doi.org/10.1007/3-540-48405-1_24
12. Gamal, T.E.: A public key cryptosystem and a signature scheme based on discrete logarithms. IEEE Trans. Inf. Theor. **31**(4), 469–472 (1985)
13. Goldwasser, S., Micali, S.: Probabilistic encryption. J. Comput. Syst. Sci. **28**(2), 270–299 (1984)
14. Harn, L., Chang, C., Wu, H.: An anonymous multi-receiver encryption based on RSA. Int. J. Netw. Secur. **15**(4), 307–312 (2013)
15. He, D., Bu, J., Chan, S., Chen, C.: Handauth: efficient handover authentication with conditional privacy for wireless networks. IEEE Trans. Comput. **62**(3), 616–622 (2013)
16. Huang, X., Susilo, W., Mu, Y., Zhang, F.: Identity-based ring signcryption schemes: cryptographic primitives for preserving privacy and authenticity in the ubiquitous world. In: 19th International Conference on Advanced Information Networking and Applications (AINA 2005), Taipei, Taiwan, 28–30 March 2005, pp. 649–654 (2005)

17. Libert, B., Paterson, K.G., Quaglia, E.A.: Anonymous broadcast encryption: adaptive security and efficient constructions in the standard model. In: Fischlin, M., Buchmann, J., Manulis, M. (eds.) PKC 2012. LNCS, vol. 7293, pp. 206–224. Springer, Heidelberg (2012). https://doi.org/10.1007/978-3-642-30057-8_13

18. Lu, R., Lin, X., Zhu, H., Ho, P., Shen, X.: ECPP: efficient conditional privacy preservation protocol for secure vehicular communications. INFOCOM 2008, pp. 1229–1237 (2008)

19. Mohassel, P.: A closer look at anonymity and robustness in encryption schemes. In: Abe, M. (ed.) ASIACRYPT 2010. LNCS, vol. 6477, pp. 501–518. Springer, Heidelberg (2010). https://doi.org/10.1007/978-3-642-17373-8_29

20. Rackoff, C., Simon, D.R.: Non-interactive zero-knowledge proof of knowledge and chosen ciphertext attack. In: Feigenbaum, J. (ed.) CRYPTO 1991. LNCS, vol. 576, pp. 433–444. Springer, Heidelberg (1992). https://doi.org/10.1007/3-540-46766-1_35

21. Rivest, R.L., Shamir, A., Tauman, Y.: How to leak a secret. In: Boyd, C. (ed.) ASIACRYPT 2001. LNCS, vol. 2248, pp. 552–565. Springer, Heidelberg (2001). https://doi.org/10.1007/3-540-45682-1_32

22. Zhang, J., Mao, J.: An improved anonymous multi-receiver identity-based encryption scheme. Int. J. Commun. Syst. **28**(4), 645–658 (2015)

Compact Attribute-Based and Online-Offline Multi-input Inner Product Encryptions from Standard Static Assumptions (Short Paper)

Pratish Datta[✉]

NTT Secure Platform Laboratories, Tokyo 180-8585, Japan
datta.pratish@lab.ntt.co.jp

Abstract. This paper presents an *attribute-based encryption* (ABE) construction for monotone span programs achieving the *shortest* known ciphertext size under *well-studied static* complexity assumptions. Our ABE construction is built in composite order bilinear group setting and involves only 2 group elements in the ciphertexts. For proving selective security of the proposed ABE scheme under the *Subgroup Decision* assumptions, the most standard static assumptions in composite order bilinear group setting, we apply the extended version of the elegant *Déjà Q* framework, which was originally proposed as a general technique for reducing the q-type complexity assumptions to their static counter parts. Our work thus demonstrates the power of this framework in overcoming the need of q-type assumptions, which are vulnerable to serious practical attacks, for deriving security of highly expressive ABE systems with compact parameters. We further introduce the concept of *online-offline multi-input functional encryption* (OO-MIFE), which is a crucial advancement towards realizing this highly promising but computationally intensive cryptographic primitive in resource bounded and power constrained devices. We also instantiate our notion of OO-MIFE by constructing such a scheme for the multi-input analog of the *inner product* functionality, which has a wide range of application in practice. Our OO-MIFE scheme for multi-input inner products is built in asymmetric bilinear groups of prime order and is proven selectively secure under the *well-studied k-Linear* assumption.

Keywords: Attribute-based encryption · Déjà Q
Online-offline multi-input functional encryption

1 Introduction

FE: *Functional encryption* (FE) is a new vision of modern cryptography that aims to overcome the potential limitation of the traditional encryption schemes, namely, the all or nothing control over decryption capabilities. FE supports restricted decryption keys which enable a decrypter to learn specific functions

© Springer International Publishing AG 2017
J. K. Liu and P. Samarati (Eds.): ISPEC 2017, LNCS 10701, pp. 204–214, 2017.
https://doi.org/10.1007/978-3-319-72359-4_12

of encrypted messages, and nothing more. More precisely, an FE scheme for a function family $\mathfrak{f}$ involves a setup authority which holds a master secret key and publishes public system parameters. An encrypter uses the public parameters (along with a secret encryption key provided by the setup authority in case of a private key scheme) to encrypt its message $\mathcal{M}$ belonging to some supported message space $\mathbb{M}$ creating a ciphertext $\text{CT}(\mathcal{M})$. A decrypter may obtain a private decryption key $\text{SK}(\mathcal{F})$ corresponding to some $\mathcal{F} \in \mathfrak{f}$ from the setup authority provided that the authority deems that the decrypter is entitled for that key. Such a decryption key $\text{SK}(\mathcal{F})$ can be used to decrypt $\text{CT}(\mathcal{M})$ to recover $\mathcal{F}(\mathcal{M})$. The standard security notion for FE is collusion resistance, i.e., an arbitrary number of decrypters cannot jointly retrieve any more information about an encrypted message beyond the union of what they each can learn individually.

PE: An important subclass of FE is *predicate encryption* (PE) with *public index*. Consider a predicate family $\mathfrak{P} = \{\mathscr{P}_{\mathscr{Y}} : \mathbb{X} \to \{0,1\} \mid \mathscr{Y} \in \mathfrak{Y}\}$, where $\mathbb{X}$ and $\mathfrak{Y}$ are index sets. In a PE scheme for the predicate family $\mathfrak{P}$, the associated message space $\mathbb{M}$ is of the form $\mathbb{X} \times \mathbb{W}$, where $\mathbb{W}$ contains the actual payloads. The functionality $\mathscr{F}_{\mathscr{P}_{\mathscr{Y}}}$ associated with a predicate $\mathscr{P}_{\mathscr{Y}} \in \mathfrak{P}$ is defined as $\mathscr{F}_{\mathscr{P}_{\mathscr{Y}}}(\mathscr{X}, \mathscr{W}) = \mathscr{W}$, if $\mathscr{P}_{\mathscr{Y}}(\mathscr{X}) = 1$, and the empty string $\perp$, otherwise, for all $(\mathscr{X}, \mathscr{W}) \in \mathbb{M} = \mathbb{X} \times \mathbb{W}$. In the public index setting, a PE ciphertext $\text{CT}(\mathcal{M})$ encrypting some message $\mathcal{M} = (\mathscr{X}, \mathscr{W})$ includes the index $\mathscr{X}$ in the clear.

ABE: A highly expressive form of public-index PE is *attribute-based encryption* (ABE). The recent advances in cloud technology has triggered an emerging trend among individuals and organizations to outsource potentially sensitive private informations to external untrusted servers and later share various segments of the outsourced data with legitimate entities. ABE is an indispensable cryptographic tool for preserving data confidentiality in such cloud computing platforms. ABE comes in two flavors, namely, *key-policy* and *ciphertext-policy*. In a key-policy ABE system over an attribute universe $\mathbb{U}$, the index set $\mathbb{X}$ consists of all non-empty subsets of $\mathbb{U}$ and the index set $\mathfrak{Y}$ is comprised of certain access structures over $\mathbb{U}$. A predicate $\mathscr{P}_{\mathscr{A}} : \mathbb{X} \to \{0,1\}$ associated with some access structure $\mathscr{A} \in \mathfrak{Y}$ is defined for all attribute sets $\Gamma \in \mathbb{X}$ as $\mathscr{P}_{\mathscr{A}}(\Gamma) = 1$, if the access structure $\mathscr{A}$ accepts the attribute set Γ, and 0, otherwise. The ciphertext-policy variant interchanges the roles of attribute sets and access structures. In this work, we concentrate on key-policy ABE.

The notion of ABE was introduced by Sahai and Waters [12] for threshold access structures. Over time the class of access structures realizable by ABE systems has been gradually expanded by several researchers culminating into the recent state of the art constructions which can now support access structures represented by arbitrary polynomial-size circuits and even Turing machines. However, in view of the current progress in computing technology, it appears that the most expressive form of access structures supported by computationally practical ABE systems are span programs. Besides the expressiveness of supported access structures, succinctness of ciphertext headers has been an important concern towards practicality of ABE schemes.

Attrapadung et al. [5] were the first to develop a selectively secure key-policy ABE construction supporting non-monotone span programs in prime order bilinear groups featuring 3 group elements in the ciphertext headers based on a q-type assumption, namely, the Decisional Bilinear Diffie-Hellman (DBDHE) assumption parameterized by ℓ, where ℓ is the maximum number of attributes per ciphertext. Later, Yamada et al. [15] designed another selectively secure key-policy ABE scheme for non-monotone span programs in prime order bilinear group setting that further reduced the number of ciphertext header components by 1 group element. As per our knowledge, this construction involves the least number of ciphertext header components among the computationally practical key-policy ABE systems currently available in the literature. However, the underlying complexity assumption of this construction is again DBDHE parameterized by ℓ. Attrapadung [3,4] subsequently built adaptively secure key-policy ABE schemes for monotone span programs with constant number of group elements in the ciphertext headers. The construction of [3] is developed in composite order bilinear groups and it has 6 group elements in the ciphertext headers, whereas, the scheme of [4] is constructed in prime order bilinear groups and its ciphertext headers include 18 group elements. These constructions are also based on certain q-type assumptions which are even stronger than the DBDHE assumption.

However, as demonstrated by Cheon [8], the q-type complexity assumptions and thus the cryptosystems built on them are vulnerable to a serious attack. Specifically, Cheon developed an algorithm which recovers the secret involved in a q-type assumption in time inversely proportional to q. Later, Sakeme et al. [13] showed that the attack of Cheon can be a real threat to cryptosystems based on q-type assumptions by executing a successful experiment. Hence, it is clear that the parameters of q-type-assumption-based cryptographic constructions must scale with q in order to maintain a constant security level. Consequently, the principal downside of all the four ABE constructions [3–5,15] is that they suffer from Cheon's attack [8] and require parameters that scale with the number of attributes per ciphertext or in the attribute universe for preserving a fixed security level. This bottleneck of using q-type complexity assumptions for building key-policy ABE systems with constant number of ciphertext header components was first mitigated by Chen and Wee [7], who designed a key-policy ABE scheme for monotone span programs in composite order bilinear group setting based on static assumptions featuring the least number (only 2) of group elements in the ciphertext headers among existing similar constructions. However, the static assumptions used in [7] are rather non-standard. In all the ABE constructions discussed above, the number of group elements constituting the decryption keys and the public parameters are $O(m\ell)$ and $O(\ell)$ respectively, where m is the maximum number of rows of the matrix representing the span program.

Online-Offline MIFE: *Multi-input functional encryption* (MIFE), introduced by Goldwasser et al. [9], is a generalization of FE to the setting of multi-input functions. In an MIFE scheme for a family $\mathfrak{f}_m$ of m-ary functions, a decryption key $\text{SK}(\mathscr{F})$ corresponding to some function $\mathscr{F} \in \mathfrak{f}_m$ can be used to decrypt m ciphertexts $\text{CT}^{(1)}(\mathscr{M}^{(1)}), \ldots, \text{CT}^{(m)}(\mathscr{M}^{(m)})$, encrypting the messages $\mathscr{M}^{(1)}, \ldots, \mathscr{M}^{(m)}$ for the input slots $1, \ldots, m$ respectively, to retrieve $\mathscr{F}(\mathscr{M}^{(1)}, \ldots, \mathscr{M}^{(m)})$. In such systems, other than generating the public system parameters and master secret key, the setup authority also creates m encryption keys $\text{ENK}^{(1)}, \ldots,$ $\text{ENK}^{(m)}$ which are necessary for encrypting messages for the input slots $1, \ldots, m$ respectively. MIFE has a wide range of practical applications such as running SQL (structured query language) queries on encrypted databases, non-interactive differentially private data release, delegation of expensive computations to external servers and many more.

The *bounded-norm multi-input inner product* functionality, which we consider in this paper, is an extension of the usual single-input inner product function and has been explicitly defined by Abdalla et al. [1]. A multi-input inner product function $\mathscr{F}_{\vec{y}^{(1)}, \ldots, \vec{y}^{(m)}}$ over $\mathbb{Z}_n$ is specified by an m-tuple of vectors $(\vec{y}^{(1)}, \ldots, \vec{y}^{(m)})$, where for each $j \in [m]$, $\vec{y}^{(j)}$ is a vector of length ℓ over $\mathbb{Z}_n$, for some $m, n, \ell \in \mathbb{N}$. The function $\mathscr{F}_{\vec{y}^{(1)}, \ldots, \vec{y}^{(m)}}$ takes as input m vectors $\vec{x}^{(1)}, \ldots, \vec{x}^{(m)}$, where for each $j \in [m]$, $\vec{x}^{(j)}$ is again a vector of length ℓ over $\mathbb{Z}_n$, and outputs the sum of inner product values $\sum_{j \in [m]} \langle \vec{x}^{(j)}, \vec{y}^{(j)} \rangle$. In the bounded norm setting, it is required that the norm of each component inner product $\langle \vec{x}^{(j)}, \vec{y}^{(j)} \rangle$ be bounded by some fixed $\mathsf{B} \in \mathbb{N}$. Inner product and hence its multi-input variant is an extremely useful functionality in the context of descriptive statistics, e.g., for computing the weighted mean of a collection of values. It also enables the computations of conjunctions, disjunctions, and polynomial expressions, as well as determination of exact thresholds.

In recent years, as computation is moving on to resource bounded and power constrained devices like mobile phones, there has been a growing demand for *online-offline* cryptography. The basic idea of the online-offline model is to provision for an expensive preparation or offline phase, where the majority of computation is performed before the actual data become available. This is followed by an efficient online phase, which is run when the data become known.

One vital limitation of FE is that the rich functionalities often come at the expense of a serious computational load compared to traditional encryption schemes. Specifically, the decryption key generation time depends on the complexity of the functions, while the encryption time scales with the length of the message and sometime even with the complexity of the function family. The situation is evidently more severe in the context of MIFE as multi-input functionalities have much larger complexity compared to the single input ones. In fact, an exacerbating issue is that the cost for operations may vary widely between each ciphertext and decryption key, thus forcing a system to provision for a load that matches a worst case scenario. In the field of single-input FE, online-offline versions have already been considered for ABE [10] and very recently for general purpose FE supporting arbitrary polynomial-size circuits in the bounded collusion setting [2]. However, MIFE is not yet investigated in the online-offline model.

Our Contributions: Our goal in this work is to develop ABE scheme with best-known parameters under *well-studied static* complexity assumptions. Specifically, we present a selectively secure key-policy ABE scheme supporting monotone span programs in composite order bilinear groups with only 2 group elements in the ciphertexts. The security is proven under the *Subgroup decision* assumptions, which are the *most standard static* assumptions in composite order bilinear group settings. Our ABE decryption keys and public parameters involve respectively $O(m\ell)$ and $O(\ell)$ group elements which are the same as all previously known key-policy ABE construction with short ciphertexts. Here, m and ℓ respectively denotes the maximum number of rows in the matrix representing the supported span programs and the maximum number of attributes per ciphertext.

We work in the *key encapsulation* setting, where the ABE ciphertexts hide a symmetric session key that can be used to symmetrically encrypt the actual payload of arbitrary length. For proving security of our ABE construction, we employ the recent extended *Déjà Q* framework presented by Wee [14]. The Déjà Q framework was originally proposed by Chase et al. [6]. It is a general framework for reducing various q-type complexity assumptions or their generalization, namely, the family of uber assumptions to their static counter parts in composite order bilinear group setting making use of the classic dual system methodology [11].

The other contribution of this paper is to introduce the notion of *online-offline multi-input functional encryption* (OO-MIFE) and to develop the *first* OO-MIFE construction for the multi-input analog of the inner product functionality. Our construction is proven secure under the well-studied k-*Linear* assumption. Our online operations are quite fast. Our online decryption key generation algorithm costs only $m\ell(k + 1)$ modular multiplications, where m, ℓ, and k are respectively the arity of the multi-input inner product function, the length of the vectors, and the parameter of the underlying complexity assumption. Thus, for instance, if we base the security of our construction on the Symmetric External Diffie-Hellman (SXDH) assumption, then $k = 1$, so that our online decryption key generation algorithm would involve just $2m\ell$ modular multiplications. Our online encryption algorithm is even more efficient as it incurs only modular additions which is the fastest operation in bilinear group setting. Regarding communication and storage requirements, both our offline and online decryption keys contain $m(k + 1)$ additional $\mathbb{Z}_n$-component over those of the MIPE scheme of [1], while our offline and online ciphertexts both include only ℓ additional $\mathbb{Z}_n$-components over those of the MIPE construction of [1]. The increase in the ciphertext and decryption key sizes is reminiscent with those of the earlier online-offline single-input FE construction [10]. Moreover, the sizes of our public parameters and encryption keys are exactly the same as those of the MIPE construction of [1].

2   Notations

Let $\lambda \in \mathbb{N}$ denotes the security parameter and 1^λ be its unary representation. Throughout this paper we will follow notations presented in Fig. 1.

Symbol	Explanation
$\aleph \xleftarrow{\$} \mathbb{S}$	$\aleph$ is uniformly sampled from a set $\mathbb{S}$.
$\varkappa \xleftarrow{\$} \mathcal{Z}(\varUpsilon)$	$\varkappa$ is a random variable representing the output of a randomized algorithm $\mathcal{Z}$ on input $\varUpsilon$.
$\varkappa = \mathcal{Z}(\varUpsilon)$	$\varkappa$ is the output of a deterministic algorithm $\mathcal{Z}$ on input $\varUpsilon$.
$[\hbar]$	$\{1, \ldots, \hbar\} \subset \mathbb{N}$, where $\hbar \in \mathbb{N}$.
$\vec{v}$	a vector $(v_1, \ldots, v_\hbar) \in \mathbb{Z}_n^\hbar$ of length $\hbar$, for some $n, \hbar \in \mathbb{N}$.
$\boldsymbol{B} = (B_{\iota,\iota'})_{\hbar \times \hbar'}$	a member of $\mathbb{Z}_n^{\hbar \times \hbar'}$, i.e., a matrix of size $\hbar \times \hbar'$ with entries $B_{\iota,\iota'} \in \mathbb{Z}_n$, for $\iota \in [\hbar]$, $\iota' \in [\hbar']$, where $\hbar, \hbar' \in \mathbb{N}$.
$\boldsymbol{B}^\intercal$ $(\vec{v}^\intercal)$	the transpose of the matrix $\boldsymbol{B} \in \mathbb{Z}_n^{\hbar \times \hbar'}$ (the vector $\vec{v} \in \mathbb{Z}_n^\hbar$).
$\langle \vec{v}, \vec{w} \rangle$ or $\vec{v}\vec{w}^\intercal$	the inner product $\sum_{i \in [\hbar]} v_i w_i$ of vectors $\vec{v}, \vec{w} \in \mathbb{Z}_n^\hbar$.
$\boldsymbol{z} = g^{\vec{v}}$	a $\hbar$-length vector of group elements, $(z_1 = g^{v_1}, \ldots, z_\hbar = g^{v_\hbar}) \in \mathbb{G}^\hbar$, for some cyclic group $\mathbb{G}$ of order n and some $g \in \mathbb{G}$, where $\vec{v} \in \mathbb{Z}_n^\hbar$.
$g^{\delta \vec{v}} = (g^{\vec{v}})^\delta$	$(g^{\delta v_1}, \ldots, g^{\delta v_\hbar}) \in \mathbb{G}^\hbar$, where $\delta \in \mathbb{Z}_n$, $\vec{v} \in \mathbb{Z}_n^\hbar$, and $g \in \mathbb{G}$.
$g^{\vec{v}+\vec{w}} = g^{\vec{v}} g^{\vec{w}}$	$(g^{v_1+w_1}, \ldots, g^{v_\hbar+w_\hbar}) \in \mathbb{G}^\hbar$, where $\vec{v}, \vec{w} \in \mathbb{Z}_n^\hbar$ and $g \in \mathbb{G}$.
$\boldsymbol{Z} = g^{\boldsymbol{B}}$	a matrix $(g^{B_{\iota,\iota'}})_{\hbar \times \hbar'} \in \mathbb{G}^{\hbar \times \hbar'}$, where $\boldsymbol{B} = (B_{\iota,\iota'})_{\hbar \times \hbar'} \in \mathbb{Z}_n^{\hbar \times \hbar'}$ and $g \in \mathbb{G}$.
$(\boldsymbol{Z})^{\vec{v}} = (g^{\boldsymbol{B}})^{\vec{v}}$	$g^{\vec{v}\boldsymbol{B}^\intercal} \in \mathbb{G}^\hbar$, where $\vec{v} \in \mathbb{Z}_n^{\hbar'}$, $\boldsymbol{B} \in \mathbb{Z}_n^{\hbar \times \hbar'}$, and $g \in \mathbb{G}$.

Fig. 1. Notations

3 Our Attribute-Based Encryption Scheme

In this section, we present our ABE scheme for monotone span programs. The necessary backgrounds on monotone access structures (MAS) and linear secret-sharing (LSS) schemes can be found in the full version.

ABE.Setup($1^\lambda, \mathbb{U}$) $\rightarrow$ (MPK, MSK): The setup authority takes as input the unary encoded security parameter 1^λ along with an attribute universe $\mathbb{U} = \{1, \ldots, \ell\}$. It proceeds as follows:

1. It first generates $(n = p_1 p_2 p_3, \mathbb{G}, \mathbb{G}_T, e) \xleftarrow{\$} \mathcal{G}(1^\lambda, \mathsf{symmetric}, \mathsf{composite})$.
2. Next, it selects $\mu, \alpha, \gamma \xleftarrow{\$} \mathbb{Z}_n$, $g \xleftarrow{\$} \mathbb{G}_{p_1}$, and $\breve{g}, \breve{r}_0, \breve{r}_1, \ldots, \breve{r}_{\ell+1} \xleftarrow{\$} \mathbb{G}_{p_3}$.
3. Then, it computes $h_0 = g^\gamma \breve{r}_0$, $u = g^\mu$, $\widetilde{u}_{\iota'} = u^{\alpha^{\iota'}} \breve{r}_{\iota'}$, for $\iota' \in [\ell+1]$, and $e(g, \widetilde{u}_{\ell+1})$.
4. After that, it uniformly samples $\mathcal{H} : \mathbb{G}_T \rightarrow \{0,1\}^\lambda$ from a pairwise independent hash family $\mathbb{H}_2$.
5. It publishes the public parameters MPK $= ((n, \mathbb{G}, \mathbb{G}_T, e), g, \breve{g}, h_0, \{\widetilde{u}_{\iota'}\}_{\iota' \in \mathbb{U}}, e(g, \widetilde{u}_{\ell+1}), \mathcal{H})$, while keeps the master secret key MSK $= (p_1 p_2 p_3, \mu, \alpha, \gamma)$.

ABE.KeyGen(MPK, MSK, $\mathscr{A}$) $\rightarrow$ SK($\mathscr{A}$): On input the public parameters MPK $= ((n, \mathbb{G}, \mathbb{G}_T, e), g, \breve{g}, h_0, \{\widetilde{u}_{\iota'}\}_{\iota' \in \mathbb{U}}, e(g, \widetilde{u}_{\ell+1}), \mathcal{H})$, the master secret key MSK $= (p_1 p_2 p_3, \mu, \alpha, \gamma)$, and an MAS $\mathscr{A} = (\boldsymbol{M}, \rho)$ belonging to the family $\mathfrak{A}$ of MAS's over $\mathbb{U}$, where $\boldsymbol{M} \in \mathbb{Z}_n^{m \times m'}$ and $\rho : [m] \to \mathbb{U}$ is the labeling of the rows of $\boldsymbol{M}$ with attributes in $\mathbb{U}$, the setup authority executes the following steps:

1. It first computes m shares $\{\kappa_\iota\}_{\iota \in [m]} \xleftarrow{\$} \mathsf{LSS.Distribute}(\mathscr{A} = (\boldsymbol{M}, \rho), \varsigma = \mu \alpha^{\ell+1})$ of the secret $\varsigma = \mu \alpha^{\ell+1}$.

2. For $\iota \in [m]$, it performs the following:

   (a) It picks $\wp_\iota \xleftarrow{\$} \mathbb{Z}_n$, $\breve{r}'_\iota, \breve{r}'_{\iota,\iota'} \xleftarrow{\$} \mathbb{G}_{p_3}$, for $\iota' \in \mathbb{U} \backslash \{\rho(\iota)\}$.

   (b) It computes $k_\iota = g^{\kappa_\iota} g^{(\gamma + \mu \alpha^{\rho(\iota)}) \wp_\iota} \breve{r}'_\iota$, $k'_\iota = g^{\wp_\iota}$, $k''_{\iota,\iota'} = g^{\mu \alpha^{\iota'} \wp_\iota} \breve{r}'_{\iota,\iota'}$, for $\iota' \in \mathbb{U} \backslash \{\rho(\iota)\}$.

3. It provides the decryption key $\mathsf{SK}(\mathscr{A}) = (\mathscr{A}, \{k_\iota, k'_\iota, \{k''_{\iota,\iota'}\}_{\iota' \in \mathbb{U} \backslash \{\rho(\iota)\}}\}_{\iota \in [m]})$ to a legitimate decrypter.

ABE.Encrypt$(\mathsf{MPK}, \Gamma) \to (\mathsf{CT}(\Gamma), \mathsf{EK})$: On input the public parameters $\mathsf{MPK} = ((n, \mathbb{G}, \mathbb{G}_T, e), g, \breve{g}, h_0, \{\tilde{u}_{\iota'}\}_{\iota' \in \mathbb{U}}, e(g, \tilde{u}_{\ell+1}), \mathcal{H})$ along with an attribute set $\Gamma \subseteq \mathbb{U}$, an encrypter operates as follows:

1. It picks $\theta, \breve{\nu}_\Gamma \xleftarrow{\$} \mathbb{Z}_n$, and sets $\breve{r}_\Gamma = \breve{g}^{\breve{\nu}_\Gamma}$.

2. It sets $c_1 = g^\theta$, $c_2 = (h_0 \prod_{\iota' \in \Gamma} \tilde{u}_{\iota'})^\theta \breve{r}_\Gamma = g^{(\gamma + \mu \sum_{\iota' \in \Gamma} \alpha^{\iota'})\theta} (\breve{r}_0 \prod_{\iota' \in \Gamma} \breve{r}_{\iota'})^\theta \breve{r}_\Gamma$, and $T = e(g, \tilde{u}_{\ell+1})^\theta$.

3. It outputs the ciphertext $\mathsf{CT}(\Gamma) = (\Gamma, c_1, c_2)$ and the session key $\mathsf{EK} = \mathcal{H}(T)$.

ABE.Decrypt$(\mathsf{MPK}, \mathsf{SK}(\mathscr{A}), \mathsf{CT}(\Gamma)) \to \mathsf{EK}'$ or $\bot$: A decrypter takes as input the public parameters $\mathsf{MPK} = ((n, \mathbb{G}, \mathbb{G}_T, e), g, \breve{g}, h_0, \{\tilde{u}_{\iota'}\}_{\iota' \in \mathbb{U}}, e(g, \tilde{u}_{\ell+1}), \mathcal{H})$, its decryption key $\mathsf{SK}(\mathscr{A}) = (\mathscr{A}, \{k_\iota, k'_\iota, \{k''_{\iota,\iota'}\}_{\iota' \in \mathbb{U} \backslash \{\rho(\iota)\}}\}_{\iota \in [m]})$ corresponding to its legitimate MAS $\mathscr{A} = (\boldsymbol{M}, \rho) \in \mathfrak{A}$, where $\boldsymbol{M} \in \mathbb{Z}_n^{m \times m'}$ and $\rho : [m] \to \mathbb{U}$ is a labeling of the rows of $\boldsymbol{M}$ with attributes in $\mathbb{U}$, together with a ciphertext $\mathsf{CT}(\Gamma) = (\Gamma, c_1, c_2)$ prepared for some attribute set $\Gamma \subseteq \mathbb{U}$. If $\mathscr{A}$ does not accept Γ, then it outputs $\bot$. Otherwise, it executes the following steps:

1. It first determines $(\mathbb{I}_\Gamma, \{\eta_\iota\}_{\iota \in \mathbb{I}_\Gamma}) \xleftarrow{\$} \mathsf{LSS.Reconstruct}(\mathscr{A} = (\boldsymbol{M}, \rho), \Gamma))$.

2. Next, it computes $b_1 = \prod_{\iota \in \mathbb{I}_\Gamma} (k_\iota \prod_{\iota' \in \Gamma \backslash \{\rho(\iota)\}} k''_{\iota,\iota'})^{\eta_\iota}$, $b_2 = \prod_{\iota \in \mathbb{I}_\Gamma} (k'_\iota)^{\eta_\iota}$, and
$$T' = \frac{e(c_1, b_1)}{e(c_2, b_2)}.$$

3. It retrieves the session key as $\mathsf{EK}' = \mathcal{H}(T')$.

Theorem 3.1 (Security of Our ABE Scheme). *The proposed* ABE *scheme is selectively secure under the Subgroup Decision assumptions.*

The proof of Theorem 3.1 is provided in the full version.

4 Our Online-Offline Multi-input Inner Product Encryption Scheme

Definition 4.1 (Multi-Input Bounded-Norm Inner Product Functionality [1]). A multi-input bounded-norm inner product function family $\mathfrak{f}_m^{\ell, \mathsf{B}}$ over $\mathbb{Z}_n$, for some $n, \ell, m, \mathsf{B} \in \mathbb{N}$ with $n \gg m\mathsf{B}$, consists of functions $\mathscr{F}_{\vec{y}^{(1)}, \dots, \vec{y}^{(m)}}$:

$(\mathbb{Z}_n^\ell)^m \to \mathbb{Z}_n$ associated with a tuple of vectors $(\vec{y}^{(1)}, \ldots, \vec{y}^{(m)}) \in (\mathbb{Z}_n^\ell)^m$, where $\mathscr{F}_{\vec{y}^{(1)}, \ldots, \vec{y}^{(m)}}(\vec{x}^{(1)}, \ldots, \vec{x}^{(m)}) = (\sum_{j \in [m]} \langle \vec{x}^{(j)}, \vec{y}^{(j)} \rangle) \mod n$, for $\vec{x}^{(1)}, \ldots, \vec{x}^{(m)} \in \mathbb{Z}_n^\ell$ with the norm of component inner products, $|\langle \vec{x}^{(j)}, \vec{y}^{(j)} \rangle| \leq B$, for $j \in [m]$.

In order to simplify naming conventions, we will omit "bounded-norm" for the rest of the paper. We now present our OO-MIPE scheme.

OO-MIPE.Setup$(1^\lambda, \ell, m, B) \to (\text{PP}, \{\text{ENK}^{(j)}\}_{j \in [m]}, \text{MSK})$: The setup authority takes as input the unary encoded security parameter 1^λ, the length ℓ of vectors, the arity m of the multi-input inner product function, and the bound B. It proceeds as follows:

1. It first generates $(n, \mathbb{G}_1, \mathbb{G}_2, \mathbb{G}_T, e) \xleftarrow{\$} \mathcal{G}(1^\lambda, \text{asymmetric}, \text{prime})$ such that $n \gg mB$.

2. Next it selects $\boldsymbol{A}^{(1)}, \ldots, \boldsymbol{A}^{(m)} \xleftarrow{\$} \mathbb{Z}_n^{(k+1) \times k}$, $\boldsymbol{W}^{(1)}, \ldots, \boldsymbol{W}^{(m)} \xleftarrow{\$} \mathbb{Z}_n^{\ell \times (k+1)}$, $\boldsymbol{N}^{(1)}, \ldots, \boldsymbol{N}^{(m)} \xleftarrow{\$} \mathbb{Z}_n^{k \times (k+1)}$, $\vec{f}^{(1)}, \ldots, \vec{f}^{(m)} \xleftarrow{\$} \mathbb{Z}_n^k$, for some appropriate $k \in \mathbb{N}$, $g_1 \xleftarrow{\$} \mathbb{G}_1$, and $g_2 \xleftarrow{\$} \mathbb{G}_2$.

3. Then, it computes $\boldsymbol{A}_1^{(j)} = g_1^{\boldsymbol{A}^{(j)}}$, $\boldsymbol{D}_1^{(j)} = g_1^{\boldsymbol{W}^{(j)} \boldsymbol{A}^{(j)}}$, $\boldsymbol{F}_1^{(j)} = g_1^{\boldsymbol{N}^{(j)} \boldsymbol{A}^{(j)}}$, for $j \in [m]$, and $G = e(g_1, g_2)$.

4. It sets the public parameters $\text{PP} = ((n, \mathbb{G}_1, \mathbb{G}_2, \mathbb{G}_T, e), g_1, g_2, G, \{\boldsymbol{A}_1^{(j)}, \boldsymbol{D}_1^{(j)}, \boldsymbol{F}_1^{(j)}\}_{j \in [m]})$, the encryption keys $\text{ENK}^{(j)} = \vec{f}^{(j)}$, for $j \in [m]$, and master secret key $\text{MSK} = (\{\boldsymbol{W}^{(j)}, \boldsymbol{N}^{(j)}\}_{j \in [m]}, \sum_{j \in [m]} \vec{f}^{(j)})$. It publishes PP, provides $\text{ENK}^{(j)}$ to the jth encrypter, for $j \in [m]$, while keeps MSK to itself.

OO-MIPE.OfflineKeyGen$(\text{PP}, \text{MSK}) \to \text{IT}_{\text{SK}}$: Taking as input the public parameters $\text{PP} = ((n, \mathbb{G}_1, \mathbb{G}_2, \mathbb{G}_T, e), g_1, g_2, G, \{\boldsymbol{A}_1^{(j)}, \boldsymbol{D}_1^{(j)}, \boldsymbol{F}_1^{(j)}\}_{j \in [m]})$ and the master secret key $\text{MSK} = (\{\boldsymbol{W}^{(j)}, \boldsymbol{N}^{(j)}\}_{j \in [m]}, \sum_{j \in [m]} \vec{f}^{(j)})$, the setup authority executes the following steps:

1. It first picks $\vec{z}^{(1)}, \ldots, \vec{z}^{(m)} \xleftarrow{\$} \mathbb{Z}_n^{k+1}$, and $\vec{h} \xleftarrow{\$} \mathbb{Z}_n^k$.

2. After that, it computes $\widetilde{\boldsymbol{k}}^{(1,j)} = g_2^{\vec{z}^{(j)} + \vec{h} \boldsymbol{N}^{(j)}}$, for $j \in [m]$, $\widetilde{\boldsymbol{k}}^{(2)} = g_2^{\vec{h}}$, and $\widetilde{K}^{(3)} = G^{\langle \sum_{j \in [m]} \vec{f}^{(j)}, \vec{h} \rangle}$.

3. It stores the intermediate decryption key $\text{IT}_{\text{SK}} = (\{\widetilde{\boldsymbol{k}}^{(1,j)}\}_{j \in [m]}, \widetilde{\boldsymbol{k}}^{(2)}, \widetilde{K}^{(3)}, \{\vec{z}^{(j)}\}_{j \in [m]})$.

OO-MIPE.OnlineKeyGen$(\text{PP}, \text{MSK}, \text{IT}_{\text{SK}}, (\vec{y}^{(1)}, \ldots, \vec{y}^{(m)})) \to \text{SK}(\vec{y}^{(1)}, \ldots, \vec{y}^{(m)})$:
On input the public parameters $\text{PP} = ((n, \mathbb{G}_1, \mathbb{G}_2, \mathbb{G}_T, e), g_1, g_2, G, \{\boldsymbol{A}_1^{(j)}, \boldsymbol{D}_1^{(j)}, \boldsymbol{F}_1^{(j)}\}_{j \in [m]})$, the master secret key $\text{MSK} = (\{\boldsymbol{W}^{(j)}, \boldsymbol{N}^{(j)}\}_{j \in [m]}, \sum_{j \in [m]} \vec{f}^{(j)})$, a fresh intermediate decryption key $\text{IT}_{\text{SK}} = (\{\widetilde{\boldsymbol{k}}^{(1,j)}\}_{j \in [m]}, \widetilde{\boldsymbol{k}}^{(2)}$,

$\widetilde{K}^{(3)}, \{\vec{z}^{(j)}\}_{j\in[m]})$ formed in the offline phase, along with an m-tuple of vectors $(\vec{y}^{(1)}, \ldots, \vec{y}^{(m)}) \in (\mathbb{Z}_n^\ell)^m$, the setup authority performs the following steps:

1. It sets $\boldsymbol{k}^{(1,j)} = \widetilde{\boldsymbol{k}}^{(1,j)}$, for $j \in [m]$, $\boldsymbol{k}^{(2)} = \widetilde{\boldsymbol{k}}^{(2)}$, $K^{(3)} = \widetilde{K}^{(3)}$, and $\vec{k}^{(4,j)} = \vec{y}^{(j)}\boldsymbol{W}^{(j)} - \vec{z}^{(j)}$, for $j \in [m]$.

2. It gives a legitimate decrypter with the decryption key $\mathrm{SK}(\vec{y}^{(1)}, \ldots, \vec{y}^{(m)}) = ((\vec{y}^{(1)}, \ldots, \vec{y}^{(m)}), \{\boldsymbol{k}^{(1,j)}\}_{j\in[m]}, \boldsymbol{k}^{(2)}, K^{(3)}, \{\vec{k}^{(4,j)}\}_{j\in[m]})$.

OO-MIPE.OfflineEncrypt$(\mathrm{PP}, j, \mathrm{ENK}^{(j)}) \rightarrow \mathrm{IT}_{\mathrm{CT}^{(j)}}$: The jth encrypter takes as input the public parameters $\mathrm{PP} = ((n, \mathbb{G}_1, \mathbb{G}_2, \mathbb{G}_T, e), g_1, g_2, G, \{\boldsymbol{A}_1^{(j)}, \boldsymbol{D}_1^{(j)}, \boldsymbol{F}_1^{(j)}\}_{j\in[m]})$, its index $j \in [m]$, along with its private encryption key $\mathrm{ENK}^{(j)} = \vec{f}^{(j)}$. It operates as follows:

1. It first selects $\vec{u}^{(j)} \xleftarrow{\$} \mathbb{Z}_n^\ell$ and $\vec{s}^{(j)} \xleftarrow{\$} \mathbb{Z}_n^k$.

2. Next, it computes $\widetilde{\boldsymbol{c}}^{(1,j)} = g_1^{\vec{u}^{(j)}}(\boldsymbol{D}_1^{(j)})^{\vec{s}^{(j)}} = g_1^{\vec{u}^{(j)} + \vec{s}^{(j)}\boldsymbol{A}^{(j)\intercal}\boldsymbol{W}^{(j)\intercal}}$, $\widetilde{\boldsymbol{c}}^{(2,j)} = g_1^{\vec{f}^{(j)}}(\boldsymbol{F}_1^{(j)})^{\vec{s}^{(j)}} = g_1^{\vec{f}^{(j)} + \vec{s}^{(j)}\boldsymbol{A}^{(j)\intercal}\boldsymbol{N}^{(j)\intercal}}$, and $\widetilde{\boldsymbol{c}}^{(3,j)} = (\boldsymbol{A}_1^{(j)})^{\vec{s}^{(j)}} = g_1^{\vec{s}^{(j)}\boldsymbol{A}^{(j)\intercal}}$.

3. It stores the intermediate ciphertext $\mathrm{IT}_{\mathrm{CT}^{(j)}} = (\widetilde{\boldsymbol{c}}^{(1,j)}, \widetilde{\boldsymbol{c}}^{(2,j)}, \widetilde{\boldsymbol{c}}^{(3,j)}, \vec{u}^{(j)})$.

OO-MIPE.OnlineEncrypt$(\mathrm{PP}, j, \mathrm{IT}_{\mathrm{CT}^{(j)}}, \vec{x}^{(j)}) \rightarrow \mathrm{CT}^{(j)}(\vec{x}^{(j)})$: An encrypter upon input the public parameters $\mathrm{PP} = ((n, \mathbb{G}_1, \mathbb{G}_2, \mathbb{G}_T, e), g_1, g_2, G, \{\boldsymbol{A}_1^{(j)}, \boldsymbol{D}_1^{(j)}, \boldsymbol{F}_1^{(j)}\}_{j\in[m]})$, its own index $j \in [m]$, a fresh intermediate ciphertext $\mathrm{IT}_{\mathrm{CT}^{(j)}} = (\widetilde{\boldsymbol{c}}^{(1,j)}, \widetilde{\boldsymbol{c}}^{(2,j)}, \widetilde{\boldsymbol{c}}^{(3,j)}, \vec{u}^{(j)})$ created in the offline phase, and a vector $\vec{x}^{(j)} \in \mathbb{Z}_n^\ell$, proceeds as follows:

1. It sets $\boldsymbol{c}^{(1,j)} = \widetilde{\boldsymbol{c}}^{(1,j)}$, $\boldsymbol{c}^{(2,j)} = \widetilde{\boldsymbol{c}}^{(2,j)}$, $\boldsymbol{c}^{(3,j)} = \widetilde{\boldsymbol{c}}^{(3,j)}$, and $\vec{c}^{(4,j)} = \vec{x}^{(j)} - \vec{u}^{(j)}$.

2. It outputs the ciphertext $\mathrm{CT}^{(j)}(\vec{x}^{(j)}) = (j, \boldsymbol{c}^{(1,j)}, \boldsymbol{c}^{(2,j)}, \boldsymbol{c}^{(3,j)}, \vec{c}^{(4,j)})$.

OO-MIPE.Decrypt$(\mathrm{PP}, \mathrm{SK}(\vec{y}^{(1)}, \ldots, \vec{y}^{(m)}), \{\mathrm{CT}^{(j)}(\vec{x}^{(j)})\}_{j\in[m]}) \rightarrow \sum_{j\in[m]} \langle \vec{x}^{(j)}, \vec{y}^{(j)} \rangle$ or $\perp$: A decrypter takes as input the public parameters $\mathrm{PP} = ((n, \mathbb{G}_1, \mathbb{G}_2, \mathbb{G}_T, e), g_1, g_2, G, \{\boldsymbol{A}_1^{(j)}, \boldsymbol{D}_1^{(j)}, \boldsymbol{F}_1^{(j)}\}_{j\in[m]})$, a decryption key $\mathrm{SK}(\vec{y}^{(1)}, \ldots, \vec{y}^{(m)}) = ((\vec{y}^{(1)}, \ldots, \vec{y}^{(m)})\{\boldsymbol{k}^{(1,j)}\}_{j\in[m]}, \boldsymbol{k}^{(2)}, K^{(3)}, \{\vec{k}^{(4,j)}\}_{j\in[m]})$ corresponding to an m-tuple of vectors $(\vec{y}^{(1)}, \ldots, \vec{y}^{(m)}) \in (\mathbb{Z}_n^\ell)^m$, and m ciphertexts $\{\mathrm{CT}^{(j)}(\vec{x}^{(j)}) = (j, \boldsymbol{c}^{(1,j)}, \boldsymbol{c}^{(2,j)}, \boldsymbol{c}^{(3,j)}, \vec{c}^{(4,j)})\}_{j\in[m]}$. It executes the following:

1. It first computes

$$\widetilde{T} = \prod_{j\in[m]} \left[\frac{E_\ell(\boldsymbol{c}^{(1,j)} g_1^{\vec{c}^{(4,j)}}, g_2^{\vec{y}^{(j)}}) E_k(\boldsymbol{c}^{(2,j)}, \boldsymbol{k}^{(2)})}{E_{k+1}(\boldsymbol{c}^{(3,j)}, \boldsymbol{k}^{(1,j)} g_2^{\vec{k}^{(4,j)}})} \right]. \tag{1}$$

2. Next, it computes $T = \dfrac{\widetilde{T}}{K^{(3)}}$.

3. Finally, it attempts to determine a value $\psi \in \mathbb{Z}_n$ such that $T = G^\psi$, by exhaustively searching a polynomial size range of possible values and outputs ψ, if successful. Otherwise, it outputs $\perp$ indicating failure.

Theorem 4.1 (Security of Our OO-MIPE Scheme). *The proposed* OO-MIPE *scheme is selectively secure under the k-Linear assumption.*

The proof of Theorem 4.1 is given in the full version.

References

1. Abdalla, M., Gay, R., Raykova, M., Wee, H.: Multi-input inner-product functional encryption from pairings. In: Coron, J.-S., Nielsen, J.B. (eds.) EUROCRYPT 2017. LNCS, vol. 10210, pp. 601–626. Springer, Cham (2017). https://doi.org/10.1007/978-3-319-56620-7_21
2. Agrawal, S., Rosen, A.: Online-offline functional encryption for bounded collusions. Cryptology ePrint Archive, Report 2016/361 (2016)
3. Attrapadung, N.: Dual system encryption via doubly selective security: framework, fully secure functional encryption for regular languages, and more. In: Nguyen, P.Q., Oswald, E. (eds.) EUROCRYPT 2014. LNCS, vol. 8441, pp. 557–577. Springer, Heidelberg (2014). https://doi.org/10.1007/978-3-642-55220-5_31
4. Attrapadung, N.: Dual system encryption framework in prime-order groups via computational pair encodings. In: Cheon, J.H., Takagi, T. (eds.) ASIACRYPT 2016. LNCS, vol. 10032, pp. 591–623. Springer, Heidelberg (2016). https://doi.org/10.1007/978-3-662-53890-6_20
5. Attrapadung, N., Libert, B., de Panafieu, E.: Expressive key-policy attribute-based encryption with constant-size ciphertexts. In: Catalano, D., Fazio, N., Gennaro, R., Nicolosi, A. (eds.) PKC 2011. LNCS, vol. 6571, pp. 90–108. Springer, Heidelberg (2011). https://doi.org/10.1007/978-3-642-19379-8_6
6. Chase, M., Meiklejohn, S.: Déjà Q: using dual systems to revisit q-type assumptions. In: Nguyen, P.Q., Oswald, E. (eds.) EUROCRYPT 2014. LNCS, vol. 8441, pp. 622–639. Springer, Heidelberg (2014). https://doi.org/10.1007/978-3-642-55220-5_34
7. Chen, J., Wee, H.: Semi-adaptive attribute-based encryption and improved delegation for boolean formula. In: Abdalla, M., De Prisco, R. (eds.) SCN 2014. LNCS, vol. 8642, pp. 277–297. Springer, Cham (2014). https://doi.org/10.1007/978-3-319-10879-7_16
8. Cheon, J.H.: Security analysis of the strong Diffie-Hellman problem. In: Vaudenay, S. (ed.) EUROCRYPT 2006. LNCS, vol. 4004, pp. 1–11. Springer, Heidelberg (2006). https://doi.org/10.1007/11761679_1
9. Goldwasser, S., Gordon, S.D., Goyal, V., Jain, A., Katz, J., Liu, F.-H., Sahai, A., Shi, E., Zhou, H.-S.: Multi-input functional encryption. In: Nguyen, P.Q., Oswald, E. (eds.) EUROCRYPT 2014. LNCS, vol. 8441, pp. 578–602. Springer, Heidelberg (2014). https://doi.org/10.1007/978-3-642-55220-5_32
10. Hohenberger, S., Waters, B.: Online/offline attribute-based encryption. In: Krawczyk, H. (ed.) PKC 2014. LNCS, vol. 8383, pp. 293–310. Springer, Heidelberg (2014). https://doi.org/10.1007/978-3-642-54631-0_17
11. Lewko, A., Waters, B.: New techniques for dual system encryption and fully secure HIBE with short ciphertexts. In: Micciancio, D. (ed.) TCC 2010. LNCS, vol. 5978, pp. 455–479. Springer, Heidelberg (2010). https://doi.org/10.1007/978-3-642-11799-2_27
12. Sahai, A., Waters, B.: Fuzzy identity-based encryption. In: Cramer, R. (ed.) EUROCRYPT 2005. LNCS, vol. 3494, pp. 457–473. Springer, Heidelberg (2005). https://doi.org/10.1007/11426639_27

13. Sakemi, Y., Hanaoka, G., Izu, T., Takenaka, M., Yasuda, M.: Solving a discrete logarithm problem with auxiliary input on a 160-bit elliptic curve. In: Fischlin, M., Buchmann, J., Manulis, M. (eds.) PKC 2012. LNCS, vol. 7293, pp. 595–608. Springer, Heidelberg (2012). https://doi.org/10.1007/978-3-642-30057-8_35
14. Wee, H.: Déjà Q: encore! Un Petit IBE. In: Kushilevitz, E., Malkin, T. (eds.) TCC 2016. LNCS, vol. 9563, pp. 237–258. Springer, Heidelberg (2016). https://doi.org/10.1007/978-3-662-49099-0_9
15. Yamada, S., Attrapadung, N., Hanaoka, G., Kunihiro, N.: A framework and compact constructions for non-monotonic attribute-based encryption. In: Krawczyk, H. (ed.) PKC 2014. LNCS, vol. 8383, pp. 275–292. Springer, Heidelberg (2014). https://doi.org/10.1007/978-3-642-54631-0_16

Symmetric Encryption

Optimizing Online Permutation-Based AE Schemes for Lightweight Applications

Yu Sasaki[✉] and Kan Yasuda[✉]

NTT Secure Platform Laboratories, Tokyo, Japan
{sasaki.yu,yasuda.kan}@lab.ntt.co.jp

Abstract. We explore ways to optimize online, permutation-based authenticated-encryption (AE) schemes for lightweight applications. The lightweight applications demand that AE schemes operate in resource-constrained environments, which raise two issues: (1) implementation costs must be low, and (2) ensuring proper use of a nonce is difficult due to its small size and lack of randomness. Regarding the implementation costs, recently it has been recognized that permutation-based (rather than block-cipher-based) schemes frequently show advantages. However, regarding the security under nonce misuse, the standard permutation-based duplex construction cannot ensure confidentiality. There exists one permutation-based scheme named APE which offers certain robustness against nonce misuse. Unfortunately, the APE construction has several drawbacks such as ciphertext expansion and bidirectional permutation circuits. The ciphertext expansion would require more bandwidth, and the bidirectional circuits would require a larger hardware footprint. In this paper, we propose new constructions of online permutation-based AE that require less bandwidth, a smaller hardware footprint and lower computational costs. We provide security proofs for the new constructions, demonstrating that they are as secure as the APE construction.

Keywords: AEAD · Permutation-based · Sponge · APE · Bandwidth Hardware footprint · Inverse-free

1 Introduction

With the rise of Internet of Things (IoT), *lightweight* cryptography is drawing more and more attentions today [9,15,18]. This is because many of the IoT devices need to operate within tight resource constraints and hence may not be able to accommodate conventional cryptographic algorithms. The constraints include, for example, limited amount of storage, power and bandwidth.

The lightweight cryptography aims for essentially the same type of security goal as the conventional cryptography, with two most important security notions being confidentiality and integrity. The two notions can be simultaneously achieved by a symmetric-key primitive called *authenticated encryption* (AE) [4,5,11]. Hence it becomes one of the most fundamental problems in

© Springer International Publishing AG 2017
J. K. Liu and P. Samarati (Eds.): ISPEC 2017, LNCS 10701, pp. 217–236, 2017.
https://doi.org/10.1007/978-3-319-72359-4_13

lightweight cryptography to come up with an AE scheme that can be efficiently run in resource-constrained environments.

Although the type of security goal is the same, appropriate design approaches may differ between lightweight cryptography and conventional one, due to the low-resource conditions in the former. Of the existing AE designs, some become more suitable for lightweight cryptography, while others remain less suitable. In recent years, it is recognized that *permutation-based* (rather than block-cipher-based) designs have comparative advantages in lightweight cryptography, owing to their small RAM footprint [3,8,13].

Unfortunately, naively building an AE scheme from permutations would not give us one that is workable in resource-constrained environments, because there is a major security issue inherent in lightweight AE: the initializing vector (IV) needs to be a *nonce* [20]. In general, the security of an AE scheme gets compromised if the same value of IV is used twice under the same key. However, in many resource-constrained scenarios it is difficult for devices to ensure their IV to be a nonce, as explained below.

Two typical methods to realize a nonce are *counter* and *randomization*. A counter IV would require a secure writable memory, which also needs to be non-volatile if the device is supplied with a weak battery or reboots frequently, because the IV may get reset due to loss of power or rebooting. Such memory tends to be costly to be securely implemented [16], and it is unlikely that devices with such a weak battery or unstable system would come with such rich memory. The other type, a randomized IV, is not easily realizable in lightweight environments, either. It is difficult for low-resource devices to ensure a source of randomness [10], which implies that a randomized IV may have insufficient entropy and produce collisions.

A related issue with nonce misuse is the fact that fully nonce-misuse-resistant AE schemes [14,21] require "two-pass" or "three-pass" operations on data, which result in a larger state size. This may make these schemes unsuitable for severely resource-constrained environments, even if the data size is relatively small. There is a "one-pass" permutation-based AE construction called the duplex construction [7], but it does not provide security under nonce misuse. Hence we aim at *online* permutation-based AE schemes [12], that is to say, when the same nonce is repeated, the only information leaked to adversaries is that the new message and associated data are the same as the previous ones up to the block where different data is processed for the first time. This onlineness provides us with a good tradeoff between performance (still "one-pass") and security.

There is previous work of online permutation-based AE called APE [2], but it requires relatively high bandwidth and large hardware footprint. The large footprint comes from the decryption process that uses both forward and inverse permutations, requiring independent circuits for the two permutation calls. Moreover, the computational costs of APE tend to be higher, because the technique called concurrent absorption [22] or full-state absorption [19], which reduce computational costs in the duplex construction, is not applicable to APE. A small note on APE is that it is equipped with backward decryption, which can be problematic for high-end use involving streaming data. Fortunately this should not be problematic in our setting, because in most lightweight applications the data and state sizes remain small and latency is not an issue.

Contributions of This Paper. We provide online permutation-based AE schemes with minimal bandwidth, hardware footprint and computational cost. Our constructions improve those over APE by a few to several dozens of bytes, which make a big difference in the resource-constrained environments. We provide three different constructions, APE^{RI}, APE^{OW} and APE^{CA}, which can be chosen depending on the situations.

1. The APE^{RI} scheme optimizes the hardware footprint, so that developers need to implement only the forward permutation f for the encryption circuit and only the inverse f^{-1} for the decryption circuit. Recall that APE required implementation of both f and f^{-1} for decryption. The bandwidth, computational cost and security are exactly the same as APE, hence APE^{RI} simply improves APE in the hardware footprint. The core idea is replacing the standard nonce-based AE framework of APE with the protected-IV (PIV) framework formalized by Shrimpton and Terashima [23], which converts nonce N to other value called reconstruction information (RI) and sends RI to the receiver instead of N.

2. The APE^{OW} scheme further modifies APE^{RI} in order to improve bandwidth while it inherits improved hardware footprint of APE^{RI}. The most interesting feature of APE^{OW} is that it adopts the overwrite-mode of the sponge construction instead of the XOR-absorbing mode for processing N. Namely after absorbing N, we replace r bits (called rate) with the first block of associated data A. This allows the receiver to verify authenticity and privacy of received (A, C, T) without N. Hence, it saves bandwidth for sending N and computational cost for processing N in decryption.

3. The APE^{CA} scheme improves bandwidth in different approach from APE^{OW}. APE^{OW} improves bandwidth by not sending N. The advantage of APE^{OW} becomes bigger as the size of N increases. APE^{CA} improves bandwidth even if N is small or even users choose not to use N. The idea here is avoiding the expansion of ciphertext or tag. Namely, when the input data size to encryption is $|N| + |A| + |M|$, we aim to achieve the output size of $|N| + |A| + |M| + c/2$ where $c/2$ is proven security level, i.e. $|C| = |M|$ and tag size is $c/2$ bits. This is the optimal bandwidth in the nonce based AE framework because $|C|$ cannot be smaller than $|M|$ and using $c/2$-bit tag is inevitable to ensure $c/2$-bit security. In other words, even by being based on the permutation, APE^{CA} achieves the competitive bandwidth with standard AE schemes.

Paper Outline. Section 2 summarizes specification of APE and its disadvantages. Section 3 introduces AE framework by Shrimpton and Terashima [23] and defines security under this framework. Our three new constructions APE^{RI}, APE^{OW}, and APE^{CA} are proposed in Sects. 4, 5, and 6, respectively. Finally, we compare the performance of those schemes and APE in Sect. 7.

2 Previous Work: APE

In this section, we introduce the specification of APE in Sect. 2.1 and explains several drawbacks of APE in Sect. 2.2.

2.1 Specification of APE

The APE scheme is the only existing permutation based AE mode which satisfies onlineness and offers a certain level of robustness against nonce-misuse, which is often called "up to prefix security," i.e. even if nonce is repeated, the scheme only leaks the information that the new message and associated data are the same as the previous ones up to the block where different data is processed for the first time. The mode of operation was firstly proposed at FSE 2014 [2], then it was later submitted to CAESAR with a specific primitive [1]. In this paper, we only focus our attention on the mode of operation.

The APE scheme adopts a b-bit permutation f as its underlying primitive. The b-bit state is further divided into r bits called *rate* and c bits called *capacity* like the well-known sponge or duplex constructions [6,7].

Encryption of APE. The APE scheme uses a c-bit key K. It takes an associated data A, a nonce N, a message M as input and computes the corresponding ciphertext C and a tag T. If the user compromises security to be "up to prefix security," the nonce input is not necessary. In order to unify the description, it is assumed that the nonce is a part of associated data A, thus N is not explicitly written even if N is used. In this paper, N is an important factor to minimize the bandwidth, thus N is often explicitly written independently of A.

The APE scheme initializes the state to r bits of zeros and c bits of K. Then A and M are divided into r bits of $A_0, A_1, A_2, \cdots$ and $M_0, M_1, M_2, \cdots$. Here, the designers limit that A and M must be a multiple of r.

To process A, the scheme first xors A_0 to rate and updates the state by computing f. This is iterated until all the associated data blocks are processed. In the end, the scheme xors a single bit one to capacity, which makes a border between A and M. Then, the scheme xors M_0 to rate, updates the state by f, and outputs r bits of rate as the corresponding ciphertext block C_0. This is iterated until all the message blocks are processed. Finally, c bits of K is xored to capacity, and the resulted c bits are output as tag T.

A typical choice of the ratio of r and c is $r = c/2$, which comes from $c/2$-bit security of the construction. The encryption of APE for $r = c/2$ is illustrated in Fig. 1.

Decryption of APE. The decryption of APE is a bit tricky, which is often called *backward decryption*. By concatenating the last ciphertext block and $K \oplus T$, the receiver constructs the b-bit state. Then, the receiver updates the state by f^{-1}, outputs the XOR of the rate and the next ciphertext block as the last plaintext block and replaces the rate with the next ciphertext block. This

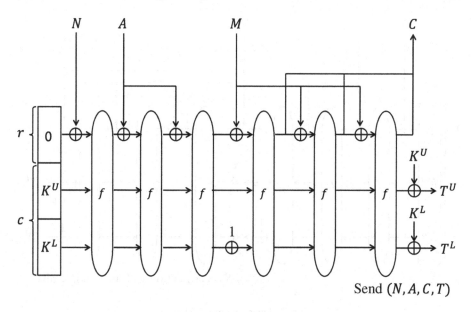

Fig. 1. Encryption of APE

is iterated until the second message block M_1 is recovered. The scheme then replaces rate by C_0 and updates the state by f^{-1}, but M_0 is not recovered at this stage. Let rate and capacity of the resulted state be S_r and S_c, respectively.

Procedures to recover the first message block M_0 and verification are very different. The receiver processes A as the encryption process (in the forward direction). Let rate and capacity of the resulted state be S'_r and S'_c. The receiver checks the match of S_c and S'_c for verification. If they match, the scheme computes $M_0 \leftarrow S_r \oplus S'_r$ and outputs the recovered M. If they do not match, the scheme returns the failure symbol $\perp$. The decryption process of APE for $r = c/2$ is illustrated in Fig. 2.

Security of APE. Intuitively, both of privacy and integrity of APE are proven to be secure up to $2^{c/2}$ queries in both of the nonce-respect and nonce-repeat settings.

2.2 Drawbacks of APE

Requiring High Bandwidth. Although integrity of APE is secure up to $2^{c/2}$ queries, owing to its computational structure, it is necessary to output a c-bit tag T, which increases communication cost compared to ordinary AE schemes that produce a $c/2$-bit tag for $c/2$-bit security.

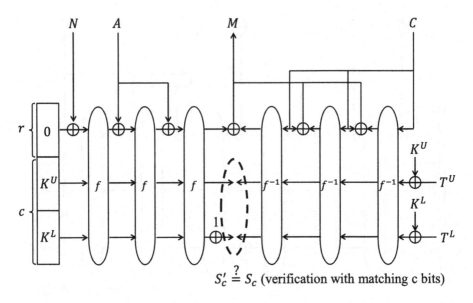

$$S'_c \stackrel{?}{=} S_c \text{ (verification with matching c bits)}$$

Fig. 2. Decryption of APE

Large Hardware Footprint. As illustrated in Figs. 1 and 2, the encryption of APE only requires to implement f, while the decryption of APE requires to implement both f and f^{-1}. This forces bigger hardware footprint for decryption devices.

High Computational Cost. The number of calls of f or f^{-1} is $(|N| + |A| + |M|)/r$, where $|X|$ represents the size of the variable X. At a glance this seems optimal. However, for the duplex construction, it is known that M and A can be processed simultaneously, e.g. *the concurrent absorption* [22], thus the number of permutation calls can be $(|N| + |A| + |M|)/b$. From a security reason, such an optimization cannot be applied to APE. (Intuitively, a tag reveals some information on the capacity value, which makes impossible to prove its security when the direct modification of any capacity value is allowed to the adversary.)

Remarks on Backward Decryption. The backward decryption of APE recovers the message from the last block to the first block. It is often said that this can be a drawback when the message length is big because it cannot be used for data streaming. In fact, APE was designed as a general-purpose AE scheme, hence the criticism makes sense. On the other hand, we point out that the backward decryption is not a problem at all in lightweight applications for IoT because the packet size is designed to be very short. For example, LoRa [17], a popular standard for Low Power Wide Area (LPWA), specifies that the maximum packet size is around 40 bytes, which is easy to store even for resource-restricted devices.

3   Security Definitions

In this section we first give a syntactical definition of authenticated encryption. Then we provide a security model for online authenticated encryption scheme.

3.1   Authenticated Encryption

Put $\mathbf{R} := \{0,1\}^r$ and $\mathbf{C} := \{0,1\}^c$, corresponding to the rate r and the capacity c. We use the notation $\mathbf{R}^* := \cup_{i=0}^{\ell} \mathbf{R}^i$ and $\mathbf{R}^+ := \cup_{i=1}^{\ell} \mathbf{R}^i$ where ℓ is the maximum length of queries that an adversary (an oracle machine) makes to its oracles. Here by the usual convention we regard $\mathbf{R}^0 = \varnothing$.

We adopt the generalized framework of authenticated encryption formalized by Shrimpton and Terashima [23]. An AE scheme is a triplet $(\mathcal{K}, \mathcal{E}, \mathcal{D})$. The key generation algorithm $\mathcal{K}$ simply draws a key $K \xleftarrow{\$} \mathbf{C}$ uniformly at random. Given a key $K \leftarrow \mathcal{K}(\cdot)$, the encryption algorithm $\mathcal{E}_K$ takes as its input a nonce $N \in \mathbf{R}^n$ for some fixed n, associate data $A \in \mathbf{R}^+$ and a message $M \in \mathbf{R}^+$ and outputs reconstruction information $RI \in \mathbf{R}^*$, ciphertext $C \in \mathbf{R}^*$ and a tag $T \in \mathbf{C}$ as $(RI, C, T) \leftarrow \mathcal{E}_K(N, A, M)$. Similarly, given a key K, the decryption algorithm $\mathcal{D}_K$ takes as its input reconstruction information $RI \in \mathbf{R}^*$, associated data $A \in \mathbf{R}^+$, ciphertext $C \in \mathbf{R}^*$ and a tag $T \in \mathbf{C}$, and outputs either the reject symbol $\perp$ or a message $M \in \mathbf{R}^+$ as $M \leftarrow \mathcal{D}_K(RI, A, C, T)$ where M may be equal to $\perp$. Optionally, an AE scheme may be equipped with a nonce recovery algorithm $\mathcal{R}_K$ which takes as its input reconstruction information $RI \in \mathbb{R}^*$, associated data $A \in \mathbf{R}^+$, ciphertext $C \in \mathbf{R}^*$ and a tag $T \in \mathbf{C}$, and outputs a (possibly partial) nonce $N[1] \in \mathbf{R}$ as $N[1] \leftarrow \mathcal{R}_K(RI, A, C, T)$, irrespective of the verification result. In this case the AE scheme is a quadruplet $(\mathcal{K}, \mathcal{E}, \mathcal{D}, \mathcal{R})$.

3.2   Security of Online AE Schemes

We prove the security of our schemes in the random-permutation model, regarding the underlying permutation $f : \mathbf{B} \to \mathbf{B}$ as an ideal. Here $\mathbf{B} := \{0,1\}^{r+c} = \mathbf{R} \times \mathbf{C}$. We consider the strongest adversaries possible, namely computationally unbounded ones. Hence we limit the power of adversaries only by query complexity. Let q, ℓ, σ denote the maximum number of queries, the maximum length of each query, and the total number of blocks of queries, respectively.

An adversary is given access to three oracles. Two of them are offline oracles $y \leftarrow f(x)$ and $x \leftarrow f^{-1}(y)$ where f is drawn uniformly at random from permutations on $\mathbf{B}$. They correspond to the underlying permutation. The remaining two are an encryption oracle $\mathcal{E}(\cdot, \cdot, \cdot)$ and a decryption oracle $\mathcal{D}(\cdot, \cdot, \cdot, \cdot)$. The goal of the adversary is to distinguish, by outputting a bit $b \in \{0,1\}$ after its interaction with oracles, between two worlds. In the real game, the encryption oracle is the real oracle $(RI, C, T) \leftarrow \mathcal{E}_K(N, A, M)$, and similarly the decryption oracle is the real oracle $M \leftarrow \mathcal{D}_K(RI, A, C, T)$. In the ideal game, the encryption oracle $\$(N, A, M)$ is defined as follows, and the decryption oracle is simply $\perp(RI, A, C, T)$ which always returns the reject symbol $\perp$.

The ideal encryption oracle $(RI, C, T) \leftarrow \$(N, A, M)$ is defined as follows. The value RI is computed in exactly the same way as the real world, i.e. $(RI, \cdot, \cdot, \cdot) \leftarrow \mathcal{E}_K(N, A, M)$. To describe how C and T are generated in the ideal world, write $M = M[1]M[2]\cdots M[w]$. We choose functions $g : \mathbf{R}^+ \times \mathbf{R}^* \to \mathbf{R}$ and $g' : \mathbf{R}^+ \times \mathbf{R}^+ \to \mathbf{C}$ uniformly at random, and define

$$C[i] := g(NA, M[1]M[2]\cdots M[i]) \qquad \text{for } i = 1, 2, \ldots, w$$
$$T := g'(NA, M).$$

When there is a nonce recovery algorithm $N[1] \leftarrow \mathcal{R}_K(RI, A, C, T)$, in the ideal world this is replaced with a random oracle $\$'$ which chooses an independently random function $g'' : \mathbf{R} \times \mathbf{R}^+ \times \mathbf{R}^* \times \mathbf{C} \to \mathbf{R}$ and outputs

$$N[1] \leftarrow g''(RI, A, C, T).$$

Now formally we define the advantage of an adversary D as

$$\mathrm{Adv}(D) := \Pr\left[D^{f, f^{-1}, \mathcal{E}_K, \mathcal{D}_K, \mathcal{R}_K} = 1\right] - \Pr\left[D^{f, f^{-1}, \$, \bot, \$'} = 1\right],$$

where $D^{\cdots} = 1$ denotes the event that D outputs 1 after interacting with its oracles $\cdots$. The probabilities are defined over random coins used by the oracles, and those used by D if any.

We assume that adversary D does not repeat a query or make a trivial-win query. That is, if D makes a query $(RI, C, T) \leftarrow \mathcal{E}_K(N, A, M)$, then D makes neither a $\mathcal{D}$-query (RI, A, C, T) nor an $\mathcal{R}$-query (RI, A, C, T).

4 APE^{RI}: Minimizing Hardware Footprint

In this section we present our first scheme, APE^{RI}, which offers a smaller hardware footprint than the original APE by its encryption algorithm making calls only to the forward permutation f while its decryption algorithm only to the inverse f^{-1}. The construction follows the generalized AE framework that utilizes reconstruction information RI. See Figs. 3 and 4 for illustration of the scheme.

The encryption algorithm of APE^{RI} is very similar to that of APE. We assume $N \in \mathbf{R}$. The main difference is that it additionally outputs r bits of the internal state as RI. The user (who has performed the encryption algorithm) does not send N but sends RI instead, together with C, T. Note that $|RI| = |N|$, and hence the communication cost of APE^{RI} is exactly the same as that of APE. Also note that the encryption of APE only calls f and not f^{-1}, and APE^{RI} inherits this good property. A small remark here is that the position of xoring 1 in the capacity is moved 1-block earlier in the new scheme than in APE. This is because APE^{RI} starts outputting the rate value 1-block earlier than APE, and in this way we can "reuse" the known results of APE for proving the security of APE^{RI}.

A major difference between APE^{RI} and APE comes in the decryption process. To decrypt (RI, A, C, T), the process is exactly the same up to the recovery

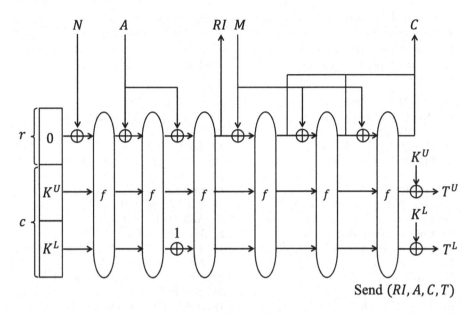

Fig. 3. Illustration of APE^{RI} encryption

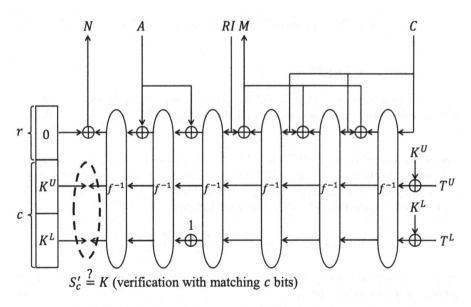

Fig. 4. Illustration of APE^{RI} decryption

of $M[2]$. In APE^{RI}, $M[1]$ can be recovered in a continuous way thanks to the presence of RI. After M is recovered, the decryption procedure continues to backtrack the computation by using A. After finishing absorbing all blocks of A, the capacity should match the value of K for verification. Formally, the encryption and decryption algorithms of APE^{RI} are defined in Fig. 5.

```
 1: M[1]M[2] ··· M[w] ← M            17: C[1]C[2] ··· C[w] ← C
 2: A[1]A[2] ··· A[u] ← A            18: A[1]A[2] ··· A[u] ← A
 3: V ← (0^r, K^U, K^L)              19: V ← (0^r, T^U ⊕ K^U, T^L ⊕ K^L)
 4: V ← f(N ⊕ V^r, V^U, V^L)         20: for i = w to 2 do
 5: for i = 1 to u − 1 do            21:     V ← f^{-1}(C[i], V^U, V^L)
 6:     V ← f(A[i] ⊕ V^r, V^U, V^L)  22:     M[i] ← V^r ⊕ C[i − 1]
 7: end for                         23: end for
 8: V ← f(A[u] ⊕ V^r, V^U, V^L ⊕ 1)  24: V ← f^{-1}(C[1], V^U, V^L)
 9: RI ← V^r                        25: M[1] ← V^r ⊕ RI
10: for i = 1 to w do               26: V ← f^{-1}(RI, V^U, V^L)
11:     V ← f(M[i] ⊕ V^r, V^U, V^L)  27: V ← f^{-1}(A[u] ⊕ V^r, V^U, V^L ⊕ 1)
12:     C[i] ← V^r                  28: for i = u − 1 to 2 do
13: end for                         29:     V ← f^{-1}(A[i] ⊕ V^r, V^U, V^L)
14: T^U ← V^U ⊕ K^U                 30: end for
15: T^L ← V^L ⊕ K^L                 31: if V^U ‖ V^T = K then
16: return (RI, C, T)               32:     return M
                                    33: else
                                    34:     return ⊥
                                    35: end if
```

Fig. 5. Encryption and decryption algorithms of APE^{RI}

4.1 Security of APE^{RI}

In this section we prove that APE^{RI} is as secure as the original APE as an authenticated encryption scheme. Recall that for APE^{RI} we assume $N \in \mathbf{R}$ (i.e. $n = 1$).

Theorem 1. *Let $\Pi = (\mathcal{K}, \mathcal{E}, \mathcal{D})$ be APE^{RI}. Then Π is at least as secure as the original APE scheme $\Pi' = (\mathcal{K}, \mathcal{E}', \mathcal{D}')$ that uses the same underlying permutation f and the parameters r, c. Specifically, for any adversary D attacking Π, there exists an adversary D' that attacks Π' and satisfies*

$$\text{Adv}_\Pi(D) \leq \text{Adv}_{\Pi'}(D') + \frac{4\sigma^2}{2^{r+c}} + \frac{4\sigma(2\sigma + 1)}{2^c},$$

where σ denotes the query complexity of D and D' makes at most twice many queries to its oracles as D.

Proof. Consider an intermediate scheme $\tilde{\Pi} := (\mathcal{K}, \mathcal{E}, \mathcal{D}')$. We first show that $\tilde{\Pi}$ is as secure as the original APE $\Pi' = (\mathcal{K}, \mathcal{E}', \mathcal{D}')$. Given an adversary $\tilde{D}$ that attacks $\tilde{\Pi}$, we construct an adversary D' that attacks Π'. Simply, D' runs $\tilde{D}$. When $\tilde{D}$ makes queries to its $f/f^{-1}/\mathcal{D}'$ oracles, the adversary D' forwards the queries to its $f/f^{-1}/\mathcal{D}'$ oracles, respectively, and returns to $\tilde{D}$ whatever D' gets from its oracles. When $\tilde{D}$ makes an $\mathcal{E}$-query (N, A, M), the adversary D' makes an $\mathcal{E}'$-query $(N, A[1] \cdots A[u-1], A[u]M)$ and receives a reply (C, T) from its $\mathcal{E}'$-oracle. Then D' returns (RI, C', T) to $\tilde{D}$, where $RI := C[1]$ and $C' = C[2] \cdots C[w+1]$. Eventually, the adversary D' outputs the bit b that $\tilde{D}$ outputs. We see that

$$\mathrm{Adv}_{\tilde{\Pi}}(\tilde{D}) \leq \mathrm{Adv}_{\Pi'}(D'), \tag{1}$$

where the query complexity of D' is the same as that of $\tilde{D}$.

Next we consider another intermediate scheme $\Pi^+ := (\mathcal{K}, \mathcal{E}, \mathcal{D}', \mathcal{R})$ which is nothing but the above $\tilde{\Pi}$ now equipped with the recovery function $N \leftarrow \mathcal{R}_K(A, RI, C, T)$. Given D^+ that attacks Π^+, we can construct an adversary $\tilde{D}$ that attacks $\tilde{\Pi}$ by simulating the $\mathcal{R}$-oracle with a random function. The simulation fails only when the recovery function $\mathcal{R}_K$ does not behave random, and such a probability can be bounded by $\sigma^2/2^{r+c} + 2\sigma(\sigma+1)/2^c$ (Andreeva et al. [2, Theorem 2]) where σ denotes the query complexity of D^+. Therefore, we have

$$\mathrm{Adv}_{\Pi^+}(D^+) \leq \mathrm{Adv}_{\tilde{\Pi}}(\tilde{D}) + \frac{\sigma^2}{2^{r+c}} + \frac{2\sigma(\sigma+1)}{2^c}, \tag{2}$$

where the query complexity of $\tilde{D}$ is no more than that of D^+.

Finally, given an adversary D that attacks $\Pi = (\mathcal{K}, \mathcal{E}, \mathcal{D})$, we construct an adversary D^+ that attacks Π^+ as follows. The adversary D^+ runs D as its subroutine and forwards all $f/f^{-1}/\mathcal{E}$ queries and replies. When D makes a $\mathcal{D}$-query (A, RI, C, T), the adversary D^+ first makes an $\mathcal{R}$-query (A, RI, C, T) and receives $N \leftarrow \mathcal{R}(A, RI, C, T)$. Then D^+ makes a $\mathcal{D}$-query (N, A, C, T). We see that D^+ perfectly simulates the real and ideal worlds for D and hence

$$\mathrm{Adv}_{\Pi}(\tilde{D}) \leq \mathrm{Adv}_{\Pi^+}(D^+), \tag{3}$$

where the query complexity of D^+ is at most twice that of D. Combining (1), (2) and (3) proves the theorem. $\square$

5 APE^{OW}: Lower Bandwidth via Nonce-Less Decryption

APE^{RI} introduced in the previous section could improve the hardware footprint, while another strong drawback of APE, namely bandwidth, was untouched with APE^{RI}. The main purpose of this section is modifying APE^{RI} to improve the bandwidth by keeping the same hardware footprint of APE^{RI}.

The most interesting feature in this construction is using the *overwrite-mode* of the sponge hash construction for processing N. During encryption, we process N as the standard keyed sponge construction to make a b-bit state. We then replace r-bit rate with zeros. The remaining c bits of the state inherit the result of processing N. Intuitively, the r bits of zeros are the bit-string used for authentication. Hence, the sender does not need to communicate N to the

1: $M[1]M[2]\cdots M[w] \leftarrow M$
2: $A[1]A[2]\cdots A[u] \leftarrow A$
3: $N[1]N[2]\cdots N[v] \leftarrow N$
4: $V \leftarrow (0^r, K^U, K^L)$
5: **for** $i = 1$ to v **do**
6:     $V \leftarrow f(N[i] \oplus V^r, V^U, V^L)$
7: **end for**
8: $V \leftarrow (0^r, V^U, V^L)$
9: **for** $i = 1$ to $u - 1$ **do**
10:     $V \leftarrow f(A[i] \oplus V^r, V^U, V^L)$
11: **end for**
12: $V \leftarrow f(A[u] \oplus V^r, V^U, V^L \oplus 1)$
13: $RI \leftarrow V^r$
14: **for** $i = 1$ to w **do**
15:     $V \leftarrow f(M[i] \oplus V^r, V^U, V^L)$
16:     $C[i] \leftarrow V^r$
17: **end for**
18: $T^U \leftarrow V^U \oplus K^U$
19: $T^L \leftarrow V^L \oplus K^L$
20: **return** (RI, C, T)

21: $C[1]C[2]\cdots C[w] \leftarrow C$
22: $A[1]A[2]\cdots A[u] \leftarrow A$
23: $V \leftarrow (0^r, T^U \oplus K^U, T^L \oplus K^L)$
24: **for** $i = w$ to 2 **do**
25:     $V \leftarrow f^{-1}(C[i], V^U, V^L)$
26:     $M[i] \leftarrow V^r \oplus C[i-1]$
27: **end for**
28: $V \leftarrow f^{-1}(C[1], V^U, V^L)$
29: $M[1] \leftarrow V^r \oplus RI$
30: $V \leftarrow f^{-1}(RI, V^U, V^L)$
31: $V \leftarrow f^{-1}(A[u] \oplus V^r, V^U, V^L \oplus 1)$
32: **for** $i = u - 1$ to 2 **do**
33:     $V \leftarrow f^{-1}(A[i] \oplus V^r, V^U, V^L)$
34: **end for**
35: **if** $V^r \oplus A[1] = 0$ **then**
36:     **return** M
37: **else**
38:     **return** $\bot$
39: **end if**

Fig. 6. Encryption and decryption algorithms of APE^{OW}

receiver, which contributes to improve the bandwidth. In order to decrypt the first message block without implementing f^{-1}, we need r-bits of RI as introduced in APE^{RI}. The construction is named APE^{OW}, and the encryption and decryption procedures of APE^{OW} are defined in Fig. 6. Their illustrations for $r = c/2$ are given in Figs. 7 and 8.

Advantages of APE^{OW}. Advantages of APE^{OW} can be summarized as follows.

Requiring Low Bandwidth. The amount of communicated data is reduced by a factor of $|N|$ bits due to the omission of sending N, while it is increased by a factor of r bits due to RI. Thus, the bandwidth is improved from the original APE by a factor of $|N| - r$ bits. Obviously, if $|N|$ is so small that $|N| - r$ is negative, users should use APE^{RI} instead of APE^{OW}. If $|N| > r$, APE^{OW} simply outperforms APE^{RI}.

Small Hardware Footprint. APE^{OW} inherits the advantage of APE^{RI}, namely users need to implement only f for encryption devices and only f^{-1} for decryption devices.

Low Computational Cost. The encryption procedure of APE^{OW} is exactly the same as APE^{RI} but for overwriting the rate after processing N with 0^r instead of directly xoring A. Hence the computational cost of encryption of APE^{OW} is the same as one for APE^{RI} and even for the original APE. Computational cost of decryption is greatly improved from APE^{RI} and APE owing to the omission of processing N. This is another big advantage of APE^{OW}.

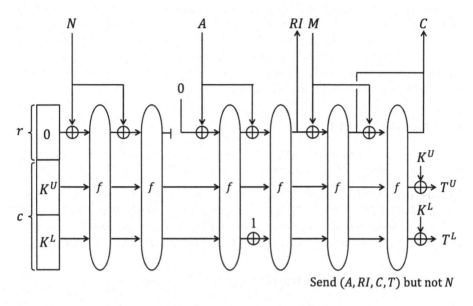

Fig. 7. Encryption of APE^{OW}

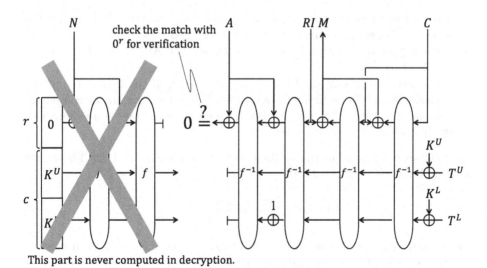

Fig. 8. Decryption of APE^{OW}

Recommended Parameters of APE^{OW}. As defined in Fig. 6, verification is performed by matching the r-bit information, thus security for tag guessing is up to r bits. When $r = c/2$, this matches the security of APE. When $r > c/2$, this part is not the bottleneck and thus security is standard $c/2$ bits. When $r < c/2$, this part lowers the security of the entire construction. Hence, we do not recommend using APE^{OW} when $r < c/2$. Instead, we recommend another construction, which will be explained in Sect. 6.

5.1   Security of APE^{OW}

In this section we prove that APE^{OW} is secure as an AE scheme. The scheme is secure up to $\min\{2^r, 2^{c/2}\}$ queries, which becomes $2^{c/2}$ when $r \geq c/2$.

Theorem 2. *Let $\Pi = (\mathcal{K}, \mathcal{E}, \mathcal{D})$ be APE^{OW}. Then Π is secure as an AE scheme. Specifically, let $\Pi' = (\mathcal{K}, \mathcal{E}', \mathcal{D}')$ be the original APE scheme that uses the same underlying permutation f and the parameters r, c. Then, for any adversary D attacking Π, there exists an adversary D' that attacks Π' and satisfies*

$$\mathrm{Adv}_\Pi(D) \leq \mathrm{Adv}_{\Pi'}(D') + \frac{2\sigma^2}{2^{r+c}} + \frac{3\sigma(2\sigma+1)}{2^c} + \frac{\sigma}{2^r},$$

where σ denotes the query complexity of D and D' makes at most twice many queries to its oracles as D.

Proof. We consider an intermediate scheme $\tilde{\Pi} = (\tilde{\mathcal{K}}, \tilde{\mathcal{E}}, \tilde{\mathcal{D}})$ which is a modification of APE^{RI}, as follows:

1. Two independent keys $K_1, K_2 \in \mathbf{C}$ are used for the initialization and the masking of tags, respectively. So we have $(K_1, K_2) \leftarrow \tilde{\mathcal{K}}(\cdot)$.
2. The encryption algorithm $\tilde{\mathcal{E}}$ generates RI just like APE^{RI}, as $(RI, C, T) \leftarrow \tilde{\mathcal{E}}_{K_1, K_2}(N, A, M)$.
3. The decryption algorithm $\tilde{\mathcal{D}}$ takes as its input both the nonce N and the reconstruction information RI, and the verification is done not by comparing the capacity state value with K_1 but by comparing the rate state value with the first block $N[1]$ of the nonce.

Now the security proof of the original APE by Andreeva et al. [2, Theorem 2] also applies to $\tilde{\Pi}$, and we obtain

$$\mathrm{Adv}(\tilde{D}) \leq \frac{\sigma^2}{2^{r+c}} + \frac{2\sigma(\sigma+1)}{2^c} + \frac{\sigma}{2^r} \tag{4}$$

for any adversary $\tilde{D}$ that attacks $\tilde{\Pi}$ and makes queries of complexity at most σ.

Now we consider intermediate scheme $\Pi^* = (\mathcal{K}^*, \mathcal{E}^*, \mathcal{D}^*)$ which operates as follows:

1. Choose a random function $g : \mathbf{R}^n \to \mathbf{C}$. This is used for generating the initialization key as $K_1 \leftarrow g(N)$.

2. An independent key $K_2 \xleftarrow{\$} \mathbf{C}$ is used for masking tags.
3. The encryption algorithm $\mathcal{E}^*$ and the decryption algorithm $\mathcal{D}^*$ are exactly the same as those of $\tilde{\Pi}$, except the key K_1 is generated as above.

Now let D^* be an adversary attacking Π^*, and then by a hybrid argument we get

$$\mathrm{Adv}(D^*) \leq \frac{\sigma^2}{2^{r+c}} + \frac{2\sigma(\sigma+1)}{2^c} + \frac{\sigma}{2^r}, \tag{5}$$

where again σ denotes the total query complexity of the adversary.

Lastly, we compare Π and Π^*. In the former the "keys" are generated from N and K_1 through the calls of permutation f, whereas in the latter the "keys" are generated as $g(N)$. Hence by the same argument as the privacy proof of APE by Andreeva et al. [2, Theorem 1], we get

$$\mathrm{Adv}(D) \leq \mathrm{Adv}(D^*) + \frac{\sigma^2}{2^{r+c}} + \frac{\sigma(\sigma+1)}{2^c}, \tag{6}$$

where σ denotes the total query complexity of D. From (4), (5) and (6) we see that the theorem is proved. □

6   APE^{CA}: Lower Bandwidth via Absorption in Capacity

The idea of improving bandwidth by APE^{OW} is omitting the communication of N between encryption and decryption players. In this section, we present another construction to improve bandwidth from a different point of view. Recall that one of the drawbacks of APE is that the tag size (c bits) is always bigger than the security parameter ($c/2$ bits) owing to its decryption procedure. In this section, our goal is minimizing the expansion of ciphertext or expansion of tag in order to make the bandwidth to be competitive as standard AE schemes, i.e. when the input data size to encryption is $|N| + |A| + |M|$, we aim to achieve the output size of $|N| + |A| + |M| + c/2$ by making $|C| = |M|$ and $|T| = c/2$.

The overall idea is as follows. In the original APE, verification is performed by checking the match of c bits as illustrated in Fig. 2. The same applies to the verification of APE^{RI}. Considering that the security of the entire construction is $c/2$ bits, using a c-bit string for verification can be regarded as the waste of the information. Hence, our idea is separating the c-bit string used for verification of APE^{RI} (K) into two $c/2$-bit strings (K^U and K^L), and use one of them for verification and use the other one for encrypting $c/2$ bits of M denoted by $M^{c/2}$. Differently from APE^{RI}, we now send N in clear, thus do not need to hide r bits of N at the very beginning by using 0^r in the initial state. Instead, we encrypt r bits of M denoted by M^r at this position. In the end, r bits of RI in APE^{RI} can be a ciphertext of M^r and $c/2$ bits of T^U in APE^{RI} can be a ciphertext of $M^{c/2}$, which achieves $|M| = |C|$. The remaining tag size is $c/2$ bits, thus $|T| = c/2$ is achieved.

Our idea of absorbing M both in rate and (a half of) capacity can be regarded as a variant of the concurrent absorption [22], which absorbs M in rate and A in capacity. We call this scheme APE^{CA}, and the encryption and decryption algorithms are defined in Fig. 9. They are also illustrated in Figs. 10 and 11.

1: $M^r M^{c/2} M[1]M[2]\cdots M[w] \leftarrow M$
2: $A[1]A[2]\cdots A[u] \leftarrow A$
3: $V \leftarrow (0^r, K^U, K^L)$
4: $V \leftarrow f(M^r \oplus V^r, M^{c/2} \oplus V^U, V^L)$
5: $V \leftarrow f(N \oplus V^r, V^U, V^L)$
6: **for** $i = 1$ to $u - 1$ **do**
7:     $V \leftarrow f(A[i] \oplus V^r, V^U, V^L)$
8: **end for**
9: $V \leftarrow (A[u] \oplus V^r, V^U, V^L \oplus 1)$
10: $C^r \leftarrow V^r$
11: **for** $i = 1$ to w **do**
12:     $V \leftarrow f(M[i] \oplus V^r, V^U, V^L)$
13:     $C[i] \leftarrow V^r$
14: **end for**
15: $C^{c/2} \leftarrow V^U \oplus K^U$
16: $T \leftarrow V^L \oplus K^L$
17: $C \leftarrow C^r C^{c/2} C[1]C[2]\cdots C[w]$
18: **return** (C, T)

19: $C^r C^{c/2} C[1]C[2]\cdots C[w] \leftarrow C$
20: $A[1]A[2]\cdots A[u] \leftarrow A$
21: $V \leftarrow (0^r, K^U \oplus C^{c/2}, K^L \oplus T)$
22: **for** $i = w$ to 2 **do**
23:     $V \leftarrow f^{-1}(C[i], V^U, V^L)$
24:     $M[i] \leftarrow V^r \oplus C[i-1]$
25: **end for**
26: $V \leftarrow f^{-1}(C[1], V^U, V^L)$
27: $M[1] \leftarrow V^r \oplus C^r$
28: $V \leftarrow f^{-1}(C^r, V^U, V^L)$
29: $V \leftarrow f^{-1}(A[u] \oplus V^r, V^U, V^L \oplus 1)$
30: **for** $i = u - 1$ to 1 **do**
31:     $V \leftarrow f^{-1}(A[i] \oplus V^r, V^U, V^L)$
32: **end for**
33: $V \leftarrow f^{-1}(N \oplus V^r, V^U, V^L)$
34: **if** $V^L = K^L$ **then**
35:     $M^r \leftarrow V^r$
36:     $M^{c/2} \leftarrow V^U \oplus K^U$
37:     $M \leftarrow M^r M^{c/2} M[1]M[2]\cdots M[w]$
38:     **return** M
39: **else**
40:     **return** $\perp$
41: **end if**

Fig. 9. Encryption and decryption algorithms of APE^{CA}

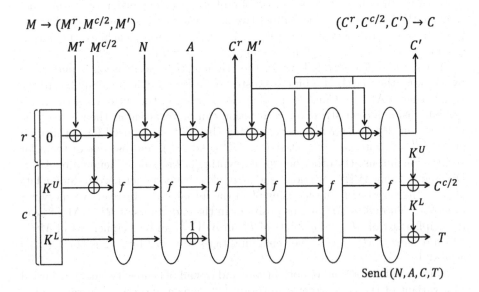

Fig. 10. Encryption of APE^{CA}

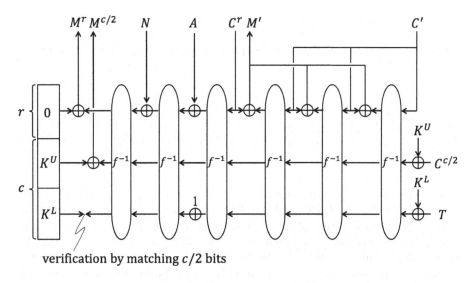

Fig. 11. Decryption of APE^{CA}

Advantages of APE^{CA}. Advantages of APE^{CA} can be summarized as follows.

Requiring Low Bandwidth. The amount of communicated data is reduced by a factor of $r + c/2$ bits due to the omission of sending M^r and $M^{c/2}$, while it is increased by a factor of r bits due to C^r. Thus, the bandwidth is improved from the original APE or APE^{RI} by a factor of $c/2$ bits.

Small Hardware Footprint. APE^{OW} inherits the advantage of APE^{RI}, namely users need to implement only f for encryption devices and only f^{-1} for decryption devices.

Low Computational Cost. At the very beginning, $r + c/2$ bits of M are absorbed accordingly to the line of concurrent absorption. When $r = c/2$, this corresponds to reducing the number of f or f^{-1} calls by 1. Differently from APE^{OW}, improvement of the computational cost can be exploited both in encryption and decryption algorithms.

7 Comparisons of Proposed Schemes

In this section, we compare the performance of APE, APE^{RI}, APE^{OW}, and APE^{CA}. Let $|N|$, $|A|$ and $|M|$ be nonce size, associated data size, and message size, respectively. We then compare the bandwidth and computational cost for encrypting this message and for decrypting its ciphertext. Hardware footprint is simply measured by the types of permutations to be implemented. The comparison is given in Table 1.

When the message length is $|M|$ and security level is $c/2$ bits, the bandwidth should ideally be $|N|+|A|+|M|+c/2$, while APE requires $|N|+|A|+|M|+c$ for

Table 1. Performance comparison of our AE schemes. We put $X := |N| + |A| + |M|$.

Scheme	Bandwidth	Hardware footprint		Computational cost		Security
		Enc	Dec	Enc	Dec	
APE	$X + c$	f	f, f^{-1}	X/r	X/r	$c/2$
APE^{RI}	$X + c$	f	f^{-1}	X/r	X/r	$c/2$
APE^{OW}	$X - |N| + r + c$	f	f^{-1}	X/r	$(X - |N|)/r$	$\min\{r, c/2\}$
APE^{CA}	$X + c/2$	f	f^{-1}	$(X - c)/r$	$(X - c)/r$	$c/2$

the expanded tag. APE requires both f and f^{-1} for decryption, and the computational cost is standard $(|N| + |A| + |M|)/r$ in both encryption and decryption.

APE^{RI} simply improves APE by removing the necessity of f in decryption. APE^{OW} omits sharing N between the sender and the receiver. It should be stressed that security of APE^{OW} also depends on b. The condition to ensure the standard $c/2$-bit security is $r \geq c/2$. In APE^{OW}, the bandwidth is reduced from APE when $|N| \geq r$. For example, when the permutation size is 256 bits and $r = 96$, $c = 160$ for 80-bit security, APE^{OW} has better bandwidth than APE to process the nonce which is longer than or equal to 96 bits. Another advantage of APE^{OW} is that N does not have to be processed during decryption. APE^{CA} always outperforms APE with respect to all of bandwidth, hardware footprint, computational cost.

The better choice between APE^{OW} and APE^{CA} depends on the nonce length and the choice of the rate and capacity sizes. Considering that communication speed is slower than computation speed, minimizing the bandwidth is likely to be the most important issue.

Condition 1: To ensure $c/2$-bit security, APE^{CA} should be chosen when $r < c/2$.
Condition 2a: If $r \geq c/2$, compare the size of $r + c/2$ and N. If $N < r + c/2$, APE^{CA} offers better bandwidth than APE^{OW}.
Condition 2b: Otherwise, APE^{OW} offers better bandwidth than APE^{CA}.

For example, when the ratio of a rate size to a capacity size is one to two, $|N| < c$ is the border to choose APE^{OW} or APE^{CA}. Considering the practical parameters, APE^{OW} should be chosen when $|N| = 64$ for a 80-bit permutation, or $|N| = 48$ for a 64-bit permutation.

References

1. Andreeva, E., Bilgin, B., Bogdanov, A., Luykx, A., Mendel, F., Mennink, B., Mouha, N., Wang, Q., Yasuda, K.: PRIMATEs v1. Submission to CAESAR (2014)
2. Andreeva, E., Bilgin, B., Bogdanov, A., Luykx, A., Mennink, B., Mouha, N., Yasuda, K.: APE: authenticated permutation-based encryption for lightweight cryptography. In: Cid, C., Rechberger, C. (eds.) FSE 2014. LNCS, vol. 8540, pp. 168–186. Springer, Heidelberg (2015). https://doi.org/10.1007/978-3-662-46706-0_9

3. Aumasson, J.-P., Henzen, L., Meier, W., Naya-Plasencia, M.: QUARK: a lightweight hash. In: Mangard, S., Standaert, F.-X. (eds.) CHES 2010. LNCS, vol. 6225, pp. 1–15. Springer, Heidelberg (2010). https://doi.org/10.1007/978-3-642-15031-9_1

4. Bellare, M., Namprempre, C.: Authenticated encryption: relations among notions and analysis of the generic composition paradigm. In: Okamoto, T. (ed.) ASI-ACRYPT 2000. LNCS, vol. 1976, pp. 531–545. Springer, Heidelberg (2000). https://doi.org/10.1007/3-540-44448-3_41

5. Bernstein, D.: CAESAR Competition (2013). http://competitions.cr.yp.to/caesar.html

6. Bertoni, G., Daemen, J., Peeters, M., Van Assche, G.: On the indifferentiability of the sponge construction. In: Smart, N. (ed.) EUROCRYPT 2008. LNCS, vol. 4965, pp. 181–197. Springer, Heidelberg (2008). https://doi.org/10.1007/978-3-540-78967-3_11

7. Bertoni, G., Daemen, J., Peeters, M., Van Assche, G.: Duplexing the sponge: single-pass authenticated encryption and other applications. In: Miri, A., Vaudenay, S. (eds.) SAC 2011. LNCS, vol. 7118, pp. 320–337. Springer, Heidelberg (2012). https://doi.org/10.1007/978-3-642-28496-0_19

8. Bogdanov, A., Knežević, M., Leander, G., Toz, D., Varıcı, K., Verbauwhede, I.: SPONGENT: a lightweight hash function. In: Preneel, B., Takagi, T. (eds.) CHES 2011. LNCS, vol. 6917, pp. 312–325. Springer, Heidelberg (2011). https://doi.org/10.1007/978-3-642-23951-9_21

9. CRYPTREC Lightweight Cryptography Working Group: CRYPTREC cryptographic technology guideline (lightweight cryptography) (2017). https://www.cryptrec.go.jp/report/cryptrec-gl-0001-2016-e.pdf

10. Dinca, L.M., Hancke, G.: Behavioural sensor data as randomness source for IoT devices. In: ISIE 2017, pp. 2038–2043. IEEE (2017)

11. Dworkin, M.: Recommendation for block cipher modes of operation: Galois/Counter Mode (GCM) and GMAC. NIST Special Publication 800-38D (2007)

12. Fleischmann, E., Forler, C., Lucks, S.: McOE: a family of almost foolproof online authenticated encryption schemes. In: Canteaut, A. (ed.) FSE 2012. LNCS, vol. 7549, pp. 196–215. Springer, Heidelberg (2012). https://doi.org/10.1007/978-3-642-34047-5_12

13. Guo, J., Peyrin, T., Poschmann, A.: The PHOTON family of lightweight hash functions. In: Rogaway, P. (ed.) CRYPTO 2011. LNCS, vol. 6841, pp. 222–239. Springer, Heidelberg (2011). https://doi.org/10.1007/978-3-642-22792-9_13

14. Hoang, V.T., Krovetz, T., Rogaway, P.: AEZ v1: Authenticated-encryption by enciphering. Submission to CAESAR (2014)

15. JTC 1/SC 27: Information technology–Security techniques–Lightweight cryptography–Part 1: General. ISO/IEC 29192-1 (2012)

16. Kannan, S., Karimi, N., Sinanoglu, O., Karri, R.: Security vulnerabilities of emerging nonvolatile main memories and countermeasures. IEEE Trans. CAD Integr. Circ. Syst. **34**(1), 2–15 (2015)

17. LoRa Alliance: LoRa specification (2015). https://www.lora-alliance.org/

18. McKay, K.A., Bassham, L., Turan, M.S., Mouha, N.: Report on lightweight cryptography. NISTIR 8114 (2017). http://nvlpubs.nist.gov/nistpubs/ir/2017/NIST.IR.8114.pdf

19. Mennink, B., Reyhanitabar, R., Vizár, D.: Security of full-state keyed sponge and duplex: applications to authenticated encryption. In: Iwata, T., Cheon, J.H. (eds.) ASIACRYPT 2015. LNCS, vol. 9453, pp. 465–489. Springer, Heidelberg (2015). https://doi.org/10.1007/978-3-662-48800-3_19

20. Rogaway, P.: Nonce-based symmetric encryption. In: Roy, B., Meier, W. (eds.) FSE 2004. LNCS, vol. 3017, pp. 348–358. Springer, Heidelberg (2004). https://doi.org/10.1007/978-3-540-25937-4_22

21. Rogaway, P., Shrimpton, T.: A provable-security treatment of the key-wrap problem. In: Vaudenay, S. (ed.) EUROCRYPT 2006. LNCS, vol. 4004, pp. 373–390. Springer, Heidelberg (2006). https://doi.org/10.1007/11761679_23

22. Sasaki, Y., Yasuda, K.: How to incorporate associated data in sponge-based authenticated encryption. In: Nyberg, K. (ed.) CT-RSA 2015. LNCS, vol. 9048, pp. 353–370. Springer, Cham (2015). https://doi.org/10.1007/978-3-319-16715-2_19

23. Shrimpton, T., Terashima, R.S.: A modular framework for building variable-input-length tweakable ciphers. In: Sako, K., Sarkar, P. (eds.) ASIACRYPT 2013. LNCS, vol. 8269, pp. 405–423. Springer, Heidelberg (2013). https://doi.org/10.1007/978-3-642-42033-7_21

Dual Relationship Between Impossible Differentials and Zero Correlation Linear Hulls of SIMON-Like Ciphers

Xuan Shen[1], Ruilin Li[2], Bing Sun[1(✉)], Lei Cheng[1], Chao Li[1(✉)],
and Maodong Liao[3]

[1] College of Science, National University of Defense Technology,
Changsha 410073, People's Republic of China
shenxuan_08@163.com, happy_come@163.com, chenglei_1111@163.com,
academic_lc@163.com
[2] School of Electronic Science, National University of Defense Technology,
Changsha 410073, People's Republic of China
securitylrl@163.com
[3] Academy of Mathematics and Systems Science, Chinese Academy of Sciences,
Beijing 100190, People's Republic of China
liaomd278@163.com

Abstract. As far as we know, for impossible differentials and zero correlation linear hulls of SIMON-like ciphers (denoted as SIMON in our paper), the distinguishers previously constructed by the miss-in-the-middle technique are all based on bit-level contradictions. Under this condition, our results on the two kinds of distinguishers are presented as follows:

Firstly, by introducing both the diffusion matrix and the dual cipher of SIMON, we establish some links between impossible differentials and zero correlation linear hulls for SIMON and its dual cipher. For SIMON, we prove that there is a one-to-one correspondence between impossible differentials and zero correlation linear hulls. Meanwhile, for SIMON and its dual cipher, we show that there is also a one-to-one correspondence between impossible differentials of one cipher and zero correlation linear hulls of the dual one. Secondly, we show that impossible differentials and zero correlation linear hulls of SIMON can be constructed by a matrix calculation approach. Finally, when applying our method to SIMON with some specific parameters, we show that SIMON with parameter (1,0,2) recommended at CRYPTO 2015 is worse than the original SIMON with respect to security against impossible differential and zero correlation linear cryptanalysis.

Keywords: SIMON-like ciphers · Impossible differential
Zero correlation linear hull

The work in this paper is supported by National Key R&D Program of China (No: 2017YFB0802000), the National Natural Science Foundation of China (No: 61672530, 61402515, 61772545), the Project of Hunan Province Department of Education (No: 16B086) and Open Research Fund of Hunan Provincial Key Laboratory of Network Investigational Technology (No: 2016WLZC018).

© Springer International Publishing AG 2017
J. K. Liu and P. Samarati (Eds.): ISPEC 2017, LNCS 10701, pp. 237–255, 2017.
https://doi.org/10.1007/978-3-319-72359-4_14

1   Introduction

With the development of network techniques, information security has been increasingly important. Due to the restrictions in constrained environments like RFID tags, many lightweight block ciphers have been designed to protect data confidentiality in those devices, such as PRESENT [1], LED [2], LBlock [3], PICCOLO [4], PRINCE [5].

In 2013, SIMON [6] was designed by National Security Agency (NSA) as a lightweight block cipher. It uses only simple operations such as XOR, bitwise AND and bit rotation to improve its implementation performance. After it was published, a large number of cryptanalysis on SIMON were proposed [7–16].

To investigate the design principle of the rotation number selection of SIMON, some cryptanalysts focused on SIMON-like ciphers that only differ at the rotation number. At CRYPTO 2015, Kölbl et al. [22] studied the differential and linear properties of SIMON-like ciphers with block sizes no more than 64-bit. They recommended three parameters (12,5,3), (1,0,2) and (7,0,2). Among them, SIMON-like ciphers with parameters (12,5,3) and (1,0,2) have better differential and linear properties than those of the original SIMON. Moreover, the parameter (7,0,2) cipher has the best diffusion when it is restricted to $b = 0$ for all possible choices. At ACNS 2016, Kondo et al. [20] constructed some impossible differential and integral distinguishers of SIMON-like ciphers whose block sizes are only restricted to 32-bit. They found the parameter (12,5,3) may be a good alternative parameter to the original one against differential, linear, impossible differential as well as integral attacks. Recently, Zhang et al. [21] presented a security evaluation for SIMON-like ciphers against integral attack and showed that among all possible choices of the rotation numbers, there exist 120 parameters that are equal or superior to the original one with respect to the length of integral distinguishers.

As far as we know, for SIMON-like ciphers with arbitrary rotation number and all block sizes, there is no literature on impossible differentials and zero correlation linear hulls. We mainly focus on these two kinds of distinguishers in this paper. Impossible differential cryptanalysis was independently proposed by Knudsen [23] and Biham et al. [24]. The most popular impossible differential is the so-called truncated impossible differential, which is independent of the choices of S-boxes. Several approaches have been proposed to derive truncated impossible differentials of a block cipher effectively such as $\mathcal{U}$-method [25], UID-method [26] and the extended tool of the former two methods generalized by Wu and Wang [27]. To search impossible differential distinguishers we mainly use the *miss-in-the-middle* method, by which the contradictions are obtained in the middle matching from the encryption and decryption directions. Zero correlation linear cryptanalysis was firstly proposed by Bogdanov and Rijmen [28]. The main idea is to construct some linear characteristics with correlation exactly zero, which is similar to impossible differential cryptanalysis.

At CRYPTO 2015, Sun et al. proposed the concept of "structure", which contains all ciphers that only differ at the nonlinear parts, to characterize those cryptanalytic methods that are independent of the details of the S-boxes [29].

Furthermore, with the help of "dual structure", they built a link between impossible differential and zero correlation linear cryptanalysis, e.g., *an impossible differential of a structure always implies a zero correlation linear hull of the corresponding dual structure.* However, the nonlinear component of SIMON-like ciphers is made up of XOR, bit-wise AND and rotation, which often have a weak confusion and diffusion. When applying the concept of "structure" to SIMON-like ciphers, we can only get 4-round impossible differentials and 4-round zero correlation linear hulls, respectively, which are far less than the known results. Therefore, the concept of "structure" can not be directly applied to get an accurate security margin for SIMON-like ciphers and the link built by Sun *et al.* can not be applied to SIMON-like ciphers. Thus, it motives us to study how to get a relatively tight security evaluation and build the link between impossible differentials and zero correlation linear hulls of SIMON-like ciphers in a new way.

For most ciphers which adopt S-boxes, the contradiction is found when the difference/mask is zero from encryption/decryption direction and non-zero from the other direction. However, for SIMON-like ciphers, the contradiction sometimes could be built at the bit level, e.g., we could compute the exact values of some bits of the difference/mask from both the encryption and decryption directions. To the best of our knowledge, all impossible differentials and zero correlation linear hulls of SIMON-like ciphers found so far are constructed based on the bit-level contradictions. Therefore, we are going to investigate the properties of impossible differential and zero correlation linear distinguishers for SIMON-like ciphers based on bit-level contradictions.

Our Contribution. In this paper, we use SIMON to denote the family of SIMON-like ciphers with the rotation number (a, b, c). Furthermore, with the diffusion matrix defined in our paper, we build some links between impossible differentials and zero correlation linear hulls for SIMON and Dual-SIMON (see Definition 1 in Sect. 2.2) based on bit-level contradictions in Fig. 1.

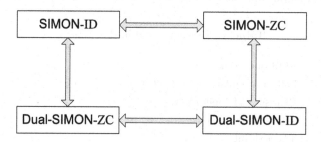

Fig. 1. Links between impossible differentials (ID) and zero correlation linear hulls (ZC) for SIMON and Dual-SIMON

(1) With the diffusion matrix, for SIMON, we prove that there is a one-to-one correspondence between impossible differentials and zero correlation linear

hulls. Meanwhile, for SIMON and Dual-SIMON, we show that there is also a one-to-one correspondence between impossible differentials of one cipher and zero correlation linear hulls of the dual one, which extends the link built by Sun *et al.* at CRYPTO 2015 for Sbox-based ciphers.

(2) With our method, we can construct impossible differentials and zero correlation linear hulls of SIMON based on bit-level contradictions. Furthermore, when applying our method to SIMON with some specific parameters, some results are obtained.

- We show that SIMON with parameter (12,5,3) may not be a good alternative to the original SIMON against impossible differential and zero correlation linear attack when the block size is larger than 32-bit.
- We present that SIMON with parameter (1,0,2) is worse than the original SIMON with respect to the resistance against impossible differential and zero correlation linear attacks.

Organization. The remainder of this paper is organized as follows. In Sect. 2, we give some notations and concepts that will be used in this paper. Moreover, we also present the brief description of SIMON-like ciphers. Then, we introduce the definition of the diffusion matrix and give some properties about it in Sect. 3. After that, some links between impossible differentials and zero correlation linear hulls of SIMON-like ciphers are presented in Sect. 4. In Sect. 5, we apply our matrix-based method to SIMON with some parameters. Finally, Sect. 6 concludes this paper.

2 Preliminary

2.1 Notations and Concepts

In this subsection, we give some notations in Table 1, which will be used in the rest of this paper. Note that all vectors used in our paper are *row vectors* and X_0 is the least significant bit for a vector $X = (X_{n-1}, X_{n-2}, \cdots, X_1, X_0)$.

Table 1. Notations used in this paper

$\oplus$	XOR operation
$\lll l, \ggg l$	Left and right rotation for l bits, respectively
$\&$	Bitwise AND operation
X^i	The i-th round state
X^i_j	The j-th bit of X^i
X_j	The j-th bit of vector X
K^i	The i-th round subkey
Y^T	Transpose of vector Y
M^T	Transpose of matrix M
$\varepsilon_{\{i_1, i_2, \cdots, i_t\}}$	The $\{i_1, i_2, \cdots, i_t\}$-th bits of vector ε are 1 and the others are 0

We recall the concepts of impossible differential and zero correlation linear hull of a vectorial function.

Given a function $G: \mathbb{F}_2^n \to \mathbb{F}_2^k$, let $\delta \in \mathbb{F}_2^n$ and $\Delta \in \mathbb{F}_2^k$. The differential probability $\delta \to \Delta$ is defined as

$$p(\delta \xrightarrow{G} \Delta) \triangleq \frac{\#\{X \in \mathbb{F}_2^n | G(X) \oplus G(X \oplus \delta) = \Delta\}}{2^n}.$$

If $p(\delta \xrightarrow{G} \Delta) = 0$, then $\delta \to \Delta$ is called an *impossible differential* of G [23,24].

Let $\Gamma X = (\Gamma X_{n-1}, \Gamma X_{n-2}, \cdots, \Gamma X_1, \Gamma X_0) \in \mathbb{F}_2^n, X \in \mathbb{F}_2^n$. Then

$$\Gamma X \cdot X \triangleq \bigoplus_{i, \Gamma X_i = 1} X_i$$

denotes the inner product of ΓX and X. It is notable that the inner product of ΓX and X can be written as $(\Gamma X) X^T$ where the multiplication is defined as matrix multiplication.

For a function $G: \mathbb{F}_2^n \to \mathbb{F}_2^k$, the correlation of the linear approximation for an n-bit input mask ΓX and a k-bit output mask ΓY is defined by

$$c(\Gamma X \cdot X \oplus \Gamma Y \cdot G(X)) \triangleq \frac{1}{2^n} \sum_{X \in \mathbb{F}_2^n} (-1)^{\Gamma X \cdot X \oplus \Gamma Y \cdot G(X)}.$$

If $c(\Gamma X \cdot X \oplus \Gamma Y \cdot G(X)) = 0$, then $\Gamma X \to \Gamma Y$ is called an *zero correlation linear hull* of G [28].

2.2 Brief Description of SIMON-Like Ciphers

SIMON-like ciphers are based on Feistel structures. Let $X^i = (X_L^i \| X_R^i) = (X_{2n-1}^i, X_{2n-2}^i, \ldots, X_n^i \| X_{n-1}^i, X_{n-2}^i, \ldots, X_0^i)$, where $2n$ denotes the block size and $2n \in \{32, 48, 64, 96, 128\}$.

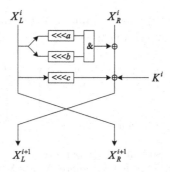

Fig. 2. The round function of SIMON-like ciphers

According to the Feistel structure described in Fig. 2, the round function is given below

$$\begin{cases} X_L^{i+1} = f(X_L^i) \oplus X_R^i \oplus K^i, \\ X_R^{i+1} = X_L^i, \end{cases}$$

where the f-function is defined by

$$f(X) = (X_{\lll a} \& X_{\lll b}) \oplus X_{\lll c}, 0 \le a, b, c \le n - 1.$$

Note that when $(a, b, c) = (1, 8, 2)$, it is the original SIMON.

In this paper, we are going to investigate impossible differentials and zero correlation linear hulls of SIMON-like ciphers which are often independent of the details of the key schedule. We refer to [6] for the details of the key schedule. Moreover, we give the following definition to study the links between impossible differentials and zero correlation linear hulls of SIMON-like ciphers.

Definition 1. *For any specific instance of the SIMON-like ciphers with rotation number (a, b, c), the dual cipher is defined as the one with rotation number $(n - a, n - b, n - c)$. If n and (a, b, c) are clear from the context, we simply use SIMON and Dual-SIMON as the specific instance SIMON-like cipher and its dual cipher.*

3   Diffusion Matrix and Its Properties

For a vectorial boolean function $F : \mathbb{F}_2^n \to \mathbb{F}_2^n$, we can always associate F with a graph $\mathcal{G}$ which has $2n$ vertices, denoted by $X_0, \ldots, X_{n-1}, Y_0, \ldots, Y_{n-1}$. There are 3 types of edges e_{ij} in $\mathcal{G}$:

   $e_{ij} = 0$ means that Y_j is not inverted when the value of X_i is changed;
   $e_{ij} = 1$ means that Y_j is always inverted when the value of X_i is changed;
   $e_{ij} = \lambda$ means that Y_j is sometimes inverted and sometimes not inverted when the value of X_i is changed.

If we do not investigate the exact value of F but only focus on the 3 types of relations between X_i and Y_j, we can get that

$$\begin{pmatrix} Y_{n-1} \\ Y_{n-2} \\ \vdots \\ Y_0 \end{pmatrix} \triangleq \begin{pmatrix} e_{(n-1)(n-1)} & e_{(n-2)(n-1)} & \cdots & e_{0(n-1)} \\ e_{(n-1)(n-2)} & e_{(n-2)(n-2)} & \cdots & e_{0(n-2)} \\ \vdots & \vdots & \cdots & \vdots \\ e_{(n-1)0} & e_{(n-2)0} & \cdots & e_{00} \end{pmatrix}_{n \times n} \begin{pmatrix} X_{n-1} \\ X_{n-2} \\ \vdots \\ X_0 \end{pmatrix} = E \begin{pmatrix} X_{n-1} \\ X_{n-2} \\ \vdots \\ X_0 \end{pmatrix}.$$

Note that all vectors used in our paper are *row vectors*. The above equation could be written as $Y^T = EX^T$, where $X = (X_{n-1}, X_{n-2}, \cdots, X_0)$, $Y = (Y_{n-1}, Y_{n-2}, \cdots, Y_0)$. The matrix E is used to characterize the *bit pattern* propagation from the bit pattern of X to the bit pattern of Y. We give the following example to describe the matrix E.

Example 1. Let $F : \mathbb{F}_2^3 \to \mathbb{F}_2^3$ be a boolean function which is presented below

$$\begin{cases} Y_2 = X_2 \oplus X_1 X_0, \\ Y_1 = X_2 X_1, \\ Y_0 = X_2 X_0 \oplus X_1 \oplus X_0. \end{cases}$$

Then,

$$E = \begin{pmatrix} e_{22} & e_{12} & e_{02} \\ e_{21} & e_{11} & e_{01} \\ e_{20} & e_{10} & e_{00} \end{pmatrix} = \begin{pmatrix} 1 & \lambda & \lambda \\ \lambda & \lambda & 0 \\ \lambda & 1 & \lambda \end{pmatrix}.$$

For the matrix E, it is called the diffusion matrix of F as follows.

Definition 2 (Diffusion matrix of F). *For a vectorial boolean function $F :$ $\mathbb{F}_2^n \to \mathbb{F}_2^n$, the diffusion matrix of F is defined as*

$$E = (a_{ij})_{n \times n}, \quad a_{ij} = e_{(n-1-j)(n-1-i)}, 0 \le i, j \le (n-1).$$

There are 3 kinds of elements $\{0, 1, \lambda\}$ in the diffusion matrix E, and addition and multiplication tables are shown in Tables 2 and 3, respectively.

Table 2. Addition table

+	0	1	λ
0	0	1	λ
1	1	0	λ
λ	λ	λ	λ

Table 3. Multiplication table

$\times$	0	1	λ
0	0	0	0
1	0	1	λ
λ	0	λ	λ

Many block ciphers adopt S-boxes as their nonlinear components, which could be also regarded as the vectorial boolean functions. Due to the principle of designing S-boxes, there should not be 1 or 0 in the diffusion matrix of S-boxes. However, for lower diffusion block ciphers, such as SIMON-like ciphers, there are many entries of 1 and 0 in the diffusion matrices.

For each component boolean function of the f-function used in the SIMON-like ciphers, say $Y_j = (X_{i_1} \& X_{i_2}) \oplus X_{i_3}$, it is obvious for e_{ij} that

$$e_{ij} = \begin{cases} \lambda & i = i_1, i_2; \\ 1 & i = i_3; \\ 0 & i \ne i_1, i_2, i_3. \end{cases}$$

We recall the definition of $circ[x_0 x_1 \cdots x_{n-1}]$, which is defined as

$$circ[x_0 x_1 \cdots x_{n-1}] \triangleq \begin{pmatrix} x_0 & x_1 & \cdots & x_{n-1} \\ x_{n-1} & x_0 & \cdots & x_{n-2} \\ \vdots & \vdots & \ddots & \vdots \\ x_1 & x_2 & \cdots & x_0 \end{pmatrix}.$$

For SIMON, we define $L_{[n,a,b,c]} = circ[x_0 x_1 \cdots x_{n-1}]$, where

$$x_j = \begin{cases} \lambda & j = a, b; \\ 1 & j = c; \\ 0 & j \neq a, b, c. \end{cases}$$

In the following theorem, we show that $L_{[n,a,b,c]}$ could be used to characterize the diffusion matrix of the f-function.

Theorem 1. *For* SIMON, *we use* E_f *to denote the diffusion matrix of the f-function. Then,*

$$E_f = L_{[n,a,b,c]}.$$

Example 2. For SIMON with parameter $(0,1,2)$ and 8-bit block size, the f-function is defined by

$$f(X) = (X \& X_{\lll 1}) \oplus X_{\lll 2}.$$

Then,

$$\begin{cases} Y_3 = X_3 X_2 \oplus X_1, \\ Y_2 = X_2 X_1 \oplus X_0, \\ Y_1 = X_1 X_0 \oplus X_3, \\ Y_0 = X_0 X_3 \oplus X_2. \end{cases}$$

Thus,

$$E_f = L_{[4,0,1,2]} = circ[\lambda\lambda 10] = \begin{pmatrix} \lambda & \lambda & 1 & 0 \\ 0 & \lambda & \lambda & 1 \\ 1 & 0 & \lambda & \lambda \\ \lambda & 1 & 0 & \lambda \end{pmatrix}$$

Remark 1. Let ΔX and ΔY be the input and output differences of the f-function, respectively. Obviously, we have $\Delta Y^T = E_f \Delta X^T = L_{[n,a,b,c]} \Delta X^T$ with the definition of E_f and Theorem 1.

Remark 2. The method illustrated above could be extended to linear cases: Let ΓX and ΓY be the input and output masks of the f-function, respectively. Since $Y^T = E_f X^T = L_{[n,a,b,c]} X^T$, we have $(\Gamma X) X^T = (\Gamma Y) Y^T = \Gamma Y (L_{[n,a,b,c]} X^T)$. Thus, $\Gamma X = \Gamma Y L_{[n,a,b,c]}$.

Corollary 1. *For* SIMON, *we use* $D_{[2n,a,b,c]}$ *to denote the diffusion matrix of the round function. Then,*

$$D_{[2n,a,b,c]} = \begin{pmatrix} L_{[n,a,b,c]} & I_{n \times n} \\ I_{n \times n} & O_{n \times n} \end{pmatrix},$$

where $I_{n \times n}$ *is the* $n \times n$ *identity matrix and* $O_{n \times n}$ *is the* $n \times n$ *zero matrix.*

According to the definition of $D_{[2n,a,b,c]}$, we have $\left(X^{s+1}\right)^T = D_{[2n,a,b,c]}$ $(X^s)^T$, which is similar to $Y^T = L_{[n,a,b,c]}X^T$. Furthermore, $\left(X^{s+t}\right)^T = D_{[2n,a,b,c]}^t (X^s)^T$.

Let $D_{[2n,a,b,c]}^t = \left(d_{ij}^{(t)}\right)$, where $d_{ij}^{(t)}$ stands for the i-th row and j-th column element of $D_{[2n,a,b,c]}^t$. There are 3 kinds of values for $d_{ij}^{(t)}$ and their meanings are similar to those of 3 types of edges e_{ij}.

$d_{ij}^{(t)} = 0$ means that X_j^{s+t} is not inverted when the value of X_i^s is changed;

$d_{ij}^{(t)} = 1$ means that X_j^{s+t} is always inverted when the value of X_i^s is changed;

$d_{ij}^{(t)} = \lambda$ means that X_j^{s+t} is sometimes inverted and sometimes not inverted when the value of X_i^s is changed.

Remark 3. Let ΔX^s and ΔX^{s+t} be the input difference of the s-th and $(s+t)$-th round, respectively. We have $\left(\Delta X^{s+t}\right)^T = D_{[2n,a,b,c]}^t \left(\Delta X^s\right)^T$. Furthermore, this method could also be applied to characterize linear trails.

For $D_{[2n,a,b,c]}^t$, we give the following proposition.

Proposition 1. *Let*

$$D_{[2n,a,b,c]}^t = \begin{pmatrix} D_{11}^{(t)} & D_{12}^{(t)} \\ D_{21}^{(t)} & D_{22}^{(t)} \end{pmatrix}, t \geq 1.$$

Then all $D_{11}^{(t)}, D_{12}^{(t)}, D_{21}^{(t)}, D_{22}^{(t)}$ *are* $n \times n$ *circulant sub-matrices and*

$$D_{22}^{(t+2)} = D_{12}^{(t+1)} = D_{21}^{(t+1)} = D_{11}^{(t)}.$$

Proposition 1 can be directly obtained by calculating the power of $D_{[2n,a,b,c]}$. It indicates that we only need to consider $D_{22}^{(t)}$ to characterize the maximum round number r that contains 1 or 0 in $D_{[2n,a,b,c]}^t$. In other words, there does not exist 0 or 1 in $D_{[2n,a,b,c]}^t$ when $t \geq r+1$. Furthermore, we use r_1 and r_0 to denote the maximum round number that contains 1 and 0 in $D_{[2n,a,b,c]}^t$, respectively. And r_1 and r_0 are defined as

$$r_1 = \max\{t | \exists \{i, j_1, j_2, \cdots, j_k\}, \bigoplus_{j_1, j_2, \cdots, j_k} d_{ij}^{(t)} = 1\};$$

$$r_0 = \max\{t | \exists \{i, j_1, j_2, \cdots, j_k\}, \bigoplus_{j_1, j_2, \cdots, j_k} d_{ij}^{(t)} = 0\},$$

where $\bigoplus\limits_{j_1, j_2, \cdots, j_k} d_{ij}^{(t)}$ is denoted as the XOR sum of $d_{ij_1}^{(t)}, d_{ij_2}^{(t)}, \cdots, d_{ij_k}^{(t)}$ and $d_{ij}^{(t)} \in \{0,1\}, j = j_1, j_2, \cdots, j_k, 1 \leq k < n$.

According to the Feistel structure, when a bit of the output difference after r_1 rounds from the encryption direction is 1 and the same bit of the output difference after (r_0-1) rounds from the decryption direction is 0, an (r_1+r_0-1)-round impossible differential of SIMON could be constructed based on bit-level contradictions. Therefore, we give the following proposition.

Proposition 2. *For SIMON, there exist* $(r_1 + r_0 - 1)$*-round impossible differential distinguishers.*

With the definition of r_1 and r_0, we know that the longest impossible differential distinguishers based on bit-level contradictions are bounded by $r_1 + r_0 - 1$. Since r_1 and r_0 are determined by $D_{[2n,a,b,c]}$ which is only related to the block size $2n$ and the rotation number (a, b, c), the longest impossible differentials of SIMON based on bit-level contradictions are only determined by the four parameters (n, a, b, c). Moreover, all impossible differentials based on bit-level contradictions could be constructed by the matrix-based approach.

Example 3. For SIMON with parameter $(0,1,2)$ and 8-bit block size, which has been given in Example 2, we have

$$
D_{[8,0,1,2]} = \begin{pmatrix} \lambda\,\lambda\,1\,0\,1\,0\,0\,0 \\ 0\,\lambda\,\lambda\,1\,0\,1\,0\,0 \\ 1\,0\,\lambda\,\lambda\,0\,0\,1\,0 \\ \lambda\,1\,0\,\lambda\,0\,0\,0\,1 \\ 1\,0\,0\,0\,0\,0\,0\,0 \\ 0\,1\,0\,0\,0\,0\,0\,0 \\ 0\,0\,1\,0\,0\,0\,0\,0 \\ 0\,0\,0\,1\,0\,0\,0\,0 \end{pmatrix}, D_{[8,0,1,2]}^2 = \begin{pmatrix} \lambda\,\lambda\,\lambda\,\lambda\,\lambda\,\lambda\,1\,0 \\ \lambda\,\lambda\,\lambda\,0\,\lambda\,\lambda\,1 \\ \lambda\,\lambda\,\lambda\,\lambda\,1\,0\,\lambda\,\lambda \\ \lambda\,\lambda\,\lambda\,\lambda\,\lambda\,1\,0\,\lambda \\ \lambda\,\lambda\,1\,0\,1\,0\,0\,0 \\ 0\,\lambda\,\lambda\,1\,0\,1\,0\,0 \\ 1\,0\,\lambda\,\lambda\,0\,0\,1\,0 \\ \lambda\,1\,0\,\lambda\,0\,0\,0\,1 \end{pmatrix},
$$

$$
D_{[8,0,1,2]}^3 = \begin{pmatrix} \lambda\,\lambda\,\lambda\,\lambda\,\lambda\,\lambda\,\lambda\,\lambda \\ \lambda\,\lambda\,\lambda\,\lambda\,\lambda\,\lambda\,\lambda\,\lambda \\ \lambda\,\lambda\,\lambda\,\lambda\,\lambda\,\lambda\,\lambda\,\lambda \\ \lambda\,\lambda\,\lambda\,\lambda\,\lambda\,\lambda\,\lambda\,\lambda \\ \lambda\,\lambda\,\lambda\,\lambda\,\lambda\,\lambda\,1\,0 \\ \lambda\,\lambda\,\lambda\,0\,\lambda\,\lambda\,1 \\ \lambda\,\lambda\,\lambda\,\lambda\,1\,0\,\lambda\,\lambda \\ \lambda\,\lambda\,\lambda\,\lambda\,1\,0\,\lambda \end{pmatrix}, D_{[8,0,1,2]}^4 = \begin{pmatrix} \lambda\,\lambda\,\lambda\,\lambda\,\lambda\,\lambda\,\lambda\,\lambda \\ \lambda\,\lambda\,\lambda\,\lambda\,\lambda\,\lambda\,\lambda\,\lambda \\ \lambda\,\lambda\,\lambda\,\lambda\,\lambda\,\lambda\,\lambda\,\lambda \\ \lambda\,\lambda\,\lambda\,\lambda\,\lambda\,\lambda\,\lambda\,\lambda \\ \lambda\,\lambda\,\lambda\,\lambda\,\lambda\,\lambda\,\lambda\,\lambda \\ \lambda\,\lambda\,\lambda\,\lambda\,\lambda\,\lambda\,\lambda\,\lambda \\ \lambda\,\lambda\,\lambda\,\lambda\,\lambda\,\lambda\,\lambda\,\lambda \\ \lambda\,\lambda\,\lambda\,\lambda\,\lambda\,\lambda\,\lambda\,\lambda \end{pmatrix}.
$$

Therefore, $r_0 = r_1 = 3$ and a 5-round impossible differential $(0, \varepsilon_0) \rightarrow (\varepsilon_3, 0)$ is constructed as follows:

$$
(0000, 0001) \xrightarrow{D_{[8,0,1,2]}} (0001, 0000) \xrightarrow{D_{[8,0,1,2]}} (01\lambda\lambda, 0001) \xrightarrow{D_{[8,0,1,2]}} (\lambda\lambda\lambda\lambda, 01\lambda\lambda)
$$

$$
(1000, \lambda01\lambda) \xleftarrow{D_{[8,0,1,2]}} (0000, 1000) \xleftarrow{D_{[8,0,1,2]}} (1000, 0000).
$$

It should be pointed out that the differentials from decryption direction of the above 5-round impossible differential are interchanged the left and right branch differentials before working by $D_{[8,0,1,2]}$ as well as after working by $D_{[8,0,1,2]}$.

4   Links Between Impossible Differentials and Zero Correlation Linear Hulls of SIMON-Like Ciphers

In this section, we mainly study the links between impossible differentials and zero correlation linear hulls of SIMON-like ciphers. To prove our results, we give the definition of the index permutation P and present a proposition about it.

We use P to denote the index permutation mapping the index i to $(n-i)$ (mod n). It can be expressed as $Pv = P(v_{n-1}v_{n-2}\cdots v_1v_0) = (v_1v_2\cdots v_{n-1}v_0)$ and we define $Pv = v \times M$, where M is the corresponding index permutation matrix

$$M = \begin{pmatrix} 0 & 0 & \cdots & 0 & 1 & 0 \\ 0 & 0 & \cdots & 1 & 0 & 0 \\ \vdots & \vdots & \ddots & \vdots & \vdots & \vdots \\ 0 & 1 & \cdots & 0 & 0 & 0 \\ 1 & 0 & \cdots & 0 & 0 & 0 \\ 0 & 0 & \cdots & 0 & 0 & 1 \end{pmatrix}_{n\times n}.$$

Obviously, the index permutation matrix M is symmetric, i.e., $M = M^T$. Since $v = P^2v = P(vM) = vM^2$, $M^2 = I_{n\times n}$. Therefore, M is involutional. Thus, $M = M^{-1} = M^T$. Furthermore, we present the relations among $L^T_{[n,a,b,c]}$, $L_{[n,n-a,n-b,n-c]}$ and $L_{[n,a,b,c]}$ in the following proposition:

Proposition 3. *Let M be the index permutation matrix and $L_{[n,a,b,c]}$ be the diffusion matrix of the f-function. Then,*

$$L^T_{[n,a,b,c]} = L_{[n,n-a,n-b,n-c]} = M^{-1}L_{[n,a,b,c]}M.$$

Proposition 3 can be directly verified. With the definition of the index permutation P and Proposition 3, we give the following theorem to show the link between impossible differentials of SIMON and zero correlation linear hulls of SIMON based on bit-level contradictions.

Theorem 2. *Based on bit-level contradictions, $(\delta^1, \delta^0) \rightarrow (\delta^{r+1}, \delta^r)$ is an impossible differential of SIMON if and only if $(P\delta^0, P\delta^1) \rightarrow (P\delta^r, P\delta^{r+1})$ is a zero correlation linear hull of SIMON, where P is the index permutation.*

Sketch of the proof. After studying the link between one round differential characteristic and one round linear trail, we prove that there exists a one-to-one correspondence between them. Then, the relationship could be extended to iterated rounds. Finally, with the help of *miss-in-the-middle* method, Theorem 2 can be proved based on bit-level contradictions. The details of the proof are presented in Appendix A.

The above approach could be also exploited to build the link between impossible differentials and zero correlation linear hulls of SIMON and Dual-SIMON. We only need to note $L^T_{[n,a,b,c]} = L_{[n,n-a,n-b,n-c]}$ shown in Proposition 3. Then, the corollary is given below.

Corollary 2. *Based on bit-level contradictions, $(\delta^1, \delta^0) \rightarrow (\delta^{r+1}, \delta^r)$ is an impossible differential of SIMON if and only if $(\delta^0, \delta^1) \rightarrow (\delta^r, \delta^{r+1})$ is a zero correlation linear hull of Dual-SIMON.*

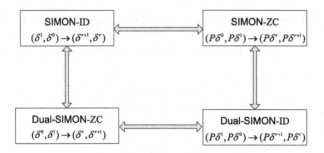

Fig. 3. Links between impossible differentials (ID) and zero correlation linear hulls (ZC) for SIMON and Dual-SIMON

Combining Theorem 2 and Corollary 2, we establish the links between impossible differentials and zero correlation linear hulls for SIMON and Dual-SIMON depicted in Fig. 3.

Especially, when $a + b = n, c = \dfrac{n}{2}$, SIMON is the same as Dual-SIMON. Thus, with Theorem 2 and Corollary 2, we get that if $(\delta^1, \delta^0) \rightarrow (\delta^{r+1}, \delta^r)$ is an impossible differential/zero correlation linear hull of SIMON, both $(P\delta^0, P\delta^1) \rightarrow (P\delta^r, P\delta^{r+1})$ and $(\delta^0, \delta^1) \rightarrow (\delta^r, \delta^{r+1})$ are zero correlation linear hulls/impossible differentials of SIMON.

Corollary 3. *For SIMON and Dual-SIMON, there exist $(r_1 + r_0 - 1)$-round impossible differentials and zero correlation linear hulls.*

Proof. With the links built in Fig. 3, for SIMON and Dual-SIMON, we get that they are the same for the length of impossible differentials and zero correlation linear hulls based on bit-level contradictions. Moreover, with Proposition 2, there are $(r_1 + r_0 - 1)$-round impossible differentials of SIMON. Therefore, there exist $(r_1 + r_0 - 1)$-round impossible differentials and zero correlation linear hulls for SIMON and Dual-SIMON.

With the definitions of r_1 and r_0, for SIMON and Dual-SIMON, the length of impossible differentials and zero correlation linear hulls based on bit-level contradictions could be bounded by $r_1 + r_0 - 1$, which is only determined by the block size $2n$ and the rotation number (a, b, c).

Example 4. For the original SIMON with 32-bit block size, we have

$$D_{[32,1,8,2]} = \begin{pmatrix} L_{[16,1,8,2]} & I_{16 \times 16} \\ I_{16 \times 16} & O_{16 \times 16} \end{pmatrix}.$$

By calculating the power of the matrix $D_{[32,1,8,2]}$, we get that $r_1 = r_0 = 6$. According to Corollary 3, there are 11-round impossible differential and zero correlation linear hull distinguishers. In [13], the authors presented the impossible differential $(0, \varepsilon_0) \xrightarrow{11} (\varepsilon_9, 0)$ and the zero correlation linear hull $(\varepsilon_0, 0) \xrightarrow{11} (0, \varepsilon_7)$, which are consistent with our result.

5   Applications

At CRYPTO 2015, Kölbl *et al.* recommended the three parameters (12,5,3), (7,0,2) and (1,0,2). SIMON with these three parameters are regarded to be promising when compared with the original SIMON for the differential and linear properties. Meanwhile, SIMECK [17–19] is a family of lightweight block ciphers proposed at CHES 2015, which could be viewed as SIMON with parameter (5,0,1).

In this section, we study SIMON with these parameters on impossible differential and zero correlation linear distinguishers. SIMON with parameter (a, b, c) is called SIMON$[a, b, c]$ for short. With our matrix-based method, we present the length of impossible differential and zero correlation linear distinguishers of the original SIMON with all block sizes in Table 4. The results are consistent with previous results.

Table 4. The length of the distinguishers for SIMON

Block size	r_1	r_0	ID/ZC
32	6	6	11
48	6	7	12
64	6	8	13
96	7	10	16
128	8	12	19

The length of impossible differentials and zero correlation linear hulls of SIMECK with all block sizes are shown in Table 5. 11/13/15-round zero correlation linear distinguishers of SIMECK32/48/64 have been presented in [30]. According to Theorem 2, we can directly prove without any search that there are also 11/13/15-round impossible differential distinguishers for SIMECK32/48/64, respectively. The results are also given in [31] where 11/13/15-round impossible differential distinguishers for SIMECK32/48/64 are searched with the help of computer search.

Table 5. The length of the distinguishers for SIMECK

Block size	r_1	r_0	ID/ZC
32	5	7	11
48	6	8	13
64	6	10	15

For SIMON with the three parameters recommended in [22], they have good performance on the differential and linear properties. However, in Table 6, the length of ID/ZC distinguishers of SIMON with the three parameters are no shorter than those of the original SIMON (SIMON[1, 8, 2]). Especially, for SIMON[1, 0, 2], the length of the distinguishers are much longer than those of the original SIMON. From this point, SIMON[1, 0, 2] is worse than the original SIMON and it is necessary to evaluate the security again. We present a 17-round impossible differential distinguisher as an example in Appendix B. For SIMON[12, 5, 3], it is considered as a good alternative to the original SIMON for differential, linear, impossible differential and integral attacks in [20]. However, the block size considered in [20] is only 32-bit. Compared with the original SIMON for various block sizes, the length of ID/ZC distinguishers of SIMON[12, 5, 3] have 1 round more than those of the original SIMON when the block size takes 48-bit and 96-bit in Table 6. Therefore, SIMON[12, 5, 3] needs to be further evaluated with all block sizes against impossible differential and zero correlation linear attacks.

Table 6. The length of the distinguishers for SIMON with different parameters

ID/ZC	32-bit	48-bit	64-bit	96-bit	128-bit
(1,8,2)	11	12	13	16	19
(12,5,3)	11	13	13	17	19
(7,0,2)	13	15	17	19	21
(1,0,2)	17	25	33	49	65

6   Conclusion

In this paper, we investigated impossible differentials and zero correlation linear hulls of SIMON. By introducing the diffusion matrix, we established some links between impossible differentials and zero correlation linear hulls for SIMON and Dual-SIMON based on bit-level contradictions. Furthermore, when applying our matrix-based method to SIMON with some specific parameters, SIMON with parameter (1,0,2) is worse than the original SIMON with respect to security against impossible differential and zero correlation linear attacks. Thus, it is necessary to evaluate the security again. In brief, our results can provide more generic security evaluation against impossible differentials and zero correlation linear hulls of SIMON-like ciphers.

Acknowledgment. The authors would like to thank the anonymous reviewers for their useful comments, and Yunwen Liu, Yi Zhang for fruitful discussions.

Appendix A. Proof of Theorem 2

Proof. The differential and linear propagations of SIMON are shown in Fig. 4.

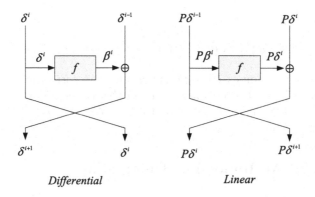

Fig. 4. Differential (left) and linear (right) propagations of SIMON

For the round function of SIMON, we prove that there is a one-to-one correspondence between the differential propagation $(\delta^i, \delta^{i-1}) \rightarrow (\delta^{i+1}, \delta^i)$ and the linear propagation $(P\delta^{i-1}, P\delta^i) \rightarrow (P\delta^i, P\delta^{i+1})$.

According to the definition of the diffusion matrix, we know that the differential propagation of the f-function is $(\beta^i)^T = L_{[n,a,b,c]} (\delta^i)^T$. Meanwhile, the linear propagation of the f-function is $P\beta^i = (P\delta^i) L_{[n,a,b,c]}$. Since $\delta^{i+1} = \delta^{i-1} \oplus \beta^i \Leftrightarrow P\delta^{i+1} = P\delta^{i-1} \oplus P\beta^i$, we could prove the one-to-one correspondence between one round differential propagation and one round linear propagation of SIMON if

$$(\beta^i)^T = L_{[n,a,b,c]} (\delta^i)^T \Leftrightarrow P\beta^i = P\delta^i L_{[n,a,b,c]}.$$

With Proposition 3, $L^T_{[n,a,b,c]} = M^{-1} L_{[n,a,b,c]} M$. Therefore,

$$(\beta^i)^T = L_{[n,a,b,c]} (\delta^i)^T \Leftrightarrow \beta^i = \delta^i L^T_{[n,a,b,c]},$$
$$\Leftrightarrow \beta^i = \delta^i M^{-1} L_{[n,a,b,c]} M,$$
$$\Leftrightarrow \beta^i M^{-1} = \delta^i M^{-1} L_{[n,a,b,c]}.$$

Since $M^{-1} = M$,

$$(\beta^i)^T = L_{[n,a,b,c]} (\delta^i)^T \Leftrightarrow \beta^i M = \delta^i M L_{[n,a,b,c]}.$$

According to the definition of P, $P\beta^i = \beta^i M, P\delta^i = \delta^i M$. Then,

$$(\beta^i)^T = L_{[n,a,b,c]} (\delta^i)^T \Leftrightarrow P\beta^i = P\delta^i L_{[n,a,b,c]}.$$

Therefore, we have proved that there is a one-to-one correspondence between the differential propagation $(\delta^i, \delta^{i-1}) \rightarrow (\delta^{i+1}, \delta^i)$ and the linear propagation $(P\delta^{i-1}, P\delta^i) \rightarrow (P\delta^i, P\delta^{i+1})$.

Naturally, considering i-round differential and linear propagations, we get that there is a one-to-one correspondence between the differential characteristic

$$\left(\delta^1, \delta^0\right) \rightarrow \left(\delta^2, \delta^1\right) \rightarrow \cdots \rightarrow \left(\delta^{i+1}, \delta^i\right)$$

and the linear trail

$$\left(P\delta^0, P\delta^1\right) \rightarrow \left(P\delta^1, P\delta^2\right) \rightarrow \cdots \rightarrow \left(P\delta^i, P\delta^{i+1}\right).$$

Since constructing impossible differentials and zero correlation linear hulls of SIMON are based on bit-level contractions in this paper, $(\delta^1, \delta^0) \rightarrow (\delta^{r+1}, \delta^r)$ is an impossible differential if and only if $(P\delta^0, P\delta^1) \rightarrow (P\delta^r, P\delta^{r+1})$ is a zero correlation linear hull.

Appendix B. An Impossible Differential

See Table 7.

Table 7. A 17-round impossible differential of SIMON[1, 0, 2] with 32-bit block size

Round	Left	Right
0	0000000000000000	0000000000000001
1	0000000000000001	0000000000000000
2	00000000000001λλ	0000000000000001
3	000000000001λλλλ	00000000000001λλ
4	0000000001λλλλλλ	000000000001λλλλ
5	00000001λλλλλλλλ	0000000001λλλλλλ
6	000001λλλλλλλλλλ	00000001λλλλλλλλ
7	0001λλλλλλλλλλλλ	000001λλλλλλλλλλ
8	01λλλλλλλλλλλλλλ	0001λλλλλλλλλλλλ
9	λλλλλλλλλλλλλλλλ	01λλλλλλλλλλλλλλ
8	λ0001λλλλλλλλλλλ	λ01λλλλλλλλλλλλλ
7	λ000001λλλλλλλλλ	λ0001λλλλλλλλλλλ
6	λ00000001λλλλλλλ	λ000001λλλλλλλλλ
5	λ0000000001λλλλλ	λ00000001λλλλλλλ
4	λ000000000001λλλ	λ0000000001λλλλλ
3	λ00000000000001λ	λ000000000001λλλ
2	1000000000000000	λ00000000000001λ
1	0000000000000000	1000000000000000
0	1000000000000000	0000000000000000

References

1. Bogdanov, A., Knudsen, L.R., Leander, G., Paar, C., Poschmann, A., Robshaw, M.J.B., Seurin, Y., Vikkelsoe, C.: PRESENT: an ultra-lightweight block cipher. In: Paillier, P., Verbauwhede, I. (eds.) CHES 2007. LNCS, vol. 4727, pp. 450–466. Springer, Heidelberg (2007). https://doi.org/10.1007/978-3-540-74735-2_31
2. Guo, J., Peyrin, T., Poschmann, A., Robshaw, M.: The LED block cipher. In: Preneel, B., Takagi, T. (eds.) CHES 2011. LNCS, vol. 6917, pp. 326–341. Springer, Heidelberg (2011). https://doi.org/10.1007/978-3-642-23951-9_22
3. Wu, W., Zhang, L.: LBlock: a lightweight block cipher. In: Lopez, J., Tsudik, G. (eds.) ACNS 2011. LNCS, vol. 6715, pp. 327–344. Springer, Heidelberg (2011). https://doi.org/10.1007/978-3-642-21554-4_19
4. Shibutani, K., Isobe, T., Hiwatari, H., Mitsuda, A., Akishita, T., Shirai, T.: *Piccolo*: an ultra-lightweight blockcipher. In: Preneel, B., Takagi, T. (eds.) CHES 2011. LNCS, vol. 6917, pp. 342–357. Springer, Heidelberg (2011). https://doi.org/10.1007/978-3-642-23951-9_23
5. Borghoff, J., et al.: PRINCE – a low-latency block cipher for pervasive computing applications. In: Wang, X., Sako, K. (eds.) ASIACRYPT 2012. LNCS, vol. 7658, pp. 208–225. Springer, Heidelberg (2012). https://doi.org/10.1007/978-3-642-34961-4_14
6. Beaulieu, R., Shors, D., Smith, J., Treatman-Clark, S., Weeks, B., Wingers, L.: The SIMON and SPECK families of lightweight block ciphers. Cryptology ePrint Archive, Report 2013/404 (2013). http://eprint.iacr.org/
7. Abed, F., List, E., Lucks, S., Wenzel, J.: Differential cryptanalysis of round-reduced SIMON and SPECK. In: Cid, C., Rechberger, C. (eds.) FSE 2014. LNCS, vol. 8540, pp. 525–545. Springer, Heidelberg (2015). https://doi.org/10.1007/978-3-662-46706-0_27
8. Biryukov, A., Roy, A., Velichkov, V.: Differential analysis of block ciphers SIMON and SPECK. In: Cid, C., Rechberger, C. (eds.) FSE 2014. LNCS, vol. 8540, pp. 546–570. Springer, Heidelberg (2015). https://doi.org/10.1007/978-3-662-46706-0_28
9. Sun, S., Hu, L., Wang, P., Qiao, K., Ma, X., Song, L.: Automatic security evaluation and (related-key) differential characteristic search: application to SIMON, PRESENT, LBlock, DES(L) and other bit-oriented block ciphers. In: Sarkar, P., Iwata, T. (eds.) ASIACRYPT 2014. LNCS, vol. 8873, pp. 158–178. Springer, Heidelberg (2014). https://doi.org/10.1007/978-3-662-45611-8_9
10. Abdelraheem, M.A., Alizadeh, J., Alkhzaimi, H.A., Aref, M.R., Bagheri, N., Gauravaram, P.: Improved linear cryptanalysis of reduced-round SIMON-32 and SIMON-48. In: Biryukov, A., Goyal, V. (eds.) INDOCRYPT 2015. LNCS, vol. 9462, pp. 153–179. Springer, Cham (2015). https://doi.org/10.1007/978-3-319-26617-6_9
11. Chen, H., Wang, X.: Improved linear hull attack on round-reduced SIMON with dynamic key-guessing techniques. In: Peyrin, T. (ed.) FSE 2016. LNCS, vol. 9783, pp. 428–449. Springer, Heidelberg (2016). https://doi.org/10.1007/978-3-662-52993-5_22
12. Raddum, H.: Algebraic analysis of the simon block cipher family. In: Lauter, K., Rodríguez-Henríquez, F. (eds.) LATINCRYPT 2015. LNCS, vol. 9230, pp. 157–169. Springer, Cham (2015). https://doi.org/10.1007/978-3-319-22174-8_9

13. Wang, Q., Liu, Z., Varıcı, K., Sasaki, Y., Rijmen, V., Todo, Y.: Cryptanalysis of reduced-round SIMON32 and SIMON48. In: Meier, W., Mukhopadhyay, D. (eds.) INDOCRYPT 2014. LNCS, vol. 8885, pp. 143–160. Springer, Cham (2014). https://doi.org/10.1007/978-3-319-13039-2_9

14. Sun, L., Fu, K., Wang, M.: Improved zero-correlation cryptanalysis on SIMON. In: Lin, D., Wang, X.F., Yung, M. (eds.) Inscrypt 2015. LNCS, vol. 9589, pp. 125–143. Springer, Cham (2016). https://doi.org/10.1007/978-3-319-38898-4_8

15. Todo, Y., Morii, M.: Bit-based division property and application to SIMON family. In: Peyrin, T. (ed.) FSE 2016. LNCS, vol. 9783, pp. 357–377. Springer, Heidelberg (2016). https://doi.org/10.1007/978-3-662-52993-5_18

16. Xiang, Z., Zhang, W., Bao, Z., Lin, D.: Applying MILP method to searching integral distinguishers based on division property for 6 lightweight block ciphers. In: Cheon, J.H., Takagi, T. (eds.) ASIACRYPT 2016. LNCS, vol. 10031, pp. 648–678. Springer, Heidelberg (2016). https://doi.org/10.1007/978-3-662-53887-6_24

17. Yang, G., Zhu, B., Suder, V., Aagaard, M.D., Gong, G.: The Simeck family of lightweight block ciphers. In: Güneysu, T., Handschuh, H. (eds.) CHES 2015. LNCS, vol. 9293, pp. 307–329. Springer, Heidelberg (2015). https://doi.org/10.1007/978-3-662-48324-4_16

18. Bagheri, N.: Linear cryptanalysis of reduced-round SIMECK variants. In: Biryukov, A., Goyal, V. (eds.) INDOCRYPT 2015. LNCS, vol. 9462, pp. 140–152. Springer, Cham (2015). https://doi.org/10.1007/978-3-319-26617-6_8

19. Kölbl, S., Roy, A.: A brief comparison of Simon and Simeck. Cryptology ePrint Archive, Report 2015/706 (2015). http://eprint.iacr.org/

20. Kondo, K., Sasaki, Y., Iwata, T.: On the design rationale of SIMON block cipher: integral attacks and impossible differential attacks against SIMON variants. In: Manulis, M., Sadeghi, A.-R., Schneider, S. (eds.) ACNS 2016. LNCS, vol. 9696, pp. 518–536. Springer, Cham (2016). https://doi.org/10.1007/978-3-319-39555-5_28

21. Zhang, H., Wu, W.: Structural evaluation for Simon-like designs against integral attack. In: Bao, F., Chen, L., Deng, R.H., Wang, G. (eds.) ISPEC 2016. LNCS, vol. 10060, pp. 194–208. Springer, Cham (2016). https://doi.org/10.1007/978-3-319-49151-6_14

22. Kölbl, S., Leander, G., Tiessen, T.: Observations on the SIMON block cipher family. In: Gennaro, R., Robshaw, M. (eds.) CRYPTO 2015. LNCS, vol. 9215, pp. 161–185. Springer, Heidelberg (2015). https://doi.org/10.1007/978-3-662-47989-6_8

23. Knudsen, L.R.: DEAL-a 128-bit block cipher. Technical report, Department of Informatics, University of Bergen, Norway (1998)

24. Biham, E., Biryukov, A., Shamir, A.: Cryptanalysis of Skipjack reduced to 31 rounds using impossible differentials. In: Stern, J. (ed.) EUROCRYPT 1999. LNCS, vol. 1592, pp. 12–23. Springer, Heidelberg (1999). https://doi.org/10.1007/3-540-48910-X_2

25. Kim, J., Hong, S., Lim, J.: Impossible differential cryptanalysis using matrix method. Discrete Math. **310**(5), 988–1002 (2010)

26. Luo, Y., Lai, X., Wu, Z., Gong, G.: A unified method for finding impossible differentials of block cipher structures. Inf. Sci. **263**, 211–220 (2014)

27. Wu, S., Wang, M.: Automatic search of truncated impossible differentials for word-oriented block ciphers. In: Galbraith, S., Nandi, M. (eds.) INDOCRYPT 2012. LNCS, vol. 7668, pp. 283–302. Springer, Heidelberg (2012). https://doi.org/10.1007/978-3-642-34931-7_17

28. Bogdanov, A., Rijmen, V.: Linear hulls with correlation zero and linear cryptanalysis of block ciphers. Des. Codes Crypt. **70**(3), 369–383 (2014)

29. Sun, B., Liu, Z., Rijmen, V., Li, R., Cheng, L., Wang, Q., Alkhzaimi, H., Li, C.: Links among impossible differential, integral and zero correlation linear cryptanalysis. In: Gennaro, R., Robshaw, M. (eds.) CRYPTO 2015. LNCS, vol. 9215, pp. 95–115. Springer, Heidelberg (2015). https://doi.org/10.1007/978-3-662-47989-6_5

30. Zhang, K., Guan, J., Hu, B., Lin, D.: Security evaluation on Simeck against zero correlation linear cryptanalysis. Cryptology ePrint Archive, Report 2015/911 (2015). http://eprint.iacr.org/

31. AlTawy, R., Rohit, R., He, M., Mandal, K., Yang, G., Gong, G.: sLiSCP: Simeck-based permutations for lightweight sponge cryptographic primitives. Cryptology ePrint Archive, Report 2017/747 (2017). http://eprint.iacr.org/

Block Cipher Modes of Operation
for Heterogeneous Format Preserving
Encryption

Toshiya Shimizu[(✉)] and Takeshi Shimoyama

Fujitsu Laboratories Ltd., 1-1, Kamikodanaka 4-chome,
Nakahara-ku, Kawasaki 211-8588, Japan
shimizu.toshiya@jp.fujitsu.com

Abstract. Format-preserving encryption (FPE), a kind of symmetric encryption, has caught a great deal of attention of late years. FPE, as the name suggests, does not change the format of inputs which may include the length of inputs, coding of characters or data size of inputs. It is very useful to encrypt or generate some data with fixed format such as credit card numbers (CCN), social security numbers (SSN) or even address. With this encryption, we can add encryption to existing applications without changing structures including input-output format or decreasing those performance. In this work we develop and discuss block cipher modes of operation for FPE which are applicable for messages consisting of multibyte characters and their securities. This paper also gives a way to implement these modes for the format consisting of characters encoded by EUC or UTF-8 and its performance. Formats consisting of multibyte characters – we call those "heterogeneous formats" – are very important in many countries including Japan where "Kanji" or other multibyte characters are used. In addition, this paper gives an efficient way to encrypt messages of such formats and modes of operations to realize a high performance encryption algorithm.

Keywords: Block ciphers · Format-preserving encryption
Heterogeneous format · Modes of operation · Symmetric encryption
Provable security

1 Introduction

In recent years, a kind of block ciphers called format-preserving encryption (FPE) has attracted a lot of attention and has been developed. FPE, as the name suggests, preserves the format of the message after encrypting. With this encryption, we don't have to change the data scheme or interfaces of inputs or outputs if the messages are encrypted. There are many applications with fixed input-output format in the world. We can add encryption to such existing applications without changing those structures or decreasing those performances. Therefore it is very useful when we treat some data with fixed format like CCN (Credit Card Number), date or address.

© Springer International Publishing AG 2017
J. K. Liu and P. Samarati (Eds.): ISPEC 2017, LNCS 10701, pp. 256–275, 2017.
https://doi.org/10.1007/978-3-319-72359-4_15

Related Works. There are some previous works for FPE. Brightwell and Smith [7] give an encryption scheme which preserves the datatype of the plaintext such as four alphabets or twelve digits. This scheme uses indexing of characters constituting messages, modulo operations and usual streaming encryption scheme. Bellare and Rogaway [3] developed cipher schemes on arbitrary finite domains including $\mathbb{Z}_N = \{0, 1, ..., N - 1\}$, finite fields and groups of rational points of elliptic curves over finite fields. They gave three ways to treat finite domains, namely prefix cipher, cycle-walking cipher and Feistel cipher which is widely used for current FPEs. Spies [12] proposed practical constructions for encrypting CCNs or SSNs (Social Security Numbers) extending the construction in [3]. In [13], he also gives a way called FFSEM to encrypt finite set using Feistel structure. The paper [4] gives a way to formulate FPE scheme. Some encryption algorithms including one with Feistel structure are also discussed in this paper where the securities are carefully considered. Moreover, in [5], the FPE algorithm called FFX is developed based on algorithms in [4] which enables us to encrypt messages consisting of a single kind of character like n decimal digits, n bits or n alphabets. The standardizations of FPE called FF1 and FF3 based on FFX are proposed to NIST in [10] for which we can use any 128-bit block cipher. The security of Feistel structure used for these schemes in common for small domains is analyzed in [8]. Another example of construction of FFX called VAES3 or FF2 using AES is given in [14,15]. An evaluation of the performance of these schemes FF1, FF2 and FF3 is studied in [1] with respect to entropy and operational latency. The block cipher modes of operation are also developed. For example, in [6], a block cipher mode of operation for FPE following the usual CBC mode is studied assuming that there are FPE schemes like FFX for short messages. Many FPE constructions including those mentioned above are described and studied in [11].

Discussion. However, many algorithms mentioned above including FFX give us only encryptions for "homogeneous" strings as its inputs. That is, they can only be applicable for messages consisting of a single kind of character, fixed length or specific formats. Still, there are many data or strings the formats of which are not homogeneous. In Japan or other many Asian countries, for example, addresses consist of concatenation of numbers as postal code and "Kanji" as details. The day and month of Japanese is also one of those formats. In addition to these dependent on languages, formats used for databases like XML data which have tags or CSV data which have commas cannot be treated as homogeneous messages. To make matters worse, there are a lot of data consisting of a nest of many formats. Of course, it is one solution to use some encodes such as base64 to reduce such formats to homogeneous case. But, in general, the data size using base64 encoding will get 33.3% bigger and the data format as cipher data will be different from that of plain data. Namely, it is very important to develop FPE schemes which can treat messages of "heterogeneous" formats.

Of course, there are works of FPE schemes for general formats. In [16], a generalized FPE scheme is suggested to encrypt messages consisting of many given formats like finite integral domains, CCNs, SSNs or dates. They describe general formats as a concatenation of some primitive formats, and then encrypt. Moreover, a general FPE scheme called C-FFX following FFX for general formats is considered in [9]. They also use Feistel structure and enables us to encrypt messages consisting of "heterogeneous" characters including 1-byte character, 2-byte character or any other kind of characters.

In these works, FPEs for heterogeneous formats were carefully developed, but modes of operation were not considered. In homogeneous cases, modes of operations have been developed [6]. For encrypting long and various size of messages by using block ciphers, block cipher modes of operation are necessary. The core encryption algorithms of block ciphers like AES are only applicable to small fixed domains like 128-bit strings, and modes of operation give us to encrypt strings of any length securely and efficiently. Similarly, it's not practical to use (heterogeneous) FPE without modes of operation for any data from the view point of performance as the processing efficiency decreases if the block size becomes bigger. As mentioned above, there are a lot of heterogeneous strings of a large size such as XML data, strings consisting of multibyte characters or even unknown size like streaming data. Many applications including legacy ones may have fixed input-output format with heterogeneous characters and unknown (streaming) data size. It is necessary to develop modes of operation for heterogeneous FPEs in order to encrypt such data efficiently. As the size of characters in a message with a heterogeneous format may be different from each other, the usual way of dividing a message into blocks based on fixed block size is not applicable, which makes difficult to construct modes of operation and to prove those securities.

Our Contributions. In this paper, we develop block cipher modes of operation of FPEs for heterogeneous characters and give some usual security evaluations. We introduce two modes of operation following CBC mode and CTR mode respectively as these modes are frequently and widely used among a lot of modes. Security proofs of these two modes for left-or-right chosen-plaintext-attack are also carefully considered. At first glance, security proofs are drawn from the proofs for ordinary modes of operation. However, in constructing modes of operation for heterogeneous FPE, we have to divide a string into blocks the size of which may vary in order not to destroy the structure of the format. Therefore, we cannot use a fixed block size parameter such as 128-bit and have to treat such dynamic parameters for security proofs. We carefully treat such parameters, use probability calculation over different-sized sets and give security evaluations based on given security parameters and the size of character consisting messages. Moreover, we discuss its implementation using AES for its core algorithm and performance for some concrete characters. We also give real performance (19 Mbps on our regular machine) of our proposed modes. With this implementation, we can easily encrypt messages of any length including "Kanji" or other multibyte characters encoded by EUC or UTF-8. We also introduce a permutation function to reduce the semantic risks which are essentially hidden in format itself.

Contents. Our contents are just as follows. In Sect. 2, we fix some notations for FPE and summarize the FPE algorithms in previous works. The developed modes and its algorithms are described in Sect. 3 and the details of securities are written in Sect. 4. Implementations, including the machine spec, configurations for definitions of characters and security parameters, are discussed and mentioned in Sect. 5.

2   Preliminary

In this section, we fix some notations to introduce format preserving encryptions or block cipher modes of operation. And then we introduce some previous works for FPE and those algorithms following the fixed notations. The works also include the securities of its scheme including CCA security and meet-in-the-middle (MITM) attack security.

2.1   Notation

We assume that every character belongs to one finite non-empty set. Let us denote such a set by $\mathrm{Ch}(c)$ for a character c. For each such a set $\mathrm{Ch}(c)$, we need a bijection called the *rank* function between $\mathrm{Ch}(c)$ and $\mathbb{Z}_{|\mathrm{Ch}(c)|}$, where $\mathbb{Z}_{|\mathrm{Ch}(c)|}$ is the set of non-negative integers smaller than $|\mathrm{Ch}(c)|$ (cardinality of $\mathrm{Ch}(c)$). The inverse function of a rank function is called the *chara* function. We shall identify a character as an integer by rank function and we use this identification without notice in this paper. A *format* Ω is defined as a finite product of character sets $C_1 := \mathrm{Ch}(c_1), \ldots, C_n := \mathrm{Ch}(c_n)$, i.e. $\Omega = \prod_{i=1}^{n} C_i$ and an element of Ω is called a string of length n. Conversely, given a string x, we shall use $\mathrm{Form}(x)$ as the format of x and $\mathrm{len}(x)$ as the length of x. Its entropy $S(x)$ is defined as the bit size of the format of x, that is $S(x) := \log_2(|\mathrm{Form}(x)|)$. For a string $x = x[1] \ldots x[n]$, we denote x by $(x[i])_{i=1}^{n}$ or more simply by $(x[i])_i$.

For each format Ω, we can construct a bijection $\mathrm{NUM}_\Omega \colon \Omega \to \mathbb{Z}_{|\Omega|}$ by dictionary order using rank functions of characters. To be more specific, NUM function is recursively defined as follows;

$$\mathrm{NUM}_\Omega((x[i])_{i=1}^{n}) = \mathrm{NUM}_{\Omega'}((x[i])_{i=1}^{n-1})|C_n| + x[n],$$

$$\Omega' = \prod_{i=1}^{n-1} C_i, \ \mathrm{NUM}(x[1]) = x[1]$$

Let us denote the inverse function of NUM_Ω by STR_Ω. The function STR_Ω is easily extended to the function on the whole positive integer by $\mathrm{STR}_\Omega(M) = \mathrm{STR}_\Omega(M \bmod |\Omega|)$. A format $\Omega = \prod_{i=1}^{n} C_i$ is called homogeneous if $C_i = C_j$ for all $i, j \in \{1, \ldots, n\}$. Otherwise the format is called heterogeneous.

2.2   Previous Works

Homogeneous FPE. We summarize the core algorithm of homogeneous format preserving encryption in [5], used for both FF1 and FF3. First of all, fix following parameters; a key K, a 128-bit block cipher CIPH_K, a tweak T, the round number r and the set of characters defining the input space. The encryption algorithm using Feistel structure for a string $x = x_1 x_2 \ldots x_n$ is as follows;

1. Set $\text{CTR} = 0$ which means the round number in the Feistel network.
2. Divide x into two strings $u \,\|\, v$ and let $A = u$ and $B = v$.
3. Let S be a big byte string (the size depends on the security parameters) determined by CIPH_K with $\text{NUM}(B), T, \text{CTR}$ as its inputs.
4. Set $C = \text{STR}_{\text{Form}(m)}(\text{NUM}(A) + \text{NUM}(S) \bmod |\text{Form}(m)|)$, where $m = v$ if CTR is an odd number and $m = u$ if even number.
5. If $\text{CTR} < r$, set $A = B, B = C, \text{CTR} = \text{CTR} + 1$ and go back to the step 3. Otherwise output $B \,\|\, C$.

The NUM function used in this algorithm is uniquely determined by the set of characters for inputs.

Heterogeneous FPE. In [9], the above algorithm is extended to that for heterogeneous formats called C-FFX by assuming that there exists a random function F_K^T with tweak T and key K from all strings of length l to those of length $n - l$. The construction of this function depends on the format of the block and it is a little difficult to construct such functions together. If we can construct, F_K^T performs a function as CIPH_K in the homogeneous case, and then step 4 in the above algorithm is realized as integer addition of strings having the same format. Specifically, the encryption E_K^T is described in Algorithm 1. Note that this encryption preserves the whole format of a message. That is, it preserves not only the total data size of an input message but also the order of characters appeared in the message.

Algorithm 1. Calculate $E_K^T(X)$

Input: X, K, T, F_K^T, l
Output: $Y = E_K^T(X)$
  $\text{CTR} \leftarrow 0$
  $n \leftarrow \text{len}(X)$
  $L \leftarrow X[0]X[1] \ldots X[l-1]$
  $R \leftarrow X[l]X[l+1] \ldots X[n-1]$
  while $\text{CTR} < r$ **do**
    $L' \leftarrow ((R[i] + F_K^T(L)[i]) \bmod |\text{Ch}(R[i])|)_{i=0}^{n-l-1}$
    $R' \leftarrow L$
    $Y = L' \| R'$
    $L \leftarrow Y[0]Y[1] \ldots Y[l-1]$
    $R \leftarrow Y[l]Y[l+1] \ldots Y[n-1]$
    $\text{CTR} \leftarrow \text{CTR} + 1$
  end while
  return Y

---

3   Block Cipher Mode of FPE

We give two modes of operation called Mode 1 and Mode 2 following the usual CBC mode and CTR mode, respectively. Both modes need the same new block partition algorithm which is essentially different from that used in typical block cipher modes like CBC. If we divide a string (regarded as a bit sequence) into blocks by the usual way using a security parameter like 128-bit, we may destroy not only the structure of the format of the string but also the character itself. So we need a good partition algorithm which preserves the data structure of messages.

Overview of Algorithms. We roughly summarize our proposed algorithms. Given a string X, first, all characters in X are assigned integers using rank functions to map the sparse spaces of character sets to dense sets. Then, we divide X into blocks by calculating entropies of characters and using the security parameter. For each block, we use Heterogeneous FPE to encrypt. Note that we can interpret the input space of each block as consecutive integers using NUM functions. Finally, we follow the classical modes to stir the next block. Note that, as input spaces of each block are mapped to consecutive integers, we can interpret block messages as integers, and we can use integer modulo operation to mix two blocks.

3.1   Algorithm

Block Partition. To describe the block partition algorithm, let us fix a security parameter[1] $s \in \mathbb{N}$. This parameter determines the minimum size of blocks and depends on the security of the format preserving encryption algorithm or pseudo random functions used for these modes. The detail of the block partition algorithm is described in Algorithm 2. Roughly speaking, this algorithm calculates the entropy of a given string character by character, and divides it into blocks with their entropies bigger than s. Note that the partitioned blocks may have different sizes, but the entropies of blocks are bigger than s and smaller than $2s$ except the last block[2]. In the following, we describe the details of the algorithms of Mode 1 and Mode 2 for encrypting the block messages.

Mode 1. In this paragraph, we describe the encryption algorithm Mode 1 for each block generated in the previous paragraph. Let us fix the format preserving encryption $(E_K^{T,\Omega}, D_K^{T,\Omega})$ defined by a key K and a tweak T, where $E_K^{T,\Omega}$ and $D_K^{T,\Omega}$ mean the encryption and the decryption, respectively, and these two functions are both bijections on Ω. In addition, we need to give an initial vector IV. The initial vector can be chosen from any space we desire like 128-bit strings or strings of a fixed format. In the following, we fix a natural number l and the IV vector will be chosen from $\mathbb{Z}_{2^l}$. Denote the m-th plain block by P_m, its format by $\Omega_m = \text{Form}(P_m)$,

---

[1] We assume that the maximum entropy described in Sect. 2.1 of characters in plaintexts is smaller than s.

[2] The entropy of the last block may be a little bigger than $2s$ with a little possibility.

Algorithm 2. Calculate blocks of $X = X[1]...X[n]$

Input: X and security parameter s
Output: the block number m and the set of blocks $B_1, \ldots, B_m$
    if $S(X) < s$ **then**
        $B_1 \leftarrow X$
        return $1, (B_1)$
    end if
    $i \leftarrow 0$
    while $S(X) \geq s$ **do**
        if $i \neq 0$ **then**
            $B_i \leftarrow C$
        end if
        find j such that $(S(X[1]...X[j-1]) < s) \wedge (S(X[1]...X[j]) \geq s)$
        $C \leftarrow X[1]...X[j]$
        $X \leftarrow X[j+1]...X[len(X)]$
        $i \leftarrow i+1$
    end while
    $B_i \leftarrow C \,\|\, X$
    $m \leftarrow i$
    return $m, (B_1, ..., B_m)$

$(m-1)$-th cipher block by C_{m-1} and its format by $\Omega_{m-1} = \text{Form}(P_{m-1})$. For $i = 1, \ldots, \text{len}(P_m)$, let $I_m[i]$ be the character defined by

$$I_m[i] := P_m[i] + \text{STR}_{\Omega_m}(\text{NUM}_{\Omega_{m-1}}(C_{m-1}))[i] \bmod |\text{Ch}(P_m[i])|$$

Then the m-th cipher block can be computed as follows;

$$C_m = E_K^{T, \Omega_m}(I_m[1]\|| \cdots \|I_m[\text{len}(P_m)]).$$

However, for the first block, we use IV instead of $\text{NUM}_{\Omega_{m-1}}(C_{m-1})$. The decryption algorithm is easily given by the following equation for all $i = 1, \ldots, \text{len}(C_m)$;

$$P_m[i] = D_K^{T, \Omega_m}(C_m)[i] - \text{STR}_{\Omega_m}(\text{NUM}_{\Omega_{m-1}}(C_{m-1}))[i] \bmod |\text{Ch}(C_m[i])|$$

Here we also use IV for the first block. Figure 1 shows schematic views of these algorithms.

Mode 2. Again, we fix a key K, tweak T, pseudo random generator F_K^T the output bit size of which is s, the initial vector IV and the variable CTR which stands for the block number. Then the computation of the i-th character of the ciphertext block for all $i = 1, \ldots, \text{len}(P_m)$ is as follows;

$$C_m[i] = P_m[i] + \text{STR}_{\Omega_m}(F_K^T(\text{IV} + \text{CTR}))[i] \bmod |\text{Ch}(P_m[i])|$$

If we have an ideal random function from $\mathbb{Z}_{2^l}$ to Ω_m, we may use that function instead of $\text{STR}_{\Omega_m} \circ F_K^T$. More generally, we simply refer to these sets of PRF

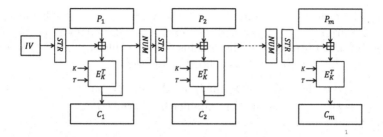

Fig. 1. Overview of mode 1 (CBC-like mode)

functions associated to the format appeared in blocks as the family of Mode 2. We call the family consisting of ideal random functions the random family of Mode 2. This family is used in Sect. 4.

The decryption is easily given in a similar way. The view of these algorithms is showed in Fig. 2.

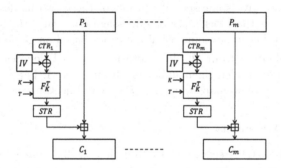

Fig. 2. Overview of mode 2 (CTR-like mode)

3.2 Permutation

In some formats including Japanese encoding, format itself may have the information about strings. For example, if a string x of length 6 consists of two 1-byte characters, one 2-byte character, two 1-byte characters and one 2-byte character, then one might guess that string expresses the day and month in Japanese language. To reduce such a semantic risk, we suggest the permutation algorithm for these modes of operation, which can be realized as a streaming process on a block-by-block basis. We can use block-then-encipher algorithm in [3] for implementation of permutation functions on small domains.

Fix a key K and we need a pseudo random permutation $\mathrm{Perm}_{K,M}$ on $\mathbb{Z}_M$ for small M. Its inverse is denoted by $\mathrm{Perm}_{K,M}^{-1}$. For an integer $i \in \mathbb{Z}_M$, $\mathrm{Perm}_{K,M}(i)$ is the i-th element of the permutation $\mathrm{Perm}_{K,M}$. Let $C_m = c_m[1]c_m[2]\ldots c_m[n_m+1]$ be the m-th ciphertext block given in previous paragraphs, t_m be

the number of characters from the first block to the $(m-1)$-th block, then
$\text{Perm} := \text{Perm}_{K,t_m+n_m}$ is applied to C_m except for the final character and the
resulting block is outputted as the conclusive cipher block. That is, the output
$C'_m = c'_m[1]c'_m[2]\dots c'_m[n_m+1]$ is defined as follows;

1. Let $\text{ord}(i)$ be the order of $\text{Perm}(i)$ in the set $\{\text{Perm}(i)\}_{i=t_m+1}^{n_m}$. That is,
   $\text{Perm}(i)$ is the $\text{ord}(i)$-th smallest number in $\{\text{Perm}(i)\}_{i=t_m+1}^{t_m+n_m}$.
2. Then, C'_m is defined as;

$$c'_m[i] = \begin{cases} c_m[\text{ord}(i)] & i \le n_m \\ c_m[n_m+1] & i = n_m+1 \end{cases}$$

Note that we excluded the final character. As we use entropy for dividing messages into blocks, we can preserve the character acting as the block separator by this exclusion.

4   Security Evaluation

In this section, we give some security proofs of these two modes and the core
FPE algorithm. As the block sizes of a message may vary, the security proofs
are not so trivial. Let us fix some usual notations based on game-playing proofs
for security evaluation from [2]. The notation $a \xleftarrow{R} A$ denotes the operation
of selecting a random element a uniformly from a set A. Let $\text{Rand}(A,B)$ and
$\text{Perm}(A)$ be the set of all maps from A to B and all bijections on A, respectively.

4.1   LoR-CPA Security

We define the LoR-CPA security based on that in [2]. Conventionally, we use
$(\mathcal{K},\mathcal{E},\mathcal{D})$ for symmetric encryption scheme, where $\mathcal{K},\mathcal{E},\mathcal{D}$ means the key space,
encryption functions and decryption functions, respectively. If we fix a key $K \in$
$\mathcal{K}$, we define the left-or-right oracle $\mathcal{E}_K(\mathcal{LR}(\cdot,\cdot,b))$ as an oracle which does the
following; it takes (x_0,x_1) for its input and returns $\mathcal{E}_K(x_0)$ if $b = 0$, $\mathcal{E}_K(x_1)$ if
$b = 1$. Then, for an adversary A which has access to the left-or-right oracle, we
consider the following experiment of A;

1. $K \xleftarrow{R} \mathcal{K}$
2. $d \leftarrow A^{\mathcal{E}_K(\mathcal{LR}(\cdot,\cdot,b))}$
3. **Return** d

Note that we require that the two messages queried of $\mathcal{E}_K(\mathcal{LR}(\cdot,\cdot,b))$ always
have equal format. We may also define the advantage of A as follows;

$$\mathbf{Adv}_A^{\text{LoR-CPA}} = \Pr[\mathbf{Exp}_A^{\text{LoR-CPA-1}} = 1] - \Pr[\mathbf{Exp}_A^{\text{LoR-CPA-0}} = 1]$$

The maximum advantage for time complexity t, number of queries q and total
bits μ is defined as the maximum advantage over all advantages with such conditions.

Mode 2. We now prove the general security bound for Mode 2 operation.

Lemma 1. *Suppose that the random family for Mode 2 is used. Then, for any* $t, q, \mu,$

$$\mathbf{Adv}_{\mathrm{mode2}}^{\mathrm{LoR\text{-}CPA}}(t, q, \mu) \leq \frac{\mu(q-1)}{2^{s+l}}$$

where l is the input length of the random family and s is the security parameter mentioned above, respectively.

Proof. In the following, we may regard all messages as integers using NUM functions as usual. This proof is very influenced by that of Lemma 10 in [2]. Let $(M_1, N_1), ..., (M_q, N_q)$ be the oracle queries of the adversary A, each consisting of a pair of equal formats, and $r_i \in \mathbb{Z}_{2^l}$ be the associated nonce. Let n_i be the number of blocks in the i-th query. Denote the formats of blocks in i-th query by $\Omega_{i,1}, ..., \Omega_{i,n_i}$.

As usual, let D be the following event, defined for either game: $r_i + k \neq r_j + k'$ whenever $(i, k) \neq (j, k')$ for all i, j, k, k'. D means that there are no collisions in the inputs of random family among all of the queries. We call strings $r_i + 1, ..., r_i + n_i$ the i-th sequence, and $r_i + k$ the k-th point in i-th sequence. If we define $\mathrm{Pr}_i[\cdot]$ to be the probability of an event in game i, we may prove $\mathrm{Pr}_0[\overline{D}] = \mathrm{Pr}_1[\overline{D}]$ as D for either game depends only on the nonces which are chosen randomly and independent of the game. We may also prove $\mathrm{Pr}_0[A = 1|D] = \mathrm{Pr}_1[A = 1|D]$. This is because, we use the random family for Mode 2 and, given the event D, the random functions are evaluated at new points each time they are invoked, and therefore the outputs are randomly and uniformly distributed over their format space. Thus each cipher block is a message block added by a random value and we get the equality.

Now, we can give an upper bound of the advantage as follows;

$$\begin{aligned}
\mathbf{Adv}^{\mathrm{LoR\text{-}CPA}}(\cdot) &= \mathrm{Pr}_1[A = 1] - \mathrm{Pr}_0[A = 1] \\
&= \mathrm{Pr}_1[A = 1|\overline{D}] \cdot \mathrm{Pr}_1[\overline{D}] + \mathrm{Pr}_1[A = 1|D] \cdot \mathrm{Pr}_1[D] \\
&\quad - \mathrm{Pr}_0[A = 1|\overline{D}] \cdot \mathrm{Pr}_0[\overline{D}] - \mathrm{Pr}_0[A = 1|D] \cdot \mathrm{Pr}_0[D].
\end{aligned}$$

Then we have,

$$\mathbf{Adv}^{\mathrm{LoR\text{-}CPA}}(\cdot) \leq \mathrm{Pr}_1[\overline{D}] = \mathrm{Pr}_0[\overline{D}].$$

Let p_i be the probability of the i-th sequence colliding with any of the previous sequences. Obviously, we can show that $\mathrm{Pr}_i[\overline{D}] \leq \sum_{i=1}^{q} p_i$ We also have,

$$p_i \leq \frac{\sum_{j=1}^{i-1}(n_j + n_i - 1)}{2^l} = \frac{(i-1)(n_i - 1) + \sum_{j=1}^{i-1} n_j}{2^l}.$$

Putting everything together and by the assumption that the entropy of $\Omega_{i,j}$ is larger than s for all i, j, we have,

$$\mathbf{Adv}^{\mathrm{LoR\text{-}CPA}}(\cdot) \leq \frac{(q-1)\sum_{i=1}^{q} n_i - \frac{q(q-1)}{2}}{2^l} \leq \frac{\mu(q-1)}{2^{s+l}}.$$

$\square$

We may also prove the following real security.

Theorem 1. *Suppose that the family* (F_i) *of Mode 2 consists of a PRF families with input space* $\mathbb{Z}_l$ *and output space* Ω_i. *Then, for any* t, q *and* $\mu = q'2^s$,

$$\mathbf{Adv}_{\mathrm{mode2}}^{\mathrm{LoR\text{-}CPA}}(t, q, \mu) \leq 2\,\mathbf{Adv}_{(F_i)}^{\mathrm{PRF}}(t, q') + \frac{\mu(q-1)}{2^{s+l}}$$

where s *is the security parameter.*

Proof. The proof is a simple contradiction argument. That is, if we have an adversary attacking Mode 2 in the LoR-CPA sense, we may build a distinguisher which have an advantage better than $\mathbf{Adv}_{(F_i)}^{\mathrm{PRF}}$ for some reasonable queries. The distinguisher simply runs the adversary who has an advantage greater than $\mathbf{Adv}_{(F_i)}^{\mathrm{PRF}}(t, q')$ and checks whether he breaks the encryption scheme or not. All we must be careful is that the total number of oracle queries made by distinguisher is at most $\mu/2^s$ and the proof is omitted.   □

Mode 1. We can also prove the security bound for Mode 1 operation. This proof is based on the proof of securities for CBC in [2].

Lemma 2. *Suppose the family* $(E_K^{T,\Omega})_\Omega$ *is* $(\mathrm{Perm}(\Omega))_\Omega$. *Let* ϵ *be the max entropy of character used in queries. Then, for any* t, q, μ, *we have*

$$\mathbf{Adv}_{\mathrm{mode1}}^{\mathrm{LoR\text{-}CPA}}(t, q, \mu) \leq \left(\frac{\mu^2}{s^2} - \frac{\mu}{s}\right) \cdot \frac{\epsilon}{2^s}$$

where s *is the security parameter mentioned above, respectively.*

Proof. Again, note that we may regard all messages as integers using NUM functions in the following. We use the same notations as above, i.e. (M_1, M_1'), ..., (M_q, M_q') for the oracle queries of the adversary A, each consisting of a pair of equal formats, n_i for the number of blocks in the i-th query and $\Omega_{i,1}, ..., \Omega_{i,n_i}$ for the formats of blocks in the i-th query. We let $M_{i,j}$ and $M_{i,j}'$ denote the j-th blocks of i-th queries, so that $M_i = M_{i,1} \ldots M_{i,n_i}$ and $M_i' = M_{i,1}' \ldots M_{i,n_i}'$. Let $C_i = C_{i,0} \ldots C_{i,n_i}$ be the random variable which is the response of oracle to the i-th query.

Similar to the way in [2], we can define the block-based event called distinct which tells us all we want to know about the advantage of the adversary. First, for a pair (i, j) and (i', j') which are indexes of message blocks, we define the event $Col_{(j,k),(j',k')}$ called collision to be true if either $(C_{j,k-1} + M_{j,k} \equiv C_{j',k'-1} + M_{j',k'} \bmod |\Omega_{j,k}|$ and $\Omega_{j,k} = \Omega_{j',k'})$ or $(C_{j,k-1} + M_{j,k}' \equiv C_{j',k'-1} + M_{j',k'}' \bmod |\Omega_{j,k}|$ and $\Omega_{j,k} = \Omega_{j',k'})$ holds. Then we can define the event called distinct which is true if there are no collisions before a fixed index. Namely, the event $D_{i,u}$ is defined to be false if there exists a pair (j, k), (j', k') such that

$Col_{(j,k),(j',k')}$ holds and

$$\sum_{t=1}^{j-1}(n_t + 2) + k < \sum_{t=1}^{j'-1}(n_t + 2) + k' \text{ and}$$

$$\sum_{t=1}^{j'-1}(n_t + 2) + k' \le \sum_{t=1}^{i-1}(n_t + 2) + u.$$

Finally, set $D := D_{q,n_q}$. Then, using the fact that we use the random permutation family for block ciphers, we may prove that the adversary never have an advantage as long as D holds.

Next, for a fixed index (i, u), we have to compute the probability of $C_{i,u-1}$ which may cause a collision $D_{i,u}$ under $D_{i,u-1}$. We define two sets as follows;

$$MV_{i,u} := \{C_{j,k-1} + M_{j,k} - M_{i,u} \bmod |\Omega_{i,u}| \text{ for all } (j,k) \text{ such that}$$

$$\Omega_{j,k} = \Omega_{i,u} \text{ and } \sum_{t=1}^{j-1}(n_t + 2) + k < \sum_{t=1}^{i-1}(n_t + 2) + u\},$$

$$MV'_{i,u} := \{C_{j,k-1} + M'_{j,k} - M'_{i,u} \bmod |\Omega_{i,u}| \text{ for all } (j,k) \text{ such that}$$

$$\Omega_{j,k} = \Omega_{i,u} \text{ and } \sum_{t=1}^{j-1}(n_t + 2) + k < \sum_{t=1}^{i-1}(n_t + 2) + u\}.$$

Then, the collision occurs when $C_{i,u-1}$ falls in a set $MV \cup MV'$. Note that $|MV_{i,u} \cup MV'_{i,u}| \le 2(n_1 + \cdots + n_{i-1} + u - 1)$.

There are two cases. The easy one is $|\Omega_{i,u-1}| \le |\Omega_{i,u}|$. In this case, we can check that the probability is bounded by $2(n_1 + \cdots + n_{i-1} + u - 1)/|\Omega_{i,u-1}|$. Next, we deal with the case with $|\Omega_{i,u-1}| > |\Omega_{i,u}|$. Then there is some modulo bias and we have to compute it. Let Q, R be integers defined by $|\Omega_{i,u-1}| = |\Omega_{i,u}| \cdot Q + R$. Then, the probability is bounded by $2(n_1 + \cdots + n_{i-1} + u - 1) \cdot (Q+1)/|\Omega_{i,u-1}|$. By construction, Q is bounded by ϵ and the denominator is bounded by the security parameter. Namely, we have the bound $2(n_1 + \cdots + n_{i-1} + u - 1) \cdot \epsilon/2^s$. Then, computing the sum, the probability of $\overline{D}$ is bounded by

$$\sum_{i=1}^{q}\sum_{u=1}^{n_i} \Pr[\overline{D_{i,u}} \mid D_{i,u-1}] \le \sum_{i=1}^{q}\sum_{u=1}^{n_i} \frac{2\epsilon(n_1 + \cdots + n_{i-1} + u - 1)}{2^s}$$

$$\le \frac{\epsilon}{2^s}\left(\frac{\mu^2}{s^2} - \frac{\mu}{s}\right).$$

$\square$

The following theorem tells the real security of Mode 1.

Theorem 2. *Suppose the family* $(F_i) = (E_K^{T,\Omega_i})$ *is a family of PRP families. Then, for any* t, q, μ,

$$\mathbf{Adv}_{\mathrm{model}}^{\mathrm{LoR\text{-}CPA}}(t, q, \mu) \le 2\,\mathbf{Adv}_{(F_i)}^{\mathrm{PRP}}(t, 1) + q^2 2^{-s-1} + \left(\frac{\mu^2}{s^2} - \frac{\mu}{s}\right) \cdot \frac{1}{2^s}$$

where s is the security parameter mentioned above, respectively.

Proof. The proof is very similar to the one given for Theorem 1. All we must be careful is that we use PRP families instead of PRF families in Theorem 1. But the difference of these two families can be computed by the following well-known inequality;

$$\mathbf{Adv}^{\mathrm{PRF}}(t, q) \leq \mathbf{Adv}^{\mathrm{PRP}}(t, q) + q^2 2^{-l-1}.$$

between $\mathrm{Perm}(\mathbb{Z}_{2^l})$ and $\mathrm{Rand}(\mathbb{Z}_{2^l}, \mathbb{Z}_{2^l})$.   □

4.2   MITM Security for Implementation

In this subsection, we discuss concrete round number for implementation of the core heterogeneous FPE algorithm. This is already discussed and computed in [9], but we give a more precise evaluation which can be used for its implementation. This evaluation only depends on the size of the entropy of the plain text. Namely, that is independent of a division of message for Feistel structure or entropies of characters appeared in the plain text.

Theorem 3. *Suppose that heterogeneous FPE described in Sect. 2 is an r round Feistel on a format Ω. Let $E := |\Omega|$ and $r' := \lfloor r/4 \rfloor$. Then the time cost of the MITM attack as a PRP one is bounded by below as follows;*

$$t \geq (E/2)^{r'} \cdot \sqrt{E}.$$

Note that this is a very rough evaluation but enough for implementations. For instance, if we let the block size be 128-bit and the round of Feistel be 8, the time for MITM attack is at least 2^{318}.

Proof. First of all, let us begin with describing the whole table of the adversary queries. Fix a splitting of the Feistel structure, namely the left side format Ω_1 with its entropy E_1 and the right side format Ω_2 with its entropy E_2. Then a round function for the i-th round is regarded as a map $f \colon \Omega_2 \to \Omega_1$ if i is even and $f \colon \Omega_1 \to \Omega_2$ if i is odd. Adversary queries make two tables which consist of values applied round functions and inverse functions of round functions, respectively. The size of the first table is $E_2^{E_1 \cdot \lceil r/4 \rceil} \cdot E_1^{E_2 \cdot r'}$ and then, neglecting the second table, the time to make the first is at least $t = (E_2^{E_1} \cdot E_1^{E_2})^{r'} \cdot (E_1 + E_2)$. Define a function f on $[1, E]$ as $f(x) = (x^{E/x} \cdot (E/x)^x)^{r'} \cdot (x + E/x)$. As E_1 and E_2 are the splitting of E, the equations $t = f(E_1) = f(E_2)$ hold.

   Let us bound f by below. The inequality of arithmetic and geometric means easily tells us that $f(x) \geq (x^{E/x} \cdot (E/x)^x)^{r'} \cdot \sqrt{E}$. Now, all we need is to evaluate $x^{E/x} \cdot (E/x)^x$. But this is obviously larger than $E/2$ on $[1, 2]$ and $2^{\sqrt{E}} \cdot E$ on $[2, \sqrt{E}]$. As $f(x) = f(E/x)$, we just have the evaluation to prove.   □

5   Implementation

In this section, we discuss an implementation of our modes including its core FPE algorithm. The characters we used for this implementation are EUC-JP and some of UTF-8. As core algorithms are independent of the kind of characters in messages, if we define rank functions for characters as configurations, our implementation is easily applicable for another characters. Our machine spec and the language of the implementation are showed in Table 1.

Table 1. Specification of our machine

OS	Windows 7
Processor	Intel Core i7-6700, 3.40 Ghz
Memory	16.0 GB
Language	go 1.6.2

5.1   Parameter Setting and Performance

The security parameter s is set to be 128 following the usual block cipher. For the core block cipher used in FPE which encrypts blocks of messages, we use AES with 128-bit keys. The round number of FPE is 8, which is enough secure as mentioned in Sect. 4.

We encrypted 100-Kb random data 2000 times and take the average. As a result, eliminating system functions like garbage collection or sleep, our cipher encrypts messages by 19 Mbps. Note that we use a lot of arithmetic functions for this algorithm and AES only 32 times every block as showed in the next subsection. AES used in our **golang** is AES-NI and has about 50 clocks/block performance in the environment. Therefore, analyzing the profile, about 6% of the execution time is occupied by AES. Remaining parts of the execution are expended by arithmetic functions such as addition, subtraction, multiplication, division, rank functions or NUM functions.

5.2   Example

In this subsection, we discuss the concrete implementation for EUC coding which is heavily used by Japanese Unix operating systems. Using EUC coding, strings may have two kind of characters which are characters expressed by 1-byte and those by 2-byte. A sample encrypted data is described in Appendix A. The implementation for UTF-8 which is the dominant character encoding for the web is discussed in Appendix B. First of all, we construct the block cipher used in modes of operation using AES and following the construction of FFX in [10]. Fix a format Ω of inputs, number of characters u determining the splitting of block, a key K for AES, a pseudo random function PRF based on K with 128-bit output. For example, we use the following algorithm as the implementation of $\text{PRF}(X)$ based on AES.

1. Apply bit padding to X, if necessary.
2. Let $X_1, \ldots, X_m$ be the blocks for which $X = X_1 || \ldots || X_m$.

Table 2. EUC-JP 2-byte codes

index	$c_{i,1}$	num	prefix: p_i	index	$c_{i,1}$	num	prefix: p_i
C_1	0xa1a1	94	0	C_{14}	0xa6c1	24	402
C_2	0xa2a1	14	94	C_{15}	0xa7a1	33	426
C_3	0xa2ba	8	108	C_{16}	0xa3e1	33	459
C_4	0xa2ca	7	116	C_{17}	0xa8a1	32	492
C_5	0xa2dc	15	123	C_{18}	0xb0a1	94	524
C_6	0xa2f2	8	138	$\vdots$	$\vdots$	$\vdots$	$\vdots$
C_7	0xa2fe	1	146				
C_8	0xa3b0	10	147	C_{48}	0xcea1	94	3344
C_9	0xa3c1	26	157	C_{49}	0xcfa1	51	3438
C_{10}	0xa3e1	26	183	C_{50}	0xd0a1	94	3489
C_{11}	0xa4a1	83	209	$\vdots$	$\vdots$	$\vdots$	$\vdots$
C_{12}	0xa5a1	86	292	C_{85}	0xf3a1	94	6779
C_{13}	0xa6a1	24	378	C_{86}	0xf4a1	6	6873

3. Let $Y_0 = 0^{128}$, amd for j from 1 to m define $Y_j = \mathrm{AES}(Y_{j-1} \oplus X_j)$
4. Return Y_m.

Let Ω_L, Ω_R be the left side format of the block and the right side format, respectively. For a natural number n, we denote the l-byte string representation of n by $[n]^l$. Then, the algorithm with security parameter 128 is constructed as showed in Algorithm 3.

Now, all we have to do is to construct the rank function and chara function. We describe a sample implementation of these functions for EUC. We define two sets $C_{\mathrm{euc},1}, C_{\mathrm{euc},2}$ consisting of 1-byte characters and 2-byte characters, respectively, the sizes of which are 95 and 6879. As the first 31 characters in 1-byte code are control characters, the functions $\mathrm{rank}_{\mathrm{euc},1} : C_{\mathrm{euc},1} \to \mathbb{Z}_{95}$ and $\mathrm{chara}_{\mathrm{euc},1}$ are simply constructed as follows;

$$\mathrm{rank}_{\mathrm{euc},1}(c) = c - 32, \quad \mathrm{chara}_{\mathrm{euc},1}(n) = n + 32$$

As the addresses of two byte characters are not continuous and there are a lot of unused byte code, the construction of the functions for $C_{\mathrm{euc},2}$ is a little complicated. To define the functions, we use the Table 2 which classifies the 2-byte characters into some blocks. In Table 2, *num* and *prefix* of C_i means the number of characters in C_i, the number of characters in $\bigcup_{j=1}^{i-1} C_j$, respectively. Let $c_{i,1}$ be the byte code of the first character of C_i. Then, we can define the rank and chara functions described in Algorithms 4 and 5.

Algorithm 3. Algorithm of block cipher

Input: X, K, T

Output: the cipher text Y

  1. Let $A = X[1\ldots u], B = X[u+1\ldots n]$

  2. Let $b = \lceil\lceil\log_2|\Omega_R|\rceil/8\rceil$

  3. Let $d = 4\lceil b/4\rceil + 4$

  4. Let $P = [1]^1||[2]^1||[1]^1||[|\Omega_L| \bmod 2^8]^1||[|\Omega_R| \bmod 2^{16}]^2||[8]^1||[u]^1||[n]^8$

for i *from* 0 *to* 7 **do**

    5.1. Let $Q = [0]^{(-b-1) \bmod 16}||[i]^1||[\mathrm{NUM}(B)]^b$

    5.2. Let $R = \mathrm{PRF}(P||Q||T)$

    5.3. Let s be the first d bytes integer of the following string (*):

        $R||\mathrm{AES}_K(R \oplus [1]^{16})||\mathrm{AES}_K(R \oplus [2]^{16})\ldots \mathrm{AES}_K(R \oplus [\lceil d/16\rceil - 1]^{16})$

    5.4. If i is even, let $\Phi = \Omega_L$; else, let $\Phi = \Omega_R$

    5.5. Let $c = (\mathrm{NUM}(A) + s) \bmod |\Phi|$

    5.6. Let $C = \mathrm{STR}^\Phi(c)$

    5.7. Let $A = B, B = C$

end for

$Y \leftarrow A \,||\, B$

return Y

(*): interpret byte string as integer using BigEndian

Algorithm 4. Calculate $\mathrm{rank}_{\mathrm{euc},2}(c)$

Input: c and $C_i, c_{i,1}$ for $i = 1, \ldots, 86$

Output: $\mathrm{rank}_{\mathrm{euc},2}(c)$

  $i \leftarrow 0$

  while c not in C_i **do**

    $i \leftarrow i + 1$

  end while

  return $(c - c_{i,1}) + p_i$

Algorithm 5. Calculate $\mathrm{chara}_{\mathrm{euc},2}(n)$

Input: n and $C_i, c_{i,1}$ for $i = 1, \ldots, 86$

Output: $\mathrm{chara}_{\mathrm{euc},2}(n)$

  $i \leftarrow 0$

  while $n < p_i$ **do**

    $i \leftarrow i + 1$

  end while

  return $c_{i,1} + (n - p_i)$

---

6 Conclusion

In this work, we constructed CBC-like, CTR-like block cipher modes of operation for heterogeneous FPEs for dealing with any length of messages, and gave the security proofs and some concrete implementation. With these algorithms, we can get practical implementations for arbitrary formats only by defining rank and chara functions for characters. In addition, we don't have to fix a base character of messages or care about the size of messages.

However there are still some problems to consider. One problem for these algorithms (or implementations) is the amount of operations. It's not so big problem in the aspect of the number of AES which is less than or equal to 16 for block ciphers in our implementation with 128-bit security parameter of any formats. But, if we consider in terms of other operations like multiplication or division, we use a lot of operations to compute NUM or STR. There is a room for argument about decreasing the number of such operations or replacing those by higher performance operations like bitwise operations. We think that we can use a character hex or bit code itself instead of its rank, NUM and other functions for one-way functions like PRFs in these algorithms. The block partition algorithm must also be considered more. With the algorithm suggested in this paper, a block may be decided not only by its size but with that of the next one. This gives us sufficiently secure modes and the common structure between encryption and decryption schemes even if we use permutation option, but clearly decreases the performance.

A   Example of Encryption

Here, we give an example of an encryption data with EUC coding. Parameter settings are just as mentioned in Sect. 5 and the mode is 2. The key K, initial vector IV, tweak T, plaintext and ciphertext are as follows;

> K : 0x000102030405060708090a0b0c0d0e0f
> IV : 0x0...0 (32-byte zero sequence)
> T : null
> **plaintext** : 〒 100-8111 日本東京都千代田区千代田 1-1
> **ciphertext** : 僑 0!eQ6~sR 念蛡斑益桛股巤杣籬玕沾兊 IXI

Note that we didn't use the permutation option for this encryption.

B   Implementation for UTF-8

We give a way to construct an FPE algorithm for UTF-8 encoding. As mentioned in Sect. 5, all we have to do is to define rank functions and chara functions for UTF-8. Other algorithms do not depend on the character codes once we define such functions. Here we give an example of such constructions.

We use only 1-byte characters, 2-byte characters and 3-byte characters for simplification. Accordingly, we define three sets $C_{\text{utf8,1}}$, $C_{\text{utf8,2}}$, $C_{\text{utf8,3}}$ consisting of 1-byte, 2-byte and 3-byte characters, respectively, the sizes of which are 95, 127 and 27880.

Table 3. UTF-8 2- byte codes

index	$c_{i,1}^{\text{utf8},2}$	num	prefix: $p_i^{\text{utf8},2}$
$C_1^{\text{utf8},2}$	0xc2a2	2	0
$C_2^{\text{utf8},2}$	0xc2a6	2	2
$C_3^{\text{utf8},2}$	0xc2ac	1	4
$C_4^{\text{utf8},2}$	0xc2b0	2	5
$C_5^{\text{utf8},2}$	0xc2b4	1	7
$C_6^{\text{utf8},2}$	0xc2b6	1	8
$C_7^{\text{utf8},2}$	0xc397	1	8
$C_8^{\text{utf8},2}$	0xc3a7	1	10
$C_9^{\text{utf8},2}$	0xce91	25	11
$C_{10}^{\text{utf8},2}$	0xceb1	25	36
$C_{11}^{\text{utf8},2}$	0xd081	1	61
$C_{12}^{\text{utf8},2}$	0xd090	64	62
$C_{13}^{\text{utf8},2}$	0xd191	1	126

Table 4. UTF-8 3 byte "Kanji" codes

index	$c_{i,1}^{\text{utf8},3.2}$	num	prefix: p_i
$C_1^{\text{utf8},3.2}$	0xe39080	64	0
$C_2^{\text{utf8},3.2}$	0xe39180	64	64
$C_3^{\text{utf8},3.2}$	0xe39280	64	128
⋮	⋮	⋮	⋮
$C_{48}^{\text{utf8},3.2}$	0xe3bf80	64	3008
$C_{49}^{\text{utf8},3.2}$	0xe48080	64	3072
$C_{50}^{\text{utf8},3.2}$	0xe48180	64	3136
⋮	⋮	⋮	⋮
$C_{102}^{\text{utf8},3.2}$	0xe4b580	64	6464
$C_{103}^{\text{utf8},3.2}$	0xe4b680	54	6528
$C_{104}^{\text{utf8},3.2}$	0xe4b880	64	6582
$C_{105}^{\text{utf8},3.2}$	0xe4b980	64	6646
⋮	⋮	⋮	⋮
$C_{429}^{\text{utf8},3.2}$	0xe9bd80	64	27382
$C_{430}^{\text{utf8},3.2}$	0xe9be80	38	27446

1-Byte. Rank and chara functions for $C_{\text{utf8},1}$ are constructed in the exactly similar way as those for EUC-JP.

2-Byte. To avoid the use of platform dependent characters, we use only characters appeared in 2-byte characters in EUC-JP. Then we can give a table for defining the rank and chara functions for $C_{\text{utf8},2}$. The algorithm for these functions is the same as shown in Algorithms 4 and 5. An example of table is given in Table 3

3-Byte. It is a little more complicated to define a table for 3-byte characters. We define two subsets $C_{\text{utf8},3.1}$, $C_{\text{utf8},3.2}$ of $C_{\text{utf8},3}$ which are a set containing no "Kanji" and set containing only "Kanji". For simplification, we use only characters appeared in 2-byte characters in EUC-JP for $C_{\text{utf8},3.1}$. The table for this set is given in Table 5. We also use only CJK "Kanji" and CJK "Kanji" A appeared in Unicode 1.1 for simplification. The table for this set is showed in Table 4. The rank and chara functions are easily constructed from these tables.

Table 5. UTF-8 3-byte codes

index	$c_{i,1}^{utf8,3.1}$	num	prefix: $p_i^{utf8,3.1}$	index	$c_{i,1}^{utf8,3.1}$	num	prefix: $p_i^{utf8,3.1}$
$C_1^{utf8,3.1}$	0xe28090	1	0	$C_{41}^{utf8,3.1}$	0xe294a0	1	70
$C_2^{utf8,3.1}$	0xe28095	1	1	$C_{42}^{utf8,3.1}$	0xe294a3	3	71
$C_3^{utf8,3.1}$	0xe28098	2	2	$C_{43}^{utf8,3.1}$	0xe294a8	1	74
$C_4^{utf8,3.1}$	0xe2809c	2	4	$C_{44}^{utf8,3.1}$	0xe294ab	2	75
$C_5^{utf8,3.1}$	0xe280a0	2	6	$C_{45}^{utf8,3.1}$	0xe294af	2	77
$C_6^{utf8,3.1}$	0xe280a5	2	8	$C_{46}^{utf8,3.1}$	0xe294b3	2	79
$C_7^{utf8,3.1}$	0xe280b0	1	10	$C_{47}^{utf8,3.1}$	0xe294b7	2	81
$C_8^{utf8,3.1}$	0xe280b2	2	11	$C_{48}^{utf8,3.1}$	0xe294bb	2	83
$C_9^{utf8,3.1}$	0xe280bb	1	13	$C_{49}^{utf8,3.1}$	0xe294bf	1	85
$C_{10}^{utf8,3.1}$	0xe28483	1	14	$C_{50}^{utf8,3.1}$	0xe29582	1	86
$C_{11}^{utf8,3.1}$	0xe284ab	1	15	$C_{51}^{utf8,3.1}$	0xe2958b	1	87
$C_{12}^{utf8,3.1}$	0xe28690	4	16	$C_{52}^{utf8,3.1}$	0xe296a0	2	88
$C_{13}^{utf8,3.1}$	0xe28792	1	20	$C_{53}^{utf8,3.1}$	0xe296b2	2	90
$C_{14}^{utf8,3.1}$	0xe28794	1	21	$C_{54}^{utf8,3.1}$	0xe296bc	2	92
$C_{15}^{utf8,3.1}$	0xe28880	1	22	$C_{55}^{utf8,3.1}$	0xe29786	2	94
$C_{16}^{utf8,3.1}$	0xe28882	2	23	$C_{56}^{utf8,3.1}$	0xe2978b	1	96
$C_{17}^{utf8,3.1}$	0xe28887	2	25	$C_{57}^{utf8,3.1}$	0xe2978e	2	97
$C_{18}^{utf8,3.1}$	0xe2888b	1	27	$C_{58}^{utf8,3.1}$	0xe297af	1	99
$C_{19}^{utf8,3.1}$	0xe28892	1	28	$C_{59}^{utf8,3.1}$	0xe29885	2	100
$C_{20}^{utf8,3.1}$	0xe2889a	1	29	$C_{60}^{utf8,3.1}$	0xe29980	1	102
$C_{21}^{utf8,3.1}$	0xe2889d	2	30	$C_{61}^{utf8,3.1}$	0xe29982	1	103
$C_{22}^{utf8,3.1}$	0xe288a0	1	32	$C_{62}^{utf8,3.1}$	0xe299aa	1	104
$C_{23}^{utf8,3.1}$	0xe288a5	1	33	$C_{63}^{utf8,3.1}$	0xe299ad	1	105
$C_{24}^{utf8,3.1}$	0xe288a7	6	34	$C_{64}^{utf8,3.1}$	0xe299af	1	106
$C_{25}^{utf8,3.1}$	0xe288b4	2	40	$C_{65}^{utf8,3.1}$	0xe38080	4	107
$C_{26}^{utf8,3.1}$	0xe288bd	1	42	$C_{65}^{utf8,3.1}$	0xe38085	15	111
$C_{27}^{utf8,3.1}$	0xe28992	1	43	$C_{67}^{utf8,3.1}$	0xe38181	63	126
$C_{28}^{utf8,3.1}$	0xe289a0	2	44	$C_{68}^{utf8,3.1}$	0xe38280	20	189
$C_{29}^{utf8,3.1}$	0xe289a6	2	46	$C_{69}^{utf8,3.1}$	0xe3829b	4	209
$C_{30}^{utf8,3.1}$	0xe289aa	2	48	$C_{70}^{utf8,3.1}$	0xe382a1	31	213
$C_{31}^{utf8,3.1}$	0xe28a82	2	50	$C_{71}^{utf8,3.1}$	0xe38380	55	244
$C_{32}^{utf8,3.1}$	0xe28a86	2	52	$C_{72}^{utf8,3.1}$	0xe383bb	4	299
$C_{33}^{utf8,3.1}$	0xe28aa5	1	54	$C_{73}^{utf8,3.1}$	0xefbc81	1	303
$C_{34}^{utf8,3.1}$	0xe28c92	1	55	$C_{74}^{utf8,3.1}$	0xefbc83	4	304
$C_{35}^{utf8,3.1}$	0xe29480	4	56	$C_{75}^{utf8,3.1}$	0xefbc88	5	308
$C_{36}^{utf8,3.1}$	0xe2948c	1	60	$C_{76}^{utf8,3.1}$	0xefbc8e	50	313
$C_{37}^{utf8,3.1}$	0xe2948f	2	61	$C_{77}^{utf8,3.1}$	0xefbd80	31	363
$C_{38}^{utf8,3.1}$	0xe29493	2	63	$C_{78}^{utf8,3.1}$	0xefbfa3	1	394
$C_{39}^{utf8,3.1}$	0xe29497	2	65	$C_{79}^{utf8,3.1}$	0xefbfa5	1	395
$C_{40}^{utf8,3.1}$	0xe2949b	3	67				

References

1. Agbeyibor, R., Butts, J., Grimaila, M., Mills, R.: Evaluation of format-preserving encryption algorithms for critical infrastructure protection. In: Butts, J., Shenoi, S. (eds.) ICCIP 2014. IAICT, vol. 441, pp. 245–261. Springer, Heidelberg (2014). https://doi.org/10.1007/978-3-662-45355-1_16
2. Bellare, M., Desai, A., Jokipii, E., Rogaway, P.: A concrete security treatment of symmetric encryption. In: Proceedings of The 38th Annual Symposium on Foundations of Computer Science (FOCS 1997), pp. 394–405. IEEE (1997)
3. Black, J., Rogaway, P.: Ciphers with arbitrary finite domains. In: Preneel, B. (ed.) CT-RSA 2002. LNCS, vol. 2271, pp. 114–130. Springer, Heidelberg (2002). https://doi.org/10.1007/3-540-45760-7_9
4. Bellare, M., Ristenpart, T., Rogaway, P., Stegers, T.: Format-preserving encryption. In: Jacobson, M.J., Rijmen, V., Safavi-Naini, R. (eds.) SAC 2009. LNCS, vol. 5867, pp. 295–312. Springer, Heidelberg (2009). https://doi.org/10.1007/978-3-642-05445-7_19
5. Bellare, M., Ristenpart, T., Rogaway, P., Stegers, T.: The FFX mode of operation for Format-preserving encryption. NIST submission (2010)
6. Brier, E., Peyrin, T., Stern, J.: BPS: a format-preserving encryption proposal. NIST submission (2010)
7. Brightwell, M., Smith, H.: Using datatype-preserving encryption to enhance data warehouse security. In: Proceedings of the Twentieth National Information Systems Security Conference (1997)
8. Morris, B., Rogaway, P., Stegers, T.: How to encipher messages on a small domain. In: Halevi, S. (ed.) CRYPTO 2009. LNCS, vol. 5677, pp. 286–302. Springer, Heidelberg (2009). https://doi.org/10.1007/978-3-642-03356-8_17
9. Ma, H.Y., Liu, Z.L., Jia, C.F., Yuan, K.: Generalized format-preserving encryption for character data. Science paper Online (2013)
10. NIST Special Publication 800–38G: Recommendation for Block Cipher Modes of Operation - Methods for Format-Preserving Encryption, March 2016
11. Rogaway, P.: A Synopsis of Format-Preserving Encryption (2010)
12. Spies, T.: Format Preserving Encryption. Voltage Security, Cupertino, California (2008)
13. Spies, T.: Feistel Finite Set Encryption Mode. National Institute of Standards and Technology, Gaithersburg (2008)
14. Vance, J.: VAES3 Scheme for FFX: An Addendum to the FFX Mode of Operation for Format Preserving Encryption. National Institute of Standards and Technology, Gaithersburg (2011)
15. Vance, J., Bellare, M.: An extension of the FF2 FPE Scheme. Submission to NIST, July 2014
16. Weiss, M., Rozenberg, B., Barham, M.: Practical solutions for format-preserving encryption. arXiv:1506.04113

Lattice-Based Cryptography

Compact Lossy and All-but-One Trapdoor Functions from Lattice

Leixiao Cheng[1], Quanshui Wu[1], and Yunlei Zhao[2(✉)]

[1] School of Mathematical Sciences, Fudan University, Shanghai, China
{14110180004,qswu}@fudan.edu.cn
[2] School of Computer Science, Fudan University, Shanghai, China
ylzhao@fudan.edu.cn

Abstract. Lossy trapdoor functions (LTDF) and all-but-one trapdoor functions (ABO-TDF) are fundamental cryptographic primitives. And given the recent advances in quantum computing, it would be much desirable to develop new and improved lattice-based LTDF and ABO-TDF. In this work, we provide more compact constructions of LTDF and ABO-TDF based on the learning with errors (LWE) problem. In addition, our LWE-based ABO-TDF can allow smaller system parameters to support super-polynomially many injective branches in the construction of CCA secure public key encryption. As a core building tool, we provide a more compact homomorphic symmetric encryption schemes based on LWE, which might be of independent interest. To further optimize the ABO-TDF construction, we employ the full rank difference encoding technique. As a consequence, the results presented in this work can substantially improve the performance of all the previous LWE-based cryptographic constructions based upon LTDF and ABO-TDF.

Keywords: Lossy trapdoor functions · All-but-one trapdoor functions Homomorphic symmetric encryption · Lattice · Learning with errors

1 Introduction

Injective one-way trapdoor function (TDF) F specifies, for each public key pk, a *deterministic* map F_{pk} that can be inverted given an associated trapdoor. It was one of the first abstract cryptographic primitives, allowing us to go back to the seminal paper of Diffie and Hellman [5]. TDFs had been realized only from problems related to factoring [13,18,21] prior to the seminal work [16].

The notion of lossy trapdoor functions (LTDF) was proposed by Peikert and Waters at STOC 2008 [16], which can be viewed as a strictly stronger powerful primitive than TDF. Informally speaking, a family of lossy trapdoor functions contains two computationally indistinguishable types of functions: injective

This research was supported in part by NSFC (Grant Nos. 61472084 and U1536205), National Key R&D Program of China (No. 2017YFB0802000), Shanghai innovation action project No. 16DZ1100200, and Shanghai science and technology development funds No. 16JC1400801.

© Springer International Publishing AG 2017
J. K. Liu and P. Samarati (Eds.): ISPEC 2017, LNCS 10701, pp. 279–296, 2017.
https://doi.org/10.1007/978-3-319-72359-4_16

functions with a trapdoor, and lossy functions that statistically lose information about their input. Furthermore, Lossiness implies one-wayness [16]. They imply many cryptographic primitives such as one-way trapdoor function [5], collision resistant hash function [8], oblivious transfer protocol [9], chosen ciphertext secure public key encryption scheme [6,12,16,19], deterministic public key encryption scheme [3], OAEP based public key encryption scheme [11], and selective opening secure public key encryption scheme [10]. LTDF can be constructed based on many assumptions [7,11,16,22,23] and, in particular, lattice-based assumption (specifically, the LWE assumption) [16]. Lattice-based constructions are especially desirable in the post-quantum era, since lattice-based cryptosystems are commonly believed to be resistant to quantum attacks.

In order to construct CCA-secure cryptosystem from LTDF, it is more convenient to consider a new notion called *all-but-one* trapdoor functions (ABO-TDF) [16]. In an ABO-TDF collection, each function has a lot of branches: only a single branch is lossy, while super-polynomially many branches are injective trapdoor functions owning the same trapdoor. In the construction of CCA-secure cryptosystems from ABO-TDF [16], an injective branch of ABO-TDF corresponds to the verification key of a one-time signature that is, in turn, used in forming the ciphertext. As a consequence, we expect to allow smaller parameters to support enough branches since super-polynomially many branches are needed in construction of CCA secure PKE. The basic relation between the two notions is revealed in [16]: lossy and ABO trapdoor functions are equivalent on appropriately chosen parameters. In this work, following the general paradigm proposed in [16] we provide improved and more compact constructions of LTDF and ABO-TDF based on the LWE problem. As a core building tool we provide a more compact homomorphic symmetric encryption schemes based on LWE, which might be of independent interest. To further reduce the size of the encrypted matrix of function indices of ABO-TDF, we make use of the full rank difference encoding (FRD) proposed in [4] (instead of the pairwise independent hash function originally used in [16]); The FRD technique not only reduces the matrix size, but also can allow smaller system parameters to support super-polynomially many injective branches in the construction of CCA secure public key encryption, which further optimize the construction of ABO-TDF. As a consequence, the results presented in this work can substantially improve the performance of all the previous LWE-based cryptographic constructions based upon LTDF and ABO-TDF.

2   Preliminaries

For a vector $\mathbf{x}$, $\mathbf{x}[i]$ denotes its i-th coordinate. For $x \in \mathbb{R}$, let $\lceil x \rceil$ denote the smallest integer greater than or equal to x, let $\lfloor x \rfloor$ denote the largest integer less than or equal to x, let $\lfloor x \rceil = \lfloor x + 1/2 \rfloor$ denotes the nearest integer to x. For any $x, y \in \mathbb{R}$ with $y > 0$ we define $x \bmod y$ to be $x - \lfloor x/y \rfloor y$.

The (i, j)-th entry of a 2 dimensional matrix $\mathbf{M}$ is denoted by $m_{i,j}$. For any $i, j \in \mathbb{Z}$ such that $i < j$, denote by $[i, j]$ the set of integers $\{i, i+1, \cdots j-1, j\}$.

For any positive integer a, denote by $[a]$ the set of integers $\{1, \cdots, a\}$, let $\mathbb{Z}_a$ denote $\mathbb{Z}/a\mathbb{Z}$, the elements of which are represented, by default, as $[0, a-1]$. We define $\mathbb{T} = \mathbb{R}/\mathbb{Z}$, i.e., the group of reals $[0, 1)$ with modulo 1 addition.

If S is a finite set then $|S|$ is its cardinality, and $x \leftarrow S$ is the operation of choosing an element randomly from S. For any random variable X over $\mathbb{R}$, denote $\mathrm{supp}(X) = \{x \in \mathbb{R}|\Pr[X = x] > 0\}$. We use standard notations and conventions below for writing probabilistic algorithms and experiments. For a probability distribution $\mathcal{D}$, $x \leftarrow \mathcal{D}$ denotes the operation of choosing an element according to $\mathcal{D}$.

We use standard asymptotic (O, o, Ω, ω) notation to denote the growth of positive functions. We say that $f(n) = \tilde{O}(g(n))$ if $f(n) = O(g(n) \log^c n)$ for some constant c. Let λ denote the security parameter (for constructions and analyses of LWE-based scheme, we also use the dimension, denoted l, of the underlying matrix as the security parameter). We say that a function $f(\lambda)$ is *negligible*, if for every $c > 0$, there exists a λ_c, such that $f(\lambda) < 1/\lambda^c$ for all $\lambda > \lambda_c$. For two distribution ensembles $\{X(\lambda, z)\}_{\lambda \in \mathbb{N}, z \in \{0,1\}^*}$ and $\{Y(\lambda, z)\}_{\lambda \in \mathbb{N}, z \in \{0,1\}^*}$, we say that they are computationally indistinguishable, denoted $\{X(\lambda, z)\} \overset{c}{\approx} \{Y(\lambda, z)\}$, if for any probabilistic polynomial-time (PPT) algorithm D, and for sufficiently large λ and any $z \in \{0, 1\}^*$, it holds $|\Pr[D(\lambda, z, X)] = 1 - \Pr[D(\lambda, z, Y)] = 1|$ is *negligible* in λ.

2.1 Definitions of LTDF and ABO-TDF

Here we describe the notions of lossy trapdoor functions (LTDF), and all-but-one trapdoor functions (ABO-TDF).

Let $n(\lambda) = \mathrm{poly}(\lambda)$ denote the input length of the function, and let $k(\lambda) \leq n(\lambda)$ denote the *lossiness* of the collection. For presentation simplicity, we usually omit the dependence on λ for convenience.

Definition 1. *A collection of (n, k)-lossy trapdoor functions is described by tuple of (possibly probabilistic) polynomial-time algorithms $(S_{\mathrm{ltdf}}, F_{\mathrm{ltdf}}, F_{\mathrm{ltdf}}^{-1})$, having the properties below.*

1. Easy to sample an injective function with trapdoor: $S_{\mathrm{inj}}(1^\lambda)$ *outputs* (s, t) *where s is a function index and t is its trapdoor, $F_{\mathrm{ltdf}}(s, \cdot)$ computes a (deterministic) injective function $f_s(\cdot)$ over the domain $\{0, 1\}^n$, and $F_{\mathrm{ltdf}}^{-1}(t, \cdot)$ computes $f_s^{-1}(\cdot)$. If a value y is not in the image $f_s(\{0, 1\}^n)$, i.e., if $f_s^{-1}(y)$ does not exist, then the behavior of $F_{\mathrm{ltdf}}^{-1}(t, y)$ is unspecified. Note that some applications may need to check the output of F_{ltdf}^{-1} for correctness.*
2. Easy to sample a lossy function: $S_{\mathrm{loss}}(1^\lambda)$ *outputs* $(s, \bot)$ *where s is a function index, and $F_{\mathrm{ltdf}}(s, \cdot)$ computes a (deterministic) function $f_s(\cdot)$ over the domain $\{0, 1\}^n$ whose image has size at most 2^{n-k}.*
3. Hard to distinguish injective from lossy: *the first outputs of $S_{\mathrm{inj}}(1^\lambda)$ and $S_{\mathrm{loss}}(1^\lambda)$ are computational indistinguishable. More formally, letting X_λ denote the distribution of s from $S_{\mathrm{inj}}(1^\lambda)$, and letting Y_λ denote the distribution of s from $S_{\mathrm{loss}}(1^\lambda)$, then $\{X_\lambda\} \overset{c}{\approx} \{Y_\lambda\}$.*

As shown in [16], for constructing lattice-based of LTDF a slightly relaxed definition of lossy TDF is considered, which is called *almost-always* lossy TDF. That is, the output of S_{inj} describes an injective function f_s that F_{ltdf}^{-1} inverts correctly on all values in the image of f_s *with overwhelming probability*. Namely, the probability (over the choice of s) that f_s is not injective or that $F_{\mathrm{ltdf}}^{-1}(t, \cdot)$ computes $f_s^{-1}(\cdot)$ on some input incorrectly is *negligible*. Moreover, the image size of the lossy function f_s generated by S_{loss} is required to be, with overwhelming probability, at most 2^{n-k}. In general, the function sampler cannot check these conditions (i.e., whether $f_s(\cdot)$ is injective, or whether $F_{\mathrm{ltdf}}^{-1}(t, \cdot)$ correctly computes $f_s^{-1}(\cdot)$ for all input), because they are associated with global probabilities of the generated function. Since the generation of trapdoor/lossy functions does not under the control of the adversary, we may make use of almost-always lossy TDF without affecting security of all the applications (e.g., CCA-secure encryption). Therefore the potential advantage of the adversary due to sampling an improper function is bounded by a negligible quantity.

The combination of the lossiness and indistinguishability properties implies that the injective function is one-wayness, as shown in the following lemma given in [16].

Lemma 1. *Let* $(S_{\mathrm{ltdf}}, F_{\mathrm{ltdf}}, F_{\mathrm{ltdf}}^{-1})$ *give a collection of* (n, k)-*LTDF with* $k = \omega(\log \lambda)$. *Then* $(S_{\mathrm{inj}}, F_{\mathrm{ltdf}}, F_{\mathrm{ltdf}}^{-1})$ *gives a collection of injective trapdoor function. (The analogous result applies for almost-always collections.)*

In order to construct CCA-secure cryptosystem from LTDF, it is more convenient to consider a new notion called *all-but-one* trapdoor function (ABO-TDF) [16]. In an ABO-TDF collection, each function has multiple branches. One branch is lossy, while (super-polynomially) many others are injective trapdoor functions owning the same trapdoor.

Definition 2. *Let* $\mathcal{B} = \{B_\lambda\}_{\lambda \in \mathbb{N}}$ *denote a collection of sets whose elements represent the branches. A collection of* (n, k)-all-but-one *trapdoor functions with branch collection* $\mathcal{B}$ *is described by a tuple of (possible probabilistic) polynomial-time algorithms* $(S_{\mathrm{abo}}, G_{\mathrm{abo}}, G_{\mathrm{abo}}^{-1})$, *having the following properties:*

1. Sampling a trapdoor function with given lossy branch: *for any* $b^* \in B_\lambda$, $S_{\mathrm{abo}}(1^\lambda, b^*)$ *outputs* (s, t), *where* s *is a function index and* t *is its trapdoor. For any* $b \in B_\lambda$ *distinct from* b^*, $G_{\mathrm{abo}}(s, b, \cdot)$ *computes a (deterministic) injective function* $g_{s,b}(\cdot)$ *over the domain* $\{0, 1\}^n$, *and* $G_{\mathrm{abo}}^{-1}(t, b, \cdot)$ *computes* $g_{s,b}^{-1}(\cdot)$. *As above, the behavior of* $G_{\mathrm{abo}}^{-1}(t, b, y)$ *is unspecified if* $g_{s,b}^{-1}(y)$ *does not exist.*

   Additionally, $G_{\mathrm{abo}}(s, b^*, \cdot)$ *computes a function* $g_{s,b^*}(\cdot)$ *on the domain* $\{0, 1\}^n$ *whose image has size at most* 2^{n-k}.
2. Hidden lossy branch: *for any* $b_0^*, b_1^* \in B_\lambda$, *the first output* s_0 *of* $S_{\mathrm{abo}}(1^\lambda, b_0^*)$ *and the first output* s_1 *of* $S_{\mathrm{abo}}(1^\lambda, b_1^*)$ *are computationally indistinguishable.*

Similar to LTDF, for lattice-based constructions we consider almost-always ABO-TDF [16], i.e., the injective, invertible, and lossy properties are required to hold only with overwhelming probability over the choice of the function index s.

Remark 1. The basic relation between the two notions is revealed in [16]: lossy and ABO trapdoor functions are equivalent if we choose parameters appropriately. The reader is referred to [16] for more details.

2.2   Probability Distributions

We present the notions of *normal distribution* over $\mathbb{R}$, the *discrete distribution* over $\mathbb{Z}_q$, and a standard *tail inequality*. Given a positive real number $\sigma > 0$, the *normal distribution* with mean 0 and variance σ^2 (or standard deviation σ) is the distribution having density function $\rho_\sigma(x) = \exp(-x^2/2\sigma^2)/\sqrt{2\pi\sigma^2}$ for $x \in \mathbb{R}$. In fact, the sum of two independent normal variables with mean 0 and variances σ_1^2 and σ_2^2, respectively, is a normal variable with mean 0 and variance $\sigma_1^2 + \sigma_2^2$.

For a positive real number $\alpha > 0$, we define Ψ_α to be the distribution on $\mathbb{T}$ of a normal variable with mean 0 and standard deviation $\alpha/\sqrt{2\pi}$, reduced modulo 1. For any probability distribution $\phi : \mathbb{T} \to \mathbb{R}_{>0}$ and a positive integer $q > 0$, we define its *discretization* $\bar{\phi} : \mathbb{Z}_q \to \mathbb{R}_{>0}$ to be the *discrete distribution* over $\mathbb{Z}_q$ of the random variable $\lfloor q \cdot X_\phi \rceil \bmod q$, where X_ϕ has distribution ϕ.

For a positive real number $\sigma > 0$ and $t > 0$, let X be a normal variable with variance σ^2, a standard *tail inequality* tells that $\Pr[|X| \le t\sigma] = 1 - \exp(-t^2/2)/t$.

2.3   The Learning with Errors Problem

The *learning with errors* (LWE) problem is a classic hard lattice problem proposed in [20]. The LWE problem can be viewed as an average-case "unique encoding" on a certain family of random lattices under a natural error distribution, and is believed to be hard on the average even against quantum computer. The following is almost verbatim from [16,20].

On input security parameter λ, for positive integers l and q, a vector $\mathbf{s} \in \mathbb{Z}_q^l$ and some probability distribution χ on $\mathbb{Z}_q$, let $A_{q,\mathbf{s},\chi}$ be the distribution over $\mathbb{Z}_q^l \times \mathbb{Z}_q$, obtained by choosing $\mathbf{a} \in \mathbb{Z}_q^l$ uniformly at random as well as $e \leftarrow \chi$ independently, outputting the pair $(\mathbf{a}, \langle \mathbf{a}, \mathbf{s} \rangle + e)$, where all the above are operated in $\mathbb{Z}_q$. The error distribution χ is taken to be the discrete distribution as specified in Sect. 2.2.

The goal of the (decisional) *learning with errors* problem $\mathrm{LWE}_{q,\chi}$ in dimension l is to distinguish the distribution $A_{q,\mathbf{s},\chi}$ for some secret random $\mathbf{s} \leftarrow \mathbb{Z}_q^l$ from the uniform distribution over $\mathbb{Z}_q^l \times \mathbb{Z}_q$ with non-negligible probability, even if the adversary sees polynomially many samples and even if the secret vector $\mathbf{s}$ is drawn randomly from χ^l [2].

The dimension l is the main parameter for the hardness of LWE. In the rest of this paper, for the constructions and analysis of LWE-based schemes we simply let l instead of λ be the security parameter, and let other parameters like q, α, n, etc., be function of l. When $\alpha q \ge 2\sqrt{l}$, this decision problem is at least as hard as approximating several problems on l-dimensional lattices in the worst-case to within $\widetilde{O}(l/\alpha)$ factors with a *quantum* algorithm [20], or via a *classical* algorithm for a subset of these problems [15]. We state a fact from [20] below:

Proposition 1. *Let $\alpha = \alpha(l) \in (0,1)$ and let $q = q(l)$ be a prime such that $\alpha \cdot q > 2\sqrt{l}$. If there exists an efficient (possibly quantum) algorithm such that solves $\text{LWE}_{q, \bar{\Psi}_\alpha}$, then there exists an efficient quantum algorithm for solving the following worst-case lattice problems:*

- *SIVP: In any lattice Λ of dimension l, find a set of l linearly independent lattice vectors of length within at most $\tilde{O}(l/\alpha)$ of optimal.*
- *GapSVP: In any lattice Λ of dimension l, approximate the length of a shortest nonzero lattice vector to within a $\tilde{O}(l/\alpha)$ factor.*

In fact, there is no efficient or even subexponential-time quantum algorithms known for the above worst-case lattice problems. Moreover, for lattice problem in any ℓ_p norm, $p > 2$, the proposition still holds for substantially the same $\tilde{O}(l/\alpha)$ approximation factors [14].

In the following, we construct our compact lossy trapdoor functions in terms of LWE problem, without considering the connection to lattices or the restrictions of the parameters. Later in Sect. 6, we will instantiate the parameters properly to invoke Proposition 1 to guarantee security, assuming the quantum worst-case hardness of lattice problems.

3   Compact (Homomorphic) Symmetric Encryption Scheme Based on LWE

We now construct compact symmetric encryption scheme based on the hardness of the LWE problem. This basic scheme has certain limited homomorphic properties over a small message space, which is enough for the purpose of constructing LTDF.

3.1   Encrypting Elements

The message space is $\mathbb{Z}_p$ for some $p \geq 2$. For every message $m \in \mathbb{Z}_p$, define $c_m = \frac{m}{p} \in \mathbb{T}$. Let $q > p$ and $g \geq 2$ be integers, and let χ denote an unspecified error distribution that we will instantiate later. The scheme is as follows:

- **Gen(1^l):** The secret key is a uniform $\mathbf{s} \leftarrow \mathbb{Z}_q^l$.
- **Enc($m \in \mathbb{Z}_p$):** It chooses uniform $\mathbf{a} \leftarrow \mathbb{Z}_q^l$ and an error term $e \leftarrow \chi$. Denote $\hat{c}_m = \langle \mathbf{a}, \mathbf{s} \rangle + e + \lfloor qc_m \rceil \bmod q \in \mathbb{Z}_q$. Define the *rounding errors*: $u = \lfloor qc_m \rceil - qc_m \in [-1/2, 1/2]$ and $u' = \lfloor g\hat{c}_m/q \rceil - g\hat{c}_m/q \in [-1/2, 1/2]$. The ciphertext is

$$E_{\mathbf{s}}(m, u, u'; \mathbf{a}, e) := (\mathbf{a}, g(\langle \mathbf{a}, \mathbf{s} \rangle + e + qc_m + u)/q + u') \in \mathbb{Z}_q^l \times \mathbb{Z}_g. \quad (1)$$

The reason that we treat u and u' as explicit input to the encryption algorithm, even though they are usually determined by m, is that we can treat $E_{\mathbf{s}}(m, u, u'; \mathbf{a}, e)$ as a well-defined expression even for either $u \notin [-1/2, 1/2]$ or $u' \notin [-1/2, 1/2]$. We can also omit them and denote the ciphertext as

$$E_{\mathbf{s}}(m; \mathbf{a}, e) := (\mathbf{a}, \lfloor g(\langle \mathbf{a}, \mathbf{s} \rangle + e + \lfloor qc_m \rceil)/q \rceil). \quad (2)$$

- **Dec(s, c):** For $c = (\mathbf{a}, c')$, compute

$$m' = \lfloor p(c'/g - \langle \mathbf{a}, \mathbf{s} \rangle / q) \rceil \bmod p. \tag{3}$$

Proposition 2. *The above encryption scheme is correct.*

Proof. For any ciphertext $c = E_{\mathbf{s}}(m, u, u'; \mathbf{a}, e)$, we have

$$m' = \lfloor p(c'/g - \langle \mathbf{a}, \mathbf{s} \rangle / q) \rceil \bmod p \tag{4}$$

$$= \left\lfloor m + \frac{p}{q}(\langle \mathbf{a}, \mathbf{s} \rangle + e - \langle \mathbf{a}, \mathbf{s} \rangle) + \frac{p}{q}u + \frac{p}{g}u' \right\rceil \bmod p \tag{5}$$

$$= \left\lfloor m + \frac{p}{q}e + \frac{p}{q}u + \frac{p}{g}u' \right\rceil \bmod p. \tag{6}$$

As long as the absolute $|pe/q + pu/q + pu'/g| \le p|e|/q + p/2q + p/2g < 1/2$, i.e., $(2|e| + 1)p < q(1 - \frac{p}{g})$, the decryption $\mathbf{Dec}(c, \mathbf{s})$ is correct. $\qquad \square$

Proposition 3. *The above scheme is homomorphic.*

Proof. By a simple calculation, we have

$$E_{\mathbf{s}}(m_1, u_1, u_1'; \mathbf{a}_1, e_1) + E_{\mathbf{s}}(m_2, u_2, u_2'; \mathbf{a}_2, e_2) \tag{7}$$

$$= E_{\mathbf{s}}(m_1 + m_2, u_1 + u_2, u_1' + u_2'; \mathbf{a}_1 + \mathbf{a}_2, e_1 + e_2). \tag{8}$$

Furthermore, even without knowing the secret key under which a ciphertext was created, one can add any scalar value $v \in \mathbb{Z}_p$ to its plaintext. Let $c = (\mathbf{a}, c') = E_{\mathbf{s}}(m, u, u'; \mathbf{a}, e)$, define $u'' = \lfloor qc_v \rceil - qc_v \in [-1/2, 1/2]$ and $u''' = \lfloor g\lfloor qc_v \rceil / q \rceil - g\lfloor qc_v \rceil / q \in [-1/2, 1/2]$, then

$$c \boxplus v := (\mathbf{a}, c' + \lfloor g\lfloor qc_v \rceil / q \rceil) = E_{\mathbf{s}}(m + v, u + u'', u' + u'''; \mathbf{a}, e). \tag{9}$$

$$\square$$

3.2   Encrypting Matrices

The message space is $\mathbb{Z}_p^{h \times w}$ for arbitrary positive integers h and w. For every message $\mathbf{M} = (m_{i,j}) \in \mathbb{Z}_p^{h \times w}$, we describe an extension of the symmetric encryption scheme from encrypting elements to encrypting matrices.

- **Gen(1^l):** For every column $j \in [w]$, choose independently $\mathbf{s}_j \in \mathbb{Z}_q^l$. The secret key is the tuple $\mathbf{S} = (\mathbf{s}_1, \cdots, \mathbf{s}_w)$.
- **Enc($\mathbf{M} \in \mathbb{Z}_p^{h \times w}$):** For every row $i \in [h]$, choose independently $\mathbf{a}_i \leftarrow \mathbb{Z}_q^l$, forming a matrix $\mathbf{A} \in \mathbb{Z}_q^{h \times l}$ whose i-th row is $\mathbf{a}_i$. For every $i \in [h]$ and every $j \in [w]$, choose independently error terms $e_{i,j} \leftarrow \chi$, forming an error matrix $\mathbf{E} = (e_{i,j}) \in \mathbb{Z}_q^{h \times w}$. Denote $\hat{c}_{m_{i,j}} = \langle \mathbf{a}_i, \mathbf{s}_j \rangle + e_{i,j} + \lfloor qc_{m_{i,j}} \rceil \bmod q \in \mathbb{Z}_q$. Define $\mathbf{U} = (u_{i,j})$ and $\mathbf{U}' = (u_{i,j}')$ to be matrices of rounding errors, where $u_{i,j} =$

$\lfloor qc_{m_{i,j}} \rceil - qc_{m_{i,j}} \in [-1/2, 1/2]$ and $u'_{i,j} = \lfloor g\hat{c}_{m_{i,j}}/q \rceil - g\hat{c}_{m_{i,j}}/q \in [-1/2, 1/2]$. The encryption of $\mathbf{M}$ is

$$\mathbf{C} = E_{\mathbf{S}}(\mathbf{M}, \mathbf{U}, \mathbf{U}'; \mathbf{A}, \mathbf{E}), \tag{10}$$

where $c_{i,j} = E_{\mathbf{s}_j}(m_{i,j}, u_{i,j}, u'_{i,j}; \mathbf{a}_i, e_{i,j})$. Note that the i-th row shares the same randomness $\mathbf{a}_i$, while the j-th column shares the same secret key $\mathbf{s}_j$. The ciphertext can be expressed as $(\mathbf{A}, \mathbf{C}')$, where $c'_{i,j} = g(\langle \mathbf{a}_i, \mathbf{s}_j \rangle + e_{i,j} + qc_{m_{i,j}} + u_{i,j})/q + u'_{i,j}$.

- **Dec(S,C):** For $\mathbf{C} = (c_{i,j})$, the decrypted matrix is $\mathbf{M} = (m_{i,j}) \in \mathbb{Z}_p^{h \times w}$, where $m_{i,j} = \mathbf{Dec}(\mathbf{s}_j, c_{i,j})$.

Correctness: The correctness is direct from that of the basic scheme for encrypting elements.

Homomorphism: All linear operations, including addition of ciphertexts, multiplication and addition by scalars, can be extended to encrypted matrices based on the homomorphism of the underlying symmetric encryption scheme of elements.

In particular, for any $\mathbf{x} \in \mathbb{Z}_p^h$, for an encryption $\mathbf{C} = E_{\mathbf{S}}(\mathbf{M}, \mathbf{U}, \mathbf{U}'; \mathbf{A}, \mathbf{E})$ of some $\mathbf{M} \in \mathbb{Z}_p^{h \times w}$, we have

$$\mathbf{x}\mathbf{C} = E_{\mathbf{S}}(\mathbf{x}\mathbf{M}, \mathbf{x}\mathbf{U}, \mathbf{x}\mathbf{U}'; \mathbf{x}\mathbf{A}, \mathbf{x}\mathbf{E}). \tag{11}$$

Furthermore, for any matrix of scalars $\mathbf{V} \in \mathbb{Z}_p^{h \times w}$ inducing two matrices of rounding errors $\mathbf{U}''$ and $\mathbf{U}'''$, we have

$$\mathbf{C} \boxplus \mathbf{V} = E_{\mathbf{S}}(\mathbf{M} + \mathbf{V}, \mathbf{U} + \mathbf{U}'', \mathbf{U}' + \mathbf{U}'''; \mathbf{A}, \mathbf{E}). \tag{12}$$

Lemma 2. *For any height and width $h, w = \mathrm{poly}(l)$, the matrix encryption scheme described above produces indistinguishable ciphertexts under the assumption that $\mathrm{LWE}_{q,\chi}$ is hard.*

Proof. The proof is almost the same as Lemma 6.2 in [16], and we omit details here. □

Lemma 3. *For some positive integer r and α, let $\mathbf{E} = (e_{i,j}) \in \mathbb{Z}_q^{n \times w}$ be an error matrix generated by choosing independent error terms $e_{i,j} \leftarrow \bar{\Psi}_\alpha$. Then except with probability at most $w \cdot 2^{-r}$ over the choice of $\mathbf{E}$, every entry of $\mathbf{x}\mathbf{E}$ has absolute value less than $2q(n + r)\alpha + n/2$ for all $\mathbf{x} \in \{0, 1\}^n$.*

Proof. The proof is almost the same as Lemma 6.3 in [16], so we omit it. □

Remark 2. With our compact encryption scheme, when encrypting an element m the resulting ciphertext is $E_{\mathbf{s}}(m; \mathbf{a}, e) = (\mathbf{a}, \lfloor g(\langle \mathbf{a}, \mathbf{s} \rangle + e + \lfloor qc_m \rceil)/q \rceil) \in \mathbb{Z}_q^l \times \mathbb{Z}_g$, while the ciphertext is $E_{\mathbf{s}}(m; \mathbf{a}, e) = (\mathbf{a}, \langle \mathbf{a}, \mathbf{s} \rangle + e + \lfloor qc_m \rceil) \in \mathbb{Z}_q^l \times \mathbb{Z}_q$ in [16], where

$q \approx gO(n^c)$, $c > 0$ is a constant. The length of our compact LTDF ciphertext is $\log q - \log g$ bits shorter than that of the scheme given in [16].

Similarly, when encrypting an matrix $\mathbf{M} \in \mathbb{Z}_p^{n \times m}$, the ciphertext in this paper is $E_{\mathbf{S}}(\mathbf{M}; \mathbf{A}, \mathbf{E}) \in \mathbb{Z}_q^{n \times l} \times \mathbb{Z}_g^{n \times m}$, which reduces $nm \log(q/g)$-bit length than that of $E_{\mathbf{S}}(\mathbf{M}; \mathbf{A}, \mathbf{E}) \in \mathbb{Z}_q^{n \times l} \times \mathbb{Z}_q^{n \times m}$ in [16], where $q \approx gO(n^c)$, $c > 0$ is a constant and $m = n/\lfloor \log p \rfloor$.

4   Compact LTDF Based on LWE

Let $a = \lfloor \lg p \rfloor$, assume without loss of generality that n is divisible by a, and let $m = n/a$. Define a matrix $\mathbf{G} \in \mathbb{Z}_p^{n \times m}$ as follows: in column $j \in [m]$, the $((j-1)a + k)$th entry is $2^{k-1} \in [1, p]$ for $k \in [a]$. All other entries are zero. Formally, $\mathbf{G}$ is the tensor product $\mathbf{I}_m \otimes \mathbf{g}$, where $\mathbf{I}_m$ is the identity matrix and $\mathbf{g} = (1, 2, \cdots, 2^{a-1})^T \in \mathbb{Z}_p^{a \times 1}$ (we can also use other integer base $b \geq 2$).

For any input vector $\mathbf{x} \in \{0, 1\}^n$, we may correspond $\mathbf{x}$ to an unique vector $\mathbf{v} = (v_1, \cdots, v_m) \in \mathbb{Z}_p^m$ using the matrix $\mathbf{G}$; That is, $\mathbf{x}\mathbf{G} = \mathbf{v}$, and vice versa.

Evaluating the function on $\mathbf{x} \in \{0, 1\}^n$ involves homomorphically computing an encrypted linear product $\mathbf{x}\mathbf{M}$, where $\mathbf{M}$ is some matrix being encrypted in the sampling algorithm. In the injective case, let $\mathbf{M} = \mathbf{G}$, then $\mathbf{x}\mathbf{G} = \mathbf{v}$, which allows us to recover the entire input by decrypting $\mathbf{v}$ and producing the corresponding $\mathbf{x}$. In the lossy case, we have $\mathbf{M} = \mathbf{0}$, then $\mathbf{x}\mathbf{M} = \mathbf{0} \in \mathbb{Z}_p^m$, which means the output contains only $m = n/a$ ciphertexts, i.e., less information is leaked via the error terms.

In order to obtain a lossy TDF, we need to ensure that each decrypted plaintext contains more information than what might be carried by the error terms of the corresponding ciphertext. In the following, we describe our lossy TDF generation, evaluation, and inversion algorithms formally.

- *Sampling an injective/lossy function.* The generator of injective function $S_{\text{inj}}(1^l)$ outputs a matrix encryption

$$\mathbf{C} = E_{\mathbf{S}}(\mathbf{G}, \mathbf{U}, \mathbf{U}'; \mathbf{A}, \mathbf{E}), \tag{13}$$

  where $\mathbf{S}$, $\mathbf{U}$, $\mathbf{U}'$, $\mathbf{A}$, $\mathbf{E}$ are chosen as described in Sect. 3.2. The function index s is the encryption $\mathbf{C}$, and the trapdoor information t consists of the tuple of secret keys $\mathbf{S} = (\mathbf{s}_1, \cdots, \mathbf{s}_m)$.

  The generator of lossy function $S_{\text{loss}}(1^l)$ generates a matrix encryption

$$\mathbf{C} = E_{\mathbf{S}}(\mathbf{0}, \mathbf{U}, \mathbf{U}'; \mathbf{A}, \mathbf{E}), \tag{14}$$

  which is the encryption of the all-zeros matrix $\mathbf{0} \in \mathbb{Z}_p^{n \times m}$. The function index s is $\mathbf{C}$, and there is no trapdoor output.
- *Evaluation algorithm.* On input $(\mathbf{C}, \mathbf{x})$ where $\mathbf{C}$ is the function index (an encryption of either $\mathbf{M} = \mathbf{G}$ or $\mathbf{M} = \mathbf{0}$) and $\mathbf{x} \in \{0, 1\}^n$ is an n-bit input interpreted as a vector, the evaluation function F_{ltdf} outputs the vector of ciphertexts $\mathbf{y} = \mathbf{x}\mathbf{C}$.

By the properties of homomorphism, the output $\mathbf{y}$ is

$$\mathbf{y} = E_{\mathbf{S}}(\mathbf{xM}, \mathbf{xU}, \mathbf{xU}'; \mathbf{xA}, \mathbf{xE}), \tag{15}$$

where every ciphertext y_j is of the form $(\mathbf{xA}, y_j') \in \mathbb{Z}_q^l \times \mathbb{Z}_g$.

- *Inversion algorithm.* On input $(\mathbf{S}, \mathbf{y})$ where $\mathbf{S}$ is the trapdoor, the inversion function F_{ltdf}^{-1} computes $\mathbf{v} = \mathbf{Dec}(\mathbf{S}, \mathbf{y}) \in \mathbb{Z}_p^m$, and outputs the unique $\mathbf{x} \in \{0, 1\}^n$ such that $\mathbf{xG} = \mathbf{v}$.

Similar to [16], we now instantiate the parameters of the above scheme to prove that, conditioned on the assumption $\text{LWE}_{q,\chi}$ is hard, our construction describe a collection of almost-always (n, k)-lossy TDF.

Theorem 1. *Let $n = l^{c_3}$ for some constant $c_3 > 1$, and let $p = n^{c_1}$ for some constant c_1. Let $q \in [4pn, O(pn^{c_2})]$ for some constant c_2 where $1 < c_2 < c_1$ and let $m = n/\lfloor \lg p \rfloor$. Let $g \in [4pn, q]$, and let $\chi = \bar{\Psi}_\alpha$ where $\alpha \le 1/(32pn)$.*

Then the algorithms described above give a collection of almost-always (n,k)-lossy TDF under the assumption that $\text{LWE}_{q,\chi}$ is hard, where the residual leakage $n - k$ is

$$n - k \le \left(\frac{c_2}{c_1} + o(1)\right) \cdot n. \tag{16}$$

Proof. First we claim that the inversion algorithm F_{ltdf}^{-1} satisfies, with overwhelming probability over the choice of $\mathbf{C}$ by S_{inj}, the correctness requirement on all inputs $\mathbf{y} = F_{\text{ltdf}}(\mathbf{C}, \mathbf{x})$. We note that

$$\mathbf{y} = E_{\mathbf{S}}(\mathbf{xM}, \mathbf{xU}, \mathbf{xU}'; \mathbf{xA}, \mathbf{xE}), \tag{17}$$

by the homomorphic properties.

Letting $r = n$ in Lemma 3, we have $|(\mathbf{xE})_j| < 2q(n + r)\alpha + n/2 \le q/4p$ for every $\mathbf{x}$ and $j \in [m]$, except with probability at most $m \cdot 2^n = \text{negl}(l)$ over the choice of $\mathbf{E}$. Moreover, note that $|(\mathbf{xU})_j| \le n/2 \le q/8p$ and $|(\mathbf{xU}')_j| \le n/2 \le q/8p$ for all $j \in [m]$ by the size of $\mathbf{U}$'s and $\mathbf{U}'$'s entries. Therefore we have

$$\left|\frac{p}{q}(\mathbf{xE})_j + \frac{p}{q}(\mathbf{xU})_j + \frac{p}{g}(\mathbf{xU}')_j\right| < \frac{p}{q} \cdot \frac{q}{4p} + \frac{p}{q} \cdot \frac{q}{8p} + \frac{p}{g} \cdot \frac{n}{2} \le \frac{1}{4} + \frac{1}{8} + \frac{1}{8} = \frac{1}{2}. \tag{18}$$

The correctness requirement is satisfied.

We now analyze the lossiness of a lossy function. For any input $\mathbf{x} \in \{0, 1\}^n$, we have

$$\mathbf{y} = E_{\mathbf{S}}(\mathbf{0} = \mathbf{x0}, \mathbf{xU}, \mathbf{xU}'; \mathbf{xA}, \mathbf{xE}). \tag{19}$$

For every $j \in [m]$, y_j is a ciphertext $(\mathbf{xA}, y_j') \in \mathbb{Z}_q^l \times \mathbb{Z}_g$, where $\mathbf{xA}$ is the same randomness for all j and $y_j' = g(\langle \mathbf{xA}, \mathbf{s}_j \rangle + (\mathbf{xE})_j + 0 + 0)/q + (\mathbf{xU}')_j)$. Fixing $\mathbf{A}, \mathbf{x}$ and $j \in [m]$, we have

$$\left|\frac{g}{q}(\mathbf{xE})_j + (\mathbf{xU}')_j\right| < \frac{g}{q} \cdot \frac{q}{4p} + \frac{n}{2} \le \frac{q}{4p} + \frac{q}{8p} = \frac{q}{2p}. \tag{20}$$

Obviously, the total number of outputs of the lossy function is at most $q^l(q/p)^m$, the logarithm of which gives an upper bound on the residual leakage $n - k$:

$$n - k \leq l \cdot \lg q + m \cdot \lg O(n^{c_2}) \tag{21}$$

$$\leq O(n^{1/c_3} \lg n) + m \cdot (O(1) + c_2 \lg n) \tag{22}$$

$$\leq o(n) + n \cdot \frac{O(1) + c_2 \lg n}{\lfloor c_1 \lg n \rfloor} \tag{23}$$

$$\leq n \cdot \left(\frac{c_2}{c_1} + o(1) \right), \tag{24}$$

where the third inequality is because of the fact that $m = n/\lfloor \lg p \rfloor = n/\lfloor c_1 \lg n \rfloor$.

Finally, note that $\mathbf{C} = E_{\mathbf{S}}(\mathbf{G}, \mathbf{U}, \mathbf{U}'; \mathbf{A}, \mathbf{E})$ is indistinguishable from $\mathbf{C} = E_{\mathbf{S}}(\mathbf{0}, \mathbf{U}, \mathbf{U}'; \mathbf{A}, \mathbf{E})$ by Lemma 2 on the security of matrix encryption; That is, we can not distinguish lossy function from injective one. $\qquad \square$

5 Compact ABO-TDF

In order to yield enough branches, the construction of ABO-TDF in [16] makes use of a family of pairwise independent hash functions $\mathcal{H} = \{h : \mathbb{Z}_p^l \to \mathbb{Z}_p^{m \times w}\}$, where $w = m + 2l$, to generate the matrix $\mathbf{M} = -h(b^*) \otimes \mathbf{g}$ for the desired branch b^*. The properties of the pairwise independent function h ensure that $\mathbf{H} = h(b) - h(b^*)$ have full row rank for any $b \neq b^*$, which suffices for recovering $\mathbf{v}$ from the product $\mathbf{vH}$. The branch set is $B = B_l = \mathbb{Z}_p^l$. Note that, with this approach, the encrypted matrix of function indices of ABO-TDF is larger than that of LTDF in [16]. We are wondering whether we can further reduce it? The answer is yes. To solve this problem, we make use of the full rank difference (FRD) encoding [4] (instead of the pairwise independent hash function originally used in [16]), which not only reduces the matrix size in our ABO-TDF to get equal to that of our compact LTDF, but also can allow smaller system parameters to support super-polynomially many injective branches in the construction of CCA secure public key encryption. We first briefly review the full rank difference encoding technique proposed in [4].

5.1 Full Rank Difference Encoding $\mathsf{G}_{\mathbf{FRD}}$ of $\mathbb{Z}_p^m$ to $\mathbb{Z}_p^{m \times m}$

In fact, Cramer and Damgård [4] introduced an encoding function maps a superpolynomially-sized domain $\mathbb{F}^m$ to matrices in $\mathbb{F}^{m \times m}$ with some strongly injective properties. This encoding notion has then been updated by [1] to the name "Full-Rank Difference Encoding". We uses FRD in a similar way to [17].

Definition 3. *Let p be a prime and m a positive integer. We say that a function $\mathsf{G}_{\mathrm{FRD}} : \mathbb{Z}_p^m \to \mathbb{Z}_p^{m \times m}$ is an encoding with full-rank difference (FRD) if:*

1. *for all distinct $\mathbf{x}, \mathbf{y} \in \mathbb{Z}_p^m$, the matrix $\mathsf{G}_{\mathrm{FRD}}(\mathbf{x}) - \mathsf{G}_{\mathrm{FRD}}(\mathbf{y})$ is full rank.*
2. *$\mathsf{G}_{\mathrm{FRD}}$ is computable in polynomial time.*

The goal in designing $\mathsf{G}_{\mathrm{FRD}}$ is to construct an additive subgroup $\mathcal{G}$ of $\mathbb{Z}_p^{m \times m}$ of size p^m with all non-zero matrices in $\mathcal{G}$ of full rank. Since for all distinct $\mathbf{A}, \mathbf{B} \in \mathcal{G}$, the difference $\mathbf{A}\text{-}\mathbf{B}$ is also in $\mathcal{G}$, it follows that $\mathbf{A}\text{-}\mathbf{B}$ is full rank.

For a polynomial $g \in \mathbb{Z}_p[X]$ of degree at most $m - 1$, let $\mathsf{coeff}(g) \in \mathbb{Z}_p^{1 \times m}$ be the m-row of the coefficient of g. If g is of degree less than $m - 1$ we pad the coefficients vector with zeroes on the right to make it a m-vector. Let f be some polynomial of degree m, irreducible in $\mathbb{Z}_p[X]$. Note that for a polynomial $g \in \mathbb{Z}_p[X]$, the polynomial $(g \bmod f)$ has degree less than m, thus $\mathsf{coeff}(g \bmod f) \in \mathbb{Z}_p^m$.

For any integer $m \geq 2$, any input $\mathbf{h} = (h_0, \cdots, h_{m-1}) \in \mathbb{Z}_p^m$, define $g_{\mathbf{h}}(X) = \sum_{i=0}^{m-1} h_i x^i \in \mathbb{Z}_p[X]$, then define $\mathsf{G}_{\mathrm{FRD}}(\mathbf{h})$ as

$$\mathsf{G}_{\mathrm{FRD}}(\mathbf{h}) := \begin{bmatrix} \mathsf{coeff}(g_{\mathbf{h}} \bmod f) \\ \mathsf{coeff}(X \cdot g_{\mathbf{h}} \bmod f) \\ \mathsf{coeff}(X^2 \cdot g_{\mathbf{h}} \bmod f) \\ \vdots \\ \mathsf{coeff}(X^{(m-1)} \cdot g_{\mathbf{h}} \bmod f) \end{bmatrix} \in \mathbb{Z}_p^{m \times m}. \tag{25}$$

The following theorem in [4] proves that the above function $\mathsf{G}_{\mathrm{FRD}}$ is an FRD.

Theorem 2. *Let $\mathbb{F}$ be a field and f a polynomial in $\mathbb{F}[X]$. If f is irreducible in $\mathbb{F}[X]$ then the function $\mathsf{G}_{\mathrm{FRD}}$ defined above is an encoding with full-rank differences.*

Moreover, the function $\mathsf{G}_{\mathrm{FRD}}$ has the following properties:

1. ($\mathsf{G}_{\mathrm{FRD}}$ is linear) $\mathsf{G}_{\mathrm{FRD}}(a\mathbf{h}_1 + b\mathbf{h}_2) = a \cdot \mathsf{G}_{\mathrm{FRD}}(\mathbf{h}_1) + b \cdot \mathsf{G}_{\mathrm{FRD}}(\mathbf{h}_2)$ for any $a, b \in \mathbb{Z}_p, \mathbf{h}_1, \mathbf{h}_2 \in \mathbb{Z}_p^m$.
2. (The image of $\mathsf{G}_{\mathrm{FRD}}$ is invertible or zero) For any vector $\mathbf{h} \neq \mathbf{0}$, $\mathsf{G}_{\mathrm{FRD}}(\mathbf{h})$ is invertible, and $\mathsf{G}_{\mathrm{FRD}}(\mathbf{0}) = \mathbf{0}$.

5.2   Construction and Analysis of Compact ABO-TDF

As above, let $a = \lfloor \lg p \rfloor$, assume without loss of generality that n is divisible by a, and let $m = n/a$. Define a matrix $\mathbf{G} := \mathbf{I}_m \otimes \mathbf{g}$, where $\mathbf{I}_m$ is the identity matrix and $\mathbf{g} = (1, 2, \cdots, 2^{a-1})^T \in \mathbb{Z}_p^{a \times 1}$ (we can also use other integer base $b \geq 2$). Using matrix $\mathbf{G}$ allows us to correspond each the input vector $\mathbf{x} \in \{0, 1\}^n$ to a unique vector $\mathbf{v} = (v_1, \cdots, v_m) \in \mathbb{Z}_p^m$ by $\mathbf{x}\mathbf{G} = \mathbf{v}$.

In our construction, instead of using the family of pairwise independent hash functions, we consider the full rank difference encoding function $\mathsf{G}_{\mathrm{FRD}}$ described in Sect. 5.1, to generate the matrix $\mathbf{M} = -\mathsf{G}_{\mathrm{FRD}}(b^*) \otimes \mathbf{g}$ for the desired branch b^*. The properties of the FRD function guarantees that $\mathbf{H} = \mathsf{G}_{\mathrm{FRD}}(b) - \mathsf{G}_{\mathrm{FRD}}(b^*)$ is invertible for all $b^* \neq b$, which is enough for the purpose of recovering $\mathbf{v}$ from $\mathbf{v}\mathbf{H}$. It turns out to be a larger branch set $B = \mathbb{Z}_p^m$ if we fix parameter p, where $m = n/\lfloor \lg p \rfloor > l$, according to the following instantiated parameters. This means that we can choose smaller p in order to support super-polynomially many injective branches in the construction of CCA secure public key encryption.

Evaluating the ABO function on an input $\mathbf{x} \in \{0, 1\}^n$ involves computing an encrypted linear product $\mathbf{vM}$, where $\mathbf{M}$ is some matrix deciding by the branch b^* of the function being evaluated. The explicit fact that $\mathbf{x}(\mathbf{M} \otimes \mathbf{g}) = \mathbf{vM}$ for any $\mathbf{M} \in \mathbb{Z}_p^{m \times m}$ plays an important role in our construction of ABO-TDF. Let $\mathbf{M} = -\mathsf{G}_{\mathrm{FRD}}(b^*) \otimes \mathbf{g}$, then $\mathbf{x}((\mathsf{G}_{\mathrm{FRD}}(b) - \mathsf{G}_{\mathrm{FRD}}(b^*)) \otimes \mathbf{g}) = \mathbf{v}(\mathsf{G}_{\mathrm{FRD}}(b) - \mathsf{G}_{\mathrm{FRD}}(b^*))$, which allows us to recover the entire input by decrypting $\mathbf{v}(\mathsf{G}_{\mathrm{FRD}}(b) - \mathsf{G}_{\mathrm{FRD}}(b^*))$ and recovering $\mathbf{v}$, then producing the corresponding $\mathbf{x}$.

Let the branch set $B = \mathbb{Z}_p^m$. Let $\mathsf{G}_{\mathrm{FRD}}$ denote a full rank difference encoding from $B = \mathbb{Z}_p^m$ to $\mathbb{Z}_p^{m \times m}$ as introduced in Sect. 5.1. In the following, we describe our ABO-TDF generation, evaluation, and inversion algorithms formally.

- *Sampling an ABO function.* The function generator $S_{\mathrm{abo}}(1^l, b^* \in B)$ outputs a matrix encryption

$$\mathbf{C} = E_{\mathbf{S}}(-\mathsf{G}_{\mathrm{FRD}}(b^*) \otimes \mathbf{g}, \mathbf{U}, \mathbf{U}'; \mathbf{A}, \mathbf{E}), \tag{26}$$

where $\mathbf{S}, \mathbf{U}, \mathbf{U}', \mathbf{A}, \mathbf{E}$ are chosen as described in Sect. 3.2. The function index s is the encryption $\mathbf{C}$, and the trapdoor information t consists of the tuple of secret keys $\mathbf{S} = (\mathbf{s}_1, \cdots, \mathbf{s}_m)$ and the lossy branch value b^*.

- *Evaluation algorithm.* On input $(\mathbf{C}, b, \mathbf{x})$ where $\mathbf{C}$ is the function index, $b \in B$ is the desired branch, and $\mathbf{x} \in \{0, 1\}^n$ is an n-bit input interpreted as a vector, the evaluation function G_{abo} outputs the vector of ciphertexts

$$\mathbf{y} = \mathbf{x}(\mathbf{C} \boxplus (\mathsf{G}_{\mathrm{FRD}}(b) \otimes \mathbf{g})). \tag{27}$$

Let $\mathbf{H} = \mathsf{G}_{\mathrm{FRD}}(b) - \mathsf{G}_{\mathrm{FRD}}(b^*)$. Then by the properties of homomorphism, the output $\mathbf{y}$ is

$$\mathbf{y} = E_{\mathbf{S}}(\mathbf{vH} = \mathbf{x}(\mathbf{H} \otimes \mathbf{g}), \mathbf{x}(\mathbf{U} + \mathbf{U}''), \mathbf{x}(\mathbf{U}' + \mathbf{U}'''); \mathbf{xA}, \mathbf{xE}), \tag{28}$$

where $\mathbf{U}''$ and $\mathbf{U}'''$ are the matrices of rounding errors induced by the scalar matrix.

- *Inversion algorithm.* The function G_{abo}^{-1} takes as input $((\mathbf{S}, b^*), b, \mathbf{y})$, where $(\mathbf{S}, b^*)$ is the trapdoor information, b is the evaluated branch, and $\mathbf{y}$ is the function output. It first computes $\mathbf{m} = \mathbf{Dec}(\mathbf{S}, \mathbf{y}) \in \mathbb{Z}_p^m$. It then computes $\mathbf{H} = \mathsf{G}_{\mathrm{FRD}}(b) - \mathsf{G}_{\mathrm{FRD}}(b^*)$, if $\mathbf{H}$ is invertible, it computes $\mathbf{v} = \mathbf{mH}^{-1}$. Finally, it outputs the unique $\mathbf{x} \in \{0, 1\}^n$ such that $\mathbf{xG} = \mathbf{v}$.

Theorem 3. *Let $n = l^{c_3}$ for some constant $c_3 > 1$ and let $p \in [n^{c_1}, (n+1)^{c_1}]$ be a prime for some constant c_1. Let $q \in [20pn/3, O(pn^{c_2})]$ for some constant c_2 where $1 < c_2 < c_1$ and let $m = n/\lfloor \lg p \rfloor$. Let $g \in [20pn/3, q]$, and let $\chi = \bar{\Psi}_\alpha$ where $\alpha \le 1/(32pn)$.*

Then the algorithms described above give a collection of almost-always (n, k)-ABO-TDF with branch set $\mathbb{Z}_p^m$, under the assumption that $\mathrm{LWE}_{q,\chi}$ is hard, where the residual leakage $n - k$ is

$$n - k \le \left(\frac{c_2}{c_1} + o(1) \right) \cdot n. \tag{29}$$

Proof. The proof is similar to that of Theorem 1. First we claim that the inversion algorithm G_{abo}^{-1} satisfies, with overwhelming probability over the choice of $\mathbf{C}$ by $S_{\text{abo}}(1^l, b^*)$, the correctness requirement for all branches $b \neq b^*$ and on all inputs $\mathbf{y} = G_{\text{abo}}(\mathbf{C}, b, \mathbf{x})$. We note that

$$\mathbf{y} = E_{\mathbf{S}}(\mathbf{vH} = \mathbf{x}(\mathbf{H} \otimes \mathbf{g}), \mathbf{x}(\mathbf{U} + \mathbf{U}''), \mathbf{x}(\mathbf{U}' + \mathbf{U}'''); \mathbf{xA}, \mathbf{xE}), \qquad (30)$$

by the homomorphic properties. For every $j \in [m]$, y_j is a ciphertext $(\mathbf{xA}, y_j') \in \mathbb{Z}_q^l \times \mathbb{Z}_g$, where $\mathbf{xA}$ is the same randomness for all j and $y_j' = g(\langle \mathbf{xA}, \mathbf{s}_j \rangle + (\mathbf{xE})_j + q(\mathbf{vH})_j/p + (\mathbf{xU})_j + (\mathbf{xU}'')_j)/q + (\mathbf{xU}')_j + (\mathbf{xU}''')_j$.

Letting $r = n$ in Lemma 3, we have $|(\mathbf{xE})_j| < 2q(n + r)\alpha + n/2 \leq q/5p$ for every $\mathbf{x}$ and $j \in [m]$, except with probability at most $m \cdot 2^n = \text{negl}(l)$ over the choice of $\mathbf{E}$. Moreover, note that $|(\mathbf{xU})_j| \leq n/2 \leq 3q/40p$ and so do $|(\mathbf{xU}')_j|, |(\mathbf{xU}'')_j|, |(\mathbf{xU}''')_j|$, for all $j \in [m]$ by the size of their entries. Therefore we have

$$\left| \frac{p}{q}(\mathbf{xE})_j + \frac{p}{q}((\mathbf{xU})_j + (\mathbf{xU}'')_j) + \frac{p}{g}((\mathbf{xU}')_j + (\mathbf{xU}''')_j) \right| \qquad (31)$$

$$< \frac{p}{q} \cdot \frac{q}{5p} + \frac{p}{q} \cdot \left(\frac{3q}{40p} + \frac{3q}{40p} \right) + \frac{p}{g} \cdot \left(\frac{n}{2} + \frac{n}{2} \right) \qquad (32)$$

$$\leq \frac{1}{5} + \frac{3}{20} + \frac{3}{20} = \frac{1}{2}. \qquad (33)$$

Hence the decryption $\mathbf{Dec}(\mathbf{S}, \mathbf{y})$ outputs $\mathbf{m} = \mathbf{vH}$. We have $\mathbf{v} = \mathbf{mH}^{-1}$, since $\mathbf{H} = \mathsf{G}_{\text{FRD}}(b) - \mathsf{G}_{\text{FRD}}(b^*)$ is invertible for all $b \neq b^*$. The input vector $\mathbf{x} \in \{0, 1\}^n$ can be recover correctly from the vector $\mathbf{v}$.

We now analyze the lossiness. For any input $\mathbf{x} \in \{0, 1\}^n$, we have

$$\mathbf{y} = E_{\mathbf{S}}(\mathbf{0} = \mathbf{x}(\mathbf{0} \otimes \mathbf{g}), \mathbf{x}(\mathbf{U} + \mathbf{U}''), \mathbf{x}(\mathbf{U}' + \mathbf{U}'''); \mathbf{xA}, \mathbf{xE}). \qquad (34)$$

For every $j \in [m]$, y_j is a ciphertext $(\mathbf{xA}, y_j') \in \mathbb{Z}_q^l \times \mathbb{Z}_g$, where $\mathbf{xA}$ is the same randomness for all j and $y_j' = g(\langle \mathbf{xA}, \mathbf{s}_j \rangle + (\mathbf{xE})_j + 0 + 0)/q + (\mathbf{xU}')_j + (\mathbf{xU}''')_j)$. Fixing $\mathbf{A}$, $\mathbf{x}$ and $j \in [m]$, we have

$$\left| \frac{g}{q}(\mathbf{xE})_j + (\mathbf{xU}')_j + (\mathbf{xU}''')_j \right| < \frac{g}{q} \cdot \frac{q}{5p} + n \leq \frac{q}{5p} + \frac{3q}{20p} < \frac{q}{2p}. \qquad (35)$$

Obviously, the total number of outputs of the lossy function is at most $q^l(q/p)^m$, the logarithm of which gives an upper bound on the residual leakage $n - k \leq n \cdot \left(\frac{c_2}{c_1} + o(1) \right)$ as Theorem 1 does.

Finally, note that the hidden lossy branch property follows from Lemma 2 on the security of matrix encryption. □

6   Parameter Instantiation and Worst-Case Connection

We now associate the security of our constructions with the worst-case quantum hardness of lattice problems, by properly instantiating all the parameters n, p,

q, etc., and by invoking Proposition 1. The relationship between any desired constant lossiness rate $K \in (0,1)$, where larger K means more information is lost, and the corresponding approximation factor of the lattice problems is what we are interested in.

The following theorem is similar to the one in [16], except that the parameters we choose might not be the same as that of [16]. For completeness, the proof is presented here.

Theorem 4. *For any constant $K \in (0,1)$, the construction of Sect. 4 with prime q gives a family of almost-always (n, Kn)-lossy TDF for all sufficiently large n, assuming that SIVP and GapSVP are hard for quantum algorithms to approximate to within $\tilde{O}(l^c)$ factors, where $c = 2 + \frac{3}{2(1-K)} + \delta$ for any desired $\delta > 0$.*

The same applies for the construction in Sect. 5.2, with prime q and p, of almost-always (n, Kn)-all-but-one TDF.

Proof. Using the notation from Theorem 1 (likewise Theorem 3), we let $p = n^{c_1}$ ($p \in [n^{c_1}, (n+1)^{c_1}]$ is a prime) and let $n = l^{c_3}$ for some constant $c_1 > 1$, $c_3 > 1$ respectively that we will be set later, and let $r = n$, $\alpha = 1/(32pn)$. In order to invoke Proposition 1 (connecting LWE to lattice problems), we need to use some

$$q > 2\sqrt{l}/\alpha = 64pn\sqrt{l} = 64pn^{1+1/(2c_3)}. \tag{36}$$

Therefore we set $c_2 = 1 + 1/(2c_3)$, so we may take $q = O(pn^{c_2})$.

Now invoking Theorem 1 (likewise Theorem 3), we get that the lossy function has $n - k$ at most

$$n \cdot \left(\frac{c_2}{c_1} + \epsilon \right) = n \cdot \left(\frac{1 + 2c_3}{2c_1 c_3} + \epsilon \right), \tag{37}$$

for any $\epsilon > 0$ and sufficiently large n. By Proposition 1, LWE is hard for our choice of parameters, assuming the lattice problems are hard to approximate within $\tilde{O}(l/\alpha) = \tilde{O}(l^{1+c_3(c_1+1)})$ factors for quantum algorithms. With the constraint on the residual leakage as $\frac{1+2c_3}{2c_1 c_3} < 1 - K$, we get that $c_1 > \frac{1+2c_3}{2c_3(1-K)}$. This implies that the exponent in the lattice approximation factor may be brought arbitrarily close to $1 + c_3 + \frac{1+2c_3}{2(1-K)}$. Then under the constraint that $c_3 > 1$, the exponent may be brought arbitrarily close to $2 + \frac{3}{2(1-K)}$. □

7   Comparison

Let the parameters n, p, q, g, r, α be chosen as above. Compared to the LWE-based LTDF and ABO-TDF proposed in [16], our compact LTDF and ABO-TDF constructions reduce both the size of public key (i.e. the function index matrices) and that the vector of ciphertexts. Furthermore, the number of branches in our ABO-TDF is larger that of [16] if we fix p, which means that we can choose smaller p in order to support super-polynomially many injective branches in the

Table 1. Comparison between LTDF/ABO-TDF in [PW08] and those in this paper.

	[PW08]	This paper	D-value
Size of pk (LTDF)	$(nl + nm)\log q$	$nl\log q + nm\log g$	$nm\log(q/g)$
Size of pk (ABO-TDF)	$(nl + nw)\log q$	$nl\log q + nm\log g$	$2nl\log q + nm\log(q/g)$
Size of ciphertexts (LTDF)	$m(l+1)\log q$	$m(l\log q + \log g)$	$m\log(q/g)$
Size of ciphertexts (ABO-TDF)	$w(l+1)\log q$	$m(l\log q + \log g)$	$(2l^2 + 2l)\log q + m\log(q/g)$
Number of branches (ABO-TDF)	p^l	p^m	$p^m - p^l$

construction of CCA secure public key encryption. The comparison is summa-rized in Table 1, where D-value stands for the corresponding difference value.

In [16], the construction of LWE-based LTDF yields public key $\mathbf{C} \in \mathbb{Z}_q^{n\times l} \times \mathbb{Z}_q^{n\times m}$ and m-dimension vector of ciphertexts $\mathbf{y}$ where $y_j \in \mathbb{Z}_q^l \times \mathbb{Z}_q$. While the construction of LWE-based ABO-TDF in [16] yields public key $\mathbf{C} \in \mathbb{Z}_q^{n\times l} \times \mathbb{Z}_q^{n\times w}$, where $w = m + 2l$, and w-dimension vector of ciphertexts $\mathbf{y}$ where $y_j \in \mathbb{Z}_q^l \times \mathbb{Z}_q$. The branch set is $B = \mathbb{Z}_p^l$.

In this paper, the construction of LTDF yields public key $\mathbf{C} \in \mathbb{Z}_q^{n\times l} \times \mathbb{Z}_g^{n\times m}$ and m-dimension vector of ciphertexts $\mathbf{y} = \mathbf{xC}$ where $y_j \in \mathbb{Z}_q^l \times \mathbb{Z}_g$. While the construction of ABO-TDF yields public key $\mathbf{C} \in \mathbb{Z}_q^{n\times l} \times \mathbb{Z}_g^{n\times m}$ and m-dimension vector of ciphertexts $\mathbf{y}$ where $y_j \in \mathbb{Z}_q^l \times \mathbb{Z}_g$. The branch set is $B = \mathbb{Z}_p^m$.

Take the size of public key as example, the difference value (D-value) between [PW08] and this paper is $nm\log(q/g)$ bits. When $p = n^{c_1}$, $q = O(pn^{c_2})$, $g = 4pn$ and $m = n/\lfloor \lg p \rfloor$, we have $nm\log(q/g) > n\log O(n^{c_2-1})$, which can substan-tially improve the performance. As for the number of branches, under the same choice of p, the difference value between ABO-TDF in [16] and that in this paper is $p^m - p^l$. When prime $p \in [n^{c_1}, (n+1)^{c_1}]$, $n = l^{c_3}$ for some constants $c_1 > 1$ and $c_3 > 1$, we have $m = \frac{n}{\lceil \log p \rceil} \approx \frac{l^{c_3}}{c_3 c_1 \log l} = l \cdot \frac{l^{c_3-1}}{c_3 c_1 \log l} > l$, which means more branches under the same p. Alternatively, we only need smaller p (in turn smaller l since $p \in [l^{c_3 c_1}, (l^{c_3} + 1)^{c_1}]$) to support enough branches.

References

1. Agrawal, S., Dan, B., Boyen, X.: Efficient Lattice (H)IBE in the Standard Model. DBLP (2010)
2. Applebaum, B., Cash, D., Peikert, C., Sahai, A.: Fast cryptographic primitives and circular-secure encryption based on hard learning problems. In: Advances in Cryptology - CRYPTO 2009, International Cryptology Conference, Santa Barbara, CA, USA, 16–20 August 2009, Proceedings, pp. 595–618 (2009)
3. Boldyreva, A., Fehr, S., O'Neill, A.: On notions of security for deterministic encryption, and efficient constructions without random Oracles. In: Wagner, D. (ed.) CRYPTO 2008. LNCS, vol. 5157, pp. 335–359. Springer, Heidelberg (2008). https://doi.org/10.1007/978-3-540-85174-5_19

4. Cramer, R., Damgård, I., Pastro, V.: On the amortized complexity of zero knowledge protocols for multiplicative relations. In: Smith, A. (ed.) ICITS 2012. LNCS, vol. 7412, pp. 62–79. Springer, Heidelberg (2012). https://doi.org/10.1007/978-3-642-32284-6_4

5. Diffie, W., Hellman, M.E.: New directions in cryptography. IEEE Trans. Inf. Theory **22**(6), 644–654 (1976)

6. Dolev, D., Dwork, C., Naor, M.: Nonmalleable cryptography. SIAM J. Comput. **30**(2), 391–437 (2000). https://doi.org/10.1137/S0097539795291562

7. Freeman, D.M., Goldreich, O., Kiltz, E., Rosen, A., Segev, G.: More constructions of lossy and correlation-secure trapdoor functions. In: International Workshop on Public Key Cryptography, pp. 279–295 (2010)

8. Goldreich, O.: The Foundations of Cryptography, vol. 1. Basic Techniques, DBLP (2001)

9. Goldreich, O.: Foundations of Cryptography, vol. 2, Basic Applications. Cambridge University Press (2004)

10. Hofheinz, D.: Possibility and impossibility results for selective decommitments. J. Cryptol. **24**(3), 470–516 (2011)

11. Kiltz, E., O'Neill, A., Smith, A.: Instantiability of RSA-OAEP under chosen-plaintext attack. In: Rabin, T. (ed.) CRYPTO 2010. LNCS, vol. 6223, pp. 295–313. Springer, Heidelberg (2010). https://doi.org/10.1007/978-3-642-14623-7_16

12. Naor, M., Yung, M.: Public-key cryptosystems provably secure against chosen ciphertext attacks. In: Proceedings of the Twenty-Second Annual ACM Symposium on Theory of Computing, STOC 1990, pp. 427–437. ACM, New York (1990). https://doi.org/10.1145/100216.100273

13. Paillier, P.: Public-key cryptosystems based on composite degree residuosity classes. In: International Conference on Theory and Application of Cryptographic Techniques, pp. 223–238 (1999)

14. Peikert, C.: Limits on the hardness of lattice problems in ℓ_p norms. In: IEEE Conference on Computational Complexity, pp. 333–346 (2007)

15. Peikert, C.: Public-key cryptosystems from the worst-case shortest vector problem: extended abstract. In: ACM Symposium on Theory of Computing, pp. 333–342 (2009)

16. Peikert, C., Waters, B.: Lossy trapdoor functions and their applications. In: Fortieth ACM Symposium on Theory of Computing, pp. 187–196 (2008)

17. Peikert, C., Waters, B.: Lossy trapdoor functions and their applications. SIAM J. Comput. **40**(6), 1803–1844 (2011). https://doi.org/10.1137/080733954

18. Rabin, M.O.: Digitalized signatures and public-key functions as intractable as factorization. Massachusetts Institute of Technology (1979)

19. Rackoff, C., Simon, D.R.: Non-interactive zero-knowledge proof of knowledge and chosen ciphertext attack. In: International Cryptology Conference on Advances in Cryptology, pp. 433–444 (1991)

20. Regev, O.: On lattices, learning with errors, random linear codes, and cryptography. In: Proceedings of the Thirty-Seventh Annual ACM Symposium on Theory of Computing, STOC 2005, pp. 84–93. ACM, New York (2005). https://doi.org/10.1145/1060590.1060603

21. Rivest, R.L., Shamir, A., Adleman, L.: A method for obtaining digital signatures and public-key cryptosystems. Commun. ACM **21**(2), 120–126 (1978)

22. Seurin, Y.: On the lossiness of the rabin trapdoor function. In: Krawczyk, H. (ed.) PKC 2014. LNCS, vol. 8383, pp. 380–398. Springer, Heidelberg (2014). https://doi.org/10.1007/978-3-642-54631-0_22

23. Xue, H., Li, B., Lu, X., Jia, D., Liu, Y.: Efficient lossy trapdoor functions based on subgroup membership assumptions. In: Abdalla, M., Nita-Rotaru, C., Dahab, R. (eds.) CANS 2013. LNCS, vol. 8257, pp. 235–250. Springer, Cham (2013). https://doi.org/10.1007/978-3-319-02937-5_13

A Lattice-Based Approach to Privacy-Preserving Biometric Authentication Without Relying on Trusted Third Parties

Trung Dinh$^{(\boxtimes)}$, Ron Steinfeld, and Nandita Bhattacharjee

Monash University, Clayton, VIC 3800, Australia
{Trung.Dinh,Ron.Steinfeld,Nandita.Bhattacharjee}@monash.edu

Abstract. We propose a two-factor authentication protocol that uses a cryptographic authentication factor (secret key) to add biometric template privacy security against server exposure attack, to any given (non-private, one-factor) biometric authentication scheme based on Hamming-Distance (HD) comparison of stored and queried binary biometric templates. Our protocol provides provable privacy under the hardness of a standard cryptographic lattice problem (Ring-LWE), and provable two-factor impersonation security under malicious client model.

1 Introduction

1.1 Background

User authentication is the process of verifying the claimed identity of a user, which is an important aspect in the big picture of information and network security. Generally, there are three factors that can be used for this purpose: Something You Know, such as password; Something You Have, such as smartcard and Something You Are, such as iris or fingerprint. The last factor, also known as biometrics, can be considered the most usable factor as one does not have to carry or remember anything during authentication. In this approach, generally a user first enrols his biometric template with a server, later he can use a query template to authenticate: The server compares the distance between the stored and query templates with some pre-defined threshold value to decide the authentication result. Biometric authentication is lately deployed widely in many platforms thanks to the reduced cost of hardware. However, the main drawback of this method is lack of biometric privacy against server exposure. If biometric data is ever revealed or stolen, the victims may be vulnerable to impersonation attacks for the rest of their life, as it is nearly impossible to change one's fingerprints or iris, unlike password or smartcard approaches. Hence there is a strong motivation to develop authentication systems that protect the privacy of biometric data. Designing such a system is challenging due to following desirable requirements:

Privacy against server exposure. The biometric data should be securely encrypted prior to uploading to the server, using a key stored only to the biometric owner. This is important to avoid similar incident to [37], where

© Springer International Publishing AG 2017
J. K. Liu and P. Samarati (Eds.): ISPEC 2017, LNCS 10701, pp. 297–319, 2017.
https://doi.org/10.1007/978-3-319-72359-4_17

millions of plaintext fingerprint data was leaked. Ideally, the server storing the encrypted biometric should not be able to comprehend the data, in other words, it does not have the encryption key.

Quantum resistant privacy. Considering quantum computing is developing fast and the biometric data will persist over the lifetime of a user, the encrypted biometric data should have long term security against quantum computing attacks.

No reliance on trusted third parties. With the wide exposure of cloud computing to potential attacks, the protocol should not rely on one or more cloud-based trusted third parties to help with the authentication process.

Security against malicious client. An attacker attempting to impersonate the real client to the server should not be able to authenticate without a genuine biometric, even if the attacker is malicious and does not follow the authentication protocol, i.e. the impersonation attacker cannot be assumed to be 'honest but curious' (HBC).

Two factor security. If the client is responsible for decrypting biometric-related data, the protocol should be multi-factor secure: an attacker with a compromised key should not be able to authenticate without a genuine biometric.

Practical performance. The computation time and communication size of the whole protocol should be within practical time frame.

Previous protocols in the literature do not meet one or more of our requirements. In particular, many previous protocols [8,12,34] assume honest-but-curious clients and are insecure in the authentication context that involves malicious clients. The few protocols involving malicious clients [43,44] are not quantum-resistant. Previous practical quantum-resistant protocols [31,52] are not secure against malicious client and involve the use of a trusted third-party verification server and therefore client privacy is not completely achieved.

1.2   Contribution

We propose a protocol to support all of the above features. Our technique combines state-of-the-art cryptographic tools such as Homomorphic Encryption (HE) and Zero-Knowledge-Proof (ZKP) to balance security and usability of the system. The techniques are all lattice-based, which is currently the best candidate for long term security against quantum attacks. Our protocol also achieves privacy against server exposure without relying on a trusted third party. The contributions include:

- A quantum resistant and provable-secure biometric authentication protocol that does not rely on trusted third-parties (Sect. 3). The server stores the encrypted data and does homomorphic operations to compute the distance (HD) to decide the authentication result. It does not need a third party to decrypt the encrypted HD but sending it to the client for decryption. The client uses ZKP to convince the server that the ciphertext was decrypted correctly.

- The protocol provides security under malicious client model, this is done by a new ZKP technique that we design specifically for the ciphertext packing method of [52] (Sect. 4.1). It is also applicable to do proof of plaintext knowledge for the BV Homomorphic Encryption scheme [7] that we adapted, the ZKP technique is based on [48].
- Due to the noise inherent inside lattice-based homomorphic encryption and its correlation with the evaluated ciphertext, we observe that there can be information leakage about the original plaintexts used in the homomorphic computations to a two-factor attacker that exposed the client's secret key. We propose an approach to cover such leakage without significantly reducing the efficiency of the protocol: the approach is a new application of Renyi Divergence (RD) based analysis to show the security of the protocol with a small 'imperfect' one-time pad (Sect. 4.2). This correlation of Homomorphic Encryption noise with the original plaintext before homomorphic evaluation was observed as a problem of "circuit privacy" in theoretical HE literature [21,41], but the proposed solutions [15,16,35] involves 'smudging' (imperfect masking) with an exponentially large noise or bootstrapping techniques (in the security parameter) that reduces efficiency. In contrast, our Renyi-based method can use much smaller imperfect masks leading to better efficiency. This is the first application of Renyi divergence techniques to circuit privacy of HE to our knowledge.

2   Preliminaries

2.1   Notations

We use R and r to denote a ring and its element (e.g., $r \in R$). Specific rings R used in this work include ring of integers $\mathbb{Z}$ and ring of polynomials $R_q = \mathbb{Z}_q[x]/(x^n + 1)$ for n a power of 2 and $\mathbb{Z}_q$ to be the ring of integers modulo q. We write elements of polynomial rings in boldface (e.g. $\mathbf{x} \in R_q$), a polynomial ring element can be represented interchangeably by a vector of integers (e.g. $\overrightarrow{x} = \mathbf{x} = (x_1, x_2, \ldots, x_n)$). Standard vector notation is used in different rings (e.g. $\overrightarrow{v} \in \mathbb{Z}_q^n$ or $\overrightarrow{\mathbf{v}} \in R_q^n$). Ring operations are denoted as $(+, \cdot)$, inner product of vector is denoted as $\langle \overrightarrow{a}, \overrightarrow{b} \rangle$. The output of an algorithm is denoted as $x \leftarrow A$, a uniform random sample from a distribution is written as $u \xleftarrow{r} \mathcal{D}$. D_{id} is used to denote the distribution of templates sampled from one specific user $\mathcal{U}_{id}$ and D_{bio} is the collection of many D_{id}s over the biometric population. We denote $HD_{x,y}$ to be the Hamming Distance of two bitstring x and y.

2.2   Homomorphic Encryption

Homomorphic Encryption (HE) is a family of cryptosystems that allows operations on encrypted data. The idea was introduced since late 1970s [40] and has been actively researched lately ([17,45,46,51], etc.) since the break through work of Gentry [15]. Although the idea of Fully Homomorphic Encryption (arbitrary number of operations) is feasible, its performance has not been considered practical enough. We only present a Somewhat Homomorphic Encryption system, the BV system by [7], it allows additions and some levels of multiplications on the ciphertexts, and it serves well our purpose. The security of this cryptosystem is based on the hardness of the Ring-Learning With Error (RLWE) problem [30], we present the polynomial variant (PLWE) of RLWE [47].

The Ring Learning with Errors Problem

Definition 1 (RWLE). *Given parameters q, n define the ring $R_q = \frac{\mathbb{Z}_q[x]}{x^n+1}$ and a distribution $\chi_{\alpha q}$ defines a small noise distribution, the $RWLE_{q,n,\chi_{\alpha q}}$ problem asks to distinguish two distributions. In the first distribution, one samples uniformly $(\mathbf{a}_i, \mathbf{b}_i)$ from R_q^2. In the second distribution, one first samples $\mathbf{s} \xleftarrow{r} R_q$, $\mathbf{e}_i \xleftarrow{r} \chi_{\alpha q}$ and generates $(\mathbf{a}_i, \mathbf{b}_i)$ by sampling $\mathbf{a}_i \xleftarrow{r} R_q$ and compute $\mathbf{b}_i = \mathbf{a}_i \cdot \mathbf{s} + \mathbf{e}_i$.*

SHE Scheme construction. The BV cryptosystem is as follows.

Setup. Initiate (n, m, q, t, χ) to define the ciphertext space R_q, the plaintext space $R_t = \frac{\mathbb{Z}_t[x]}{x^n+1}$, and the error distribution, note that $t << q$.

KeyGen. The secret key sk can be chosen by select a small element $\mathbf{s} \in R_q$, one can sample $\mathbf{s} \xleftarrow{r} \chi^n$. The public key pk is a pair of ring element $(\mathbf{p}_0, \mathbf{p}_1)$ where $\mathbf{p}_1 \xleftarrow{r} R_q$ and $\mathbf{p}_0 = -(\mathbf{p}_1\mathbf{s} + t\mathbf{e})$ with $\mathbf{e} \xleftarrow{r} \chi^n$.

Encryption. Given a plaintext $\mathbf{m} \in R_t$ and a public key $pk = (\mathbf{p}_0, \mathbf{p}_1)$, the encryption first samples $\mathbf{u}, \mathbf{f}, \mathbf{g} \xleftarrow{r} \chi$ and compute a fresh ciphertext by

$$Enc_{pk}(\mathbf{m}) = (\mathbf{c}_0, \mathbf{c}_1) = (\mathbf{p}_0\mathbf{u} + t\mathbf{g} + \mathbf{m}, \mathbf{p}_1\mathbf{u} + t\mathbf{f})$$

Conventionally, we use $\llbracket P \rrbracket$ to denote the encryption of a plaintext P under BV scheme with the public key and we do not take into account the randomness. When we want to specify also the noise used in the encryption, we write $\llbracket (P, e) \rrbracket$, where e is the noise.

Decryption. Although the above encryption generates ciphertexts of 2 elements only in R_q, the homomorphic operations (discussed next) will make the ciphertext longer. We can write the decryption for ciphertext $c = (\mathbf{c}_0, \mathbf{c}_1, \ldots, \mathbf{c}_L)$ with the extended secret key $sk = (1, \mathbf{s}, \mathbf{s}^2, \ldots, \mathbf{s}^L)$ as $Dec(c, sk) = \left[[\langle \mathbf{c}, \mathbf{sk} \rangle]_Q \right]_t$.

Homomorphic Operations. Given 2 ciphertext $c = (\mathbf{c}_0, \mathbf{c}_1, \ldots, \mathbf{c}_L)$ and $c' = (\mathbf{c'}_0, \mathbf{c'}_1, \ldots, \mathbf{c'}_L)$. The homomorphic addition $add(c, c')$ is computed by component wise addition $add(c, c') = (\mathbf{c}_0 + \mathbf{c'}_0, \ldots, \mathbf{c}_L + \mathbf{c'}_L)$. The homomorphic multiplication $mult(c, c')$ is computed by $mult(c, c') = (\hat{\mathbf{c}}_0, \hat{\mathbf{c}}_1, \ldots, \hat{\mathbf{c}}_{2L-2})$ with $\sum_{i=0}^{2L-2} \hat{\mathbf{c}}_i z^i = \sum_{i=0}^{L-1} \mathbf{c}_i z^i \times \sum_{j=0}^{L-1} \mathbf{c'}_j z^j$, where z denotes a symbolic variable.

2.3   Ciphertext Packing

Given a bit string plaintext $m \in \{0, 1\}^*$, there are several ways that one can encode it to a polynomial, or a ring element $\mathbf{m} \in R_t$ before encryption. A recent popular approach for BV cryptosystem is called CRT packing method, which is based on Chinese Remainder Theorem [45]. The method allows Single Instruction, Multiple Data (SIMD) operations on encrypted data. However, we do not use this packing technique as there is not yet known efficient method to compute HD based on it. We instead apply the method from [52], which is an extension of [27], the technique allow HD computation in just one level of multiplication. The definition follows.

Definition 2. *For* $\mathbf{T} = (t_0, \ldots, t_{n-1})$ *and* $\mathbf{Q} = (q_0, \ldots, q_{n-1})$, *we define two types of polynomials in the ring* R_Q *of the SHE scheme:* $pm_1(\mathbf{T}) = \sum_{i=0}^{n-1} t_i x^i$ *and* $pm_2(\mathbf{Q}) = -\sum_{j=0}^{n-1} q_j x^{n-j}$. *The two types of packed ciphertexts are defined as* $[\![pm_1(\mathbf{T})]\!]$ *and* $[\![pm_2(\mathbf{Q})]\!]$.

In the ring R_Q we have $x^n = -1$, then when we do multiplication between $pm_1(\mathbf{T})$ and $pm_2(\mathbf{Q})$, the constant term of the result would be the inner product $\langle \mathbf{T}, \mathbf{Q} \rangle$. We can also do homomorphic multiplication on the ciphertexts and get the ciphertext of the inner product similarly. Furthermore, we can use this result to compute HD as follows, this operation costs one level of multiplication with 3 additions and 3 multiplications on ciphertexts.

Theorem 1 ([52]). *Let* $C_1 = -\sum_{i=0}^{n-1} x^{n-i}$ *and* $C_2 = 2 - C_1 = \sum_{i=0}^{n-1} x^i$. *Let* $Enc(HD)$ *be a ciphertext given by*

$$[\![pm_1(\mathbf{T})]\!] * [\![C_1]\!] + [\![pm_2(\mathbf{Q})]\!] * [\![C_2]\!] - 2 * [\![pm_1(\mathbf{T})]\!] * [\![pm_2(\mathbf{Q})]\!]$$

Then, the constant term of $Dec(Enc(HD))$ *gives the Hamming Distance of* $\mathbf{T}$ *and* $\mathbf{Q}$.

2.4   Zero Knowledge Proofs and ISIS Problem

Zero Knowledge Proofs (ZKP), first introduced in [18], is a strong cryptographic tool, a beautiful notion that goes beyond the limits of traditional proofs: In a ZKP system, a *Prover* P convinces a *Verifier* P that some statement is true without leaking any thing but the validity of the assertion. There are several types of ZKP, which are the building blocks in many cryptographic protocols (anonymous credential systems, identification schemes, group signatures, etc.). In this work, we focus on ZKP of knowledge (ZKPoK) [5,18], where P needs to also convince V that he knows a "witness" for the given statement, we then apply such proof to enforce the user to follow the authentication protocol transcript and therefore claim that the protocol is secure against malicious clients. ZKPoK has been actively studied in the last 30 years [13,28,32,38], we focus our work on techniques to do ZKPoK for an important hard-on-average problem in lattice-based cryptography: the Inhomogeneous Small Integer Solution (ISIS) problem. The proof relation is

$$R_{ISIS_{n,m,Q,\beta}} = \{((\mathbf{A}, \mathbf{y}); \mathbf{x}) \in \mathbb{Z}_Q^{n \times m} \times \mathbb{Z}_Q^n \times \mathbb{Z}^m : (\|\mathbf{x}\|_\infty \leq \beta) \wedge (\mathbf{A}\mathbf{x} = \mathbf{y} \mod Q)\}$$

The secret witness of P is $\boldsymbol{x}$ and the public parameters for V are $(\mathbf{A}, \boldsymbol{y})$. One of the main research directions was initiated by Stern [48], he proposed the protocol for a simpler relation (Syndrome Decoding Problem). Ling et al. [28] developed a scheme to fully support ISIS proofs. The proof is a 3-move interactive protocol: P starts the protocol by computing and sends to V three commitments; V then sends to P a random challenge; P reveals two of the three commitments according to the challenge. The *Prover*'s witness is the secret vector $\boldsymbol{x}$, the public inputs are $\mathbf{A}$ and $\boldsymbol{y}$. The protocol is detailed in [28]. We refer readers to the original paper for correctness and statistical zero-knowledge proofs. We note that from their result, each round of communication costs $\log \beta \tilde{O}(n \log Q)$ bits and we denote **SternExt(A,x,y)** for the whole run.

3   The Protocol

3.1   The Syntax and Security Model

We first describe the protocol and its security model in generic form. We then can use them as a framework to apply and analyze in our specific proposal.

The Generic Two-Party Model

Entities: There can be 2 or 3 typical entities involved in a secure biometric authentication system. The user $\mathcal{U}$, an authentication server $\mathcal{S}$, and a decryptor, who is a third party trusted by both of the users and the server. The decryptor presents in some systems [19,20,31], with the assumption that there is no collusion between this entity and $\mathcal{U}$ or $\mathcal{S}$. In our work, we aim to avoid the assumption of trusted decryptor party, so we only have two parties, $\mathcal{U}$ and $\mathcal{S}$.

Biometrics Features in non-private setting. In biometric authentication systems (e.g., fingerprint authentication system), a user $\mathcal{U}$ first enrolls his finger-gerprint template X with the server $\mathcal{S}$. $\mathcal{U}$ later authenticates with $\mathcal{S}$ using the same finger with a template Y, $\mathcal{S}$ uses an algorithm $Verify(X, Y)$ to obtain the result of the authentication: **Accept** or **Reject**. Different fingerprint system might use different features of fingers such as minutia or fingercode to compute this distance Δ between X and Y in the algorithm $Verify$. The distance Δ is compared to some predefined threshold value τ to determine the result of the authentication. We refer the reader to [22] for biometric feature extraction and comparison techniques. Our protocol assumes that Hamming Distance is used in $Verify(x, y)$.

Unlike password based system where $\mathcal{U}$ always uses one same query for many authentication, all biometric systems have the concept of False Acceptance Rate (FAR), where the system **Accept** an incorrect template; and False Rejection Rate (FRR), where the system **Reject** a genuine one. Balancing these 2 rates while keeping good performance is one of the main challenges that fingerprint verification algorithms [14] are trying to solve. We also reflect these two rates in our models.

Algorithms and Procedures in privacy-preserving setting: We describe the high level constructions of the protocol as follows

Enroll: This procedure inserts records into the server's database.
- Input: Client: identity k, a registered template X_k; Server: Parameters of the cryptographic tools used.
- Output: A public-private key pair (sk_k, pk_k) for the user $\mathcal{U}_k$. The server learns the protected template of T_k of X_k.

Auth: This procedure allows a user to authenticate with the system.
- Input: Client: identity k, a query template Y_k and the secret key sk_k; Server: record (k, T_k, pk_k)
- Output: The server learns the authentication result $res = \{$**Accept,Reject**$\}$

Correctness Requirement: A genuine user $\mathcal{U}_k$ runs $(sk_k, T_k) \leftarrow$ **Enroll**(k, X_k) using a $X_k \in Supp(D_k)$ and later uses his biometric template $Y_k \xleftarrow{r} D_k$ to do $res \leftarrow$ **Auth**$((k, Y_k, sk_k), (k, T_k, pk_k))$ The privacy-preserving protocol works correctly if FRR under this system is exactly equal to FRR of the non-privacy preserving system:

$$Pr[res = Verify(X_k, Y_k)] = 1$$

The Security Model

Privacy against an Honest But Curious server: The security model is defined in terms of following security games.

The real game Real$_\mathcal{A}(D_k, X_k)$: This is the game for a privacy attack against the privacy-preserving protocol for the underlying biometric system, between an attacker $\mathcal{A}$ and a challenger $\mathcal{C}$. The input to the game is an attacked $\mathcal{U}_k$ with biometric distribution $D_k \in D_{bio}$ and a user template $X_k \in Supp(D_k)$.
1. $\mathcal{C}$ runs $(T_k, sk_k) \leftarrow$ **Enrol**(k, X_k) and sends T_k to $\mathcal{A}$.
2. For $i = 1 \ldots q$:
   - $\mathcal{C}$ samples $Y_i \xleftarrow{r} D_k$
   - $\mathcal{C}$ simulates the **Auth** protocol, playing the roles of both the client and the server: $res \leftarrow$ **Auth$_i$**$((k, Y_i, sk_k), (k, T_k, pk_k))$
   - Let V_i denotes the ith view of $\mathcal{S}$ when $\mathcal{C}$ runs **Auth$_i$**. $\mathcal{C}$ sends the view V_i to $\mathcal{A}$.
3. $\mathcal{A}$ outputs a bit β, representing some information that $\mathcal{A}$ has learned about (D_k, X_k). The game output is **Real**$_\mathcal{A}(D_k, X_k) = \beta$.

The ideal game Ideal$_{\mathcal{A}'}(D_k, X_k)$: This is the game for a privacy attack against an ideal privacy scenario for the underlying biometric authentication system, where the attacker $\mathcal{A}'$ interacts with a challenger $\mathcal{C}'$. The input to the game is an attacked $\mathcal{U}_k$ with biometric distribution $D_k \in D_{bio}$ and a user template $X_k \in Supp(D_k)$. In this ideal game, the information $\mathcal{A}'$ can learn about (D_k, X_k) is the value of HD_{X_k, Y_k} which implies the bit $Verify(X_k, Y_i)$.
1. For $i = 1 \ldots q$:
   - $\mathcal{C}'$ samples query template $Y_i \xleftarrow{r} D_k$.
   - $\mathcal{C}'$ sends HD_{X, Y_i} to $\mathcal{A}'$.

2. $\mathcal{A}'$ output a bit β', representing some information that $\mathcal{A}'$ has learned about (D_k, X_k). The game output is $\mathbf{Ideal}_{\mathcal{A}'}(D_k, X_k) = \beta'$.

Definition 3 (Privacy Security against Server). *We say that a biometric authentication protocol is q-private in the sense of biometric template privacy against an honest but curious server $\mathcal{S}$ if for every efficient real-game attacker $\mathcal{A}$, there exists an efficient ideal-game attacker $\mathcal{A}'$ such that, for all (D_k, X_k) we have:*

$$|\Pr[\mathbf{Real}_{\mathcal{A}}(D_k, X_k) = 1] - \Pr[\mathbf{Ideal}_{\mathcal{A}'}(D_k, X_k) = 1]| \leq negl(\lambda).$$

Security against the malicious client: In this work, we aim for security against active client, where an attacker $\mathcal{A}$ is assumed not to follow the protocol transcript.

  Biometric Impersonation: FAR is the usual biometric impersonation probability, it is inherent to the biometrics themselves without any cryptographic protocols. We first discuss this security game (which will be referred to as *biometric impersonation*).

  Setup: $\mathcal{C}$ samples $X_k \xleftarrow{r} D_k$ from a random $\mathcal{U}_k$ ($D_k \xleftarrow{r} D_{bio}$).

  Query: $\mathcal{A}$ is given access to the authentication oracle $Verify(X_k, Y)$ that returns the authentication result of $\mathcal{U}_k$ with a query template Y. $\mathcal{A}$ has q attempts to make queries, in each attempt, $\mathcal{A}$ chooses a Y_q by himself and does $Verify(X_k, Y_q)$.

  Guess: $\mathcal{A}$ outputs $Y_{q'}$ such that $Verify(X_k, Y_{q'}) = \mathbf{Accept}$.

  The advantage of $\mathcal{A}$ in the game is defined as

$$\mathbf{Adv}_{\mathcal{A}}^{bio}(\lambda) = Pr[Verify(X_k, Y_{q'}) = \mathbf{Accept}]$$

  In this basic model, when $q = 1$, the advantage of $\mathcal{A}$ is FAR. Therefore, we can say the advantage of $\mathcal{A}$ for q queries is $\mathbf{Adv}_{\mathcal{A}}^{bio}(\lambda) \leq q \times FAR$.

  Privacy-Preserving Protocol: This model extend the above protocol and captures the client side attacks.

  Setup: The setup phase includes 2 steps:
  - $\mathcal{C}$ samples $X_k \xleftarrow{r} D_k$ from a random $\mathcal{U}_k$ ($D_k \xleftarrow{r} D_{bio}$).
  - $\mathcal{C}$ runs **Enroll**(k, X_k) that returns (sk_k, T_k).

  Query: In the query phase:
  - $\mathcal{A}$ is given access to the authentication oracle **Auth**(Y) that returns the authentication result of $\mathcal{U}_k$ with a query template Y.
  - $\mathcal{A}$ chooses the attack type $t \in \{I, II\}$ which specifies the scenario of key exposed or template exposed.
  - $\mathcal{C}$ gives sk_k if $t = I$ or T_k if $t = II$ to $\mathcal{A}$. Note that, this model reflects the 2-factors authentication (the secret key and the biometric template), if $\mathcal{A}$ requests both factors, he loses the game.
  - $\mathcal{C}$ and $\mathcal{A}$ runs **Auth**$()$ q times, For the ith run, $\mathcal{A}$ plays the client's role that chooses and sends Y_i to $\mathcal{C}$, $\mathcal{C}$ plays the server's role that replies with $res_i = \mathbf{Auth}(Y_i)$.

Guess: $\mathcal{A}$ wins the game if it outputs Y such that **Auth**$(Y) =$ **Accepted**.

The advantage of $\mathcal{A}$ in this game is defined as

$$\mathbf{Adv}_{\mathcal{A}}^{Imp}(\lambda) = Pr[\mathcal{A} \ wins]$$

We would want this advantage value not to be too large compared to the non-privacy-preserving biometric impersonation model's advantage $\mathbf{Adv}_{\mathcal{A}}^{bio}(\lambda)$, which was bounded by $q \times FAR$.

Definition 4 (Impersonation Security). *We say that a biometric authentication protocol is c-secure in the sense of template protection against the malicious user $\mathcal{U}$ if $\mathbf{Adv}_{\mathcal{A}}^{Imp}(\lambda)$ is not greater than $\mathbf{Adv}_{\mathcal{A}}^{bio}(\lambda)$ in some factor c (if $c = 1$ we would have perfectly the same security level as the non-privacy-preserving system):*

$$\mathbf{Adv}_{\mathcal{A}}^{Imp}(\lambda) \leq c \times \mathbf{Adv}_{\mathcal{A}}^{bio}(\lambda)$$

3.2 Our Protocol

We denote $\mathcal{U}$ to be the client and $\mathcal{S}$ to be the server. There are 3 main submodules in the protocol: Setup, Enrol, and Authenticate

Setup. $\mathcal{U}$ and $\mathcal{S}$ initialize the parameters, there are several categories:

Biometric Authentication System Parameters. These parameters are standard ones used by non privacy preserving biometric authentication systems:

– False Acceptance Rate (FAR) and False Rejection Rate (FRR)
– τ: Threshold for comparing the Hamming Distance to decide the authentication result.
– n': The bit-length of the encoded biometric data.

Ring-LWE based techniques parameters. These parameters are used in the lattice-based cryptosystem which provide client privacy against long term quantum attacks.

– λ: General security parameter of the cryptosystem
– n: Integer n defining the plaintext and ciphertext spaces rings.
– t: Integer t defining the plaintext space ring $R_t = \mathbb{Z}_t[x]/x^n + 1$.
– q: Integer q defining the ciphertext space ring $R_q = \mathbb{Z}_q[x]/x^n + 1$
– $\chi_{\alpha q}$: A distribution which is used to sample noises for LWE-based techniques. We choose $\chi_{\alpha q}$ to be a discrete Gaussian distribution with standard deviation αq.
– δ: Renyi Divergence parameter for the security of noise masking. (Section 4.2)

Keygen. Keys are generated for $\mathcal{U}$:

– Secret key: $\mathbf{s} \xleftarrow{r} \chi_{\alpha q}^n$
– Public key: $pk = (\mathbf{p}_0, \mathbf{p}_1)$, where $\mathbf{p}_0 = -\mathbf{p}_1\mathbf{s} - t\mathbf{e}$ with $\mathbf{p}_1 \xleftarrow{r} R_q$ and $\mathbf{e} \xleftarrow{r} \chi_{\alpha q}^n$.

Enrolment. $\mathcal{U}$ extracts the biometric template $\mathbf{x} \in \{0,1\}^t$, note that the bit string $\mathbf{x}$ can be represented as a ring element of R_t. The encryption is done by $[\![\mathbf{x}]\!] = (\mathbf{c}_0, \mathbf{c}_1)$ and sends to $\mathcal{S}$.

Authentication. This is done in following steps:

1. $\mathcal{U}$ extracts his biometric again $\mathbf{y}$ to use as the query. $\mathcal{U}$ sends $[\![\mathbf{y}]\!] = (\mathbf{c}'_0, \mathbf{c}'_1)$ to $\mathcal{S}$.

2. ZKP for the first relation: $\mathcal{U}$ has to prove that $[\![\mathbf{y}, \tilde{e}_y]\!]$ is a valid encryption, that is, it encrypts a bit string under the BV cryptosystem using the corresponding secret key. This is done by module **SternBV(A, y, x)** described in Sect. 4.1, where $\mathbf{A} = \begin{bmatrix} \mathbf{c}'_0, t, 0, 1 \\ \mathbf{p}_0, 0, t, 0 \end{bmatrix}$, $\mathbf{X} = [\mathbf{s}, \tilde{e}_y, \mathbf{e}, \mathbf{y}]^T$ and $\mathbf{Y} = [\mathbf{c}'_1, \mathbf{p}_1]^T$.

3. HD Computation: $\mathcal{S}$ computes $[\![HD_{\mathbf{x},\mathbf{y}}]\!]$ using procedure in Sect. 2.3 where the constant coefficient of HD is the Hamming Distance $HD_{X,Y}$. We note that this noise term $\mathbf{e}_{HD}$ of $[\![\mathbf{HD}, \mathbf{e}_{HD}]\!]$ can leak information about $\mathbf{x}$ when $\mathbf{HD}$ is decrypted. Therefore, we need to do an extra step to secure this operation.

   - Sample $\mathbf{e}_r \xleftarrow{r} \chi_\sigma^n$ such that σ is big enough compared to $\|\mathbf{e}_{HD}\|_\infty$ (Sect. 4.2).
   - Sample $\mathbf{r} = \{r_1, ..., r_n\} \xleftarrow{r} \mathbb{Z}_q^n$ and compute $[\![\mathbf{r}, \mathbf{e}_r]\!]$ and do one homomorphic addition operation to mask both the values of **HD** and the noise $\mathbf{e}_{HD}$: $[\![\mathbf{HD}', \mathbf{e}'_{HD}]\!] = [\![\mathbf{HD}, \mathbf{e}_{HD}]\!] + [\![\mathbf{r}, \mathbf{e}_r]\!]$

   The result $[\![\mathbf{HD}']\!]$ is then sent to $\mathcal{U}$.

4. $\mathcal{U}$ decrypts $[\![\mathbf{HD}']\!]$ and derive the actual value HD' from the first coefficient of the plaintext:$dec[\![\mathbf{HD}']\!] = (HD', r'_1, r_2, \ldots, r'_{n-1})$ for some r'_i. $\mathcal{U}$ sends HD' to $\mathcal{S}$.

5. $\mathcal{U}$ proves that it computes the decryption honestly, this is done similarly to step 2.

6. $\mathcal{S}$ unmasks HD' by computing $HD = HD' - r_1$ and output the authentication result **Accept** if $HD < \tau$ and **Reject** else.

Correctness. We start with the noise sampled during key generation: $e_0 \xleftarrow{r} \chi_{\alpha q}$ where $\chi_{\alpha q}$ is a Gaussian distribution with standard deviation αq. When sampling the noise, we can tail-cut the coefficients of the noise vector at $3\alpha q$ and set the noise vector infinity norm bound when doing key generation to be $B_\chi \leq 3\alpha q$. Denote B_0 to be the noise bound of the first level ciphertext $c = (\mathbf{c}_0, \mathbf{c}_1)$. We have

$$[\langle \mathbf{c}, \mathbf{s} \rangle]_q = m + t(\mathbf{g} + \mathbf{fs} - \mathbf{e}_0\mathbf{u})$$

So we can bound $B_0 \leq t(1 + B_\chi + 2nB_\chi^2)$. From Theorem 1, we can derive the noise of the HD ciphertext (unmask) $B_{HD} \leq 2nB_0 + nB_0^2$. The noise of the final masked ciphertext is

$$B_{HDMasked} \leq (4\pi kn + 1)n(B_0^2 + 2B_0)$$

where $k = 1 + \sqrt{\frac{1}{\pi \log 4nFAR^{-1}}}$ (Sect. 4.2). For correct decryption, we want this noise to be less than $q/2t$, the final correctness condition is: $q > 4\pi n^2 t(B_0^2 + 2B_0)$.

Lemma 1 (Condition for Correct Decryption of HD). *For the BV encrypted Hamming Distance $[\![HD]\!]$, the decryption recovers the correct result if $\langle [\![HD]\!], s \rangle$ does not wrap around mod q, namely, if $q > 4\pi n^2 t(B_0^2 + 2B_0)$.*

Security. The proposed scheme satisfies the security notions defined in Sect. 3.1, proofs are provided in the full version of the paper.

Theorem 2 (Server side security). *Under the IND-CPA security of BV cryptosystem, and the zero-knowledge property of the Stern protocol, the proposed scheme satisfies (Honest But Curious) Server Privacy Security.*

Theorem 3 (Client side security). *Under the IND-CPA security of BV cryptosystem and the soundness property of the underlying Stern protocol, the proposed scheme satisfies Impersonation Security. Concretely, for $\delta > 0$, the protocol is (q, c)-secure against impersonation with $c \le c(\delta) + 3 \cdot c_1$, assuming the underlying non-private biometric protocol has impersonation probability ε_{bio} and the underlying Stern ZK protocols have knowledge error $\varepsilon_{ZK1}, \varepsilon_{ZK2}$ such that $q(\varepsilon_{ZK1} + \varepsilon_{ZK2}) + \delta \le c_1 \cdot \varepsilon_{bio}$, $c(\delta) = 2e^{1+2\delta}$, and the condition $\sigma/r_0 \ge 4\pi knq$ holds, with $k = 1 + \sqrt{1/\pi \ln(2nq/\delta)}$ and r_0 an upper bound on the size of the noise in C_{HD}.*

4 Zero Knowledge Proofs and Noise Masking Analysis

Our main technical contributions in this work include a variant of the Stern-based Zero Knowledge Proof technique and a security improvement by applying Renyi Divergence (RD) to mask the noise of result ciphertexts. We discuss these techniques in this section.

4.1 Stern-Based ZKP

Recall that we need to construct a proof for the ISIS relation:

$$R_{ISIS_{n,mq,\beta}} = \{((\mathbf{A}, \mathbf{y}); \mathbf{x}) \in \mathbb{Z}_q^{n \times m} \times \mathbb{Z}_q^n \times \mathbb{Z}^m : (\|\mathbf{x}\|_\infty \le \beta) \wedge (\mathbf{A}\mathbf{x} = \mathbf{y} \mod q)\}$$

There are several approaches to construct such proof (e.g. [29, 32, 48]). We discuss an approach based on [48] in this work. We refer our readers to the original paper for the detailed steps of the protocol and we denote **Stern**$_{A,x,y}$ for the whole proof. Provided such a proof, it can be applied to do a Zero Knowledge Proof of Plaintext Knowledge (ZKPoPK) for latticed-based cryptosystems. For example, in the work of [28] with an extension (denoted by **SternExt**), plaintext knowledge proof was done by proving the encryption relation of Regev's cryptosystem [39]:

$$R_{Regev}^{q,m,n,t,\chi} = \{((p_0, p_1), (c_0, c_1); \mathbf{r} \| M) \in (\mathbb{Z}_q^{m \times n} \times \mathbb{Z}_q^m) \times (\mathbb{Z}_q^n \times \mathbb{Z}_q) \times \mathbb{Z}_q^{n+1} :$$
$$(c_0 = p_0 \mathbf{r}) \wedge (c_1 = p_1 \mathbf{r} + M)\}$$

The proof worked by letting $\mathbf{A}' = \begin{bmatrix} p_1, 1 \\ p_0, 0 \end{bmatrix}$ and $\mathbf{y} = \begin{bmatrix} c_1 \\ c_0 \end{bmatrix}$ being the public

parameters and let $\mathbf{x} = \begin{bmatrix} r \\ M \end{bmatrix}$ be the *Prover*'s witness. We observe that $\mathbf{A}'\mathbf{x} = \mathbf{y}$ mod q, that is, $\mathbf{x}$ is a solution to the ISIS problem, provided that $\|r\|_\infty \approx |M|$ AND the *Prover* must know r. This solution only works in the symmetric key setting, in many other contexts, the client does not know r as encryption is done by other parties using public key. For such situation, we can look at the decryption equation:

$$c_1 - c_0 s = t\tilde{e} + M$$

Therefore, we can write the decryption relation as:

$$R_{Regev,dec}^{q,m,n,t,\chi} = \{((p_0,p_1),(c_0,c_1),s,e,\tilde{e},M) \in (\mathbb{Z}_q^{m\times n} \times \mathbb{Z}_q^m) \times (\mathbb{Z}_q^n \times \mathbb{Z}_q) \times \chi^n \times \chi^n \times \chi \times \mathbb{Z}_q :$$
$$(p_1 = p_0 s + te) \wedge (c_1 = c_0 s + t\tilde{e} + M)\}$$

Similarly, we can let $\mathbf{A}_{Stern} = \begin{bmatrix} c_0, t, 0, 1 \\ p_0, 0, t, 0 \end{bmatrix}$ to be the public parameters and $\mathbf{X}_{Stern} = [s, \tilde{e}, e, M]^T$ and try applying **SternExt** to obtain the ZKPoPK. However, it will not work because the original protocol proves that $\|\mathbf{X}_{Stern}\|_\infty < \beta$. In this situation, we want to prove the bound of separate components differently: in our above example, $\|\tilde{e}\|_\infty > \|e\|_\infty$. In Regev cryptosystem, the problem might not be clear enough as the norm of each vector in $\mathbf{X}_{Stern}$ is quite close to each other but for other latticed-based system, we can see a big difference. For example, if we look at the BV system's decryption relation:

$$R_{BV}^{q,n,t,\chi} = \{((\mathbf{c}_0,\mathbf{c}_1),(\mathbf{p}_0,\mathbf{p}_1),\mathbf{s},\mathbf{e}',\mathbf{e},\mathbf{m} \in (R_q \times R_q) \times (R_q \times R_q) \times \chi^n \times \chi^n \times \chi^n \times R_t :$$
$$(\mathbf{p}_1\mathbf{s} + t\mathbf{e} = -\mathbf{p}_0) \wedge (\mathbf{c}_1\mathbf{s} - t\mathbf{e}' - \mathbf{m} = -\mathbf{c}_0)\}$$

Our *Prover*'s witness in this situation is $\mathbf{X}_{Stern} = [\mathbf{s}, \mathbf{e}', \mathbf{e}, \mathbf{m}]^T$ with $\|\mathbf{m}\|_\infty \ll \|\mathbf{s}\|_\infty \approx \|\mathbf{e}\|_\infty < \|\mathbf{e}'\|_\infty$. Therefore, instead of proving $\|\mathbf{X}_{Stern}\|_\infty < \beta$, we need a proof with different constraints on the witness's components. We present a solution for this problem.

Our construction

The idea. Our first observation is, instead of proving $\|x_i\|_\infty < \beta_i$, or all the coefficients x_i of $\mathbf{x}$ is in the range $\{-\beta_i, \ldots, \beta_i\}$, we can also prove $x_i + \beta_i.f(x)$ is in the range $\{0, \ldots, 2\beta_i\}$, where $f(x) = 1 + x + x^2 + \cdots + x^{n-1}$. Secondly, if we decompose $x_i + \beta_i.f(x)$ to their binary representation and applying the Stern's variant of [25] to prove the relation

$$R_{KTX} = \{((\mathbf{A},\mathbf{y}),\mathbf{x}) \in \mathbb{Z}_q^{n\times m} \times \mathbb{Z}_q^n \times \{0,1\}^m : wt(\mathbf{x}) \wedge \mathbf{A}.\mathbf{x} = \mathbf{y} \mod q\}$$

Then we can obtain the prove for the original relation $R_{BV}^{q,n,t,\chi}$. Note that at this point the *Prover*'s witness is a binary vector, that is, if we need to prove some part of the message is binary, we obtain that goal at this point as well. It is important if we use such proof for latticed-based cryptosystem where the message space is R_2: a proof for ISIS relation is not useful in this situation because it only proves that the infinity norm of the whole witness is less than some $\beta > 2$.

Protocol description. The protocol **SternBV(A,y,x)** works as follows. Let A be a matrix of $m \times l$ ring element ($A \in R_q^{m \times l}$), $\mathbf{x}$ be a vector of l ring elements $\mathbf{x} = \{\mathbf{x}_1, \mathbf{x}_2, \ldots, \mathbf{x}_l\}$ and similarly $\mathbf{y} = \{\mathbf{y}_1, \ldots, \mathbf{y}_m\}$. The protocol includes the following steps.

Step 1. Normalizing the bound of each component x_i of $\mathbf{x}$ from $\{-\beta_i, \ldots, \beta_i\}$ to $\{0, \ldots, 2^{l_i}\}$, where l_i is the smallest integer satisfying $2^{l_i} > (2\beta_i - 1)$. This step is done by one ring multiplication for each $\mathbf{x}_i$, let $x_i' = x_i + \beta_i.\mathbf{f}(x)$, where $f(x) = 1 + x + x^2 + \cdots + x^{n-1}$. After this normalization step, instead of proving the relation $\mathbf{a}_i \mathbf{x}_i = \mathbf{y}_i$ with $\|x_i\|_\infty \in \{-\beta_i, \ldots, \beta_i\}$, we prove $\mathbf{a}_i \mathbf{x}_i' = \mathbf{y}_i'$ with $\|x_i'\|_\infty \in \{0, \ldots, 2^{l_i}\}$, where $\mathbf{y}_i' = \mathbf{y}_i + \mathbf{a}_i \beta_i f(x)$.

Step 2. Decompose $x_i' = x_i + \beta_i$ into their binary representation

$$\mathbf{x}_i'' = \sum_{j=0}^{l_i - 1} 2^j b_j$$

Let $\mathbf{x}''$ be the result ring element that concatenates all $\mathbf{x}_i''$ and has $L = \sum l_i$ coefficients. In this step we need to hide the Hamming Weight of the secret vector $\mathbf{x}_i'$. This hiding task is done by padding:

1. Let ζ_0 and ζ_1 be the number of coefficients of $\mathbf{x}''$ that equal to 0 or 1, respectively.
2. Sample a random vector $\zeta \in \{0, 1\}^L$ that has $(L - \zeta_0)$ coefficients 0 and $(L - \zeta_1)$ coefficients 1.
3. Output $\mathbf{x}_{Stern} = \mathbf{x}''||\zeta$.

The result binary vector $\mathbf{x}_{Stern}$ has length $2L$ and the total number of 0s and 1s in the $\mathbf{x}_{Stern}$ are the same.

Step 3. We denote $rot(\mathbf{c}) \in \mathbb{Z}_Q^{n \times n}$ to be an anti-circulant square matrix, whose first column is $\mathbf{c}$ and the other columns are the cyclic rotations of $\mathbf{c}$ with the cycled entries negated

$$rot(\mathbf{c}) = \begin{bmatrix} c_0 & -c_{n-1} & -c_{n-2} & \cdots \\ c_1 & c_0 & -c_{n-1} & \cdots \\ \cdots & \cdots & \cdots & \cdots \\ c_{n-1} & c_{n-2} & c_{n-3} & \cdots \end{bmatrix}$$

and reconstruct the matrix A with the rot matrices:

$$\forall \mathbf{a}_{i,j} \in \mathbf{A} : \mathbf{a}_{i,j}' = rot(\mathbf{a}_{i,j})$$

The result expanded matrix is denoted $\mathbf{A}'$. We also need to pad the resulting matrix with corresponding number of 0s to make sure $\mathbf{A}'$ complying with all x_i'. Let $\mathbf{A}_{Stern}$ be the padded result.

Step 4. Modify $\mathbf{y}_i$: Let $\mathbf{y}'_i = \mathbf{y}_i + \mathbf{a}_i \beta_i f(x)$ and let $\mathbf{y}_{Stern}$ be the concatenation of all $\mathbf{y}'_i$.

Step 5. Run the Stern protocol as in [28] for the proof of $\mathbf{A}_{Stern} \mathbf{x}_{Stern} = \mathbf{y}_{Stern}$.

Result. Our protocol has the following properties:

- The knowledge extractor produces different x_i with $\|x_i\|_\infty \leq \beta_i$. Inheriting from the original Stern protocol, the extraction gap is $\gamma = 1$.
- The communication cost is $2(n \log q) \sum l_i + commitmentSize$ for each round.
- In the full version of the paper, we also show a variant of this ZKP that allows relations where some coefficients of the witness are unbounded. This is used in the last step of the protocol where we need to prove only the first coefficient of the authentication result.

4.2   Renyi Divergence and Its Application in Noise Masking

Consider the a product ciphertexts result in BV cryptosystem (Sect. 2.2).

$$mult(c, c') = (\mathbf{c}_0 \mathbf{c}'_0, \mathbf{c}_0 \mathbf{c}'_1 + \mathbf{c}_1 \mathbf{c}'_0, \mathbf{c}_1 \mathbf{c}'_1)$$

The noise term of this result ciphertext correlates to both $\mathbf{s}$ and $\mathbf{m}$. In many contexts, this leakage might be fine for a genuine user with a secret key because s/he is supposed to know the key and decrypt the message. However, in many other contexts, especially in multi-factor authentication scenarios, this is not the case. For instance, in our system, we do not want the client to know the Hamming Distance result, so that an attacker with a stolen device and a secret key cannot derive information about the data stored in the server. We propose to mask this leakage by homomorphically adding the ciphertext $Enc(HD)$ with $Enc(r)$ to refresh the noise terms, together with masking the Hamming Distance. The question is how much we need to shift the original noise distribution to preserve correctness while providing the new security measure. We use Renyi Divergence analysis to answer the question.

Let D_1 and D_2 be the probability distributions of the original noise in the ciphertext $Enc(HD)$ and the new shifted noise of $Enc(HD+r)$. We observe that the 2 distributions are identical Gaussian distribution with the same standard deviation σ and different means. Let r_0 be the shifted in means of D_1 and D_2. Our goal is to set up parameter r_0 such that D_1 and D_2 are statistically indistinguishable while keeping other parameters of the cryptosystem within practical performance thresholds. Statistical Distance (SD) is normally used to measure the difference of distributions and is generally bounded by

$$SD(D_1, D_2) = \frac{1}{2} \sum_{x \in X} |D_1(x) - D_2(x)| \leq K \times \frac{r_0}{\sigma}$$

where K is a constant. We quickly see that in order for SD to be indistinguishable ($SD < \epsilon \approx \frac{1}{2^\lambda}$, where λ is the security parameter), the standard deviation of the initial noise needs to be really large, which is $\sigma \geq K r_0 2^\lambda$.

In the work of [3], the authors proposed Renyi Divergence (RD) as an alternative to measure distributions closeness and its applications to security proofs. $R_a(D_1\|D_2)$ of order a between D_1 and D_2 is defined as the expected value of $(D_1(x)/D_2(x))^{a-1}$ over the randomness of x sampled from D_1.

$$R_a(D_1\|D_2) = \left(\sum_{x \in D_1} \frac{D_1(x)^a}{D_2(x)^{a-1}} \right)^{\frac{1}{a-1}}$$

Similar to SD, RD is useful in our context with its *Probability Preservation* property (we refer readers to [3] for detailed formal descriptions): Given D_1 and D_2 as described, for any event E, for instance, we want to look at $D_2(E)$ is the winning probability of the attacker in the distinguishing game, the probability of the event with respect to D_2 is bounded by

$$D_2(E) \geq D_1(E)^{\frac{a}{a-1}} / RD_a(D1\|D2) \tag{1}$$

Particularly, if we look at the second order $(a = 2)$ of RD like previous work [26], we would have $D_2(E) \geq D_1(E)^2/RD_2(D1\|D2)$. Provided that the distribution functions of D_1 and D_2 are discrete Gaussian on lattices, which are of the form $\rho_\sigma(x) = \frac{1}{\sigma}e^{-\pi \frac{x^2}{\sigma^2}}$, we have $RD_2(D_1\|D_2) = e^{2\pi \frac{r_0^2}{\sigma^2}} \approx e^{2\pi}$, when r_0 is much smaller than σ. That means when switching from D_1 to D_2, the success probability of E will be at least the old probability to the power of 2 divided by some constant. This squaring factor brings a big trade-off, for example, in our protocol, we would need to use $FAR = 2^{-20}$ in the non-privacy biometric settings to get $FAR = 2^{-10}$ in our scheme.

We aim at a solution to remove this factor. The idea is to look at RD_∞ instead of RD_2: from Eq. (1), we can see that when a is large, $\frac{a}{a-1}$ becomes 1. However, for usual Gaussian distributions, RD_∞ is also infinity (not a constant $e^{2\pi}$ like in RD_2 when $a = 2$). This is due to the ratios $\frac{D_1(x)}{D_2(x)}$ becoming large when samplings are in the extreme tails of the distributions. Our idea is to truncate the distribution when doing noise sampling: if we get a noise value that is too far in the tail, we reject and sample again. As a result, the truncated distribution grows slightly, that means, the small noises have a bit higher probability when sampling, which does not have a big impact in security.

For the following analysis, let D_1 to be a discrete Gaussian on $\mathbb{Z}$ with deviation parameter σ shifted by the constant $r_0 \in \mathbb{Z}$, while D_2 is a discrete Gaussian on $\mathbb{Z}$ with dev. par. σ centered on zero, i.e. $D_1 = D_{\mathbb{Z},\sigma} + r_0$ and $D_2 = D_{\mathbb{Z},\sigma}$, where $D_{\mathbb{Z},\sigma}(x) = e^{-\pi \cdot x^2/\sigma^2} / \sum_{z \in \mathbb{Z}} e^{-\pi \cdot z^2/\sigma^2}$ for $x \in \mathbb{Z}$. To allow us to use RD_∞ we use tail-cut variants $D_1^{(cut)}$ and $D_2^{(cut)}$ of D_1 and D_2, respectively with parameter k. The parameter k defines where D_1 and D_2 are cut at, for example, we can set $k = 3$ to cut the distributions at 3 deviation parameters from the mean. So, we let $D_{\mathbb{Z},\sigma}^{(cut)}$ denote distribution $D_{\mathbb{Z},\sigma}$ tail-cutted to the interval $[-k\cdot\sigma, k\cdot\sigma]$ by rejection sampling. We let $D_1^{(cut)} = D_{\mathbb{Z},\sigma}^{(cut)} + r_0$ and $D_2^{(cut)} = D_{\mathbb{Z},\sigma}^{(cut)}$. Notice that the supports of $D_1^{(cut)}$ and $D_2^{(cut)}$ are different, namely $Supp(D_1^{(cut)}) = [-k\sigma+r_0, k\sigma+r_0]$

while $Supp(D_2^{(cut)}) = [-k\sigma, k\sigma]$. We assume, without loss of generality, that $r_0 > 0$. We would like to switch from distribution $D_1^{(cut)}$ to $D_2^{(cut)}$, but unfortunately $R_\infty(\overline{D}_1^{(cut)} \| D_2^{(cut)})$ is not finite since $Supp(D_1^{(cut)})$ is not a subset of $Supp(D_2^{(cut)})$. To satisfy the latter condition, we first switch from $D_1^{(cut)}$ to $\overline{D}_1^{(cut)}$ by further cutting (by rejection sampling) the positive tail of $D_1^{(cut)}$ to ensure it does not go beyond the $k\sigma$ upper bound on tail of $D_2^{(cut)}$, and use a (mild condition) statistical distance step to lower bound $\overline{D}_1^{(cut)}(E)$. Then, in a second step using $Supp(\overline{D}_1^{(cut)}) = [-k\sigma + r_0, k\sigma] \subseteq [-k\sigma, k\sigma] = Supp(D_2^{(cut)})$, we derive a finite upper bound on $R_\infty(\overline{D}_1^{(cut)} \| D_2^{(cut)})$ to lower bound $D_2^{(cut)}(E)$. Details follow.

First SD Step. Since $Supp(D_1^{(cut)})$ is transformed into $\overline{D}_1^{(cut)}$ by rejection and resampling if a sample of $Supp(D_1^{(cut)})$ falls in $(k\sigma, k\sigma + r_0]$, we have $SD(D_1^{(cut)}, \overline{D}_1^{(cut)}) \le D_1^{(cut)}((k\sigma, k\sigma + r_0]) = D_2^{(cut)}((k\sigma - r_0, k\sigma]) = D_{\mathbb{Z},\sigma}((k\sigma - r_0, k\sigma])/C_2$, where $C_2 = D_{\mathbb{Z},\sigma}([-k\sigma, k\sigma])$. Now, we have

$$\Delta \overset{\text{def}}{=} \frac{D_{\mathbb{Z},\sigma}((k\sigma - r_0, k\sigma])}{C_2} = \frac{\sum_{z \in (k\sigma - r_0, k\sigma]} e^{-\pi z^2/\sigma^2}}{\sum_{z \in [-k\sigma, k\sigma]} e^{-\pi z^2/\sigma^2}}.$$

For the numerator, we have an upper bound $\sum_{z \in (k\sigma - r_0, k\sigma]} e^{-\pi z^2/\sigma^2} \le \int_{k\sigma - r_0}^\infty e^{-\pi z^2/\sigma^2} dz \le \sigma \cdot e^{-\pi(k\sigma - r_0)^2/\sigma^2}$, using the standard normal distribution upper bound $\int_\gamma^\infty \frac{1}{\sqrt{2\pi}\sigma} \cdot e^{-z^2/\sigma^2} dz \le e^{-\gamma^2/(2\sigma^2)}$ for $\gamma \ge 0$. For the denominator, we have a lower bound $\sum_{z \in [-k\sigma, k\sigma]} e^{-\pi z^2/\sigma^2} \ge 2 \cdot \sum_{z \in [0, k\sigma]} e^{-\pi z^2/\sigma^2} \ge 2 \cdot (\int_0^\infty e^{-\pi z^2/\sigma^2} dz - \int_{k\sigma}^\infty e^{-\pi z^2/\sigma^2} dz) \ge \sigma \cdot (1 - 2 \cdot e^{-\pi(k\sigma - r_0)^2/\sigma^2})$. Therefore, $SD(D_1^{(cut)}, \overline{D}_1^{(cut)}) \le \Delta \le \delta'/(1 - 2\delta') \le 2\delta'$ if $\delta' \le 1/4$, where $\delta' = e^{-\pi(k\sigma - r_0)^2/\sigma^2}$. Defining $\delta = 2\delta'$, we have $\Delta \le \delta$ if $\delta \le 1/8$ and the conditions $r_0 \le \sigma$ and $k \ge 1 + \sqrt{1/\pi \cdot \ln(2/\delta)}$ hold. Therefore, for any event E we have $\overline{D}_1^{(cut)}(E) \ge D_1^{(cut)}(E) - \delta$.

Second RD step. The desired RD of order ∞ is defined by

$$R_\infty(\overline{D}_1^{(cut)} \| D_2^{(cut)})) = \max_{x \in [-k\sigma + r_0, k\sigma]} \frac{\overline{D}_1^{(cut)}}{D_2^{(cut)}(x)}.$$

Observe that, for each $x \in [-k\sigma + r_0, k\sigma]$, we have $\overline{D}_1^{(cut)}(x) = C \cdot D_1^{(cut)}(x)$, where the normalization constant $C = \frac{1}{1 - D_1^{(cut)}((k\sigma, k\sigma + r_0])} = \frac{1}{1 - D_2^{(cut)}((-k\sigma + r_0, k\sigma])} = \frac{1}{1 - \Delta}$, where Δ is defined and upper bounded by δ above under the assumed conditions on k and δ. Since the $D_1^{(cut)}(x)$ and $D_2^{(cut)}(x)$ are shifts of each other, they have the same rejection sampling normalization constant with respect to D_1 (resp. D_2). Therefore, $D_1^{(cut)}(x)/D_2^{(cut)}(x) =$

$D_1(x)/D_2(x)$ for each x in the support of both $D_1^{(cut)}$ and $D_2^{(cut)}$, and we have

$$R_\infty(\overline{D}_1^{(cut)} \| D_2^{(cut)}) \leq \frac{1}{1-\delta} \cdot \max_{x \in [-k\sigma+r_0, k\sigma]} \frac{D_1(x)}{D_2(x)}$$

$$= \max_{x \in [-k\sigma, k\sigma]} \frac{e^{\frac{-\pi(x-r_0)^2}{\sigma^2}}}{e^{-\pi \frac{x^2}{\sigma^2}}}$$

$$= e^{\pi \cdot r_0^2/\sigma^2} \cdot \max_{x \in [-k\sigma+r_0, k\sigma]} e^{\frac{2\pi r_0}{\sigma^2} x}$$

This is an exponential function and we get the max value at $x = k\sigma$:

$$R_\infty(\overline{D}_1^{(cut)} \| D_2^{(cut)}) = e^{1/(1-\delta)} \cdot e^{\pi \cdot r_0^2/\sigma^2 + 2\pi k \cdot r_0/\sigma}.$$

Since $0 < \delta \leq 1/8$, the first factor above is $\leq 1 + 2\delta \leq e^{2\delta}$. Also, a simple computation shows that the second factor is $\leq e$ if the condition $\sigma/r_0 \geq 4\pi \cdot k$ is satisfied using $k \geq 1$. We conclude, under the assumed parameter conditions that $R_\infty(\overline{D}_1^{(cut)} \| D_2^{(cut)})) \leq e^{1+2\delta} = c'(\delta)$ is constant for constant $\delta > 0$, so that, by the RD probability preservation property $D_2^{(cut)}(E) \geq \frac{1}{c(\delta)} \cdot \overline{D}_1^{(cut)}(E) \geq \frac{1}{c(\delta)} \cdot (D_1^{(cut)}(E) - \delta)$. Note that if $D_1^{(cut)}(E) = \varepsilon$, then by choosing $\delta = \varepsilon/2$, we get $D_2^{(cut)}(E) \geq \frac{1}{2c(\delta)} \cdot \varepsilon$, and we only need $k \geq 1 + \sqrt{1/\pi \cdot \ln(2/\delta)}$ and σ/r_0 logarithmic in $1/\delta$, much smaller than σ/r_0 linear in $1/\delta$, which we would need if we were to use the 'SD only' analysis approach.

The above discussion immediately generalizes from the one-dimensional case of discrete Gaussian samples over $\mathbb{Z}$ to the m-dimensional case of discrete Gaussian samples over $\mathbb{Z}^m$ due to the independence of the m coordinates. The only changes to the above argument is that the statistical distance in the 'SD step' can multiply by at most a factor m, whereas the RD in the 'RD step' above gets raised to the m'th power, where we replace r_0 by $\|r_0\|_\infty$. We compensate for this by replacing the bound δ on Δ in the above analysis by the bound δ/m. We have therefore proved the following result used in our impersonation security proof, which improved upon the R_2-based analogue result for shifted Gaussians stated in [26].

Lemma 2. *For integer $m \geq 1$, real $\sigma > 0$, $k \geq 1$, real $0 < \delta \leq 1/8$ and vector $r_0 \in \mathbb{Z}^m$, let $D_1^{(cut)} = D_{\mathbb{Z}^m, \sigma}^{(cut)} + r_0$ and $D_2^{(cut)} = D_{\mathbb{Z}^m, \sigma}^{(cut)}$ be relatively shifted tail-cut discrete Gaussian distributions, where $D_{\mathbb{Z}^m, \sigma}^{(cut)}$ is the discrete Gaussian $D_{\mathbb{Z}^m, \sigma}$ with its tails cut to the support $[-k\sigma, k\sigma]^m$ by rejection sampling. If the conditions $k \geq 1 + \sqrt{1/\pi \cdot \ln(2m/\delta)}$ and $\sigma/\|r_0\|_\infty \geq 4\pi \cdot k \cdot m$ hold, then, for any event E defined over the support of $D_1^{(cut)}$ we have*

$$D_2^{(cut)}(E) \geq \frac{1}{2e^{1+2\delta}} \cdot \left(D_1^{(cut)}(E) - \delta \right).$$

5   Result Evaluation

5.1   Parameters

We consider how to set concrete parameters. According to the best known lattice attack [2] and the result of Lemma 1, we can choose ($\alpha q = 3, t = 4096, n = 4096, q \approx 2^{71}$) to have security level $\lambda \approx 156$ for classical attack and $\lambda \approx 142$ for quantum attack. The plaintext space ring R_t should cover enough biometrics data upto 4096 bits. The proposed scheme works with only 1 level of homomorphic multiplication, computation time is approximately 0.01 s and communication size is approximately 12 MB. The experiments ran on an Intel core i7 at 3.1 GHz with 16 GB memory, the computations in the ring R_q were done with Sagemath.

5.2   Limitations and Open Problems

We expose the HD to the server in the last step of the protocol and let the server do the threshold comparison operation in the plaintext domain. We assume that given such value, the server should not be able to learn any information about the original bit strings template. This assumption may hold in practice if HD between registered and queried templates corresponds to biometric measurement noise with a probability distribution that is independent of the templates themselves, but needs further investigation for specific biometric systems. Doing the comparison of HD with threshold homomorphically is much less efficient and removing this assumption is left as an open problem.

Also, we assume honest but curious server, that is reasonable against passive exposure attacks. Active attacks are harder to do undetected and slower provided that the server can be audited regularly. We emphasize that previous quantum resistant protocols also made this assumption, and did not even defend against passive honest but curious trusted party. Defending against malicious server privacy is left as an open problem.

Finally, the communication size of Stern-based ZKP protocol is large due to the round soundness error 2/3 (many communication rounds will be needed for security). We leave the problem of how to reduce such overhead for future works.

6   Related Work

In a biometric authentication system, a user $\mathcal{U}$ first enrols his fingerprint template X with the server $\mathcal{S}$. $\mathcal{U}$ later authenticates with $\mathcal{S}$ using the same finger with a template Y, $\mathcal{S}$ uses an algorithm $Verify(X, Y)$ to obtain the result of the authentication: **Accept** or **Reject**. Different biometric system might use different methods to compute the distance Δ between X and Y in the algorithm $Verify$. The distance Δ is compared to some predifined threshold value τ to determine the result of the authentication. We refer the reader to [22] for biometric feature extraction and comparison techniques. In this work, we consider the biometric data are represented as binary codes and HD is used to measure the similarity between two of them. We refer the readers to [11] or [1] for examples of 2048-bit iris codes generation and HD comparison.

There are three main approaches for privacy-preserving biometric authentication [4,23,24]. In the *Feature transformation approach* (cancelable biometrics or biohashing, such as [9,49]), the template data are encrypted using a client's key, it is single factor and not secure if the key is leaked. The *Biometric cryptosystem approach* (fuzzy vault and fuzzy commitment, [33,50]) is based on error correcting codes and it is not well understood the tradeoff between biometric accuracy and security. We focus our work on the last approach, *Homomorphic Encryption*, which seems to be the best candidate to provide all of the system design requirements mentioned.

The idea was first proposed in 2006 ([42]) using addictive homomorphic system Paillier [36]. In 2010, Osadchy et al. [34] providing privacy-preserving feature by combining Paillier system with oblivious transfer protocol. SCiFI uses 900-bit vector to represent face image data and Hamming Distance (HD) to compare two vectors. [6] developed a similar system for iris and fingerprints but using DGK cryptosystem [10] and garble circuit technique instead, they represented biometric data as 2048-bit vectors and also used HD for threshold comparison. [52] proposed an approach based on Somewhat Homomorphic Encryption (SHE) [7], they introduced a ciphertext packing technique to speed up the HD computation operation. There have been variations and improvements over time ([31,44], etc.). However, most of the protocols are only secure against a semi-honest client, many relied on one or more trusted third parties with the client's secret key to decrypt the HD.

7   Conclusion

We defined the formal model of secure biometric authentication and proposed a protocol that satisfies such definition. Our scheme does not rely on a trusted third party to do the verification but does both of distance computation and comparison homomorphically on ciphertexts of templates. Such setting require stronger security requirements, especially on the client-side of the protocol. The application of ZKP techniques let the system work in malicious client, HBC server model with the assumption that the server can be audited periodically. We also introduced Renyi Divergence in the security analysis to allow practical settings for the scheme. Future works include optimizing the algorithms, parameters, and implementation for practical applications and security levels, extending the method to other low-FRR biometric verification algorithms or applying the homomorphic and ZKP techniques to provide malicious client model for lattice-based protocols.

References

1. Fujitsu develops world's first slide-style vein authentication technology based on palm veins - Fujitsu global. http://www.fujitsu.com/global/about/resources/news/press-releases/2017/0110-01.html. Accessed 23 Jan 2017
2. Alkim, E., Ducas, L., Pöppelmann, T., Schwabe, P.: Post-quantum key exchange-a new hope. In: USENIX Security Symposium, pp. 327–343 (2016)
3. Bai, S., Langlois, A., Lepoint, T., Stehlé, D., Steinfeld, R.: Improved security proofs in lattice-based cryptography: using the Rényi divergence rather than the statistical distance. In: Iwata, T., Cheon, J.H. (eds.) ASIACRYPT 2015. LNCS, vol. 9452, pp. 3–24. Springer, Heidelberg (2015). https://doi.org/10.1007/978-3-662-48797-6_1
4. Belguechi, R., Alimi, V., Cherrier, E., Lacharme, P., Rosenberger, C., et al.: An overview on privacy preserving biometrics. In: Recent Application in Biometrics, pp. 65–84 (2011)
5. Bellare, M., Goldreich, O.: On defining proofs of knowledge. In: Brickell, E.F. (ed.) CRYPTO 1992. LNCS, vol. 740, pp. 390–420. Springer, Heidelberg (1993). https://doi.org/10.1007/3-540-48071-4_28
6. Blanton, M., Gasti, P.: Secure and efficient protocols for iris and fingerprint identification. In: Atluri, V., Diaz, C. (eds.) ESORICS 2011. LNCS, vol. 6879, pp. 190–209. Springer, Heidelberg (2011). https://doi.org/10.1007/978-3-642-23822-2_11
7. Brakerski, Z., Vaikuntanathan, V.: Fully homomorphic encryption from ring-lwe and security for key dependent messages. In: Rogaway, P. (ed.) CRYPTO 2011. LNCS, vol. 6841, pp. 505–524. Springer, Heidelberg (2011). https://doi.org/10.1007/978-3-642-22792-9_29
8. Bringer, J., Chabanne, H., Izabachène, M., Pointcheval, D., Tang, Q., Zimmer, S.: An application of the Goldwasser-Micali cryptosystem to biometric authentication. In: Pieprzyk, J., Ghodosi, H., Dawson, E. (eds.) ACISP 2007. LNCS, vol. 4586, pp. 96–106. Springer, Heidelberg (2007). https://doi.org/10.1007/978-3-540-73458-1_8
9. Cappelli, R., Ferrara, M., Maltoni, D.: Minutia cylinder-code: a new representation and matching technique for fingerprint recognition. IEEE Trans. Pattern Anal. Mach. Intell. 32(12), 2128–2141 (2010)
10. Damgard, I., Geisler, M., Kroigard, M.: Homomorphic encryption and secure comparison. Int. J. Appl. Cryptography 1(1), 22–31 (2008)
11. Daugman, J.: The importance of being random: statistical principles of iris recognition. Pattern Recogn. 36(2), 279–291 (2003)
12. Erkin, Z., Franz, M., Guajardo, J., Katzenbeisser, S., Lagendijk, I., Toft, T.: Privacy-preserving face recognition. In: Goldberg, I., Atallah, M.J. (eds.) PETS 2009. LNCS, vol. 5672, pp. 235–253. Springer, Heidelberg (2009). https://doi.org/10.1007/978-3-642-03168-7_14
13. Feige, U., Fiat, A., Shamir, A.: Zero-knowledge proofs of identity. J. Cryptol. 1(2), 77–94 (1988)
14. FVC-ongoing. https://biolab.csr.unibo.it/FVCOnGoing/UI/Form/Home.aspx. Accessed 12 Apr 2016
15. Gentry, C.: A fully homomorphic encryption scheme. Ph.D. thesis, Stanford University (2009). crypto.stanford.edu/craig
16. Gentry, C., Halevi, S., Vaikuntanathan, V.: i-Hop homomorphic encryption and rerandomizable Yao circuits. In: Rabin, T. (ed.) CRYPTO 2010. LNCS, vol. 6223, pp. 155–172. Springer, Heidelberg (2010). https://doi.org/10.1007/978-3-642-14623-7_9

17. Gentry, C., Sahai, A., Waters, B.: Homomorphic encryption from learning with errors: conceptually-simpler, asymptotically-faster, attribute-based. In: Canetti, R., Garay, J.A. (eds.) CRYPTO 2013. LNCS, vol. 8042, pp. 75–92. Springer, Heidelberg (2013). https://doi.org/10.1007/978-3-642-40041-4_5

18. Goldwasser, S., Micali, S., Rackoff, C.: The knowledge complexity of interactive proof systems. SIAM J. Comput. **18**(1), 186–208 (1989)

19. Higo, H., Isshiki, T., Mori, K., Obana, S.: Privacy-preserving fingerprint authentication resistant to hill-climbing attacks. In: Dunkelman, O., Keliher, L. (eds.) SAC 2015. LNCS, vol. 9566, pp. 44–64. Springer, Cham (2016). https://doi.org/10.1007/978-3-319-31301-6_3

20. Hirano, T., Hattori, M., Ito, T., Matsuda, N.: Cryptographically-secure and efficient remote cancelable biometrics based on public-key homomorphic encryption. In: Sakiyama, K., Terada, M. (eds.) IWSEC 2013. LNCS, vol. 8231, pp. 183–200. Springer, Heidelberg (2013). https://doi.org/10.1007/978-3-642-41383-4_12

21. Ishai, Y., Paskin, A.: Evaluating branching programs on encrypted data. In: Vadhan, S.P. (ed.) TCC 2007. LNCS, vol. 4392, pp. 575–594. Springer, Heidelberg (2007). https://doi.org/10.1007/978-3-540-70936-7_31

22. Jain, A., Flynn, P., Ross, A.A.: Handbook of Biometrics. Springer, New York (2007)

23. Jain, A.K., Nandakumar, K., Nagar, A.: Biometric template security. EURASIP J. Adv. Sig. Process. **2008**, 113 (2008)

24. Jain, A.K., Nandakumar, K., Ross, A.: 50 years of biometric research: accomplishments, challenges, and opportunities. Pattern Recogn. Lett. **79**, 80–105 (2016)

25. Kawachi, A., Tanaka, K., Xagawa, K.: Concurrently secure identification schemes based on the worst-case hardness of lattice problems. In: Pieprzyk, J. (ed.) ASIACRYPT 2008. LNCS, vol. 5350, pp. 372–389. Springer, Heidelberg (2008). https://doi.org/10.1007/978-3-540-89255-7_23

26. Langlois, A., Stehlé, D., Steinfeld, R.: GGHLite: more efficient multilinear maps from ideal lattices. In: Nguyen, P.Q., Oswald, E. (eds.) EUROCRYPT 2014. LNCS, vol. 8441, pp. 239–256. Springer, Heidelberg (2014). https://doi.org/10.1007/978-3-642-55220-5_14

27. Lauter, K., Naehrig, M., Vaikuntanathan, V.: Can homomorphic encryption be practical? Cryptology ePrint Archive, Report 2011/405 (2011). http://eprint.iacr.org/2011/405

28. Ling, S., Nguyen, K., Stehlé, D., Wang, H.: Improved zero-knowledge proofs of knowledge for the ISIS problem, and applications. In: Kurosawa, K., Hanaoka, G. (eds.) PKC 2013. LNCS, vol. 7778, pp. 107–124. Springer, Heidelberg (2013). https://doi.org/10.1007/978-3-642-36362-7_8

29. Lyubashevsky, V.: Lattice-based identification schemes secure under active attacks. In: Cramer, R. (ed.) PKC 2008. LNCS, vol. 4939, pp. 162–179. Springer, Heidelberg (2008). https://doi.org/10.1007/978-3-540-78440-1_10

30. Lyubashevsky, V., Peikert, C., Regev, O.: On ideal lattices and learning with errors over rings. In: Gilbert, H. (ed.) EUROCRYPT 2010. LNCS, vol. 6110, pp. 1–23. Springer, Heidelberg (2010). https://doi.org/10.1007/978-3-642-13190-5_1

31. Mandal, A., Roy, A., Yasuda, M.: Comprehensive and improved secure biometric system using homomorphic encryption. In: Garcia-Alfaro, J., Navarro-Arribas, G., Aldini, A., Martinelli, F., Suri, N. (eds.) DPM/QASA -2015. LNCS, vol. 9481, pp. 183–198. Springer, Cham (2016). https://doi.org/10.1007/978-3-319-29883-2_12

32. Micciancio, D., Vadhan, S.P.: Statistical zero-knowledge proofs with efficient provers: lattice problems and more. In: Boneh, D. (ed.) CRYPTO 2003. LNCS, vol. 2729, pp. 282–298. Springer, Heidelberg (2003). https://doi.org/10.1007/978-3-540-45146-4_17

33. Nagar, A., Nandakumar, K., Jain, A.K.: A hybrid biometric cryptosystem for securing fingerprint minutiae templates. Pattern Recogn. Lett. 31(8), 733–741 (2010)

34. Osadchy, M., Pinkas, B., Jarrous, A., Moskovich, B.: SCiFI-a system for secure face identification. In: 2010 IEEE Symposium on Security and Privacy (SP), pp. 239–254. IEEE (2010)

35. Ostrovsky, R., Paskin-Cherniavsky, A., Paskin-Cherniavsky, B.: Maliciously circuit-private FHE. In: Garay, J.A., Gennaro, R. (eds.) CRYPTO 2014. LNCS, vol. 8616, pp. 536–553. Springer, Heidelberg (2014). https://doi.org/10.1007/978-3-662-44371-2_30

36. Paillier, P.: Public-key cryptosystems based on composite degree residuosity classes. In: Stern, J. (ed.) EUROCRYPT 1999. LNCS, vol. 1592, pp. 223–238. Springer, Heidelberg (1999). https://doi.org/10.1007/3-540-48910-X_16

37. Peterson, A.: OPM says 5.6 million fingerprints stolen in cyberattack, five times as many as previously thought. The Washington Post, 23 September 2015

38. Rackoff, C., Simon, D.R.: Non-interactive zero-knowledge proof of knowledge and chosen ciphertext attack. In: Feigenbaum, J. (ed.) CRYPTO 1991. LNCS, vol. 576, pp. 433–444. Springer, Heidelberg (1992). https://doi.org/10.1007/3-540-46766-1_35

39. Regev, O.: On lattices, learning with errors, random linear codes, and cryptography. J. ACM (JACM) 56(6), 34 (2009)

40. Rivest, R.L., Adleman, L., Dertouzos, M.L.: On data banks and privacy homomorphisms. Found. Secure Comput. 4(11), 169–180 (1978)

41. Sander, T., Young, A., Yung, M.: Non-interactive cryptocomputing for NC/SUP 1. In: 40th Annual Symposium on Foundations of Computer Science, pp. 554–566. IEEE (1999)

42. Schoenmakers, B., Tuyls, P.: Efficient binary conversion for Paillier encrypted values. In: Vaudenay, S. (ed.) EUROCRYPT 2006. LNCS, vol. 4004, pp. 522–537. Springer, Heidelberg (2006). https://doi.org/10.1007/11761679_31

43. Šeděnka, J., Govindarajan, S., Gasti, P., Balagani, K.S.: Secure outsourced biometric authentication with performance evaluation on smartphones. IEEE Trans. Inf. Forensics Secur. 10(2), 384–396 (2015)

44. Shahandashti, S.F., Safavi-Naini, R., Ogunbona, P.: Private fingerprint matching. In: Susilo, W., Mu, Y., Seberry, J. (eds.) ACISP 2012. LNCS, vol. 7372, pp. 426–433. Springer, Heidelberg (2012). https://doi.org/10.1007/978-3-642-31448-3_32

45. Smart, N.P., Vercauteren, F.: Fully homomorphic SIMD operations. Des. Codes Crypt. 71(1), 1–25 (2014)

46. Stehlé, D., Steinfeld, R.: Faster fully homomorphic encryption. Cryptology ePrint Archive, Report 2010/299 (2010). http://eprint.iacr.org/2010/299

47. Stehlé, D., Steinfeld, R., Tanaka, K., Xagawa, K.: Efficient public key encryption based on ideal lattices. In: Matsui, M. (ed.) ASIACRYPT 2009. LNCS, vol. 5912, pp. 617–635. Springer, Heidelberg (2009). https://doi.org/10.1007/978-3-642-10366-7_36

48. Stern, J.: A new identification scheme based on syndrome decoding. In: Stinson, D.R. (ed.) CRYPTO 1993. LNCS, vol. 773, pp. 13–21. Springer, Heidelberg (1994). https://doi.org/10.1007/3-540-48329-2_2

49. Teoh, A.B., Kuan, Y.W., Lee, S.: Cancellable biometrics and annotations on biohash. Pattern Recogn. 41(6), 2034–2044 (2008)

50. Uludag, U., Pankanti, S., Prabhakar, S., Jain, A.K.: Biometric cryptosystems: issues and challenges. Proc. IEEE **92**(6), 948–960 (2004)
51. van Dijk, M., Gentry, C., Halevi, S., Vaikuntanathan, V.: Fully homomorphic encryption over the integers. In: Gilbert, H. (ed.) EUROCRYPT 2010. LNCS, vol. 6110, pp. 24–43. Springer, Heidelberg (2010). https://doi.org/10.1007/978-3-642-13190-5_2
52. Yasuda, M., Shimoyama, T., Kogure, J., Yokoyama, K., Koshiba, T.: Practical packing method in somewhat homomorphic encryption. In: Garcia-Alfaro, J., Lioudakis, G., Cuppens-Boulahia, N., Foley, S., Fitzgerald, W.M. (eds.) DPM/SETOP -2013. LNCS, vol. 8247, pp. 34–50. Springer, Heidelberg (2014). https://doi.org/10.1007/978-3-642-54568-9_3

Enhancement for Secure Multiple Matrix Multiplications over Ring-LWE Homomorphic Encryption

Pradeep Kumar Mishra[1], Dung Hoang Duong[2], and Masaya Yasuda[2(✉)]

[1] Graduate School of Mathematics, Kyushu University,
744 Motooka Nishi-ku, Fukuoka 819-0395, Japan
p-mishra@math.kyushu-u.ac.jp
[2] Institute of Mathematics for Industry, Kyushu University,
744 Motooka Nishi-ku, Fukuoka 819-0395, Japan
duong@math.kyushu-u.ac.jp, yasuda@imi.kyushu-u.ac.jp

Abstract. Homomorphic encryption allows to perform various calculations on encrypted data without decryption. In this paper, we propose an efficient method for secure multiple matrix multiplications over the somewhat homomorphic encryption scheme proposed by Brakerski and Vaikuntanathan. Our method is a generalization of Duong et al.'s method, which computes only one multiplication between two matrices. In order to minimize both the ciphertext size and the computation cost, our method packs every matrix into a single ciphertext so that it enables efficient matrix multiplications over the packed ciphertexts. We also propose several modifications to obtain practical performance of secure multiplications among matrices with larger size and entries. We show implementation results of our packing method with modifications for secure multiplications among two and three matrices with 32×32 and 64×64 sizes and entries from 16-bit to 64-bit.

Keywords: Ring-based somewhat homomorphic encryption
Secure matrix multiplications · Packing methods · CRT method

1 Introduction

The development of cloud computing in recent years allows users to outsource their data in the cloud. However, security and privacy concerns for both consumers and businesses have risen at the same time. An excellent way to address such issues is to store all the data in encrypted format and perform computations on the encrypted data. Homomorphic encryption can support meaningful operations on encrypted data, and it has been expected to give a powerful tool in cloud computing. The concept of homomorphic encryption was first introduced by Rivest et al. in 1978 [17]. The first scheme of fully homomorphic encryption (FHE) that supports arbitrary operations on encrypted data was constructed by Gentry in 2009 [8]. After Gentry's breakthrough, a number of FHE schemes

© Springer International Publishing AG 2017
J. K. Liu and P. Samarati (Eds.): ISPEC 2017, LNCS 10701, pp. 320–330, 2017.
https://doi.org/10.1007/978-3-319-72359-4_18

have been proposed and improved. However, currently known FHE schemes are yet impractical (e.g., the state-of-the-art bootstrapping [5] takes less than 0.1 s to refresh the error of a ciphertext for arbitrary operations). On the other hand, the Paillier scheme [14] and the BGN scheme [1] are practical but their functionality is very limited. Actually, the Paillier scheme (resp., the BGN scheme) can support only additions (resp., additions and one-depth multiplications). In contrast, somewhat homomorphic encryption (SHE) schemes, initially used as building blocks for FHE construction, have recently attracted a lot of attention from various communities. Compared to FHE, such SHE schemes can support only a limited number of additions and multiplications, but they are applicable in various scenarios with reasonable performance.

Costache and Smart [6] compared several features of ring-based SHE schemes such as the BGV [3], FV [10], YASHE [2], and NTRU [13] schemes (see also [12] for a comparison of FV and YASHE). They showed that the BGV scheme is more efficient for large plaintext space than other schemes. In this paper, we choose to use the BV scheme proposed by Brakerski and Vaikuntanathan [4] as an alternative of the BGV scheme for secure multiplications among matrices with large entries, since both schemes have similar structure and the BV scheme is much easier to understand and implement. The security of the BV scheme relies on a simplified version of ring-LWE (Learning with Errors) assumption. Over the BV scheme, Lauter et al. [11] proposed a method to pack an integer of large size into a single ciphertext so that it enables to efficiently compute secure sums and products over the integers. After that, Yasuda et al. [18] proposed a new packing method for secure multiple inner products, and it is efficient only for very small entries so they modified their method for large size entries [19]. Later, Duong et al. [7] proposed several packing methods for secure matrix multiplication, using the idea of Yasuda et al.'s methods [18,19]. (A very similar method to [7] is presented in [15, Sect. 6], but no implementation result is reported.)

Our Contributions. While the method of [7] enables secure multiplication between two matrices only, we generalize the method for secure *multiple matrix multiplications*. The BV scheme uses $R = \mathbb{Z}[x]/(x^n + 1)$ as the base ring and $R_t = R/tR$ as the plaintext space for two parameters n and t. For a secure multiplication between two matrices $\mathbf{A}$ and $\mathbf{B}$, a main ingredient of [7] is to pack $\mathbf{A}$ and $\mathbf{B}$ into two types of polynomial over R, and then encrypt the polynomials. Homomorphic property of the BV scheme enables to compute all the entries of $\mathbf{A} \times \mathbf{B}$ over packed ciphertexts. Our basic strategy for multiple matrix multiplications $\mathbf{A}_1 \times \cdots \times \mathbf{A}_\ell$ is to adopt the two types of polynomial transformation of [7] for $\mathbf{A}_1 \times \cdots \times \mathbf{A}_{\ell-1}$ and $\mathbf{A}_\ell$. More specifically, we pack $\mathbf{A}_1$ by the first transformation of [7], and flip the columns of $\mathbf{A}_2, \ldots, \mathbf{A}_{\ell-1}$ and pack them using a method similar to $\mathbf{A}_1$ to obtain the entries of $\mathbf{A}_1 \times \cdots \times \mathbf{A}_{\ell-1}$ in polynomial format. In contrast, we make use of the second transformation of [7] for $\mathbf{A}_\ell$. But we take an appropriate jump for exponents of the variable x greater than the total degree of polynomials over R corresponding to the matrices $\mathbf{A}_1, \ldots, \mathbf{A}_{\ell-1}$, in order to avoid overlapping the coefficients of the decryption polynomial which are equal to the entries of our desired result $\mathbf{A}_1 \times \cdots \times \mathbf{A}_\ell$.

The method of [7] has another obstacle that it requires large t and n for matrices with large size and entries, which makes the BV scheme very slow. To address the obstacle, we give several modifications for efficiency. In particular, for large entries, we split the plaintext parameter t as $t = \prod_{i=1}^{k} t_i$ with small t_i for some k. Then we encrypt a message modulo every t_i so that after decryption we can recover the original message from every message modulo t_i using CRT (Chinese Remainder Theorem) over the integers. Different from the double-CRT representation in [9] for SIMD (single instruction multiple data), our CRT method just splits the plaintext space R_t into small spaces R_{t_i}. However, this method requires k ciphertexts for encrypting a message. Our modifications enable us to flexibly select parameters of the BV scheme for both enough security and efficiency. For example, while the method of [7] took about 7.27 s for secure multiplication between two matrices with 16×16 size and 10-bit entries, it took only about 0.50 (resp., 0.75 and 1.70) seconds due to our modifications for 32×32 size with 16-bit (resp., 32-bit and 64-bit) entries (our implementation level and security level of chosen parameters seem almost same as in [7]).

Notation. The symbols $\mathbb{Z}$ and $\mathbb{Z}_t$ denote the ring of integers and the ring of integers modulo a positive integer t, respectively. For two integers z and d, let $[z]_d$ denote the reduction of z modulo d included in the interval $[-d/2, d/2)$. Let A_i (resp., A_i^T) denote the i-th row (resp., column) of a matrix $\mathbf{A}$. Let $\langle A, B \rangle$ be the inner product between two vectors A and B. Let $\lg(a)$ denote the logarithm value of an integer a with base 2.

2 Preliminaries

In this section, we briefly review the construction of the SHE scheme proposed by Brakerski and Vaikuntanathan [4], simply called the BV scheme. We also review previous methods for secure matrix multiplication over the BV scheme.

2.1 Construction of BV Scheme

The BV scheme requires the following four parameters:

- n: an integer of 2-power defining the base ring $R = \mathbb{Z}[x]/(f(x))$ with the cyclotomic polynomial $f(x) = x^n + 1$ of degree n.
- q: a prime number with $q \equiv 1 \mod 2n$ defining the ciphertext space $R_q = R/qR = \mathbb{Z}_q[x]/(x^n + 1)$.
- t: a positive integer with $t < q$ defining the plaintext space $R_t = R/tR = \mathbb{Z}_t[x]/(x^n + 1)$.
- σ: the parameter defining a discrete Gaussian error distribution $\chi = D_{\mathbb{Z}^n, \sigma}$ over $\mathbb{Z}^n$ with mean 0 and standard deviation $\sigma > 0$.

We identify elements of $\mathbb{Z}^n$ as elements of R by $(a_0, \ldots, a_{n-1}) \mapsto \sum_{i=0}^{n-1} a_i x^i$. In the below, we present the construction of the BV scheme from [11, Sect. 3.2]:

- **KeyGen**: Choose $s \leftarrow \chi$, sample $p_1 \in R_q$ (uniformly) and an error $e \leftarrow \chi$. Set a public key pk $= (p_0, p_1)$ with $p_0 = -(p_1 s + te)$ and a secret key sk $= s$.
- **Encryption**: For a message $m \in R_t$, sample $u, f, g \leftarrow \chi$ and compute

$$\text{Enc}(m, \text{pk}) = (c_0, c_1) = (p_0 u + tg + m, p_1 u + tf) \in (R_q)^2$$

as a fresh ciphertext, where m is considered as an element of R_q since $t < q$.
- **Decryption**: For a ciphertext ct $= (c_0, c_1, \ldots, c_\xi)$, the decryption is computed by $\text{Dec}(\text{ct}, \text{sk}) = [\tilde{m}]_q \bmod t$, where $\tilde{m} = \sum_{i=0}^{\xi} c_i s^i \in R$.
- **Homomorphic operations**: Let ct $= (c_0, \ldots, c_\xi)$ and ct$' = (c_0', \ldots, c_\eta')$ be two ciphertexts. The homomorphic addition "$\dotplus$" is computed by component-wise addition (we pad with zeros if $\xi \neq \eta$)

$$\text{ct} \dotplus \text{ct}' = (c_0 + c_0', \ldots, c_{\max(\xi,\eta)} + c_{\max(\xi,\eta)}') \in R_q^{\max(\xi,\eta)+1}.$$

The homomorphic multiplication "$*$" is defined as ct $*$ ct$' = (\tilde{c}_0, \ldots, \tilde{c}_{\xi+\eta})$ with (here z denotes just a symbolic variable)

$$\sum_{i=0}^{\xi+\eta} \tilde{c}_i z^i = \left(\sum_{i=0}^{\xi} c_i z^i \right) \left(\sum_{j=0}^{\eta} c_j' z^j \right) \in R_q[z].$$

The next lemma gives a condition for the homomorphic correctness (see [4] for details). It enables to choose parameters to avoid decryption failure.

Lemma 1. *For a ciphertext* ct, *the decryption* $\text{Dec}(\text{ct}, \text{sk})$ *recovers the correct plaintext if it satisfies* $\|\langle \text{ct}, \mathbf{s} \rangle\|_\infty < \frac{q}{2}$. *Here for a* $a = \sum_{i=0}^{n-1} a_i x^i \in R$ *let* $\|a\|_\infty = \max |a_i|$ *denote the* ∞-*norm of its coefficient representation.*

2.2 Previous Methods for Secure Matrix Multiplication

By using packing methods of Yasuda et al. [18,19], one needs m^2 secure inner product computations (i.e., m^2 homomorphic multiplications) to compute a matrix multiplication between two $m \times m$ matrices. Here we introduce Duong et al.'s methods [7], generalizing the methods of Yasuda et al. [18,19] for secure matrix multiplication. The methods of [7] require only one homomorphic multiplication.

First Packing Method. Let $\mathbf{A}$ and $\mathbf{B}$ be two matrices of size $m \times m$ whose entries are positive integers. We pack each row $A_i = (a_{i1}, \ldots, a_{im})$ and column $B_j^T = (b_{1j}, \ldots, b_{mj})$ of matrices $\mathbf{A}$ and $\mathbf{B}$, respectively, as follows:

$$\text{pm}^{(1)}(A_i) := \sum_{u=1}^{m-1} a_{iu} x^{u-1}, \quad \text{pm}^{(2)}(B_j^T) := -\sum_{v=1}^{m} b_{vj} x^{n-v+1}.$$

Define the following two types of polynomial in $R = \mathbb{Z}[x]/(x^n + 1)$ associated to two matrices $\mathbf{A}$ and $\mathbf{B}$:

$$\text{Pol}^{(1)}(\mathbf{A}) := \sum_{i=1}^{m} \text{pm}^{(1)}(A_i) x^{(i-1)m}, \quad \text{Pol}^{(2)}(\mathbf{B}) := \sum_{j=1}^{m} \text{pm}^{(2)}(B_j^T) x^{(j-1)m^2}.$$

Define two types of packed ciphertext for a matrix $\mathbf{A}$ as

$$\text{ct}^{(i)}(\mathbf{A}) := \text{Enc}\left(\text{Pol}^{(i)}(\mathbf{A}), \text{pk}\right) \text{ for } i = 1, 2. \tag{1}$$

Theorem 1 (Theorem 7 in [7]). *Assume* $n \geq m^3$. *Let*

$$\text{ct} = \text{ct}^{(1)}(\mathbf{A}) * \text{ct}^{(2)}(\mathbf{B})$$

and let $\text{Dec}(\text{ct}, \text{sk}) \in R_t$ *denote its decryption result. Then under the condition of Lemma 1 for the ciphertext* ct, *for each* $i, j \in \{1, \ldots, m\}$, *the inner product* $\langle A_i, B_j^T \rangle$ *is the coefficient of* $x^{(j-1)m^2 + (i-1)m}$ *in* $\text{Dec}(\text{ct}, \text{sk})$.

This method is efficient only for small entries. For large entries, it forces to take very large size of the plaintext parameter t. Assume that all entries of A_i and B_j^T are p-bit. In order to obtain the correct result after decryption, one should take $t > \langle A_i, B_j^T \rangle = \sum_{k=1}^{m} a_{ik} b_{kj}$ so that the decryption result can not wrap around (mod t)-operation. Therefore one should set $t > m2^{2p}$, which becomes very large for large p. Such large t also forces to take huge q in order to avoid decryption failure. To resolve this issue, Duong et al. [7, Sect. 4.2] adopted Yasuda et al.'s [19] modification for large entries as follows.

Second Packing Method. Let $\mathbf{A}$ and $\mathbf{B}$ be two $m \times m$ matrices whose entries are positive integers of less than p-bit. We pack each row $A_i = (a_{i1}, \ldots, a_{im})$ and $B_j^T = (b_{1j}, \ldots, b_{mj})$ of matrices $\mathbf{A}$ and $\mathbf{B}$, respectively. For a chosen integer $r > 0$, write each integral entry a_{ik} in the base-r representation, namely $a_{ik} = \sum_{u=1}^{d} a_{iku} r^{u-1}$ with $a_{iku} \in \{0, 1, \ldots, r-1\}$, where $d = \lceil \log_r 2^p \rceil$ (in particular, we have $d = p$ when $r = 2$). Pack each a_{ik} as

$$a_{ik}(x) := \sum_{u=1}^{d} a_{iku} x^{u-1} \in R = \mathbb{Z}[x]/(x^n + 1).$$

In the same manner, we pack each $b_{\ell j}$ as $b_{\ell j}(x) \in R$. Associate each row A_i and B_j^T of $\mathbf{A}$ and $\mathbf{B}$ respectively to the following polynomials in the ring R:

$$\begin{cases} \text{pm}_{m,p,r}^{(1)}(A_i) := \sum_{k=1}^{m} a_{ik}(x) x^{2(k-1)d}, \\ \text{pm}_{m,p,r}^{(2)}(B_j^T) := -\sum_{\ell=1}^{m} b_{\ell j}(x) x^{n-2(\ell-1)d}. \end{cases} \tag{2}$$

Define the following polynomials in R associated to $\mathbf{A}$ and $\mathbf{B}$:

$$
\begin{cases}
\mathrm{Pol}^{(1)}(\mathbf{A}) := \sum_{i=1}^{m} \mathrm{pm}_{m,p,r}^{(1)}(A_i) x^{(i-1)2md}, \\[2mm]
\mathrm{Pol}^{(2)}(\mathbf{B}) := \sum_{j=1}^{m} \mathrm{pm}_{m,p,r}^{(2)}\left(B_j^T\right) x^{(j-1)2m^2 d}.
\end{cases}
$$

Define two types of packed ciphertext for a matrix $\mathbf{A}$ in the same manner as (1).

Theorem 2 (Theorem 10 in [7]). *Assume $n \geq 2m^3 d + 2md + 2d$. Let*

$$
\mathrm{ct} = \mathrm{ct}^{(1)}(\mathbf{A}) * \mathrm{ct}^{(2)}(\mathbf{B})
$$

and let $\mathrm{Dec}(\mathrm{ct}, \mathrm{sk}) \in R_t$ denote its decryption result. Then under the condition of Lemma 1 for ct, for each $i, j \in \{1, \ldots, m\}$, the inner product $\langle A_i, B_j^T \rangle$ is the sum of the terms of degree greater than or equal to $(i-1)2md + (j-1)2m^2 d$ and less than $(i-1)2md + (j-1)2m^2 d + 2d$ in $\mathrm{Dec}(\mathrm{ct}, \mathrm{sk})$ evaluated at $x = r$.

From the construction (2), we have

$$
\mathrm{pm}_{m,p,r}^{(1)}(A_i) \times \mathrm{pm}_{m,p,r}^{(2)}\left(B_j^T\right) = \sum_{k=1}^{m} a_{ik}(x) b_{kj}(x) + \text{terms of degree} \geq 2d,
$$

which is equal to the decryption result of ct. The polynomial $\sum_{k=1}^{m} a_{ik}(x) b_{kj}(x)$ has degree at most $2(d-1)$, and by substituting r for the variable x, we have

$$
\sum_{k=1}^{m} a_{ik}(r) b_{kj}(r) = \sum_{k=1}^{m} \left(\sum_{u=1}^{d} a_{iku} r^{u-1} \right) \left(\sum_{v=1}^{d} b_{kjv} r^{v-1} \right) = \langle A_i, B_j^T \rangle.
$$

Every coefficient of $\sum_{k=1}^{m} a_{ik}(x) b_{kj}(x)$ is up to $m(r-1)^2 d$ by the base-r representation. In order to obtain the correct inner product between A_i and B_j^T, it requires $t \geq m(r-1)^2 d$. In particular, when $r = 2$, it requires $t \geq mp$ since $d = \lceil \log_r 2^p \rceil$ whereas the first packing method requires $t \geq m2^{2p}$.

3   Our Improvements

Methods proposed by Duong et al. [7] (described in Subsect. 2.2) are only for one time secure multiplication between two matrices. Moreover, their methods enforce to take very large size of t or n for large entries (see [7, Table 2]). In this section, we extend their methods from just one matrix multiplication to multiple matrix multiplications, and then give some modifications for efficiency.

3.1 Extension for Secure Multiple Matrix Multiplications

In this subsection, we present a packing method for secure multiple matrix multiplications. Specifically, we generalize methods of [7] to secure multiplications among matrices. Due to space restriction, we only consider the case of three matrices without a proof. (The proof will be presented in the full version paper, and a general case of secure matrix multiplications will be also discussed in the paper.) Let $\mathbf{A}$ be a matrix with size $m \times m$ whose entries are positive entries. As in the previous section, we give two types of polynomial in $R = \mathbb{Z}[x]/(x^n + 1)$ for each row $A_i = (a_{i1}, \ldots, a_{im})$ of $\mathbf{A}$ as follows:

$$
\begin{cases}
\mathrm{pm}_{m,3}^{(1)}(A_i) := \sum_{u=1}^{m} a_{iu} x^{u-1}, \\
\mathrm{pm}_{m,3}^{(2)}(A_i) := -\sum_{u=1}^{m} a_{iu} x^{n-(u-1)m^2 - m + 1},
\end{cases}
$$

where the indices "$m, 3$" represent the size of matrix and the number of matrices being multiplied, respectively. Note that the first polynomial transformation $\mathrm{pm}_{m,3}^{(1)}(A_i)$ is same as that in the method of [7]. Now we define three types of polynomial in R associated with three matrices $\mathbf{A}, \mathbf{B}$ and $\mathbf{C}$ as follows:

$$
\begin{cases}
\mathrm{Pol}_{m,3}^{(1)}(\mathbf{A}) := \sum_{i=1}^{m} \mathrm{pm}_{m,3}^{(1)}(A_i) \, x^{(i-1)m}, \\
\mathrm{Pol}_{m,3}^{(2)}(\mathbf{B}) := \sum_{j=1}^{m} \mathrm{pm}_{m,3}^{(1)}\left(\overline{B}_j^T\right) x^{(j-1)m^2}, \\
\mathrm{Pol}_{m,3}^{(3)}(\mathbf{C}) := \sum_{k=1}^{m} \mathrm{pm}_{m,3}^{(2)}\left(C_k^T\right) x^{(k-1)m^3},
\end{cases}
$$

where $B_j^T = (b_{1j}, \ldots, b_{mj})$ and C_k^T are the jth and the kth columns of $\mathbf{B}$ and $\mathbf{C}$ respectively, and $\overline{B}_j^T = (b_{mj}, \ldots, b_{1j})$ (i.e., flipping the column B_j^T). Define three types of packed ciphertext for a matrix $\mathbf{A}$ to be

$$
\mathrm{ct}^{(i)}(\mathbf{A}) := \mathrm{Enc}\left(\mathrm{Pol}_{m,3}^{(i)}(\mathbf{A}), \mathrm{pk}\right) \text{ for } i = 1, 2, 3.
$$

Theorem 3. *Assume* $n \geq m^4$. *Let*

$$
\mathrm{ct} = \mathrm{ct}^{(1)}(\mathbf{A}) * \mathrm{ct}^{(2)}(\mathbf{B}) * \mathrm{ct}^{(3)}(\mathbf{C}),
$$

and let $\mathrm{Dec}(\mathrm{ct}, \mathrm{sk}) \in R_t$ *denote its decryption result. Then under the condition of Lemma 1 for the ciphertext* ct, *for each* $i, k \in \{1, \ldots, m\}$, *the* $(i, k)^{th}$ *entry of the matrix* $\mathbf{A} \times \mathbf{B} \times \mathbf{C}$ *is the coefficient of* $x^{(i-1)m+(k-1)m^3}$ *in* $\mathrm{Dec}(\mathrm{ct}, \mathrm{sk})$.

3.2 Other Modifications

For matrices with large entries, the packing method in Subsect. 2.2 needs very large t and hence huge q for successful decryption. Such parameter setting makes the BV scheme very slow. On the other hand, the packing method in Subsect. 2.2 enables to take small t. However, it forces to set very large n since it requires $n \geq 2m^3p + 2mp + 2p$ from Theorem 2 (in which $d = p$ when $r = 2$) for matrices with p-bit entries. In the below, we give two modifications to get rid of these two problems:

CRT Method. To solve the problem with the packing method in Subsect. 2.2, we split the parameter t as $t = \prod_{i=1}^{k} t_i$ with small t_i's (assume that $\mathrm{GCD}(t_i, t_j) = 1$ for $i \neq j$). Given a message modulo t, we encrypt the message modulo every t_i. After decryption modulo every t_i, we can recover the original message by the CRT method. This enables us to use $\mathbb{Z}_{t_i}[x]/(x^n + 1)$ with small t_i as the plaintext space. However, it requires k ciphertexts for encrypting a message.

Block-Matrix Method. Let $\mathbf{A}$ be a matrix of size $M \times M$. For a block size m, assume $M = bm$ for some $b \in \mathbb{Z}$ for simplicity. Consider $\mathbf{A}$ as a matrix with b^2 sub-matrices $\mathbf{A}_{ij}$ with size $m \times m$ for $i, j = 1, \ldots, b$. In this method, we pack each sub-matrix $\mathbf{A}_{ij}$ into a single polynomial by our packing method, and encrypt the polynomial. This enables us to take small n for packing every $m \times m$ sub-matrix $\mathbf{A}_{ij}$, instead of the whole matrix $\mathbf{A}$. However, it requires more homomorphic operations for secure matrix multiplications. For example, it requires b^3 homomorphic multiplications and $b^2(b - 1)$ homomorphic additions for secure matrix multiplication between two matrices.

4 Implementation Results

In this section, we show performance of our packing method with modifications for secure multiplications among two and three matrices with size $M \times M$ and p-bit entries for $M = 32, 64$ and $p = 16, 32, 64$. Note that our packing method for two matrices is the same as Duong et al.'s method [7]. Our experiments ran on an Intel Core i7-4790 CPU with 3.60 GHz and 8.00 GB RAM, using PARI library [16] (version 2.9.2) in C programs. In Tables 1 and 2, we show our chosen parameters of the BV scheme and running time for secure matrix multiplications. In the tables, let δ denote the root Hermite factor for the distinguishing attack against LWE, and we choose parameters (n, q, t, σ) of the BV scheme so that δ is less than 1.006 for 80-bit security level with an enough margin.

For two matrices with 16×16 size and 10-bit entries, Duong et al. [7] adopted the second packing method in Subsect. 2.2. They needed to set $n = 131072$ from Theorem 2, and it took about 7.27 s from [7, Table 2]. In contrast, we adopted the first packing method in Subsect. 2.2 for secure multiplication between two matrices with $M \times M$ size for $M = 32$ and 64. We divided every matrix into sub-matrices with size 16×16 by our block-matrix method, and then set $n = 4096$

Table 1. Performance (seconds) of secure multiplication between two matrices **A** and **B** with size $M \times M$ and p-bit entries (We divide every matrix into sub-matrices with size 16×16, and take $n = 4096$ for our packing method. We split t as $t = \prod_{i=1}^{k} t_i$ with $t_1 \approx \cdots \approx t_k$ by our CRT method, and we use a prime q for all t_i's)

	p	k	$(\lg(q), \lg(t_i), \delta)$	Encryption	Sec Matrix Mul.	Decryption	Total time
$M = 32$	16	1	$(115, 37, 1.0048)$	0.1109	0.2970	0.0940	0.5019
	32	3	$(85, 23, 1.0035)$	0.1726	0.4210	0.1570	0.7506
	64	3	$(135, 45, 1.0056)$	0.3430	1.0490	0.3280	1.7020
$M = 64$	16	1	$(115, 37, 1.0048)$	0.3900	2.3910	0.3740	3.1550
	32	3	$(85, 23, 1.0035)$	0.7502	3.8600	0.8280	5.4382
	64	3	$(135, 45, 1.0056)$	1.8440	8.8590	1.4530	12.1560

Table 2. Performance (seconds) of secure multiplications among three matrices **A**, **B** and **C** with size $M \times M$ and p-bit entries (As in Table 1, we divide every matrix into sub-matrices with size 16×16, and take $n = 65536$ for our packing method. But we did not use our CRT method due to such large n)

	p	$(\lg(q), \lg(t), \delta)$	Encryption	Sec Matrix Mul.	Decryption	Total time
$M = 32$	16	$(250, 58, 1.0006)$	3.5780	32.9690	9.2960	45.8430
	32	$(400, 106, 1.0010)$	4.4380	42.4990	11.7820	58.7190
	64	$(700, 202, 1.0018)$	7.4384	74.7500	19.6090	101.7974
$M = 64$	16	$(250, 60, 1.0006)$	13.1570	240.4850	31.4690	285.1110
	32	$(400, 108, 1.0010)$	17.8750	397.6090	46.9370	462.4210
	64	$(700, 204, 1.0018)$	29.7500	799.6880	104.7810	934.2190

from Theorem 1. From Table 1, our method took only about 0.50 (resp., 0.75 and 1.70) seconds for $M = 32$ and p-bit entries for $p = 16$ (resp., $p = 32$ and 64). Our method is much faster than [7] due to taking smaller n, and our method for large p does not reduce the performance due to our CRT method. Actually, our CRT method enables to take small size of plaintext space and then we can take practical q for large p (however, it requires more ciphertexts and additional homomorphic operations). Comparing Table 1 with Table 2, our method for three matrices is about $80 \sim 100$ times slower than two matrices case. For three matrices, we took $n = 65536$ and it is unnecessary to use our CRT method for such large n. We expect that as the number of matrices increases, the running time would be at least about 80 times slower. (We will discuss such a magnitude about the running time in a full version paper.)

Acknowledgments. This work was supported by JST CREST Grant Number JPMJCR14D6, Japan. This work was also supported by JSPS KAKENHI Grant Numbers 16K17644 and 16H02830.

References

1. Boneh, D., Goh, E.-J., Nissim, K.: Evaluating 2-DNF formulas on ciphertexts. In: Kilian, J. (ed.) TCC 2005. LNCS, vol. 3378, pp. 325–341. Springer, Heidelberg (2005). https://doi.org/10.1007/978-3-540-30576-7_18

2. Bos, J.W., Lauter, K., Loftus, J., Naehrig, M.: Improved security for a ring-based fully homomorphic encryption scheme. In: Stam, M. (ed.) IMACC 2013. LNCS, vol. 8308, pp. 45–64. Springer, Heidelberg (2013). https://doi.org/10.1007/978-3-642-45239-0_4

3. Brakerski, Z., Gentry, C., Vaikuntanathan, V.: (Leveled) fully homomorphic encryption without bootstrapping. ACM Trans. Comput. Theory (TOCT) **6**(3) (2014). Article No. 13, Special issue on innovations in theoretical computer science 2012-Part II

4. Brakerski, Z., Vaikuntanathan, V.: Fully homomorphic encryption from ring-LWE and security for key dependent messages. In: Rogaway, P. (ed.) CRYPTO 2011. LNCS, vol. 6841, pp. 505–524. Springer, Heidelberg (2011). https://doi.org/10.1007/978-3-642-22792-9_29

5. Chillotti, I., Gama, N., Georgieva, M., Izabachène, M.: Faster fully homomorphic encryption: bootstrapping in less than 0.1 seconds. In: Cheon, J.H., Takagi, T. (eds.) ASIACRYPT 2016. LNCS, vol. 10031, pp. 3–33. Springer, Heidelberg (2016). https://doi.org/10.1007/978-3-662-53887-6_1

6. Costache, A., Smart, N.P.: Which ring based somewhat homomorphic encryption scheme is best? In: Sako, K. (ed.) CT-RSA 2016. LNCS, vol. 9610, pp. 325–340. Springer, Cham (2016). https://doi.org/10.1007/978-3-319-29485-8_19

7. Duong, D.H., Mishra, P.K., Yasuda, M.: Efficient secure matrix multiplication over LWE-based homomorphic encryption. Tatra Mountains Math. Publ. **67**(1), 69–83 (2016)

8. Gentry, C.: Fully homomorphic encryption using ideal lattices. In: Symposium on Theory of Computing-STOC 2009, pp. 169–178. ACM (2009)

9. Gentry, C., Halevi, S., Smart, N.P.: Homomorphic evaluation of the AES circuit. In: Safavi-Naini, R., Canetti, R. (eds.) CRYPTO 2012. LNCS, vol. 7417, pp. 850–867. Springer, Heidelberg (2012). https://doi.org/10.1007/978-3-642-32009-5_49

10. Fan, J., Vercauteren, F.: Somewhat practical fully homomorphic encryption. IACR Cryptology ePrint 2012/144 (2014). https://eprint.iacr.org/2012/144

11. Naehrig, M., Lauter, K.E., Vaikuntanathan, V.: Can homomorphic encryption be practical? In: ACM Workshop on Cloud Computing Security Workshop-CCSW 2011, pp. 113–124. ACM (2011)

12. Lepoint, T., Naehrig, M.: A comparison of the homomorphic encryption schemes FV and YASHE. In: Pointcheval, D., Vergnaud, D. (eds.) AFRICACRYPT 2014. LNCS, vol. 8469, pp. 318–335. Springer, Cham (2014). https://doi.org/10.1007/978-3-319-06734-6_20

13. Lòpez-Alt, A., Tromer, E., Vaikuntanathan, V.: On-the-fly multiparty computation on the cloud via multikey fully homomorphic encryption. In: Symposium on Theory of Computing-STOC 2012, pp. 1219–1234. ACM (2012)

14. Paillier, P.: Public-key cryptosystems based on composite degree residuosity classes. In: Stern, J. (ed.) EUROCRYPT 1999. LNCS, vol. 1592, pp. 223–238. Springer, Heidelberg (1999). https://doi.org/10.1007/3-540-48910-X_16

15. Pedrouzo-Ulloa, A., Troncoso-Pastoriza, J.R., Pérez-González, F.: Number theoretic transforms for secure signal processing. IEEE Trans. Inf. Forensics Secur. **12**(5), 1125–1140 (2017)

16. The PARI Group, Bordeaux, PARI/GP. http://pari.math.u-bordeaux.fr/doc.html
17. Rivest, R.L., Shamir, A., Adleman, L.: A method for obtaining digital signatures and public-key cryptosystems. Commun. ACM **21**(2), 120–126 (1978)
18. Yasuda, M., Shimoyama, T., Kogure, J., Yokoyama, K., Koshiba, T.: New packing method in somewhat homomorphic encryption and its applications. Secur. Commun. Netw. (SCN) **8**(13), 2194–2213 (2015)
19. Yasuda, M., Shimoyama, T., Kogure, J., Yokoyama, K., Koshiba, T.: Secure statistical analysis using RLWE-based homomorphic encryption. In: Foo, E., Stebila, D. (eds.) ACISP 2015. LNCS, vol. 9144, pp. 471–487. Springer, Cham (2015). https://doi.org/10.1007/978-3-319-19962-7_27

Searchable Encryption

Verifiable Range Query Processing for Cloud Computing

Yanling Li[1], Junzuo Lai[1,2], Chuansheng Wang[1(✉)], Jianghe Zhang[1], and Jie Xiong[1]

[1] Department of Computer Science, Jinan University, Guangzhou, China
chueng0828@126.com
[2] State Key Laboratory of Cryptology, Beijing, China

Abstract. With the popularity of cloud computing technology, the clients usually store a mass of data in the cloud server. Because of the untrusted cloud servers, the massive data query raises privacy concerns. To prevent sensitive data on the cloud from hostile attacking, and obtain the query result timely, users usually use the searchable encryption technology to store encrypted data on the cloud. In the prior work, there are many privacy-preserving schemes for cloud computing, but the verification of these schemes cannot be ensured. Due to software errors, communication transmission failure or the dishonest features of the public cloud servers, only part of the data set was searched. So the integrity is also an urgent problem to be solved. In this paper, we propose a verifiable range query processing scheme with the ability to verify the correctness of query result. The key idea of this paper is to add additional information to a complete binary tree, which is used to organize indexing elements. The result returned by the cloud server will be accompanied by validation information so that the user can verify whether the result is complete. Finally, we confirm that the storage overhead of the verifiable scheme is $O(n \log n)$, where n is the total number of data items, and implement our scheme to testify to its practicability.

Keywords: Cloud computing · Range query · Verification

1 Introduction

1.1 Background

In recent years, as the Internet developed at a high rate of speed, our life and work affected by the Internet have become more convenient. Following the prevalent, the cloud computing is being integrated into our life and work. Instead of storing data in the hardware devices, increasing popularity, data and computing are outsourced to clouds for many factors. First, it does not require spending money on purchasing equipment, and it is wise to delegate the heavy computation workloads into the powerful servers. Obviously, outsourcing can reduce the cost effectively. Additionally, since the most resources that may be used in our

© Springer International Publishing AG 2017
J. K. Liu and P. Samarati (Eds.): ISPEC 2017, LNCS 10701, pp. 333–349, 2017.
https://doi.org/10.1007/978-3-319-72359-4_19

work are existing in the cloud, we can transfer what we need from the cloud. It greatly improves the efficiency of our work. Because of these advantages, the cloud servers are favored by many businesses. At present, there are many companies with outsourcing computation, such as Google App Engine [10], IBM Blue Cloud Computing Platform [15], Amazon Web Services [1], and Microsoft Azure [19]. These service providers bring convenience to the cloud users.

Meanwhile, there is an obvious weakness for outsourcing computation [8]. In some special scenarios, secure outsourcing computation is significant. Yet, the data on the public cloud takes a high risk due to many causes. For instance, provided that data users try to request our data in the cloud, and our information would be leaked. Of course, that is not what we are willing to face. For example, last year, Apples iCloud leaked private photos uploaded by users, this issue given rise to people to consider whether the cloud storage is secure, especially for the confidential institutions, such as the national governments, securities traders, investment banks and others. Privacy becomes an urgent issue to be solved [20]. Beyond that, it is possible that the cloud may intercept data between users' transaction or return erroneous results to users. Therefore, we should strengthen data privacy protection at the same time to enhance the verification of computing and other security technology.

1.2 Motivation

Cloud server becomes more popular for people to store data, one person's data may be used by others. So, in this paper, we adopt a model as following: a data owner stores data on the cloud, and multiple data users could query the interested data on the cloud. For the most simple example, a data user stores his own data on the cloud and queries what he is interested from these data in the cloud. Figure 1 shows the three parties in our model: a data owner, multiple data users and a cloud. Data users usually protect sensitive data by encryption. Before uploading data on the cloud, the data owner encrypts data in order to data security. This operation ensures the confidentiality of the data, but all of these come at a price. For example, it becomes hard to query data on the ciphertext. When user queries data, first, he should download all data he stored on the cloud, decrypt these data, after that search out the required data. Obviously, it is infeasible when the data size is extremely large. Our motivation is to achieve verification of the query results in the case of ensuring data security.

1.3 Related Work

Prior works have made many contributions to data security. Here we just talk about the security for range query. The existing privacy-preserving query schemes are divided into two categories according to their query types: range queries [13] and key-word queries [5,7]. Rang queries which query all data items that fall into the given range, can also be called range searchable symmetric encryption schemes. Prior range searchable symmetric encryption schemes can be divided into two kinds: bucketing schemes [12–14] and order-preserving

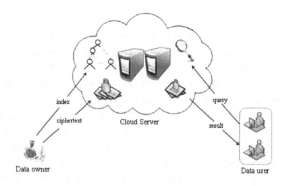

Fig. 1. Storing computing model

schemes [3,4,17]. In bucketing schemes, data owner partitions the data domain
into various sizes. For example, the range [0, 150] represents the age of human, we
divide it into many ranges like that [0, 12], [13, 22], [23, 60], [61, 150]. Data owner
constructs index by the ID of a bucket and all encrypted data items in this field.
The trapdoor of a range query consists of the IDs of the buckets that overlap a
query range. For instance, for query range [10, 20], the corresponding trapdoor
consists of ID1 and ID2. All data items in the buckets will be returned to data
user on condition that the buckets overlap the query ranges. In this example,
the cloud will return ranges [0, 12], [13, 22] to the data user. From the above, we
can get a conclusion that the prior encryption schemes still have many shortcomings. The weakness of private-preserving is the most significant. The Cloud
could estimate the actual values according to historical query results. In addition
to this, the communication cost of this scheme is very high, as there are many
data items which are not gratified the query. Reducing the size of every bucket
leads to lower cost, but weakens privacy at the same time. Because, in this case,
the number of buckets approximates to the number of data items. It is easy to
estimate the size of our data set.

In order-preserving schemes, data order keeps consistent after encryption. For
example, for any two data items a and b, as well as a function f which is used
to keep the order unchanged, called order-preserving encryption function. $a < b$
if and only if $f(a) < f(b)$. In order-preserving schemes, the index for data items
$d_1, \ldots, d_n$ is $f(d_1), \ldots, f(d_n)$, and the trapdoor of range $[a, b]$ is $[f(a), f(b)]$. It is
obvious that order-preserving is also weak for privacy, since they allow the cloud
to estimate the actual values of the data items and the query in a statistical way.

The above mentioned schemes prove that the fundamental cause of the weak
privacy preserving is that these data have different distributions when they have
the same number of encrypted data items, in other words, they have index
distinguished. In bucketing schemes, for different numbers of data items, different
distributions in the data values will result in the regions to have different size
distributions as to they require the number of data items in the equilibrium
area. In order-preserving schemes, in the case of the same number of data items,

the different distributions in the data values will lead to the ciphertexts to have different distributions in the space. Using the domain knowledge about the data distribution, the bucketing schemes and the order-preserving schemes can be used by the cloud to statistically estimate the values of the data and queries.

In view of the weak privacy protection caused by index distinguished, Li et al. [18] proposed a range query processing scheme that achieves index indistinguishability under the indistinguishability against chosen keyword attack (IND-CKA). They achieve index indistinguishability by complete binary tree, that is to say, when the number of data items is equal, they have the same data structure that can not be distinguished. And the nodes are indistinguishable, thanks to the randomness. They proved their scheme is privacy preserving under the widely adopted IND-CKA security model, but there are also existing many uncertain factors. Because the cloud is not credible, it may not try its best to query what the users interested, the results returned by the cloud may be wrong or incomplete. Nevertheless, for users, they can not judge what they have got is good or bad. Thus it needs operation operated by data users to verify the correctness of the results.

1.4 Our Contribution

At present, according to the study of the searchable encryption scheme, they are not exceedingly convenient for range query. For instance, users can not verify the integrality of the returned results in range query. Unreliable server may take incomplete data to users, and this problem would bring annoyance to the following work. To solve this question is an urgent issue for us.

In this paper, we proposed a leveled verifiable range queries scheme based on a private-preserving scheme which is proposed by Li et al. in [18]. We reserve the security and high efficiency of the original scheme, and obtain verification by storing additional information in the leaf nodes. Our main works as follows: firstly, analyzing [18], pointing out deficiency in the original scheme, its main defect is that users can not verify the correct and integrity of the results. This paper proposed a modified scheme aiming at these shortcomings. Not only do we analyze the security of our scheme, but we have done a comparison with the original scheme, and shown the advantage of our scheme by theoretical analysis and experiments. In our scheme, we need space is $O(n \log n)$ as before, but it has verification at the same time.

Next, we give a brief overview of the searchable encryption technology, hash function and Bloom filter that we utilize in Sects. 2 and 3, we describe our verifiable scheme in detail; In Sects. 4 and 5, we analyse security of our scheme and implement it respectively.

2 Preliminaries

2.1 Searchable Encryption Technology

Searchable encryption technology allows the client to store, on an untrusted server, message encrypted by a private or public key. The client could query related information from the untrusted server by a trapdoor, which is constructed by some key words, while the trapdoor does not reveal keywords or ciphertexts anymore. Searchable encryption technology is divided into two categories: symmetric searchable encryption [22] and asymmetric searchable encryption [5]. The searchable encryption technology can be divided into four steps:

(1) Encryption: A user encrypts messages with the private key, afterward uploads the ciphertext on an external server.
(2) Trapdoor Construction: Users with search permission construct trapdoor by encrypting query keywords, while the trapdoor does not leak any information about the keywords.
(3) Query: External server queries according to the trapdoor, after that returns the result to the data user. While the server only knows whether the files contain these keywords, but does not know other additional information.
(4) Decryption: The user receives the query results returned by the server, then decrypts ciphertext with private key to obtain related information.

2.2 Hash Function

Hash functions, also called compression functions, have many applications in cryptography and computer security. In general, hash functions are just functions that take arbitrary-length strings and compress them into shorter strings. Hash functions have many useful properties. Hash functions have security, since the rival can not restore the original data according to the output value in any polynomial time, namely, unipolarity. For example, the rival knows $H(x)$, but it is unlikely for the rival to compute x in any polynomial time. Besides that the adversary can not find two different input values and the output values are the same in any polynomial time. For instance, there is a pair of values x and x', and no polynomial-time adversary can compute $H(x) = H(x')$, that is to say that hash functions have Collision-Resistant. Typical hash functions are such as CR32, MD5, SHA1 [21] and so on. The hash functions exert a great influence on integrity and digital signatures.

2.3 Bloom Filter

Bloom filters are usually used to retrieve whether an element is in a collection [2]. It is actually a very long binary vector (each bit is set to be 0) and a series of random mapping functions. We compute every data item using hash functions to get the corresponding position in the hash table, secondarily we set this position to be 1. When judging one element whether in the collection, we just need to compute the hash functions, and find the corresponding position in the hash table, and check the value in the position. If the value is 1, it reveals that the element is in the collection, else we get the opposite consequence. We can affirm that the element is included by the collection while the corresponding positions are all set to be 1.

Comparing with other data structure, Bloom filter has a huge advantage in space and time. The most prominent advantage is that storage space and insert query time are all constant. Beyond that, hash function is independent, and it brings convenience to hardware to achieve parallel processing. Bloom filter does not store data items, hence it has great advantages in the occasion that has confidentiality requirements. Meanwhile, the shortcomings of Bloom filter are apparent as its advantages. False positive is one of them. As the number of deposited elements increases, the rate of false positive increases. When the number of data items more than a certain number, the element that is not included in set will obtain the same result as it is in the collection. The solution to the false positive is to create a small list which is called white lists that store elements that may be misjudged. In addition, it is unable to delete elements in Bloom filter, for the reason that it must ensure that the deleted element is indeed inside the Bloom filer, but it is not easily guaranteed. Bloom filter is generally used to query and filter spam.

2.4   Adversary Model

In this paper, we assume that the cloud is semi-honest (also called honest-but-curious) [6] as original scheme. That is to say that the cloud could execute our protocol and compute algorithm correctly to help us obtain the result. But at the same time, the cloud may try to analysis information obtained by the distribution or result before acquiring many useful messages. For example, in bucketing schemes, the cloud may according to the number of buckets to evaluate the number of data items when reducing communication. For the data owners and users, we assume that they are all trusted.

3   Verifiable Scheme

3.1   Prefix Encoding

As proposed in [18], we should first encode prefix as described in [5]. Through prefix encoding, we could check whether the data sets have the same elements instead of judging whether a data belong to a range. Next, we explain how to encode the data properly to submit it to the server. Given a number x, let the binary representation of x is $x_1 x_2 \ldots x_w$, where x_w is the least significant bit. Each number corresponds to a prefix family, denoted as $F(x)$, including $w + 1$ prefixes: $\{x_1 x_2 \ldots x_w, x_1 x_2 \ldots x_{w-1}*, \ldots, x_1 * \ldots *, ** \ldots *\}$, where the ith prefix is $x_1 x_2 \ldots x_{w-i+1} * \ldots *$. For example, the prefix set of number 6 of 5 bits is $F(6) = F(00110) = \{00110, 0011*, 001**, 00***, 0****, *****\}$. Given a range $[a, b]$, firstly, we transfer it into a smallest prefix encoding set, represented as $S([a, b])$. In this way, the range represented by prefix encoding is same as range $[a, b]$. For example, $S([0, 8]) = \{00***, 01000\}$. In the given range $[a, b]$, a and b are two numbers of w bits, respectively, so the number of prefixes in $S([a, b])$ is at most $2w - 2$ [11]. For any x and range $[a, b]$, when $x \in [a, b]$, $x \in p$ if and only if the prefix $p \in S([a,b])$. For any x and prefix p, $x \in p$ is same as $p \in F(x)$. So, for any x and range $[a,b]$, $x \in [a,b]$ if and only if $F(x) \in S([a,b])$. According to the example above, $6 \in [0,8]$ and $F(6) \cap S([0,8]) = \{00 * **\}$. In this paper, for n data $d_1, d_2, \ldots, d_n$, the data owner computes prefix families $F(d_1), \ldots, F(d_n)$, and the data user can compute prefix family $S([a,b])$ of range $[a,b]$.

Before uploading data to the cloud server, the user should sort the data and record the values before and after the data. For example, if the uploaded data set is $S = \{1,9,4,8,14,11,16,21,26,10\}$. After sorting, the set S is transferred into $S' = \{1,4,8,9,10,11,14,16,21,26\}$. We denote $P(x)$ as the value x and the values of its before and after. For example, $P(4) = \{1,4,8\}$. When the value is the head or tail of the sequential queue, we denote as ∞ or $-\infty$, such as $P(1) = \{-\infty, 1, 4\}$, $P(26) = \{21, 26, \infty\}$.

3.2   PBtree Construction

In order to achieve the efficient query, we store $F(d_1) \ldots F(d_n)$ in a complete binary tree, called PBtree. Here, "P" means privacy and "B" means Bloom filter. We do not use existing database indexing structures (such as $b+$ tree) for two reasons as follows: when the two numbers are relatively large, query in the $b+$ tree also need do some testing work; $b+$ tree storing different data items has different structures, even they have the same number of data items. While two different data sets that have equal size are stored on the PBtree respectively, then two PBtree have same data structures, that is to say the two PBtrees are indistinguishable.

Definition 1 (PBtree). *The PBtree used to store n data items is a full binary tree, which has n terminal nodes and $n - 1$ non-terminal nodes. In PBtree, n terminal nodes form a linked list from left to right, and every node is represented by a Bloom filter. Each leaf node stores a data item, and each non-terminal node stores the union set of its left and right subtrees. For any non-terminal node, the number of data items in its left subtree either equals that of its right subtree or exceeds only by one.*

According to this definition, we can easily know that PBtree is a highly balanced binary research tree. The height of the PBtree storing n data items is $\lfloor \log n \rfloor + 1$. We construct a PBtree adopting a top-down fashion. Firstly, we construct the root node. The root node contains the set of prefix $\{F(d_1), \ldots, F(d_n)\}$. Then, we divide the prefix set $\{F(d_1), \ldots, F(d_n)\}$ into two subsets S_{left} and S_{right}. If n is even, $|S_{left}| = |S_{right}|$, else $|S_{left}| = |S_{right}| - 1$. The two subsets are the root nodes of the left and right childtree respectively. For any left subtree and right subtree, we recursively apply the above steps until the terminal node. Each terminal node contains prefix set of one data item. Figure 2 shows the PBtree for prefix set $S = \{F(d_1), F(d_2), F(d_3), F(d_4), F(d_5), F(d_6), F(d_7), F(d_8), F(d_9)\}$.

In Theorem 1, the key properties of PBtree are simply described according to their construction algorithm. Constraint $0 \leq |S_{left}| - |S_{right}| \leq 1$ makes the structure of PBtree completely dependent on the number of data contained.

Theorem 1 (Structure indistinguishable). *For any two data sets S_1 and S_2, they have the same constructions of PBtrees if and only if $|S_1| = |S_2|$.*

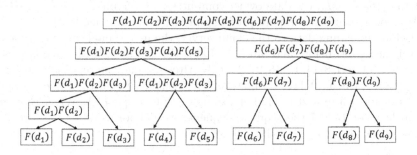

Fig. 2. PBtree example

3.3   Data Encryption

In this paper, we have two parts to be encrypted, data items and prefixes.

For data items, we adopt asymmetric encryption. Here our encryption is based on a n bit RSA modulus. The encryption process as follows.

(1) Generate a n bit RSA modulus $n = pq$ for primes p, q;
(2) Choose an integer e satisfying $gcd(g(n), e) = 1$ and $1 < e < g(n)$, where $g(n) = (p-1)(q-1)$;
(3) Compute $d \equiv e^{-1} mod\ g(n)$;
(4) The public key is now $pk = (e, n)$, and the secret key is $sk = (d, n)$. For all ordered data items $d_1, \ldots, d_n$, the encryption term of the ith data item d_i is $C_i = (d_{i-1}||d_i||d_{i+1})^e (mod\ n)$.

The encryption of prefixes is still implemented by secure hash function and Bloom filter. For each node v, the prefix family of node v is stored by Bloom filter, represented as $v.B$. Assuming r secret keys $k_1, \ldots, k_r$ have been shared between the data owner and the data user. $L(v)$ is a label of node v, which contains prefix sets. $U(v)$ represents a union set of prefix sets in $L(v)$. For example, if the two prefix families $F(x)$ and $F(x')$ are in the node v, then the set $L(v) = \{F(x), F(x')\}$, and the set $U(v) = \{F(x) \cup F(x')\}$. Each data is a w-bits binary data.

For prefix p_i, we compute p_i with r keys using hash functions: $HMAC(k_1, p_i), \ldots, HMAC(k_r, p_i)$. This step is to achieve one-wayness. That is to say that we can easily compute $HMAC(k_j, p_i)$ with r keys and p_i, but it is hard to obtain p_i and r keys even the adversary knows $HMAC(k_j, p_i)$, where $1 \leq j \leq r$. For any node v, generating a random number $v.R$ which has the same size with keys. Then using $v.R$ to compute r hash functions: $HMAC(v.R, HMAC(k_1, p_i)), \ldots, HMAC(v.R, HMAC(k_r, p_i))$. For each prefix p_i and for each key k_j, we set $v.B[HMAC(v.R, HMAC(k_j, p_i))\ mod\ M] := 1$, where M is the length of the Bloom filter.

So far, the PBtree has been constructed by the data owner, then the data owner sends encrypted data and PBtree to the cloud server.

3.4   Trapdoor Computation

Before querying data from the cloud server, it is necessary for the data user to computing trapdoor. Given a range $[a, b]$ that used to be queried. Suppose $S[a, b]$ contains z prefixes $p_1, \ldots, p_z$. For any prefix, the data user computes r results of hash functions $HMAC(k_1, p_i), \ldots, HMAC(k_r, p_i)$. The trapdoor of the range $[a, b]$ is represented as a matrix $M_{[a,b]}$ that is consist of $z * r$ hashes.

$$\begin{pmatrix} HMAC(k_1, p_1) & \cdots & HMAC(k_r, p_1) \\ \cdots & \ddots & \cdots \\ HMAC(k_1, p_z) & \cdots & HMAC(k_r, p_z) \end{pmatrix}$$

The ith prefix p_i corresponds to the ith row of the matrix of the trapdoor. Then data user sends the matrix $M_{[a,b]}$ to the cloud server (Fig. 3).

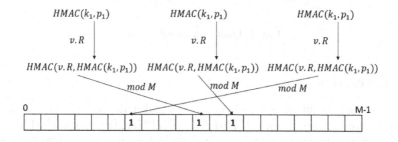

Fig. 3. Bloom filter

3.5   Query Processing

After receiving the trapdoor sent by the data user, the cloud server uses the trapdoor to search on the PBtree. Firstly, the cloud checks whether $v.B[HMAC(v.R, HMAC(k_j, p_i)) \bmod M] := 1$ for every j ($1 \leq j \leq r$) in ith row in the matrix $M_{[a,b]}$. If there exists a row i ($1 \leq i \leq z$) in $M_{[a,b]}$ satisfying $v.B[HMAC(v.R, HMAC(k_j, p_i)) \bmod M] := 1$, then it indicates that there may exists p_i in the PBtree. If there has at least one equation as $v.B[HMAC(v.R, HMAC(k_j, p_i)) \bmod M] := 0$, then we can infer that $U(v) \cap p_i = \phi$. For any subtree node v' of node v, there exists $U(v') \cap p_i = \phi$, because $U(v') \subset U(v)$. Then we can remove ith row of the matrix $M_{[a,b]}$ from $M_{[a,b]}$. We take new matrix to search on the PBtree. We continue that operation on the PBtree, until the matrix $M_{[a,b]}$ becomes empty or we finish searching terminal nodes.

Now, we analyze the time complexity of this algorithm. The number of PBtree index items is n, the query range is $[a, b]$, and the number of query result is R.

The average runtime of query algorithm depends on the size of query result $|R|$, if $|R| = 0$, then it will only need check the root node of PBtree, so the time complex is $O(1)$ in this case. While n is usually much larger than $|R|$ in the real word. So as to querying every item in the result set R, we need to traverse at least $2(\log n) - 1$ nodes. Therefore, the time complex of this algorithm above is $O(|R| \log n)$ generally (Fig. 4).

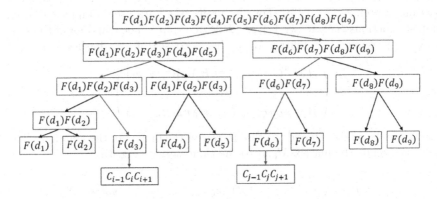

Fig. 4. Query for cloud server

3.6 Decryption

If the finishing condition is searching on terminal node, there exists ith row of $M_{[a,b]}$ for every p_i satisfying $v.B[HMAC(v.R, HMAC(k_j, p_i)) \ mod \ M] := 1$. It shows that the number in this terminal node falls into the range $[a, b]$ that the data user queries. The ciphertext of this number in the terminal node is $C_i = (d_{i-1}, d_i, d_{i+1})^e (mod \ n)$. Here, the secret key is $sk = (d, n)$. The data user computes C_i with secret key sk to obtain plaintext, the plaintext is $(d_{i-1}, d_i, d_{i+1}) = C_i^d (mod \ n)$. Then, the data user obtains interested number d_i. So far, the query operation is implemented.

3.7 Verification

Prior work is completed at the end of the query, they can not ensure the integrity of the query results. But, in our scheme, we have added additional information into PBtree. The data user gets the result which not only contains what the data user wants, but adjacent data items, which would be used to verify whether the result is really integrated or not.

If the cloud server did not query the matching results, it will return the whole PBtree to the data user for verification. On the other hand, if the cloud server has got the related data set, it will return the result to the data user. Supposing that the range of data user queried is $[a, b]$, after querying in the cloud server, the result is $\{d_i, d_j, d_k\}$. But the data set returned to the data user includes other adjacent data items, it is $\{d_{i-1}, d_i, d_{i+1}, d_{j-1}, d_j, d_{j+1}, d_{k-1}, d_k, d_{k+1}\}$. The data user could use these additional data items to judge whether the result returned by the cloud server is complete.

3.8   False Positive Analysis

Because of the property of the Bloom filter, there always exists false positive when we use Bloom filter to judge whether a prefix is concluded in a set. In order to improve the accuracy of the query results, we need to estimate the rate of false positive to make the query optimal. We always set the number of hash functions is $(m/n) \times \ln 2$, and it will minimize the false positive rate on this condition. As analysed in [18], we can easily get the relationship between a and M_a as follows:

$$M_a = af \times \frac{1 - (2f)^{h - \lceil log\ a \rceil}}{1 - 2f} + (2^{\lceil log\ a \rceil} - a) f(2f)^{h - \lceil log\ a \rceil}$$

where a is the size of all possible query result sets and M_a is denoted as the maximum expected number of false positives. When $f = 0.05$ and $h = 13$, the relationship between M_a and a is as shown in Fig. 5.

Fig. 5. Relationship of M_a and a

4   Security Analysis

4.1   Security Model

PBtree achieves IND-CKA security by pseudo-random function. There is no unavoidable advantage to distinguish it from the random function [16]. This pseudo-random function is: $g : \{0,1\}^n \times \{0,1\}^s \rightarrow \{0,1\}^m$. It means that inputting a string of n bit and a string of s bit maps a m bit string. And the random function is $G : \{0,1\}^n \rightarrow \{0,1\}^m$. This function is used to map a n bit string to a m bit string. For the pseudo-random function g, selecting a fixed scalar $k \in \{0,1\}^s$, and it can efficiently compute $g(x, k)$ for any $x \in \{0,1\}^n$. In polynomial time, the rival has no negligible probability to distinguish $g\{x, k\}$ and the output of the random function G. We use $HMAC()$ as the pseudo-random function. When the adversary does not have negligible probability in polynomial time to distinguish between the actual index generated using the pseudo-random function and the simulated index generated by the random function, then it demonstrates that this symmetric searchable encryption scheme is secure.

4.2   Security Proof

We treat PBtree as a series of Bloom filters, each of them storing a set of different prefixes that respond to user queries. Therefore, it can be observed that the safety proof of PBtree can be equivalent to proving that the Bloom filter is compliant with IND-CKA and satisfies the following conditions: (1) It can not be leaked any information about data items stored in Bloom filters; (2) the adversaries can not distinguish two Bloom filters storing different size of data sets. We consider a non-adaptive adversary who has finite original query results, including a set of security trapdoors and their corresponding query results. To help proving, we assume a probabilistic polynomial time simulator S, it can simulate the creation of a security index, which retains only a small number of history search query traces. The rival using S as using a real index to query, the challenge of the adversary is whether there is a negligible probability to make a distinction between the results returned by two different indexes. In the following definition, let the security parameter s be the length of the secret key.

Records of historical query H_q. The set $D = \{D_1, D_2, \ldots, D_n\}$ represents a set of data, and D_i is the ith data item. The set $R_{1:q} = \{R_1, R_2, \ldots, R_q\}$ represents the range query for q times, and the format of each query is $R_i = \{a_i, b_i\}(a_i, b_i, q \in N)$. Historical records is defined as $H_q = \{D, R_{1:q}\}$, where D contains at least one query that satisfies $R_{1:q}$. In order to limit the adversary to be solvable in the polynomial time, q must be a polynomial of the safe parameter s.

Advantage of the adversary A_v. For each range query $R_i = \{a_i, b_i\}$, there will be a generation of r_i trapdoors $T_i = \{t_{i,1}, t_{i,2}, \ldots, t_{i,r_i}\}$, then we encrypt them with secret key K. The advantages of the adversary include the trapdoor that satisfies the range query, security index I of the data set D, and the set of encrypted data items $Enc_K(D) = \{Enc_K(D_1), Enc_K(D_2), \ldots, Enc_K(D_n)\}$. Here, $A_v(H_q) = \{T; I; Enc_K(D)\}$. In addition, the adversary may also know the approximate amount of encrypted data.

Trace of the query. Defined as an adversary to match in index I after using T access and search model. The data items matching the access pattern are $M(T) = \{m(t_1), m(t_2), \ldots, m(t_q)\}$. $m(t_i)$ represents the data item that matches the trapdoor t_i. Search model is an asymmetric binary matrix $\prod_T$ defined on T, and when $t_p = t_q$, $\prod_T [p, q] = 1$. The trace $M_{(Hq)} = \{M(R_{1:q}), \prod_T [p, q]\}$ is defined on H_q. In the two modes, the adversary obtains only one set of matching data for each trap. Thus, each Bloom filter can be treated as a different match(which may be the same in PBtree). Each range query can not match to multiple different trapdoors.

Theorem 2. *PBtree scheme is IND-CKA security base on the pseudo-random function f and the encryption algorithm Enc.*

Proof. The adversary can construct a polynomial time simulator $S = \{S_0, S_q\}$ with the advantage $A_v(H_q)$ and a real result query trace M_{H_q}. $A_v^*a(H_q)$ denotes the advantage of rival simulation, I^* denotes the index of the simulation, $Enc_K(D^*)$ denotes the simulated encrypted data, and T^* denotes the trapdoor. According to definition, each Bloom filter matches a different trapdoor, and the query results are visible. ID_j represents a unique identifier for a Bloom filter. The final output of the simulator is a trapdoor created by the historical traces of the query range that the adversary selected, assuming that the adversary can not know the index and the trapdoor before selecting range.

First: simulate index. It is known that the length and number of Bloom filters are related to I, and generate a string B^* with the same length as I^* to simulate the index I^*, set to 1 in the random bit, and ensure that the number of position set to 1 is similar in each Bloom filter of each layer. Then, we generate random $Enc_K(D^*)$, each of which has the same length as the original encrypted data $Enc_K(D)$, $|Enc_K(D^*)| = |Enc_K(D)|$.

In the index I^*, we store the entire set of $Enc_K(D^*)$ in the first Bloom filter representing the PBtree root node. In the next two Bloom filters store two subsets of $Enc_K(D^*)$, and for each data, it is assigned to one of the Bloom filters through throwing coins. We take this operation in turn, so that the number of data for each subset is differ by no more than one.

Second: Simulator state S_0. In h_q, when $q = 0$, it represents that the simulator state is S_0. We define the adversary's advantage is $A_v^*(H_0) = \{T^*; I^*; Enc_K(D^*)\}$. In the trapdoor set T^*, each data item in $Enc_K(D^*)$ corresponds to a matching trapdoor. The length of each trapdoor is calculated by the random function g, and the maximum length of the trapdoor may depend on the length of the data in the prefix set(when the length of data is n, the length of the trapdoor is $n + 1$). Therefore, we generate $(n + 1) * |Enc_K(D^*)|$ trapdoors with the length of $|g(.)|$, and each data in $Enc_K(D^*)$ is associated with no more than $n + 1$ trapdoors. The distribution of each trapdoor in index I^* is the same as in the original index I, and the structure of the index generated by the simulation is exactly as same as the index structure generated in PBtree. Since g is a random function and the distribution probability of the trapdoor is uniform, this distribution is indistinguishable for the adversary in probability polynomial time.

Third: simulator state S_q. In h_q, when $q \geq 1$, it represents that the simulator state is S_q. We define the advantage of the adversary is $A_v^*(H_q) = \{T^*; T_q; Enc_K(D^*)\}$. T_q is the historical query of the corresponding trapdoor. Considering that data set in each trapdoor is $M(T) = m(t_1), m(t_2), \ldots, m(t_q)$, $M(R_{1:q})$ contains p unique data. In each data $Enc_K(D_p)$, simulator combines the trapdoors and the corresponding data items of $M(T_i)$. Because of $p < |D|$, simulator generates i random strings($1 \leq i \leq |D| - q + 1$). And we associate $Enc_K^*(D_i)$ with $n + 1$ trapdoors as the second step to ensure that the strings do not match the strings in $M(T_i)$. The simulator state ST_q records trapdoors and the matching data. For the first Bloom filter, we map identifiers of all data: $Enc_K(D^*) = M(R_{1:q}) \cup Enc_K^*(D_i)$, the Bloom filter of child node are operated in the way that we have described above. The output of simulator is $\{T^*; T_q; Enc_K(D^*)\}$. All steps are made by the simulator in polynomial time.

If data queried by the adversary is matched with the set $M(R_{1:q})$ in the probability polynomial time, the simulator will provide the correct trap. For other data, because of the random function g, the trapdoors provided by the simulator are indistinguishable. Since each Bloom filter contains random bits that are set to 1, our scheme is proved safe under the IND-CKA model.

5   Experiment Evaluation

5.1   Experiment

In this section, we implement our verifiable scheme, and evaluate it in terms of computational cost, query cost, security and verification. Specifically, in our experiments, we develop our scheme on Ubuntu 16.04 with 8 GB memory and an intel core i7-6700 processor. We use HAMC-SHAI as the pseudo-random function in the Bloom filter. For the Bloom filter, its length m and the stored data amount n satisfy such a relationship: $m/n = 10$. We use the virtual machine to simulate the operation of the server. The data used for presentation and performance test are randomly generated by the $random()$ function.

First, data owner transfers the data to cloud server by a client. The client reads and orders these data, then records every data item as a triplet. Its duties also include encryption, and it encrypts data items and prefixes with AES algorithm. After constructing PBtree, the client sends encrypted data and PBtree to the cloud server. We chose random datasets which consist of 10000 to 100000 records. Next, when someone wants to query data from the server, he should input the query range to the client, then the trapdoor will be computed and sent to server by the client. Last, when the server receives the trapdoor, it will use the method we mentioned before to match the data on the server. When the matching is success, the server returns the result data set, and when it fails to match the corresponding data, the server returns all the data stored on PBtree to the client for users verifying.

5.2   Evaluation

To evaluate our work, we compared our work with existing range query scheme on ciphertext including the private-preserving range query scheme, bucketing schemes and order-preserving schemes. In evaluation of the performance of our scheme, we consider five factors: local computing overhead, server query computing overhead, server storing overhead, security and verification. The table shows the result. In this comparing work, we set the data size is n, and the query size is R.

According to the table, our scheme increases a little computing and storing overhead, but compared to the paper [5,9], it has better private-preserving.

Besides, our scheme not only has the same algorithm complexity as the original project, but also has the significate property of verification (Table 1).

Table 1. Performance comparison

Schemes	Local computation	Query computation	Storage	Security	Verification
Rang query	$O(n \log n)$	$O(|R| \log n)$	$O(n \log n)$	Strong	No
Bucketing	$O(n^2)$	$O(|R| \cdot n)$	$O(n)$	Weak	No
Order-preserving	$O(n \log n)$	$O(n)$	$O(n)$	Weak	No
Our scheme	$O(n \log n)$	$O(|R| \log n)$	$O(n \log n)$	Strong	Yes

In this section, we answer the running time of our verifiable scheme. For the time of the assessment, we mainly take into account two phases: a construction phase and a query phase.

In the construction phase, this process includes three interactive steps, which are data ordering, prefix encoding and PBtree construction. The results are as Fig. 6(a).

In the second phase, query process consists of generating and transmitting the trapdoor, matching the prefix, and decrypting the data. The results of this phase are shown in Fig. 6(b).

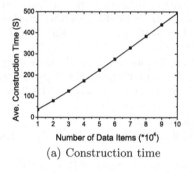
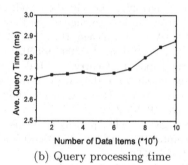

(a) Construction time   (b) Query processing time

Fig. 6. Performance evaluation

6   Conclusion

In this paper, we present that although the private-preserving range query scheme proposed by Li et al. is security under the IND-CKA model, but it is not satisfied verification. Data users receive the result that the cloud server returns, but it is trouble for data users that they cannot be sure whether the query result is completely correct. Our scheme is based on the private-preserving range query scheme, and achieves the property of verification by adding additional information into the query result, and data users utilize additional information to verify the query result.

References

1. Amazon: Amazon Web Services. http://aws.amazon.com
2. Bloom, B.H.: Space/time trade-offs in hash coding with allowable errors. Commun. ACM **13**(7), 422–426 (1970). http://doi.acm.org/10.1145/362686.362692
3. Boldyreva, A., Chenette, N., Lee, Y., O'Neill, A.: Order-preserving symmetric encryption. In: Joux, A. (ed.) EUROCRYPT 2009. LNCS, vol. 5479, pp. 224–241. Springer, Heidelberg (2009). https://doi.org/10.1007/978-3-642-01001-9_13
4. Boldyreva, A., Chenette, N., O'Neill, A.: Order-preserving encryption revisited: improved security analysis and alternative solutions. In: Rogaway, P. (ed.) CRYPTO 2011. LNCS, vol. 6841, pp. 578–595. Springer, Heidelberg (2011). https://doi.org/10.1007/978-3-642-22792-9_33
5. Boneh, D., Di Crescenzo, G., Ostrovsky, R., Persiano, G.: Public key encryption with keyword search. In: Cachin, C., Camenisch, J.L. (eds.) EUROCRYPT 2004. LNCS, vol. 3027, pp. 506–522. Springer, Heidelberg (2004). https://doi.org/10.1007/978-3-540-24676-3_30
6. Canetti, R., Feige, U., Goldreich, O., Naor, M.: Adaptively secure multi-party computation. In: Proceedings of the Twenty-Eighth Annual ACM Symposium on the Theory of Computing, Philadelphia, Pennsylvania, USA, 22–24 May 1996, pp. 639–648 (1996). http://doi.acm.org/10.1145/237814.238015
7. Chang, Y., Mitzenmacher, M.: Privacy preserving keyword searches on remote encrypted data. IACR Cryptology ePrint Archive 2004, 51 (2004). http://eprint.iacr.org/2004/051
8. Chow, R., Golle, P., Jakobsson, M., Shi, E., Staddon, J., Masuoka, R., Molina, J.: Controlling data in the cloud: outsourcing computation without outsourcing control. In: Proceedings of the First ACM Cloud Computing Security Workshop, CCSW 2009, Chicago, IL, USA, 13 November 2009, pp. 85–90 (2009). http://doi.acm.org/10.1145/1655008.1655020
9. van Dijk, M., Gentry, C., Halevi, S., Vaikuntanathan, V.: Fully homomorphic encryption over the integers. In: Gilbert, H. (ed.) EUROCRYPT 2010. LNCS, vol. 6110, pp. 24–43. Springer, Heidelberg (2010). https://doi.org/10.1007/978-3-642-13190-5_2
10. Google: Google App Engine. https://en.softonic.com/
11. Gupta, P., Mckeown, N.: Algorithms for packet classification. IEEE Netw. **15**(2), 24–32 (2002)
12. Hacigümüs, H., Iyer, B.R., Li, C., Mehrotra, S.: Executing SQL over encrypted data in the database-service-provider model. In: Proceedings of the 2002 ACM SIGMOD International Conference on Management of Data, Madison, Wisconsin, 3-6 June 2002, pp. 216–227 (2002). http://doi.acm.org/10.1145/564691.564717
13. Hore, B., Mehrotra, S., Canim, M., Kantarcioglu, M.: Secure multidimensional range queries over outsourced data. VLDB J. **21**(3), 333–358 (2012). https://doi.org/10.1007/s00778-011-0245-7
14. Hore, B., Mehrotra, S., Tsudik, G.: A privacy-preserving index for range queries. In: Proceedings of the Thirtieth International Conference on Very Large Data Bases, Toronto, Canada, August 31 - September 3 2004, pp. 720–731 (2004). http://www.vldb.org/conf/2004/RS19P2.PDF
15. IBM: IBM Blue Cloud Computing Platform. https://www.ibm.com/cloud-computing/
16. Katz, J., Lindell, Y.: Introduction to Modern Cryptography. Chapman and Hall/CRC Press, Boca Raton (2007)

17. Li, J., Omiecinski, E.R.: Efficiency and security trade-off in supporting range queries on encrypted databases. In: Jajodia, S., Wijesekera, D. (eds.) DBSec 2005. LNCS, vol. 3654, pp. 69–83. Springer, Heidelberg (2005). https://doi.org/10.1007/11535706_6

18. Li, R., Liu, A.X., Wang, A.L., Bruhadeshwar, B.: Fast and scalable range query processing with strong privacy protection for cloud computing. IEEE/ACM Trans. Netw. **24**(4), 2305–2318 (2016). https://doi.org/10.1109/TNET.2015.2457493

19. Microsoft: Microsoft Azure. `http://.microsoft.com/azure`

20. Ren, K., Wang, C., Wang, Q.: Security challenges for the public cloud. IEEE Internet Comput. **16**(1), 69–73 (2012). https://doi.org/10.1109/MIC.2012.14

21. Rivest, R.: The MD5 Message-Digest Algorithm. RFC Editor (1992)

22. Song, D.X., Wagner, D.A., Perrig, A.: Practical techniques for searches on encrypted data. In: 2000 IEEE Symposium on Security and Privacy, Berkeley, California, USA, May 14-17, 2000, pp. 44–55 (2000). https://doi.org/10.1109/SECPRI.2000.848445

Ranked Searchable Symmetric Encryption Supporting Conjunctive Queries

Yanjun Shen[1]([✉]) and Peng Zhang[2]

[1] Faculty of Information Technology, Monash University,
Melbourne, VIC 3800, Australia
olivia.shen@monash.edu
[2] College of Information Engineering, Shenzhen University, Shenzhen 518060, China
zhangp@szu.edu.cn

Abstract. Searchable symmetric encryption allows searching over the encrypted data directly without decryption, which is particularly useful in cloud computing as users can outsource the data to cloud servers without privacy leakage while retaining the ability to search. To meet users' specific needs, searching supporting conjunctive queries and ranking is considered. Based on the searchable symmetric encryption protocol OXT of Cash et al., we propose a ranked searchable symmetric encryption scheme by integrating order preserving encryption, so that the matching documents returned to the client are ordered by keyword occurrences. It retains OXT's efficiency and supports ranked search. The security analysis shows that the proposed scheme is secure against chosen plaintext attacks.

Keywords: Searchable symmetric encryption · Conjunctive queries
Order preserving encryption · Ranked search

1 Introduction

With data boosting in modern businesses and trending cloud database solutions, data specialists are constantly facing advanced requirements from aspects including but not limited to data availability and integrity, query processing efficiency, and especially impending security concerns when businesses consider transferring databases and data warehouses from an on-premise server to an untrusted external online server, in other words, outsourcing data storage. Therefore, encryption techniques have never been as challenged as before so as to protect confidential sensitive data from being compromised by malicious or honest-but-curious adversaries.

As an efficient and dominant security technique, data encryption, which encodes data from plaintext into ciphertext that only authorised people with a secret key can read, on the one hand enables parties to communicate messages over a security bridge; however, on the other hand, sacrifices query performance to some extend for security robustness because data has to be decrypted first for further processing.

© Springer International Publishing AG 2017
J. K. Liu and P. Samarati (Eds.): ISPEC 2017, LNCS 10701, pp. 350–360, 2017.
https://doi.org/10.1007/978-3-319-72359-4_20

In order to improve capabilities such like searching or computing over ciphertext to fulfil fundamental business needs, new methods and approaches are proposed to address both data efficiency and security, as a result of which, searchable symmetric encryption (SSE) schemes, firstly introduced by Song et al. [1], have been continuously revised and extended (e.g., [2–5]) to strike a balance between privacy and performance from a technical viewpoint. Meanwhile, with respect to business scenarios, directions for flexible keyword search that supports Boolean queries (both conjunctive and disjunctive), sorting and range queries have been proposed (e.g., [6–10]) to enhance real-world utilisation.

1.1 Our Contributions

In this paper, we follow a searchable symmetric encryption scheme called Oblivious Cross-Tags (OXT) protocol developed by Cash et al. in 2013 [5], and integrate an order preserving encryption scheme into the OXT protocol. As a result, an order preserving searchable encryption scheme in the symmetric key setting is put forward, which allows conjunctive queries over multiple keywords. The proposed scheme returns matching documents ordered by keyword occurrences. In other words, the document with the largest number of occurrences that all keywords appear together is returned first.

As a rigorous extension of Cash et al.'s OXT protocols [5], this proposed scheme retains OXT's performance efficiency, to be precise, optimal server computation and storage as well single round of communication; on the basis of which, it also improves OXT by supporting ranked search to offer a more satisfactory result set.

1.2 The Related Work

In this section, the related studies about searchable symmetric encryption, conjunctive and Boolean queries, and order preserving encryption will be introduced.

Searchable symmetric encryption. Song et al. constructed an SSE solution in 2000 [1] at a price of weakened security guarantee, after which, Goh in 2003 [2] and Chang and Mitzenmacheret in 2005 [3] proposed secure indexes to tackle the above security limitations, whose computation complexity is linear to the number of documents. In 2011, Curtmola et al. [4] provided two solutions whose server computation is linear in the number of documents containing the keyword hence optimal, which was then most secure and efficient and the first sublinear SSE scheme. In addition, they also proposed SSE in the multi-user setting. However, all the above SSE schemes focus on single-keyword search, which results in a large number of matching documents, and a naive solution of conjunctive queries is to run a single-keyword SSE scheme for each keyword thus is not efficient.

Conjunctive and Boolean queries. An SSE solution with supporting for conjunctive and Boolean queries is of practical essence, at least the scheme should be able to support conjunctive searches that return matching documents containing all queried keywords (e.g., "female" and "master degree"). Conjunctive searches in the symmetric key setting was first considered by Golle, Staddon and Waters in 2004 [6], which is suited for structured data only and leaks the attributes searched, whose complexity is linear in the number of all documents in the database. Ballard et al. in 2005 [7] and Byun et al. in 2006 [8] furthered efficient conjunctive keyword searches, both of which as before apply to structured data only and are linear in the size of the database. Besides, none of the solutions supports disjunctive Boolean queries.

The OXT protocol built by Cash et al. [5] extends to general Boolean queries not only supporting conjunctions but also disjunctions, negations, and more. It also addresses limitations of previous SSE schemes by applying to arbitrarily-structured data, including both attribute-value data and free text. Furthermore, this solution has significant advantages over previous SSE schemes because it scales to large database at a realistic price of allowing leakage of access patterns (but never searched attributes) that is explicitly and precisely defined, whose complexity is linear in the number of documents that contain the least frequent keyword in the query. This protocol can also be extended to support range queries (e.g., "age < 30") and the multi-user setting.

Order preserving encryption (OPE). OPE was first introduced by Agrawal et al. in 2004 [11], which was formally performed and analysed by Boldyreva et al. in 2009 [12] for the first time. Several other OPE schemes were proposed (e.g., [13–15]) but provided no or little security guarantees while leaking most of the plaintext until Popa et al. [16] proposed an ideal-security OPE scheme that satisfies the minimum security requirement, which is to reveal nothing about the plaintext values other than their relative order. OPE enhances searchable encryption to support range queries containing operators such like greater than ($>$) or less than ($<$) in addition to equal to ($=$), meanwhile enables ranked search over encrypted data. Wang et al. [10,17] proposed ranked searchable symmetric encryption schemes adapted from [12], which supports single-keyword search only. Cao et al. [18] defined a multi-keyword ranked search encryption scheme using "coordinate matching" that ranks documents by as many keyword matches as possible which is not ideal considering varied presence frequency and significance of different keywords. Other feasible multi-keyword ranked search encryption schemes (e.g., [19–21]) have been proposed recently using vector space model.

1.3   Organisation

The rest of this paper is organised as follows. Section 2 introduces the preliminaries, including notations, the OXT protocol, and order preserving encryption. Next, our order preserving SSE is defined and proposed in Sect. 3, after which we analyse the security of the proposed algorithm in Sect. 4. At last, this paper is concluded in Sect. 5.

2   Preliminaries

2.1   Notations

In the rest of the sections, some notations are continuously quoted and are essential denoting concepts and terminologies. Following is a list of fundamental notations involved in this paper.

- $[c]$: a set from 1 to c, which is the same as $\{1, 2, ..., c\}$
- $|t|$: the size or length of t
- $t[i]$: the i-th elements of t
- d: the number of documents in a database DB
- ind_i: the identifier of the i-th document
- W_i: a set of keywords in the i-th document
- $W = \cup_{i=1}^{d} W_i$: the keyword set of the entire database
- $DB = (\text{ind}_i, W_i)_{i=1}^{d}$: a database is parsed as a list of key (document identifier ind_i) - value (corresponding keyword set W_i) pairs
- $DB(w)$: a set of identifiers of documents that contain the keyword w
- *sterm*: a term (or keyword) estimated to have the least frequency, which is denoted by w_1 for simplicity, that will return a *smallest* $|DB(w_1)|$
- *xterm*: other terms (or keywords) that are queried, where x stands for *cross*.
- TSet: a tuple set that presents a list of equal-length data tuples with each keyword in the database
- XSet: a set data structure that contains elements computed from each keyword - document pair

2.2   The OXT Protocol

The Oblivious Cross-Tags (OXT) protocol is proposed in the highly-scalable SSE scheme by Cash et al. [5], which consists of an EDB Setup algorithm and a Search protocol. The output from the protocol are encrypted identifiers, which are used by the client to retrieve encrypted documents. The OXT protocol can support Boolean queries of multiple keywords, achieve better security performance by preventing the server from knowing the identifiers of queried *sterm* (the term or keyword that is evaluated to have the least frequency), and reduce the communication between the client and the server to a single round. In order to present our order preserving SSE in an approachable manner, the syntax of OXT is depicted as follows.

In the EDB Setup algorithm described in the following Algorithm 1, function EDBSetup works by taking DB as input and outputting secret keys K along with EDB. K is given to the client, while EDB is given to the server. At this stage, for each keyword in the database, a list of encrypted document pointers is generated, which is then added to an array **T** indexed by all keywords of W. During EDBSetup, TSet is initialised taking **T** as an output, assembling EDB together with XSet.

Algorithm 1. Cash - EDB Setup Algorithm

Input: DB
Output: EDB, K
  function EDBSetup(DB)
    Select key K_S for PRF F. Select keys K_X, K_I, K_Z for PRF F_p with range $\mathbb{Z}_p^*$.
    DB $= (\text{ind}_i, \mathsf{W}_i)_{i=1}^d$
    Initialise $\mathbf{T} \leftarrow \{\}$ indexed by $w \in \mathsf{W}$.
    Set XSet $\leftarrow \emptyset$
    for $w \in \mathsf{W}$ **do**
      Initialise $\mathbf{t} \leftarrow \{\}$.
      Set $K_e \leftarrow F(K_S, w)$.
      for ind $\in$ DB(w) **do**
        Set a counter $c \leftarrow 0$
        $e \leftarrow \mathsf{Enc}(K_e, \text{ind})$.
        Compute xind $\leftarrow F_p(K_I, \text{ind})$, $z \leftarrow F_p(K_Z, w||c)$, and $y \leftarrow \text{xind} z^{-1}$.
        Append (e, y) to $\mathbf{t}$.
        Set xtag $\leftarrow g^{F_p(K_X, w) \cdot \text{xind}}$ and XSet $\leftarrow$ XSet $\cup \{\text{xtag}\}$
        Let $c \leftarrow c + 1$.
      end for
      $\mathbf{T}[w] \leftarrow \mathbf{t}$
    end for
    Set (TSet, K_T) $\leftarrow$ TSetSetup($\mathbf{T}$).
    return EDB $=$ (TSet, XSet), $K = (K_S, K_X, K_I, K_Z, K_T)$
  end function

For ease of understanding, the Search protocol running between the client and the server is split into two parts: Token Generation algorithm and Search algorithm. The Token Generation algorithm described in Algorithm 2 computes and outputs a tag of *sterm* as well as a set of tokens of *xterms* using K and w_1 at the client, and then the Search algorithm described in Algorithm 3 checks existence of *xterms* in the XSet of *sterms* at the server. In other words, the client takes responsibility to choose *sterm* which is basically the least frequent keyword that exists in the smallest number of satisfied documents, and the server returns encrypted identifiers of all satisfied documents to the client, which is then decrypted at the client to retrieve documents, and then stops the client from sending tokens.

Algorithm 2. Cash - Token Generation Algorithm

Input: $\bar{w} = (w_1 \wedge \cdots \wedge w_n), K$
Output: stag, xtoken
  function TokenGeneration($\bar{w}, K$)
    Computes stag $\leftarrow$ TSetGetTag(K_T, w_1).
    for $c = 1, 2, \ldots$ until stopped by the server **do**
      for $i = 2, \ldots, n$ **do**
        xtoken$[c, i] \leftarrow g^{F_p(K_Z, w_1||c) \cdot F_p(K_X, w_i)}$
      end for
      xtoken$[c] \leftarrow$ (xtoken$[c, 2], \ldots,$ xtoken$[c, n]$)
    end for
    return stag, xtoken
  end function

Algorithm 3. Cash - Search Algorithm

Input: stag, xtoken, EDB
Output: e
  function Search(stag, xtoken, EDB)
    Set $t \leftarrow$ TSetRetrieve(TSet, stag)
    for $c = 1, \ldots, |t|$ **do**
      Retrieve (e, y) from the c-th tuple in t
      if $\forall i = 2, \ldots, n : \mathsf{xtoken}[c, i]^y \in \mathsf{XSet}$ **then**
        Send e to the client until the last tuple in t then sends stop
      end if
    end for
  end function

Please refer to [5] to obtain more details about the used parameters and T-set implementation $\Sigma = \{\mathsf{TSetSetup}, \mathsf{TSetGetTag}, \mathsf{TSetRetrieve}\}$.

2.3 Order Preserving Encryption

The order preserving encryption scheme $\Pi = \{KeyGen, Enc, Dec\}$ is a deterministic symmetric-key encryption scheme that maintains order relations of plaintexts. A detailed description of each algorithm follows.

$KeyGen(\lambda) \to s$. This algorithm inputs the security parameter λ and generates a secret key s.

$Enc(s, x) \to y$. This algorithm computes a ciphertext y for plaintext x based on the secret key s.

$Dec(s, y) \to x$. This algorithm computes the plaintext x for ciphertext y based on the secret key s.

We say the scheme Π is correct if $\Pi.Dec(s, \Pi.Enc(s, x)) = x$ for any valid s and x. We say it is order preserving if for any valid s, $x < x' \implies \Pi.Enc(s, x) < \Pi.Enc(s.x')$.

So far, the strongest definition of security of order-preserving encryption is indistinguishability under ordered chosen plaintext attack (IND-OCPA), which is achieved by the encryption schemes of [22].

3 Order Preserving SSE Supporting Conjunctive Queries

In this section, the order preserving extension of SSE, which searches the encrypted database based on a conjunctive query and returns satisfied documents ordered by the number of occurrences of all keywords, will be presented and elaborated in detail. This scheme comprises four algorithms as follows, three of which are altered to introduce keyword(s) occurrences.

EDB Setup Algorithm. As described in Algorithm 4, it takes the database DB as an input and outputs the encrypted database EDB along with keys K by the data owner. For each keyword w of interest, an encrypted identifier e of each of all mapped documents, an order preserving encryption result $e^{\cdot}$ of keyword occurrence o in each mapped document, as well as a word-document pointer y that is a function result of the keyword w, each counter c (which is the number of mapped documents), and the corresponding document identifier ind are all stored in $\mathbf{T}[w]$. The array $\mathbf{T}$ indexed by all keywords is then used by TSetSetup as an input to initialise TSet and outputs K_T. Meanwhile, the function result of each keyword w and associated identifiers ind are stored in XSet. The encrypted database EDB = (TSet, XSet) is given to the server, and all keys K are given to the data owner.

Algorithm 4. EDB Setup Algorithm

Input: DB
Output: EDB, K
  function EDBSetup(DB)
    • Select key K_S for PRF F and $K_{e'}$ for OPE scheme Π. Select keys K_X, K_I, K_Z for PRF F_p (with range $\mathbb{Z}_p^*$).
    • Initialise $\mathbf{T}$ to an empty array indexed by keywords from W.
    • Initialise XSet $\leftarrow \{\}$.
    for $w \in$ W do
      Initialise $\mathbf{t} \leftarrow \{\}$; and let $K_e \leftarrow F(K_S, w)$.
      for ind $\in$ DB(w) do
        Initialise a counter $c \leftarrow 0$.
        Set xind $\leftarrow F_p(K_I, \text{ind})$, $z \leftarrow F_p(K_Z, w||c)$, $y \leftarrow$ xind $\cdot z^{-1}$.
        Compute $e \leftarrow$ Enc(K_e, ind).
        Compute $e' \leftarrow \Pi.Enc(K_{e'}, o)$.
        Append (y, e, e') to $\mathbf{t}$.
        Set xtag $\leftarrow g^{F_p(K_X, w) \cdot \text{xind}}$ and append (xtag, e') to XSet.
        $c \leftarrow c + 1$.
      end for
      $\mathbf{T}[w] \leftarrow \mathbf{t}$
    end for
    • (TSet, K_T) $\leftarrow$ TSetSetup($\mathbf{T}$).
    • return EDB = (Tset, XSet), $K = (K_S, K_{e'}, K_X, K_I, K_Z, K_T)$
  end function

Token Generation Algorithm. This algorithm runs at the client side by generating *stag* and *xtoken*, using keywords $\bar{w}$ from a query and keys K from the data owner. *stag* is computed against keyword w_1 that is assumed to result in a relatively small number of mapped documents among all keywords in the query, and *xtoken* is the function result of w_1, counter c, and each other keyword w_i. *stag* and *xtoken* are sent to the server. The details are described in the following Algorithm 5.

Algorithm 5. Token Generation Algorithm

Input: K, $\bar{w} = (w_1 \wedge \cdots \wedge w_n)$
Output: stag, xtoken
  function TokenGeneration(K, $\bar{w}$)
    • Computes stag $\leftarrow$ TSetGetTag(K_T, w_1).
    for $c = 1, 2, \ldots$ until the server stops do
      for $i = 2, \ldots, n$ do
        xtoken$[c, i] \leftarrow g^{F_p(K_Z, w_1||c) \cdot F_p(K_X, w_i)}$
      end for
      Set xtoken$[c] \leftarrow$ (xtoken$[c, 2]$, $\ldots$, xtoken$[c, n]$)
    end for
    • return stag, xtoken
  end function

Search Algorithm. This algorithm described in Algorithm 6 runs at the server, which first retrieves $\mathbf{T}[w_1]$ using $stag$ from the client and TSet from the data owner, further retrieves the encrypted identifier e of each document that contains w_1 and the corresponding number of occurrences e_1'. It then uses $xtoken$ to verify whether other keywords exist in XSet for each satisfying document and get their encrypted number of occurrences e_i' accordingly. Following that, the smallest of e' denoted as e_{min}' is chosen to be the overall number of occurrences that all keywords appear together. In the end, encrypted identifiers e of all satisfying documents along with their number of occurrences e_{min}' are sent to the client sorted by e_{min}'.

Algorithm 6. Search Algorithm

Input: stag, xtoken, EDB
Output: ERS
  function Search(TSet, XSet, stag, xtoken)
    • Initialise ERS $\leftarrow$ {}
    • Set $\mathbf{t} = \mathbf{T}[w_1] \leftarrow$ TSetRetrieve(TSet, stag)
    for $c = 1, \ldots, |\mathbf{t}|$ **do**
      Retrieve (y, e, e_1') from the c-th tuple in $\mathbf{t}$
      if $\forall i = 2, \ldots, n :$ xtoken$[c, i]^y \in$ XSet **then**
        Retrieve $e_2', \ldots, e_n'$.
        $e_{min}' \leftarrow \min(e_1', e_2', \ldots, e_n')$ and append (e, e_{min}') to ERS
      end if
    end for
    • $\forall e$ in ERS, order e by e_{min}'.
    • return ERS
  end function

Retrieve Algorithm. This algorithm described in Algorithm 7 runs at the client side after receiving ERS from the server, which is decrypted using keys K_S and $K_{e'}$ to get document identifiers and corresponding number of occurrences accordingly. Encrypted documents are retrieved and returned in order (i.e., the document with largest keyword occurrences is returned first).

Algorithm 7. Retrieve Algorithm

Input: K, ERS
Output: ind, o
  function Retrieve(ERS)
    • $K_e \leftarrow F(K_S, w_1)$
    for $(e, e_{min}') \in$ ERS **do**
      Compute ind $\leftarrow$ Dec(K_e, e), $o \leftarrow \Pi.\text{Dec}(K_{e'}, e_{min}')$
    end for
    • return (ind, o) sorted by o.
  end function

---

4 Security Analyses

In this section we describe the scheme leakage profile $\mathcal{L}$ and analyse its security. We use the definition of semantic security for SSE as Cash et al.

Definition. Let $\varUpsilon = \{\text{EDBSetup}, \text{TokenGeneration}, \text{Search}, \text{Retrieve}\}$ be an SSE scheme and let $\mathcal{L}$ be an algorithm. For efficient algorithms A and S, we define experiments $Real_A^\varUpsilon(\lambda)$ and $Ideal_{A,S}^\varUpsilon(\lambda)$ as follows.

$Real_A^\varUpsilon(\lambda)$: Chooses DB and a list of queries q. The experiment then runs $(\text{EDB}, K) \leftarrow \text{EDBSetup(DB)}$. For each $i \in |q|$, it runs $\text{TokenGeneration}(K, q[i])$ by the client and $\text{Search}(\text{EDB}, stag, xtoken)$ by the server. Finally the game gives EDB and $\mathbf{t}$ to A, which returns a bit that the game uses as its own output.

$Ideal_{A,S}^\varUpsilon(\lambda)$: Chooses DB and a list of queries q. The experiment runs $S(\mathcal{L}(\text{DB}, q))$ and gives its output to A, which returns a bit that the game used as its own output.

We say that is $\mathcal{L}$-semantically-secure against non-adaptive attacks if for all efficient adversaries A there exists an algorithm S such that $\Pr[Real_A^\varUpsilon(\lambda) = 1] - \Pr[Ideal_{A,S}^\varUpsilon(\lambda)] \leq neg(\lambda)$.

Theorem. $\varUpsilon$ is $\mathcal{L}$-semantically-secure against non-adaptive attacks where $\mathcal{L}$ is defined as above, assuming that the DDH assumption holds in G, that F and F_p are secure PRFs, that (Enc, Dec) is an IND-CPA secure symmetric encryption scheme, that Σ is a $\mathcal{L}$-secure and computationally correct T-set implementation, and that $\varPi$ is an IND-OCPA secure order preserving encryption scheme.

Proof. This proof is same with the one in [5] except a new game G_N is added after all games G_{Cash}.

Game G_N. During Initialize mentioned in [5], the ciphertext e' is generated with an encryption of keyword occurrence o. We define there exists an efficient adversary B_N such that
$$Pr[G_N = 1] - Pr[G_{Cash} = 1] \leq \mathbf{Adv}_{\varPi, B_N}^{IND-OCPA}(\lambda)$$
So we say the proposed $\varUpsilon$ is $\mathcal{L}$-semantically-secure against non-adaptive attacks.

5   Conclusion

Based on the work in [5], by setting keyword-occurrence parameters and integrating an order preserving encryption scheme, an order preserving searchable symmetric encryption supporting conjunctive queries is proposed. Not only all matching documents with keywords are returned to clients, the documents are also ordered by keyword occurrences where the document with the largest number of occurrences is returned first, which may be the most desirable answer for users. The security analysis indicates that the proposed scheme is IND-CPA secure based on the DDH assumptions, secure PRFs, secure symmetric encryption scheme, secure T-set implementation, and secure order preserving encryption scheme.

There are several directions of improvement we can make in the future following the current work. The most promising one is to extend the solution to support Boolean queries, which not only supports conjunctive keyword search but also disjunctions, negations, and more. However, the current relevance score of a matching document is defined as the number of occurrences of the least frequently occurring keyword of all queried keywords contained, which needs further investigation to cooperate with more general Boolean search.

Acknowledgments. This work was supported by the Science and Technology Plan of Shenzhen, China (JCYJ20160307150216309, JCYJ20170302151321095), and Tencent Rhinoceros Birds - Scientific Research Foundation for Young Teachers of Shenzhen University, China.

References

1. Song, D.X., Wagner, D., Perrig, A.: Practical techniques for searches on encrypted data. In: IEEE Symposium on Security & Privacy, pp. 44–55 (2000)
2. Goh, E.: Secure indexes. Cryptology ePrint Archive, Report 2003/216 (2003). http://eprint.iacr.org/2003/216
3. Chang, Y.-C., Mitzenmacher, M.: Privacy preserving keyword searches on remote encrypted data. In: Ioannidis, J., Keromytis, A., Yung, M. (eds.) ACNS 2005. LNCS, vol. 3531, pp. 442–455. Springer, Heidelberg (2005). https://doi.org/10.1007/11496137_30
4. Curtmola, R., Garay, J., Kamara, S., Ostrovsky, R.: Searchable symmetric encryption: improved definitions and efficient constructions. J. Comput. Secur. **19**(5), 895–934 (2011)
5. Cash, D., Jarecki, S., Jutla, C., Krawczyk, H., Roşu, M.-C., Steiner, M.: Highly-scalable searchable symmetric encryption with support for boolean queries. In: Canetti, R., Garay, J.A. (eds.) CRYPTO 2013. LNCS, vol. 8042, pp. 353–373. Springer, Heidelberg (2013). https://doi.org/10.1007/978-3-642-40041-4_20
6. Golle, P., Staddon, J., Waters, B.: Secure conjunctive keyword search over encrypted data. In: Jakobsson, M., Yung, M., Zhou, J. (eds.) ACNS 2004. LNCS, vol. 3089, pp. 31–45. Springer, Heidelberg (2004). https://doi.org/10.1007/978-3-540-24852-1_3
7. Ballard, L., Kamara, S., Monrose, F.: Achieving efficient conjunctive keyword searches over encrypted data. In: Qing, S., Mao, W., López, J., Wang, G. (eds.) ICICS 2005. LNCS, vol. 3783, pp. 414–426. Springer, Heidelberg (2005). https://doi.org/10.1007/11602897_35
8. Byun, J.W., Lee, D.H., Lim, J.: Efficient conjunctive keyword search on encrypted data storage system. In: Atzeni, A.S., Lioy, A. (eds.) EuroPKI 2006. LNCS, vol. 4043, pp. 184–196. Springer, Heidelberg (2006). https://doi.org/10.1007/11774716_15
9. Shi, E., Bethencourt, J., Chan, T.H.H., Song, D., Perrig, A.: Multi-dimensional range query over encrypted data. In: IEEE Symposium on Security & Privacy, pp. 350–364 (2007)
10. Wang, C., Cao, N., Li, J., Ren, K., Lou, W.: Secure ranked keyword search over encrypted cloud data. In: IEEE 30th International Conference on Distributed Computing Systems, pp. 253–262 (2010)
11. Agrawal, R., Kiernan, J., Srikant, R., Xu, Y.: Order preserving encryption for numeric data. In: The 2004 ACM SIGMOD International Conference on Management of Data, pp. 563–574 (2004)

12. Boldyreva, A., Chenette, N., Lee, Y., O'Neill, A.: Order-preserving symmetric encryption. In: Joux, A. (ed.) EUROCRYPT 2009. LNCS, vol. 5479, pp. 224–241. Springer, Heidelberg (2009). https://doi.org/10.1007/978-3-642-01001-9_13
13. Lee, S., Park, T.J., Lee, D., Nam, T., Kim, S.: Chaotic order preserving encryption for efficient and secure queries on databases. IEICE Trans. Inf. Syst. 92(11), 2207–2217 (2009)
14. Yum, D.H., Kim, D.S., Kim, J.S., Lee, P.J., Hong, S.J.: Order-preserving encryption for non-uniformly distributed plaintexts. In: Jung, S., Yung, M. (eds.) WISA 2011. LNCS, vol. 7115, pp. 84–97. Springer, Heidelberg (2012). https://doi.org/10.1007/978-3-642-27890-7_7
15. Boldyreva, A., Chenette, N., O'Neill, A.: Order-preserving encryption revisited: improved security analysis and alternative solutions. In: Rogaway, P. (ed.) CRYPTO 2011. LNCS, vol. 6841, pp. 578–595. Springer, Heidelberg (2011). https://doi.org/10.1007/978-3-642-22792-9_33
16. Popa, R.A., Li, F.H., Zeldovich, N.: An ideal-security protocol for order-preserving encoding. In: IEEE Symposium on Security & Privacy, pp. 463–477 (2013)
17. Wang, C., Cao, N., Ren, K., Lou, W.: Enabling secure and efficient ranked keyword search over outsourced cloud data. IEEE Trans. Parallel Distrib. Syst. 23(8), 1467–1479 (2012)
18. Cao, N., Wang, C., Li, M., Ren, K., Lou, W.: Privacy-preserving multi-keyword ranked search over encrypted cloud data. IEEE Trans. Parallel Distrib. Syst. 25(1), 222–233 (2014)
19. Sun, W., Wang, B., Cao, N., Li, M., Lou, W., Hou, Y.T., Li, H.: Privacy-preserving multi-keyword text search in the cloud supporting similarity-based ranking. In: Proceedings of the 8th ACM SIGSAC Symposium on Information, Computer and Communications Security, pp. 71–82. ACM (2013)
20. Fu, Z., Sun, X., Liu, Q., Zhou, L., Shu, J.: Achieving efficient cloud search services: multi-keyword ranked search over encrypted cloud data supporting parallel computing. IEICE Trans. Commun. 98(1), 190–200 (2015)
21. Xia, Z., Wang, X., Sun, X., Wang, Q.: A secure and dynamic multi-keyword ranked search scheme over encrypted cloud data. IEEE Trans. Parallel Distrib. Syst. 27(2), 340–352 (2016)
22. Kerschbaum, F., Schroepfer, A.: Optimal average-complexity ideal-security order-preserving encryption. In: CCS, pp. 275–286 (2014)

A New Functional Encryption
for Multidimensional Range Query
(Short Paper)

Jia Xu[1(✉)], Ee-Chien Chang[2], and Jianying Zhou[3]

[1] Singapore Telecommunications Limited, Singapore, Singapore
jia.xu@singtel.com
[2] National University of Singapore, Singapore, Singapore
changec@comp.nus.edu.sg
[3] Singapore University of Technology and Design, Singapore, Singapore
jianying_zhou@sutd.edu.sg

Abstract. Functional encryption, which emerges in the community recently, is a generalized concept of traditional encryption (e.g. RSA and AES). In traditional encryption scheme, decrypting a ciphertext with a correct decryption key will output the original plaintext associated to the ciphertext. In contrast, in functional encryption scheme, decrypting a ciphertext with a correct decryption key will output a value that is derived from both the plaintext and the decryption key, and the decryption output would change when different correct decryption key is used to decrypt the same ciphertext. We propose a new functional encryption scheme for multidimensional range query. Given a ciphertext that is the encryption of some secret plaintext under a public attribute (a multidimensional point), and a decryption key corresponding to a query range and a function key. If the public attribute point is within the query range, a user is able to decrypt the ciphertext with the decryption key to obtain a value, which is the output of a pre-defined *one-way* function with the secret plaintext and the function key as input. In comparison, in previous functional encryption for range query, a decryption will simply output the original secret plaintext when the attribute point is within the query range.

Keywords: Functional encryption · Multidimensional range query
Polymorphic property

1 Introduction

The concept of functional encryption emerges recently, as a generalization of traditional encryption. Informally, in traditional encryption scheme (e.g. public

The first two authors are supported by the National Research Foundation, Prime Minister's Office, Singapore under its Corporate Laboratory@University Scheme, National University of Singapore, and Singapore Telecommunications Ltd. The third author is supported by SUTD start-up research grant SRG-ISTD-2017-124.

J. K. Liu and P. Samarati (Eds.): ISPEC 2017, LNCS 10701, pp. 361–372, 2017.
https://doi.org/10.1007/978-3-319-72359-4_21

key cipher like RSA and private key cipher like AES), decrypting a ciphertext CT of a secret plaintext Msg with correct decryption key will output the original plaintext Msg. In a functional encryption scheme, decrypting a ciphertext CT with "correct decryption key" SK_k will obtain only a function value $f(k, Msg)$ of the plaintext Msg and the function key k, and nothing more. It will be more interesting when the function f is one-way, such that the original plaintext Msg remains secret after several function values $f(k_j, Msg)$'s for different function keys k_j are revealed.

To the best of our knowledge, almost all previous instances of functional encryption schemes (for example, attribute-based encryption or predicate encryption) implements a functionality F of the following type:

$$F(k, (\mathbf{x}, Msg)) = \begin{cases} Msg & (\text{if } \text{PREDICATE}(\mathbf{x}, k) = \text{True}); \\ \bot & (\text{otherwise}) \end{cases} \tag{1}$$

where PREDICATE is pre-defined. In this paper, we are interested in a more general functionality:

$$F(k, (\mathbf{x}, Msg)) = \begin{cases} f(k, Msg) & (\text{if } \text{PREDICATE}(\mathbf{x}, k) = \text{True}); \\ \bot & (\text{otherwise}) \end{cases} \tag{2}$$

where f is some one-way function. Few works have been devoted to the latter type of functionality (Eq. (2)). Very recently, Gorbunov et al. [1] proposed a function encryption method for any multi-variable polynomial function, using Secure Multi-party Computation. The supported functionality belongs to the latter style (Eq. (2)). In this paper, we will propose a more efficient functional encryption scheme which implements functionality in Eq. (2) for a particular one-way function f (defined later) with PREDICATE replaced by multidimensional range query, using a novel technique.

1.1 Overview of Our Technique

We observe that some (HIBE) encryption scheme (KeyGen, Enc, Dec), e.g. BBG HIBE scheme [2], satisfies a *polymorphic property*: From a pair of keys $(pk, sk) \in$ KeyGen(1^κ), a plaintext M, an identity id, and a random coin r, one can efficiently find multiple tuples $(pk_j, sk_j, M_j, r_j), 1 \le j \le n$, such that for any $1 \le j \le n$, $(pk_j, sk_j) \in$ KeyGen(1^κ) is a valid key pair and

$$\text{Enc}_{pk}(\text{id}, M; r) = \text{CT} = \text{Enc}_{pk_j}(\text{id}, M_j; r_j).$$

From the opposite point of view, a ciphertext CT can be decrypted into value M_j using the decryption key $sk_j, 1 \le j \le n$. We can view these decrypted values M_j's as a function of the original plaintext M which is used to produce the ciphertext CT, i.e. decrypting CT using decryption key sk_j will generate the function value $f(j, M) := M_j$ of the plaintext M. Hence, such polymorphic property may lead to a new way to construct functional encryption schemes [3–6].

1.2   Application

Besides the theoretical merit as an example of a new kind of functional encryption paradigm, our proposed scheme can also be used to authenticate multidimensional range queries. Here we give a brief description in a nutshell: A data owner encrypts his multidimensional data points $(\mathsf{Msg}, \mathbf{x})$ (e.g. netflow, log, or sensor data in a cyber-physical system) using our functional encryption scheme, and outsources all ciphertexts to a cloud. Later, the data owner could choose a multidimensional query range $\mathbf{R}$ and a nonce[1] ρ, and sends a delegation key w.r.t. $(\mathbf{R}, \rho)$ to the cloud. Then the cloud tries to decrypt each ciphertext using this delegation key. If the corresponding point $\mathbf{x}$ is within the query range $\mathbf{R}$, then decryption will succeed and the cloud is able to obtain a one-way function value $f(\rho, \mathsf{Msg})$, which could serve as a proof that $\mathbf{x} \in \mathbf{R}$. The cloud could find and count all ciphertexts of data points within the query range, and sends corresponding proofs to the data owner. This is the basic idea how our proposed scheme can be used to authenticate multidimensional count queries. How to aggregate all individual proofs to reduce total proof size using some homomorphism, and how to prevent miss-counting or double counting, requires other non-trivial techniques. More details are provided in the full version [7,8].

1.3   Contribution

- We propose a functional encryption scheme, by exploiting a special property (we call it "polymorphic property") of the BBG HIBE scheme [2]. Under this functional encryption scheme, given a secret message Msg and a public identity $\boldsymbol{x}$, which is a d-dimensional point in domain $[1, \mathcal{Z}]^d$ where system parameter $\mathcal{Z}$ is an integer, a ciphertext can be generated using the *private*[2] key. A decryption key w.r.t. a d-dimensional rectangular range $\mathbf{R}$ and a random nonce ρ can also be derived from the private key. With this decryption key and the ciphertext for message Msg under identity $\boldsymbol{x}$, the decryption algorithm will output $\Omega^{\rho \cdot \mathsf{Msg}}$ iff $\boldsymbol{x} \in \mathbf{R}$, where Ω is a part of key of the functional encryption scheme. The size[3] of a public/private key is in $O(1)$, the size of a ciphertext is in $O(d)$, and the size of a decryption key is in $O(d \log^2 \mathcal{Z})$.
- We define weak-IND-sID-CPA security following the IND-sID-CPA security formulation given by Boneh *et al.* [2]. We prove that the proposed functional encryption scheme is weak-IND-sID-CPA secure (as defined in Sect. 3.3), if BBG HIBE scheme [2] is IND-sID-CPA secure (See Theorem 2).

---

[1] Here the nonce ρ is crucial to prevent cloud from abusing delegation keys across different queries.

[2] Unlike [3,4], our functional encryption scheme is a symmetric key encryption system.

[3] Since the private key contains $O(d)$ random elements from $\mathbb{Z}_p^*$ and $O(\ell)$ random elements from $\widetilde{\mathbb{G}}$, its size can be reduced from $O(\ell + d)$ to $O(1)$ (precisely, $O(1)$ number of secret seeds, and each seed with length equal to the security parameter κ), using a pseudorandom function.

1.4   Organization

The rest of this paper is organized as below. Section 2 reviews related works. Section 3 constructs a new functional encryption scheme for multidimensional range query, and Sect. 4 presents the security formulation and analyzes the correctness and security of the proposed scheme. At the end, Sect. 5 concludes this paper.

2   Related Works

Functional encryption [1,3–6,9–12] is a new and more general notion to capture all of previous public encryption (e.g. RSA), private encryption (e.g. AES), identity based encryption (e.g. [13]), attribute-based encryption (e.g. [14]), and predicate encryption (e.g. [15]). Some works [3,4,10] aimed to formulate the security of generic functional encryption, some [1,9,12] constructed functional encryption for a somewhat generic class of functionalities, and some [11] analyzed the lower bound of functional encryption scheme.

In particular to functional encryption supporting multidimensional range query, Shi *et al.* [16] proposed a predicate encryption scheme called MRQED (Multi-dimensional Range Query over Encrypted Data). Under their scheme, given a message and an identity, which is a d-dimensional point, a ciphertext can be generated. A short decryption key for a d-dimensional rectangular range can be generated from the master secret key. From this decryption key and the ciphertext, the original message can be decrypted, iff the identity point associated with the ciphertext is within the query range. There is a subtle but crucial difference between MRQED scheme and our implementation of functional encryption scheme: After a successful decryption, MRQED scheme reveals the message, whereas our functional encryption scheme reveals only a function value of the message. Precisely, the functionalities supported by MRQED [16] and this paper are given in Eqs. (3) and (4), respectively.

$$\text{MRQED:} \quad F(k = (\mathbf{R}), (\mathbf{x}, \mathsf{Msg})) = \begin{cases} \mathsf{Msg} & (\text{if } \mathbf{x} \in \mathbf{R}); \\ \bot & (\text{otherwise}) \end{cases} \quad (3)$$

$$\text{This paper:} \quad F(k = (\rho, \mathbf{R}), (\mathbf{x}, \mathsf{Msg})) = \begin{cases} f(\rho, \mathsf{Msg}) & (\text{if } \mathbf{x} \in \mathbf{R}); \\ \bot & (\text{otherwise}) \end{cases} \quad (4)$$

where f is some one-way function and will be defined later.

On the other hand, MRQED has its own advantages over our proposed functional encryption scheme—MRQED [16] is a public key encryption scheme and has a stronger security model.

Other recent works in functional encryption include [17–21].

3   Construction of a New Functional Encryption Scheme

3.1   Polymorphic Property of **BBG HIBE** Scheme

We observe that the BBG HIBE scheme [2] satisfies the polymorphic property: An encryption of a message M can be viewed as the encryption of another message $\widehat{M}$ under different key. Precisely, let CT and $\widehat{\mathsf{CT}}$ be defined as follows, we have $\mathsf{CT} = \widehat{\mathsf{CT}}$:

$$\mathsf{CT} = \mathsf{Encrypt}(\mathsf{params}, \mathsf{id}, M; s) = \left(\Omega^s \cdot M, \ g^s, \ \left(h_1^{I_1} \cdots h_k^{I_k} \cdot g_3 \right)^s \right)$$

under key: $\mathsf{params} = (g, g_1, g_2, g_3, h_1, \ldots, h_\ell, \Omega = e(g_1, g_2))$, $\mathsf{master\text{-}key} = g_2^\alpha$

$$\widehat{\mathsf{CT}} = \mathsf{Encrypt}(\widehat{\mathsf{params}}, \mathsf{id}, \widehat{M}; sz) = \left(\Omega^{sz} \cdot \widehat{M}, \ \widehat{g}^{sz}, \ \left(\widehat{h}_1^{I_1} \cdots \widehat{h}_k^{I_k} \cdot \widehat{g}_3 \right)^{sz} \right),$$

under key: $\widehat{\mathsf{params}} = (\widehat{g}, g_1, g_2, \widehat{g}_3, \widehat{h}_1, \ldots, \widehat{h}_\ell, \Omega = e(g_1, g_2))$, $\widehat{\mathsf{master\text{-}key}} = g_2^{\alpha z}$ \hfill (5)

where ℓ is the maximum depth of the HIBE scheme, $k \le \ell$ is the length of identity id, $\widehat{M} = M\Omega^{s(1-z)}$, $\widehat{g} = g^{z^{-1} \bmod p}$, $\widehat{g}_3 = g_3^{z^{-1} \bmod p}$, $\widehat{h}_i = h_i^{z^{-1} \bmod p}$ for $1 \le i \le \ell$ and identity $\mathsf{id} = (I_1, \ldots, I_k) \in \left(\mathbb{Z}_p^* \right)^k$. One can verify the above equality easily.

3.2 Define Identities Based on Binary Interval Tree

An identity is a sequence of elements from $\mathbb{Z}_p^*$. To apply HIBE scheme, we intend to construct two mappings, named ID and IdSet, to associate identities to integers or integer intervals:

- $\mathsf{ID}(\cdot)$ maps an integer $x \in [\mathcal{Z}]$ into an identity $\mathsf{ID}(x) \in \left(\mathbb{Z}_p^* \right)^\ell$, where $\ell = \lceil \log \mathcal{Z} \rceil$ is the height of identity hierarchy tree of the BBG HIBE scheme.
- $\mathsf{IdSet}(\cdot)$ maps an integer interval $[a, b] \subseteq [\mathcal{Z}]$ into a set of $O(\ell)$ identities, where each identity is a sequence of at most ℓ elements from $\mathbb{Z}_p^*$.

The two mappings ID and IdSet are required to satisfy this property: *For any $x \in [a, b] \subseteq [\mathcal{Z}]$, there is a unique identity id in the set $\mathsf{IdSet}([a, b])$, such that identity id is a prefix of identity $\mathsf{ID}(x)$. If $x \notin [a, b]$, then there is no such identity id in $\mathsf{IdSet}([a, b])$. For each dimension $\iota \in [d]$, we will construct such mappings ID_ι and IdSet_ι using a binary interval tree [16]. The resulting mappings are made public.*

Binary Interval Tree. The binary interval tree is constructed as below: First, we build a complete ordered binary tree with 2^ℓ leaf nodes. Next, we associate an integer interval to each tree node in a bottom-up manner: (1) Counting from the leftmost leaf, the j-th leaf is associated with interval $[j, j]$; (2) For any internal node, the associated interval is the union of the two intervals associated to its left and right children respectively. As a result, the interval associated to the root node is $[1, 2^\ell]$. An example of binary interval tree with size 8 is showed in Fig. 1.

Constructions of Mappings ID_ι and IdSet_ι for dimension ι. Let $\mathcal{H} : \mathbb{Z}_{2^\ell+1} \times \mathbb{Z}_{2^\ell+1} \times [d] \to \mathbb{Z}_p^*$ be a collision resistant hash function. Let $(\mathsf{v}_1, \mathsf{v}_2, \ldots, \mathsf{v}_m)$ be the path from the root node v_1 to the node v_m in the binary interval tree. We associate to node v_m the identity $(\mathcal{H}(a_1, b_1, \iota), \ldots, \mathcal{H}(a_m, b_m, \iota)) \in \left(\mathbb{Z}_p^* \right)^m$, where $[a_j, b_j]$ is the interval associated to node v_j, $1 \le j \le m$.

For any $x \in [\mathcal{Z}]$, we define $\mathsf{ID}_\iota(x)$ as the identity associated to the x-th leaf node (counting from the left). For any interval $[a, b] \subseteq [\mathcal{Z}]$, we find the minimum covering set $\mathsf{MCS}_{a,b}$, which is a set $\{v_j : v_j$ is a tree node, $1 \leq j \leq n\}$ with minimal size such that the intervals associated to v_j's form a partition of the interval $[a, b]$, and define $\mathsf{IdSet}_\iota([a,b]) := \{id_j : id_j$ is the identity associated to nodev_j, $v_j \in \mathsf{MCS}_{a,b}\}$. One can verify that the newly constructed mappings ID_ι and IdSet_ι satisfy the property mentioned in the beginning of Sect. 3.2. Furthermore, the set $\mathsf{IdSet}_\iota([a, b])$ contains $O(\ell)$ identities and each identity is a sequence of at most ℓ elements from $\mathbb{Z}_p^*$.

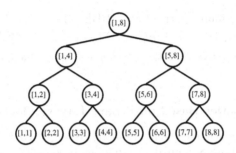

Fig. 1. Binary interval tree with 8 leaf nodes.

3.3   Construction of Functional Encryption Scheme

Let (Setup, KeyGen, Encrypt, Decrypt) be the BBG Hierarchical Identity Based Encryption (HIBE) scheme proposed by Boneh, Boyen and Goh [2] (the description of this scheme is in the appendix of the full version [7,8]). Based on this HIBE scheme, we construct a functional encryption scheme $\mathsf{FE} = (f\mathsf{Setup}, f\mathsf{Enc}, f\mathsf{KeyGen}, f\mathsf{Dec})$ as below.

$f\mathsf{Setup}(1^\lambda, d, \mathcal{Z})$:   `security parameter` λ`, dimension` d`, maximum integer` $\mathcal{Z}$`;`
`the domain of points is` $[\mathcal{Z}]^d$

1. Let $\ell = \lceil \log \mathcal{Z} \rceil$. Run algorithm $\mathsf{Setup}(\ell, \lambda)$ to obtain bilinear groups $(p, \mathbb{G}, \widetilde{\mathbb{G}}, e)$, public parameter $\mathbf{params} = (g, g_1, g_2, g_3, h_1, \ldots, h_\ell, \Omega = e(g_1, g_2))$ and master private key $\mathbf{master\text{-}key} = g_2^\alpha$, such that p is a λ bits prime, $\mathbb{G}, \widetilde{\mathbb{G}}$ are cyclic multiplicative groups of order p, $e : \mathbb{G} \times \mathbb{G} \to \widetilde{\mathbb{G}}$ is a bilinear map, g is a generator of $\mathbb{G}$, $\alpha \in \mathbb{Z}_p$, $g_1 = g^\alpha \in \mathbb{G}$, and $g_2, g_3, h_1, \ldots, h_\ell \in \mathbb{G}$.
2. Let ID_ι and IdSet_ι, $\iota \in [d]$, be the mappings as in Sect. 3.2.
3. Choose d random elements $\tau_1, \ldots, \tau_d$ from $\mathbb{Z}_p^*$ and let $\boldsymbol{\tau} = (\tau_1, \ldots, \tau_d)$.
4. Let $pk = (p, \mathbb{G}, \widetilde{\mathbb{G}}, e, \Omega)$ and $sk = (pk, \mathbf{params}, \mathbf{master\text{-}key}, \boldsymbol{\tau})$. Make ID_ι's and IdSet_ι's public and output (pk, sk).

$f\mathsf{Enc}(\mathsf{Msg}, \boldsymbol{x}, sk)$:   `message` $\mathsf{Msg} \in \mathbb{Z}_p^*$`,` d`-dimensional point` x

1. Treat the d-dimensional point $\boldsymbol{x}$ as $(x_1, \ldots, x_d) \in [\mathcal{Z}]^d$; recall that the private key sk is $(pk, \mathbf{params}, \mathbf{master\text{-}key}, \boldsymbol{\tau})$, where $\boldsymbol{\tau} = (\tau_1, \ldots, \tau_d)$.

2. Choose d random elements $s_1, \ldots, s_d$ from $\mathbb{Z}_p$ with constraint $\mathsf{Msg} = -\sum_{j=1}^{d} s_j \cdot \tau_j \pmod{p}$.

3. Choose d random elements $\sigma_1, \ldots, \sigma_d$ from $\widetilde{\mathbb{G}}$ with constraint $\prod_{j=1}^{d} \sigma_j = \Omega^{-\sum_{j=1}^{d} s_j}$.

4. For each $j \in [d]$, encrypt σ_j under identity $\mathsf{ID}_j(x_j)$ with random coin s_j to obtain ciphertext c_j as follows

$$c_j \leftarrow \mathsf{Encrypt}(\mathsf{params}, \mathsf{ID}_j(x_j), \sigma_j; s_j). \tag{6}$$

5. Output ciphertext $\mathsf{CT} = (c_1, \ldots, c_d)$.

$f\mathsf{KeyGen}(\mathbf{R}, \rho, sk)$: d-dimensional rectangular range $\mathbf{R}$, function key $\rho \in \mathbb{Z}_p^*$

1. Treat the d-dimensional rectangular range $\mathbf{R} \subseteq [\mathcal{Z}]^d$ as Cartesian product $\mathbf{A}_1 \times \mathbf{A}_2 \ldots \times \mathbf{A}_d$, where $\mathbf{A}_j \subseteq [\mathcal{Z}]$ for each $j \in [d]$; recall that the private key sk is $(pk, \mathsf{params}, \mathsf{master\text{-}key}, \boldsymbol{\tau})$, where $\boldsymbol{\tau} = (\tau_1, \ldots, \tau_d)$.

2. For each dimension $j \in [d]$, generate a set δ_j in this way:
   (a) For each identity $\mathsf{id} \in \mathsf{IdSet}_j(\mathbf{A}_j)$, generate the private key d_{id}, using algorithm KeyGen and taking the value $\mathsf{master\text{-}key}^{\rho \tau_j}$ as the master key.
   (b) Set $\delta_j \leftarrow \{d_{\mathsf{id}} : \mathsf{id} \in \mathsf{IdSet}_j(\mathbf{A}_j)\}$.

3. Output delegation key $\boldsymbol{\delta} = (\delta_1, \delta_2, \ldots, \delta_d)$.

$f\mathsf{Dec}(\mathsf{CT}, \boldsymbol{x}, \mathbf{R}, \boldsymbol{\delta}, pk)$: ciphertext CT, d-dimensional point $\boldsymbol{x}$, d-dimensional rectangular range $\mathbf{R}$, delegation key $\boldsymbol{\delta}$

1. Treat the d-dimensional rectangular range $\mathbf{R} \subseteq [\mathcal{Z}]^d$ as Cartesian product $\mathbf{A}_1 \times \mathbf{A}_2 \ldots \times \mathbf{A}_d$, where $\mathbf{A}_j \subseteq [\mathcal{Z}]$ for each $j \in [d]$. Let us write the ciphertext CT as $(c_1, \ldots, c_d)$, and the d-dimensional point $\boldsymbol{x}$ as $(x_1, \ldots, x_d)$.

2. For each dimension $j \in [d]$, generate $\widetilde{t}_j$ in this way: If $x_j \notin \mathbf{A}_j$, then output $\perp$ and abort. Otherwise, do the followings:
   (a) Find the unique identity $\mathsf{id}^* \in \mathsf{IdSet}_j(\mathbf{A}_j)$ such that id^* is a prefix of identity $\mathsf{ID}_j(x_j)$.
   (b) Parse $\boldsymbol{\delta}$ as $(\delta_1, \ldots, \delta_d)$ and find the private key $d_{\mathsf{id}^*} \in \delta_j = \{d_{\mathsf{id}} : \mathsf{id} \in \mathsf{IdSet}_j(\mathbf{A}_j)\}$ for identity id^*.
   (c) Generate the private key d_j for the identity $\mathsf{ID}_j(x_j)$ from private key d_{id^*}, using algorithm KeyGen.
   (d) Decrypt c_j using algorithm $\mathsf{Decrypt}$ with decryption key d_j, and denote the decrypted message as $\widetilde{t}_j$.

3. Output $\widetilde{t} = \prod_{1 \leq j \leq d} \widetilde{t}_j \in \widetilde{\mathbb{G}}$.

4 The Constructed Functional Encryption Scheme Is Correct and Secure

In this section, we analyze the correctness and security of the newly constructed functional encryption scheme.

4.1 Correctness

Let us define a key-ed function family $\{f_\rho : \mathbb{Z}_p^* \to \widetilde{\mathbb{G}}\}_{\rho \in \mathbb{Z}_p^*}$ as below: Let $\Omega \in \widetilde{\mathbb{G}}$ be as in $f\mathsf{Setup}$ of Sect. 3.3.

$$f_1(\mathsf{Msg}) = \Omega^{\mathsf{Msg}}; \quad \forall \rho \in \mathbb{Z}_p^*, \ f_\rho(\mathsf{Msg}) = f_1(\mathsf{Msg})^\rho \in \widetilde{\mathbb{G}}. \tag{7}$$

Lemma 1 (FE is correct). *The functional encryption scheme* FE *described in Sect. 3.3 satisfies this property: For any public-private key pair* $(pk, sk) \leftarrow f\mathsf{Setup}(1^\lambda, d, \mathcal{Z})$, *for any message* $\mathsf{Msg} \in \mathbb{Z}_p^*$, *for any point* $\boldsymbol{x} \in [\mathcal{Z}]^d$, *for any rectangular range* $\mathbf{R} \subseteq [\mathcal{Z}]^d$, *for any* $\rho \in \mathbb{Z}_p^*$, *if* $\mathsf{CT} \leftarrow f\mathsf{Enc}(\mathsf{Msg}, \boldsymbol{x}, sk)$ *and* $\boldsymbol{\delta} \leftarrow f\mathsf{KeyGen}(\mathbf{R}, \rho, sk)$, *then*

$$f\mathsf{Dec}(\mathsf{CT}, \ \boldsymbol{x}, \ \mathbf{R}, \ \boldsymbol{\delta}, \ pk) = \begin{cases} f_\rho(\mathsf{Msg}) & (if \ \boldsymbol{x} \in \mathbf{R}) \\ \perp & (otherwise) \end{cases} \tag{8}$$

Most of previous functional encryption schemes [5] (e.g. attribute-based encryption [14], and predicate encryption [15]), if not all, allow the decryptor to obtain the original plaintext Msg from a ciphertext of Msg in "good" case (e.g. if the attribute of plaintext and/or the decryption key satisfy the designated predicate), and nothing otherwise. In contrast, our functional encryption scheme FE only allows the decryptor to obtain $f_1(\mathsf{Msg})^\rho$ in "good" case, from a ciphertext of Msg, where f_1 is a one-way function. Unlike [3,4], our functional encryption scheme is a symmetric key system. Our security formulation is weaker than previous works (e.g. [3,4]).

4.2 Proof of Correctness

Proof (of Lemma 1). We observe that the BBG HIBE scheme [2] satisfies the polymorphic property: An encryption of a message M can be viewed as the encryption of another message $\widehat{M}$ under different key. Precisely, let CT and $\widehat{\mathsf{CT}}$ be defined as follows, we have $\mathsf{CT} = \widehat{\mathsf{CT}}$:

$$\mathsf{CT} = \mathsf{Encrypt}(\mathsf{params}, \mathsf{id}, M; s) = \left(\Omega^s \cdot M, \ g^s, \ \left(h_1^{I_1} \cdots h_k^{I_k} \cdot g_3 \right)^s \right)$$

under key: $\mathsf{params} = (g, g_1, g_2, g_3, h_1, \ldots, h_\ell, \Omega = e(g_1, g_2))$, $\ \mathsf{master\text{-}key} = g_2^\alpha$

$$\widehat{\mathsf{CT}} = \mathsf{Encrypt}(\widehat{\mathsf{params}}, \mathsf{id}, \widehat{M}; sz) = \left(\Omega^{sz} \cdot \widehat{M}, \ \widehat{g}^{sz}, \ \left(\widehat{h}_1^{I_1} \cdots \widehat{h}_k^{I_k} \cdot \widehat{g}_3 \right)^{sz} \right),$$

under key: $\widehat{\mathsf{params}} = (\widehat{g}, g_1, g_2, \widehat{g}_3, \widehat{h}_1, \ldots, \widehat{h}_\ell, \Omega = e(g_1, g_2))$, $\ \widehat{\mathsf{master\text{-}key}} = g_2^{\alpha z} \tag{9}$

where identity $\mathsf{id} = (I_1, \ldots, I_k) \in (\mathbb{Z}_p^*)^k$, $\widehat{M} = M\Omega^{s(1-z)}$, $\widehat{g} = g^{z^{-1} \bmod p}$, $\widehat{g}_3 = g_3^{z^{-1} \bmod p}$ and $\widehat{h}_i = h_i^{z^{-1} \bmod p}$ for $1 \leq i \leq \ell$. One can verify the above equality easily.

Let $(pk, sk) \leftarrow f\mathsf{Setup}(1^\lambda)$, message $\mathsf{Msg} \in \mathbb{Z}_p^*$, point $\boldsymbol{x} \in [\mathcal{Z}]^d$, $\mathbf{R}$ be a d-dimensional rectangular range, and $\rho \in \mathbb{Z}_p^*$. Let $\mathsf{CT} \leftarrow f\mathsf{Enc}(\mathsf{Msg}, \boldsymbol{x}, sk)$, $\boldsymbol{\delta} \leftarrow f\mathsf{KeyGen}(\mathbf{R}, \rho, sk)$, and $y \in \widetilde{\mathbb{G}}$.

We consider dimension $j \in [d]$ and apply the polymorphic property of BBG scheme (Eq. (9)): Take $M = \sigma_j, s = s_j$ and $z = \rho\tau_j$. Then $\widehat{M} = M\Omega^{s(1-z)} = \sigma_j\Omega^{s_j(1-\tau_j\rho)}$.

In case $\boldsymbol{x} \in \mathbf{R}$. If $\boldsymbol{x} \in \mathbf{R}$, then the HIBE decryption will succeed in the process of $f\mathsf{Dec}$ (Sect. 3.3). Note that during decryption for dimension j, we use decryption key derived from $\mathsf{master\text{-}key}^{\rho\tau_j}$. Let $\tilde{t}_j$ be as in Step 2(d) of $f\mathsf{Dec}$ for decrypting ciphertext CT. We have

$$\tilde{t}_j = \widehat{M} = \sigma_j\Omega^{s_j(1-\tau_j\rho)}, j \in [d]. \tag{10}$$

Combining all d dimensions, and applying the two equalities (see algorithm $f\mathsf{Enc}$ in Sect. 3.3) $\mathsf{Msg} = -\sum_{j=1}^{d} s_j\tau_j \bmod p$ and $\prod_{j=1}^{d} \sigma_j = \Omega^{-\sum_{j=1}^{d} s_j}$ we have,

$$f\mathsf{Dec}(\mathsf{CT},\ \boldsymbol{x},\ \mathbf{R},\ \boldsymbol{\delta},\ pk) = \tilde{t} = \prod_{j=1}^{d} \tilde{t}_j = \prod_{j=1}^{d} \left(\sigma_j\Omega^{s_j(1-\tau_j\rho)}\right)$$

$$= \prod_{j=1}^{d} \sigma_j \cdot \prod_{j=1}^{d} \Omega^{s_j} \cdot \left(\prod_{j=1}^{d} \Omega^{-s_j\tau_j}\right)^{\rho}$$

$$= \Omega^{-\sum_{j=1}^{d} s_j} \cdot \prod_{j=1}^{d} \Omega^{s_j} \cdot \left(\Omega^{\mathsf{Msg}}\right)^{\rho}$$

$$= \Omega^{\rho\mathsf{Msg}} = f_{\rho}(\mathsf{Msg}).$$

In case $\boldsymbol{x} \notin \mathbf{R}$. Let $\mathbf{R} = \mathbf{A}_1 \times \mathbf{A}_2 \dots \times \mathbf{A}_d$ as in Step 1 of $f\mathsf{Dec}$. If $\boldsymbol{x} \notin \mathbf{R}$, then for some dimension $j \in [d]$, $\boldsymbol{x}[j] \notin \mathbf{A}_j$, and $f\mathsf{Dec}$ will output $\perp$ (Step 2 of $f\mathsf{Dec}$ in Sect. 3.3).

4.3   Security

We formulize the security requirement of our functional encryption scheme by modifying the IND-sID-CPA security game [2]. The resulting weak-IND-sID-CPA security game between an adversary $\mathcal{A}$ and a challenger $\mathcal{C}$ is defined as below:

Commit: The adversary $\mathcal{A}$ chooses the target point $\boldsymbol{x}^*$ from the space $[\mathcal{Z}]^d$ and sends it to the challenger $\mathcal{C}$.

Setup: The challenger $\mathcal{C}$ runs the setup algorithm $f\mathsf{Setup}$ and gives $\mathcal{A}$ the resulting system parameters pk, keeping the secret key sk to itself.

Challenge: The challenger $\mathcal{C}$ chooses two plaintexts $\mathsf{Msg}_0, \mathsf{Msg}_1$ at random from the message space $\mathbb{Z}_p^*$, and chooses a random bit $b \in \{0, 1\}$. $\mathcal{C}$ sets the challenge ciphertext to $\mathsf{CT} = f\mathsf{Enc}(\mathsf{Msg}_b, \boldsymbol{x}^*, sk)$, and sends $(\mathsf{CT}, f_1(\mathsf{Msg}_0), f_1(\mathsf{Msg}_1))$ to the adversary $\mathcal{A}$.

Learning Phase: The adversary $\mathcal{A}$ adaptively issues queries to the challenger $\mathcal{C}$, where each query is one of the following:

- Delegation key query $(\mathbf{R}, \rho)$, where $\boldsymbol{x}^* \notin \mathbf{R}$: In response to this query, $\mathcal{C}$ runs algorithm $f\mathsf{KeyGen}(\mathbf{R}, \rho, sk)$ to generate the delegation key $\boldsymbol{\delta}$, and sends $\boldsymbol{\delta}$ to $\mathcal{A}$.
- Anonymous delegation key query $(\mathbf{R})$: In response to this query, $\mathcal{C}$ chooses ρ at random from the space $\mathbb{Z}_p^*$ and runs algorithm $f\mathsf{KeyGen}(\mathbf{R}, \rho, sk)$ to generate the delegation key $\boldsymbol{\delta}$, and sends $\boldsymbol{\delta}$ to $\mathcal{A}$.
- Encryption query $(\mathsf{Msg}, \boldsymbol{x})$: In response to this query, $\mathcal{C}$ runs $f\mathsf{Enc}(\mathsf{Msg}, \boldsymbol{x}, sk)$ to obtain a ciphertext, and sends the ciphertext to $\mathcal{A}$.

Guess: Finally, the adversary $\mathcal{A}$ outputs a guess $b' \in \{0, 1\}$ and wins if $b = b'$.

We refer to the above adversary $\mathcal{A}$ as a weak-IND-sID-CPA adversary. We define the advantage of the adversary $\mathcal{A}$ in attacking the scheme FE as

$$\mathsf{Adv}_{\mathsf{FE}, \mathcal{A}}^{\mathsf{weak\text{-}IND\text{-}sID\text{-}CPA}} = \left| \Pr[b = b'] - \frac{1}{2} \right|.$$

We will show in the following theorem that: if the BBG HIBE scheme is IND-sID-CPA secure (as defined in [2]), then the functional encryption scheme FE constructed in Sect. 3.3 is weak-IND-sID-CPA secure. Note that the above security definition is *weak* in the sense that the two challenged messages Msg_0 and Msg_1 are chosen randomly instead of adversarially. Compared to Gorbunov *et al.* [1] which only allows a pre-defined number of delegation queries (they called "q-Collusions"), the above security definition allows practically unlimited number of delegation key queries.

Theorem 2. *Suppose there exists a* weak-IND-sID-CPA *adversary* $\mathcal{A}_{\mathsf{FE}}$, *which runs in time* t_{FE} *and has non-negligible advantage* ϵ *against the functional encryption scheme* FE *(constructed in Sect. 3.3) with one chosen delegation key query and* N_{aq} *chosen anonymous delegation key queries and* N_{enc} *chosen encryption queries. Then there exists an* IND-sID-CPA *adversary* $\mathcal{A}_{\mathsf{BBG}}$, *which has advantage* $\frac{\epsilon}{2d}$ *against the BBG HIBE scheme [2] with* $O(d\ell)$ *chosen private key queries and zero chosen decryption query, and runs in time* $t_{\mathsf{FE}} + O(d\ell \cdot t_{max} \cdot (N_{aq} + N_{enc}))$, *where* t_{max} *is the maximum time for a random sampling (within a space of size at most* p*), a BBG encryption* Encrypt, *or a BBG key generation* KeyGen. *(The proof of security is in the full version [7, 8].*

5   Conclusion

In this paper, we constructed a new functional encryption scheme for multidimensional range query, using a new technique. The proposed functional encryption scheme allows a user with a valid ciphertext and a correct decryption key to obtain only a one-way function value of the plaintext, where the plaintext remains secure, assuming that the multidimensional point associated to the ciphertext is within the query range associated to the decryption key. Our functional encryption scheme is designed by exploiting the polymorphic property of existing BBG HIBE scheme: encryption of a message can be viewed as encryption of another message under a different key.

References

1. Gorbunov, S., Vaikuntanathan, V., Wee, H.: Functional encryption with bounded collusions via multi-party computation. In: Safavi-Naini, R., Canetti, R. (eds.) CRYPTO 2012. LNCS, vol. 7417, pp. 162–179. Springer, Heidelberg (2012). https://doi.org/10.1007/978-3-642-32009-5_11
2. Boneh, D., Boyen, X., Goh, E.-J.: Hierarchical identity based encryption with constant size ciphertext. In: Cramer, R. (ed.) EUROCRYPT 2005. LNCS, vol. 3494, pp. 440–456. Springer, Heidelberg (2005). https://doi.org/10.1007/11426639_26
3. Boneh, D., Sahai, A., Waters, B.: Functional encryption: definitions and challenges. In: Ishai, Y. (ed.) TCC 2011. LNCS, vol. 6597, pp. 253–273. Springer, Heidelberg (2011). https://doi.org/10.1007/978-3-642-19571-6_16
4. O'Neill, A.: Definitional issues in functional encryption. Cryptology ePrint Archive, Report 2010/556 (2010). http://eprint.iacr.org/
5. Lewko, A., Okamoto, T., Sahai, A., Takashima, K., Waters, B.: Fully secure functional encryption: attribute-based encryption and (hierarchical) inner product encryption. In: Gilbert, H. (ed.) EUROCRYPT 2010. LNCS, vol. 6110, pp. 62–91. Springer, Heidelberg (2010). https://doi.org/10.1007/978-3-642-13190-5_4
6. Okamoto, T., Takashima, K.: Fully secure functional encryption with general relations from the decisional linear assumption. In: Rabin, T. (ed.) CRYPTO 2010. LNCS, vol. 6223, pp. 191–208. Springer, Heidelberg (2010). https://doi.org/10.1007/978-3-642-14623-7_11
7. Xu, J., Chang, E.C.: Authenticating aggregate range queries over multidimensional dataset. Cryptology ePrint Archive, Report 2010/050 (2010). http://eprint.iacr.org/
8. Xu, J., Chang, E.C., Zhou, J.: A new functional encryption for multidimensional range query. Cryptology ePrint Archive, Report 2017/970 (2017). http://eprint.iacr.org/2017/970
9. Waters, B.: Functional encryption for regular languages. In: Safavi-Naini, R., Canetti, R. (eds.) CRYPTO 2012. LNCS, vol. 7417, pp. 218–235. Springer, Heidelberg (2012). https://doi.org/10.1007/978-3-642-32009-5_14
10. Barbosa, M., Farshim, P.: Semantically secure functional encryption, revisited. Cryptology ePrint Archive, Report 2012/474 (2012). http://eprint.iacr.org/
11. Agrawal, S., Gorbunov, S., Vaikuntanathan, V., Wee, H.: Functional encryption: new perspectives and lower bounds. Cryptology ePrint Archive, Report 2012/468 (2012). http://eprint.iacr.org/
12. Sahai, A., Seyalioglu, H.: Worry-free encryption: functional encryption with public keys. In: ACM Conference on Computer and Communications Security, CCS 2010, pp. 463–472
13. Boneh, D., Franklin, M.: Identity-based encryption from the Weil pairing. SIAM J. Comput. 32(3), 586–615 (2003)
14. Sahai, A., Waters, B.: Fuzzy identity-based encryption. In: Cramer, R. (ed.) EUROCRYPT 2005. LNCS, vol. 3494, pp. 457–473. Springer, Heidelberg (2005). https://doi.org/10.1007/11426639_27
15. Katz, J., Sahai, A., Waters, B.: Predicate encryption supporting disjunctions, polynomial equations, and inner products. In: Smart, N. (ed.) EUROCRYPT 2008. LNCS, vol. 4965, pp. 146–162. Springer, Heidelberg (2008). https://doi.org/10.1007/978-3-540-78967-3_9
16. Shi, E., Bethencourt, J., Chan, T.H.H., Song, D., Perrig, A.: Multi-dimensional range query over encrypted data. In: IEEE Symposium on Security and Privacy, SP 2007, pp. 350–364 (2007)

17. Garg, S., Gentry, C., Halevi, S., Raykova, M., Sahai, A., Waters, B.: Candidate indistinguishability obfuscation and functional encryption for all circuits. SIAM J. Comput. **45**(3), 882–929 (2016)
18. Garg, S., Gentry, C., Halevi, S., Zhandry, M.: Functional encryption without obfuscation. In: Kushilevitz, E., Malkin, T. (eds.) TCC 2016. LNCS, vol. 9563, pp. 480–511. Springer, Heidelberg (2016). https://doi.org/10.1007/978-3-662-49099-0_18
19. Waters, B.: A punctured programming approach to adaptively secure functional encryption. In: Gennaro, R., Robshaw, M. (eds.) CRYPTO 2015. LNCS, vol. 9216, pp. 678–697. Springer, Heidelberg (2015). https://doi.org/10.1007/978-3-662-48000-7_33
20. Goldwasser, S., Gordon, S.D., Goyal, V., Jain, A., Katz, J., Liu, F.-H., Sahai, A., Shi, E., Zhou, H.-S.: Multi-input functional encryption. In: Nguyen, P.Q., Oswald, E. (eds.) EUROCRYPT 2014. LNCS, vol. 8441, pp. 578–602. Springer, Heidelberg (2014). https://doi.org/10.1007/978-3-642-55220-5_32
21. Fisch, B.A., Vinayagamurthy, D., Boneh, D., Gorbunov, S.: Iron: functional encryption using Intel SGX. Cryptology ePrint Archive, Report 2016/1071 (2016). http://eprint.iacr.org/2016/1071

Signature

Linearly Homomorphic Signatures
with Designated Entities

Cheng-Jun Lin, Xinyi Huang$^{(\boxtimes)}$, Shitang Li, Wei Wu, and Shao-Jun Yang

Fujian Provincial Key Laboratory of Network Security and Cryptology,
School of Mathematics and Informatics, Fujian Normal University, Fuzhou, China
cjlin1241@outlook.com, {xyhuang,tangshili,weiwu}@fjnu.edu.cn,
shaojunyang@outlook.com

Abstract. As a kind of homomorphic signatures, linearly homomorphic signatures allow any entity to linearly combine the signed data and produce a valid signature of the new data. Motivated by the open problem given by Rivest in 2000, we introduce the notion of linearly homomorphic signatures with designated entities (LHSDE). In the new notion, only one entity (designated combiner) can perform the homomorphic operations, and only one entity (designated verifier) can be convinced by the validity of the signature. We initiate a foundational study on LHSDE including definitions and security requirements, namely, unforgeability against the designated combiner, unforgeability against the designated verifier and indistinguishability. In addition, we present a specific design of LHSDE with provable security in the random oracle model.

Keywords: Linearly homomorphic signatures · Designated combiner
Designated verifier · Random oracle model

1 Introduction

The notion of digital signatures, put forth by Diffie and Hellman in 1976 [11], aims at providing integrity, authenticity and non-repudiation of the signed messages. In order to achieve the properties mentioned above, digital signatures should satisfy certain security requirements. The traditional security of a digital signature scheme requires that it should be existentially unforgeable under adaptively chosen message attacks. In such attacks, an adversary is allowed to request the signer for signatures of some messages. These messages depend on not only the signer's public key but also the signatures that the adversary has obtained. A signature scheme is called existentially unforgeable if no adversary succeeds in forging a signature for a message which was not previously signed by the signer. Although this security requirement of digital signatures (i.e., existential unforgeability) is widely used, it would be too strong in some scenarios such as network coding.

In traditional routing, each node can only store and forward incoming packets, and an output (input) link only forwards (receives) one packet every time.

© Springer International Publishing AG 2017
J. K. Liu and P. Samarati (Eds.): ISPEC 2017, LNCS 10701, pp. 375–390, 2017.
https://doi.org/10.1007/978-3-319-72359-4_22

Network coding as a new routing mechanism [1,17], in contrary, allows the intermediate node to produce a new packet by combining incoming packets in order to increases throughput. However, a major concern on network coding is that malicious nodes can execute pollution attacks by introducing error packets. Even one error packet can propagate and rapidly pollute a large amount of packets, and eventually the destination node cannot recover original packets. Although ordinary existentially unforgeable signature schemes can provide integrity verification, it would be impossible to produce a valid signature for a new valid packet (i.e., a packet obtained by combining the valid incoming packets). In situations such as the network coding, existential unforgeability is too strong and computations on authenticated data is necessary. This feature is provided by homomorphic signatures.

The notion of homomorphic signatures is firstly introduced by Rivest in 2000 [19] and then redefined by Johnson et al. in 2002 [16]. In the talk [19], Rivest presented two instances of homomorphic signatures: prefix aggregation signatures and transitive signatures. Prefix aggregation signatures allow any entity, without the knowledge of the signer's private key, to compute the signature $\sigma(x)$ from signatures $\sigma(x \parallel 0)$ and $\sigma(x \parallel 1)$. Transitive signatures allow any entity, without the knowledge of the signer's private key, to compute the edge signature $\sigma(A, C)$ from edge signatures $\sigma(A, B)$ and $\sigma(B, C)$. Johnson et al. [16] gave the formal definition of secure homomorphic signatures, and then constructed a homomorphic signature scheme which allows any entity, without the knowledge of the signer's private key, to compute the signature $\sigma(w)$ on any subset w of x from the signature $\sigma(x)$.

There are various types of homomorphic signatures with different homomorphic operations. Among them, linearly homomorphic signatures allow any entity to linearly combine authenticated data and obtain a valid signature of the new data without the signer private key. Boneh et al. [6] designed a linearly homomorphic signature scheme to improve the security of the network coding. In their scheme [6], data packs are viewed as a linear vector space over a prime field, and a modification of the received vectors is viewed as a linear combination of vectors with some integer coefficients. Besides, each node can verify the authenticity of the packets and create a valid signature for a new valid packet. Boneh et al. proved that their scheme is secure based on the co-CDH assumption in the random oracle model. In the years that followed, linearly homomorphic signature schemes with various properties were proposed.

In the random oracle model, Gennaro et al. [15] put forth a homomorphic network coding signature scheme over the integers, and proved its security under the RSA assumption. In addition, they pointed out that intermediate nodes can choose small coefficients to implement linear combination, and therefore greatly reduces the computational overhead.

The first linearly homomorphic signature scheme with provable security in the standard model is put forth by Attrapadung and Libert in 2011 [2]. Their scheme is defined over the bilinear group of composite order N, and the coefficient of linear combination and the coordinate of vectors belong to $\mathbb{Z}_N$. In 2012,

Catalano *et al.* [8] presented two linearly homomorphic signature schemes to further improve the efficiency of linearly homomorphic signatures in the standard model. Their first scheme works over the group of composite order and the security is based on the strong-RSA assumption. Their second scheme works over a bilinear group of prime order and the security is based on the q-SDH assumption.

Boneh and Freeman [5] proposed the first linearly homomorphic signature scheme from complexity assumptions on lattices. They formulate a new complexity problem called k-SIS problem which is also used in other cryptographic schemes. Furthermore, Boneh and Freeman [4] constructed a polynomial homomorphic signature scheme based on ideal lattice. Both of these schemes are proven secure in the random oracle model. There are no lattice-based linearly homomorphic signature scheme in the standard model, until Chen *et al.* [9] proposed the first design that authenticates vectors over small field. Other designs of linearly homomorphic signatures include the schemes in [3, 10, 12, 14, 18].

1.1 Motivation and Contributions

The motivation of this paper is to design a homomorphic signature scheme with designated entities, only who is able to perform the homomorphic operations. This is first raised by Rivest in [19], namely, how to design a transitive signature scheme (a specific kind of homomorphic signatures) such that only one entity can create the edge signature $\sigma(A, C)$ from edge signatures $\sigma(A, B)$ and $\sigma(B, C)$. We investigate a similar problem in the setting of linearly homomorphic signatures. Our goal is to design a linearly homomorphic signature scheme such that only one entity can combine signatures from the existing ones. As a result, homomorphic signatures are no longer publicly known and a designated verifier is introduced. To the best of our knowledge, this is the first formal study on linearly homomorphic signatures with designated entities (LHSDE).

In order to satisfy the goal of LHSDE, we revise the **Sign**, **Verify** and **Combine** algorithms in an ordinary linearly homomorphic signature scheme, and introduce two new algorithms **DVerify** and **Simulation**. The newly defined **Sign** (resp. **Verify**) takes the public key (resp. private key) of the designated combiner as an additional input, and the revised **Combine** needs the private key of the designated combiner and the public key of the designated verifier. **DVerify** is used to convince the designated verifier about the validity of the signature. With **Simulation**, one can generate a signature designated to himself/herself.

Accordingly, we define three essential security requirements of LHSDE. First, the scheme must be existentially unforgeable against the malicious designated combiner. Second, no entity can serve as the role of the designated combiner. Last, only the designated verifier can be convinced by the signatures generated by the honest combiner. Then we show a construction meeting these requirements, and the security is proved in the random oracle model under the co-Bilinear Diffie-Hellman assumption and the Gap Bilinear Diffie-Hellman assumption.

Organization of the Paper. Section 2 presents the definition and the security model of LHSDE. In Sect. 3.1, we introduce the complexity assumptions which are needed in our scheme. We construct a concrete LHSDE scheme in Sect. 3.2 and prove its security in the random oracle model in Sect. 3.3. Section 4 concludes this paper.

2 Definitions and Preliminaries

We regard a document as an ordered sequence of n-dimensional vectors $\overline{\mathbf{v}}_1, \ldots, \overline{\mathbf{v}}_m \in \mathbb{F}_p^n$ where p is a prime. At the beginning, the signer transforms these n-dimensional vectors into the properly augmented basis vectors of the subspace $V \subset \mathbb{F}_p^N$ such that:

$$
\mathbf{v}_i = (-\overline{\mathbf{v}}_i -, \overbrace{0, \ldots, 0, \underbrace{1}_{i}, 0, \ldots, 0}^{m}) \in \mathbb{F}_p^N,
$$

where $N = n+m$ and m is the dimension of subspace V. Intuitively, every vector $\mathbf{v}_i$ is equal to vector $\overline{\mathbf{v}}_i$ appended with a m-dimensional unit vector which only has a single 1 at the i'th position and other $m - 1$ positions are 0.

2.1 Syntax of LHSDE

This subsection focuses on the definition and the security model of linearly homomorphic signatures with designated entities (LHSDE).

We assume that every document is associated with an identifier id (the identifier can be viewed as the document's name) that is chosen by the signer. Every entity uses identifiers to recognise packets of the same document.

Before presenting the definition of LHSDE, we denote the signer as Alice, the designated combiner as Bob (combining the signatures produced by Alice) and the designated verifier as Cindy (the receiver whom Bob want to convince that he has a valid signature). Below is the definition of LHSDE.

Definition 1. *A linearly homomorphic signature scheme with designated entities consists of the following probabilistically polynomial-time (PPT) algorithms* $\mathcal{S} = $ (**Setup, KeyGen, Sign, Verify, Combine, DVerify, Simulation**).

- **Setup**($1^k, N$). This algorithm takes as input a security parameter k and a positive integer N, where N is the dimension of a vector to be signed. It outputs the public parameter cp.
- **KeyGen**(cp). The signer Alice runs this algorithm to generate a public key PK_A and a private key SK_A. Bob, the combiner designated by Alice, runs this algorithm to generate his key pair (PK_B, SK_B). Cindy, the verifier designated by Bob, also runs this algorithm to generate her key pair (PK_C, SK_C).
- **Sign**($SK_A, PK_B, id, m, \mathbf{v}$). This algorithm takes as input a private key SK_A, a public key PK_B (of the designated combiner), a document identifier id which is randomly chosen from a samplable set $\mathcal{I} = \{0, 1\}^k$, a positive integer $m < N$ representing the vector subspace's dimension, and a vector $\mathbf{v} \in \mathbb{F}_p^N$. It outputs a signature σ of the vector $\mathbf{v}$.

- **Verify**$(PK_A, SK_B, id, m, \mathbf{v}, \sigma)$. This algorithm takes as input a public key PK_A, a private key SK_B, a document identifier id, a positive integer $m < N$ representing the vector subspace's dimension, a vector $\mathbf{v} \in \mathbb{F}_p^N$, and a signature σ. It outputs 1 (accept) or 0 (reject).
- **Combine**$(PK_A, PK_C, SK_B, id, \{(\mathbf{v}_k, \sigma_k)\}_{k=1}^l)$. This algorithm takes as input two public keys PK_A and PK_C (of the designated verifier), a private key SK_B, a document identifier id, and l pairs of $\{(\mathbf{v}_k, \sigma_k)\}_{k=1}^l$ where σ_k is a signature of the vector $\mathbf{v}_k \in \mathbb{F}_p^N$. It outputs a new signature σ and a new vector $\mathbf{v}$.
- **DVerify**$(PK_A, SK_C, id, m, \mathbf{v}, \sigma)$. This algorithm takes as input a public key PK_A, a private key SK_C, a document identifier id, a positive integer $m < N$ representing the vector subspace's dimension, a vector $\mathbf{v} \in \mathbb{F}_p^N$, and a signature σ. It outputs 1 (accept) or 0 (reject).
- **Simulation**$(PK_A, SK_C, id, m, \mathbf{v})$. This algorithm takes as input a public key PK_A, a private key SK_C, a document identifier id, a positive integer $m < N$ representing the vector subspace's dimension, and a vector $\mathbf{v}$. It outputs a signature $\hat{\sigma}$ of the vector $\mathbf{v}$.

In addition to the above seven algorithms, we require other obvious properties of LHSDE.

- **Correctness of the Sign algorithm.** For any identifier $id \in \mathcal{I}$ and vector $\mathbf{v} \in \mathbb{F}_p^N$, if $\sigma \leftarrow$ **Sign**$(SK_A, PK_B, id, m, \mathbf{v})$, then

$$\textbf{Verify}(PK_A, SK_B, id, m, \mathbf{v}, \sigma) = 1.$$

- **Correctness of the Combine algorithm.** For any identifier $id \in \mathcal{I}$ and the set of pairs $\{(\mathbf{v}_k, \sigma_k)\}_{k=1}^l$, if **Verify**$(PK_A, SK_B, id, m, \mathbf{v}_k, \sigma_k) = 1$ for $k = 1, \ldots, l$, then

$$\textbf{DVerify}(PK_A, SK_C, id, m, \mathbf{v}, \sigma) = 1,$$

where $(\sigma, \mathbf{v}) \leftarrow$ **Combine**$(PK_A, PK_C, SK_B, id, \{(\mathbf{v}_k, \sigma_k)\}_{k=1}^l)$.
- **Correctness of the Simulation algorithm.** For any identifier $id \in \mathcal{I}$ and vector $\mathbf{v} \in \mathbb{F}_p^N$, if $\hat{\sigma} \leftarrow$ **Simulation**$(PK_A, SK_C, id, m, \mathbf{v})$, then

$$\textbf{DVerify}(PK_A, SK_C, id, m, \mathbf{v}, \hat{\sigma}) = 1.$$

2.2   Security

An adversary can break an LHSDE scheme from two aspects. First, he can create a valid signature on a non-zero vector which dose not belong to any vector space signed by Alice. Second, he can replace the designated combiner to combine signatures and convince other entities. As a result, we introduce two types of unforgeability for LHSDE.

UF$_1$: Type 1 Unforgeability

The first type (UF$_1$) requires no efficient adversary can forge a non-zero new vector which does not appear previously. Obviously, the designated combiner has more knowledge than other entities. Thus we only need to define UF$_1$ against the malicious designated combiner. This is defined using the following game between an adversary $\mathcal{A}$ and a challenger $\mathcal{C}$.

Definition 2 (UF$_1$). *A linearly homomorphic signature scheme with designated entities* $\mathcal{S}$ *satisfies UF$_1$ if the success probability of any PPT adversary* $\mathcal{A}$ *in the following game is negligible with the security parameter* k:

- **Setup$_1$.** $\mathcal{C}$ chooses a positive integer N and runs **Setup**$(1^k, N)$ to obtain cp, and then runs **KeyGen**(cp) to obtain the signer's key pair (SK_A, PK_A) and the designated verifier's key pair (SK_C, PK_C). The tuple (cp, PK_A, PK_C) is sent to $\mathcal{A}$. As response, $\mathcal{A}$ sends a public key PK_B to $\mathcal{C}$.
- **Query$_1$.** Proceeding adaptively, $\mathcal{A}$ submits a vector subspace $V_i \subset \mathbb{F}_p^N$ (V_i can be described by the properly augmented basis vectors $\mathbf{v}_{i1}, \ldots, \mathbf{v}_{im} \in \mathbb{F}_p^N$) to $\mathcal{C}$. $\mathcal{C}$ then selects an identifier $id_i \xleftarrow{R} \mathcal{I}$ and runs **Sign**$(SK_A, PK_B, id_i, m, \mathbf{v}_{ij})$ to generate signature σ_{ij} for $j = 1, \ldots, m$. Finally, $\mathcal{C}$ sends (id_i, σ_i) to the adversary $\mathcal{A}$, where $\sigma_i = (\sigma_{i1}, \ldots, \sigma_{im})$ is the signature of the vector subspace V_i.
- **Output$_1$.** $\mathcal{A}$ outputs an identifier id^*, a vector $\mathbf{v}^* \in \mathbb{F}_p^N$, and a signature σ^*.

The adversary $\mathcal{A}$ wins the above game if **DVerify**$(PK_A, SK_C, id^*, m, \mathbf{v}^*, \sigma^*) = 1$, and satisfies one of the following requirements.

1. Type 1.1 forgery: $id^* \neq id_i$ for any i and $\mathbf{v}^* \neq \mathbf{0}$ (which means that $\mathcal{A}$ can produce a valid signature on the vector $\mathbf{v}^*$ of a new vector space).
2. Type 1.2 forgery: $id^* = id_i$ for some i and $\mathbf{v}^* \notin V_i$ (which means that $\mathcal{A}$ can inject malicious vector into a signed vector space).

We define $Succ_{\mathcal{A},\mathcal{S}}^{UF_1}$ as the probability of $\mathcal{A}$ wins the above game.

UF$_2$: Type 2 Unforgeability

The second type (UF$_2$) requires that no entity except the signer can serve as the role of the designated combiner. Obviously, the designated verifier has more knowledge than other entities except the signer and the combiner. We only need to show that the designated verifier Cindy cannot produce even one signature to convince the challenging entity David (we assume his private/public key pair is (SK_D, PK_D)), even if Cindy has received a number of pairs $\{(\mathbf{v}_k, \sigma_k)\}_{k=1}^l$ from the designated combiner.

Note that Cindy can convince David means that she eventually produces a pair of vector/signature $(\mathbf{v}, \sigma)$ such that **DVerify**$(PK_A, SK_D, id, m, \mathbf{v}, \sigma) = 1$. This type of unforgeability aims at convincing the designated combiner that only he can perform the **Combine** algorithm. This is defined using the following game between an adversary $\mathcal{A}$ and a challenger $\mathcal{C}$.

Definition 3 (UF₂). *A linearly homomorphic signature scheme with designated entities S satisfies UF_2 if the success probability of any PPT adversary A in the following game is negligible with the security parameter k:*

- **Setup₂.** C chooses a positive integer N and runs **Setup**$(1^k, N)$ to obtain cp, and then runs **KeyGen**(cp) to generate the signer's key pair (SK_A, PK_A), the designated combiner's key pair (SK_B, PK_B) and the challenging key pair (SK_D, PK_D). The tuple (cp, PK_A, PK_B, PK_D) is sent to A. As response, A sends a public key PK_C to C.
- **Sign Query₂.** Proceeding adaptively, A sends C a vector subspace $V_i \subset \mathbb{F}_p^N$ (V_i can be described by the properly augmented basis vectors $\mathbf{v}_{i1}, \ldots, \mathbf{v}_{im} \in \mathbb{F}_p^N$). C then selects an identifier $id_i \xleftarrow{R} \mathcal{I}$, and runs **Sign**$(SK_A, PK_B, id_i, m, \mathbf{v}_{ij})$ to generate signature σ_{ij} for $j = 1, \ldots, m$. Finally, C sends (id_i, σ_i) to A, where $\sigma_i = (\sigma_{i1}, \ldots, \sigma_{im})$ is the signature of the vector subspace V_i.
- **Combine Query₂.** Proceeding adaptively, A sends C $(id_i, \{(\mathbf{v}_{ik}, \sigma_{ik}, \beta_k)\}_{k=1}^l)$. C runs **Combine**$(PK_A, PK_C, SK_B, id_i, \{(\mathbf{v}_{ik}, \sigma_{ik})\}_{k=1}^l)$ to generate a vector/signature pair $(\mathbf{v}, \sigma)$, where the combination coefficients are $\beta_1, \ldots, \beta_l$ in order. The pair $(\mathbf{v}, \sigma)$ is sent to A.
- **Output₂.** The adversary A outputs an identifier id^*, a vector $\mathbf{v}^* \in \mathbb{F}_p^N$, and a signature σ^*.

The adversary wins the above game if **DVerify**$(PK_A, SK_D, id^*, m, \mathbf{v}^*, \sigma^*) = 1$, where $id^* = id_i$ for some i and $\mathbf{0} \neq \mathbf{v}^* \in V_i$ (Type 2 forgery).

We define $Succ_{A,S}^{UF_2}$ as the probability of the adversary A wins the above game.

Definition 4. *A linearly homomorphic signature scheme with designated entities S is unforgeable against adaptively chosen message attacks if both $Succ_{A,S}^{UF_1}$ and $Succ_{A,S}^{UF_2}$ are negligible with the security parameter k.*

Indistinguishability

In addition to unforgeability, another goal of our scheme is that only the designated verifier can be convinced by the signautures. So we require that the verifier must be unable to show that he has a valid signature of Alice to any other entity, even sharing his private key among others. In order to achieve this requirement, we need to show that the outputs of the **Simulation** algorithm are indistinguishable from those of the **Combine** algorithm. This notion is defined using the following game between a distinguisher D and a challenger C.

Definition 5 (IND). *A linearly homomorphic signature scheme with designated entities S satisfies IND if the advantage of any PPT distinguisher D in the following game is negligible with the security parameter k:*

- **Setup.** C chooses a positive integer N and runs **Setup**$(1^k, N)$ to obtain cp, and then runs **KeyGen**(cp) to generate the signer's key pair

(SK_A, PK_A), and the designated combiner's key pair (SK_B, PK_B). The tuple (cp, PK_A, PK_B) is sent to the distinguisher $\mathcal{D}$. As response, $\mathcal{D}$ sends the designated verifier's public key PK_C to $\mathcal{C}$.

- **Sign Query.** Proceeding adaptively, $\mathcal{D}$ submits a vector space $V_i \subset \mathbb{F}_p^N$ (V_i can be described by the properly augmented basis vectors $\mathbf{v}_{i1}, \ldots, \mathbf{v}_{im} \in \mathbb{F}_p^N$) to $\mathcal{C}$. $\mathcal{C}$ then selects an identifier $id_i \xleftarrow{R} \mathcal{I}$, and runs **Sign**$(SK_A, PK_B, id_i, m, \mathbf{v}_{ij})$ to generate signature σ_{ij} for $j = 1, \ldots, m$. Finally, $\mathcal{C}$ sends (id_i, σ_i) to $\mathcal{D}$, where $\sigma_i := (\sigma_{i1}, \ldots, \sigma_{im})$ is the signature of the vector subspace V_i.
- **Combine Query.** Proceeding adaptively, $\mathcal{D}$ sends $\mathcal{C}$ $(id_i, \{(\mathbf{v}_{ik}, \sigma_{ik}, \beta_k)\}_{k=1}^l)$. $\mathcal{C}$ runs **Combine**$(PK_A, PK_C, SK_B, id_i, \{(\mathbf{v}_{ik}, \sigma_{ik})\}_{k=1}^l)$ to generate a vector/signature pair $(\mathbf{v}, \sigma)$, where the combination coefficients are $\beta_1, \ldots, \beta_l$ in order. The pair $(\mathbf{v}, \sigma)$ is sent to $\mathcal{D}$.
- **Challenge.** $\mathcal{D}$ chooses $(id_i, \{(\mathbf{v}_{ik}, \sigma_{ik}, \beta_k)\}_{k=1}^l)$ (which does not appear in the combine query and id_i is chosen in the sign queries) and then sends this tuple to $\mathcal{C}$. $\mathcal{C}$ computes $\mathbf{v} = \sum_{k=1}^l \beta_k \mathbf{v}_{ik}$ and chooses a random bit b from $\{0, 1\}$. If $b = 0$, $\mathcal{C}$ runs $(\sigma, \mathbf{v}) \leftarrow$ **Combine**$(PK_A, PK_C, SK_B, id_i, \{(\mathbf{v}_{ik}, \sigma_{ik})\}_{k=1}^l)$; otherwise, runs $\sigma \leftarrow$ **Simulation**$(PK_A, SK_C, id_i, m, \mathbf{v})$. The signature σ is given to $\mathcal{D}$ as the challenge.
- **Output.** $\mathcal{D}$ outputs a bit b' from $\{0, 1\}$ and wins the game if $b' = b$.

We define the advantage of $\mathcal{D}$ in the above game as $Adv_{\mathcal{A}, \mathcal{S}}^{IND} = |Pr[b' = b] - \frac{1}{2}|$.

3   Our Design of LHSDE

In this section, we describe a specific and secure LHSDE scheme based on the network coding signature scheme proposed by Boneh *et al.* [6].

3.1   Bilinear Groups and Complexity Assumptions

We briefly describe the group with efficiently computable bilinear maps and the complexity assumptions of our scheme.

Definition 6. *Let* $\mathbb{G}_1$, $\mathbb{G}_2$ *and* $\mathbb{G}_T$ *be three cyclically multiplicative groups of the same prime order* p, *and let* $e : \mathbb{G}_1 \times \mathbb{G}_2 \to \mathbb{G}_T$ *be a bilinear map. Then we define a tuple of* $(\mathbb{G}_1, \mathbb{G}_2, \mathbb{G}_T, e, \varphi)$ *as a bilinear group tuple which has the following properties:*

1. Computability: For any $g \in \mathbb{G}_1$, $h \in \mathbb{G}_2$, we can efficiently compute $e(g, h)$.
2. Bilinearity: For any $a, b \in \mathbb{Z}_p$, $g \in \mathbb{G}_1$, and $h \in \mathbb{G}_2$, $e(g^a, h^b) = e(g, h)^{ab} = e(g^b, h^a)$.
3. Non-degeneracy: If g is a generator of $\mathbb{G}_1$, and h is a generator of $\mathbb{G}_2$, then $e(g, h)$ is a generator of $\mathbb{G}_T$, i.e., $e(g, h) \neq 1_{\mathbb{G}_T}$.
4. $\varphi : \mathbb{G}_2 \to \mathbb{G}_1$ is an efficient, computable isomorphism.

Definition 7 (co-BDH Problem). *Given a randomly chosen element $g_1 \in \mathbb{G}_1$, as well as $g_2 \in \mathbb{G}_2$, g_2^a and g_2^b for some unknown $a, b \in \mathbb{Z}_p$, compute $e(g_1, g_2)^{ab} \in \mathbb{G}_T$.*

The probability that a PPT adversary $\mathcal{A}$ solves the co-BDH problem is $\Pr[e(g_1, g_2)^{ab} \leftarrow \mathcal{A}(g_1, g_2, g_2^a, g_2^b)]$, which is defined as $Adv_{\mathcal{A},(\mathbb{G}_1,\mathbb{G}_2)}^{co-BDH}$.

Definition 8 (co-BDH Assumption). *We say that the co-BDH problem is hard in $(\mathbb{G}_1, \mathbb{G}_2, \mathbb{G}_T)$ if for any PPT adversary the probability $Adv_{\mathcal{A},(\mathbb{G}_1,\mathbb{G}_2)}^{co-BDH}$ is negligible.*

Definition 9 (Decisional Bilinear Diffie-Hellman (DBDH) Problem). *Given a randomly chosen element $g_1 \in \mathbb{G}_1$, as well as $g_2 \in \mathbb{G}_2$, $w \in \mathbb{G}_T$, g_2^a and g_2^b for some unknown $a, b \in \mathbb{Z}_p$, decide whether $w \stackrel{?}{=} e(g_1, g_2)^{ab}$.*

A DBDH oracle $\mathcal{O}_{DBDH}$ is that takes as input $g_1 \in \mathbb{G}_1$, $g_2 \in \mathbb{G}_2$, g_2^a, g_2^b and $w \in \mathbb{G}_T$, outputs 1 if $w = e(g_1, g_2)^{ab}$ and 0 otherwise.

Definition 10 (Gap Bilinear Diffie-Hellman (GBDH) Problem). *Given a randomly chosen element $g_1 \in \mathbb{G}_1$, as well as $g_2 \in \mathbb{G}_2$, g_2^a and g_2^b for some unknown $a, b \in \mathbb{Z}_p$, compute $e(g_1, g_2)^{ab} \in \mathbb{G}_T$ with the help of $\mathcal{O}_{DBDH}$.*

The probability that an adversary $\mathcal{A}$ solves the GBDH problem is $\Pr[e(g_1, g_2)^{ab} \leftarrow \mathcal{A}(g_1, g_2, g_2^a, g_2^b, \mathcal{O}_{DBDH})]$, which is defined as $Adv_{\mathcal{A},(\mathbb{G}_1,\mathbb{G}_2)}^{GBDH}$.

Definition 11 (GBDH Assumption). *We say that the GBDH problem is hard in $(\mathbb{G}_1, \mathbb{G}_2, \mathbb{G}_T)$ if for any PPT adversary the probability $Adv_{\mathcal{A},(\mathbb{G}_1,\mathbb{G}_2)}^{GBDH}$ is negligible.*

3.2   Our LHSDE Scheme

Our LHSDE scheme has two goals. First, only the combiner Bob, designated by the signer Alice, can combine signatures. Second, Bob uses the combined signature to convince the verifier Cindy (Bob can specify any entity in the system as the verifier), and only Cindy can believe the authenticity of the combined signature. However, no other third party can believe it because the designated verifier can use her private key to create a valid signature, which is indistinguishable from the one created by the designated combiner. Therefore, one cannot distinguish whether the signature is created by the designated combiner or by the designated verifier. The details of our design are given below.

- **Setup($1^k, N$).** On input a security parameter k and an integer $N > 0$:
    1. Generate $\mathcal{G} = (\mathbb{G}_1, \mathbb{G}_2, \mathbb{G}_T, e, \varphi)$ such that $\mathbb{G}_1$, $\mathbb{G}_2$, and $\mathbb{G}_T$ have the same prime order $p > 2^k$, $e : \mathbb{G}_1 \times \mathbb{G}_2 \to \mathbb{G}_T$ is an efficient bilinear map, and $\varphi : \mathbb{G}_2 \to \mathbb{G}_1$ is an efficiently computable isomorphism.
    2. Choose a generator $h \xleftarrow{R} \mathbb{G}_2 \setminus \{1\}$.
    3. Choose generators $g_1, g_2, \ldots, g_N \xleftarrow{R} \mathbb{G}_1 \setminus \{1\}$.

4. Choose three hash functions $H_1 : \{0,1\}^* \to \mathbb{G}_1$, $H_2 : \mathbb{F}_p^N \to \mathbb{G}_1$ and $H_3 : \mathbb{G}_T \to \mathbb{G}_1$.
5. Output the common parameter $cp = (\mathcal{G}, p, H_1, H_2, H_3, h, g_1, g_2, \ldots, g_N)$.

- **KeyGen**(cp). The signer Alice generates his private/public key as following:

  1. Chooses $\alpha_A \xleftarrow{R} \mathbb{F}_p$, and sets $u_A = h^{\alpha_A}$.
  2. Outputs the signer's public key $PK_A = u_A$ and private key $SK_A = \alpha_A$.

  Accordingly, the combiner Bob (the receiver Cindy) generates his private/pubic key as following:

  1. Chooses $\alpha_B \xleftarrow{R} \mathbb{F}_p$ ($\alpha_C \xleftarrow{R} \mathbb{F}_p$), and sets $u_B = h^{\alpha_B}$ ($u_C = h^{\alpha_C}$).
  2. Outputs Bob's (Cindy's) public key $PK_B = u_B$ ($PK_C = u_C$) and private key $SK_B = \alpha_B$ ($SK_C = \alpha_C$).

- **Sign**$(SK_A, PK_B, id, m, \mathbf{v})$. This algorithm takes as input a private key SK_A, a public key PK_B, an identifier $id \in \{0,1\}^k$, a positive integer $m < N$, and a vector $\mathbf{v} \in \mathbb{F}_p^N$. It outputs the signature

$$\sigma = \left(\prod_{i=1}^m H_1(id, i)^{v_{n+i}} \prod_{j=1}^n g_j^{v_j} \right)^{\alpha_A} H_3(e(H_2(\mathbf{v}), u_B)^{\alpha_A}).$$

- **Verify**$(PA_A, SK_B, id, m, \sigma, \mathbf{v})$. This algorithm takes as input a public key PK_A, a private key SK_B, an identifier id, a positive integer $m < N$, a signature σ and a vector $\mathbf{v}$, and then define $\gamma_1(PK_A, \sigma) \overset{\text{def}}{=} e(\sigma, h)$ and $\gamma_2(SK_B, PA_A, id, m, \mathbf{v}) \overset{\text{def}}{=} e(\prod_{i=1}^m H_1(id, i)^{v_{n+i}} \prod_{j=1}^n g_j^{v_j}, u_A) e(H_3(e(H_2(\mathbf{v}), u_A)^{\alpha_B}), h)$. It outputs 1 (accept) if $\gamma_1(PK_A, \sigma) = \gamma_2(SK_B, PA_A, id, m, \mathbf{v})$; Otherwise, outputs 0 (reject).

- **Combine**$(PK_A, PK_C, SK_B, id, \{(\mathbf{v}_k, \sigma_k)\}_{k=1}^l)$. This algorithm takes as input two public keys PK_A and PK_C, a private key SK_B, an identifier id, and l pairs of $\{(\mathbf{v}_k, \sigma_k)\}_{k=1}^l$ where $\mathbf{v}_i \in \mathbb{F}_p^N$ is a vector and σ_i is a signature. It outputs a vector $\mathbf{v} = \sum_{k=1}^l \beta_k \mathbf{v}_k$ and a signature $\sigma = e(\prod_{k=1}^l (\sigma_k \cdot [H_3(e(H_2(\mathbf{v}_k), u_A)^{\alpha_B})]^{-1})^{\beta_k}, u_C)$, where $\beta_1, \ldots, \beta_l \in \mathbb{F}_p$ are chosen by the combiner.

- **DVerify**$(PK_A, SK_C, id, m, \mathbf{v}, \sigma)$. This algorithm takes as input a public key PK_A, a private key SK_C, an identifier id, a positive integer $m < N$, a vector $\mathbf{v} \in \mathbb{F}_p^N$, and a signature σ. It outputs 1 (accept) if $\sigma = e(\prod_{i=1}^m H_1(id, i)^{v_{n+i}} \prod_{j=1}^n g_j^{v_j}, u_A)^{\alpha_C}$; Otherwise, output 0 (reject).

- **Simulation**$(PK_A, SK_C, id, m, \mathbf{v})$. This algorithm takes as input a public key PK_A, a private key SK_C, a document identifier id, a positive integer $m < N$, and a vector $\mathbf{v}$. It outputs a signature

$$\hat{\sigma} = e\left(\prod_{i=1}^m H_1(id, i)^{v_{n+i}} \prod_{j=1}^n g_j^{v_j}, u_A \right)^{\alpha_C}.$$

We will now demonstrate the correctness of our scheme.

- **Correctness of the Sign Algorithm.** We assume that $(\mathbf{v}, \sigma)$ is a valid pair of vector/signature signed by the signer. Then we have

$$\gamma_1(PK_A, \sigma)$$
$$= e(\sigma, h)$$
$$= e\left(\left(\prod_{i=1}^{m} H_1(id, i)^{v_{n+i}} \prod_{j=1}^{n} g_j^{v_j}\right)^{\alpha_A} H_3\left(e(H_2(\mathbf{v}), u_B)^{\alpha_A}\right), h\right)$$
$$= e\left(\prod_{i=1}^{m} H_1(id, i)^{v_{n+i}} \prod_{j=1}^{n} g_j^{v_j}, u_A\right) e(H_3(e(H_2(\mathbf{v}), u_A)^{\alpha_B}), h)$$
$$= \gamma_2(SK_B, PA_A, id, m, \mathbf{v}).$$

- **Correctness of the Combine Algorithm.** We assume that $\{(\mathbf{v}_k, \sigma_k)\}_{k=1}^{l}$ are l pairs of vector/signature with the same identifier such that $\gamma_1(PK_A, \sigma_k)=\gamma_2(SK_B, PA_A, id, m, \mathbf{v}_k)$ for all $k \in \{1, \ldots, l\}$. $\mathbf{v} = \sum_{k=1}^{l} \beta_k \mathbf{v}_k$ and $\sigma = e(\prod_{k=1}^{l}(\sigma_k \cdot [H_3(e(H_2(\mathbf{v}_k), u_A)^{\alpha_B})]^{-1})^{\beta_k}, u_C)$ are output by the **Combine** algorithm. Then we have

$$\sigma = e\left(\prod_{k=1}^{l}(\sigma_k \cdot [H_3(e(H_2(\mathbf{v}_k), u_A)^{\alpha_B})]^{-1})^{\beta_k}, u_C\right)$$
$$= e\left(\prod_{k=1}^{l}\left(\prod_{i=1}^{m} H_1(id, i)^{v_{k,n+i}} \prod_{j=1}^{n} g_j^{v_{k,j}}\right)^{\beta_k}, u_A\right)^{\alpha_C}$$
$$= e\left(\prod_{i=1}^{m} H_1(id, i)^{\sum_{k=1}^{l} \beta_k v_{k,n+i}} \prod_{j=1}^{n} g_j^{\sum_{k=1}^{l} \beta_k v_{k,j}}, u_A\right)^{\alpha_C}$$
$$= e\left(\prod_{i=1}^{m} H_1(id, i)^{v_{n+i}} \prod_{j=1}^{n} g_j^{v_j}, u_A\right)^{\alpha_C}.$$

- **Correctness of the Simulation Algorithm.** We assume that $\hat{\sigma} \leftarrow$ **Simulation**$(PK_A, SK_C, id, m, \mathbf{v})$. Then we have

$$\hat{\sigma} = e\left(\prod_{i=1}^{m} H_1(id, i)^{v_{n+i}} \prod_{j=1}^{n} g_j^{v_j}, u_A\right)^{\alpha_C},$$

which means that **DVerify**$(PK_A, SK_C, id, m, \mathbf{v}, \hat{\sigma}) = 1$.

Efficiency. The computation overhead of the signer consists of three map-to-point operations, one multi-exponentiation in $\mathbb{G}_1$ and one pairing. The designated combiner's computation overhead of verifying a vector consists of $m + 2$ map-to-point operations, one multi-exponentiation in $\mathbb{G}_1$ and four pairings, whereas other entity needs m map-to-point operations, one multi-exponentiation in $\mathbb{G}_1$ and one pairing to verify a signature.

3.3   Security Proof

Now we prove that our design satisfies the definitions of unforgeability and indistinguishability.

Theorem 1. *Our LHSDE scheme satisfies UF_1 in the random oracle model if co-BDH assumption holds in $(\mathbb{G}_1, \mathbb{G}_2, \mathbb{G}_T)$. If there exists a PPT adversary $\mathcal{A}$ with success probability $Succ^{UF_1}_{\mathcal{A},\mathcal{S}}$, then there exists a PPT algorithm $\mathcal{B}$ that solves co-BDH problem in $(\mathbb{G}_1, \mathbb{G}_2, \mathbb{G}_T)$ with success probability*

$$Adv^{co-BDH}_{\mathcal{B},(\mathbb{G}_1,\mathbb{G}_2)} \geq Succ^{UF_1}_{\mathcal{A},\mathcal{S}} - \frac{q_s(q_s + q_{h_1}) + 1}{2^k},$$

where q_s and q_{h_1} are the numbers of signature and hash H_1 queries, respectively, made by $\mathcal{A}$.

Proof. The proof is similar to **Theorem 6** in [6], so we omit it.   □

Theorem 2. *Our LHSDE scheme satisfies IND.*

Proof. For any vector $\mathbf{v}$, the corresponding signature output by the **Combine** algorithm is exactly the same as that of the **Simulation** algorithm. So our LHSDE scheme satisfies IND.   □

Theorem 3. *Our LHSDE scheme satisfies UF_2 in the random oracle model if GBDH assumption holds in $(\mathbb{G}_1, \mathbb{G}_2, \mathbb{G}_T)$. If there exists a PPT adversary $\mathcal{A}$ with the probability $Succ^{UF_2}_{\mathcal{A},\mathcal{S}}$, then there exists a PPT algorithm $\mathcal{B}$ that solves GBDH in $(\mathbb{G}_1, \mathbb{G}_2, \mathbb{G}_T)$ with the success probability*

$$Adv^{GBDH}_{\mathcal{B},(\mathbb{G}_1,\mathbb{G}_2)} \geq Succ^{UF_2}_{\mathcal{A},\mathcal{S}} - \frac{1}{2^k}.$$

Proof. We assume that $\mathcal{A}$ is a successful adversary that breaks the UF_2 of our scheme, and our goal is to construct an algorithm $\mathcal{B}$ that solves GBDH problem in $(\mathbb{G}_1, \mathbb{G}_2, \mathbb{G}_T)$: given $g \in \mathbb{G}_1$ and $h, w_1, w_2 \in \mathbb{G}_2$ with $w_1 = h^{\alpha_A}$, $w_2 = h^{\alpha_B}$ for some unknown $\alpha_A, \alpha_B \in \mathbb{F}_p^*$, outputs an element $e(g, h)^{\alpha_A \alpha_B} \in \mathbb{G}_T$ with the help of the oracle $\mathcal{O}_{DBDH}$.

First of all, $\mathcal{B}$ maintains four lists H_1-List, H_2-List, H_3-List and σ-List which are used to record H_1 queries, H_2 queries, H_3 queries and signature queries, respectively. H_1-List consists of tuples $(id, i, H_1(id, i))$. H_2-List consists of pairs $(\mathbf{v}, H_2(\mathbf{v}))$, where $\mathbf{v}$ is the signed data. H_3-List consists of tuples $(E, \mathbf{v}, H_3(E))$, where E is the input of H_3 (whether $E^{s^{-1}} \overset{?}{=} e(g, h)^{\alpha_A \alpha_B ab}$ is determined by the DBDH oracle, and the values of s, a and b will be introduced later). σ-List consists of tuples (V, id, σ), where σ is the signature of $V \subset \mathbb{F}_p^N$, id is the identifier of vector subspace V.

Setup. $\mathcal{B}$ chooses a positive integer N, then

1. Chooses $k_1, \ldots, k_N \overset{R}{\leftarrow} \mathbb{F}_p$, and sets $g_j := \varphi(h)^{k_j}$ for $j = 1, \ldots, N$.

2. Sets the common parameter $cp := (\mathcal{G}, p, h, g_1, \ldots, g_N)$.

3. Chooses $a \xleftarrow{R} \mathbb{F}_p^*$ and sets $u_A := w_1^a$ as the signer's public key.

4. Chooses $b \xleftarrow{R} \mathbb{F}_p^*$ and sets $u_B := w_2^b$ as the designated combiner's public key.

5. Chooses $d \xleftarrow{R} \mathbb{F}_p^*$ and sets $u_D := w_2^d$ as the challenging public key.

6. Sends (cp, PK_A, PK_B, PK_D) to the adversary $\mathcal{A}$.

Then, $\mathcal{A}$ sends the verifier's public key $PK_C = u_C$ ($u_C := h^{\alpha_C}$) to the challenger $\mathcal{C}$.

H_1 Query. Upon receiving a request of the value of $H_1(id, i)$ from $\mathcal{A}$, $\mathcal{B}$ chooses random $l_i \in \mathbb{F}_p^*$ and sets $H_1(id, i) := g^{l_i}$. Then, the tuple $(id, i, H_1(id, i))$ is added into H_1-List.

H_2 Query. Upon receiving a request of the value of $H_2(\mathbf{v})$ from $\mathcal{A}$, $\mathcal{B}$:

1. If there exists a pair $(\mathbf{v}, H_2(\mathbf{v}))$ in the H_2-List, returns h_2 to $\mathcal{A}$.

2. Otherwise, chooses $s \xleftarrow{R} \mathbb{F}_p^*$ and computes $H_2(\mathbf{v}) := g^s$. Then, $\mathcal{B}$ adds $(\mathbf{v}, H_2(\mathbf{v}))$ into the H_2-List and sends $H_2(\mathbf{v})$ to $\mathcal{A}$.

H_3 Query. Upon receiving a request of $(E, \mathbf{v})$ from $\mathcal{A}$, $\mathcal{B}$ checks whether there exists a pair $(\mathbf{v}, H_2(\mathbf{v}))$ in the H_2-List. If not, let the simulation of $H_2(\mathbf{v})$ be the same as the H_2 query. Then, $\mathcal{B}$ submits the tuple $(g, u_A, u_B, E^{s^{-1}})$ to the DBDH oracle. The DBDH oracle will tell $\mathcal{B}$ whether $E^{s^{-1}} = e(g, h)^{\alpha_A \alpha_B ab}$.

1. If $E^{s^{-1}} = e(g, h)^{\alpha_A \alpha_B ab}$, $\mathcal{B}$ computes $E^{s^{-1} a^{-1} b^{-1}} := e(g, h)^{\alpha_A \alpha_B}$ which means that $\mathcal{B}$ can solve the given instance of the GBDH problem.

2. If $E^{s^{-1}} \neq e(g, h)^{\alpha_A \alpha_B ab}$, $\mathcal{B}$ chooses $h_3 \xleftarrow{R} \mathbb{G}_1$ such that there is no tuple $(\cdot, \cdot, h_3)$ in the H_3-List. Then, $\mathcal{B}$ adds $(E, \perp, h_3)$ ($\perp$ means that $\mathcal{B}$ does not know this value) into the H_3-List and returns h_3 to $\mathcal{A}$.

Sign. Upon receiving a request of a signature on a vector space $V \subset \mathbb{F}_p^N$ ($\mathbf{v}_1, \ldots, \mathbf{v}_m \in \mathbb{F}_p^N$ are the properly augmented basis vectors of V) from $\mathcal{A}$, $\mathcal{B}$:

1. Chooses $id \xleftarrow{R} \{0, 1\}^k$ as V's identifier.

2. Computes $H_1(id, i)$ for $i = 1, \ldots, m$ as in the H_1 query.

3. For $i = 1, \ldots, m$, chooses $\sigma_i \xleftarrow{R} \mathbb{G}_1$.

4. Sets $\sigma = (\sigma_1, \ldots, \sigma_m)$, and records tuple (V, id, σ) into σ-List.

5. Sends id and σ to $\mathcal{A}$.

Combine. Theorem 2 shows that $\mathcal{A}$ can implement the **Simulation** algorithm that outputs the identical values as the **Combine** algorithm. So, there is no need to simulate the **Combine** algorithm.

Output. $\mathcal{A}$ eventually outputs an identifier id^* (there exists an id_i in the signature queries satisfies $id^* = id_i$), a nonzero vector $\mathbf{v}^* \in V_i$, and a signature σ^* (a type 2 forgery) such that **DVerify**($PK_A, SK_D, id^*, m, \mathbf{v}^*, \sigma^*$) = 1. We have

$$\sigma^* = e\left(\prod_{i=1}^{m} H_1(id^*, i)^{v_{n+i}^*} \prod_{j=1}^{n} g_j^{v_j^*}, h\right)^{ad\alpha_A\alpha_B}$$

$$= e\left(\prod_{i=1}^{m} g^{l_i v_{n+i}^*} \prod_{j=1}^{n} \varphi(h)^{k_j v_j^*}, h\right)^{ad\alpha_A\alpha_B}$$

$$= e\left(g^{\sum_{i=1}^{m} l_i v_{n+i}^*}, h\right)^{ad\alpha_A\alpha_B} e\left(\varphi(h)^{\sum_{j=1}^{n} k_j v_j^*}, h\right)^{ad\alpha_A\alpha_B}$$

$$= e\left(g^{\sum_{i=1}^{m} l_i v_{n+i}^*}, h\right)^{ad\alpha_A\alpha_B} e\left(\varphi(u_A)^{\sum_{j=1}^{n} k_j v_j^*}, u_D\right).$$

If $\sum_{i=1}^{m} l_i v_{n+i}^* \neq 0$, $\mathcal{B}$ can further compute

$$e(g, h)^{\alpha_A\alpha_B} = \frac{\sigma^*}{e\left(\varphi(u_A)^{\sum_{j=1}^{n} k_j v_j^*}, u_D\right)}^{(\sum_{i=1}^{m} l_i v_{n+i}^*)^{-1} a^{-1} d^{-1}}.$$

As we can see, the values of $l_1, \ldots, l_m$ are independent of $\mathcal{A}$'s view, and $\mathbf{v}^* \in V_i$ is a non-zero vector. So the probability of $\sum_{i=1}^{m} l_i v_{n+i}^* = 0$ is $1/p$ which is at most $1/2^k$.

Therefore, $\mathcal{B}$ successfully solves an instance of the GBDH problem with success probability

$$Adv_{\mathcal{B},(\mathbb{G}_1,\mathbb{G}_2)}^{GBDH} \geq Succ_{\mathcal{A},\mathcal{S}}^{UF_2} - \frac{1}{2^k}.$$

This completes the proof of Theorem 3.   □

4   Conclusion

In this paper, we introduce designated entities into linearly homomorphic signatures. Only the designated combiner is able to produce signatures of linearly-combined signed data, and only the designated verifier can be convinced about the validity of those signatures. We formally define the new notion "linearly homomorphic signatures with designated entities" and the relevant security requirements. A specific and secure design is given to show that our definitions are achievable. Our scheme is motivated by the open problem given by Rivest in the setting of transitive signatures (a specific kind of homomorphic signatures). It is our future work to study designated entities in other variants of homomorphic signatures.

Acknowledgements. The authors would like to thank anonymous reviewers for their helpful comments. This work is supported by National Natural Science Foundation of China (61472083, 61402110, 61771140), Distinguished Young Scholars Fund of Fujian (2016J06013), and Fujian Normal University Innovative Research Team (NO. IRTL1207).

References

1. Ahlswede, R., Cai, N., Li, S.R., Yeung, R.W.: Network information flow. IEEE Trans. Inf. Theory **46**(4), 1204–1216 (2000). https://doi.org/10.1109/18.850663
2. Attrapadung, N., Libert, B.: Homomorphic network coding signatures in the standard model. In: Catalano et al. [7], pp. 17–34. https://doi.org/10.1007/978-3-642-19379-8_2
3. Attrapadung, N., Libert, B., Peters, T.: Computing on authenticated data: new privacy definitions and constructions. In: Wang, X., Sako, K. (eds.) ASIACRYPT 2012. LNCS, vol. 7658, pp. 367–385. Springer, Heidelberg (2012). https://doi.org/10.1007/978-3-642-34961-4_23
4. Boneh, D., Freeman, D.M.: Homomorphic signatures for polynomial functions. In: Paterson, K.G. (ed.) EUROCRYPT 2011. LNCS, vol. 6632, pp. 149–168. Springer, Heidelberg (2011). https://doi.org/10.1007/978-3-642-20465-4_10
5. Boneh, D., Freeman, D.M.: Linearly homomorphic signatures over binary fields and new tools for lattice-based signatures. In: Catalano et al. [7], pp. 1–16. https://doi.org/10.1007/978-3-642-19379-8_1
6. Boneh, D., Freeman, D., Katz, J., Waters, B.: Signing a linear subspace: signature schemes for network coding. In: Jarecki, S., Tsudik, G. (eds.) PKC 2009. LNCS, vol. 5443, pp. 68–87. Springer, Heidelberg (2009). https://doi.org/10.1007/978-3-642-00468-1_5
7. Catalano, D., Fazio, N., Gennaro, R., Nicolosi, A. (eds.): PKC 2011. LNCS, vol. 6571. Springer, Heidelberg (2011). https://doi.org/10.1007/978-3-642-19379-8
8. Catalano, D., Fiore, D., Warinschi, B.: Efficient network coding signatures in the standard model. In: Fischlin et al. [13], pp. 680–696. https://doi.org/10.1007/978-3-642-30057-8_40
9. Chen, W., Lei, H., Qi, K.: Lattice-based linearly homomorphic signatures in the standard model. Theor. Comput. Sci. **634**, 47–54 (2016). https://doi.org/10.1016/j.tcs.2016.04.009
10. Cheng, C., Jiang, T., Liu, Y., Zhang, M.: Security analysis of a homomorphic signature scheme for network coding. Secur. Commun. Netw. **8**(18), 4053–4060 (2015). https://doi.org/10.1002/sec.1321
11. Diffie, W., Hellman, M.E.: New directions in cryptography. IEEE Trans. Inf. Theory **22**(6), 644–654 (1976). https://doi.org/10.1109/TIT.1976.1055638
12. Fiore, D., Mitrokotsa, A., Nizzardo, L., Pagnin, E.: Multi-key homomorphic authenticators. In: Cheon, J.H., Takagi, T. (eds.) ASIACRYPT 2016. LNCS, vol. 10032, pp. 499–530. Springer, Heidelberg (2016). https://doi.org/10.1007/978-3-662-53890-6_17
13. Fischlin, M., Buchmann, J., Manulis, M. (eds.): PKC 2012. LNCS, vol. 7293. Springer, Heidelberg (2012). https://doi.org/10.1007/978-3-642-30057-8
14. Freeman, D.M.: Improved security for linearly homomorphic signatures: a generic framework. In: Fischlin et al. [13], pp. 697–714. https://doi.org/10.1007/978-3-642-30057-8_41
15. Gennaro, R., Katz, J., Krawczyk, H., Rabin, T.: Secure network coding over the integers. In: Nguyen, P.Q., Pointcheval, D. (eds.) PKC 2010. LNCS, vol. 6056, pp. 142–160. Springer, Heidelberg (2010). https://doi.org/10.1007/978-3-642-13013-7_9
16. Johnson, R., Molnar, D., Song, D., Wagner, D.: Homomorphic signature schemes. In: Preneel, B. (ed.) CT-RSA 2002. LNCS, vol. 2271, pp. 244–262. Springer, Heidelberg (2002). https://doi.org/10.1007/3-540-45760-7_17

17. Li, S.R., Yeung, R.W., Cai, N.: Linear network coding. IEEE Trans. Inf. Theory **49**(2), 371–381 (2003). https://doi.org/10.1109/TIT.2002.807285
18. Libert, B., Peters, T., Joye, M., Yung, M.: Linearly homomorphic structure-preserving signatures and their applications. Des. Codes Cryptogr. **77**(2–3), 441–477 (2015). https://doi.org/10.1007/s10623-015-0079-1
19. Rivest, R.L.: Two signature schemes. Talk at Cambridge University, October 2000. http://people.csail.mit.edu/rivest/pubs/Riv00.slides.pdf

Efficient Certificate-Based Signature
and Its Aggregation

Xinxin Ma[1], Jun Shao[1(✉)], Cong Zuo[2], and Ru Meng[3]

[1] School of Computer and Information Engineering, Zhejiang Gongshang University,
Hangzhou, Zhejiang, China
`wangdax@126.com, chn.junshao@gmail.com`
[2] Faculty of Information Technology, Monash University, Clayton Campus,
Melbourne, VIC 3800, Australia
`cong.zuo1@monash.edu`
[3] Shaanxi Normal University, Xi'an, Shaanxi, China
`mengru@snnu.edu.cn`

Abstract. The certificate-based cryptography is proposed to eliminate the key escrow problem of ID-based public key cryptography and simplify certificate management procedures of traditional public key infrastructure (PKI) in the same time. Since its invention, many certificate-based signature have been proposed. However, the existing schemes either only support partial aggregateability, or require a pre-negotiated one-time-use nonce. To solve this problem, in this paper, we propose a new certificate-based signature scheme where signatures on the same message signed by different users can be aggregated into a single signature without the pre-negotiated one-time-use nonce. Furthermore, verification in our proposal only involves four pairing operations. Our proposed certificate-based (aggregate) signature scheme can be considered as the combination of Gentry-Ramzan identity-based aggregate signature scheme and Boneh-Lynn-Shacham short signature scheme. Similar to their schemes, our proposal can be also proven secure in the random oracle model based on the computational Diffie-Hellman assumption.

1 Introduction

In traditional public key infrastructure (PKI), the user's public key is usually a random string that is unrelated to the user's identity information. Hence, the public key should be authenticated before its use. To solve this problem, PKI introduces a trusted third party, named certificate authority (CA), whose responsibility is to issue certificates. The certificate can provide an unforgeable and trusted link between the public key and the user's identity information. However, this solution has a side effect: bring a heavy certificate management duty to the CA.

To simplify certificate management in PKI, Shamir [29] proposed the concept of ID-based cryptography (IBC) in 1984. The main idea is to use the user's identity information as the public key, and a trusted third party, named private

© Springer International Publishing AG 2017
J. K. Liu and P. Samarati (Eds.): ISPEC 2017, LNCS 10701, pp. 391–408, 2017.
https://doi.org/10.1007/978-3-319-72359-4_23

key generator (PKG), who can generate the user's private key corresponding to the user's identity information. Nevertheless, this solution still has its side effect: key escrow. It is easy to see that the PKG knows all the private keys of all the users; hence, it can impersonate anyone in the system.

To efficiently overcome the complexity and costs of the certificate management in PKI and the key escrow issue in IBC, Al-Riyami and Paterson [1] proposed a new kind of cryptographic technique called certificateless cryptography (CLC) at Asiacrypt 2003. In CLC, there also exists a trusted third party that is called key generator center (KGC) like IBC. However, KGC in this system can only generate the partial private key for users. The full private key is computed by combining the partial private key and a secret key that is only known to the user. Hence, CL-PKC avoid the key escrow problem in ID-PKC, and no certificate exists in this system.

Another kind of cryptographic technique, similar to CLC named certificate-based encryption (CBE), is proposed by Gentry [10] at Eurocrypt 2003. CBE aims to import the advantages of IBE into conventional PKI. Generally speaking, a CBE scheme mixes a PKI scheme with an IBE scheme. In particular, the trusted third party (called the certifier) in the CBE system generates the certificate as in a conventional PKI system. This certificate not only has all the functionalities of a conventional PKI certificate but also has an additional functionality that acts as a part of decryption key. The private key of the user in CBE is composed of the certificate and a secret key chosen by the user. In parallel to CBE, Kang et al. [15] proposed the notion of certificate-based signature (CBS) following the idea of CBE in 2004. Since then, many certificate-based signatures have been proposed. However, the existing schemes either only support partial aggregateability, (i.e., only a part of signature can be aggregated), or are lack of efficient verification (i.e., tons of pairing operations are required).

However, the full aggregateability and efficient verification are quite desired in resource constraint environments, like Internet of Things [9]. As we know, the IoT network is composed by lots of resource-limited network nodes that are restricted in electric power, communication bandwidth, and storage. When we request service from this network, each node should return the newest information, and each message has to be signed to immune forgery or other attacks. However, the regular signatures need to be saved and verified individually. Tons of messages and signatures would transmitted and verified over in this resource-limited network, which significantly decrease the efficiency of this network. This situation asks for the efficient signature with full aggregateability to save bandwidth and computational cost.

1.1   Related Work

In this part, we will review the work that related to our proposal.

Certificate-Based Signature. In 2004, Kang et al. [15] proposed the definition of certificate-based signature (CBS) and gave the first two certificate-based signature schemes. However, Li *et al.* [17] pointed out that the scheme in [15] which used the idea of the multisignature was insecure against key replacement attack. To overcome this attack, Li *et al.* firstly gave an improved security model, and then proposed a new certificate-based signature scheme secure in their new security model by using random oracles method. Later, a new scheme secure in the standard model given in [18]. However, the latter one broken by Yang and Li [25]. To improve the efficiency and security of certificate-based signature, Liu *et al.* [22] proposed two new certificate-based signature schemes. One is pair-free, the other is secure in the standard model. However, they broken by Zhang [40] and Yang and Li [25], respectively. Later, in 2009, Wu *et al.* [35,36] proposed new security model to model the key replacement attack. In their new security model, there exist three types of adversaries: normal adversary, strong adversary and super adversary. A generic construction of certificate-based signature from certificateless signature along with the security proof in the random oracle were also given by Wu *et al.* [35,36]. To obtain more efficient scheme, Ming and Wang [38] proposed a new pairing-free scheme, and its improvement was given by Li *et al.* [20]. Later on, Li *et al.* [19] and Liu [24] independently proposed short certificate-based signature schemes where the signature only contains one element. Unfortunately, their schemes suffers from the attacks proposed by Cheng [6]. In 2013, Feng and Li [7,8] proposed a new certificate-based signature schemes. Most recently, Gao *et al.* [34] proposed a generic construction of certificate-based signature from certificateless signature as well as its security proof in the standard model. To the best of our knowledge, the above schemes can only support partial aggregateability at most.

Certificate-Based Aggregate Signature. To reduce the bandwidth cost by many certificate-based signatures, the concept of certificate-based aggregate signature is proposed. However, there are only two papers dealing with the certificate-based aggregate signature [4,23]. However, none of them can efficiently provide full aggregateability and efficient verification at the same time.

To make this part complete, we further review certificateless aggregate signature in the below. As mentioned above certificateless aggregate cryptography is quite similar with certificate-based aggregate cryptography.

By using bilinear pairings, Gong *et al.* [12] proposed the first two certificateless aggregate signature schemes secure in random oracle model. However, the first one can only provide partial aggregateability, where only a part of signature can be aggregated. The second one requires the pre-negotiated one-time-use nonce and has an inefficient verification. To improve the efficiency in verification, Zhang and Zhang [42] proposed a new certificateless aggregate signature scheme. However, it suffers from the coalition attacks [32]. New certificateless aggregate signature scheme with constant pairing computation was proposed by Zhang *et al.* [16]. However, their scheme still requires the pre-negotiated one-time-use nonce. Later on, Xiong *et al.* [37] proposed a new certificateless aggregate signature scheme with efficient verification. Nevertheless, He *et al.* [13] showed that their scheme was not secure. An improvement was proposed later in [33], but the resulting scheme only supports partial aggregateability. In 2014, Liu *et al.* [21] proposed another new certificateless aggregate signature scheme with efficient verification. Unfortunately, it was broken by Chen *et al.* [5] and Shen *et al.* [30]. An improved certificateless aggregate signature scheme was also proposed by Chen *et al.* [5]. However, it has been shown to be insecure in [31,39,41]. In 2015, Malhi and Batra [26] proposed an efficient certificateless aggregate signature scheme for vehicular ad-hoc networks. However, it only supports partial aggregateability. In 2016, Nie *et al.* [27] proposed an efficient certificateless aggregate signature scheme, but it is not secure [28]. Recently, Kang *et al.* [14] proposed another certificateless aggregate signature scheme. However, their scheme only supports partial aggregateability like the scheme in [42].

1.2   Our Contribution

In this paper, we propose a new certificate-based signature based on the identity-based aggregate signature in [11] and short signature in [3]. Our proposal allows anyone to aggregate signatures on the same message by different signers into a single signature, while it does not require the pre-negotiated one-use-time nonce. Furthermore, the verification in our proposal only needs four pairing operations. Our proposal can significantly reduce the bandwidth and verification cost by large number of CBS signatures, and widen the spectrum of the applications of CBS. The security proofs of our proposed CBS scheme and its aggregate version are also given in the random oracle based on the computational Diffie-Hellman assumption.

1.3   Organization

The rest of the paper is organized as follows. In Sect. 2, we give the definitions of certificate-based signature (CBS), and certificate-based aggregate signature (CBAS) as well as their security models and some preliminaries on which our scheme relies. In Sect. 3, we construct a new certificate-based signature scheme and give its security analysis. Next, we propose a concrete CBAS Scheme based on our CBS scheme above together with its security proof in Sect. 4.2. At last, we give conclusion and outlook in Sect. 5.

2   Preliminaries

In this section, we will give the definitions related to certificate-based signature (CBS), and certificate-based aggregate signature (CBAS) and their security models. Furthermore, in this section we will also give the definitions related to the computational Diffie-Hellman (CDH) assumption that we will use in the security proofs of our proposals.

2.1 Definitions of Certificate-Based Signature (CBS)

The Concept of CBS. In a certificate-based signature scheme, there exist the following five algorithms.

- $\mathtt{Setup}(1^\lambda) \to (msk, mpk)$: In this algorithm, the certifier takes the security parameter 1^λ as input, and outputs the corresponding master secret key msk and master public key mpk. The master public key mpk is published and implicitly involved in the following algorithms, while the master secret key msk is kept secret by the certifier.
- $\mathtt{UKeyGen}(1^\lambda) \to (sk, pk)$: This algorithm takes the security parameter 1^λ as input, and outputs the corresponding secret key sk and public key pk. The public key pk is published, while the secret key sk is kept secret by the user.
- $\mathtt{Certify}(msk, pk_{\mathrm{ID}}, \mathrm{ID}) \to d_{\mathrm{ID}}$: In this algorithm, upon receiving the identity information ID and its public key pk_{ID}, the certifier uses its master secret key msk to generate the corresponding certificate d_{ID} of the signer ID.
- $\mathtt{Sign}(m, d_{\mathrm{ID}}, sk_{\mathrm{ID}}) \to \sigma_{\mathrm{ID}, pk}$: By using its private key sk_{ID} and certificate d_{ID}, the signer ID can generate the signature σ on message m from the message space.
- $\mathtt{Verify}(m, \sigma_{\mathrm{ID}, pk}, pk, \mathrm{ID}) \to 1$ or 0: Given a signature σ_{ID} corresponding to identity ID and public key pk, and the underlying message m, the algorithm outputs 1 if it is valid, or 0 otherwise.

Correctness. We say a CBS scheme is correct if for $(msk, mpk) \leftarrow \mathtt{Setup}(1^\lambda)$, $(sk_{\mathrm{ID}}, pk_{\mathrm{ID}}) \leftarrow \mathtt{Setup}(1^\lambda)$, and $d_{\mathrm{ID}} \leftarrow \mathtt{Certify}(msk, pk_{\mathrm{ID}}, \mathrm{ID})$, we have that

$$\mathtt{Verify}(m, \mathtt{Sign}(m, d_{\mathrm{ID}}, sk_{\mathrm{ID}}), pk_{\mathrm{ID}}, \mathrm{ID}) = 1.$$

Existential Unforgeability of CBS. The security of CBS is defined by two different games and the adversary should decide which game to play before start. Game 1 models the attack where the adversary can obtain the user's private key but not the corresponding certificate, while Game 2 models the attack where the adversary can obtain all certificates (by holding the master secret key of the certifier) but not the private key of the targeted user.

Game 1.

Setup In this phase, $\mathcal{C}$ runs algorithm $\mathtt{Setup}(1^\lambda)$ to generate (msk, mpk), and sends mpk to $\mathcal{A}$, while keeping msk secret.
Find In this phase, $\mathcal{A}$ can issue a number of different queries to $\mathcal{A}$ adaptively. Each query can be one of the followings.
- Key generation oracle $\mathcal{O}_{pk}$: On receiving an identity ID from $\mathcal{A}$, $\mathcal{C}$ first checks whether $(\mathrm{ID}, sk_{\mathrm{ID}}, pk_{\mathrm{ID}})$ exists in List L_k. If it does exist, $\mathcal{C}$ returns pk_{ID}. If it does not exist, $\mathcal{C}$ runs algorithm $\mathtt{UKeyGen}(1^\lambda)$ to get the corresponding key pair $(sk_{\mathrm{ID}}, pk_{\mathrm{ID}})$, and sends pk_{ID} to $\mathcal{A}$. At last, $\mathcal{C}$ records $(\mathrm{ID}, sk_{\mathrm{ID}}, pk_{\mathrm{ID}})$ in List L_k.

- Secret key oracle $\mathcal{O}_{sk}$: On receiving an identity ID from $\mathcal{A}$, $\mathcal{C}$ first checks whether $(\text{ID}, sk_{\text{ID}}, pk_{\text{ID}})$ exists in List L_k. If it does exist, $\mathcal{C}$ returns sk_{ID}. If it does not exist, $\mathcal{C}$ returns $\perp$.
- Certificate oracle $\mathcal{O}_c$: On receiving an identity ID and a public key pk_{ID} from $\mathcal{A}$, $\mathcal{C}$ responds with $\mathcal{A}$ with the corresponding certificate d_{ID}. Note that pk_{ID} should exist in List L_k.
- Key-replace oracle $\mathcal{O}_r$: On receiving an identity ID and a key pair $(sk'_{\text{ID}}, pk'_{\text{ID}})$ from $\mathcal{A}$, $\mathcal{C}$ checks whether $(\text{ID}, sk_{\text{ID}}, pk_{\text{ID}})$ exists in List L_k and whether $(sk'_{\text{ID}}, pk'_{\text{ID}})$ is a valid key pair. If both are yes, $\mathcal{C}$ updates $(\text{ID}, sk_{\text{ID}}, pk_{\text{ID}})$ with $(\text{ID}, sk'_{\text{ID}}, pk'_{\text{ID}})$ in List L_k; otherwise, $\mathcal{C}$ responds with $\perp$.
- Signing oracle $\mathcal{O}_s$: On receiving a message m, an identity ID and its corresponding public key pk_{ID}, $\mathcal{C}$ checks whether $(\text{ID}, sk_{\text{ID}}, pk_{\text{ID}})$ exists in List L_k. If it exists, $\mathcal{C}$ returns the corresponding signature by running algorithm Sign.

Output Finally, $\mathcal{A}$ decides to finish Find phase, and outputs a forgery σ^* on message m^* under identity ID^* and public key pk^*. We say $\mathcal{A}$ wins if the following requirements are satisfied.

- σ^* is a valid signature.
- $(\text{ID}^*, pk^*, \star)$ exists in List L_k.
- ID^* has never been queried to the certification oracle.
- (m^*, ID^*, pk^*) has never been queried to the signing oracle.

Definition 1. *We say a CBS scheme is existentially unforgeable against in Game 1 of CBS if there is no probabilistic polynomial-time adversary A that can win Game 1 of CBS with a non-negligible probability.*

Game 2.

Setup. In this phase, $\mathcal{C}$ runs algorithm $\text{Setup}(1^\lambda)$ to generate (msk, mpk), and sends mpk to $\mathcal{A}$. $\mathcal{A}$ can also ask $\mathcal{C}$ to sends msk to it.

Find. In this phase, $\mathcal{A}$ can issue a number of different queries to $\mathcal{A}$ adaptively. Each query can be one of the followings.

- Key generation oracle $\mathcal{O}_{pk}$: Identical to that in Game 1.
- Secret key oracle $\mathcal{O}_{sk}$: Identical to that in Game 1.
- Certificate oracle $\mathcal{O}_c$: Identical to that in Game 1.
- Signing oracle $\mathcal{O}_s$: Identical to that in Game 1.

Output. Finally, $\mathcal{A}$ decides to finish Find phase, and outputs a forgery σ^* on message m^* under identity ID^* and public key pk^*. We say $\mathcal{A}$ wins if the following requirements are satisfied.

- σ^* is a valid signature.
- pk^* exists in List L_k.
- pk^* has never been queried to the secret key oracle.
- (m^*, ID^*, pk^*) has never been queried to the signing oracle.

Definition 2. *We say a CBS scheme is existentially unforgeable against in Game 2 if there is no probabilistic polynomial-time adversary A that can win Game 2 with a non-negligible probability.*

2.2   Definitions of Certificate-Based Aggregate Signature (CBAS)

The Concept of CBAS. In a certificate-based aggregate signature scheme, there exist the following six algorithms.

- $\mathtt{Setup}(1^\lambda) \rightarrow (msk, mpk)$: Identical to that in CBS.
- $\mathtt{UKeyGen}(1^\lambda) \rightarrow (sk, pk)$: Identical to that in CBS.
- $\mathtt{Certify}(msk, pk_{\mathtt{ID}}, \mathtt{ID}) \rightarrow d_{\mathtt{ID}}$: Identical to that in CBS.
- $\mathtt{Sign}(m, d_{\mathtt{ID}}, sk_{\mathtt{ID}}) \rightarrow \sigma_{\mathtt{ID},pk}$: Identical to that in CBS.
- $\mathtt{Aggr}\left(\{m_{0i}, \mathtt{ID}_{0i}, pk_{0i}\}_{i=1}^{n_i}, \sigma_0\right), (\{m_{1j}, \mathtt{ID}_{1j}, pk_{1j}\}_{j=1}^{n_j}, \sigma_1)\right) \rightarrow \sigma$: This algorithm takes two (message set, identity/public key set, signature) pairs as input, the aggregator can aggregate these two signatures into an aggregated signature σ corresponding to $\left\{\{m_{0i}, \mathtt{ID}_{0i}, pk_{0i}\}_{i=1}^{n_i}, \{m_{1j}, \mathtt{ID}_{1j}, pk_{1j}\}_{j=1}^{n_j}\right\}$ if both of these signatures are valid by running $\mathtt{Verify}$. Otherwise, the aggregator outputs $\perp$. Note that n_i and n_j are integers greater than 0, and anyone can be the aggregator.
- $\mathtt{Verify}(\{m_i, pk_i, \mathtt{ID}_i\}_{i=1}^{n}, \sigma) \rightarrow 1$ or 0: Given a signature σ corresponding to $\{m_i, pk_i, \mathtt{ID}_i\}_{i=1}^{n}$, the algorithm outputs 1 if it is valid, or 0 otherwise. Note that n is an integer greater than 0.

Correctness. Besides the correctness of CBS, CBAS needs the following requirement.

For $(msk, mpk) \leftarrow \mathtt{Setup}(1^\lambda)$, $(sk_i, pk_i) \leftarrow \mathtt{Setup}(1^\lambda)$, $d_{\mathtt{ID}_i} \leftarrow \mathtt{Certify}(msk, pk_i, \mathtt{ID}_i)$, and $\sigma \leftarrow \mathtt{Aggr}\left((\{m_{0i}, \mathtt{ID}_{0i}, pk_{0i}\}_{i=1}^{n_i}, \sigma_0), (\{m_{1j}, \mathtt{ID}_{1j}, pk_{1j}\}_{j=1}^{n_j}, \sigma_1)\right)$, we have that

$$\mathtt{Verify}\left(\left\{\{m_{0i}, \mathtt{ID}_{0i}, pk_{0i}\}_{i=1}^{n_i}, \{m_{1j}, \mathtt{ID}_{1j}, pk_{1j}\}_{j=1}^{n_j}\right\}, \sigma\right) = 1.$$

Remark 1. Our proposal only supports aggregateability on signatures on the same message. But the whole signature in our proposal can be aggregated, and the verification in our proposal is quite efficient. See the details in Sect. 4.2.

Existential Unforgeability of CBAS. Like CBS, the security of CBAS is also defined by two different games.

Game 1.

Setup Identical to that in the CBS case.

Find Identical to that in the CBS case.

Output Finally, $\mathcal{A}$ decides to finish Find phase, and outputs a forgery σ^* on message set $\{m_i^*\}_{i=1}^{n}$ under a set of pairs $\{\mathtt{ID}_i^*, pk_i^*\}_{i=1}^{n}$. We say $\mathcal{A}$ wins if the following requirements are satisfied.

- σ^* is a valid signature.
- All pk_i^* exist in List L_k.
- Not all $\mathtt{ID}_i^*$ have been queried to the certification oracle.
- σ^* cannot be aggregated or directly from the responses of the queries that have been queried to the signing oracle.

Definition 3. *We say a CBAS scheme is existentially unforgeable against in Game 1 of CBAS if there is no probabilistic polynomial-time adversary A that can win Game 1 of CBAS with a non-negligible probability.*

Game 2.

Setup Identical to that in Game 1 of CBAS.

Find In this phase, $\mathcal{A}$ can issue a number of different queries to $\mathcal{A}$ adaptively. Each query can be one of the followings.

– Key generation oracle $\mathcal{O}_{pk}$: Identical to that in Game 2.
– Secret key oracle $\mathcal{O}_{sk}$: Identical to that in Game 2.
– Certificate oracle $\mathcal{O}_c$: Identical to that in Game 2.
– Signing oracle $\mathcal{O}_s$: Identical to that in Game 2.

Output Finally, $\mathcal{A}$ decides to finish Find phase, and outputs a forgery σ^* on message set $\{m_i^*\}_{i=1}^n$ under a set of pairs $\{\text{ID}_i^*, pk_i^*\}_{i=1}^n$. We say $\mathcal{A}$ wins if the following requirements are satisfied.

– σ^* is a valid signature.
– Not all pk_i^* have been queried to the secret key oracle. Among the public key pk_i^* not queried to the secret key oracle, there exists at least one public key in List L_k.
– σ^* cannot be aggregated or directly from the responses of the queries that have been queried to the signing oracle.

Definition 4. *We say a CBAS scheme is existentially unforgeable against in Game 2 of CBAS if there is no probabilistic polynomial-time adversary A that can win Game 2 of CBAS with a non-negligible probability.*

2.3   Complexity Assumption

Bilinear Maps. Let $\mathbb{G}$ and $\mathbb{G}_T$ be two (multiplicative) cyclic groups of prime order q, and g be a generator of $\mathbb{G}$. We call a bilinear map $e : \mathbb{G} \times \mathbb{G} \to \mathbb{G}_T$ as an admissible bilinear map, if it satisfies the following properties.

– Bilinearity: $e(g^a, g^b) = e(g, g)^{ab}$ for any $a, b \in \mathbb{Z}_q^*$.
– Non-degeneracy: $e(g, g)$ is a generator of group $\mathbb{G}_T$.
– Computability: e can be computed efficiently.

For simplicity, we denote $\mathtt{BSetup}$ as an algorithm that takes as input the security parameter 1^λ and outputs the parameters for an admissible bilinear map as $(q, g, \mathbb{G}, \mathbb{G}_T, e)$.

Computational Diffie-Hellman Assumption. Let $e : \mathbb{G} \times \mathbb{G} \to \mathbb{G}_T$ be a bilinear map, both $\mathbb{G}$ and $\mathbb{G}_T$ are cyclic groups of prime order q. Choose a random generator g of $\mathbb{G}$ and random a, b from $\mathbb{Z}_q^*$. The computational Diffie-Hellman (CDH) problem is to compute g^{ab}, given (g, g^a, g^b). The CDH assumption is that for any efficient $\mathcal{A}$, the probability $\Pr[\mathcal{A}(g, g^a, g^b) \to g^{ab}]$ is negligible.

3   The Proposed Certificate-Based Signature

3.1   The Description of Our CBS Scheme

In this section, we will give the description of our CBS scheme that is based on the identity-based aggregate signature in [11]. The details are as follows.

- **Setup:** Given the security parameter 1^λ, the certifier firstly runs $\texttt{BSetup}(1^\lambda)$ to obtain $(q, g, \mathbb{G}, \mathbb{G}_T, e)$, and then selects a random x from $\mathbb{Z}_q^*$ as the master secret key msk, and sets $y = g^x$. The certifier also chooses cryptographically secure hash functions: $H_i : \{0,1\}^* \to \mathbb{G}$, $(i = 1, 2, 3, 4)$, and $H_j : \{0,1\}^* \to \mathbb{Z}_q^*$, $j = 5, 6$. At last, the certifier publishes the master public key $(q, g, y, \mathbb{G}, \mathbb{G}_T, e, H_i(\cdot), i = 1, 2, 3, 4, 5, 6)$, while keeping msk secret.
- **UKeyGen:** The users choose a random sk from $\mathbb{Z}_q^*$ and computes $pk = g^{sk}$.
- **Certify:** Given an identity ID and a public key pk, the certifier uses the master secret key msk to compute the corresponding certificate $d_{\mathtt{ID}} = (d_{1,\mathtt{ID}}, d_{2,\mathtt{ID}})$ by the following equation

$$d_{1,\mathtt{ID}} = H_1(\mathtt{ID}\|pk)^{msk}, \qquad d_{2,\mathtt{ID}} = H_2(\mathtt{ID}\|pk)^{msk}$$

- **Sign:** Given a message m, the secret key sk and the corresponding certificate $d_{\mathtt{ID}} = (d_{1,\mathtt{ID}}, d_{2,\mathtt{ID}})$, the signer ID computes the signature $\sigma = (S, T)$ by the following equation

$$S = H_3(m)^r H_4(m)^{sk} \cdot d_{1,\mathtt{ID}} \cdot d_{2,\mathtt{ID}}^{H_5(\mathtt{ID}\|pk\|m)}, \quad T = g^r,$$

where $r = H_6(\mathtt{ID}\|pk\|m\|d_{1,\mathtt{ID}}\|d_{2,\mathtt{ID}}\|sk)$. It is easy to see that for the same message under the same signer, the signature is always the same. In other words, the signing algorithm is deterministic.
- **Verify:** Given a signature $\sigma = (S, T)$ under identity ID and public key pk, the algorithm outputs 1 if the following equality holds, or 0 otherwise.

$$e(S, g) = e(H_3(m), T) \cdot e(H_4(m), pk) \cdot e\left(H_1(\mathtt{ID}\|pk) \cdot H_2(\mathtt{ID}\|pk)^{H_5(\mathtt{ID}\|pk\|m)}, y\right).$$

Correctness. We can have the correctness of our proposed CBS scheme by the following equations.

$$
\begin{aligned}
e(S, g) &= e\left(H_3(m)^r H_4(m)^{sk} \cdot d_{1,\mathtt{ID}} \cdot d_{2,\mathtt{ID}}^{H_5(\mathtt{ID}\|pk\|m)}, g\right) \\
&= e\left(H_3(m)^r, g\right) \cdot e(H_4(m)^{sk}, g) \cdot e\left(d_{1,\mathtt{ID}} \cdot d_{2,\mathtt{ID}}^{H_5(\mathtt{ID}\|pk\|m)}, g\right) \\
&= e\left(H_3(m), T\right) \cdot e(H_4(m), pk) \cdot e\left(H_1(\mathtt{ID}\|pk) \cdot H_2(\mathtt{ID}\|pk)^{H_5(\mathtt{ID}\|pk\|m)}, y\right)
\end{aligned}
$$

3.2   Security Analysis of Proposed CBS Scheme

Theorem 1. *The proposed CBS scheme is existentially unforgeable in Game 1 of CBS if the CDH assumption holds in $\mathbb{G}$.*

Proof. Assume we have an adversary $\mathcal{A}$ that can break our proposal in Game 1 of CBS, then we can build an algorithm $\mathcal{B}$ that can solve the CDH problem (given (g, g^a, g^b), to compute g^{ab}) by interacting with $\mathcal{A}$ as follows.

Setup $\mathcal{B}$ sets $y = g^a$, and chooses cryptographically secure hash functions H_i, $(i = 1, 2, 3, 4, 5, 6)$ that will be treated as random oracles later. $\mathcal{B}$ also initializes lists L_k, $L_{H_{1,2}}$, L_{H_3}, L_{H_4}, L_{H_5} and L_{H_6}.

Find $\mathcal{B}$ builds the following oracles for $\mathcal{A}$.

- $\mathcal{O}_{H_1}$ and $\mathcal{O}_{H_2}$: Given an identity $\mathtt{ID}_i$ and a public key pk_i, $\mathcal{B}$ first checks whether $(\mathtt{ID}_i, pk_i, \mathtt{coin}_{\mathtt{ID},i}, \alpha_{1,i}, \alpha'_{1,i}, \alpha_{2,i}, \alpha'_{2,i}, R_{1,i}, R_{2,i})$ exists in List $L_{H_{1,2}}$. If it does exist, $\mathcal{B}$ returns $R_{1,i}$ and $R_{2,i}$ to $\mathcal{A}$. Otherwise, $\mathcal{B}$ does the following steps.
  - $\mathcal{B}$ chooses random $\alpha_{1,i}$, $\alpha'_{1,i}$, $\alpha_{2,i}$ and $\alpha'_{2,i}$ from $\mathbb{Z}_q^*$.
  - $\mathcal{B}$ decides the value of $\mathtt{coin}_{\mathtt{ID},i} \in \{0, 1\}$ that satisfies $\Pr[\mathtt{coin}_{\mathtt{ID},i} = 0] = \delta_{\mathtt{ID}}$.
  - If $\mathtt{coin}_{\mathtt{ID},i} = 1$, $\mathcal{B}$ responds with $R_{1,i} = (g^b)^{\alpha_{1,i}} \cdot g^{\alpha'_{1,i}}$ and $R_{2,i} = (g^b)^{\alpha_{2,i}} \cdot g^{\alpha'_{2,i}}$. Otherwise, $\mathcal{B}$ responds with $R_{1,i} = g^{\alpha_{1,i}}$ and $R_{2,i} = g^{\alpha_{2,i}}$.
  - $\mathcal{B}$ records $(\mathtt{ID}_i, pk_i, \mathtt{coin}_{\mathtt{ID},i}, \alpha_{1,i}, \alpha_{2,i}, \alpha'_{1,i}, \alpha'_{2,i}, R_{1,i}, R_{2,i})$ in List $L_{H_{1,2}}$.
- $\mathcal{O}_{H_3}$: Given a message m_i, $\mathcal{B}$ first checks whether $(m_i, \alpha_{3,i}, R_{3,i})$ exists in List L_{H_3}. If it does exist, $\mathcal{B}$ returns $R_{3,i}$ to $\mathcal{A}$. Otherwise, $\mathcal{B}$ chooses a random $\alpha_{3,i}$ from $\mathbb{Z}_q^*$ and returns $R_{3,i} = g^{\alpha_{3,i}}$ to $\mathcal{A}$. At last, $\mathcal{B}$ records $(m_i, \alpha_{3,i}, R_{3,i})$ in List L_{H_3}.
- $\mathcal{O}_{H_4}$: Given a string m_i, $\mathcal{B}$ first checks whether $(m_i, R_{4,i})$ exists in List L_{H_4}. If it does exist, $\mathcal{B}$ returns $R_{4,i}$ to $\mathcal{A}$. Otherwise, $\mathcal{B}$ chooses a random $R_{4,i}$ from $\mathbb{G}$ and returns it to $\mathcal{A}$. At last, $\mathcal{B}$ records $(m, R_{4,i})$ in List L_{H_4}.
- $\mathcal{O}_{H_5}$: Given an identity $\mathtt{ID}_i$, a public key pk_i, and a message m_i, $\mathcal{B}$ first checks whether $(\mathtt{ID}_i, pk_i, m_i, \mathtt{coin}_{m,i}, \alpha_{5,i})$ exists in List L_{H_5}. If it does exist, $\mathcal{B}$ returns $\alpha_{5,i}$ to $\mathcal{A}$. Otherwise, $\mathcal{B}$ does the following steps.
  - $\mathcal{B}$ queries $\mathcal{O}_{H_1}$ or $\mathcal{O}_{H_2}$ with $(\mathtt{ID}_i, pk_i)$, and obtains $\mathtt{coin}_{\mathtt{ID},i}$, $\alpha_{1,i}$ and $\alpha_{2,i}$.
  - $\mathcal{B}$ decides the value of $\mathtt{coin}_{m,i} \in \{0, 1\}$ that satisfies $\Pr[\mathtt{coin}_{m,i} = 0] = \delta_m$.
  - If $\mathtt{coin}_{m,i} = 0$ and $\mathtt{coin}_{\mathtt{ID},i} = 1$, then $\mathcal{B}$ sets $\alpha_{5,i} = -\alpha_{1,i}/\alpha_{2,i}$. Otherwise, $\mathcal{B}$ chooses a random $\alpha_{5,i}$ from $\mathbb{Z}_q^*$.
  - $\mathcal{B}$ returns $\alpha_{5,i}$ to $\mathcal{A}$.
  - $\mathcal{B}$ records $(\mathtt{ID}_i, pk_i, m_i, \mathtt{coin}_{m,i}, \alpha_{5,i})$ in List L_{H_5}.
- $\mathcal{O}_{H_6}$: Given the string $\mathtt{ID}_i \| pk_i \| m_i \| d_{1,\mathtt{ID}_i} \| d_{2,\mathtt{ID}_i} \| sk_i$, $\mathcal{B}$ firstly checks whether $(\mathtt{ID}_i \| pk_i \| m_i \| d_{1,\mathtt{ID}_i} \| d_{2,\mathtt{ID}_i} \| sk_i, \alpha_{6,i})$ exists in List L_{H_6}. If it does exist, $\mathcal{B}$ returns $\alpha_{6,i}$ to $\mathcal{A}$. Otherwise, $\mathcal{B}$ checks whether $pk_i = g^{sk_i}$, $e(d_{1,\mathtt{ID}_i}, g) = e(H_1(\mathtt{ID}_i \| pk_i), y)$, $e(d_{2,\mathtt{ID}_i}, g) = e(H_2(\mathtt{ID}_i \| pk_i), y)$ and $\mathtt{coin}_{\mathtt{ID},i} = 1$ hold. If not all hold, $\mathcal{B}$ chooses a random $\alpha_{6,i}$ from $\mathbb{Z}_q^*$, and

returns it to $\mathcal{A}$. Furthermore, $\mathcal{B}$ records $(\text{ID}_i\|pk_i\|m_i\|d_{1,\text{ID}_i}\|d_{2,\text{ID}_i}\|sk_i, \alpha_{6,i})$ in List L_{H_6}. If all hold, then $\mathcal{B}$ can get g^{ab} from d_{1,ID_i} by using $\alpha_{1,i}$ corresponding to (ID_i, pk_i).

- $\mathcal{O}_{pk}$: Given an identity ID_i, $\mathcal{B}$ checks whether $(\text{ID}_i, pk_i, \star)$ exists in List L_k. If it exists, $\mathcal{B}$ returns pk_i. Otherwise, $\mathcal{B}$ chooses a random sk_i from $\mathbb{Z}_q^*$, and sets $pk_i = g^{sk_i}$. At last, $\mathcal{B}$ records $(\text{ID}_i, pk_i, sk_i)$ into List L_k and returns pk_i to $\mathcal{A}$.

- $\mathcal{O}_{sk}$: Given an identity ID_i, $\mathcal{B}$ checks whether $(\text{ID}_i, pk_i, sk_i)$ exists in List L_k. If it does not exist, $\mathcal{B}$ returns $\perp$. Otherwise, $\mathcal{B}$ returns sk_i to $\mathcal{A}$.

- $\mathcal{O}_c$: Given an identity ID_i and a public key pk_i, $\mathcal{B}$ checks whether $(\text{ID}_i, pk_i, \star)$ exists in List L_k. If it does not exist, $\mathcal{B}$ returns $\perp$. Otherwise, $\mathcal{B}$ does the following steps.
  - $\mathcal{B}$ queries $\mathcal{O}_{H_1}$ and $\mathcal{O}_{H_2}$ with (ID_i, pk_i) to obtain $\text{coin}_{\text{ID},i}$, $\alpha_{1,i}$ and $\alpha_{2,i}$.
  - If $\text{coin}_{\text{ID}_i} = 0$, $\mathcal{B}$ returns $((g^a)^{\alpha_{1,i}}, (g^a)^{\alpha_{2,i}})$ to $\mathcal{A}$.
  - If $\text{coin}_{\text{ID}_i} = 1$, $\mathcal{B}$ reports fail and aborts.

- $\mathcal{O}_r$: Given $(\text{ID}_i, pk_i', sk_i')$, $\mathcal{B}$ updates $(\text{ID}_i, pk_i, sk_i)$ with $(\text{ID}_i, pk_i', sk_i')$ in List L_k if (pk_i', sk_i') is a valid key pair.

- $\mathcal{O}_s$: Given an identity ID_i, public key pk_i and a message m_i, $\mathcal{B}$ queries $\mathcal{O}_{H_1}$, $\mathcal{O}_{H_5}$ as well as $\mathcal{O}_{sk}$ with (ID_i, pk_i), (ID_i, pk_i, m_i) and (ID_i, pk_i), respectively. After that, $\mathcal{B}$ can obtain $\text{coin}_{\text{ID},i}$, $\text{coin}_{m,i}$, $\alpha_{1,i}$, $\alpha_{1,i}'$, $\alpha_{2,i}$, $\alpha_{2,i}'$, $\alpha_{5,i}$ and sk_i. $\mathcal{B}$ also chooses a random r from $\mathbb{Z}_q^*$.
  - If $\text{coin}_{\text{ID},i} = 0$, $\mathcal{B}$ returns the signature as follows.

$$S = H_3(m_i)^r \cdot H_4(m_i)^r \cdot (g^a)^{\alpha_{1,i}} \cdot (g^a)^{\alpha_{2,i}\cdot H_5(\text{ID}_i\|pk_i\|m_i)}, \quad T = g^r.$$

Note that r is the hash value from $\mathcal{O}_{H_6}$, and we have $H_1(\text{ID}_i\|pk_i) = g^{\alpha_{1,i}}$, $H_2(\text{ID}_i\|pk_i) = g^{\alpha_{2,i}}$ and $pk_i = g^{sk_i}$; hence, the signature $\sigma = (S,T)$ is valid.

  - If $\text{coin}_{\text{ID},i} = 1$ and $\text{coin}_{m,i} = 0$, $\mathcal{B}$ returns the signature as follows.

$$S = H_3(m_i)^r \cdot H_4(m_i)^{sk_i}(g^a)^{\alpha_{1,i}'} \cdot (g^a)^{-\alpha_{2,i}'\cdot\alpha_{m,i}}, \quad T = g^r.$$

Note that we have that

$$\sigma = H_3(m_i)^r \cdot H_4(m_i)^{sk} \cdot (g^a)^{\alpha_{1,i}'} \cdot (g^a)^{-\alpha_{2,i}'\cdot\alpha_{m,i}}$$
$$= H_3(m_i)^r \cdot H_4(m_i)^{sk} \cdot g^{a\cdot b\cdot\alpha_{1,i}}(g^a)^{\alpha_{1,i}'} \cdot g^{-a\cdot b\cdot\alpha_{1,i}}(g^a)^{-\alpha_{2,i}'\cdot\alpha_{1,i}/\alpha_{2,i}}$$
$$= H_3(m_i)^r \cdot H_4(m_i)^{sk} \cdot ((g^b)^{\alpha_{1,i}} \cdot g^{\alpha_{1,i}'})^a \cdot ((g^b)^{\alpha_{2,i}} \cdot g^{\alpha_{2,i}'})^{-a\cdot\alpha_{1,i}/\alpha_{2,i}}$$
$$= H_3(m_i)^r \cdot H_4(m_i)^{sk} \cdot H_1(\text{ID}_i\|pk_i)^{msk} \cdot H_2(\text{ID}_i\|pk_i)^{-msk\cdot H_5(\text{ID}_i\|pk_i\|m_i)}$$
$$= H_3(m_i)^r \cdot H_4(m_i)^{sk} \cdot d_{1,\text{ID}} \cdot d_{2,\text{ID}}^{H_5(\text{ID}_i\|pk_i\|m_i)}$$

Hence, $\sigma = (S,T)$ is a valid signature.
  - If $\text{coin}_{\text{ID},i} = \text{coin}_{m,i} = 1$, $\mathcal{B}$ reports fail and aborts.

Output At last, $\mathcal{A}$ outputs a forgery $\sigma^* = (w^*, S^*, T^*)$ on message m^* under identity ID^* and public key pk^*. If $\text{coin}_{\text{ID}^*} = \text{coin}_{m^*} = 0$, $\mathcal{B}$ reports fail and aborts. Otherwise, we have that

$$S^* = (g^{\alpha_{3,i}^*})^{r^*} \cdot R_{4,i}^{sk^*}(g^{ab})^{\alpha_{1,i}^* + \alpha_{2,i}^*\cdot\alpha_{5,i}^*} \cdot (g^a)^{\alpha_{1,i}'^* + \alpha_{2,i}'^*\cdot\alpha_{5,i}^*}, \quad T = g^{r^*}.$$

It is easy to see that $\mathcal{B}$ can obtain g^{ab} from σ^*. Note that $\alpha_{1,i}^*$, $\alpha_{2,i}^*$, $\alpha_{1,i}'^*$, $\alpha_{2,i}'^*$, $\alpha_{3,i}^*$, $R_{4,i}^*$, $\alpha_{5,i}^*$ and sk^* are the values corresponding to (ID^*, pk^*), m^*, m^*, (ID^*, pk^*, m^*), and (ID^*, pk^*) in lists $L_{H_{1,2}}$, L_{H_3}, L_{H_4}, L_{H_5} and L_k, respectively.

By using the similar method in [11], we have that $\mathcal{B}$ can succeed in the above game with a non-negligible probability.   □

Theorem 2. *The proposed CBS scheme is existentially unforgeable in Game 2 of CBS if the CDH assumption holds in* $\mathbb{G}$.

Proof. Assume we have an adversary $\mathcal{A}$ that can break our proposal in Game 2 of CBS, then we can build an algorithm $\mathcal{B}$ that can solve the CDH problem (given (g, g^a, g^b), to compute g^{ab}) by interacting with $\mathcal{A}$ as follows.

Setup $\mathcal{B}$ chooses random u from Z_q^*, sets $y = g^u$, and chooses cryptographically secure hash functions H_i, $(i = 1, 2, 3, 4, 5, 6)$ that will be treated as random oracles later. $\mathcal{B}$ also initializes lists L_k, $L_{H_{1,2}}$, L_{H_3}, L_{H_4}, L_{H_5} and L_{H_6}.

Find $\mathcal{B}$ builds the following oracles for $\mathcal{A}$.

- $\mathcal{O}_{H_1}$: Given an identity ID_i and a public key pk_i, $\mathcal{B}$ first checks whether $(\text{ID}_i, pk_i, R_{1,i})$ exists in List L_{H_1}.
  - If it does exist, $\mathcal{B}$ returns $R_{1,i}$.
  - If it does not exist, $\mathcal{B}$ chooses a random $R_{1,i}$ from $\mathbb{G}$, and responds with $R_{1,i}$. At last, $\mathcal{B}$ records $(\text{ID}_i, pk_i, R_{1,i})$ into List L_{H_1}.
- $\mathcal{O}_{H_2}$: Given an identity ID_i and a public key pk_i, $\mathcal{B}$ first checks whether $(\text{ID}_i, pk_i, R_{2,i})$ exists in List L_{H_2}.
  - If it does exist, $\mathcal{B}$ returns $R_{2,i}$.
  - If it does not exist, $\mathcal{B}$ chooses a random $R_{2,i}$ from $\mathbb{G}$, and responds with $R_{2,i}$. At last, $\mathcal{B}$ records $(\text{ID}_i, pk_i, R_{2,i})$ into List L_{H_2}.
- $\mathcal{O}_{H_3}$: Given a string m_i, $\mathcal{B}$ first checks whether $(m_i, \alpha_{3,i}, R_{3,i})$ exists in List L_{H_3}. If it does exist, $\mathcal{B}$ returns $R_{3,i}$ to $\mathcal{A}$. Otherwise, $\mathcal{B}$ chooses a random $\alpha_{3,i}$ from Z_q^* and returns $R_{3,i} = g^{\alpha_{3,i}}$ to $\mathcal{A}$. At last, $\mathcal{B}$ records $(m_i, \alpha_{3,i}, R_{3,i})$ in List L_{H_3}.
- $\mathcal{O}_{H_4}$: Given a message m_i, $\mathcal{B}$ first checks whether $(m_i, \text{coin}_{m,i}, \alpha_{4,i}, R_{4,i})$ exists in List L_{H_4}. If it does exist, $\mathcal{B}$ returns $R_{4,i}$ to $\mathcal{A}$. Otherwise, $\mathcal{B}$ chooses a random $\alpha_{4,i}$ from Z_q^* and decides the value of $R_{4,i} = \text{coin}_{m,i} \in \{0,1\}$ with $\Pr[\text{coin}_{m,i} = 0] = \delta_m$. $\mathcal{B}$ returns $R_{4,i} = g^{\alpha_{4,i}}$ if $\text{coin}_{m,i} = 0$, or $R_{4,i} = (g^b)^{\alpha_{4,i}}$ otherwise. At last, $\mathcal{B}$ records $(m_i, \text{coin}_{m,i}, \alpha_{4,i}, R_{4,i})$ in List L_{H_4}.
- $\mathcal{O}_{H_5}$: Given an identity ID_i, a public key pk_i, a message m_i, $\mathcal{B}$ first checks whether $(m_i, \alpha_{5,i})$ exists in List L_{H_5}. If it does exist, $\mathcal{B}$ returns $\alpha_{5,i}$ to $\mathcal{A}$. Otherwise, $\mathcal{B}$ chooses a random $\alpha_{5,i}$ from Z_q^* and returns it $\mathcal{A}$. At last, $\mathcal{B}$ records $(m_i, \alpha_{5,i})$ in List L_{H_5}.
- $\mathcal{O}_{H_6}$: Given the string $\text{ID}_i \| pk_i \| m_i \| d_{1,\text{ID}_i} \| d_{2,\text{ID}_i} \| sk_i$, $\mathcal{B}$ firstly checks whether $(\text{ID}_i \| pk_i \| m_i \| d_{1,\text{ID}_i} \| d_{2,\text{ID}_i} \| sk_i, \alpha_{6,i})$ exists in List L_{H_6}. If it does exist, $\mathcal{B}$ returns $\alpha_{6,i}$ to $\mathcal{A}$. Otherwise, $\mathcal{B}$ checks whether $pk_i = g^{sk_i}$, $e(d_{1,\text{ID}_i}, g) = e(H_1(\text{ID}_i \| pk_i), y)$, $e(d_{2,\text{ID}_i}, g) = e(H_2(\text{ID}_i \| pk_i), y)$ and

$\text{coin}_{\text{ID},i} = 1$ hold. If not all hold, $\mathcal{B}$ chooses a random $\alpha_{6,i}$ from $\mathbb{Z}_q^*$, and returns it to $\mathcal{A}$. Furthermore, $\mathcal{B}$ records $(\text{ID}_i\|pk_i\|m_i\|d_{1,\text{ID}_i}\|d_{2,\text{ID}_i}\|sk_i, \alpha_{6,i})$ in List L_{H_6}. If all hold, then $\mathcal{B}$ can get a from sk_i by using w_i corresponding to pk_i.

- $\mathcal{O}_{pk}$: Given an identity ID_i, $\mathcal{B}$ checks whether $(\text{ID}_i, pk_i, \star)$ exists in List L_k. If it exists, $\mathcal{B}$ returns pk_i. Otherwise, $\mathcal{B}$ does the following steps.
  - $\mathcal{B}$ decides the value of $\text{coin}_{pk,i} \in \{0, 1\}$ that satisfies $\Pr[\text{coin}_{pk,i} = 0] = \delta_{pk}$.
  - $\mathcal{B}$ chooses a random w_i from $\mathbb{Z}_q^*$.
  - If $\text{coin}_{pk,i} = 0$, $\mathcal{B}$ sets $pk_i = g^{w_i}$; otherwise, $\mathcal{B}$ sets $pk_i = (g^a)^{w_i}$.
  - At last, $\mathcal{B}$ records $(\text{ID}_i, pk_i, \text{coin}_{pk,i}, w_i)$ into List L_k, respectively.

- $\mathcal{O}_{sk}$: Given an identity ID_i, $\mathcal{B}$ checks whether $(\text{ID}_i, pk_i, \text{coin}_{pk,i}, w_i)$ exists in List L_k. If it does not exist, $\mathcal{B}$ returns $\perp$. Otherwise, $\mathcal{B}$ does the following steps. If $\text{coin}_{pk,i} = 0$, $\mathcal{B}$ returns w_i. If $\text{coin}_{pk,i} = 1$, $\mathcal{B}$ reports fail and aborts.

- $\mathcal{O}_c$: Given an identity ID_i and a public key pk_i, $\mathcal{B}$ returns $H_1(\text{ID}_i\|pk_i)^u$.

- $\mathcal{O}_s$: Given an identity ID_i, public key pk_i and a message m_i, $\mathcal{B}$ queries $\mathcal{O}_{H_4}$ as well as $\mathcal{O}_{sk}$ with m_i and (ID_i, pk_i), respectively. After that, $\mathcal{B}$ can obtain $\text{coin}_{m,i}$, $\alpha_{4,i}$, $\text{coin}_{pk,i}$ and w_i.
  - If $\text{coin}_{pk,i} = 0$, $\mathcal{B}$ returns the signature as follows.

$$S = H_3(m)^r \cdot H_4(m)^{w_i} \cdot H_1(\text{ID}_i\|pk_i)^u \cdot H_2(\text{ID}_i\|pk_i)^{uH_5(\text{ID}_i\|pk_i\|m_i)}, \quad T = g^r.$$

  Note that r is the hash value from $\mathcal{O}_{H_6}$, $y = g^u$ and $pk_i = g^{w_i}$; hence, the signature $\sigma = (S, T)$ is valid.
  - If $\text{coin}_{pk,i} = 1$ and $\text{coin}_{m,i} = 0$, $\mathcal{B}$ returns the signature as follows.

$$S = H_3(m)^r \cdot (g^a)^{\alpha_{4,i} \cdot w_i} \cdot H_1(\text{ID}_i\|pk_i)^u \cdot H_2(\text{ID}_i\|pk_i)^{uH_5(\text{ID}_i\|pk_i\|m_i)}, \quad T = g^r.$$

  Note that we have that

$$\begin{aligned}\sigma &= H_3(m)^r \cdot (g^a)^{\alpha_{4,i} \cdot w_i} \cdot H_1(\text{ID}_i\|pk_i)^u \cdot H_2(\text{ID}_i\|pk_i)^{uH_5(\text{ID}_i\|pk_i\|m_i)}\\ &= H_3(m)^r \cdot H_4(m)^{sk_i} \cdot H_1(\text{ID}_i\|pk_i)^u \cdot H_2(\text{ID}_i\|pk_i)^{uH_5(\text{ID}_i\|pk_i\|m_i)}\end{aligned}$$

  Note that, r is the hash value from $\mathcal{O}_{H_6}$, $y = g^u$ and $pk_i = g^{aw_i}$ Hence, $\sigma = (S, T)$ is a valid signature.
  - If $\text{coin}_{pk,i} = \text{coin}_{m,i} = 1$, $\mathcal{B}$ reports fail and aborts.

Output At last, $\mathcal{A}$ outputs a forgery $\sigma^* = (S^*, T^*)$ on message m^* under identity ID^* and public key pk^*. If $\text{coin}_{pk^*} = \text{coin}_{m^*} = 0$, $\mathcal{B}$ reports fail and aborts. Otherwise, we have that

$$S^* = (g^{\alpha_{3,i}^*})^{r^*} \cdot (g^{ab})^{\alpha_{4,i}^* \cdot w^*} \cdot H_1(\text{ID}_i\|pk_i)^u \cdot H_2(\text{ID}_i\|pk_i)^{uH_5(\text{ID}_i\|pk_i\|m_i)}$$

and

$$T^* = g^{r^*}.$$

It is easy to see that $\mathcal{B}$ can obtain g^{ab} from σ^*. Note that $\alpha_{3,i}^*, \alpha_{4,i}^*$ and w^* are the values corresponding to m^*, m^* and (ID^*, pk^*) in lists L_{H_3}, L_{H_4} and L_k, respectively.

By using the similar method in [2], we have that $\mathcal{B}$ can succeed in the above game with a non-negligible probability.   □

4   The Proposed CBAS Scheme

4.1   The Description of Proposed CBAS Scheme

In this section, we will give our CBAS scheme that is directly from our CBS scheme. Compared to our CBS scheme, our CBAS additionally has algorithm `Aggr`, and algorithm `Verify` is changed accordingly.

- `Aggr`:   Given   two   signatures $(m, \{\text{ID}_{0i}, pk_{0i}\}_{i=1}^{n_i}, (S_0, T_0))$,   and $(m, \{\text{ID}_{1j}, pk_{1j}\}_{j=1}^{n_j}, (S_1, T_1))$, where

$$S_0 = \prod_{i=1}^{n_i} H_3(m)^{r_{0i}} \cdot H_4(m)^{sk_{0i}} H_1(\text{ID}_{0i}||pk_{0i})^{msk} \cdot (H_2(\text{ID}_{0i}||pk_{0i})^{msk})^{H_5(\text{ID}_{0i}||pk_{0i}||m)},$$

$$T_0 = \prod_{i=1}^{n_i} g^{r_{0i}}$$

and

$$S_1 = \prod_{j=1}^{n_j} H_3(m)^{r_{0j}} \cdot H_4(m)^{sk_{0j}} H_1(\text{ID}_{0j}||pk_{0j})^{msk} \cdot (H_2(\text{ID}_{0j}||pk_{0j})^{msk})^{H_5(\text{ID}_{0j}||pk_{0j}||m)},$$

$$T_1 = \prod_{j=1}^{n_j} g^{r_{0j}}$$

the aggregator first runs `Verify` to check the validity of the two signatures. If both of them are valid, the aggregator outputs the aggregated signature $\sigma = (S, T)$.

$$S = S_0 \cdot S_1, \quad T = T_0 \cdot T_1.$$

- `Verify`: Given a signature $(m, \{\text{ID}_i, pk_i\}_{i=1}^{n}, (S, T))$, the verify checks its validity by using the following equality.

$$e(S, g) = e(H_3(m), T) \cdot e\left(H_4(m), \prod_{i=1}^{n} pk_i\right) e\left(\prod_{i=1}^{n} H_1(\text{ID}_i||pk_i) \cdot H_2(\text{ID}_i||pk_i)^{H_5(\text{ID}_i||pk_i||m_i)}, y\right).$$

Correctness. The correctness can be easily obtained by the followings.

$$e(S, g)$$

$$= e\left(\prod_{i=1}^{n} H_3(m)^{r_i} \cdot H_4(m)^{sk_i} \cdot H_1(\text{ID}_i||pk_i)^{msk} \cdot (H_2(\text{ID}_i||pk_i)^{msk})^{H_5(\text{ID}_i||pk_i||m)}, g\right)$$

$$= e\left(\prod_{i=1}^{n} H_3(m)^{r_i}, g\right) \cdot e\left(\prod_{i=1}^{n} H_4(m)^{sk_i}, g\right) \cdot e\left(\prod_{i=1}^{n} H_1(\text{ID}_i||pk_i)^{msk} \cdot (H_2(\text{ID}_i||pk_i)^{msk})^{H_5(\text{ID}_i||pk_i||m)}, g\right)$$

$$= e\left(H_3(m), \prod_{i=1}^{n} g^{r_i}\right) \cdot e\left(H_4(m), \prod_{i=1}^{n} g^{sk_i}\right) \cdot e\left(\prod_{i=1}^{n} H_1(\text{ID}_i||pk_i) \cdot (H_2(\text{ID}_i||pk_i))^{H_5(\text{ID}_i||pk_i||m)}, g^{msk}\right)$$

$$= e(H_3(m), T) \cdot e\left(H_4(m), \prod_{i=1}^{n} pk_i\right) e\left(\prod_{i=1}^{n} H_1(\text{ID}_i||pk_i) \cdot H_2(\text{ID}_i||pk_i)^{H_5(\text{ID}_i||pk_i||m_i)}, y\right)$$

4.2   Security Analysis of Proposed CBAS Scheme

Theorem 3. *The proposed CBAS scheme is existentially unforgeable in Game 1 of CBAS if the CDH assumption holds in* $\mathbb{G}$.

Proof. It is almost the same as that in the proof of Theorem 1, except the followings.

Output. At last, $\mathcal{A}$ outputs a forgery $\sigma^* = (S^*, T^*)$ corresponding to $\{m^*, \text{ID}_i^*, pk_i^*\}_{i=1}^n$. If $\text{coin}_m^* = 0$ or $\text{coin}_{\text{ID},i}^* = 0$ $(i = 1, \cdots, n)$, $\mathcal{B}$ reports fail and aborts. Otherwise, $\mathcal{B}$ does the followings.

- Let $\mathcal{S}_u$ be the set of indices for $\{\text{ID}_j^*, pk_j^*, m^*\}$ where $\text{coin}_{\text{ID},j}^* = 0$ and $j \in \{1, \cdots, n\}$. Accordingly, let $\mathcal{S}_h = \{1, \cdots, n\}/\mathcal{S}_u$.

- $\mathcal{B}$ can obtain $\{H_4(m^*)^{sk_j^*} \cdot d_{1,\text{ID}_j^*} \cdot d_{2,\text{ID}_j^*}^{H_5(\text{ID}_j^* \| pk_j^* \| m^*)}\}_{j \in \mathcal{S}_u}$ by using the method in $\mathcal{O}_s$.

- $\mathcal{B}$ computes $\widehat{S^*} = S^* / \prod_{j \in \mathcal{S}_u} H_4(m^*)^{sk_j^*} \cdot d_{1,\text{ID}_j^*} \cdot d_{2,\text{ID}_j^*}^{H_5(\text{ID}_j^* \| pk_j^* \| m^*)}$.

- $\mathcal{B}$ can compute g^{ab} from σ^*. Note that

$$S^* = \prod_{j \in \mathcal{S}_h} (g^{\alpha_{3,j}})^{r^*} \cdot R_{4,i}^{sk_j^*} \cdot (g^{ab})^{\alpha_{1,j}^* + \alpha_{2,j}^* \cdot \alpha_{4,j}^*} \cdot (g^a)^{\alpha_{1,j}^{'*} + \alpha_{2,j}^{'*} \cdot \alpha_{4,j}^*}$$

and

$$T^* = \prod_{j \in \mathcal{S}_h} g^{r^*}$$

where $\{\alpha_{1,j}, \alpha_{1,j}', \alpha_{2,j}, \alpha_{2,j}', sk_j^*, R_{4,j}, \alpha_{3,j}^*, \alpha_{5,j}^*\}_{j \in \mathcal{S}_h}$, are the values corresponding to $\{\text{ID}_j^*, pk_j^*\}_{j \in \mathcal{S}_h}$, $\{\text{ID}_j^*, pk_j^*\}_{j \in \mathcal{S}_h}$, m^*, $\{\text{ID}_j^*, pk_j^*, m_j^*\}_{j \in \mathcal{S}_h}$ in list $L_{H_{1,2}}$, L_k, L_{H_4} and L_{H_3}, L_{H_5} respectively.

By using the similar method in [2], we have that $\mathcal{B}$ can succeed in the above game with a non-negligible probability.   □

Theorem 4. *The proposed CBAS scheme is existentially unforgeable in Game 2 of CBAS if the CDH assumption holds in* $\mathbb{G}$.

Proof. It is almost the same as that in the proof of Theorem 1, except the followings.

Output. At last, $\mathcal{A}$ outputs a forgery $\sigma^* = (S^*, T^*)$ corresponding to $\{m^*, \text{ID}_i^*, pk_i^*\}_{i=1}^n$. If $\text{coin}_m^* = 0$ or $\text{coin}_{pk,i}^* = 0$ $(i = 1, \cdots, n)$, $\mathcal{B}$ reports fail and aborts. Otherwise, $\mathcal{B}$ does the followings.

- Let $\mathcal{S}_u$ be the set of indices for $\{\text{ID}_j^*, pk_j^*, m^*\}$ where $\text{coin}_{\text{ID},j}^* = 0$ and $j \in \{1, \cdots, n\}$. Accordingly, let $\mathcal{S}_h = \{1, \cdots, n\}/\mathcal{S}_u$.
- $\mathcal{B}$ can obtain $\{H_4(m^*)^{sk_j^*} \cdot d_{1,\text{ID}_j^*} \cdot d_{2,\text{ID}_j^*}^{H_5(\text{ID}_j^* \| pk_j^* \| m^*)}\}_{j \in \mathcal{S}_u}$ by using the method in $\mathcal{O}_s$.

- $\mathcal{B}$ computes $\widehat{S^*} = S^* / \prod_{j \in \mathcal{S}_u} H_4(m^*)^{sk_j^*} \cdot d_{1,\mathrm{ID}_j^*} \cdot d_{2,\mathrm{ID}_j^*}^{H_5(\mathrm{ID}_j^* \| pk_j^* \| m^*)}$.
- $\mathcal{B}$ computes g^{ab} from σ^*. Note that

$$S^* = \prod_{j \in \mathcal{S}_h} (g^{\alpha_{3,j}^*})^{r^*} (g^{ab})^{\alpha_{4,j}^* \cdot w_j^*} \cdot H_1(\mathrm{ID}_j^* \| pk_j^*)^u \cdot (H_2(\mathrm{ID}_j^* \| pk_j^*)^u)^{H_5(\mathrm{ID}_j^* \| pk_j^* \| m^*)}$$

and

$$T^* = \prod_{j \in \mathcal{S}_h} g^{r^*}$$

where $\{\alpha_{3,j}^*, \alpha_{4,j}^*, w_j^*\}_{j \in \mathcal{S}_h}$, are the values corresponding to $m^*, \{\mathrm{ID}_j^*, pk_j^*\}_{j \in \mathcal{S}_h}$ in list L_{H_3} and L_{H_4}, L_k respectively.

By using the similar method in [2], we have that $\mathcal{B}$ can succeed in the above game with a non-negligible probability.   □

5   Conclusion and Outlook

In this paper, we propose a new certificate-based signature scheme where signatures on the message signed by different users can be aggregated into a single signature without a pre-negotiated one-time-use nonce. Furthermore, only four pairing operations are required in the verification. These properties make our proposal useful in bandwidth and computation constraint environments.

Acknowledgement. Xinxin Ma and Jun Shao were supported in part by the National Natural Science Foundation of China under Grant 61472364, Grant 61472365, and Grant 61379121, and in part by the Science Plan Project of Zhejiang under Grant 2017C01091. Cong Zuo was supported by Data61 Research Collaborative Project (Enhancing Security and Privacy in IoT).

References

1. Al-Riyami, S.S., Paterson, K.G.: Certificateless public key cryptography. In: Laih, C.-S. (ed.) ASIACRYPT 2003. LNCS, vol. 2894, pp. 452–473. Springer, Heidelberg (2003). https://doi.org/10.1007/978-3-540-40061-5_29
2. Boneh, D., Franklin, M.: Identity-based encryption from the Weil pairing. In: Kilian, J. (ed.) CRYPTO 2001. LNCS, vol. 2139, pp. 213–229. Springer, Heidelberg (2001). https://doi.org/10.1007/3-540-44647-8_13
3. Boneh, D., Lynn, B., Shacham, H.: Short signatures from the Weil pairing. In: Boyd, C. (ed.) ASIACRYPT 2001. LNCS, vol. 2248, pp. 514–532. Springer, Heidelberg (2001). https://doi.org/10.1007/3-540-45682-1_30
4. Chen, J.N., Chen, Q.S., Zou, F.M.: Certificate-based aggregate signature scheme without bilinear pairings. J. Inf. Hid. Multimedia Sig. Process. **7**(6), 1330–1336 (2016)
5. Chen, Y.-C., Tso, R., Mambo, M., Huang, K., Horng, G.: Certificateless aggregate signature with efficient verification. Secur. Commun. Netw. **8**(13), 2232–2243 (2015)

6. Cheng, L., Xiao, Y., Wang, G.: Cryptanalysis of a certificate-based on signature scheme. Proc. Eng. **29**(4), 2821–2825 (2012)
7. Feng, J., Li, J.: A new certificate-based digital signature scheme. In: 2013 Fourth International Conference on Emerging Intelligent Data and Web Technologies (EIDWT), pp. 547–549 (2013)
8. Feng, J., Li, J.: A new certificate-based digital signature scheme in bilinear group. Int. J. Embed. Syst. **6**(1), 44–49 (2014)
9. Floerkemeier, C., Langheinrich, M., Fleisch, E., Mattern, F., Sarma, S.E. (eds.): IOT 2008. LNCS, vol. 4952. Springer, Heidelberg (2008). https://doi.org/10.1007/978-3-540-78731-0
10. Gentry, C.: Certificate-based encryption and the certificate revocation problem. In: Biham, E. (ed.) EUROCRYPT 2003. LNCS, vol. 2656, pp. 272–293. Springer, Heidelberg (2003). https://doi.org/10.1007/3-540-39200-9_17
11. Gentry, C., Ramzan, Z.: Identity-based aggregate signatures. In: Yung, M., Dodis, Y., Kiayias, A., Malkin, T. (eds.) PKC 2006. LNCS, vol. 3958, pp. 257–273. Springer, Heidelberg (2006). https://doi.org/10.1007/11745853_17
12. Gong, Z., Long, Y., Hong, X., Chen, K.: Two certificateless aggregate signatures from bilinear maps. In: SNPD, vol. 3, pp. 188–193. IEEE Computer Society (2007)
13. He, D., Tian, M., Chen, J.: Insecurity of an efficient certificateless aggregate signature with constant pairing computations. Inf. Sci. **268**, 458–462 (2014)
14. Kang, B., Mu, W., Jing, D.: An efficient certificateless aggregate signature scheme. Wuhan Univ. J. Nat. Sci. **22**(2), 165–170 (2017)
15. Kang, B.G., Park, J.H., Hahn, S.G.: A certificate-based signature scheme. In: Okamoto, T. (ed.) CT-RSA 2004. LNCS, vol. 2964, pp. 99–111. Springer, Heidelberg (2004). https://doi.org/10.1007/978-3-540-24660-2_8
16. Wu, Q., Zhang, F., Zhang, L., Qin, B.: Efficient many-to-one authentication with certificateless aggregate signatures. Comput. Netw. **54**, 2481–2491 (2010)
17. Li, J., Huang, X., Mu, Y., Susilo, W., Wu, Q.: Certificate-based signature: security model and efficient construction. In: Lopez, J., Samarati, P., Ferrer, J.L. (eds.) EuroPKI 2007. LNCS, vol. 4582, pp. 110–125. Springer, Heidelberg (2007). https://doi.org/10.1007/978-3-540-73408-6_8
18. Li, J., Huang, X., Yi, M., Susilo, W., Wu, Q.: Constructions of certificate-based signature secure against key replacement attacks. J. Comput. Secur. **18**(3), 421–449 (2010)
19. Li, J., Huang, X., Zhang, Y., Xu, L.: An efficient short certificate-based signature scheme. J. Syst. Softw. **85**(2), 314–322 (2012)
20. Li, J., Wang, Z., Zhang, Y.: Provably secure certificate-based signature scheme without pairings. Inf. Sci. **233**, 313–320 (2013)
21. Liu, H., Liang, M., Sun, H.: A secure and efficient certificateless aggregate signature scheme. IEICE Trans. Fundam. Electron. Commun. Comput. Sci. **E97.A**(4), 991–995 (2014)
22. Liu, J.K., Baek, J., Susilo, W., Zhou, J.: Certificate-based signature schemes without pairings or random oracles. In: Wu, T.-C., Lei, C.-L., Rijmen, V., Lee, D.-T. (eds.) ISC 2008. LNCS, vol. 5222, pp. 285–297. Springer, Heidelberg (2008). https://doi.org/10.1007/978-3-540-85886-7_20
23. Liu, J.K., Baek, J., Zhou, J.: Certificate-based sequential aggregate signature. In: Proceedings of the Second ACM Conference on Wireless Network Security, WISEC 2009, Zurich, Switzerland, 16–19 March 2009, pp. 21–28 (2009)

24. Liu, J.K., Bao, F., Zhou, J.: Short and efficient certificate-based signature. In: Casares-Giner, V., Manzoni, P., Pont, A. (eds.) NETWORKING 2011. LNCS, vol. 6827, pp. 167–178. Springer, Heidelberg (2011). https://doi.org/10.1007/978-3-642-23041-7_17

25. Yang, L., Li, J.: Improved certificate-based signature scheme without random oracles. IET Inf. Secur. **10**(2), 80–86 (2016)

26. Malhi, A.K., Batra, S.: An efficient certificateless aggregate signature scheme for vehicular ad-hoc networks. Discrete Math. Theor. Comput. Sci. **17**(1), 317–338 (2015)

27. Nie, H., Li, Y., Chen, W., Ding, Y.: NCLAS: a novel and efficient certificateless aggregate signature scheme. Secur. Commun. Netw. **9**(16), 3141–151 (2016)

28. Pakniat, N., Noroozi, M.: Cryptanalysis of a certificateless aggregate signature scheme. In: The 9th Conference of Command, Control, Communications and Computer Intelligence (2016)

29. Shamir, A.: Identity-based cryptosystems and signature schemes. In: Blakley, G.R., Chaum, D. (eds.) CRYPTO 1984. LNCS, vol. 196, pp. 47–53. Springer, Heidelberg (1985). https://doi.org/10.1007/3-540-39568-7_5

30. Shen, H., Chen, J., Hu, H., Shen, J.: Insecurity of a certificateless aggregate signature scheme. IEICE Trans. Fund. Electron. Commun. Comput. Sci. **E99.A**(2), 660–662 (2014)

31. Shen, H., Chen, J., Shen, J., He, D.: Cryptanalysis of a certificateless aggregate signature scheme with efficient verification. Secur. Commun. Netw. **9**(13), 2217–2221 (2016)

32. Shim, K.-A.: On the security of a certificateless aggregate signature scheme. IEEE Commun. Lett. **15**(8), 1136–1138 (2011)

33. Tu, H., He, D., Huang, B.: Reattack of a certificateless aggregate signature scheme with constant pairing computations. Sci. World J. 10 pages (2014). Article ID 343715

34. Chen, K., Wang, X., Gao, W., Wang, G.: Generic construction of certificate-based signature from certificateless signature with provable security. Informatica **28**(2), 215–235 (2017)

35. Wu, W., Mu, Y., Susilo, W., Huang, X.: Certificate-based signatures: new definitions and a generic construction from certificateless signatures. In: Chung, K.-I., Sohn, K., Yung, M. (eds.) WISA 2008. LNCS, vol. 5379, pp. 99–114. Springer, Heidelberg (2009). https://doi.org/10.1007/978-3-642-00306-6_8

36. Wei, W., Yi, M., Susilo, W., Huang, X.: Certificate-based signatures revisited. J. UCS **15**(8), 1659–1684 (2009)

37. Xiong, H., Guan, Z., Chen, Z., Li, F.: An efficient certificateless aggregate signature with constant pairing computations. Inf. Sci. **219**, 225–235 (2012)

38. Wang, Y., Ming, Y.: Efficient certificate-based signature scheme. In: Fifth International Conference on Information Assurance and Security, pp. 87–90 (2009)

39. Zhang, H.: Insecurity of a certificateless aggregate signature scheme. Secur. Commun. Netw. **9**(11), 1547–1552 (2016)

40. Zhang, J.: On the security of a certificate-based signature scheme and its improvement with pairings. In: Bao, F., Li, H., Wang, G. (eds.) ISPEC 2009. LNCS, vol. 5451, pp. 47–58. Springer, Heidelberg (2009). https://doi.org/10.1007/978-3-642-00843-6_5

41. Zhang, J., Zhao, X., Mao, J.: Attack on chen et al.'s certificateless aggregate signature scheme. Secur. Commun. Netw. **9**(1), 54–59 (2016)

42. Zhang, L., Zhang, F.: A new certificateless aggregate signature scheme. Comput. Commun. **32**(6), 1079–1085 (2009)

Recovering Attacks Against Linear Sketch in Fuzzy Signature Schemes of ACNS 2015 and 2016

Masaya Yasuda[1]([⊠]), Takeshi Shimoyama[2], Masahiko Takenaka[2],
Narishige Abe[2], Shigefumi Yamada[2], and Junpei Yamaguchi[3]

[1] Institute of Mathematics for Industry, Kyushu University,
744 Motooka Nishi-ku, Fukuoka 819-0395, Japan
yasuda@imi.kyushu-u.ac.jp
[2] FUJITSU LABORATORIES LTD.,
1-1, Kamikodanaka 4-chome, Nakahara-ku, Kawasaki 211-8588, Japan
[3] Graduate School of Mathematics, Kyushu University,
744 Motooka Nishi-ku, Fukuoka 819-0395, Japan

Abstract. In biometrics, template protection aims to protect the confidentiality of templates (i.e., enrolled biometric data) by certain conversion. At ACNS 2015, as a new approach of template protection, Takahashi et al. proposed a new concept of digital signature, called "fuzzy signature", that uses biometric data as a private key for securely generating a signature. After that, at ACNS 2016, Matsuda et al. modified the original scheme with several relaxing requirements. A main ingredient of fuzzy signature is "linear sketch", which incorporates a kind of linear encoding and error correction process to securely output only the difference of signing keys without revealing any biometric data. In this paper, we give recovering attacks against the linear sketch schemes proposed at ACNS 2015 and 2016. Specifically, given encoded data by linear sketch (called a "sketch"), our attacks can directly recover both the signing key and the biometric data embedded in the sketch. Our attacks make use of the special structure that a sketch has the form of a sum of an integral part and a decimal part, and biometric data is embedded in the decimal part. On the other hand, we give a simple countermeasure against our attacks and discuss the effect in both theory and practice.

Keywords: Template protection · Fuzzy signature · Linear sketch

1 Introduction

Biometric authentication (or biometrics) is authentication of users by using their physiological (e.g., fingerprint, iris, face and vein) or behavioral characteristics (e.g., signature, keystroke dynamics, and gait). Compared to the commonly used ID/password authentication, it does not require users to remember long and complex passwords, and hence it is now expanding in various applications ranging from international border crossings to securing information in databases.

© Springer International Publishing AG 2017
J. K. Liu and P. Samarati (Eds.): ISPEC 2017, LNCS 10701, pp. 409–421, 2017.
https://doi.org/10.1007/978-3-319-72359-4_24

With widespread development of biometric authentication, concerns about the security and the privacy have been rapidly increasing.

Template Protection. In biometrics, it is the most important to protect *templates* which are enrollment biometric features, since once leaked templates can be neither revoked nor replaced. During rapid expansion of biometrics, template protection technology has been intensively investigated (e.g., see [1,3]), and its basic method is to store biometric features transformed by certain conversion, instead of storing raw ones. According to [3, Sect. 3], an ideal biometric template protection scheme should satisfy the following four requirements (see also [6]); (1) *Diversity*: secure templates (i.e., transformed templates) must not allow cross-matching across databases. (2) *Revocability*: it should be straightforward to revoke a compromised template and reissue a new secure template based on the same biometric data. (3) *Security*: it must be computationally hard to obtain the original biometric template from a secure template. (4) *Performance*: the scheme should not degrade the recognition performance (e.g., FAR = False Acceptance Rate and FRR = False Rejection Rate). At present, there are four main approaches for template protection [3, Sect. 3]; (i) salting (e.g., biohashing [11]), (ii) non-invertible transform (e.g., robust hashing [9]), (iii) key-binding (e.g., fuzzy vault [4] and fuzzy commitment [5]), and finally (iv) key-generation (e.g., secure sketch-fuzzy extractor [2]). Homomorphic encryption is often regarded as yet another approach. Each approach has both advantages and limitations, and no approach can achieve an ideal scheme.

Fuzzy Signature Schemes [7,10]. As a new approach for template protection, a new concept of digital signature, called *fuzzy signature*, was first introduced in 2015 by Takahashi et al. [10]. It is a signature scheme that uses fuzzy data (such as biometric data) as a private key for securely generating a signature. Different from the context of fuzzy-extractor-based digital signature, it does not require auxiliary data (see [10, Fig. 1] for a comparison), and hence it is expected to be applied to various applications. As a typical application, the authors of [10] discussed how fuzzy signature can be used to realize a biometric-based public key infrastructure (PKI), called the *public biometric infrastructure (PBI)*, in which biometric data of each user is used as his or her specific cryptographic key. In 2016, Matsuda et al. [7] modified the fuzzy signature scheme of [10] with relaxing requirements of building blocks of the scheme. One of the main ingredients of fuzzy signature is *linear sketch*, which incorporates a kind of linear encoding and error correction process. More specifically, linear sketch is a one-way encoding $c = \mathtt{Sketch}(s, x)$ of a secret key s by fuzzy data x (the encoded data c is called a *sketch*). Given two sketches $c = \mathtt{Sketch}(s, x)$ and $\tilde{c} = \mathtt{Sketch}(\tilde{s}, \tilde{x})$, it enables to securely reconstruct the exact difference $s - \tilde{s}$ of secret keys (without revealing x and $\tilde{x}$) if two fuzzy data x and $\tilde{x}$ are sufficiently close with respect to certain distance. These properties are useful to combine with certain cryptographic signature schemes in order to construct a fuzzy signature scheme.

Our Contributions. Concrete linear sketch schemes were presented in [10, Sect. 5] and [7, Sect. 5.2] to construct concrete fuzzy signature schemes. In this paper, we give recovering attacks against the linear sketch schemes of [7,10]. More specifically, from a sketch $\mathbf{c} = \texttt{Sketch}(\mathbf{s}, \mathbf{x})$, our attacks can recover both the secret key $\mathbf{s}$ and the fuzzy data $\mathbf{x}$ exactly. In both schemes of [7,10], fuzzy data are represented by vectors $\mathbf{x} \in [0, 1)^n$. In order to tolerate the fuzziness of $\mathbf{x}$, given secret data $\mathbf{s} \in \mathbb{Z}^n$, a sketch $\mathbf{c}$ basically has the form $\mathbf{s} + E(\mathbf{x}) \bmod q$ for some positive integer q and scaler function E (e.g., $E(\mathbf{x}) = T\mathbf{x}$ for some $T > 0$). For $\mathbf{y} := \mathbf{s} + E(\mathbf{x}) = (y_1, \ldots, y_n) \in \mathbb{R}^n$, each component of $\mathbf{y} \bmod q$ is represented as a sum of the "integral part" modulo q and the "decimal part" of $y_i \in \mathbb{R}$. The basic strategy of our attacks is to multiply the sketch $\mathbf{c}$ by a factor $f > 0$ so that $f\mathbf{c} \in \mathbb{Z}^n$. After that, we make use of several modulo operations for $f\mathbf{c} \in \mathbb{Z}^n$ and the linearity of E to recover either $\mathbf{s}$ or $\mathbf{x}$ exactly. Once either $\mathbf{s}$ or $\mathbf{x}$ is obtained, it is straightforward to recover the other data from the sketch $\mathbf{c}$. The linear sketch schemes of [7,10] are vulnerable against our recovering attacks. The security proof of each fuzzy signature scheme is given in [7,10] under the assumption that fuzzy data $\mathbf{x}$ are uniform real numbers. Despite the security proof, our attacks can recover both $\mathbf{s}$ and $\mathbf{x}$ embedded in any sketch $\mathbf{c}$ with known denominator of $\mathbf{x}$, and our attacks are independent of the uniform assumption on $\mathbf{x}$. (Security requirement of indistinguishability for linear sketch are given in [10, Definition 5 in Sect. 4.1]. However, in the security proof of [7,10], there is no careful discussion about whether specific linear sketch schemes satisfy the security requirement or not.)

As another work, we propose a countermeasure against our recovering attacks. Our countermeasure is very simple, and it just adds noisy data ε to a sketch $\mathbf{c} = \texttt{Sketch}(\mathbf{s}, \mathbf{x})$. For the sketch $\mathbf{c}_\varepsilon = \mathbf{c} + \varepsilon$ with noise, our attacks can recover fuzzy data $\mathbf{x}'$ close enough to the original fuzzy data $\mathbf{x}$ in theory. But in practice, this countermeasure might often prevent from recovering $\mathbf{x}'$ due to lack of the accuracy of floating point numbers. In this paper, we discuss the effect of our simple countermeasure.

Notation. The symbols $\mathbb{Z}$, $\mathbb{Q}$ and $\mathbb{R}$ denote the ring of integers, the field of rational numbers, and the field of real numbers, respectively. For a positive integer q, we always represent representatives of integers modulo q by elements in the set $\{0, 1, 2, \ldots, q-1\}$. For $a \in \mathbb{R}$, let $\lfloor a \rceil$ denote its nearest integer, and $\lfloor a \rfloor$ its round-off integer. This notation can be naturally extended to vectors. The ∞-norm of a vector $\mathbf{x} = (x_1, \ldots, x_n) \in \mathbb{R}^n$ is defined as $\|\mathbf{x}\|_\infty := \max_{1 \le i \le n} |x_i|$.

2 Overview of Fuzzy Signature

In this section, we give an overview of fuzzy signature [7,10]. Specifically, we present building blocks and a generic construction of a fuzzy signature scheme. From the construction, we see what role linear sketch plays in fuzzy signature.

2.1 Building Blocks

A fuzzy signature scheme $\mathcal{F} = (\Sigma, \mathcal{S})$ basically consists of a cryptographic signature scheme Σ and a linear sketch scheme $\mathcal{S}$ as follows:

- $\varSigma = (\mathsf{Setup}, \mathsf{KG}, \mathsf{Sign}, \mathsf{Ver})$: It is a cryptographic signature scheme consisting of a setup algorithm Setup, a key generation algorithm KG, a signing algorithm Sign, and a verification algorithm Ver.
  - $pp \leftarrow \mathsf{Setup}(1^k)$: It takes 1^k as input (k is determined by a threshold t of a fuzzy signature scheme), and outputs a public parameter pp.
  - $vk \leftarrow \mathsf{KG}(pp, sk)$: It takes as input pp and a signing key sk, and outputs a verification key vk.
  - $\sigma \leftarrow \mathsf{Sign}(pp, sk, m)$: It takes as input pp, sk and a message m, and outputs a signature σ.
  - $\top$ or $\bot \leftarrow \mathsf{Ver}(pp, vk, m, \sigma)$: It takes as input pp, vk, m and σ, and outputs either $\top$ ("valid") or $\bot$ ("invalid").
  Certain *homomorphic property* (formally described in [10, Definition 3]) is required for $\varSigma$ to construct the fuzzy signature scheme $\mathcal{F}$. As concrete schemes for $\varSigma$, a variant of the Waters signature scheme [12] and the Schnorr signature scheme [8] are adopted in [7,10], respectively.
- $\mathcal{S} = (\mathsf{Sketch}, \mathsf{DiffRec})$: It is a linear sketch scheme consisting of a "sketching" algorithm Sketch and a "difference reconstruction" algorithm $\mathsf{DiffRec}$.
  - $\mathbf{c} \leftarrow \mathsf{Sketch}(\mathbf{s}, \mathbf{x})$: It takes as input a secret key $\mathbf{s}$ (e.g., a signing key sk of $\varSigma$) and fuzzy data $\mathbf{x}$ (e.g., biometric data), and outputs a sketch $\mathbf{c}$. Note that the sketch $\mathbf{c}$ is a kind of encoded data, but it does not require to decrypt $\mathbf{c}$ to recover the secret key $\mathbf{s}$ in fuzzy signature.
  - $\Delta \leftarrow \mathsf{DiffRec}(\mathbf{c}, \tilde{\mathbf{c}})$: It takes as input two sketches $\mathbf{c} = \mathsf{Sketch}(\mathbf{s}, \mathbf{x})$ and $\tilde{\mathbf{c}} = \mathsf{Sketch}(\tilde{\mathbf{s}}, \tilde{\mathbf{x}})$, and outputs the "difference" Δ. In particular, the difference Δ is equal to $\mathbf{s} - \tilde{\mathbf{s}}$ if certain distance $\mathrm{dist}(\mathbf{x}, \tilde{\mathbf{x}})$ between two fuzzy data $\mathbf{x}$ and $\tilde{\mathbf{x}}$ is less than the threshold t of $\mathcal{F}$.
  See [10, Definition 5] for the formal definition of a linear sketch scheme $\mathcal{S}$. Compared to the formal definition, we omit the information of the base abelian group for secret keys $\mathbf{s}$ and $\tilde{\mathbf{s}}$. For the sake of simplicity, we here assume that we can subtract $\tilde{\mathbf{s}}$ from $\mathbf{s}$. In Sect. 3 below, we shall present concrete constructions of linear sketch schemes $\mathcal{S}$, described in [10, Sect. 5] and [7, Sect. 5.2].

2.2 Generic Construction

In Fig. 1, we show an overview of a generic construction of a fuzzy signature scheme $\mathcal{F} = (\varSigma, \mathcal{S})$ in case of biometric authentication between a user $\mathcal{U}$ and an authentication server $\mathcal{A}$ (see also [10, Sects. 1.3 and 4] for an overview). The authentication server $\mathcal{A}$ first prepares a public parameter $pp \leftarrow \mathsf{Setup}(1^k)$. Then the following two phases are performed for biometric authentication:

Enrollment Phase

1. The user $\mathcal{U}$ randomly generates a signing key sk, and computes the corresponding verification key $vk \leftarrow \mathsf{KG}(pp, sk)$.
2. The user $\mathcal{U}$ extracts fuzzy data $\mathbf{x}$ from his or her biometric image (e.g., fingerprint and vein), and computes a sketch $\mathbf{c} \leftarrow \mathsf{Sketch}(sk, \mathbf{x})$.

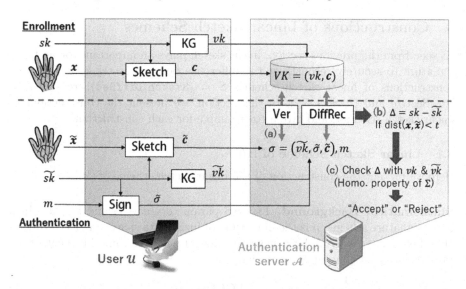

Fig. 1. An overview of a generic construction of a fuzzy signature scheme for biometric authentication ($sk, \tilde{sk}$: signing keys, $vk, \tilde{vk}$: verification keys, $\mathbf{x}, \tilde{\mathbf{x}}$: fuzzy data extracted from biometric images, $\mathbf{c} = \texttt{Sketch}(sk, \mathbf{x}), \tilde{\mathbf{c}} = \texttt{Sketch}(\tilde{sk}, \tilde{\mathbf{x}})$: sketches, m: message, $\tilde{\sigma}$: signature)

3. Then $\mathcal{U}$ sends $VK = (vk, \mathbf{c})$ as a verification key of the fuzzy signature scheme $\mathcal{F}$ to the authentication server $\mathcal{A}$.

Authentication Phase

1. As in the registration phase, the user $\mathcal{U}$ randomly generates a new signing key $\tilde{sk}$, and computes $\tilde{vk} \leftarrow \texttt{KG}(pp, \tilde{sk})$.
2. For authentication, the user $\mathcal{U}$ extracts fuzzy data $\tilde{\mathbf{x}}$ from his or her biometric image, and computes a sketch $\tilde{\mathbf{c}} \leftarrow \texttt{Sketch}(\tilde{sk}, \tilde{\mathbf{x}})$.
3. Given a message m, the user $\mathcal{U}$ computes a signature $\tilde{\sigma} \leftarrow \texttt{Sign}(pp, \tilde{sk}, m)$. Then $\mathcal{U}$ sends $\sigma = (\tilde{vk}, \tilde{\sigma}, \tilde{\mathbf{c}})$ and m as a signature of $\mathcal{F}$ to $\mathcal{A}$.
4. The authentication server $\mathcal{A}$ verifies the signature $\sigma = (\tilde{vk}, \tilde{\sigma}, \tilde{\mathbf{c}})$ with m by using the verification key $VK = (vk, \mathbf{c})$ of $\mathcal{F}$ as follows:
   (a) Check the validity of $\tilde{\sigma}$ under $\tilde{vk}$ by computing $\texttt{Ver}(pp, \tilde{vk}, m, \tilde{\sigma})$.
   (b) Compute $\Delta \leftarrow \texttt{DiffRec}(\mathbf{c}, \tilde{\mathbf{c}})$, and recover $\Delta = sk - \tilde{sk}$ if $\text{dist}(\mathbf{x}, \tilde{\mathbf{x}}) < t$.
   (c) Finally check whether the difference vk and $\tilde{vk}$ corresponds to $\Delta = sk - \tilde{sk}$. This can be done by the homomorphic property of Σ.

Features of Fuzzy Signature. In Fig. 1, neither $\mathbf{x}$ nor $\tilde{\mathbf{x}}$ is revealed in the authentication server $\mathcal{A}$. Different from the key-generation approach (e.g., secure-sketch fuzzy extractor [2]), a main feature of fuzzy signature is that it does not require to extract the signing key sk from the sketch $\mathbf{c} = \texttt{Sketch}(sk, \mathbf{x})$ and the fuzzy data $\tilde{\mathbf{x}}$ close to $\mathbf{x}$. Alternatively, it requires another sketch $\tilde{\mathbf{c}} = \texttt{Sketch}(\tilde{sk}, \tilde{\mathbf{x}})$ to securely reconstruct the difference $\Delta = sk - \tilde{sk}$ in $\mathcal{A}$ only when two fuzzy data $\mathbf{x}$ and $\tilde{\mathbf{x}}$ are sufficiently close.

3   Constructions of Linear Sketch Schemes

As seen from the previous section, linear sketch plays an important role in fuzzy signature to securely reconstruct the difference between secret keys. Concrete constructions of linear sketch schemes $\mathcal{S} = (\texttt{Sketch}, \texttt{DiffRec})$ are shown in [10, Sect. 5] and [7, Sect. 5.2]. In this section, we present the constructions of linear sketch schemes, and give a toy example for each construction.

3.1   Linear Sketch Scheme of [10]

Here we present the construction of the linear sketch scheme of [10].

Mathematical Background. Fix two parameters $n \in \mathbb{N}$ and $t \in \mathbb{R}$. (In a fuzzy signature scheme, n is the dimension of fuzzy data space, and t is a threshold.) Let $w_1, \ldots, w_n \in \mathbb{N}$ be n positive integers with the same bit length (i.e., $\lceil \log_2 w_1 \rceil = \cdots = \lceil \log_2 w_n \rceil$), such that

$$w_i \le \frac{1}{2t} \ (1 \le \forall i \le n) \text{ and } \mathrm{GCD}(w_i, w_j) = 1 \ (\forall i \ne \forall j). \tag{1}$$

Set $\mathbf{w} = (w_1, \ldots, w_n) \in \mathbb{N}^n$, and define two spaces by

$$\mathbb{Z}_{\mathbf{w}}^n := \prod_{i=1}^n \mathbb{Z}/w_i\mathbb{Z} \quad \text{and} \quad \mathbb{R}_{\mathbf{w}}^n := \mathbb{Z}_{\mathbf{w}}^n \otimes_{\mathbb{Z}} \mathbb{R}.$$

In particular, the space $\mathbb{R}_{\mathbf{w}}^n$ can be represented as the quotient set $\mathbb{R}^n / \sim$ of $\mathbb{R}^n$ by the equivalence relation '$\sim$', where for $\mathbf{y} = (y_i), \mathbf{z} = (z_i) \in \mathbb{R}^n$ we define

$$\mathbf{y} \sim \mathbf{z} \iff y_i = n_i w_i + z_i \text{ for some } n_i \in \mathbb{Z} \ (\forall 1 \le i \le n).$$

Therefore each component y_i of any element $\mathbf{y} = (y_i) \in \mathbb{R}_{\mathbf{w}}^n$ can be uniquely represented as $y_i = p_i + q_i$ for some $p_i \in \mathbb{Z}$ and $q_i \in \mathbb{R}$ with $0 \le p_i < w_i$ and $0 \le q_i < 1$ (p_i is the integral part modulo w_i, and q_i the decimal part). Now define two functions:

$$\begin{cases} E_{\mathbf{w}} : \mathbb{R}^n \longrightarrow \mathbb{R}_{\mathbf{w}}^n, & \mathbf{x} = (x_i) \mapsto (w_1 x_1, \ldots, w_n x_n) \in \mathbb{R}_{\mathbf{w}}^n, \\ C_{\mathbf{w}} : \mathbb{R}_{\mathbf{w}}^n \longrightarrow \mathbb{Z}_{\mathbf{w}}^n, & \mathbf{y} = (y_i) \mapsto (\lfloor y_1 + 0.5 \rfloor, \ldots, \lfloor y_n + 0.5 \rfloor) \in \mathbb{Z}_{\mathbf{w}}^n. \end{cases}$$

Since $E_{\mathbf{w}}(\mathbf{x} + \mathbf{e}) = E_{\mathbf{w}}(\mathbf{x}) + E_{\mathbf{w}}(\mathbf{e}) \bmod \mathbf{w}$ for any $\mathbf{x}, \mathbf{e} \in \mathbb{R}^n$, the function $E_{\mathbf{w}}$ can be regarded as a kind of linear coding. In contrast, the round-off operation $\lfloor y_i + 0.5 \rfloor$ in $C_{\mathbf{w}}$ can be regarded as a kind of error correction. Actually, for $\mathbf{x}, \tilde{\mathbf{x}} \in \mathbb{R}^n$ with $\|\mathbf{x} - \tilde{\mathbf{x}}\|_\infty < t$, we have

$$\|E_{\mathbf{w}}(\mathbf{x}) - E_{\mathbf{w}}(\tilde{\mathbf{x}})\|_\infty < t \cdot \max_{1 \le i \le n} |w_i| \le 0.5.$$

by condition (1). Therefore, for such $\mathbf{x}, \tilde{\mathbf{x}}$, it holds that

$$C_{\mathbf{w}}\left(E_{\mathbf{w}}(\mathbf{x}) - E_{\mathbf{w}}(\tilde{\mathbf{x}})\right) = \mathbf{0}. \tag{2}$$

Furthermore, for any $\mathbf{x} \in \mathbb{R}^n$ and $\mathbf{s} \in \mathbb{Z}_{\mathbf{w}}^n$, we clearly have

$$C_{\mathbf{w}}(\mathbf{x} + \mathbf{s}) = C_{\mathbf{w}}(\mathbf{x}) + \mathbf{s} \bmod \mathbf{w}. \tag{3}$$

Scheme Construction. Now we are ready to present the linear sketch scheme $\mathcal{S} = (\texttt{Sketch}, \texttt{DiffRec})$ of [10]. Given $\mathbf{s} \in \mathbb{Z}_{\mathbf{w}}^n$ and $\mathbf{x} \in [0,1)^n$, we define

$$\mathbf{c} = \texttt{Sketch}(\mathbf{s}, \mathbf{x}) := \mathbf{s} + E_{\mathbf{w}}(\mathbf{x}) \bmod \mathbf{w} \in \mathbb{R}_{\mathbf{w}}^n.$$

On the other hand, for two sketches $\mathbf{c}, \tilde{\mathbf{c}} \in \mathbb{R}_{\mathbf{w}}^n$, we define

$$\varDelta = \texttt{DiffRec}(\mathbf{c}, \tilde{\mathbf{c}}) := C_{\mathbf{w}}(\mathbf{c} - \tilde{\mathbf{c}}) \in \mathbb{Z}_{\mathbf{w}}^n.$$

Write $\mathbf{c} = \texttt{Sketch}(\mathbf{s}, \mathbf{x})$ and $\tilde{\mathbf{c}} = \texttt{Sketch}(\tilde{\mathbf{s}}, \tilde{\mathbf{x}})$. By Eq. (3) and the linearity of $E_{\mathbf{w}}$, we clearly have

$$\begin{cases} \mathbf{c} - \tilde{\mathbf{c}} = (\mathbf{s} - \tilde{\mathbf{s}}) + E_{\mathbf{w}}(\mathbf{x} - \tilde{\mathbf{x}}) \bmod \mathbf{w}, \\ \varDelta = C_{\mathbf{w}}(\mathbf{c} - \tilde{\mathbf{c}}) \\ \qquad = (\mathbf{s} - \tilde{\mathbf{s}}) + C_{\mathbf{w}}(E_{\mathbf{w}}(\mathbf{x}) - E_{\mathbf{w}}(\tilde{\mathbf{x}})) \bmod \mathbf{w}. \end{cases}$$

Furthermore, if $\|\mathbf{x} - \tilde{\mathbf{x}}\|_\infty < t$, we have $\varDelta = \mathbf{s} - \tilde{\mathbf{s}} \bmod \mathbf{w}$ by Eq. (2). This error correction property plays a central role to combine with certain cryptographic signature scheme in fuzzy signature.

Example 1. As a toy example, we fix $n = 3$ and $t = 0.005$. We also choose $w_1 = 97$, $w_2 = 89$, $w_3 = 91$ such that $w_i \leq \frac{1}{2t} = 100$ for $i = 1, 2, 3$. Set $\mathbf{w} = (97, 89, 91) \in \mathbb{Z}^3$. Given fuzzy data $\mathbf{x} = (0.11, 0.63, 0.71) \in [0,1)^3$, we compute $E_{\mathbf{w}}(\mathbf{x}) = (w_1 x_1, w_2 x_2, w_3 x_3) = (10.67, 56.07, 64.61) \in \mathbb{R}^3$. Set $\mathbf{s} = (11, 45, 41) \in \mathbb{Z}^3$ as a secret key. Then a sketch $\mathbf{c} \in \mathbb{R}_{\mathbf{w}}^3$ is obtained as

$$\begin{aligned} \mathbf{c} = \texttt{Sketch}(\mathbf{s}, \mathbf{x}) &= (21.67, 101.07, 105.61) \bmod \mathbf{w} \\ &= (21.67, 12.07, 14.61). \end{aligned}$$

Note that the decimal part of each component of $\mathbf{c}$ is equal to that of $E_{\mathbf{w}}(\mathbf{x})$. Since $\mathbf{w}$ is a public information in fuzzy signature, some information of the fuzzy data $\mathbf{x}$ (e.g., biometric data) can be leaked from $\mathbf{c}$. This is remarked in [10, Sect. 5.3], and it states that it does not affect the security (the EUF-CMA-security, defined in [10, Definition 4]) of the fuzzy signature scheme of [10].

3.2 Construction of [7]

In this subsection, we present the construction of the linear sketch scheme of [7]. Compared to the construction of [10], this construction is very simple (here we give a simpler construction of the linear sketch scheme than the original construction presented in [7, Sect. 5.2]). Given a threshold $t \in \mathbb{R}$ of the fuzzy signature scheme, set $T = \frac{1}{2t} \in \mathbb{N}$ and choose a prime number p with $p \geq T$. Given $\mathbf{s} \in \mathbb{F}_p^n$ and $\mathbf{x} \in [0,1)^n$, we define

$$\mathbf{c} = \texttt{Sketch}(\mathbf{s}, \mathbf{x}) := \mathbf{s} + T\mathbf{x} \bmod p \in \mathbb{R}_p^n,$$

where let $\mathbb{R}_p^n = \mathbb{F}_p^n \otimes_{\mathbb{Z}} \mathbb{R}$. Similar to the space $\mathbb{Z}_{\mathbf{w}}^n$ in the previous subsection, each component y_i of any element of $\mathbb{R}_p^n$ is uniquely represented as a sum of the integral part modulo p and the decimal part of y_i. On the other hand, for two sketches $\mathbf{c} = \texttt{Sketch}(\mathbf{s}, \mathbf{x})$ and $\tilde{\mathbf{c}} = \texttt{Sketch}(\tilde{\mathbf{s}}, \tilde{\mathbf{x}})$, we define

$$\Delta = \texttt{DiffRec}(\mathbf{c}, \tilde{\mathbf{c}}) := \lfloor \mathbf{c} - \tilde{\mathbf{c}} \rceil \bmod p \in \mathbb{F}_p^n.$$

In particular, if $\|\mathbf{x} - \tilde{\mathbf{x}}\|_\infty < t$, we have $\Delta = \mathbf{s} - \tilde{\mathbf{s}} \bmod p \in \mathbb{F}_p^n$ since $\mathbf{c} - \tilde{\mathbf{c}} = (\mathbf{s} - \tilde{\mathbf{s}}) + T(\mathbf{x} - \tilde{\mathbf{x}})$ and $T(\mathbf{x} - \tilde{\mathbf{x}}) \in \left(-\frac{1}{2}, \frac{1}{2}\right)^n$ by the setting of T. This error correction property is useful to combine with the Schnorr signature scheme [8].

Example 2. In this example, we fix $n = 3$, $T = 203$ and $p = 211$ (conversely, we have $t = \frac{1}{406}$). Choose $\mathbf{s} = (153, 43, 198) \in \mathbb{F}_p^3$ as a secret key. Given fuzzy data $\mathbf{x} = (0.11, 0.63, 0.71) \in [0, 1)^3$, a sketch $\mathbf{c} \in \mathbb{R}_p^n$ is obtained as

$$\begin{aligned} \mathbf{c} = \texttt{Sketch}(\mathbf{s}, \mathbf{x}) &= (175.33, 170.89, 342.13) \bmod p \\ &= (175.33, 170.89, 131.13). \end{aligned}$$

4   Recovering Attacks Against Linear Sketch Schemes

In this section, we give recovering attacks against linear sketch schemes of [7, 10]. Specifically, from a sketch $\mathbf{c} = \texttt{Sketch}(\mathbf{s}, \mathbf{x})$ and public information, our attacks enable us to directly recover both the secret key $\mathbf{s}$ and the fuzzy data $\mathbf{x}$.

4.1   Attack Against Linear Sketch Scheme of [10]

Here we give our recovering attack against the linear sketch scheme of [10]. We use the same notation as in Subsect. 3.1. Given a sketch $\mathbf{c} = \texttt{Sketch}(\mathbf{s}, \mathbf{x}) = \mathbf{s} + E_{\mathbf{w}}(\mathbf{x}) \bmod \mathbf{w} \in \mathbb{R}_{\mathbf{w}}^n$ and a public information $\mathbf{w} = (w_1, \ldots, w_n) \in \mathbb{Z}^n$ (but $\mathbf{s} \in \mathbb{Z}_{\mathbf{w}}^n$ and $\mathbf{x} \in [0, 1)^n$ are unknown). Here we assume $\mathbf{x} \in \mathbb{Q}^n$ for simplicity (this assumption is required for practical implementation). Under this assumption, we show a method how to recover both the secret key $\mathbf{s}$ and the fuzzy data $\mathbf{x}$ as follows: Take $f \in \mathbb{Z}$ such that $f\mathbf{c} \in \mathbb{Z}^n$. Then we clearly have $E_{\mathbf{w}}(f\mathbf{x}) \bmod \mathbf{w} = \mathbf{0}$ since $f\mathbf{x} \in \mathbb{Z}^n$. From the construction of the sketch $\mathbf{c}$, we also have

$$f\mathbf{c} = f\mathbf{s} + E_{\mathbf{w}}(f\mathbf{x}) \bmod \mathbf{w} = f\mathbf{s} \bmod \mathbf{w} \in \mathbb{Z}_{\mathbf{w}}^n,$$

in which we make use of the linearity of the scaling function $E_{\mathbf{w}}$ so that $fE_{\mathbf{w}}(\mathbf{x}) \equiv E_{\mathbf{w}}(f\mathbf{x}) \bmod \mathbf{w}$. Then we can recover the secret key $\mathbf{s} \in \mathbb{Z}_{\mathbf{w}}^n$ as

$$\mathbf{s} = f^{-1}(f\mathbf{c}) \bmod \mathbf{w},$$

where we denote $f^{-1} \bmod \mathbf{w} = (f^{-1} \bmod w_1, \ldots, f^{-1} \bmod w_n)$. We also obtain $E_{\mathbf{w}}(\mathbf{x}) = \mathbf{c} - \mathbf{s} \bmod \mathbf{w}$. Since the i-th component $w_i x_i$ of $E_{\mathbf{w}}(\mathbf{x})$ is included in the range $[0, w_i)$ for every $1 \le i \le n$, we can recover the exact $E_{\mathbf{w}}(\mathbf{x}) \in \mathbb{R}^n$ (without modulo $\mathbf{w}$). Then we can also recover the fuzzy data $\mathbf{x} \in [0, 1)^n$ by dividing each component $w_i x_i$ of $E_{\mathbf{w}}(\mathbf{x})$ by w_i for every $1 \le i \le n$.

Example 3. In this example, we apply our recovering attack against the sketch $\mathbf{c} = (21.67, 12.07, 14.61) \in \mathbb{Z}_{\mathbf{w}}^3$ with $\mathbf{w} = (97, 89, 91)$, generated in Example 1. Here take $f = 100$, then we have

$$f\mathbf{c} = (2167, 1207, 1461) \bmod \mathbf{w} = (33, 50, 5).$$

Then we can recover

$$\mathbf{s} = f^{-1}(f\mathbf{c}) \bmod \mathbf{w} = (11, 45, 41).$$

This is the same secret key as in Example 1. Moreover, we compute

$$\begin{aligned} E_{\mathbf{w}}(\mathbf{x}) = \mathbf{c} - \mathbf{s} \bmod \mathbf{w} &= (21.67, 12.07, 14.61) - (11, 45, 41) \bmod \mathbf{w} \\ &= (10.67, -32.93, -26.39) \bmod \mathbf{w} \\ &= (10.67, 56.07, 64.61). \end{aligned}$$

Therefore we can recover the same fuzzy data $\mathbf{x}$ as in Example 1:

$$\mathbf{x} = \left(\frac{10.67}{w_1}, \frac{56.07}{w_2}, \frac{64.61}{w_3} \right) = (0.11, 0.63, 0.71).$$

4.2   Attack Against Linear Sketch Scheme of [7]

Here we give our recovering attack against the linear sketch scheme of [7]. We use the same notation as in Subsect. 3.2. Given a sketch $\mathbf{c} = \mathtt{Sketch}(\mathbf{s}, \mathbf{x}) = \mathbf{s} + T\mathbf{x} \bmod p \in \mathbb{R}_p^n$ and public information p and T with $p \geq T$ (but $\mathbf{s} \in \mathbb{F}_p^n$ and $\mathbf{x} \in [0, 1)^n$ are unknown). For the fuzzy data $\mathbf{x} = (x_1, \ldots, x_n) \in [0, 1)^n$, we assume that each component x_i is represented as

$$x_i = \frac{x_i^{(1)}}{10} + \frac{x_i^{(2)}}{10^2} + \cdots + \frac{x_i^{(r)}}{10^r} \text{ with } 0 \leq x_i^{(j)} \leq 9$$

for some fixed $r \geq 1$ (length r is independent of $1 \leq i \leq n$). This assumption is reasonable since each component of $\mathbf{x} \in [0, 1)^n$ should be represented as a floating point number in practical implementation. Under this assumption, we show a method how to recover both the fuzzy data $\mathbf{x} = (x_1, \ldots, x_n) \in [0, 1)^n$ and the secret data $\mathbf{s}$ from the sketch $\mathbf{c}$ as follows: Set $\mathbf{x}^{(j)} = (x_1^{(j)}, \ldots, x_n^{(j)}) \in \mathbb{Z}^n$ for $1 \leq j \leq r$, and then we can simply represent

$$\mathbf{x} = \frac{\mathbf{x}^{(1)}}{10} + \frac{\mathbf{x}^{(2)}}{10^2} + \cdots + \frac{\mathbf{x}^{(r)}}{10^r}. \tag{4}$$

For the sketch $\mathbf{c}$, we can also write $\mathbf{c} = \mathbf{s} + T\mathbf{x} + p\mathbf{z}$ for some $\mathbf{z} \in \mathbb{Z}^n$. Now consider

$$10^r \mathbf{c} = 10^r (\mathbf{s} + p\mathbf{z}) + T \left(10^{r-1}\mathbf{x}^{(1)} + 10^{r-2}\mathbf{x}^{(2)} + \cdots + \mathbf{x}^{(r)} \right). \tag{5}$$

By performing modulo 10 for $10^r \mathbf{c} \in \mathbb{Z}^n$, we can recovery $\mathbf{x}^{(r)}$ as

$$\mathbf{x}^{(r)} = T^{-1} (10^r \mathbf{c}) \bmod 10$$

if $\mathrm{GCD}(10, T) = 1$ (even in the case $\mathrm{GCD}(10, T) \neq 1$, we can easily modify Eq. (5) to obtain $\mathbf{x}^{(r)}$). Next we consider

$$\frac{10^r \mathbf{c} - T\mathbf{x}^{(r)}}{10} = 10^{r-1}(\mathbf{s} + p\mathbf{z}) + T\left(10^{r-2}\mathbf{x}^{(1)} + 10^{r-3}\mathbf{x}^{(2)} + \cdots + \mathbf{x}^{(r-1)}\right).$$

In the same manner as above, we can recover $\mathbf{x}^{(r-1)}$. By performing the same procedure recursively, we can recover all $\mathbf{x}^{(j)}$ and hence $\mathbf{x} \in [0, 1)^n$. More specifically, from $j = r - 1$ down to $j = 1$, we perform

$$\mathbf{x}^{(j)} = T^{-1}\left(\frac{10^r \mathbf{c} - T\left(\mathbf{x}^{(r)} + 10\mathbf{x}^{(r-1)} + \cdots + 10^{r-j-1}\mathbf{x}^{(j+1)}\right)}{10^{r-j}}\right) \bmod 10$$

in order to recover $\mathbf{x}^{(j)}$. Once the exact fuzzy data $\mathbf{x} \in [0, 1)^n$ is obtained, we can also recover $\mathbf{s} \in \mathbb{F}_p$ by computing $\mathbf{c} - T\mathbf{x} \bmod p$.

Example 4. In this example, we apply our recovering attack against the sketch $\mathbf{c} = (175.33, 170.89, 131.13)$ with public information $T = 203$ and $p = 211$, generated in Example 2. For this example, write $\mathbf{x} = \dfrac{\mathbf{x}^{(1)}}{10} + \dfrac{\mathbf{x}^{(2)}}{10^2}$. Then our recovering attack against $\mathbf{c}$ perform the following:

$$\begin{cases} \mathbf{x}^{(2)} = T^{-1}(10^2\mathbf{c}) \bmod 10 = (1, 3, 1), \\ \mathbf{x}^{(1)} = T^{-1}\left(\dfrac{10^2\mathbf{c} - T\mathbf{x}^{(2)}}{10}\right) \bmod 10 = (1, 6, 7). \end{cases}$$

From this, we can recover $\mathbf{x} = (0.11, 0.63, 0.71) \in [0, 1)^3$, which is the same as in Example 2. Furthermore, we can also recover the secret key correctly as

$$\mathbf{s} = \mathbf{c} - T\mathbf{x} \bmod p = (153, 43, -13) \bmod p = (153, 43, 198).$$

5   Discussion on Simple Countermeasure

A simple countermeasure against our recovering attacks is to add noisy data ε to a sketch $\mathbf{c} = \mathtt{Sketch}(\mathbf{s}, \mathbf{x})$ to prevent from recovering the secret data $\mathbf{s}$ and the fuzzy data $\mathbf{x}$. On the other hand, small ε is only acceptable for error tolerance of fuzzy data. In this section, we consider the effect of this countermeasure.

Here we consider the case of the linear sketch scheme of [7]. We use the same notation in Subsects. 3.2 and 4.2. Let $\mathbf{c} = \mathtt{Sketch}(\mathbf{s}, \mathbf{x}) = \mathbf{s} + T\mathbf{x} \bmod p$ be a sketch with public information p and T satisfying $p \geq T$. Consider to add small noisy data $\varepsilon = (\varepsilon_1, \ldots, \varepsilon_n) \in [0, 1)^n$ to the sketch $\mathbf{c}$ as $\mathbf{c}_\varepsilon := \mathbf{c} + \varepsilon \in \mathbb{R}_p^n$. For the sketch $\mathbf{c}_\varepsilon$ with noise ε, we cannot recover the original $\mathbf{x} \in [0, 1)^n$ by our recovery attack presented in Subsect. 4.2. However, as described in Subsect. 4.2, for some $\mathbf{z} \in \mathbb{Z}^n$, we now have

$$\mathbf{c}_\varepsilon = \mathbf{s} + T\mathbf{x} + p\mathbf{z} + \varepsilon = (\mathbf{s} + p\mathbf{z}) + T\left(\mathbf{x} + \frac{\varepsilon}{T}\right).$$

By performing our recovering attack against $\mathbf{c}_\varepsilon$, we can recover

$$\mathbf{x}_\varepsilon := \mathbf{x} + \frac{\varepsilon}{T}$$

in theory and hence $\mathbf{s} \in \mathbb{F}_p$. As mentioned in the first paragraph of this section, small ε is only acceptable, and hence we might obtain the fuzzy data $\mathbf{x}_\varepsilon$ close enough to the original data $\mathbf{x}$. However, as the below example shows, our recovering attack against $\mathbf{c}_\varepsilon$ might fail *in practice* due to lack of the accuracy of floating point numbers:

Example 5. As an example of the above discussion, we consider the sketch $\mathbf{c} = (175.33, 170.89, 131.13)$ with public information $T = 203$ and $p = 211$, generated in Example 2. We take $\varepsilon = (0.021, 0.009, 0.017)$ as a noisy data. Consider $\mathbf{c}_\varepsilon = \mathbf{c} + \varepsilon = (175.351, 170.899, 131.147)$. Write

$$\mathbf{x}_\varepsilon = \frac{\mathbf{x}_\varepsilon^{(1)}}{10} + \frac{\mathbf{x}_\varepsilon^{(2)}}{10^2} + \frac{\mathbf{x}_\varepsilon^{(3)}}{10^3}$$

as in Example 4. Now we apply our recovering attack against $\mathbf{c}_\varepsilon$:

$$
\begin{cases}
\mathbf{x}_\varepsilon^{(3)} = T^{-1} \left(10^3 \mathbf{c}_\varepsilon\right) \bmod 10 = (7, 3, 9), \\[2mm]
\mathbf{x}_\varepsilon^{(2)} = T^{-1} \left(\dfrac{10^3 \mathbf{c}_\varepsilon - T\mathbf{x}_\varepsilon^{(3)}}{10}\right) \bmod 10 = (1, 3, 4), \\[3mm]
\mathbf{x}_\varepsilon^{(1)} = T^{-1} \left(\dfrac{10^3 \mathbf{c}_\varepsilon - T\left(\mathbf{x}_\varepsilon^{(3)} + 10\mathbf{x}_\varepsilon^{(2)}\right)}{10^2}\right) \bmod 10 = (3, 4, 4).
\end{cases}
$$

Then we have $\mathbf{x}_\varepsilon = (0.317, 0.433, 0.449)$ from the above computation. But this $\mathbf{x}_\varepsilon$ is neither equal nor close to the correct vector

$$
\mathbf{x} + \frac{\varepsilon}{T} = (0.11, 0.63, 0.71) + \frac{1}{T}(0.021, 0.009, 0.017)
$$
$$
= (0.1101034482\cdots, 0.6300443349\cdots, 0.7100837438\cdots).
$$

This failure is due to lack of the accuracy of floating point numbers.

Remark 1. Note that our recovering attack works correctly against the sketch $\mathbf{c}_\varepsilon$ with noise ε as long as the fuzzy data $\mathbf{x}_\varepsilon = \mathbf{x} + \dfrac{\varepsilon}{T}$ can be represented as

$$\mathbf{x}_\varepsilon = \frac{\mathbf{x}_\varepsilon^{(1)}}{10} + \frac{\mathbf{x}_\varepsilon^{(2)}}{10^2} + \cdots + \frac{\mathbf{x}_\varepsilon^{(r)}}{10^r}$$

for some length $r > 0$ and $\mathbf{x}_\varepsilon^{(j)} = (y_1^{(j)}, \ldots, y_n^{(j)}) \in \mathbb{Z}^n$ with $0 \le y_i^{(j)} \le 9$. More generally, if the fuzzy data $\mathbf{x}_\varepsilon$ can be represented as

$$\mathbf{x}_\varepsilon = \frac{\mathbf{z}^{(1)}}{q} + \frac{\mathbf{z}^{(2)}}{q^2} + \cdots + \frac{\mathbf{z}^{(s)}}{q^s}$$

for some positive integer q (e.g., $q = T$), length $s > 0$ and $\mathbf{z}^{(j)} = (z_1^{(j)}, \ldots, z_n^{(j)}) \in \mathbb{Z}^n$ with $0 \le z_i^{(j)} < q$, our recovering attack with modulus q (instead of modulus 10) can recover $\mathbf{x}_\varepsilon$. However, it seems difficult to find such q only from $\mathbf{c}_\varepsilon$.

Remark 2. Given a sketch $\mathbf{c} = (c_1, \ldots, c_n)$, we can consider $\mathbf{c}' = (c_1', \ldots c_n')$ as a new sketch with noise, where set

$$c_i' = \frac{\lfloor \theta c_i + 0.5 \rfloor}{\theta} \text{ for } 1 \le i \le n$$

for a pre-defined threshold $t = 10^{-r}$ with $\theta = 1/t = 10^r$ (i.e., it is just the rounding off operation at $1/10^r$). We expect that this procedure would not affect the authentication accuracy for large r. For example, when we set $r = 10$ and $n = 10^3$, we estimate that the probability to affect the authentication performance is about $10^{-10} \cdot 10^3 = 1/10^7$.

6   Conclusion

In this paper, we gave a recovering attack against each construction of the linear sketch schemes of [7, 10]. Our attacks are critical against fuzzy signature schemes of [7, 10]. Actually, in Fig. 1, our attacks enable us to directly recover both the signing key sk and biometric data $\mathbf{x}$ from a sketch $\mathbf{c} = \texttt{Sketch}(sk, \mathbf{x})$. The security of fuzzy signature schemes is proved in [7, 10] under the assumption that biometric data $\mathbf{x}$ are uniform over $[0, 1)^n$. Despite the security proof, our attacks can easily recover both sk and $\mathbf{x}$ embedded in any sketch $\mathbf{c} = \texttt{Sketch}(sk, \mathbf{x})$ with known denominator of $\mathbf{x}$, and our attacks are independent of the uniform assumption for $\mathbf{x}$. Furthermore, the denominator of biometric data $\mathbf{x} \in [0, 1)^n$ should be known in practical implementation, and hence our attacks give a practical threat against fuzzy signature schemes of [7, 10].

On the other hand, we might avoid our attacks in practice by just adding noisy data ε to a sketch $\mathbf{c}$. Since the failure of our attacks depends on the accuracy of floating point numbers, there must exist a trade-off between the size (or the form) of ε for failure of our attacks and the error tolerance of biometric fuzzy data for authentication. Such trade-off is an open problem, and it should be carefully discussed for practical use of fuzzy signature schemes with our simple countermeasure.

References

1. Belguechi, R., Alimi, V., Cherrier, E., Lacharme, P., Rosenberger, C.: An overview on privacy preserving biometrics. In: Yang, J. (ed.) Recent Application in Biometrics. InTech (2011)
2. Dodis, Y., Reyzin, L., Smith, A.: Fuzzy extractors: how to generate strong keys from biometrics and other noisy data. In: Cachin, C., Camenisch, J.L. (eds.) EUROCRYPT 2004. LNCS, vol. 3027, pp. 523–540. Springer, Heidelberg (2004). https://doi.org/10.1007/978-3-540-24676-3_31. Full version in SIAM J. Comput. **38**(1), 97–139 (2008)

3. Jain, A.K., Nandakumar, K., Nagar, A.: Biometric template security. EURASIP J. Adv. Signal Process. **2008**, 113:1–113:17 (2008). http://dx.doi.org/10.1155/2008/579416
4. Juels, A., Sudan, M.: A fuzzy vault scheme. Des. Codes Crypt. **38**(2), 237–257 (2006)
5. Juels, A., Wattenberg, M.: A fuzzy commitment scheme. In: Proceedings of the 6th ACM Conference on Computer and Communications Security, pp. 28–36. ACM (1999)
6. Maltoni, D., Maio, D., Jain, A.K., Prabhakar, S.: Handbook of Fingerprint Recognition, 2nd edn. Springer, Heidelberg (2009)
7. Matsuda, T., Takahashi, K., Murakami, T., Hanaoka, G.: Fuzzy signatures: relaxing requirements and a new construction. In: Manulis, M., Sadeghi, A.-R., Schneider, S. (eds.) ACNS 2016. LNCS, vol. 9696, pp. 97–116. Springer, Cham (2016). https://doi.org/10.1007/978-3-319-39555-5_6
8. Schnorr, C.P.: Efficient signature generation by smart cards. J. Cryptology **4**(3), 161–174 (1991)
9. Sutcu, Y., Sencar, H.T., Memon, N.: A secure biometric authentication scheme based on robust hashing. In: Proceedings of the 7th Workshop on Multimedia and Security, pp. 111–116. ACM (2005)
10. Takahashi, K., Matsuda, T., Murakami, T., Hanaoka, G., Nishigaki, M.: A signature scheme with a fuzzy private key. In: Malkin, T., Kolesnikov, V., Lewko, A.B., Polychronakis, M. (eds.) ACNS 2015. LNCS, vol. 9092, pp. 105–126. Springer, Cham (2015). https://doi.org/10.1007/978-3-319-28166-7_6
11. Teoh, A.B., Goh, A., Ngo, D.C.: Random multispace quantization as an analytic mechanism for biohashing of biometric and random identity inputs. IEEE Trans. Pattern Anal. Mach. Intell. **28**(12), 1892–1901 (2006)
12. Waters, B.: Efficient identity-based encryption without random oracles. In: Cramer, R. (ed.) EUROCRYPT 2005. LNCS, vol. 3494, pp. 114–127. Springer, Heidelberg (2005). https://doi.org/10.1007/11426639_7

Fast and Adaptively Secure Signatures in the Random Oracle Model from Indistinguishability Obfuscation (Short Paper)

Bei Liang$^{(\boxtimes)}$ and Aikaterini Mitrokotsa

Chalmers University of Technology, Gothenburg, Sweden
{lbei,aikmitr}@chalmers.se

Abstract. Indistinguishability obfuscation ($i\mathcal{O}$) is a powerful cryptographic tool often employed to construct a variety of core cryptographic primitives such as public key encryption and signatures. In this paper, we focus on the employment of $i\mathcal{O}$ in order to construct short signatures with strong security guarantees (*i.e.*, adaptive security) that provide a very efficient signing process for resource-constrained devices. Sahai and Waters (SW) (STOC 2014) initially explored the construction of $i\mathcal{O}$-based short signature schemes but their proposal provides selective security. Ramchen and Waters (RW) (CCS 2014) attempted to provide stronger security guarantees (*i.e.*, adaptive security) but their proposal is much more computationally expensive than the SW proposal.

In this work, we propose an $i\mathcal{O}$-based short signature scheme that provides adaptive security, fast signing for resource-constrained devices and is much more cost-efficient than the RW signature scheme. More precisely, we employ a puncturable PRF with a fixed length input to get a fast and adaptively secure signature scheme without any additional hardness assumption as in the SW signature scheme. To achieve this goal, we employ the technique of Hofheinz *et al.* called *"delayed backdoor programming"* using a random oracle, which allows to embed an execution thread that will only be invoked by special inputs generated using secret key information. Furthermore, we compare the cost of our signature scheme in terms of the cost of the underlying PRG used by the puncturable PRF. Our scheme has a much lower cost than the RW scheme, while providing strong security guarantees (*i.e.*, adaptive security).

Keywords: Signature scheme · Indistinguishability obfuscation · Puncturable pseudo-random functions

1 Introduction

The notion of indistinguishability obfuscation ($i\mathcal{O}$), initially introduced by Barak *et al.* [1], requires that the obfuscation of any two distinct (equal-size) programs that implement identical functionalities, renders them computationally

© Springer International Publishing AG 2017
J. K. Liu and P. Samarati (Eds.): ISPEC 2017, LNCS 10701, pp. 422–431, 2017.
https://doi.org/10.1007/978-3-319-72359-4_25

indistinguishable from each other. However, the problem of whether or not indistinguishability obfuscation exists and how useful it is, has been unclear until the breakthrough result of Garg et al. [2] when they proposed the first candidate construction of an efficient indistinguishability obfuscator for general programs [3]. This initial breakthrough by Garg et al. has motivated a new line of research focusing on re-exploring the construction of existing cryptographic primitives through the lens of obfuscation. For instance, Sahai and Waters [9] performed a systematic study of employing indistinguishability obfuscation to public-key encryption, short signatures, non-interactive zero-knowledge proofs, injective trapdoor functions, and oblivious transfer. This line of research is of great importance since it may lead to unexpected results and qualitatively different ways of settling cryptographic problems.

In this paper, we explore the employment of $i\mathcal{O}$ to build new signature schemes with two main properties: *(i)* they are short signatures with strong security guarantees (*i.e.*, adaptive security), and *(ii)* they provide a fast signing process suitable for resource-constrained devices (*e.g.*, sensors). The latter objective naturally leads to an *imbalanced* scheme, where the signing process is fast, while the verification process is longer; this guarantees that resource-constrained devices can sign, while computationally powerful devices will be employed for the verification. Such imbalanced schemes have been explored before *e.g.*, the research area of *delegation of computation* schemes focus on saving resources in computationally weak devices.

Although current obfuscation candidates may lead to very slow verification process, current work on obfuscation techniques (esp. on implementing specific functionalities) is under development, rendering plausible the realisation of systems with reasonable performance in the near future.

SW short signature. We begin by reviewing the selectively-secure signature scheme of Sahai-Waters (SW) based on $i\mathcal{O}$ and puncturable pseudorandom functions (PRFs) as well as one-way functions [9]. In this approach, the secret signing key is simply a key k for a puncturable PRF $F_k(\cdot)$, and a message m is signed by simply evaluating $\sigma = F_k(m)$. The public verification key is an indistinguishability obfuscation $\hat{C} \leftarrow i\mathcal{O}(C_k)$ of a circuit C_k that on input a message/signature pair (m, σ), verifies that the value $f(\sigma)$ is equal to the value $f(F_k(m))$. Verifying any σ for m is simply done by executing the program $\hat{C}$ on input (m, σ). One significant limitation of this scheme is that it only satisfies unforgeability against a *selective* attacker. In this notion of security, the attacker is forced to preselect the message m^*, he will attempt to forge, before seeing the verification key and before querying for signatures on other messages.

RW short signature. In CCS'14, Ramchen and Waters (RW) [8] explored methods for achieving *adaptively secure* obfuscation-derived signatures in the standard model. More precisely, they employed the prefix-guessing technique of Hohenberger-Waters [6]. Their signature scheme consists of two main pieces. The first piece is a one-time signature for a tag t, which is the value of a puncturable PRF on the tag t. The second signature piece is the ability to sign the tag t according to the prefix-guessing technique [6]. A signature on the message is the tag along with the xor of these two parts. To generate the first piece, they choose a tag t of λ bits and compute $s_1 = \oplus_{i=1}^{\ell} F_1(K_1, t\|i\|m(i))$, where $F_1(K_1, \cdot)$ is a puncturable PRF with appropriate input length and $m(i)$ is the i-th bit of an ℓ-bit message m. To generate the second piece they choose λ puncturable PRFs $F_{2,i}(K_{2,i}, \cdot)$ for $i \in [1, \lambda]$ which takes inputs of i bits, and they compute $s_2 = \oplus_{i=1}^{\lambda} F_{2,i}(K_{2,i}, t^{(i)})$ where $t^{(i)}$ denotes the first i bits of t. A signature for the message m is $(t, s = s_1 \oplus s_2)$.

To improve the signing process (i.e., fast sign) of their scheme, they also give a slightly modified second construction. The primary change is that instead of using λ different punctured PRF systems, each with a different domain size, a punctured PRF with a variable length domain is used in the second piece of the signature. Ramchen and Waters [8] have shown that the variable-input-length punctured PRF can be created by a length tripling PRG. We note that in the generation of the first piece of the signature, ℓ values of one fixed-input-length punctured PRF must be evaluated, and in the generation of the second piece of signature, either values of λ different fixed-input-length punctured PRFs or λ values of one variable-input-length punctured PRF must be evaluated. All these require many more computations than the SW signature scheme.

Our contribution. This state of affairs has motivated us to explore the following ambitious question: *Is it possible to construct an efficient (i.e., fast signing) and adaptively secure short signature scheme, in which the signature for a message m is a value of a puncturable PRF on m?* More precisely, in this paper we consider the problem of modifying the SW signature scheme [9] to accommodate adaptive security, where the attacker can adaptively choose which message he will forge on, and provide a positive answer to the above question. Instead of resorting to the tag-based technique of the RW scheme, which requires using either λ different fixed-input-length punctured PRFs or one variable-input-length punctured PRF, we explore to simply use one puncturable PRF with a fixed length input to get a fast signature as the SW signature scheme does, while at the same time providing strong security guarantees[1]. In particular, we present a fast signing, short signature scheme that is adaptively secure in the random oracle model relying on $i\mathcal{O}$, puncturable pseudorandom functions (PRFs) and one-way functions.

In the random oracle (RO) model, a trivial generic way to transform the selective security of the SW signature scheme to adaptive security is by hashing the message prior to signing. That is the signature for a message m is the value $\sigma = F_k(H(m))$. Now the public verification key is an indistinguishability obfuscation of a new circuit C'_k that on input a hash-value/signature pair $(H(m), \sigma)$, verifies that $f(\sigma) = f(F_k(H(m)))$. Let q_H be the number of hash queries during the game. Since with probability $1/q_H$ the simulator correctly guesses the i-th hash query i.e., the query for m^*, it can then use the punctured key $k\{h^*\}$ to answer the signing queries (let h^* is the value of i-th hash query).

One could consider that the above hash-then-sign method is very trivial by employing the hash function on the message to obtain a value $h = H(m)$ with

---

[1] Contrary to our scheme the SW signature scheme provides weaker security guarantees (i.e., selective security).

uniform distribution, thus resulting in the pseudorandomness of PRF $\sigma = F_k(h)$. However, we are motivated to seek another non-trivial method that can lead to the pseudorandomness of σ in the SW signature scheme in the random oracle model. Namely, we are taking advantage of a hash function in order to produce a new PRF key k' and thus to obtain the signature $\sigma = F_{k'}(m)$ on the message m. To achieve this goal, we employ Hofheinz et al.'s technique [5], called *"delayed backdoor programming"* using a programmable random oracle.

At a high level, in our construction the secret signing key is still a key $\tilde{K}$ for a puncturable PRF $F_{\tilde{K}}$, where $\tilde{K}$ is computed by a puncturable PRF F_K on input $w = H(m)$ and the signature σ on the message m is still $\sigma = F_{\tilde{K}}(m)$. The public verification key VK consists of an obfuscated program as well as a hash function H modelled as a random oracle. Let us see how to create a program Verify, that will be obfuscated to create VK. The program will actually follow a similar structure as the program of Hofheinz et al.'s [5] universal parameters scheme, which allows to embed an execution thread that will only be invoked by special inputs generated by using secret key information. Informally speaking, the program Verify takes as input a random string w and consists of two main stages. In the first stage, it checks to see if the random string is an encoding, which is produced by a "hidden trigger" using secret key information. This step will either output a string $\alpha \in \{0,1\}^n$ or it will output $\perp$ to indicate failure. For a uniformly randomly chosen string w, this step will output $\perp$ with very high probability, since the trigger values are encoded sparsely. Moreover, without the secret information it should be difficult to distinguish an encoding from a uniformly sampled string. If the first step fails, it will move into its second stage. At this point the program will compute the signing key $\tilde{K} = F_K(w)$ from a puncturable PRF F_K. Now instead of directly comparing the value of $f(\sigma)$ with the value $f(F_{\tilde{K}}(m))$, we add a level of indirection as Hofheinz et al. does. The program Verify will output the obfuscated program of the $C_{\tilde{K}}$ as in the SW signature scheme.

Our proof of adaptive security proceeds by a sequence of hybrids. Let any PPT adversary $\mathcal{A}$ make at most a polynomial number $Q = Q(\lambda)$ (unique) queries $m_1, \ldots, m_Q$ to the RO with outputs $w_1, \ldots, w_Q$. We will perform a hybrid of Q outer steps, where at outer step i, we move from using the puncturable PRF key K to output the obfuscated program $i\mathcal{O}(C_{\tilde{K}_i})$ (which is the output of the program Verify on input w_i), to having $i\mathcal{O}(C_{\tilde{K}_i})$ being encoded in w_i itself for $\tilde{K}_i = F_K(w_i)$. More precisely, following the pseudorandomness of the puncturable PRF F_K, we can let a program g to be $i\mathcal{O}(C_{\tilde{K}_i})$, where $\tilde{K}_i$ is chosen independently and then set w_i to be a "hidden trigger" encoding of g. Next, we use punctured programming techniques to replace the normal computation of the program $C_{\tilde{K}_i}$ with a hardwired and randomly sampled value for $\hat{p}_i = f(F_{\tilde{K}_i}(m_i))$. At this point on computing $i\mathcal{O}(\text{Verify})(w_i)$ the output will be the program $g = i\mathcal{O}(C_{\tilde{K}_i, \hat{p}_i, m_i})$. In the final hybrid any poly-time attacker $\mathcal{A}$ that succeeds in outputting a forgery (m^*, σ^*) with non-negligible probability can be used to find a preimage of $\hat{p}_i$ for the one-way function f–that is σ^*, which breaks the security of one way functions.

Comparison of Cost. We compare the cost of the SW [9], the RW [8] schemes and our proposed signature in terms of the cost of the underlying PRG used by the puncturable PRF and the provided security.

Table 1. Comparison of our short signature scheme to the SW and RW schemes.

Scheme	Security	Model	Employed primitives	Cost
SW14 [9]	Selective	Standard	$i\mathcal{O}$ & fixed-length input PRF	$g_D \cdot \ell$
RW14 [8]	Adaptive	Standard	$i\mathcal{O}$ & fixed-length input PRF variable-length input PRF	$g_D \cdot (\lambda + 2\ell - 1) + g_T \cdot \lambda$
Ours	Adaptive	Random oracle	$i\mathcal{O}$ & fixed-length input PRF	Less than $g_D \cdot (2\ell)$

We note (as seen in Table 1) that although the RW scheme is proven to be adaptively secure in the standard model, their proposal is quite heavy computationally. We have chosen to provide a more efficient (fast signing), adaptively secure solution suitable for resource-constrained devices at the cost of employing the random oracle model.

2   Preliminaries

2.1   Signature Schemes

Definition 1. *A signature scheme with message space $\mathcal{M}(\lambda)$, signature key space $\mathcal{SK}(\lambda)$ and verification key space $\mathcal{VK}(\lambda)$ consists of the PPT algorithms $SIG = (SIG.Setup, SIG.Sign, SIG.Verify)$:*

- *Key generation. SIG.Setup is a randomized algorithm that takes as input the security parameter 1^λ and outputs the signing key $sk \in \mathcal{SK}$ and the verification key $vk \in \mathcal{VK}$.*
- *Signature generation. SIG.Sign takes as input the signing key $sk \in \mathcal{SK}$ and a message $m \in \mathcal{M}$ and outputs a signature σ.*
- *Verification. SIG.Verify takes as input a verification key $vk \in \mathcal{VK}$, a message $m \in \mathcal{M}$ and a signature σ and outputs either 0 or 1.*

Correctness. *For all $\lambda \in \mathbb{N}$, $(vk, sk) \leftarrow SIG.Setup(1^\lambda)$, messages $m \in \mathcal{M}(\lambda)$, we require that $SIG.Verify(vk, m, SIG.Sign(sk, m)) = 1$.*
We say that a signature scheme $SIG = (SIG.Setup, SIG.Sign, SIG.Verify)$ is existentially unforgeable under adaptively chosen message attacks if

$$\Pr[Exp_{SIG,\mathcal{A}}^{uf\text{-}cma}(\lambda) = 1] \leq negl(\lambda)$$

for some negligible function negl and for all PPT attackers $\mathcal{A}$, where $Exp_{SIG,\mathcal{A}}^{uf\text{-}cma}(\lambda)$ is the following experiment with the scheme SIG and an attacker $\mathcal{A}$:

1. *$(vk, sk) \leftarrow SIG.Setup(1^\lambda)$.*
2. *$(m^*, \sigma^*) \leftarrow \mathcal{A}^{Sign(sk,\cdot)}(1^\lambda, vk)$.*

If $SIG.Verify(vk, m^*, \sigma^*) = 1$ and m^* was not queried to the $Sign(sk, \cdot)$ oracle, then return 1, else return 0.

2.2 Indistinguishability Obfuscation

Definition 2 (Indistinguishability obfuscation [2]). *A probabilistic polynomial time (PPT) algorithm $i\mathcal{O}$ is said to be an indistinguishability obfuscator for a circuits class $\{\mathcal{C}_\lambda\}$, if the following conditions are satisfied:*

- *For all security parameters $\lambda \in \mathbb{N}$, for all $C \in C_\lambda$, for all inputs x, we have that:*

$$\Pr[C'(x) = C(x) : C' \leftarrow i\mathcal{O}(\lambda, C)] = 1.$$

- *For any (not necessarily uniform) PPT adversaries (Samp, D), there exists a negligible function $negl(\cdot)$ such that the following holds: if $\Pr[\forall x, C_0(x) = C_1(x) : (C_0, C_1, \sigma) \leftarrow \mathsf{Samp}(1^\lambda)] > 1 - negl(\lambda)$, then we have:*

$$\big| \Pr[D(\sigma, i\mathcal{O}(\lambda, C_0)) = 1 : (C_0, C_1, \sigma) \leftarrow \mathsf{Samp}(1^\lambda)]$$
$$- \Pr[D(\sigma, i\mathcal{O}(\lambda, C_1)) = 1 : (C_0, C_1, \sigma) \leftarrow \mathsf{Samp}(1^\lambda)] \big| \leq negl(\lambda).$$

2.3 Puncturable PRFs

Definition 3. *A puncturable family of PRFs F mapping is given by a triple of Turing Machines $(\mathsf{Key}_F, \mathsf{Puncture}_F, \mathsf{Eval}_F)$, and a pair of computable functions $\tau_1(\cdot)$ and $\tau_2(\cdot)$, satisfying the following conditions:*

- *[**Functionality preserved under puncturing**]. For every PPT adversary $\mathcal{A}$ such that $\mathcal{A}(1^\lambda)$ outputs a point $x^* \in \{0,1\}^{\tau_1(\lambda)}$, then for all $x \in \{0,1\}^{\tau_1(\lambda)}$ where $x \neq x^*$, we have that:*

$$\Pr[\mathsf{Eval}_F(K, x) = \mathsf{Eval}_F(K_{x^*}, x) :$$
$$K \leftarrow \mathsf{Key}_F(1^\lambda), K_{x^*} \leftarrow \mathsf{Puncture}_F(K, x^*)] = 1.$$

- *[**Pseudorandom at punctured point**]. For every PPT adversary $(\mathcal{A}_1, \mathcal{A}_2)$ such that $\mathcal{A}_1(1^\lambda)$ outputs a point $x^* \in \{0,1\}^{\tau_1(\lambda)}$ and a state σ, consider an experiment where $K \leftarrow \mathsf{Key}_F(1^\lambda)$ and $K_{x^*} \leftarrow \mathsf{Puncture}_F(K, x^*)$. Then, we have:*

$$\big| \Pr[\mathcal{A}_2(\sigma, K_{x^*}, x^*, \mathsf{Eval}_F(K, x^*)) = 1]$$
$$- \Pr[\mathcal{A}_2(\sigma, K_{x^*}, x^*, U_{\tau_2(\lambda)}) = 1] \big| = negl(\lambda),$$

where $negl(\cdot)$ is a negligible function and $U_{\tau_2(\lambda)}$ denotes the uniform distribution over $\tau_2(\lambda)$ bits.

Theorem 1 [9]. *If one-way functions exist, then for all efficiently computable functions $\tau_1(\lambda)$ and $\tau_2(\lambda)$, there exists a puncturable family of PRFs that maps $\tau_1(\lambda)$ bits to $\tau_2(\lambda)$ bits.*

3   Adaptively Secure Short Signatures in the RO Model

The proposed construction is parameterized over a security parameter λ and has message space $\mathcal{M} = \mathcal{M}(\lambda) = \{0,1\}^{\ell(\lambda)}$ for some polynomial function $\ell(\cdot)$. We use a random oracle $H : \{0,1\}^\ell \to \{0,1\}^{n^2+n}$, a PRG mapping n-bit inputs to $2n$-bit outputs, a one way function $f(\cdot)$ mapping ℓ'-bit inputs to $\hat{\ell}$-bit outputs, and a hash function $H : \{0,1\}^\ell \to \{0,1\}^{n^2+n}$. We also make use of four different puncturable PRFs in our construction:

- $F_1^{(n)}$ is a sequence of $2n$ puncturable PRFs $\{F_1^{1,0}, F_1^{1,1}, \ldots, F_1^{n,0}, F_1^{n,1}\}$ that each maps n-bit inputs to n-bit outputs. The corresponding key sequence is denoted by $K_1^{(n)} = \{K_1^{1,0}, K_1^{1,1}, \ldots, K_1^{n,0}, K_1^{n,1}\}$. Then, on an n-bit input v, the output of the function $F_1^{(n)}$ is denoted by $F_1^{(n)}(K_1^{(n)}, v)$.
- $F_2(K_2, \cdot)$ is a puncturable PRF mapping (n^2+n)-bit inputs to n_1-bit outputs, where n_1 is the size of K_3 for the puncturable PRF $F_3(K_3, \cdot)$.
- $F_2'(K_2', \cdot)$ is a puncturable PRF mapping (n^2+n)-bit inputs to n_2-bit outputs, where n_2 is the size of the randomness r used by the $i\mathcal{O}$.
- $F_3(K_3, \cdot)$ is a puncturable PRF mapping ℓ-bit inputs to ℓ'-bit outputs.

Setup(1^λ): On input 1^λ, the Setup algorithm firstly samples the PRF keys $K_1^{(n)}, K_2, K_2'$. Next, it creates an obfuscation of the program Verify as depicted in Fig. 1(a). The size of the program is padded to be the maximum of the size of itself and the corresponding programs Verify in the various hybrid games, as described in the full version of our article [7]. The verification key, VK, is the obfuscated program $i\mathcal{O}([\text{Verify}])$. The secret key SK is $(K_1^{(n)}, K_2, K_2')$.

Sign$(SK, m \in \mathcal{M})$: To sign a message m, the Sign algorithm queries the random oracle H to obtain $H(m) = u\|v$ and computes $K_3 = F_2(K_2, u\|v)$. It outputs $\sigma = F_3(K_3, m)$.

Verify(VK, m, σ): To verify a signature σ on message m, the Verify algorithm queries the random oracle H to get $H(m) = u\|v$ and then evaluates the obfuscated program $i\mathcal{O}(\text{Verify})$ with inputs $H(m) = u\|v$ to obtain the obfuscated program $i\mathcal{O}(P_{K_3}; r')$. Then, it runs the program $i\mathcal{O}(P_{K_3}; r')$ on inputs (m, σ) and returns its output.

Theorem 2. *If $i\mathcal{O}$ is a secure indistinguishability obfuscator, $F_1^{(n)}$, F_2, F_2', F_3 are secure puncturable PRFs, $f(\cdot)$ is a one way function, and PRG is a secure pseudo-random generator, then our signature scheme given above is existentially unforgeable under chosen message attacks in the random oracle model.*

Our proof of adaptive security proceeds by a sequence of hybrids. Let any PPT adversary $\mathcal{A}$ make at most a polynomial number $Q = Q(\lambda)$ (unique) queries $m_1, \ldots, m_Q$ to the RO with outputs $w_1, \ldots, w_Q$. We will perform a hybrid of Q outer steps, where at outer step i, we move from using the puncturable PRF key K to output the obfuscated program $i\mathcal{O}(C_{\tilde{K}_i})$ (which is the output of the program Verify on input w_i), to having $i\mathcal{O}(C_{\tilde{K}_i})$ being encoded in w_i itself for $\tilde{K}_i = F_K(w_i)$. More precisely, following the pseudorandomness of the

---

Verify

Hardwired into the circuit: $K_1^{(n)}, K_2, K_2'$.

Input to the circuit: $u = u[1]\| \ldots \|u[n] \in \{0,1\}^{n^2}$, $v \in \{0,1\}^n$.

Algorithm:
1. Compute $F_1^{(n)}(K_1^{(n)}, v) = (y_{1,0}, y_{1,1}), \ldots, (y_{n,0}, y_{n,1})$.
2. For $i = 1, \ldots, n$, if $u[i] = y_{i,0}$ set $\alpha_i = 0$ else if $u[i] = y_{i,1}$ set $\alpha_i = 1$ else set $\alpha_i = \bot$.
3. If $\alpha \in \{0,1\}^n$ contains no $\bot$s, output α.
4. Else set $K_3 = F_2(K_2, u\|v)$, $r' = F_2'(K_2', u\|v)$. Output $i\mathcal{O}(P_{K_3}; r')$ of the program a P_{K_3} of Figure 1(b).

(a) The program **Verify**

P_{K_3}

Hardwired into the circuit: K_3.

Input to the circuit: $m \in \{0,1\}^\ell$, $\sigma \in \{0,1\}^{\ell'}$.

Algorithm:
1. Test if $f(\sigma) = f(F_3(K_3, m))$. Output accept if true, reject if false.

(b) The program P_{K_3}

Fig. 1. The description of the programs Verify and P_{K_3}

puncturable PRF F_K, we can let a program g to be $i\mathcal{O}(C_{\tilde{K}_i})$, where $\tilde{K}_i$ is chosen independently and then set w_i to be a "hidden trigger" encoding of g. Next, we use punctured programming techniques to replace the normal computation of the program $C_{\tilde{K}_i}$ with a hardwired and randomly sampled value for $\hat{p}_i = f(F_{\tilde{K}_i}(m_i))$. At this point on computing $i\mathcal{O}(\text{Verify})(w_i)$ the output will be the program $g = i\mathcal{O}(C_{\tilde{K}_i, \hat{p}_i, m_i})$. In the final hybrid any poly-time attacker $\mathcal{A}$ that succeeds in outputting a forgery (m^*, σ^*) with non-negligible probability can be used to find a preimage of $\hat{p}_i$ for the one-way function f–that is σ^*, which breaks the security of one way functions. The complete proof is provided in the full version of this article [7].

4   Analysis of Costs

In this section, we evaluate the cost of the Sahai-Waters signature [9] (selectively secure), Ramchen and Waters signature [8] (adaptively secure in the standard model) and our proposed signature (adaptively secure in the random oracle model) in terms of the computation of the puncturable PRFs involved in the signing algorithm, which can be constructed by a pseudorandom generator based on GGM [4] trees. We express the cost of the computation of puncturable PRFs involved in the signing algorithm of each scheme in terms of the underlying length-doubling and length-tripling PRGs.

Let g_D be the cost of the length-doubling PRG and g_T be the cost of the length-tripling PRG. We assume that the messages to be signed are ℓ-bits and the size of the image range of the hash function is $|H(\cdot)|$.

Sahai-Waters signature [9]. This scheme makes a single call to the fixed-input-length puncturable PRF on an ℓ-bit message. This call traverses the GGM tree according to the message bits, requiring ℓ invocations of the length-doubling PRG. The cost is therefore $g_D \cdot \ell$.

Ramchen and Waters signature [8]. This scheme calls the fixed-length puncturable PRF once on each of $\lambda + \lg \ell + 1$ inputs. Since each input has the same λ-bit suffix, the GGM tree can be first traversed to a depth of λ, and then a depth-first search is performed to an additional $\lg \ell + 1$ depth. Thus, $\lambda + 2(2^{\lg \ell} - 1) + 1 = \lambda + 2\ell - 1$ calls are made to the length-doubling PRG. In addition the scheme evaluates the variable-length puncturable PRF once on an λ-bit input, which requires λ calls to the length-tripling PRG. Therefore the total cost is $g_D \cdot (\lambda + 2\ell - 1) + g_T \cdot \lambda$.

Our signature scheme. Our adaptively secure scheme makes a call to the puncturable PRF on an $|H(\cdot)|$-bits input and a call to the puncturable PRF on an ℓ-bit message. This call traverses the GGM tree according to the message bits, requiring $|H(\cdot)|$ invocations of the length-doubling PRG. The cost is therefore $g_D \cdot (|H(\cdot)| + \ell)$. Since the hash function is a one-way compression function, then it holds that $|H(\cdot)| < \ell$. Therefore, the total cost of our scheme is less than $g_D \cdot (2\ell)$, which is slightly more than the cost of the SW scheme and a lot less than the cost of RW scheme.

Table 1 (Sect. 1) summarises the comparison between our proposed scheme and the SW and RW schemes. We note that although the RW scheme is proven to be adaptively secure in the standard model, their proposal is quite heavy computationally. We have chosen to provide a more efficient (fast signing), adaptively secure solution suitable for resource-constrained devices at the cost of employing the random oracle model.

We note that, although the RW scheme is proven to be adaptively secure in the standard model, while our scheme is secure in the random oracle, the efficiency gain made by our scheme is outweighed by the loss in security.

5   Conclusion

In this paper, we explore the methods for achieving adaptively secure obfuscation-derived signatures. In particular, relying on iO and puncturable pseudorandom functions (PRFs) as well as one-way functions we present a signature scheme that is adaptively secure in the random oracle model.

Acknowledgements. This work was partially supported by the People Programme (Marie Curie Actions) of the European Union's Seventh Framework Programme (FP7/2007-2013) under REA grant agreement no. 608743.

References

1. Barak, B., Goldreich, O., Impagliazzo, R., Rudich, S., Sahai, A., Vadhan, S., Yang, K.: On the (im)possibility of obfuscating programs. In: Kilian, J. (ed.) CRYPTO 2001. LNCS, vol. 2139, pp. 1–18. Springer, Heidelberg (2001). https://doi.org/10.1007/3-540-44647-8_1
2. Garg, S., Gentry, C., Halevi, S., Raykova, M., Sahai, A., Waters, B.: Candidate indistinguishability obfuscation and functional encryption for all circuits. In: FOCS (2013)
3. Garg, S., Gentry, C., Halevi, S.: Candidate multilinear maps from ideal lattices. In: Johansson, T., Nguyen, P.Q. (eds.) EUROCRYPT 2013. LNCS, vol. 7881, pp. 1–17. Springer, Heidelberg (2013). https://doi.org/10.1007/978-3-642-38348-9_1
4. Goldreich, O., Goldwasser, S., Micali, S.: How to construct random functions. J. ACM **33**(4), 792–807 (1986)
5. Hofheinz, D., Jager, T., Khurana, D., Sahai, A., Waters, B., Zhandry, M.: How to generate and use universal parameters. Cryptology ePrint Archive, Report 2014/507 (2014). http://eprint.iacr.org/
6. Hohenberger, S., Waters, B.: Short and stateless signatures from the RSA assumption. In: Halevi, S. (ed.) CRYPTO 2009. LNCS, vol. 5677, pp. 654–670. Springer, Heidelberg (2009). https://doi.org/10.1007/978-3-642-03356-8_38
7. Liang, B., Mitrokotsa, A.: Fast and adaptively secure signatures in the random oracle model from indistinguishability obfuscation. Cryptology ePrint Archive: Report 2017/969
8. Ramchen, K., Waters, B.: Fully secure and fast signing from obfuscation. In: Proceedings of the 2014 ACM SIGSAC Conference on Computer and Communications Security, pp. 659–673. ACM (2014)
9. Sahai, A., Waters, B.: How to use indistinguishability obfuscation: deniable encryption, and more. In: STOC, pp. 475–484 (2014)

Authentication

EyeSec: A Practical Shoulder-Surfing Resistant Gaze-Based Authentication System

Na Li[1], Qianhong Wu[1](✉), Jingwen Liu[2], Wei Hu[2], Bo Qin[3], and Wei Wu[4]

[1] School of Electronic and Information Engineering,
Beihang University, Beijing 100191, China
lina_buaa_work@163.com, qianhong.wu@buaa.edu.cn
[2] Potevio Information Technology Co., Ltd., Beijing, China
[3] Key Laboratory of Data Engineering and Knowledge Engineering,
Ministry of Education, School of Information, Renmin University of China,
Beijing 100872, China
bo.qin@ruc.edu.cn
[4] Fujian Provincial Key Laboratory of Network Security and Cryptology,
School of Mathematics and Informatics, Fujian Normal University,
Fuzhou 350117, Fujian, China

Abstract. With ubiquitous use of electronic devices where personal information is often stored, secure authentication is greatly underscored. As conventional password entry approaches are vulnerable to shoulder-surfing, gaze-based authentication approaches have been developed, but most of them require extra eye trackers which usually rely on special hardware and are too expensive for ordinary people. Aimed at both shoulder-surfing resistance and practicality, we present EyeSec, a gaze-based authentication system which exploits state-of-art gaze tracking technology without requirement for additional hardware except for a webcam. EyeSec offers three kinds of authentications, i.e., gaze-based PIN, gaze-based pattern and gaze-based captcha. According to the results of experiment, the best-performing participants, aged between 21 and 35, achieve average 76.2%, 90.0%, 100.0% success rate for passing the three kinds of authentications, respectively, which makes gaze-based authentication from theory to practice.

Keywords: Gaze-based authentication · Gaze tracking
Shoulder-surfing · Usable security · Gaze-based captcha

1 Introduction

With the ubiquitous utilization of electronic devices such as PC, smartphone and tablet, personal data and important information are often stored in these devices to make electronic access easier. There are usually solely vulnerable log-in passwords to keep others outdoor, which underscores the security of the passwords. Conventional password entry methods, especially those based on keyboard or touchscreen, are susceptible to shoulder-surfing attacks, i.e., attackers

© Springer International Publishing AG 2017
J. K. Liu and P. Samarati (Eds.): ISPEC 2017, LNCS 10701, pp. 435–453, 2017.
https://doi.org/10.1007/978-3-319-72359-4_26

may obtain users' passwords by observing the input process through a camera or binoculars or just watching through users' shoulders.

In spite of the ease-of-use to log in the systems with PINs or graphical pattern passwords in daily life, shoulder-surfing attacks against user passwords is a tricky problem. A lot of information about the passwords is exposed via finger movements and can be easily acquired by attackers when users input passwords by typing or mouse-clicking. As one may notice, the finger positions on the keyboard or the feedback on the interactive screen reveal the input content and cause information leakage when users type text or click objects. In contrast, eye movements are much more inconspicuous when applying gaze interaction. With proper design for feedback, gaze-based password entry can effectively reduce shoulder-surfing.

Several gaze-based authentication schemes have been proposed to mitigate shoulder-surfing, where the key idea is to substitute the traditional password entry by gaze-based password entry [3,7,13,17,21]. Nevertheless, most previous research remains at theoretical level due to the requirement for highly accurate eye trackers when implementing the schemes. Commercial eye trackers which provide high precision usually rely on tailored hardware and are not affordable to ordinary people. The high expense of commercial eye trackers might not come from the production cost of special hardware but be paid for the scientific research investment, which exactly indicates the prospect demanding for research about low-cost as well as precise gaze tracking technologies.

In recent years, gaze tracking technologies have been developed due to the dramatic advance in computer science and the growing attention attracted to the emerging gaze interaction [12,14,15,18,19]. As mentioned above, the most promising work is to devise gaze tracking methods which are non-invasive, accurate, low-cost, easy-to-use, calibration-free and head-free. Unfortunately, until now there have been no existing applications or systems meeting all the requests for accuracy, cost and user experience simultaneously. Although a number of pervasive low-cost gaze tracking methods eliminate tailored hardware and can be implemented on universal electronic devices, like PC and smartphone, lack of precision is a formidable obstacle for widespread, which make sense that precision becomes the most vital factor to assess the quality of them [22,24,25].

Fortunately, compared to some accurate human-computer interactive applications, gaze-based authentication like gaze-based PIN and gaze-based graphical pattern password usually have less and larger interactive objects displayed on the screen which compensates for the lack of precision of the underlying gaze tracking technologies.

In this paper, we present EyeSec, a practical versatile shoulder-surfing resistant gaze-based authentication system that provides gaze-based PIN, gaze-based pattern and gaze-based captcha authentication schemes. The underlying gaze tracking technology requires no special hardware and can be easily implemented in common electronic devices. Moreover, with password authentication retained, the approach proposed can be incorporated in multi-factor authentication schemes [9,10]. Multi-threshold deciding mechanism is also proposed to tackle Midas Touch problem [11] in gaze interaction. A 2-phase experiment is conducted to evaluate the usability and security of EyeSec where the PHASE 1 contains overall analysis and human factors estimation and the PHASE 2 assesses the capability in shoulder-surfing reduction of gaze-based PIN and gaze-based pattern through a guessing-password study.

2   Related Work

Passwords have been indispensable in daily human-computer interaction. Password owners are likely to get into big trouble when encountering important passwords stealing. However, conventional password input approaches, especially keyboard-based and touchscreen-based, can be vulnerable to shoulder-surfing attacks. According to research of [5], the lowest average success rate of smartphone unlocking shoulder-surfing attacks is 10.9% with 6-digit PIN in the single view treatment which is fairly high for password security. And the success rate with respect to smartphone 4-length pattern with lines authentication is 94.67% in the in-person study. That means the conventional pattern passwords nearly have no capability to be a secure shield in front of skilled shoulder-surfing attackers.

The first line of research addresses such security issues by applying gaze-based authentication approaches. While amounts of shoulder-surfing resistant gaze-based authentication schemes are proposed, few of them provide practical systems owing to the reliance on commercial eye trackers. Manu Kumar et al. present EyePassword, a novel gaze-based password entry approach implemented with Tobii 1750 eye tracker [13]. EyeDent adopts another password entry scheme in which user's selections are determined through automatic clustering of gaze points, but it still depends on the EyeTech Digital Systems TM3 eye tracker [21]. Gaze-based cued-recall graphical passwords are presented and improved in [3,7] to mitigate shoulder-surfing while Tobii eye trackers are utilized to estimate gaze. Commercial eye trackers with high accuracy require special hardware, such as glasses, head-mounted devices, or remote control bar, and are too expensive, so they are usually used in laboratory research and market investigation. In consequence, gaze-based password entry remains novel because there are no low-cost gaze tracking technologies require no special hardware and provide as high precision as commercial eye trackers do.

Another category of related work can be incorporated into the research of reliable, economical and easy-to-use eye tracking technologies. Gaze tracking algorithms are basically divided into model-based approaches and appearance-based approaches [8]. The best-performing systems including commercial eye trackers are mostly model-based [12,18,22]. However, model-based approaches usually rely on special equipment like light sources, infrared camera or multiple cameras to achieve sufficient data. Despite quantities of research in building versatile model-based eye trackers attempting to remove the special equipment, they lost the advantage in reliable gaze estimation. In contrast, appearance-based approaches concern the whole pixels and estimate gaze direction or gaze position without explicitly reconstructing 3D facial model [14,15,19,24,25]. Two remarkable works in gaze tracking are OpenFace [2] and Webgazer [16]. Open-Face is an open-source toolkit for detecting facial landmarks, head pose and eye gaze in images or videos as well as through a webcam, where the main technologies are based on state-of-the-art facial detection algorithm [1]. Webgazer is an online eye tracking library which performs real-time eye tracking through continuous self-calibration. Compared to commercial eye trackers, those freely available tools are far more inexpensive, and therefore can be affordable for most ordinary users although they exhibit lower accuracy in gaze estimation.

3   The Proposed EyeSec

We introduce EyeSec, a shoulder-surfing resistant gaze-based authentication system with only a single webcam or a common USB camera needed. Without requirement for special hardware like infrared lights, special glasses, head-mounted devices and so on, the system can be deployed on universal electronic devices. For instance, such system can be redesigned for vehicle drivers to securely communicate with each other even when they are driving and certainly a secure vehicle network is required [23]. Moreover, taking advantage of publicity of research in related realm, the cost for gaze-based authentication might be cut down to almost zero. EyeSec might be the first step towards affordable widespread gaze-based authentication system.

3.1   System Model

EyeSec consists of a gaze tracking module and an user authentication module (see Fig. 1). The user authentication module is further composed of three independent sub-modules each of which provides an authentication scheme corresponding to a certain usage scenario. Gaze-based PIN and gaze-based pattern password simulate the prevalent simple password input schemes to reduce shoulder-surfing as well as retain the ease-of-use of the PIN and the pattern password. Gaze-based captcha is devised to perform separation between human and machine and can be a candidate for next generation of captcha.

3.2   Real-Time Gaze Estimation

The main idea of gaze-based authentication is exploiting users' gazes for password entry to get rid of finger movements in conventional password entry methods. Traditional human-computer interaction comprises two categories of activities, localization and activation. Localization is implemented by moving eye fixations on the screen while activation usually achieved through a period of dwelling. A look & shoot gaze-interactive method is presented in [6], where users fixate at an interactive object for localization and hit an additional button to activate interaction. We conceive that extra buttons for activation is inconvenient and unnecessary considering that it is easier for users to fixate on a point for a moment after they find it than to distract their attention to buttons.

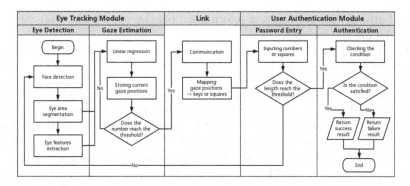

Fig. 1. The global structure and workflow of EyeSec. EyeSec comprises a Gaze Tracking Module performing gaze estimation and an User Authentication Module checking if the users pass the authentication. The Link part creates an information bridge connecting two modules. The User Authentication Module provides three gaze-based authentication schemes with different functions and passing rules. In terms of gaze-based PIN and gaze-based pattern, users pass the authentication through password match, whereas gaze-based captcha requires correct squares selection certain times.

The underlying gaze estimation technology of EyeSec resembles Webgazer which predicts real-time gaze positions on the screen based on the continuously collected interactive data. The self-calibration method presented in Webgazer is not suitable for our case since the mouse is forbidden during the period of password entry. We redesign the training and prediction process of the model to rearrange a preliminary model training procedure for the calibration stage and a following gaze prediction procedure for the input stage. Specifically, users fixate their gazes on predefined points and mouse-click the points for calibration where the point positions and users' data are collected for training, and users input passwords solely using their eyes since all mouse-related events are eliminated and no training data are added to the model.

3.3 Gaze-Based PIN

PIN is widely used for authentication through keyboard typing, mouse clicking and screen touching. Nevertheless, since finger movements that occur during password input stage are noticeable and thus easily to be recognized by observers, all those input approaches are vulnerable to should-surfing attacks. Gaze-based PIN is presented to be an alternative to traditional PIN while gaze interaction is more unobtrusive and remains simplicity and ease of use.

The interface of gaze-based PIN consists of 9 interactive keys with a 3×3 style that are evenly arranged horizontally and vertically. To help users focusing as close as possible to the center point of the key, the size of the key drawn on the screen is designed to be much smaller than the actual available area for interaction. To mitigate the impact caused by lack of precision of the gaze tracking technology, we maximize the interactive space through the following ways:

1. No buttons, dialogue boxes or information bars except for 9 keys are displayed on the interactive area.
2. The digit number 0 is excluded from the password set and the rest numbers 1–9 are attached on the keys.

Note that this is not negligible because the area size of the interactive key has significant influence on system's correct recognition for key selection.

In addition to common PIN keyboard layout in which the numbers are usually arranged from the smallest to the biggest, we provide an optional random keyboard where the numbers are randomly arranged. Figure 2 shows 2 example interfaces of gaze-based PIN with conventional and random keyboard. Users have choices to select one type of keyboard for password entry. Although there is no strict security proof that the random keyboard is more secure than the common keyboard, we recommend the former. The random keyboard updates the arrangement of the numbers in pseudorandom order each time users input the entire password rather than users input a number. That is, the random keyboard updates before users input password and keeps no change until the end. By this way, an adversary needs to observe both users' eye movements and the keyboard layout to commit a shoulder-surfing attack, if the adversary can infer gaze positions from eye movements.

In the input stage, right after the on-screen keyboard shows up, users get an alert saying that the gaze entry begins and the interaction is triggered at the very moment. Users fixate their gaze on the key for a so-called dwell time to select a number. The selected key will change its color to inform users that one key is successfully activated which means that one number has been selected and appended to the pre-entered number sequence. When users complete gaze entry, all the numbers are concatenated together to form a number sequence which is exactly the password for gaze-based PIN authentication. In practice, the feedback can be redesigned as a whole-screen color conversion to suggest that a number is successfully selected instead of changing the form of the selected number while keeping the others fixed. This approach will not reveal any details about the exact selected number. Since users know exactly which number they are looking at, they only need to be notified when the number is triggered so that they can step forward.

3.4 Gaze-Based Pattern Password

Compared to PIN, pattern password is easier to remember and normally used in smartphone and tablet. A pattern password is fully determined by the dot sequences without the lines and can be represented with a number code once all the dots are labeled by digital numbers. Differing from conventional touchscreen-based pattern where users touch the screen and move fingers to select dots while maintain physical contact with the screen throughout the input, gaze-based pattern does not require users to draw the lines with so-called gaze smooth-pursuit, i.e., eye movement along specified continuous traces on the screen. Therefore

(a) An example interface of gaze-based PIN with conventional keyboard.

(b) An example interface of gaze-based PIN with random keyboard.

Fig. 2. Two example interfaces of gaze-based PIN. The right part of the screen is inter-active area available for gaze-based PIN entry. The small orange dot on the interface is located based on current predicted gaze position. The left part is a data-display panel for monitoring present situation of the system, where real-time frames captured by camera, occurring frequency of each key, current gaze position on the screen, number of frames per second and the preset password are displayed from top to bottom. (Color figure online)

gaze-based pattern resembles gaze-based PIN in regard with alleviating shoulder-surfing since no more eye-related actions added.

As Fig. 3 shows, the interface of gazed-based pattern has the identical layout to gaze-based PIN as 9 keys replaced by 9 dots. Users input pattern password by draw a pattern composed of a series of dots with their eyes. Each dot is selected through dwelling and the dot sequence forms a pattern password. Slightly different from gaze-based PIN, gaze-based pattern requires no-repeat key selection and supports variable lengths of password. The system does not always accept a successfully activated dot unless it differs from all the previously selected dots.

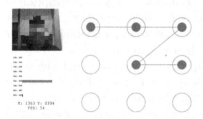

Fig. 3. An example interface of gaze-based pattern. The right part of the screen is interactive area available for gaze-based pattern password entry. The left part is the same data-display panel as in gaze-based PIN interface.

Fig. 4. An example interface of gaze-based captcha. The right part of the screen is interactive area available for gaze-based captcha entry. The left part is the same data-display panel as in gaze-based PIN interface (Color figure online)

3.5 Gaze-Based Captcha

Captcha [20] is a test to tell human beings and machines apart. Contemporary visual-perception captcha is software that automatically produces distorted images for humans to recognize the objects or text contents. However, due to the contribution of machine learning technologies in promoting image understanding, it is more and more hard to defend computer attacks against captcha system. Consequently, the images employed in captcha become more and more twisted, vague and obscure, sometimes even difficult for humans to recognize. What's worse, the visual-perception captcha might either lost its capability to separate humans and computers or take users a very long time to pass the authentication.

A typical captcha system usually works following a 3-step routine that first the system produces images for users to recognize, then users type characters or click some objects to submit the answer, and finally the system receives and checks the answer. When analyzing the entire procedure, we can see that visual-perception captcha relies on the difficulty for computers to produce correct answers. But the barriers can be erected in different place. We propose gaze-based captcha that only accepts from users the frame streams captured by camera rather than electrical pulses produced by mouse or touch screen in traditional visual-perception captcha system. That means, even if a computer knows the answer, it cannot correctly submit the answer to the system. By this way, the gaze-based captcha sets a task that is easy for humans but difficult for computers to fulfill. The data transferred to captcha system from users completely changes although what users feel is no more than alternating clicking or touching with eye fixating.

As showed in Fig. 4, the gaze-based captcha interface comprises 9 squares with a 3×3 matrix format one of which is green and the others are gray. The green square is denoted as T-square that is for selection and the other gray squares are denoted as F-squares which are distractors to T-square. Users are given 10 chances each round to pick up the T-square 3 times (interruption is permitted) with the dwell method. Each time users select one square, no matter T-square or F-square, the system rearranges the squares in pseudorandom order till users pass the captcha authentication or chances run out.

To analyze the security of gaze-based captcha, we presume that the communication throughout the captcha system is secure, i.e., an adversary cannot hack into the system and is only allowed to convey information through interface. There are usually two ways to attack the gaze-based captcha. One is called video-based attack and the other is called simulation-based attack. Video-based attack is that the adversary exploits previously recorded videos to interact with the system and tries to deceive it. Simulation-based attack is that the adversary intercepts the frame streams from camera and swap out them with real-time simulated frames which generate corresponding human facial pictures based on the present instructions. Since the system updates the arrangement of the squares each time users choose one square, pre-recorded video is impossible to match all the gaze positions correctly to the randomly generated T-squares, and thus video-based attack fails. If a malicious software wants to pass the gaze-based captcha authentication, it is supposed to be constructed in this way: produce a real-time video containing a human face and alter the gazes to obey orders sent by the system. Since simulation of human faces including gaze change in real time remains to be laborious for contemporary computers, simulation-based attack fails. To sum up, gaze-based captcha does have the capability to tell humans and computers apart.

3.6 Multi-threshold Deciding Mecanism

The underlying gaze tracking technology of EyeSec produces gaze positions on the screen at pixel level that can be represented with screen coordinates. Since gaze estimation is performed by the trained regression model predicting current gaze positions on the screen, the estimated gaze positions not always coincide with users' real fixation points but are located around them with some displacements. We divide uniformly the whole interactive screen into 9 areas for 9 keys and the key that will be triggered is determined by the statistical data of gaze positions in each area. It is obvious that the larger the area is the more possible the corresponding key can be correctly identified. However, although the statistical method compensates the lack of precision of gaze estimation, there is still an unsettled problem called Midas Touch effect influencing the correctness of key selection, that is, you cannot tell which gazes are attentive fixation and which gazes are perceptive saccades. Since there is no mouse or button or gaze gesture etc. to control the interactive duration, the input process might contain effective gazes corresponding to interactive dwelling and unwanted gazes corresponding to information-acquiring scanning or just useless glancing, and both will participate in determining the selected key.

Some gaze-based interactive schemes deal with the Midas Touch effect by setting a dwell time and users are supposed to interact with the systems among this session. However, these methods usually suffer from uncertainty of interactive time and inflexibility for different users. Instead of using a timer, we prefer counting the number of frames to determine the duration for interaction. While the processing speed and frame rate might vary greatly among different devices, exploiting the number of frames as the timing reference guarantees the constancy of information.

Concerning the gaze-based interaction in EyeSec, these unwanted gazes usually occur when users look for the correct key or T-square within the entire screen, namely, after users successfully select a key or a square and before users fixate on next key or square. To tackle this problem, we devise a multi-threshold deciding mechanism (MTDM) that excludes as many unwanted gazes as possible to enhance the system performance. The MTDM contains 5 key parameters to jointly determine the situation of current gazes. They are effective-frame counter, ineffective-frame counter, effective-frame threshold, ineffective-frame threshold, occurring-ratio threshold and are denoted as c_{EF}, c_{IF}, t_{EF}, t_{IF}, t_{OR}, respectively. EyeSec constantly receives and processes frames from camera following the same procure, and it can be comprehended as a periodic process. Detailed description in one cycle with MTDM deployed is provided below.

MTDM consists of the following five steps.

- **Step 0:** Initialize t_{EF}, t_{IF} both to be 0.
- **Step 1:** Receive a frame from camera and c_{IF} adds 1.
- **Step 2:** Check if c_{IF} is equal to t_{IF}. If yes, reset c_{IF} to be 0 and go to **Step 3**, otherwise go back to **Step 1**.
- **Step 3:** Receive a frame from camera and estimates current gaze position based on the frame, meanwhile c_{EF} adds 1.
- **Step 4:** Check if c_{EF} is equal to t_{EF}. If yes, go to **Step 5**, otherwise go back to **Step 3**.
- **Step 5:** Calculate the occurring frequencies of all the keys or squares and check if the maximum frequency is equal to t_{OR}. If yes, decide the key or square corresponding to the maximum frequency as the selected one and then reset c_{EF} to 0, otherwise go back to **Step 3**.

Here c_{IF} and t_{IF} are used to define the situation where users are searching a key or a square on the screen. Note that when c_{IF} is smaller than t_{IF}, the frames are regarded as useless and are thrown away without gaze estimation. c_{EF} and t_{EF} are used to control the total amount of data from users in each key-selecting cycle where the value of t_{EF} is the minimum number of frames to decide a key. t_{IF} is appropriately set to fit general interactive time, but unwanted gazes might still arise and likely not be clearly excluded since t_{IF} is fixed and cannot adjust automatically to occasional conditions. Thus, t_{OR} is the second way to eliminate impact of unwanted gazes, i.e., though unwanted gazes exist, the occurring frequency of the key on which users fixate increases as time pass by until the predominant frequency reaches t_{OR}. Through properly threshold setting, the multi-threshold deciding mechanism permits the system to differentiate between effective gazes and unwanted gazes and considerably increases the correctness of key selection.

4 Implementation

4.1 Hardware

EyeSec is a software that only requires single ordinary USB camera or webcam. Since webcam is presently on almost all the laptops, users don't need any additional equipment to execute our system. We implement EyeSec on a PC with an i7-6500U 8G CPU, a 13-inch monitor with a resolution of 1920×1080 pixels, and an embedded $1280 \times 720\,\text{p}/30\,\text{fps}$ webcam on the top center of the monitor. No extra device is needed.

4.2 Calibration

EyeSec requires a preliminary calibration stage to provide training data for subsequent gaze prediction since users ought not to use a mouse during password input. But mouse-click is required during the calibration stage. Since the accuracy of gaze estimation in EyeSec essentially relies on model training, sufficient training data are required to produce more reliable gaze prediction.

On the Calibration interface, 4×3, totally 12 small icons are placed uniformly on the screen and take turns to show up for users to fixate on. When calibrating, users are required to move the mouse slowly to the small icon that displayed on the screen while keeping their gazes focused on the mouse pointer. When the mouse pointer arrives at the icon, users are supposed to click the icon with the mouse after approximately 0.5 s delay. At this moment, the system collects current frames and corresponding mouse-click positions to enrich the training dataset. Then the clicked icon disappears while another icon shows up and users repeat above activities until all the icons are clicked. Throughout the calibration stage, the system updates its parameters hence optimizes the model whenever new data added.

Though lots of efforts devoted to the removal of calibration stage, calibration remains inevitable because that is the very source of training data for regression models. And 12 calibration points turns out to be the least amount to guarantee accuracy for subsequent gaze prediction.

4.3   Input and Authentication

Once the calibration completed, users are free to interact with computers using solely their eyes. In general, users choose a key or square by fixate on it for a dwell time and the system will decide which key to activate based on the statistical data of gaze position. The gaze tracking module provides gaze positions on the screen at pixel level, so we map gaze positions to keys by simply dividing the interactive screen into 9 uniform areas each of which contains a key in the center. On the 1920×1080 pixels monitor, the 1080×1080 pixels area on the right screen is used for interaction and thus the area encompassing 1–270 pixels horizontally and 1–270 pixels vertically is interactive filed for the first key, and so on. The gaze-based PIN and gaze-based pattern have nearly identical interfaces and the only difference is that the gaze-based PIN has numbers attached on the keys whereas the keys of gaze-based pattern only contain a dot in the center. Based on the gaze-based pattern, the gaze-based captcha substitutes squares for the keys and keeps the same configurations.

For convenience, EyeSec supports 4-digit PIN and arbitrary length of pattern password. Gaze-based PIN can be easily extended to 6-digit or arbitrary length with slight alteration. Users are required to preset passwords through mouse clicking or keyboard typing ahead of gaze-based authentication. We attach the numerical labels 1–9 sequentially to the dots in gaze-based pattern so that a pattern password can be represented with a no-repeat number code. With the knowledge of the preset password, input behavior stops on the condition where the length of the entered password is equal to the preset password. Then the system compares the entered password to the preset password and gives the authentication result. In terms of gaze-based captcha, the authentication result is provided when users pass the authentication or run out all 10 chances.

5   Experiment Design

The experiment was conducted in two phases. The goal of PHASE 1 was to evaluate the usability of EyeSec, specifically, interaction time and success rate of authentication. PHASE 2 assessed the security of gaze-based PIN and gaze-based pattern against shoulder-surfing attacks through a guessing-password study.

While some usability-assessing experiments were conducted in laboratorial environment and the subjects were usually well educated college students and staffs who were proficient at computer, the experimental results might lack of universality among ordinary people. Instead, we recruited from society participants that vary in age, occupation, educational level and computer skill. Additionally, the experimental places were not strictly constrained, so they could use EyeSec in non-laboratory places such as home, library, classroom, office etc. But quiet and neat environment was recommended so that participants might be more concentrated on the experiment. After contacting with some participants, we took the equipment of EyeSec to visit them and carried out experiment at agreed places. It turned out that the participants preferred to choose indoor personal places for the experiment.

PHASE 1: 16 participants (8 females, 8 males, 3 with glasses, 13 without glasses), aged between 13 and 51 years ($mean = 25.3$, $sd = 11.1$), were asked to use three gaze-based authentication schemes provided by EyeSec. Since almost all the participants had no idea about EyeSec or gaze-based authentication, we first explained the main functions and the purpose of experiment and then instructed them in EyeSec manipulation and permitted them to try the system again and again until they were ready for the experiment.

During experiment, participants could place their heads in convenient space within the system's working domain, about 25–45 cm distant from the screen. Each of them was allowed to use each authentication scheme as many times as they wanted. Their personal information such as gender, age, vision condition, educational level and computer skill was recorded for exploring human factors in EyeSec. For gaze-based PIN and gaze-based pattern authentication, calibration time, input time, preset passwords, entered passwords and the authentication results were measured and recorded. And for gaze-based captcha, calibration time, input time, number of consumed chances and authentication results were measured and recorded.

PHASE 2: While gaze-based authentication aimed at reducing shoulder-surfing, we designed a guessing-password study to evaluate the security of EyeSec. In our case, as mentioned at Sect. 3.4, gaze-based PIN and gaze-based pattern had similar qualities in shoulder-surfing mitigation, thus we evaluated the security of gaze-based PIN and extended the conclusion to the gaze-based pattern. Among all shoulder-surfing attacks with variable view angles, a frontal-face attack is the worst case, i.e., the attackers obtained some frontal-face videos demonstrating users' eye movements during the interactive process. To simulate this attack, we placed a video camera close to embedded webcam on the monitor to record gaze-based PIN authentication process. The recorded videos contained users' fontal faces and pretty approximated the interactive videos. Figure 5 showed synchronal snaps of a recorded video and an interactive video.

According to the results in Sect. 6.2, college students generally had higher success rate in authentication which implied their capability of controlling Eye-Sec. So we recruited 2 college students who were skilled in computer to play a role as attackers to guess passwords from the recorded videos. They were not only well educated but also received sufficient detailed instruction in shoulder-surfing attacks. They either spectated or participated in PHASE 1 so they were familiar with EyeSec both in principle and in practice. The impersonated attackers both had the recorded video and the corresponding keyboard arrangement information. They could play the videos unlimited times to analyze the eye movements and further exact passwords from them. Then they were asked to write down and submit the guessed passwords.

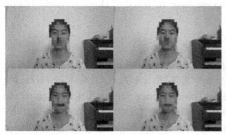 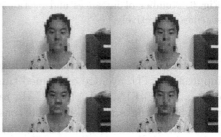

(a) Snaps of a sample interactive video.   (b) Snaps of a sample recorded video.

Fig. 5. The synchronal snaps of the interactive videos and the recorded videos. Two pictures from (a) and (b) with the same position were captured at the same moment and exhibited similarity in view angle to each other.

6   Experimental Analysis

For simplicity, we will use the following abbreviations when referring to the authentication schemes: gaze-based PIN (G-PIN), gaze-based pattern (G-PAT), gaze-based captcha (G-CAP). Totally 85 authentication instances (40 G-PIN, 31 G-PAT, 14 G-CAP) are collected where the maximum and the minimum number of instances per authentication scheme per participant were 6, 0, respectively.

6.1   Overall Analysis

Figure 6 shows the comparison of the number of success and failure instances as well as success rate among three authentication schemes. G-PIN has the lowest success rate (52.5%) while G-CAP has the highest success rate (85.7%), and the variance between them is 33.2%. This might result from the difference of requirement for passing the authentication, i.e., G-PIN requires users correctly input all the numbers whereas G-CAP gives users 10 chances to input correctly 3 times. To sum up, tolerance for input error raises the success rate of authentication.

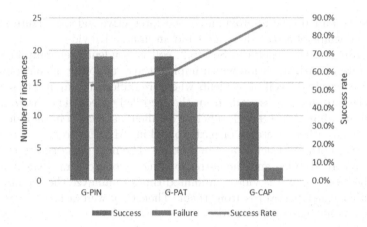

Fig. 6. Number of instances and overall success rate in passing three authentication schemes respectively.

Figure 7 shows the distribution of consumed time in calibration stage and in input stage. The average consumed time are 20.41 s, 14.36 s, 16.63 s, 19.67 s for calibration, G-PIN, G-PAT, G-CAP, respectively. Since the calibration is done through looking and clicking, the consumed time is completely controlled by users whereas the consumed time in input stage chiefly depends on MDTM (see Sect. 3.6). This explains the scattered distribution of consumed time in calibration stage as illustrated in Fig. 7. According to the reported results in [4], image captchas takes around 7–13 s while audio captchas takes 12–25 s. Average 19.67s consumed by gaze-based captcha is acceptable.

To get insight into the accuracy of EyeSec, we introduce displacement error (d_{error}) to measure the average Euclidean displacement of the recognized password from the preset password. Each element in a password is represented by a discrete coordinate (x, y), $x, y \in \{1, 2, 3\}$, based on its position on the screen. And displacement error is calculated by

$$d_{error} = \frac{1}{m} \Sigma \sqrt{(x_p - x_r)^2 + (y_p - y_r)^2} \tag{1}$$

where (x_p, y_p) and (x_r, y_r) are the coordinates of the preset password and the recognized password, respectively. m is the number of instances.

Entry confidence (*confidence*) is derived as

$$confidence = 1 - d_{error}/d_{average} \tag{2}$$

where $d_{average}$ is the average distance between two keys on the screen.

Figure 8 presents the data distribution of displacement between the recognized password and the preset password. Displacement error and confidence with respect to three authentication schemes are listed in Table 1.

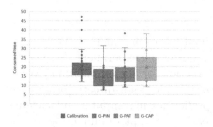

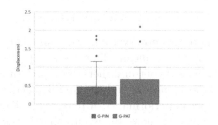

Fig. 7. Distributions of consumed time in calibration and three gaze-based entry process.

Fig. 8. Distributions of displacement between recognized password and preset password in G-PIN and G-PAT.

In PHASE 2, as showed in Table 2, the success rate of guessing password are both 0.0% for 2 attackers. To inspect the relationship between guessed password and real password, d_{error} and $confidence$ are calculated and the results are listed in Table 2. Although the attackers have frontal-face videos recording gaze-based authentication process and keyboard arrangement information, no one password is correctly guessed. This inspiring result might benefit from the dwell method for gaze interaction. That is, since no extra buttons or eye gestures are used to determine the gaze interaction period, it is difficult for attackers to correctly recognize all the key-selection process. Furthermore, the relatively lower overall confidence in guessing password (23.7%) compared to that in G-PIN password entry (89.2% for the best) also demonstrates the security of gaze-based password entry in shoulder-surfing resistance.

Table 1. Displacement error between preset password and recognized password; Confidence of password entry in G-PIN and G-PAT authentication schemes. Note that users always attempt to pass the authentication by inputting the preset password but the system might incorrectly recognize the input due to technical issues, which causes the difference between the preset password and recognized password.

	d_{error}	$Confidence$
G-PIN	0.304	89.2%
G-PAT	0.337	88.0%

Table 2. Success rate for guessing password from frontal-face videos recorded in G-PIN authentication process; Displacement error between guessed password and real password; Confidence of guessing password. These results can be extended to G-PAT since G-PAT has similar quality in shoulder-surfing mitigation with G-PIN.

	Success rate	d_{error}	$Confidence$
Guess 1	0.0%	1.087	32.9%
Guess 2	0.0%	1.387	14.4%
Overall	0.0%	1.237	23.7%

6.2   Human Factors Estimation

Through observation, we find that participants within different age ranges exhibit significant differences in performance during the experiment. In general, youths do better either in comprehending instructions or in manipulating EyeSec than teenagers and the middle-aged. However, age does not directly bring variance in performance, it reflects participants' proficiency in computer and learning ability for new things and that is the real reason. To explore human factors in EyeSec, we divided data into three groups according to participants' age and estimate success rate over these groups separately. The results are suggested in Fig. 9. Predictably, users aged between 21 and 35, mainly college students and graduated students, achieve significantly higher success rate in authentication (76.2% in G-PIN, 90.0% in G-PAT, 100.0% in G-CAP) compared to the others.

Moreover, the participants' behavior in the experiment reveals some interesting findings. In the beginning, users who are inexperienced with computers spend much more time in calibration compared to these proficient, but after several trails, they speed up until reaching a steady level. Therefore, calibration time is record for 3 times for each participant. Figure 10 demonstrates the declining trend of consumed time in calibration stage, especially obvious for users aged from 36 to 55. In contrast, the other 2 groups have nearly constant consumed time with slight decrease. Consistent with the performance in authentication, the consumed time for calibration indicates, at some degree, the capability of passing authentication. However, due to the limitation in time, no more calibration time is collected, but it can be inferred that users within other age groups might spend less time in calibration and achieve higher success rate in authentication through enough training and practice.

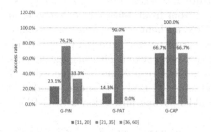
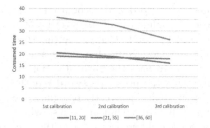

Fig. 9. Success rate in passing three authentication schemes over three age groups.

Fig. 10. Average consumed time over 3 age groups for calibration. Calibration time is recorded 3 times per participant.

7   Conclusion

EyeSec offers a practical gaze-based authentication system both aimed at shoulder-surfing resistance and versatility and becomes the first-of-its-kind to apply state-of-art gaze tracking technology in gaze-based authentication. Eye-Sec provides 3 authentication schemes, of which gaze-based PIN and gaze-based pattern are designed to be shoulder-surfing resistant alternatives to conventional keyboard-based, mouse-based or touchscreen-based password entry schemes, and gaze-based captcha exploits the difficulty for computers in simulating real-time human faces and gazes to tell human and computer apart.

In the usability-estimating experimental phase, 16 participants, recruited from society, varying in age, occupation, educational level and computer skill, achieve overall 52.5%, 61.3%, 85.7% success rate for passing gaze-based PIN, gaze-based pattern, gaze-based captcha, respectively. The average consumed time are 20.41 s, 14.36 s, 16.63 s, 19.67 s for calibration, G-PIN entry, G-PAT entry, G-CAP entry, respectively.

In human-factors study, the results demonstrate strong correlation between the performance of EyeSec and the age of participants. Participants aged between 21 to 35, achieve average 76.2%, 90.0%, 100.0% in success rate for gaze-based PIN, gaze-based pattern, gaze-based captcha, respectively. Since the calibration procedure is mainly controlled by participants themselves, we notice that the consumed time in calibration stage have a negative correlation with proficiency of participants in computer. Moreover, for participants aged between 36 and 45, the consumed time shows downward trend in successive calibration process, which implies increasing proficiency in computer and familiarity of EyeSec. Therefore, we predict that these participants would achieve higher success rate in authentication with sufficient training and practice. Unfortunately, with time limited, no more data is collected. Hope this prediction can be verified in further work.

In the guessing-password study, the worst case of shoulder-surfing attack is simulated—skillful shoulder-surfing attackers obtaining frontal-face videos recorded during authentication process along with keyboard arrangement information. The success rate of guessing password is 0.0% and the confidence is 23.7% which suggests high security of EyeSec when encountering shoulder-surfing attacks. Plus, without information of keyboard arrangement, attackers are unable to do anything about guessing password in the random-keyboard gaze-based PIN scheme.

To sum up, EyeSec is the first implementation of gaze-based authentication system without requirement for extra eye trackers or special hardware. Through usability evaluation among different people, the system's usability, especially suggested by the college students, is potentially acceptable. Moreover, the gaze-based captcha realized through gaze interaction, with average 19.67 s consumed time, might be an alternative to contemporary visual-perception captcha schemes.

Acknowledgements. Qianhong Wu is the corresponding author. This paper is supported by the National High Technology Research and Development Program of China (863 Program) through project 2015AA017205, the Natural Science Foundation of China through projects 61772538, 61672083 and 61370190, and by the National Cryptography Development Fund through project MMJJ20170106. This work is supported by National Natural Science Foundation of China (61472083, 61402110, 61771140).

References

1. Baltrusaitis, T., Robinson, P., Morency, L.P.: Constrained local neural fields for robust facial landmark detection in the wild. In: Proceedings of the IEEE International Conference on Computer Vision Workshops, pp. 354–361 (2013)
2. Baltrušaitis, T., Robinson, P., Morency, L.P.: Openface: an open source facial behavior analysis toolkit. In: 2016 IEEE Winter Conference on Applications of Computer Vision (WACV), pp. 1–10. IEEE (2016)
3. Bulling, A., Alt, F., Schmidt, A.: Increasing the security of gaze-based cued-recall graphical passwords using saliency masks. In: Proceedings of the SIGCHI Conference on Human Factors in Computing Systems, pp. 3011–3020. ACM (2012)
4. Bursztein, E., Bethard, S., Fabry, C., Mitchell, J.C., Jurafsky, D.: How good are humans at solving CAPTCHAs? A large scale evaluation. In: 2010 IEEE Symposium on Security and Privacy (SP), pp. 399–413. IEEE (2010)
5. Davin, J.T.: Baseline measurements of shoulder surfing analysis and comparability for smartphone unlock authentication. Technical report, Naval Academy Annapolis MD Annapolis (2017)
6. De Luca, A., Weiss, R., Drewes, H.: Evaluation of eye-gaze interaction methods for security enhanced pin-entry. In: Proceedings of the 19th Australasian Conference on Computer-Human Interaction: Entertaining User Interfaces, pp. 199–202. ACM (2007)
7. Forget, A., Chiasson, S., Biddle, R.: Shoulder-surfing resistance with eye-gaze entry in cued-recall graphical passwords. In: Proceedings of the SIGCHI Conference on Human Factors in Computing Systems, pp. 1107–1110. ACM (2010)
8. Hansen, D.W., Ji, Q.: In the eye of the beholder: a survey of models for eyes and gaze. IEEE Trans. Pattern Anal. Mach. Intelligence 32(3), 478–500 (2010)
9. Huang, X., Xiang, Y., Bertino, E., Zhou, J., Xu, L.: Robust multi-factor authentication for fragile communications. IEEE Trans. Dependable Secure Comput. 11(6), 568–581 (2014)
10. Huang, X., Xiang, Y., Chonka, A., Zhou, J., Deng, R.H.: A generic framework for three-factor authentication: preserving security and privacy in distributed systems. IEEE Trans. Parallel Distrib. Syst. 22(8), 1390–1397 (2011)
11. Jacob, R.J.: Eye tracking in advanced interface design. In: Virtual Environments and Advanced Interface Design, pp. 258–288 (1995)
12. Kassner, M., Patera, W., Bulling, A.: Pupil: an open source platform for pervasive eye tracking and mobile gaze-based interaction. In: Proceedings of the 2014 ACM International Joint Conference on Pervasive and Ubiquitous Computing: Adjunct Publication, pp. 1151–1160. ACM (2014)
13. Kumar, M., Garfinkel, T., Boneh, D., Winograd, T.: Reducing shoulder-surfing by using gaze-based password entry. In: Proceedings of the 3rd Symposium on Usable Privacy and Security, pp. 13–19. ACM (2007)
14. Lu, F., Chen, X., Sato, Y.: Appearance-based gaze estimation via uncalibrated gaze pattern recovery. IEEE Trans. Image Process. 26(4), 1543–1553 (2017)
15. Lu, F., Sugano, Y., Okabe, T., Sato, Y.: Inferring human gaze from appearance via adaptive linear regression. In: 2011 IEEE International Conference on Computer Vision (ICCV), pp. 153–160. IEEE (2011)
16. Papoutsaki, A., Sangkloy, P., Laskey, J., Daskalova, N., Huang, J., Hays, J.: WebGazer: scalable webcam eye tracking using user interactions. In: Proceedings of the Twenty-Fifth International Joint Conference on Artificial Intelligence (IJCAI 2016) (2016)

17. Rajanna, V., Polsley, S., Taele, P., Hammond, T.: A gaze gesture-based user authentication system to counter shoulder-surfing attacks. In: Proceedings of the 2017 CHI Conference Extended Abstracts on Human Factors in Computing Systems, pp. 1978–1986. ACM (2017)

18. Santini, T., Fuhl, W., Geisler, D., Kasneci, E.: EyeRecToo: open-source software for real-time pervasive head-mounted eye tracking. In: VISIGRAPP (6: VISAPP), pp. 96–101 (2017)

19. Sugano, Y., Matsushita, Y., Sato, Y.: Appearance-based gaze estimation using visual saliency. IEEE Trans. Pattern Anal. Mach. Intell. **35**(2), 329–341 (2013)

20. von Ahn, L., Blum, M., Hopper, N.J., Langford, J.: CAPTCHA: using hard AI problems for security. In: Biham, E. (ed.) EUROCRYPT 2003. LNCS, vol. 2656, pp. 294–311. Springer, Heidelberg (2003). https://doi.org/10.1007/3-540-39200-9_18

21. Weaver, J., Mock, K., Hoanca, B.: Gaze-based password authentication through automatic clustering of gaze points. In: 2011 IEEE International Conference on Systems, Man, and Cybernetics (SMC), pp. 2749–2754. IEEE (2011)

22. Wood, E., Bulling, A.: EyeTab: model-based gaze estimation on unmodified tablet computers. In: Proceedings of the Symposium on Eye Tracking Research and Applications, pp. 207–210. ACM (2014)

23. Wu, Q., Domingo-Ferrer, J., González-Nicolás, U.: Balanced trustworthiness, safety, and privacy in vehicle-to-vehicle communications. IEEE Trans. Veh. Technol. **59**(2), 559–573 (2010)

24. Zhang, X., Sugano, Y., Fritz, M., Bulling, A.: Appearance-based gaze estimation in the wild. In: Proceedings of the IEEE Conference on Computer Vision and Pattern Recognition, pp. 4511–4520 (2015)

25. Zhang, X., Sugano, Y., Fritz, M., Bulling, A.: It's written all over your face: full-face appearance-based gaze estimation. arXiv preprint arXiv:1611.08860 (2016)

Enhanced Remote Password-Authenticated Key Agreement Based on Smart Card Supporting Password Changing

Jian Shen[1,2](✉), Meng Feng[1], Dengzhi Liu[1], Chen Wang[1], Jiachen Jiang[1], and Xingming Sun[1]

[1] Jiangsu Engineering Center of Network Monitoring,
Nanjing University of Information Science & Technology, Nanjing 210044, China
s_shenjian@126.com, fengmeng1031@163.com, liudzdh@126.com,
wangchennuist@126.com, 1577870352@qq.com, sunnudt@163.com
[2] State Key Laboratory of Information Security, Institute of Information
Engineering, Chinese Academy of Sciences, Beijing 100093, China

Abstract. Cryptographic scheme is the safeguard for achieving secure communication in networks and distributed systems. Smart card-based password authentication has become a common authentication method to enhance the security of a system. So far, many schemes about smart card-based password authentication have been proposed for preventing various kinds of attacks. In this paper, we first analyze Sun *et al.*'s scheme and find out that it may be vulnerable to malicious server attack, password guessing attack, user impersonation attack. And then, we propose an enhanced remote password-authenticated key agreement scheme based on smart card to thwart the above security threats. Through the security analysis and performance comparison, our enhanced scheme is proved to be secure and efficient.

Keywords: Cryptography · Authentication · Key agreement
Relay attack · Smart card

1 Introduction

With computer and network technologies developing rapidly, users can share various resources and convenient services to remote sever via the network, which makes our life more intelligent and convenient. Although remote service and communication bring many benefits to us, many important and urgent security issues are raised. Data stored in the computer needs to be protected and messages transmitted in network are necessary to be encrypted for defending against attacking and eavesdropping [15,23,24,26]. Many schemes and protocols [12,17,18,22] have been proposed to make systems or networks more secure. Lamport first introduces a remote user authentication scheme in 1981 [1]. Then a great many authentication schemes [2–11,13,14,16,19,21,25,27–29] have been proposed for enhancing the security of the system.

© Springer International Publishing AG 2017
J. K. Liu and P. Samarati (Eds.): ISPEC 2017, LNCS 10701, pp. 454–467, 2017.
https://doi.org/10.1007/978-3-319-72359-4_27

Smart card-based password authentication key agreement is an effective authentication mechanism for enhancing the security of the system. Note that a secure authentication can guarantee a smart card-based password-authenticated key agreement. Usually, there are two entities involved in a smart card password authentication scheme: a user and a server. And the scheme includes three phases: the registration phase, the login phase and the password changing phase. In the first phase, the server sends a smart card containing some information to the user. Once the user completes the registration, he/she is able to login the server by using the smart card. If the faulty information exists or attackers obtain message successfully, the authentication process will be terminated. In the last phase, the user can change his password freely. Note that, in this paper, the proposed scheme includes four phases: the registration phase, the login phase, the authentication phase and the password changing phase. In particular, the authentication phase plays a very important role in key agreement in the scheme.

It is necessary for us to take all possible attacks into account with regard to an improved security model when we design a smart card-based password authenticated scheme. In this paper, we find that Sun *et al.*'s scheme [11] may be vulnerable to password guessing attack [20], and user impersonation attack. Moreover, the initial password installed by a server may be attacked by a malicious server. Hence, we propose an enhanced scheme to resist the security issues and enhance the security of the system.

1.1 Our Contributions

In this paper, we first review Sun *et al.*'s scheme and present the security analysis. Then, we propose an enhanced scheme which has the following enhancements:

- The initial password is installed by a user, which can resist malicious server attack.

    If the server is malicious in a system, the initial password installed by the server may be leaked by the malicious server. Then, attackers may obtain the password and damage the security of the system. Hence, installing the initial password by a user can improve the security of the system.
- The enhanced scheme can resist the attacker with different private data stored in the smart card at different times [20].

    An attacker with the smart card may obtain the different data stored in the smart card at time T_1 and time T_2, then it can do the special operation with the obtained data. The output is only related to the password and the attacker is able to guess the password in the password dictionary. The enhanced scheme adds the user's secret information to the data stored in the smart card. The output is related to the password and the secret information. Then the attacker cannot guess the password.
- Wrong password can be detected by a smart card in the beginning of login phase.

    In the registration phase, a user provides his password and biometric information. Then the password and biometric information will be encrypted by the special device. Then, the user sends the encrypted data to the server. The server stores the encrypted data in the smart card and sends the smart card to the user. When the user wants to login to the server by inputting his password and biometric information, the smart card will do corresponding computation to verify the password. If the password is wrong, the login phase will be terminated before the smart card being sent to the server, which can reduce the unnecessary communication cost and computational cost during the login and authentication phases. Moreover, it can avoid more attacks with the smart card in communication channels.

1.2 Related Works

Many smart card-based password authentication schemes have been put forward for improving the security of systems. However, due to the different of the security model and the system model, the most perfect secure scheme is not trivial to design. In 1981, a remote password authentication scheme [1] was proposed by Lamport, which employs a one-way hash chain and Haller later used the hash chain to design the well-known S/KEY one-time password system [2]. The weakness of Haller's scheme is that the remote server need have a verification table for validating that whether the registered users are legal. If the server is destroyed by an adversary, the table may be easily modified or damaged [3]. After that, an efficient mutual authentication scheme [4] using smart cards was proposed by Chien et al. The scheme realizes the mutual authentication to strength the privacy, but the limitation is the high computation cost. In addition, it cannot resist the parallel session attack, which was proposed by Hsu [6]. Lee et al. [7] improved Chien et al.'s scheme and proposed a scheme that can resist the parallel session attack. However, their scheme was destroyed by the attackers with the smart card [8]. Then, a robust and efficient user authentication and key agreement scheme using smart card [10] was proposed by Juang et al. The scheme has some properties such as no password table, server authentication. In Juang et al.'s scheme, the pre-computation phase is added to reduce the cost of computation. But the crucial data for the session key stored in the smart card is exposed to the attackers. The pre-computation phase was removed by Sun et al. [11] and their scheme could resist attacks with the smart card in their assumed security model. Moreover, Huang et al. [20] reviewed Juang et al.'s scheme [10] and Sun et al.'s scheme [11]. Two new types of security threats [20] were proposed in their paper: pre-computed data may be attacked by attackers, and different data (at different time slots) may be attacked by attackers. They proposed some countermeasures to resist the security issues and enhance the security of the system. In this paper, we make some enhancements on Sun et al.'s scheme [11] and we propose an enhanced scheme which can also resist password guessing attack mentioned in Huang et al.'s scheme [20].

1.3   Organization

The remaining of this paper is organized as follows. Preliminary works are presented in Sect. 2. After that, the adversary model and security model are briefly illustrated in Sect. 3. In Sect. 4, the review and security analysis of Sun et al.'s scheme [11] are shortly described. The proposed scheme is depicted in detail in Sect. 5 and the security analysis and comparison are described in Sect. 6. Finally, the conclusion is covered in Sect. 7.

2   Preliminaries

2.1   One-Way Hash Function

One-way hash function transforms an arbitrarily long input message string into a fixed length output string and it is difficult to obtain an input string according to the output string. Hash function is mainly used for integrity checking and improving the validity of digital signature. Among common hashing algorithms, SHA is a relatively new hashing algorithm that generates a 160-bit value for any length of data operation and MAC is a one-way function using keys that can be used to validate files or messages between systems and users.

2.2   Symmetric Cryptography

Symmetric cryptography uses the same secret key to encrypt and decrypt messages. The sender will make special operations with the data and secret key. Then the encrypted data will be sent to the recipient. The recipient needs to decrypt the received data with the same secret key. The algorithm has small amount of calculation, fast encryption speed and high encryption efficiency.

2.3   Elliptic Curve Cryptography

ECC (Elliptic Curve Cryptography) is a public key encryption technology based on elliptic curve theory. It makes use of the intractability of Abel group discrete logarithm formed by the points of elliptic curve in finite field to realize encryption, decryption and digital signature. Corresponding the adding operation of elliptic curve to the modular multiplication in discrete logarithm, then the cryptography system based on elliptic curve can be established.

2.4   Timestamp

Timestamp refers to the identification of text added to a series of data, such as time or date, to ensure that the update sequence of the local data is consistent with the remote server. A secret document is consisted of three ingredients: a summary of a document with timestamp, the data and the time of the destination receiving the document, and the destination's digital signature. The user will first need to encode the file with hash function and the file needs to be added the time stamp to form the digest. Then the digest is sent to the destination. The destination encrypts the file after he receives the file that contains the digest's date and time. And then the file will be sent back to the user.

3   Adversary Model and Security Model

3.1   Adversary Model

Attackers are divided into two categories on the basis of the password and the smart card. They are attackers with the password and attackers with the smart card. The former attackers are such attackers that they have the password of the user but cannot access the smart card. Attackers with smart card can obtain the data in the smart card. Such attackers may steal the smart card of the user and then extract the private data in the smart card, which may help attackers guess the password. It is obvious that attackers can launch a login request or send messages to the user with the identity of the server when the smart card and password were stolen in the meantime.

To analyze the security of Sun *et al.*'s scheme and our enhanced scheme, we give the following adversary model.

- An attacker may guess the password by using the password dictionary.
- An attacker may steal a user's smart card and then extract the secret values stored in the smart card more than once, but it cannot obtain the password at the same time. Moreover, the attacker can launch a login request instead of the user, or send messages to the user with the identity of the server and make mutual authentication with the server using the password and the smart card.
- An attacker cannot obtain the user's the biometric information [18].
- An attacker can extract the secret values stored in the smart card, but it cannot modify the secret values and store new data in the smart card.

3.2   Security Model

The special security requirements of password-authenticated key agreement scheme using smart cards are defined as follows.

In our password-authenticated key agreement scheme, each participant is either a user or a server. The server keeps a master secret key K, and each user holds the password PW and the biometric information BIO. PW is chosen from the small dictionary and BIO will not be available for attackers. The server in the system is secure. Additionally, we assume channels in the registration phase are secure.

4   Review of Sun *et al.*'s Scheme

This section briefly reviews Sun *et al.*'s scheme and makes the security analysis.

4.1   Sun *et al.*'s Scheme

The scheme is composed of three phases: the registration phase, the authentication phase, and the password changing phase.

Registration Phase. When a user wants to register to the remote server, the registration phase will be started. The user selects the sub-identifier ID_U that is defined specially in [11]. The user sends $\{ID_U\}$ to the server, if ID_U is valid, the server selects the sub-identifier ID_S and generates $ID = ID_U||ID_S$ for the server. Then, the server sends PW, smart card to the user and the smart card $= \{D, M\}$, where $D = h(ID||K) \oplus h(PW)$, $M = E_K(ID||r)$, and PW is the initial password chosen by the server.

Authentication Phase. The user is able to login the server with the help of his password and smart card when the registration is completed. At first, the smart card sends $\{M, G_C\}$ to the server, where $G_C = r_c \cdot G$, r_c is a random number chosen by the smart card. Then the user decrypts M and checks the output. The session will be terminated if the verification is wrong. Otherwise it will continue. Then, the server sends $\{G_S, M_S\}$ to the user, where $G_S = r_s \cdot G$, $M_S = h(K_{SU}||G_C||G_S)$, and $K_{SU} = h(h(ID||K)||(r_s \cdot G_C))$. The smart card computes $D' = D \oplus h(PW)$ and $K_{SU} = h(D'||(r_c \cdot G_S))$. The process will be ended if $M_S \neq h(K_{SU}||G_C||G_S)$. Otherwise, the smart card sends $\{M_U = h(K_{SU}||G_S)\}$ to the server. Finally, the server checks that whether $M_U = h(K_{SU}||G_S)$, if positive, the authentication is successful. K_{SU} is the session key.

Password Changing Phase. The user should enter the old password PW and a new password PW' when he/she wants to change his password. Then the smart card will compute $D'' = D \oplus h(PW) \oplus h(PW') = h(ID||K) \oplus h(PW')$.

4.2 Security Analysis of Sun *et al.*'s Scheme

In this section, we analyze the security weaknesses of Sun *et al.*'s scheme [11]. We assume that an attacker could get the different private data stored in the smart card at different times.

Password Guessing Attack. Sun *et al.* [11] pointed that an adversary can not corrupt the user's authentication session only using $D = h(ID||K) \oplus h(PW)$. Because the adversary has no access to the server's secret key K. However, Huang *et al.* [20] makes the security analysis and proposes that the adversary can guess the password with more than one D generated at different times. The user changes the password at the different time and the message stored in the smart card also changes. The attacker with the smart card can obtain the different data stored in the smart card. Then it can do the special operation with the obtained data. The output is only related to the password and the attacker is able to guess the password in the password dictionary.

User Impersonation Attack. With the guessed password and the secret data fetched in the user's smart card in an illegal way, the attacker is able to login to the server with the user's identity. The attacker can launch a login request instead of the user and make mutual authentication with the server using the password and the smart card, which may destroy the authentication session.

Malicious Server Attack. In Sun *et al.*'s scheme, the initial password is chosen by the server. If the server in the system is malicious, the password will be leaked. Then the leaked password may be obtained by attackers and attackers can damage the security of the system with the password.

5 Our Enhanced Scheme

Our scheme is presented in this section in detail, which consists of four phases: the registration phase, the login phase, the authentication phase and the password changing phase. The description of the four phases are depicted in Fig. 1. At the beginning of the scheme, the server first chooses an elliptic curve E over a finite field Fp such that the discrete logarithm problem is hard in $E(Fp)$. The set of all the points on E is denoted by $E(Fp)$. The server also chooses a point $G \in E(F_p)$ such that the subgroup generated by G has a large order q. The server produces the parameters (p, q, E, G, h) but keeps his private key $K \in Z_q^*$ secret. Here, p and q are two prime numbers, and h is a hash function. The notations used in the proposed scheme are shown in Table 1.

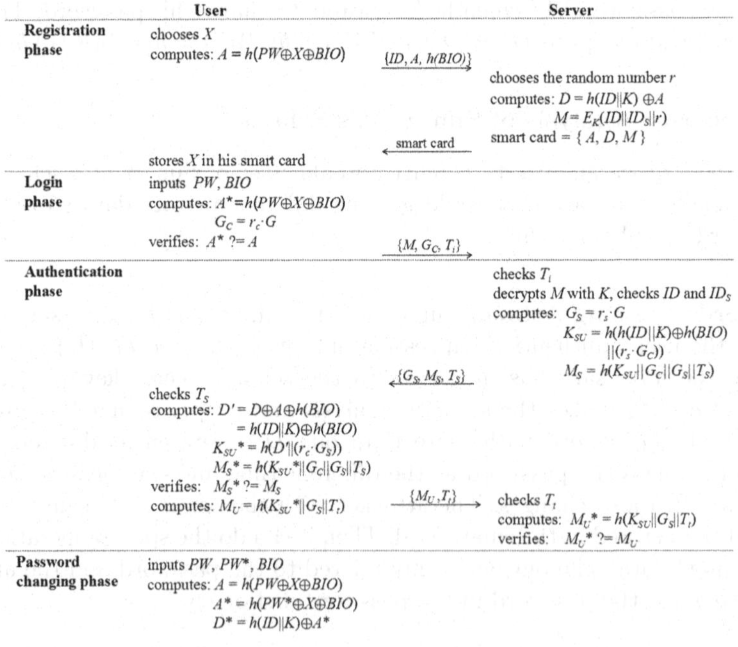

	User		Server
Registration phase	chooses X		
	computes: $A = h(PW \oplus X \oplus BIO)$	$\{ID, A, h(BIO)\} \longrightarrow$	
			chooses the random number r
			computes: $D = h(ID\|K) \oplus A$
			$M = E_K(ID\|ID_S\|r)$
		$\longleftarrow$ smart card	smart card = $\{A, D, M\}$
	stores X in his smart card		
Login phase	inputs PW, BIO		
	computes: $A^* = h(PW \oplus X \oplus BIO)$		
	$G_C = r_c \cdot G$		
	verifies: $A^* ?= A$	$\{M, G_C, T_i\} \longrightarrow$	
Authentication phase			checks T_i
			decrypts M with K, checks ID and ID_S
			computes: $G_S = r_s \cdot G$
			$K_{SU} = h(h(ID\|K) \oplus h(BIO)$
			$\|(r_s \cdot G_C))$
		$\longleftarrow \{G_S, M_S, T_S\}$	$M_S = h(K_{SU}\|G_C\|G_S\|T_S)$
	checks T_S		
	computes: $D' = D \oplus A \oplus h(BIO)$		
	$= h(ID\|K) \oplus h(BIO)$		
	$K_{SU}^* = h(D'\|(r_c \cdot G_S))$		
	$M_S^* = h(K_{SU}^*\|G_C\|G_S\|T_S)$		
	verifies: $M_S^* ?= M_S$		
	computes: $M_U = h(K_{SU}^*\|G_S\|T_i)$	$\{M_U, T_i\} \longrightarrow$	checks T_i
			computes: $M_U^* = h(K_{SU}\|G_S\|T_i)$
			verifies: $M_U^* ?= M_U$
Password changing phase	inputs PW, PW^*, BIO		
	computes: $A = h(PW \oplus X \oplus BIO)$		
	$A^* = h(PW^* \oplus X \oplus BIO)$		
	$D^* = h(ID\|K) \oplus A^*$		

Fig. 1. The process of our enhanced scheme

Table 1. Notations

Symbol	Description
$h\,()$	A public one-way hash function
$\|$	String concatenation operator
K	The secret key of the server
$E_K\,()$	A secure symmetric encryption algorithm with the secret k
$D_K\,()$	A secure symmetric decryption algorithm with the secret k
G	A generator of a group on an elliptic curve generated by the server
K_{SU}	The session key
r_c	A random number chosen by the smart card
r	A random number chosen by the server
r_s	A random number chosen by the server
x	A random number chosen by the user
BIO	The biometric information of the user
PW	The password of the user
ID	The identity of the user
ID_S	The identity of the server

5.1 Registration Phase

When a user needs to register to the remote server, the registration phase will be started. We use the biometric information BIO applied in [18] to construct our scheme.

- The user computes $A = h(PW \oplus X \oplus BIO)$ and submits ID, A, $h(BIO)$ to the server via a secure channel, where ID is the user's identity, PW is the password chosen by the user, $X \in Z_q{}^*$ is the random number chosen by the user and BIO is the biometric information of the user.
- The server receives the message and computes $D = h\,(ID\|K) \oplus A$, $M = E_K\,(ID\|ID_S\|r)$. Then, the server sends the smart card that contains A, D and M to the user via a secure channel. Here, $r \in Z_q{}^*$ is a random number chosen by the server, K is the secret key of the server and ID_S is the server's identity.
- Then, the user stores X in the smart card.

5.2 Login Phase

When the user wants to login to the remote server, the login phase will be started. The server inputs his PW and inserts his smart card. Also, the user inputs his BIO on the specific device. In this phase, we use explicit verification of the user's input password. Note that, another technique of fuzzy verification can well deal with the "security-usability" dilemma, which was proposed in some previous studies [30–33]. In the future work, we will try to use the fuzzy-verifier technique instead of explicit verification. In this paper, the login phase will perform the following steps.

- The smart card first computes $A^* = h(PW \oplus X \oplus BIO)$. If the computed value A^* is equal to A stored in the smart card, the following steps of the login phase will continue. Otherwise, the session will be ended.
- The smart card then sends $\{M, G_C, T_i\}$ to the server, where $r_c \in Z_q^*$ is randomly chosen by the smart card, G_C $(G_C = r_c \cdot G)$ is a point on the elliptic curve and T_i is the current timestamp.

5.3   Authentication Phase

Upon receiving the message from the user, the server performs the following steps after the server receives the user's login request message.

- The server checks T_i. If it is valid, the server obtains ID^* and ID_S^* by the decryption of the $E_K(M)$ with K. If ID^* is equal to ID and ID_S is equal to ID_S^*, going on the next step. Otherwise, the process is terminated.
- The server sends $\{G_S, M_S, T_S\}$ to the smart card, where $r_s \in Z_q^*$ is randomly chosen by the server, G_S $(G_S = r_s \cdot G)$ is a point on the elliptic curve and T_S is the current timestamp.

$$M_S = h(K_{SU} \| G_C \| G_S \| T_S) \tag{1}$$

$$K_{SU} = h(h(ID\|K) \oplus h(BIO) \| (r_s \cdot G_C)) \tag{2}$$

- The smart card checks T_S. If it is valid, the smart card calculates the following equations, then the smart card checks if M_S^* is equal to M_S. If the output is correct, going on the next step. Otherwise, the process is terminated.

$$D' = D \oplus A \oplus h(BIO) = h(ID\|K) \oplus h(BIO) \tag{3}$$

$$K_{SU}^* = h(D'\|(r_c \cdot G_S)) = h(h(ID\|K) \oplus h(BIO) \| (r_c \cdot G_S)) \tag{4}$$

$$M_S^* = h(K_{SU}^* \| G_C \| G_S \| T_S) \tag{5}$$

$$M_S^*? = M_S \tag{6}$$

- The smart card sends $\{MU, Tt\}$ to the server, where $M_U = h(K_{SU}^* \| G_S \| T_t)$, T_t is the current timestamp.
- The server checks T_t. If it is valid, the server calculates the following equation and checks whether M_U^* is equal to M_U. If the output is correct, the authentication phase is completed successfully and the K_{SU} is the session key. Otherwise, the process is terminated.

$$M_U^* = h(K_{SU} \| G_S \| T_t) \tag{7}$$

$$M_U^*? = M_U \tag{8}$$

5.4   Password Changing Phase

When the user needs to change the password, he should input his old password PW, BIO and new password PW^*. Then, the smart card replaces D with D^* and A^* with A.

$$A = h(PW \oplus X \oplus BIO) \tag{9}$$

$$A^* = h(PW^* \oplus X \oplus BIO) \tag{10}$$

$$D^* = D \oplus A \oplus A^* = h(ID\|K) \oplus A \oplus A \oplus A^* = h(ID\|K) \oplus A^* \tag{11}$$

6   Security Analysis and Comparison

In this section, we present the security analysis of the enhanced scheme, and we compare it with other schemes in terms of the security. The comparison is shown in Table 2. The result shows that the enhanced scheme is more secure and efficient than other related schemes.

6.1   Correctness Analysis

There are two main verification processes in our scheme. The correctness of Eq. (6) is elaborated as follow.

$$
\begin{aligned}
&M_S{}^* \\
&= h(K_{SU}{}^*\|G_C\|G_S\|T_S) \\
&= h(h(D\|(r_c \cdot G_S))\|G_C\|G_S\|T_S) = h(h(D\|(r_c \cdot G_S))\|G_C\|G_S\|T_S) \\
&= h(h(h(ID\|K) \oplus h(BIO)\|(r_c \cdot G_S))\|G_C\|G_S\|T_S) \\
&= h(h(h(ID\|K) \oplus h(BIO)\|(r_c \cdot r_s \cdot G))\|G_C\|G_S\|T_S) \\
&= h(h(h(ID\|K) \oplus h(BIO)\|(r_s \cdot G_C))\|G_C\|G_S\|T_S) \\
&= h(K_{SU}\|G_C\|G_S\|T_S) \\
&= M_S
\end{aligned}
$$

The correctness of Eq. (8) is elaborated as follow.

$$
\begin{aligned}
&M_U{}^* \\
&= h(K_{SU}\|G_S\|T_t) \\
&= h(h(h(ID\|K) \oplus h(BIO)\|(r_s \cdot G_C))\|G_S\|T_t) \\
&= h(h(h(ID\|K) \oplus h(BIO)\|(r_s \cdot r_c \cdot G))\|G_S\|T_t) \\
&= h(h(h(ID\|K) \oplus h(BIO)\|(r_c \cdot G_S))\|G_S\|T_t) \\
&= h(K_{SU}{}^*\|G_S\|T_t) \\
&= M_U
\end{aligned}
$$

6.2   Security Analysis

Prompt Detection of Wrong Password. In the enhanced scheme, the user's password can be verified quickly in the beginning of the login phase. In the login phase, the user inputs his BIO, PW and inserts his smart card. Then, the smart card computes $A^* = h(PW \oplus X \oplus BIO)$. If A^* is equal to A stored in the smart card, the following steps of the login phase will continue. Otherwise, the smart card terminates the session because the user inputs a wrong password.

Detecting the wrong password promptly can terminate the authentication session before the smart card being sent to the server, which can resist more attacks with the smart card in communication channels. In addition, it can diminish the unnecessary communication cost and computational cost during the login and authentication phases.

Password Guessing Attack. The enhanced scheme can also resist the attacker with different data stored in the smart card at different times, which is demonstrated by Huang et al. in [20]. Huang et al. proposed some efficient countermeasures to resist such attack. They change $D = h(ID\|K) \oplus h(PW)$ into $D = h(ID\|K\|PW) \oplus h(PW)$. The attacker with the card can get the private values from the smart card at time T_1 and T_2. The attacker can do the following computation.

$$D_1 \oplus D_2 = h(ID\|K\|PW_1) \oplus h(PW_1) \oplus h(ID\|K\|PW_2) \oplus h(PW_2) \quad (12)$$

Obviously, the attacker can not guess the password without K. The enhanced scheme can also resist such attack. We also assume that the attacker with the card can get the private values from the smart card at time T_1 and T_2. The attacker can compute the value of $D_1 \oplus D_2$, but it can not obtain PW_1 and PW_2 without X and BIO. Although the attack may steal X from the smart card, it has no access to the user's BIO, which we have assumed in our security model.

$$D_1 = h(ID\|K) \oplus h(PW_1 \oplus X \oplus BIO) \quad (13)$$

$$D_2 = h(ID\|K) \oplus h(PW_2 \oplus X \oplus BIO) \quad (14)$$

$$D_1 \oplus D_2 = h(PW_1 \oplus X \oplus BIO) \oplus h(PW_2 \oplus X \oplus BIO) \quad (15)$$

Moreover, with extracted secret values A in the user's smart card, the attacker may attempt to acquire the user's password in the way of computing $A = h(PW \oplus X \oplus BIO)$. But the attacker cannot succeed because it has no access to the user's BIO.

Malicious Server Attack. In the enhanced scheme, the initial password is chosen by the user. On the contrary, if the initial password is chosen by the server when the server is malicious, the password may be leaked by the malicious server. Then the leaked password may be obtained by attackers and attackers can damage the security of the system with the password.

User Impersonation Attack. When the attacker wants to login to the server, he needs to forge the message $\{M, G_C, T_i\}$. But the attacker is unable to success due to the attacker cannot obtain M, G_C without the server's secret key and the random number chosen by the smart card. Although the attacker may extract M and G_C from the smart card and make a login request message $\{M, G_C, T_i\}$, the authentication will fail because the BIO is not available to the attacker.

Relay Attack. The attacker may retransmit the previous login request messages and mutual authentication messages to the server and user. In the enhanced scheme, we add the current timestamp to messages. The retransmitted messages can be detected quickly by checking the timestamp. The session will be terminated by the server or the smart card if the verification fails.

6.3 Security Comparison

The comparison of our enhanced scheme with the related schemes is summarized in Table 2. The enhanced scheme can withstand parallel session attack, relay attack, password guessing attack, user impersonation attack and attack with session key. Additionally, the enhanced scheme provides mutual authentication and session key agreement, which is relatively more secure than the related schemes.

Table 2. Security comparison with the related schemes

Securities	Scheme [4]	Scheme [10]	Scheme [11]	Scheme [18]	Our enhanced scheme
Quickly detect wrong password	No	No	No	Yes	Yes
Password guessing attack	Possible	Possible	Possible	Possible	Impossible
User impersonation attack	Possible	Possible	Possible	Possible	Impossible
Parallel session attack	Possible	Possible	Impossible	Possible	Impossible
Relay attack	Impossible	Possible	Impossible	Impossible	Impossible
Mutual authentication	No	Yes	Yes	Yes	Yes
Session key agreement	No	Yes	Yes	Yes	Yes

7 Conclusion

In this paper, we propose an enhanced remote password authentication key agreement scheme based on smart card. In the enhanced scheme, password verification is added in the beginning of the login phase. In addition, the communication cost and computational cost can be reduced in the login and authentication phases due to the use of the password verification. The initial password is installed by the user rather than the server, which can prevent the malicious server from leaking the password. In addition, attackers with the smart card cannot guess the password by obtaining the different private data from the smart card at different times. Moreover, the enhanced scheme can also resist relay attack.

Acknowledgment. This work is supported by the National Science Foundation of China under Grant No. 61672295, No. 61672290 and No. U1405254, the State Key Laboratory of Information Security under Grant No. 2017-MS-10, the 2015 Project of six personnel in Jiangsu Province under Grant No. R2015L06, the CICAEET fund, and the PAPD fund.

References

1. Lamport, L.: Password authentication with insecure communication. Commun. ACM **24**, 770–772 (1981)
2. Haller, N.M.: The S/KEY one-time password system. In: Proceedings of the Internet Society Symposium on Network and Distributed Systems, pp. 151–157 (1995)
3. Chen, C.M., Ku, W.C.: Stolen-verifier attack on two new strong-password authentication protocol. IEICE Trans. Commun. **85**, 2519–2521 (2002)
4. Chien, H., Jan, J., Tseng, Y.: An efficient and practical solution to remote authentication: smart card. Comput. Secur. **21**(4), 372–375 (2002)
5. Yoon, E.J., Ryu, E.K., Yoo, K.Y.: Further improvements of an efficient password based remote user authentication scheme using smart cards. IEEE Trans. Consum. Electron. **50**(2), 612–614 (2004)
6. Hsu, C.L.: Security of Chien et al.'s remote user authentication scheme using smart cards. Comput. Stand Interfaces **26**(3), 167–169 (2004)
7. Lee, S.W., Kim, H.S., Yoo, K.Y.: Improvement of Chien et al.'s remote user authentication scheme using smart cards. Comput. Stand Interfaces **27**(2), 181–183 (2005)
8. Lin, C.W., Tsai, C.S., Hwang, M.S.: A new strong-password authentication scheme using one-way hash functions. J. Comput. Syst. Sci. Int. **45**(4), 623–626 (2006)
9. Choo, K.-K.R., Boyd, C., Hitchcock, Y.: The importance of proofs of security for key establishment protocols: formal analysis of Jan-Chen, Yang-Shen-Shieh, Kim-Huh-Hwang-Lee, Lin-Sun-Hwang Yeh-Sun protocols. Comput. Commun. **29**(15), 2788–2797 (2006)
10. Juang, W.S., Chen, S.T., Liaw, H.T.: Robust and efficient password authenticated key agreement using smart cards. IEEE Trans. Ind. Electron. **55**(6), 2551–2556 (2008)
11. Sun, D., Huai, J., Sun, J., Li, J., Zhang, J., Feng, Z.: Improvements of Juang et al.'s password-authenticated key agreement scheme using smart card. IEEE Trans. Ind. Electron. **56**(6), 2284–2291 (2009)
12. Shen, J., Chang, S., Shen, J., Liu, Q., Sun, X.: A lightweight multi-layer authentication protocol for wireless body area networks. Future Gener. Comput. Syst. **78**, 956–963 (2016)
13. Sun, H.: An efficient remote user authentication scheme using smart cards. J. Netw. Comput. Appl. **46**(4), 958–961 (2000)
14. Li, C.T., Hwang, M.S.: An efficient biometrics-based remote user authentication scheme using smart cards. J. Netw. Comput. Appl. **33**, 1–5 (2010)

15. Shen, J., Shen, J., Chen, X., Huang, X., Susilo, W.: An efficient public auditing protocol with novel dynamic structure for cloud data. IEEE Trans. Inf. Forensics Secur. **12**(10), 2402–2415 (2017)
16. Song, R.: Advanced smart card-based password authentication protocol. Comput. Stand. Interfaces **32**(5), 321–325 (2010)
17. Das, A.K.: Analysis and improvement on an efficient biometric-based remote user authentication scheme using smart cards. IET Inf. Secur. **5**(3), 541–552 (2011)
18. An, Y.H.: Security enhancements of smart card-based remote user password authentication scheme with session key agreement. In: International Conference on Advanced Communication Technology (2015)
19. Shen, J., Liu, D., Liu, Q., Sun, X., Zhang, Y.: Secure authentication in cloud big data with hierarchical attribute authorization structure. IEEE Trans. Big Data (2017). https://doi.org/10.1109/TBDATA.2017.2705048
20. Huang, X., Chen, X., Li, J.: Further observations on smart-card-based password-authenticated key agreement in distributed systems. IEEE Trans. Parallel Distribut. Syst. **25**(7), 1767–1775 (2014)
21. Madhusudhan, R., Mittal, R.C.: Dynamic ID-based remote user password authentication scheme using smart cards: a review. J. Netw. Comput. Appl. **35**, 1235–1248 (2012)
22. Xie, Q., Zhao, J., Yu, X.: Chaotic maps-based three-party password-authenticated key agreement scheme. Nonlinear Dyn. **74**(4), 1021–1027 (2013)
23. Bellare, M., Pointcheval, D., Rogaway, P.: Authenticated key exchange secure against dictionary attacks. Tecnologia Electronica E Informatica, 139–155 (2000)
24. Messerges, T.S., Dabbish, E.A., Sloan, R.H.: Examining SmartCard security under the threat of power analysis attacks. IEEE Trans. Comput. **51**(5), 541–552 (2002)
25. Li, X., Niu, J., Khan, M.K.: An enhanced smart card based remote user password authentication scheme. J. Netw. Comput. Appl. **36**(5), 1365–1371 (2013)
26. Shen, J., Zhou, T., He, D., Zhang, Y., Sun, X., Xiang, Y.: Block design-based key agreement for group data sharing in cloud computing. IEEE Trans. Dependable Secure Comput. (2017). https://doi.org/10.1109/TDSC.2017.2725953
27. Zhang, L., Tang, S., Cai, Z.: Efficient and flexible password authenticated key agreement for voice over internet protocol session initiation protocol using smart card. Int. J. Commun. Syst. **27**(11), 2691–2702 (2015)
28. Jiang, Q., Ma, J., Tian, Y.: Cryptanalysis of smart-card-based password authenticated key agreement protocol for session initiation protocol of Zhang et al. Int. J. Commun. Syst. **28**(7), 1340–1351 (2015)
29. Odelu, V., Das, A.K., Goswami, A.: An efficient ECC-based privacy-preserving client authentication protocol with key agreement using smart card. J. Inf. Secur. Appl. **21**(C), 1–19 (2015)
30. Wang, D., Wang, P.: Two-factor authentication with security beyond conventional bound. IEEE Trans. Dependable Secure Comput. (2016). https://doi.org/10.1109/TDSC.2016.2605087
31. Wang, D., He, D., Wang, P., Chu, C.H.: Anonymous two-factor authentication in distributed systems: certain goals are beyond attainment. IEEE Trans. Dependable Secure Comput. **12**(4), 228–442 (2015)
32. Jiang, Q., Wei, F., Ma, J., Li, G.: Robust extended chaotic maps-based three-factor authentication scheme preserving biometric template privacy. Nonlinear Dyn. 83, 2085–2011 (2016)
33. Chaturvedi, A., Das, A.K., Mishra, D.: Design of a secure smart card-based multi-server authentication scheme. J. Inf. Secur. Appl. **30**, 64–80 (2016)

A Practical Authentication Protocol for Anonymous Web Browsing

Xu Yang[1]([⊠]), Xun Yi[1], Hui Cui[1], Xuechao Yang[1], Surya Nepal[2],
Xinyi Huang[3], and Yali Zeng[3]

[1] School of Science, RMIT University, Melbourne, VIC 3000, Australia
s3629637@student.rmit.edu.au
[2] CSIRO Data61, Sydney, NSW 2122, Australia
[3] School of Mathematics and informatics, Fujian Normal University, Fuzhou, China

Abstract. Authentication protocols with anonymity attract wide attention in recent years since they could protect users' privacy. Anonymous web browsing refers to utilization of the World Wide Web that hides a user's personally identifiable information from the websites visited. Even if a user can hide the IP address and other physical information with anonymity programs such as Tor, the web server can always monitor the user on the basis of the identity. In this paper, we propose a practical authentication protocol for anonymous web browsing. In the proposed protocol, we take the advantages of a pseudo identity mechanism and an identity-based elliptic curve cryptography algorithm to achieve the user anonymity, robust security as well as high efficiency. The results of security analysis and performance evaluation indicate the feasibility and practicality of our proposed anonymous authentication protocol.

Keywords: Authentication · Anonymous web browsing · Privacy
Security · Efficiency

1 Introduction

When a user opens a web page, his or her IP address and other computer information (e.g. device fingerprint) become visible to the target web page's server. This information can be used to track the user. Anonymous web browsing refers to the utilization of the World Wide Web that hides a user's personally identifiable information from the websites visited. Anonymous web browsing can be achieved via proxy servers, virtual private networks and other anonymity programs such as Tor [3].

These programs work by sending information through a series of routers in order to hide the source and destination. For example, Tor directs the Internet traffics through a free, worldwide, volunteer network consisting of more than seven thousand relays to conceal a user's location and usage from anyone conducting network surveillance or traffic analysis. Using Tor makes it more difficult for Internet activities to be traced back to the user: this includes visits to Web

J. K. Liu and P. Samarati (Eds.): ISPEC 2017, LNCS 10701, pp. 468–482, 2017.
https://doi.org/10.1007/978-3-319-72359-4_28

sites, online posts, instant messages, and other communication forms. Tor's use is intended to protect the personal privacy of users, as well as their freedom and ability to conduct confidential communication by keeping their Internet activities from being monitored.

Before a user can get access to some web services, he or she usually needs to register to a web server at first and is provided with a username and a password, with which the user is allowed to surf the web sites. Consider, for example, the Forrester Research or IBM patent server web sites. These sites are heavily used by many companies. Once you become a registered user, you gain access to a large volume of information. On the flip side, it is feasible for Forrester Research and IBM to determine who you are. And even worse, by examining your reading habits, they may be able to infer your company's corporate strategy and the new markets you are considering. Imagine if this information found its way to your competitors. Such a user tracking can also occur when subscribing to newspapers, magazines, stock databases, pay per view movies, and many other resources. The behavior of users might be aggregated and used in a potentially malicious manner.

Even if the user can hide his or her IP address and other computer information with anonymity programs such as Tor, the web server can always monitor the user on the basis of the username. Therefore, in order to protect the user privacy in this kind of applications, an anonymous web authentication mechanism is required.

In this paper, we consider a scenario where there exist some mobile users (MUs), an authentication server (AS) and several websites (WSs), where MUs include personal computers, smart phones, personal digital assistants and so on. A mobile user needs to register to the authentication server to access web services. Once the user becomes a registered user, he or she can get access to several websites via an anonymous channel implemented with anonymous programs such as Tor. The scenario in Fig. 1 can be illustrated as follows.

In order to provide a secure anonymous authentication scenario for mobile users, there are some key requirements that need to be taken into account. Anonymity is an important property of authentication. A privacy information leakage of mobile user could cause great inconvenience and the information could be utilized by an attacker in the future computer crimes. Apart from anonymity, efficiency and security of the authentication protocol are also of great importance. The computation and communication complexity of authentication protocol should be low and the protocol should stand against various attacks.

The early methods [4,10,12] in providing a mutual authentication between the user and the server are based on public-key cryptosystems (PKC), such as RSA and ElGamal. However, PKC needs to compute the time-consuming modular exponential operations and an extra key management system for certificate control [13]. Therefore, the traditional PKC-based authentication protocols are not suitable to mobile users with constrained capability.

Compared with traditional PKC-based authentication protocols, ID-based cryptography (IBC) authentication protocols show great advantages for mobile

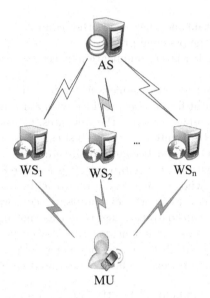

Fig. 1. A formal web authentication scenario

application scenarios. He et al. [5] present a secure and efficient anonymous authentication protocol based on bilinear pairing functions. However, He et al. [6] point out that [5] is not secure at all since it can not resist compromised key attack. Though they also propose an improved scheme, Yeo et al. [16] point out that He et al.' protocol [6] still suffers from the compromised key problem. Due to the complexity and inefficiency of the bilinear pairing operations, it is attractive to design authentication protocols without utilizing bilinear pairing.

In order to improve the efficiency, some anonymous authentication protocols [8,9,11,14,15] have been proposed based on Elliptic Curve Cryptography (ECC). Both Yang et al. [15] and Islam et al. [9] proposes an identity based scheme for MU authentication based on ECC. Unfortunately, their protocols suffer from a number of issues such as security attack and lack of user anonymity. To enhance the security, Hsieh et al. [8] also propose an improved anonymous authentication protocol based on ECC. However, He et al. [7] reveal that their protocol could easily obtain other users' identities, which means Hsieh et al.'s protocol [8] cannot preserve the user anonymity. Also, Li et al. [11] design an efficient privacy-aware roaming authentication protocol using ECC. However, Xie et al. [14] point out that Li et al.'s protocol is vulnerable to the impersonation attack and propose an improved protocol to enhance the security. Though the improvement on the security can resist impersonation attack, the original deficiency in [11] is not completely eliminated so that an attacker can still send a forged message and will be authenticated by an access point.

Taking into account the weaknesses in recent authentication protocols, in this paper, we take the advantage of identity-based elliptic curve algorithm [2] and propose a practical efficient authentication protocol for web browsing. In a nutshell, our main contributions can be summarized as follows.

(1) Our protocol is able to provide the user anonymity when a mobile user requires an authentication with the web server. The user anonymity is achieved using the pseudo identity mechanism. Any mobile user can be easily revoked by the system if it wishes to be revoked from the system or its secret key has been compromised.
(2) Except the mobile user and the web server, there is no need of an additional third party during the process of web authentication. And there are only two messages exchanged between the mobile user and the web server in the web authentication phase.
(3) By utilizing an elliptic curve cryptography algorithm, our authentication protocol achieves a higher efficiency and a robust security. Through the simulation analysis and comparison with other protocols, it shows that our protocol has a good performance in terms of computation and communication costs.

The remainder of this paper is organized as follows. Section 2 discusses some preliminaries, including the elliptic curve group, mathematical problems and the security requirements. In Sect. 3, we present a new web authentication protocol. Sections 4 and 5 provide the security analysis and performance evaluation of our protocol, respectively. At last, we conclude the paper in Sect. 6.

2   Preliminaries

In this section, we briefly introduce the elliptic curve cryptography, the corresponding mathematical problems over it, and the security requirements for an authentication protocol.

2.1   Elliptic Curve Cryptography

Let F_q be a prime finite field, $E/F_q : y^2 = x^3 + a \cdot x + b$ is an elliptic curve defined over F_q, where $a, b \in F_q$ and $\Delta = 4a^3 + 27b^2 \neq 0 \bmod q$. Let P be an element of a large prime order q in E/F_q. The points on E/F_q together with an extra point Θ, called the point at infinity, form a group $G = \{(x, y) : x, y \in F_q; (x, y) \in E/F_q\} \cup \{\Theta\}$. G is a cyclic additive group of composite order q. Besides, a scalar multiplication over E/F_q can be computed as follows: $tP = \underbrace{P + P + \cdots + P}_{t \ times}$,

where t is an integer.

2.2 Mathematical Problems

There exist the following problems over the elliptic curve group which have been widely used in the design of authentication protocols.

Discrete Logarithm (DL) Problem: For a random chosen value $a \in \mathbb{Z}_q^*$ and the generator P of G, given aP, it is computationally intractable to compute the value a.

Computational Diffie-Hellman (CDH) Problem: For random chosen values $a, b \in \mathbb{Z}_q^*$ and the generator P of G, given aP and bP, it is computationally intractable to compute the value abP.

2.3 Security Requirements

To guarantee a secure communication, the design of an authentication protocol should satisfy the following requirements:

(1) **Mutual authentication:** In order to ensure that only the legitimate users can access into the web service, the authentication protocol should provide a mutual authentication between MU and WS.

(2) **User anonymity:** To protect users' privacy, the legitimate users should be anonymous to any WS in a process of web authentication. Any adversary or curious WS should not be able to extract MU's real identity or trace MU's activities.

(3) **Conditional privacy preserving:** If there exists some users' actions that cause harm to the system, then the AS should be able to extract the real identity of MU via the messages exchanged in the process of web authentication.

(4) **Forward secrecy:** The session key shared between MU and WS may be known by an adversary through a compromised MU or WS. To address the potential threat of this compromised session key, the process of an authentication should be able to provide the forward secrecy to prevent an adversary from extracting the previous session keys.

(5) **Attack resistance:** Under various types of attacks (e.g., replay, impersonation, modification, man-in-the-middle, etc.), the security of the web authentication protocol should be able to withstand those aforementioned attacks so that it has a practical application value.

3 Proposed Protocol

In this section, we propose a new anonymous web browsing authentication protocol. Our protocol consists of four phases: system initialization phase, key pre-distribution phase, anonymous web authentication phase and user revocation phase. To facilitate the presentation, we list some related notations in Table 1.

Table 1. Notations in the protocol

Notation	Description
q	A k-bit prime
F_q	A prime finite field
E/F_q	An elliptic curve E over F_q
G	A cyclic additive group, $G = \{(x,y) : x,y \in E/F_q\} \cup \{\Theta\}$
P	Generator for the group G
ID_x	Identity of entity x
ts	A time stamp
$H_1()$	A secure hash function $H_1 : \{0,1\}^* \times G \to Z_q^*$
$H_2()$	A secure hash function $H_2 : \{0,1\}^* \times \{0,1\}^* \times G \to \{0,1\}^k$
$H_3()$	A secure hash function $H_3 : \{0,1\}^k \times G \to \{0,1\}^k$
$H_4()$	A secure hash function $H_4 : \{0,1\}^k \times G \times G \to Z_q^*$
PK	Public key
S_x	Entity x's private key
Ver_x	A verification value generated by entity x

3.1 System Initialization Phase

Here we assume that the AS is a trusted third party and it performs the process of system initialization to generate the system parameters. The AS executes the following operations:

(1) Properly chooses a k-bit prime q and determines the tuple $\{F_q, E/F_q, G, P\}$.
(2) Chooses random number $s \in Z_q^*$ as the master key, and compute the system public keys $PK = s \cdot P$.
(3) Chooses four secure hash functions H_1, H_2, H_3 and H_4.
(4) Publishes $\{F_q, E/F_q, G, P, PK, H_1, H_2, H_3, H_4\}$ as system parameters and keeps the master key secret.

3.2 Key Pre-distribution Phase

As is shown in Fig. 2, in this phase, both MU and WS send their identities to AS, then the AS responds with long-term secret key tuples for each MU and WS.

(1) When receiving ID_{WS} from a WS, the AS first checks the validity of this identity. If valid, the AS selects random numbers $r_{WS} \in Z_q^*$, then computes $R_{WS} = r_{WS} \cdot P$ and the private key $S_{WS} = r_{WS} + H_1(ID_{WS}\|R_{WS}) \cdot s$. Finally, it sends a long-term secret key tuple $(ID_{WS}, R_{WS}, S_{WS})$ to the WS using a secure transmission protocol (e.g., a wired transport layer security protocol). Upon receiving the private key S_{WS}, the WS can validate the

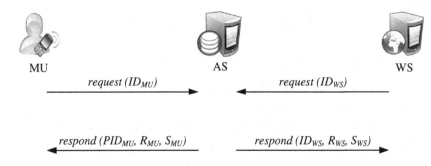

Fig. 2. Key pre-distribution phase

received private key by checking whether $PK_{WS} = S_{WS} \cdot P = R_{WS} + H_1(ID_{WS}\|R_{WS}) \cdot PK$ holds or not.

(2) Similarly, when an MU sends the request message to the AS with its real identity ID_{MU}, the AS first checks the validity. If the MU is valid, the AS selects random numbers $r_{MU} \in Z_q^*$, and then computes a pseudo-ID $PID_{MU} = ID_{MU} \oplus H_3(r_{MU}\|PK)$. For this pseudo-ID, the AS computes $R_{MU} = r_{MU} \cdot P$ and a corresponding private key $S_{MU} = r_{MU} + H_1(PID_{MU}\|R_{MU}) \cdot s$. At last, the AS securely sends the tuple $(PID_{MU}, R_{MU}, S_{MU})$ back to the MU. Upon receiving the tuples, the MU can check the received private key by $PK_{MU} = S_{MU} \cdot P = R_{MU} + H_1(PID_{MU}\|R_{MU}) \cdot PK$. By doing this, an MU can constantly change its pseudo-ID to achieve the user anonymity in the web authentication phase.

3.3   Anonymous Web Authentication Phase

In order to access wireless networks for web browsing, an MU needs to execute a web authentication process when it accesses a new WS. As shown in Fig. 3, a mutual authentication between the MU and the new WS shall be accomplished in this phase. The session key should be directly established between them during the web authentication phase. Here are the messages to be exchanged in the web authentication phase.

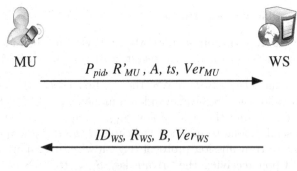

Fig. 3. Web authentication phase

(1) $MU \rightarrow WS : P_{pid}, R'_{MU}, A, ts, Ver_{MU}$

The MU first chooses the random values $a, c \in Z_q^*$, and computes $A = a \cdot P$, $P_{pid} = c \cdot H_1(PID_{MU} \| R_{MU})$, $R'_{MU} = c \cdot R_{MU}$ and $S'_{MU} = c \cdot S_{MU}$. Besides, let $H_{MU} = H_4(P_{pid} \| ts \| R'_{MU} \| A)$, where a time stamp ts is added by the MU to resist replay attacks (we assume that all network entities keep loose time synchronization via some existing time synchronization mechanisms). Then, the MU computes a verification value $Ver_{MU} = a + S'_{MU} \cdot H_{MU}$. After the executions, the MU sends the request message $\{P_{pid}, R'_{MU}, A, ts, Ver_{MU}\}$ to the WS.

(2) $WS \rightarrow MU : ID_{WS}, R_{WS}, B, Ver_{WS}$

Upon receiving the message, the WS first checks the time stamp ts to prevent the replay attack. If this time stamp ts is beyond the service expiration time, the WS drops this message. Otherwise, it computes $PK_{MU} = R'_{MU} + P_{pid} \cdot PK$ and $H_{MU} = H_4(P_{pid} \| ts \| R'_{MU} \| A)$. In order to verify the correctness of Ver_{MU}, the WS checks whether the equation $Ver_{MU} \cdot P = A + PK_{MU} \cdot H_{MU}$ holds. If it does not hold, WS drops this message. Otherwise, the MU will be authenticated by the WS. Then the WS chooses a random value $b \in Z_q^*$ to compute $B = b \cdot P$ and it also calculates a key $K_{WS-MU} = S_{WS} \cdot A + b \cdot PK_{MU}$ in order to generate the session key $SK_{WS-MU} = H_2(P_{pid} \| ID_{WS} \| K_{WS-MU})$. Similarly, for the purpose of being authenticated by the MU, the WS also generates a verification value $Ver_{WS} = H_1(SK_{WS-MU} \| A)$ and sends the response message $\{ID_{WS}, R_{WS}, B, Ver_{WS}\}$ to the MU.

(3) MU

When the MU receives the message sent back from the WS, it will calculate a key $K_{MU-WS} = S'_{MU} \cdot B + a \cdot PK_{WS}$ and generate the session key $SK_{MU-WS} = H_2(P_{pid} \| ID_{WS} \| K_{MU-WS})$. Then it checks whether $H_1(SK_{MU-WS} \| A)$ is equal to the received Ver_{WS}. The WS is successfully authenticated by the MU only if the confirmation value is correct. Otherwise, it terminates this authentication process. At the end of executions, the session key SK_{MU-WS} (SK_{WS-MU}) is established between the MU and the WS. This completes the mutual web authentication.

Key agreement: The session key shares between the MU and the WS can be checked by the following equations.

$$
\begin{aligned}
K_{WS-MU} &= S_{WS} \cdot A + b \cdot PK_{MU} \\
&= S_{WS} \cdot a \cdot P + b \cdot (P_{pid} \cdot PK + R'_{MU}) \\
&= a \cdot PK_{WS} + b \cdot (c \cdot H(PID_{MU} \| R_{MU}) \cdot s \cdot P + c \cdot r_{MU} \cdot P) \\
&= a \cdot PK_{WS} + (c \cdot (H(PID_{MU} \| R_{MU}) \cdot s + r_{MU})) \cdot b \cdot P \\
&= a \cdot PK_{WS} + (c \cdot S_{MU}) \cdot B \\
&= a \cdot PK_{WS} + S'_{MU} \cdot B \\
&= K_{MU-WS}
\end{aligned}
$$

$$SK_{WS-MU} = H(P_{pid}\|ID_{WS}\|K_{WS-MU})$$
$$= H(P_{pid}\|ID_{WS}\|K_{MU-WS})$$
$$= SK_{MU-WS}$$

Due to the random number a, b, c and the private key S_{MU}, S_{WS} are secret information, and the calculation of session key is based on CDH problem, only the legitimate MU and WS can generate the valid secret key to achieve the mutual authentication and establish the secret session key.

3.4   User Revocation Phase

If an MU wishes to revoke itself from the system or the secret key has been compromised, the AS will check it and revoke the MU from the system. The AS publishes a revocation list (RL) of all revoked users' identities and this RL can be updated periodically. The contents in this RL are listed as follows: $\{\{PID_{MU_1}, R_{MU_1}\}, \{PID_{MU_2}, R_{MU_2}\}, \ldots, \{PID_{MU_i}, R_{MU_i}\}, \ldots\}$.

When a WS receives the first message from MU, which includes its pseudo identity P_{pid} and the parameter R'_{MU}, the WS will first verify the verification value. If this message is valid, then the WS will check the identity on the RL by repeatedly checking whether $P_{pid} \cdot H_1(PID_{MU_i}\|R_{MU_i})^{-1} \cdot R_{MU}$ is equal to R'_{MU}. Due to $P_{pid} = c \cdot H_1(PID_{MU_j}\|R_{MU_j})$ and $R'_{MU} = c \cdot R_{MU_j}$, it is easy to match the equation $P_{pid} \cdot R_{MU} = H_1(PID_{MU_i}\|R_{MU_i}) \cdot R'_{MU}$ if $i = j$. If this equation matches, it means the corresponding $\{PID_{MU_j}, R_{MU_j}\}$ is revoked and the tuple $\{P_{pid}, R'_{MU}\}$ is invalid now. Otherwise, this MU is a legitimate user and has not been revoked.

4   Security Analysis

In this section, we discuss the security of our proposed protocol.

Mutual authentication: Here we only discuss the mutual authentication between the MU and the WS in the proposed protocol. The mutual authentication can be divided into two aspects, one is MU-to-WS authentication and another is WS-to-MU authentication.

- MU-to-WS authentication:
  When a WS receives the message $\{P_{pid}, R'_{MU}, A, ts, Ver_{MU}\}$ from an MU, the WS can authenticate this MU by verifying the key information in the message, which is the verification value Ver_{MU}. So we assume that an attacker $\mathcal{A}$ can forge a valid verification value Ver'_{MU} which can be successfully verified by the WS with a non-negligible advantage. The forged message of $\mathcal{A}$ should be like $\{P_{pid}, R'_{MU}, A, ts', Ver'_{MU}\}$ to satisfy the equation $Ver'_{MU} \cdot P = A + S'_{MU} \cdot H'_{MU} \cdot P$. Because the real verification value satisfies $Ver_{MU} \cdot P = A + S'_{MU} \cdot H_{MU} \cdot P$, we can get $(Ver'_{MU} - Ver_{MU}) \cdot P = (H'_{MU} - H_{MU}) \cdot S'_{MU} \cdot P$. Thus the attacker $\mathcal{A}$ can get the value $(Ver'_{MU} - Ver_{MU}) \cdot (H'_{MU} - H_{MU})^{-1} mod \ q$ as the answer of the given DL problem. However, it contradicts with the

assumption of the DL problem. That is, an attacker $\mathcal{A}$ can not be successfully authenticated by the WS. Therefore, our proposed protocol can provide the MU-to-WS authentication.

- WS-to-MU authentication:
  When an MU gets the response message $\{ID_{WS}, R_{WS}, B, Ver_{WS}\}$ from a WS, the MU can authenticate this WS by generating the valid session key to check the verification value Ver_{WS}. The key information to complete WS-to-MU authentication is the secret key $K_{WS-MU} = S_{WS} \cdot A + b \cdot PK_{MU}$. So the security analysis of WS-to-MU authentication is actually similar to that of key agreement. We assume that an attacker $\mathcal{A}$ can forge a valid secret key $K'_{WS-MU} = V + b' \cdot PK_{MU}$ to generate the verification value and then can be successfully verified by the MU with a non-negligible advantage. That is, $\mathcal{A}$ can use $PK_{WS} = S_{WS} \cdot P$ and $A = a \cdot P$ to obtain the value of V which is equal to $S_{WS} \cdot a \cdot P$. However, it contradicts with the assumption of the CDH problem. Therefore, an attacker $\mathcal{A}$ can not be successfully authenticated by the MU. Our proposed protocol can provide the secure WS-to-MU authentication.

User anonymity and conditional privacy preserving: In our protocol, the MU gets a pseudo identity PID_{MU} and the corresponding parameter R_{MU} from the AS. Before the process of web authentication, the MU generates a new pseudo identity P_{pid} and the corresponding R'_{MU} with a random number c. Therefore, the MU can ensure every pseudo identity P_{pid} and the corresponding R'_{MU} are just used once. The attacker can not identify the real identity of MU or track this MU by two different pseudo identities. Furthermore, if there is an MU in the system who has been compromised or just broken the rules, the AS can track this MU by collecting its pseudo identity P_{pid} and the corresponding R'_{MU}. The AS can extract the user's initial identity PID_{MU} and the corresponding R_{MU} from the stored user list. Then it can do a cycle verification on computing $c' = P_{pid} \cdot H_1(PID_{MU} \| R_{MU})^{-1}$ and checking whether $c' \cdot R_{MU}$ is equal to R'_{MU}. If equal, then the AS can extract the real identity ID_{MU} of the MU from the stored user list. Therefore, our authentication protocol can provide the user anonymity and achieve the conditional privacy preserving.

Forward secrecy: The session key in our protocol is generated by a hash function $SK_{WS-MU} = H_2(P_{pid} \| ID_{WS} \| K_{WS-MU}) \to \{0,1\}^k$, so this session key has no relation with other session keys. Therefore, even if an attacker can obtain a session key, it does not impact the security of the process of web authentication.

Attack resistance: Our scheme can resist the following attacks.

- Replay attack: A replay attack is infeasible in our scheme because we use a time stamp ts to prevent the replay attacks; that is, any replay messages does not go beyond the service expiration time. Even if the time stamp ts can be updated by an attacker in the replay message, the attacker can not generate a valid verification value Ver_{MU} related to this new ts. So it is not possible to successfully pass the verification due to the different ts.

- Impersonation attack: As is analyzed in the mutual authentication, impersonating an authorized MU or WS for sending or receiving information are prevented since an impersonate attacker can not generate the valid verification values and the session key. As a consequence, our protocol is able to resist the impersonation attack.
- Modification attack: The verification value Ver_{MU} is calculated by the MU's private key and the one-way hash function. The one-way hash function in the authentication message can ensure the data integrity. Therefore, it is impossible to modify a valid message during authentication.
- Man-in-the-middle attack: As the key agreement in our scheme is based on the CDH problem, both MU and WS send the packets by checking the Diffie-Hellman public components and generate session keys via the long-term secret keys, which makes our protocol secure against the attacker who would like to cheat by eavesdropping in the middle to forge or replay the messages.

5   Performance Evaluation

In this section, we discuss the performance of our web authentication protocol and compare with a most recent authentication protocol [14]. We analyze the performance of our protocol in terms of computation and communication costs. All tests are performed on a laptop with the following specifications: CPU: 2.2 GHz Intel Core i7, Memory: 16 GB 1600 MHz DDR3, and we also used a high performing implementation from libgmp via the gmpy2 python module (https://gmpy2.readthedocs.io/en/latest/).

The computation overhead represents the processing delays of the cryptography operations at each entity. We only consider the cost of operations listed as (T_M, T_A, T_H), where we denote the time for one elliptic curve scalar multiplication operation as T_M, the time for one elliptic curve point addition operation as T_A and the time for a hash operation as T_H. According to NIST recommended key size [1], we test the computation time and communication size in 5 rounds based on the key sizes of ECC: 160 bits, 224 bits, 256 bits, 384 bits and 512 bits. As is known, with the increase of the key size, the security of ECC operations will be enhanced, but it also will result in the low efficiency of computation and communication costs. The time cost of executing ECC operations on different key sizes is shown in Table 2.

We also assume that the sizes of an MU's pseudo identity, a WS's identity, timestamp, and general hash functions output are 32 bits, 32 bits, 32 bits, and 160 bits, respectively. Based on these facts, we analyze the computation and communication costs of the key pre-distribution and the anonymous web authentication phase in our protocol. Table 3 shows the computation and communication consumption results of our evaluation.

In the key pre-distribution phase of our protocol, the computation costs on both MU and WS are the same and consist of two scalar multiplication operations, one point addition operation and one hash operation, i.e., the total execution time is $2T_M + T_A + T_H$. The computation costs on AS consist of two

Table 2. The time cost of executing ECC operations on different key sizes

Key size (bits)	T_M (ms)	T_A (ms)
160	1.541	0.009
224	4.241	0.016
256	5.461	0.018
384	19.777	0.044
512	56.963	0.088

Table 3. Computation and communication consumption

		Computation cost	Communication cost
Key pre-distribution	MU:	$2T_M + T_A + T_H$	32
	WS:	$2T_M + T_A + T_H$	32
	AS:	$2T_M + 2T_H$	$160 + 2s^{\text{a}}$
Web authentication	MU:	$4T_M + T_A + 4T_H$	$352 + 4s$
	WS:	$6T_M + 3T_A + 3T_H$	$192 + 4s$

[a] s denotes the key size of ECC.

scalar multiplication operations and two point addition operation, i.e., the total execution time is $2T_M + 2T_A$. Therefore, the total computation costs in key pre-distribution phase are $6T_M + 4T_A + 2T_H$. Similarly, in the anonymous web authentication phase of our protocol, the computation costs on the MU consist of four scalar multiplication operations, one point addition operation and four hash operations, i.e., the total execution time of MU is $4T_M + T_A + 4T_H$. The computation costs on the WS consist of six scalar multiplication operations, three point addition operations and three hash operations, i.e., the total execution time of WS is $6T_M + 3T_A + 3T_H$. Therefore, the total computation costs in the anonymous web authentication phase are $10T_M + 4T_A + 7T_H$. The total computation costs of the key pre-distribution phase and the anonymous web authentication phase on different key sizes of ECC are shown in Fig. 4(a). Similarly, the total communication costs of the key pre-distribution phase and the anonymous web authentication phase on different key sizes of ECC are shown in Fig. 4(b). From these two figures, we can find that when the key size of ECC is 160 bits, the computation costs in both web authentication and key pre-distribution phases are less than 20 ms, and the computation costs are less than 2000 bits. Even if the key size of ECC is 512 bits, the computation and communication costs are less than 600 ms and 5000 bits, respectively.

Comparison: Our protocol is compared with the most recent authentication protocol [14]. Xie et al.'s protocol is also based on the elliptic curve cryptography. Apart from the security problem, here we mainly evaluate the computation and

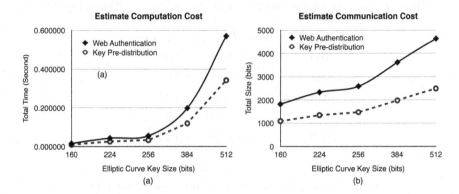

Fig. 4. (a) Total computation costs of our protocol on different key sizes; (b) Total communication costs of our protocol on different key sizes.

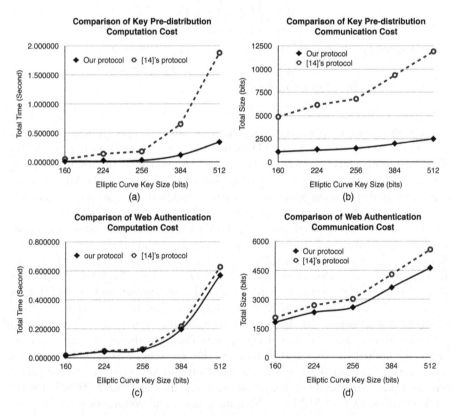

Fig. 5. (a) Comparison on the computation cost of key pre-distribution phase; (b) Comparison on the communication cost of key pre-distribution phase; (c) Comparison on the computation cost of authentication phase; (d) Comparison on the communication cost of authentication phase.

communication costs of the protocols. We assume that an MU gets 10 pseudo-identities in the key pre-distribution phase in [14]. The total computation costs of the key pre-distribution phase and authentication phase in [14] are $33T_M + 11T_A + 22T_H$ and $11T_M + 5T_A + 8T_H$, respectively. Also, the total communication costs of the key pre-distribution phase and the authentication phase in [14] are $1664 + 20s$ and $416 + 10s$, respectively. As is shown in Fig. 5, we compare the communication and computation costs of both key pre-distribution phase and authentication phase based on on different key sizes of ECC.

Overall, the simulation results show that our authentication protocol only incurs little computation and communication costs and achieves much better performance in comparison with other proposed protocol.

6   Conclusion

In this paper, we have proposed a practical and efficient authentication protocol based on the identity-based elliptic curve cryptography for the anonymous web browsing. User anonymity is fulfilled in key pre-distribution phase by using the pseudo identity mechanism. The web authentication phase is efficient with only two messages exchanged. Besides, our protocol also provides a user revocation mechanism for mobile users. Both the security analysis and performance evaluation indicate the feasibility and practicality of our proposed authentication protocol.

Acknowledgement. This work is partial supported by Australian Research Council Discovery Project (DP160100913: Security and Privacy of Individual Data Used to Extract Public Information) and Data61 Research Collaborative Project (Enhancing Security and Privacy in IoT).

References

1. BlueKrypt: Nist key length recommended (2016). https://www.keylength.com/en/4/
2. Cao, X., Kou, W., Du, X.: A pairing-free identity-based authenticated key agreement protocol with minimal message exchanges. Inf. Sci. **180**(15), 2895–2903 (2010)
3. Dingledine, R., Mathewson, N., Syverson, P.: Tor: the second-generation onion router. Technical report, DTIC Document (2004)
4. Halevi, S., Krawczyk, H.: Public-key cryptography and password protocols. ACM Trans. Inf. Syst. Secur. (TISSEC) **2**(3), 230–268 (1999)
5. He, D., Chen, C., Chan, S., Bu, J.: Secure and efficient handover authentication based on bilinear pairing functions. IEEE Trans. Wirel. Commun. **11**(1), 48–53 (2012)
6. He, D., Khan, K.M., Kumar, N.: A new handover authentication protocol based on bilinear pairing functions for wireless networks. Int. J. Ad Hoc Ubiquitous Comput. **18**(1–2), 67–74 (2015)

7. He, D., Zhang, Y., Chen, J.: Cryptanalysis and improvement of an anonymous authentication protocol for wireless access networks. Wirel. Pers. Commun. **74**(2), 229–243 (2014)
8. Hsieh, W.B., Leu, J.S.: Anonymous authentication protocol based on elliptic curve Diffie-Hellman for wireless access networks. Wirel. Commun. Mobile Comput. **14**(10), 995–1006 (2014)
9. Islam, S.H., Biswas, G.: A more efficient and secure id-based remote mutual authentication with key agreement scheme for mobile devices on elliptic curve cryptosystem. J. Syst. Softw. **84**(11), 1892–1898 (2011)
10. Krawczyk, H.: HMQV: a high-performance secure Diffie-Hellman protocol. In: Shoup, V. (ed.) CRYPTO 2005. LNCS, vol. 3621, pp. 546–566. Springer, Heidelberg (2005). https://doi.org/10.1007/11535218_33
11. Li, G., Jiang, Q., Wei, F., Ma, C.: A new privacy-aware handover authentication scheme for wireless networks. Wirel. Pers. Commun. **80**(2), 581–589 (2015)
12. Neuman, B.C., Ts'o, T.: Kerberos: an authentication service for computer networks. IEEE Commun. Mag. **32**(9), 33–38 (1994)
13. Wang, D., Cheng, H., He, D., Wang, P.: On the challenges in designing identity-based privacy-preserving authentication schemes for mobile devices. IEEE Syst. J. **PP**(99), 1–10 (2016)
14. Xie, Y., Wu, L., Kumar, N., Shen, J.: Analysis and improvement of a privacy-aware handover authentication scheme for wireless network. Wirel. Pers. Commun. **93**(2), 523–541 (2017)
15. Yang, J.H., Chang, C.C.: An ID-based remote mutual authentication with key agreement scheme for mobile devices on elliptic curve cryptosystem. Comput. Secur. **28**(3), 138–143 (2009)
16. Yeo, S.L., Yap, W.S., Liu, J.K., Henricksen, M.: Comments on "analysis and improvement of a secure and efficient handover authentication based on bilinear pairing functions". IEEE Commun. Lett. **17**(8), 1521–1523 (2013)

Cloud Security

Dynamic Provable Data Possession Protocols with Public Verifiability and Data Privacy

Clémentine Gritti[1]([⊠]), Rongmao Chen[2], Willy Susilo[3], and Thomas Plantard[3]

[1] EURECOM, Sophia Antipolis, France
clementine.gritti@eurecom.fr
[2] College of Computer, National University of Defense Technology, Changsha, China
chromao@nudt.edu.cn
[3] School of Computing and Information Technology, University of Wollongong, Wollongong, Australia
{wsusilo,thomaspl}@uow.edu.au

Abstract. Cloud storage services have become accessible and used by everyone. Nevertheless, stored data are dependable on the behavior of the cloud servers, and losses and damages often occur. One solution is to regularly audit the cloud servers in order to check the integrity of the stored data. The Dynamic Provable Data Possession scheme with Public Verifiability and Data Privacy presented in ACISP'15 is a straightforward design of such solution. However, this scheme is threatened by several attacks. In this paper, we carefully recall the definition of this scheme as well as explain how its security is dramatically menaced. Moreover, we proposed two new constructions for Dynamic Provable Data Possession scheme with Public Verifiability and Data Privacy based on the scheme presented in ACISP'15, one using Index Hash Tables and one based on Merkle Hash Trees. We show that the two schemes are secure and privacy-preserving in the random oracle model.

Keywords: Provable Data Possession · Dynamicity
Public verifiability · Data privacy · Index Hash Tables
Merkle Hash Trees

1 Introduction

Storage systems allow everyone to upload his/her data on cloud servers, and thus avoid keeping them on his/her own devices that have often limited storage capacity and power. Nevertheless, storage services are susceptible to attacks or failures, and lead to possible non-retrievable losses of the stored data. Indeed, storage systems are vulnerable to internal and external attacks that harm the data integrity even being more powerful and reliable than the data owner's personal computing devices. A solution is to construct a system that offers an efficient, frequent and secure data integrity check process to the data owner such that the frequency of data integrity verification and the percentage of audited

© Springer International Publishing AG 2017
J. K. Liu and P. Samarati (Eds.): ISPEC 2017, LNCS 10701, pp. 485–505, 2017.
https://doi.org/10.1007/978-3-319-72359-4_29

data should not be limited by computational and communication costs on both cloud server's and data owner's sides.

A Provable Data Possession (PDP) enables a data owner, called the *client*, to verify the integrity of his/her data stored on an untrusted cloud server, without having to retrieve them. Informally, the client first divides his/her data into blocks, generates tags on each block, and then forwards all these elements to the server. In order to check whether the data are correctly stored by the server, the client sends a challenge such that the server replies back by creating a proof of data possession. If the proof is correct, then this means that the storage of the data is correctly done by the server; otherwise, this means that the server is actually cheating somehow. Natural extension features of PDP include: (1) Dynamicity (D) that enables the client to update his/her data stored on the server via three operations (insertion, deletion and modification); (2) Public verifiability (PV) that allows a client to indirectly check that the server correctly stores his/her data by enabling a Third Party Auditor (TPA) or everyone else to do the audit; (3) Data privacy (DP) preservation that ensures that the contents of the stored data are not leaked to neither the TPA nor anyone else. We require that a Dynamic PDP (DPDP) with PV and DP system is secure at untrusted server, which means that the server cannot successfully generate a proof of data possession that is correct without actually storing all the data. In addition, a DPDP with PV and DP system should be data privacy-preserving, which means that the TPA should not learn anything about the client's data even by having access to the public information.

Gritti et al. [9] recently constructed an efficient and practical DPDP system with PV and DP. However, we have found three attacks threatening this construction: (1) The *replace attack* enables the server to store only one block of a file m and still pass the data integrity verification on any number of blocks; (2) The *replay attack* permits the server to keep the old version of a block m_i and the corresponding tag T_{m_i}, after the client asked to modify them by sending the new version of these elements, and still pass the data integrity verification; (3) The *attack against data privacy* allows the TPA to distinguish files when proceeding the data integrity check without accessing their contents. We then propose two solutions to overcome the adversarial issues threatening the DPDP scheme with PV and DP in [9]. We give a first new publicly verifiable DPDP construction based on Index Hash Tables (IHT) in the random oracle model. We prove that such scheme is secure against replace and replay attacks as well as is data privacy-preserving according to a model differing from the one proposed in [9]. We present a second new publicly verifiable DPDP construction based on Merkle Hash Trees (MHT) in the random oracle model. We demonstrate that such scheme is not vulnerable against the three attacks mentioned above. In particular, we use the existing model given in [9] to prove that the MHT-based scheme is data privacy-preserving.

1.1 Related Work

Ateniese et al. [1] introduced the notion of Provable Data Possession (PDP) which allows a client to verify the integrity of his/her data stored at an untrusted server without retrieving the entire file. Their scheme is designed for static data and used homomorphic authenticators as tags based on public key encryption for auditing the data file. Subsequently, Ateniese et al. [2] improved the efficiency of the aforementioned PDP scheme by using symmetric keys. The resulting scheme gets lower overhead and partially supports partial dynamic data operations. Thereafter, various PDP constructions were proposed in the literature [10,20,23, 24]. Moreover, PDP schemes with the property of full dynamicity were suggested in [4,18,19,25,26]. An extension of DPDP includes version control [3,6] where all data changes are recorded into a repository and any version of the data can be retrieved at any time. DPDP protocols with multi-update capability were suggested in [5]. More recently, data privacy-preserving and publicly verifiable PDP schemes were presented in [7,9,14–17].

2 Preliminaries

Let $\mathbb{G}_1$, $\mathbb{G}_2$ and $\mathbb{G}_T$ be three multiplicative cyclic groups of prime order $p \in \Theta(2^\lambda)$ (where λ is the security parameter). Let g_k be a generator of $\mathbb{G}_k$ for $k \in \{1, 2\}$, that we denote $< g_k > = \mathbb{G}_k$.

Bilinear Maps: Let $e : \mathbb{G}_1 \times \mathbb{G}_2 \to \mathbb{G}_T$ be a bilinear map with the following properties: (1) *Bilinearity:* $\forall u \in \mathbb{G}_1, \forall v \in \mathbb{G}_2, \forall a, b \in \mathbb{Z}_p, e(u^a, v^b) = e(u, v)^{ab}$. (2) *Non-degeneracy:* $e(g_1, g_2) \neq 1_{\mathbb{G}_T}$. $\mathbb{G}_1$ and $\mathbb{G}_2$ are said to be bilinear groups if the group operation in $\mathbb{G}_1 \times \mathbb{G}_2$ and the bilinear map e are both efficiently computable. Let GroupGen denote an algorithm that on input the security parameter λ, outputs the parameters $(p, \mathbb{G}_1, \mathbb{G}_2, \mathbb{G}_T, e, g_1, g_2)$.

Discrete Logarithm (DL) Assumption: Let $a \in_R \mathbb{Z}_p$. If $\mathcal{A}$ is given an instance (g_1, g_1^a), it remains hard to extract $a \in \mathbb{Z}_p$. The DL assumption holds if no polynomial-time adversary $\mathcal{A}$ has non-negligible advantage in solving the DL problem.

Computational Diffie-Hellman (CDH) Assumption: Let $a, b \in_R \mathbb{Z}_p$. If $\mathcal{A}$ is given an instance (g_1, g_1^a, g_1^b), it remains hard to compute $g_1^{ab} \in \mathbb{G}_1$. The CDH assumption holds if no polynomial-time adversary $\mathcal{A}$ has non-negligible advantage in solving the CDH problem.

Decisional Diffie-Hellman Exponent (DDHE) Assumption: Let $\beta \in_R \mathbb{Z}_p$. If $\mathcal{A}$ is given an instance $(g_1, g_1^\beta, \cdots, g_1^{\beta^{s+1}}, g_2, g_2^\beta, Z)$, it remains hard to decide if either $Z = g_1^{\beta^{s+2}}$ or Z is a random element in $\mathbb{G}_1$. The $(s+1)$-DDHE assumption holds if no polynomial-time adversary $\mathcal{A}$ has non-negligible advantage in solving the $(s+1)$-DDHE problem.

2.1   Definition of the DPDP Scheme with PV and DP

Let m be a data file to be stored that is divided into n *blocks* m_i, and then each block m_i is divided into s *sectors* $m_{i,j} \in \mathbb{Z}_p$, where p is a large prime. A DPDP scheme with PV and DP is made of the following algorithms:

• KeyGen$(\lambda) \rightarrow (pk, sk)$. On input the security parameter λ, output a pair of public and secret keys (pk, sk).

• TagGen$(pk, sk, m_i) \rightarrow T_{m_i}$. TagGen is independently run for each block. Therefore, to generate the tag T_m for a file m, TagGen is run n times. On inputs the public key pk, the secret key sk and a file $m = (m_1, \cdots, m_n)$, output a tag $T_m = (T_{m_1}, \cdots, T_{m_n})$ where each block m_i has its own tag T_{m_i}. The client sets all the blocks m_i in an ordered collection $\mathbb{F}$ and all the corresponding tags T_{m_i} in an ordered collection $\mathbb{E}$. He/she sends $\mathbb{F}$ and $\mathbb{E}$ to the server and removes them from his/her local storage.

• PerfOp$(pk, \mathbb{F}, \mathbb{E}, info = (\text{operation}, l, m_l, T_{m_l})) \rightarrow (\mathbb{F}', \mathbb{E}', \nu')$. On inputs the public key pk, the previous collection $\mathbb{F}$ of all the blocks, the previous collection $\mathbb{E}$ of all the corresponding tags, the type of the data operation to be performed, the rank l where the data operation is performed in $\mathbb{F}$, the block m_l to be updated and the corresponding tag T_{m_l} to be updated, output the updated block collection $\mathbb{F}'$, the updated tag collection $\mathbb{E}'$ and an updating proof ν'. For the operation: (1) *Insertion:* $m_l = m_{\frac{i_1+i_2}{2}}$ is inserted between the consecutive blocks m_{i_1} and m_{i_2} and $T_{m_l} = T_{m_{\frac{i_1+i_2}{2}}}$ is inserted between the consecutive tags $T_{m_{i_1}}$ and $T_{m_{i_2}}$. We assume that $m_{\frac{i_1+i_2}{2}}$ and $T_{m_{\frac{i_1+i_2}{2}}}$ were provided by the client to the server, such that $T_{m_{\frac{i_1+i_2}{2}}}$ was correctly computed by running TagGen. (2) *Deletion:* $m_l = m_i$ is deleted, meaning that m_{i_1} is followed by m_{i_2} and $T_{m_l} = T_{m_i}$ is deleted, meaning that $T_{m_{i_1}}$ is followed by $T_{m_{i_2}}$, such that i_1, i, i_2 were three consecutive ranks. (3) *Modification:* $m_l = m_i'$ replaces m_i and $T_{m_l} = T_{m_i'}$ replaces T_{m_i}. We assume that m_i' and $T_{m_i'}$ were provided by the client to the server, such that $T_{m_i'}$ was correctly computed by running TagGen. After operations, the set of ranks becomes $(0, n+1) \cap \mathbb{Q}$.

• CheckOp$(pk, \nu') \rightarrow 0/1$. On inputs the public key pk and the updating proof ν' sent by the server, output 1 if ν' is a correct updating proof; output 0 otherwise.

• GenProof$(pk, F, chal, \Sigma) \rightarrow \nu$. On inputs the public key pk, an ordered collection $F \subset \mathbb{F}$ of blocks, a challenge $chal$ and an ordered collection $\Sigma \subset \mathbb{E}$ which are the tags corresponding to the blocks in F, output a proof of data possession ν for the blocks in F that are determined by $chal$.

• CheckProof$(pk, chal, \nu) \rightarrow 0/1$. On inputs the public key pk, the challenge $chal$ and the proof of data possession ν, output 1 if ν is a correct proof of data possession for the blocks determined by $chal$; output 0 otherwise.

Correctness. We require that a DPDP with PV and DP is *correct* if for $(pk, sk) \leftarrow$ KeyGen(λ), $T_m \leftarrow$ TagGen(pk, sk, m), $(\mathbb{F}', \mathbb{E}', \nu') \leftarrow$ PerfOp$(pk, \mathbb{F}, \mathbb{E}, info)$, $\nu \leftarrow$ GenProof$(pk, F, chal, \Sigma)$, then $1 \leftarrow$ CheckOp(pk, ν') and $1 \leftarrow$ CheckProof$(pk, chal, \nu)$.

2.2   Security and Privacy Models

Security Model Against the Server. The model follows the ones in [1,4,9]. We consider a DPDP with PV and DP as defined above. Let a data possession game between a challenger $\mathcal{B}$ and an adversary $\mathcal{A}$ (acting as the server) be as follows:

$\diamond$ *Setup.* $\mathcal{B}$ runs $(pk, sk) \leftarrow \mathsf{KeyGen}(\lambda)$ such that pk is given to $\mathcal{A}$ while sk is kept secret.

$\diamond$ *Adaptive Queries.* First, $\mathcal{A}$ is given access to a tag generation oracle $\mathcal{O}_{TG}$. $\mathcal{A}$ chooses blocks m_i and gives them to $\mathcal{B}$, for $i \in [1, n]$. $\mathcal{B}$ runs $\mathsf{TagGen}(pk, sk, m_i) \rightarrow T_{m_i}$ and gives them to $\mathcal{A}$. Then, $\mathcal{A}$ creates two ordered collections $\mathbb{F} = \{m_i\}_{i \in [1,n]}$ of blocks and $\mathbb{E} = \{T_{m_i}\}_{i \in [1,n]}$ of the corresponding tags. Then, $\mathcal{A}$ is given access to a data operation performance oracle $\mathcal{O}_{DOP}$. For $i \in [1, n]$, $\mathcal{A}$ gives to $\mathcal{B}$ a block m_i and $info_i$ about the operation that $\mathcal{A}$ wants to perform. $\mathcal{A}$ also submits two new ordered collections $\mathbb{F}'$ of blocks and $\mathbb{E}'$ of tags, and the updating proof ν'. $\mathcal{B}$ runs $\mathsf{CheckOp}(pk, \nu')$ and replies the answer to $\mathcal{A}$. If the answer is 0, then $\mathcal{B}$ aborts; otherwise, it proceeds. The above interaction between $\mathcal{A}$ and $\mathcal{B}$ can be repeated. Note that the set of ranks has changed after calls to the oracle $\mathcal{O}_{DOP}$.

$\diamond$ *Challenge.* $\mathcal{A}$ chooses blocks m_i^* and $info_i^*$, for $i \in \mathcal{I} \subseteq (0, n+1) \cap \mathbb{Q}$. Adaptive queries can be again made by $\mathcal{A}$, such that the first $info_i^*$ specifies a full re-write update (this corresponds to the first time that the client sends a file to the server). $\mathcal{B}$ still checks the data operations. For $i \in \mathcal{I}$, the final version of m_i is considered such that these blocks were created regarding the operations requested by $\mathcal{A}$, and verified and accepted by $\mathcal{B}$ beforehand. $\mathcal{B}$ sets $\mathbb{F} = \{m_i\}_{i \in \mathcal{I}}$ of these blocks and $\mathbb{E} = \{T_{m_i}\}_{i \in \mathcal{I}}$ of the corresponding tags. It then sets two ordered collections $F = \{m_{i_j}\}_{i_j \in \mathcal{I}, j \in [1,k]} \subset \mathbb{F}$ and $\Sigma = \{T_{m_{i_j}}\}_{i_j \in \mathcal{I}, j \in [1,k]} \subset \mathbb{E}$. It computes a resulting challenge $chal$ for F and Σ and sends it to $\mathcal{A}$.

$\diamond$ *Forgery.* $\mathcal{A}$ computes a proof of data possession ν^* on $chal$. Then, $\mathcal{B}$ runs $\mathsf{CheckProof}(pk, chal, \nu^*)$ and replies the answer to $\mathcal{A}$. If the answer is 1 then $\mathcal{A}$ wins.

The advantage of $\mathcal{A}$ in winning the data possession game is defined as $Adv_{\mathcal{A}}(\lambda) = Pr[\mathcal{A} \text{ wins}]$. The DPDP with PV and DP is *secure against the server* if there is no PPT (probabilistic polynomial-time) adversary $\mathcal{A}$ who can win the above game with non-negligible advantage $Adv_{\mathcal{A}}(\lambda)$.

Data Privacy Model Against the TPA. In a DPDP protocol, we aim to ensure that data privacy is preserved at the verification step, meaning that data are accessible to all but protected only via a non-cryptographic access control, and the verification process does not leak any information on the data blocks.

First Data Privacy Model. The model is found in [17,20]. We consider a DPDP with PV and DP as defined above. Let the first data privacy game between a challenger $\mathcal{B}$ and an adversary $\mathcal{A}$ (acting as the TPA) be as follows:

$\diamond$ *Setup.* $\mathcal{B}$ runs $\mathsf{KeyGen}(\lambda)$ to generate (pk, sk) and gives pk to $\mathcal{A}$, while sk is kept secret.

◇ *Queries.* $\mathcal{A}$ is allowed to make queries as follows. $\mathcal{A}$ sends a file $m = (m_1, \cdots, m_n)$ to $\mathcal{B}$. $\mathcal{B}$ computes $T_m = (T_{m_1}, \cdots, T_{m_n})$ and gives it back to $\mathcal{A}$. Then, two ordered collections $\mathbb{F} = \{m_i\}_{i \in [1,n]}$ of blocks and $\mathbb{E} = \{T_{m_i}\}_{i \in [1,n]}$ of tags are created.

◇ *Challenge.* $\mathcal{A}$ submits a challenge *chal* containing $k \leq n$ ranks, the k corresponding blocks in F and their k tags in Σ.

◇ *Generation of the Proof.* $\mathcal{B}$ computes a proof of data possession $\nu^* \leftarrow$ GenProof($pk, F, chal, \Sigma$) such that the blocks in F are determined by *chal* and Σ contains the corresponding tags.

$\mathcal{A}$ succeeds in the first data privacy game if $F \not\subseteq \mathbb{F}$ and $\Sigma \not\subseteq \mathbb{E}$, and CheckProof($pk, chal, \nu^*$) $\rightarrow 1$. The advantage of $\mathcal{A}$ in winning the first data privacy game is defined as $Adv_{\mathcal{A}}(\lambda) = Pr[\mathcal{A}$ succeeds]. The DPDP with PV and DP is *data privacy-preserving* if there is no PPT adversary $\mathcal{A}$ who can win the above game with non-negligible advantage $Adv_{\mathcal{A}}(\lambda)$. This implies that there is no $\mathcal{A}$ who can recover the file from a given tag tuple with non-negligible probability.

Second Data Privacy Model. The model follows the ones in [7,9,24]. We consider a DPDP with PV and DP as defined above. Let a second data privacy game between a challenger $\mathcal{B}$ and an adversary $\mathcal{A}$ (acting as the TPA) be as follows:

◇ *Setup.* $\mathcal{B}$ runs KeyGen(λ) to generate (pk, sk) and gives pk to $\mathcal{A}$, while sk is kept secret.

◇ *Queries.* $\mathcal{A}$ is allowed to make queries as follows. $\mathcal{A}$ sends a file m to $\mathcal{B}$. $\mathcal{B}$ computes the corresponding T_m and gives it to $\mathcal{A}$.

◇ *Challenge.* $\mathcal{A}$ submits two different files m_0 and m_1 of equal length, such that they have not be chosen in the phase Queries, and sends them to $\mathcal{B}$. $\mathcal{B}$ generates T_{m_0} and T_{m_1} by running TagGen, randomly chooses a bit $b \in_R \{0,1\}$ and forwards T_{m_b} to $\mathcal{A}$. Then, $\mathcal{A}$ sets a challenge *chal* and sends it to $\mathcal{B}$. $\mathcal{B}$ generates a proof of data possession ν^* based on m_b, T_{m_b} and *chal*, and replies to $\mathcal{A}$ by giving ν^*.

◇ *Guess.* Finally, $\mathcal{A}$ chooses a bit $b' \in \{0,1\}$ and wins the game if $b' = b$.

The advantage of $\mathcal{A}$ in winning the second data privacy game is defined as $Adv_{\mathcal{A}}(\lambda) = |Pr[b' = b] - \frac{1}{2}|$. The DPDP with PV and DP is *data privacy-preserving* if there is no PPT adversary $\mathcal{A}$ who can win the above game with non-negligible advantage $Adv_{\mathcal{A}}(\lambda)$.

3   The Three Attacks

3.1   DPDP Construction with PV and DP in [9]

The DPDP scheme with PV and DP construction presented in [9] is as follows:
• KeyGen(λ) $\rightarrow (pk, sk)$. The client runs GroupGen(λ) $\rightarrow (p, \mathbb{G}_1, \mathbb{G}_2, \mathbb{G}_T, e, g_1, g_2)$ such that on input the security parameter λ, GroupGen generates the cyclic groups $\mathbb{G}_1$, $\mathbb{G}_2$ and $\mathbb{G}_T$ of prime order $p = p(\lambda)$ with the bilinear map $e : \mathbb{G}_1 \times \mathbb{G}_2 \rightarrow \mathbb{G}_T$. Let $< g_1 > = \mathbb{G}_1$ and $< g_2 > = \mathbb{G}_2$. Then, $h_1, \cdots, h_s \in_R \mathbb{G}_1$ and $a \in_R \mathbb{Z}_p$ are randomly chosen. Finally, he/she sets the public key $pk = (p, \mathbb{G}_1, \mathbb{G}_2, \mathbb{G}_T, e, g_1, g_2, h_1, \cdots, h_s, g_2^a)$ and the secret key $sk = a$.

- TagGen$(pk, sk, m_i) \rightarrow T_{m_i}$. A file m is split into n blocks m_i, for $i \in [1, n]$. Each block m_i is then split into s sectors $m_{i,j} \in \mathbb{Z}_p$, for $j \in [1, s]$. Therefore, the file m can be seen as a $n \times s$ matrix with elements denoted as $m_{i,j}$. The client computes $T_{m_i} = (\prod_{j=1}^{s} h_j^{m_{i,j}})^{-sk} = \prod_{j=1}^{s} h_j^{-a \cdot m_{i,j}}$. Yet, he/she sets $T_m = (T_{m_1}, \cdots, T_{m_n}) \in \mathbb{G}_1^n$.

- PerfOp$(pk, \mathbb{F}, \mathbb{E}, info = (\text{operation}, l, m_l, T_{m_l})) \rightarrow (\mathbb{F}', \mathbb{E}', \nu')$. The server first selects at random $u_j \in_R \mathbb{Z}_p$, for $j \in [1, s]$, and computes $U_j = h_j^{u_j}$. It also chooses at random $w_l \in_R \mathbb{Z}_p$ and sets $c_j = m_{l,j} \cdot w_l + u_j$, $C_j = h_j^{c_j}$, and $d = T_{m_l}^{w_l}$. Finally, it returns $\nu' = (U_1, \cdots, U_s, C_1, \cdots, C_s, d, w_l) \in \mathbb{G}_1^{2s+1}$ to the TPA. For the operation: (1) *Insertion:* $(l, m_l, T_{m_l}) = (\frac{i_1+i_2}{2}, m_{\frac{i_1+i_2}{2}}, T_{m_{\frac{i_1+i_2}{2}}})$; (2) *Deletion:* $(l, m_l, T_{m_l}) = (i, \_, \_)$, meaning that m_l and T_{m_l} are not required (the server uses m_i and T_{m_i} that are kept on its storage to generate ν'); (3) *Modification:* $(l, m_l, T_{m_l}) = (i, m_i', T_{m_i'})$.

- CheckOp$(pk, \nu') \rightarrow 0/1$. The TPA has to check whether the following equation holds:

$$e(d, g_2^a) \cdot e(\prod_{j=1}^{s} U_j, g_2) \stackrel{?}{=} e(\prod_{j=1}^{s} C_j, g_2) \tag{1}$$

If Eq. 1 holds, then the TPA returns 1 to the client; otherwise, it returns 0 to the client.

- GenProof$(pk, F, chal, \Sigma) \rightarrow \nu$. The TPA first chooses $I \subseteq (0, n+1) \cap \mathbb{Q}$, randomly chooses $|I|$ elements $v_i \in_R \mathbb{Z}_p$ and sets $chal = \{(i, v_i)\}_{i \in I}$. After receiving $chal$, the server sets $F = \{m_i\}_{i \in I} \subset \mathbb{F}$ of blocks and $\Sigma = \{T_{m_i}\}_{i \in I} \subset \mathbb{E}$ which are the tags corresponding to the blocks in F. It then selects at random $r_j \in_R \mathbb{Z}_p$, for $j \in [1, j]$, and computes $R_j = h_j^{r_j}$. It also sets $b_j = \sum_{(i,v_i) \in chal} m_{i,j} \cdot v_i + r_j$, $B_j = h_j^{b_j}$ for $j \in [1, s]$, and $c = \prod_{(i,v_i) \in chal} T_{m_i}^{v_i}$. Finally, it returns $\nu = (R_1, \cdots, R_s, B_1, \cdots, B_s, c) \in \mathbb{G}_1^{2s+1}$ to the TPA.

- CheckProof$(pk, chal, \nu) \rightarrow 0/1$. The TPA has to check whether the following equation holds:

$$e(c, g_2^a) \cdot e(\prod_{j=1}^{s} R_j, g_2) \stackrel{?}{=} e(\prod_{j=1}^{s} B_j, g_2) \tag{2}$$

If Eq. 2 holds, then the TPA returns 1 to the client; otherwise, it returns 0 to the client.

Correctness. Given the proof of data possession ν and the updating proof ν', we have:

$$e(c, g_2^a) \cdot e(\prod_{j=1}^{s} R_j, g_2) = e(\prod_{\substack{(i,v_i) \\ \in chal}} T_{m_i}^{v_i}, g_2^a) \cdot e(\prod_{j=1}^{s} h_j^{r_j}, g_2) = e(\prod_{j=1}^{s} h_j^{b_j}, g_2) = e(\prod_{j=1}^{s} B_j, g_2)$$

$$e(d, g_2^a) \cdot e(\prod_{j=1}^{s} U_j, g_2) = e(T_{m_i}^{w_i}, g_2^a) \cdot e(\prod_{j=1}^{s} h_j^{u_j}, g_2) = e(\prod_{j=1}^{s} h_j^{c_j}, g_2) = e(\prod_{j=1}^{s} C_j, g_2)$$

N.B. In the construction in [9], the definition of the tag T_{m_i} corresponding to the block m_i and enabling to remotely verify the data integrity is independent of the rank i; thus, this begs for being used for an attack. Note that if $m_i = 0$, then $T_{m_i} = 1$ and thus, one can trivially cheat since the tag is independent of the file.

3.2   Replace Attack

Let the server store only one block (e.g. m_1) instead of n blocks as the client believes. The TPA audits the server by sending it a challenge *chal* for blocks with ranks in $I \subseteq [1, n]$ such that $|I| \le n$. The server generates a proof of data possession on the $|I|$ blocks m_1 (instead of the blocks defined by *chal*) by using $|I|$ times the block m_1 to obtain the proof of data possession. The attack is successful if the server manages to pass the verification process and has its proof of data possession being accepted by the TPA.

The client computes $T_m = (T_{m_1}, \cdots, T_{m_n}) \in \mathbb{G}_1^n$ for a file $m = (m_1, \cdots, m_n)$ where $T_{m_i} = (\prod_{j=1}^s h_j^{m_{i,j}})^{-sk} = (\prod_{j=1}^s h_j^{m_{i,j}})^{-a}$ for s public elements $h_j \in \mathbb{G}_1$ and the secret key $sk = a \in \mathbb{Z}_p$. Then, the client stores all the blocks m_i in $\mathbb{F}$ and the tags T_{m_i} in $\mathbb{E}$, forwards these collections to the server and deletes them from his/her local storage. Yet, the server is asked to generate a proof of data possession ν. We assume that it only stores m_1 while it has deleted $m_2, \cdots, m_n$ and we show that it can still pass the verification process. The TPA prepares a challenge *chal* by choosing a set $I \subseteq [1, n]$ (without loss of generality, we assume that the client has not requested the server for data operations yet). The TPA then randomly chooses $|I|$ elements $v_i \in_R \mathbb{Z}_p$ and sets $chal = \{(i, v_i)\}_{i \in I}$. Second, after receiving *chal*, the server sets $F = \{m_1\}_{i \in I} \subset \mathbb{F}$ of blocks (instead of $F = \{m_i\}_{i \in I}$) and $\Sigma = \{T_{m_1}\}_{i \in I} \subset \mathbb{E}$ (instead of $\Sigma = \{T_{m_i}\}_{i \in I}$). The server finally forwards $\nu = (R_1, \cdots, R_s, B_1, \cdots, B_s, c) \in \mathbb{G}_1^{2s+1}$ to the TPA, where $R_j = h_1^{r_j}$ for $r_j \in_R \mathbb{Z}_p$ and $B_j = h_j^{\sum_{(i,v_i) \in chal} m_{1,j} \cdot v_i + r_j}$ (instead of $B_j = h_j^{\sum_{(i,v_i) \in chal} m_{i,j} \cdot v_i + r_j}$) for $j \in [1, s]$, and $c = \prod_{(i,v_i) \in chal} T_{m_1}^{v_i}$ (instead of $c = \prod_{(i,v_i) \in chal} T_{m_i}^{v_i}$). The TPA has to check whether the following equation holds:

$$e(c, g_2^a) \cdot e(\prod_{j=1}^s R_j, g_2) \overset{?}{=} e(\prod_{j=1}^s B_j, g_2) \tag{3}$$

If Eq. 3 holds, then the TPA returns 1 to the client; otherwise, it returns 0 to the client.

Correctness. Given the proof of data possession ν, we have:

$$e(c, g_2^a) \cdot e(\prod_{j=1}^s R_j, g_2) = e(\prod_{(i,v_i) \in chal} T_{m_1}^{v_i}, g_2^a) \cdot e(\prod_{j=1}^s h_j^{r_j}, g_2)$$

$$= e\left(\prod_{(i,v_i)\in chal} \prod_{j=1}^{s} h_j^{m_{1,j}\cdot(-a)\cdot v_i}, g_2^a \right) \cdot e\left(\prod_{j=1}^{s} h_j^{r_j}, g_2 \right)$$

$$= e\left(\prod_{j=1}^{s} h_j^{b_j}, g_2 \right) = e\left(\prod_{j=1}^{s} B_j, g_2 \right)$$

Therefore, Eq. 3 holds, although the server is actually storing one block only.

3.3 Replay Attack

The client asks the server to replace m_i with m_i'. However, the server does not proceed and keeps m_i on its storage. Then, the TPA has to check that the operation has been correctly done and asks the server for an updating proof ν'. The server generates it, but using m_i instead of m_i'. The attack is successful if the server manages to pass the verification process and has ν' being accepted by the TPA.

A client asks the server to modify the block m_i by sending m_i' and $T_{m_i'}$. However, the server does not follow the client's request and decides to keep m_i and T_{m_i}, and deletes m_i' and $T_{m_i'}$. The server receives i, m_i' and $T_{m_i'}$ from the client but deletes them, and generates the updating proof $\nu' = (U_1, \cdots, U_s, C_1, \cdots, C_s, d) \in \mathbb{G}_1^{2s+1}$ by using m_i and T_{m_i} such that $U_j = h_1^{u_j}$ where $u_j \in_R \mathbb{Z}_p$ and $C_j = h_j^{m_{i,j}\cdot w_i + u_j}$ (instead of $C_j = h_j^{m_{i,j}'\cdot w_i + u_j}$) for $j \in [1, s]$, and $d = T_{m_i}^{w_i}$ (instead of $d = T_{m_i'}^{w_i}$). It gives ν' to the TPA. The TPA has to check whether the following equation holds:

$$e(d, g_2^a) \cdot e\left(\prod_{j=1}^{s} U_j, g_2 \right) \overset{?}{=} e\left(\prod_{j=1}^{s} C_j, g_2 \right) \tag{4}$$

If Eq. 4 holds, then the TPA returns 1 to the client; otherwise, it returns 0 to the client.

Correctness. Given the updating proof ν', we have:

$$e(d, g_2^a) \cdot e\left(\prod_{j=1}^{s} U_j, g_2 \right) = e(T_{m_i}^{w_i}, g_2^a) \cdot e\left(\prod_{j=1}^{s} h_j^{u_j}, g_2 \right) = e\left(\prod_{j=1}^{s} h_j^{m_{i,j}\cdot(-a)\cdot w_i}, g_2^a \right) \cdot e\left(\prod_{j=1}^{s} h_j^{u_j}, g_2 \right)$$

$$= e\left(\prod_{j=1}^{s} h_j^{c_j}, g_2 \right) = e\left(\prod_{j=1}^{s} C_j, g_2 \right)$$

Therefore, Eq. 4 holds, although the server has not updated the block m_i' and the corresponding tag $T_{m_i'}$.

3.4 Attack against Data Privacy

The adversarial TPA and the server play the second data privacy game. The TPA gives two equal-length blocks m_0 and m_1 to the server and the latter replies by sending T_{m_b} of m_b where $b \in_R \{0, 1\}$ is a random bit. Then, the TPA selects a bit $b' \in \{0, 1\}$. The attack is successful if using $m_{b'}$, the TPA can discover which block $m_b \in \{m_0, m_1\}$ was chosen by the server.

Let $m_0 = (m_{0,1}, \cdots, m_{0,n})$ and $m_1 = (m_{1,1}, \cdots, m_{1,n})$. The server computes $T_{m_b,i} = (\prod_{j=1}^{s} h_j^{m_{b,i,j}})^{-sk} = (\prod_{j=1}^{s} h_j^{m_{b,i,j}})^{-a}$, for $b \in_R \{0, 1\}$ and $i \in [1, n]$, and gives them to the TPA. Note that $e(T_{m_b,i}, g_2) = e((\prod_{j=1}^{s} h_j^{m_{b,i,j}})^{-a}, g_2) = e(\prod_{j=1}^{s} h_j^{m_{b,i,j}}, (g_2^a)^{-1})$. The computation of $e(\prod_{j=1}^{s} h_j^{m_{b,i,j}}, (g_2^a)^{-1})$ requires only public elements. Therefore, for $b' \in \{0, 1\}$, the TPA is able to generate the pairing $e(\prod_{j=1}^{s} h_j^{m_{b',i,j}}, (g_2^a)^{-1})$ given pk and the block that it gave to the server, and $e(T_{m_b,i}, g_2)$ given the tag sent by the server. Finally, the TPA compares them. If these two pairings are equal, then $b' = b$; otherwise $b' \neq b$.

N.B. This attack is due to the public verifiability property of the scheme in [9] based on the definition of the second data privacy game. Moreover, in the proof for data privacy in [9], the analysis is wrong: the affirmation "The probability $Pr[b' = b]$ must be equal to $\frac{1}{2}$ since the tags $T_{m_b,i}$, for $i \in [1, n]$, and the proof ν^* are independent of the bit b." is incorrect since $T_{m_b,i}$ and ν^* actually depend on b.

4   IHT-based DPDP Scheme with PV and DP

A solution to avoid the replace attack is to embed the rank i of m_i into T_{m_i}. When the TPA on behalf of the client checks ν generated by the server, it requires to use all the ranks of the challenged blocks to process the verification. Such idea was proposed for the publicly verifiable scheme in [13]. A solution to avoid the replay attack is to embed the version number vnb_i of m_i into T_{m_i}. The first time that the client sends m_i to the server, $vnb_i = 1$ (meaning that the first version of the block is uploaded) and is appended to i. When the client wants to modify m_i with m_i', he/she specifies $vnb_i = 2$ (meaning that the second version of the block is uploaded) and generates $T_{m_i'}$ accordingly. When the TPA on behalf of the client checks that the block was correctly updated by the server, it has to use both i and vnb_i of m_i. Moreover, we stress that the rank i of the block m_i is unique. More precisely, when a block is inserted, a new rank is created that has not been used and when a block is modified, the rank does not change. However, when a block is deleted, its rank does not disappear to ensure that it won't be used for another block and thus, to let the scheme remain secure.

4.1   IHT-based Construction

The IHT-based DPDP scheme with PV and DP construction is as follows:
• KeyGen(λ) $\rightarrow$ (pk, sk). The client runs Group- Gen(λ) $\rightarrow$ $(p, \mathbb{G}_1, \mathbb{G}_2, \mathbb{G}_T, e, g_1, g_2)$ such that on input the security parameter λ, GroupGen generates the cyclic groups $\mathbb{G}_1$, $\mathbb{G}_2$ and $\mathbb{G}_T$ of prime order $p = p(\lambda)$ with the bilinear map $e : \mathbb{G}_1 \times \mathbb{G}_2 \rightarrow \mathbb{G}_T$. Let $< g_1 >= \mathbb{G}_1$ and $< g_2 >= \mathbb{G}_2$. Let the hash

function $H : \mathbb{Q} \times \mathbb{N} \to \mathbb{G}_1$ be a random oracle. Then, $h_1, \cdots, h_s \in_R \mathbb{G}_1$ and $a \in_R \mathbb{Z}_p$ are randomly chosen. Finally, he/she sets the public key $pk = (p, \mathbb{G}_1, \mathbb{G}_2, \mathbb{G}_T, e, g_1, g_2, h_1, \cdots, h_s, g_2^a, H)$ and the secret key $sk = a$.

• TagGen$(pk, sk, m_i) \to T_{m_i}$. A file m is split into n blocks m_i, for $i \in [1, n]$. Each block m_i is then split into s sectors $m_{i,j} \in \mathbb{Z}_p$, for $j \in [1, s]$. Therefore, the file m can be seen as a $n \times s$ matrix with elements denoted as $m_{i,j}$. The client computes $T_{m_i} = (H(i, vnb_i) \cdot \prod_{j=1}^{s} h_j^{m_{i,j}})^{-sk} = H(i, vnb_i)^{-a} \cdot \prod_{j=1}^{s} h_j^{-a \cdot m_{i,j}}$. Yet, he/she sets $T_m = (T_{m_1}, \cdots, T_{m_n}) \in \mathbb{G}_1^n$.

• PerfOp$(pk, \mathbb{F}, \mathbb{E}, info = (operation, l, m_l, T_{m_l})) \to (\mathbb{F}', \mathbb{E}', \nu')$. The server first selects at random $u_j \in_R \mathbb{Z}_p$, for $j \in [1, s]$, and computes $U_j = h_j^{u_j}$. It also chooses at random $w_l \in_R \mathbb{Z}_p$ and sets $c_j = m_{l,j} \cdot w_l + u_j$, $C_j = h_j^{c_j}$ for $j \in [1, s]$, and $d = T_{m_l}^{w_l}$. Finally, it returns $\nu' = (U_1, \cdots, U_s, C_1, \cdots, C_s, d, w_l) \in \mathbb{G}_1^{2s+1}$ to the TPA. For the operation: (1) *Insertion:* $(l, m_l, T_{m_l}) = (\frac{i_1+i_2}{2}, m_{\frac{i_1+i_2}{2}}, T_{m_{\frac{i_1+i_2}{2}}})$ and $vnb_l = vnb_{\frac{i_1+i_2}{2}} = 1$; (2) *Deletion:* $(l, m_l, T_{m_l}) = (i, \_, \_)$ and $vnb_l = vnb_i = \_$, meaning that m_l, T_{m_l} and vnb_l are not required (the server uses m_i, T_{m_i} and vnb_i that are kept on its storage to generate ν'); (3) *Modification:* $(l, m_l, T_{m_l}) = (i, m_i', T_{m_i'})$ and $vnb_l = vnb_i' = vnb_i + 1$.

• CheckOp$(pk, \nu') \to 0/1$. The TPA has to check whether the following equation holds:

$$e(d, g_2^a) \cdot e(\prod_{j=1}^{s} U_j, g_2) \stackrel{?}{=} e(H(l, vnb_l)^{w_l}, g_2) \cdot e(\prod_{j=1}^{s} C_j, g_2) \tag{5}$$

If Eq. 5 holds, then the TPA returns 1 to the client; otherwise, it returns 0 to the client.

• GenProof$(pk, F, chal, \Sigma) \to \nu$. The TPA first chooses $I \subseteq (0, n+1) \cap \mathbb{Q}$, randomly chooses $|I|$ elements $v_i \in_R \mathbb{Z}_p$ and sets $chal = \{(i, v_i)\}_{i \in I}$. After receiving $chal$, the server sets $F = \{m_i\}_{i \in I} \subset \mathbb{F}$ of blocks and $\Sigma = \{T_{m_i}\}_{i \in I} \subset \mathbb{E}$ which are the tags corresponding to the blocks in F. It then selects at random $r_j \in_R \mathbb{Z}_p$, for $j \in [1, s]$, and computes $R_j = h_j^{r_j}$. It also sets $b_j = \sum_{(i, v_i) \in chal} m_{i,j} \cdot v_i + r_j$, $B_j = h_j^{b_j}$ for $j \in [1, s]$, and $c = \prod_{(i, v_i) \in chal} T_{m_i}^{v_i}$. Finally, it returns $\nu = (R_1, \cdots, R_s, B_1, \cdots, B_s, c) \in \mathbb{G}_1^{2s+1}$ to the TPA.

• CheckProof$(pk, chal, \nu) \to 0/1$. The TPA has to check whether the following equation holds:

$$e(c, g_2^a) \cdot e(\prod_{j=1}^{s} R_j, g_2) \stackrel{?}{=} e(\prod_{\substack{(i, v_i) \\ \in chal}} H(i, vnb_i)^{v_i}, g_2) \cdot e(\prod_{j=1}^{s} B_j, g_2) \tag{6}$$

If Eq. 6 holds, then the TPA returns 1 to the client; otherwise, it returns 0 to the client.

Correctness. Given the proof of data possession ν and the updating proof ν', we have:

$$e(c, g_2^a) \cdot e(\prod_{j=1}^{s} R_j, g_2) = e(\prod_{(i,v_i) \in chal} T_{m_i}^{v_i}, g_2^a) \cdot e(\prod_{j=1}^{s} h_j^{r_j}, g_2)$$

$$= e(\prod_{(i,v_i) \in chal} (H(i, vnb_i) \cdot \prod_{j=1}^{s} h_j^{m_{i,j}})^{-a \cdot v_i}, g_2^a) \cdot e(\prod_{j=1}^{s} h_j^{r_j}, g_2)$$

$$= e(\prod_{(i,v_i) \in chal} H(i, vnb_i)^{v_i}, g_2) \cdot e(\prod_{j=1}^{s} B_j, g_2)$$

$$e(d, g_2^a) \cdot e(\prod_{j=1}^{s} U_j, g_2) = e(T_{m_l}^{w_l}, g_2^a) \cdot e(\prod_{j=1}^{s} h_j^{u_j}, g_2)$$

$$= e(H(l, vnb_l) \cdot \prod_{j=1}^{s} h_j^{m_{l,j}}, g_2^a)^{-a \cdot w_l} \cdot e(\prod_{j=1}^{s} h_j^{u_j}, g_2)$$

$$= e(H(l, vnb_l)^{w_l}, g_2) \cdot e(\prod_{j=1}^{s} C_j, g_2)$$

N.B. The client or TPA must store the values vnb locally. However, this does not incur more burden if we consider the values vnb as bit strings.

4.2   Security and Privacy Proofs

Security Proof Against the Server

Theorem 1. *Let $\mathcal{A}$ be a PPT adversary that has advantage ϵ against the IHT-based DPDP scheme with PV and DP. Suppose that $\mathcal{A}$ makes a total of $q_H > 0$ queries to H. Then, there is a challenger $\mathcal{B}$ that solves the Computational Diffie-Hellman (CDH) and Discrete Logarithm (DL) problems with advantage $\epsilon' = \mathcal{O}(\epsilon)$.*

We give the security proof in the Appendix A.

First Data Privacy Proof Against the TPA

Theorem 2. *Let $\mathcal{A}$ be a PPT adversary that has advantage ϵ against the IHT-based DPDP scheme with PV and DP. Suppose that $\mathcal{A}$ makes a total of $q_H > 0$ queries to H. Then, there is a challenger $\mathcal{B}$ that solves the CDH problem with advantage $\epsilon' = \mathcal{O}(\epsilon)$.*

We give the first data privacy proof in the full version of this paper [8].

4.3   Performance

We compare the IHT-based scheme with the original scheme proposed in [9]. First, the client and TPA obviously have to store more information by keeping the IHT. Nevertheless, we stress that in any case, the client and TPA should maintain a rank list. Indeed, they need some information about the stored data in order to select some data blocks to be challenged. We recall that the challenge consists of pairs of the form "(rank, random element)". By appending an integer and sometimes an auxiliary comment (only in case of deletions) to each rank, the extra burden is not excessive. Therefore, such table does slightly affect the client's as well as TPA's local storages. The communication between the client and TPA rather increases since the client should send more elements to the TPA in order to keep the table updated. Second, the client has to perform extra computation when generating the verification metadata: for each file block m_i, he/she has to compute $H(i, vnb_i)$. However, the communication between the client and server overhead does not increase. Third, the TPA needs to compute an extra pairing $e(H(i, vnb_i), g_2)^{w_i}$ in order to check that the server correctly performed a data operation requested by the client. The TPA also has to compute $|I|$ multiplications in $\mathbb{G}_1$ and one extra pairing when checking the proof of data possession: for each challenge $chal = \{(i, v_i)\}_{i \in I}$, it calculates $\prod_{(i,vi) \in chal} H(i, vnb_i)$ as well as the pairing $e(\prod_{(i,vi) \in chal} H(i, vnb_i)^{v_i}, g_2)$. This gives a constant total of four pairings in order to verify the data integrity instead of three, that is not a big loss in term of efficiency and practicality. Finally, apart the storage of a light table and computation of an extra pairing by the TPA for the verification of both the updating proof and proof of data possession, the new construction for the DPDP scheme with PV and DP is still practical by adopting asymmetric pairings to gain efficiency and by still reducing the group exponentiation and pairing operations. In addition, this scheme still allows the TPA on behalf of the client to request the server for a proof of data possession on as many data blocks as possible at no extra cost, as in the scheme given in [9].

5   MHT-based DPDP Scheme with PV and DP

A second solution to avoid the three attacks is to implement a MHT [12] for each file. In a MHT, each internal node has always two children. For a leaf node nd_i based on the block m_i, the assigned value is $H'(m_i)$, where the hash function $H' : \{0,1\}^* \rightarrow \mathbb{G}_1$ is seen as a random oracle. Note that the hash values are affected to the leaf nodes in the increasing order of the blocks: nd_i and nd_{i+1} correspond to the hash of the blocks m_i and m_{i+1} respectively. A parent node of nd_i and nd_{i+1} has a value computed as $H'(H'(m_i)||H'(m_{i+1}))$, where $||$ is the concatenation sign (for an odd rank i). The Auxiliary Authentication Information (AAI) Ω_i of a leaf node nd_i for m_i is a set of hash values chosen from its upper levels, so that the root rt can be computed using (m_i, Ω_i).

5.1   MHT-based Construction

Let DPDP be a DPDP construction with PV and DP such as defined in Sect. 3.1 and [9]. Let $\mathsf{SS} = (\mathsf{Gen}, \mathsf{Sign}, \mathsf{Verify})$ be a strongly unforgeable digital signature scheme. The MHT-based DPDP scheme with PV and DP construction is as follows:

- $\mathsf{MHT.KeyGen}(\lambda) \rightarrow (\mathsf{pk}, \mathsf{sk})$. Let $\mathsf{GroupGen}(\lambda) \rightarrow (p, \mathbb{G}_1, \mathbb{G}_2, \mathbb{G}_T, e, g_1, g_2)$ be run as follows. On input the security parameter λ, $\mathsf{GroupGen}$ generates the cyclic groups $\mathbb{G}_1$, $\mathbb{G}_2$ and $\mathbb{G}_T$ of prime order $p = p(\lambda)$ with the bilinear map $e : \mathbb{G}_1 \times \mathbb{G}_2 \rightarrow \mathbb{G}_T$. Let $< g_1 >= \mathbb{G}_1$ and $< g_2 >= \mathbb{G}_2$. The client runs $\mathsf{Gen}(\lambda) \rightarrow (pk_{\mathsf{SS}}, sk_{\mathsf{SS}})$ and $\mathsf{KeyGen}(\lambda) \rightarrow (pk, sk) = ((p, \mathbb{G}_1, \mathbb{G}_2, \mathbb{G}_T, e, g_1, g_2, h_1, \cdots, h_s, g_2^a), a)$, where $h_1, \cdots, h_s \in_R \mathbb{G}_1$ and $a \in_R \mathbb{Z}_p$ are randomly chosen. The client sets his/her public key $\mathsf{pk} = (pk, pk_{\mathsf{SS}})$ and his/her secret key $\mathsf{sk} = (sk, sk_{\mathsf{SS}})$.
- $\mathsf{MHT.TagGen}(\mathsf{pk}, \mathsf{sk}, m_i) \rightarrow T_{m_i}$. The client runs n times $\mathsf{TagGen}(pk, sk, m_i) \rightarrow T'_{m_i} = (\prod_{j=1}^s h_j^{m_{i,j}})^{-sk} = (\prod_{j=1}^s h_j^{m_{i,j}})^{-a}$ for $i \in [1, n]$ and obtains $T'_m = (T'_{m_1}, \cdots, T'_{m_n}) \in \mathbb{G}_1^n$. He/she also chooses a hash function $H' : \{0,1\}^* \rightarrow \mathbb{G}_1$ seen as a random oracle. Then, he/she creates the MHT regarding the file $m = (m_1, \cdots, m_n)$ as follows. He/she computes $H'(m_i)$ and assigns it to the i-th leaf for $i \in [1, n]$. He/she starts to construct the resulting MHT, and obtains the root rt. Finally, the client runs $\mathsf{Sign}(sk_{\mathsf{SS}}, rt) \rightarrow \sigma_{rt}$. Using the hash values, he/she computes the tags as $T_{m_i} = H'(m_i)^{-sk} \cdot T'_{m_i} = H'(m_i)^{-a} \cdot \prod_{j=1}^s h_j^{-a \cdot m_{i,j}}$ for $i \in [1, n]$. Then, the client stores all the blocks m_i in an ordered collection $\mathbb{F}$ and the corresponding tags T_{m_i} in an ordered collection $\mathbb{E}$. He/she forwards these two collections and (H', σ_{rt}) to the server. Once the server receives $(\mathbb{F}, \mathbb{E}, H')$, it generates the MHT. It sends the resulting root rt_{server} to the client. Upon getting the root rt_{server}, the client runs $\mathsf{Verify}(pk_{\mathsf{SS}}, \sigma_{rt}, rt_{server}) \rightarrow 0/1$. If 0, then the client aborts. Otherwise, he/she proceeds, deletes $(\mathbb{F}, \mathbb{E}, \sigma_{rt})$ from his/her local storage and keeps H' for further data operations.
- $\mathsf{MHT.PerfOp}(\mathsf{pk}, \mathbb{F}, \mathbb{E}, R = (\text{operation}, i), info = (m_i, T_{m_i}, \sigma_{rt'})) \rightarrow (\mathbb{F}', \mathbb{E}', rt'_{server})$. First, the client sends a request $R = (\text{operation}, i)$ to the server, that contains the type and rank of the operation. Upon receiving R, the server selects the AAI Ω_i that the client needs in order to generate the root rt' of the updated MHT, and sends it to the client. Once the client receives Ω_i, he/she first constructs the updated MHT. He/she calculates the new root rt' and runs $\mathsf{Sign}(sk_{\mathsf{SS}}, rt') \rightarrow \sigma_{rt'}$. Then, the client sends $info = (m_i, T_{m_i}, \sigma_{rt'})$ (note that m_i and T_{m_i} are not needed for a deletion). After receiving $info$ from the client, the server first updates the MHT, calculates the new root rt'_{server} and sends it to the client. Upon getting the root rt'_{server}, the client runs $\mathsf{Verify}(pk_{\mathsf{SS}}, \sigma_{rt'}, rt'_{server}) \rightarrow 0/1$. If 0, then the client aborts. Otherwise, he/she proceeds and deletes $(m_i, T_{m_i}, \sigma_{rt'})$ from his/her local storage. For the operation: (1) *Insertion:* m_{i_0} is added before m_i by placing m_{i_0} at the i-th leaf node, and all the blocks from m_i are shifted to leaf nodes by 1 to the right; (2) *Deletion:* m_i is removed from the i-th leaf node and all the blocks from m_{i+1} are shifted to leaf nodes by 1 to the left; (3) *Modification:* m'_i simply replaces m_i at the i-th leaf node.

- MHT.GenProof$(pk, F, chal, \Sigma) \rightarrow (\nu, rt_{server}, \{H'(m_i), \Omega_i\}_{i \in I})$. The TPA chooses a subset $I \subseteq [1, n_{max}]$ (n_{max} is the maximum number of blocks after operations), randomly chooses $|I|$ elements $v_i \in_R \mathbb{Z}_p$ and sets the challenge $chal = \{(i, v_i)\}_{i \in I}$. Then, after receiving $chal$ and given $F = \{m_i\}_{i \in I} \subset \mathbb{F}$ and $\Sigma = \{T_{m_i}\}_{i \in I} \subset \mathbb{E}$, the server runs GenProof$(pk, F, chal, \Sigma) \rightarrow \nu$ such that $\nu = (R_1, \cdots, R_s, B_1, \cdots, B_s, c) \in \mathbb{G}_1^{2s+1}$, where $r_j \in_R \mathbb{Z}_p$, $R_j = h_1^{r_j}$, $b_j = \sum_{(i,v_i) \in chal} m_{i,j} \cdot v_i + r_j \in \mathbb{Z}_p$ and $B_j = h_j^{b_j}$ for $j \in [1, s]$, and $c = \prod_{(i,v_i) \in chal} T_{m_i}^{v_i}$. Moreover, the server prepares the latest version of the stored root's signature σ_{rt} provided by the client, the root rt_{server} of the current MHT, the $H'(m_i)$ and AAI Ω_i for the challenged blocks, such that current MHT has been constructed using $\{H'(m_i), \Omega_i\}_{i \in I}$. Finally, it returns $(\nu, \sigma_{rt}, rt_{server}, \{H'(m_i), \Omega_i\}_{i \in I})$ to the TPA.
- MHT.CheckProof$(pk, chal, \nu, \sigma_{rt}, rt_{server}, \{H'(m_i), \Omega_i\}_{i \in I}) \rightarrow 0/1$. After receiving $\{H'(m_i), \Omega_i\}_{i \in I}$ from the server, the TPA first constructs the MHT and calculates the root rt_{TPA}. It then checks that $rt_{server} = rt_{TPA}$. If not, then it aborts; otherwise, it runs Verify$(pk_{SS}, \sigma_{rt}, rt_{server}) \rightarrow 0/1$. If 0, then the TPA aborts. Otherwise, it proceeds and checks whether the following equation holds:

$$e(c, g_2^a) \cdot e(\prod_{j=1}^{s} R_j, g_2) \stackrel{?}{=} e(\prod_{(i,v_i) \in chal} H'(m_i)^{v_i}, g_2) \cdot e(\prod_{j=1}^{s} B_j, g_2) \qquad (7)$$

If Eq. 7 holds, then the TPA returns 1 to the client; otherwise, it returns 0 to the client.

Correctness. We suppose that the correctness holds for DPDP and SS protocols. Given the proof of data possession ν, we have:

$$e(c, g_2^a) \cdot e(\prod_{j=1}^{s} R_j, g_2) = e(\prod_{(i,v_i) \in chal} T_{m_i}^{v_i}, g_2^a) \cdot e(\prod_{j=1}^{s} h_j^{r_j}, g_2)$$

$$= e(\prod_{(i,v_i) \in chal} (H'(m_i) \cdot \prod_{j=1}^{s} h_j^{m_{i,j}})^{-a \cdot v_i}, g_2^a) \cdot e(\prod_{j=1}^{s} h_j^{r_j}, g_2)$$

$$= e(\prod_{(i,v_i) \in chal} H'(m_i)^{v_i}, g_2) \cdot e(\prod_{j=1}^{s} B_j, g_2)$$

N.B. In MHT.GenProof, since I is a subset of ranks, the server has to be given the appropriate $\{\Omega_i\}_{i \in I}$ along with $\{H'(m_i)\}_{i \in I}$ to obtain the current MHT and thus complete the proof generation. Otherwise, the TPA won't get the proper MHT.

5.2   Security and Privacy Proofs

We give the proofs in the full version of this paper [8].

Security Proof Against the Server

Theorem 3. *Let $\mathcal{A}$ be a PPT adversary that has advantage ϵ against the MHT-based DPDP scheme with PV and DP. Suppose that $\mathcal{A}$ makes a total of $q_{H'} > 0$ queries to H'. Then, there is a challenger $\mathcal{B}$ that solves the CDH and DL problems with advantage $\epsilon' = \mathcal{O}(\epsilon)$.*

Second Data Privacy Proof Against the TPA

Theorem 4. *Let $\mathcal{A}$ be a PPT adversary that has advantage ϵ against the MHT-based DPDP scheme with PV and DP. Suppose that $\mathcal{A}$ makes a total of $q_{H'} > 0$ queries to H'. Then, there is a challenger $\mathcal{B}$ that solves the $(s+1)$-DDHE problem with advantage $\epsilon' = \mathcal{O}(\epsilon)$.*

5.3   Performance and Discussion with Other Existing Works

We first compare the MHT-based scheme with the original one presented in [9]. The MHT-based construction seems less practical and efficient than the construction in [9]. Communication and computation burdens appear in order to obtain the desired security standards against the server and TPA. The communication overheads increase between the client and server. The computation overheads for the client raise also, although the client is limited in resources. The storage space of the server should be bigger, since it has to create and possibly stores MHTs for each client. The TPA has to provide more computational resources for each client in order to ensure valid data integrity checks. Nevertheless, experiments might show that the time gap between the algorithms in the scheme proposed in [9] and the ones in the MHT-based scheme is acceptable.

The MHT is an Authenticated Data Structure (ADS) that allows the client and TPA to check that the server correctly stores and updates the data blocks. Erway et al. [4] proposed the first DPDP scheme. The verification of the data updates is based on a modified ADS, called Rank-based Authentication Skip List (RASL). This provides authentication of the data block ranks, which ensures security in regards to data block dynamicity. However, public verifiability is not reached. Note that such ADS with bottom-up leveling limits the insertion operations. For instance, if the leaf nodes are at level 0, any data insertion that creates a new level *below* the level 0 will bring necessary updates of all the level hash values and the client might not be able to verify. Wang et al. [21] first presented a DPDP with PV using MHT. However, security proofs and technical details lacked. The authors revised the aforementioned paper [21] and proposed a more complete paper [22] that focuses on dynamic and publicly verifiable PDP systems based on BLS signatures. To achieve the dynamicity property, they employed MHT. Nevertheless, because the check of the block ranks is not done, the server can delude the client by corrupting a challenged block as follows: it is able to compute a valid proof with other non-corrupted blocks. Thereafter, in a subsequent work [20], Wang et al. suggested to add randomization to the above system [22], in order to guarantee that the server cannot deduce the contents of the data files from the proofs of data possession. Liu et al. [11] constructed a PDP protocol based on MHT with top-down leveling. Such protocol satisfies dynamicity and public verifiability. They opted for such design to let leaf nodes be on different levels. Thus, the client and TPA have both to remember the total number of data blocks and check the block ranks from two directions (leftmost to rightmost and vice versa) to ensure that the server does not delude the client with another node on behalf of a file block during the data integrity checking process. In this paper, the DPDP scheme with PV and DP is based on MHT with bottom-up leveling, such that data block ranks are authenticated. Such tree-based construction guarantees secure dynamicity and public verifiability processes as well as preservation of data privacy, and remains practical in real environments.

6 Conclusion

We provided two solutions to solve the adversarial issues encountered in the DPDP scheme with PV and DP proposed in [9]. These solutions manage to overcome replay attacks, replace attacks and attacks against data privacy by embedding IHT or MHT into the construction in [9]. We proved that the two new schemes are both secure against the server and data privacy-preserving against the TPA in the random oracle.

Acknowledgments. This work was partially supported by the TREDISEC project (G.A. no 644412), funded by the European Union (EU) under the Information and Communication Technologies (ICT) theme of the Horizon 2020 (H2020) research and innovation programme.

A Security Proof Against the Server for the IHT-based Scheme

For any PPT adversary $\mathcal{A}$ who wins the game, there is a challenger $\mathcal{B}$ that wants to break the CDH and DL problems by interacting with $\mathcal{A}$ as follows:

$\diamond$ *KeyGen.* $\mathcal{B}$ runs $\mathsf{GroupGen}(\lambda) \rightarrow (p, \mathbb{G}, \mathbb{G}_T, e, g)$. Then, it is given the CDH instance tuple (g, g^a, g^b) where $< g >= \mathbb{G}$, chooses two exponents $x, y \in \mathbb{Z}_p$ and computes $g_1 = g^x$ and $g_2 = g^y$. It also sets $\mathbb{G}_1 =< g_1 >$ and $\mathbb{G}_2 =< g_2 >$. Note that $(g^a)^x = g_1^a$, $(g^b)^x = g_1^b$, $(g^a)^y = g_2^a$ and $(g^b)^y = g_2^b$. $\mathcal{B}$ chooses $\beta_j, \gamma_j \in_R \mathbb{Z}_p$ and sets $h_j = g_1^{\beta_j} \cdot (g_1^b)^{\gamma_j}$ for $j \in [1, s]$. Let a hash function $H : \mathbb{Q} \times \mathbb{N} \rightarrow \mathbb{G}_1$ be controlled by $\mathcal{B}$ as follows. Upon receiving a query $(i_{l'}, vnb_{i_{l'}})$ to H for some $l' \in [1, q_H]$, if $((i_{l'}, vnb_{i_{l'}}), \theta_{l'}, W_{l'})$ exists in L_H, return $W_{l'}$; otherwise, choose $\beta_j, \gamma_j \in_R \mathbb{Z}_p$ and set $h_j = g_1^{\beta_j} \cdot (g_1^b)^{\gamma_j}$ for $j \in [1, s]$. For each $i_{l'}$, choose $\theta_{l'} \in_R \mathbb{Z}_p$ at random and set $W_{l'} = \dfrac{g_1^{\theta_{l'}}}{g_1^{\sum_{j=1}^{s} \beta_j m_{i_{l'}, j}} (g_1^b)^{\sum_{j=1}^{s} \gamma_j m_{i_{l'}, j}}}$ for a given block $m_{i_{l'}} = (m_{i_{l'}, 1}, \cdots, m_{i_{l'}, s})$. Put $((i_{l'}, vnb_{i_{l'}}), \theta_{l'}, W_{l'})$ in L_H and return $W_{l'}$. $\mathcal{B}$ sets the public key $pk = (p, \mathbb{G}_1, \mathbb{G}_2, \mathbb{G}_T, e, g_1, g_2, h_1, \cdots, h_s, g_2^a, H)$ and forwards it to $\mathcal{A}$. $\mathcal{B}$ keeps g_1^a, g_1^b and g_2^b secret.

◇ *Adaptive Queries.* $\mathcal{A}$ has first access to $\mathcal{O}_{TG}$ as follows. It first adaptively selects blocks $m_i = (m_{i,1}, \cdots, m_{i,s})$, for $i \in [1,n]$. Then, $\mathcal{B}$ computes $T_{m_i} = (W \cdot \prod_{j=1}^{s} h_j^{m_{i,j}})^{-sk} = (W \cdot \prod_{j=1}^{s} h_j^{m_{i,j}})^{-a}$, such that if $((i, vnb_i), \theta, W)$ exists in L_H, then W is used to compute T_{m_i}. Otherwise, $\theta \in_R \mathbb{Z}_p$ is chosen at random, $W = \dfrac{g_1^\theta}{g_1^{\sum_{j=1}^{s} \beta_j m_{i,j}} (g_1^b)^{\sum_{j=1}^{s} \gamma_j m_{i,j}}}$ is computed for $h_j = g_1^{\beta_j} \cdot (g_1^b)^{\gamma_j}$, $((i, vnb_i), \theta, W)$ is put in L_H and W is used to compute T_{m_i}. Note that we have $\prod_{j=1}^{s} h_j^{m_{i,j}} \cdot H(i, vnb_i) =$

$$\left(\prod_{j=1}^{s} h_j^{m_{i,j}}\right) \cdot \frac{g_1^\theta}{g_1^{\sum_{j=1}^{s} \beta_j m_{i,j}} \cdot (g_1^b)^{\sum_{j=1}^{s} \gamma_j m_{i,j}}} = \frac{g_1^{\sum_{j=1}^{s} \beta_j m_{i,j}} (g_1^b)^{\sum_{j=1}^{s} \gamma_j m_{i,j}} \cdot g_1^\theta}{g_1^{\sum_{j=1}^{s} \beta_j m_{i,j}} \cdot (g_1^b)^{\sum_{j=1}^{s} \gamma_j m_{i,j}}} = g_1^\theta \text{ and}$$

so, $T_{m_i} = (H(i, vnb_i) \cdot \prod_{j=1}^{s} h_j^{m_{i,j}})^{-sk} = (H(i, vnb_i) \cdot \prod_{j=1}^{s} h_j^{m_{i,j}})^{-a} = (g_1^a)^{-\theta}$.
$\mathcal{B}$ gives the blocks and tags to $\mathcal{A}$. The latter sets an ordered collection $\mathbb{F} = \{m_i\}_{i \in [1,n]}$ of blocks and an ordered collection $\mathbb{E} = \{T_{m_i}\}_{i \in [1,n]}$ which are the tags corresponding to the blocks in $\mathbb{F}$.

$\mathcal{A}$ has also access to $\mathcal{O}_{DOP}$ as follows. Repeatedly, $\mathcal{A}$ selects a block m_l and the corresponding $info_l$ and forwards them to $\mathcal{B}$. Here, l denotes the rank where $\mathcal{A}$ wants the data operation to be performed: l is equal to $\frac{i_1 + i_2}{2}$ for an insertion and to i for a deletion or a modification. We recall that only the rank is needed for a deletion and the version number vnb_l increases by 1 for a modification. Then, $\mathcal{A}$ outputs two new ordered collections $\mathbb{F}'$ and $\mathbb{E}'$, and a corresponding updating proof $\nu' = (U_1, \cdots, U_s, C_1, \cdots, C_s, d, w_l)$, such that $w_l \in_R \mathbb{Z}_p$, $d = T_{m_l}^{w_l}$, and for $j \in [1,s]$, $u_j \in_R \mathbb{Z}_p$, $U_j = h_j^{u_j}$, $c_j = m_{l,j} \cdot w_l + u_j$ and $C_j = h_j^{c_j}$. $\mathcal{B}$ runs CheckOp on ν' and sends the answer to $\mathcal{A}$. If the answer is 0, then $\mathcal{B}$ aborts; otherwise, it proceeds.

◇ *Challenge.* $\mathcal{A}$ selects m_i^* and $info_i^*$, for $i \in \mathcal{I} \subseteq (0, n+1) \cap \mathbb{Q}$, and forwards them to $\mathcal{B}$ who checks the data operations. In particular, the first $info_i^*$ indicates a full re-write. $\mathcal{B}$ chooses a subset $I \subseteq \mathcal{I}$, randomly selects $|I|$ elements $v_i \in_R \mathbb{Z}_p$ and sets $chal = \{(i, v_i)\}_{i \in I}$. It forwards $chal$ as a challenge to $\mathcal{A}$.

◇ *Forgery.* Upon receiving $chal$, the resulting proof of data possession on the correct stored file m should be $\nu = (R_1, \cdots, R_s, B_1, \cdots, B_s, c)$ and pass the Eq. 6. However, $\mathcal{A}$ generates a proof of data possession on an incorrect stored file $\tilde{m}$ as $\tilde{\nu} = (\tilde{R}_1, \cdots, \tilde{R}_s, \tilde{B}_1, \cdots, \tilde{B}_s, \tilde{c})$, such that $\tilde{r}_j \in_R \mathbb{Z}_p$, $\tilde{R}_j = h_j^{\tilde{r}_j}$, $\tilde{b}_j = \sum_{(i,v_i) \in chal} \tilde{m}_{i,j} \cdot v_i + \tilde{r}_j$ and $\tilde{B}_j = h_j^{\tilde{b}_j}$, for $j \in [1,s]$. It also sets $\tilde{c} = \prod_{(i,v_i) \in chal} T_{\tilde{m}_i}^{v_i}$. Finally, it returns $\tilde{\nu}$ to $\mathcal{B}$. If $\tilde{\nu}$ still pass the verification, then $\mathcal{A}$ wins. Otherwise, it fails.

Analysis. We define $\Delta r_j = \tilde{r}_j - r_j$, $\Delta b_j = \tilde{b}_j - b_j = \sum_{(i,v_i) \in chal} (\tilde{m}_{i,j} - m_{i,j}) v_i + \Delta r_j$ and $\Delta \mu_j = \sum_{(i,v_i) \in chal} (\tilde{m}_{i,j} - m_{i,j}) v_i$, for $j \in [1,s]$. Note that r_j and b_j are the elements of a honest proof of data possession ν such that $r_j \in_R \mathbb{Z}_p$ and $b_j = \sum_{(i,v_i) \in chal} m_{i,j} \cdot v_i + r_j$ where $m_{i,j}$ are the actual sectors (not the ones that $\mathcal{A}$ claims to have).

We prove that if $\mathcal{A}$ can win the game, then solutions to the CDH and DL problems are found, which contradicts the assumption that the CDH and DL problems are hard in $\mathbb{G}$ and $\mathbb{G}_1$ respectively. Let assume that $\mathcal{A}$ wins the game. We recall that if $\mathcal{A}$ wins then $\mathcal{B}$ can extract the actual blocks $\{m_i\}_{(i,v_i) \in chal}$ in polynomially-many interactions with $\mathcal{A}$. Wlog, suppose that $chal = \{(i, v_i)\}$, meaning the challenge contains only one block.

○ *First case* ($\tilde{c} \neq c$): According to Eq. 6, we have $e(\frac{\tilde{c}}{c}, g_2) = e\left(\frac{T_{\tilde{m}_i}}{T_{m_i}}, g_2\right)^{v_i} = e(\prod_{j=1}^{s} h_j^{\Delta\mu_j}, g_2^{-a}) = e(\prod_{j=1}^{s}(g_1^{\beta_j} \cdot (g_1^b)^{\gamma_j})^{\Delta\mu_j}, g_2^{-a})$ and so, we get that $e(\frac{\tilde{c}}{c} \cdot (g_1^a)^{\sum_{j=1}^{s} \beta_j \Delta\mu_j}, g_2) = e(g_1^b, g_2^{-a})^{\sum_{j=1}^{s} \gamma_j \Delta\mu_j}$ meaning that we have found the solution to the CDH problem, that is $(g_1^b)^a = (g^x)^{ab} = (\frac{\tilde{c}}{c} \cdot (g_1^a)^{\sum_{j=1}^{s} \beta_j \Delta\mu_j})^{\frac{-1}{\sum_{j=1}^{s} \gamma_j \Delta\mu_j}}$ unless evaluating the exponent causes a divide-by-zero. Nevertheless, we notice that not all of the $\Delta\mu_j$ can be zero (indeed, if $\mu_j = m_{i,j}v_i = \tilde{\mu}_j = \tilde{m}_{i,j}v_i$ for $j \in [1, s]$, then $c = \tilde{c}$ which contradicts the hypothesis), and the γ_j are information theoretically hidden from $\mathcal{A}$ (Pedersen commitments), so the denominator is zero only with probability $1/p$, which is negligible. Finally, since $\mathcal{B}$ knows the exponent x such that $g_1 = g^x$, it can directly compute $((\frac{\tilde{c}}{c} \cdot (g_1^a)^{\sum_{j=1}^{s} \beta_j \Delta\mu_j})^{\frac{-1}{\sum_{j=1}^{s} \gamma_j \Delta\mu_j}})^{\frac{1}{x}}$ and obtains g^{ab}. Thus, if $\mathcal{A}$ wins the game, then a solution to the CDH problem can be found with probability equal to $1 - 1/p$.

○ *Second Case* ($\tilde{c} = c$): According to Eq. 6, we have $e(\tilde{c}, g_2^a) = e(H(i, vnb_i)^{v_i}, g_2) \cdot e(\prod_{j=1}^{s} \tilde{B}_j, g_2) \cdot e(\prod_{j=1}^{s} \tilde{R}_j, g_2)^{-1}$. Since the proof $\nu = (R_1, \cdots, R_s, B_1, \cdots, B_s, c)$ is a correct one, we also have $e(c, g_2^a) = e(H(i, vnb_i)^{v_i}, g_2) \cdot e(\prod_{j=1}^{s} B_j, g_2) \cdot e(\prod_{j=1}^{s} R_j, g_2)^{-1}$. We recall that $chal = \{(i, v_i)\}$. From the previous analysis step, we know that $\tilde{c} = c$. Therefore, we get that $\prod_{j=1}^{s} \tilde{B}_j \cdot (\prod_{j=1}^{s} \tilde{R}_j)^{-1} = \prod_{j=1}^{s} B_j \cdot (\prod_{j=1}^{s} R_j)^{-1}$. We can re-write as $\prod_{j=1}^{s} h_j^{\tilde{b}_j - \tilde{r}_j} = \prod_{j=1}^{s} h_j^{b_j - r_j}$ or even as $\prod_{j=1}^{s} h_j^{\Delta b_j - \Delta r_j} = \prod_{j=1}^{s} h_j^{\Delta\mu_j} = 1$. For $g_1, h \in \mathbb{G}_1$, there exists $\xi \in \mathbb{Z}_p$ such that $h = g_1^\xi$ since $\mathbb{G}_1$ is a cyclic group. Wlog, given $g_1, h \in \mathbb{G}_1$, each h_j could randomly and correctly be generated by computing $h_j = g_1^{y_j} \cdot h^{z_j} \in \mathbb{G}_1$ such that y_j and z_j are random values in $\mathbb{Z}_p$. Then, we have $1 = \prod_{j=1}^{s} h_j^{\Delta\mu_j} = \prod_{j=1}^{s}(g_1^{y_j} \cdot h^{z_j})^{\Delta\mu_j} = g_1^{\sum_{j=1}^{s} y_j \cdot \Delta\mu_j} \cdot h^{\sum_{j=1}^{s} z_j \cdot \Delta\mu_j}$. Clearly, we can find a solution to the DL problem. More specifically, given $g_1, h = g_1^\xi \in \mathbb{G}_1$, we can compute $h = g_1^{\frac{\sum_{j=1}^{s} y_j \cdot \Delta\mu_j}{\sum_{j=1}^{s} z_j \cdot \Delta\mu_j}} = g_1^\xi$ unless the denominator is zero. However, not all of the $\Delta\mu_j$ can be zero and the z_j are information theoretically hidden from $\mathcal{A}$, so the denominator is only zero with probability $1/p$, which is negligible. Thus, if $\mathcal{A}$ wins the game, then a solution to the DL problem can be found with probability equal to $1 - 1/p$. Therefore, for $\mathcal{A}$, it is computationally infeasible to win the game and generate an incorrect proof of data possession which can pass the verification.

The simulation of $\mathcal{O}_{TG}$ is perfect. The simulation of $\mathcal{O}_{DOP}$ is almost perfect unless $\mathcal{B}$ aborts. This happens when the data operation was not correctly performed. As previously, we can prove that if $\mathcal{A}$ can pass the updating proof, then solutions to the CDH and DL problems are found. Following the above analysis and according to Eq. 5, if $\mathcal{A}$ generates an incorrect updating proof which can pass the verification, then solutions to the CDH and DL problems can be found with probability equal to $1 - \frac{1}{p}$ respectively. Therefore, for $\mathcal{A}$, it is computationally infeasible to generate an incorrect updating proof which can pass the verification. The proof is completed.

References

1. Ateniese, G., Burns, R., Curtmola, R., Herring, J., Kissner, L., Peterson, Z., Song, D.: Provable data possession at untrusted stores. In: Proceedings of CCS 2007, pp. 598–609 (2007)
2. Ateniese, G., Di Pietro, R., Mancini, L.V., Tsudik, G.: Scalable and efficient provable data possession. In: Proceedings of SecureComm 2008, pp. 1–10 (2008)
3. Chen, B., Curtmola, R.: Auditable version control system. In: Proceedings of NDSS 2014 (2014)
4. Erway, C., Küpçü, A., Papamanthou, C., Tamassia, R.: Dynamic provable data possession. In: Proceedings of CCS 2009, pp. 213–222 (2009)
5. Esiner, E., Küpçü, A., Özkasap, O.: Analysis and optimization on flexDPDP: a practical solution for dynamic provable data possession. In: Proceedings of ICC 2014 (2014)
6. Etemad, M., Küpçü, A.: Tranparent, distributed, and replicated dynamic provable data possession. In: Proceedings of ACNS 2013 (2013)
7. Fan, X., Yang, G., Mu, Y., Yu, Y.: On indistinguishability in remote data integrity checking. Comput. J. $58(4)$, 823–830 (2015)
8. Gritti, C., Chen, R., Susilo, W., Plantard, P.: Dynamic provable data possession protocols with public verifiability and data privacy (2015). https://arxiv.org/abs/1709.08434
9. Gritti, C., Susilo, W., Plantard, T.: Efficient dynamic provable data possession with public verifiability and data privacy. In: Foo, E., Stebila, D. (eds.) ACISP 2015. LNCS, vol. 9144, pp. 395–412. Springer, Cham (2015). https://doi.org/10.1007/978-3-319-19962-7_23
10. Hao, Z., Zhong, S., Yu, N.: A privacy-preserving remote data integrity checking protocol with data dynamics and public verifiability. IEEE Trans. Knowl. Data Eng. $23(9)$, 1432–1437 (2011)
11. Liu, C., Ranjan, R., Yang, C., Zhang, X., Wang, L., Chen, J.: MuR-DPA: top-down levelled multi-replica merkle hash tree based secure public auditing for dynamic big data storage on cloud. IEEE Trans. Comput. $64(9)$, 2609–2622 (2015)
12. Merkle, R.C.: Secrecy, authentication, and public key systems. Ph.D. thesis, Stanford University (1979)
13. Shacham, H., Waters, B.: Compact proofs of retrievability. In: Proceedings of ASIACRYPT 2008, pp. 90–107 (2008)
14. Wang, B., Li, B., Li, H.: Knox: privacy-preserving auditing for shared data with large groups in the cloud. In: Bao, F., Samarati, P., Zhou, J. (eds.) ACNS 2012. LNCS, vol. 7341, pp. 507–525. Springer, Heidelberg (2012). https://doi.org/10.1007/978-3-642-31284-7_30
15. Wang, B., Li, B., Li, H.: Oruta: privacy-preserving public auditing for shared data in the cloud. IEEE Trans. Cloud Comput. $2(1)$, 43–56 (2012)
16. Wang, B., Li, B., Li, H.: Panda: public auditing for shared data with efficient user revocation in the cloud. IEEE Trans. Serv. Comput. $8(1)$, 92–106 (2015)
17. Wang, C., Chow, S., Wang, Q., Ren, K., Lou, W.: Privacy-preserving public auditing for secure cloud storage. IEEE Trans. Comput. $62(2)$, 362–375 (2013)
18. Wang, C., Wang, Q., Ren, K., Cao, N., Lou, W.: Toward secure and dependable storage services in cloud computing. IEEE Trans. Serv. Comput. $5(2)$, 220–232 (2012)
19. Wang, C., Wang, Q., Ren, K., Lou, W.: Ensuring data storage security in cloud computing. In: Proceedings of IWQoS 2009 (2009)

20. Wang, C., Wang, Q., Ren, K., Lou, W.: Privacy-preserving public auditing for data storage security in cloud computing. In: Proceedings of INFOCOM 2010, pp. 525–533 (2010)
21. Wang, Q., Wang, C., Li, J., Ren, K., Lou, W.: Enabling public verifiability and data dynamics for storage security in cloud computing. In: Backes, M., Ning, P. (eds.) ESORICS 2009. LNCS, vol. 5789, pp. 355–370. Springer, Heidelberg (2009). https://doi.org/10.1007/978-3-642-04444-1_22
22. Wang, Q., Wang, C., Ren, K., Lou, W., Li, J.: Enabling public auditability and data dynamics for storage security in cloud computing. IEEE Trans. Parallel Distrib. Syst. 22(5), 847–859 (2011)
23. Yu, S., Wang, C., Ren, K., Lou, W.: Achieving secure, scalable, and fine-grained data access control in cloud computing. In: Proceedings of INFOCOM 2010, pp. 534–542 (2010)
24. Yu, Y., Au, M.H., Mu, Y., Tang, S., Ren, J., Susilo, W., Dong, L.: Enhanced privacy of a remote data integrity-checking protocol for secure cloud storage. IJIS 14, 1–12 (2014)
25. Zhu, Y., Ahn, G.-J., Hu, H., Yau, S.S., An, H.G., Hu, C.-J.: Dynamic audit services for outsourced storages in clouds. IEEE Trans. Serv. Comput. 6(2), 227–238 (2013)
26. Zhu, Y., Wang, H., Hu, Z., Ahn, G.-J., Hu, H., Yau, S.S.: Dynamic audit services for integrity verification of outsourced storages in clouds. In: Proceedings of SAC 2011, pp. 1550–1557 (2011)

Outsourcing Encrypted Excel Files

Ya-Nan Li[1,2], Qianhong Wu[1(✉)], Wenyi Tang[3], Bo Qin[3,4], Qin Wang[1],
and Meixia Miao[5]

[1] School of Electronics and Information Engineering,
Beihang University, Beijing, China
{yanan_li,qianhong.wu}@buaa.edu.cn, wangqin0409@foxmail.com
[2] State Key Laboratory of Cryptology, P. O. Box 5159, Beijing 100878, China
[3] Key Laboratory of Data Engineering and Knowledge Engineering,
Ministry of Education, School of Information, Renmin University of China,
Beijing, China
tangwenyi@foxmail.com, bo.qin@ruc.edu.cn
[4] State Key Laboratory of Information Security, Institute of Information
Engineering, Chinese Academy of Sciences, Beijing 100093, China
[5] State Key Laboratory of Integrated Service Networks,
Xidian University, Xi'an 710071, China
miaofeng415@163.com

Abstract. With the development of cloud computing, the enterprises
tend to outsource their data to the third party for saving cost and mobile
access. However, simultaneously achieving the security and the operability of the outsourced data becomes a real challenge. Existing solutions
mainly deal with the security of the outsourced data, but cannot support
the operation of encrypted data at the same time, except for few kinds
of operations. In this paper, we propose an outsourcing encrypted Excel
file scheme, which supports most operations of the encrypted data, as if
it were not encrypted in Excel. Based on extensive experimental tests,
the system achieves the function of summing, seeking mean, searching,
indexing. The analysis shows that our scheme can provide proper security
in practice.

Keywords: Outsource data · Excel · Privacy · Operability

1 Introduction

With the popularity of the Internet and the development of cloud computing,
mobile office becomes more and more important. According to the research published by the International Data Corporation (IDC) in 2016, the growth of mobile
office has exploded since 2015, and the entire market still exists a vast space for
development. Mobile office will keep rapid growth in the next 2–3 years [11].

In order to provide the mobile office service, the enterprises outsource their
data resources to large cloud service providers and rent partial storage resources
and related data services for their needs. This is because the modern enterprises

© Springer International Publishing AG 2017
J. K. Liu and P. Samarati (Eds.): ISPEC 2017, LNCS 10701, pp. 506–524, 2017.
https://doi.org/10.1007/978-3-319-72359-4_30

have more and more data needed to store and deal with, and the technical limitations on rebuilding cloud infrastructures and the high cost of management and maintenance make it impossible [10] to enterprises if their main business is not information services. Then the technology of outsourcing data has been widely applied in the cloud computing era.

The enterprises outsource their data and receive the convenient services, but they are still under the risk of sensitive data loss and privacy leakage. The threat of private information exposure has become an inescapable problem, especially for online applications [14]. Cloud service provider can snoop on enterprise's private data [25]; attackers with physical access to servers can access all data on cloud storage [17]. And then a large number of scholars have researched on how to achieve the security of outsourcing data. Many schemes (e.g., [33,34]) have been proposed to achieve the confidentiality of outsourcing data through access control. Some schemes employ the traitor tracing method to achieve the confidentiality of outsourcing data for example [15,21]. In the meanwhile, many papers like [22,32] studied the provable data possession (PDP for short) to achieve the integrity of outsourcing encrypted data. However, few of them can achieve functional operations on outsourced encrypted data except for few kinds of operations.

With the popularization of Database as a Service (DBaaS for short), researchers have done many studies on outsourcing encrypted database which supports some query functions so far (e.g., [13,25]). However, to the best of our knowledge, there has been no research on outsourcing encrypted Excel in the public literatures. Compared with the database mainly used for storing, Excel is a kind of spreadsheet which combines the data storage with the data analysis within obvious advantages (e.g., strong visibility with graphical interface, easy to operate, easy to get started, low entry requirement). The report published by the market-research firm Forrester shows that not including other Office versions, only Office 2010 can keep up to 85 percent market share [18], that is, Microsoft Office has been a preferred productivity suite for enterprises among similar products. Excel has innate advantages as one part of Microsoft Office. Excel's distiguishing market share provides the importance and necessity of doing research on outsourcing Excel. Because Excel files may contain much private information, such as financial data, staff information, and so on. Hence, we have to pay attention to private information protection when outsourcing Excel files.

1.1 Our Contribution

In this paper, we propose an outsourcing encrypted Excel scheme which simultaneously protects private information of the Excel file owners and supports the most often-used data processing functions in Excel. The system contains three entities, i.e., data users, data owners and the third proxy. The system can be coarsely described as follows. The data owner encrypts Excel data before outsourcing to the third proxy. The data user submits a request in the form of Excel plaintext formula to the data owner. Then the data owner translates the plaintext formula into the cipher form, which is executable directly for the third proxy. The third proxy receives the ciphertext formula from the data owner and performs the formula on the ciphertext Excel. Then it returns the results in ciphertext to the data owner, who is responsible for decrypting and returning the final result in plaintext to the data user. The third proxy can only store and operate ciphertext, so an enterprise can outsource data securely. Data user's interface is just an empty table with standard architecture and necessary index information. We provide the data user with an input box used for submitting formula requests. In this way, we can prevent data users and the proxy from accessing information without authorization.

We are inspired by the idea of achieving some query functions on outsourcing encrypted database. We study the characteristics of Excel, and build conversion module to adapt to the original structure of Excel, and eventually support partial Excel functions in outsourced ciphertext Excel. Based on a large amount of experiments, our outsourcing encrypted Excel system can operate eight of the ten most popular Excel functions and some other common functions, including calculating the summation, calculating the mean value, sifting, matching and indexing, and so on. Experiments show that we can get more secure operation on encrypted data at the small price of extra storage and processing time. The secrecy of the Excel file outsourced is well protected.

1.2   Related Work

Numerous proposals have been proposed to achieve secure data outsourcing. Existing outsourced data security schemes have well guaranteed the confidentiality, integrity of the outsourced data through access control and traitor tracing, provable data possess (PDP for short).

To achieve access control, some early works adopt traditional public-key encryption. For example, the work [26] uses digital signature with RSA algorithm to achieve access control. They are complicated regarding key management and public-key validation before encryption. To circumvent these problems, attribute-based encryption (ABE for short) has been widely applied to design fine-grained access control system, e.g., [19,23,34]. Castiglione et al. [9] proposed a hierarchical access control scheme. Some other proposals, e.g., [7,8] achieve access control supporting dynamic updates.

Access control only provides a priori approach to achieve data confidentiality. Traitor tracing gives a posteriori approach to achieve data confidentiality. For tracing traitors who leaked decryption keys, Boneh et al. [3,4] constructed two collusion-resistant public-key broadcast encryption schemes. For the leakage of sensitive data in cloud computing, Chow et al. [12] proposed a dynamic secure provenance scheme which can record the data ownership as an evidence if there is a dispute later. Deng et al. [15] proposed an a posteriori approach for tracing and revoking leaked credentials, which can trace, in a black-box manner, at least one traitor who illegally distributed a credential, without any help from the cloud service provider.

PDP proves the integrity of data stored at untrusted servers [16]. Ateniese *et al.* [1] introduced a model for PDP that allows a client that has stored data at an untrusted server to verify that the server possesses the original data without retrieving it. Erway *et al.* [16] presented efficient constructions for dynamic provable data possession (DPDP), which extends the PDP model to support provable updates to stored data. To solve the problem that existing publicly verifiable PDP schemes require the user to perform expensive computations, Wang *et al.* [32] proposed an efficient online/offline PDP (OOPDP) model, which is practical to speed-up PDP schemes.

All the aforementioned works on the secure data outsourcing consider the security of data itself, including confidentiality and integrity. But they do not achieve any meaningful data manipulation on encrypted data. As for data functions, most works only support searchability. Boneh *et al.* [2] proposed the first searchable encryption scheme using the asymmetric encryption scheme, which only supported the single keyword search over the encrypted data. To enrich the search functionality, some schemes (e.g., [5,6,27]) supporting multiple keywords search have been proposed. However, none of the schemes can support fuzzy keyword search. Li *et al.* [20] proposed a wildcard based fuzzy search over encrypted data. Then Wang *et al.* [30] proposed a novel multikeyword fuzzy search scheme by exploiting the locality-sensitive hashing technique. Tahir *et al.* [29] presented a novel ranked searchable encryption scheme preserving the privacy by the probabilistic trapdoor.

In this paper, we explore more versatile ways to operate outsourced data securely. Our outsourcing encrypted Excel system supports most function manipulations over encrypted data.

1.3   Paper Organization

The rest of this paper is organized as follows. In Sect. 2, we introduce the outsourcing encrypted Excel system model and the data flow. We state the threat model and related security goals. Section 3 gives a detailed description of our proposal. In Sect. 4, we compare the feasible performance and efficiency between the plaintext Excel and the encrypted one. Besides, we conduct detailed security analyses of the system. Section 5 concludes the paper.

2   System Description

In this section, we briefly introduce the outsourcing encrypted Excel system model and the data flow. Then we present a description of possible attack behaviors. Finally we show the security goals that this system tends to achieve.

2.1   System Model

We not only outsource the data stored in Excel and the architecture formed by spreadsheets, but also implement the processing capacity over the encrypted data. In the premise of supporting mobile office, remote and multiple information sharing, the main design objectives of outsourcing encrypted Excel are to minimize the cost of local storage and maintenance, to enhance information security, and to maximize the supported outsourcing functions. Our outsourcing encrypted Excel implementation scheme realizes the efficient combination of the three aspects. Outsourcing data to the third proxy saves the local storage and the maintenance cost. Outsourcing encrypted Excel to the third proxy who stores and processes encrypted data guarantees the security of sensitive data. The third proxy can implement the function operation on ciphertext, which maximizes the outsourcing function.

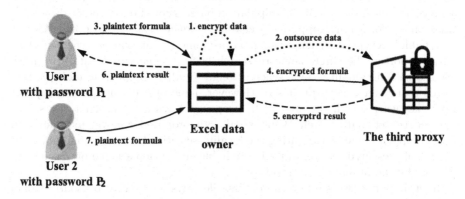

Fig. 1. System architecture of outsourced encrypted Excel. Dotted arrows represent initialization process. Solid arrows indicate the sent to the third proxy and short solid arrows represent the reply from the third proxy.

As Fig. 1 shows, the system model contains three entities, data users, data owner and the third proxy. At the beginning of the system operation, the data owner encrypts the data and outsources the ciphertext Excel data to the third proxy. After the completion of initial deployment, a data user first sends clear formula request to the data owner. Then the data owner encrypts clear data and converts Excel built-in function into the corresponding user defined function (UDF for short), which can be carried out by the third proxy. After receiving the ciphertext Excel formula from the data owner, the third proxy executes it on the ciphertext Excel, and returns the encrypted result to the data owner. Finally, the data owner decrypts it back to the data user. In this way, the data user makes a plain-text operation request, and successfully obtains the plain-text result. The third proxy gives the real information, which the data user wants to obtain, to the data user, without knowing what it is.

2.2   Data Flow

In our outsourcing encrypted Excel system, the secure outsourcing works by directly executing various Excel-based data manipulations over encrypted data.

The overall architecture based on the system model consists of three layers, as shown in Fig. 2.

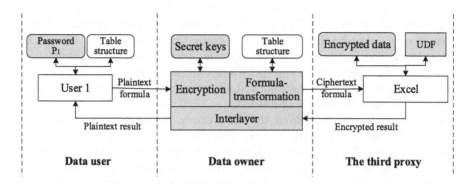

Fig. 2. Data flow in outsourcing encrypted Excel system. Rectangular and rounded boxes represent processes and data, respectively. Shading indicates components added by our outsouring encrypted Excel system. Dashed lines are used to separate the scope of different participants, the data user, the data owner and the third proxy.

The procedure of secure outsourcing for the plaintext Excel files is shown as follows:

1. During the pre-processing period, the data owner generates secret keys and saves them. An encrypted Excel file is outsourced just after encryption. The data owner preserves the original table structure and some necessary indexes, without any copy of the plaintext data or the encrypted data.
2. The third proxy receives and stores the encrypted Excel file. Some UDFs for ciphertext Excel are also built and optimized in advance.

The procedure of data processing on the encrypted data is offered as follows:

1. The user 1 uses his private password P_1 to login the system, and submits a plaintext formula request to the data owner.
2. According to the access control policies, the data owner checks whether the formula request that comes from the active user 1 has been authorized. If it is an unauthorized access, then this manipulation is refused and a security warning is returned.
3. The data owner translates the plaintext formula request into ciphertext formula with the same conversion rules, and sends them to the third proxy.
4. Appropriate ciphertext Excel UDFs are invoked by the third proxy to execute ciphertext formula over the encrypted Excel and the encrypted results are returned.
5. The data owner receives and decrypts the results, and returns the plaintext results to the end user 1.

2.3 Security Model

At present, the security of the enterprise's data mainly confronts two threats. (1) When the enterprise's data is outsourced to the third proxy, the information is likely to be disclosed to the third proxy. On the one hand, the compromised third proxy may reveal secret data for various reasons. On the other hand, an attacker might break the third-party storage system, and obtain data stored there. (2) Information leakage from enterprise's internal employees or authorized personnel. Internal employees or authorized personnel may disclose the information they have to the attacker out of interest.

For information leakage from the third proxy, outsourcing encrypted data prevents the third proxy from directly accessing and operating sensitive information. If an attacker breaches the third-party storage (including obtaining the data stored in the third-party storage through compromising the administrator), he can gain the outsourced ciphertext data. Then the attacker can make a ciphertext-only attack and conjecture its clear information on the basis of ciphertext. In this case, the security of information depends on the length of the secret key used for encrypting. When deploying data, the data owner needs to balance tradeoffs between the security and the cost of space and operating time.

Our scheme also takes measures to address information leakage from enterprise's internal employees or authorized personnel. In our system, the data user can only see the frame structure of the table and necessary index information without any substantial content, which avoids the data user knowing clear information and disclosing it. If the users want to obtain information, the only way is to make a formula request to the data owner. But malicious users can make a continuous request to infer the actual internal data. In order to handle this problem, we can set up some access control policies for the system, restricting the user's requests for malicious intent. In this paper, we don't consider this kind of security protection but leave to the future work.

3 The Proposal

In this section, we describe the encryption algorithm of our scheme, introduce the methods for processing different types of data, and state the specific implementation of the transformation layer.

3.1 Building Block

Encryption scheme. In our scheme, we use the order preserving encryption algorithm with additivity (OPEA for short) that Wang *et al.* [31] presents, for encryption. The OPEA encryption function $E : X \rightarrow Y$ should meet the following two conditions:

1. Order-preservation: $\forall a, b \in X$, **if** $a < b$, **then** $E(a) < E(b)$;
2. Additive order-preservation: $\forall a, b, c \in X$, **if** $a + b < c$, **then** $E(a) + E(b) < E(c)$;

where X, Y represent the plaintext domain and the ciphertext domain of the OPEA algorithm, respectively.

The OPEA algorithm in the paper [31] can be summarized formally as a symmetric encryption algorithm, including the following three sub-algorithms: the boundary generation algorithm GenBoundary, the encryption algorithm Encrypt, and the decryption algorithm Decrypt. When the ciphertext is summed, two extended algorithms, the extended encryption algorithm Encrypt' and the extended decryption algorithm Decrypt' are also necessary. For more information of the OPEA algorithm, please refer to the paper [31].

3.2   Data Type and Processing Method

Generally speaking, the plaintext domain of OPEA is defined as a part of positive integers, that is $X \subseteq N^+$. But by preprocessing, plain-text data type can be easily extended to other types, not limited to integers. The data in different columns are preprocessed and encrypted according to the data type and the required operation:

Number type. Integers can be encrypted directly with the OPEA algorithm. For a float data, a simple approach is to divide encryption according to its data range. For floating point type data, the minimum precision of the plaintext space can be used to divide a ciphertext-space by the least precision on plaintext-space. Their lower and upper boundaries are recomputed on the basis of partition distribution.

A numerical data is usually used in the process of sorting or calculating. Since OPEA is order preserving, sorting and comparing operations can be done in conjunction with ciphertext size and ciphertext judgment functions. As for calculations, this scheme is mainly concerned with the linear calculation, including the addition and the multiplication with integer, which can be seen as multiple additions. For data columns with calculated requirements, they are encrypted into two columns with the same system keys, using the OPEA and OPEA extension algorithms respectively. Linear calculation in the ciphertext domain can be achieved via the ciphertext sum calculation protocol.

Character type. Character type data is primarily used in lookup and reference functions, and text functions. Generally the operations performed on the data of the character type are matching, including exact matching and fuzzy matching. Compared with the literature [25] using SEARCH algorithm to achieve full keyword fuzzy matching, in this paper, the columns that store character-type data encrypted with the OPEA algorithm can theoretically support all types of fuzzy matching, including wildcards and regular expressions.

To support the use of lookup and reference functions and text functions in ciphertext Excel, we need to take the following measures on character data. The first step is converting the character data to the numeric data with the smallest matching unit, e.g., converting English characters to ASCII, converting Chinese characters to Unicode, etc. The second step is encrypting the numeric data in turn. For example, the string "*abc*" is encrypted as:

$$E(\text{int}(a)); E(\text{int}(b)); E(\text{int}(c)); v,$$

where $E(\cdot)$ represents OPEA encryption function; $int(\cdot)$ means the conversion function of character data to ASCII; ";" denotes standard separator; the ciphertext string ends with the tail "v". We have to admit that this encryption method will inevitably leak data length.

Column name hidden. Both a simple symmetric encryption algorithm and a collision-resistant hash function can be used to hide column names. Since the smallest unit of operation in Excel is a cell rather than a record, the column name is not necessary for each file. We can even omit the column name, only by the data owner to maintain a column index and column name mapping file. This also prevents the attacker from obtaining the column name information by attacking the symmetric encryption algorithm or the hash function.

3.3 Transformation Implementation

Next we give the design principles of the transformation layer, as well as the conversion of specific operators and commonly used functions.

Transformation layer design. The data owner is responsible for converting the plaintext formula request to a ciphertext formula which the third proxy can execute directly on encrypted Excel. In our scenario, the data owner completes the conversion through the Formula-transformation module. The module is entered as a standard plaintext Excel formula, and the goal is to output a formula that the third party agent can execute directly on the ciphertext Excel.

Excel's formula contains all of the following or one of them: functions, references, operators, and constants. The general form of a formula is $= \text{SUM}(A1 : A10)$ or $= IF(A1 > 0)$. For more Excel formula syntax rules, please refer to [28]. The Formula-transformation module designs conversion rules for each function and operator. A rule matching function is defined in the module to complete the conversion rule match. The rule matching function finds the rules converted into the corresponding ciphertext formula according to the specific function used in the plaintext formula, and then calls the corresponding rule conversion function to complete the formula conversion.

For cell references, the formula-transformation module holds a mapping table with plaintext columns to the corresponding ciphertext columns, as the mapping is not a one-to-one mapping. For columns that need to be summed, each column will be encrypted into two columns of ciphertext.

Operator conversion rules. The operators in Excel are divided into four different types: comparison, arithmetic, text, and reference. Ciphertext-based operations require appropriate adjustments to the operator to achieve the same effect as the plaintext-based operations. This article uses Excel user-defined function (UDF for short) to achieve the adjustment of the required operators. In ciphertext Excel, the concrete implementations of the four types of operators are as follows:

Comparison operator. Plaintext-based comparison operators, such as $>, <,$ $=, ...$ are used to compare two values directly. A formula with the comparison operator, such as $= A1 > B1$, outputs a logical value of TRUE or FALSE. As this paper adopts the probability encryption algorithm, the size of two ciphertexts obtained by the same plaintext encryption may not be equal. Therefore it is necessary to adjust the comparison operator based on plaintext to adapt to the ciphertext comparison.

We define two ciphertext comparison functions to obtain the plaintexts size relationship by comparing the corresponding ciphertexts. The following are detail descriptions:

Ciphertext comparison function $\mathsf{EquCom}(E(value_1), E(value_2), x)$: Directly determine the size relationship between the two ciphertext values.

Input The input parameters $E(value_1), E(value_2)$ represent the ciphertext values involved in the comparison or their cell references. The input parameter x is randomly selected by the data owner with the secret key, requiring $R_T < x < Sigma$.

Calculate: Calculate whether $|E(value_1) - E(value_2)| \leq x$ is established. If it is true, the plaintext $value_1$ is equal to $value_2$. Otherwise the relationship between ciphertext size and plaintext size is consistent

Output The function output is 1, indicating that the plaintext $value_1$ is greater than $value_2$; the function outputs 0, indicating that the plaintext $value_1$ is equal to $value_2$; the function outputs -1, indicating that the plaintext $value_1$ is less than $value_2$;

Here's an example of a formula conversion that compares two values using the comparison operator:

$$= A1 > B1 \quad \Longrightarrow \quad = \mathsf{EquCom}(A1, B1, x_1),$$

where the plaintext A, B columns are mapped to the ciphertext A, B columns, respectively. x_1 is the specific value selected randomly by the owner.

Ciphertext-Sum comparison function $\mathsf{SumEquCom}(\mathsf{SUM}(E(\varsigma)), \mathsf{SUM} - (E'(\varsigma)), L[n], U'[n])$: Determine the size relationship between the SUM function value and the constant n in ciphertext.

Input: $\mathsf{SUM}(E'(varsigma))$ is the sum of the dataset's ciphertexts. $\mathsf{SUM}(E'(varsigma))$ is the sum of the dataset's extended ciphertexts. $L[n]$ denotes the lower bound of the integer n, and $U'[n]$ denotes the extended upper bound of the integer n. Where $E'(\cdot)$ represents the extended encryption function.

Calculate: Determine whether $\mathsf{SUM}(E(\varsigma)) \leq L[n]$ and $\mathsf{SUM}(E'(\varsigma)) \geq U'[n]$ is true or not

Output If the result is true, the function returns 0, indicating that the sum of the ciphertext is within the bounds of the corresponding plaintext. Otherwise, if $\mathsf{SUM}(E'(\varsigma)) > U'[n]$, the function returns 1, indicating that the sum of the ciphertexts is greater than the corresponding plaintext threshold; if $\mathsf{SUM}(E(\varsigma)) < L[n]$, the function returns -1, indicating the SUM of the ciphertexts is less than corresponding plaintext threshold.

Here's an example of a formula conversion that compares the SUM function value to the constant using the comparison operator:

$$= \mathsf{SUM}(A1 : A3) > 100$$
$$\implies = \mathsf{SumEquCom}(\mathsf{SUM}(A1 : A3), \mathsf{SUM}'(A1 : A3), L[100], U'[100]) = 1,$$

where the plaintext A column is mapped to the ciphertext A column.

Arithmetic operator. The arithmetic operators are used for basic mathematical operations (addition, subtraction, multiplication, or division), merging numbers, and generating numerical results. Since the encryption scheme used in this article only supports additions, we give the conversion rule for the plaintext addition operator $(+)$.

The data owner first converts the formula containing the $+$ operator into the formula of SUM function. As for the conversion rule of the SUM function, we will introduce later.

Here's an example of a formula conversion using the $+$ operator:

$$= A1 + A2 + A3 \implies = \mathsf{SUM}(A1, A2, A3),$$

where the plaintext A column is mapped to the ciphertext A column.

Text operator. In plaintext Excel, one can use a text operator $(\&)$ to connect (join) one or more text strings to generate a piece of text. In the ciphertext Excel, the direct use of the operator $(\&)$ does not conform to the ciphertext character representation. According to the text string encryption rules, when the connection of two plaintext strings is converted into connecting two strings of ciphertext, one needs to delete the end of the first ciphertext.

Here's an example of a formula conversion using the $\&$ operator:

$$= A1\&A2 \implies = \mathsf{LEFT}(A1, \mathsf{LEN}(A1) - 1)\&A2,$$

where the plaintext A column is mapped to the ciphertext A column.

Reference operator. The plaintext Excel uses a reference operator to merge the cell ranges. The reference operators include the area operator $(:)$, union operator $(,)$ and intersection operator (space). These three operators are equally applicable in ciphertext Excel and do the same functionality. For detail information, please refer to Microsoft's official website [28]. Here we'll not repeat them.

Conversion rules of commonly used functions. Microsoft official website gives the most commonly used 10 functions in Excel [28]. All the most commonly used functions can be achieved in the ciphertext Excel, except for the two date functions. Next we introduce the conversion rules of the most commonly used plaintext Excel functions.

SUM function. Converting the SUM function to the operation on the ciphertext domain requires both the data owner and the third proxy to perform a secure ciphertext SUM computation protocol.

Ciphertext-Sum calculation protocol: The data user submits the SUM function request $SUM(\varsigma)$ to the data owner. The data owner returns the correct plaintext result to the data user. The steps are as follows:

1. The data owner submits $SUM(E(\varsigma))$ and $SUM(E'(\varsigma))$ to the proxy (If the average is required, $COUNT(\varsigma)$ is also needed). The third proxy returns the result. Among them, $SUM(E(\varsigma)$ is the corresponding OPEA ciphertext of the dataset ς and, $SUM(E'(\varsigma))$ is the corresponding OPEA extended ciphertext of the dataset ς.

2. The data owner calls the two decryption functions to calculate $d = Decrypt(SUM(E(\varsigma)))$ and $d' = Decrypt'(SUM(E'(\varsigma)))$, where Decrypt and Decrypt' represents OPEA's decryption algorithm and OPEA extended decryption algorithm.

3. The data owner perform a judgment. If $d = d'$, then it returns d to the data user, that is, the correct plaintext, (If the average is calculated, the data owner returns $d/COUNT(\varsigma)$) otherwise turn to 4.

4. The data owner find out an integer $i(i = 1, 2, ..., d' - d)$ which meets the equation

$$SumEquCom(SUM(E(\varsigma)), SUM(E'(\varsigma)), L[d + i], U'[d + i]) = 0,$$

then returns $d + i$ to user, that is, the correct plaintext result (If the average is required, then $d/COUNT(\varsigma)$ is returned).

When the SUM function participates in the comparison operation in the formula submitted by the data user, only the comparison operator is directly converted, as described in the previous section: comparing the size relationship between the SUM function and the constant.

When the data user submits the SUM function and asks the data owner to return the specific value of the summation, the data owner and the third proxy need to co-execute the ciphertext SUM computation protocol to get the result.

IF function. The IF(*logical_test*, [*value_if_true*], [*value_if_false*]) function is one of the most commonly used functions in Excel, and it can compare the logical values and the expected values. The IF function syntax makes reference to [28]. Here's an example of a simple conversion using the IF function:

$$= IF(C2 > B2, \text{``Over Budget''}, \text{``Within Budget''})$$
$$\implies = IF(EquCom(C2, B2) = 1, E(\text{``Over Budget''}), E(\text{``Within Budget''}))$$

where $E(\text{"Over Budget"})$ and $E(\text{"Within Budget"})$ represent the corresponding ciphertexts of the "Over Budget" and "Within Budget", respectively; the plaintext B, C columns are mapped to the ciphertext B, C column, respectively.

CHOOSE function. The CHOOSE$(index\_num, value1, [value2], ...)$ function is used to return the specified value in the numeric argument list. It is available in both plaintexts and ciphertexts of the Excel. Here is an example of the CHOOSE function conversion:

$$= \text{CHOOSE}(2, A1, B1, C1) \quad \Longrightarrow \quad = \text{CHOOSE}(2, A1, B1, C1),$$

where the plaintext A, B, C columns are mapped to the ciphertext A, B, C column, respectively.

INDEX function. The INDEX$(reference, row\_num, [column\_num], [area\_num])$ function is used to return the cell reference at the intersection of the specified row and column. If the reference consists of a discontinuous selected area, you can select a selected area. As the reference operator is common in the ciphertext Excel and the plaintext Excel, the INDEX function is also available in the ciphertext Excel.

4 Experiments and Evaluation

This chapter compares the realizations of the calculation operators in both plaintexts and ciphertexts of the Excel. Then we count the time of the operations in the ciphertext Excel and make a comparison in the plaintext Excel. Finally, we analyze the security of the outsourcing encrypted Excel implementation.

4.1 Function Comparison

Calculation operators. In Excel, calculation operators are divided into four categories, each of which contains several specific operators. As showed in Table 1, In ciphertext Excel, we can implement all operators except for subtraction, multiplication and division, which is consistent with what we have discussed earlier. The most important reason is that our employed encryption algorithm only supports ciphertext addition.

Table 1. Realization of calculation operators in plaintext and ciphertext Excel, where "Y" denotes that the operator can be achieved, "N" represents that the operator can not be accomplished.

Calculation operators	Arithmetic				Comparison				Text	Reference		
	+	−	*	\	=	>	<	<>	&	:	,	Space
Plaintext Excel	Y	Y	Y	Y	Y	Y	Y	Y	Y	Y	Y	Y
Ciphertext Excel	Y	Y	N	N	Y	Y	Y	Y	Y	Y	Y	Y

Function. Microsoft lists the ten most popular functions of Excel, and the following table shows the comparison of the most popular functions. In the ciphertext Excel, we can achieve the other eight most popular functions in addition to the DATE function and the DAYS function. Besides, we can also achieve some other functions, e.g., the LEN function, the LEFT function, the MID function (Table 2).

Table 2. The comparison of the implementation of the ten most popular functions in plaintext Excel and ciphertext Excel, where "Y" denotes that the function can be achieved, "N" represents that the function can not be accomplished.

Function	SUM	IF	LOOKUP	VLOOKUP	MATCH	CHOOSE	DATE	DAYS	FIND	INDEX
Plaintext Excel	Y	Y	Y	Y	Y	Y	Y	Y	Y	Y
Ciphertext Excel	Y	Y	Y	Y	Y	Y	N	N	Y	Y

4.2 Efficiency Comparison

The test data for this article is from TPC-H 2.17.2, a set of database benchmarks defined by the TPC[1]. The operation platform is the Microsoft Excel 2016 and the programming language is Bisual basic for Applications (VBA). As showed in the following table, we preprocess 150,000 lines of data. When the plaintext space is 0-150,000, we need about 0.15 s to generate keys and 0.03 s to calculate boundaries. In the 0-150,000 plaintext space, we encrypt and decrypt 150,000 lines of integers and strings, respectively. The results are showed in the first row of data in the table. As for the second row of data in the table, we expand the plaintext space to 0-1200,000 and add encryption and decryption on the 150,000 lines of float numbers (Table 3).

Table 3. 150,000 lines of data encryption and decryption processing statistics, where "–" denotes that we did not perform the corresponding operations (Unit: second).

Plaintext space	Generate keys	Calculate boundaries	Encrypt integer	Decrypt integer	Encrypt string	Decrypt string	Encrypt float	Decrypt float
0-15w	0.15	0.03	9	9.4	17.7	19	–	–
0-120w	1.2	0.25	9	9.4	17.8	19	9.2	9.7

For the operating time of specific functions, we also make comparisons through some experiments. In the plaintext Excel, built-in functions' implementation efficiency is very high. The time of function execution in the ciphertext Excel is over 20 times of that in the plaintext Excel.

---

[1] downloaded from http://www.tpc.org/tpc_documents_current_versions/current_specifications.asp.

Now we states some examples of a few typical functions. According to the experiment in the ciphertext Excel, the time-consuming of the SUM function is almost 0.07 s, as well as the AVERAGE function. However, in the plaintext Excel, the execution time of the SUM function is close to 0 s, and the AVERAGE function is the same.

The implementation of the MATCH function in the ciphertext Excel requires defining the new UDF: MATCH$_E$ to complete. Because the realization of the new function MATCH$_E$ needs to traverse the contents of each cell in the selected region, so the function execution time is approximately proportional to the size of the selected region. As shown in the following figure, the execution time is proportional to the number of selected cells. When the number of cells is controlled within 150,000, the execution time is less than 1.5 s (Fig. 3).

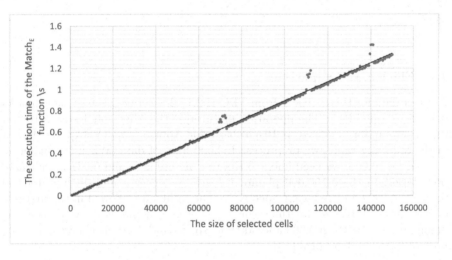

Fig. 3. The relationship between the execution time of the Match$_E$ function and the size of the selected cells. The blue points represent the experiment data, and the black slash represents the trend line. (Color figure online)

As for the LEFT, MID, RIGHT and LEN functions, we also need to define new UDFs (e.g., LEFT$_E$, MID$_E$, RIGHT$_E$, LEN$_E$) to complete the same functions. These functions can be performed in the ciphertext Excel as efficiently as in the plaintext Excel.

4.3   Security Analysis

In this paper, our scheme realizes the complete isolation of the third proxy from the plaintext, in the case where the third proxy does not communicate with the data user in private. The third proxy completes the operation on the ciphertext data via the built-in functions, operators, and reference in the ciphertext Excel. The input parameters of the function are ciphertext. And the third party agent does not perform the decryption operation throughout the operation. Therefore, the third proxy does not touch the plaintext in the whole process, which ensures that the data owner's data privacy will not be leaked by the third proxy.

Our proposal achieves that not all data are fully open to the data user. On the one hand, the data user cannot see the complete Excel data, only some column names and necessary indexes. On the other hand, the data user can only submit the authorized requests.

As for the security of encryption algorithm, Papa *et al.* [24] proved that to achieve the optimal security definition, i.e., indistinguishability under ordered chosen-plaintext attack (IND-OCPA for short), the existing Order Preserving Encryption (OPE) scheme requires the ciphertext space to be at least the exponential level of the plaintext space. The literature [31] proves that its scheme based on the OPEA algorithm is indistinguishability under ordered chosen-plaintext attack (IND-AOCPA for short). It has one more constraint to the adversary compared to previous IND-OCPA, i.e., the plaintexts in queries are bounded by a proportional relation. This article uses the same encryption algorithm, OPEA algorithm, as the literature [31]. Assuming that the data owner in the system safely saves the encryption key and the third proxy performs the operation on the ciphertext as required, our scheme is also IND-AOCPA.

5 Conclusion

In this paper, we presented an outsourcing encrypted Excel scheme and implement it. We mainly use OPEA encryption algorithm and take measures to adjust and encrypt different types of data. Eventually we made it possible to perform various Excel function operations on encrypted data. Data users can only see the table structure and the vital index information, and obtain the desired results and information by submitting the formula request. The third proxy only accesses the outsourced ciphertext data and completes the processing of the ciphertext data by executing the ciphertext formula. The data owner acts as a bridge. Only the data owner has the secret key, who is in charge of encryption and decryption and translation from plaintext formulas to ciphertext formulas.

Our scheme addresses serval critical issues in outsourcing private Excel files. It solves the problem that the third proxy spies the company's private information over the outsourced data. It supports the implementation of function operations over the outsourced ciphertext data, which is conducive to the enterprise's outsourced data flexibly. It has a bright application prospect as our scheme is based on the Microsoft Excel which is widely used in the world.

In the outsourcing encrypted Excel system, the third proxy can perform all operator operations on the ciphertext in addition to subtracting, multiplying, and dividing, and implement the most commonly used 10 built-in functions on the ciphertext except for the two date functions. Besides, we can use UDFs to implement the functionality of some other built-in functions.

We utilized the data provided by TPC-H to complete the experimental test in the outsourcing encrypted Excel system. The test results show that the system goals proposed in this paper are reached, and the statistics of the average operation time are given in the test, which shows that our scheme is also efficient.

Acknowledgment. Qianhong Wu is the corresponding author. This paper is supported by the National Key Research and Development Program of China through project 2017YFB0802505, the Natural Science Foundation of China through projects 61772538, 61672083, 61370190, 61532021, 61472429 and 61402029, and by the National Cryptography Development Fund through project MMJJ20170106.

References

1. Ateniese, G., Burns, R.C., Curtmola, R., Herring, J., Kissner, L., Peterson, Z.N.J., Song, D.X.: Provable data possession at untrusted stores. In: Proceedings of CCS 2007, pp. 598–609. ACM (2007)
2. Boneh, D., Di Crescenzo, G., Ostrovsky, R., Persiano, G.: Public key encryption with keyword search. In: Cachin, C., Camenisch, J.L. (eds.) EUROCRYPT 2004. LNCS, vol. 3027, pp. 506–522. Springer, Heidelberg (2004). https://doi.org/10.1007/978-3-540-24676-3_30
3. Boneh, D., Sahai, A., Waters, B.: Fully collusion resistant traitor tracing with short ciphertexts and private keys. In: Vaudenay, S. (ed.) EUROCRYPT 2006. LNCS, vol. 4004, pp. 573–592. Springer, Heidelberg (2006). https://doi.org/10.1007/11761679_34
4. Boneh, D., Waters, B.: A fully collusion resistant broadcast, trace, and revoke system. In: Proceedings CCS 2006, pp. 211–220. ACM (2006)
5. Boneh, D., Waters, B.: Conjunctive, subset, and range queries on encrypted data. In: Vadhan, S.P. (ed.) TCC 2007. LNCS, vol. 4392, pp. 535–554. Springer, Heidelberg (2007). https://doi.org/10.1007/978-3-540-70936-7_29
6. Cao, N., Wang, C., Li, M., Ren, K., Lou, W.: Privacy-preserving multi-keyword ranked search over encrypted cloud data. IEEE Trans. Parallel Distrib. Syst. **25**(1), 222–233 (2014)
7. Castiglione, A., De Santis, A., Masucci, B., Palmieri, F., Huang, X., Castiglione, A.: Supporting dynamic updates in storage clouds with the akl-taylor scheme. Inf. Sci. **387**, 56–74 (2017)
8. Castiglione, A., Santis, A.D., Masucci, B., Palmieri, F., Castiglione, A., Huang, X.: Cryptographic hierarchical access control for dynamic structures. IEEE Trans. Inf. Forensics Secur. **11**(10), 2349–2364 (2016)
9. Castiglione, A., Santis, A.D., Masucci, B., Palmieri, F., Castiglione, A., Li, J., Huang, X.: Hierarchical and shared access control. IEEE Trans. Inf. Forensics Secur. **11**(4), 850–865 (2016)
10. Chen, X., Li, J., Weng, J., Ma, J., Lou, W.: Verifiable computation over large database with incremental updates. IEEE Trans. Comput. **65**(10), 3184–3195 (2016)
11. China, I.: China's social mobile office software market in 2015. https://www.idc.com.cn/about/press.jsp?id=OTUw. Accessed 10 Mar 2016
12. Chow, S.S.M., Chu, C., Huang, X., Zhou, J., Deng, R.H.: Dynamic secure cloud storage with provenance. In: Cryptography and Security: From Theory to Applications - Essays Dedicated to Jean-Jacques Quisquater on the Occasion of His 65th Birthday, pp. 442–464 (2012)

13. Ciriani, V., De Capitani di Vimercati, S., Foresti, S., Jajodia, S., Paraboschi, S., Samarati, P.: Keep a few: outsourcing data while maintaining confidentiality. In: Backes, M., Ning, P. (eds.) ESORICS 2009. LNCS, vol. 5789, pp. 440–455. Springer, Heidelberg (2009). https://doi.org/10.1007/978-3-642-04444-1_27

14. Clearinghouse, P.R.: Chronology of data breaches. https://www.privacyrights.org/data-breaches

15. Deng, H., Wu, Q., Qin, B., Chow, S.S.M., Domingo-Ferrer, J., Shi, W.: Tracing and revoking leaked credentials: accountability in leaking sensitive outsourced data. In: Proceedings ASIA CCS 2014, pp. 425–434. ACM (2014)

16. Erway, C.C., Küpçü, A., Papamanthou, C., Tamassia, R.: Dynamic provable data possession. ACM Trans. Inf. Syst. Secur. 17(4), 15:1–15:29 (2015)

17. Halderman, J.A., Schoen, S.D., Heninger, N., Clarkson, W., Paul, W., Calandrino, J.A., Feldman, A.J., Appelbaum, J., Felten, E.W.: Lest we remember: cold-boot attacks on encryption keys. Commun. ACM 52(5), 91–98 (2009)

18. Karcher, P., Burris, P., Keitt, T.: Market update: Office 2013 and productivity suite alternatives. Forrester Research, Inc (2013)

19. Li, J., Chen, X., Li, J., Jia, C., Ma, J., Lou, W.: Fine-grained access control system based on outsourced attribute-based encryption. In: Crampton, J., Jajodia, S., Mayes, K. (eds.) ESORICS 2013. LNCS, vol. 8134, pp. 592–609. Springer, Heidelberg (2013). https://doi.org/10.1007/978-3-642-40203-6_33

20. Li, J., Wang, Q., Wang, C., Cao, N., Ren, K., Lou, W.: Fuzzy keyword search over encrypted data in cloud computing. In: Proceedings of INFOCOM 2010, pp. 441–445. IEEE (2010)

21. Li, J., Zhao, G., Chen, X., Xie, D., Rong, C., Li, W., Tang, L., Tang, Y.: Fine-grained data access control systems with user accountability in cloud computing. In: Cloud Computing, Second International Conference, CloudCom 2010, 30 November - 3 December 2010, Indianapolis, Indiana. Proceedings, pp. 89–96 (2010)

22. Liu, H., Mu, Y., Zhao, J., Xu, C., Wang, H., Chen, L., Yu, Y.: Identity-based provable data possession revisited: security analysis and generic construction. Computer Stand. Interfaces 54, 10–19 (2017)

23. Liu, J.K., Au, M.H., Huang, X., Lu, R., Li, J.: Fine-grained two-factor access control for web-based cloud computing services. IEEE Trans. Inf. Forensics Secur. 11(3), 484–497 (2016)

24. Popa, R.A., Li, F.H., Zeldovich, N.: An ideal-security protocol for order-preserving encoding. In: 2013 IEEE Symposium on Security and Privacy SP 2013, Berkeley, CA, 19–22 May 2013, pp. 463–477 (2013)

25. Popa, R.A., Redfield, C.M.S., Zeldovich, N., Balakrishnan, H.: Cryptdb: protecting confidentiality with encrypted query processing. In: Proceedings of SOSP 2011, pp. 85–100. ACM (2011)

26. Somani, U., Lakhani, K., Mundra, M.: Implementing digital signature with RSA encryption algorithm to enhance the data security of cloud in cloud computing. In: 2010 1st International Conference on Parallel Distributed and Grid Computing (PDGC), pp. 211–216. IEEE (2010)

27. Sun, W., Wang, B., Cao, N., Li, M., Lou, W., Hou, Y.T., Li, H.: Privacy-preserving multi-keyword text search in the cloud supporting similarity-based ranking. In: Proceedings of ASIA CCS 2013, pp. 71–82. ACM (2013)

28. Support, M.: Excel help center. https://support.office.com/en-us/excel

29. Tahir, S., Rajarajan, M., Sajjad, A.: A ranked searchable encryption scheme for encrypted data hosted on the public cloud. In: 2017 International Conference on Information Networking, ICOIN 2017, Da Nang, Vietnam, 11–13 Jan 2017, pp. 242–247 (2017)

30. Wang, B., Yu, S., Lou, W., Hou, Y.T.: Privacy-preserving multi-keyword fuzzy search over encrypted data in the cloud. In: Proceedings of INFOCOM 2014, pp. 2112–2120. IEEE (2014)
31. Wang, X., Wu, Q., Zhang, Y.: T-DB: toward fully functional transparent encrypted databases in dbaas framework. CoRR abs/1708.08191 (2017)
32. Wang, Y., Wu, Q., Qin, B., Tang, S., Susilo, W.: Online/offline provable data possession. IEEE Trans. Inf. Forensics Secur. **12**(5), 1182–1194 (2017)
33. Yu, S., Wang, C., Ren, K., Lou, W.: Achieving secure, scalable, and fine-grained data access control in cloud computing. In: IEEE INFOCOM 2010, pp. 534–542 (2010)
34. Zhou, J., Duan, H., Liang, K., Yan, Q., Chen, F., Yu, F.R., Wu, J., Chen, J.: Securing outsourced data in the multi-authority cloud with fine-grained access control and efficient attribute revocation. Comput. J. **60**(8), 1210–1222 (2017)

Outsourced Privacy-Preserving Random Decision Tree Algorithm Under Multiple Parties for Sensor-Cloud Integration

Ye Li[1], Zoe L. Jiang[1(✉)], Xuan Wang[1], S. M. Yiu[3], and Junbin Fang[2]

[1] Harbin Institute of Technology Shenzhen Graduate School, Shenzhen 518055, China
zoeljiang@gmail.com
[2] Jinan University, Guangzhou, China
[3] The University of Hong Kong, HKSAR, China

Abstract. The emerging trends in cloud computing have facilitated the integration of existing technologies towards achieving new and innovative applications for the betterment of humans. Remote health monitoring, a bi-product of technology integration, assists in minimizing human mortality through continuous health monitoring using low-cost sensors. However, privacy and security concerns have become a bottleneck in this process. The secure multi-party computation (SMC)-based privacy-preserving data mining algorithm has emerged as a solution to this problem. However, traditional cryptography-based PPDM solutions are too inefficient and infeasible for analysis on large-scale datasets for data owners. Previous work on random decision trees (RDTs) shows that it is possible to generate equivalent and accurate models at substantially lower costs. In this paper, we focus on the outsourced privacy-preserving random decision tree (OPPRDT) algorithm for multiple parties. We outsource most of the protocol computation to the cloud and propose secure sub-protocols to protect users' data privacy. As a result, we show that our method can achieve similar results as the original RDT algorithm while also preserving the privacy of the data. We prove that there is a sub-linear relationship between the computational cost of the user side and the number of participating parties.

Keywords: Secure multi-party computation · Outsourced computing
Privacy-preserving random decision tree

1 Introduction

The emerging trends in cloud computing have facilitated the integration of existing technologies towards achieving new and innovative applications for the betterment of humans. Remote health monitoring, a bi-product of technology integration, assists in minimizing human mortality through continuous health monitoring using low-cost sensors. However, privacy and security concerns have become a bottleneck in this process. The secure multi-party computation (SMC)-based privacy-preserving data mining algorithm has emerged as a solution to this

© Springer International Publishing AG 2017
J. K. Liu and P. Samarati (Eds.): ISPEC 2017, LNCS 10701, pp. 525–538, 2017.
https://doi.org/10.1007/978-3-319-72359-4_31

problem. Traditional SMC solutions are infeasible due to the efficiency problem facing large-scale data analytics [23]. Therefore, it is important to reduce the computational costs of traditional SMC methods. Cloud-based outsourcing methods provide data owners with the opportunity to allow third parties to process the data. We can reduce the computational cost of the SMC methods for the user's side by outsourcing most of the computations to the cloud server [19].

The random decision tree method, developed by Fan et al. [5], can be used for multiple data mining tasks and achieves better performance than traditional data mining algorithms (such as ID3 and C4.5). In addition, an additional security advantage of RDTs is that they can be very easily made differentially private [23].

1.1   Our Idea

In this paper, we develop methods to outsource the privacy-preserving random decision tree algorithm for multiple parties over horizontally partitioned data sets. In a horizontally distributed data set, two or more parties hold different objects for the same set of attributes. To realize our solutions, we proposed a secure outsourced electronic voting protocol and modified some other subprotocols; then, we proposed an outsourced privacy-preserving random decision tree algorithm based on the protocols.

2   Related Work

Recently, many techniques, which can be classified into two categories according to the existence of a cloud, have been proposed to address the SMC-based privacy-preserving data mining problem.

(1) No-Cloud-Exists Methods: In no-cloud-exists methods, the computations are distributed among the parties. In 2002, Lindell and Pinkas [13] proposed the first cryptography-based approach to build a decision tree over horizontally partitioned data among two parties. Later, similar works were conducted to address the privacy-preserving decision tree construction problem. Zhan et al. [10], Emekci et al. [6], Samet and Miri [20], and Xiao et al. [16] discussed the ID3 decision tree on a horizontally distributed database, whereas Vaidya and Clifton [22] and Zhan et al. [11] addressed the same problem on a vertically distributed database. Xiao et al. [24] discussed the C4.5 decision tree on a horizontally distributed database, whereas Shen et al. [21] and Gangrade et al. [8] addressed the C4.5 algorithm on a vertically distributed database.

(2) Cloud-Exist Methods: In cloud-exist methods, the computations are outsourced to the cloud server. However, it is important to ensure the security and privacy of the outsourced data. In 2005, Hohenberger et al. [9] provided a formal security definition for securely outsourcing computations and presented a scheme securely outsourcing cryptographic computations. In 2011, Kamara et al. [12] designed a general outsourced multiparty computation protocol for a server-aided two-party scheme. In 2013,

Peter et al. [19] proposed an efficiently outsourced multi-party computation construction under multiple keys that can be applied in our case. In 2014, Liu et al. [3] applied a new encryption scheme for outsourcing privacy-preserving k-means data mining. In this scheme, most of the computations were finished on the cloud, thereby reducing the computational work of the data owner, but this scheme was a one-party data mining scheme. Xiaoyan et al. [14] extended that scheme to the two-party case.

A characteristic comparison among different schemes is described in Table 1. In this paper, we focus on the outsourced privacy-preserving random decision tree algorithm with a cloud-exist method. Unlike existing work, we propose the protocol over horizontally partitioned data sets, and we extend the algorithm to address multiple parties.

Table 1. The characteristic comparison among different schemes

Paper	Algorithm	Data partition	Num. of parties	With cloud?
[13, 16, 18]	ID3	Horizontally	2	No
[10]	ID3	Horizontally	2	No
[6, 20]	ID3	Horizontally	n	No
[22]	ID3	Vertically	n	No
[11]	ID3	Vertically	n	No
[24]	C4.5	Horizontally	2	No
[21]	C4.5	Vertically	2	No
[8]	C4.5	Vertically	n	No
[3]	K-Means	Horizontally	1	Yes
[7]	K-Means	Horizontally	2	Yes
Our scheme	RDT	Horizontally	n	Yes

2.1 Organization

The remainder of this paper is organized as follows: In Sect. 3, the Secure Multi-Party Computation, the Random Decision Trees, the BCP homomorphic encryptions, our Outsourced Secure Electronic Voting Protocol (OSEVP) and the other sub-protocols are presented. In Sect. 4, our outsourced privacy-preserving random decision tree algorithm (OPPRDT) is presented. Section 5 gives the analysis of our OPPRDT algorithm, and finally, Sect. 6 presents the conclusions of the paper.

3 Background and Definitions

3.1 Secure Multi-party Computation

SMC [1] is mainly concerned with the problem of evaluating a function using the private input from two or more parties. Therefore, after running the protocol, each party holds a share of the output with no additional information revealed. There are two primary security models: the semi-honest model and the malicious model.

In this study, we mainly focus on solving the SMC problem of the semi-honest model, a model far more widely adopted than the malicious model. In the semi-honest adversary model, even corrupted parties correctly follow protocol specifications. However, the adversary can acquire the internal state of all corrupted parties (including transcripts of all messages received), which can be misused to acquire private information of other parties. Thus, private user data are leaked.

3.2 Random Decision Trees

The random decision tree was introduced by Fan et al. [5] and can simply randomly generate a set of trees from its database. This method can randomly choose an attribute A and set that as a current node; if A has m valid values, it then constructs m child nodes for each attribute value a_i. This algorithm achieves a better performance than traditional decision tree algorithms (such as ID3 and C4.5).

The random decision tree algorithm is summarized in Algorithm 1.

Algorithm 1. The random decision tree algorithm

TreeTrain(S, A, m)
Require: S is the training dataset from the participant.
Require: $A = A_1 \cup A_2 \cup ... \cup A_n$ is the set of attributes.
Require: m is the number of random trees.
for $1 \geq i \geq m$ **do**
    if $A = \emptyset$ **then**
    | establish the node as a leaf
    end
    else
        randomly choose an attribute A_i for set A;
        set A_i as a current node;
        if A has m valid values, it then constructs m child nodes for each
          attribute value a_i;
        TreeTrain$(S - S_A, A - A_i, m)$;
    end
end
Return $\{T_1, ..., T_m\}$
Classify$(\{T_1, ..., T_m\}, x)$
For tree T_i, $P_i(y|x) = \frac{n[y]}{\sum_y n[y]}$, where $n[y]$ is the count at the leaf node that x
    ultimately reaches;
Return $\frac{1}{m} \sum_{i=1}^{m} P_i(y|x)$ for all class labels y;

3.3   The BCP Homomorphic Cryptosystem

The **BCP** homomorphic cryptosystem [2] is an additive homomorphic cryptosystem, which was introduced by Bresson, Catalano, and Pointcheval in 2003. This system has the following property:

$$Enc_{pk}(m_1 + m_2) = Enc_{pk}(m_1) \odot Enc_{pk}(m_2) \tag{1}$$

where m_1 and m_2 are two messages and $\odot$ is an arithmetic multiplication operation in the encrypted domain under the same public key.

In contrast to traditional homomorphic cryptosystems (such as Paillier [17] and ElGamal [4]), the **BCP** cryptosystem can support arithmetic operations in the encrypted domain under multiple parties' public keys. This can be performed by the cloud server after generating a public parameter; then, every party generates its key pairs based on the public parameter. Next, all the parties' public keys can be transformed into a uniform public key, and the ciphertext under each party's public key can be transformed into the ciphertext under the uniform public key.

The BCP cryptosystem employs two non-colluding, semi-honest cloud servers C and S, and the cryptosystem is constructed as follows:

$Setup(\lambda)$: Given a security parameter λ, a server S chooses $N = pq$ of bit length λ, where $p = 2p' + 1$ and $q = 2q' + 1$ for distinct primes p' and q'. Then, S selects a random element $g \in \mathbb{Z}_{N^2}^*$ such that $g^{p'q'} \mod N^2 = 1 + \lambda N$ for $\lambda \in [1, N-1]$. Then, S generates the public parameter PP and the master key MK

$$PP = (N, \lambda, g) \ and \ MK = (p', q'). \tag{2}$$

$KeyGen(PP)$: After each party obtains PP, they select a random $a_i \in \mathbb{Z}_{N^2}$ and generate both its public key pk_i and private key sk_i:

$$public \ key \ pk_i = g^{a_i} \ and \ secret \ key \ sk_i = a_i. \tag{3}$$

$Enc_{pk_i}(m_i)$: Given a plaintext $m_i \in \mathbb{Z}_N$, each party selects a random $r_i \in \mathbb{Z}_{N^2}$ and outputs the ciphertext (A_i, B_i) as

$$A_i = g^{r_i} \mod N^2, \ \ B_i = g^{a_i r_i}(1 + m_i N) \mod N^2. \tag{4}$$

$Dec_{sk_i}(A_i, B_i)$: Given a ciphertext (A_i, B_i) and secret key $sk_i = a_i$, each party can output the plaintext m_i as

$$m_i = \frac{B_i/(A_i^{a_i}) - 1 \mod N^2}{N}. \tag{5}$$

We refer the interested reader to [2,19] for the detailed construction of the **BCP** cryptosystem.

3.4   The TransDec Protocol

The task of the sub-protocol $TransDec$ is to take the result encrypted under $Prod.pk$ and to transform it back into n encryptions of the same plaintext under each party's public key [19].

Algorithm 2. The Sub-protocol of TransDec

---

1. C picks a random number ρ for the input ciphertext (A, B) under Prod.pk, calculates $(C, D) \leftarrow Add((A, B), Enc_{Prod.pk}(\rho))$, and sends them to S.
2. S decrypts them using the master key and obtains $z \leftarrow mDec_{(Prod.pk, MK)}$ (C, D); then, S re-encrypts them with $(X_i, Y_i) \leftarrow Enc_{pk_i}(z)$ under each client public key pk_i. In addition, S sends (X_i, Y_i) back to C.
3. C calculates $Enc_{pk_i}(-\rho)$ and obtains the result as
$$(\bar{A}, \bar{B}) \leftarrow Add((X_i, Y_i), Enc_{pk_i}(-\rho))$$

Then, C outputs the result to each party.

3.5 Secure Addition Protocol (SAP)

Our **SAP** is designed for plaintext addition over encrypted data with different keys. In other words, we suppose that there are n parties $\{P_i \mid 1 \leq i \leq n\}$, each of whom has private input x_i and encrypts its data $Enc_{pk_i}(x_i)$ under its public key. The goal of the **SAP** protocol is to calculate $Enc_{Prod.pk}(\sum_{i=1}^{n} x_i)$, Prod.pk $:= \prod_{i=1}^{n} pk_i \mod N^2$, which can encrypt all the P_i data under a single public key.

The **SAP** protocol can be described as follows:

Algorithm 3. Secure Addition Protocol (SAP)

Require: $\{P_i \mid 1 \leq i \leq n\}$, each of whom has a private input x_i.
1. The server S chooses the BCP homomorphic encryption scheme and distributes its public parameters $PP = (N, k, g)$ to C and P_i.
2. After this initial setup, P_i can use the cryptosystem's $KeyGen$ to generate its respective pair of public and private keys (pk_i, sk_i). It then uploads the public keys pk_i and the ciphertext $Enc_{pk_i}(x_i)$ to C.
3. C chooses n random numbers $r_i \in Z_N$ for each participant and calculates
$$X_i = Enc_{pk_i}(x_i) \cdot Enc_{pk_i}(r_i) = Enc_{pk_i}(x_i + r_i),$$

4. C then calculates the product Prod.pk $:= \prod_{i=1}^{n} pk_i \mod N^2$, which can encrypt all the P_i data under a single public key. Then, C sends Prod.pk and each X_i to S.
5. S calculates both $X_i' = mDec_{MK}(X_i)$ and $T = \sum_{i=1}^{n} X_i'$, encrypts T with $Prod.pk$, and sends the encrypted data to C.
6. C calculates $R = \sum_{i=1}^{n} r_i$, uses $Prod.pk$ to encrypt R as $Enc_{Prod.pk}(R)$, and calculates

$$Enc_{Prod.pk}(T) \cdot Enc_{Prod.pk}(R)^{N-1} = Enc_{Prod.pk}(T - R) = Enc_{Prod.pk}(\sum_{i=1}^{n} x_i).$$

7. C uses the **TransDec** protocol to transform it back into n encryptions of the same plaintext under each participant's public key pk_i; then, it sends the result back to each participant.
8. P_i can decrypt all these ciphertexts received using its corresponding private key sk_i and obtain the final result.

3.6 Secure Multiplication Protocol (SMD)

Given two encrypted numbers $Enc_{pk_a}(x)$ and $Enc_{pk_b}(y)$ under different keys pk_a and pk_b, respectively, the goal of **SMD** is to calculate $Enc_{Prod.pk}(x \cdot y)$ under $Prod.pk$ [15].

Algorithm 4. Secure Multiplication Protocol (SMD)

---

1. C chooses a random number $r_x, r_y, R_x, R_y \in Z_N$, calculates
$$X = Enc_{pk_a}(x) \cdot Enc_{pk_a}(r_a) = Enc_{pk_a}(x + r_a),$$
$$Y = Enc_{pk_b}(y) \cdot Enc_{pk_b}(r_b) = Enc_{pk_b}(y + r_b),$$
$$S = Enc_{pk_a}(R_x) \cdot [Enc_{pk_a}(x)]^{N-r_y} = Enc_{pk_a}(R_x - r_y \cdot x),$$
$$T = Enc_{pk_b}(R_y) \cdot [Enc_{pk_b}(y)]^{N-r_x} = Enc_{pk_b}(R_y - r_x \cdot y).$$

and sends X, Y, and S and T to S.

2. S calculates $h = mDec_{MK}(X) \cdot mDec_{MK}(Y)$, $S_2 = mDec_{MK}(S)$, and $T_2 = mDec_{MK}(T_1)$; then, it encrypts h, S_2 and T_2 with $Prod.pk$ as $H = Enc_{Prod.pk}(h), S_3 = Enc_{Prod.pk}(S_2)$, and $T_3 = Enc_{Prod.pk}(T_2)$. Then, it sends the encrypted data to C.

3. Once the encrypted data are received, C encrypts r_x, r_y, R_x and R_y with $Prod.pk$ as $S_4 = Enc_{Prod.pk}(r_x \cdot r_y)^{N-1}, S_5 = Enc_{Prod.pk}(R_x)^{N-1}$ and $S_6 = Enc_{Prod.pk}(R_y)^{N-1}$. Then, it calculates the following to recover the encrypted $x \cdot y$:

$$H \cdot T_3 \cdot S_3 \cdot S_4 \cdot S_5 \cdot S_6 =$$
$$Enc_{Prod.pk}(h + R_x - r_y \cdot x + R_y - r_x \cdot y - r_x \cdot r_y - R_x - R_y) = Enc_{Prod.pk}(x \cdot y)$$

3.7 Secure Sign Bit Acquisition Protocol (SSBA)

Given encrypted data $Enc_{Prod.pk}(x)$, the goal of the **SSBA** protocol [15] is to obtain the encrypted sign bit $Enc_{Prod.pk}(t^*)$ whereby $t^* = 1$ when $x \geq 0$ and $t^* = 0$ when $x < 0$.

3.8 Secure Less Than Protocol (SLT)

The goal of the **SLT** protocol [15] is to obtain the encrypted data $Enc_{Prod.pk}(u^*)$ to determine which of two encrypted values $Enc_{Prod.pk}(x)$ and $Enc_{Prod.pk}(y)$ is larger, that is, $x \geq y$ or $x < y$. Liu et al. [15] proposed the **SLT** protocol for encrypted data under different keys, and we simply use it for the ciphertext under the same public key $Prod.pk$. We modified this protocol as follows:

Algorithm 5. Secure Sign Bit Acquisition Protocol (SSBA)

---

1. C flips a coin t and chooses a random number r s.t. $\mathcal{L}(r) < \mathcal{L}(N)/4$. ($\mathcal{L}(r)$ denotes the length of r in bits of the modulus n). If $t = 1$, C calculates
$$Enc_{Prod.pk}(l) = ((Enc_{Prod.pk}(x))^2 \cdot Enc_{Prod.pk}(1))^r = Enc_{Prod.pk}[r(2x+1)]$$

If $t = 0$, C calculates

$$Enc_{Prod.pk}(l) = ((Enc_{Prod.pk}(x))^2 \cdot Enc_{Prod.pk}(1))^{N-r} = Enc_{Prod.pk}[-r(2x+1)]$$

Then, C sends $L = Enc_{pk_i}(l)$ to S.
2. S calculates $mDec_{MK}(Enc_{Prod.pk}(l))$ to obtain l. If $\mathcal{L}(l) < 3/8 \cdot \mathcal{L}(N)$, let $u = 1$; otherwise, $u = 0$. Then, u is encrypted using $Prod.pk$ and sends $Enc_{Prod.pk}(u)$ to C.
3. If $t = 1$, C calculates

$$Enc_{Prod.pk}(t^*) = CR(Enc_{Prod.pk}(u));$$

otherwise, it calculates
$$Enc_{Prod.pk}(t^*) = CR(Enc_{Prod.pk}(1) \cdot Enc_{Prod.pk}(u)^{N-1}).$$

Algorithm 6. Secure Less Than Protocol (SLT)

---

1. C calculates
$$Enc_{Prod.pk}(l) \leftarrow SAD(Enc_{Prod.pk}(x), (Enc_{Prod.pk}(y))^{N-1}).$$

2. C uses the **SSBA** protocol to obtain the encrypted sign bit $Enc_{Prod.pk}(t^*)$.
3. C uses the **TransDec** protocol to transform the $Enc_{Prod.pk}(t^*)$ into ciphertext under each party's public key.
4. Each party decrypts it and obtains the result.
If $t^* = 1$, then $x \geq y$; if $t^* = 0$, then $x < y$.

Algorithm 7. Outsourced Secure Electronic Voting Protocol (OSEVP)

Require: $\{P_i \mid 1 \leq i \leq n\}$, each of which has a private input $x_i(x_i = 0\,or\,1)$.
1. The server S chooses the BCP homomorphic encryption scheme and distributes its public parameters $PP = (N, k, g)$ to C and P_i.
2. P_i can use the $KeyGen$ based on the PP to generate its key pair (pk_i, sk_i). It then uploads public keys pk_i and the ciphertext $Enc_{pk_i}(x_i)$ to C.
3. C uses the **SAD** protocol to calculate $Enc_{Prod.pk}(\sum\limits_{i=1}^{n} x_i)$.
4. C uses the **SLT** protocol to determine whether
$$Enc_{Prod.pk}(\sum\limits_{i=1}^{n} x_i) \geq Enc_{Prod.pk}(\lceil n/2 \rceil + 1).$$
5. C uses the **TransDec** protocol to transform the result under each party's public key and sends it to each party.
6. Each party decrypts the ciphertext and obtains the result.

3.9   Outsourced Secure Electronic Voting Protocol (OSEVP)

We propose the OSEVP protocol based on the above sub-protocols. We assume that there are n voters, and each action is assigned to the Authorities. At least $\lceil n/2 \rceil + 1$ out of n voters perform the operation property. Then, every party can obtain the result without disclosing their secret ballot.

4   Outsourced Privacy Preserving Random Decision Tree Algorithm (OPPRDT)

The system model consists of $n(n \geq 2)$ parties and the cloud servers C and S. Each party P_i has a private database $D_i, (1 \leq i \leq n)$. Each party collaborates with the cloud servers to process the RDT algorithm and obtain the result without losing any privacy information. We assume that the two cloud servers S and C are semi-honest and not colluding with each other. Each party P_i is also considered semi-honest in this paper. We assume that each P_i knows the attribute names and sizes of the other parties' private databases.

4.1   Horizontally Partitioned Data

When data are horizontally partitioned, parties hold different objects for the same set of attributes. Assume that there are n parties, and each party P_i has a database $D_i, (1 \leq i \leq n)$ (we denote the whole database as $D, D = D_1 \cup \cdots \cup D_n$). They share the set of general attributes $A = A_1 \cup A_2 \cup \ldots \cup A_n$ and the class attribute $C = \{c_1, ..., c_m\}$. However, the number of records in the databases $|D_i|$ and the true record values $v_j \in A_i$ are unknown for the other parties.

First, if we calculate the distributed random decision tree in a non-private setting, one party can send the other parties any information that they want from its database. Then, each party can independently create a few random trees based on their own datasets. The structure of the trees can be shared with other parties or held by the party itself. Thus, there are two cases to be considered:

(1) If the structure of the trees is known to each participant, the party owning the instance can identify all the leaf nodes that it reaches and can obtain the sum of the class distribution vectors.
(2) If the structure of the trees is unknown to each participant, the party owning the instance can send the instance to other parties. Every party identifies the leaf nodes that it reaches, sends the class distribution vectors to the other parties, and obtains the final result.

4.2   The Structure of the Tree Is Known to Each Participant

In this case, each party first creates a set of random trees for its own databases and then sends the structure to the other parties. However, if a party thinks that a tree reveals too much information, it can use our **OSEVP** in Sect. 3.9 to reject that particular tree and ask for alternatives. After that, we can use the **SAP** in Sect. 3.5 to calculate the class vector components together. Finally, the cloud server uses the **TransDec** protocol in Sect. 3.4 to send the data to each party, and every party decrypts the data and obtains the result.

Algorithm 8 gives the details.

Algorithm 8. Building the random trees for horizontally partitioned data

---

Require: $\{P_i \mid 1 \le i \le n\}$, each of which has a private database D_i.

Require: n_i, the number of random trees to be created by each participant such that $\sum_i n_i = m$, the total number of random trees.

1. The server S chooses the BCP homomorphic encryption scheme and distributes its public parameters $PP = (N, k, g)$ to C and P_i.
2. After this initial setup, P_i can use the cryptosystem's $KeyGen$ to generate its respective pair of public and private keys (pk_i, sk_i). It then sends public keys pk_i to C and other parties.
3. Each party creates a set of random trees from its databases.
4. Each party cooperates with C to use the **OSEVP** to determine if all the parties agree to all the random trees. Then, the structure of every tree is communicated to all the parties.
5. Each party P_i computes the class distribution vectors for each leaf node in the random trees and then encrypts the class distribution vectors for all leaf nodes using pk_i.
6. All parties cooperate with C to use the **SAP** to calculate the corresponding encrypted class distribution vector elements that they receive for each leaf node to obtain the encrypted global value for that node.
7. C uses the **TransDec** protocol to transform the result into the ciphertext under each party's public key and then sends them to each party.
8. Each party decrypts the ciphertext and obtains the result.

4.3 The Structure of the Trees Is Unknown to Each Participant

In this case, every party dose not communicate the structure of the random trees to the other parties. Each party simply needs to encrypt its leaf nodes. In addition, they calculate the encrypted class vector components together with the other parties. We can simply use the **SAP** from Sect. 3.5.

4.4 Classify the New Instance

When a new instance needs to be classified, the instance is sent to each party, and every party identifies all the leaf nodes that it reaches from its trees. Then, each party encrypts the class distribution vectors and uses the **SAP** with the cloud servers to multiply the encrypted class vector components together. After that, each party can decrypt the data to obtain the results. Algorithm 9 gives the relevant steps.

Algorithm 9. Classify Instance(x)

Require: x, the new instance that needs to be classified.

Require: m, the total number of random trees.

1. **for** $j = 1 \cdots m$ **do**

   Each party P_i counts the number $n_j[y]$ of the leaf node that x finally reaches;

   Then, each P_i encrypts $n_j[y]$ and sends it to the server C.

   end

2. C uses the **SAP** to calculate the encrypted sum of $Enc_{Prod.pk}(\sum_y n[y])$ and $Enc_{Prod.pk}(\sum_j n[y])$.

3. C uses the **TransDec** protocol to transform the result and send it to each party.

4. Each party decrypts $Enc_{pk_i}(\sum_y n[y])$ and $Enc_{pk_i}(\sum_j n[y])$ and divides by m to obtain the actual statistics.

---

5 Analysis

5.1 Complexity and Communication Analysis

The performance of our contribution depends on the security parameter k and the number of participants n. In the discussed OPPRDT for the horizontally partitioned data algorithm, each party should encrypt the leaf nodes of its random trees. If there are m attributes, there are $2^{m/2-1}$ leaf nodes. In addition, we assume that there are n participants, and the number of class attribute values is c. Each party generates t random trees, and there will be $O(ntc2^{m/2-1})$ encryption leaf nodes. Before computing, the data owners should encrypt their own data and transfer the data to the server to compute. Subsequently, the server computes over the encrypted data. The Setup step performs the computation for $O(k^5/\log k^2)$. A full overview of the complexity of each protocol is given in Table 2.

5.2 Security Analysis

In the case of the structure of the trees being known to each participant, although the leaf class distribution vector is known to everyone, the leaf class distribution vectors for all trees are encrypted using the BCP cryptosystem. Because semantically secure homomorphic encryption is used, this reveals no information to any of the parties or the cloud servers about the values. In addition, if a party thinks that a tree reveals too much information, it can use the **OSEVP** to reject that particular tree and ask for alternatives. The **OSEVP** uses the sub-protocols based on the BCP cryptosystem and also does not reveal any information to other parties or the cloud servers.

Table 2. Complexity and runtime analysis of the protocol

Algorithm	Time	Traffic in bits
Setup	$O(k^5/\log k^2)$ on S	$4k$
SAP	$O(k^2)$ on C	$2k$
SLT	$O(k^2)$ on C $O(k^2)$ on S	$12k$
SMD	$O(k^3)$ on C $O(k^3)$ on S	$12k$
SSBA	$O(k^3)$ on client $O(nk^3)$ on C $O(nk^5/\log k^2)$ on S	$4(n+1)k$
TransDec	$O(nk^3)$ on C $O(nk^3)$ on S	$4(n+1)k$
OSEVP	$O(k^3)$ on client $O(tk^2)$ on C $O(tk^3)$ on S	$6(n+1)k$
OPPRDT	$O(ntc2^{m/2-1})$ on client $O(nm^2k^2)$ on C $O(nmk^3)$ on S	$12(n+1)k$

In the case of the structure of the trees being unknown to each participant, each party simply uses the **SAP** to calculate the class vector components together to obtain the sum of the class distribution vectors for each tree. The **SAP** is also based on the BCP cryptosystem and does not reveal any information to other parties or the cloud servers.

When a new instance needs to be classified, the parties also use the **SAP** to multiply the encrypted class vector components together to obtain the encrypted sum of the class distribution vectors for each tree. This also does not reveal any information to other parties or the cloud servers.

6   Conclusion

In this paper, we proposed an outsourced privacy-preserving random decision tree algorithm over horizontally partitioned databases for multiple parties. To realize our solutions, we proposed a secure outsourced electronic voting protocol and modified some other sub-protocols; then, we proposed an outsourced privacy-preserving random decision tree algorithm based on the protocols. We considered two cases: the case where the structure of the tree is known to each participant and the case where the structure of the tree is unknown to each participant. The proposed algorithm shows its safety in the semi-honest adversary model. In the future, we plan to extend all three partitioned datasets in the malicious model. We also aim to extend the OSEVP and other sub-protocols into a general multi-party privacy-preserving framework that is suitable for other machine learning algorithms, for example, k-means [14] and deep learning.

Acknowledgment. This work is supported by National High Technology Research and Development Program of China (No. 2015AA016008).

References

1. Yao, A.: How to generate and exchange secrets. In: Proceedings of Annual Symposium on Foundations of Computer Science, pp. 162–167 (1986)
2. Bresson, E., Catalano, D., Pointcheval, D.: A simple public-key cryptosystem with a double trapdoor decryption mechanism and its applications. In: Laih, C.-S. (ed.) ASIACRYPT 2003. LNCS, vol. 2894, pp. 37–54. Springer, Heidelberg (2003). https://doi.org/10.1007/978-3-540-40061-5_3
3. Liu, D., Bertino, E., Yi, X.: Privacy of outsourced k-means clustering. In: Proceedings of ACM Symposium on Information, Computer and Communications Security, pp. 123–134 (2014)
4. Elgamal, T.: A public key cryptosystem and a signature scheme based on discrete logarithms. In: CRYPTO 1984, Proceedings of Advances in Cryptology, pp. 10–18 (1985)
5. Fan, W., Wang, H., Yu, P.S., et al.: Is random model better? On its accuracy and efficiency. In: IEEE International Conference on Data Mining, pp. 51–58. DBLP (2003)
6. Emekci, F., Sahin, O.D., et al.: Privacy preserving decision tree learning over multiple parties. Data Knowl. Eng. **63**(2), 348–361 (2007)
7. Jagannathan, G., Wright, R.N.: Privacy-preserving distributed K-means clustering over arbitrarily partitioned data. In: Proceedings of ACM International Conference on Knowledge Discovery, pp. 593–599 (2005)
8. Gangrade, A., Patel, R.: Building privacy-preserving C4.5 decision tree classifier on multi-parties. Int. J. Comput. Sci. Eng. **1**(3), 199–205 (2009)
9. Hohenberger, S., Lysyanskaya, A.: How to securely outsource cryptographic computations. In: Kilian, J. (ed.) TCC 2005. LNCS, vol. 3378, pp. 264–282. Springer, Heidelberg (2005). https://doi.org/10.1007/978-3-540-30576-7_15
10. Zhan, J., Matwin, S., et al.: Privacy preserving decision tree classiffcation over horizontally partitioned data. In: Proceedings of International Conference on Electronic Business, pp. 470–476 (2005)
11. Zhan, J., Matwin, S., Chang, L.W.: Privacy-preserving decision tree classification over vertically partitioned data. In: Proceedings of IEEE International Conference on Data Mining Workshop on Multiagent Data Warehousing (MADW) and Multiagent Data Mining (MADM), pp. 27–35 (2005)
12. Kamara, S., Mohassel, P., Raykova, M.: Outsourcing multi-party computation. In: IACR Cryptology Eprint Archive, vol. 2011(3), pp. 435–451 (2011)
13. Lindell, Y., Pinkas, B.: Pinkas.: privacy preserving data mining. J. Cryptol. **15**(3), 177–206 (2002)
14. Liu, X., Jiang, Z.L., Yiu, S.M., Wang, X.: Outsourcing two-party privacy preserving k-means clustering protocol in wireless sensor networks. In: Proceedings of International Conference on Mobile Ad-Hoc and Sensor Networks, pp. 124–133 (2015)

15. Liu, X., Deng, R., Choo, K.K.R., et al.: An efficient privacy-preserving outsourced calculation toolkits with multiple keys. IEEE Trans. Inf. Forensics Secur. **11**(11), 1–1 (2016)
16. Xiao, M., Huang, L., et al.: Privacy preserving ID3 algorithm over horizontally partitioned data. In: Proceedings of International Conference on Parallel and Distributed Computing, Applications and Technologies, pp. 239–243 (2005)
17. Paillier, P.: Public-key cryptosystems based on composite degree residuosity classes. In: Stern, J. (ed.) EUROCRYPT 1999. LNCS, vol. 1592, pp. 223–238. Springer, Heidelberg (1999). https://doi.org/10.1007/3-540-48910-X_16
18. Lory, P.: Enhancing the efficiency in privacy preserving learning of decision trees in partitioned databases. In: Domingo-Ferrer, J., Tinnirello, I. (eds.) PSD 2012. LNCS, vol. 7556, pp. 322–335. Springer, Heidelberg (2012). https://doi.org/10.1007/978-3-642-33627-0_25
19. Peter, A., Tews, E., Katzenbeisser, S.: Efficiently outsourcing multiparty computation under multiple keys. IEEE Trans. Inf. Forensics Secur. **8**(12), 2046–2058 (2013)
20. Samet, S., Miri, A.: Privacy preserving ID3 using Gini index over horizontally partitioned data. In: Proceedings of IEEE/ACS International Conference on Computer Systems and Applications, pp. 645–651 (2008)
21. Shen, Y., Shao, H., Yang, L.: Privacy preserving C4.5 algorithm over vertically distributed datasets. In: Proceedings of IEEE International Conference on Networks Security, Wireless Communications and Trusted Computing, pp. 446–448 (2009)
22. Vaidya, J., Clifton, C.: Privacy-preserving decision trees over vertically partitioned data. In: Jajodia, S., Wijesekera, D. (eds.) DBSec 2005. LNCS, vol. 3654, pp. 139–152. Springer, Heidelberg (2005). https://doi.org/10.1007/11535706_11
23. Vaidya, J., Shafiq, B., Fan, W., et al.: A random decision tree framework for privacy-preserving data mining. IEEE Trans. Dependable Secure Comput. **11**(5), 399–411 (2014)
24. Xiao, M.J., Han, K., Huang, L.S., et al.: Privacy preserving C4.5 algorithm over horizontally partitioned data. In: Proceedings of International Conference on Grid and Cooperative Computing, pp. 78–85 (2006)

Effective Security Analysis for Combinations of MTD Techniques on Cloud Computing (Short Paper)

Hooman Alavizadeh[1]([✉])[iD], Dong Seong Kim[2][iD], Jin B. Hong[2][iD], and Julian Jang-Jaccard[1][iD]

[1] Institute of Natural and Mathematical Sciences, Massey University, Auckland, New Zealand
{h.alavizadeh,j.jang-jaccard}@massey.ac.nz
[2] Department of Computer Science and Software Engineering, University of Canterbury, Christchurch, New Zealand
{dongseong.kim,jin.hong}@canterbury.ac.nz

Abstract. Moving Target Defense (MTD) is an emerging security solution based on continuously changing attack surface thus makes it unpredictable for attackers. Cloud computing could leverage such MTD approaches to prevent its resources and services being compromised from an increasing number of attacks. Most of the existing MTD methods so far have focused on devising subtle strategies for attack surface mitigation, and only a few have evaluated the effectiveness of different MTD techniques deployed in systems. We conducted an in-depth study, based on realistic simulations done on a cloud environment, on the effects of *security* and *reliability* for three different MTD techniques: (*i*) *Shuffle*, (*ii*) *Redundancy*, and (*iii*) the combination of *Shuffle* and *Redundancy*. For comparisons, we use a formal scalable security model to analyse the effectiveness of the MTD techniques. Moreover, we adopt Network Centrality Measures to enhance the performance of security analysis to overcome the exponential computational complexity which is often seen in a large networked mode.

Keywords: Cloud computing · Graphical Security Models
Moving Target Defense · Security analysis

1 Introduction

Cloud computing is an on-demand network access model and offers benefits including scalability, resilience, availability, and cost reduction. Cloud providers (e.g., Amazon Web Services, Windows Azure Platform, Google App Engine, *etc.*) offering various services are responsible for providing security or their services. This is because, despite cloud computing benefits, security-related issues would affect customer's trust on cloud. Although many security mechanisms are implemented in the cloud, cyber criminals can still exploit software vulnerabilities to

© Springer International Publishing AG 2017
J. K. Liu and P. Samarati (Eds.): ISPEC 2017, LNCS 10701, pp. 539–548, 2017.
https://doi.org/10.1007/978-3-319-72359-4_32

penetrate into a cloud system [9] using tools and techniques easily available on the Internet. Moving Target Defense (MTD) is an emerging security solution that confuses the attackers by continuously changing the attack surface [11,14]. Unlike traditional security solutions that focused on removing vulnerabilities, MTD techniques increase the attack efforts by changing attack surfaces. However, it is difficult to assess their effectiveness in various systems, especially when they are used in combinations. MTD techniques are mainly classified into three main categories [6]: *Shuffle*, *Redundancy*, and *Diversity*. Those techniques can be used either independently or in a combination. The latter is used to provide an insight if it is more effective if different categories of MTD techniques used together. In this paper, we evaluate the effectiveness of the MTD techniques and their combinations using *security* and *dependability* metrics.

Many graphical security models (GSM) (such as Attack Trees (ATs) and Attack Graphs (AGs)) in conjunction with security metrics, have been proposed and used. They provide formal methods to analyse the security of a networked system [10]. Various security metrics can be used with the GSMs (e.g., system risk, attack costs and *etc.*), providing different perspectives of the system security. Hence, incorporating MTD techniques into GSMs could allow formulating an optimal MTD deployment solution through security analyses. Moreover, these models can also be used to find how effective the deployed MTD techniques are by comparing the results obtained through the models and the metrics. Analysing security through GSMs suffers from scalability issue, especially in the enterprise networks [4].

We address the aforementioned problem by using a scalable security model named Hierarchical Attack Representation Model (HARM) [7]. The HARM can evaluate the security-related effects of a particular MTD technique before deploying it. The strength of the HARM is that the security analysis is more scalable and it also provides heuristic methods such as using Importance Measures (IMs) [5] to overcome the exponential computational complexity issues. We further detail the usage and application of IMs to analyse the effectiveness of MTD techniques in combinations, which was not previously taken into account.

To the best of our knowledge, there is no prior work to evaluate and compare the effectiveness of the combination of MTD techniques via a formal GSM. Our main contributions are:

- Analyse and compare the effects of each MTD technique, *shuffle*, *redundancy* and their combinations in term of both *system risk* and *reliability*.
- Investigate the use of IMs on different properties of Network Centrality Measures (NCMs) to understand the effects of such properties to assess the effectiveness of MTD techniques;
- Analyse the correlation of IMs, *Betweenness* and *Closeness*, with the result of deployed MTD techniques using an Exhaustive Search (ES) method in a HARM to observe the mathematical relation between the metrics;

The rest of this paper is organised as follow. We define the methods and metrics used in Sect. 2. In Sect. 3, we analyse the MTD techniques and combined them, then further discussion and limitations are given in Sect. 4. Related work is summarised in Sect. 5. Finally, we conclude the paper in Sect. 6.

2   Preliminaries

Importance Measures. IMs are computed to find a set of network components that serves a critical role in an event of an attack without exhausting all possible attack paths. We use NCMs in the upper layer of the HARM to compute the IMs [5], where we consider two types of NCMs; *Betweenness* and *Closeness*. However, there are other NCMs measures which can be used (e.g., Harmonic Closeness, PageRank *etc.*), which are out of scope of this paper.

System Risk Analysis. A risk of an asset (here, a VM) can be defined as a the product of probability of an attack success of a VM and the impact of the attack on that VM. Given above, we can define the *system risk* as a cumulative sum of all the risk associated with VMs in all possible attack paths. To compute the *system risk*, the HARM is first generated using the reachability and vulnerability information. Then, we first show the probability of an attack success calculation steps. We assume there is a set of VMs VM, an N number of VMs in the upper layer HARM where $N = |VM|$, and each VM $VM_i \in VM$ has up to a $|V|$ number of vulnerabilities for a set of vulnerabilities V. Let V_i be the set of vulnerabilities for a VM VM_i, then there exists a vulnerability $v_j \in V_i \mid 0 \le i \le |N|, 0 \le j \le |V|$. There are two logical gates AND and OR-gates, which connect the vulnerabilities in the lower layer of the HARM. AND_k represents a set of vulnerabilities and other logical gates connected by the AND-gate$_k$, and the OR_k represents a set of vulnerabilities and other logical gates connected by the OR-gate$_k$. Let $p(VM_i)$ be the probability of compromising the VM_i, and $p(v_j)$ is the probability of attack success when exploiting the vulnerability v_j. Also, we let $p(AND_k)$ be the probability of attack success for exploiting all vulnerabilities grouped for that AND-gate$_k$, and similarly for $p(OR_i)$. Then, the probability of attack success based on AND_i or OR_i can be calculated as follows.

$$p(AND_k) = \prod p(v_j) \mid v_j \in AND_k \tag{1}$$

$$p(OR_k) = 1 - \prod \left(1 - p(v_j)\right) \mid v_j \in OR_k \tag{2}$$

Using Eqs. (1) and (2), we can calculate the probability of an attack success to compromise VM_i as shown in Eq. (3) denoted by the top-gate, TOP.

$$p(VM_i) = p(TOP) \mid TOP \in \{AND_j, OR_k\} \tag{3}$$

We define the impact of an attack exploiting a vulnerability v_j as I_{v_j}. Then, we define the impact of an attack exploiting VM_i as denoted as I_{VM_i}, which is shown in Eq. (4).

$$I_{VM_i} = max(I_{v_j}) \mid v_j \in VM_i \tag{4}$$

Then, we denote the risk associated with VM_i as R_{VM_i}, which is calculated by the product of the probability of an attack success and the impact of an attack to VM_i as shown in Eq. 5.

$$R_{VM_i} = p(VM_i) \times I_{VM_i}, \tag{5}$$

Here, we assume that each attack path is independent to other attack paths in the system. All possible attack paths, *paths*, is a set of attack paths $path \in paths$ where $path = (VM_1, VM_2, \ldots, VM_N) \in VM \times VM \times \ldots \times VM \mid path \in paths$, where a series of VMs that form an attack path such that VM_i is adjacent to VM_{i+1} for $1 \le i < |N|$. Finally, the *system risk*, R_{system}, can be calculated as shown in Eq. 6.

$$R_{system} = \sum_{VM_i \in path \in paths} R_{VM_i} \tag{6}$$

Reliability Analysis. We use SHARPE (Symbolic Hierarchical Automated Reliability and Performance Evaluator) [12] to assess the reliability of the cloud. In detail, we can compute the probability of the existence of a path from start point to target using a reliability graph in SHARPE. We utilise this feature by defining the upper layer of the HARM as a reliability graph. This allows us to determine the robustness of the system over the time given attack rates. We can compute the probability of the existence of a path from a start point (entry of a network) to a target using the reliability graph. Reliability of the networked system was computed assuming the attack rates follow an exponential distribution. We vary the attack rate, indicated by λ value over time t, to observe the change in reliability of the network. Hence, estimating the probability of attack success, p(AS) (component failure) at time t can be obtained by a cumulative exponential distribution. Then, the reliability of each component (a VM in here) can be defined as the probability of an attack failure under certain attack rate and a given time, $R(t) = 1 - p(AS)$. Finally, to expand the *reliability* analysis for the whole system, we fed the reliability graph constructed through the upper layer of HARM to SHARPE with an assumed attack rate ($\lambda = 0.2$, one attack per five hours) and different time t to evaluate the overall *reliability* of system.

3   MTD Technique Analysis Through HARM

In order to evaluate the effectiveness of different MTD techniques, we simulated a large Cloud-band model as shown in Fig. 1. This model includes two cloud-band nodes that can hold up to 450 VMs. Only a few VMs in the Cloud-band are connected to the Internet (i.e., front-end servers). We assume there is an attacker outside the cloud, and the attack goal is to compromise the resource node by compromising VMs in the attack paths. We also assume that VMs can migrate between the Cloud-band nodes if there is an available space, which rearranges the logical connections between the VMs. All VMs in the Cloud-bands are using the same OS. We measure the changes in *system risk* and *reliability* to evaluate the effectiveness of MTD techniques. In the following sections, we show that how the MTD techniques may affect *security* and *reliability* factors. The *system risk* and *reliability* of the current system have been evaluated based on different number of VMs in each cloud-band node and reported in Fig. 2 for further comparison with the results of MTD deployment strategies.

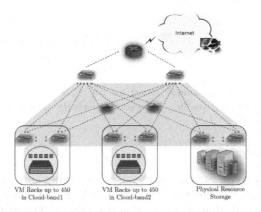

Fig. 1. A Cloud-band model consisting up to 450 VMs in each Cloud-band nodes.

3.1   Shuffle

In this paper, we only focus on shuffling the VM through the VM live migration (VM-LM), where we use the HARM to assess the effectiveness of deploying the *shuffle*.

If we consider all possible migration scenarios and analyse the effectiveness of each movement separately through an exhaustive search (ES) method, we can obtain an optimal solution. However, this method is time consuming and impractice for large sized networks. Alternatively, we use IMs for discovering the most important nodes in the network [5]. We analyse the relation of each IMs, *betweenness* and *closeness*, with deploying *shuffle*. We then compare the results obtained from ES with those of found through a portion of IMs. The effects of deploying *shuffle* on each node are investigated by both ES method and using IMs (two NCMs are used, *betweenness* and *closeness*). Figure 2a illustrates (*i*) how deploying *shuffle* can enhance *system security*, (*ii*) whether the best scenario for deployed MTD technique can be obtained through IMs. The results show that the best *shuffle* deployment scenario minimising the *system risk* can be found through analysing only the top 10 percent of the most important nodes based on *betweenness*, but this method does not guarantee the best *reliability* value. As shown in Fig. 2a, the result of this analysis is equivalent with ES to find the optimal *shuffle* deployment. However, deploying *shuffle* so that it minimises the *system risk* leads a mild decrement on the *system reliability*. Figure 2b demonstrates the *reliability* values before and after deploying *shuffle*.

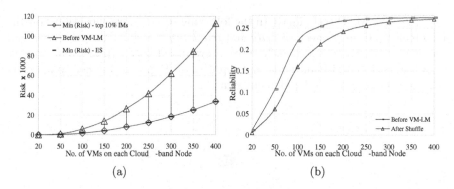

Fig. 2. Deploying *shuffle* technique based on top 10% of *betweenness* and ES. (a) System *risk* after deploying shuffle. (b) System *reliability* after deploying shuffle.

3.2 Redundancy

For *redundancy*, we replicate the number of VMs k times and connect the replicas to the same adjacent nodes with the original VM. We denote the number of replicated VMs as k-R. However, any other component of the network can also be replicated (e.g., a service, server *etc*). In this section, (i) we perform a regression analysis to compare *system risk* and *reliability* against the IMs. We first calculate the values of *reliability* and *system risk* after deploying *redundancy* technique (with 3-R) for each VM through the ES. The upper layer of HARM is used by the SHARPE to obtain *reliability*, then perform a regression analysis to show the correlation of each IMs with the corresponding *system risk* and *reliability* values. Despite correlation analysis, and for evaluation of deploying *redundancy*, (ii) we investigate if the optimal values for the *system risk* and *reliability* can be found using the IMs, and (iii) to investigate how IMs can affect the *system risk* and *reliability* when deploying *redundancy*.

The results of regression analysis on deploying *redundancy* in HARM's nodes are considered through comparing the correlation of *system risk* and *reliability* against *betweenness* and *closeness*. We construct the HARM consisting of overall 50 VMs based on the Cloud-band model. Then, the behaviour of system are monitored after passing three hours in order to calculate *reliability*. We deploy three replicas (3-R) for each VM in the top layer of HARM in order to perform regression analysis. However, other VM sizes and different replicas are tested to compare the effects of *redundancy* on both *system risk* and *reliability* separately.

The results shown in Fig. 3 indicates that deploying the *redundancy* technique increases the *reliability*. The best deployment scenario can be found through analysing *closeness*. It is noticeable that the *reliability* obtained through this deployment grows logarithmic while if we use *betweenness*, it causes an exponential growth in the *system risk* and in the best case (using *closeness*) we have linear increment in the *system risk*. Hence, one should deploy *redundancy* precisely based on the network's size and specifications. Next, we investigate the combinations of the *shuffle* and *redundancy*.

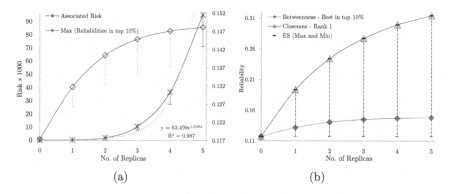

Fig. 3. *System risk* and *reliability* based on IMs after deploying *redundancy*. (a) compares deploying *redundancy* on the top 10% of *betweenness* nodes. (b) compares deploying *redundancy* on the top 10% of *betweenness* and *closeness*.

3.3   Combination of Shuffle and Redundancy

The *shuffle* technique improves the security while the *redundancy* improves the *reliability* as shown in previous sections. Thus both aforementioned measures would be necessary in a network, especially in large sized networks or cloud environments. In this section, we explore the effectiveness of the combination of *Shuffle(S)* and *Redundancy(R)*, denoted as $S+R$ technique. Based on the experimental results obtained from the previous sections, we develop the $S+R$ together with IMs so that we deploy *shuffle* among the top 10% of VMs having the highest *betweenness* values and we deploy *redundancy* on the most important VM opted by on *closeness* measure. The obtained results of $S+R$ are compared with the *suffle* only, *redundancy* only, and no MTD deployed configurations of the network. Figure 4a compares the growth trend in the *system risk* against different cloud-band sizes and replicas by deploying all combinations of foregoing MTD strategies. Furthermore, in order to analyse the effects of deploying $S+R$ on *system reliability* and compare it with other deployment scenarios, we duplicate the most important VM in the term of *closeness* and find the best *shuffle* scenario through *betweenness* (as in Sect. 3.1), see Fig. 4b).

As it can be seen in Fig. 4a, deploying *shuffle-only* can decrease the *system risk* (compare *S-Only* with *No-R-No-S* in chart). Next, deploying *redundancy-only* decreases system security. Nevertheless, deploying $S+R$ causes a gentle increment on the *system risk* which is not comparable with the same values cased by deploying *redundancy* only. In Fig. 4b, comparing current system with the results of deploying both *redundancy* and $S+R$, we obviously observe that both of these techniques enhance the *system reliability*, while *shuffle* decreases *reliability*.

Finally, we conclude that the two important *security* and *reliability* measures have a negative correlation toward MTD techniques. Although increasing the *system reliability* through deploying *redundancy* may deteriorate security and vice versa, one can benefit from a combination strategy to find a reliable

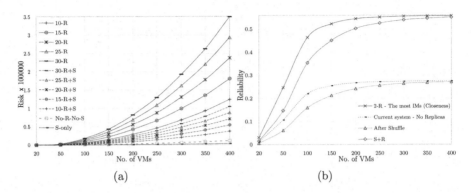

Fig. 4. Combinations of MTD techniques with regard to *system risk* and *reliability*. (a) compares the combinations of MTD techniques based on different cloud-band sizes and replicas over the *system risk*. (b) compares deploying *Shuffle, Redundancy (2-R), and S+R* techniques on the *system reliability*

threshold between those two measures based on the a particular system and networked environment.

4   Discussion and Limitations

In this section, we discuss the main findings of the deployed methods as well as the limitations and future work. Experimental analysis in Sect. 3 showed that the best *shuffle* technique that minimised the *system risk* can be found using the IMs with only the top 10% of VMs. Although deploying the shuffle decreased the *system reliability*, this decrement was neglectable (especially in the larger cloud-bands) as shown in Figs. 2a and 4b. When deploying the *redundancy* technique, *betweenness* measure has a strong exponential correlation with the *system risk*. It shows that deploying *redundancy* technique on the nodes with higher *betweenness* values increases *system risk* exponentially. As the redundancy technique aims to improve the the *system reliability*, we observed a trade-off between the *system risk* and the *reliability* when using the redundancy technique. The second finding is that, the *betweenness* had no correlation with the *reliability*; thus, replication of a VM with highest *betweenness* centrality does not guarantee the best *reliability*. However, one can deploy *redundancy* on a VM with the highest *closeness* rate to achieve the best *reliability* value while *system risk* grows linearly. Finally, through combination of both *shuffle* and *redundancy* and utilising the pros and cons of each, we can find an appropriate threshold between those with regard to the security and performance-related requirements and the networked environment. The observed results are valid based on our cloud-band model and may vary on different type of networks and cloud models. Other MTD combinations including *Diversity* should also be considered with more analysis related to time and complexity of the methods. We only focused on two criteria for assessing our methods, *system risk* and *reliability*, while there are many security metrics, such as attack cost, probability, *etc.*

For our future work, we will conduct experiments using a real testbed, which we are currently working on implementing a private cloud named Unitecloud [3]. Further, we will incorporate other combinations of MTD techniques to evaluate their effectiveness, as well as to incorporate more vulnerabilities from other layers in the system (e.g., application vulnerabilities).

5   Related Work

Many research efforts are made to improve the MTD systems in the last decade, including frameworks [14], strategies and techniques [1,8], and applications [2]. Jafarian *et al.* [8] developed a MTD technique to proactively change the IP addresses of the hosts. Similarly, the concept of Random Route Mutation (RRM) has been introduced by Al-Shaer [1] to find an optimal randomised path between the source and the target. Zhang *et al.* [13] proposed an end-to-end defence strategy to secure VMs in a cloud data centre at a hypervisor level. Zhang *et al.* [14] proposed a MTD method to cope with the problem resulting from co-residency in the virtualised environment.

On the other hand, there are only a few work to evaluate the effectiveness of the MTD techniques. Peng *et al.* [11] investigated the effectiveness of MTD techniques for securing cloud-based services with a heterogamous or dynamic attack surface. However, they did not utilise a rational and formal security model and analysis tool. Hong *et al.* [6] analysed the security changes when MTD techniques are deployed, by introducing a formal method to model *Shuffle*, *Redundancy*, and *Diversity* individually. We extended this work by combining *Shuffle* and *Redundancy* measuring the *system risk* and *reliability*, as well as incorporating to use the IMs for better scalability.

6   Conclusion

MTD techniques have been proposed to enhance the cyber security by changing the network surface continuously, therefore making the attack surface unpredictable for attackers. However, the effectiveness of deploying multiple MTD techniques has not been evaluated. To address this problem, we first incorporated MTD techniques, namely *Shuffle*, *Redundancy*, and the combination of both, into a scalable graphical security model named HARM, in order to evaluate the effectiveness of MTD techniques by comparing the changes in the *system risk* and *reliability*. Moreover, we used IMs to find the most effective MTD techniques in a scalable manner. Finally, our experimental results showed the effectiveness and the trade-off using the proposed MTD techniques in order to maximise the *reliability* while minimising the *system risk*.

Acknowledgment. This paper was made possible by Grant NPRP 8-531-1-111 from Qatar National Research Fund (QNRF). The statements made herein are solely the responsibility of the authors.

References

1. Al-Shaer, E.: Toward network configuration randomization for moving target defense. In: Jajodia, S., Ghosh, A., Swarup, V., Wang, C., Wang, X. (eds.) Moving Target Defense - Creating Asymmetric Uncertainty for Cyber Threats, vol. 54, pp. 153–159. Springer, New York (2011). https://doi.org/10.1007/978-1-4614-0977-9_9

2. Chatfield, B., Haddad, R.: Moving Target Defense Intrusion Detection System for IPv6 based smart grid advanced metering infrastructure. In: Proceedings of the IEEE SoutheastCon 2017, pp. 1–7, March 2017

3. He, M., Pang, S., Lavrov, D., Lu, D., Zhang, Y., Sarrafzadeh, A.: Reverse Replication of Virtual Machines (rRVM) for mow latency and high availability services. In: Proceedings of the 9th International Conference on Utility and Cloud Computing (UCC 2016), pp. 118–127. ACM (2016)

4. Hong, J.B., Kim, D.S.: Performance analysis of scalable attack representation models. In: Janczewski, L.J., Wolfe, H.B., Shenoi, S. (eds.) SEC 2013. IAICT, vol. 405, pp. 330–343. Springer, Heidelberg (2013). https://doi.org/10.1007/978-3-642-39218-4_25

5. Hong, J.B., Kim, D.S.: Scalable security analysis in hierarchical attack representation model using centrality measures. In: Proceedings of the 43rd Annual IEEE/IFIP International Conference on Dependable Systems and Networks Workshop (DSN-W 2013), pp. 1–8 (2013)

6. Hong, J.B., Kim, D.S.: Assessing the effectiveness of moving target defenses using security models. IEEE Trans. Dependable Secure Comput. 13(2), 163–177 (2016)

7. Hong, J.B., Kim, D.S.: Towards scalable security analysis using multi-layered security models. J. Netw. Comput. Appl. 75(C), 156–168 (2016)

8. Jafarian, J., Al-Shaer, E., Duan, Q.: Openflow random host mutation: transparent moving target defense using software defined networking. In: Proceedings of the 1st Workshop on Hot Topics in Software Defined Networks (HotSDN 2012), pp. 127–132. ACM, New York (2012)

9. Jia, Q., Wang, H., Fleck, D., Li, F., Stavrou, A., Powell, W.: Catch me if you can: a cloud-enabled DDoS defense. In: Proceedings of the Annual IEEE/IFIP International Conference on Dependable Systems and Networks (DSN 2014), pp. 264–275 (2014)

10. Kaynar, K., Sivrikaya, F.: Distributed attack graph generation. IEEE Trans. Dependable Secure Comput. 13(5), 519–532 (2016)

11. Peng, W., Li, F., Huang, C., Zou, X.: A moving-target defense strategy for cloud-based services with heterogeneous and dynamic attack surfaces. In: Proceedings of the IEEE International Conference on Communications (ICC 2014), pp. 804–809 (2014)

12. Sahner, R., Trivedi, K., Puliafito, A.: Performance and Reliability Analysis of Computer Systems: An Example-Based Approach Using the SHARPE Software Package. Springer, US (2012)

13. Zhang, L., Shetty, S., Liu, P., Jing, J.: Rootkitdet: practical end-to-end defense against kernel rootkits in a cloud environment. In: Proceedings of the European Symposium on Research in Computer Security (ESORICS 2014), pp. 475–493 (2014)

14. Zhang, Y., Li, M., Bai, K., Yu, M., Zang, W.: Incentive compatible moving target defense against VM-colocation attacks in clouds. In: Proceedings of the 27th IFIP Information Security and Privacy Conference (SEC 2012), pp. 388–399 (2012)

Network Security

Fast Discretized Gaussian Sampling and Post-quantum TLS Ciphersuite

Xinwei Gao[1], Lin Li[1(✉)], Jintai Ding[2(✉)], Jiqiang Liu[1], R. V. Saraswathy[2], and Zhe Liu[3]

[1] Beijing Key Laboratory of Security and Privacy in Intelligent Transportation, Beijing Jiaotong University, Beijing 100044, People's Republic of China
{xinweigao,lilin,jqliu}@bjtu.edu.cn
[2] Department of Mathematical Sciences, University of Cincinnati, Cincinnati 45219, USA
jintai.ding@gmail.com, rvsaras86@gmail.com
[3] APSIA, Interdisciplinary Centre for Security, Reliability and Trust (SnT), University of Luxembourg, Luxembourg City, Luxembourg
sduliuzhe@gmail.com

Abstract. LWE/RLWE-based cryptosystems require sampling error term from discrete Gaussian distribution. However, some existing samplers are somehow slow under certain circumstances therefore efficiency of such schemes is restricted. In this paper, we introduce a more efficient discretized Gaussian sampler based on ziggurat sampling algorithm. We also analyze statistical quality of our sampler to prove that it can be adopted in LWE/RLWE-based cryptosystems. Compared with ziggurat-based sampler by Buchmann et al. related samplers by Peikert, Ducas et al. and Knuth-Yao, our sampler achieves more than 2x speedup when standard deviation is large. This can benefit constructions rely on noise flooding (e.g., homomorphic encryption). We also present two applications: First, we use our sampler to optimize the RLWE-based authenticated key exchange (AKE) protocol by Zhang et al. We achieve 1.14x speedup on total runtime of this protocol over major parameter choices. Second, we give practical post-quantum Transport Layer Security (TLS) ciphersuite. Our ciphersuite inherits advantages from TLS and the optimized AKE protocol. Performance of our proof-of-concept implementation is close to TLS v1.2 ciphersuites and one post-quantum TLS construction.

Keywords: Post-quantum cryptography · Lattice · RLWE · Sampling · TLS

1 Introduction

1.1 Backgrounds

Various public key algorithms had been proposed and widely deployed in real world since the ground-breaking Diffie-Hellman key exchange protocol [6].

© Springer International Publishing AG 2017
J. K. Liu and P. Samarati (Eds.): ISPEC 2017, LNCS 10701, pp. 551–565, 2017.
https://doi.org/10.1007/978-3-319-72359-4_33

With the advent of quantum computers however, it is believed that most current public key cryptographic constructions are no longer secure while lattice-based algorithms can survive. Best known attacks on current cryptosystems are Shor's algorithm [20] and Grover's algorithm [11]. Shor's algorithm can break most public key algorithms efficiently when practical quantum computers are available. Grovers algorithm can speedup attacks against most symmetric ciphers and hash functions, but they are considered to be relatively secure [3]. Bennett et al. proved that a quantum computer may provide quadratic speedup on brute-force key search [2] and this attack can be defeated by doubling key length. However, increasing key size while remain practical does not work for public key cryptosystems.

During the past years, lattice-based cryptographic primitives had been recognized for their attractive properties, including resistant to quantum attacks, strong provable security and efficiency. Currently, no public algorithms can efficiently solve hard lattice problems. During the past decade, Learning With Errors (LWE) [19] and Ring-LWE (RLWE) [15] underlie as foundation for numerous modern lattice-based cryptosystems. Constructions based on these hard problems enjoy strong provable security and high efficiency. The secret, fresh and random error term e in LWE/RLWE makes both problems very hard to solve when parameters are properly chosen. For common practices, e and secret key s are sampled from discrete Gaussian distribution, therefore efficient sampling algorithm is essential towards practical LWE/RLWE-based cryptographic constructions. However, some papers have pointed out that sampling may take up too much time in practice. Weiden et al. [21] reported that sampling time takes up $> 50\%$ of total runtime when they implement Lyubashevskys signature scheme [14]. In the authenticated key exchange from ideal lattices protocol proposed at EUROCRYPT 2015 [22], they report that sampling operations may take up $> 60\%$ of total runtime. Therefore, design and implement Gaussian sampler with high efficiency and nice statistical quality become a major technical challenge.

1.2   Related Works

Buchmann et al. proposed the first ziggurat-based discrete Gaussian sampler at SAC 2013 in [5]. This work adapts original ziggurat sampling algorithm designed for continuous Gaussian distribution to discrete case. They claimed that when standard deviation σ is large, their sampler outperforms several common sampling methods. Peikert introduced a sampler using cumulated distribution tables (CDT) at CRYPTO 2010 [18]. This sampler has been proven to be extremely efficient when σ is small, but rather inefficient for large σ. Ducas et al. gave a new sampler that has better trade-off between time and memory at CRYPTO 2013 [9]. It does not use precomputed tables and they claim that sampler is efficient even when σ is large. Knuth-Yao algorithm [12] can sample from Gaussian distribution using binary tree search technique. It is efficient but might cost too much memory. There are various constructions (e.g., homomorphic encryption) that require samples from discrete Gaussian distribution with large σ. This technique is known as noise-flooding.

A RLWE-based authenticated key exchange protocol was proposed at EURO-CRYPT 2015 [22] (denoted as AKE15). This protocol behaves in HMQV [13] manner and its hardness is directly based on RLWE problem. It is mutual authenticated, proven secure under Bellare-Rogaway model [1] and forward secure. Bos et al. proposed an implementation of RLWE key exchange protocol at IEEE Symposium on Security and Privacy 2015 [4] (denoted as BCNS15) and integration into TLS. Their ciphersuites adopt RSA or ECDSA as signing algorithm which are vulnerable to quantum computers. Moreover, their ciphersuites cannot achieve mutual authentication.

1.3 Contributions

Our contributions are summarized as follows: First, we introduce a much faster discretized ziggurat Gaussian sampler. We discretize original ziggurat sampling algorithm with several improvement techniques to make it more efficient. We prove that the statistical distance between distribution generated by our sampler and discrete Gaussian distribution is smaller than 2^{-80}, therefore it can be used in lattice-based cryptosystems. Performance of our optimized implementation shows that our sampler is more than 2x speedup over [5,9,18] when σ is large. This could benefit constructions that using distributions with large standard deviations to flood small noises (e.g., homomorphic encryption etc.).

Second, we optimize a RLWE-based authenticated key exchange protocol [22]. We replace the sampler for sampling from distribution with large standard deviation in original AKE15 with our efficient discretized Gaussian sampler. We achieve 1.14x speedup on total runtime of this protocol over major parameter choices.

Third, we integrate our optimized AKE implementation into TLS v1.2 as post-quantum TLS ciphersuite. We also present proof-of-concept implementation and benchmark. Our ciphersuite inherits advantages from both AKE15 and TLS v1.2, including mutual authentication, resistant to quantum attacks and forward secrecy. Performance of our ciphersuite is close to standard TLS v1.2 ciphersuites and BCNS15.

1.4 Organization

In Sect. 2, we recall background knowledge. In Sect. 3, we present our efficient discretized ziggurat-based Gaussian sampler, security proofs, implementation, benchmark and comparison with related works. In Sect. 4.1, we show how our sampler optimizes AKE15 and report benchmarks on 6 parameter choices ranging from 80 to 256-bit security. Section 4.2 introduces our post-quantum TLS ciphersuite, implementation, runtime and comparisons with related works. We conclude the paper in Sect. 5.

2 Preliminaries

2.1 Notation

Let ring $R = Z[x]/(x^n + 1)$ and $R_q = Z_q[x]/(x^n + 1)$. Polynomial $x^n + 1$ is n-th cyclotomic polynomial where n is a power of 2. χ is a probability distribution on R_q, $\leftarrow \chi$ denotes sampling according to distribution χ, $\leftarrow_r$ denotes randomly choosing an element from a finite set. A discrete Gaussian distribution over Z with standard deviation $\sigma > 0$ and mean $c \in Z$ is denoted as $D_{Z,\sigma,c}$. If c is 0, we denote $D_{Z,\sigma,c}$ as $D_{Z,\sigma}$. log denotes natural logarithm. Let L be a discrete subset of Z^m. For any vector $c \in R^m$ and any positive parameter $\sigma \in R > 0$, let $\rho_{\sigma,c}(x) = e^{-\frac{\|x-c\|^2}{2\sigma^2}}$ be the Gaussian function on R^m with center c and parameter σ. Denote $\rho_{\sigma,c}(L) = \sum_{x \in L} \rho_{\sigma,c}(x)$ be the discrete integral of $\rho_{\sigma,c}$ over L, and $D_{L,\sigma,c}$ be the discrete Gaussian distribution over L with center c and parameter σ. Specifically, for all $y \in L$, we have $D_{L,\sigma,c}(y) = \frac{\rho_{\sigma,c}(y)}{\rho_{\sigma,c}(L)}$ [7].

2.2 LWE and RLWE

LWE and its ring variant RLWE are hard problems when parameters are properly chosen. The core idea of these two problems is to perturb random linear equations with small noise. Due to perturbation from error terms, it is very hard to distinguish these equations from truly uniform ones. There are quantum [19] and classical reduction [17] between LWE problem in average-case and worst-case hard lattice problems. If there exists a polynomial-time algorithm to solve LWE/RLWE problem, then there exists algorithms to solve hard lattice problems. Hardness of LWE/RLWE serves as the solid foundation to numerous cryptographic schemes. In practice, RLWE-based schemes are more preferable than LWE-based ones since LWE has an inherent quadratic overhead in computation and communication (large matrix) and this leads to inefficiency. RLWE sample is constructed as polynomial pair (a, b), where $a \in R_q$ is uniformly random, $b = a \cdot s + e \in R_q$, s is small and secret term, e is sampled from discrete Gaussian distribution. Search-RLWE problem is to recover s given many RLWE samples. Decision-RLWE problem is to distinguish b from uniform random. There are similar variants for search-LWE and decision-LWE therefore we ignore details. Cryptographic constructions based on RLWE (e.g., public key encryption, signature, key exchange, homomorphic encryption etc.) can be made truly efficient and practical for real-world deployment.

2.3 Statistical Distance

Since discrete Gaussian distribution has infinitely long tail and high precision for the probabilities of sampled points, it is impossible to generate a truly discrete Gaussian distribution within finite computations. Therefore, it is required that the statistical distance between distribution generated by sampler and discrete Gaussian distribution to be very small.

Statistical distance is defined as follows: If X and Y are two random variables corresponding to given distributions on L, the statistical difference is defined as:

$$\Delta(X, Y) = \frac{1}{2} \sum_{x \in L} |\Pr(X = x) - \Pr(Y = x)| \tag{1}$$

If the statistical distance between two distributions is very small (e.g., $< 2^{-80}$), the difference between these two distributions is negligible.

3   Faster Discretized Gaussian Sampler

Generally, secret key s and error term e of LWE/RLWE-based schemes are sampled from discrete Gaussian distribution. Sampling takes up large portion of runtime in implementation, therefore efficiency of sampling algorithm is very crucial. Ziggurat sampling algorithm [16] can sample from Gaussian distribution very efficiently. However, ziggurat algorithm is designed for continuous distribution and lattice-based schemes require discretized version.

Our sampler is discretized version of [16] and we improve efficiency of our sampler by eliminating computations in sampling operations. We prove that our sampler has very close statistical distance to discrete Gaussian distribution, therefore our sampler can be used in LWE/RLWE-based cryptosystems securely. We also introduce optimized implementation. We explain the construction of our sampler, analyze its statistical quality with proofs, present implementation details, benchmark, discussion and comparisons with several samplers in the following sections.

3.1   Ziggurat Gaussian Sampling Algorithm

We recall the ziggurat Gaussian sampling algorithm [16]: Area A encloses the probability density function $\rho_\sigma(x)$ with n rectangles. Rectangles are chosen in a way such that they have equal area. (x_i, y_i) denotes the coordinate of the lower right corner of each rectangle R_i. R_i^l lies within the area of $\rho_\sigma(x)$ and R_i^r is partly covered by $\rho_\sigma(x)$. We first randomly select $i \in [1, n]$ to select one rectangle, then randomly sample x-coordinate inside R_i by choosing $x' \in [0, x_i]$. If $x' \leq x_{i-1}$, x' is accepted and returned, otherwise we sample a value $\gamma \in [y_{i+1}, y_i]$. If $\gamma + y_{i+1} \leq \rho_\sigma(x')$, x' is accepted and returned, otherwise it is rejected and start over again. The probability of sampling a point in these rectangles are equal since they have same size and rectangle is randomly chosen. Marsaglia also suggested an algorithm for tail region: The following procedure is repeated until $2y > x^2$: uniformly sample $a \in (-1, 0) \cup (0, 1)$ and $b \in (0, 1)$, $x = -\frac{1}{r} \log |a|$, $y = -\log b$. If $a > 0$, return $(r + x)$, else return $-(r + x)$.

3.2   Our Fast Discretized Gaussian Sampling and Statistical Quality Analysis

Our sampler is designed directly based on original ziggurat sampling algorithm, which is designed for continuous Gaussian distribution. We discretize it and improve the efficiency of this algorithm with several optimization techniques. The result is our sampler can get samples subjected to discrete Gaussian distribution efficiently with high statistical quality.

We notice that the most expensive part in original ziggurat algorithm is exponential computation since original ziggurat algorithm requires large amount of exponential computations. This computation is directly related to certain σ, therefore it is more inefficient when σ is large. We improve this by sampling from normal continuous Gaussian distribution ($\sigma = 1$, instead of distribution with certain σ), then multiply the sampled value to σ and a randomly generated sign. Finally, we round it to nearest integer to get discretized value. Our approach effectively avoid the inefficiency where plenty of samplers cannot handle large σ efficiently.

We optimize our sampler even further. We use 3 precomputed tables: $ytab$, $ktab$ and $wtab$ to reduce online computations. Computations on generating these tables are irrelevant from both sampling computation and different standard deviations, since it is a once-for-all computation. Value of precomputed tables are hard-coded in implementation. We can comfortably use same tables when dealing with different standard deviations. Precomputed tables are generated as follows: $ytab = \rho_1(x_i)$ which stores tabulated values for the height of each ziggurat. $ktab$ is for quick acceptance check with $ktab_0 = \lfloor 2^{128} \cdot r \cdot \rho_1(r)/v \rfloor$, $ktab_i = \lfloor 2^{128} \cdot (x_{i-1}/x_i) \rfloor$, $r = x_{127} \approx 3.444286476761$, v is the size of each rectangle. $wtab$ is for quick value conversion with $wtab_0 = 0.5^{128} \cdot v/\rho_1(r)$ and $wtab_i = 0.5^{128} \cdot x_i$. We note that other samplers may need to generate precomputed tables again when σ changes while our sampler does not.

Pseudocode of our sampler is given in Algorithm 1 (urandom() refers to generate a uniformly distributed 128-bit precision random float number between 0 and 1):

Here we prove that statistical distance between distribution generated by our sampler and discrete Gaussian distribution is very small. We approximate statistical distance between the distribution generated by our sampler and discrete Gaussian distribution to be less than 2^{-80} for $n = 1024$ samples and $\sigma = 869.632$. We utilize a similar approach as [5] since our sampler takes n samples from discrete Gaussian on Z to get discrete Gaussian distribution samples on Z^n. Conclusion still holds for other parameter choices. We first recall two useful lemmas from [10] for our proofs:

Lemma 1. Let $\sigma > 0$ and $n \in N$ be fixed. Consider distribution $D_{Z^n,\sigma}$. Let $k \in N$ and suppose $c \geq 1$ is such that:

$$c > \sqrt{1 + 2\log c + 2(k/n)\log 2} \tag{2}$$

Then:

$$\Pr_{v \leftarrow D_{Z^n,\sigma}} (\|v\| > c\sqrt{n}\sigma) < \frac{1}{2^k} \tag{3}$$

Algorithm 1. Fast Discretized Gaussian Sampling

Input: $ytab, ktab, wtab, r, \sigma$
Output: Integer distributed according to discrete Gaussian distribution
1: **while** true **do**
2:     $i \leftarrow_r \{0, \cdots, 127\}, s \leftarrow_r \{-1, 1\}$
3:     $r \leftarrow_r \text{urandom}(), j \leftarrow r \cdot 2^{128}, x \leftarrow j \cdot wtab_i$
4:     **if** $j < ktab_i$ **then**
5:         **break**
6:     **end if**
7:     **if** $i < 127$ **then**
8:         $y0 \leftarrow ytab_i, y1 \leftarrow ytab_{i+1}$
9:         $y \leftarrow y1 + (y0 - u1) \cdot \text{urandom}()$
10:    **else**
11:        $x \leftarrow r - \log(1 - \text{urandom}())/r$
12:        $y \leftarrow e^{-r(x-0.5r)} \cdot \text{urandom}()$
13:    **end if**
14:    **if** $y < e^{-0.5x^2}$ **then**
15:        **break**
16:    **end if**
17: **end while**
18: **if** $s = 1$ **then**
19:    **return** $\lfloor s \cdot \sigma \rceil$
20: **else**
21:    **return** $-\lfloor s \cdot \sigma \rceil$
22: **end if**

Next lemma gives us a way to approximate distributions in Z based on the approximation we need for Z^n:

Lemma 2. *Let $\sigma > 0, \epsilon > 0$ be given. Let $k \in N$ and $t > 0$ be such that the tail bound $\Pr(\|v\| > t\sigma)$ as in Lemma 1 is at most $1/2^k$. For $x \in Z$, denote ρ_x as the probability of sampling x from the distribution D_σ. Suppose one has computed approximations $0 \le p_x \le Q$ for $x \in Z$, $-t\sigma \le x \le t\sigma$ such that:*

$$|p_x - \rho_x| < \epsilon \tag{4}$$

and such that $\sum_{x=-t\sigma}^{t\sigma} = 1$. Let D' be the distribution on $[-t\sigma, t\sigma] \cap Z$ corresponding to the probabilities p_x.

Denote by D'' the distribution on Z^n corresponding to taking n independent samples v_i from D' and forming the vector $v = (v_1, \cdots, v_n)$. Then:

$$\Delta(D'', D_{Z^n,\sigma}) < 2^{-k} + 2nt\sigma\epsilon \tag{5}$$

Let χ_β denote the distribution generated by our sampler, $D_{Z^n,\beta}$ denote the discrete Gaussian distribution on Z^n. We show the approximation for our sampler using parameters from parameter choice I in Table 3. In order to use Lemma 2, we first need to compute the value of c for $k = 81$ and $n = 1024$ in Lemma 1, thus we have $c = 1.242617$ and this gives us tail $t = c\sqrt{n} \approx 40$. Note that this tail cut is much larger than most samplers (e.g., [5] has tail cut $t = 13$). For our sampler, we have $\Delta(\chi, D_{Z^n, \beta}) < 2^{-k} + 2nt\beta\epsilon$. By choosing the precision level to be 128 for the precomputed tables, we can approximate p_x in the lemma, for the tail cut to be close to discrete Gaussian in Z with the error-constant ϵ as 2^{-128}, therefore we have $\Delta(\chi, D_{Z^n, \beta}) < 2^{-81} + 2 \cdot 1024 \cdot 40 \cdot 869.632 \cdot 2^{-128} < 2^{-80}$. The efficiency of rejection procedure is estimated to be 98.78% [16] which contributes to the performance of our sampler.

3.3   Implementation and Runtime

We use MPFR, GMP and NTL library implement our sampler. We set precision to 128-bit to achieve highly accurate computations. We use 128-bit seed and 128-bit random numbers to remain secure against brute-force quantum attacks. Each value in precomputed tables has 40 significant figures. In one execution, a vector with 2048 samples is generated. Each sampled value mod to a 78-bit prime p and stored in a vec_ZZ_p type vector. We test on a Lenovo ThinkCentre M8500t equipped with 3.6 GHz Intel Core i7-4790 processor running Ubuntu 14.04 64-bit version with 3 GB memory. Our implementation is compiled by g++ 4.8.4 with '-O3 -m64' compilation flags and only runs on single core. We report average runtime of 1,000 times execution of our sampler with different standard deviations σ in Table 1:

Table 1. Performance of our sampler

σ	Million samples/s	σ	Million samples/s	σ	Million samples/s
5	2.94	10^6	2.95	10^{12}	2.91
50	3.01	10^7	2.92	10^{13}	2.89
10^2	2.99	10^8	2.93	10^{14}	2.87
10^3	3.02	10^9	2.90	10^{15}	2.88
10^4	2.97	10^{10}	2.88	10^{16}	2.85
10^5	2.99	10^{11}	2.89	10^{17}	2.84

We also use Valgrind to profile memory cost. Our implementation costs maximum of 11.07 MB memory to generate 2048 samples. Each precomputed table consumes nearly 6 KB of memory. Generate three precomputed tables costs 0.173 s but they are computed offline and values are hard-coded in our implementation. In each execution, same precomputed tables are used and they are irrelevant to different standard deviation. We report this timing for completeness.

3.4   Comparisons and Discussions

We present detailed introduction, analysis and comparison with other samplers in [5, 9, 12, 18]. We also test actual performance of these samplers using same test environment, compiler and compilation flags as Sect. 3.3 with various σ.

A ziggurat-based discrete Gaussian sampler was proposed in [5]. Their approach of adapting original ziggurat algorithm to discrete case is different from ours. Compared with their work, our sampler has following improvements and differences:

1. We effectively avoid expensive computation caused by standard deviation. This major contributes to efficiency of our sampler.
   Bottlenecks of their sampler are:
   - More than 50% of total runtime is spent on computing $e^{-x^2/2\sigma^2}$ (x is also related to σ) in constructing each rectangle.
   - Computation in rejection judgement (calculate $e^{-0.5x^2}$ when judging y is smaller than $e^{-0.5x^2}$ or not).
   - Computation in tail region ($y = e^{-r(x-0.5r)}$·urandom(), line 12 of Algorithm 1).
   It is clear that when σ is large, large amount of time is spent on exponential computation. Our sampler avoids this by sampling from normal distribution first and this is much more efficient.
2. We use 3 precomputed tables to store the values required in sampling procedure, compared to only 1 table to store x_i in their implementation. Our sampler can fetch results from these tables directly instead of online computation, therefore the performance is further improved. In our implementation, multiplication, conversion and generating random numbers take up most time. We use their implementation to test their sampler using same environment and precision with various σ. They claimed that their sampler is the fastest when $\sigma = 1.6 \cdot 10^5$. In our test environment, their sampler produces 1.34 million samples/s and 1.23 s to generate precomputed tables, while our sampler produces 2.97 million samples/s with no additional time cost. We fail to test $\sigma > 10^8$ cases since their code crashes.
3. Their implementation needs to compute precomputed tables again when σ is different. This increases total sampling time significantly. Time spent on generating these tables is not even counted when comparing sampling performance in Table 2. If this part is also included, their sampler is much slower. Our sampler can generate precomputed tables within 0.2 s. These tables are hard-coded in implementation and irrelevant with different σ.
4. Their sampler has statistical distance $< 2^{-100}$ at 106-bit precision and it is better than ours. We are able to achieve much faster sampling at the expense of statistical quality to some extent, but statistical quality of our sampler is still good enough to be adopted in LWE/RLWE-based constructions.

At CRYPTO 2010, Peikert gave a very efficient Gaussian sampler (denoted as PKT) using cumulated distribution table (CDT) [18]. We implement it and benchmark shows that PKT is extremely efficient and much faster than all others when $\sigma < 10^6$, but it can be very slow when σ is large, thus it is more preferable to deal with distributions with smaller σ. We did not count time spent on generating precomputed tables in Table 2 when comparing sampling speed.

Ducas et al. presented a sampling algorithm that offered better trade-off between time and memory at CRYPTO 2013 (denoted as DDLL) [9]. It can sample efficiently without using precomputed tables. We implement DDLL and it is faster than all other samplers (except ours) when σ is large, but our sampler is twice as fast when $\sigma > 10^8$. We note that DDLL consumes less memory than our sampler, thus it is more suitable in resource-constrained devices.

Knuth-Yao algorithm (denoted as KY) [12] can sample from Gaussian distribution efficiently. According to [5], their KY implementation outputs nearly 5.8, 4.9, 3.2 and 1.2 million samples/s when $\sigma = 10, 32, 1000$ and $1.6 \cdot 10^5$ respectively. However, when $\sigma = 1.6 \cdot 10^5$, KY consumes 424 times more memory but only 4.26% faster than ziggurat sampler in [5], where their ziggurat implementation consumes 30.57 MB memory with 2048 samples by our profiling. We use another KY implementation and test in same environment to verify their results. When $\sigma = 10^3$, it outputs 7.85 million samples/s but costs more than 200 MB memory. When $\sigma = 10^4$, the process is terminated by operating system because it costs too much memory.

The importance for developing efficient samplers for large standard deviation is that various constructions require sampling from such distributions. For constructions like homomorphic encryption, it is required to use noise-flooding technique to preserve security and privacy of circuit etc. However, various current samplers cannot deal with large standard deviation efficiently. Our efficient sampler solve this problem. This is very important for efficiency and practicality of such constructions.

We implement [9,18] fairly to test their performance. Implementation of [5] we use is what they provided in the paper. We test all implementations on same machine, compiled with same compilation flags, executes same number of times and report average performance in Table 2. Sampling speed is given in million samples per second. Time spent on generating precomputed tables is given in second.

Table 2. Performance comparison between our sampler and related works

Standard deviation	This work	Discrete zigguart ([5])		PKT ([18])		DDLL([9])
		Sampling speed	Generate CDT (s)	Sampling speed	Generate CDT (s)	
10^2	2.99	1.67	1.11	10.41	0.017	4.86
10^3	3.02	1.61	1.12	8.36	0.166	3.29
10^4	2.97	1.52	1.14	6.76	1.61	2.69
10^5	2.99	1.46	1.09	4.95	16.07	2.22
10^6	2.95	1.25	1.12	2.35	163.79	1.84
10^7	2.92	1.17	1.22	1.33	1620.8	1.64
10^8	2.93	1.04	1.11	Cost too much time		1.47

We can see that our sampler is much more efficient than [5,9,18] when standard deviation $> 10^4$. It is known that noise-flooding use much larger standard deviation than 10^4, therefore our sampler has an advantage. Moreover, our sampler and DDLL do not require additional precomputations except sampling. Before sampling operation, [5,18] first need to compute ziggurat tables and CDT respectively. This costs additional time and it is inefficient.

4 Applications: Optimizing RLWE Key Exchange and Post-quantum TLS Ciphersuite

4.1 Optimizing AKE15

Bottleneck and Our Approach. AKE15 [22] is a RLWE-variant of HMQV. It is mutual authenticated and proven secure under Bellare-Rogaway model with enhancements to capture weak perfect forward secrecy. Communicating parties do not need to encrypt or sign messages. One major bottleneck of this protocol is sampling from Gaussian distribution. According to [22], sampling operation may take up > 60% of total runtime for some parameter choices. In their implementation, generating long-term static key, polynomial c and d adopt PKT sampler. DDLL sampler is adopted in generating ephemeral keys and computing shared session key. As we discussed in Sect. 3.4, DDLL sampler is less efficient than our sampler when σ is large, thus we replace DDLL sampler with ours to sample from $D_{Z^n,\beta}$ to reduce total runtime. In one complete execution of key exchange, it requires 3 online sampling operations from $D_{Z^n,\beta}$: 2 in ephemeral key generation and 1 in shared key computation, thus our sampler can improve the efficiency of their implementation. Sampling from $D_{Z^n,\alpha}$ and $D_{Z^n,\gamma}$ still uses PKT sampler as original work. Parameter choices of the protocol remain the same and we recall them in Table 3:

Table 3. Parameter choices of AKE15 protocol

Parameter choice	Security (bits)	n	α	γ	β	Bit-length of q
I	80	1024	3.397	101.919	$8.7 \cdot 10^2$	40
II	80	2048	3.397	161.371	$4.56 \cdot 10^8$	78
III	128	2048	3.397	161.371	$1.78 \cdot 10^6$	63
IV	128	4096	3.397	256.495	$3.82 \cdot 10^{15}$	125
V	192	4096	3.397	256.495	$2.33 \cdot 10^{11}$	97
VI	256	4096	3.397	256.495	$9.12 \cdot 10^8$	81

Implementation and Performance. We report average runtime of our preliminary implementation of original AKE15 and our optimized version. Our implementation uses NTL 9.6.2, MPFR 3.1.3 and GMP 6.1.0 library with 128-bit precision. Implementation of AKE15 is executed 1,000 times and use same test environment as Sect. 3.3. Average runtime is reported in Table 4:

Table 4. Sampling and runtime of original and optimized AKE15 protocol

Parameter choice	DDLL (ms)	This work (ms)	Sampling speedup	Original AKE15 runtime (ms)	Optimized AKE15 runtime (ms)	Runtime speedup
I	0.312	0.355	0.88x	2.993	4.687	0.64x
II	1.635	0.694	2.36x	11.673	10.361	1.13x
III	1.269	0.721	1.76x	9.963	9.132	1.09x
IV	2.591	1.397	1.85x	26.741	21.964	1.22x
V	2.514	1.394	1.80x	22.865	21.457	1.07x
VI	3.349	1.394	2.40x	24.887	21.064	1.18x

By adopting our sampler, we achieve nearly 1.14x speedup of total runtime of this protocol for last 5 parameter choices. We fail to optimize parameter choice I since when σ is not large enough, our sampler is outperformed by DDLL and this leads to deceleration.

4.2   Practical Post-quantum TLS Ciphersuite

Introduction. TLS is designed to ensure secure communications over adversary controlled network, providing secrecy and data integrity between two communicating parties. It is widely deployed in real world and it already comprises more than 50% of total web traffic. It supports various algorithms for key exchange, authentication, encryption and message integrity check. Since TLS is so important and we are moving into the era of quantum computing, we consider TLS should also adopt post-quantum cryptographic primitives. However, most ciphersuites in the latest version of TLS fail to meet the demands since available key exchange and signature algorithms can be broken by quantum computers.

Our Post-quantum TLS Ciphersuite. We integrate optimized AKE15 into TLS v1.2 and this forms our post-quantum TLS ciphersuite. We give detailed cryptographic primitive combination of our ciphersuite:

- Key exchange and authentication: We integrate optimized AKE15 to achieve post-quantum key exchange and authentication. Quantum-insecure digital signatures are no longer necessary. Parameter choices follow Table 3.
- Authenticated encryption: We choose AES-128-GCM. It provides confidentiality, integrity and authenticity assurances on data.
- Hash function: We choose SHA-256. Our choice followed the principle proposed by NIST of deprecating SHA-1.

Implementation and Runtime. We use mbedTLS 1.3.10, WinNTL 9.6.2, MPFR 3.1.1 and MPIR 2.6.0 to implement our ciphersuite. Test programs simulate a TLS session between client and server. Server listens on localhost at port 443 and client communicates with local server. We measure runtime of session initiation and handshake. Test programs run in the following environment:

Lenovo ThinkCentre M8500t equipped with a 3.6 GHz Intel Core i7-4790 processor and 8 GB RAM running Windows 7 SP1 64-bit version. Test programs are compiled by Visual Studio 2010 with optimization flags and execute 1,000 times using single core. For parameter choices aimed at 80, 128, 192 and 256-bit security, average time cost is 24.417 ms, 51.224 ms, 123.443 ms and 98.842 ms respectively, communication overhead for key exchange messages is 33.125 KB, 102.25 KB, 312.25 KB and 264.5 KB respectively. In our ciphersuite, most time is spent on sending/receiving public key and key exchange messages since they are much larger than standard TLS. This might be a bottleneck of our ciphersuite.

Comparison. We compare performance of some ciphersuites in standard TLS and the post-quantum TLS ciphersuite proposed at IEEE S&P 2015 with our work. Our ciphersuite is faster in some cases but slower in others.

- Standard TLS v1.2: We choose two standard TLS ciphersuites: 0x9F (1024-bit DH+2048-bit RSA) and 0xC030 (elliptic curve secp521r1+2048-bit RSA). Test environment and procedure remain the same as Sect. 4.2. Runtime of these two ciphersuites are 30.959 ms and 49.742 ms respectively. For comparison, our 80-bit parameter choice I is faster than ciphersuite 0x9F, 256-bit parameter choice VI is slower than ciphersuite 0xC030.
- BCNS15: This work introduced implementation of an unauthenticated post-quantum key exchange aimed at 128-bit security and integration in TLS protocol. We implement client/server side test programs using code in [8] and test these ciphersuites: RLWE-RSA-AES128-GCM-SHA256 and RLWE-ECDSA-AES128-GCM-SHA256. Test environment remain the same as Sect. 3.3. For first ciphersuite, server adopts a self-signed 3072-bit RSA certificate and average execution time is 44.536 ms. For the second ciphersuite, server adopts a self-signed ECDSA certificate using curve secp256k1 and average execution time is 41.539 ms. Our post-quantum TLS ciphersuite at same 128-bit security is slower and average runtime is 51.224 ms. Our ciphersuite has much larger communication overhead than this work (around 10 KB). Another difference is that our ciphersuite can achieve mutual authentication while this work only authenticates the server. Furthermore, we use different library and operating system to test, thus it is harder to compare directly and fairly. We believe their ciphersuites have better performance and smaller communication cost, but ours is more closer to a fully post-quantum TLS ciphersuite.

5 Conclusion

In this paper, we introduce a much faster discretized Gaussian sampler based on the ziggurat sampling algorithm. We utilize several optimization techniques to improve our sampler, so that our sampler has advantage on computation efficiency. We prove that the statistical distance between distribution generated by our sampler and discrete Gaussian distribution is very small so that our sampler is suitable for lattice-based cryptography. We also present optimized implementation and comparisons with several related samplers. Results show that our sampler is very computational efficient, especially when σ is large. This can benefit constructions using noise-flooding technique (e.g., homomorphic encryption). We also give two applications: first is optimizing RLWE-based authenticated key exchange protocol. We achieve 1.14x speedup on total runtime of this protocol over major parameter choices. Another application is we present our practical post-quantum TLS ciphersuite. Performance of ciphersuite is close to standard TLS v1.2 ciphersuites and BCNS15. We believe our sampler and post-quantum TLS ciphersuite will have further optimizations and more applications.

Acknowledgement. We would like to thank Jiang Zhang for valuable help and discussions, Chen Feng for the support on this paper. We also thank anonymous reviewers for valuable feedbacks. Implementation for testing Knuth-Yao sampler is from Rachid El Bansarkhani. This work is supported by National Natural Science Foundation of China (Grant No. 61402035) and Fundamental Research Funds for the Central Universities (Grant No. 2014JBM033, No. 2015YJS039 and No. 2017YJS038).

References

1. Bellare, M., Rogaway, P.: Entity authentication and key distribution. In: Stinson, D.R. (ed.) CRYPTO 1993. LNCS, vol. 773, pp. 232–249. Springer, Heidelberg (1994). https://doi.org/10.1007/3-540-48329-2_21
2. Bennett, C.H., Bernstein, E., Brassard, G., Vazirani, U.: Strengths and weaknesses of quantum computing. SIAM J. Comput. **26**(5), 1510–1523 (1997)
3. Bernstein, D.J., Buchmann, J., Dahmen, E.: Post-Quantum Cryptography. Springer, Heidelberg (2009). https://doi.org/10.1007/978-3-540-88702-7
4. Bos, J.W., Costello, C., Naehrig, M., Stebila, D.: Post-quantum key exchange for the TLS protocol from the ring learning with errors problem. In: IEEE Symposium on Security and Privacy (SP), 2015, pp. 553–570. IEEE (2015)
5. Buchmann, J., Cabarcas, D., Göpfert, F., Hülsing, A., Weiden, P.: Discrete ziggurat: a time-memory trade-off for sampling from a Gaussian distribution over the integers. In: Lange, T., Lauter, K., Lisoněk, P. (eds.) SAC 2013. LNCS, vol. 8282, pp. 402–417. Springer, Heidelberg (2014). https://doi.org/10.1007/978-3-662-43414-7_20
6. Diffie, W., Hellman, M.: New directions in cryptography. IEEE Trans. Inf. Theory **22**(6), 644–654 (1976)
7. Ding, J., Xie, X., Lin, X.: A simple provably secure key exchange scheme based on the learning with errors problem. IACR Cryptology EPrint Archive, 2012:688 (2012)
8. Douglas, S.: dstebila/openssl-rlwekex
9. Ducas, L., Durmus, A., Lepoint, T., Lyubashevsky, V.: Lattice signatures and bimodal Gaussians. In: Canetti, R., Garay, J.A. (eds.) CRYPTO 2013. LNCS, vol. 8042, pp. 40–56. Springer, Heidelberg (2013). https://doi.org/10.1007/978-3-642-40041-4_3
10. Dwarakanath, N.C., Galbraith, S.D.: Sampling from discrete Gaussians for lattice-based cryptography on a constrained device. Appl. Algebra Eng. Commun. Comput. **25**(3), 159–180 (2014)

11. Grover, L.K.: A fast quantum mechanical algorithm for database search. In: Proceedings of the Twenty-eighth Annual ACM Symposium on Theory of Computing, pp. 212–219. ACM (1996)
12. Knuth, D.: The complexity of nonuniform random number generation. In: Algorithms and Complexity, New Directions and Results, pp. 357–428 (1976)
13. Krawczyk, H.: HMQV: A high-performance secure Diffie-Hellman protocol. In: Shoup, V. (ed.) CRYPTO 2005. LNCS, vol. 3621, pp. 546–566. Springer, Heidelberg (2005). https://doi.org/10.1007/11535218_33
14. Lyubashevsky, V.: Lattice signatures without trapdoors. In: Pointcheval, D., Johansson, T. (eds.) EUROCRYPT 2012. LNCS, vol. 7237, pp. 738–755. Springer, Heidelberg (2012). https://doi.org/10.1007/978-3-642-29011-4_43
15. Lyubashevsky, V., Peikert, C., Regev, O.: On ideal lattices and learning with errors over rings. In: Gilbert, H. (ed.) EUROCRYPT 2010. LNCS, vol. 6110, pp. 1–23. Springer, Heidelberg (2010). https://doi.org/10.1007/978-3-642-13190-5_1
16. Marsaglia, G., Tsang, W.W., et al.: The ziggurat method for generating random variables. J. Stat. Softw. 5(8), 1–7 (2000)
17. Peikert, C.: Public-key cryptosystems from the worst-case shortest vector problem. In: Proceedings of the forty-first annual ACM symposium on Theory of computing, pp. 333–342. ACM (2009)
18. Peikert, C.: An efficient and parallel Gaussian sampler for lattices. In: Rabin, T. (ed.) CRYPTO 2010. LNCS, vol. 6223, pp. 80–97. Springer, Heidelberg (2010). https://doi.org/10.1007/978-3-642-14623-7_5
19. Regev, O.: On lattices, learning with errors, random linear codes, and cryptography. J. ACM (JACM) 56(6), 34 (2009)
20. Shor, P.W.: Algorithms for quantum computation: discrete logarithms and factoring. In: 35th Annual Symposium on Foundations of Computer Science, 1994 Proceedings, pp. 124–134. IEEE (1994)
21. Weiden, P., Hülsing, A., Cabarcas, D., Buchmann, J.A.: Instantiating treeless signature schemes. IACR Cryptology ePrint Archive, 2013:65 (2013)
22. Zhang, J., Zhang, Z., Ding, J., Snook, M., Dagdelen, Ö.: Authenticated key exchange from ideal lattices. In: Oswald, E., Fischlin, M. (eds.) EUROCRYPT 2015. LNCS, vol. 9057, pp. 719–751. Springer, Heidelberg (2015). https://doi.org/10.1007/978-3-662-46803-6_24

Automatic Encryption Schemes Based on the Neural Networks: Analysis and Discussions on the Various Adversarial Models (Short Paper)

Yidan Zhang[1], Marino Anthony James[1], Jiageng Chen[1(✉)], Chunhua Su[2], and Jinguang Han[3,4]

[1] Central China Normal University, Wuhan 430079, China
allenzyd1997@gmail.com, silver7017@gmail.com,
jiageng.chen@mail.ccnu.edu.cn
[2] University of Aizu, Aizuwakamatsu, Japan
suchunhua@gmail.com
[3] University of Surrey, Guildford, UK
jghan22@gmail.com
[4] State Key Laboratory of Information Security, Institute of Information Engineering, Chinese Academy of Sciences, Beijing, China

Abstract. Modern cryptographic schemes have been focusing on protecting attacks from computational bounded adversaries. The various cryptographic primitives are designed concretely following some randomization design strategies, so that one of the goals is to make it hard for the attacker to distinguish between the real ciphers and the randomly distributed ones. Recently, Google Brain team proposed the idea to build cryptographic scheme automatically based on the neural network, and they claim that the scheme can defeat neural network adversaries. While it is a whole new direction, the security of the underlined scheme is remained unknown. In this paper, we investigate their basic statistical behavior from traditional cryptography's point of view and extend their original scheme to discuss how the encryption protocol behave under a much more stronger adversary.

1 Introduction

Modern cryptography are widely deployed to protect the digital communications. Complicated cryptographic protocols are usually built from more simple components such as block ciphers, hash functions, message authentication code and so on. During the past 20 years, researchers have proposed a lot of concrete algorithms, among which the block cipher AES is one of the most well known one. Similar to other proposed cryptographic schemes, researchers also try hard to analyze their security margin. In most of the cases, in order to make the

J. K. Liu and P. Samarati (Eds.): ISPEC 2017, LNCS 10701, pp. 566–575, 2017.
https://doi.org/10.1007/978-3-319-72359-4_34

scheme practical, only computational bounded adversaries are considered in the design stage. Under this big assumption, lots of security models are proposed such as semantic security [3], chosen plaintext attack, chosen ciphertext attack and so on. Each cryptographic scheme are analyzed under these different models to ensure their security.

In 2016, Google Brain team proposed the idea [2] to build cryptographic scheme automatically without manually designing any concrete algorithms. In this new direction, all parties joining the computation are actually neural networks. In order to achieve the security goal, the core idea of the paper is to introduce an adversarial neural network, and let it compete with the legal users. This is however not a brand new idea, which has appeared in several previous works [4,5,9]. It shares the similarity to the well known model called generative adversarial network (GAN), which was originally proposed to determine whether a sample value was generated by a model or drawn from a given data distribution. As we will see in Sect. 2 that the introducing of the adversarial neural network is the key part to make the communication secure from the eavesdropper. Before [2], there are several other works which took advantage of the machine learning techniques to protect communication such as [6–8], which focused more on the other fundamental issues such as how the secret keys can be established and so on.

The work [2] provided a whole new insights on how to construct cryptographic primitives in an intelligent way. The machine learning and the techniques of neural networks have already found massive applications in the areas such as image recognition, voice generation and so on, it seems that finally the they come to the area of cryptography. However, a lot of questions still remain untouched such as the security margin of the underlined scheme as well as how the model will behave under other much more stronger adversaries. In this paper, we follow the work of [2] by first providing some fundamental statistical analysis of the scheme, and then we try to recognize the structure of the learned network. Also other encryption protocols are evaluated under the different and stronger adversarial models. We discussed the key recovery models as well as the key or plaintext leakage models. Finally, we try to enhance the encryption scheme by introducing two adversary models simultaneously.

This paper is organized as follows. In Sect. 2, we briefly introduce the work [2] reproduce and improve their results, as well as a short description on the statistical behavior and the shape of the learned cipher. In Sect. 3, other models are discussed including the key recovery model, leakage model and the dual adversary model. And finally we conclude our paper in Sect. 4.

2 Preliminary

Martin Abadi and David G. Andersen's paper [2] presented a multi-agent system, where the communication between the two parties needs to be protected. The setting is very similar to the symmetric key encryption, where there are two legal parties Alice and Bob who want to communicate with each other. And there is an adversary Eve who wants to understand the content of the communication without knowing the secret key that is shared between Alice and Bob. In their paper, the ability of the adversary Eve is limited to knowing the ciphertext generated by Alice only. So comparing with the adversarial model in the traditional cryptography, it is a ciphertext only attack, which is the weakest model. Different from the traditional symmetric key model, all the participants in this protocol are neural networks including the adversary Eve. Each neural network has its own purpose, which is expected to be achieved after the training stage. For example, the goal of Alice and Bob is to minimize the distance between P and P_{Bob}, which are the input and output plaintexts by Alice and Bob respectively. In order to train the model to be useful an adversarial neural network has to be introduced, which is Eve in our setting. In the training stage, Eve's goal is to minimize the distance between P and P_{Eve}. As a legal party, however, Alice and Bob would like to maximize the plaintext distance, which is obviously against Eve's goal. The competition mechanism introduced here borrows the idea from the generative adversarial network (GAN) [4]. Notice that no specific algorithms are specified beforehand, so our protection goal is rather flexible which depends on the adversarial neural network. The model is shown in Fig. 1. By using Tensorflow [1], we rebuilt their encryption systems and the results are shown in Fig. 2.

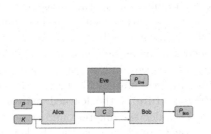

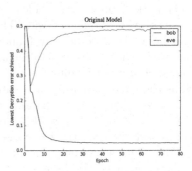

Fig. 1. Original model in paper [2]   **Fig. 2.** Batch size: 1024, epochs: 80

The result we derived is similar to [2]. The x-axis denotes the training epoch with batch size 1024. The y-axis denotes the decryption error which is a little bit different from the work [2]. The decryption error is calculated by using the mean of the differences in every output bit. Therefore we would expect the decryption error of Eve to be 0.5, which indicates that she only guesses the result randomly. On the other hand, we would like the decryption error of Bob to be as close as possible to 0 to guarantee the correctness. As we can see from the experimental result, as the number of training steps increases, Bob can successfully decrypt messages. Eve has some advantages in decrypting the ciphertext at the beginning, but soon Alice and Bob changed their strategies to better defeat Eve such that she does not have any advantages in the end. Although the authors did not put their effort in making the cipher indistinguishable from a random chosen one just as the design of the traditional symmetric key ciphers do, we would like to know its statistical behavior.

Since the ciphertext generated by Alice is floating point numbers, we need to first transfer the floating point number to integer first and then we can apply the NIST statistical test suit. From the test result, we found that the proportion of passing for some of the tests is very low. Especially, with 50% chance we failed to pass the frequency test, which tests the ratio between the number of 0 and 1. We further confirmed that the ratio of 1 and 0 is a fixed number 0.942. As long as the hyper-parameter of the neural network remains unchanged, the ratio is not changed no matter how many times we trained the neural networks. Thus the trained model is far from being statistically indistinguishable, which is required by the modern cryptography. How to improve the model to close the gap is worth further investigation.

The training process is very intelligent and we do not control what kind of functions it will learn. Compare to the modern cryptography where concrete algorithms are specified, we are also interested in knowing the learned function. Xor logic is one of the most widely used operation in modern cryptography and it is famous for its application in the one time pad. So we would like to know whether the learned functions share some similarities with the xor logic. In our experiment we randomly choose some message and the key to generate the ciphertext using the stabilized neural network. We also derive the second result by xoring the same plaintext and the key. Then the two results are xored together to generate the test statistic. If the learned function is indeed an xor function, then the distribution of the value 0 will show a peak while other values will be flat. However, the distribution we derived showed a bell shape which indicates the violation of our assumption.

3 Discussions on Various Models

We enhance the original encryption scheme by introducing different attackers with various abilities. Since the strength of the scheme depends on the ability of the attacker during the training stage, some of the models showed in this Section will be more stronger and more flexible in resisting against various attacks. A first straightforward idea is to feed the attacker the plaintext and ciphertext pair, or the ciphertext only and to see if he or she can recover the secret key. This model resembles the known plaintext attack and the ciphertext only attack in the modern cryptography. In the experiment which is omitted here, we found that the adversary Eve does not have any advantage since the beginning of the training. As a result, the competitive model does not have any effect in improving the quality of the encryption scheme since Alice and Bob could just exclude the involvement of the secret key in the encryption scheme.

Sometimes we need to consider what advantage can the adversary gain when he or she has already obtained part of the information such as the secret key or the plaintext. Leakage resilient cryptography was proposed to investigate this issue, and we are also interested to see how the model will behave in the neural network setting. We exploit several models and use "Info1(L) + Info2 → Info3" to denote the corresponding type. Here the information on the left hand side of $\rightarrow$ is given to the attacker, and the information on the other side is the target of the attacker. If "(L)" is appended after some information, it means that this information is partially leaked to the attacker. The filters' sizes of CNN and the batch size remain the same as the previous models.

3.1   One-Eve Model

This section provides various models assuming that there is one type of attacker Eve. The attacker has only one target, for example, to either recover the plaintext or the secret key.

Key(L) + Ciphertext → Plaintext

In this model, we use two inputs. One is the ciphertext in the communication between the Alice and Bob, the other one is part of the shared secret key. Eve's goal to derive the plaintext. We change the input bits of the key from 0 to 16. The model is shown in Fig. 3. When the number of leaked key bits increases, the loss-rate of Eve and Bob could not go convergence. As shown in the experiment, when the amount of bits leaked to Eve is below 5, the curve can converge at a certain point. Figure 4 shows situation that Bob finally defeats the attacker, while Fig. 5 shows you the situation that the curve cannot be convergent even we trained it with 500 epochs.

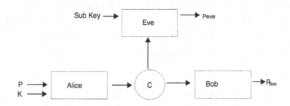

Fig. 3. Key(L) + Ciphertext → Plaintext

Considering that we increase the leaked key bits to Eve, Bob gradually loses the ability decoding the ciphertext that he received. The advantage that Eve hold can not directly help her to generate the correct plaintext from the ciphertext. However, the advantage can help her prevent Bob from decoding the information from the ciphertext. It is evident that Eve can successfully damage the communication between Alice and Bob.

Key(L) + Ciphertext → Key

In this model, Eve's goal is to recover the secret key instead of the plaintext. This model has the same input as the previous model as shown in Fig. 6. We show one of the experiment results in Fig. 7 and the trend between the leakage bits and the loss rate in Fig. 8.

The loss rate of Eve in Fig. 8 is very close to the baseline which is the straight line in the figure. The baseline shows the information about key that Eve has

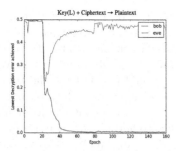

Fig. 4. Eve gets 4 bits key. Trained with 80 epochs while test with 80 epochs.

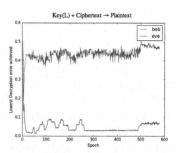

Fig. 5. Eve gets 8 bits key. We deliberately train the model 500 epochs here.

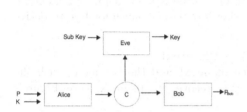

Fig. 6. Key(L) + Ciphertext → Key

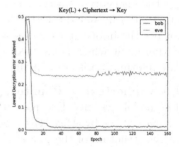

Fig. 7. 8 bits key is leaked. Epoch is 80 for both training and testing.

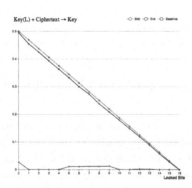

Fig. 8. The trend between the leakage bit and the decryption error

known before we trained this system. Obviously, Eve do not know more information about the key than we told her before the training. From this result, we can make a hypothesis that the Alice will reduce the involvement of the secret key when Alice find that Eve's goal is to generate the whole secret key. If Alice do not use the key to generate the output, Eve would not find out the key for sure. Therefore, the loss rate of Eve should be a straight line, which means the amount of the key that we told Eve is all what she knows about key. Therefore, we could consider using new models forcing Alice to add the key material when generating the ciphertext. And this inspires us designing the "Two-Eve model" that would be described later.

Also we can design the model "Key(L) + Plaintext + Ciphertext → Key", and in this model, Alice is smart enough to reduce the influence of the secret key during the encryption process. Even Eve knows all the information about the plaintext, she can not derive the key used in the communication because Alice do not use the information of the key to derive the ciphertext in the beginning. The experiment which is omitted here shows that the chance for Eve to derive the key information is very small.

Key + Ciphertext + Plaintext(L) → Plaintext

In this model, we give Eve part of the plaintext and the key along with the ciphertext output by Alice, Eve's goal is to recover the plaintext here. Figure 9 shows the structure of the model.

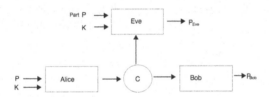

Fig. 9. Key + Ciphertext + Plaintext(L) → Plaintext

The experiment shows an opposite performance compared with the previous model. While the amount of leaked plaintext to Eve is small, both Bob and Eve can not easily converge to a certain point as shown in Fig. 12. However when the leaked bits is 16, Eve and Bob can get a good performance as shown in Fig. 13. When the amount of bits leaked is larger than 9, Eve and Bob can gradually get the convergence as shown in Figs. 10 and 11.

In this model, Alice wants to prevent Eve from recovering the correct plaintext. However, she cannot ignore the involvement of the plaintext because Bob needs to decrypt the ciphertext correctly. In this disadvantage circumstance, Alice and Bob can also prevent the attack from Eve even she knows most part of the plaintext information. Alice and Bob also pay for a price for reducing the decoding accuracy of Bob, therefore both Bob and Eve cannot get a convergence easily as shown in Fig. 12. When Eve obtains rich information about the plaintext, then Alice and Bob cannot efficiently prevent the attack from Eve,

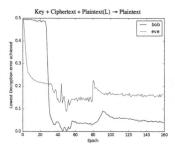

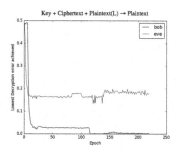

Fig. 10. Leaked plaintext bits is 9. Epoch is set to 80.

Fig. 11. Leaked plaintext bits is 10. Epoch is set to 140.

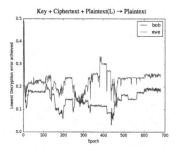

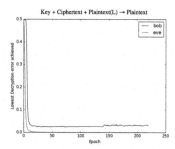

Fig. 12. Leaked plaintext bits is 8. Epoch is set to 600.

Fig. 13. Leaked plaintext bits is 16. Epoch is set to 140.

and finally Alice and Bob give up protection. System will reach an agreement to ensure that Bob can get the correct information without defeating Eve. In this situation, both Bob and Eve can get a convergence as shown in Fig. 13.

3.2 Two-Eve Model

From the discussion in the previous models, we can see that the strength of the encryption scheme depends largely on the ability of the adversary. Inspiring from the fact that recovering the key or the plaintext only cannot make the encryption protocol stronger (Alice can reduce the involvement of the key), we introduce a two-eve adversarial model to further enhance the encryption protocol. In this new model, we have two attackers Eve1 and Eve2 with different attacking goals. Eve1 focuses on recovering the plaintext and Eve2's goal is to recover the secret key. In this model, Alice cannot simply ignore the involvement of the secret key due to the existence of Eve1. We further divide into the following two categories.

Key(L) + Ciphertext → Plaintext(Eve1) + Key(Eve2)

In this model, Eve1 and Eve2 have two inputs, which are part of the leaked key and the ciphertext. Eve1 outputs the plaintext and Eve2 outputs the secret key. The other structure and parameters are same as the previous model. Figure 14 shows the model and the experiment results including the decryption error and

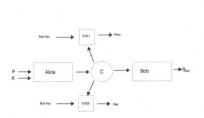

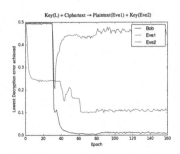

Fig. 14. Key(L)+Ciphertext → Plain-text(Eve1)+Key(Eve2)

Fig. 15. 8 bits key is leaked. Epoch is set to 80.

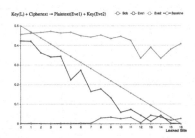

Fig. 16. The trend between the leakage bit and the decryption error

the trend of the loss rate are shown in Figs. 15 and 16. 8 bits key is leaked to Eve 8, and we train the model using 80 epochs data, and 80 for testing. The batch size of each epoch is 256.

The curve of Eve is entirely below the baseline in the Fig. 16, which reflect that Eve2 is helping Eve1 to gain more advantages. Eve2 forces Alice to use the key when she generate the ciphertext, and meanwhile, Eve1 has an advantage when she decrypt the ciphertext. Also the attack from Eve1 and Eve2 make Bob impossible to recover the plaintext accurately when Eve1 and Eve2 have already obtained most of the key information. In Fig. 16, after Eve1 and Eve2 gained more than 7 bits of key, the loss-rate of Bob begins to rise. For testing, the batch size of each epoch of data is set to 256.

Key(L) + Ciphertext + Plaintext → Plaintext(Eve1) + Key(Eve2)
In this model, Eve1 and Eve2 have three inputs, which are the plaintext, cipher-text and part of the key. Other settings are the same as the previous models. We give Eve 8 bits of the secret key and use 80 epochs for training the model and 80 for testing. Eve in this model behaves very similar to the model "Key(L) + Ciphertext → Key". It is reasonable to assume that Eve2 has already known what she want, which makes the adversary too strong, thus Alice gives up fight-ing back finally. We omit the experiment details for this model.

4   Conclusion

In this paper, we investigate the techniques of building an automatic encryption scheme based on the neural networks. Starting from the basic symmetric key model, we first show that learned function is not an Xor logic, and it cannot provide random statistical behavior. Then we extend the original model by investigating other more powerful adversaries. Except for a few models where the attackers are too strong, most of the models can be stabilized after the training stage. The new proposed encryption scheme is more strong and flexible in resisting against various attacks. Future works include how to further optimize the neural networks to make the legal party communication more efficient given less training steps. Also how to choose the appropriate hyper-parameters to improve the statistical randomness to resist against distinguishing attack is worth further investigating.

Acknowledgment. This work has been partly supported by the National Natural Science Foundation of China under Grant No. 61702212 and the research funds of CCNU from colleges' basic research and operation of MOE under Grant No. CCNU16A05040.

References

1. Abadi, M., Agarwal, A., Barham, P., Brevdo, E., Chen, Z., Citro, C., Corrado, G.S., Davis, A., Dean, J., Devin, M., et al.: Tensorflow: large-scale machine learning on heterogeneous distributed systems. arXiv preprint arXiv:1603.04467 (2016)
2. Abadi, M., Andersen, D.G.: Learning to protect communications with adversarial neural cryptography. arXiv preprint arXiv:1610.06918 (2016)
3. Goldwasser, S., Micali, S.: Probabilistic encryption. J. Comput. Syst. Sci. **28**(2), 270–299 (1984)
4. Goodfellow, I., Pouget-Abadie, J., Mirza, M., Xu, B., Warde-Farley, D., Ozair, S., Courville, A., Bengio, Y.: Generative adversarial nets. In: Advances in Neural Information Processing Systems, pp. 2672–2680 (2014)
5. Goodfellow, I.J., Shlens, J., Szegedy, C.: Explaining and harnessing adversarial examples. arXiv preprint arXiv:1412.6572 (2014)
6. Klimov, A., Mityagin, A., Shamir, A.: Analysis of neural cryptography. In: Zheng, Y. (ed.) ASIACRYPT 2002. LNCS, vol. 2501, pp. 288–298. Springer, Heidelberg (2002). https://doi.org/10.1007/3-540-36178-2_18
7. Mislovaty, R., Klein, E., Kanter, I., Kinzel, W.: Security of neural cryptography. In: Proceedings of the 2004 11th IEEE International Conference on Electronics, Circuits and Systems, ICECS 2004, Tel Aviv, Israel, 13–15 December 2004, pp. 219–221 (2004)
8. Ruttor, A.: Neural synchronization and cryptography. Ph.D. thesis, Julius Maximilians University Würzburg, Germany (2006)
9. Szegedy, C., Zaremba, W., Sutskever, I., Bruna, J., Erhan, D., Goodfellow, I.J., Fergus, R.: Intriguing properties of neural networks. CoRR abs/1312.6199 (2013)

Relevance Filtering for Shared Cyber Threat Intelligence
(Short Paper)

Thomas D. Wagner$^{(\boxtimes)}$, Esther Palomar, Khaled Mahbub, and Ali E. Abdallah

Birmingham City University, Birmingham, West Midlands B4 7XG, UK
{thomas.wagner,esther.palomar,khaled.mahbub,ali.abdallah}@bcu.ac.uk

Abstract. Cyber threat intelligence sharing is an imperative process to survive current and future attacks. The received information may protect stakeholders from being attacked by utilizing the course of action to remedy on-site vulnerabilities. Automating this process has shown to be challenging because several processes have to be synchronized and orchestrated to achieve the goal of automated information sharing. Organizations are inundated with threat information generated on site and received through crowd sourcing. This work presents a novel component for automated sharing, i.e. the content relevance filter.

Keywords: Threat intelligence platform · Advanced persistent threat
Cyber threat intelligence · Threat sharing · Relevance

1 Introduction

Traditional ways of defending IT infrastructures have been insufficient, due to daily increasing attacks which are more sophisticated than ever. For instance, Tactics, Techniques, and Procedures (TTP), especially the detection, capture, and sharing have become a conundrum for threat analysts. Attackers find more elaborate and efficient ways to infiltrate IT systems. These attacks are sometimes not immediately noticed and linger in the systems for years. Daily reports of successful security attacks have demonstrated that current defending methods, such as intrusion detection and prevention methods, are failing to address adequate security.

In addition, even the most diverse industries accept similar importance of improving resilience to cyber incidents and mitigating cyber threats. Underlying these efforts is the need to acquire the best possible information about the health of systems and networks, and the capabilities and intentions of cyber adversaries [2,8]. It is in the knowledge acquisition where perhaps the biggest challenge lies when identifying relevant cyber indicators for data analysis, protection, and sharing.

This work focuses on the prototype implementation of the relevance filter to contribute to the automated sharing of threat intelligence. Our preliminary

© Springer International Publishing AG 2017
J. K. Liu and P. Samarati (Eds.): ISPEC 2017, LNCS 10701, pp. 576–586, 2017.
https://doi.org/10.1007/978-3-319-72359-4_35

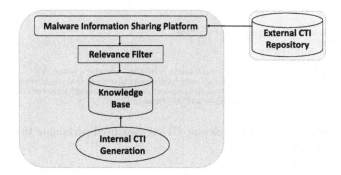

Fig. 1. Threat intelligence platform architecture

working prototype, relevance filter, is based on the Malware Information Sharing Platform (MISP).

The rest of the paper is organized as follows. Section 2 introduces the relevance architecture. Section 3 presents the relevance filter prototype. Section 4 analyzes existing solutions for relevance filtering. Section 5 concludes our work.

2 A Threat Sharing Architecture with Focus on Relevance

This section provides an architectural overview of the proposed platform, namely a novel approach to implement a relevance filter (Fig. 1).

The open-source and community driven MISP, current version 2.4.55, is used to manage and exchange cyber threat intelligence in human and machine readable form [7]. The platform is installed on Oracle's Virtual Box with Linux Ubuntu Server version 14.04 and stores Cyber Threat Intelligence (CTI) in the industry standard Structured Threat Information Expression (STIX) format (XML and JSON). To develop Threat Intelligence Platform (TIP) independent functions, the tool is developed outside the MISP environment and connects remotely to MISP's SQL database. This gives us the option to scale and apply the tools to other TIP's in the future. The Virtual Box is used for the testing environment, organizations like a bank would install the system in a production environment.

2.1 Content Relevance Filter

The content relevance filter automatically downloads CTI from the MISP database[1] into a temporary storage and screens through the data. Content relevant information will be stored in an external knowledge base. 1,000 mock data

---

[1] The cyber threat sharing platform connects to repositories on the cloud to exchange intelligence. To ensure that no information pertaining to the system is revealed, the MISP platform downloads all available information and stores it in its database.

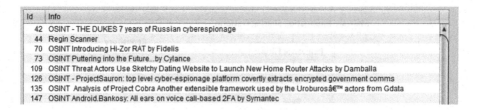

Id	Info
42	OSINT - THE DUKES 7 years of Russian cyberespionage
44	Regin Scanner
70	OSINT Introducing Hi-Zor RAT by Fidelis
73	OSINT Puttering into the Future...by Cylance
109	OSINT Threat Actors Use Sketchy Dating Website to Launch New Home Router Attacks by Damballa
126	OSINT - ProjectSauron: top level cyber-espionage platform covertly extracts encrypted government comms
135	OSINT Analysis of Project Cobra Another extensible framework used by the Uroburosâ€™ actors from Gdata
147	OSINT Android.Bankosy: All ears on voice call-based 2FA by Symantec

Fig. 2. Content relevance filter: relevant CTI is visualized pertaining to the filter settings in the SQL query.

sets and 700 open source data sets from the CIRCL[2] and Botvrij[3] repositories are used for database population and experimentation. The relevance filter is a structured process to identify which CTI is relevant to the stakeholder pertaining to the content. The filtering process identifies the content relevance, whether the CTI is complete or under ongoing/initial analysis, and verifies the threat level.

We are using SQL queries for the automated filtering process. The query creates an inner join between the "events" and "events_tags" tables of the MISP database. The query is stored in an external properties file which allows the system administrator to adjust the query according to the stakeholder's preferences. MISP's tagging system is utilized to filter the content. For example, the filter parameters are set to only accept CTI which is tagged as Traffic Light Protocol (TLP)[4] red and green, must have a high threat level, and must have its analysis completed. Everything else is ignored as shown in this query:

SELECT DISTINCT e FROM Events e INNER JOIN EventTags t on e.id = t.eventId WHERE t.tagId = (3,45) AND e.threatLevelId = 1 AND e.analysis = 2; Some query results are shown in Fig. 2.

To make the content relevance more precise in the future, we are going to suggest a scalable IT infrastructure taxonomy to extend the tagging system. It will relate to operating systems, applications, databases, and hardware. Phishing attacks and DDoS attacks qualify automatically as relevant because they are system unspecific.

Received CTI is normally already tagged with undefined, low, medium, or high priority. These predefined threat levels mirror the submitting stakeholder's or source's views but not automatically the receivers perception of the threat (Fig. 3).

---

[2] Computer Incident Response Center Luxembourg (https://www.circl.lu/doc/misp/feed-osint): A government initiative to collect, analyze, report, and respond to cyber threats.

[3] Botvrij (http://www.botvrij.eu/data/feed-osint): An open source repository for CTI.

[4] TLP is defined into four colors namely white (no restrictions), green (sharing with peers and partners, not publicly), amber (sharing only inside own organization on who need to know basis), and red (no sharing).

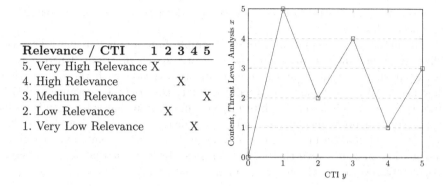

Relevance / CTI	1	2	3	4	5
5. Very High Relevance	X				
4. High Relevance			X		
3. Medium Relevance					X
2. Low Relevance		X			
1. Very Low Relevance				X	

Fig. 3. Relevance matrix: demonstrates 5 records of CTI and their relevance to our system.

Content relevance is subjective and stakeholders have to decide which information they consider relevant. For our model we define relevance as very high (91% – 100%), high (81% – 90%), medium (61% – 80%), low (50% – 60%), and very low (0% – 49%). These figures have been compiled from the following criteria: Content Relevance (CR) 50% (relevant 50%, irrelevant 0%), Threat Level (TL) 30% (high 30%, medium 15%, low 0%), Threat Analysis (TA) 20% (complete 20%, ongoing 10%, initial 5%, unknown 0%). The following 2 examples demonstrate how CTI 1 and 2 have been evaluated:

- **CTI 1:** Reached very high relevance (100%) because the content is relevant to the system (50%), the threat level is high (30%), and the analysis is complete (20%).
- **CTI 2:** Reached low relevance (55%) because the content was relevant (50%), but the threat level was low (0%), and the threat analysis is initial (5%).

3   Relevance Filter: First Prototype

At present, few vendors provide security and threat information sharing platforms. These platforms seek the elimination of manual processes and a rapid detection and analysis of security threats, while helping reduce the cost of defense. For example, NC4's "CTX/Soltra Edge" automates sharing in the way of peer to peer exchange using existing trust relationships and also supporting community defense models such as inter-sector sharing (e.g. FS-ISAC) and cross-sector sharing (e.g. with other critical entities). This solution can be accessed through a web-browser and makes use of crowd sourcing letting the user connect to different threat intelligence repositories. Another solution namely NECOMAtter disseminates cyber intelligence in a Twitter style [3].

In [4], a threat sharing model bases such an analysis on a Bayesian game where participants decide how much threat intelligence is shared. The research defines a two level status: full and no sharing and presents a monetary-free threat sharing mechanism.

Threat intelligence platforms provide simple functions regarding relevance. These functions include browsing and keyword search functions. Current relevance filtering is insufficient to provide an organization with the information they need. An analyst has to manually evaluate the content relevance and risk priority. The focus has to lie on filtering out information that is irrelevant to the stakeholder on both, mechanism and communication point of view [5]. [6] discuss that CTI sharing faces similar hurdles in data quality compared to regular information sharing. Nevertheless, the authors also suggest that it may need a completely new approach on how to manage data quality.

3.1   A Note on Relevance Techniques

Current TIP's establish relevance by keyword search or browsing through specific groups of CTI, i.e. malware, Phishing attacks, etc. Another relevance functionality uses a ticking system where the user enables certain feeds. Stakeholders can establish a more relevant approach to only receive specific information from vendors. This presupposes that the environment is trusted because infrastructure specific information is revealed. This may be a disadvantage if this information gets into the wrong hands and may facilitate an attack. CTI has to fulfill certain attributes to be considered relevant. Relevance is a challenging endeavour because it is inherently subjective and unique. [1] use the term quality instead of actionable to describe CTI. One quality aspect of CTI is the relevance to the community members.

Relevance can only be achieved if stakeholders know their IT infrastructure. The inventory ranges from software to hardware components and their pertaining versions. This has to be well maintained and continuously kept up-to date. Current relevance filtering is conducted manually by the analyst and depends completely on the knowledge of each individual to decide whether the information will be considered. This approach is time consuming and may be error prone if inexperienced analysts oversee the selective process.

3.2   System Model

This subsection describes the system model of the content relevance filter (Fig. 4). The objective of the relevance filter is to provide system relevant intelligence to the stakeholder. For instance, information that is relevant and can be acted upon. The data input is derived from threat monitoring and detection tools. The CTI has then manually to be labeled pertaining to its group. For example, type of operating system, software, database, or hardware. The intelligence is then shared with other stakeholders through the MISP instance. Received intelligence is stored in the MISP instance's database. The relevance filter accesses the database and screens through the data records. It utilizes the SQL queries from an external properties file. The query searches for the following pre-defined attributes:

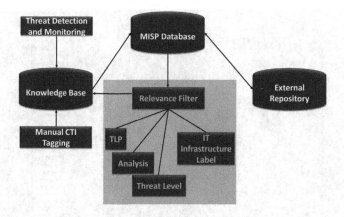

Fig. 4. Relevance filter architecture

- Analysis complete from events table where analysis equals 2
- Threat level high (id 1) from threat levels table
- TLP from tags table amber (id 44) and red (id 45)

Figure 5 shows some tags that are used to identify for which part of the IT infrastructure the CTI is intended to. The list shows an initial set of tagging attributes but is completely scalable. E.g., stakeholders can tag their CTI according to their own IT infrastructure such as specific versions of operating systems, databases, software, or hardware. Depending on which component is affected by the threat.

The model scenario provides the following processes to render CTI relevant to the stakeholder. There are 2 different directions for relevance, e.g., dispatch and reception.

The dispatching process involves firstly, the detection of a threat that has to be analyzed, evaluated, and then transformed into actionable CTI. Secondly, the intelligence is stored in the local knowledge base where internal analysts can make use of the information. Thirdly, the information is labeled according to which asset is vulnerable to the attack. The labeled intelligence is then uploaded to the MISP instance where it is shared with other stakeholders.

The reception process involves the following processes. Firstly, the MISP instance receives intelligence from various sources. The relevance filter accesses the MISP instance's database and pulls all information into temporary storage. Secondly, the filter screens the intelligence for the TLP, completeness, threat level, and whether the threat information is a risk to the stakeholder's system. Thirdly, the filtered intelligence is then stored in the local knowledge base for analysts to use.

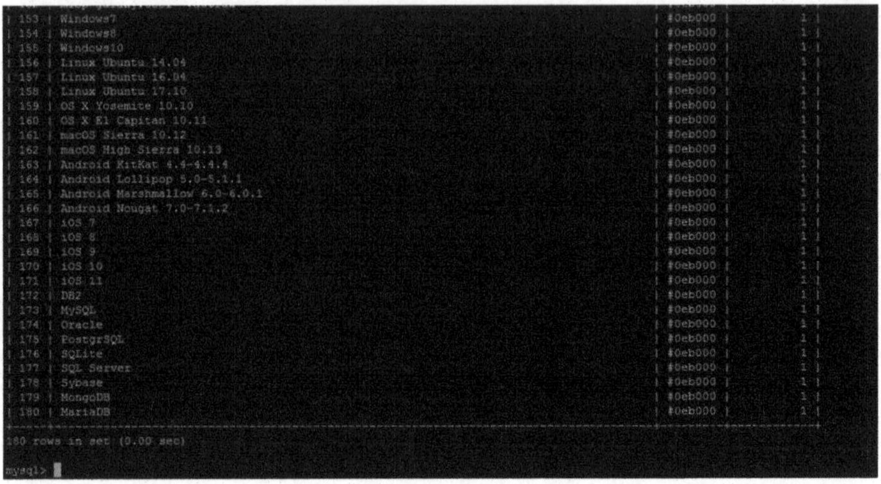

Fig. 5. Extended IT infrastructure taxonomy in MISP database: the taxonomy allows stakeholders to receive system specific relevance by utilizing low level tags.

3.3 Preliminary Evaluation and Threat Model

The test run of the relevance filter has shown a precise output of relevant information pertaining to the system as shown in Table 1. The SQL queries were modified several times to ensure the flexibility of the tool. The modifications were for example, also accepting ongoing analysis, medium threat levels, and other tags that may be considered relevant.

Table 1. Relevance filter results

Relevance	Data sets	Accuracy	False negatives
Traffic light protocol	832	832 (100%)	0
Analysis complete	832	832 (100%)	0
Threat level	832	832 (100%)	0
IT infrastructure label	832	832 (100%)	0

The latency of the prototype is depicted in Fig. 6. The speed of providing relevant information to the stakeholder was with 1,000 data set less than 2.5 s.

The requirements for content relevant information were realized by the prototype. The following steps were conducted for the reception of CTI:

- The MISP instance synchronizes available CTI from several repositories.
- The Relevance filter prototype transfers all new intelligence into temporary storage.

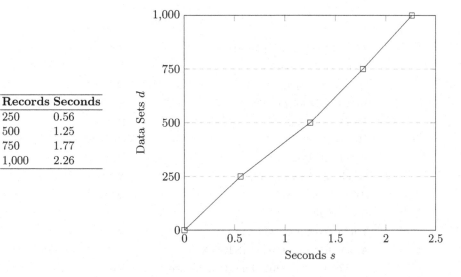

Records	Seconds
250	0.56
500	1.25
750	1.77
1,000	2.26

Fig. 6. Latency results relevance filter

- The intelligence is scanned for the tags that describe TLP, analysis, threat level, and the IT infrastructure.
- Relevant information is transferred and stored in the local knowledge base.
- Irrelevant intelligence stays in the MISP instance's database for future correlation which may render it relevant.

The following steps were conducted for the dispatch of CTI:

- Detected threats are analyzed and transformed into actionable CTI.
- The intelligence is stored in the local knowledge base, labeled, and uploaded to the local MISP instance.
- The MISP instance shares the intelligence with trusted repositories.

4   Analysis of Threat Intelligence Platforms for Relevance

30 threat intelligence platforms have been analyzed and compared, to the best of our knowledge, pertaining to relevance filtering methods (Table 2). One of the methods used for the evaluation was direct testing where possible. We did not have access to all platforms, therefore the second method was the analysis of academic literature, white/gray literature such as technical reports, and company websites for the evaluation. Platforms labeled with R_1 are using tags and/or search functions to improve content relevance. Platforms labeled with R_2 provide stakeholders with customized information.

A number of 6 threat intelligence providers dispense their paid services to customers. Information about an organization's infrastructure is collected and

Table 2. Threat intelligence platforms.

Threat intelligence platforms	Relevance
Malware information	
Sharing platform (MISP)[1]	R_1
NC4 CTX/Soltra Edge[1]	R_1
ThreatConnect[1]	R_1
Microsoft interflow[2]	R_1
HP threat Central[2]	R_1
Facebook threat exchange[2]	R_1
IBM X-Force exchange[1]	R_1
Alien vault open	
Threat exchange (OTX)[1]	R_1
Anomali threat stream (STAXX)[2]	R_1
LookingGlass scoutPrime (Cyveillance)[2]	R_2
Cisco Talos[2]	R_1
Crowd strike falcon platform[2]	R_1
Norm shield[2]	R_2
ServiceNow - bright point security[2]	R_2
NECOMAtter (NECOMAtome)[2]	R_1
Splunk[1]	R_2
CyberConnector[2]	R_1
Last quarter mile toolset (LQMT)[2]	R_1
Health information trust alliance	
- Cyber Threat XChange (CTX)[2]	R_2
Defense security information exchange[2]	R_1
Retail cyber intelligence sharing	
Center (R-CISC) intelligence sharing portal[2]	R_1
Accenture cyber intelligence platform[2]	R_1
Anubis networks cyberfeed[2]	R_1
Comilion[2]	R_1
McAfee threat intelligence exchange[2]	R_1
ThreatQuotient[2]	R_2
ThreatTrack threatIQ[2]	R_1
Eclectic IQ[2]	R_1
Infoblox threat intelligence data exchange[2]	R_1
Cyber-security information sharing	
Partnership[1]	R_1

[1]Denotes direct access,
[2]Denotes white/gray literature.

the intelligence is then customized. Another identified process is that the service provider bases the impact of a threat posed towards an organization and thus ensures relevance. "LookingGlass" utilizes their Threat Intelligence Confidence (TIC) score to provide threat relevancy to stakeholders. The "Norm Shield" solution collects and analyzes information about a client to render the CTI feed relevant. "Service Now" supports stakeholders with prioritized CTI based on impact level. "Splunk" uses its analytical capabilities to feed relevant information to the stakeholder and its correct teams. "Cyber Threat XChange" is focused on vulnerabilities to the health care system in the United States. It provides alerts for suspicious domain registrations linked to the stakeholder's domain, and alerts for compromised credentials. Furthermore, the premium subscription provides more detailed analysis and content. "ThreatQuotient" enables relevance by letting the customer define its parameters. The platform calculates relevance for external and internal CTI using the provided aggregated context. 24 threat intelligence platforms yield browse/search functions to make the content relevant. Most platforms group their intelligence according to types and predefined threat levels. The platforms provide high-level relevance filtering systems that identify general threats for stakeholders. None of the analyzed tools provide low-level relevance in form of threat information about specific operating systems, applications, databases, or hardware.

Our relevance tool provides an improved functionality on how to receive relevant information by utilizing tags. Content relevance filtering is only provided in its basic functionality such as search and browsing options in the analyzed tools.

5   Conclusion

This paper introduced a sharing platform based on MISP with focus on relevance filtering. Relevance is an important attribute to establish actionable threat intelligence sharing. As in many other domains that suffer from an overflow of information, threat sharing has similar hurdles to overcome. CTI is currently filtered on a high level, e.g., such as malware, phishing, etc. This paper presents an idea to render threat information more relevant to the stakeholder by using various tags. Furthermore, 30 popular threat intelligence sharing platforms were analyzed pertaining to how relevance is established.

References

1. Al-Ibrahim, O., Mohaisen, A., Kamhoua, C., Kwiat, K., Njilla, L.: Beyond free riding: quality of indicators for assessing participation in information sharing for threat intelligence. arXiv preprint arXiv:1702.00552 (2017)
2. Friedman, J., Bouchard, M.: Definitive Guide to Cyber Threat Intelligence. CyberEdge Press (2015)
3. Iimura, T., Miyamoto, D., Tazaki, H., Kadobayashi, Y.: NECOMAtter: curating approach for sharing cyber threat information. In: Proceedings of The Ninth International Conference on Future Internet Technologies, p. 19. ACM (2014)

4. Khouzani, M.H.R., Pham, V., Cid, C.: Strategic discovery and sharing of vulnerabilities in competitive environments. In: Poovendran, R., Saad, W. (eds.) GameSec 2014. LNCS, vol. 8840, pp. 59–78. Springer, Cham (2014). https://doi.org/10.1007/978-3-319-12601-2_4
5. Lu, S., Kokar, M.M.: A situation assessment framework for cyber security information relevance reasoning. In: 2015 18th International Conference on Information Fusion (Fusion), pp. 1459–1466. IEEE (2015)
6. Sillaber, C., Sauerwein, C., Mussmann, A., Breu, R.: Data quality challenges and future research directions in threat intelligence sharing practice. In: Proceedings of the 2016 ACM on Workshop on Information Sharing and Collaborative Security, pp. 65–70. ACM (2016)
7. Wagner, C., Dulaunoy, A., Wagener, G., Iklody, A.: MISP: the design and implementation of a collaborative threat intelligence sharing platform. In: Proceedings of the 2016 ACM on Workshop on Information Sharing and Collaborative Security, pp. 49–56. ACM (2016)
8. Zheng, D.E., Lewis, J.A.: Cyber Threat Information Sharing: Recommendations for Congress and the Administration (2015)

Design and Implementation of a Lightweight Kernel-Level Network Intrusion Prevention System for Virtualized Environment (Short Paper)

Mei-Ling Chiang[1]([⊠]), Jian-Kai Wang[2], Li-Chi Feng[2],
Yang-Sen Chen[1], You-Chi Wang[2], and Wen-Yu Kao[1]

[1] Department of Information Management, National Chi-Nan University,
545 Puli, Nantou, Taiwan, R.O.C.
joanna@ncnu.edu.tw,
{s102213542, s103213525}@maill.ncnu.edu.tw
[2] Department of Computer Science and Information Engineering,
Chang Gung University, 333, Tao-Yuan, Taiwan, R.O.C.
tn0024@gmail.com, lcfeng@mail.cgu.edu.tw,
eddiewang539@gmail.com

Abstract. Cloud platforms often take advantage of virtualization technology and make their actual hosts virtualized. As network attack events occur frequently, providing system security in a virtualized environment is the focus of this study. We have designed and implemented a lightweight network-based intrusion prevention system (IPS) named VMM-IPS for the virtual machine (VM) execution environment. To ensure the system safety of VMs and the host system at the same time, VMM-IPS is operated in the Linux kernel of the host system and co-located with the Kernel-based Virtual Machine that turns Linux kernel into a hypervisor. As packets enter the system, no matter destined to VMs or passing through the host, they are detected by VMM-IPS. Unlike user-level IPS that needs switching protection domain and copying packets to user buffer for inspection, VMM-IPS is more efficient because of the capability to perform in-place packet inspection. It adopts signature-based detection and is implemented with the multiple-pattern search algorithm AC-BM for efficient string matching. Besides, VMM-IPS can protect the system against attacks using packet splitting and reassembly to evade introduction detection system (IDS). The experimental results demonstrate VMM-IPS can achieve system safety effectively and efficiently.

Keywords: Intrusion prevention system · Network security · Kernel level
Virtual machine monitor · Virtualization technology

1 Introduction

The intrusion detection system (IDS) is a network security monitoring system for maintaining system and network security. By inspecting the file system audit records or network activities, it detects attacks carried out on the system and then returns alerts to

© Springer International Publishing AG 2017
J. K. Liu and P. Samarati (Eds.): ISPEC 2017, LNCS 10701, pp. 587–598, 2017.
https://doi.org/10.1007/978-3-319-72359-4_36

the administrator. The network-based IDS (NIDS) examines network packets and analyzes network traffic to detect attacks over the network. As network traffic increases, detection efficiency becomes very critical.

Cloud platforms often take advantage of virtualization technology and make their actual hosts virtualized. Virtualization technology allows a physical machine to provide multiple execution environments and run multiple operating systems concurrently, each in its own virtual machine (VM). The virtual machine monitor (VMM) provides an abstract layer of underlying hardware for each operating system running on it and is responsible for managing the hardware resources of the actual machine and monitoring the activity of each virtual machine. Since the operating system and the underlying VMM belong to different protection domains, and the communication between the operating system and the VMM are subject to more stringent control, the relevant studies [1–5] indicated VMM is the most appropriate level for providing security-related mechanisms and is less likely to become the subject of attacks.

This paper presents the design and implement of a lightweight network-based intrusion prevention system (IPS) named VMM-IPS for virtualized environment. The virtualization software we use is Kernel-based Virtual Machine (KVM) [6] due to its prominent performance [7]. KVM is a virtualization infrastructure for the Linux kernel, which turns it into a hypervisor. KVM is also adopted for VM creation in OpenStack [8] that is popularly used for building virtualized cloud computing platforms.

The proposed VMM-IPS is a network-based IPS with signature-based detection. As network packets received, they are intercepted and examined by VMM-IPS. Once malicious packets are detected, they are dropped and their associated connections are reset by VMM-IPS. Therefore, only normal packets are allowed to enter the system. For such type of NIPS with on-line packet inspection, detection efficiency is especially important as each network packet is examined and network traffic increases greatly.

To be efficient in packet inspection, VMM-IPS adopts kernel-level implementation and network packets are directly examined in the kernel. Unlike the most NIPSs that are operated at the user level, user-level intrusion detection systems need to copy packets from the kernel buffer to the user-space buffer for packet inspection. This copy operation and the switch of protection domains between kernel mode and user mode degrade system performance [4]. Besides, VMM-IPS is more secure because it operates at the kernel-level with the virtual machine monitor. If intrusion detection systems operate at the user level, they are more susceptible to attack through various techniques once an attacker has gained privileged access to a system [1].

To be efficient in packet inspection, using an efficient algorithm is important because the performance of a signature-based NIDS is dominated by the string matching of packets against many signatures. The multiple-pattern search algorithm AC-BM [9] that takes the best characteristics of both the Boyer-Moore [10] and Aho-Corasick [11] string search algorithms is implemented in VMM-IPS for faster string matching.

On the other hand, recently some technologies about evading intrusion detection and prevention systems (i.e. IDS Evasion [12]) have been developed. Our system can also perform multi-packet detection and protect the system against attacks using the concept of packet splitting and reassembly to evade IDS [12].

To ensure system safety of the entire system, all incoming packets should be captured and examined, no matter they are destined for VMs or the host system.

The implementation of our VMM-IPS employs the technology of Netfilter [13] which is a Linux kernel subsystem for packets filtering. Therefore, our VMM-IPS can detect packets forwarded to each VM and packets passing through the host.

VMM-IPS also provides flexible responding actions. Once malicious packets are detected, VMM-IPS can either drop them, log this event and notify the administrator, or reset the connection, according to the configuration. Particularly, different reactions can be set in the detection rules for different VMs and for different connections.

Through the practical implementation of VMM-IPS as a loadable Linux kernel module that can be dynamically inserted into the Linux kernel at run time, the experimental results demonstrate VMM-IPS can achieve system safety effectively and efficiently. It also obtains better performance and incurs less system overhead than the famous and popularly used open-source IPS Snort [14]. This is because VMM-IPS does not need to switch protection domains and copy received packets to user buffer for packet inspection, so it obtains better performance.

2 Background and Related Works

Most NIDSs are operated at the user level and use the pcap library [15] or raw socket system calls to receive packets captured under the promiscuous mode in the kernel. To allow NIDS to inspect network packets at the user-level, a large number of packets are duplicated from the kernel buffer to the user-space buffer in NIDS. As NIDS obtains these packets, it needs to analyze them to detect network attacks by comparing these data with the signature database. However, this duplication of packets and the required overhead for switching protection domains between kernel mode and user mode always greatly decrease system performance. In contrast, we adopt kernel-level approach in the implementation to escape from these overhead.

For network-based IDSs/IPSs, Snort [14] and Suricata [16] are the two major open-source network-based IDSs/IPSs. By analyzing all packets passing through the network, they check for malicious packets that match the detection rule sets and then generate alerts to the administrator. Users are also allowed to add or customize their detection rules. Because of lots of benefits, Snort has been widely deployed and utilized as the intrusion detection engine in many researches for distributed or cloud environments. Suricata is developed with multi-threading capabilities.

Other researches related to IDSs/IPSs in virtualized environments are introduced as follows. Garfinkel and Rosenblum [1] discussed the methods of IDS implementation and indicated IDS implementation in the VMM layer has the benefits of combining the advantages of host-based IDS and NIDS. Besides, it is less likely to become the subject of attacks. They proposed the idea of Virtual Machine Introspection (VMI), which co-locates an IDS on the same machine as the monitored host and leverages the VMM technology to isolate the IDS from the monitored host. The VMM they used is a modified version VMware Workstation for Linux version 3.1. With modification to the VMM, they implemented a prototype VMI-based IDS named Livewire that can obtain the required information from the VMM and issue commands to the VMM for examining VM states. The VMI-based IDS consists of the OS interface library that provides an OS-level view of the VM's states and the policy engine to execute IDS policies using the OS interface library and the VMM interface.

Azmandian et al. [2] implemented their IDS in the VMM layer to guard against malicious attacks. The VMM they used is VirtualBox. Their IDS consists of two key components: a front-end and a back-end. The front-end component at the VMM-level is responsible for event extraction and feature construction. These features are then passed on to the back-end component which performs the operations including feature reduction, normal model creation, anomaly detection, and raising an alarm. Data mining algorithms are utilized for model creation and anomaly detections.

Tupakula and Varadharajan [3] also implemented a VMM-based IDS named VICTOR at the VMM level. The VICTOR contains several components including entity validation, an intrusion detection engine, and a dynamic analyzer. Each component is designed to deal with different types of malicious behaviors or attacks on VMs. They indicated that an IDS implemented in the VMM can not only monitor the activity of VMs but also examine the internal VM state. Besides, the isolation between the VMM and VMs makes it more difficult for intruders to attack the VMM.

Jin et al. [4] developed a VMM-based IPS named VMFence in a virtualization-based cloud computing environment. VMFence monitors network flow and file modification operations in real time. It then prevents malicious attacks and provides file integrity protection. The system was built on Xen. Its main process runs in the privileged VM (i.e. Dom0) to detect all VMs' activities because the privileged VM is able to capture all network packets to and from other service VMs. Besides, it adopts Snort [14] as its IDS and iptables [17] as a firewall in the implementation.

Bharadwaja et al. [5] developed a distributed intrusion detection platform named Collabra. Collabra works in a virtualized environment based on Xen hypervisors to maintain the security of the cloud. Collabra instances are integrated with the VMM of each host. Collabra dynamically monitors each hyper-call from guest VMs to VMM and then filters out malicious hyper-calls. If an intrusion is detected, it notifies all other Collabra instances and notifies the specific VMM to be sanitized. Besides, this system is used to detect anomaly based intrusions.

3   System Design and Implementation

3.1   The VMM-IPS Overview

VMM-IPS is a lightweight intrusion detection and prevention system for virtual machine execution environment. It is implemented as a kernel module that can be dynamically inserted/removed into/from the Linux kernel during system runtime. Its implementation employs the Netfilter [13], a packet filtering framework within the Linux kernel, to intercept all packets entering the system. Only the normal packets destined to virtual machines or host system are then forwarded. Therefore, VMM-IPS can protect both the host system and the VMs. In fact, VMM-IPS can be deployed in the Linux-based networking devices, such as gateways, router, servers, etc.

In the implementation, we mainly use the Kernel-based Virtual Machine (KVM) [6] to set up VMs for the virtualized environment. KVM is an open-source virtualization infrastructure for Linux and requires a processor with hardware virtualization extensions. It allows users to create multiple VMs that run unmodified guest operating systems. KVM consists of a loadable kernel module providing the core virtualization infrastructure and a processor specific module. It runs within the Linux kernel and needs user-mode QEMU [18] to provide full hypervisor functionality, such that each VM running as a single Linux process has its own separate virtual address space.

Figure 1 shows the networking architecture of the VMM-IPS. The VMM-IPS is located between the Linux Ethernet bridge and virtual NICs (TAP). As packets enter the system before being transmitted to the virtual NICs for KVM's processing, they are processed by the VMM-IPS for packet inspection. It then decides to either accept or drop the packet, or even interrupts the connection, according to the detection rules.

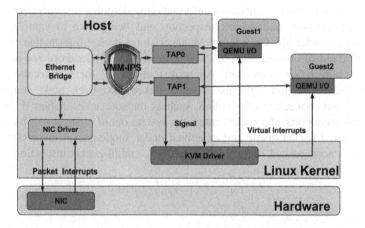

Fig. 1. The VMM-IPS networking architecture.

Netfilter [13] provides different hooks to allow kernel modules to register their callback functions for handling packets. For each packet received by NIC, the kernel would trigger the registered callback functions to process the packet in the flow of packet processing. The VMM-IPS is registered and hooked at the PREROUTING hook, so the VMM-IPS can inspect all packets entering the system or to be forwarded.

3.2   The VMM-IPS System Architecture and Components

VMM-IPS consists of four modules. The Manager module is responsible for controlling the operation of the entire system and the communication between each module. The Connection Manager module is responsible for connection tracking and maintaining information about the tracked connection. The Pattern Matching module is responsible for packet inspection to find malicious payloads, while the Reaction module performs the reaction according to the detection result and reaction mechanism.

The Connection Manager Module. In addition to maintaining the information for connection tracking, the Connection Manager module is also responsible for determining whether a received packet is to be inspected under the single-packet inspection mode or multi-packet inspection mode. The implementation of multi-packet inspection is due to attackers being able to exploit the concept of packet splitting and reassembling to evade IDS [12], by which malicious attacks or string information are disassembled and hidden in two or more consecutive packets. Those payload are disguised as harmless and are not detected if an IDS supports only single-packet inspection. After packets are reassembled and received, these seemingly harmless safe packets will become a malicious payload and lead the system to a dangerous state.

The Connection Manager module maintains three linked lists, in which the connection state linked list is used to store connection information for each connection established through three-way handshaking. The information stored in the connection transmission data linked list is used for determining whether a data packet should be examined under single-packet or multi-packet inspection. The disconnection state linked list is used to store connection information undergoing disconnection.

For implementing multi-packet inspection and being able to examine packets received out of order, the Connection Manager stores packet information for dealing with received out-of-ordered packets. Packets are accumulated and ordered in a circular buffer for multi-packet inspection. As shown in Fig. 2, the Connection Manager maintains the connection transmission data linked list. Each node stores packet information and connection information, such as the source/destination IP addresses, source/destination ports. If a packet enters the system out of order, it will be enqueued in the unordered packet queue and examined under single-packet inspection. On the contrary, it is accumulated in the circular buffer for multi-packet inspection.

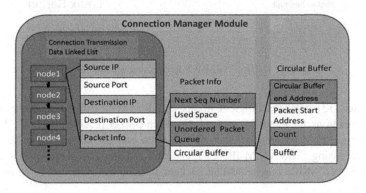

Fig. 2. The structure of connection transmission data linked list.

The Pattern Matching Module. This module consists of the detection engine and the rule database storing detection rules. For efficient string matching, the multiple-pattern search algorithm AC-BM [9] is implemented. During the system startup time, the VMM-IPS imports all the detection rules and builds a rule tree to speed up the subsequent rule-matching operation as shown in Fig. 3. The rule tree includes the rule tree node (RTN) and the pattern tree node (PTN). Each RTN stores the source/destination IPs and source/destination ports extracted from detection rules, and it is unique. The PTN is a tree constructed by the characteristic strings extracted from detection rules, which stores the required information used in AC-BM algorithm.

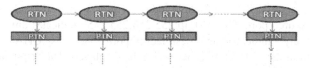

(a) The schematic diagram of the rule tree.

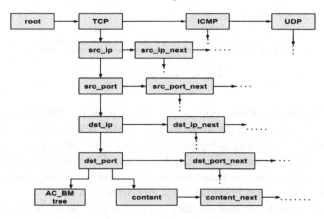

(b) The rule tree structure.

Fig. 3. The rule tree for detection.

The Reaction Module. The Reaction module is responsible for performing the reaction once a malicious packet is detected. There are four reaction methods shown in Table 1. In the design, the reaction module can respond differently according to the setting of each rule. Therefore, different VM systems with different IP/port can have rules and reaction methods suitable for their own systems.

Table 1. Reaction methods.

	Method	Description
1.	Send reset packet	Send a reset packet to the client and the server to interrupt the connection
2.	Drop packet	Drop the malicious packet, which is possible to cause TCP retransmission
3	Send reset packet & log file	Send a reset packet to the client and the server to interrupt the connection. This event is recorded in the VMM-IPS log file
4.	Drop packet & log file	Drop the malicious packet and record this event in the VMM-IPS log file

The rule database stores many detection rules and Fig. 4 shows one rule as an example. The first column indicates which reaction method should be performed for this detection rule. In this example, the second column "t" indicates this is a TCP packet. The "src_ip:255.255.255.255" indicates any source IP and "src_port:any" indicates any source port. The "dst_ip:255.255.255.255" indicates any destination IP and "dst_port:any" indicates any destination port. The "msg:CHAT ICQ access" indicates the message "CHAT ICQ access" to be displayed. The "content:User-Agent| 3A|ICQ" indicates the characteristic string to be matched.

Fig. 4. An example rule.

The Packet Inspection Flow. For each incoming packet, VMM-IPS first checks its type. If the packet belongs to the command type, VMM-IPS performs the processing of the connection establishment using the connection state linked list or performs disconnection using the disconnection state linked list. If the packet is a data packet, it then looks up the connection transmission data linked list to find the corresponding node that stores the packet information for this connection.

VMM-IPS then determines whether a data packet should be examined under single-packet or multi-packet inspection. If the system is set to perform single-packet inspection, it directly performs single-packet inspection. For performing multi-packet inspection, VMM-IPS examines whether this packet arrives out of order by comparing the sequence number of the packet with the expected sequence number stored in the connection transmission data linked list. The out-of-ordered packet will be enqueued in the unordered packet queue and examined under single-packet inspection. For multi-packet inspection, packets are accumulated and ordered in the circular buffer for inspection.

4   Performance Evaluation

Our experimental environment consists of a server and three client machines, as shown in Table 2. The VMM-IPS which is a Linux kernel module operates within the host OS, while the KVM-based VM running on top of the host OS. In contrast, the Snort is a user-level IPS operating on top of the host OS with the KVM-based VM. In the VM, the Apache Web server [19] is installed to provide Web services.

We measure the performance impact on the Web server when VMM-IPS or Snort is deployed in the system. To compare the performance fairly, both VMM-IPS and Snort should adopt the same detection rules. For this purpose, we develop a rule transformation tool to convert Snort rules to the right format for VMM-IPS. The Snort rules (i.e. snortrules-snapshot-2982 [14]) are used and there are a total of 8217 rules. To evaluate the performance impact when VMM-IPS or Snort is deployed, we use an open-source tool, i.e. Apache Bench [20], to measure the performance of the Apache Web server. The Web server is installed and runs on top of the guest OS. A large amount of requests through different amounts of concurrent connections are sent to the Web server to drive the stress test.

Table 2. Hardware and software specification.

	Server	VM	Client 1,2,3
CPU	Intel xeon E5-2620 2.4 GHz	KVM Virtual CPU	Intel i5-3470 3.2 GHz
RAM	16G	2G	4G
NIC	Intel I210	KVM Virtual NIC	RTL 8111/8168B
OS	Ubuntu 12.04	Ubuntu 12.04	Ubuntu 12.04
Linux kernel version	3.7.9	3.13.0	3.13.0
Apache version	X	2.2.22	X

The following command is issued on each client machine to send one million requests through 750 concurrent connections to the Web server: "ab -n 1000000 -c 750 http://192.168.3.15/localhost". We also test setting different numbers of concurrent connections, such as 250, 500, 750, and 1000. The requested Web page is 1 K bytes. The same experiment is also performed on the system without deploying any IDS.

We found under such a large number of incoming network packets, VMM-IPS still can effectively handle and inspect each packet. In contrast, the packet drop rate as reported by Snort is 48.1%, which affects the ability to protect the system under heavy network traffic load. Despite the high drop rate of Snort, Fig. 5 shows the performance result, in which the "Base" case represents the system without deploying any IDS. Compared with the Base case, the average number of requests processed per second of the VMM-IPS is decreased by up to 1.8%, while that of Snort is decreased by 12–16.3%. The average response time of VMM-IPS is increased by up to 2%, while that of Snort is increased by 13.7–19.7%. The transfer rate of VMM-IPS is 12.3–19.4% higher than that of Snort. Under such a large amount of requests, the number of failed requests is less than 0.5% for each system.

The performance of Snort and VMM-IPS are lower than the Base case, mainly due to the processing overhead such as packet inspection and performing reaction. VMM-IPS incurs less overhead than Snort. This is because Snort is a user-level IDS, so packets received are copied from the kernel buffer to the user buffer in Snort for packet inspection. In contrast, VMM-IPS operates at the kernel-level and examines packets directly, so no additional copy operation and switching protection domain are needed. Besides, under these high network traffic loads, VMM-IPS inspects each packet, whereas, the packet drop rate is 48% for Snort.

We also measure the performance impact when different sized Web pages are requested. Each client machine sends one million requests to the Web server through 750 concurrent connections to drive the stress test. The file sizes are 177 bytes (i.e. the default Web page in Apache Bench [20]), 1 K bytes, and 4 K bytes. VMM-IPS still can effectively handle and inspect each incoming network packet. In contrast, the packet drop rate as reported by Snort is substantially high and ranges from 45.9%–48.1%. Compared with the Base case, the average number of requests processed per second of VMM-IPS is decreased by 0.6–1%, while that of Snort is decreased by 14.6–18.4%. The average response time per request of VMM-IPS is increased by 0.6–0.9%, while

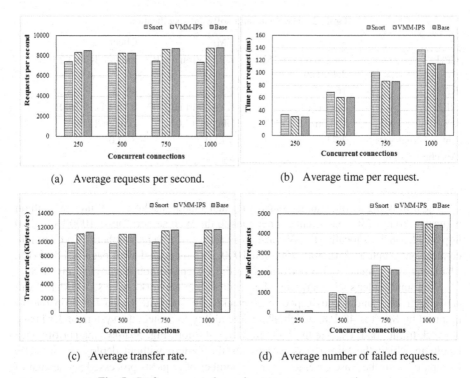

(a)   Average requests per second.   (b)   Average time per request.

(c)   Average transfer rate.   (d)   Average number of failed requests.

Fig. 5. Performance under various concurrent connections.

that of Snort is increased by 17.1–22.6%. The number of failed requests is less than 0.3% for each system and the transfer rate of VMM-IPS is 15.9–22.2% higher than that of Snort.

5   Conclusions and Future Works

We have designed and implemented a lightweight network-based IPS for virtualized environment. The virtualization software we use is the Kernel-based Virtual Machine (KVM) that turns Linux kernel into a hypervisor. VMM-IPS is implemented as a loadable kernel module that can be dynamically loaded into the Linux kernel during run time. Therefore, VMM-IPS is operated at the kernel level with KVM module. VMM-IPS employs Netfilter technology and is registered at the PREROUTING hook, so VMM-IPS can perform in-place packet inspection and inspect all packets entering the system. In contrast, the user-level IDS needs the overhead of coping packets to user buffer for inspection and switching protection domain between user mode and kernel mode for processing. The experimental results demonstrate that VMM-IPS incurs less overhead and effectively ensures the system safety. Besides, under heavy network traffic loads, VMM-IPS still can effectively handle and inspect packets. Whereas, the packet drop rate as reported by Snort is substantially high.

Currently, VMM-IPS adopts signature-based detection that inspects network packets to find malicious patterns in known attacks. We plan to add the detection of abnormal behaviors to make VMM-IPS more complete in protecting the system. We also will extend VMM-IPS to become distributed IPS and explore the security issues for clouds, such that it can be more suitable for operating in a cloud environment.

Acknowledgments. This research was supported in part by grant MOST 105-2221-E-260-015 and MOST 106-2221-E-260-001 from the Ministry of Science and Technology, Taiwan, Republic of China. We would also like to thank M. L. Wang, H. Cheng, C. W. Huang and members in the Computer System laboratory of Chang Gung University for their efforts in this study.

References

1. Garfinkel, T., Rosenblum, M.: A virtual machine introspection based architecture for intrusion detection. In: Proceeding of Network and Distributed Systems Security Symposium, pp. 191–206 (2003)
2. Azmandian, F., Moffie, M., Alshawabkeh, M.: Virtual machine monitor-based lightweight intrusion detection. ACM SIGOPS Operating Syst. Rev. **45**(2), 38–53 (2011)
3. Tupakula, U.K., Varadharajan, V.: Dynamic state-based security architecture for detecting security attacks in virtual machines. Comput. J. **55**(4), 397–409 (2012)
4. Jin, H., Xiang, G., Zou, D., Wu, S., Zhao, F., Li, M., Zheng, W.: A VMM-based intrusion prevention system in cloud computing environment. J. Supercomputing **66**(3), 1133–1151 (2013)
5. Bharadwaja, S., Weiqing, S., Niamat, M., Fangyang, S.: Collabra: a Xen hypervisor based collaborative intrusion detection system. In: Proceedings of the Eighth International Conference on Information Technology: New Generations, pp. 695–700 (2011)
6. KVM: http://www.linux-kvm.org/. Accessed 5 Oct 2017
7. Chierici, A., Veraldi, R.: A quantitative comparison between Xen and KVM. J. Phys. (2010). Conference Series 219, https://doi.org/10.1088/1742-6596/219/4/042005
8. OpenStack cloud software: https://www.openstack.org/. Accessed 5 Oct 2017
9. Coit, C.J., Staniford, S., McAlemey, J.: Towards faster string matching for intrusion detection or exceeding the speed of Snort. In: Proceedings of DARPA Information Survivability Conference & Exposition II, vol. 1, pp. 367–373 (2001)
10. Boyer, R.S., Moore, J.S.: A fast string searching algorithm. Commun. ACM **20**(10), 762–772 (1977)
11. Aho, A.V., Corasick, M.J.: Efficient string matching: an aid to bibliographic search. Commun. ACM **18**(6), 333–340 (1975)
12. Cheng, T.H., Lin, Y.D., Lai, Y.C., Lin, P.C.: Evasion techniques: sneaking through your intrusion detection/prevention systems. IEEE Commun. Surv. Tutorials **14**(4), 1011–1020 (2012)
13. Netfilter: http://www.netfilter.org. Accessed 5 Oct 2017
14. Snort: http://www.snort.org. Accessed 5 Oct 2017
15. TCPDump/Libpcap: http://www.tcpdump.org. Accessed 5 Oct 2017
16. Suricata: http://www.suricata-ids.org. Accessed 5 Oct 2017
17. Iptables: http://www.netfilter.org/projects/iptables/index.html. Accessed 5 Oct 2017

18. Bellard, F.: QEMU, a fast and portable dynamic translator. In: Proceedings of the Annual Conference on USENIX Annual Technical Conference, pp. 41–46 (2005)
19. Apache web server: https://httpd.apache.org/. Accessed 5 Oct 2017
20. Apache Bench: https://httpd.apache.org/docs/2.4/programs/ab.html. Accessed 5 Oct 2017

Cyber-Physical Security

Secure Communications in Unmanned Aerial Vehicle Network

Shuangyu He[1], Qianhong Wu[1(✉)], Jingwen Liu[2], Wei Hu[2], Bo Qin[3], and Ya-Nan Li[1]

[1] School of Electronic and Information Engineering,
Beihang University, Beijing, China
{shaungyuhe,qianhong.wu}@buaa.edu.cn
[2] Potevio Information Technology Co., Ltd., Beijing, China
[3] Key Laboratory of Data Engineering and Knowledge Engineering,
School of Information, Ministry of Education, Renmin University of China,
Beijing, China
bo.qin@ruc.edu.cn

Abstract. The unmanned aerial vehicle (UAV) network has attracted much attention in industry and academia. However, a UAV as a vital information carrier and data relay platform is prone to various attacks. In this paper, we propose a secure communication scheme for UAV network. In our scheme, each drone maintains and manages an area in which the authorized devices can obtain a broadcast key without an online centralized authority. By employing the hierarchical identity-based broadcast encryption and pseudonym mechanism, all the devices in this system can broadcast encrypted messages anonymously and decrypt the legal ciphertext. The analysis shows that our scheme satisfies four important security properties of confidentiality, authentication, partial privacy-preservation and resistance to denial of service attacks. Experiments show that our scheme incurs a delay of only a couple of milliseconds.

Keywords: Unmanned aerial vehicle · Secure communication
Mutual authentication

1 Introduction

Unmanned aerial vehicles (UAV), also called drones, were initially used for military purposes such as mapping, surveillance, search and target tracking. Recently, drones, as extensions of the human body, have been used in civil applications. In 2016, Facebook's solar-powered unmanned plane *Aquila* completed its first test flight as an alternative Internet delivery platform for remote parts of the world. The communications payload that *Aquila* carries uses lasers to transfer data more than 10 times faster than existing systems [17]. Moreover, Qualcomm Technologies, a subsidiary of Qualcomm Incorporated and AT&T, announced that it would test Unmanned aircraft systems (UAS), or drones, on commercial

© Springer International Publishing AG 2017
J. K. Liu and P. Samarati (Eds.): ISPEC 2017, LNCS 10701, pp. 601–620, 2017.
https://doi.org/10.1007/978-3-319-72359-4_37

4G LTE networks [24]. UAV networks are used today in many areas such as disaster relief [2,9], public services [18], agriculture [20], and infrastructure damage assessment [15].

Compared with an infrastructure based overlay network, using UAVs to deploy a wireless network is beneficial to adapt the network topology efficiently and to assigning wireless parameters dynamically. Moreover, UAVs are able to carry hardware with sufficient computation capability to perform complex operations, while running such hardware on land-based devices is expensive and inefficient due to the hardness of deployment of infrastructure in ruinate regions. Indeed, Using UAVs to build a temporary network is far less expensive and requires much less time than implementing an equivalent wired infrastructure in a remote area.

Although UAV networks have so many benefits, security risks hinder their deployment. In 2011, Iranian forces captured an American RQ-170 unmanned aerial vehicle, which caused concern regarding drone security. The applications of UAV networks, such as for battlefield communication and scouting forces in the hostile environment, always encounter the risk of adversaries launching network attacks. Furthermore, due to the openness of wireless networks, the attackers can more easily access them, launch various attacks, e.g., intercept, modify transmitted messages and even take over communication flows.

To address the security threats to UAV networks, Kong et al. [11] proposed a symmetric key distribution scheme in which each device should store all its neighbors' public keys and symmetric session keys. But when the number of end devices increases, the storage and communication costs begin to plan an intolerable burden in practice. To establish secure channels between drones and end devices more efficiently, Won et al. [25] proposed a secure communication protocol between drone and end devices with a certificateless signcryption tag key encapsulation mechanism. Unfortunately, the scheme cannot support group communication among end devices. It still remains a significant challenge to construct a secure communication protocol with efficiency, security, and availability.

1.1   Our Contribution

To meet the needs of wide message broadcast, end-device identity authentication, and partial device privacy-preservation, we propose a scheme that employs a hierarchical identity-based broadcast encryption (HIBBE) technique and device and UAVs identity based on signcryption to remove an online remote management center when a temporary communication network based on UAVs is constructed. Our scheme improves three of the main security concerns referred to in the security requirements as follows.

- We propose fast batch-encrypted packet transitions by using the HIBBE approach. Messages for broadcast are encrypted by a broadcast key pre-assigned by the device's relevant UAV. Our scheme achieves complete message confidentiality that uses a scale-tolerant key size and a session key delegate algorithm without requiring an online remote management center.

- We present mutual authentication using identity-based signcryption. Using this approach, drones can verify whether an end device is authorized by verifying the signature generated by the device. Similarly, an end device can verify whether a drone is a real master or an imitation using the same techniques.
- We achieve privacy-preservation by pseudonym and ciphertext transition mechanism. With the pseudonym mechanism, the end device cuts the link between its real and broadcast identities. Namely, any device can generate a temporary identity in the broadcast system such that the only ones who know its real identity are itself and its master drone. Through the ciphertext transition mechanism and the HIBBE characteristics, the master drone can transmit a HIBBE ciphertext to a hierarchical identity based encryption (HIBE) ciphertext that will take over the broadcast set information.
- We realize the resistance against denial of service (DoS) attack by prove of work mechanism with which drones dynamic control access numbers and the interval of time for each login.

1.2 Paper Organization

The remainder of this paper is organized as follows. We review the related work in Sect. 1. We formalize the model of a UAV network system and the system security requirements in Sect. 3. Section 4 discusses our proposed secure communication system for UAV networks. We demonstrate the system's security in Sect. 5 and evaluate the performance of our protocols in Sect. 6. Finally, Sect. 7 provides concluding remarks.

2 Related Work

UAV communication network has far-reaching prospects, and has attracted increasing research attention from both academia and industry. Researchers are working to solve technical issues and challenges in UAV network system, some of which involve communication and networking. Gupta et al. [10] introduced a series of communication and network requirements for UAV networks. These requirements include characteristics such as dynamic networking, quality of wireless communications, flight control and so forth. More specifically, to consider the dynamic networking requirement, in 2010, Li et al. [14] proposed a multi-source cooperative communication system that used small UAVs to relay the source signals to the destination nodes. To adapt UAV network in rapidly changing environments, Li et al. [13] proposed four kinds of communication architectures. To ensure the quality of wireless communications, there are varies achievements. On physical layer, some studies have focused on spectrum management [3] and signal coverage [30] problems for the UAV networks. On network layer, to ensure the wireless link reliable, Rosati et al. [22] proposed an extension of the optimized link-state routing protocol (OLSR) that efficiently computed routing in dynamic conditions. The proposed protocol computes the routing by weighting the expected transmission count (ETX) metric. In 2016, different from upon distributed routing protocol, Lee et al. [12] proposed a centralized routing protocol utilizing ground control system for efficiently network construction. To address the lack of effective joint UAV flight control and management in multi-UAV networks, Vachtsevanos et al. [23] employed game theory to control multiple UAVs and avoid UAV crashes. In 2015, Nodland et al. [19] used a neural network to achieve optimal flight path tracking of a helicopter UAV. Xu et al. [29] proposed an online finite horizon optimal flocking control and optimal co-design for efficient UAV networks.

While UAV networks are becoming increasingly popular and have already been applied in some fields, the increasing security risks cannot be ignored. Without the security mechanisms, a hacker could easily capture users' private or sensitive personal information. In 2016, Nils Rodday performed a live hack by exploiting a professional drone's vulnerabilities to compromises a system and take control of UAV system [21]. The real consequences of such intrusions are harsh. In 2009, a terrorist organization captured an unencrypted UAV video being transmitted from a US drone to a US military satellite using SkyGrabber [1].

The primary security mechanisms for UAV networks focuses on the privacy, confidentiality, integrity of data via cryptography. A well-designed data protection mechanism can guarantee that an attacker can get no useful information regardless of the attack technique used. A few studies have donated to data protection for UAV networks. Kong et al. [11] proposed a new secure communication scheme for an MBN-UAV network that used certificate-based encryption. Benefiting from the use of certificates, the proposed scheme supports UAVs by authenticating the identity of end devices and supports end devices using a negotiated session key and then transmitting messages encrypted with a symmetric key. However, this scheme cannot support broadcasting encrypted messages because the scheme only allows secure end-to-end communication; the involved devices must spend considerable computational resources to establish many individual session keys. Moreover, they also need sufficient storage space to store the certificates and session keys, which is unaffordable to resource-limited end devices. To overcome this disadvantage, Won et al. [25] designed the efficient Certificateless Signcryption Tag Key Encapsulation Mechanism, which is a secure communication protocol for drones and smart objects. However, this protocol still cannot transmit large amounts of encrypted messages to receivers efficiently while preserving the privacy of end devices.

Besides the above specific schemes, there are some other novel cryptographic key management mechanisms. To assign symmetric encryption keys to a set of classes, Arcangelo et al. [8] proposed a novel hierarchical key assignment scheme using a symmetric encryption scheme and a perfect secret sharing scheme. In this scheme, the system master can generate a symmetric key for a set of entities satisfied a complicated access structure. Soon after, to reach the goal of making dynamic updates to the hierarchy, Arcangelo et al. [7] construct a hierarchical key assignment scheme with dynamic updates, in which each user only needs to store a single private key. The above two scheme are symmetric encryption schemes, so in order to reduce stress of symmetric key management, Wu et al. [26] proposed a new cryptographic asymmetric primitive denoted asymmetric group key agreement. Based on this new primitive, Wu *et al.* [28] proposed a new asymmetric group key agreement scheme which overcome the obstacles of the potentially limited communication from the group to the sender with the absence of a fulltime trusted third party and also support dynamic key update. However, the group structure in [28] is a circuit, in order to support hierarchical group structure, Wu *et al.* [27] proposed a contributory broadcast encryption in which the degree of group is unlimited. In this scheme, some group members can generate a corporate public key by coalescing each member's public key to encrypt messages and decrypt ciphertext with his private key without an online trusted third party. Although these novel cryptographic mechanisms are efficient and proven secure, they are always used in the group communication where the computation capability of nodes are equal. However, in UAV networks, the drones can carry a powerful data processing platform and extra energy, which means that the UAV network is not a pure decentralized network. So the traditional key management for distributed network cannot take full advantages of the UAV network.

3   Problem Statement

3.1   System Model

The entire system mainly consists of three types of entities: a Remote management centre (RMC), a set of subnetwork master drones, and groups of end devices. The system architecture is depicted in Fig. 1.

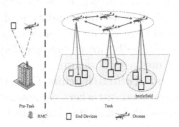

Fig. 1. Network model

- RMC is a trusted third party and its task is to manage drones and end-user devices. Besides it initializes the system parameters, and generate private keys of end devices and drones according to their identity and then extract the broadcast key to drones.
- A drone denoted by $\mathcal{D}$ is a drone equipped with wireless communication modules and high-speed processors. The drone communicates with other drones and the subgroup members via radio. The $\mathcal{D}$ obtains its private key from the RMC and uses it to show its identity legitimacy. After verifying $\mathcal{U}$'s validity, $\mathcal{D}$ generates the broadcast key pair and provides the message transmit service for users.

- A subgroup member device denoted by $\mathcal{U}$ moves within the area covered by the wireless signal of $\mathcal{D}$. $\mathcal{U}$ gets its private key from RMC and uses it to prove its identity to $\mathcal{D}$. After getting the permission to access the network from $\mathcal{D}$, it uses the broadcast key getting from $\mathcal{D}$ to generate a secure channel with other end devices.

3.2   Security Requirements

To guarantee the communication security of UAV network, the security protocol should satisfy the following security requirements:

- *Message Confidentiality.* For wireless networks in complex environments, message confidentiality is an essential security requirement. Without message confidentiality, any adversary may obtain sensitive information by simply intercepting the wireless channel.
- *Mutual Authentication.* In a drone network environment, an attacker may act as other participants and use ingenuous device to control communication. Thus an eligible scheme should provide mutual authentication to verify the participants' identities.
- *Identity Anonymity.* Using a long term identity may lead to privacy leakage. An eligible scheme should provide identity anonymity to ensure that the attacker cannot obtain the user's real identity from eavesdropped or captured messages.
- *Session Key Security.* Once the session key leaks, attackers can easily decrypt transmitted messages, which leads to breaking message confidentiality. So session key security is the foundation of message confidentiality. For further secure communication, an eligible scheme should ensure that the established shared session key between some participants which will be used to encrypt transmitted messages is secure.
- *Message Integrity and Authentication.* Once the secure group communication channel is established, attackers cannot get any useful information from encrypted messages. But attackers can still affect the communication by sending forged messages, truncate encrypted messages. Hence an eligible scheme should ensure message integrity and authentication.
- *Resistance against Denial of Service Attack.* With the above security requirements, attackers cannot get useful information from the protocol, while they can lower the quality of wireless communication or even cut down the communication links among end devices and drones by launching wireless network attack such as DoS attack For the robust of the UAV network, an eligible scheme should resist various popular network attacks.

4   Secure Communications in UAV Networks

Our system can be described with the following three protocols: system setup, register and secure communication among entities in the entire drone network.

During the offline phase, the RMC runs the system setup and then initializes all the system global parameters and generates the system's master key. All the entities in the drone network must first register with the RMC to obtain the necessary information. In detail, the RMC generates a long-term identity and a corresponding private key for each end device and drone in this phase. During the task execute period, if end devices want to access the network, the drones should first authenticate and account for the devices before they provide services. In the registration, we introduces an ID-based signcryption scheme to generate a secure channel between drones and devices in such a subnetwork. To guard against DoS attacks by malicious devices, we use the experience gained using a proven of work mechanism. The third protocol can guarantee secure communications among devices in different subnetworks. Using this protocol, an ordinary device can encrypt messages intended for other subnetwork devices using those devices' pseudonyms, which can be obtained through the subnetwork master drones. For preventing receive devices from obtaining other receives' identity, we proposed a ciphertext transformation method that drones whose members are the real receivers will transform the HIBBE ciphertext to the HIBE ciphertext which will hide the broadcast receivers' identities.

4.1   Computational Assumptions

Our scheme is implemented in bilinear groups widely used in modern cryptosystems. A bilinear group consists of two cycle groups $\mathbb{G}_1, \mathbb{G}_2$, a multiplicative cycle group $\mathbb{G}_T$ where g_1 is the generator of $\mathbb{G}_1$ and g_2 is the generator of $\mathbb{G}_2$. Let q be a large prime number. A map $e : \mathbb{G}_1 \times \mathbb{G}_2 \rightarrow \mathbb{G}_T$ is called a bilinear group if it satisfies the following properties: (1) Bilinear: $e(g_1^a, g_2^b) = e(g_1, g_2)^{(ab)}$ where $g_1 \in \mathbb{G}_1$, $g_2 \in \mathbb{G}_2$ and $a, b \in \mathbb{Z}_p$. (2) Non-degenerate: $e(g_1, g_2) \neq 1$ for all $g_1 \in \mathbb{G}_1, g_2 \in \mathbb{G}_2$. (3) Computable: There is an efficient algorithm to compute this map e.

Our scheme relies on the hardness of two computational problems, which are briefly reviewed below. Let $(\mathbb{G}_1, \mathbb{G}_2, \mathbb{G}_T)$ be a bilinear group where g_1, g_2 are the generators of $\mathbb{G}_1, \mathbb{G}_2$.

q-**Strong Diffie-Hellman problem** (q-SDHP) [6]. For any random chosen $x \in Z_p^*$, given a bilinear group $(\mathbb{G}_1, \mathbb{G}_2, \mathbb{G}_T)$ where g_1, g_2 are the generators of $\mathbb{G}_1, \mathbb{G}_2$, respectively, and a $(q + 2)$ instance: $(g_1, g_2^x, g_2^{x^2}, \ldots, g_2^{x^q}) \in \mathbb{G}_1 \times \mathbb{G}_2^{q+1}$, find a pair $(c, g_2^{\frac{1}{x+c}})$ with $c \in \mathbb{Z}_p^*$.

q-**Bilinear Diffie-Hellman Inversion problem** (q-BDHIP) [5]. For any random chosen $x \in \mathbb{Z}_p$, given a bilinear group $(\mathbb{G}_1, \mathbb{G}_2, \mathbb{G}_T)$ where g_1, g_2 are the generators of $\mathbb{G}_1, \mathbb{G}_2$ and a $(q + 2)$ instance: $(g_1, g_2^x, g_2^{x^2}, \ldots, g_2^{x^q}) \in \mathbb{G}_1 \times \mathbb{G}_2^{q+1}$, computing $e(g_1, g_2)^{1/x} \in \mathbb{G}_T$.

4.2   System Setup

System Initialization. The system first creates an empty list called ML and initializes the entire system as follows.

- Upon input of a security parameter λ, generate a cyclic additive group G and a cyclic multiplicative group $\mathbb{G}_T$ with the same large prime p. Consider g to be the generator of G and g_T to be the generator of $\mathbb{G}_T$. There is a bilinear map $e : G \times G \to \mathbb{G}_T$. Pick two random elements $g_2, u' \in G$
- Generate the RMC's master key $\alpha \in \mathbb{Z}_p^*$ and then compute the value $g^\alpha \in G$
- Select four hash functions: $H_1 : \{0,1\}^* \to \mathbb{Z}_p^*$, $H_2 : \{0,1\}^* \times \{0,1\}^* \to \mathbb{Z}_p^*$, $H_3 : \mathbb{G}_T \to \mathbb{Z}_p^*$, and $H_4 : \mathbb{Z}_p^* \times \mathbb{G}_T \to \mathbb{Z}_p^*$.
- Publish the system parameters: $PP = \{g_2, u', e, p, g, G, g_T, H_1, H_2, H_3, H_4\}$

Pre-mission. We assume that $(n-1)$ pieces of equipment are participating in a mission. The RMC initializes the broadcast system's formalization $BSK_{ID_0} = (\nu_0, \nu_1, \{z_j\}_{j \in [1,n]})$ using its own identity ID_0. Then, it picks a random number $r \in \mathbb{Z}_p^*$ and a random element $u_0 \in G$. For all $j \in [1, n]$ it computes $u_j \xleftarrow{R} G$. Therefore, the initial broadcast is as follows.

$$BSK_{ID_0} = (g^r, g_2^\alpha (u' \cdot \prod_{i \in \phi_{ID}} u_0^{H(ID_0)})^r, \{u_j^r\}_{j \in [1,n]})$$

$$= (\nu_0, \nu_1, \{z_j\}_{j \in [1,n]})$$

Any device in this system should preload the system parameters and register with the RMC. The RMC completes identity registration for any device with ID_u as follows.

1. The RMC first checks whether an entry exists in the ML corresponding to the submitted identity ID_u. If so, the RMC responds to the requesting user with the existing entry; otherwise, it executes the following steps.
2. The RMC Computes the device's private keys $K_{ID_u} = g^{\frac{1}{\alpha + H_1(ID_u)}}$. Next, it sets a validity period T_u for the new identity. Then, it distributes the message $M = (T_u, K_u)$ to device ID_u and adds the message to the ML.

Similarly, any drone with an identity ID_k in this system should preload the system parameters and register with the RMC as follows.

1. The RMC first checks whether an entry exits in the ML corresponding to the requested identity ID_k. If so, the RMC responds with the existing entry; otherwise, it executes the following steps.
2. It computes the drone's private keys $K_{ID_k} = g^{\frac{1}{\alpha + H_1(ID_k)}}$.
3. The RMC delegates the broadcast SK to the drone. First, we assume that the $\mathbf{ID}$ vector in our system is in the form of (ID_0, ID_k, ID_u) and that the whole system has only three levels. Here, ID_0 is the root of the ID vector. Thus, the broadcast key delegates to the i-th drone using the ID vector $\mathbf{ID} = (ID_0, ID_k)$ following the steps described in [16]. First, pick a random exponent $t_k \in \mathbb{Z}_p^*$.

Next, compute BSK_{ID_k} as follows.

$$BSK_{ID_k} = \left(\nu_0 g^{t_k}, \nu_1(z_k^{H_1(ID_k)})(u' u_0^{H_1(ID_0)} u_k^{H_1(ID_k)})^{t_k}, \{z_j u_j^t\}_{j \in [1,n]\setminus\{k\}} \right)$$

$$= \left(a_k, a_{0,k}, \{a_{j,k}\}_{j \in [1,n]\setminus\{k\}} \right)$$

By implicitly setting $r' = r + t_k$, it easy to transform the preceding formula to the following form.

$$BrSK_{ID_k} = \left(g^{r'}, g_2^{\alpha}(u' \cdot \prod_{i \in \phi_{f(ID_k)}} u_i^{ID_i})^{r'}, \{u_j^{r'}\}_{j \in [1,n]\setminus\{k\}} \right)$$

4. Next, the RMC sets a validity period T_k for the new identity. Then, it distributes the message $M = (T_k, K_{D_i}, BSK_{ID_k})$ to drone D_i and adds the message to the ML.

4.3   Registration

The entire phase consists of 4 phases: Req, Res, Dis, and Fin. Assume that a device's identity is ID_u and the subnetwork it belongs to is managed by a drone whose identity is ID_k. The device's ID vector in the broadcast system is (ID_0, ID_k, ID_u).

Req The drone chooses a random number γ in $\mathbb{Z}_p^*$ and computes a $puzzle = H_2(s_0\|\gamma)$ where s_0 is a short bit string. Then, it sets $M_0 = (ID_k, puzzle, \gamma)$ and sends (M_0) to the device.

Res When the end-user device receives the message M_0. It first runs the hash function H_2 several times to find a value s_1 that satisfies the equation $H_2(s_1\|\gamma) = puzzle$. Next, it computes the response message using an ID-based signcryption [4] procedure as follows.

1. Device ID_u picks a random number, $\eta_1, \eta_2, \eta_3 \in \mathbb{Z}_p^*$ and computes $R_1 = g_t^{\eta_3}$, $M_1 = (ID_u\|\eta_2\|s_1\|\gamma + \eta_1)$, $T_1 = M_1 \oplus H_3(R_1)$.
2. It sets $h_2 = H_2(M_1, R_1)$, computes $T_2 = K_{ID_u}^{(\eta_3 + h_2)}$ and then computes $T_3 = (g^{H_1(ID_k)} g^{\alpha})^{\eta_3}$.
3. Finally, the device sends (s_1, T_1, T_2, T_3) to the master drone ID_k.

Ver When the master drone ID_k receives the message, it first checks whether s_1 is the correct answer to the $puzzle$. If so, it extracts the temporarily stored message and checks whether the signature sent by ID_u is available. The drone computes $r_d = e(T_3, K_{ID_k})$, $M_d = T_1 \oplus H_3(r_d)$ and $h_d = H_d(M_d, r_d)$. Then, it encrypts the message and recovers the random value η_2 used to generate end device's pseudonym. Finally, it accepts the message if $r_d = e(T_2, g^{\alpha} g^{H_1(ID_u)}) g_t^{-h_d}$ and records (ID_u, η_2) in its UL, which it will exchange with other drones through a secure broadcast channel.

Dis After the device's identity has been verified, the drone generates a broadcast key pair for its subnetwork device as follows.

1. ID_k updates the device's temporary ID by computing $P_u = (ID_u)^{\eta_2}$. The new ID vector is (ID_0, ID_k, P_u); consequently, the broadcast private key can be calculated in the same way as the RMC delegate broadcast private key for ID_k. The final broadcast key is formed as follows. ID_k chooses a random number $t_u \in \mathbb{Z}_p^*$. Then, it computes

$$a_u = a_k g^{t_u}, a_{0,u} = a_{0,k}(b_u^{H_1(P_u)})(u'u_0^{H_1(ID_0)}u_k^{H_1(ID_k)}u_u^{H_1(P_u)})^{t_u}$$

$$\{a_{j,u}\} = \{b_j u_u^{t_u}\}_{j \in [1,n]\backslash\{u\}}, BSK_{P_u} = (a_u, a_{0,u}, \{a_{j,u}\}_{j \in [1,n]\backslash\{u\}})$$

2. Following the procedure in [4], the drone generates a signcryption ciphertext using the same scheme described in the **rep** phase.
   (a) ID_k picks a random number $\eta_4 \in \mathbb{Z}_p^*$ and computes $R_2 = g_t^{\eta_4}$ and $T_4 = (M) \oplus H_3(R_2)$ where $M_2 = (BSK_{P_u}\|\eta_1 + 1)$.
   (b) It sets $h_2 = H_2(M_2, R_2)$, computes $T_5 = K_{ID_k}^{(\eta_4 + h_2)}$ and then computes $T_6 = (g^{H_1(ID_u)}g^\alpha)^{\eta_4}$.
   (c) Finally. ID_k sends (T_4, T_5, T_6) to device ID_u.

Fin After receiving the ciphertext, ID_u checks if $r_f = e(T_6, K_{ID_u})$ holds. If so, it then computes $M_f = T_4 \oplus H_3(r_f)$ and $h_f = H_2(M_f, r_f)$. After recovering the message, it checks $q_f = \eta_1 + 1$ and $r_f = e(T_5, g^\alpha g^{H_1(ID_k)})g_t^{-h_f}$. If so, the device completes the session and obtains its broadcast key BSK_{P_u}.

4.4 Message Broadcast

In this part we introduce two message broadcast method called basic broadcast and broadcast with ciphertext transformation. In the former method following the method described in [16] some one in our system can encrypt message to any subgroup members in system and any receiver can decrypted the received ciphertext with his own private key and a public receiver set. While sometimes in the hostile environment senders or receivers wants to hide the receiver set. So we propose the second method by utilizing the drones which have dual identity of a subgroup key generator and a router to transform a HIBBE ciphertext to a HIBE ciphertext which the receivers can decrypt the ciphtertext without knowing the receiver set.

Basic Broadcast. When all users have completed the registration phase, they can exchange encrypted messages with each other via a secure broadcast channel. The drones can share management messages through both identity-based encryption and broadcast encryption. All the UL lists with the new pseudonym identities are shared among the drones' networks, which makes it easy for users in different subnetworks to obtain the ID vector of the person or persons they want to communicate with. A secure broadcast communication is established as follows.

- $\mathcal{E}(PP, M, \mathbb{V})$. For a receiver identity vector set $\mathbb{V}$, the encryption algorithm picks a random number ζ and computes the ciphertext as follows.

$$C = (c_0, c_1, c_2) = \left(g^\zeta, (u' \prod_{i \in f(\mathbb{V})} u_i^{H_1(ID_i)})^\zeta, Me(g, g_2)^{\zeta\alpha} \right)$$

- $\mathcal{D}(\mathbb{V}, C_0, BSK_{P_u}) \to M$. For a given ciphertext CT, any device whose ID belongs to the receiver identity vector can use its private key to compute the decryption key as follows.

$$K = a_1 \prod_{j \in f(\mathbb{V} \backslash \mathbb{V}_k)} b_j^{H_1(ID_j)}$$

where the message M is equal to the value of $e(c_1, a_0)/e(K, c_0)$.

Broadcast with Ciphertext Transformation. When a sender wants to hide its broadcast set so that no receiver can get any information from the received ciphertext and guess the other receivers' identities, a ciphertext transformation method can be used. This is a difficult task for most general ad hoc network broadcast system structures, but it is easily achieved by our scheme. The receiver set can easily be preserved among different users as follows.

- $\mathcal{EN}(PP, M, \mathbb{V})$. Unlike the preceding encryption phase, in this phase, the message is encrypted using an identity set consisting of the receiver's and its master drone's identities $\mathbb{V}_D$. The ciphertext is formed as follows.

$$C_0 = (c_{0,0}, c_{1,0}, c_{2,0}) = (g^{\zeta_1}, u' \cdot \prod_{i \in \mathbb{V}_D} u_i^{H_1(ID_i)})^{\zeta_1}, Me(g_1, g_2)^{\zeta_1})$$

- $\mathcal{T}(CT, BSK_{ID_k}, V)$. When any drone receives the message, it checks whether any of its members is in the receiver set. If so, for any of these members U_m, it transforms the ciphertext as follows.

$$X = e((b_m u_m^{t_m})^{H_1(p_u)} / \prod_{i \in f(V_D \backslash \mathbb{V}_k)} (b_i u_i^{t_m})^{H_1(ID_i)}, c_{0,0})$$

where t is the random value used in the registration's distribution phase to generate the BSK for ID_m. Let $c_{0,1} = c_{0,0}$, $c_{1,1} = c_{1,0}$ and $c_{2,1} = X \cdot c_{2,0}$. Finally, the new ciphertext the drone transforms for the ID_m is: $C_1 = (c_{0,1}, c_{1,1}, c_{2,1})$.
- $\mathcal{TD}(CT_1, BSK_{P_m})$. Given a ciphertext, using its BSK_{ID_m}, the receiver ID_m can obtain the message M by computing $M = c_{2,1} e(c_{1,1}, a_0)/e(a_1, c_{0,1})$. The receiver cannot acquire sufficient message content from the ciphertext to guess the identities of the other receivers.

5   Security Analysis

In this section, we analyse the security of the proposed protocol and show that it satisfies the security requirements defined in Sect. 3.2.

5.1   Security Model

We define the model using the following game strategy. This game is played between a challenger C and an adversary A who has full control over all network communications. This means that the adversary has the ability to eavesdrop on or even modify communicated messages. Each user can run the protocol several times with different drones; consequently, we model this using the concept of instances. We denote instance i for member U as Π_U^i. During the *Setup* process, C runs a setup in which the security parameter λ acts as the *RMC*. The setup outputs the system parameter pp and then sends pp to A. During the *Query* phase, according to the protocol registration process, C provides a sequence of oracles to A, giving A the necessary information to attack the protocol. The query oracles work as follows.

- Q_1: This query will help A obtain the transmitted messages generated in the **Res** or **Dis** phases.
- Q_2: This query will help A obtain detailed messages generated in **Ver** phase (this situation is possible because in the real world, a drone may be captured and used as a decryption oracle to help the adversary win the games.)
- Q_{H_i}: This query will return the result of hash function H_i to A.
- $Corrupt(ID_i)$: A can execute the this query to obtain the long-term key pair of some identity ID_i (other than the target identity).
- $Reveal(\Pi_U^i)$: A can execute the this query to obtain the session key invoked in π_U^i.
- $Test()$: A can execute the $Test()$ query only once. A chooses two messages, m_0 and m_1, using an identity which it has never performed the Corrupt query before and using the same D identity. The C chooses a random bit b and executes the protocol with $\pi_{u_b}^b$.

Finally, A guesses bit $b' \in \{0,1\}$. If $b = b'$, A wins in the game. The advantage for A in breaking session key secure (SKS) of registration Σ with system parameters λ is defined by

$$Adv_{A,\Sigma}^{SKS}(1^\lambda) = |2Pr[b = b'] - 1|$$

Definition 1. *(SKS) The registration is session key secure, if for any polynomial time adversary A, we have the $Adv_{A,\Sigma}^{SKS}(1^\lambda)$ is negligible.*

We say that A can break the mutual authentication (MA) secure of registration Σ, if he can generate a legal **res** message denoted as E_{Res} or **Dis** message denoted as E_{Dis}. The advantage for A to break mutual authentication(MA) secure of registration Σ with system parameters λ is defined as follows.

$$Adv_{A,\Sigma}^{MA}(1^\lambda) = Pr[E_{Res}] + Pr[E_{Dis}]$$

Definition 2. *(MA-secure) The registration is sMA-secure, if for any polynomial time adversary $\mathcal{A}$, the $Adv_{\mathcal{A},\Sigma}^{MA}(1^\lambda)$ is negligible.*

5.2 Provable Security

Lemma 1. *Suppose that the underlying signcryption used in the registration is (ϵ', t)-secure against existentially unforgeable signature against adaptive chosen messages attack. The registration is (ϵ, t)-MA-secure provided that $\epsilon = 2\epsilon$.*

Proof. It's easy to find that the Res and Dis messages are also standard ID-based signcryption [4] ciphertext. If $\mathcal{A}$ can forge a legal signature message with probability ϵ', according to the Definition 2, we can come to a conclusion easily that $\mathcal{A}$ can break the MA-secure of registration with probability $\epsilon = 2\epsilon'$.   □

Theorem 1. *Assume that there exists an $\mathcal{A}$ that makes q_{h_i} queries for Q_{H_i}, q_1 queries for Q_1 and q_2 queries for Q_2, $\mathcal{A}$ can break MA-secure of the registration with probability $\epsilon \leq 10(q_1 + 1)(q_1 + q_{h_2})/2^\lambda$. Then, there exists an algorithm $\mathcal{B}$ to solve the q-SDHP [4] with probability ϵ*

Proof. Based on the Theorem 3 given in [4] and Lemma 1 above, no polynomial adversary can forge a legal Req message or a legal Dis message if the q-SDHP is hard. Therefore, it concludes that the proposed registration is MA-secure.   □

Theorem 2. *Assume that there exists an $\mathcal{A}$ that make q_{h_i} queries for Q_{H_i}, q_1 queries for Q_1 and q_2 queries for Q_2, $\mathcal{A}$ can break session key secure of registration with probability $\frac{1}{q_{h_1}}(1 - (q_1\frac{q_1+q_{h_2}}{2^k})(1 - \frac{q_2}{2^\lambda}))$. Then, there exists an algorithm $\mathcal{B}$ to solve the q-BDHIP [4] with probability ϵ.*

Proof. The detailed proof is given in Appendix A.   □

Our scheme also obtains confidentiality and partial identity anonymity. From the broadcast protocol, all the transmitted messages are encrypted by the user's broadcast key. According to the Theorem 2, a polynomial time attacker can get no advantage to distinguish a real broadcast key from a random number, so we can say that broadcast key encrypted by drones with end device identity is secure. In [16], the encryption we employed has been proven secure against chosen-plaintext attacks (CPA). Hence, our scheme can satisfy the message confidentiality.

Partial identity anonymity guarantees that when an end device finishes register to one drone, it cannot be recognized, even if an attacker can take over all communication flows. According to the specification of our scheme, the end device real identity ID_u, only appear in res messages, $T_1 = (ID_u\|\eta_2\|s_1\|\gamma + \eta_1) \bigoplus H_3(R_1)$. To recover the real identity, the adversary should compute $R_1 = e(g^{\alpha+H_1(ID_k)}, g^{\frac{1}{\alpha+H_1(ID_k)}})$ which means that without knowing the user's private key, the adversary should solve the q-BDHI problem. The confidentiality provided by signcryption [4] guarantees that the end device real identity can be hidden by upon pseudonym mechanism. But the pseudonym mechanism is associated to the corresponding end devices, so it cannot obtain full identity anonymity. Hence, we claim that our scheme can satisfy partial identity anonymity.

Our scheme can be resistant of network attacks. During the registration, we introduce a prove of work mechanism by computing a target hash value. This mechanism is similar to the proof-of-work mechanism that involves scanning for a value that the hash begins with small integers. The average required computation grows exponentially with the bit length of the puzzle. Different from the hardness of scan the answer of the puzzle, verification only execute a value comparison operator. So the drone can control the access request by adjusting the bit length of the puzzle and fast reject the venomous request with an false answer. When a drone is under a DoS attack, it will decrease the concurrent access request by enhancing the length of hash value. Hence, we claim that our scheme can be resistant to network attack.

One may also be interested in message integrity and message authentication. Although our proposed protocol is not cover these requirements, there are general solutions that mostly hash functions such as SHA-256, can easily obtain message integrity and mostly signatures such as DSA, can guarantee message authentication to reach these requirements. We do not describe these methods to our scheme due to space limited.

6   Performance Analysis

In this section, we further evaluate the efficiency and applicability of our protocol with broadcast encryption in a real-world environment by using the Network Simulator-3 (NS3) simulator to show the relationship between performance, the traffic conditions, and the number of broadcasts.

We analyse the simulation results to evaluate the efficiency and applicability of the proposed broadcast scheme. We use NS3 to perform this simulation. The area of this simulation is approximate $500 \times 500\,\mathrm{m}^2$. Five Ds are uniformly distributed in the simulation area. In this section, we assume that the Ds have a static elevation of 5 m and can move horizontally within a small range. The users are uniformly divided into 5 subgroups that initially are randomly positioned within 2 m around their corresponding D. The motion model applied is the random2Dwalkmodel with a constant speed of 2 m/s. The wireless protocol between users and Ds is IEEE 802.11a and the channel bandwidth is set to 6 Mb/s. In addition, the packet size ranges from 64 Byte to 512 Bytes. We use multicast to deliver messages for normal broadcast schemes and unicast to simulate the re-encryption scheme. All the simulation times are set to 100 s. The time interval between two broadcast messages from one user is 5 s.

We use two performance measure indexes to assess the simulation performances: the average message loss rate L_m and the average message delay D_m. The average message delay is the average time latency for a message to be received by all users in the broadcast sets after it is generated. The average time delay is defined as follows.

$$D_m = \frac{1}{L_{\mathcal{D}}} \Sigma_{L \in \mathcal{D}} (\frac{1}{M_{l_\rightarrow}} \Sigma_{m=1}^{M_{l_\rightarrow}} \frac{1}{S_l} (T_{Enc}^{lm} + \Sigma_{k=1}^{S_l} T_{trans}^{lmk}))$$

where $\mathcal{D}$ denotes the simple area in this simulation, $L_{\mathcal{D}}$ denotes the l-th user in this area, $M_{l_\rightarrow}$ is the number of broadcast messages generated by the l-th user, S_l is the size of the broadcast set, T_{Enc}^{lm} is the time when the l-th user encrypted the m-th message, and $T_t^{lmk} rans$ is the transmission time at which message m was delivered from the l-th user to the k-th user in the broadcast set.

The average message loss rate is the probability that a message cannot be received or processed, and it is defined as follows.

$$L_m = 1 - \frac{1}{L_{\mathcal{D}}} \Sigma_{l=1}^{L_{\mathcal{D}}} \frac{M_{consumed}^l * S_l}{\Sigma_{s=1}^{S_l} M_{arrived}^s}$$

where $M_{consumed}^l$ represents the number of packets consumed by the l-th user and $M_{arrived}^s$ denotes the number of packets received by the s-th user (Fig. 2).

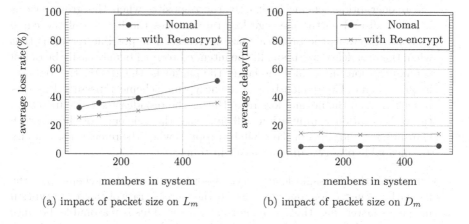

(a) impact of packet size on L_m (b) impact of packet size on D_m

Fig. 2. Performance of broadcast 1

(1) The impact of packet size. In the first simulation set, to analyze the impact of different packet sizes from 64 Bytes to 512 Bytes we fixed the number of the broadcast set to 25 and the user speed to 2 m/s. Figure 3 shows that packet size has only a small impact on both the basic broadcast method and the ciphertext transformation mechanism. In other words, the message loss rate is not influenced by the size of packets. However, the average time delay increases.

(2) The impact of the number of group members. As Fig. 3a shows, given a fixed packet size, the average message delay increases as the broadcast group size increases. In addition, the message loss rate of the normal broadcast scheme increases as the broadcast size increases, and it tends to be Small fluctuations when the group size grows. However, the message loss rate for

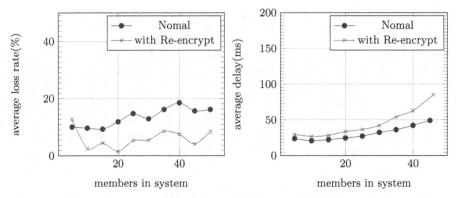

(a) impact of broadcast group size on L_m;   (b) impact of broadcast group size on D_m

Fig. 3. Performance of broadcast 2

the re-encryption scheme is exactly the opposite; when the group size is between 40 and 45 the message loss rate reaches the bottom of the curve and then grows as the broadcast size increases. The possible reason is that when the broadcast size is small, the intended recipients may easily be out of communication range, and the larger the packet is, the greater the loss rate in this scheme. Consequently, the re-encryption scheme's message loss rate is smaller than the normal loss rate. But as the broadcast set size increases, the re-encryption computation will influence the efficiency of the network transmission and some packets will be dropped when the re-encryption nodes are incapable of forwarding a packet in time.

Comparing the message delay curves between the regular scheme and the scheme with re-encryption, one can see that the increase rate of the re-encryption scheme grows faster than that of the normal scheme. This is reasonable, because although the packet size of the normal scheme is larger than that of the re-encryption scheme for the same message, the re-encryption computation requires considerably more time to transform larger packets. However because using the re-encryption can hide the identities of the members of the broadcast set, it is beneficial for protecting user privacy.

7   Conclusion

In this paper, we proposed a secure communication system to balance security and performance in a UAV network. We achieve security goals by combining identity-based signcryption and hierarchical identity-based broadcast encryption. We posed the problem of finding a hash value's preimage as a restriction in our registration phase to control access device number. By adopting the hierarchical cryptosystem, a device in our protocol uses its broadcast key and its public pseudonym identity to send and receive encoded broadcast messages to others.

Combined with the common security group communication scheme, there is no need to store each group's encryption keys which is an practical benefit because of the limited storage space in typical environments. The simulation demonstrates that our scheme can adapt to a variety of different traffic conditions.

Acknowledgment. Qianhong Wu is the corresponding author. This paper is supported by the National High Technology Research and Development Program of China (863 Program) through project 2015AA017205, the Natural Science Foundation of China through projects 61772538, 61672083 and 61370190, and by the National Cryptography Development Fund through project MMJJ20170106.

A   Proof of Theorem 2

In each result, we assume that $\mathcal{A}$ makes q_{h_i} queries to the hash function H_i for $i \in \{0,1\}$. The numbers of queries for Q_1 and Q_2 are denoted by q_1 and q_2, respectively.

Proof. The $\mathcal{C}$ first obtains a q-BDHIP problem instance, $(g, g^\alpha, g^{\alpha^2}, \ldots, g^{\alpha^{q-1}})$, to generate some pairs $(c_i, g^{\frac{1}{c_i+\alpha}})$ to use as key pairs. Then, $\mathcal{C}$ proceeds as follows.

1. $\mathcal{C}$ first randomly picks $w_1, w_2, \ldots, w_{q-1} \in \mathbb{Z}_p^*$ and expands $f(z) = \prod_{i=1}^{q-1}(z + w_i)$ to $f(z) = \Sigma_{i=0}^{q-1} a_i w^i$, where a_i is the coefficient of expansion. Then, $\mathcal{C}$ randomly chooses an $\ell \in \{1, \ldots, q_{h1}\}$ and let $I_i = I_\ell - w_i$.
2. $\mathcal{C}$ sets $\tilde{g} = g^{\prod_{i=0}^{q-1} c_i \alpha^i} = g^{f(\alpha)} \in G$ and generates the value $\tilde{g}^\alpha = g^{\prod_{i=1}^{q} c_i \alpha^i}$.
3. For any $1 \leq i \leq q-1$, $\mathcal{C}$ defines $f_i(z) = f(z)/(z + w_i)$; therefore,

$$\tilde{g}^{\frac{1}{w_i+\alpha}} = g^{f(\alpha)\frac{1}{w_i+\alpha}} = g^{f_i(\alpha)}$$

And the key pair can be computed as $(w_i, \tilde{g}^{\frac{1}{\alpha+w_i}})$ where $i \in \{0, 1, \ldots, q_{h_1}\ell\}$ in the initial phase. The system public key can be computed as $\tilde{g}^{-\alpha-I_\ell}$. Set $x = -\alpha - I_\ell$ which is also a secret value for $\mathcal{C}$. For $i \in [0, q] \setminus \ell$, we have $(I_i, \tilde{g}^{\frac{-1}{w_i+\alpha}}) = (I_i, \tilde{g}^{\frac{1}{I_i+x}})$.

Then, $\mathcal{C}$ prepares for $\mathcal{A}$'s queries. For simplicity, we assume that the queries for hash functions are distinct and that any queries involving an ID have been made to the H_1 in advance. The $\mathcal{C}$ simulates the hash function H_1, H_2, H_3 as follows.

- H_1 query: $\mathcal{C}$ maintains a list L_1 for this random oracle. For the ι-th query of any user or drone(we denote this identity as ID_ι), $\mathcal{C}$ responds with I_ι and records (ID, I_ι, ι) as the ι-th entity in L_1.
- H_2 query: $\mathcal{C}$ maintains a list L_2 for this random oracle. For an input (M, r), CH chooses a random number h_2. For subsequent queries, $\mathcal{C}$ runs the random oracle H_3 to obtain $H_3(r) = h_3$ and stores $(M, r, c = M \oplus H_3, h_2, \gamma = re(g,g)^{h_2})$ as an entity in L_2.

- H_3 query: The C maintains a list L_3 for this random oracle. For an input $r \in \mathbb{G}_T$, C chooses a random number h_3 and responds. C then stores (h_3, r) in L_3.

The Corrupt query for identities is simulated as follows. For a user's identity, C first checks whether the input ID_ι satisfies the condition that ι is equal ℓ. If so, it aborts; otherwise, it outputs $I_\iota = H_1(ID_\iota)$ and $\tilde{g}^{\frac{1}{T_\iota + x}}$, as the user ID's long-term key pair. For a D's identity, C checks whether the input ID_ι is equal to ℓ. If so, it aborts; otherwise, it outputs $I_\iota = H_1(ID_\iota)$ and $\tilde{g}^{\frac{1}{T_\iota + x}}$ as the D's long-term key pair.

For Q_1 query, the identity is defined as (ID_u), respectively, for any $u \in [1, q_{h_1}]$. If $u \neq \ell$, C can generate the sign-encrypted messages according to the protocol specification because C knows ID_u's private key. When $u = \ell$, C knows the ID_ι's private key $\tilde{g}^{\frac{1}{T_\iota + x}}$. C first picks two random numbers $t, h \in \mathbb{Z}_p^*$ and computes $S = g^{t \frac{1}{T_\iota + x}}$, $T = g^{t\alpha - h(I_\iota - \alpha - I_\ell)}$.

It is easy to verify the equality

$$e(T, \tilde{g}^{\frac{1}{T_i + x}}) = e(S, \tilde{g}^\alpha)e(g, \tilde{g})^{-h}$$

We should note that, in this step, the value $r = e(T, \tilde{g}^{\frac{1}{T_i + x}})$ is different in the hash function H_2; consequently, C will fail if this message has been queried to H_2 previously. The ciphertext C is defined as $(M \oplus h_3(r), S, T)$.

We describe how to simulate the Q_2 query as follows. We assume that the ciphertext is (c, S, T) and the identities is (ID_u, ID_ι). If $\iota \neq ell$, then C can decrypt the messages because it knows ID_D's private key. Then, C can generate the response by following the response phase procedure. If $\iota = \ell$, because $u \neq \ell$, C has the user's private key and, for all valid ciphertext, $h = H_2(M, r)$ and ID_D's public key is $\tilde{g}^\alpha$. Therefore, the following equation holds:

$$e(T, \tilde{g}^{\frac{1}{T_u + x}}) = e(S, \tilde{g}^\alpha)e(g^{I_u - \alpha - I_\ell}, \tilde{g}^{\frac{1}{T_u + x}})^{-h}$$

C next computes the value $\gamma = e(S, \tilde{g}^{\frac{1}{T_u + x}})$ and then searches the L_2 to find the entities $(M_i, r_i, h_{2,i}, c_i, \gamma)$ where $i \in [1, \ldots, q_{h_2}]$. If no entity is found, C rejects this ciphertext. Then, for any entity satisfying this condition, C checks whether the entity satisfies the following equation:

$$e(T, \tilde{g}^{\frac{1}{T_u + x}}) = e(S, \tilde{g}^\alpha)e(g^{I_u - \alpha - I_\ell}, \tilde{g}^{\frac{1}{T_u + x}})^{-h_{2,i}}.$$

If any unique i is found, then it outputs $(M_i, h_{2,i})$ and generates a response based on the decrypted message $(M_i, h_{2,i})$. We should note that the Reveal query can be responded to with the value $(M_i, h_{2,i})$.

To run a $Reveal(\pi_U^i)$ query, C returns the session key to A invoked in π_U^i.

To run a Test query for some instances $\pi_{U_i}^i$ with a D identity of ID_D, if $ID_D \neq ID_\ell$, C aborts. Otherwise, C pick a random $\zeta \in \mathbb{Z}_p^*$, $c \in 0, 1^n$, $S \in G$, $T = g^{-\zeta}$ and returns the ciphertext (c, S, T). Because $\zeta = \rho\alpha$, it is easy to see that $T = g^{-\alpha\rho} = g^{(I_\ell + x)\rho}$. Consequently, the r corresponding to this T satisfies

$r = e(g, \tilde{g})^{\rho}$. The $\mathcal{A}$ cannot distinguish whether this ciphertext is valid unless he can query H_2 or H_3 with the value r. Therefore, if $\mathcal{A}$ can win in the game with a non-negligible probability, he has queried this value (probably from H_2 or H_3). Therefore, $\mathcal{C}$ can guess the right r in H_2 or H_3 with probability $1/(q_{h_2} + q_{h_3})$ and solve the q-BDHIP by computing $e(g,g)^{\frac{1}{\alpha}} = (r^{\frac{1}{\zeta}}/(\prod_{i=1}^{q-1} e(g, g^{\alpha^{i-1}})^{c_i}))^{\frac{1}{c_0}} = (e(g,g)^{\frac{f(\alpha)}{\alpha}}/e(g, g^{\prod_{i=1}^{q-1} c_i \alpha^{i-1}}))^{\frac{1}{c_0}}$.

In conclusion, we note that the simulation will fail under the following conditions. Event1: The $\mathcal{D}$'s identity for the Test query is not ID_ℓ, with probability $1 - 1/q_{h_1}$. Event2: The $\mathcal{C}$ aborts because an H_2 collision occurs in a Q_1 query; this probability is $q_1 \frac{q_1 + q_{h_2}}{2^k}$. Event3: The $\mathcal{C}$ rejects a valid ciphertext because it cannot simulate the corresponding private key; the probability is $\frac{q_2}{2^\lambda}$. Consequently, the overall probability that $\mathcal{A}$'s advantage will win the game is

$$Pr[\neg\text{Event1} : |\neg\text{Event2} : |\neg\text{Event3} :] = \frac{1}{q_{h_1}}(1 - (q_1 \frac{q_1 + q_{h_2}}{2^k})(1 - \frac{q_2}{2^\lambda}))$$ □

References

1. Arthur, C.: SkyGrabber: the \$26 software used by insurgents to hack into US drones (2009). https://www.theguardian.com/technology/2009/dec/17/skygrabber-software-drones-hacked

2. Asadpour, M., Giustiniano, D., Hummel, K.A., Egli, S.: UAV networks in rescue missions. In: Proceedings of the 8th ACM International Workshop on Wireless Network Testbeds, Experimental Evaluation and Characterization, pp. 91–92. ACM (2013)

3. Athukoralage, D., Guvenc, I., Saad, W., Bennis, M.: Regret based learning for UAV assisted LTE-U/WiFi public safety networks. In: GLOBECOM 2016, pp. 1–7. IEEE (2016)

4. Barreto, P.S.L.M., Libert, B., McCullagh, N., Quisquater, J.-J.: Efficient and provably-secure identity-based signatures and signcryption from bilinear maps. In: Roy, B. (ed.) ASIACRYPT 2005. LNCS, vol. 3788, pp. 515–532. Springer, Heidelberg (2005). https://doi.org/10.1007/11593447_28

5. Boneh, D., Boyen, X.: Efficient selective-ID secure identity-based encryption without random oracles. In: Cachin, C., Camenisch, J.L. (eds.) EUROCRYPT 2004. LNCS, vol. 3027, pp. 223–238. Springer, Heidelberg (2004). https://doi.org/10.1007/978-3-540-24676-3_14

6. Boneh, D., Boyen, X.: Short signatures without random oracles. In: Cachin, C., Camenisch, J.L. (eds.) EUROCRYPT 2004. LNCS, vol. 3027, pp. 56–73. Springer, Heidelberg (2004). https://doi.org/10.1007/978-3-540-24676-3_4

7. Castiglione, A., De Santis, A., Masucci, B., Palmieri, F., Castiglione, A., Huang, X.: Cryptographic hierarchical access control for dynamic structures. IEEE Trans. Inf. Forensics Secur. **11**(10), 2349–2364 (2016)

8. Castiglione, A., De Santis, A., Masucci, B., Palmieri, F., Castiglione, A., Li, J., Huang, X.: Hierarchical and shared access control. IEEE Trans. Inf. Forensics Secur. **11**(4), 850–865 (2016)

9. Erdelj, M., Natalizio, E., Chowdhury, K.R., Akyildiz, I.F.: Help from the sky: leveraging UAVs for disaster management. IEEE Pervasive Comput. **16**(1), 24–32 (2017)

10. Gupta, L., Jain, R., Vaszkun, G.: Survey of important issues in UAV communication networks. IEEE Commun. Surv. Tutor. **18**(2), 1123–1152 (2016)
11. Kong, J., Luo, H., Xu, K., Gu, D.L., Gerla, M., Lu, S.: Adaptive security for multilevel ad hoc networks. Wirel. Commun. Mob. Comput. **2**(5), 533–547 (2002)
12. Lee, J., Kim, K., Yoo, S., Chung, A.Y., Lee, J.Y., Park, S.J., Kim, H.: Constructing a reliable and fast recoverable network for drones. In: ICC 2016, pp. 1–6. IEEE (2016)
13. Li, J., Zhou, Y., Lamont, L.: Communication architectures and protocols for networking unmanned aerial vehicles. In: GC Wkshps 2013, pp. 1415–1420. IEEE (2013)
14. Li, X., Zhang, Y.D.: Multi-source cooperative communications using multiple small relay UAVs. In: GC Wkshps, 2010, pp. 1805–1810. IEEE (2010)
15. Lim, G.J., Kim, S., Cho, J., Gong, Y., Khodaei, A.: Multi-UAV pre-positioning and routing for power network damage assessment. IEEE Trans. Smart Grid (2016)
16. Liu, W., Liu, J., Wu, Q., Qin, B., Li, Y.: Practical chosen-ciphertext secure hierarchical identity-based broadcast encryption. Int. J. Inf. Secur. **15**, 35–50 (2016)
17. Mark, Z.: The technology behind Aquila (2016). https://www.facebook.com/notes/mark-zuckerberg/the-technology-behind-aquila/10153916136506634
18. Merwaday, A., Guvenc, I.: UAV assisted heterogeneous networks for public safety communications. In: WCNCW 2015, pp. 329–334. IEEE (2015)
19. Nodland, D., Zargarzadeh, H., Jagannathan, S.: Neural network-based optimal adaptive output feedback control of a helicopter UAV. IEEE Trans. Neural Netw. Learn. Syst **24**(7), 1061–1073 (2013)
20. Polo, J., Hornero, G., Duijneveld, C., García, A., Casas, O.: Design of a low-cost wireless sensor network with UAV mobile node for agricultural applications. Comput. Electron. Agric. **119**, 19–32 (2015)
21. Rodday, N.: Hacking a professional drone (2016). https://www.rsaconference.com/events/us16/agenda/sessions/2273/hacking-a-professional-drone
22. Rosati, S., Krużelecki, K., Heitz, G., Floreano, D., Rimoldi, B.: Dynamic routing for flying ad hoc networks. IEEE Trans. Veh. Technol. **65**(3), 1690–1700 (2016)
23. Vachtsevanos, G., Tang, L., Reimann, J.: An intelligent approach to coordinated control of multiple unmanned aerial vehicles. In: Proceedings of the American Helicopter Society 60th Annual Forum, Baltimore, MD (2004)
24. Vanian, J.: Qualcomm and AT&T are joining forces on a new drone project (2016). http://fortune.com/2016/09/06/qualcomm-att-drone-tests/
25. Won, J., Seo, S.H., Bertino, E.: A secure communication protocol for drones and smart objects. In: ASIA CCS 2015, pp. 249–260. ACM (2015)
26. Wu, Q., Mu, Y., Susilo, W., Qin, B., Domingo-Ferrer, J.: Asymmetric group key agreement. In: Joux, A. (ed.) EUROCRYPT 2009. LNCS, vol. 5479, pp. 153–170. Springer, Heidelberg (2009). https://doi.org/10.1007/978-3-642-01001-9_9
27. Wu, Q., Qin, B., Zhang, L., Domingo-Ferrer, J., Farràs, O., Manjon, J.A.: Contributory broadcast encryption with efficient encryption and short ciphertexts. IEEE Trans. Comput. **65**(2), 466–479 (2016)
28. Wu, Q., Qin, B., Zhang, L., Domingo-Ferrer, J., Manjón, J.A.: Fast transmission to remote cooperative groups: a new key management paradigm. IEEE/ACM Trans. Netw. **21**(2), 621–633 (2013)
29. Xu, H., Carrillo, L.: Fast reinforcement learning based distributed optimal flocking control and network co-design for uncertain networked multi-UAV system. In: SPIE Defense Security, p. 1019511. International Society for Optics and Photonics (2017)
30. Yanmaz, E.: Connectivity versus area coverage in unmanned aerial vehicle networks. In: ICC 2012, pp. 719–723. IEEE (2012)

On the Security of In-Vehicle Hybrid Network: Status and Challenges

Tianxiang Huang[1(✉)], Jianying Zhou[2(✉)], Yi Wang[3],
and Anyu Cheng[1]

[1] Chongqing University of Posts and Telecommunications, Chongqing, China
petterhuang92@gmail.com
[2] Singapore University of Technology and Design, Singapore, Singapore
jianying_zhou@sutd.edu.sg
[3] Continental Automotive, Singapore, Singapore
estelle.wang@Continental-Corporation.com

Abstract. In-Vehicle Network (IVN) is composed of many communication nodes and Electronic Control Units (ECUs). The complex and interactive hybrid IVN expose more vulnerabilities of the system as it connects to the external network environment and opens up more attacking surface. In this paper, we first show a complete structure of the in-vehicle hybrid network. Then, we propose a three-layer network structure model, analyze the security threats of each layer, and compare the state-of-the-art countermeasures in detail. Finally, we identify the challenges and future research directions for the security of the in-vehicle hybrid network.

Keywords: Automobiles · In-Vehicle Network Security
Cyber security · IDS

1 Introduction

Controller Area Network (CAN) has become the main control bus in a vehicle, which simplifies the in-vehicle communication network with the efficient and fault-tolerant mechanism. CAN bus keeps evolving, as more functions and services are added by vehicle manufacturers. In modern vehicles, there are up to 70 electronic control units (ECUs) in each car. Meanwhile, the network topology becomes more complex supporting different types of communication buses.

These feature-rich networks are designed to provide users with a more comfortable driving experience. On the other hand, it also exposes more attack surfaces to access the CAN network which may cause serious safety issues to the targeted vehicle. As the CAN network provides most of the vehicle control, Koscher et al. utilized CAN bus vulnerabilities to demonstrate serious threats even when the car moves at high speed [1]. In a modern vehicle, IVN (In-Vehicle Network) gateway connects different buses and ECUs and supports more remote services to access the in-vehicle network. Potentially, the structure of a hybrid network also provides multiple intrusion paths for attackers. Once an ECU is hacked remotely, it can be exploited to attack other nodes in the network. Miller et al. used the Jeep Cherokee WIFI open port to invade the Uconnect system and reprogram firmware of ECU, then control the critical functions through the CAN network intrusion [23], which resulted in a recall of 1.4 million cars.

© Springer International Publishing AG 2017
J. K. Liu and P. Samarati (Eds.): ISPEC 2017, LNCS 10701, pp. 621–637, 2017.
https://doi.org/10.1007/978-3-319-72359-4_38

There are intensive researches on the security of the in-vehicle network, The EVITA (E-Safety Vehicle Intrusion Protected Applications) project [4] focused on solving hardware security issue. The AUTOSAR (AUTOmotive Open System Architecture) architecture proposed Secure On-Board Communication to regulate the secure transmission between the ECUs [5] which has been used by many vehicle manufacturers. Some security companies had also proposed a security module that can be integrated into the gateway directly for intrusion detection [6].

In this paper, we take a systematic approach to illustrate the state-of-the-art vulnerabilities in the in-vehicle hybrid network. This will become a basic for the future work in this domain. In addition, we also analyze and compare existing countermeasures in the in-vehicle network. Through this study, it helps us to identify the open security challenges as future research directions.

The rest of this paper is organized as follows: Sect. 2 introduces the in-vehicle hybrid network topology and hierarchical structure. Section 3 analyses vulnerabilities in different network layers. Section 4 investigates the state-of-the-art countermeasures in different layers. Section 5 discusses the future research directions on the security of the in-vehicle hybrid network, and Sect. 6 concludes the paper.

2   In-Vehicle Hybrid Network

In a modern vehicle, there are several kinds of vehicle communication buses, e.g. CAN, LIN (Local Interconnect Network), CAN-FD (CAN with Flexible Data Rate), FlexRay, Ethernet, MOST (Media Oriented System Transport) and so on. These buses are used in different control fields of an automobile according to their communication speed and transmission mode. Figure 1 shows a typical onboard hybrid network architecture.

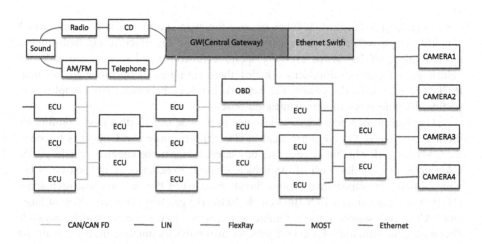

Fig. 1. In-vehicle hybrid network topology

The network in the vehicle can be divided into several domains according to the bus feature.

Powertrain Domain

The vehicle's powertrain domain mainly contains the engine control and chassis control components, such as ECM (Engine Control Module), ABS (Anti-skid Brake System), EPS (electric steering system) and so on. To ensure the real-time communication rate, it usually has high bandwidth and stable communication capabilities. It is mainly composed of the high-speed CAN (up to 1 Mbps), CAN-FD (up to 5 Mbps), FlexRay bus (up to 10 Mbps). CAN bus in the powertrain domain is also known as CAN C (critical). Instead, manufacturers are turning to use a higher communication rate and larger data load (64 bytes) bus CAN-FD. Figure 2 is the data frame structure comparison between classical CAN and CAN-FD bus.

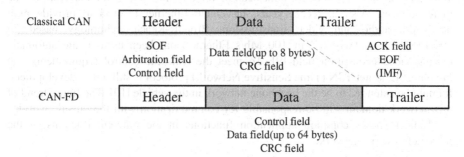

Fig. 2. CAN and CAN-FD data construct

FlexRay is a high-speed, critical, fault tolerance bus. Its cycle time traffic includes the static segment (periodic messages) and the dynamic segment (event message) which ensures the critical real-time communication performance. Many premium class vehicles are equipped with this bus.

Body Domain

The body domain is mainly composed of components that do not have high requirement for data rate and real-time capability. It is used for non-critical component control and information services in the non-powertrain domain, with low-speed CAN bus or LIN bus to achieve the corresponding function control. The speed of CAN network in this domain ranges from 125 kbps to 250 kbps. The components mounted on this bus usually have headlamp, electric windows and doors, seats and HVAC (Heating, Ventilating, and Air Conditioning). Some ECUs with a wireless function connect to this bus too, such as PKE (Passive Keyless Enter), PATS (Passive Anti-Theft System) and so on. The LIN bus is usually combined with the CAN bus to control the electric windows or seat and other components. LIN bus connects multiple devices through a single line. For example, when the keyless entry ECU receives the unlock command, it sends the CAN message to the BCM (body controller). Then the BCM controls the door operation via the LIN bus.

High-Speed Information Service Domain

The domain of high-speed information service refers to the communication that has a large stream of data transmission capability but does not have control function. It is generally used for the transmission of the service information of corresponding features or the collection and output of audio and video information. With the increase of infotainment system communication equipment, the form of communication is becoming more and more complicated. For example, the MOST bus with the highest bandwidth up to 150 Mbps is connected through a ring transmission mode. Video device, camera, radio equipment, handheld telephone and even GPS navigation can be linked up by this bus [7]. Now the MOST bus integrates more intelligent communication functions, INIC (Intelligent Network Interface bandwidth Controller) is developed by Microchip, which is based on the MOST using 150 Mbps. It integrates the MOST Ethernet Packets (MEPs) based on the Ethernet protocol and USB protocol [8]. With this function, the network nodes can be directly mount over the bus and provide more services. Also in recent years, in-vehicle Ethernet is used to provide high bandwidth audio and video transmission. BroadR-Reach technology based on 100BASE-T1 (1 Twisted Pair 100 Mb/s Ethernet) has been used in the automatic driving video acquisition field [9]. To meet the real-time control requirements, the in-vehicle Ethernet TSN (Time Sensitive Network) protocol is still under development. It might be extended to be the backbone network in the vehicle [10]. The future trend of this network domain will be responsible for communication with the outside world.

Table 1 shows common application functions in the different domains of the in-vehicle hybrid network.

Table 1. Common application functions in the different domains.

Domain	Powertrain domain	Body domain	High speed information service domain
Bus type	CAN/CAN-FD/ Flex Ray	CAN/LIN	MOST/Ethernet
Data rate	1 Mbps–10 Mbps	20 kbps–250 kbps	$\geq$ 100 Mbps
Application	Engine Driving assistants Steer-by-Wire ABS ...	Door locking Power windows Headlamp ...	Infotainment services Surround view system Audio ...

Communications among these different domains are through a central gateway. In the early stage, the structure of vehicle network was not complex, the vehicle gateway was used for CAN bus packet routing of different rate bus. In the more complex network structure, the function of the gateway is not limited to CAN data forwarding. It becomes a critical part of the communication system [19]. Figure 3 is a schematic diagram of a hybrid gateway.

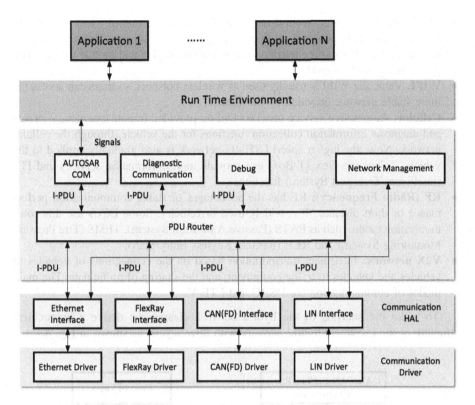

Fig. 3. A brief structure of general vehicular central gateway

An in-vehicle gateway mainly supports the following functions:

- **Communication driver:** Abstract different communications bus hardware, so that the software can directly invoke the API to get the PDU (Protocol Data Unit) through the physical layer.
- **Routing:** Protocol routing layer is mainly responsible for the extraction, repackaging and routing of messages, which is the key function of the gateway.
- **Application processing:** When routing, some data needs to be extracted and analyzed in the application.
- **Network management:** Ensure the stability of the entire network with a monitoring of the wrong nodes.

The External interface in the vehicle is a part of the hybrid network. There are physical interface and wireless interface. The typical physical surface is OBD (On-Board Diagnostics). It connects to the CAN bus both in powertrain domain and body domain directly or through the gateway bridge. It is used to identify and report fault. The vehicular wireless interface is multifarious. These devices parse the external network data into the in-vehicle network. The modern vehicle wireless communication function mainly includes the following kinds of remote communication.

- **Bluetooth:** It is a common short-range communication technology with 2.4 GHz to 1 Mbps data rate in personal smart devices. Its protocol supports data transmission and audio play. Hands-free telephone, wireless music play and mobile wireless key are all based on Bluetooth.
- **WIFI:** Vehicular WIFI is usually used as wireless hotspots, so users can access the more stable network provided by the vehicle.
- **Cellular:** Automotive service provider OnStar provided remote emergency service and diagnosis information collection functions for the vehicle, through the cellular network. Now, the higher speed LTE 4G network is also gradually applied to the vehicle. Telematics Box (T-Box) can provide more information services and ITS (Intelligent Transport System) functions.
- **RF (Radio Frequency):** RF has the advantages of stable communication performance in short distance. It is widely used in vehicles. Some ECUs use this communication mode, such as PATS (Passive Anti-Theft System), TPMS (Tire Pressure Monitoring System) and RKE (Remote Keyless Entry/Start).
- **V2X network:** Intelligent transportation based on the connections of vehicles to vehicles and vehicles to traffic equipment, and the sharing of traffic data. The main modes of communication are DSRC and LTE-V.

To make the analysis of the hybrid network clearer, we derive a hierarchical structure of the in-vehicle hybrid network with three layers, as shown in Fig. 4.

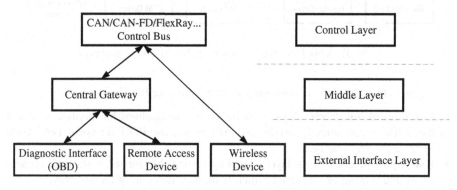

Fig. 4. In-vehicle hybrid network 3-layer model

The top control layer is the final target for attackers, because CAN network is responsible for most of the data acquisition and control tasks in the vehicle, so we call this layer as the Control Layer. In the Middle Layer, there is a central gateway because it is the essential node that connects internal nodes and it is also the bridge between the external network and internal network. The bottom layer is External Interface Layer, which could be accessed through the physical interface and different remote surface. Some devices in this layer connect to control units and others connect to the gateway.

We will use this 3-layer model to discuss the vulnerabilities and countermeasures in the in-vehicle hybrid network.

3   Security Analysis of In-Vehicle Hybrid Network

This section discusses security vulnerabilities of the in-vehicle hybrid network based on our 3-layer model. Some of these vulnerabilities are verified in real vehicles while others are theoretical.

3.1   Vulnerabilities at Control Layer

The control layer network vulnerabilities are mainly related to the CAN and CAN-FD network. The attacks can be divided into three categories, DoS (Denial of Service) attack, fuzzing attack, and attack based on error handling of the bus.

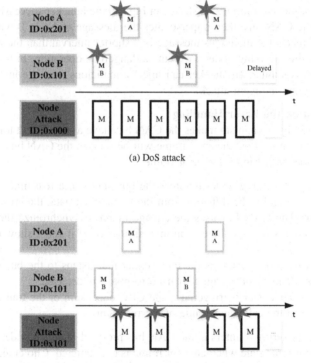

(a) DoS attack

(b) Fuzzing attack

Fig. 5. DoS and fuzzing attacks in CAN network

DoS Attack
Both CAN and CAN-FD provide multi-master capability. When the bus is idle, any node can send messages on the bus. When several nodes access the bus at the same time, only the frame with lower ID gains the arbitration and maintains in transmission mode. The arbitration rule of CAN bus reduces the message conflict. However, the ID

0x000 message has the highest priority, if an attacker has access to the CAN bus or cracks an ECU node, it is easy to flood lots of messages with ID 0x000 on the bus. Malicious adversaries can interfere the network without understanding the contents of the CAN bus. When sending high priority messages into the bus continuously, eventually leading to the high busload, it will affect the stability of the system seriously. In Fig. 5a, the messages of Node A with an ID 0x201 and of Node B with an ID 0x101 are delayed by the continuous attacking messages with an ID 0x000. Mukherjee et al. verified that the network can be disrupted by DoS attack [3].

Fuzzing Attack

CAN bus has the characteristics of broadcast communication. Once an attacker has access to the bus, it is easy to sniff the CAN message and analyze the contents. After marking the control field in a control frame, it is easy to use a reverse engineering. To some extent, this operation is dangerous to the vehicle and driver if it attacks the key components in the automobile. As shown in Fig. 5b the attacker successfully sniffs the message on the CAN bus, then impersonates the message of Node B with an ID 101, The attacker injects the malicious message in a shorter interval than the normal nodes, which causes the receiving node to execute a dangerous operation. In the FlexRay the attack method is similar, an attacker can inject a malicious message into the dynamic segment to trigger an event attack.

Attack Based on the Error Handling

The error handling mechanism makes the CAN bus have a strong fault tolerance, and if there is an error on the bus, the error frame will be sent. In the CAN bus, the following typical situations will trigger the error frame:

- *Bit error:* The sending node monitors the bus status in a real time while sending data. If it is found to be different from the transmitted data, the error is triggered.
- *Stuff error:* The CAN bus uses the change of bit to synchronize the clock. After each five same state bits, there is an inversion level. If it is not shown, triggers this error.
- *ACK response error:* ACK is the data sender that listens to the bus state after the data is sent. This error is triggered if no response is detected.
- *CRC error:* This error is triggered if the CRC checksum of the transmitted data is different from the calculated value of the recipient.

There are two error counters in the CAN bus protocol in which nodes could switch among different error state when an error frame is encountered. Cho et al. showed how attackers use a CAN node to fake error conditions based on error handling, resulting in the bus-off [11]. As the CAN-FD retained the CAN definition of error handling mechanism, this attack is also applicable for CAN-FD network. The malicious node in FlexRay bus could leverage error handling during synchronisation to jam the network.

3.2   Vulnerabilities at Middle Layer

As shown in the topology above, the vehicular gateway is very important in a hybrid network, but there are some security vulnerabilities in the current gateway.

The gateway connects most ECUs in the vehicle and the remote access network. When an attacker succeeds in cracking one node of a hybrid network, the attacker can get control of the whole network through the gateway. For example, an attacker can counterfeit an ECU using the gateway as a bridge and sends the data to implement a dangerous operation etc.

The gateway also supports some nodes with the FOTA (Firmware update Over the Air) function. The attacker can obtain control nodes which support download service and crack the weak key/pass pair. By controlling the gateway node to start corresponding ECU bootloader service, the attacker can intrude the node, and thus pose a threat.

3.3   Vulnerabilities at External Interface Layer

The OBD is an external physical interface. Usually, OBD devices will access multi-line CAN bus. Although OBD is not easy to be accessed physically by the attacker, now there are many aftermarket products called OBD-Box which provides network service function. It enables background system remote access the in-vehicle network through the cellular. Foster et al. showed how to crack an OBD II device through remote connect vulnerabilities and intrude the CAN network [24].

There are many remote devices. Table 2 shows general remote interfaces and the attack methods of current vehicles and some accidents happen due to these vulnerabilities. Checkoway et al. have verified the potential security holes in the remote surface [2].

Table 2. The external interface in the vehicle and its vulnerabilities.

Remote access type	Attack method	Example
Bluetooth	Attack weak stack and crack PIN code, connect device	BYD Qin, weak Bluetooth pair mode
WIFI	Attach through open port	Jeep Cherokee, WIFI D-bus port 6667 [23]
Cellular	Intrude the backend system	Nissan Connect 2016, Mobile App attack
RF	Sniff and send the fake data in the same frequency	TPMS Packet Spoof, University of South Carolina [12]
V2X/V2I	Attack the Ad hoc networks of the intelligent vehicle, fake traffic information	Vehicular Ad hoc Networks (VANETs) [13]

3.4   Further Discussions

Based on the above analysis of the vulnerabilities at different layers, the most serious problem is that the interoperability features of the hybrid network allow for a lot of paths for attackers. It may be difficult to access the interior vehicular nodes physically, but the combination of multi-layer network attacks will reduce the difficulty. Table 3 is a combinatorial analysis. With the integration of the gateway and external access surface, the system will become more insecure. If any of these three layers is cracked, the attacker will be able to access and control the entire network.

Table 3. Comparison of different attack combination.

Threat	Attack object			Probability of access
	Controller (Control Layer)	Center gateway	External interface nodes	
Control of single ECU or single bus line	✔			Difficult
Access of entire network		✔		Difficult
Access of privacy information and injection			✔	Easy
Access and control of entire network	✔	✔		Difficult
Remote control of some ECUs	✔		✔	Easy
Remote access of entire network		✔	✔	Easy
Remote access and control of entire network	✔	✔	✔	Easy

4   State-of-the-Art Countermeasures

4.1   Countermeasures at Control Layer

Hardware Secure Module

The hardware encryption module can support secure communication and guarantee the real-time control. For example, a FPGA based hardware encryption method is used in the vehicular embedded system [14]. A fault tolerance and flexibility security mechanism were implemented in a novel hardware architecture to achieve a faster and lower energy performance on FlexRay bus [28]. Several ECU manufactories adopt the Secure Hardware Extension (SHE) such as Fujitsu etc. [21].

Authentication

Authentication method can effectively avoid the dangerous operations caused by impersonating the data. Because classical CAN bus is used in the embedded system, it has an efficient synchronous communication capability. However, its useful data load is very limited, so it is unrealistic to add adequate communication authentication field or set encryption under this condition. Some researchers proposed to authenticate the data with truncated MAC (message authentication code) for secure transmission. They proposed a key-chain based authentication protocol, with truncated MAC. This approach can enable the real-time data transmission in the embedded system [15]. In the AUTOSAR latest version 4.2 Specification of Module Secure Onboard Communication [5], it also proposed a countermeasure by using random MAC code. Because this authentication will occupy part of the communication payload, it is more suitable for CAN-FD network authentication, as shown in Fig. 6. Han et al. proposed an efficient authentication for the FlexRay [26].

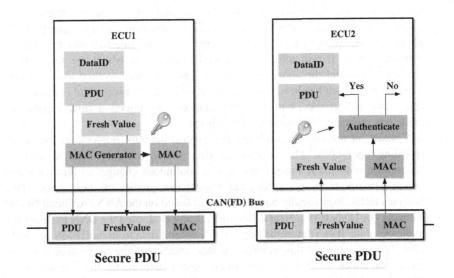

Fig. 6. Secure data transmission with MAC in CAN(FD) bus

IDS (Intrusion Detection System)

Although the bus communication is exposed to all nodes on the bus, it also makes the intrusion detection method possible, which can be divided into the following three categories. Different methods have their own merits and limitations.

(1) *IDS based on the key monitoring parameters.* The in-vehicle network is different from the event communication in the computer network as most of the messages in the car is periodical. When the attacker invades the network, there are some changes of the network signal, which could be detected through the following ways.

    (a) In CAN bus, when a node receives a remote frame, it will respond with a message to the sending node. When an attacker sends lots of fraudulent messages, the offset ratio of the response frame can reflect the suspicious activity.

    (b) Transmission intervals of a message among different ECUs can be detected and compared against the established baseline. When the period is shorter than the normal value, it will alert an abnormal state [16].

    (c) Different devices have their own hardware fingerprints. Even if the interval of cycle time messages is same, the hardware attributes may cause a small clock skew. Normally, the integration increases linearly with a constant slope. If an attacker injects excess messages or replace the original device, the slope will change. This method is effective at hardware substitution detection [29].

All those three methods have a low error rate. However, the last two methods need a fast sampling frequency to get time parameter for analysis. Detecting the intervals may not be effective for new and unknown attacks, and the parameters might be different in different vehicle networks.

(2) *IDS based on the information entropy.* In a normal vehicle, the communications among each ECU are orderly, so systematic information entropy should be relatively stable. When lots of malicious messages are injected into the normal communication, it will affect the network stability in which the information entropy can reflect the anomaly. There are entropy-based method to detect network attacks which has been tested in practice [17, 22]. This method is efficient to detect the DoS attacks, but when the attacker only injects a small number of malicious messages, it is hard to recognise.

(3) *IDS based on the content analysis.* The control network implements the corresponding operations. The changes of data values must be handled with in accordance with the relevant rules. It is a continuous change, so through some neural network training method, the system can predict the next value. This analyses technology usually builds the model based on the ANN (Artificial Neural Network) or DNN (Deep Neural Network). Kang et al. used the DNN to detect the malicious data. It can detect the bogus CAN control data from the TPMS precisely [27]. The advantage of this technique is that detection at the application level can reduce the attack which has a very strong intent to execute the threat instructions. But its disadvantages are also obvious, as the decision process is offline and needs high-performance computing resources.

4.2   Countermeasures at Middle Layer

As shown in the topology of Fig. 1, the vehicular gateway is very important in a hybrid network. The gateway connects different types of buses in the network so that it can monitor most data package according to certain specifications. There are several ways to protect the network.

(1) *Firewall.* Setting network firewall to restrict the external interface access of internal data and the control permission. For some controllers that implement MAC authentication, it needs to authorize operations based on the certificate inside the controller. Only authorized controllers can send control commands to the control layer. Moreover, the gateway should prevent MOST, Ethernet bus from sending direct control operation instructions.

(2) *Whitelist.* Setting whitelist routing table mechanism, so that a node can only communicate with another appointed node.

(3) *Separate operating system.* Using an isolation operating system, such as PikeOS with separation micro-kernel. This system can be divided into different business services and different interface and data only exchange using their services.

(4) *IDS system*. Using an IDS system which is mounted on the gateway, it can detect abnormal network behaviours. Compared with the intrusion detection scheme in the CAN(FD) network of control layer, this detection mechanism is more precise with the existing hybrid network traffic scheme. Based on the description of the network communication rules inside the CANdb database file, it can be converted into XML files and configurated as restrictions in the gateway. When the gateway forwards the data, it can rapidly detect the message which has an abnormal circle or exclusive ID in the network according to the preset conditions [18].

These methods could be integrated into a cental gateway as an intrusion prevention system (IPS). Firewall takes responsibility for the primary protection. IDS system could give a reactive protection when a malicious message bypasses the firewall and enters the network.

4.3   Countermeasures at External Interface Layer

An important protection for remote communication is to reduce the opening ports or the debug ports to the outside world. For the physical interface OBD, it should connect to the gateway through a single CAN bus and enhance the authentication property. For Bluetooth communication, manufacturers should strengthen the authentication and encrypt the data when transmitting the key control data, as some tools can sniff the wireless package of Bluetooth device. For the cellular network communication, it is necessary for the ISP (Internet Service Provider) to build a security system in the service platform including mobile application and the background system. It must have a strict authentication mechanism before the user sends control command. In addition, the machine learning based detection techniques also provide some solution in abnormal network detection. Alheeti et al. used the artificial neural network to analyze the trace file of the wireless network to detect the anomal intention of the traffic [20].

4.4   Further Discussions

Since most of the ECUs integrated by Original Equipment Manufacturers (OEM) come from different suppliers and have high control over production costs, it is very important to make systematic and operational security decisions. The implementation of the above security countermeasures has certain limitations to some extent. For example, the hardware security encryption module needs to be deployed between the different ECUs, which should be planned in the network design phase. Another example is intrusion detection method based on machine learning, which requires pretty large computational capability. In addition, if the contents need to be uploaded to the cloud for analysis, real-time communication and secure data transmission are tough to achieve. There is a comparison among the protection mechanisms in control layer through multiple vectors in Table 4. *Cost* refers to the expenses of extra equipment and system integration. *Compatibility* means the compatibility of software and hardware in the entire network. *Operability* refers to the technical difficulty to implement. *Low* means it's easy to realize in practical use, while *high* means hard to do it.

Table 4. Comparison among different protection mechanisms a control layer.

Protection mechanisms	Cost	Compatibility	Operability
Hardware secure module	High	Low	Low
Authentication	Low	Low	High
IDS based on the key monitoring parameters	Low	High	Relatively low
IDS based on the information entropy	Relatively high	High	Relatively high
IDS based on the content analysis	High	High	High

As can be seen from the analysis, the hardware encryption method is difficult to realize in the whole network, but it can be used in the key parts of the system to realize the hardware encryption of critical data. Although data authentication methods are based on software implementation, they need to ensure that vendors develop under the same standards. Because the intrusion detection mechanism will not affect the communication among the nodes, it is very good in compatibility. However, the maneuverability of the more advanced IDS methods should be optimized.

To achieve a comprehensive protection in the hybrid network, the most important is that efficient security methods of each layer are combined with their respective advantages. It is more efficient and accurate to combine data authentication and intrusion detection in the control layer and integrate in the central gateway.

5 Challenges and Future Work

In the near future, attackers will exploit vulnerabilities in multiple layers, to form a more complete attack path due to the complexity of the network. Therefore, it is necessary to combine the protection functions of multiple network layers to build a comprehensive defense system, which is different from just protecting a single network domain. In our analysis, the existing IDS systems are deployed separately in each layer. It is a trend to integrate IDS into other countermeasures. How to properly design a novel IDS to recognize the boundary of normal and malicious traffic is a challenge.

Meanwhile, with the rapid development of car networking and intelligent vehicle, the structure of the hybrid network in the car will also change. The future trends of communication network will be In-vehicle Ethernet based network. Thus, it will be similar to the IoT structure and bring more threats. How to defend attacks from the Internet, how to partition the network structure of new in-vehicle hybrid network model, and how to implement the corresponding security strategy to solve the security problems are still open questions.

In SAE 3061 standard [25], it advises manufacturers to define the network security using standardized assessment rules. For hybrid networks, manufacturers should fully evaluate and analyze all kinds of threats at the beginning of their designs.

It recommends using attack tree model to analyze the network security vulnerabilities, which is very important for the E/E Architecture design in the future.

In addition, under the restrictions of the vehicle system environment, the common practice is to integrate the security solutions into the vehicle embedded system, without affecting other functions. If it changes the message contents of transmission or requires detecting messages in the network, it should consider the compatibility. The future security mechanisms, such as encryption algorithms or IDS systems, need to consider the following capabilities: accuracy, efficiency, portability, modular insertion, off-line processing.

6 Conclusion

In this paper, we investigated the security of in-vehicle hybrid network. As such a network in the vehicle becomes more complex and plays more critical roles, it is important to consider the security solutions in a systematic approach. We classified the in-vehicle hybrid network into 3 layers, discussed various vulnerabilities at each layer, and further analyzed the state-of-the-art security solutions. Based on our investigation, we also identified open security challenges as future work.

Acknowledgments. This work was partially supported by SUTD start-up research grant SRG-ISTD-2017-124. The first author's work was done during his internship in SUTD.

References

1. Koscher, K., Czeskis, A., Roesner, F., Patel, S., Kohno, T., Checkoway, S., McCoy, D., Kantor, B., Anderson, D., Shacham, H., Savage, S.: Experimental security analysis of a modern automobile. In: 2010 IEEE Symposium on Security and Privacy (SP), pp. 447–462. IEEE (2010)
2. Checkoway, S., McCoy, D., Kantor, B., Anderson, D., Shacham, H., Savage, S., Koscher, K., Czeskis, A., Roesner, F., Kohno, T.: Comprehensive experimental analyses of automotive attack surfaces. In: USENIX Security Symposium (2011)
3. Mukherjee, S., Shirazi, H., Ray, I., Daily, J., Gamble, R.: Practical DoS attacks on embedded networks in commercial vehicles. In: Ray, I., Gaur, M.S., Conti, M., Sanghi, D., Kamakoti, V. (eds.) ICISS 2016. LNCS, vol. 10063, pp. 23–42. Springer, Cham (2016). https://doi.org/10.1007/978-3-319-49806-5_2
4. Apvrille, L., El Khayari, R., Henniger, O., Roudier, Y., Schweppe, H., Seudié, H.,Weyl, B., Wolf, M.: Secure automotive on-board electronics network architecture. In: FISITA 2010 World Automotive Congress, Budapest, Hungary, vol. 8 (2010)
5. Specification of Module Secure Onboard Communication AUTOSAR Release 4.2.2. https://www.autosar.org/standards/classic-platform/release-42/software-architecture/general/. Accessed 3 Aug 2017
6. Symantec anomaly detection for automotive. https://www.symantec.com/products/anomaly-detection-for-automotive. Accessed 29 July 2017
7. Lee, S.Y., Park, S.H., Choi, H.S., Lee, C.D.: MOST network system supporting full-duplexing communication. In: 2012 14th International Conference on Advanced Communication Technology (ICACT), pp. 1272–1275. IEEE (2012)

8. MOST150 intelligent network interface controller. http://www.microchip.com/wwwpro ducts/en/OS81118. Accessed 23 July 2017

9. Steinbach, T., Lim, H.T., Korf, F., Schmidt, T.C., Herrscher, D., Wolisz, A.: Tomorrow's in-car interconnect? A competitive evaluation of IEEE 802.1 AVB and time-triggered ethernet (AS6802). In: 2012 IEEE Vehicular Technology Conference (VTC Fall), pp. 1–5. IEEE (2012)

10. Brunner, S., Roder, J., Kucera, M., Waas, T.: Automotive E/E-architecture enhancements by usage of ethernet TSN. In: 2017 13th Workshop on Intelligent Solutions in Embedded Systems (WISES), pp. 9–13. IEEE (2017)

11. Cho, K.T., Shin, K.G.: Error handling of in-vehicle networks makes them vulnerable. In: Proceedings of the 2016 ACM SIGSAC Conference on Computer and Communications Security, pp. 1044–1055. ACM (2016)

12. Ishtiaq Roufa, R.M., Mustafaa, H., Travis Taylora, S.O., Xua, W., Gruteserb, M., Trappeb, W., Seskarb, I.: Security and privacy vulnerabilities of in-car wireless networks: a tire pressure monitoring system case study. In: 19th USENIX Security Symposium, Washington DC, pp. 11–13 (2010)

13. Al-Kahtani, M.S.: Survey on security attacks in vehicular ad hoc networks (VANETs). In: 2012 6th International Conference on Signal Processing and Communication Systems (ICSPCS), pp. 1–9. IEEE (2012)

14. Wolf, M., Gendrullis, T.: Design, implementation, and evaluation of a vehicular hardware security module. In: Kim, H. (ed.) ICISC 2011. LNCS, vol. 7259, pp. 302–318. Springer, Heidelberg (2012). https://doi.org/10.1007/978-3-642-31912-9_20

15. Komala, G.K.: Secure broadcast in controller area networks using efficient protocols. Imp. J. Interdisc. Res. 3(1), 868 (2016)

16. Song, H.M., Kim, H.R., Kim, H.K.: Intrusion detection system based on the analysis of time intervals of CAN messages for in-vehicle network. In: 2016 International Conference on Information Networking (ICOIN), pp. 63–68. IEEE (2016)

17. Müter, M., Asaj, N.: Entropy-based anomaly detection for in-vehicle networks. In: 2011 IEEE Intelligent Vehicles Symposium (IV), pp. 1110–1115. IEEE (2011)

18. Seifert, S., Obermaisser, R.: Secure automotive gateway—secure communication for future cars. In: 2014 12th IEEE International Conference on Industrial Informatics (INDIN), pp. 213–220. IEEE (2014)

19. Integrated automotive gateway can enable connected cars. http://articles.sae.org/13711/. Accessed 23 July 2017

20. Alheeti, K.M.A., Gruebler, A., McDonald-Maier, K.D.: An intrusion detection system against malicious attacks on the communication network of driverless cars. In: 2015 12th Annual IEEE Consumer Communications and Networking Conference (CCNC), pp. 916–921. IEEE (2015)

21. Fujitsu Semiconductor Europe: Fujitsu announces powerful MCU with secure hardware extension (SHE) for automotive instrument clusters (2012)

22. Marchetti, M., Stabili, D., Guido, A., Colajanni, M.: Evaluation of anomaly detection for in-vehicle networks through information-theoretic algorithms. In: 2016 IEEE 2nd International Forum Research and Technologies for Society and Industry Leveraging a better tomorrow (RTSI), pp. 1–6. IEEE (2016)

23. Miller, C., Valasek, C.: Remote exploitation of an unaltered passenger vehicle. Black Hat USA (2015)

24. Foster, I.D., Prudhomme, A., Koscher, K., Savage, S.: Fast and vulnerable: a story of telematic failures. In: WOOT (2015)

25. SAE Std J3061_201601, Cybersecurity Guidebook for Cyber-Physical Vehicle Systems. http://standards.sae.org/j3061_201601/

26. Han, G., Zeng, H., Li, Y., Dou, W.: SAFE: security-aware flexray scheduling engine. In: Design, Automation and Test in Europe Conference and Exhibition (DATE), pp. 1–4. IEEE (2014)
27. Kang, M.J., Kang, J.W.: A novel intrusion detection method using deep neural network for in-vehicle network security. In: 2016 IEEE 83rd Vehicular Technology Conference (VTC Spring), pp. 1–5. IEEE (2016)
28. Poudel, B., Giri, N.K., Munir, A.: Design and comparative evaluation of GPGPU-and FPGA-based MPSoC ECU architectures for secure, dependable, and real-time automotive CPS. In: 2017 IEEE 28th International Conference on Application-Specific Systems, Architectures and Processors (ASAP), pp. 29–36. IEEE (2017)
29. Cho, K.-T., Shin, K.G.: Fingerprinting electronic control units for vehicle intrusion detection. In: USENIX Security Symposium, pp. 911–927 (2016)

IoVShield: An Efficient Vehicular Intrusion Detection System for Self-driving (Short Paper)

Zhuo Wei[1]([✉]), Yanjiang Yang[1], Yasmin Rehana[1], Yongdong Wu[2],
Jian Weng[3], and Robert H. Deng[4]

[1] Huawei Shield Lab, Singapore, Singapore
{wei.zhuo,yang.yanjiang,rehana.yasmin}@huawei.com
[2] Astar, I2R, Singapore, Singapore
wydong@i2r.a-star.edu.sg
[3] JiNan University, Guangzhou, China
cryptweng@gmail.com
[4] Singapore Management University, Singapore, Singapore
robertdeng@smu.edu.sg

Abstract. In recent years, a lot of vehicle attacks have been reported and demonstrated by researchers and whitehat hackers indicating vehicle cyber security as an important issue particularly for self-driving cars. The reason behind this extended attack vector is the multiple external interfaces of vehicles and minimal internal security protection. Hence, it is totally possible for adversaries to take full control of connected cars. In this paper, we propose an efficient Vehicular Intrusion Detection System (IDS), named as VIDS, which consists of a lightweight domain-based detection model for ECU devices and a comprehensive crossdomain-based detection model for a gateway or domain controller. The former makes use of specification periodic features of Controller Area Network (CAN) frames, while the latter exploits stream bit value features with deep learning techniques. With the use of real vehicular normal datasets and synthesized abnormal datasets for experimenting, the experimental results indicate that the proposed VIDS can achieve better detection rate over existing IDS systems. In addition, VIDS is compatible with vehicle internal CAN network.

Keywords: Intrusion detection system (IDS)
Automotive cyber security · Deep learning

1 Introduction

Self-driving car and the Internet of Vehicles (IoV) are emerging technologies which are the current focus of automotive industry. Research and Markets, a largest market research store, forecasts the global connected car market to grow at a compound annual growth rate of 32.26% during the period of 2016 – 2017.

© Springer International Publishing AG 2017
J. K. Liu and P. Samarati (Eds.): ISPEC 2017, LNCS 10701, pp. 638–647, 2017.
https://doi.org/10.1007/978-3-319-72359-4_39

Vehicles with self-driving and IoV features make an open environment and connect with outside world unlike traditional vehicles that constitute a closed environment and are isolated. Vehicles in IoV are analogous to smartphones on wheels who have connections with other vehicles, infrastructure, pedestrians, cloud services, mobile devices etc. Meanwhile, infrastructure and mobile devices have connections with cloud services as well.

However, in recent years, there are numerous attacks reported and demonstrated by both industry and academia which indicate vehicle cyber security a very important issue, particularly for self-driving cars. Similar to Internet of Things (IoT), attackers can explore vulnerabilities in IoV system in order to remotely monitor and control vehicles. It does not only pose safety and privacy threats to drivers but OEMs (Original Equipment Manufactures) also bear customers loss as well as financial loss. System vulnerability may cause serious problems. For example, attacks on CAN (Controller Area Networks) bus can make cars out of control, which may lead to safety issues. A car can be tracked and even hacked if insecure and improperly configured telematics system is deployed. Moreover, vulnerability in one domain can expose the whole car system to the advanced attackers. The problems can be essentially traced back to the fact that ECU devices have no means to verify if a received CAN message is genuine. Internal network of vehicle consists of a large number of ECU (Electronic Control Unit) devices, deployed over CAN bus to communicate to each other.

In order to verify the source and the data value of received CAN messages inside internal networks, an intrusion detection system (IDS) monitoring vehicle networks can automatically detect any kind of known or unknown attacks. Generally, IDSs are divided into two main categories based on their intrusion detection methods, i.e., signature-based IDS and anomaly-based IDS. The former exploits known attacks behaviours to extract features from attacks dataset and generates IDS models to match an attack to a signature. Signature-based detection is a black listed approach since it is not capable of detection of unknown or new attacks. The latter utilizes statistics analysis to define normal and baseline features of behaviours and events to generate IDS models. Anomaly-based detection is a white listed approach, which focuses on measuring anomalous behaviours by comparing with baseline of normal behaviour. Since IoV is also connected with Internet, the attacks are endless and unpredictable in nature. Hence, it is hard to define and extract features for signature-based IDS. Anomaly-based IDS is therefore more suitable for IoV than signature-based IDS because of its stable baseline features. Indeed, Hoppe et al. in [1] proposed that all ECUs listen for CAN messages with their own IDs. If any ECU received a CAN frame message with its own ID but it did not actually send the message, the system detects it as an intrusion and sends an error CAN frame; Michael et al. in [2] defined eight anomaly "detection sensors" and six weighted "applicability criteria" with statistical modelling to detect anomalies. However, the existing IDS systems just consider partial abnormal situations only, and hence cannot completely observe the CAN network and detect maximum possible abnormal behaviors.

In this paper, we propose an efficient dual layers Vehicular Intrusion Detection System, named as VIDS, belonging to our IoVShield system[1]. It consists of a lightweight domain-based model and a comprehensive crossdomain-based model. They make use of specification and value features of CAN messages, respectively. The lightweight domain-based model is deployed at critical ECU devices while crossdomain-based model is deployed at the Gateway device or domain controller. In order to check CAN messages appearing at CAN bus, domain-based model works in an easy manner to process feature (CAN protocol specification) so that it is suitable for resource constrained devices, such as ECU devices having limited computation power and memory storage. On the other hand, crossdomain-based IDS analyzes CAN message streams from different domains such as the chassis domain, the powertrain domain, the body control domain and so on, in order to check that if the received CAN message data values are legitimate. In this paper, real vehicles data are collected and used for training and testing. Experimental results indicate that the proposed IDS system is better in performance over existing IDS systems and is compatible with vehicle internal CAN network. Our contributions of this paper are as follows:

- Gives an attack model under an assumed vehicle architecture which has a centre gateway or domain controller.
- Proposes the lightweight domain-based and comprehensive crossdomain-based IDS models based on the static and dynamic features of CAN message networks, respectively.
- Collects CAN bus data from real vehicles and generates abnormal CAN bus data based on the attack model, then implements the proposed VIDS with the above mixed CAN bus data.

Following is the organization of the paper: Sect. 2 introduces CAN protocol and surveys the existing vehicle IDSs. Section 3 give our architecture and attack model, then Sect. 4 describes proposed intrusion detection system. Section 5 explain implementation and performance comparison. Lastly, Sect. 6 draws the conclusion of this paper.

2   Related Works

2.1   CAN

CAN protocol is a low-level protocol which does not support any security feature in its current form. There is no encryption in standard CAN implementations, which leaves these networks open to packet interception. The ECUs broadcast messages to the entire network, and each ECU determines which of the broadcast messages it handles. Every message contains the sender message ID, but there

---

[1] IoVShield is multiple layers defense system for IoV, which consists of external network security, secure gateway, and internal network security.

is no destination message ID. Each frame is consisted of the following fields: identifier, data, CRC, ACK and few others. The identifier field (the message ID) is 11 or 29 bits value, and the data field is a 64-bit value, whose semantics are for ECU and generally proprietary.

2.2 Intrusion Detection Systems for Vehicles

The existing IDS systems are categorized based on the techniques they use for intrusion detection as the periodicity-based IDSs and deep learning-based IDSs of vehicles.

Periodicity-based IDSs. ECUs broadcast CAN messages with their specific frequency which are defined by manufacturers, such as 10–20 ms. Song et al. [3] proposed a lightweight domain-based intrusion detection system for in-vehicle network by analyzing the time intervals of CAN messages. It is a hybrid IDS that can detect both the known attack signatures and anomalous events. When a new CAN message appears on CAN bus, their proposed system checks the CAN ID and checks the arrival time of the last message with same CAN ID to see if the message came during the acceptable time interval. However, if the threshold for calculating the anomaly is not correct, there will be high false rate. In addition, if the attacker injects CAN messages with the original frequency by compromising ECUs, proposed system cannot detect injected messages. Otsuka et al. [4] designed a delayed-decision cycle detection method which does not require any modification in ECUs. Their proposed system alerts an error only if more than one packet with the same CAN ID are received within the maximum cycle time, and hence it can reduce false positive rate. Taylor et al. [7] presented an algorithm that measures inter-packet timing over a sliding window. The average frequency intervals are compared to historical averages to yield an anomaly signal. A one-class support vector machine (OCSVM) uses this frequency information to detect anomalies with high confidence. However, like [3], both [4,7] also fail to detect injected messages which are sent by the attacker with the original frequency. Cho et al. [6] proposed an anomaly-based IDS, called clock-based IDS (CIDS). If an attack is detected, CIDS's fingerprinting of ECUs also facilitates a root cause analysis, identifying which ECU exactly mounted the attack, i.e., identifying fabrication, suspension and masquerade attacks. The experimental evaluations show that CIDS detects various types of in-vehicle network intrusions with a low false-positive rate of 0.055%. However, it is based on clock skew, a factor that might change from time to time due to external factors like temperature.

Deep learning-based IDSs. Roland et al. [5] provided an approach together with implementation for in-vehicle processing of event streams to identify anomalous behavior with respect to sequences of events and not only a single event. The normal behavior should be filtered out thus leaving only a small percentage of abnormal behavior that might be caused by malicious agents and might lead to safety critical actions in the actuators of the car. Only the unanticipated behavior will be sent to the global operations center for further analysis. However, the model takes longer time in training when the number of events is high. Moreover, the data is not taken into consideration, hence an attack with wrong data but correct sequence is not detected. Sandeep et al. [8] used Hidden Markov Model to detect anomalous states from real data collected from vehicles. It is not only used for detecting attack states but also anomalous states. Furthermore, in [9] they designed a rule based approach for context detection in vehicles. It collects data from the CAN bus and uses it to generate SWRL rules, then uses these rules to build vehicule context. A multi-tier mechanism to extract context is proposed. The IoT-lite Ontology is used to model the system with new instances added for use with vehicular system. Proposed system contains three layers: Local context detection layer, Cross component context inferencing engine, and Rule mining engine layer. However, similar to a specification based approach of machine learning is not used to construct the SWRL URLs.

3   Architecture and Attack Model

3.1   Vehicle Architecture

There are more and more ECU devices in modern vehicles and these ECUs may require different network bandwidths and transmission speeds. Meanwhile, ECUs generally have different functions, therefore they are always organized into specified groups based on their roles. For example, modern vehicle contains four ECU domains, such as chassis, entertainment, body control, and power domains. These ECU domains are connected via a central gateway or domain controller constituting the internal vehicle network.

3.2   Attack Model

Based on the architecture mentioned in Sect. 3.1, there are several attack interfaces. Although previous researchers demonstrated CAN message injection from OBD interface, it is not feasible for adversaries to directly connect an OBD device to a targeted vehicle. Hence, we don't consider the attacks from OBD interface in this paper.

For self-driving vehicle, normally, there are three categories of CAN messages: Periodic, Event, and POE (Periodic and Event) at the internal network of vehicles. Periodic messages indicate those CAN messages which are broadcasted with a constant (periodic) as well as high frequency, such as broadcasting motor and wheel speeds in each 10 ms period during self-driving. Events messages refer to those CAN messages which correspond to remote control commands, such as body control. The last POE type indicates CAN messages with low frequency, such as broadcasting unlock/lock status to vehicle door in each 1000 ms.

Assume that ECU_r, ECU_s and $ECU_{s'}$ are a receiver, a sender and another ECU, respectively. Sender and receiver can be located at the same or different domains. In addition, sender ECUs can be normal ECU devices, TBox, Advanced Driving Assistance System (ADAS), or Human Machine Interface (HMI), and Immobilizer. Adversaries may launch specification (periodic and priority) and value manipulation attacks as described below.

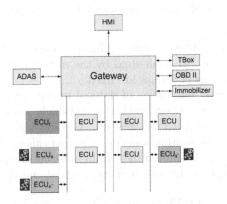

Fig. 1. Specification manipulation.

Specification manipulation. Specification manipulation is related to Periodic and POE CAN messages as shown in Fig. 1. Adversary might inject false periodic CAN messages to internal network in the following ways. Firstly, adversary compromises the ECU_s, then ECU_s sends an unspecified CAN message to ECU_r. Here, unspecified message means that attackers injects a CAN message with original CAN ID but with different priority and periodicity. Secondly, adversary compromises both ECU_s and $ECU_{s'}$. ECU_s is disabled so that it does not send normal CAN messages, while $ECU_{s'}$ generates unspecified CAN messages with the same CAN ID but with different priority and periodicity.

Value manipulation. Value manipulation attacks can launched on any CAN message, i.e., on Periodic, Event or POE. Similar to the above specification manipulation, adversary can compromise ECU_s and $ECU_{s'}$, and generate spoofed and unsafe CAN messages to the target ECU_r. Here, unsafe message means that injected CAN message's payload value is out of the range of a safety value. For example, suddenly sending unanticipated high speed value, applying sudden brake, or unlocking the vehicle door while driving.

4   Proposed VIDS

The proposed VIDS is consisted of two components, i.e., a lightweight domain-based model and a comprehensive crossdomain-based model. For our proposed VIDS, we consider both specification and data value features of CAN messages. Before elaborating on our proposed VIDS, we first describe the IoV traffic characteristics utilized by VIDS.

IoV traffic characteristics. IDS systems are widely adopted in computer networks by utilizing network baseline features. However, existing IDS models for computer networks have a high rate of false positives due to the fact that there are various kinds of Internet protocols and network frames, and they are not limited in strict manners. Unlike computer network traffics, characteristics of traffic in IoV networks are much restricted. In this paper, VIDS makes use of the following features.

- Frame periodicity of internal network frames is specified. The frequency and relativity of messages are configured by the manufacturers in the beginning, i.e., the time intervals of frames are fixed.
- The contents, types, and values of data of internal network are predefined, confirmed, and stable. Every packet in a vehicle network and its possible data contents are specified beforehand. The identifier of a CAN message, which determines the destination(s) of a packet, also specifies which kind of payload this message is allowed to contain in terms of signals and values. The permitted value range, the length of every signal and the packet function are all defined.
- Transmission mode of CAN bus protocol is broadcast. Every ECU on the bus listens for messages with the IDs designated to it, and detects a fake message circulating on the bus with an ID supposedly owned by the ECU itself.

4.1 Lightweight Domain-Based Model

The lightweight domain-based component of VIDS makes use of the frequency features of periodic CAN messages. This component for critical ECU devices on a domain in order to protect important CAN ID messages. Specifically, we utilize Long Short-Term Memory (LSTM) model to train the system using a dataset collected from a real car; the dataset contains the arrival time sequence of CAN frames for one CAN ID. **Steps of algorithms are as following:**

- For each periodic CAN ID message, we collect CAN messages data from Tesla Model X and obtain its arrival time.
- LSTM, a Recurrent Neural Network, takes time frequency difference between CAN messages as input to learn the hidden logic (predicting the next time the CAN ID going to appear in the CAN Bus message).
- The training of the neural network is done and the prediction accuracy is calculated. The statistical measure increases the accuracy of neural network prediction in each training iteration and a well-trained LSTM neural network is obtained.
- The testing data is given and the prediction accuracy is calculated. The error score is calculated for evaluation of LSTM model.

4.2 Comprehensive Crossdomain-Based Model

Comprehensive crossdomain-based model makes use of the data value features of CAN messages, which is to be deployed on a central gateway or domain controller. It detects abnormal data values utilizing Artificial Neural Network (ANN).

Crossdomain-based model detects anomalies CAN messages based on the bit positions of the CAN data values. **Steps of algorithms are as following:**

- Generate value dataset for each CAN ID, including normal data and simulated attack data.
- Artificial Neural Network consists of three hidden layers with eight neurons and 100 iterations.
- Input 64 bits of data into ANN model and output classifier: 1-Normal; 0-Attack.
- The testing data is given and the prediction accuracy is calculated.

5   Experimental Evaluation

In this paper, we collect CAN bus messages from Tesla Model X under normal driving status, and implement the lightweight domain-based and comprehensive crossdomain-based models by using Python with **pandas**[2] and **sklearn**[3] Python packages.

5.1   Datasets

For each CAN ID, we create arrival time dataset for lightweight domain-based model. Assume t_i is the time at which one CAN ID is received, t_{i+1} is the time when the same CAN ID is received next time on the CAN Bus network. The dataset contains 32498 data, 60% of which is used for training while 40% is used for testing.

For each CAN ID, we create value dataset for crossdomain-based model. In this paper, the data used to train this model is the data pertaining to the Speed of vehicle data belonging to one CAN ID. Every bit in the 64 bits of a CAN ID gives some information, such as **motor speed, estimation of motor torque, motor speed active, estimated the motor torque valid bit, active discharge state active bit, active short circuit state active bit**, and so on. The total number of dataset is 15000, normal data is 10000 and attack data is 5000. The attack data is simulated using the following three methods [7]: (1) reversing the entire 64 bits; (2) changing an unused bit in the CAN frame, e.g., the 49th bit is unused in our experiments; (3) changing a correct bit to reverse its bit value, e.g., the 33rd bit is changed in our experiments.

5.2   Experimental Results of Lightweight Domain-Based Model

We implemented lightweight domain-based model in Python. Firstly, it should reshape the training and testing data into **Numpy**[4] array. Secondly, it designs

---

[2] pandas is a software library written for Python programming language for data manipulation and analysis.

[3] sklearn is a free software library for machine learning implementations for Python programming language.

[4] Numpy is a library for the Python programming language, adding support for large, multi-dimensional arrays and matrices, along with a large collection of high-level mathematical functions to operate on these arrays.

lightweight domain-based model with four input nodes and one dense layer, and configures the parameters loss error calculation as "**Mean Squared Error**" and the optimizer as "**adam**" from the **sklearn** libraries. Lastly, the model is fit to the training and testing data with 25 training iterations.

The training score of 0.49 indicates that only round 0.5% error while training the Neural Network with 19496 data. The Test score of 6.73 means that only round 7% is error in prediction of next sequence value while testing with the Neural Network with 13002 data. Hence, the model is efficient and can be accepted to achieve a better prediction model for predicting the periodic data when next time the CAN ID is going to appear on the CAN Bus in vehicular network. We used a new value to verify lightweight domain-based model. The experimental results indicate that the proposed model predicted approximately a good value 27.384 as the expected value of the next CAN message from our training datset is 27.388 to 27.391.

5.3   Experimental Results of Crossdomain-Based Model

Once we setup Python environment and install required Python packages, we execute the program file (".py"). The program firstly reads the input data set (".csv") and separates them into training and testing subsets in the ratio of 70% and 30%. Then the system prompts for the training of the model to start. With the training model, 30% of the test data is verified and the system outputs the accuracy scores and the accuracy rate is about 95%. At last, we furthermore use the new test data ("new_data.csv") to test the training model. Experimental results indicated that proposed crossdomain-based model provided very efficient results of low false positive rate, its accuracy is about 95.207%.

5.4   Evaluation

Compared with existing IDSs, proposed VIDS considers both periodic and value features of CAN messages. Hence, it can efficiently detect CAN messages injection attacks described in Sect. 3.2. In addition, lightweight domain-based and crossdomain-based models are compatibly with current vehicle architecture, VIDS does not require extra hardware. Furthermore, proposed lightweight domain-based model exploits deep learning scheme to predict next arrival time, while most of periodic-based IDSs make use of statistic algorithms to obtain a fixed threshold. However, since predefined threshold is fixed value, it may be error. Hence, lightweight domain-based model is flexible and robust. Lastly, compared with existing deep learning IDSs which had to parse data value of each CAN message, proposed crossdomain-based model which is deployed at a central gateway or domain controller only analyze the bits distributions. Hence crossdomain-based model is efficient and real time.

6   Conclusion and Future Works

In this paper, we proposed an efficient Vehicular Intrusion Detection System (IDS), named VIDS, which consists of the lightweight domain-based model over

ECU devices and the comprehensive crossdomain-based model over a gateway or domain controller. In order to check CAN messages appearing at CAN bus, lightweight domain-based model makes use of simple and easy-to-process features (CAN protocol specification) such that it is suitable for source constrained devices, such as ECU devices having limited computation power and memory storage. On the other hand, the comprehensive crossdomain-based model detects abnormal CAN messages based on the bit positions of the CAN values in order to detect that if received CAN message data value is reasonable. For experiments, real vehicles data are collected and used for training and testing. The experimental results indicate that the proposed VIDS has better performance over existing IDS systems and is compatible with vehicle internal CAN network.

As a future work, since the comprehensive crossdomain-based model's results are only for a specific CAN ID, we need to test the model for other CAN IDs as well. In addition, VIDS should consider the logical relationship among data values.

Acknowledgments. This work is supported by National Natural Science Funds of China (Grant No. 61402199, Grant No. U1636209) and Natural Science Funds of Guangdong (Grant No. 2015A030310017).

References

1. Hoppe, T., Kiltz, S., Dittmann, J.: Security threats to automotive CAN networks-Practical examples and selected short-term countermeasures. Reliab. Eng. Syst. Saf. **96**(1), 11–25 (2011)
2. Mter, M., Groll, A., Freiling, F.C.: A structured approach to anomaly detection for in-vehicle networks. In: 2010 Sixth International Conference on Information Assurance and Security (IAS), pp. 92–98. IEEE (2010)
3. Song, H.M., Kim, H.R., Kim, H.K.: Intrusion detection system based on the analysis of time intervals of CAN messages for in-vehicle network. In: 2016 International Conference on Information Networking (ICOIN), pp. 63–68. IEEE (2016)
4. Otsuka, S., Ishigooka, T., Oishi, Y., Sasazawa, K.: CAN security: cost-effective intrusion detection for real-time control systems. No. 2014–01-0340. SAE Technical Paper (2014)
5. Rieke, R., Seidemann, M., Talla, E.K., Zelle, D., Seeger, B.: Behavior analysis for safety and security in automotive systems. In: 2017 25th Euromicro International Conference on Parallel, Distributed and Network-based Processing (PDP), pp. 381–385. IEEE (2017)
6. Cho, K.-T., Shin, K.G.: Fingerprinting electronic control units for vehicle intrusion detection. In: USENIX Security Symposium, pp. 911–927 (2016)
7. Taylor, A., Leblanc, S., Japkowicz, N.: Anomaly detection in automobile control network data with long short-term memory networks. In: 2016 IEEE International Conference on Data Science and Advanced Analytics (DSAA), pp. 130–139. IEEE (2016)
8. Narayanan, S.N., Mittal, S., Joshi, A.: Using data analytics to detect anomalous states in vehicles. arXiv preprint arXiv:1512.08048 (2015)
9. Nair, S., Mittal, S., Joshi, A.: Using semantic technologies to mine vehicular context for security. In: 37th IEEE Sarnoff Symposium (2016)

Enforcing Security in Artificially Intelligent Robots Using Monitors (Short Paper)

Orhio Mark Creado[✉] and Phu Dung Le

Monash University, Caulfield East, VIC, Australia
{mark.creado,phu.dung.le}@monash.edu

Abstract. Domestic robots are vulnerable to hi-jacking and industrial robots are vulnerable to cyber-attacks. This paper proposes the integration of a security component into a robots' system to minimise security risks. This objective is achieved through the inclusion of several monitors such as functional monitor, communication monitor and behavioural monitor, which assess the internal operations of the system at low levels of operation. Through this approach, the paper proposes a novel framework which will make it hard for robots to be hi-jacked or, at the very least, make it more difficult for attacks on their behaviour.

Keywords: Security architecture
Secure artificially intelligent systems · Secure robots

1 Introduction

Robotics and artificial intelligence have been a dominant force for many years within computer science. Today, robots can be any computational devices which can assimilate information, process it, and make decisions to affect the final outcome.

The biggest fear in mainstream adoption of robotics technology is that of unprecedented cataclysmic failure. Due to this reason, most computer controlled systems still mandate human input. Let us consider the example of the self-driving car. The technology is fascinating and offers the potential to maximize our utility of time. However, the real question, how many of us would actually consider letting a computer drive us at over 100 kms/h without having any fail-safe control over the vehicle? Yet we are comfortable using parking assist and self-parking automation in newer vehicles. Do we trust and use these features just because the risk of cataclysmic failure is small?

Modern day robots need an assurance guarantee of safe operations so as to ensure the end user that they aren't susceptible to false commands from external sources which can lead to a security compromise. Complex robotic systems can be broken down in terms of function, behavior, and communication. Many moving parts need to communicate effectively and securely. Only through effective

© Springer International Publishing AG 2017
J. K. Liu and P. Samarati (Eds.): ISPEC 2017, LNCS 10701, pp. 648–659, 2017.
https://doi.org/10.1007/978-3-319-72359-4_40

communication can the overall behavior be classified as deterministic or non-deterministic. But do most modern-day robots offer this level of confidence in their operations? The quest for performance oriented computing has come at a cost of security. Visiting our previous example, would you prefer a car which emphasizes performance over security or one which can offer a higher probability of secure operations at a reduced level of performance?

The rest of this paper is organized as follows. Section 2 outlines relevant literature and the motivation behind this research undertaking. Section 3 outlines a high level conceptual definition of the proposed framework. Section 4 proposes a concise theoretical evaluation with a brief discussion. Section 5 provides a conclusion and directions for future research.

2   Background

2.1   Reviewing Robotics and Artificially Intelligent Systems

Not much available literature actually addresses the secure operations of a robotic system. Most existing approaches can be categorized as follows:

- Application Based: Highly specific in niche areas. Some examples include Alemzadeh et al. [1], who applied fault tolerance to ensure that highly complex surgical robots do not cause accidental safety violations. Laughton [2], who applied genetic and fuzzy algorithms to secure power systems. Frank [3], who applied algorithms for intrusion detection and prevention
- Analytic Based: Quantitative or qualitative studies within specific domains. Some examples include Guiochet et al. [4] in the analysis of safety aspects within advanced robots. Guiochet [5] in the impact of human interactions with robotic operations. Lamddi [6], in decision making for complex systems via a safety and security based domain model.

2.2   Monitors to Enhance Security

The use of monitors to ensure computer system security was first proposed by Hansen [7]. Initially designed as mechanisms to structure the operating system [8], defined with administrative data and hierarchically nested to allow for inter-monitor calls. A key challenge was the result of a deadlock scenario due to monitors at the same level within the hierarchy [9], but realizable security was practically achievable through structured implementations [10, 11].

Modern implementations include the reference monitor concept to enforce access control lists and capability based systems [12, 13], trusted computing through the Trusted Platform Module [14–16], microkernels [17–19], a Virtual Machine Microkernel [20], a TPM based implementation of the Bell-LaPadula model [21], a TPM Microkernel model [22], a TPM model to enforce hardware security [23], and capability based systems with multiple independent kernels [24–26].

2.3 Motivation

The main motivation stems from the lack of a security architecture for evaluating the operations of programmed devices which are geared towards automated transactions. Our research takes into account that *AIS* need security enforced from an architectural perspective. With automation and decision support systems, for highly complex operations, now becoming more and more mainstream, there is a rising need to address security at a fundamental level of operation rather than as an add-on at the application level.

With information being transacted on a global scale by automated machines, security and privacy will soon become requirements which cannot be compromised within any automated system. As such, the proposed work aims to define security as a fundamental inclusion within the architecture of a more complex system which is made up of several components that work together to fulfil a higher objective. The main contributions our paper aims to make are as follows:

– A novel approach towards including security as part of the core operating procedures within modern day robots and *AIS* via means of structured monitors to ensure safe and secure operations.
– A robust and scalable security architecture which can be adapted to all modern day programmed robots at the right operating level without restricting the existing operating conditions.
– A new direction for future research to enhance security within the domain of robotics and *AIS*.

3 Proposed Theory

Over the years, while robotics has made many great advancements, the underlying core which defines many modern day robots still remains the same. Most, if not all, can be broken down from a large complex system into their underlying components as shown in Fig. 1.

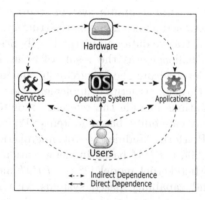

Fig. 1. Components within AI robots and their interdependence

The five main components which comprise any functional *AIS* include the Hardware, Operating System, Services, Applications, and Users. In this context, the users refer to any remotely operated controller which can operate or pass operation commands to the *AIS*. Logically, each of these five components can be evaluated individually as high-level components which can then be further broken down into the same five components. This facilitates for a recursive breakdown of any complex system into a subset of these five key elements.

With this proposed view, we can stipulate that the defined components are essential for macro level functionality, and due to their direct or indirect interdependence, vulnerabilities which affect any single subcomponent can propagate and affect the entire operation of the *AIS* as a whole. The next subsection addresses the strong need to compartmentalize all subcomponents.

3.1 Compartmentalizing Smaller Independent Systems

Component operations can only be compartmentalized and isolated, if and only if:

- Operations can be unambiguously identified.
- Operations conform to specific rules which govern their execution within the system.

This logic allows the disintegration of independent components based on their underlying mode of operation. The commonality between the various functional components within an *AIS*, is that all components must execute digitally compiled code in order to provide functionality and to fulfil their operational objectives. As such, we define the following:

Definition 1. *Block(s) of Code (BoC) - Is a self-contained set of low level instructions which can be interpreted and executed, one at a time, at the processor level within a computing system. Within the proposed work, each instruction contained within a BoC is defined as per an instruction set architecture. Collectively as a unit, a BoC can accept inputs, produce outputs, and has an associated manifest which stores an integrity signature, indication of ownership, a set of trust levels, a set of resources which need to be accessed along with associated permissions in order for it to complete its execution, and a set of states which define the valid range of possible states for each instruction executed.*

The requirement and importance of this definition is paramount as no previous or current literature has proposed a segmentation of executed instructions in this manner. Some previous approaches towards partially addressing executed instructions includes the use of ordinary procedures, functions or methods which can form self-contained set of instructions provided all embedded function calls have their code unrolled. Some examples include programming languages such as Eiffel, which allows logical annotations of inputs and outputs past on pre and post conditions; and Rust, which attaches ownership labels to data belonging to procedures. While many of these aspects allow for signed operations at the application level, these requirements for enforcing security are not applied to the *BoC* assigned to a component within the system.

3.2 Structuring Monitors to Compartmentalize Components

Defining Monitors.

Definition 2. *Monitor: Is a self-contained, independently operating, programmed unit with a strictly defined operation boundary specified by a set of attributes which govern its underlying behavior.*

Each monitor can be represented as a set of the following attributes.

Operational Attributes: Define operations to enforce a specific security characteristic, defined as:
$$M_{Operational} = \{C, O, A, T, S\}$$

- Class (C): Defines the level of operation and the degree of information sharing allowed. Includes:
  - System-Only Class (C_O) - Allows operation over the entire system, but only monitors system level code and restricts information sharing to other C_O monitors only.
  - System-Wide Class (C_W) - Allows operation over the entire system and sharing of information with other secure monitors.
  - Local Class (C_L) - Allows local operations only with restricted access to system user space.
- Mode (O): Defines the operational mode to procure and store information to facilitate decision making. Includes:
  - Analysis Mode (O_A) - An active observe-react-respond mode allowing for the use of historical data to perform run time statistical analysis and make decisions accordingly.
  - Tracking Mode (O_T) - A passive observe-track-record mode only allowing the acquisition and storing of information to facilitate statistical analysis for later executions.
  - Hybrid Mode (O_H) - Defined for high level system *BoC* only. Facilitates run time switching between O_A and O_T modes.
  - User Mode (O_U) - Defined for use only in user space under any of the above modes, but only allows sharing of information to a system level monitor but not vice versa.
- Access Level (A): Defines the level of resource access permitted. Includes:
  - System Access (A_S) - Highest level, specifically for trusted system-only operations.
  - Normal Access (A_N) - Default level, for non-critical system or user operations.
  - Restricted Access (A_R) - Restricted level for *BoC* without integrity signatures, or an untrustable trust level.
- Trust Level (T): Associates the *BoC's* functional trust level to the monitor. Includes:

- Critical Trust (T_C)
- Verifiable Trust (T_V)
- Denied Trust (T_D)
- Scope (S): Defines the operational visibility to other monitors or components. Includes:
  - Global Scope (S_G) - Allows visibility across the entire system and facilitates information sharing with all other monitors in appropriate classes.
  - Local Scope (S_L) - Allows visibility only within that component's operations. Information sharing is allowed with other monitors defined at the same level or via an S_G monitor.

Functional Attributes: Define monitor functions and behaviors during BoC execution, defined as:

$$M_{Functional} = \{H, \{S^*, A^*, F, E, R\}\}$$

- Hierarchy (H): Defines the priority in the decision making process. Includes:
  - System-Only Global (H_{OG}) - Allows analysis and decision making across the entire system, and is reserved for system monitors.
  - System-Wide Global (H_{WG}) - Allows analysis and decision making across the entire system, but does not allow intervening in any system level process.
  - System-Wide Local (H_{WL}) - Allows analysis and decision making locally only. Other H_{WL} monitor operations can only be affected through the intervention of an H_{WG} monitor.
  - Local Local (H_{LL}) - Allows analysis and decision making locally only, and cannot influence the operations of any other monitor.
- Functional Metrics: Define the monitor's behavioral functions during BoC execution. Includes:
  - Trust Level (S^*): Associates the $BoC's$ transactional trust level to the monitor to facilitate the evaluation of future executions. Includes:
    * Transitional Trust (T_T)
    * Untrustable Trust (T_U)
  - Access Level (A^*): Defines the access rights to assigned resources.
  - Functions (F): Outlines the set of instructions to be performed in order to enforce the underlying security characteristic.
  - Permissions (E): Defines the rights to perform a specific action(s) within its set of functions.
  - Rules (R): Defines the specific set of conditions to be met in order to enforce the underlying security characteristic.

Monitor Operations. Each monitor is defined to operate independently in order to determine the degree of satisfaction of its assigned security characteristic. However, each monitor is capable of accepting as input the output of another monitor so as to facilitate part of that process. The $AIS's$ monitors are responsible for instantiating all other monitors, and for ascertaining the security level of the *BoC* as a combined result of all monitors. The following lists the basic operational characteristics for each defined monitor.

Functional Monitor (FM): Is responsible for ensuring that no errors are encountered during execution, specifically for handling all inputs and outputs. As a given *BoC* is a complete set of instructions, an error state can be identified when the execution of the *BoC* does not execute the identified next instruction but defaults to another instruction within the same *BoC*, thereby indicating a handled error during execution.

Behavioral Monitor (BM): Is responsible for ensuring that no unauthorized changes in the state of operation are encountered. However, unlike the *FM*, the *BM* only triggers when the next instruction being executed resulting from an error is outside of the set of instructions included within the *BoC* being executed, indicating that the error state resulted from an unhandled exception.

Communication Monitor (CM): Is responsible for facilitating inter-monitor communication between monitors assigned to various component *BoC* within the *AIS*, and has three independent phases of operation, which involve:

1. Instance creation for each monitor and associating them with the underlying *BoC* prior to execution along with security characteristic and enforcement attributes.
2. Monitors the enforcement of each security characteristic during execution. Requests inputs from the other monitors in order to ascertain the overall level of security within the *AIS*.
3. Updating errors and other metrics post execution to facilitate secure future operations.

Monitor Component Integration. To facilitate for complex system designs, the framework proposes a specific set of system only monitors which facilitate the creation and assignment of monitors to every other component, allowing for distributed control and process execution, reinforcing compartmentalized isolation, ensuring that any compromise within a component are not propagated to another. Figure 2a illustrates a high-level representation of the monitor component integration within the *AIS*.

Structuring Using Monitors. The proposed architecture addresses the nested hierarchical monitor communication and the deadlock scenario in past implementations via the defined attributes assigned to each monitor. This allows for the enforcement of each security characteristic to be independent of hierarchy

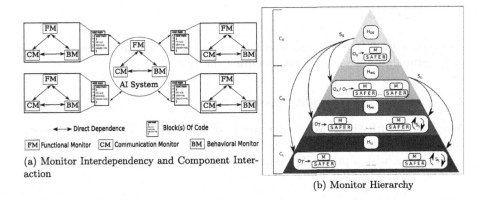

(a) Monitor Interdependency and Component Interaction

(b) Monitor Hierarchy

Fig. 2. Security as a probabilistic metric

to ensure compliance and satisfaction. The scalable hierarchy based on operational attributes also allows for deadlocks to be avoided. Figure 2b illustrates
this proposed hierarchy.

Achieving Overall System Security

Definition 3. *Security: Is the amalgamation of a set of independent character-*
istics - Function, Communication, and Behavior, associated with the BoC's of
each component within the AIS.

The overall security for an AIS Ψ, for m BoC can be defined as follows:

$$Sec\left(\Psi\right) = \{Sec\left(BoC_1\right), Sec\left(BoC_2\right), ..., Sec\left(BoC_m\right)\} \tag{1}$$

Applying the proposed framework, the security for any specific BoC_x can be
defined as follows:

$$Sec\left(BoC_x\right) = \{FM\left(BoC_x\right) \cup CM\left(BoC_x\right) \cup BM\left(BoC_x\right)\} \tag{2}$$

Applying the premise, the overall level of security can be defined as the summation of the degree of satisfaction for each of the defined security characteristics
by each BoC being executed within the system, as follows:

$$Sec\left(\Psi\right) = \bigcup_{i=0}^{m} \{Sec\left(BoC_i\right)\} \tag{3}$$

$$Sec\left(\Psi\right) = \bigcup_{i=0}^{m} \{FM\left(BoC_i\right) \cup CM\left(BoC_i\right) \cup BM\left(BoC_i\right)\} \tag{4}$$

4   Evaluation

This section presents a theoretical evaluation to analyze the architecture in terms of the probability associated with securing the system.

4.1   Defining a Probability Space

As system security is always a direct result of the presence and exploitation of a vulnerability, let us assume a probability space $\Omega \rightarrow \{0, 1\}$ for all $f \in \mathcal{F}$ where f is an event with a probability outcome of some $a | 0 \leq a \leq 1$.

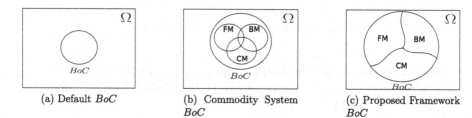

(a) Default BoC (b) Commodity System BoC (c) Proposed Framework BoC

Fig. 3. Security as a probabilistic metric

For the sake of discussion, our evaluation model assumes three hypothetical systems, on the defined premise of a BoC as the smallest foundational unit, as follows:

- Minimal System - Comprises BoC containing n instructions to provide functionality, but not including any additional security enforcing code as shown in Fig. 3a.
- Commodity AIS - Comprises BoC containing $n + X$ instructions, where X represents the total number of possible additional instructions to enforce some security aspects which are directly dependent on the number of actual security characteristics accounted for, as shown in Fig. 3b
- Proposed AIS - Comprises BoC containing $n + Y$ instructions, where Y represents the total number of mandated additional instructions to enforce each of the security characteristics within a BoC, as shown in Fig. 3c.

4.2   Security Evaluation

Applying a probabilistic model, we summarize our analysis of the assumed systems in Table 1.

Table 1. Security evaluation

$p(f)$	Commodity AI System	Proposed Framework
For any AIS executing m BoC, applying the security characteristics in conjunction with the defined probability space and the rules for probability distribution for each BoC we can establish the overall $p\,(system\ security)$ as the culmination of the enforcement of each of the defined security characteristics as follows:		
$p\left(Sec\left(\Psi\right)\right) =$	$\displaystyle\sum_{i=0}^{m}\left\{\frac{FM\left(BoC_i\right)\cap CM\left(BoC_i\right)\cap}{BM\left(BoC_i\right)}\right\}\middle| i\in\mathbb{N}$	$\displaystyle\sum_{i=0}^{m}\left\{\frac{FM\left(BoC_i\right)\cup CM\left(BoC_i\right)\cup}{BM\left(BoC_i\right)}\right\}\middle| i\in\mathbb{N}$
$p\left(Sec\left(\Psi\right)\right) =$	$\displaystyle\sum_{i=0}^{m}\left\{\frac{p\left(FM\left(BoC_i\right)\right)\cap p\left(CM\left(BoC_i\right)\right)\cap}{p\left(BM\left(BoC_i\right)\right)}\right\}\middle| i\in$ $\mathbb{N}$	$\displaystyle\sum_{i=0}^{m}\left\{\frac{p\left(FM\left(BoC_i\right)\right)\cup p\left(CM\left(BoC_i\right)\right)\cup}{p\left(BM\left(BoC_i\right)\right)}\right\}\middle| i\in$ $\mathbb{N}$
$p\left(Sec\left(\Psi\right)\right) =$	$\displaystyle\sum_{i=0}^{m}\left\{\alpha_i * \beta_i * \gamma_i\right\}\middle| i\in\mathbb{N}$	$\displaystyle\sum_{i=0}^{m}\left\{\left(\alpha_i + \beta_i + \gamma_i\right)/3\right\}\middle| i\in\mathbb{N}$

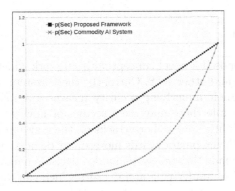

Fig. 4. Comparative analysis of p(security)

Figure 4 defines the most ideal representation of the aforementioned probabilities for the two main AIS considered. We note a strong indicative difference
between the $p(system\ security)$ for the considered systems, with the exception
of all criteria being equal to zero implying no security or all criteria being equal
to one implying perfect security, neither of which are practically realizable. Furthermore, the indicative results obtained have considered the commodity AIS
to equally enforce each of the defined security characteristics which isn't always
the case thereby resulting with the associated probability being far lower than
the ideal in most cases of commodity system operations.

4.3 Discussion

This section addresses two main arguments pertaining to the presented work -
Applicability and Evaluation.

- Applicability: The presented work, at this stage, is conceptual in nature. Begin
  logically sound, the theory is applicable to most AIS, however, a real-world

implementation or simulation has not been the focus of this paper, and is planned for future work.

– Evaluation: The presented work avoids the two extremes of complete security and no security, as these are not realizable. Additionally, the definition of the hypothetical systems is based on the most fundamental unit of operation within an AIS - a BoC, any enforcement of secure operations must be enforced through the inclusion of operating code. This extends to the commodity system in consideration, as most commodity systems may define some security characteristics although their enforcement might be left as optional add-ons at the user's discretion. By contrast, the proposed theory mandates the inclusion of code to enforce security characteristics as well as monitors to enforce secure operations. This allows for the defined characteristics within a BoC to be a partition set, thereby allowing each partition to be disjoint of others.

5   Conclusion

This paper has proposed a novel conceptual framework which can be applied to modern day robots and other AIS. Currently, these systems are becoming more predominant, but their underlying security measures are still based on dated mechanisms. And while these may seem secure for now, it is only a matter of time when vulnerabilities and cyber-attacks on these systems become more and more common. With the push towards more smart devices and more automated transactions being made through system aided decision making, there is a strong need for a more secure underlying architecture which can protect these systems while taking into account their current operating environments.

Future directions and goals of our research aim to simulate our work in order to provide some demonstrable evidence of real world applicability within modern day robots so as to justify the validity of the underlying theory and its usefulness when applied to secure AIS.

References

1. Alemzadeh, H., Chen, D., Lewis, A., Kalbarczyk, Z., Raman, J., Leveson, N., Iyer, R.: Systems-theoretic safety assessment of robotic telesurgical systems. In: Koornneef, F., van Gulijk, C. (eds.) SAFECOMP 2015. LNCS, vol. 9337, pp. 213–227. Springer, Cham (2015). https://doi.org/10.1007/978-3-319-24255-2_16
2. Laughton, M.A.: Artificial intelligence techniques in power systems. In: IEE Colloquium on Artificial Intelligence Techniques in Power Systems (Digest No: 1997/354), 1/1-119, November 1997
3. Frank, J.: Artificial intelligence and intrusion detection: current and future directions. In. Proceedings of the 17th National Computer Security Conference (1994)
4. Guiochet, J., Machin, M., Waeselynck, H.: Safety-critical advanced robots: a survey. Rob. Auton. Syst. **94**, 43–52 (2017)
5. Guiochet, J.: Hazard analysis of human-robot interactions with HAZOP-UML. Saf. Sci. **84**, 225–237 (2016)

6. Lamddi, M.A.: Developing dependability requirements engineering for secure and safe information systems with knowledge acquisition for automated specification. J. Softw. Eng. Appl. **10**(02), 211 (2017)

7. Hansen, P.B.: The nucleus of a multiprogramming system. Commun. ACM **13**(4), 238–241 (1970)

8. Hoare, C.A.R.: Monitors: an operating system structuring concept. Commun. ACM **17**(10), 549–557 (1974)

9. Howard, J.H.: Proving monitors. Commun. ACM **19**(5), 273–279 (1976)

10. Lister, A.M., Sayer, P.J.: Hierarchical monitors. Softw. Pract. Experience **7**(5), 613–623 (1977)

11. Lister, A.: The problem of nested monitor calls. ACM SIGOPS Oper. Syst. Rev. **11**(3), 5–7 (1977)

12. Department of Defense, U.S.D.: Trusted computer system evaluation criteria (1985). Accessed 15 July 2015

13. Murdoch, S., Bond, M., Anderson, R.J.: How certification systems fail: lessons from the ware report. IEEE Secur. Priv. **10**(6), 40–44 (2012)

14. Nibaldi, G.H.: Specification of a trusted computing base (TCB). Technical report ADA108831, MITRE Corporation, Bedford, Massachusetts, USA, November 1979. Accessed 15 July 2015

15. Pfitzmann, B., Riordan, J., Stüble, C., Waidner, M., Weber, A.: The PERSEUS system architecture (2001). Accessed 15 July 2015

16. DiRossi, M.: Towards a high assurance secure computing platform. In: Proceedings of the 10th IEEE High Assurance Systems Engineering Symposium, HASE 2007, pp. 381–382 (2007)

17. Tanenbaum, A., Herder, J., Bos, H.: Can we make operating systems reliable and secure? Computer **39**(5), 44–51 (2006)

18. Liedtke, J.: On μ-kernel construction. In: Proceedings of the 15th ACM Symposium on Operating System Principles, SOSP 1995, pp. 237–250. ACM, December 1995

19. Klein, G., Andronick, J., Elphinstone, K., Heiser, G., Cock, D., Derrin, P., Elkaduwe, D., Engelhardt, K., Kolanski, R., Norrish, M., Sewell, T., Tuch, H., Winwood, S.: seL4: formal verification of an operating-system kernel. Commun. ACM **53**(6), 107–115 (2010)

20. Karger, P., Zurko, M., Bonin, D., Mason, A., Kahn, C.: A retrospective on the VAX VMM security kernel. IEEE Trans. Softw. Eng. **17**(11), 1147–1165 (1991)

21. Nie, X.W., Feng, D.G., Che, J.J., Wang, X.P.: Design and implementation of security operating system based on trusted computing. In: 2006 International Conference on Machine Learning and Cybernetics, pp. 2776–2781 (2006)

22. Setapa, S., Isa, M., Abdullah, N., Manan, J.L.: Trusted computing based microkernel. In: Proceedings of the 2010 International Conference on Computer Applications and Industrial Electronics, ICCAIE 2010, pp. 1–4 (2010)

23. Hendricks, J., van Doorn, L.: Secure bootstrap is not enough: shoring up the trusted computing base. In: Proceedings of the 11th Workshop on ACM SIGOPS European Workshop, EW, p. 11. ACM (2004)

24. Gong, L.: A secure identity-based capability system. In: Proceedings of the 1989 IEEE Symposium on Security and Privacy, pp. 56–63 (1989)

25. Neumann, P.G., Watson, R.N.M.: Capabilities revisited: a holistic approach to bottom-to-top assurance of trustworthy systems. In: Proceedings of the 4th Annual Layered Assurance Workshop, LAW 2010 (2010). Accessed 15 July 2015

26. Watson, R.N.M., Anderson, J., Laurie, B., Kennaway, K.: A taste of capsicum: practical capabilities for UNIX. Commun. ACM **55**(3), 97–104 (2012)

Social Network and QR Code Security

Hello, Facebook! Here Is the Stalkers' Paradise!: Design and Analysis of Enumeration Attack Using Phone Numbers on Facebook

Jinwoo Kim[1], Kuyju Kim[1], Junsung Cho[1], Hyoungshick Kim[1(✉)], and Sebastian Schrittwieser[2]

[1] Sungkyunkwan University, Seoul, Republic of Korea
{jinwookim,kuyjukim,js.cho,hyoung}@skku.edu
[2] Josef Ressel Center for Unified Threat Intelligence on Targeted Attacks, St. Pölten University of Applied Sciences, Sankt Pölten, Austria
sebastian.schrittwieser@fhstp.ac.at

Abstract. We introduce a new privacy issue on Facebook. We were motivated by the Facebook's search option, which exposes a user profile with his or her phone number. Based on this search option, we developed a method to automatically collect Facebook users' personal data (e.g., phone number, location and birthday) by enumerating the possibly almost entire phone number range for the target area. To show the feasibility, we launched attacks for targeting the users who live in two specific regions (United States and South Korea) by mimicking real users' search activities with three sybil accounts. Despite Facebook's best efforts to stop such attempts from crawling users' data with several security practices, 214,705 phone numbers were successfully tested and 25,518 actual users' personal data were obtained within 15 days in California, United States; 215,679 phone numbers were also tested and 56,564 actual users' personal data were obtained in South Korea. To prevent such attacks, we recommend several practical defense mechanisms.

Keywords: Enumeration attack · Information leakage
User profile · Privacy · Facebook

1 Introduction

Facebook (https://www.facebook.com/) is one of the most popular online social networking service and reported more than 1.94 billion monthly active users for March 2017 [1]. Due to its popularity, Facebook has also become an attractive target of cyber criminals (spam, phishing, and misuse of personal data). For example, spammers have often used tools and bots for harvesting people's contact information (e.g., phone numbers and email addresses) in the past [8].

In this paper, we particularly focus on security concerns raised by the friend search option with phone numbers in Facebook. Facebook offers various options for searching registered users. An option is to use a user's phone number. At first

© Springer International Publishing AG 2017
J. K. Liu and P. Samarati (Eds.): ISPEC 2017, LNCS 10701, pp. 663–677, 2017.
https://doi.org/10.1007/978-3-319-72359-4_41

glance, this search option seems to be a proper compromise between privacy and utility, revealing a user's profile for his or her friends or acquaintances who only know the user's phone number. In this paper, however, we will show that this feature could potentially be misused by attackers who want to harvest Facebook users' data such as their names, phone numbers, locations, education and even photos at large scale; those stolen data can be exploited for conducting additional cyber criminal activities such as sending spam/phishing messages or creating sybil accounts. To show the security risk of the search option, we developed a method to automatically collect Facebook users' personal data (phone number, friends, current city, home town, education, family, work and relationship) by enumerating the (possibly) entire phone number range of a target area. Our main contributions are summarized as follows:

- We present a novel *enumeration* attack using the search option to enumerate entire phone number ranges to harvest Facebook users' profile information in an automatic manner at large scale (see Sect. 3).
- We describe how to bypass the defense mechanisms such as anomaly detection and CAPTCHAs provided by Facebook. We implemented an automated crawling process with a few sybil accounts to mimic normal users' activities (see Sect. 4).
- We provide a thorough evaluation of the practicality of the enumeration attack. Our evaluation is based on experiments on the actual Facebook service. In our experiments, we collected 25,518 Facebook user profiles from 214,705 phone numbers within 15 days in California, United States. Also, we collected 56,564 Facebook user profiles from 215,679 phone numbers in South Korea (see Sect. 5).
- We suggest possible defense mechanisms to mitigate such enumeration attacks and discuss their advantages and disadvantages (see Sect. 6).

While our evaluation is Facebook-specific, it could also offer important lessons for other websites which use the people search feature by phone number or email address.

2   Facebook's Profile Search

To encourage users to find their friends and acquaintances (i.e., promotional purposes), Facebook provides several options to search for people on Facebook (e.g., by name, email address, or phone number). For example, when a phone number is typed into the Facebook search bar, the results from people who registered that phone number will be displayed if the default privacy setting for the search option was not changed. We found that for a Facebook profile the default setting for the option to search for users their phone numbers is "Everyone", which means that anyone could use this feature to find that specific profile (see Fig. 1). Interestingly, even if users hide their phone numbers in profile page, they can still be searched with their phone numbers if this option is not disabled manually.

Privacy Settings and Tools			
Who can see my stuff?	Who can see your future posts?	Only me	Edit
	Who can see your friends list?	Public	Edit
	Review all your posts and things you're tagged in		Use Activity Log
	Limit the audience for posts you've shared with friends of friends or Public?		Limit Past Posts
Who can contact me?	Who can send you friend requests?	Everyone	Edit
Who can look me up?	Who can look you up using the email address you provided?	Everyone	Edit
	Who can look you up using the phone number you provided?	Everyone	Edit
	Do you want search engines outside of Facebook to link to your Profile?	Yes	Edit

Fig. 1. Privacy setting options in Facebook.

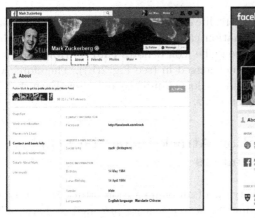
(a) Logged in

(b) Not logged in

Fig. 2. People search results ("Logged in" vs. "Not logged in").

We will exploit this feature to develop a method for performing enumeration attacks on Facebook.

We also found that the user profile information (e.g., work, education, and location) significantly changes depending on whether we are logged in or not. Figure 2 shows the differences between logged in and not logged in. When we are logged in and then try to search for a user, the search results for the user include the section called About which displays the detailed information about the user (e.g., the link to other services such as Instagram, birthday, gender, relationship

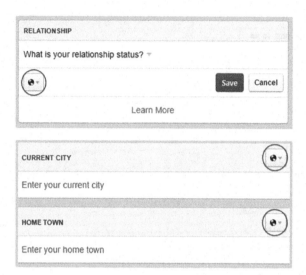

Fig. 3. Privacy settings for relationship, current city and home town in Facebook.

with the user's partner, family members, life events, etc.) (see Fig. 2(a)). To make matters worse, such personal information can be exposed to the public eye by default (see Fig. 3). In this figure, the globe icon denotes `public`. However, this section is disappeared when we are not logged in (see Fig. 2(b)). Therefore, we would perform enumeration attacks under logged in Facebook user. Each step is described in detail in the following sections.

3   Overview of Enumeration Attack Using the People Search with Phone Numbers

In this section, we present the overview of an enumeration attack to *automatically* harvest user profile data using the search feature provided by Facebook. The proposed enumeration attack involves the following three steps: (i) enumerating target phone numbers in a random or sequential order; (ii) checking whether the search results (including the user profile) are successfully returned; (iii) extracting the interesting user data from the crawled user profile web page if valid search results were returned.

To conduct the enumeration attack using the people search with phone numbers, an attacker first generates a range of phone numbers in a valid format and tries to search for people with that number. The phone numbers used for the enumeration attack can be generated for a specific target area. For example, the country code is 1 for United States; and the area codes are {209, 213, 279, 310, 323 ⋯ } for California. If the attacker wants to collect the information about Californian users, the generated phone number format would look like +1209XXXXXXX.

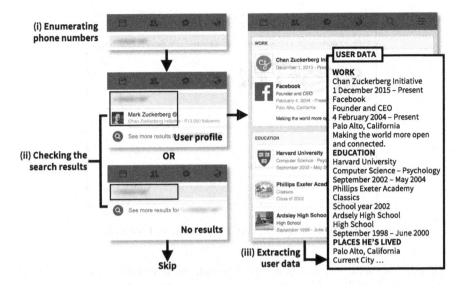

Fig. 4. Overview of the enumeration attack using the people search with phone numbers.

As described in Sect. 2, Facebook allows users to search for people with his or her phone number. Our method performs the following procedure repeatedly (see Fig. 4):

1. An attacker signs into Facebook using a sybil account. We note that a sybil account for Facebook can simply be created by a temporary email service in an automatic manner.
2. The attacker generates a phone number from a range of phone numbers in a valid format (e.g., 010XXXXXXXX, +1209XXXXXXX) and tries to search for people with that phone number on Facebook.
3. If the search results are successfully returned, the web page for user profile is crawled; otherwise, this step is skipped.
4. After the crawled web page is parsed appropriately, the user data extracted from that web page and the phone number used are stored as the output of the attack.

As a result of this attack, an attacker can harvest victims' personal data (such as phone number, name, education level, the place user are living, etc.).

Facebook is already using several defense mechanisms to protect user data from web crawling attempts. As an example, if an unusual or suspicious activity is detected, Facebook displays the "Security Check" error message, and asks the user to solve a CAPTCHA (Completely Automated Public Turing test to tell Computers and Humans Apart) [3] problem as shown in Fig. 5.

This policy seems effective against such enumeration attacks or web crawling. However, we found that this anomaly detection can be bypassed by using a few

Fig. 5. Example of CAPTCHA used in Facebook.

sybil accounts and performing attack attempts with an intentional delay. In the next section, we will explain how defense mechanisms can effectively be bypassed.

4 Evading Anomaly Detection by Mimicking Normal User Activities

In practice, a naive approach for the enumeration attack is not working. Our simple attempt failed to continuously operate the attack procedure described in Sect. 3 even when we signed in to our *normal* Facebook account. When the attack procedure was repeated around 300 times, a CAPTCHA challenge was displayed.

Unsurprisingly, the best strategy is to mimic normal user behavior by sending only a small number of search requests to evade the anomaly detection solution used by Facebook. In this case, however, the attack efficiency can be degraded significantly. To overcome this drawback, our key idea is to use multiple independent sessions to mimic multiple users' search activities rather than a single user alone.

To do this, we need to generate k temporary accounts before performing the attack procedure. We launch the attack with the first account. After repeating the user search procedure t times with the first account for as long as possible, we switch to the second account and continue this process. We note that the first account is used again after the kth account was used. Figure 6 illustrates this process visually. As shown in this figure, the attacker tries to search t consecutive phone numbers with an account (e.g., phone numbers $i, i+1, \cdots, i+(t-1)$ with account 1) and switches to another account.

It is important to use appropriate k and t for efficiently evading the anomaly detection used by Facebook. For example, if t is too large, the attack attempt can still be detected; if t is too small, switching cost will be higher. Those parameter values were determined experimentally with a small number of test samples. In Sect. 5, we will discuss how to choose proper k and t.

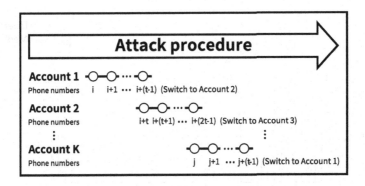

Fig. 6. Enumeration attack with k sybil accounts.

5 Experiments

We implemented a tool for performing enumeration attacks described in Sect. 3 to show the feasibility against Facebook and evaluate its attack performance in a real-world environment.

5.1 Implementation

For the enumeration attack via phone number search in Facebook, we used a virtual machine (VMware Workstation 12.0.0) installed on an Ubuntu 16.04 LTS desktop computer (with two 2.7 GHz CPU and 2.4 GB RAM) and equipped with a non-congested 100 MB WiFi connection to a LAN that was connected to the Internet. In addition, we used the software-testing framework Selenium (http://www.seleniumhq.org/) to automate our enumeration attack attempts.

It is important to choose optimal parameter values for k and t that maximize the attack performance without incurring significant costs for creating k sybil accounts and maintaining them. To practically determine the optimal threshold for the enumeration attack, we used 50 Facebook accounts as the training dataset. For each account, we counted the number of friend search requests until a CAPTCHA challenge was displayed.

Figure 7 shows the number of requests, and the mean, median and minimum values, which were 392.4 (with the standard deviation of 102.44), 366 and 300, respectively. Based on this evaluation, we selected $t = 300$ as a more conservative threshold value because 300 was the worst case in our test samples.

To minimize the cost of managing sybil accounts, it will be preferred to find the smallest k that can evade the anomaly detection mechanism. To do this, we simply tested possible k until CAPTCHA challenges were not displayed. We found that the proposed enumeration attack can be successfully performed without any delay when $k = 3$. To use fewer accounts for attack, additional delays are required between the enumeration attacks of each account. But, this delay can slow down the crawling speed.

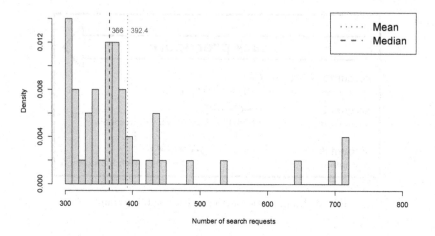

Fig. 7. Number of search requests until a CAPTCHA challenge is displayed.

We note that 300 people search operations took about 35 min on average. Thus, each account would be reused every 70 min on average. In fact, we surmise that Facebook might count the number of search operations within a specific time interval (e.g., 70 min) and then try to block additional requests if the counted number is greater than a pre-determined threshold (e.g., 300).

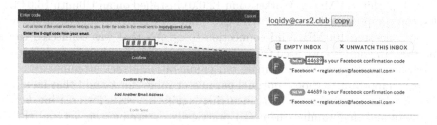

Fig. 8. Example of using a temporary email address for creating a sybil account on Facebook.

In Facebook, either email verification or phone verification is required for creating user accounts as a defense against bulk account creation. However, we figured out that this verification process does not pose a real challenge to attackers because account registration can be fully automated. Attackers can use a temporary email service such as **nada** (https://getnada.com/). Figure 8 shows an example of using a temporary email address for creating a sybil account on Facebook.

Even though Facebook does not allow users to create multiple accounts by checking their operating system and network environment and asking them to complete a security check if the same environment is used more than twice for

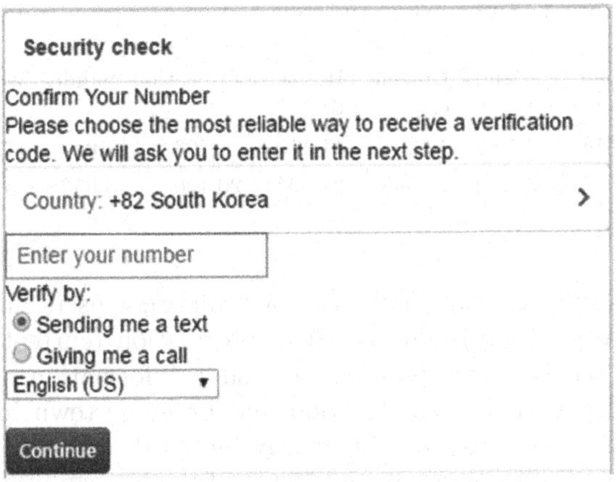

Fig. 9. Security check alert for multiple user accounts at a single machine.

creating user accounts (see Fig. 9) this restriction can also be evaded using a *rooted* Android mobile phone and a VPN connection. Whenever creating an account on Facebook, attackers can simulate a new target device by changing Android ID, International Mobile Equipment Identity (IMEI) and IP address in order to disable the security Facebook's check feature.

With this implementation, we successfully performed automated enumeration attacks without any challenges from Facebook. The experiment results are presented in the next section.

5.2 Attack Results

To show the feasibility of the enumeration attack on Facebook, we performed enumeration attacks to collect user profile data in California, United States and South Korea, respectively. The mean time required for extracting a user profile was 4.78 s if the search results were successfully returned; otherwise, the mean time to process "no search results" was 6.49 s on average. For California, we particularly tested 214,705 phone numbers for 15 days and confirmed 25,518 (11.89%) valid user profiles from those phone numbers. For South Korea, we also tested 215,679 phone numbers for the same time period and confirmed 56,564 (26.23%) valid user profiles from those numbers. Those results demonstrate that the enumeration attack using phone numbers was significantly more effective in South Korea than California, United States. We surmise that Korean users' phone numbers were likely to be denser than California users' phone numbers in Facebook. Table 1 shows the statistics for the collected user profiles. We found that several types of personal information (phone number, friends, current city, home town, education, family, work and relationship) can be accessed easily through user profiles collected by the enumeration attack developed here. From the collected user profiles using phone numbers (25,518 and 56,564 user profiles for California and South Korea, respectively), most users did not protect

Table 1. Summary of the collected users' personal data.

Region	Phone number	Friends	Current city	Home town	Education	Family	Work	Relationship
California	25,518	18,080	12,205	11,470	9,703	7,849	7,354	7,279
South Korea	56,564	42,379	25,555	22,594	20,126	3,952	13,580	8,940

their friend list information (70.9% of the California users and 74.9% of the Korean users, respectively). The location information (current city and home town) was the second most publicly accessible information; 44.9%–47.8% of the users revealed their current location and/or home town information. The users' education history was also frequently included in the collected user profiles (38.0% of the California users and 35.6% of the Korean users, respectively). Users' work information was often revealed via their user profiles (28.8% of the California users and 24.0% of the Korean users, respectively). Interestingly, California users' profiles quite frequently include the family and relationship information (30.8% of the California users for family and 28.5% of the California users for relationship, respectively) while this information was included less frequently in the Korean user profiles (only 7.0% of the Korean users for family and 15.8% of the Korean users for relationship, respectively). This implies that Korean users are expected to be more concerned about their family members and partners compared with California users. In a targeted attack scenario, such private data might be used to design sophisticated spam, spear phishing [10], or profile cloning attacks [5].

6   Countermeasures

In this section, we describe several defense mechanisms for preventing enumeration attacks on online social networking services.

6.1   Detecting Sequential Patterns of Queried Phone Numbers

An enumeration attack tries to automatically collect user information by enumerating the target phone numbers. Since the proposed enumeration attacks are performed with multiple user accounts, it might not be easy to detect suspicious patterns from a user account during a session. Our strategy is to uncover sequential patterns from enumerated phone numbers instead of focusing on user activities because phone numbers are sequentially queried from the target phone number range even with multiple user accounts.

However, attackers may effectively avoid this detection method without incurring significant additional costs by using a random permutation list (with some delay) instead of a sequential phone number order.

6.2   Deploying Honey Phone Numbers

"Honey" is the traditional term used to indicate a "decoy" or "bait" for attackers in the field of security. For example, a honeypot is a security resource, which is intended to be attacked and compromised to gain more information about an attacker [22]. Also, the technique called "honeyword" was proposed by Juels et al. [12] to detect password theft against hashed password databases.

To mitigate enumeration attacks, we suggest a novel technique called "honey phone numbers" to detect attacks against the people search with phone numbers. The system generates a large set of fake users having nonexistent phone numbers which cannot be distinguishable from real phone numbers to deceive attackers that automatically perform enumeration attacks on those phone numbers. Probably, a normal user would not try to use such nonexistent phone numbers to search for his or her friends while an attacker might try to enumerate phone numbers including honey phone numbers. Therefore, if a significant number of search requests arrive within a short period of time, this might be an unusual event for normal users and could be an evidence of enumeration attack against the friend search feature in Facebook.

6.3   Using Advanced Device Fingerprinting Techniques

Facebook already deployed security techniques that can make it difficult for attackers to create sybil accounts and use them to crawl data. However, current techniques are not sufficient to detect abusive activities used for enumeration attacks. As discussed in Sect. 5.1, email verification can be bypassed by using temporary email accounts; IP address can easily be changed by using VPN services; and device identities (e.g., UUID, IMEI or MAC address) can also be changed.

One way to overcome this limitation of existing device identification is to use some inherent characteristics of a device or web browser, which are usually hard to change. For example, web browsing history [20], network measurements [14], canvas fingerprinting [2], acoustic fingerprinting [24], plugins and fonts [17]. With some of those techniques, service providers could monitor a suspicious user (or browser) and track his or her activities. Using such advanced device (or browser) fingerprinting techniques would lead to significant cost increases of attackers.

However, those fingerprinting techniques may also raise privacy concerns because all Facebook users' activities can be tracked.

6.4   Changing the Default Privacy Settings

Even though Facebook allows users to opt-out of making their profile *searchable* using phone numbers or email addresses (see Fig. 1), users rarely change their privacy settings from the default [16]. Probably, this is an interesting feature to increase the number of users and/or friend relationships on Facebook. However, as we described in this paper, this feature now can be used for enumeration attacks. Therefore, Facebook should consider making the default privacy settings more restrictive.

6.5   Blacklisting Service Providers for Temporary Email Services

To perform the enumeration attack described in this paper, several sybil accounts must be created. In Sect. 5, we show that temporary email addresses are allowed to create these sybil accounts.

To protect the service against the described attacks using sybil accounts, Facebook needs to set more strict security policies (i.e., disallowing users to use temporary email addresses for user account creation).

However, it is likely to degrade the usability of the user account creation process because it allows email addresses from specific domains only. To make matters worse, there exist professional account generators for trustworthy email addresses (e.g., Gmail). Hence, Facebook needs to carefully blacklist email servers to effectively block sybil accounts while minimizing negative effects on normal users.

7   Ethical Issues

The main motivation of our experiments is not to obtain personal information data or to use collected data for commercial or illegal purposes. Instead, we developed a method to show the risk of enumeration attacks on Facebook and introduced reasonable countermeasures to mitigate such attacks. Therefore, we only checked Facebook's responses for our enumeration attack attempts; how-ever, actual user data were not stored.

Finally, we reported the discovered design flaws to Facebook, which acknowl-edged them.

8   Related Work

Since a huge amount of user data is shared on social network services such as Facebook, Twitter, Google+ and YouTube, user privacy is becoming ever more important in using those services. Naturally, privacy concerns about user data on social network services were often discussed. Gross et al. [9] showed that user profiles in social network services could be misused to violate people's privacy if proper measures are not taken. They observed that 77.7% of users were stalked because of the disclosure of their profiles. Zheleva and Getoor [23] showed the risk of inferring social network users' private information from their user profiles in four social network services (Facebook, Flickr, Dogster and BibSonomy). Mah-mood et al. [18] demonstrated several privacy leaks on Facebook and Twitter. For example, they showed that users' email addresses can be mapped to their real names using the Facebook's user password recovery service in Facebook. Backstrom et al. [4] introduced deanonymization attacks against an anonymized graph using the social graph mining where true node identities are replaced with pseudonyms. Mislove et al. [19] also showed that certain user profile attributes can be inferred with a high accuracy using the social network community struc-ture. To prevent such inference attacks, Heatherly et al. [11] proposed three possible defense techniques and evaluated their effectiveness. Bonneau et al. [6] demonstrated that an approximation of a social graph can be used to infer users' several sensitive properties on Facebook. Kim et al. [15] explored several sampling techniques to hide the structure of original social graph against such inference attacks.

The strategy of this attack is not new. There were several studies to design enumeration attacks. For instant messenger applications such as WhatsApp, Viber and Tango, Schrittwieser et al. [21] introduced an enumeration attack to collect active phone numbers. They showed the feasibility of the attack by collecting 21,095 valid phone numbers that are using the WhatsApp application within less than 2.5 h. Kim et al. [13] performed an enumeration attack against Kakaotalk by collecting 50,567 users' personal information (e.g., users' phone numbers, display names and profile pictures). They also proposed three possible defense strategies to mitigate enumeration attacks.

A similar problem related to enumeration attack was already reported in social network services. Balduzzi et al. [5] showed the feasibility of an enumeration attack that automatically queries about e-mail addresses to collect a list of valid e-mail addresses by uploading them to the friend-finder feature of Facebook. Based on the return value of Facebook, they were able to determine the status of an email address. They tested about 10.4 million e-mail addresses and identified more than 1.2 million user profiles associated with these addresses. After they reported the discovered design flaw, Facebook fixed this problem by limiting the number of search requests that a single user can perform. This seems a reasonable security practice because there is no normal user who submitted a million search queries within a short time interval. In this paper, however, we show that enumeration attacks can still be performed on Facebook by mimicking multiple users' search activities with a few sybil accounts.

Bonneau et al. [7] already showed that user accounts can be created anonymously by using temporary email accounts and an anonymous networking technique such as Tor (https://www.torproject.org/). To prevent such user account creation, Facebook already tried to check not only the network identity (e.g., IP address) but also the device identity (e.g., IMEI). In this paper, however, we demonstrate that this procedure can be evaded easily with a rooted Android mobile phone.

9 Conclusion

This paper analyzed a security issue in the people search functionality provided by Facebook, which is the most popular social networking service worldwide. The people search functionality with phone numbers could potentially be misused to leak user's sensitive personal data on a large scale. Based on this feature, we developed a method to automatically collect Facebook users' personal data by enumerating all the valid phone numbers for a target area. To show its feasibility, we implemented an attack for targeting users from in two specific regions (United States and South Korea) by mimicking a real users' search activities with three sybil accounts. Our implementation can evade the Facebook's defense mechanisms; 215,679 South Korean phone numbers were tested and data from 56,564 user profiles was collected in within 15 days; during the same time period 214,705 US phone numbers were tested and data from 25,518 user profiles was collected.

To mitigate such automated enumeration attacks, we suggest five possible defense mechanisms: (1) detecting sequential patterns of queried phone numbers; (2) identifying enumeration attacks with faked phone numbers; (3) using advanced device fingerprinting techniques; (4) changing the default privacy settings and (5) blacklisting service providers for temporary email services. As part of future work, we plan to implement those mechanisms and evaluate their performance against our attacks.

Acknowledgments. This research was supported by Basic Science Research Program through the National Research Foundation of Korea (NRF) funded by the Ministry of Education (2017R1D1A1B03030627), and the MSIT (Ministry of Science and ICT), Korea, under the ITRC (Information Technology Research Center) support program (IITP-2017-2015-0-00403) supervised by the IITP (Institute for Information & communications Technology Promotion). The financial support by the Austrian Federal Ministry of Science, Research and Economy and the National Foundation for Research, Technology and Development is gratefully acknowledged. The authors would like to thank all the anonymous reviewers for their valuable feedback.

References

1. Number of monthly active Facebook users worldwide as of 1st quarter 2017 (The Statistics Portal, statista). https://www.statista.com/statistics/264810/number-of-monthly-active-facebook-users-worldwide/
2. Acar, G., Eubank, C., Englehardt, S., Juarez, M., Narayanan, A., Diaz, C.: The Web never forgets: persistent tracking mechanisms in the wild. In: Proceedings of the ACM SIGSAC Conference on Computer and Communications Security (2014)
3. von Ahn, L., Blum, M., Hopper, N.J., Langford, J.: CAPTCHA: using hard AI problems for security. In: Biham, E. (ed.) EUROCRYPT 2003. LNCS, vol. 2656, pp. 294–311. Springer, Heidelberg (2003). https://doi.org/10.1007/3-540-39200-9_18
4. Backstrom, L., Dwork, C., Kleinberg, J.: Wherefore art Thou R3579x?: anonymized social networks, hidden patterns, and structural steganography. In: Proceedings of the 16th International Conference on World Wide Web (2007)
5. Balduzzi, M., Platzer, C., Holz, T., Kirda, E., Balzarotti, D., Kruegel, C.: Abusing social networks for automated user profiling. In: Jha, S., Sommer, R., Kreibich, C. (eds.) RAID 2010. LNCS, vol. 6307, pp. 422–441. Springer, Heidelberg (2010). https://doi.org/10.1007/978-3-642-15512-3_22
6. Bonneau, J., Anderson, J., Anderson, R., Stajano, F.: Eight friends are enough: social graph approximation via public listings. In: Proceedings of the 2nd ACM EuroSys Workshop on Social Network Systems (2009)
7. Bonneau, J., Anderson, J., Danezis, G.: Prying data out of a social network. In: Proceedings of the International Conference on Advances in Social Network Analysis and Mining (2009)

8. Gao, H., Hu, J., Wilson, C., Li, Z., Chen, Y., Zhao, B.Y.: Detecting and characterizing social spam campaigns. In: Proceedings of the 10th ACM SIGCOMM conference on Internet measurement (2010)

9. Gross, R., Acquisti, A.: Information revelation and privacy in online social networks. In: Proceedings of the ACM Workshop on Privacy in the Electronic Society (2005)

10. Halevi, T., Lewis, J., Memon, N.D.: Phishing, personality traits and Facebook. Social Science Research Network (2015)

11. Heatherly, R., Kantarcioglu, M., Thuraisingham, B.: Preventing private information inference attacks on social networks. IEEE Trans. Knowl. Data Eng. **25**(8), 1849–1862 (2013)

12. Juels, A., Rivest, R.L.: Honeywords: making password-cracking detectable. In: Proceedings of the ACM SIGSAC Conference on Computer and Communications Security (2013)

13. Kim, E., Park, K., Kim, H., Song, J.: Design and analysis of enumeration attacks on finding friends with phone numbers: a case study with KakaoTalk. Comput. Secur. **52**, 267–275 (2015)

14. Kim, H., Huh, J.H.: Detecting DNS-poisoning-based phishing attacks from their network performance characteristics. Electron. Lett. **47**(11), 656–658 (2011)

15. Kim, H., Bonneau, J.: Privacy-enhanced public view for social graphs. In: Proceedings of the 2nd ACM Workshop on Social Web Search and Mining (2009)

16. Krishnamurthy, B., Wills, C.E.: Characterizing privacy in online social networks. In: Proceedings of the First Workshop on Online Social Networks (2008)

17. Laperdrix, P., Rudametkin, W., Baudry, B.: Beauty and the beast: diverting modern web browsers to build unique browser fingerprints. In: Proceedings of IEEE Symposium on Security and Privacy (2016)

18. Mahmood, S.: New privacy threats for Facebook and Twitter users. In: Proceedings of the 7th International Conference on P2P, Parallel, Grid, Cloud and Internet Computing (2012)

19. Mislove, A., Viswanath, B., Gummadi, K.P., Druschel, P.: You are who you know: inferring user profiles in online social networks. In: Proceedings of the 3rd ACM International Conference on Web Search and Data Mining (2010)

20. Olejnik, L., Castelluccia, C., Janc, A.: Why Johnny can't browse in peace: on the uniqueness of web browsing history patterns. In: Proceedings of the 5th Workshop on Hot Topics in Privacy Enhancing Technologies (2012)

21. Schrittwieser, S., Kieseberg, P., Leithner, M., Mulazzani, M., Huber, M.: Guess who's texting you? Evaluating the security of smartphone messaging applications. In: Proceedings of the 19th Annual Symposium on Network and Distributed System Security (2012)

22. Spitzner, L.: Honeypots: Tracking Hackers. Addison-Wesley Longman Publishing Co., Inc., Boston (2002)

23. Zheleva, E., Getoor, L.: To join or not to join: the illusion of privacy in social networks with mixed public and private user profiles. In: Proceedings of the 18th International Conference on World Wide Web (2009)

24. Zhou, Z., Diao, W., Liu, X., Zhang, K.: Acoustic fingerprinting revisited: generate stable device ID stealthily with inaudible sound. In: Proceedings of the ACM SIGSAC Conference on Computer and Communications Security (2014)

Covert QR Codes: How to Hide in the Crowd

Yang-Wai Chow$^{(\boxtimes)}$, Willy Susilo, and Joonsang Baek

Institute of Cybersecurity and Cryptology,
School of Computing and Information Technology,
University of Wollongong, Wollongong, Australia
{caseyc,wsusilo,baek}@uow.edu.au

Abstract. This paper investigates a novel approach of distributing a hidden message via public channels. The proposed approach employs visual subterfuge to conceal secret information within a QR code. Using a QR code reader, any individual can decode the public information contained in the QR code. However, only authorized users who have the necessary credentials will be able to obtain the secret message, which is encoded in the form of a secret QR code. We call this a Covert QR (CQR) code scheme. To embed the secret information, this approach exploits the error correction mechanism inherent in the QR code structure. By using QR codes to conceal information, the proposed scheme has the advantage of reducing the likelihood of attracting the attention of potential adversaries. In addition, the information in QR codes can be scanned and decoded through the visual channel. As such, the secret information can be distributed on printed media and is not restricted to an electronic form.

Keywords: Covert message · Data hiding · Error correction · QR code
Secret sharing

1 Introduction

Consider the scenario where the Central Intelligence Agency (CIA) needs to communicate with their agents via public channels. The agency decides to put up a poster in a public place, like a train station, where everybody can see the poster. The poster has a Quick Response (QR) code, which contains innocent-looking public information along with concealed information. To a casual observer, the QR code will not raise any suspicion. Any individual who uses a QR code reader, e.g., on a mobile phone, will only be able to obtain the public information. However, CIA agents who possess the appropriate credentials will be able to obtain the secret message by decoding the contents of a secret QR code.

This paper examines a novel approach to visual subterfuge by hiding secret information within a QR code. This provides a means for secret communication over public channels using QR codes. While any member of the public can use a standard QR code reader to decode the QR code and acquire the public information, only authorized users who have the necessary credentials will be able

© Springer International Publishing AG 2017
J. K. Liu and P. Samarati (Eds.): ISPEC 2017, LNCS 10701, pp. 678–693, 2017.
https://doi.org/10.1007/978-3-319-72359-4_42

to recover the secret QR code and decode it to obtain the hidden message. In the proposed scheme, even if an adversary realizes that the QR code contains hidden information, the adversary will not be able to obtain the secret message without the correct key.

The motivation behind the proposed scheme is that in cryptography, if one were to encrypt a secret and distribute the ciphertext, the ciphertext can only be decrypted by receivers who know the encryption key. However, if the ciphertext itself were to be distributed using public channels, anybody who sees the ciphertext will immediately recognize that the text has been encrypted. The purpose of the proposed scheme is to adopt visual subterfuge to conceal this in the form of a QR code. Furthermore, in general, ciphertext is distributed via electronic means. The QR code approach presented in this paper allows for the secret information to be distributed in a visual form on printed media.

Our Contribution. This paper introduces a novel method of providing a means for secret communication via public channels, by employing visual subterfuge to conceal secret information in a QR code. We call this a Covert QR (CQR) code scheme. To embed secret information, the proposed scheme exploits an inherent feature of the QR code structure, which is its error correction mechanism. This feature allows correct decoding of a QR code even in the event that part of the QR code is damaged. In the proposed scheme, anybody can use a standard QR code reader to retrieve the public information contained in the QR code. Only authorized users who possess the necessary credentials will be able to recover a secret QR code, which is embedded within the CQR code, and decode it to obtain the secret message. The advantage of the proposed approach is that the QR code itself contains meaningful information, while at the same time it conceals secret information from casual observers.

2   Related Work

2.1   Visual Secret Sharing

Secret sharing is regarded as a mechanism that can be used to transfer secret information via public channels in cryptography [22]. A well known method of visual secret sharing is known as visual cryptography [15]. In visual cryptography, a secret in the form of an image is encoded into a number of shares and distributed to a group of participants. Only when a qualified number of shares are combined will the secret be revealed. Each share looks like a random pattern of pixels, and as such, a visual cryptography share is obvious even to a casual observer.

In a method known as extended visual cryptography, shares are created using meaningful cover images [2]. Therefore, each share looks like a meaningful, albeit noisy, image. The advantage of encoding the secret image into shares containing 'innocent-looking' meaningful cover images is that it reduces the likelihood of attracting the attention of attackers [19]. A QR code visual secret sharing scheme was introduced by Chow et al. [7], in which each share in the scheme is a valid cover QR code containing meaningful public information. As such, each share can be scanned using a standard QR code reader and decoded to obtain the meaningful information. When the secret sharing information in the cover QR code shares are combined, a secret QR code can be recovered and decoded to obtain the secret message. Wan et al. [18] also proposed a different visual secret sharing scheme using QR codes.

2.2   Data Hiding Using QR Codes

The QR code is a two-dimensional code that was invented by the company Denso Wave [9]. The use of QR codes has become ubiquitous in our everyday life. This proliferation is in part due to the QR code's convenience and ease of use. Anybody with a smartphone can obtain the information contained within a QR code. The use of QR codes has also been embraced by the information security research community. This has resulted in a variety of practical applications ranging from authenticating visual cryptography shares [20] and e-voting authentication [10], to digital watermarking [6,13] and secret sharing [7].

There are also a number of proposed schemes that employ QR codes for data hiding and steganography. For example, Wu et al. [21] proposed a data embedding approach for hiding a QR code in a digital image. Their purpose was to camouflage the appearance of a QR code in an image so as not to degrade the visual quality of the picture.

In a different approach, Huang et al. [11] developed a reversible data hiding method for images using QR codes. The problem that they were examining was that if an image contained a QR code, the QR code would obscure a portion of the image, thus degrading its quality. The aim of their proposed scheme was to avoid the QR code from degrading the quality of an image. Their approach involved the use of reversible data hiding to replace a portion of the image with a QR code and to hide the information of this portion in the rest of the image. After the QR code has been scanned, it will be removed from the image and the original image will be restored using the data that was previously hidden in the rest of the image.

Chen and Wang [5] devised a nested image steganography scheme using QR codes. In their approach, two types of secret data, in the form of text (lossless) and image (lossy), were embedded in a cover image. The text portion of the secret data is embedded using a QR code. A similar approach was also reported in Chung et al. [8]. Instead of first converting a secret into a QR code before embedding it in a cover image, Lin et al. [14] proposed a scheme for concealing secret data in a cover QR code. To conceal secret data, their approach capitalized on the QR code error correction redundancy property. The size of concealed secret data depends on the QR code version and its error correction level.

Bui et al. [4] also investigated the problem of hiding secret information in a QR code. In their work, they state that previous approaches of embedding secret messages in QR codes use bit embedding. They argue that this is vulnerable to modification attacks. As such, they proposed a method of using Reed-Solomon code and list decoding to hide a secret message in a QR code.

2.3 Others

This research is related to secret handshakes. The purpose of a secret handshake is to allow members from a group to identify each other [3]. Non-members of the group are not able to recognize group members and cannot perform the secret handshake. As such, secret handshakes can be used to perform mutual authentication between authorized parties [17]. In traditional secret handshake schemes, even if a casual observer does not have the appropriate credentials, the distributed ciphertext is easily recognizable. Examples of other related work include encryption on portable devices [1,16].

3   Background

The International Organization for Standardization (ISO) has established a standard for the QR code (ISO/IEC18004) [12]. This section outlines the basic QR code structure and error correction feature as defined by the ISO standard.[1]

3.1   The QR Code Structure

A QR code symbol consists of a two-dimensional array of light and dark squares, which are referred to as modules. There are forty sizes of QR code symbol versions (i.e. version 1 to version 40). Each version comprises of a different number of modules, and as such different QR code versions have different data capacities. The appropriate version to use depends on the amount and the type of data (i.e. alphanumeric, binary, Kanji or a combination of these) to be encoded as well as the error correction level. The error correction level will be described in Sect. 3.2 to follow.

The QR code structure is made of up of encoding regions and function patterns [12]. An example of this depicted in Fig. 1, which shows the encoding regions and function patterns of a QR code version 7 symbol. The function patterns do not encode data, but are mainly used for obtaining information from the QR code. For example, there are three identical finder patterns located at each corner of the symbol, except for the bottom right corner. These are used by a QR code reader to recognize the QR code and to determine the rotational orientation of the symbol.

---

[1] For a comprehensive description of the QR code structure and error correction mechanism, please refer to the ISO standard (ISO/IEC18004) [12].

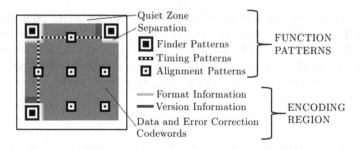

Fig. 1. QR code version 7 structure.

3.2   Encoding and Error Correction

The encoding region contains data codewords and error correction codewords. Message data is encoded as a bit stream that is divided into a sequence of codewords. Codewords are 8-bits in length. The codewords are divided into a number of error correction blocks, based on the QR code version and error correction level, and an appropriate number of error correction codewords are generated for each block. Error correction allows correct decoding of the message in the event that part of the symbol is dirty or damaged. This error correction feature has also been exploited to embed art or other information in QR code symbols. For example, the QR code symbols in Fig. 2(a) and (b)[2] can still be decoded correctly despite the embedded text and image. It can also be seen from Fig. 2(b) that modules do not have to be black and white squares.

(a)   (b)

Fig. 2. (a) QR code where part of it is obscured. (b) Artistic QR code.

The QR code employs Reed-Solomon error control coding for error detection and correction [12]. There are four error correction levels (i.e. L $\sim$ 7%, M $\sim$ 15%, Q $\sim$ 25% and H $\sim$ 30%). Each level provides a different error correction capacity. Higher error correction levels improve the recovery capacity, but also increases the amount of data to be encoded. The number of data codewords, error correction blocks and error correction codewords depend on the QR code version and error correction level.

---

[2] This QR code was generated from http://www.free-qr-code.net/.

Table 1 shows these characteristics for QR code versions 4 and 5. In the table, the error correction codewords for each block is given as (c, d, e), where c is the total number of codewords, d is the number of data codewords and e is the error correction capacity. Note that some QR code versions have blocks with different (c, d, e) values for certain error correction levels. For example, it can be seen in Table 1 that QR code version 5 with an error correction level of Q has a total of 4 error correction blocks. The (c, d, e) values for the first 2 blocks are $(33, 15, 9)$ while the values for the next 2 blocks are $(34, 16, 9)$.

The codewords from the blocks are encoded in an interleaved manner, with the error correction codewords appended to the end of the data codeword sequence. This is done to minimize the possibility that localized damage will cause the QR code to become undecodable. Figure 3 shows the data codeword and error correction codeword arrangement for QR code version 4, with an error correction level of H.

Table 1. Error correction characteristics for QR code versions 4 and 5 [12].

Version	Total codewords	Error correction level	Number of blocks	Error correction codewords per block (c, d, e)
4	100	L	1	(100, 80, 10)
		M	2	(50, 32, 9)
		Q	2	(50, 24, 13)
		H	4	(25, 9, 8)
5	134	L	1	(134, 108, 13)
		M	2	(67, 43, 12)
		Q	2	(33, 15, 9)
			2	(34, 16, 9)
		H	2	(33, 11, 11)
			2	(34, 12, 11)

4 Security Model

In this section, we define the security model of the proposed scheme. We denote assigning the output of an algorithm A, which takes $x, y, \ldots$ as input to z by $z \leftarrow A(x, y, \ldots)$. If A is particularly randomized, we write $z \leftarrow_\$ A(x, y, \ldots)$. $|Q|$ indicates the cardinality of a set Q. For the sake of clarity, we use the following notations to indicate possible inputs and outputs of various algorithms we will describe shortly:

- $\mathcal{P}$: Public message
- $\mathcal{C}$: Original public QR code
- $\mathcal{C}^*$: Covert QR code
- $\mathcal{M}$: Secret message

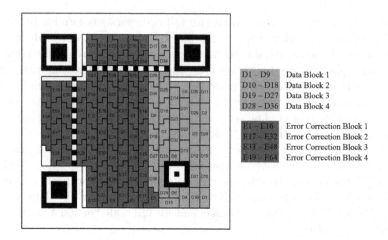

Fig. 3. Data and error correction codeword arrangement for QR code version 4 with error correction level H.

- $\mathcal{S}$: Original secret QR code
- $\mathcal{S}^*$: Recovered secret QR code

We now formally describe a covert QR (CQR) code scheme and present its security requirements.

Definition 1 (CQR). *A covert QR scheme* CQR *consists of a key generation algorithm* KeyGen, *a pseudorandom bit generator* RandGen, *a QR code encoder* QR *and decoder* InvQR, *an embedding algorithm* Emb, *an extraction algorithm* Ext *and a QR verification algorithm* QRVrfy. *The specifications of the algorithms are given as follows:*

- $k \leftarrow_\$ \mathsf{KeyGen}(\ell)$: Taking a security parameter ℓ as input, this algorithm generates a key k.
- $\hat{k} \leftarrow_\$ \mathsf{RandGen}(k, n)$: This algorithm takes a key k as input, and generates an array of pseudorandom bits $\hat{k} \in \{0, 1\}^n$, where n is the length of the array.
- $\mathcal{R} \leftarrow \mathsf{QR}(\mathcal{T})$: Taking a message $\mathcal{T}$ as input, this algorithm generates a QR code $\mathcal{R}$ for $\mathcal{T}$. Hence, $\mathcal{C} \leftarrow \mathsf{QR}(\mathcal{P})$ and $\mathcal{S} \leftarrow \mathsf{QR}(\mathcal{M})$.
- $\mathcal{T} \leftarrow \mathsf{InvQR}(\mathcal{R})$: Taking a QR code $\mathcal{R}$ as input, this algorithm converts $\mathcal{R}$ into the message $\mathcal{T}$. Hence, $\mathcal{P} \leftarrow \mathsf{QR}(\mathcal{C})$ and $\mathcal{M} \leftarrow \mathsf{QR}(\mathcal{S})$.
- $\mathcal{C}^* \leftarrow \mathsf{Emb}(k, \mathcal{S}, \mathcal{C})$: Takes a secret key k, a secret QR code $\mathcal{S}$ and a public QR code $\mathcal{C}$ as input, and generates a covert QR code $\mathcal{C}^*$.
- $\mathcal{S}^* \leftarrow \mathsf{Ext}(k, \mathcal{C}^*)$: This algorithm takes a secret key k and a covert QR code $\mathcal{C}^*$ as input, and outputs a recovered secret QR code $\mathcal{S}^*$.
- $0/1 \leftarrow \mathsf{QRVrfy}(\mathcal{R})$: Given any QR code $\mathcal{R} \in \{\mathcal{C}, \mathcal{C}^*, \mathcal{S}, \mathcal{S}^*\}$, this algorithm outputs 1 if $\mathcal{R}$ is a valid QR code, and 0 otherwise.

Definition 2 (Correctness). *For a public QR code* $\mathcal{C} \leftarrow \mathsf{QR}(\mathcal{P})$ *where* $\mathcal{P}$ *is a public message and a covert QR code* $\mathcal{C}^* \leftarrow \mathsf{Emb}(k, \mathcal{S}, \mathcal{C})$, *the following conditions should hold:*

- $\mathsf{InvQR}(\mathcal{C}) = \mathsf{InvQR}(\mathcal{C}^*) = \mathcal{P}$
- $\mathsf{QRVrfy}(\mathcal{C}) = \mathsf{QRVrfy}(\mathcal{C}^*) = 1$

Similarly, for a secret QR code $\mathcal{S} \leftarrow \mathsf{QR}(\mathcal{M})$ where $\mathcal{M}$ is a private message, and a recovered secret QR code $\mathcal{S}^* \leftarrow \mathsf{Ext}(k, \mathcal{C}^*)$, the following conditions should hold:

- $\mathsf{InvQR}(\mathcal{S}) = \mathsf{InvQR}(\mathcal{S}^*) = \mathcal{M}$
- $\mathsf{QRVrfy}(\mathcal{S}) = \mathsf{QRVrfy}(\mathcal{S}^*) = 1$

Definition 3 (Security). *Let A be an adversary whose running time is polynomial. We say that* CQR *scheme is secure if there exists a negligible function ϵ such that*

$$\Pr[\mathcal{M} \leftarrow A(\mathcal{C}^*)] \leq \epsilon(\ell),$$

where $\mathcal{C}^* \leftarrow \mathsf{Emb}(k, \mathcal{S}, \mathcal{C})$, $k \leftarrow \mathsf{GenKey}(\ell)$, $\mathcal{S} \leftarrow \mathsf{QR}(\mathcal{M})$, $\mathcal{C} \leftarrow \mathsf{QR}(\mathcal{P})$ and ℓ is the security parameter. Note that the probability is taken over the randomness used by A, the key generation algorithm and the pseudorandom bit generator.

5 Proposed Covert QR Code Scheme

In this section, we describe the proposed method of implementing a Covert QR (CQR) code scheme. Figure 4 illustrates a conceptual overview of the proposed scheme. From Fig. 4 it can be seen that first, the secret message $\mathcal{M}$ and the public message $\mathcal{P}$ are encoded in the form of QR codes, using a QR code generator, to produce $\mathcal{S}$ and $\mathcal{C}$, respectively. These QR codes along with the secret key k, will be the input of the embedding algorithm. The pseudocode for the embedding algorithm is provided in Algorithm 1, which will be described in Sect. 5.1. The output of the embedding algorithm will be the covert QR code $\mathcal{C}^*$. This CQR code contains both public and hidden information, and can be distributed via public channels.

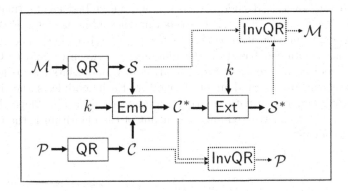

Fig. 4. Overview of the proposed CQR scheme.

Note that both C and C^* are valid QR codes. When scanned and decoded with a standard QR code reader, both QR codes will produce the public message P. The error correction mechanism in the QR code structure makes it possible to manipulate some of the codewords in C to produce C^*, while still maintaining a QR code symbol that can be decoded correctly.

For individuals who know the secret key k, the CQR code and the secret key can be provided as input to the extraction algorithm, which will be able to reconstruct a recovered secret QR code S^*. The pseudocode for the extraction algorithm is provided in Algorithm 2, which will be discussed later. Both S and S^* are valid QR codes, that when scanned and decoded will result in the secret message M. Note that even if the recovered secret QR code contains some errors, due to scanning errors or if C^* is slightly damage or obscured, the error correction mechanism inherent in the QR code symbol means that S^* can be still be decoded correctly as long as the error correction capacity has not been overwhelmed.

5.1   Algorithms

The embedding and extraction algorithms are described here. Pseudocode for the embedding algorithm is provided in Algorithm 1. The purpose of the embedding algorithm is to embed encrypted codewords from the secret QR code S into the public QR code C, using the secret key k.

The reason why only the codewords are embedded is because the function patterns, which are fixed patterns in QR codes, will leak information about the pseudorandom bits $\hat{k}$ and consequently the secret key k. As such, the codewords in S must first be extracted. Then based on the number of codewords and codeword modules (each codeword is made up of 8 modules), an array of random bits can be generated using a pseudorandom bit generator by using k as the seed value. Each codeword module is encrypted by performing an XOR operation with a corresponding random bit, before embedding it in C^*. The output of the embedding algorithm is the covert QR code C^*, which contains both the public and private information.

For the extraction algorithm, provided in Algorithm 2, the input is the secret key k and the covert QR code C^*. To extract the embedded information, the algorithm first decodes the CQR C^* to obtain the public message P. With the public message, the algorithm generates the public QR code C. The embedded information is obtained based on the differences between C^* and C. Once the embedded codewords are extracted, the array of random bits can be generated using k and the pseudorandom bit generator. Each module is the decrypted using an XOR operation with the corresponding random bit. Thus, the secret QR code can be reconstructed and the output of the algorithm is the recovered secret QR code S^*.

Algorithm 1. Pseudocode for the embedding algorithm (i.e. $\mathcal{C}^* \leftarrow \mathsf{Emb}(k, \mathcal{S}, \mathcal{C})$)

---

function EMBEDCQR(k, S, C)
   /* Extract the codewords from S */
   $num \leftarrow$ numberOfCodewords(S)
   $codewords[num][8] \leftarrow$ extractCodewords(S)

   /* Generate pseudorandom bits using k as the seed */
   $rbits[num \times 8] \leftarrow$ randomBitGenerator(k, $num \times 8$)

   /* Encrypt each codeword module */
   $b = 1$
   $\mathcal{C}^* = \mathcal{C}$
   for $i = 1$ to num **do**
      for $j = 1$ to 8 **do**
         /* Each codeword consists of 8 modules, $\oplus$ is an XOR operation */
         $encyptedModules[i][j] \leftarrow codewords[i][j] \oplus rbits[b]$
         $b = b + 1$

         /* Embed each encrypted module into $\mathcal{C}$ to produce $\mathcal{C}^*$ */
         $\mathcal{C}^* \leftarrow encryptedModules[i][j]$
      end for
   end for

   /* Output $\mathcal{C}^*$ */
   return $\mathcal{C}^*$
end function

5.2 Practical Considerations

The proposed CQR code scheme exploits the error correction mechanism in the QR code structure, by manipulating some of the codewords in $\mathcal{C}$ to produce $\mathcal{C}^*$. This will still allow the CQR code to be decoded correctly as long as the manipulated codewords does not exceed the error correction capacity. Therefore, this necessitates that the public QR code $\mathcal{C}$'s size must be large enough to accommodate the number of codewords in the secret QR code $\mathcal{S}$. In addition, based on the security discussed in Sect. 6.2 the larger the size of $\mathcal{S}$, the more difficult for an adversary to attack the CQR code. The size of a secret message that is governed by the data capacity of the secret QR code.

As described in Sect. 3.2, QR code symbols have different error correction levels. Furthermore, the different QR code versions determine the size of the QR code symbol and its data capacity. Each QR code version has different error correction characteristics. The appropriate size of $\mathcal{C}$, based on the size of $\mathcal{S}$, can be determined by referring to the QR code error correction characteristics. Refer to Table 1 for an example of this. A suitable QR code version for $\mathcal{C}$ requires that the error correction capacity per block, e, multiplied by the number of blocks for the specific error correction level, must be greater than the total number of codewords in $\mathcal{S}$. In practice, the chosen size should have an error correction

---

Algorithm 2. Pseudocode for the extraction algorithm (i.e. $\mathcal{S}^* \leftarrow \mathsf{Ext}(k, \mathcal{C}^*)$)

---

function EXTRACTCQR(k, C^*)

   /* Decode C^* to obtain the public message $\mathcal{P}$, and generate C */
   $C \leftarrow (\mathcal{P} \leftarrow \mathsf{QR}(\mathcal{C}))$

   /* Get the difference between C^* and C */
   $extracted[n][8] \leftarrow \mathrm{diff}(C^*, C)$
   $num \leftarrow \mathrm{computeSize}(extracted)$

   /* Generate pseudorandom bits using k as the seed */
   $rbits[num \times 8] \leftarrow \mathrm{randomBitGenerator}(k, num \times 8)$

   /* Construct S^* */
   $b = 1$
   for $i = 1$ to num **do**
      /* Each codeword consists of 8 modules, $\oplus$ is an XOR operation */
      for $j = 1$ to 8 **do**
         $S^* \leftarrow extracted[i][j] \oplus rbits[b]$
         $b = b + 1$
      end for
   end for

   /* Output $\mathcal{S}^*$ */
   return $\mathcal{S}^*$
end function

---

capacity which is appropriately large to accommodate the modifications. This is so that the resulting CQR code can still be decoded in the even that it is slightly damaged or obscured.

6   Analysis and Discussion

6.1   Experiment Results

An experiment to test the scheme was performed by implementing the proposed CQR code scheme. Figure 5 shows example results of the implementation. The secret QR code that contains a secret message is shown in Fig. 5(a). It is a QR code of version 2 and error correction level H. Figure 5(b) depicts the codewords that are extracted from the QR code in Fig. 5(a). The total number of codewords for a QR code version 2 is 44.

Figure 5(c) in turn shows the original public QR code, which contains the public message. It is a QR code of version 6 with error correction level H. For this version and error correction level, there are 4 encoding blocks with error correction capacity of 14. Therefore, this QR code size is suitable for the proposed scheme because $14 \times 4 > 44$. The CQR code resulting from the proposed scheme is given in Fig. 5(d). Note that the CQR shown in Fig. 5(d) is a valid QR code that can be scanned by a standard QR code reader, and will decode to the same public message as the original public QR code shown in Fig. 5(c). Finally, Fig. 5(e) shows the difference between the QR codes depicted in Fig. 5(c) and (d). Gray color indicates no difference, whereas the white and black modules are the original colors in Fig. 5(c) that differ from those in Fig. 5(d).

Fig. 5. Example results; (a) QR code containing a secret message (Contains the secret message: "Secret Message".); (b) Codewords of the QR code shown in (a); (c) Original public QR code that contains a public message (Contains the public message: "http:// www.springer.com/gp/computer-science/lncs."); (d) Covert QR code resulting from the proposed scheme (Also decodes to the public message: "http://www.springer.com/ gp/computer-science/lncs."); (e) Difference image between (c) and (d).

6.2   Security Analysis

Correctness. We first show that the proposed CQR scheme is correct in the sense of Definition 2.

Theorem 1. *The proposed covert QR code (CQR) scheme described in Sect. 5 satisfies the correctness requirement specified in Definition 2.*

Proof. By the construction of the proposed covert QR scheme CQR, $\mathcal{C}$ and $\mathcal{C}^*$ are valid QR codes. Hence, we have $\mathsf{QRVrfy}(\mathcal{C}^*) = \mathsf{QRVrfy}(\mathcal{C}) = 1$. Also, the inverses of the QR codes $\mathcal{C}$ and $\mathcal{C}^*$ point to the same public message $\mathcal{P}$. As a result, we have $\mathsf{InvQR}(\mathcal{C}^*) = \mathsf{InvQR}(\mathcal{C}) = \mathcal{P}$.

In addition, $\mathcal{S}$ and $\mathcal{S}^*$ are valid QR codes. Therefore, $\mathsf{QRVrfy}(\mathcal{S}^*) = \mathsf{QRVrfy}(\mathcal{S}) = 1$, and the inverses of the QR codes $\mathcal{S}$ and $\mathcal{S}^*$ point to the same secret message $\mathcal{M}$, i.e. $\mathsf{InvQR}(\mathcal{S}^*) = \mathsf{InvQR}(\mathcal{S}) = \mathcal{M}$.

Thus, the proposed covert QR scheme satisfies the correctness requirement.

Security Against Brute Force Attack. The security of the proposed scheme is information theoretic: If an adversary suspects that a CQR code contains secret information, the adversary can easily obtain the embedded encrypted codewords. From this, the adversary can obtain information about the size of the secret QR code based on the number of embedded codewords. However, without the secret key k, the adversary cannot decrypt the encrypted codewords.

Nevertheless, since the secret QR code $\mathcal{S}$ must be a valid QR code, an adversary can attempt to adopt a brute force strategy to infer information about $\mathcal{M}$ or k. Let S' denote a valid, or in other words 'meaningful', QR code and $\left| S' \right|$ be the cardinality of all the valid QR codes of that size. The probability of success for this attack will be bounded by $\frac{1}{\left| S' \right|}$. The space of $\left| S' \right|$ is governed by the size of data that a QR code can contain, which is determined by the specific QR code version used to encode the message. Hence, the larger the secret QR code, the larger $\left| S' \right|$ will be, which in turn lowers the success of an attack. Let d be the number of data codewords for a QR code. Since each codeword contains 8 modules, $\left| S' \right| = 2^{8d}$.

We prove this formally in the following theorem.

Theorem 2. *The proposed covert QR code scheme described in Sect. 5 satisfies the security requirement specified in Definition 3 assuming that the ℓ-bit (seed) secret key k is used to generate an array of pseudorandom bits $\hat{k} \in \{0,1\}^n$, where n is the length of the array.*

Proof. Note that by the construction of the embedding algorithm of the proposed scheme, each bit in $\hat{k}$ is XOR-ed with each codeword module in S, then embedded in C^*. This means that $\left| SP_{\mathcal{C}^*} \right| = \left| SP_{\hat{k}} \right|$, where $SP_{\mathcal{C}^*}$ and $SP_{\hat{k}}$ denote the space of the (possible) modified QR codes based on C^* and the random bit array space, respectively. Note that in the proposed scheme, $\left| SP_{\hat{k}} \right| = 2^n$. Hence,

$$\Pr[A \text{ outputs } \mathcal{M}] = \Pr[A \text{ finds correct } \hat{k}] \leq \frac{1}{2^n},$$

Thus, the probability that the adversary A will obtain a right message $\mathcal{M}$ is negligible for large n. This also implies that the larger the secret QR code, the larger n will be.

Visual Subterfuge. One of the primary advantages of the proposed scheme stems from the fact that CQR codes are meaningful innocent-looking QR codes. This will reduce the likelihood of attracting the attention of potential adversaries. In addition, since modules in QR codes do not have to be black and white squares, it would be aid in the visual subterfuge if the CQR code were to be constructed using an artistic QR code scheme, like the example shown in Fig. 2(b). The proposed CQR scheme will work as long as the contrast between light and dark modules can adequately be scanned by a QR code reader.

7   Conclusion

This paper presents a novel approach for distributing a hidden message via public channels using the proposed Covert QR (CQR) code scheme. By exploiting the error correction mechanism inherent in the QR code structure, the proposed scheme can embed encrypted codewords from a secret QR code into a covert QR code. The resulting CQR code can be scanned by a standard QR code reader to obtain the public information. However, authorized users who have the necessary credentials will be able to use the information embedded within a CQR code to reconstruct a secret QR code, which contains the secret message. The purpose of the proposed scheme is to employs visual subterfuge to conceal secret information within a QR code. In view of the fact that a CQR code contains meaningful innocent-looking information, the aim of this is to reduce the likelihood of attracting the attention of potential adversaries. This is unlike traditional ciphertext that can easily be recognized even by a casual observer. In addition, since the information in QR codes can be scanned and decoded through the visual channel, CQR codes are not restricted to an electronic form and can be distributed via printed media.

References

1. Albano, P., Bruno, A., Carpentieri, B., Palmieri, F., Pizzolante, R., Yim, K., You, I.: Secure and distributed video surveillance via portable devices. J. Ambient Intell. Humanized Comput. **5**(2), 205–213 (2014)
2. Ateniese, G., Blundo, C., De Santis, A., Stinson, D.R.: Extended capabilities for visual cryptography. Theor. Comput. Sci. **250**(1–2), 143–161 (2001)
3. Balfanz, D., Durfee, G., Shankar, N., Smetters, D.K., Staddon, J., Wong, H.: Secret handshakes from pairing-based key agreements. In: 2003 IEEE Symposium on Security and Privacy (S&P 2003), 11–14 May 2003, Berkeley, CA, USA, pp. 180–196. IEEE Computer Society (2003)
4. Bui, T.V., Vu, N.K., Nguyen, T.T., Echizen, I., Nguyen, T.D.: Robust message hiding for QR code. In: 2014 Tenth International Conference on Intelligent Information Hiding and Multimedia Signal Processing (IIH-MSP), pp. 520–523. IEEE (2014)
5. Chen, W.-Y., Wang, J.-W.: Nested image steganography scheme using QR-barcode technique. Opt. Eng. **48**(5), 057004–057004 (2009)

6. Chow, Y.-W., Susilo, W., Tonien, J., Zong, W.: A QR code watermarking approach based on the DWT-DCT technique. In: Pieprzyk, J., Suriadi, S. (eds.) ACISP 2017. LNCS, vol. 10343, pp. 314–331. Springer, Cham (2017). https://doi.org/10.1007/978-3-319-59870-3_18

7. Chow, Y.-W., Susilo, W., Yang, G., Phillips, J.G., Pranata, I., Barmawi, A.M.: Exploiting the error correction mechanism in QR codes for secret sharing. In: Liu, J.K.K., Steinfeld, R. (eds.) ACISP 2016. LNCS, vol. 9722, pp. 409–425. Springer, Cham (2016). https://doi.org/10.1007/978-3-319-40253-6_25

8. Chung, C.-H., Chen, W.-Y., Tu, C.-M.: Image hidden technique using qr-barcode. In: Fifth International Conference on Intelligent Information Hiding and Multimedia Signal Processing, IIH-MSP 2009, pp. 522–525. IEEE (2009)

9. Denso Wave Incorporated. QRcode.com, http://www.qrcode.com/en/

10. Falkner, S., Kieseberg, P., Simos, D.E., Traxler, C., Weippl, E.: E-voting authentication with QR-codes. In: Tryfonas, T., Askoxylakis, I. (eds.) HAS 2014. LNCS, vol. 8533, pp. 149–159. Springer, Cham (2014). https://doi.org/10.1007/978-3-319-07620-1_14

11. Huang, H.-C., Chang, F.-C., Fang, W.-C.: Reversible data hiding with histogram-based difference expansion for QR code applications. IEEE Trans. Consum. Electron. 57(2), 779–787 (2011)

12. International Organization for Standardization: Information technology – automatic identification and data capture techniques – QR code 2005 bar code symbology specification. ISO/IEC 18004:2006 (2006)

13. Lee, H.C., Dong, C.R., Lin, T.M.: Digital watermarking based on JND model and QR code features. In: Pan, J.S., Yang, C.N., Lin, C.C. (eds.) Advances in Intelligent Systems and Applications – Volume 2. SIST, vol 21, pp. 141–148. Springer, Heidelberg (2013). https://doi.org/10.1007/978-3-642-35473-1_15

14. Lin, P.-Y., Chen, Y.-H., Lu, E.J.-L., Chen, P.-J.: Secret hiding mechanism using QR barcode. In: 2013 International Conference on Signal-Image Technology & Internet-Based Systems (SITIS), pp. 22–25. IEEE (2013)

15. Naor, M., Shamir, A.: Visual cryptography. In: De Santis, A. (ed.) EUROCRYPT 1994. LNCS, vol. 950, pp. 1–12. Springer, Heidelberg (1995). https://doi.org/10.1007/BFb0053419

16. Pizzolante, R., Carpentieri, B., Castiglione, A., Castiglione, A., Palmieri, F.: Text compression and encryption through smart devices for mobile communication. In: 2013 Seventh International Conference on Innovative Mobile and Internet Services in Ubiquitous Computing, pp. 672–677, July 2013

17. Sorniotti, A., Molva, R.: A provably secure secret handshake with dynamic controlled matching. Comput. Secur. 29(5), 619–627 (2010). Challenges for Security, Privacy and Trust

18. Wan, S., Lu, Y., Yan, X., Wang, Y., Chang, C.: Visual secret sharing scheme for (k, n) threshold based on QR code with multiple decryptions. J. Real-Time Image Process., 1–16 (2017)

19. Wang, D., Yi, F., Li, X.: On general construction for extended visual cryptography schemes. Pattern Recogn. 42(11), 3071–3082 (2009)

20. Weir, J., Yan, W.Q.: Authenticating visual cryptography shares using 2D barcodes. In: Shi, Y.Q., Kim, H.-J., Perez-Gonzalez, F. (eds.) IWDW 2011. LNCS, vol. 7128, pp. 196–210. Springer, Heidelberg (2012). https://doi.org/10.1007/978-3-642-32205-1_17

21. Wu, W.-C., Lin, Z.-W., Wong, W.-T.: Application of QR-code steganography using data embedding technique. In: Park, J.J.J.H., Barolli, L., Xhafa, F., Jeong, H.Y. (eds.) Information Technology Convergence. LNEE, vol. 253, pp. 597–605. Springer, Dordrecht (2013). https://doi.org/10.1007/978-94-007-6996-0_63

22. Yan, W., Wier, J., Kankanhalli, M.S.: Image secret sharing. In: Cimato, S., Yang, C.-N. (eds.) Visual Cryptography and Secret Image Sharing, pp. 381–402. CRC Press, Taylor and Francis Group (2012)

Home Location Protection in Mobile Social Networks: A Community Based Method (Short Paper)

Bo Liu[1](✉), Wanlei Zhou[2], Shui Yu[2], Kun Wang[3], Yu Wang[4], Yong Xiang[2], and Jin Li[4]

[1] Department of Engineering, La Trobe University, Melbourne, Australia
b.liu2@latrobe.edu.au
[2] School of Information Technology, Deakin University, Melbourne, Australia
{wanlei.zhou,shui.yu,yong.xiang}@deakin.edu.au
[3] Nanjing University of Posts and Telecommunications, Nanjing, China
kwang@njupt.edu.cn
[4] School of Computer Science, Guangzhou University, Guangzhou, China
{yuwang,lijin}@gzhu.edu.cn

Abstract. Location privacy has drawn much attention among mobile social network users, as the geo-location information can be used by the adversaries to launch localization attacks which focus on finding people's sensitive locations such as home and office place. In this paper, we propose a community based information sharing scheme to help the users to protect their home locations. First, we study the existing home location prediction algorithms and conclude that they are all mainly based on the spatial and temporal features of the check-in data. Then we design the community based information sharing scheme which aggregates the check-ins of all community members, thus change the overall spatial and temporal features. Finally, our simulation results validate that our proposed scheme greatly reduces the home location predication accuracy and therefore can protect the user's privacy effectively.

Keywords: Location predication · Community · Mobile social network

1 Introduction

Location information is introduced into a variety of social network platforms to enrich people's interactivity and relationship [1,2]. Many people like to share activities (check-ins), thoughts (tweets, status updates, etc.), pictures, videos, or interesting articles with friends, family and the public. These shared posts often come along with location data (geo-tags). Although these information can be used to improve people's life quality, i.e., recommending famous place of interests to friends, they poses high privacy risks at the same time.

The geo-location information can be used by the adversaries to launch localization attacks which focus on finding people's position and time information.

© Springer International Publishing AG 2017
J. K. Liu and P. Samarati (Eds.): ISPEC 2017, LNCS 10701, pp. 694–704, 2017.
https://doi.org/10.1007/978-3-319-72359-4_43

A type of dangerous attack aims to find important locations such as home and work places [3,4]. There have been a number of papers investigating the home location identification problem, either based on the content of the posts [5] or the geo-tags in the check-ins [6]. And the research shows that the identification accuracy might be over 90% in many cases.

On the contrary, the research targeting on protecting sensitivity locations has been very rare. As an effort to fill this technique gap, we propose a community based home location protection scheme in this paper. Our idea is based on the fact that people sometimes only need to share precise information with certain communities, such as colleagues, family members or classmates. Therefore, when a user posts a check-in or tweets with the geo-tag, he/she can select to post this information as a member of a community which he/she belongs to. Then for the outside adversaries, the geo-location information becomes indistinguishable among the community members. We test the performance of the proposed scheme with two existing home location prediction algorithms. In summary, the contributions of this paper are as follows:

- We propose a community based scheme to deal with the challenge of sensitive location protection in mobile social networks.
- The effect of the proposed scheme on the features of the geo-location information is analyzed.
- We setup an evaluation system and validate our proposed scheme against two existing home location prediction algorithms, on the real-life dataset.

The rest of the paper is organized as follows. Section 2 lists the related work. Section 3 gives a detailed introduction on the preliminaries and system model, including the assumptions and basic notations. The proposed community based home important location prediction scheme is described and analyzed in Sect. 4. Performance analysis and extensive numerical simulations are presented in Sect. 5. Finally, Sect. 6 gives the conclusion about this paper.

2   Related Work

As there has been no work specifically targeting on home location protection, we discuss the home location identification techniques in this Section. Home Location Identification focuses on identifying home location of users in social networks. There are two types of approaches within this scope: content based approach and check-in based approach.

2.1   Content Based Approach

Content based approach infers home location of users by extracting location information from texts like tweets in social networks. Cheng et al. [5] used a classifier to identify words in tweets with a strong local geo-scope, combing with a lattice-based neighborhood smoothing model for refining a user's location estimation. Chandra et al. [7] employed a probabilistic framework to estimate the city-level location of a Twitter user, based on the content of the tweets in their dialogues. Mahumd et al. [4,8] used an ensemble of statistical and heuristic classifiers to predict Twitter users's home locations based on their tweeting behavior and content of tweets. Li et al. [9] combined user's multiple microblogs and used them to identify the location.

2.2   Check-in Based Approach

Check-in based approach infers home location of users utilizing check-in data of users. Cho et al. [6] inferred the home location by discretizing the world into 25 by 25 Km cells and defining the home location as the average position of check-ins in the cell with the most check-ins. Li et al. [10] identified home locations of users in Twitter based on the model using signals observed from friends and venues identified in tweets. Pontes et al. [11] used a majority voting scheme which takes the most popular location of a user as the home location. Liu et al. [12] obtained the estimated home locations using a hierarchical clustering method to cluster checkins at night.

Besides the content and check-in based approach, other information can also be used in home location prediction. For example, Gu et al. [3] infer home location in city scale by trusts between the friends.

The precision of the content based approaches is generally city-level, which is not as good as the check-in based approaches. Because the location information in the content is often blur. Therefore, we will use check-in based approach to test our scheme in this paper.

3   Preliminaries and System Model

As all the check-in based home location prediction methods are based on the features of users' check-in data, we will first conclude the check-in behaviour of users in mobile social networks in this section. We will also briefly describe the two location predication algorithms which will be used to test our proposed scheme. The adversary model and privacy metric are given as well, as the fundamental of the rest parts of the paper.

3.1   Check-in Behavior of Users in Mobile Social Networks

Spatial Features of Check-in Data. Cho et al. [6] explored the distribution of the check-ins numbers as a function of the distance from home and observed that the distribution follows a power law with exponential cutoff, i.e.,

$$f(d) = d^\alpha e^\beta, \tag{1}$$

where d is the check-in distance from home. α and β are the parameters vary for different datasets.

And such a phenomenon exists in different datasets including Brightkite and Gowalla.

Temporal Features of Check-in Data. Besides the spatial feature, the check-in data also have temporal feature. For example, check-ins at night (shared from 8:00 p.m. to 7:59 a.m. every day) are most likely to happen at the home location, while check-ins during work hours (from 8:00 a.m. to 6:59 p.m. on weekdays) have high probability to be linked to the office location.

3.2   Home Location Predication Algorithms

The above mentioned spatial and temporal features of the check-ins are used to predict the home locations. Here we introduce two typical algorithms based on the number of check-ins and time stamps clusterings, respectively.

Algorithm 1: Home Prediction by the Number of Check-ins. Scellato et al. [13] defined the home location as the average position of check-ins in the cell with the most check-ins. They first divide the whole area into cells $\{cell_0, cell_1, ..., cell_i, ...\}$. Then the predicted home location $l_{u,h} = avg(l_{cell_{max}})$ is the average position of check-ins locations in the cell with the most number of check-ins $cell_{max}$. Manual inspection shows that this algorithm can infer home locations with 85% accuracy [6].

Algorithm 2: Home Prediction by Clustering Check-ins Based on Time Stamps. Liu et al. [12] proposed a user home/office locations prediction algorithm by clustering check-ins shared at night and work hours respectively. First, the check-ins during the night time of user u are divided into clusters $\{cluster_{u,0}, cluster_{u,1}, ..., cluster_{u,i}, ...\}$ by a hierarchical clustering method. Then a home candidate $r_{u,h,i} = (g, n)$ is calculated from each $cluster_{u,i}$, where g is the center of all the check-in locations in $cluster_{u,i}$, and n is the number of check-ins in the cluster. Finally, the home candidates list $R_{u,h}$ is formed by $\{r_{u,h,0}, r_{u,h,1}, ..., r_{u,h,i}, ...\}$, descending by the number of check-ins in each cluster. They showed that for 98.3% of users, at least one of the first three home candidates $r_{u,h,i}, i = 1, 2, 3$ are within 2 Km of the user's true home location.

3.3   The Adversary and Attack Models

An adversary's aim in the location privacy ground is collecting location information and using it to gain benefits. Based on the two key factors of the location privacy, the adversary and his/her attack can be characterized by "how" they obtain the information, "how" the attack is launched, "what" the information they obtained (knowledge), and "what" is the target.

In this paper, we assume that the adversary obtain the information by collecting shared or published geo-location information (i.e., check-ins with timestamps). And the obtained location information is precise in the sense that it is not processed by any obfuscation schemes.

And the attack target is people's sensitive positions such as the home locations. The adversaries use data mining and machine learning tool (Alg. 1 and Alg. 2) to launch the attack.

3.4   Privacy Metrics

We use the "correctness" metric [14] to measure the performance of the proposed scheme. It is a distance based metrics quantifying the error or expected distance between the true and predicted location. For a single location, it can be computed by the posterior probability of the adversary's estimates x based on his observations o, while the true position is x_c, i.e.,

$$\sum_x Pr(x|o)d(x, x_c). \tag{2}$$

In the context of this paper, x is the predicted home location based on the observed check-ins o. $d(x, x_c)$ is the distance calculated by the coordinates.

4   Hiding Important Locations by Community-Community Based Information Sharing Scheme

4.1   Community Based Geo-Location Information Sharing Scheme

In nowadays, many people use social networking apps and websites such as facebook and tweets to share their experiences and thoughts with other people, through posts along with geo-location data. As these location data are generally available to the public, they might be collected by adversaries and used to predict a user's home location.

On the other hand, people in social networks belong to different communities, and the communities are formed based on common features such as family members, similar interests and classmates. Moreover, people may belong to multiple communities at the same time. For example, one may be in a community who graduate from the same university and another community who like to travel as well.

In reality, people sometimes only want to share precise information within certain communities. Based on this fact, we may enable the user to select to post this information as an individual or as a member of a community which he/she belongs to. The former case is the current scheme used in social networks. And the latter case can prevent possible outside adversaries from knowing the exact owner of the posts.

Figures 1 and 2 illustrate our idea of the community based geo-location information sharing scheme. As shown in Fig. 1, the user "Luke Liu" posts a check-in at a point of interest "Deakin University Library" as the member of "Deakin Staff" community, other users in this community can see that it is posted by "Luke Liu" (Fig. 2(a)), while public users who are not in this community only see that it is posted by a member of the "Deakin Staff" community (Fig. 2(b)).

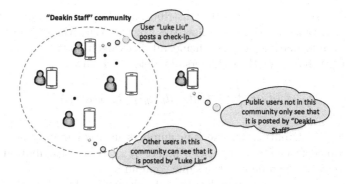

Fig. 1. Illustration of the community based geo-location information sharing scheme.

(a) Information seen by community members.

(b) Information seen by people outside the community.

Fig. 2. Example of the community based geo-location information sharing scheme.

4.2   Aggregated Check-in Behavior of Users in a Community

With this scheme, the geo-location data collected by the adversaries will be the aggregated information of different communities. We now investigate the aggregated check-in behavior of users and its impact on the prediction of home location.

As discussed in Sect. 3, all the home location predication algorithms are based on the spatial and temporal features of check-ins. The temporal feature is not changed by our scheme. Thus we focus on the change of the spatial feature under our proposed community based geo-location information sharing scheme.

Assuming that for each user, the distributions of check-in numbers as a function of the distance from home follow the Eq. (1). With the community based geo-location information sharing scheme, all check-ins from the same community are indistinguishable for the outsiders. Therefore, we have

$$f_c(d) = \int_{d_{h-h}} f(|\boldsymbol{d} - \boldsymbol{d}_{h-h}|) \cdot f_{h-h}(d_{h-h}), \tag{3}$$

where $f_c()$ is distributions of check-in numbers in a community as a function of the distance from a certain user's home. f_{h-h} is the distribution of home distances between members in the same community.

Intuitively, traditional home location algorithms are based on the precondition that each user has "one" home location. When our scheme aggregate the check-ins in communities, it hides a single user's home among all home locations of the community.

5   Performance Evaluation and Discussions

5.1   Datasets and Evaluation Setup

We evaluate our scheme using the Gowalla dataset which is collected by the authors of [15] from Gowalla which was a popular LBSN service back in 2011. The dataset was collected from February 2009 to October 2010 and it contains 6,442,892 check-ins. Besides location information, the dataset also includes the corresponding social data which contains around 1.9 million users and 9.5 million edges. Due to the large data sparsity, we take the check-in data in New York as an example, as New York is among the areas with most check-ins (138957) in the dataset. In addition, we only focus on users who have conducted at least 100 check-ins in each city and we term these users as active users (241 in total).

As our proposed scheme is based on the community structure, community detection is the first step. Community detection methods have been investigated in many papers. It is closely related to the ideas of graph partitioning in graph theory and hierarchical clustering in sociology. According to the comparative analysis [16], among all the community detection algorithms, Infomap [17] has the best performance on undirected and unweighted graphs. Therefore, we use Infomap in this work.

The Gowalla dataset contains the links among users. To detect communities of u, we first find all his/her friends as well as the links among them. Then, we delete u and all edges linked to him and apply Infomap algorithm to the remaining part of the graph. The average community numbers of each active user in our simulation is 3.215 and the average community size is 14.727.

5.2   Impact on Spatial Feature of the Check-Ins

In order to validate that our proposed scheme can protect home location, we first verify that it indeed changes the spatial features of the check-in data.

Figures 3 and 4 compare the check-in number distributions of a single user and a community. It can be seen that when calculated using the community's data, the curve becomes more flat. And when we fit the power law parameters using maximum likelihood, the parameters change a lot as well ($\alpha = -0.064$ vs -0.002, $\beta = -0.8$ vs 2.25).

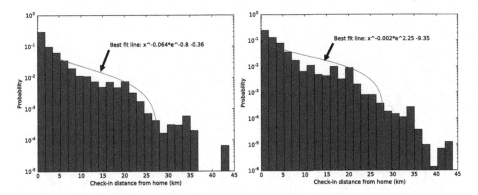

Fig. 3. Distribution of a single user's check-in distance from home.

Fig. 4. Distribution of a community's check-in distance from home.

5.3   Impact on Home Location Predication Algorithms

Now we investigate the impact on the two different home location prediction algorithms presented in Sect. 3.

Figure 5 gives an example (user id = 1940) of the home location prediction results using Alg. 1. It shows that our scheme introduces big perturbations to the predicted home location.

With regard to Alg. 2, using the user's own or the communities' check-in data results different clustering results, as shown in Figs. 6 and 7. Thus the accuracy of the home location predication is reduced accordingly, as shown in Fig. 8.

Finally, we calculate the correctness of home location prediction under our proposed community based geo-location information sharing scheme, as shown in Figs. 9 and 10. As we do not have the true home locations of users, we use the prediction results using only the user's own check-ins as his/her "actual" home. The average correctness of Alg. 1 is 1942 m and the value for Alg. 2 is 4345 m. It validates that our proposed scheme brings great obfuscation for the location predication algorithms. Moreover, the correctness of Alg. 1 is averagely smaller because of the procedure of "discretizing". The impact of the cell size on the results will be further investigated in the future works.

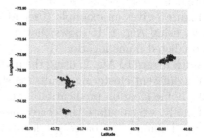

Fig. 5. Predicted home locations using Alg. 1 (the "green" is obtain by the user's own check-ins, the "red" ones obtained by the check-ins belong to the user's two communities). (Color figure online)

Fig. 6. Clustering of a single user's check-in data during night time.

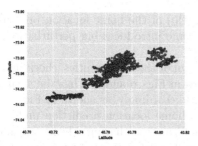

(a) Clustering results of check-ins in community 1.

(b) Clustering results of check-ins in community 2.

Fig. 7. Clustering of communities check-in data during night time.

Fig. 8. Predicted home locations by Alg. 2 (the "brone" ones are top three home location candidates obtain by the user's own check-ins, the "blue" ones are home location candidates obtained by the check-ins belong to the user's two communities). (Color figure online)

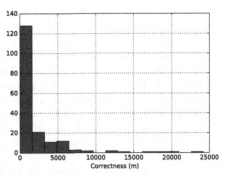

Fig. 9. Correctness of the home prediction results using Alg. 1 under the community based geo-location information sharing scheme.

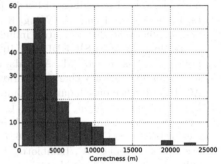

Fig. 10. Correctness of the home prediction results using Alg. 2 under the community based geo-location information sharing scheme.

6   Conclusion

In this paper, we have studied the location privacy issue in mobile social networks. Specifically, we proposed a community based information sharing scheme to prevent the user's home location to be accurately inferred by the check-in data.

References

1. Wang, K., Qi, X., Shu, L., Deng, D.-J., Rodrigues, J.J.: Toward trustworthy crowd-sourcing in the social internet of things. IEEE Wirel. Commun. **23**(5), 30–36 (2016)
2. Wang, K., Gu, L., Guo, S., Chen, H., Leung, V.C., Sun, Y.: Crowdsourcing-based content-centric network: a social perspective. IEEE Netw. **31**(5), 28–34 (2017)

3. Gu, Y., Yao, Y., Liu, W., Song, J.: We know where you are: Home location identification in location-based social networks. In: Proceedings of IEEE ICCCN, pp. 1–9 (2016)
4. Mahmud, J., Nichols, J., Drews, C.: Home location identification of twitter users. ACM Trans. Intell. Syst. Technol. (TIST) 5(3), 47 (2014)
5. Cheng, Z., Caverlee, J., Lee, K.: You are where you tweet: a content-based approach to geo-locating twitter users. In: Proceedings of ACM International Conference on Information and Knowledge Management, pp. 759–768 (2010)
6. Cho, E., Myers, S.A., Leskovec, J.: Friendship and mobility: user movement in location-based social networks. In: Proceedings of ACM SIGKDD, pp. 1082–1090 (2011)
7. Chandra, S., Khan, L., Muhaya, F.B.: Estimating twitter user location using social interactions-a content based approach. In: Proceedings of IEEE PASSAT, pp. 838–843 (2011)
8. Mahmud, J., Nichols, J., Drews, C.: Where is this tweet from? inferring home locations of twitter users. ICWSM 12, 511–514 (2012)
9. Li, G., Hu, J., Feng, J., Tan, K.-L.: Effective location identification from microblogs. In: Proceedings of ICDE, pp. 880–891 (2014)
10. Li, R., Wang, S., Deng, H., Wang, R., Chang, K.C.-C.: Towards social user profiling: unified and discriminative influence model for inferring home locations. In: Proceedings of ACM SIGKDD, pp. 1023–1031 (2012)
11. Pontes, T., Vasconcelos, M., Almeida, J., Kumaraguru, P., Almeida, V.: We know where you live: privacy characterization of foursquare behavior. In: Proceedings of ACM Conference on Ubiquitous Computing, pp. 898–905 (2012)
12. Liu, H., Zhang, Y., Zhou, Y., Zhang, D., Fu, X., Ramakrishnan, K.: Mining checkins from location-sharing services for client-independent IP geolocation. In: Proceedings of IEEE INFOCOM, pp. 619–627 (2014)
13. Scellato, S., Noulas, A., Lambiotte, R., Mascolo, C.: Socio-spatial properties of online location-based social networks. ICWSM 11, 329–336 (2011)
14. Shokri, R., Theodorakopoulos, G., Le Boudec, J.-Y., Hubaux, J.-P.: Quantifying location privacy. In: Proceedings of IEEE Security and privacy, pp. 247–262 (2011)
15. Clauset, A., Newman, M.E., Moore, C.: Finding community structure in very large networks. Phys. Rev. E 70(6), 066111 (2004)
16. Lancichinetti, A., Fortunato, S.: Community detection algorithms: a comparative analysis. Phys. Rev. E 80(5), 056117 (2009)
17. Rosvall, M., Bergstrom, C.T.: Maps of random walks on complex networks reveal community structure. Nat. Acad. Sci. 105(4), 1118–1123 (2008)

Software Security and Trusted Computing

A Formal Model for an Ideal CFI

Sepehr Minagar[(✉)], Balasubramaniam Srinivasan, and Phu Dung Le

Monash University, Melbourne, Australia
{sepehr.minagar,srini,phu.dung.le}@monash.edu

Abstract. We provide a formal model to achieve a fully precise dynamic protection of the flow of execution against control flow hijacking attacks. In more than a decade since the original Control Flow Integrity the focus of all of the proposed work in the literature has been on practical implementation of CFI. This however due to the restriction that the classic CFI poses on function return has led to the solutions that relax and bend the rules used in the proof of the original work. Some of these solutions has been shown to be completely insecure and others are hard to prove using formal methods. We use Propositional Dynamic Logic that combines actions and their consequences in a formal system which allows us to clearly express the required pre and post conditions to prevent a class of exploitation. We prove the correctness of our scheme for an abstract machine as a model of modern processors.

Keywords: Formal security model · Dynamic control flow integrity
Context-sensitive CFI · Malicious code execution prevention

1 Introduction

The focus of the research in preventing the execution of malicious code has been shifted towards the exploitation aspect in the past decade. Van der Veen et al. in [1] provide a survey of memory errors and some of the proposed protective measures in the literature. The majority of these countermeasures such as Stack Canaries and Address Space Layout Randomization (ASLR) are informal solutions in the sense that they do not provide proof of correctness and are designed for specific types of vulnerability [1]. These techniques are shown to be vulnerable to different types of attack [2,3]. The introduction of non-executable data memory and its support in modern processors is effective against code injection in data memory as long as the adversary cannot control permissions on memory pages and is vulnerable to code reuse attacks such as return-to-libc [4] and Return Oriented Programming (ROP) [5,6] and its variants [7–9]. Most of the proposed detection or prevention techniques against ROP attacks use heuristics or rely on characteristics of this type of attack [10–15]. The problem with heuristic or characteristic type of solutions is that if the behaviour of the attack or its characteristics can be changed the defensive mechanism can be bypassed [16–18].

The work of Abadi et al. [19] is among the most promising work in this area since they provide a formal model for the proposed Control Flow Integrity (CFI)

© Springer International Publishing AG 2017
J. K. Liu and P. Samarati (Eds.): ISPEC 2017, LNCS 10701, pp. 707–726, 2017.
https://doi.org/10.1007/978-3-319-72359-4_44

to assure that the execution path will follow the Control Flow Graph (CFG) of the executable code. The enforced policy however poses restrictions on function return specially with dynamically linked executables and function pointers [20]. Unfortunately besides the original work none of the proposed solutions in this area follow the formal approach. The theoretical model proposed in [19] only considered static code where the CFG of the code is known at compile time. To address the dynamic linking problem the practical work in CFI has been forced to use over-approximation of the rules by categorizing the valid destinations into equivalent classes which violates the requirement of the provided proof. The precision of these classes are used to define two broad categories of CFI policy enforcement: Coarse-Grained (CG) and Fine-Grained (FG) [21,22]. In CG policy the equivalent classes are divided to two or three classes to achieve better performance at the cost of security. The CG policy is shown to be broken due to this over-approximation [22]. The FG policy has a finer precision for the equivalent classes which nevertheless relaxes the rules of classic CFI policy. Various methods further divide this category to smaller scopes of forward-edge or backward-edge protection or hardware-assisted. A recent article by Burow et al. provides an in-depth analysis of the CFI policy enforcements with regards to precision, security and performance [23].

Although there has been an intensive research in this area with many implementations, the rules of the solid theoretical work proposed in the classic CFI [19] are relaxed which has led to inadequate security guarantees and are shown to be completely insecure in some cases [22]. In this paper we provide the first sound theoretical model that allows a fully dynamic CFI enforcement, laying the foundation for practical implementations supported by security proofs. We believe strong and provable security goals must be considered and studied in depth ahead of implementation and efficiency considerations. Our proposed model enforces a dynamic CFI policy that relies on compile time and run time information to assure that the execution flow follows the intended path by the programmer. We leave the implementation of our model and any efficiency analysis of the potential implementation for future work. Our main goal is to provide provable security measures and specify the limitations of a fully precise dynamic CFI policy enforcement in preventing exploitations.

Our contributions are as follows:

- a sound theoretical model to provide provable security guarantees against control flow hijack attacks for both code injection and code reuse, that removes the restrictions of the classic CFI
- definition of the required conditions for an ideal CFI policy enforcement within the defined model
- an extended abstract machine to model modern processors with regards to various types of control flow attack
- formal definition of control flow hijack using Propositional Dynamic Logic (PDL)

Our formal approach provides the required foundation upon which implementations for various architectures, operating systems, and compilers can be realised and formally analysed. The structure of the paper is as follows. In Sect. 2 we provide the background information and our definitions required to express the principles of our approach. In Sect. 3 we present the theorems and their proof. We discuss the related work in Sect. 4 and conclude this paper in Sect. 5.

2 Principles of an Ideal CFI

In this section we provide the necessary definitions and background information to formally express the attacks and countermeasures. An overview of the effects of different instructions on the flow of execution is discussed in Sect. 2.1. In Sect. 2.2 we define our machine model followed by the attack model in Sect. 2.3 and the verification requirements in Sect. 2.4.

2.1 Instruction Types and Flow of Execution

All machine instructions influence the execution path of an executable code and can be divided to four types: sequential, conditional branch, direct jump, and indirect jump. For sequential instructions Program Counter (PC) is incremented and for direct jump the destination is some address w embedded in the instruction. The change of the flow of execution for the conditional branch depends on a condition that when true the destination would be an address w provided in the instruction or PC+1 otherwise. For indirect jump, which includes return instruction, the destination would be an address provided as the content of a register. Other forms of change in flow of execution in more complex architectures may provide various versions of these types with more options, however it would fall in one of the aforementioned categories. We provide a formal definition for the instruction categories in Sect. 2.2, Definition 3.

Functions in high level languages have well defined boundaries, a clear entry point, and one or more return points. The labels and direct jumps in high level languages that define such control structures are only allowed within the boundary of a defined function. Although the compilers translate the high level language to an equivalent machine language code, the flexibility of instructions such as indirect jumps allows paths that where not possible in the corresponding high level program. In this sense a function call in high level language would be translated to a more permissive jump or call instruction with the memory address of the specified function as its parameter. We say it is more permissive as in high level language the function call is restricted to the start of a defined function using a unique name whereas a jump can be to any address within the address space of the program. For a program that does not rely on any external library at the end of compilation all of the virtual addresses of the defined functions are known and their names can be replaced with their addresses. While local function calls could be potentially performed with direct jump instruction, calls for dynamically linked library functions require indirect jump instructions where the address of the called function is determined at run time.

At run time before making the call to a function the return address must be recorded and the corresponding return instruction restores this recorded address to transfer the flow of execution back to the instruction after the call.

We base our formal approach on the types of the instructions and their effects on the execution path and state the preconditions that are necessary to prevent certain types of attack.

2.2   Machine Model

To make the propositions and the arguments easier to express we use a simple but realistic machine model that has been used previously in the literature for similar purpose [20,24] with modifications and in the context of PDL. The machine is comprised of a processor with a register file of 32 registers, a designated and separate register as Program Counter, and byte-addressable random access memory. The state of the machine is considered as the content of memory, register file and PC. The definition of words, memory cells, register file and machine states are as follows:

$Word :: = \{0, 1\}^*$
$Mem :: = address \rightarrow Word$
$Regnum :: = \{0, 1, ..., 31\}$
$Regfile :: = Regnum \rightarrow Word$
$State :: = Mem \times Regfile \times Word$

The machine has a load-store architecture where no direct operation is performed on memory cells as operands except for load and store instructions. The machine has six sequential instructions and one for each of direct jump, conditional branch and indirect jump and one instruction for return from a function call. The halt instruction is used to mark the end of an executable code. The instruction set is shown in Fig. 1.

$A ::= nop \mid add\ r_d, r_s, r_t \mid addi\ r_d, r_s, w \mid movi\ r_d, w \mid ld\ r_d, r_s(w) \mid st\ r_d(w), r_s \mid$
$bgt\ r_s, r_t, w \mid jd\ w \mid jmp\ r_s \mid ret\ r_s \mid halt$

Fig. 1. Machine's instruction set

The decoding function represents the notion of decoding an instruction in machine language to its semantic (Fig. 1) and is defined as follows.

Definition 1. $Decode(i) : \{0, 1\}^* \rightarrow A \cup \{illegal\}$

We omit the use of an instruction register in the definition of the $Decode()$ function as it does not contribute to the formal expressions but it can be assumed that the $Decode()$ function operates on an Instruction Register where the $fetch$ cycle of the processor transfers the instruction addressed by PC into that register.

Table 1. Notation summary

Notation	Semantic
$\leftarrow$	Assignment as $target \leftarrow value$
$Mem(x)$	Content of memory at address x
Mem	Memory state (no change)
$Reg(r_x)$	Content of register r_x in register file
Reg	The state of the register file (no change)
pc	Content of the program counter
$\in_{emb}$	Embedded as an operand (w) within the instruction (i) as $w \in_{emb} i$
dot $/$.	Partial element of the state e.g. $s.pc$: content of pc in state s
$\equiv$	Semantic equivalence
$=$	Logical comparison
$\perp$	$\neg\top$

We assume an instruction decoded as *illegal* results in *halt*. We use a byte-addressable memory and allow variable length instructions in the abstract model to address issues of complex architectures. The *Decode* function can determine the length of an instruction and for sequential instructions $pc + 1$ represents the notion of the calculated address of the next instruction based on the length of the current instruction. Table 1 provides the summary of the notation used to express the semantic of the machine instructions.

To construct a *Label Transition System* (LTS) as defined in [25], the set of states range over the machine states comprised of the content of memory, register file, and PC, the set P is the set of our propositions and the set A the set of machine instructions which will form the set of labels.

Definition 2. *For the set of propositions P and the set of atomic instructions A, the LTS is the triple $M ::= (S, R, V)$ where:*

- $S : Mem \times Reg \times pc$ *is the set of machine states*
- $R_a : \{\rightarrow^a: (s, s') \subseteq S \times S | a \leftarrow Decode(i) \in A\}$ *is a set of labelled transitions where s and s' are the states before and after the execution of the instruction i*
- $V : S \rightarrow P(p)$ *is a valuation function that determines the value of a proposition in a state*

Using the PDL language we formally define the instruction types as follows.

Definition 3. *Instruction Types: In the defined LTS $M = (S, R, V)$ the following sets can be formally defined for the atomic action a where $a \leftarrow Decode(i) \in A$:*

$SQ ::= \{a | (s, s') \in R_a \wedge [a]s'.pc = s.pc + 1\}$
$DJ ::= \{a | (s, s') \in R_a \wedge [a]s'.pc = w \in_{emb} i\}$
$CB ::= \{a | (s, s') \in R_a \wedge [a]s'.pc = w \in_{emb} i \vee s'.pc = s.pc + 1\}$
$IJ ::= \{a | (s, s') \in R_a \wedge [a]s'.pc = s.Reg(r_s)\}$

It is clear that $A = SQ \cup DJ \cup CB \cup IJ \cup \{halt\}$ and $\emptyset = SQ \cap DJ \cap CB \cap IJ \cap \{halt\}$ hence to reason about the properties of code execution we can verify the validity of the arguments for the four sets that impact the execution path and we would cover all possible transfers of the flow of execution. The three sets CB, DJ, and IJ are specifically designed to change the flow of execution beyond the normal sequential flow whereas the set SQ contains all the other instructions. Calling library functions in dynamically linked executables is one of the reasons that indirect jump instructions are required in any modern architecture as the target destination is unknown at compile-time and needs to be calculated at run-time.

The notion of instruction location in memory or the program as stored must be distinguished from the program execution. Using the definition of *finite computation sequence* of a program α as defined in [26] we can argue about possible sequences of atomic steps in the execution of a program that would belong to the set of all computation sequences of the program α denoted as $CS(\alpha)$. We use the term *memory sequence* to refer to the program as stored and *computation sequence*, which is by itself a program in the context of PDL, to refer to the order of execution of instructions that are not necessarily located in contiguous memory locations. As a simple clarification of our goal here for instance a successful code injection attack would involve a memory sequence that does not belong to the memory sequence of the program α. Since the execution of the program would allow the injection of the code and transfer of the flow of execution to the injected code then the execution of the injected code also belongs to the possible computation sequence of the program regardless of whether it was anticipated by the programmer.

2.3   Attack Model

In order to discuss countermeasures to protect against an attack we first need to formally define the attack. In general terms if we express a successful attack as proposition p for the exploitable executable α and the adversary's intended computation sequence β then the fact that at least one execution of α results in successful exploitation (hence exploitable) can be expressed in PDL as: $\langle \alpha; \beta \rangle p$.

We intend to propose measures that would result in all executions of the exploitable program α satisfy the proposition $\neg p$ expressed as: $[\alpha; \beta] \neg p$.

The proposition satisfiability depends on the type of the attack and the protective measure. We use the three types of attack described in [22] but with some modifications. We use the term *fully precise* to specify that only one valid destination is allowed for any indirect control transfer and the term *dynamic* to specify that the control flow graph is context-sensitive, meaning dynamic linking and the most recent call-sites are considered; hence a fully precise dynamic CFG would be an ideal CFG that follows the exact flow of execution intended by the programmer. The three types of attack are defined as follows:

1. *Control Data Attack* leading to control flow hijack: The adversary changes the flow of execution to a target that violates the fully precise dynamic control

flow graph. This type includes both code injection and code reuse. The key point is that the execution path of the attack contains edges that have never been part of any benign execution of the program.

2. *Non-Control Data Attack* leading to control flow bending: The adversary changes the flow of execution to a target that does not violate the fully precise dynamic control flow graph. This includes any data corruption that could influence the decision points in flow of execution (decision parameters of the conditional branch instruction) or change of parameters passed to a valid function (e.g. an edge of the fully precise dynamic CFG to execve() with corrupted parameters).

3. *Information Leakage Attack*: The adversary performs a non-control data attack that does not violate the fully precise dynamic control flow graph that leads to disclosure of sensitive information.

Our focus is the first type of attack that involves the use of an invalid edge, where as the second and third types cannot be defended against even with ideal CFG enforced since these types make use of the precise edge but with corrupted input which results in either confined code execution or information disclosure [22]. We formally define the control flow hijack attack as follows.

Definition 4. *Let the exploitable program α be comprised of the memory sequence $a_1; a_2; \ldots; a_n$, the adversary's program β be the computation sequence $b_1; b_2; \ldots; b_m$, and $CS(\alpha)$ the set of all possible computation sequences of the program α, given the program α is exploitable then there exists a partial computation sequence α_1 that leads to the execution of the adversary's intended program β and $\alpha_1; \beta \in CS(\alpha)$. We consider the proposition $p :=$ "successful control flow hijack" to be true for the computation sequence $\langle \alpha_1; \beta \rangle p$ if and only if for a_k to be the last instruction in α_1 and b_1 the first instruction of the adversary's intended computation sequence β and $b_1 \neq a_x$ where $a_x \in \alpha$ the next action under benign execution of α. We simply express the successful control flow hijack as $\langle a_k; b_1 \rangle p$ focusing on the transition from the benign execution to the adversary's computation sequence.*

The distinction between computation sequence and memory sequence is clear when comparing the user program α with the adversary's sequence β that for instance would be scattered over a much larger memory sequence(s) in case of a heap spray, or scattered over the code of the program α as ROP gadgets or be an injected memory sequence on the overflown stack, crafted to be executed as the given sequence $b_1; b_2; \ldots; b_m$. The Definition 4 expresses that if a program is exploitable then there exists a computation sequence of the program that transfers the flow of execution to the intended computation sequence of the adversary. Our focus is on the last instruction of the program where such transition occurs.

We formally define the countermeasure against the control flow hijack by focusing on the transition of the flow of execution to the first instruction of the adversary summarised as $a_k; b_1$ where $1 \leq k \leq n$. To satisfy the proposition

$p :=$ "*successful control flow hijack*" in the state transition $(s_k, s_{k+1}) \in R_{a_k}$ we will have one of the following:

1. $a_k \in SQ$
2. $a_k \in DJ$
3. $a_k \in CB$
4. $a_k \in IJ$
5. $a_k = halt$

If the proposed protective measures are expressed as the proposition ψ as a precondition to the execution of the exploitable program α under attack with the adversary's intended computation sequence β, then the notion of preventing the successful control flow hijack attack can be expressed as $\psi \implies [a_k; b_1]\bot$, that is the transition from exploitable code to the first instruction intended by the adversary will fail in all execution of the sequence $a_k; b_1$. In the next section we formally define the required precondition(s) ψ to satisfy the aforementioned expression.

2.4 Verification Requirements

To protect the integrity of the flow of execution at run time it is necessary to add the required controls that assures the flow of execution follows the intended path by the programmer. The classic CFI [19] enforces the policy as in-line and static reference monitors preceding indirect jumps to verify inserted unique label at the target of that indirect jump. Function call and return are both handled with the indirect jump instruction and the policy enforcement is the same. This however creates problems with dynamic library functions as these functions can be called from different executable code and same function may be called from different points making multiple paths available at return.

Forward Edge. An edge requires a starting point and an end point. In case of a forward edge the start is the offset of the jump instruction and the end is the called function. If the start point is omitted then the CFG will be reduced to a list of targets where any of the targets can be a valid destination for any of indirect jumps. To assure that both ends of an edge are verified in the current execution context we require that the *offset* of the indirect jump instruction and the destination of the call to be recorded at compile time. The function can be a library and dynamically linked or a local function. For analysis we assume all function calls whether local or dynamically linked are both translated to indirect jump instruction. To simplify the notation in our definitions we refer to the called function as $f_x \in local \lor lib_j$ for $0 \leq j \leq m$. At run-time the addresses will be adjusted to physical addresses which is commonly supported in hardware. This allows the code to be positioned independently. For reasons that are explained later only forward edges are translated to indirect jump instruction.

To protect the forward edges, the valid destination for each forward indirect jump instruction is uniquely specified for the executable α comprised of atomic instruction sequence $i_1; i_2; \ldots; i_n$ and the called functions $f_1; f_2; \ldots; f_m$ in its set of Authentic Calls (AC) as follows.

Definition 5. *Set of Authentic Calls* $AC ::= \{(\kappa, f_x) \mid i_\kappa \in \alpha, Decode(i_k) = jmp \; r_s \wedge f_x \in (local \vee lib_j) 0 \leq j \leq z\}$

Since each instruction has a unique address (offset at compile time), recording the indirect jump instruction address precisely specifies a forward edge. In other words an indirect jump instruction can be executed if and only if it is located at a pre-recorded address and its destination is also a registered address (AC_{foo} in Fig. 2). This will be added as a precondition to the jump instruction.

As the valid destinations are paired with the address of the indirect jumps, it can be verified whether the execution is following the defined precise edge. The incentive here is to provide precisely one valid edge for each indirect jump instruction however as it has been discussed in the literature [27–30] there are circumstances where multiple valid destinations exist at compile time. For instance in the case of a function pointer. In such cases the elements of the AC set can be defined as 3-tuples *(offset, condition, target)* where the second element specifies a verifiable condition for the target to be valid. To make this point clear we can redefine the set of Authentic Calls for the executable code α as follows:

Definition 6. *Set of Authentic Calls* $AC ::= \{(\kappa, c_j, t_j)\}$ *such that:*

- $i_\kappa \in \alpha, \wedge Decode(i_k) = jmp \; r_s$
- $\wedge Eval(c_j, t_j) = T \wedge Eval(c_{l \neq j}, t_{l \neq j}) = F$ *where Eval is the evaluate function for condition* c_j
- $\wedge t_j \in f_1; f_2; \ldots; f_m$

For the fixed *offset* κ the condition c is always true in case of normal function calls where the destination virtual address is known at compile time. In case of function pointer the condition c is the disjunction of conditions $c_1, \ldots, c_q$ for the targets $t_1, \ldots, t_q$ where only one target (t_j) is valid per condition $(c_j, j = 1 \ldots q)$. That is the condition c is evaluated at run-time for all possible conditions $c_1, \ldots, c_q$ and all valid destinations $t_1, \ldots, t_q$ and only one destination t_j is reachable. The goal is to convert a fine-grained target list to a fully precise CFG by attaching the conditions under which each of the elements in the valid target list can be reached. This is similar to the context condition discussed in [31] for pointer analysis with the difference that the attached condition is evaluated at run-time and it only involves function pointers.

From practical point of view, which is not the concern of the formal work, the implementation can vary and be specific to the circumstance as long as it could specify one valid destination. Nevertheless our theorems provide the security guarantees that are as accurate as the precision of the generated list of targets. In such cases where a precise list of multiple valid destinations exist per indirect jump, a control flow bending attack is possible by choosing a destination from the list. In our formal work we assume a verifiable set of disjunct conditions that identify a unique destination for each indirect jump at run-time can be produced.

Backward Edge. Each function $f_x \in (local \vee lib_j)$, starting at a defined offset in lib_j or executable α, has at least one or more associated return point(s). To record the location of each return instruction within the body of a function that can be used to verify a backward edge we define the set of associated return points as follows.

Definition 7. *Set of all associated return points for executable α or a library lib containing the functions: $f_1; f_2; \ldots; f_m$ is defined as:*
$$RP ::= \{(f_j, \xi) \mid f_j \text{ is the function logical address} \wedge Decode(i_\xi) = ret \ r_s \wedge i_\xi \in f_j$$
is a valid return point $\}$

The association of return point(s) for each function of executable `foo` and library `lib` is shown as RP_{foo} and RP_{lib} respectively in Fig. 2.

The set of associated return point(s) specifies the valid return instructions of a called function which prevents executing a return opcode that appears in the middle of other instructions in complex architectures in addition to other forms of control flow hijack attack. The emphasis is on specifying both ends of a valid edge.

For the forward edge it is required to check whether the tuple (instruction address, function address) belongs to the set of authentic calls. The return however requires two checks: (i) whether this is an associated return point for this function (to prevent execution of a return instruction that appears in the middle of the opcode of another instruction) and (ii) whether the destination address is authentic. These two verifications can be done by creating one run-time mapping, at the time of the call, that maps the tuple: (instruction address, authentic function x) and the corresponding return tuple(s): (function x, return point(s)) into a 3-tuple: (return address, function x, associated return point(s) of function x) where function x could be a local or external function. The forward and backward verifications are shown in Fig. 2.

The *Runtime Mapping* which associates the return point(s) of a function defined in executable code $\alpha \vee \alpha'$ (local or library) and called within the executable code α at the time of the call (run-time) is defined as follows:

Definition 8. *Runtime Mapping for executable α and set of libraries $\alpha' \equiv \wedge_{x=1..m} lib_x$ is a per call sequence (with order and repetition):*
$$RM ::= \bigwedge_{j=1...m} RM_{f_j} \text{ where } RM_{f_j} = \{(\kappa + 1, f_j, \xi) \mid (\kappa, f_j) \in AC_{\alpha \vee \alpha'}, \text{ and }$$
$(f_j, \xi) \in RP_{\alpha \vee \alpha'}\}$

This sequence is dynamic and changes according to the execution context at the time of the call and return:

- for $Decode(i_\kappa) = jmp \ r_s$
  $RM = RM \wedge RM_{f_j}$ where $(\kappa + 1, f_j, \xi_{1...x}) \in RM_{f_j}$ are the latest mappings added to the sequence
- for $Decode(i_y) = ret \ r_s$
  $RM = RM - RM_{f_j}$ where $(Reg(r_s), f_j, \xi_{1...x}) \in RM_{f_j}$ are the latest mappings removed from the sequence

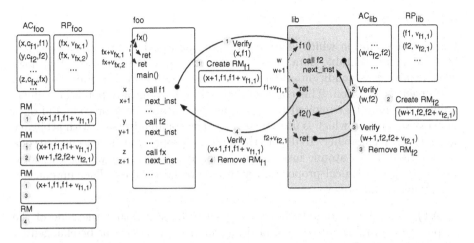

Fig. 2. Set of authentic calls used in forward-edge and runtime mapping used in backward-edge verifications

In forward jumps the verification is done before creating the mapping and in returns the verification is done before removing the mapping. The elements of this set, at the time of the call, represent: (the address to return to in the calling code α pointed to by $pc+1$, $Reg(r_s)$ pointing to the start of the called function f_j in $\alpha \vee \alpha'$, associated return point for the called function f_j recorded in $RP_{\alpha \vee \alpha'}$). For each return instruction it can be then verified, at the time of return, if there exists a 3-tuple in the sequence RM where the target address matches the first element, the address of this function matches the second element, and the address of current return instruction matches the third element (Fig. 2). This mapping entry is created per function call (steps 1 and 2 in Fig. 2) and will be removed if a match is found at the time of the authentic corresponding return (steps 3 and 4 in Fig. 2). The mapping creates the necessary execution context which helps achieve a fully precise dynamic (context-sensitive) and depth independent enforcement of the CFI policy. In the literature the shadow stack is considered a necessary condition for enforcing a fully precise CFI [22] whereas in our abstract model the data structure used for implementation could be in any form as long as it stores the specified elements used in verification and policy enforcement.

3   Theorems of ICFI

The theorems of our CFI policy enforcement specify the necessary and sufficient conditions for an abstract machine to prevent the control flow hijack of a vulnerable program. Before we state the theorems we express our assumptions in the following section.

3.1 Premises

Our first assumption which is a required precondition is expressed in the literature as non-executable data or code and data memory separation. We, however, express this condition as integrity of the code of an executable which is a stronger assumption. This condition takes into account any potential vulnerability that may be exploited to bypass non-executable data or code and data memory separation which is necessary in presence of an adversary with arbitrary memory write capability. To denote the integrity property of the executable code α comprised of the atomic instruction sequence $a_1; a_2; \ldots; a_n$ we use the notation $Int(\alpha)$ as a logical proposition with true or false values. The summary of the premises is as follows:

- **A1)** The precondition $Int(\alpha) \wedge_{j=1..m} Int(lib_j)$ states that the code of the program α and the libraries called by the program α cannot be changed by the adversary. For clarity we express this as $Int(\alpha) \wedge Int(\alpha')$ where $Int(\alpha') \equiv \wedge_{j=1..m} Int(lib_j)$.
- **A2)** The adversary cannot directly change the content of the program counter. This is represented as the post conditions on the actions, that is the only ways of affecting the content of pc is shown as part of the logical semantic of the defined atomic actions.
- **A3)** The attacker cannot modify the following sets and sequence belonging to any executable code: AC, RP, and RM. The integrity of these sets for instance could be protected with signatures or some form of secure storage, or memory bounds. We can represent this for any executable code α as $Int(RP_\alpha) \wedge Int(AC_\alpha) \wedge Int(RM_\alpha)$.
- **A4)** The end of all executable codes are marked with *halt* instruction.

3.2 Theorems

The first theorem states that the integrity precondition is a necessary and sufficient condition to prevent control flow hijack (as defined in Sect. 2.3) for a program that only contains sequential, direct jump and conditional branch type of instructions. Since function calls and returns whether local or library are done using indirect branch instruction A1 only requires $Int(\alpha)$ for the first theorem.

Theorem 1. *For the exploitable program α with memory sequence of atomic instructions: $a_1; a_2; \ldots; a_n$ and with adversary's intended computation sequence of β of atomic actions $b_1; b_2; \ldots; b_m$, a computation sequence of α that includes the partial computation sequence $a_k; b_1$ then $Int(\alpha) \implies [a_k; b_1] \perp$, where $1 \leq k \leq n$ and $a_k \in SQ \cup DJ \cup CB$.*

Proof. For computation sequence $a_k; b_1$ we have one of the following (A2):

1. $a_k \in SQ$ which always satisfies $s_{k+1}.pc = s_k.pc + 1$:
   - for $k < n$: a_k and b_1 are in consecutive memory locations (SQ property) which implies $b_1 \neq a_{k+1} \in \alpha$ (violates $Int(\alpha)$ A1)

- for $k = n$: $a_n = halt$ and $a_n \notin SQ \cup DJ \cup CB \wedge [halt; b_1] \perp$ (A4, and definition of $halt$)

2. $a_k \in DJ$ which always satisfies $s_{k+1}.pc = w'$:
   - $w' \neq w \in_{emb} a_k$ (part of a_k is overwritten with w' to point to b_1, violates $Int(\alpha)$ A1)
   - $w' = w$ hence $Mem(w) = b_1 \neq a_y \in \alpha$ (a_y is overwritten with b_1 violates $Int(\alpha)$ A1)

3. $a_k \in CB$ which always satisfies $s_{k+1}.pc = w' \vee s_{k+1}.pc = s_k.pc + 1$ and implies $a_{k+1} = b_1 \vee Mem(w) = b_1$:
   - $k < n$ implies a_k and b_1 are in consecutive memory locations and $b_1 \neq a_{k+1} \in \alpha$ (violates $Int(\alpha)$ A1)
   - $k = n$, $a_n = halt$ and $a_n \notin SQ \cup DJ \cup CB \wedge [halt; b_1] \perp$ (A4 and definition of $halt$)
   - $Mem(w') = b_1$:
     • $w' \neq w \in_{emb} a_k$ (a_k is overwritten to point to b_1 violates $Int(\alpha)$ A1)
     • $w' = w$ hence $Mem(w) = b_1 \neq a_y \in \alpha$ (a_y is overwritten with b_1 violates $Int(\alpha)$ A1)

The second theorem states that if a program contains an indirect jump instruction the integrity property is necessary but not sufficient to prevent a control flow hijack attack. Additional checks must be performed to prevent such attacks.

Theorem 2. *For the exploitable program α with memory sequence of atomic instructions: $a_1; a_2; \ldots; a_n$ with adversary's intended computation sequence of β of atomic actions $b_1; b_2; \ldots; b_m$, a computation sequence of α that contains the partial sequence of $a_k; b_1$, and $Int(\alpha') \equiv \wedge_{x=1..m} Int(lib_x)$ then:*
$$\left(Int(\alpha) \wedge Int(\alpha')\right) \wedge \left((k, \epsilon) \in AC \vee (z, \epsilon, \xi) \in RM\right) \implies [a_k; b_1] \perp, \text{ where}$$
$1 \leq k \leq n$ and $a_k \in IJ$.

Proof. For computation sequence $a_k; b_1$ where $a_k \in IJ$ which always satisfies $s_{k+1}.pc = s_k.Reg(r_s)$, we have one of the following (A2):

1. $Decode(a_k) = jmp\ r_s$ then:
   - $Reg(r_s) \neq f_j$ violates $(k, f_j) \in AC_{\alpha \vee \alpha'}$ (protected by A3)
   - $Reg(r_s) = f_j$ implies $b_1 \neq a_y \in \alpha \vee \alpha'$ (a_y the beginning of f_j is overwritten with b_1 violates $Int(\alpha) \wedge Int(\alpha')$ A1)
   Hence: $\left(Int(\alpha) \wedge Int(\alpha')\right) \wedge (k, f_j) \in AC_{\alpha \vee \alpha'} \implies [jmp\ r_s; b_1] \perp$.

2. $Decode(a_k) = ret\ r_s$ then:
   - $(Reg(r_s), f_j, pc) \notin RM$ which implies either
     $(Reg(r_s), f_j) \notin AC_{\alpha \vee \alpha'}$, (unauthentic call to local or library function)
     or $(f_j, pc) \notin RP_{\alpha \vee \alpha'}$, (unregistered return from local or library function)
   - $(Reg(r_s), f_j, pc) \in RM$ implies $b_1 \neq a_z \in \alpha \vee \alpha'$ (a_z is overwritten with b_1 violates $Int(\alpha) \wedge Int(\alpha')$ (A1)
   Hence: $A1 - A3 \wedge (z, f_j, \xi) \in RM \implies [ret\ r_s; b_1] \perp$.

4   Related Work

Preventing the execution of malicious code has long been the interest of research in computer security and the statistics of the reported vulnerabilities that could lead to arbitrary code execution [32] shows that it is still a significant problem. The focus of the research in this area is on two requirements of malicious code execution: the existence of vulnerabilities and their exploitation. There is a significant body of work regarding the detection and removal of the vulnerabilities using formal and informal techniques as well as changing high level programming languages or machine language aspects that are susceptible to errors.

The other trend of research focuses on preventing the exploitation. The work of Abadi et al. [19,20], referred to as classic CFI, is a formally described countermeasure that has clear and precise assumptions and well defined attack model. In this technique valid destinations of indirect jump instructions comprised of the start of functions and the instruction after a function call are preceded with unique labels and each jump instruction is preceded with code that verifies the label of the target. This is done by code rewriting and the association of the labels and verification code is based on a static CFG that is generated beforehand. The reliance on static CFG could be more permissive as it may contain edges to multiple destinations from a common source (e.g. return from a function that is called several times). Using multiple labels, classes of equivalent labels and code duplication are some of the discussed methods to address such difficulties where use of equivalent classes introduces imprecision [20].

Other variations of CFI in the literature can be categorized in two broad classes: Coarse-Grained (CG) and Fine-Grained (FG). Burow et al. provide an in-depth analysis of proposed CFI policy enforcements in the literature and have developed a scoring system based on various aspects such as supported direction, precision of the static analysis for forward and backward edges, performance, and supported control flow types [23].

4.1   Coarse-Grained CFI

In CG schemes a trade-off is made between the accuracy of the enforced CFG and the efficiency of implementation [21,33]. In this approach the equivalent classes are divided into two or three generic classes and a layer of indirection is added using target tables or trampolines [34–36]. The use of limited number of equivalent classes increases the efficiency of the implementation at the cost of its security. The effectiveness of the implementation is generally measured by a proposed metric called Average target or gadget Reduction (AIR) [37], where as discussed by Carlini et al. [22], the best techniques can achieve a score around 99% leaving %1 of non-negligible potential targets. To address the inaccuracy of AIR which does not take into account the number and size of equivalent classes, Burow et al. propose a quantitative measure equal to the number of equivalence classes, where the higher number signifies higher precision, multiplied by the inverse of the size of the largest class, where the larger class shows lower precision [23]. Neither AIR nor the metric of Burow et al. can provide any measure of the usefulness of the reachable targets to the attacker, meaning that there could be dangerous code among the reachable targets [22,23]. It is shown that CG solutions could result in more permissive control flow transfer and are still vulnerable to code reuse attacks [22,38,39]. The analysis of Burow et al. [23] assign the same scores for the precision of the forward edge to [29,34–37,40–46] for using ad-hoc and heuristic algorithms, context and flow insensitive analysis, or limited equivalence classes [23].

4.2 Fine-Grained CFI

In FG methods the equivalent classes for labels more accurately follow the generated CFG compared with CG schemes. The proposed FG approaches may differ in the techniques used in generating CFG but use similar guards as classic CFI to protect forward edges of CFG and shadow or dual stack to protect backward edges for return instruction [47,48]. This subclass can be further divided to forward and backward edge where some of the work in the literature only focus on either forward or backward or may provide different precision for each.

The qualitative analysis in [23] assigns a higher score than methods discussed in Sect. 4.1, for a more precise class-hierarchy analysis for the forward edge to [27,28,49–51]. The work in [30] receives a slightly higher score for producing a more precise target list for forward edge classified as context- and flow-sensitive analysis. Higher scores are assigned to [33,52–55] for context and flow sensitive analysis in determining the valid list of destination for indirect change in flow of execution.

Modular CFI also addresses the dynamic linking problem of classic CFI by using ID tables that can be updated at run-time [33]. Practical Context-Sensitive CFI performs a context-sensitive analysis to determine the valid destination for code pointers and implements the CFI policy by monitoring Last Branch Register (LBR) and verifying a given path using the generated CFG [56], however is limited by hardware resources and the scope of analysis [23]. Cryptographically enforced CFI generates Message Authentication Code (MAC) for return addresses, pointers to frames, functions, and virtual tables and exception handlers when these pointers are stored and the MAC is verified when the pointer is loaded [54]. Per-Input CFI [57] starts with a minimal active edges and adds the edges to an Enforced CFG based on the program input and the static CFG to reduce the set of reachable targets within the executable code, however the set grows over time which makes more edges available than intended. This method receives the highest score in Burow et al. qualitative analysis for the precision of the forward edge due to the dynamic enforcement of the policy as well as the highest quantitative security measurement [23].

The shadow stack is considered an ideal backward edge protection mechanism in the literature [22,23]. Various methods use the shadow stack in their implementation such as [20,40,58]. A hardware-assisted mechanism called HAFIX for backward edge protection is proposed in [50] that can improve the performance compared to software solutions. Theodorides and Wagner in [59] study and discuss the vulnerabilities of HAFIX that would allow returning to an active set of functions on the call stack.

In theory FG policy could be exploited as it introduces a level of inaccuracy or over-approximation [22,60] by using equivalent classes for labels which put various destinations in one group of valid addresses. The adversary needs to find only one chain of function calls and returns using the valid addresses at each step that satisfies the CFI policy and is suitable to launch an attack.

The proof of the classic CFI relies on the fact that all of the valid destinations have a unique label and the verification code is embedded before all of the indirect jump instructions. Both CG and FG methods relax this rule with use of equivalent classes with different level of accuracy to address the efficiency and practicality problem of the original work. This violates the very rule that supports the proof of CFI and weakens these schemes.

5   Conclusion

The flexibility of change in flow of execution in machine language allows an adversary to launch powerful exploitation. Imposing proper conditions on these types of instructions in machine language will help reduce the existing gaps between high level programming languages and the machine language which will result in stronger security guarantees. We have developed a formal basis for a fully precise dynamic CFI enforcement to counter control data attacks leading to control flow hijack. We have presented the proof of this scheme in two theorems. Any implementation that can provide the specified verification can achieve the security assurances that our theorems provide.

The CFI method proposed by Abadi et al. [19] provides a formal treatment for this problem however poses practical restrictions on function returns. These difficulties in following the rules of the classic CFI has led to the relaxation and over-approximation of the rules that were used in the proof of the formal work. CG implementations, which trade accuracy of CFG with efficiency, are shown to be broken [22,38,39] and FG methods although more restrictive still leave a small but not negligible imprecision by using equivalent classes [22].

Our work addresses the difficulties of the classic CFI in a formal framework which has been omitted in all of the works focused on implementation. The focus of our approach has been on providing the formal work to prove the correctness of the scheme and to express the required conditions and the scope and capability of the provided solution.

As it has been discussed in the literature even a fully precise static CFG cannot prevent certain types of attacks. Our method provides a fully precise dynamic CFI enforcement which is more accurate than a fully precise static CFG combined with shadow stack. It is worth mentioning that our approach cannot protect against control flow bending that uses a valid edge with corrupted data. The third defined type of attack is information leakage which cannot be prevented in our scheme if it does not involve control flow hijack. We argue that the last two types of attack cannot be prevented using CFI techniques if the rules of an ideal CFI policy is not violated and would require different protective measures such as data integrity or confidentiality policy enforcements.

We leave the implementation of our model for the future work, however some of the proposed approaches can be used in partial implementation of our model provided that the rules are not relaxed.

References

1. van der Veen, V., dutt-Sharma, N., Cavallaro, L., Bos, H.: Memory errors: the past, the present, and the future. In: Balzarotti, D., Stolfo, S.J., Cova, M. (eds.) RAID 2012. LNCS, vol. 7462, pp. 86–106. Springer, Heidelberg (2012). https://doi.org/10.1007/978-3-642-33338-5_5
2. Bulba, K.: Bypassing StackGuard and StackShield, January 2000
3. Shacham, H., Page, M., Pfaff, B., Goh, E.J., Modadugu, N., Boneh, D.: On the effectiveness of address-space randomization. In: Proceedings of the 11th ACM Conference on Computer and Communications Security, pp. 298–307 (2004)
4. Roglia, G.F., Martignoni, L., Paleari, R., Bruschi, D.: Surgically returning to randomized lib (c). In: 2009 Annual Computer Security Applications Conference, ACSAC 2009, pp. 60–69 (2009)
5. Shacham, H.: The geometry of innocent flesh on the bone: return-into-libc without function calls (on the x86). In: Proceedings of the 14th ACM Conference on Computer and Communications Security, Alexandria, Virginia, USA, pp. 552–561. ACM (2007)
6. Roemer, R., Buchanan, E., Shacham, H., Savage, S.: Return-oriented programming: Systems, languages, and applications. ACM Trans. Inf. Syst. Secur. **15**(1), 1–34 (2012)
7. Buchanan, E., Roemer, R., Shacham, H., Savage, S.: When good instructions go bad: generalizing return-oriented programming to RISC. In: Proceedings of the 15th ACM Conference on Computer and Communications Security, pp. 27–38 (2008)
8. Checkoway, S., Davi, L., Dmitrienko, A., Sadeghi, A.R., Shacham, H., Winandy, M.: Return-oriented programming without returns. In: Proceedings of the 17th ACM Conference on Computer and Communications Security, pp. 559–572. ACM (2010)
9. Bletsch, T., Jiang, X., Freeh, V.W., Liang, Z.: Jump-oriented programming: a new class of code-reuse attack. In: Proceedings of the 6th ACM Symposium on Information, Computer and Communications Security, pp. 30–40 (2011)
10. Chen, P., Xiao, H., Shen, X., Yin, X., Mao, B., Xie, L.: DROP: detecting return-oriented programming malicious code. In: Prakash, A., Sen Gupta, I. (eds.) ICISS 2009. LNCS, vol. 5905, pp. 163–177. Springer, Heidelberg (2009). https://doi.org/10.1007/978-3-642-10772-6_13
11. Chen, P., Xing, X., Han, H., Mao, B., Xie, L.: Efficient detection of the return-oriented programming malicious code. In: Jha, S., Mathuria, A. (eds.) ICISS 2010. LNCS, vol. 6503, pp. 140–155. Springer, Heidelberg (2010). https://doi.org/10.1007/978-3-642-17714-9_11
12. Onarlioglu, K., Bilge, L., Lanzi, A., Balzarotti, D., Kirda, E.: G-free: defeating return-oriented programming through gadget-less binaries. In: Proceedings of the 26th Annual Computer Security Applications Conference, Austin, Texas, pp. 49–58. ACM (2010)

13. Li, J., Wang, Z., Jiang, X., Grace, M., Bahram, S.: Defeating return-oriented rootkits with "return-less" kernels. In: Proceedings of the 5th European conference on Computer systems, Paris, France, pp. 195–208. ACM (2010)

14. Davi, L., Sadeghi, A.R., Winandy, M.: ROPdefender: a detection tool to defend against return-oriented programming attacks. In: Proceedings of the 6th ACM Symposium on Information, Computer and Communications Security, Hong Kong, China, pp. 40–51. ACM (2011)

15. Pappas, V., Polychronakis, M., Keromytis, A.: Smashing the gadgets: Hindering return-oriented programming using in-place code randomization. In: 2012 IEEE Symposium on Security and Privacy (SP), pp. 601–615 (2012)

16. Tran, M., Etheridge, M., Bletsch, T., Jiang, X., Freeh, V., Ning, P.: On the expressiveness of return-into-libc attacks. In: Sommer, R., Balzarotti, D., Maier, G. (eds.) RAID 2011. LNCS, vol. 6961, pp. 121–141. Springer, Heidelberg (2011). https://doi.org/10.1007/978-3-642-23644-0_7

17. Lu, K., Zou, D., Wen, W., Gao, D.: Packed, printable, and polymorphic return-oriented programming. In: Sommer, R., Balzarotti, D., Maier, G. (eds.) RAID 2011. LNCS, vol. 6961, pp. 101–120. Springer, Heidelberg (2011). https://doi.org/10.1007/978-3-642-23644-0_6

18. Carlini, N., Wagner, D.: ROP is still dangerous: Breaking modern defenses. In: USENIX Security Symposium (2014)

19. Abadi, M., Budiu, M., Erlingsson, Ú., Ligatti, J.: A theory of secure control flow. In: Lau, K.-K., Banach, R. (eds.) ICFEM 2005. LNCS, vol. 3785, pp. 111–124. Springer, Heidelberg (2005). https://doi.org/10.1007/11576280_9

20. Abadi, M., Budiu, M., Erlingsson, U., Ligatti, J.: Control-flow integrity principles, implementations, and applications. ACM Trans. Inf. Syst. Secur. **13**(1), 1–40 (2009)

21. Sadeghi, A.R., Davi, L., Larsen, P.: Securing legacy software against real-world code-reuse exploits: utopia, alchemy, or possible future? In: Proceedings of the 10th ACM Symposium on Information, Computer and Communications Security, Singapore, Republic of Singapore, pp. 55–61. ACM (2015)

22. Carlini, N., Barresi, A., Payer, M., Wagner, D., Gross, T.R.: Control-flow bending: On the effectiveness of control-flow integrity. In: USENIX SEC (2015)

23. Burow, N., Carr, S.A., Nash, J., Larsen, P., Franz, M., Brunthaler, S., Payer, M.: Control-flow integrity: precision, security, and performance. ACM Comput. Surv. **50**(1), 1–33 (2017)

24. Hamid, N., Shao, Z., Trifonov, V., Monnier, S., Ni, Z.: A syntactic approach to foundational proof-carrying code. In: 2002 Proceedings of the 17th Annual IEEE Symposium on Logic in Computer Science, pp. 89–100 (2002)

25. van Benthem, J., van Ditmarsch, H., van Eijck, J., Jaspars, J.: Chapter 6: Logic and Action. In: Logic in Action, February 2014. Internet electronic book

26. Harel, D., Kozen, D., Tiuryn, J.: Propositional Dynamic Logic, pp. 163–190. MIT Press, Cambridge (2000)

27. Jang, D., Tatlock, Z., Lerner, S.: SAFEDISPATCH: securing C++ virtual calls from memory corruption attacks. In: Symposium on Network and Distributed System Security (NDSS) (2014)

28. Tice, C., Roeder, T., Collingbourne, P., Checkoway, S., Erlingsson,, Lozano, L., Pike, G.: Enforcing forward-edge control-flow integrity in gcc & llvm. In: USENIX Security Symposium (2014)

29. Gawlik, R., Holz, T.: Towards automated integrity protection of C++ virtual function tables in binary programs. In: Proceedings of the 30th Annual Computer Security Applications Conference, New Orleans, Louisiana, USA, pp. 396–405. ACM (2014)

30. Prakash, A., Hu, X., Yin, H.: vfGuard: Strict protection for virtual function calls in COTS C++ binaries. In: Symposium on Network and Distributed System Security (NDSS) (2015)

31. Yu, H., Xue, J., Huo, W., Feng, X., Zhang, Z.: Level by level: making flow- and context-sensitive pointer analysis scalable for millions of lines of code. In: Proceedings of the 8th Annual IEEE/ACM International Symposium on Code Generation and Optimization, Toronto, Ontario, Canada, pp. 218–229. ACM (2010)

32. MITRE: CVE - Download CVE

33. Niu, B., Tan, G.: Modular control-flow integrity. SIGPLAN Not. **49**(6), 577–587 (2014)

34. Davi, L., Dmitrienko, A., Egele, M., Fischer, T., Holz, T., Hund, R., Nrnberger, S., Sadeghi, A.R.: MoCFI: A framework to mitigate control-flow attacks on smartphones. In: NDSS (2012)

35. Zhang, C., Wei, T., Chen, Z., Duan, L., Szekeres, L., McCamant, S., Song, D., Zou, W.: Practical control flow integrity and randomization for binary executables. In: 2013 IEEE Symposium on Security and Privacy (SP), pp. 559–573 (2013)

36. Criswell, J., Dautenhahn, N., Adve, V.: KCoFI: complete control-flow integrity for commodity operating system kernels. In: 2014 IEEE Symposium on Security and Privacy (SP), pp. 292–307 (2014)

37. Zhang, M., Sekar, R.: Control flow integrity for COTS binaries. In: Usenix Security, pp. 337–352 (2013)

38. Davi, L., Lehmann, D., Sadeghi, A.R., Monrose, F.: Stitching the gadgets: on the ineffectiveness of coarse-grained control-flow integrity protection. In: USENIX Security Symposium (2014)

39. Goktas, E., Athanasopoulos, E., Bos, H., Portokalidis, G.: Out of control: overcoming control-flow integrity. In: 2014 IEEE Symposium on Security and Privacy (SP), pp. 575–589, May 2014

40. Bletsch, T., Jiang, X., Freeh, V.: Mitigating code-reuse attacks with control-flow locking. In: Proceedings of the 27th Annual Computer Security Applications Conference, Orlando, Florida, pp. 353–362. ACM (2011)

41. Niu, B., Tan, G.: Monitor integrity protection with space efficiency and separate compilation. In: Proceedings of the 2013 ACM SIGSAC Conference on Computer & communications security, Berlin, Germany, pp. 199–210. ACM (2013)

42. Pappas, V., Polychronakis, M., Keromytis, A.D.: Transparent ROP exploit mitigation using indirect branch tracing. In: USENIX Security, pp. 447–462 (2013)

43. Cheng, Y., Zhou, Z., Miao, Y., Ding, X., DENG, H.: ROPecker: A generic and practical approach for defending against ROP attack (2014)

44. Yuan, P., Zeng, Q., Ding, X.: Hardware-assisted fine-grained code-reuse attack detection. In: Bos, H., Monrose, F., Blanc, G. (eds.) RAID 2015. LNCS, vol. 9404, pp. 66–85. Springer, Cham (2015). https://doi.org/10.1007/978-3-319-26362-5_4

45. Mohan, V., Larsen, P., Brunthaler, S., Hamlen, K., Franz, M.: Opaque control-flow integrity. In: Symposium on Network and Distributed System Security (NDSS) (2015)

46. Zhang, C., Song, C., Chen, K.Z., Chen, Z., Song, D.: VTint: defending virtual function tables integrity. In: Symposium on Network and Distributed System Security (NDSS) (2015)

47. Erlingsson, U., Abadi, M., Vrable, M., Budiu, M., Necula, G.C.: XFI: Software guards for system address spaces. In: Proceedings of the 7th Symposium on Operating Systems Design and Implementation, pp. 75–88 (2006)
48. Akritidis, P., Cadar, C., Raiciu, C., Costa, M., Castro, M.: Preventing memory error exploits with WIT. In: 2008 IEEE Symposium on Security and Privacy, SP 2008, pp. 263–277, May 2008
49. Pewny, J., Holz, T.: Control-flow restrictor: compiler-based CFI for iOS. In: Proceedings of the 29th Annual Computer Security Applications Conference, New Orleans, Louisiana, USA, pp. 309–318. ACM (2013)
50. Davi, L., Hanreich, M., Paul, D., Sadeghi, A.R., Koeberl, P., Sullivan, D., Arias, O., Jin, Y.: HAFIX: hardware-assisted flow integrity extension. In: Proceedings of the 52nd Annual Design Automation Conference, San Francisco, California, pp. 1–6. ACM (2015)
51. Bounov, D., Kc, R.G., Lerner, S.: Protecting C++ dynamic dispatch through vtable interleaving. In: Symposium on Network and Distributed System Security (NDSS) (2016)
52. Wang, Z., Jiang, X.: HyperSafe: a lightweight approach to provide lifetime hypervisor control-flow integrity. In: 2010 IEEE Symposium on Security and Privacy (SP), pp. 380–395 (2010)
53. Niu, B., Tan, G.: RockJIT: Securing just-in-time compilation using modular control-flow integrity. In: Proceedings of the 2014 ACM SIGSAC Conference on Computer and Communications Security, Scottsdale, Arizona, USA, pp. 1317–1328. ACM (2014)
54. Mashtizadeh, A.J., Bittau, A., Boneh, D., Mazières, D.: CCFI: cryptographically enforced control flow integrity. In: Proceedings of the 22nd ACM SIGSAC Conference on Computer and Communications Security, Denver, Colorado, USA, pp. 941–951. ACM (2015)
55. Ge, X., Talele, N., Payer, M., Jaeger, T.: Fine-grained control-flow integrity for kernel software. In: 2016 IEEE European Symposium on Security and Privacy (EuroS&P), pp. 179–194, March 2016
56. van der Veen, V., Andriesse, D., Goktas, E., Gras, B., Sambuc, L., Slowinska, A., Bos, H., Giuffrida, C.: Practical context-sensitive CFI. In: Proceedings of the 22nd ACM SIGSAC Conference on Computer and Communications Security, Denver, Colorado, USA, pp. 927–940. ACM (2015)
57. Niu, B., Tan, G.: Per-input control-flow integrity. In: Proceedings of the 22nd ACM SIGSAC Conference on Computer and Communications Security, Denver, Colorado, USA, pp. 914–926. ACM (2015)
58. Payer, M., Barresi, A., Gross, T.R.: Fine-grained control-flow integrity through binary hardening. In: Almgren, M., Gulisano, V., Maggi, F. (eds.) DIMVA 2015. LNCS, vol. 9148, pp. 144–164. Springer, Cham (2015). https://doi.org/10.1007/978-3-319-20550-2_8
59. Theodorides, M., Wagner, D.: Breaking active-set backward-edge CFI. In: 2017 IEEE International Symposium on Hardware Oriented Security and Trust (HOST), pp. 85–89, May 2017
60. Evans, I., Long, F., Otgonbaatar, U., Shrobe, H., Rinard, M., Okhravi, H., Sidiroglou-Douskos, S.: Control Jujutsu: on the weaknesses of fine-grained control flow integrity. In: Proceedings of the 22nd ACM SIGSAC Conference on Computer and Communications Security, Denver, Colorado, USA, pp. 901–913. ACM (2015)

Defending Application Cache Integrity
of Android Runtime

Jia Wan[1(✉)], Mohammad Zulkernine[1], Phil Eisen[2], and Clifford Liem[2]

[1] School of Computing, Queen's University, Kingston, ON, Canada
{jiawan,mzulker}@cs.queensu.ca
[2] Irdeto Corporation, Ottawa, ON, Canada
{phil.eisen,clifford.liem}@irdeto.com

Abstract. Android malware vendors profit by "piggybacking" on legitimate applications (or simply apps) and inserting malicious code that can steal users' sensitive data or display unsolicited advertisements. A piggybacked app is a repackaged legitimate app with extra code that can perform malicious acts after installation. Many researchers have put effort into signature schemes for malware detection and to develop obfuscation techniques to mitigate the effects of piggybacking. However, little has been done to protect apps after their installation. In particular, the cache, where the app actually runs, is vulnerable to tampering. Cache tampering allows for the same behavioral changes as piggybacking. Cache loading process of Android Runtime (ART) can be exploited by cache tampering attacks without rebooting the device. In this paper, we introduce an approach to protect apps by maintaining the integrity of their cache. We show that cache tampering is possible and propose a lightweight cache protection mechanism to alert users about a cache tampering attack. We describe the approach in detail and present the results of a real implementation. Our evaluation results on Android 7 (the latest version at the time of this writing) show that our cache protection system can detect the abnormal behavior effectively and efficiently.

Keywords: Android application · ART · Anti-Tampering
Mobile security

1 Introduction

Android devices remain an attractive mobile malware target in recent years [31]. Piggybacked apps are popular in third party app markets where legitimate apps are repackaged and leveraged to make profit for attackers [1]. Some research have been done to get apps repackaged for policy enforcement or software analysis [7,8], but obfuscation technology applied on original apps makes repackaging unrealistic. Also, static signature-based detection can filter out repackaged apps with malicious features and frustrates the attempts of piggybacking [14–17]. As attackers become more stealthier, an app's cache may be tampered to perform

© Springer International Publishing AG 2017
J. K. Liu and P. Samarati (Eds.): ISPEC 2017, LNCS 10701, pp. 727–746, 2017.
https://doi.org/10.1007/978-3-319-72359-4_45

the same malice as a repackaged app by exploiting the vulnerabilities in Android cache mechanism [21].

Dalvik has been replaced by ART since Android 5. ART is now the default Android Java Virtual Machine (JVM) for Android 5 and the higher versions [23]. During an app's installation, *installd* triggers *dex2oat* compiler to create app cache in Optimized ART (OAT) format. *installd* is the process in the device to receive commands from Android framework for apps' installation. The compilation operation is time-consuming and the time depends on the size of the app as compilation from Dalvik bytecode to native code takes time. An OAT format file is named `base.odex` in a specific folder and only the app is able to access (except root privilege). This folder is the app's sandbox folder. When an app starts up next time, ART will load the app's cache file into the memory of its own process rather than the reinstallation of the Android Package (APK) to reduce startup time and improve runtime performance. The cache file contains the app's Dalvik bytecode for runtime interpretation or native code for direct execution.

The reliance on app cache to load an app in ART may be exploited by attackers. Similar to repackaging an app by modifying its source code, an app's cache can be delicately crafted to achieve the same objective. A cache tampering attack can be launched without the user's notice and without restarting the device. The replacement of an app's copied APK file (`base.apk` in the app's sandbox folder) is only effective after rebooting the device and then Android framework brings notice to its user's attention. The attack may occur even the user is careful to install apps from Google's official app store. Since each installed app runs in a sandbox, the attack should break into the app's sandbox to modify the cache. The attack is effective when the target app's process restarts. Hence, when the user taps the app's icon next time, a malign cache designed to mimic the app's UI may steal the user's account information in the background. Moreover, hardened apps are made through packing services to make reverse engineering more difficult by applying dynamic loading. However, the app's cache can be generated once original Dalvik EXecutable (DEX) format file is loaded dynamically [6]. Therefore, cache protection in ART is necessary.

An OAT file is large in size, e.g., YouTube's cache file is nearly 253MB in the device. By simply encrypting or signing the cache file into hash signature as a secure store, performance overhead may affect the protected app due to CPU usage for computing, extra memory and storage space, and long app loading time that shortens device's battery lifespan. Also, to get a signature for the whole cache file is not necessary as not all parts of the cache are targeted by a cache tampering attack. Furthermore, protection should be applied for the vulnerable part that can be reached by attackers to make anti-tampering more targeted.

In this paper, we attempt to provide an anti-tampering solution for apps by protecting app cache. If a cache tampering attack happens, the original app's behavior will be modified without restarting the device on which the app is running. Cache protection is able to defeat cache tampering attacks and defend the integrity of app behavior. Our solution can be deployed easily across different

Android ART-based platforms with little effort. App developers are able to use our technique to protect the integrity of their apps' behavior. In summary, we make the following contributions:

- We perform a systematic analysis about OAT structure, factors influencing an app's cache file generation, and cache loading process to explore the possibilities of cache protection in ART. Our findings inspire the research of Android cache protection.
- We propose a defense mechanism for an app's cache protection to defend installed apps' behavior. We launch a cache tampering attack to exploit the vulnerability of ART's cache mechanism that can be leveraged to tamper the target app's behavior. The attack is used to assess the effectiveness of our proposed mechanism.
- We implement a lightweight Integrity Verification (IV) shared library integrated into the target app in the device running Android 7 and deploy the time-consuming secure store generation operation in a separate powerful server (host). On-device IV is available to detect tampering activities and generate alerts. We also do the performance evaluation of the proposed solution that shows its effectiveness and efficiency.

The rest of the paper is organized as follows. In Sect. 2, we discuss background information about ART cache in Android 7. Section 3 introduces a general overview of how a cache tampering attack can circumvent ART cache check and do malice in the device. We detail our proposed system in Sect. 4 including the implementation in both host and device. Section 5 presents the evaluation results. After introducing the related work in Sect. 6, we conclude in Sect. 7.

2 Background

Android introduced ART in Android 4 as an option and set it as default Android runtime to execute Dalvik bytecode in the later releases of Android. ART aims to improve the execution performance of Android Java apps by executing native code from `base.odex` instead of interpreting Dalvik bytecode. In Android 7, an app's compiling mode is decided by *–compiler-filter* option. Three compiling modes are introduced to save power, improve runtime performance, and reduce installation time that is mainly occupied by native code compilation on both Android 5 and 6. They are Ahead Of Time (AOT), Just In Time (JIT), and interpreter for Java runtime.

AOT translates Dalvik bytecode into native code during an app's installation by the on-device compiler *dex2oat*, while JIT is much more flexible to compile Dalvik bytecode at runtime. A compilation daemon is used to compile collected classes or methods in a profile file when the device is idle and charging [24]. The profile guided compilation will store frequently executed methods into an app's image file (`base.art`), which avoids JIT compilation again [22,25]. The interpreter interprets Dalvik byte code for execution without consuming time for compilation.

In this section, we provide background information about Android cache mechanism. Section 2.1 includes `base.odex` and `base.oat` loading procedure. OAT content varies among different Android versions. We illustrate OAT file structure in Android 7 in Sect. 2.2. Section 2.3 describes how *–compiler-filter* option for *dex2oat* influences the formation of OAT content.

2.1 Cache File

The cache file is a special Executable and Linkable Format (ELF) file with OAT structure and stored in an app's sandbox folder. For example, YouTube's cache is `/data/app/com.google.android.youtube-1/oat/arm64/base.odex` created by *dex2oat* compiler. `/data/app/com.google.android.youtube-1` is the app's sandbox folder (the app's data folder). `base.odex` is actually an OAT file with *.odex* extension. An image file `base.art` in the folder consists of compiled frequently used methods, which improves runtime class lookup performance.

A background thread is used to collect resolved classes and methods in ART and store indices of them in a profile file in `/data/misc/profiles` permanently when they are compiled by JIT or interpreted by interpreter and accessed frequently enough to exceed a threshold. The background thread is called ART's *ProfileSaver* thread [32]. The image file (`base.art`) is generated to store the compilation information of frequently used methods according to the profile by a compilation daemon triggered by many conditions, e.g., charging, idle. The compilation information includes locations of compiled classes and methods in the OAT file (`base.odex`). The compilation daemon uses *dex2oat* to compile according to the records in the profile.

Figure 1 shows how ART loads cache into memory when an app runs after its installation. For installed apps, `PathClassLoader` is the class loader to load them into memory. When cache loading is invoked from Android framework, the path of `base.apk` in the app's data folder is passed to ART that tries to load `base.odex` first. If `base.odex` does not exist, ART will roll back to load DEX content in the APK file. If `base.odex` exists, ART will check the existence of `base.art` and update `ClassTable` to accelerate linking of methods when class linker looks up classes. `ClassTable` is a sophisticated structure to record already found classes into memory. Otherwise, ART reads DEX content from `base.odex` and uses `DefineClass` (a representation to find a class by traversing all included Android framework's cache) which is slower than `ClassTable` searching to link classes in terms of runtime performance.

An attacker is able to exploit the cache loading process by removing `base.art` that is harder to tamper and by modifying static `base.odex`. The operation may incur performance penalty as `ClassTable` is removed. However, it is possible to get DEX content or native code from `base.odex` and the performance is better than an APK's reinstallation. A cache tampering attack is made to remove `base.art` and tamper `base.odex`. ART will load the modified app cache (`base.odex`) into the memory of the app's process, which may modify the target app's behavior.

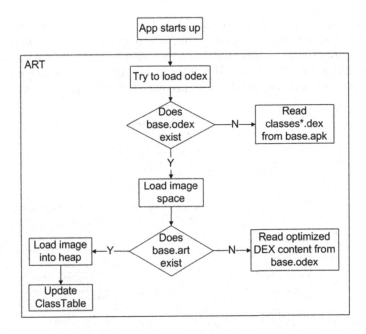

Fig. 1. Caching loading in ART

2.2   OAT Structure

As Dalvik is the JVM on older Android releases, app cache contains optimized DEX content. Now ART introduces OAT structure embedded in an ELF cache file. Figure 2 shows the OAT file format where OAT occupies two segments. *oatdata* in ELF's *.rodata* segment stores OAT data content while *oatexec* in ELF's *.text* segment is filled with platform-specific native code. The native code is generated when an app is installed and compiled by *dex2oat*. ART supports seven types of instruction architectures: Mips, Mips64, X86, X86_64, Arm, Arm64, and Thumb2. It means that cache files produced by the same Android release on different instruction architecture platforms are different.

Four kinds of sections reside in *oatdata* segment: *OATHeader*, *OatDexFile*, *DexFile*, and *OatClass*. *OATHeader* contains important fields like instruction set of the device and the number of DEX structures in the cache file that is equal to the number of *classes*.dex* files in the APK file. `adler32_checksum` in *OAT-Header* specifies the checksum of the current *OATHeader* and all DEX content. `image_file_location_oat_checksum`, the other checksum is used to verify the legitimacy of the cache file that will be discussed in Sect. 3. `key_value_store` specifies command line of *dex2oat* to create an app's cache. The command line involves many options like *–oat-file* and *–compiler-filter*.

OatDexFile is a small structure mainly to specify the offsets of both *Dex-File* and *OatClass* at *oatdata* segment. An *OatDexFile* structure also contains a checksum field (`dex_file_location_checksum`) specifying the origin of the corresponding *DexFile* structure. Multiple DEX files have been supported in Android 5 and the higher versions [26], which means that an OAT file may contain multiple *DexFile* structures and thus many *OatDexFile* structures. For example, there may be many DEX files in an APK such as *classes.dex* and *classes2.dex*. We use *classes*.dex* to represent DEX content in an APK.

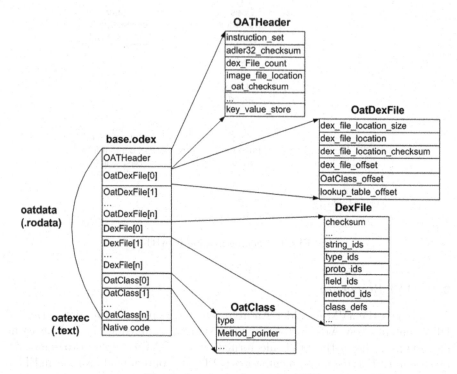

Fig. 2. App cache layout in ART

DexFile is the optimized content of *classes*.dex* [27]. Optimization happens only in the bytecode section of *DexFile*. Optimized DEX has the same DEX structure as an APK's *classes*.dex*. The checksum in *OatDexFile* is the same as the CRC32 checksum of the corresponding *classes*.dex*, even though DEX content is optimized and the checksum of the optimized DEX content is supposed to be different from the checksum of the original DEX content. A *DexFile* structure contains several fields such as constant string index list and method index list. These fields help locate methods in *OatClass* section. If the target app's behavior is expected to behave differently in a cache tampering attack, bytecode in *DexFile* needs to change. Our cache protection mechanism will extract the target app's *DexFile* structures from the app's cache as *DexFile* reflects an attack's modification. *DexFile* content is the vulnerable part of an app's cache file.

OatClass contains the description of one class with method locations to locate native code in *oatexec* segment. An *OatClass* structure describes one class in each *DexFile*. *type* in one *OatClass* indicates the compilation status of the class. There are three compilations statuses: non-compiled, some-compiled, and all-compiled. Non-compiled means that the method is interpreted by Dalvik bytecode interpreter. All-compiled means that the method is compiled by AOT. Some-compiled means that *OatClass* uses a bitmap to record compiled method index to locate native code. *method_pointer* records the offsets of methods' native code in *oatexec* segment.

2.3   Compiler Filters

The concept of compiler filter was introduced in Android 7 and will continue to exist in its higher versions. The idea is to compile apps or framework libraries in different modes with regard to Android runtime performance and device hardware conditions. Some scenarios have to be considered like AOT compilation consumes too much time during an app's installation and a mobile device may be short of space to store large cache files with compiled native code. Hence, many compilation options are provided to expedite apps' startup, improve user experience and save battery and space. An app is installed with *–compiler-filter* of *dex2oat* set to `interpret-only`, which removes compilation time and reduces app installation time for better user experience. However, it sacrifices the app's runtime performance since Dalvik bytecode interpretation is slower than native code execution. The selection of compiler filter options is a trade off between app's runtime performance, app's installation experience, and device conditions.

There are twelve compiler filters in Android 7, while four are officially supported in Android 8 [22]. This will be discussed in Sect. 4.2. There are two categories in terms of compilation options in Android 7: one is for system image configuration and the other is about app compilation. In this paper, we only discuss app compilation category that is *–compiler-filter* option. For example, `speed-profile` takes advantage of profile-guided compilation. `interpret-only` optimizes some Dalvik instructions of DEX content to get better interpreter performance. `speed` does AOT compilation for all methods to increase app execution speed [22,27].

DexFile in the cache is not the exact Dalvik bytecode in *classes*.dex* of the APK. Different *–compiler-filter* options generate different cache files. For example, `verify-profile` does not have DEX optimized and the cache file contains the exact Dalvik bytecode in the APK. `interpret-only`, `speed` and `space` do DEX-to-DEX optimization differently. The differences among all compiler filter options for DEX content optimization will not be covered in this paper.

Android uses different compiler filter options to compile apps depending on platforms' configuration. Therefore, how an app is compiled is uncertain across different devices. We deploy the time consuming compilation process in the host to generate apps' secure data (secure stores) by applying all possible compiler filter options.

3   Threat Model

ART checks the legitimacy of a cache file (`base.odex`) to ensure that the cache is generated by *dex2oat* compiler. An app's cache can be loaded into the memory of the app's process when an app starts up and its process is newly created. Figure 3 shows the cache loading check in ART.

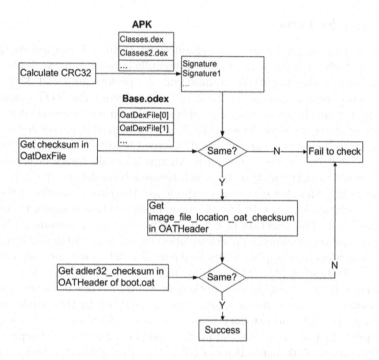

Fig. 3. Cache loading check in ART

ART calculates CRC32 for each *classes.dex* in the APK (`base.apk`) and compares them with the checksum in *OatDexFile* one by one since there may be multiple DEX files. This makes sure that the cache file is made originally from the APK. If the check passes, `image_file_location_oat_checksum` in `base.odex`'s *OATHeader* is extracted to compare with `adler32_checksum` in *OATHeader* of on-device `boot.oat` (Android framework's cache). This operation ensures that the cache file is generated in the device. If the check passes, `base.odex` is legitimate.

In Sect. 2.3, we mention that DEX-to-DEX optimization may change DEX content in an OAT file by *dex2oat*. However, checksums in `base.odex`'s *OatDexFiles* still keep the CRC32s of the original *classes*.dex* in the APK.

The checking process is vulnerable as checksums can be replaced by the right ones to satisfy the check if the attacker is proficient about OAT structure. Sabanal [21] presents an approach to launch the attack stealthily.

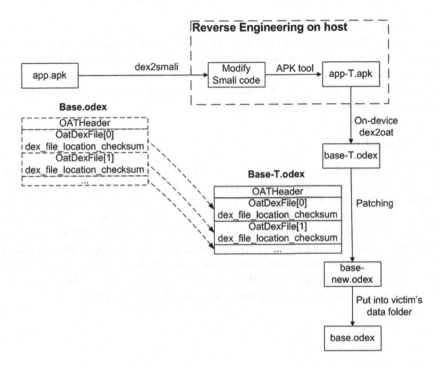

Fig. 4. Cache tampering attack operation

The attacking process is shown in Fig. 4. An attacker can do reverse engineering for one APK, modify the smali code (an intermediate code representation generated by Baksmali disassembler) as desired and repackage the modified code into `app-T.apk` by APK tool. `base-T.odex` is generated by on-device *dex2oat* to get the right `adler32_checksum` from `boot.oat` in the device. The operation can be done in the host as long as the Android Open Source Project (AOSP) environment is built to execute *dex2oat* with necessary framework *jars* in the right Android version. If *dex2oat* compiler is operated in the host, `image_file_location_oat_checksum` of *OATHeader* in the newly built `base-T.odex` should be replaced by the value of `adler32_checksum` in *OATHeader* of the target device's `boot.oat`. The next step is to modify `base-T.odex` with the original `base.odex`'s checksum of *OatDexFile*. At last, `base-T.odex` is put into the app's cache folder to replace original `base.odex`. The attacker has to acquire access to the app's sandbox folder by jailbreaking the device. As a result, when the victim app starts up with its newly created process, a cache tampering attack can be made without the user's notice.

4   Cache Protection Approach

As the vulnerable cache exploitation is demonstrated in Sect. 3, new technology should be explored to defeat cache tampering attacks effectively and efficiently and should be deployed easily across different Android platforms. In this section, we illustrate the design and implementation of such a technology that protects app behavior integrity by anti-tampering the app's cache. Section 4.1 introduces the basic concept of our proposal. We describe the compatibility for the next version of Android 8 in Sect. 4.2. Sections 4.3 and 4.4 elaborate our cache protection system implemented in both host and device.

4.1   Basic Idea

We assume that if an attacker can tamper the source code or smali code of an app after reverse engineering, *classes*.dex* (APK's Dalvik bytecode) in the tampered malicious app will be different from the ones in the original APK. The cache generated from the malicious APK by *dex2oat* compiler is different from the original cache. The difference happens in the DEX content of OAT structure. Our design goal is to get the user aware of cache tampering by making an alert. Our implementation is forward compatible and can be updated easily as ART changes in each Android release. We make performance affected tasks run in the host and do not impact an app's runtime performance too much.

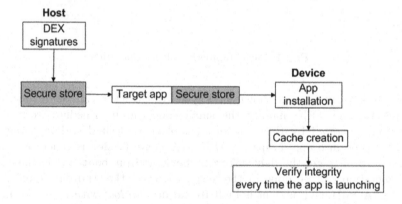

Fig. 5. App cache anti-tampering

We decide to use a secure store generated in the host which is actually a file with DEX content signature in a presumably secure format. The file will be attached with an app as an asset. Since ART is the default Android runtime in Android 5 and higher, an OAT file is generated as cache for booting the app instead of re-installing the original APK each time when the app starts up after its initial launch. The OAT file should be protected appropriately to guarantee the app's behavior integrity when the app boots up. We perform a lightweight cache IV every time the app starts up. The idea is shown in Fig. 5. The cache is `base.odex`, an OAT file which contains optimized DEX content [27].

App developers may apply app hardening technology to load sources at runtime. Packing services adopt special *ClassLoader* to dynamically load APK to assure that attackers may not take advantage of the APK file. However, ART may generate cache file for the loadee when the protected app hardened inside a shell is loaded [6]. Hence, cache file protection is still needed.

4.2 Compatibility

Our approach is based on the latest Android release (Android 7) at the time of this writing. In Android 8, three cache files are expected to be in an app's cache folder instead of two (`base.odex` and `base.art`) in Android 7. They are *.vdex*, *.odex* and *.art*, while *.vdex* has DEX code of the APK. The method of cache protection will be the same. We will keep an eye out for Android's version update and reflect the changes appropriately in our proposed system. Furthermore, four compiler filter options will be supported officially in Android 8 rather than twelve in Android 7. The work of these four app compilation modes are more definite [22]. Our protection technique may be compatible with future Android releases.

4.3 Secure Store Generation

A signing system shown in Fig. 6 is designed to generate secure stores for apps. A secure store for an app contains DEX signatures of different compiler filter options on all possible instruction architecture platforms. The signing system utilizes AOSP environments to build OAT files that need Android framework *jar* files to link classes and optimize Dalvik bytecode inside an OAT structure. The idea is to deploy AOSP environments in different Android versions in the host and generate a secure store of an app for different instruction architecture platforms such as Mips, Mips64, X86, X86_64, Arm, Arm64, and Thumb2. On-host *dex2oat* compiler generates secure stores. *oat2dex* is implemented to extract DEX content from an OAT file and may be compatible with different Android versions since OAT structure evolves gradually. The host is a server with different AOSP building environments to build framework *jar* files for different platforms.

Figure 7 demonstrates DEX signing and a secure store formation working process. The signing system runs in the host to generate DEX signatures, encrypt or hash them, and store them in a secure store. The secure store will be attached in the target app. The signing system uses the target app as an input. In our experiments, we use adler32 algorithm to get one signature for each DEX file in the target APK. *dex2oat* built in an AOSP environment runs in the host to optimize original *classes*.dex* according to different compiler filter options. Corresponding DEX signatures will be generated for IV operation in the device. From the experiments, we find that DEX content are different because of – *compiler-filter* options. For example, DEX content in `speed-profile` is different from `speed` and both are different from `verify-profile`. How compiler filters optimize DEX is not discussed in this paper.

A secure store is organized as a map involving instruction sets, compiler filter options, and corresponding DEX signatures. The target app will attach the secure store and verify the integrity of the app's cache when the app starts up. A signing system is implemented to gather OAT files of different compiler

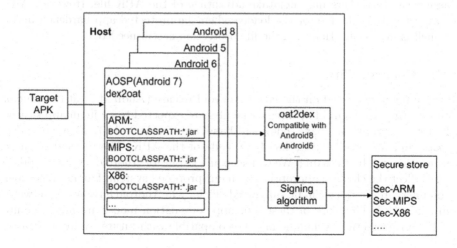

Fig. 6. Signing components in the host

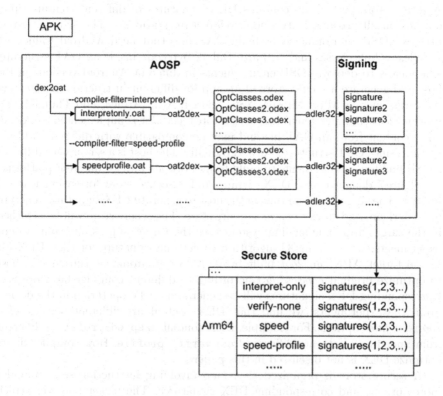

Fig. 7. Secure store generation process in the host

filter options under different instruction sets. Four bytes' signatures is used for each *DexFile* in these OAT files in our experiments.

4.4 Integrity Verification

Figure 8 illustrates an app's cache IV process. When an app is installed, Android *installd* process will trigger *dex2oat* to create a cache file in the app's cache folder. The cache file is an OAT file named `base.odex`. *oat2dex* is implemented in a native library to analyze the OAT file and extract DEX content from it. The compiler filter option and instruction set in the OAT file can be obtained from *OATHeader*. A secure store is put in the target app's asset folder. The target app uses the native library to generate DEX signatures and look up the secure store to find a match with the series of DEX signatures when it starts up. If the cache is tampered and replaced by malicious one, IV native library will check and send an alert.

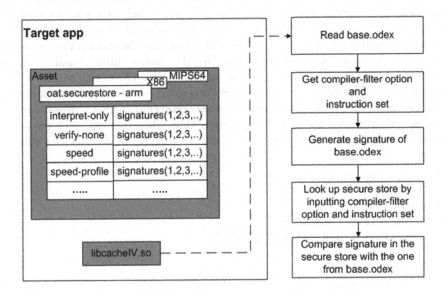

Fig. 8. Cache file IV process in the device

For example, an app owner can submit an app into our system to get a secure store which will be attached with the app. A native shared library will be delivered to the app owner to be integrated into the app. Both files will not change DEX content of the app. The app will be released with a secure store and an IV library to perform cache IV after the app is installed.

5 Evaluation

In this section, we evaluate our cache protection approach in terms of effectiveness in fending off a cache tampering attack and the overhead it introduces on the utility of an app. The signing system runs on a server as secure store generation can be done in advance and without synchronizing with the app's IV operation (Sect. 5.1). The efficiency is measured with respect to the impacts of IV operation on an app's performance (Sect. 5.2).

The device we use for the evaluation is a Google Nexus 5X phone running Android version 7.0 with kernel version 3.10.73-g43154bf. The build number is NRD90M. Our OAT file format version is 079. Our technique also considers compatibility for OAT different versions. The AOSP building environment in our signing server is `Android-7.0.0_r1`. Our signing server runs on Ubuntu 15.04 with 250 GB hard drive and 4 GB memory.

5.1 Effectiveness

We make a cache tampering attack in the device to demonstrate the effectiveness of our cache protection mechanism. The attack targets an Android app for the experiments to show that the app's behavior can be changed through cache modification. The target app is implemented to show the results of adding two numbers. `TestAdd.java` and `MainActivity.java` are Java source code of the target app. An IV native library and a secure store generated in the host are put in the APK. Once the target app is installed in the device, `base.odex` is generated in the app's cache folder `/data/app/com.testadd.experiment.testadd-1/oat/arm64/`. `base.odex` is the app's cache used to boot the app every time when the app's process is created. The following target app is designed to show "9" on the device's window view:

Example of the target app

```
TestAdd.java
  public class testAdd {
    public int add(int a, int b) {
        int c;
        c = a + b;
        return c;
    }
  }
```

```
MainActivity.java
  protected void onCreate(..) {
    ...
    testAdd t = new testAdd();
    TextView tx = new TextView(this);
    tx.setText(Integer.toString(t.add(4, 5)));
    ...
  }
```

(The target app for addition)

We tamper the target app behavior to do multiplication instead of addition by modifying the source code of the method add in class testAdd. We build the attacking app that uses on-device *dex2oat* to generate the attacking base.odex. An *oatparser* working in the host is implemented to change the attacking app's cache file with the checksum in *OatDexFile* structures obtained from the target app's cache file. The operation can pass ART cache checksum check. The checksum can also be acquired by calculating CRC32 from *classes*.dex* in base.apk that is a copy of the target APK put into the app's data folder by Android's PackageManagerService after the target app's installation. The cache of the modified attacking app replaces the target app's cache to be base.odex in the target app's cache folder. When the app starts next time (app's process is re-created), ART will load the tampered cache, which means that the attack will be successfully launched. The window view of device shows "20" after cache tampering.
Simple modification of the target app

```
TestAdd.java
  public class testAdd {
    public int add(int a, int b) {
        int c;
        c = a * b;
        return c;
    }
  }
```

(Modification to do multiplication)

Figure 9 demonstrates the experiments to show the effectiveness of cache protection. The result shows that the target app's behavior is changed after cache manipulation. We put the attacking app doing multiplication into the device. The malicious base.odex will be obtained and then changed with checksum in *OatDexFile* structures of the target app's base.odex in the host. The new base.odex will be put into the original app's cache folder to launch the attack. In our experiments, we use root privilege to manipulate the target app's cache. The malicious cache will stay effective before system upgrade that replaces all apps' OAT files.

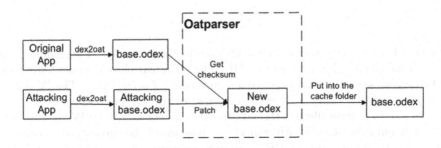

Fig. 9. Experimental cache tampering attack launching process

Cache file tampering attack can be made successfully when the checksums in headers are tampered carefully. ART will check two kinds of checksums. One is the checksum in *OATHeader* that should be equal to Android framework `boot.oat`'s checksum to make sure that the cache file is created in the device. The other one is in *OatDexFile* structures. These checksums should be the same as the ones calculated through corresponding *classes*.dex* in `/data/app/com.testadd.experiment.testadd-1/base.apk`.

The IV code is in a native library of the target app and it is not easy to reverse and modify for the safety of our protection code. We assume our cache protection code is in a safe place. When the target app starts with the secure store, IV will generate the signature for the tampered cache and check if there is a match with the one in the secure store with the same compiler filter option and instruction set. If the cache IV operation finds that there is no match in the secure store, it will send out an alert shown on the app. Since the target app's cache is tampered, no match will be found in the secure store.

Our signing server and the lightweight app's cache IV operation are able to anti-tamper and protect cache from an app's behavior modification by alerting users about the attack. However, if the target app has to include Google extra libraries like `com.google.android.maps.jar` or other libraries not included in AOSP, the secure store will not match cache's signature since AOSP environment does not contain Google extra *jar* files. We found that both Facebook and Amazon need to insert Google map *jar* as `classpath` (an environment path for reference). For a target app inserted with additional Google's *jar* files, we suggest to put the *jar* files into our signing server to get right cache signatures.

5.2   Efficiency

A target app puts the secure store into the asset folder and adds one native library to do IV operation. The performance impacts lie in the size of the secure store and the native library and the execution time of IV operation.

In our experiments, we use adler32 algorithm to sign each DEX file and get four bytes for each. Each compiler filter option occupies one byte and there are twelve compiler filter options for *dex2oat* compiler. There are seven kinds of instruction set architectures for mobile devices. It means that the size of a secure store for seven platforms with a specific instruction set is

$$7 * 12 * (1 + 4 * n)$$

bytes, where n is the number of *classes*.dex* in the target app. For example, the size of Facebook APK is nearly 75 MB. The APK has eleven *classes*.dex* files. Our signing system would produce a secure store of 3,780 bytes. The IV native library is 739 KB. They are trivial compared to the size of an app.

In the IV native library, the additional time consumed by IV operation is 20 ms in our experiments with respect to a baseline of the app's startup scenario. The time is mainly spent on DEX signature generation from an OAT cache. The time for looking up in a secure store is trivial. The adler32 algorithm is used in our experiments. However, more efficient hash algorithms can be explored and applied in our cache protection system.

6 Related Work

Finley et al. [10] presented a cache cleaner to remove apps' cache and keep users' privacy from being leaked. This app cache is about sensitive data from web browsers, network connections or emails that will not change app behavior. This kind of app data is different from Android app cache about which we are concerned. In our paper, an app's cache acts as an app's execution file once the app is installed. An app's cache contains an app's Dalvik bytecode and executable instructions.

Sabanal [21] demonstrated the possibility of replacing ART generated cache with a modified OAT file by running *dex2oat* in the device manually to change the behavior of apps and the framework. The research inspired us to defend an app's behavior integrity from ART cache. Reference hijacking [7] exploits the startup process of an Android app and repackages app to load malicious system libraries without root privilege. The attack can evade the detection of static malware analysis technology. However, our cache protection proposal can defeat reference hijacking attack since a repackaged app will result in the modification of an app's cache and breach the integrity of the original app [18].

Schulz [11] proposed obfuscation techniques to build apps that need attackers' more effort to analyze and piggyback apps [12]. Jeong et al. [13] proposed to encrypt an app's essential part to prevent the app's source code from being attacked. It makes pirating these apps more difficult, while it cannot guarantee the consistency of the app's runtime behavior. Packing services adopt obfuscation technology and dynamic loading that make static analysis more difficult, while researchers present approaches to unpack apps to dump DEX files of the apps and make it possible for attackers to reverse engineer, modify and repackage apps [2,6,19]. Moreover, instead of tempting users to install malicious apps, cache tampering attacks target installed apps by modifying target apps' cache. Even though an attacker cannot analyze a hardened app, cache tampering allows to modify the app's behavior totally by replacing the target app's cache with a malicious app's OAT file. The app's runtime behavior has been modified while the user still think the legitimate app is running in the device.

Some recent work proposed to instrument ART for apps' monitoring. Costamagna et al. [5] proposed a runtime injection approach in ART to monitor app behavior but the scope of monitoring is limited. ARTDroid diverts the execution of sensitive Android APIs for an app's behavior monitoring by method pointer replacement in class virtual table, while the app's exclusive methods are obfuscated and cannot be easily tampered. ProbeDroid achieves the same result by using *ptrace* mechanism (Linux Process Trace) to inject code into a target app's process and change the entry point of methods in the tracked app [30]. Dresel et al. proposed an instrumentation framework in ART to get the locations of Java classes and methods that are helpful for an attacker to control methods and divert their execution. However, ARTIST [3] needs to inject code into an app and repackage the app, which breaks the integrity of the original app and can be detected by our cache protection technique since repackaging the target app changes the app's cache. Backes et al. modified *dex2oat* and added compilation instrumentation for ART backend compiler, which aims to track an app's runtime execution footprint. ARTist [4] replaces *dex2oat* with the optimized one and updates the instrumented app's cache, but our cache protection may not detect such changes since backend compiler optimization impacts native code generation instead of DEX content. These technologies can be applied to tamper apps' runtime behavior. The runtime instrumentation research has influenced our work to prevent runtime methods from being tampered and employ runtime protection of methods.

We develop *oat2dex* for extracting DEX content from an OAT file in Android 7. Note that Chao [28] provides DEX content extraction from an OAT structure, but it lacks the support in OAT analysis in Android 7.

7   Conclusion

We propose to mitigate the risk of the exploitation of ART cache mechanism and thus defend app behavior integrity. We know that an app's cache is an executable file loaded into memory after the app is installed. A cache tampering attack can modify cache to change an app's behavior when the app's process restarts. Our solution is able to prevent a legitimate app's behavior from being tampered by protecting the vulnerable part of the app's cache. In this paper, we conduct a systematic investigation about an app's cache by analyzing ART cache loading process and cache structure, and by assessing the feasibility of signing an app's *classes*.dex* in the host.

We implement a lightweight and app-level cache protection mechanism against cache tampering. We deploy time-consuming compilation process in the host and implement an IV native library to defend app behavior integrity in the device. The signing host applies different compiler filter options to generate secure stores for apps. The host has to insert extra Google libraries to make sure that right secure stores can be generated if target apps need additional Google libraries that do not exist in AOSP. Furthermore, our experimental results show defense effectiveness and efficiency of our proposed approach. The cache protection system is compatible with most of the recent Android versions (5 to 8).

Our cache protection technique is able to defend by alerting users about cache tampering attacks. However, if an attack injects malicious code into an app's memory to control the app's methods in ART and diverts methods' execution to malicious code, malice would be done once a tampered method is invoked without restarting the app's process [4,5,30]. For a complete Android app anti-tampering design, defending app runtime behavior is necessary. We will extend the app protection mechanism to handle the tampering of methods at runtime.

Acknowledgments. This project is partially funded by Mitacs Canada and Irdeto Corporation.

References

1. Zhou, Y., Jiang, X.: Dissecting Android malware: characterization and evolution. In: 2012 IEEE Symposium on Security and Privacy (SP), pp. 95–109. IEEE (2012)
2. Yu, R.: Android packers: facing the challenges, building solutions. In: Proceedings of the Virus Bulletin Conference (VB 2014), pp. 266–275 (2014)
3. Dresel, L., Protsenko, M., Müller, T.: ARTIST: the Android runtime instrumentation toolkit. In: 2016 11th International Conference on Availability, Reliability and Security (ARES), pp. 107–116. IEEE (2016)
4. Backes, M., Bugiel, S., Schranz, O., von Styp-Rekowsky, P., Weisgerber, S.: ARTist: the Android runtime instrumentation and security toolkit. In: 2017 IEEE European Symposium on Security and Privacy (EuroS&P), pp. 481–495. IEEE (2017)
5. Costamagna, V., Zheng, C.: ARTDroid: a virtual-method hooking framework on Android ART runtime. In: IMPS@ ESSoS, pp. 20–28 (2016)
6. Zhang, Y., Luo, X., Yin, H.: DexHunter: toward extracting hidden code from packed android applications. In: Pernul, G., Ryan, P.Y.A., Weippl, E. (eds.) ESORICS 2015. LNCS, vol. 9327, pp. 293–311. Springer, Cham (2015). https://doi.org/10.1007/978-3-319-24177-7_15
7. You, W., Liang, B., Shi, W., Zhu, S., Wang, P., Xie, S., Zhang, X.: Reference hijacking: patching, protecting and analyzing on unmodified and non-rooted Android devices. In: Proceedings of the 38th International Conference on Software Engineering, pp. 959–970. ACM (2016)
8. Davis, B., Chen, H.: RetroSkeleton: retrofitting Android apps. In: Proceedings of the 11th Annual International Conference on Mobile Systems, Applications, and Services, pp. 181–192. ACM (2013)
9. Han, J., Yan, Q., Gao, D., Zhou, J., Deng, H.R.: Android or iOS for better privacy protection? In: International Conference on Secure Knowledge Mangagement in Big-data Era (SKM 2014) (2014)
10. Finley, S., Du, X.: Dynamic cache cleaning on Android. In: 2013 IEEE International Conference on Communications (ICC), pp. 6143–6147. IEEE (2013)
11. Schulz, P.: Code protection in Android. In: Insititute of Computer Science, Rheinische Friedrich-Wilhelms-Universitgt Bonn, Germany, 110 (2012)
12. Bichsel, B., Raychev, V., Tsankov, P., Vechev, M.: Statistical deobfuscation of Android applications. In: Proceedings of the 2016 ACM SIGSAC Conference on Computer and Communications Security, pp. 343–355. ACM (2016)
13. Jeong, Y.S., Park, Y.U., Moon, J.C., Cho, S.J., Kim, D., Park, M.: An anti-piracy mechanism based on class separation and dynamic loading for android applications. In: Proceedings of the 2012 ACM Research in Applied Computation Symposium, pp. 328–332. ACM (2012)
14. Kywe, S. M., Li, Y., Hong, J., Yao, C.: Dissecting developer policy violating apps: characterization and detection. In: 2016 11th International Conference on Malicious and Unwanted Software (MALWARE), pp. 1–10. IEEE (2016)
15. Suarez-Tangil, G., Tapiador, J. E., Peris-Lopez, P., Blasco, J.: Dendroid: a text mining approach to analyzing and classifying code structures in Android malware families. In: Malicious and Unwanted Software (MALWARE), Expert Systems with Applications, vol. 41(4), pp. 1104–1117 (2014)
16. Zhang, M., Duan, Y., Yin, H., Zhao, Z.: Semantics-aware Android malware classification using weighted contextual API dependency graphs. In: Proceedings of the 2014 ACM SIGSAC Conference on Computer and Communications Security, pp. 1105–1116. ACM (2014)

17. Deshotels, L., Notani, V., Lakhotia, A.: Droidlegacy: automated familial classification of Android malware. In: Proceedings of ACM SIGPLAN on Program Protection and Reverse Engineering Workshop 2014, p. 3. ACM (2014)
18. Li, L., Li, D., Bissyand, T.F., Klein, J., Traon, Y.L., Lo, D., Cavallaro, L.: Understanding Android app piggybacking. In: Proceedings of the 39th International Conference on Software Engineering Companion, pp. 359–361. IEEE Press (2017)
19. Xue, L., Luo, X., Yu, L., Wang, S., Wu, D.: Adaptive unpacking of Android apps. In: Proceedings of the 39th International Conference on Software Engineering, pp. 358–369. IEEE Press (2017)
20. Cheng, B., Buzbee, B.: A JIT compiler for androids Dalvik VM. In: Google I/O Developer Conference, vol. 201 (2010)
21. Sabanal, P.: Hiding behind ART. IBM, https://www.blackhat.com/docs/asia-15/materials/asia-15-Sabanal-Hiding-Behind-ART.pdf. Accessed 4 Aug 2017
22. Google Inc.: Configuring ART, https://source.android.com/devices/tech/dalvik/configure. Accessed 4 Aug 2017
23. Google Inc.: Android 5.0 Behavior Changes, https://developer.android.com/guide/practices/verifying-apps-art.html. Accessed 4 Aug 2017
24. Google Inc.: Android 7.0 for Developers, https://developer.android.com/about/versions/nougat/android-7.0.html. Accessed 4 Aug 2017
25. Google Inc.: Implementing ART Just-In-Time (JIT) Compiler, https://source.android.com/devices/tech/dalvik/jit-compiler. Accessed 4 Aug 2017
26. Google Inc.: Configure Apps with Over 64K Methods, https://developer.android.com/studio/build/multidex.html. Accessed 4 Aug 2017
27. Github.: DEX-to-DEX Optimisations, https://github.com/anestisb/oatdump_plus#dex-to-dex-optimisations. Accessed 4 Aug 2017
28. Github.: Oat2dex, https://github.com/lollipopgood/oat2dex. Accessed 4 Aug 2017
29. Dalvik and ART, http://newandroidbook.com/files/Andevcon-ART.pdf. Accessed 4 Aug 2017
30. Github.: ProbeDroid, https://github.com/ZSShen/ProbeDroid. Accessed 4 Aug 2017
31. Symantec.: Internet Security Threat ReportInternet ReportVOLUME, https://www.symantec.com/content/dam/symantec/docs/reports/istr-21-2016-en.pdf. Accessed 4 Aug 2017
32. Zhong, X.: ART JIT in Android N, http://connect.linaro.org/resource/las16/las16-201/. Accessed 4 Aug 2017

An Ensemble Learning System to Mitigate Malware Concept Drift Attacks (Short Paper)

Zhi Wang[1], Meiqi Tian[1], Junnan Wang[2,3], and Chunfu Jia[1(✉)]

[1] College of Computer and Control Engineering, Nankai University, Tianjin, China
cfjia@nankai.edu.cn
[2] Institute of Information Engineering, Chinese Academy of Sciences, Beijing, China
[3] School of Cyber Security, University of Chinese Academy of Sciences,
Beijing, China

Abstract. Machine learning is widely used in malware detection systems as a core component. However, machine learning algorithm is based on the assumption that the underlying malware concept is stable for training and testing. The assumption is vulnerable to well-crafted concept drift attacks, such as mimicry attacks, gradient descent attacks, poisoning attacks and so on. This paper proposes an ensemble learning system which combines vertical and horizontal correlation learning models. The significant diversity among vertical and horizontal correlation models increases the difficulty of concept drift attacks. And average p-value assessment is applied to fortify the system to be sensitive to hidden concept drift. The experiment results show that the hybrid system could actively recognize the concept drift among different Miuref variants.

Keywords: Malware detection · Machine learning · Concept drift
Vertical correlation · Horizontal correlation

1 Introduction

AV-Test [1] reports that over 390,000 new malicious programs are detected every day. The enormous volume of new malware variants renders manual malware analysis inefficient, time-consuming. Machine learning (ML) is widely deployed in malware detection system as a core component [2]. However, with financial motivation, attackers keep evolving their evasion techniques to bypass or poison ML detection models. Nowadays, over 70% of the advanced malware uses one or more evasion techniques to avoid detection [3].

The essential assumption of ML is that the underlying malicious data distribution is stable for training and testing datasets. The assumption is right in speech recognition, computer vision, industrial control and automation etc. However, such assumption does not stand for malware detection because the

© Springer International Publishing AG 2017
J. K. Liu and P. Samarati (Eds.): ISPEC 2017, LNCS 10701, pp. 747–758, 2017.
https://doi.org/10.1007/978-3-319-72359-4_46

malware concept is not stable but changes with time. The well-crafted malware concept drift attacker becomes more and more popular, such as new communication channel [4–7], mimicry attack [8,9], gradient descent attack [8,9], poison attack [10], and so on.

To build secure and sustainable detection system against concept drift attacks is very important. In this paper, we introduce statistical p-value to combine diverse vertical and horizontal correlation learning models. This novel system is sensitive to hidden concept drift attacks.

Vertical correlation model focuses on the life cycle of a single malware sample, such as BotHunter [11]; while horizontal correlation learning approach builds detection model based on the behavior similarity among a large number of malware variants, such as BotFinder [12]. There is a significant diversity between vertical and horizontal correlation learning models. Vertical correlation focuses on a set of behaviors of just one variant, while horizontal correlation focuses on one behavior of a set of variants. By statistical learning the prediction results given by the two diverse models, we could obtain more insights into the hidden malware concept drift. In a nutshell, this paper makes the following contributions:

- We propose a hybrid malware detection system that based on statistical p-values, which combines two diverse ML models: vertical life-cycle model and horizontal traffic similarity model.
- The p-value is more fine-grained than fixed threshold, which could identify gradual moderate concept drift earlier than threshold based detection system.
- Single learning model is vulnerable to sudden drift, because single model only observes a particular perspective of malware characteristic. Our system contains two diverse detection model which could help each other to mitigate sudden drift.

The remainder of this paper is outlined as follows. In Sect. 2, we present the related works. Section 3 presents the architecture of our hybrid malware detection system, and describes each components. Section 4 presents our experiments performed to assess the recognition of underlying concept drift. In Sect. 5, we discuss the limitations and future work, and in Sect. 6 we summarize our results.

2   Related Works

Arce [13] pointed out that machine learning itself could be the weakest link in the security chain. By exploiting the knowledge of the machine learning (ML) algorithm, many well-crafted evasion approaches have been proposed to evade or mislead ML models [14].

Botnet attackers have begun to exploit many stealthy C&C channels, such as social network [7], email protocol [15], SMS [4] and bluetooth [5]. Kartaltepe et al. [16] proposed social network based botnet to abuse trusted popular websites, such as twitter.com, as C&C server. Singh et al. [15] evaluate the viability of using harmless-looking emails to delivery botnet C&C message. Social network traffic and email traffic are beyond the data collection scope of machine learning based methods, that lack of clear mitigation strategies. What makes new protocols interesting is the introduced trusted and popular websites or email servers. First, trusted websites or email servers have very good reputation and usually are listed on the white list that all traffic to such website or server will not be monitored by botnet detection methods. Second, the trusted websites or email services are very popular and have very heavy usage volume that the light-weight occasional C&C traffic is unlikely to be noticed.

However, the new botnets use the centralized architecture that all bots communicate with C&C server directly. The central C&C server is a potential single point of failure that if the C&C server is exposed to the defender, the botnet is easy to be dismantled. Mimicry attack refers to the techniques that mimic benign behaviors to reduce the differentiation between the malicious events and benign events. Wagner and Soto [17] demonstrated the mimicry attack against a host-based IDS that mimicked the legitimate sequence of system calls. Srndic and Laskov [18] presented a mimicry attack against PDFRate [19], a system to detect malicious pdf files based on the random forest classifier.

The gradient descent is an optimization process to iteratively minimize the distance between malicious points and benign points. Šrndic and Laskov [8] applied a gradient descent-kernel density estimation attack against the PDFRate system that uses SVM and random forest classifier. Biggio et al. [9] demonstrated a gradient descent component against the SVM classifier and a neural network.

Poisoning attacks work by introducing carefully crafted noise into the training data. Biggio et al. [10] proposed poisoning attacks to merge the benign and malicious clusters that make learning model unusable.

Therefore, malware are not stable but change with time. For machine learning based malware detectors, they are designed under the assumption that the training and testing data follow the same distribution. The assumption is vulnerable to concept drift attacks that well-crafted underlying data distribution is changing with time. One of the concept drift mitigation approach is to recognize and react to concept changes. Biggio et al. [10] proposed an adversary-aware approach to proactively anticipates the attackers. Deo et al. [20] presented a probabilistic predictor to assess the underlying classifier and retraining model when it recognized concept drift. Transcend [21] is a framework to identify model aging in vivo during deployment, before the performance starts to degrade. In this paper we introduce statistical p-values to combine vertical and horizontal correlation models to mitigate model aging.

3   Ensemble Malware Detection System

Driven by financial motivation, malware authors keep evolving malware perpetually using evasion techniques to avoid detection, especially to bypass or mislead widely deployed learning-based models. Many learning-based detection models calculate a score to a new approaching sample describing the relationship between the known malware samples and the new one. Then detectors compare the score with a fixed threshold to make a decision if it is malicious. The threshold usually fits the old training dataset very well, even overfits. However, the performance degenerates to the new ever-changing malicious dataset with time. The matching scores of different ML models are not comparable directly, so it is difficult to work together with each other. In this paper, we propose a hybrid malware detection system based on statistical p-values to combine vertical life-cycle algorithm and horizontal traffic similarity algorithm as the underlying scoring classifiers. Our system is robust to malware gradual and sudden concept drift attacks.

Figure 1 depicts the framework which includes five components: non-conformity measure (NCM), conformal learning, concept drift recognition. Our system is an open system that any machine learning model based on numerical matching scores and fixed threshold could be integrated as a NCM. The diverse NCMs could describe the malware concepts from different perspectives. In this paper, we select vertical correlation based classifier BotHunter and horizontal correlation based classifier BotFinder as the underlying NCMs. The conformal learning component uses p-values to carry out the further statistical analysis based on NCM scores. The p-value is more fine-grained than threshold that can used to observe the gradual decay of detection models. P-value is comparable between different models, while the NCM matching scores are not comparable among different models. The concept drift recognition component uses the average p-value (APV) algorithm to recognize the concept drift of malware data distribution between two different time windows.

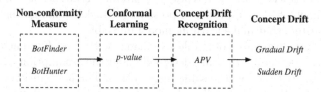

Fig. 1. The framework of hybrid detection system

3.1   Non-conformity Measure

Many machine learning algorithms are in fact scoring classifiers: when trained on a set of observations and fed with a test object x, they could calculate a prediction score $s(x)$ called scoring function. Any scoring classifiers using a fixed and empirical threshold can be introduced into our system as a underlying NCM. Each NCM uses different machine learning algorithm, such as classification, clustering, to model the malware data distribution from different perspectives. Currently, we select BotHunter and BotFinder as the NCMs. BotHunter models the malware life cycle from the vertical perspective, while BotFinder selects time related features and traffic volume features to build detection model from the horizontal perspective. The diversity of selected NCM increases the complexity of the successful sudden concept drift attack, since attackers need to obtain knowledge of more models to construct concept drift attacks than the traditional single model detection systems.

The input of the NCM is a known sample set and an unknown sample, and the output is a score that describes the similarity or dissimilarity of the unknown sample to the known sample set. This paper hybrids two different machine learning models: BotHunter and BotFinder.

BotHunter is a multi-dialog-based vertical correlation algorithm. First, BotHunter establish botnet life cycle model according to the behavior sequence pattern of botnets; Then it maps a set of host dialogues to a pre-learned life-cycle model and calculate a score to describe how close between the dialog and the model. When the dialog correlation algorithm shows that a host dialog pattern maps sufficiently close to the life-cycle model based on a threshold, the host is declared infected.

BotFinder is a detection method that does not require deep packet inspection. First, BotFinder groups netflows which share the same source IP, destination IP, destination port number, and communication protocol into trace; Then, it extracts traffic volume features, such as the average number of sent bytes, the average number of received bytes, and time related features, such as the average time interval, the average duration, and frequency calculated by Fast Fourier Transformation (FFT) algorithm. BotFinder uses the CLUES algorithm to cluster the similar traces of a botnet family, and builds detection model for each class of this family. This method can effectively identify the botnet network traffic similarity, and give a prediction based on the optimal threshold.

3.2 Conformal Learning

Once NCMs are selected, conformal learning component computes a p-value p_{z^*}, which in essence for a new object z^*, represents the percentage of objects in $\{x \in C, \forall C \in D\}$, (i.e., the whole dataset) that are equally or more estranged to C as p_{z^*}, and we will get a number between 0 and 1. The algorithm is shown in Algorithm 1.

Algorithm 1. P-value calculation used in Conformal Predictor

Require: Dataset $D = \{z_1, , z_n\}$, sequence of objects $C \subset D$, non-conformity measure A, and new object z^*
Ensure: p-value p_{z^*}
1: Set provisionally $C = C \cup \{z^*\}$
2: **for** $i \leftarrow 1$ **to** n **do**
3:     $\alpha \leftarrow A(C \setminus z_i, z_i)$
4: **end for**
5: $p_{z^*} = \frac{|\{j : \alpha_j \geq \alpha_{z^*}\}|}{n}$

P-value measures the fraction of objects within D, that are at least as different from a class C as the new object z^*. For instance, if C represents the set of malicious activities, a high p-value p_{z^*} means that there are a significant part of the objects in this set is more different than z^* with C, on the other words,

z^* is more similar to these malicious activities than the objects that already marked malicious. Therefore, the prediction result based on a high p-value shows a high credibility. P-values are directly involved in our discussion of concept drift.

The p-values are comparable for different learning models, while the NCM scores are not comparable among different models. The p-value is more fine-grained than threshold that is more sensitive to concept drift attacks. The concept drift recognition component uses the average p-value algorithm to recognize hidden concept drift.

3.3   Concept Drift Recognition

We use the average p-value (APV) algorithm based on time windows to recognize concept drift attacks. We group the malware samples into different time windows according to their time stamps in the timeline. We calculate p-values for all malware samples in a time window, and compute the APV for each time window. Note that, the number of APVs for each time window depends on the number of selected NCMs. In this paper, each time window has two APVs for the vertical and horizontal NCMs respectively.

The p-values are comparable, and the APV scores are also comparable among different time windows and even in the same window with different underlying NCMs. The change of APV value between different time window reflects the change of underlying malware data distribution with time that can identify gradual moderate drift. In the same time window, the difference between APVs calculated from different NCMs reflect the affection of concept drift to different learning models which could detect the sudden drift.

If the APV of a certain detection model decreases with time, it shows that the current concept of the malware is gradually different from the old concept learnt from previous known malware data, and indicates that the detection model is suffering from concept drift attack. But the decay of performance may not be observed immediately when concept drift is found, if it is a gradual moderate drift. Only when the variation of the underlying data distribution exceeds the boundary of the threshold, the detection model starts make poor decisions. If the APV score does not decrease in the new time window, it means in the current time window, the distribution of malware data does not drift from this observing perspective.

4   Experiment

In this paper, we use the public CTU dataset for our experiment that is provided by Malware Capture Facility project[1]. They capture long-live real botnet traffic and generate labeled netflow files that is publish for malware research.

To recognize the sudden radical concept drift between different botnet families is not the focus of this paper. We plan to recognize the hidden and gradual

---

[1] Garcia, Sebastian. Malware Capture Facility Project. Retrieved from https://stratosphereips.org.

concept drift between different variants in the same family that is not noticed by traditional models using fixed and empirical threshold. So we select the Miuref family for our experiment from CTU dataset, because Miuref has 4 variants and 8 different traffic records which is more than other families in the public CTU dataset. Miuref redirects web browser to carry out click fraud or download other malware. According to the time order of traffic records, we use $V1$, $V2$, $V3$ and $V4$ to denote the 4 variants of Miuref, which are listed in the Table 1.

Table 1. The network traffic of 4 variants in Miuref family

CTU file name	Variant	Time window
127-1	2015.06.01–2015.06.07	$V1$
127-2	2015.06.09–2015.07.08	$V1$
128-1	2015.06.01–2015.06.07	$V2$
128-2	2015.06.09–2015.07.19	$V2$
169-1	2016.08.03–2016.08.04	$V3$
169-2	2016.08.04–2016.08.04	$V3$
169-3	2016.08.03–2016.08.11	$V3$
173-1	2016.08.04–2016.08.11	$V4$

According to the time stamps of each time window, we order the variants for the experiments of concept drifting recognize and feature assessment and active reweighting. First, we split the 4 variants into 2 time windows that $V1$ and $V2$ are grouped into the first time window whose malware data is collected in 2015, and $V3$ and $V4$ are grouped into the second time window whose malware data is captured in 2016.

To assess the concept drift between different time windows and from different perspectives, we use dimension reduction algorithm tSNE [22] and statistical p-values to see the underlying data distribution.

The tSNE is a kind of reduced dimension visualization algorithm, which maps the multi-dimensional features to two or three dimensions. The goal of tSNE is to make the distance similar to the elements on the low dimension remain close to each other.

Figure 2 shows the underlying data distribution and p-value significant levels of Miuref family in two different time windows for vertical correlation model. The Fig. 2a shows the data distribution of $V1$ and $V2$ in tSNE space and the p-values for each point. The labelled colors are for the various p-values that the dark red means the point has high p-values, while the light red means the point is far from the Miuref $V1$ and $V2$ variants. The Fig. 2b shows the data distribution and p-value significant levels of all Miuref variants in the tSNE space. We can see that from the vertical perspective, the Miuref family has very slight concept drift between the two time windows in different years, because the malware data distribution and p-value significant level are almost stable without much change. In addition, the characteristics of Miuref becomes more remarkable and centralized after absorbing the malware data of $V3$ and $V4$ variants captured in 2016, because in the middle of Fig. 2a there are some points with week p-value significant level change to be almost zero in the Fig. 2b.

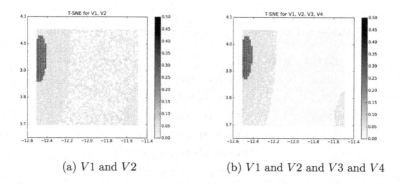

(a) $V1$ and $V2$ (b) $V1$ and $V2$ and $V3$ and $V4$

Fig. 2. The data distribution and p-value significant level for vertical correlation model in the tSNE space.

Figure 4a shows the changes of APVs of 4 Miuref variants for vertical correlation model. All 4 APVs are at high APV level, and the APV of $V4$ is even higher than 0.8 that is consistent with the Miuref data distribution and p-value significant levels in tSNE space. So from the vertical observing perspective, the Miuref family data distribution has not much concept drift, and vertical correlation model is still effective to detect Miuref variants.

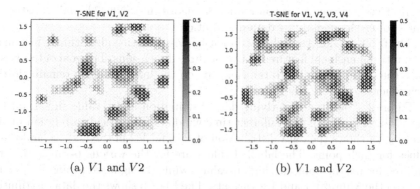

(a) $V1$ and $V2$ (b) $V1$ and $V2$

Fig. 3. The data distribution and p-value significant level for horizontal correlation model in the tSNE space.

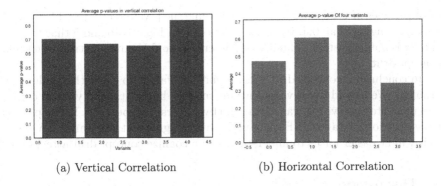

(a) Vertical Correlation   (b) Horizontal Correlation

Fig. 4. The changes of APVs of 4 variants.

Figure 3 shows the underlying data distribution and p-value significant levels of Miuref family in two different time windows for horizontal correlation model. The Fig. 3a shows the data distribution of $V1$ and $V2$ in tSNE space and the p-values for each point for horizontal model. The Fig. 3b shows the data distribution and p-value significant levels of 4 Miuref variants in the tSNE space for horizontal model. We can see that from the horizontal perspective, the Miuref family has significant concept drift between the two time windows in different years, because between the two subfigures, the malware data distribution and p-value significant level are obviously changed, especially at the upper left corner in the figure.

Figure 4b shows the changes of APVs of 4 Miuref variants for horizontal correlation model. We can see that the APV drops dramatically on $V4$ from 0.7 to 0.4, which means that the underlying $V4$ data distribution changed significantly observed from horizontal correlation perspective. Let us understand the concept drift from the cumulative distribution of p-values. As shown in Fig. 5,

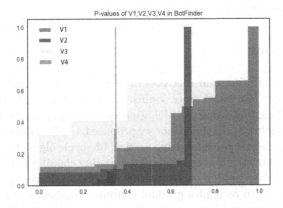

Fig. 5. The cumulative distribution of p-values of 4 variants for horizontal correlation model

most p-values of $V4$ data is less than 0.4, while the p-values of $V1$ and $V2$ and $V3$ are much higher than 0.4. It can be inferred from Figs. 3, 4b and 5 that the variant $V4$ is not consistent of family characteristics and $V4$ data distribution occurs concept drift.

In conclusion, concept drift is the significant factor to cause the model aging problem. We hybrid two diverse learning models: horizontal and vertical correlation model to observe malware data from two diverse perspectives. We map underlying malicious data to tSNE space with p-value significant levels and APV scores, so it will be easier for us to understand and recognize concept drift attacks.

5   Discussion

In the real world, malware concepts are not stable but change with time rapidly, so that ML models should quickly recognize and adapt to the hidden changes in the underlying malware data distribution. There are two types of concept drift: sudden drift and gradual moderate drift. Sudden drift means radical changes in the target concept. Single learning model is vulnerable to sudden drift, because single model only observes a particular perspective of malware data distribution.

To handle sudden drift, ensemble learning is needed that hybrid a set of diverse concept descriptions. In this paper, we maintains two much diverse learning models that observe the malware data distribution from both of vertical life-cycle perspective and horizontal traffic similarity perspective simultaneously. The hybrid model is robust to single concept drift attacks. In the future, we are going to introduce more learning models into our system based on statistical p-value against more and more sophisticated concept drift attacks.

The gradual moderate drift induce less radical changes than sudden drift, but the change is more hidden and difficult to be detected. To recognize and react gradual moderate drift, we introduce statistical p-values to enhance fixed threshold. The p-value gives us the insights of the underlying malware data distribution that is sensitive to gradual moderate drift attacks.

6   Conclusions

For the survival and financial motivation, malware keeps evolving itself perpetually to introduce more and more sophisticated evasion techniques. To build a sustainable and secure learning model, we need to quickly detect and understand the hidden concept drift. In this paper we proposed a hybrid botnet detection system based on statistical p-values using vertical life-cycle algorithm and horizontal traffic similarity algorithm as the underlying scoring classifiers. This novel system is robust to malware sudden concept drift attacks. And average p-value assessment is introduced to recognize gradual concept drift before cumulative radical drift. The experiment results show that this system could actively get insights of Miuref family hidden concept drift.

Acknowledgements. This material is based upon the work supported by the Tianjin Research Program of Application Foundation and Advanced Technology under the Grant No. 15JCQNJC41500, and by the Open Project Foundation of Information Security Evaluation Center of Civil Aviation, Civil Aviation University of China under the Grant No. CAAC-ISECCA-201701.

References

1. AV-Test: Malware statistics, September 2017. https://www.av-test.org/en/statistics/malware/
2. Demontis, A., Melis, M., Biggio, B., Maiorca, D., Arp, D., Rieck, K., Corona, I., Giacinto, G., Roli, F.: Yes, machine learning can be more secure! A case study on android malware detection. IEEE Trans. Dependable Sec. Comput. **PP**(99), 1 (2017). https://doi.org/10.1109/TDSC.2017.2700270
3. Lastline, Protect your network from advanced malware that fireeye doesn't detect (2017). https://go.lastline.com/protect-your-network-from-evasive-malware-webinar.html
4. Zeng, Y., Shin, K.G., Hu, X.: Design of SMS commanded-and-controlled and P2P-structured mobile botnets. In: Proceedings of the Fifth ACM Conference on Security and Privacy in Wireless and Mobile Networks (WISEC 2012), New York, NY, USA, pp. 137–148. ACM (2012)
5. Singh, K., Sangal, S., Jain, N., Traynor, P., Lee, W.: Evaluating bluetooth as a medium for botnet command and control. In: Kreibich, C., Jahnke, M. (eds.) DIMVA 2010. LNCS, vol. 6201, pp. 61–80. Springer, Heidelberg (2010). https://doi.org/10.1007/978-3-642-14215-4_4
6. Krombholz, K., Hobel, H., Huber, M., Weippl, E.: Advanced social engineering attacks. J. Inf. Secur. Appl. **22**, 113–122 (2015). Special Issue on Security of Information and Networks
7. Yin, T., Zhang, Y., Li, S.: DR-SNBot: a social network-based botnet with strong destroy-resistance. In: IEEE International Conference on Networking, Architecture, and Storage, pp. 191–199 (2014)
8. Šrndic, N., Laskov, P.: Practical evasion of a learning-based classifier: a case study. In: Proceedings of the 2014 IEEE Symposium on Security and Privacy (SP 2014), Washington, DC, USA, pp. 197–211. IEEE Computer Society (2014)
9. Biggio, B., Pillai, I., Rota Bulò, S., Ariu, D., Pelillo, M., Roli, F.: Is data clustering in adversarial settings secure? In: Proceedings of the 2013 ACM Workshop on Artificial Intelligence and Security (AISec 2013), New York, NY, USA, pp. 87–98. ACM (2013)
10. Biggio, B., Rieck, K., Ariu, D., Wressnegger, C., Corona, I., Giacinto, G., Roli, F.: Poisoning behavioral malware clustering. In: Proceedings of the 2014 Workshop on Artificial Intelligent and Security Workshop (AISec 2014), New York, NY, USA, pp. 27–36. ACM (2014)
11. Gu, G., Porras, P., Yegneswaran, V., Fong, M., Lee, W.: Bothunter: detecting malware infection through ids-driven dialog correlation. In: Proceedings of 16th USENIX Security Symposium. USENIX Association Berkeley, CA (2007)
12. Tegeler, F., Fu, X., Vigna, G., Kruegel, C.: Botfinder: finding bots in network traffic without deep packet inspection. In: Proceedings of the 8th International Conference on Emerging Networking Experiments and Technologies (CoNEXT 2012), France, pp. 349–360. ACM, New York, December 2012

13. Arce, I.: The weakest link revisited. IEEE Secur. Priv. **1**, 72–76 (2003)
14. Kantchelian, A., Afroz, S., Huang, L., Islam, A.C., Miller, B., Tschantz, M.C., Greenstadt, R., Joseph, A.D., Tygar, J.D.: Approaches to adversarial drift. In: Proceedings of the 2013 ACM Workshop on Artificial Intelligence and Security (AISec 2013), New York, NY, USA, pp. 99–110. ACM (2013)
15. Singh, K., Srivastava, A., Giffin, J., Lee, W.: Evaluating email feasibility for botnet command and control. In: IEEE International Conference on Dependable Systems and Networks with FTCS and DCC, Anchorage, AK, pp. 376–385. IEEE, June 2008
16. Kartaltepe, E.J., Morales, J.A., Xu, S., Sandhu, R.: Social network-based botnet command-and-control: emerging threats and countermeasures. In: Zhou, J., Yung, M. (eds.) ACNS 2010. LNCS, vol. 6123, pp. 511–528. Springer, Heidelberg (2010). https://doi.org/10.1007/978-3-642-13708-2_30
17. Wagner, D., Soto, P.: Mimicry attacks on host-based intrusion detection systems. In: Proceedings of the 9th ACM Conference on Computer and Communications Security (CCS 2002), New York, NY, USA, pp. 255–264. ACM (2002)
18. Srndic, N., Laskov, P.: Practical evasion of a learning-based classier: a case study. In: Proceedings of the 35th IEEE Symposium on Security and Privacy (S&P), San Jose, CA, May 2014
19. Smutz, C., Stavrou, A.: Malicious PDF detection using metadata and structural features. In: Proceedings of the 28th Annual Computer Security Applications Conference (ACSAC 2012), New York, NY, USA, pp. 239–248. ACM (2012)
20. Deo, A., Dash, S.K., Suarez-Tangil, G., Vovk, V., Cavallaro, L.: Prescience: probabilistic guidance on the retraining conundrum for malware detection. In: Proceedings of the 2016 ACM Workshop on Artificial Intelligence and Security (AISec 2016), New York, NY, USA, pp. 71–82. ACM (2016)
21. Jordaney, R., Sharad, K., Dash, S.K., Wang, Z., Papini, D., Nouretdinov, I., Cavallaro, L.: Transcend: detecting concept drift in malware classification models. In: Proceedings of the 26th USENIX Security Symposium (USENIX Security 2017) (2017)
22. van der Maaten, L., Hinton, G.: Visualizing data using t-SNE. J. Mach. Learn. Res. **9**, 2579–2605 (2008)

Using the B Method to Formalize Access Control Mechanism with TrustZone Hardware Isolation (Short Paper)

Lu Ren, Rui Chang[✉], Qing Yin, and Wei Wang

State Key Laboratory of Mathematical Engineering and Advanced Computing,
Zhengzhou, China
crixl021@163.com

Abstract. Successfully employed in the industry, hardware isolation environment enhances the access control of traditional operating systems and requires more rigorous analysis. This paper first applies the B method to the access control mechanism formalization and proposes an extensible formal model, which not only specifies the access control mechanism with process state transition in Linux, but also introduces the hardware isolation description. Consistent with program implementations, the B specifications can be animated and verified. The proposed B model constructs a mathematical framework for the security analysis, providing a theoretical support for mechanism enhancements. All the model components are type checked by Atelier B, with 547 proof obligations automatically generated. The current rate of model proof is 79%. The experimental results by ProB show that there is no invariant violation or deadlock. In conclusion, this paper presents a feasible solution for access control mechanism formalization and verification in the embedded system design. The access control model can be further extended and refined, with its specifications transformed into executable codes after proved.

Keywords: Access control · B method · Formal model

1 Introduction

The rapid development of new technology makes embedded equipment increasingly important in human life, whereas it also complexes the operating system ecology. Once the access control module is compromised, a system will be exposed to the permission and privacy data disclosure risk. There are two main solutions for access control vulnerabilities: optimization of access control strategy and combination with isolated execution environment. Most optimizations fully depend on the software, thus there are still large software attack surfaces. The combination with hardware isolation environment such as TrustZone [1], however, lacks a universal architecture and a formal model to theoretically support applications. According to previous studies [2, 3], it will be a challenging work to formalize the system with hardware isolation and keep the formal model amended with the system. A minimal change will largely increase the burden of proof and testing. Compared with other formal models, the B model ensures

© Springer International Publishing AG 2017
J. K. Liu and P. Samarati (Eds.): ISPEC 2017, LNCS 10701, pp. 759–769, 2017.
https://doi.org/10.1007/978-3-319-72359-4_47

the consistency between abstract model and concrete implementation. The specifications can be transformed into executable codes after proved.

In this paper, we apply the B method to formalize access control mechanisms of Linux and ARM TrustZone, conducive to security analysis and mechanism enhancement. Model components are abstracted from actual entities. The proposed B model specifies not only the access to a specific resource, but also context switch operations. Our model combines traditional access control strategies with isolation condition, establishing an extensible framework. The prover and checker results show that the model is feasible for access control mechanism formalization and verification.

This paper is organized as follows. We introduce the background in Sect. 2. Section 3 gives three basic abstract machines. The systematic access control model is presented in Sect. 4. Section 5 shows the model evaluation results and Sect. 6 summarizes the related work, followed by the conclusion in Sect. 7.

2 Background

2.1 Process Management in Linux

Operating systems generally utilize processes to manage the execution of applications. The process management of Linux includes process creation, state transition, etc. Distinct states and their transitions are useful abstractions for processes.

During the process lifecycle, there are three primary execution states closely related to a certain access of a process, including running, ready and blocked. When allocated to all necessary resources except CPU, the process is ready and awaiting execution. Once gains CPU, it moves into running state and performs the access operation. If a running process cannot be executed due to the temporary lack of required resources, it will be blocked until resources are available. Considering the process interruption and priority, realistic Linux system recognizes another three process states [4]. Traditional Linux uses Discretionary Access Control (DAC), and SELinux integrates Mandatory Access Control (MAC) strategies to protect applications.

2.2 TrustZone Isolation Environment

ARM Trustzone splits all the hardware and software into two distinct areas (secure world and normal world), granting a rigorous isolation framework for secure control solutions. The access in the system is controlled based on the isolation domain, e.g., secure resources cannot be accessed by normal world components [5]. Sensitive resources should be placed in the secure world and protected by the robust processor core. There are two main ARM TrustZone technologies applied to Cortex-A and Cortex-M processors, offering reliable protection at all critical points[1].

TrustZone introduces a secure monitor mode to control the context switch between two isolation worlds, which is triggered by the Secure Monitor Call (SMC) instruction or other exceptions (such as IRQ, FIQ and external Data Abort). Typically, IRQ is used

---

[1] This paper refers to the TrustZone technology for Cortex-A processors.

as a normal world interrupt source, FIQ as the secure interrupt. The way to enter monitor mode and context switch is crucial for access control security [5].

2.3 B Method

B method is a state-based formal method based on the set theory and first order logic. B defines many structures in model construction, such as MACHINE, REFINEMENT and IMPLEMENTATION [6]. It constructs the state characteristics and behavioral characteristics of the target system, covering the entire system development cycle.

Writing and proving formal specifications are two vital activities in B development. The former is to establish abstract machines, which contain all the defined requirements and will be finally transformed into a fault-free concrete model. The specification is composed of the data, relative invariants and operations. During the construction, the latter activity would perform lots of type checks and theorem demonstrations to prove the correctness of formulations and the conservation of security invariants. The model can be coded into C or Ada language after proved [7].

3   Basic Abstract Machine with the B Language

Three elementary entities are formalized as base abstract machines, which encapsulate primary entities and provide fundamental operations.

3.1   Process Abstract Machine

In terms of access control, each process object owns its identifier, execution state and access status. In terms of hardware isolation, each process has its security domain and enabling tag, as shown in Table 1[2]. The unique identifier is represented by a distinct element of set. Operations comprise creating a process, changing states and so on.

Table 1. Process abstract machine.

MACHINE	$Proc$
SETS	$PROC$, $AC\_STATE = \{pre,\ wait,\ acing,\ post\}$, $EXE\_STATE = \{ready,\ run,\ blocked,\ final\}$
VARIABLES	$proc$, p_ac_state, p_exe_state, p_dom, p_enable
INVARIANT	$proc \subseteq PROC \wedge p\_dom \in proc \rightarrow 0..1 \wedge p\_enable \in proc \rightarrow 0..1 \wedge$ $p\_ac\_state \in proc \rightarrow AC\_STATE \wedge p\_exe\_state \in proc \rightarrow EXE\_STATE$
OPERATIONS	create_proc, delete_proc, change_state, set_allp_enable

The set $PROC$ contains all of processes. EXE_STATE defines four execution states: *ready*, *run*, *blocked* and *final*. There are four access statuses in AC_STATE, i.e., pre-access (*pre*), waiting for access (*wait*), being in access (*acing*) and post-access (*post*).

---

[2] The abstract machine name, constants and variables are displayed in italics in this paper.

The security domain of every process is represented by 0 or 1, where 0 means secure zone and 1 means non-secure one. Similarly, the enabling tag inflects system mode.

3.2   Resource Abstract Machine

In resource abstract machine, an object consists of the unique identifier, security domain, available state and buffer capacity. Operations include adding an item, changing buffer capacity and so on.

As shown in Table 2, the set *RESS* contains all resources, each of them in free or full state. A relation variable *res_buf* is set to record buffer capability. The *res_zone* is to indicate resource location in the isolated domain, either 0 (secure world) or 1 (normal world). A resource can be accessed by a process only if their security domains match.

Table 2. Resource abstract machine.

MACHINE	*Res*
SETS	*RESS, STATUS = {free, full}*
VARIABLES	*res, res_status, res_buf, origin, res_zone*
INVARIANT	$res \subseteq RESS \wedge res\_status \in res \rightarrow STATUS \wedge res\_zone \in res \rightarrow 0..1 \wedge$
	$res\_buf \in res \rightarrow INT \wedge origin \in res \rightarrow N_1 \ldots$
OPERATIONS	add_res, sub_bf, delete_res, change_status

3.3   Control Policy Abstract Machine

DAC and MAC strategies in Linux depend on the policy inspection. The policy model sees the process and resource abstract machine to read variables, as shown in Table 3.

Table 3. Access control policy abstract machine.

MACHINE	*Policy*
SEES	*Proc, Res*
SETS	*OP = {read, write, exc}*
VARIABLES	*policy*
INVARIANT	$policy \subseteq PROC * RESS * OP$
OPERATIONS	create_policy, delete_policy

The *OP* set defines three simple access operations: read, write and execute. Every control policy limits a process to perform one legal operation on a resource.

4   Access Control Model Based on TrustZone Isolation

4.1   System Analysis

Our formal model aims at describing the formal specification of process access control with hardware isolation environment. Without considering scheduling rules and the parent-child relationship between processes, we set up process queues to record every execution state. Some state transitions are simplified in the model, e.g., a process will be blocked directly from ready state when its requested resource is unavailable. The continuous access is a complete cycle of a specified one-time access.

In view of hardware isolation environment, a symbolic domain attribute and some special exceptions should be specified in the process model. The model mainly describes the behavior of a process that encounters a certain interrupt.

4.2   Structure and Elements

Figure 1 displays the model structure. There are major attribute variables in each entity abstract machine.

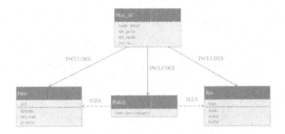

Fig. 1.   Structure of the process access control model.

Table 4.   Variables in *Proc_AC* model.

Entity code	Description
proc/res/policy	Existing process/resource/access control policy set in the system
ready_procs	A set of processes in *ready* state
run_procs	A set of running processes (during a certain interval of time)
block_set	A set of processes in *blocked* state
nw_procs/sw_procs	Existing normal/secure process set, defined as the subset of *proc*
sys_mode	Current system mode (i.e., normal, secure or monitor)
pro_ac	A real-time access relation between a process and a resource

The *Proc_AC* model includes three basic abstract machines, using their variables and encapsulated operations. It also encloses numerous variables relevant to the system management, shown in Table 4. All model variables must satisfy security invariants. For example, the established access relation must be clearly stated in the policy file. i.e., $pro\_ac \subseteq proc \times res \land pro\_ac \subseteq dom\,(policy)$.

4.3 Access Control Operations

The process state transition in *Proc_AC* merely associates with the access to certain resources. Access-related operations comprise Pre_Access, Wait_Access, Re_Access, Succ_Access, Fail_Access and End_Access, each of them concerning the access or execution state of a process. Figure 2 draws the possible state transitions scenarios.

Set the initial execution and access state of a process as *ready* and *pre*. The migrations in Fig. 2 are described as follows:

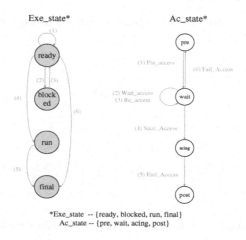

*Exe_state -- {ready, blocked, run, final}
Ac_state -- {pre, wait, acing, post}

Fig. 2. State transition of a process in *Proc_AC* model.

- Case 1. A process's access status becomes *wait* with its execution state unchanged, when it requests to access resources and waits for allocations.
- Case 2. Current access condition meets control policy, but the requested resource is unavailable. Then the process is blocked, and its access status stays the same.
- Case 3. The requested resource by a blocked process becomes available, then the process resumes executing and requests to access again, turning to case 1.
- Case 4. After the policy check, a process gains authorized access to the available resource. The process starts running, and its access status moves into *acing*.
- Case 5. A process completes its access to a certain resource. Its execution state goes into *final*, and access status becomes *post*.
- Case 6. Once access privilege checks fail, the process cannot access to target resources. Its execution state jumps to *final*, with the access status returning to *pre*.

4.4 Context Switch Specifications

The access control with TrustZone mostly relies on the secure context switch between two isolated worlds. Some relevant operations are clarified in Table 5.

Table 5. Some operations in *Proc_AC* model.

Operation code	Description
Occur_ir	An interrupt occurs during the process execution
Nw_recv_FIQ	An FIQ exception is received in the normal world
Delv_sw_FIQ	The FIQ exception is delivered to the secure world
Return_FIQ_nw	Normal world context restored, the original program is continued
Monitor_switch	In monitor mode, the context is switched
Intr_SMC	SMC instruction executed, the system comes into monitor mode

The synchronization of operations can be described according to TrustZone white paper [5]. For instance, the core traps to monitor mode when an FIQ exception occurs in normal world. Then the monitor saves normal world context and restores secure world environment. After exception is handled, secure world issues an SMC to enter monitor mode and the context is switched again, formalized as: Nw_recv_FIQ → Monitor_switch → Delv_sw_FIQ → Intr_SMC → Monitor_switch → Return_FIQ_nw. The synchronizations are dominated by state migrations of processes.

5 Model Evaluation

5.1 Property Analysis

The B model translates all security properties of access control mechanism into either invariants or operation conditions. The mechanism specification contains two strategies: security domain based and policy based access control. For a definite access, system model first matches the security domain of process and resource, and then checks the policy file to make a decision. To make sure that private resources can always be protected from non-secure processes and unauthorized accesses, there is a pre-condition in each access-related operation, i.e., $p\_dom(proc) \leq res\_zone(res)$.

Accordingly, an invariant statement should be defined to guarantee that the security level of process is always higher than that of resource in the existing access table, i.e., $pro\_ac\,[dom(pro\_ac) \cap p\_dom^{-1}[\{1\}]] \subseteq res\_zone^{-1}[\{1\}]$.

5.2 Model Verification

Our model development is based on Atelier B4.3, which supports the syntax and type check, PO (proof obligations) generation, automatic and interactive prover [8]. All model components are type checked, with 547 POs generated automatically. Table 6 summarizes the size of abstract machines, the number of POs and the rate of proofs.

Typically, the high proof rate contributes to model implementation. The results show that 79% lemmas (434 out of 547) are proved (which is a usual proof rate in the B development), 9 POs of them demonstrated interactively. In terms of the first B method based process model with hardware isolation, the verification results are promising. Actually, Atelier B automatic prover has a limited power of resolution, and it is highly

Table 6. The model proving result of process model.

Machine	Code size	POs	Proved	Unproved	Proof rate
Proc	88	21	21	0	100%
Res	74	46	39	7	85%
Policy	36	7	7	0	100%
Proc_AC	335	473	367	106	78%

improved with the interactive prover which can simplify the proof task with little cost. We are now working on demonstrating remaining POs.

Moreover, we utilize ProB to automatically animate all specifications, especially the functional operations of which the generated POs have not proven yet. ProB can also find the deadlock and violation in security invariants and operations [9]. If there is any violation in the pre-condition of operation, the corresponding unproven PO must not be proved. Load all the four abstract machines into ProB and perform the model check. Table 7 displays the number of checked states and simulated transitions in the process model.

Table 7. The model checking result of process model.

Machine	Checked states	Total distant states	Total transitions
Proc	6562	6562	170409
Res	362	362	1595
Policy	115	115	3419
Proc_AC	38516	38516	532421

Due to the uncertainty of abstract sets (i.e., *PROC*, *RESS*), the state spaces of our model are infinite and the explored nodes are large-scaled. As shown in Table 7, the state space size of *Proc* is greatly larger than *Res*, because there are more abstract sets and more possible transitions in *Proc*. The results show that there is neither invariant violation nor deadlocking node in the model. The animation results cover all the operations and guarantee that the animated system always satisfies defined properties. Particularly, we animate context switch specifications in various cases. Take the context switch from normal world to secure word for example, Fig. 3 displays the ProB animator interface. Figure 4 is the current state graph.

Fig. 3. The model animator interface.

Fig. 4. The current state of *TZ_AC* model animation (Color figure online)

The model checker and animator allow us to visually analyze the specifications. It can be regarded as a debug process for model development. As shown in Fig. 3, 19 operations have been executed, including a series of access control and context switch operations. All state properties are shown to be conflict-free during the animation, thus all state nodes in Fig. 4 are shown to be green. In summary, the verification results show that our model is feasible for access control mechanism formalization and conductive to implement a practical module.

6 Related Work

As the theoretical foundation for engineering, formal method has been studied in operating systems. Formal verification of UNIX security kernel was pioneered by Walker et al. [10]. Klein et al. [2] formalized the operating system kernel L4 and first released a verifiable embedded operating system seL4. The B method also has been utilized in the operating system modeling and verification. Hoffmann et al. [3] formalized application programming interfaces of micro-kernel L4 and evaluated the technical feasibility. Chen et al. [11] applied the B method to develop a formal operating system model called fmC/OS, including task management, task synchronization and communication functions, etc. However, these models all target at the traditional operating system without hardware isolation environment. Our model specifically discusses the access control mechanism.

For the embedded system based on the kernel separation, Kawamorita et al. [12] utilized the B method to the formal design of kernel part. Separation of the kernel structure in a single CPU creates a virtual isolation environment, so the operating system needs to provide partition-based access control, similar to the mandatory access control mechanism based on hardware isolation. However, the management module only considers the access control across different partitions, and has limited description on access objects and their relationships. Compared with the module, our formal model not only enforces policy-based mandatory access control on relevant entities, but also describes the general domain-based control specification. Sequence of operations related to context switch on TrustZone isolation environment are specified as well.

7   Conclusion

This paper proposes a formal access control model, which consists of four abstract machines and specifies access control mechanisms in both Linux and TrustZone isolation environment using the B language. The model mainly formalizes the context switch in hardware layer and two kinds of access control schemes, including security domain based and policy-based strategies. Every model specification is abstracted from actual entity and accords with defined security invariants. All the model components are type checked. 547 proof obligations are generated automatically, 434 out of them proved yet. All model specifications are animated and there is no invariant violation or deadlock. The model verification and checker results show that our model is well-defined and suitable for access control mechanism formalization and verification. We are now working on proving remaining proof obligations. Furthermore, the proposed B model supports the extension and consistency evaluation, which will inspire the development of a unified security framework for embedded system.

References

1. Sun, H., Sun, K., Wang, Y., Jing, J., Wang, H.: TrustICE: hardware-assisted isolated computing environments on mobile devices. In: 2015 45th Annual IEEE/IFIP International Conference on Dependable Systems and Networks, pp. 367–378. IEEE Press, New York (2015). https://doi.org/10.1109/DSN.2015.11
2. Klein, G., Elphinstone, K., Heiser, G., Andronick, J., Cock, D., Derrin, P., et al.: seL4: formal verification of an OS kernel. In: ACM SIGOPS 22nd Symposium on Operating Systems Principles, pp. 207–220. ACM, New York (2009). http://dx.doi.org/10.1145/1629575.1629596
3. Hoffmann, S., Haugou, G., Gabriele, S., Burdy, L.: The B-method for the construction of microkernel-based systems. In: Julliand, J., Kouchnarenko, O. (eds.) B 2007. LNCS, vol. 4355, pp. 257–259. Springer, Heidelberg (2006). https://doi.org/10.1007/11955757_23
4. Bovet, D.P., Cesati, M.: Understanding the Linux Kernel. Oreilly Media, Sebastopol (2001)
5. ARM. ARM Security Technology Building a secure system using TrustZone technology (white paper). ARM Limited (2009)
6. Abrial, J.R.: The B-Book: Assigning Programs to Meanings. Cambridge University Press, Cambridge (1996)
7. Presentation of the B method | Méthode B. http://www.methode-b.com/en/b-method/. Accessed 1 July 2017
8. Atelier B. https://www.atelierb.eu/en/. Accessed 1 July 2017
9. The ProB Animator and Modelchecker. https://www3.hhu.de/stups/prob/. Accessed 1 July 2017
10. Walker, B.J., Kemmerer, R.A., Popek, G.J.: Specification and verification of the UCLA Unix security kernel. Commun. ACM **23**(23), 118–131 (1980). https://doi.org/10.1145/358818.358825

11. Chen, D., Sun, Y., Chen, Z.: A formal specification in B of an operating system. Open Cybern. Syst. J. **9**(1), 1125–1129 (2015). https://doi.org/10.2174/1874110X01509011125
12. Kawamorita, K., Kasahara, R., Mochizuki, Y., Noguchi, K.: Application of formal methods for designing a separation kernel for embedded systems. World Acad. Sci. Eng. Technol. **68**, 506–514 (2010)

Matching Function-Call Graph of Binary Codes and Its Applications
(Short Paper)

Yong Tang[1]([✉]), Yi Wang[1], ShuNing Wei[2], Bo Yu[1], and Qiang Yang[1]

[1] School of Computer, National University of Defense Technology, Changsha, China
ytang@nudt.edu.cn
[2] College of Physics and Information Science, Hunan Normal University,
Changsha, China

Abstract. For a binary code, the function-call graph (FCG) reflects its capability, structure and intrinsic relations. In this work, we propose a FCG matching algorithm based on Hungarian algorithm which makes matching between graphs of large scale possible. Also, optimizations are proposed to improve the efficiency and accuracy of FCG matching algorithm. Finally, a series of experiments are conducted to show that FCG matching is an effective method and has huge application potentiality in software and security analysis.

1 Introduction

Graph matching aims at finding a bijective mapping that matches nodes from different graphs. In this paper, we mainly focus on matching function-call graphs of binary codes. Function-call graph (FCG) as a structural representation depicts the invocation of functions in executable files intuitively [1]. Common obfuscation of binary codes such as instruction reordering, equivalent instruction sequence substitution and branch inversion will not cause significant changes to FCG. Such merit makes FCG matching widely used in software and security analysis.

So far, most of fast algorithms [2,3] for graph matching and alignment only focus on the structural feature of graphs. Although some works have taken advantage of the local description [4] or signature [5] of node, they are still limited in the context of pattern recognition. The node in FCG has various features including mnemonic sequence, opcode sequence, function invocation, etc. Taking advantage of these features properly could achieve better FCG matching results.

In this paper, we mainly concentrate on the FCG matching of binary codes and its applications. The main contributions include: (1) We propose a metric to quantify the similarity of nodes in FCG based on instruction sequences and function invocations. (2) We propose a FCG matching algorithm based on Hungarian

Y. Wang and S. Wei—The work was partially supported by the National Natural Science Foundation of China under Grant No. 61472437 and 61402492.

J. K. Liu and P. Samarati (Eds.): ISPEC 2017, LNCS 10701, pp. 770–779, 2017.
https://doi.org/10.1007/978-3-319-72359-4_48

algorithm [6]. (3) Optimizations of FCG matching algorithm including node pairs pruning and forward matching are applied to improve the efficiency and accuracy of FCG matching algorithm. (4) We systematically investigate applications of FCG matching in reverse engineering and software plagiarism detection.

This paper is organized as follow: In Sect. 2, we give an overview of the related work. Section 3 describes the FCG matching algorithm based on Hungarian algorithm. The results of experiments are reported in Sect. 4. Section 5 demonstrates the effects of optimizations mentioned in Sect. 3. Conclusions are discussed in Sect. 6.

2   Related Work

For applications of graph matching in reverse engineering, Sartipi and Kostas (2003) modeled the software architecture recovery problem as the graph matching between query-graph and source-graph [8]. Bernardi et al. (2013) introduced an approach to detect design patterns in object oriented systems by graph matching, while the detection range is limited to the patterns specifications repository [9]. Also, graph matching can be applied to control flow graphs for constructing control flow mapping (Nagarajan et al. 2007) [10].

Identifying similar codes in programs based on finding similar subgraphs in program dependence graph (PDG) is presented by Krinke (2001) [11]. Silvio and Yang (2013) developed a online web service that identifies the similarity between executables based on the control flow graph of each binary [12]. For Android apps, the geometry characteristics of their control flow graphs can be used to detect cross-market app clone on five markets within an hour (Chen et al. 2014) [13].

3   FCG Matching Algorithm

Definition 1. (Function-call graph) a directed graph $G(V, E)$, where node $n \in V$ represents the function in program and edge $\langle u, v \rangle \in E$ represents node (function) u calls node (function) v.

The process of FCG matching algorithm is illustrated in Fig. 1. Section 3.1 introduces the computation of node similarity. Hungarian algorithm and optimizations of FCG matching algorithm are discussed in Sects. 3.2 and 3.3.

3.1   Node Similarity

Instruction Sequence Similarity. Sequence alignment technique has been used to quantify and visualize the similarity between sequences [14]. In order to compute the similarity of instruction sequences, mnemonic, an abbreviation for instruction operations, is extracted from every instruction to construct mnemonic sequence. N-gram analysis is applied to collect different subsequences of mnemonic. Then, we project them into a small set of natural numbers by hashing. The instruction sequence similarity of node n_1 and n_2 is defined as follow:

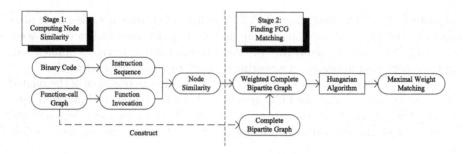

Fig. 1. Process of FCG matching algorithm

$$w_s(n_1, n_2) = \frac{|A \cap B|}{|A \cup B|} \tag{1}$$

where A, B are the hash value sets of node n_1, n_2.

Function Invocation Similarity. The definition of function invocation similarity is based on the difference in number of calling functions and called functions. Generally, the function invocation similarity of node n_1, n_2 is defined as below:

$$w_r(n_1, n_2) = \frac{1}{2} \left(\frac{\min\{p_1, p_2\}}{\max\{p_1, p_2\}} + \frac{\min\{q_1, q_2\}}{\max\{q_1, q_2\}} \right) \tag{2}$$

where p_1, p_2 represent the number of calling functions of node n_1, n_2 and q_1, q_2 represent the number of called functions.

Based on the instruction sequence and function invocation similarity, node similarity of node n_1, n_2 is defined as follow:

$$w(n_1, n_2) = p w_s(n_1, n_2) + q w_r(n_1, n_2) \tag{3}$$

where p, q are the weights of w_s, w_r and $p+q = 1$. By default, $p = q = 0.5$ in this work, which means those two kinds of similarities are of the same importance in computing node similarity.

3.2 Hungarian Algorithm

In the description of Hungarian algorithm, we will use a similarity matrix in Fig. 2 which consists of the node similarity of nodes from different FCGs. The weight of edges in weighted complete bipartite graph B, the input of Hungarian algorithm, correspond to elements in similarity matrix. Node x_i in partition X of B is connected with every node y_j in partition Y by gray dash lines in Fig. 2 which means that these nodes are not matched yet. This completes the preliminary preparation of algorithm.

The algorithm initializes the labels of nodes with l_0 in line 3 for do-while loop from line 4 to line 8, shown as below.

$$l_0(u) = \begin{cases} \max_{v \in Y} w(u,v) & , u \in X \\ 0 & , u \in Y \end{cases} \tag{4}$$

The do-while loop consists of marking subgraph, finding maximum weight matching and updating label and will not stop until all the nodes in bipartite graph B are connected by red solid lines which represent the maximum weight matching we are searching for.

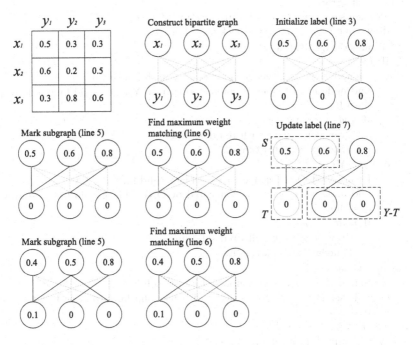

Fig. 2. A simple example of finding FCG matching by Hungarian algorithm

3.3 Optimizations

Node Pairs Pruning. The length of instruction sequence varies from tens to thousands in fact. If the difference of two sequences is so large that it is improper to match the corresponding nodes, computing their node similarity precisely becomes useless and worthless. Assigning a relative small constant as the similarity of node pairs instead will reduce the time cost. At the same time, pruning node pairs conservatively won't reduce the accuracy of FCG matching. During the process of Hungarian algorithm, the assigned constant won't bring node pairs with large difference into the final maximum weight matching.

Algorithm 1. FCG matching based on Hungarian algorithm

```
1 def Main(B):
       Input: weighted complete bipartite graph B(V_B, E_B)
       Output: maximum weight matching M of graph B
2      let X, Y the two partitions of B, initial edge ⟨u, v⟩ ∈ E_B is gray dash line.
3      initialize label l = l_0
4      repeat
5          MarkSubgraph()
6          FindMaxWeightMatch(u);      /* u can be any node in subgraph */
7          UpdateLabel(l)
8      until every node is connected by red solid line;
9 def MarkSubgraph():
10     let edge set E' = {⟨u, v⟩|w(u, v) == l(u) + l(v), ⟨u, v⟩ ∈ E_B}
11     draw edge ⟨u, v⟩ ∈ E' with black solid line.
12 def FindMaxWeightMatch(u):
13     if u ∈ X:
14         let node set P = {v|edge ⟨u, v⟩ is grey dash line, v ∈ Y}
15         find node v ∈ P which is connected by ONLY black solid line and gray
           dash line.
16         if node v exists:
17             draw edge ⟨u, v⟩ with red dash line.
18             FindMaxWeightMatch(v)
19     elif u ∈ Y:
20         let node set Q = {v|edge ⟨u, v⟩ is black solid line, u ∈ X}
21         find node v ∈ Q which is connected by ONLY black solid line and gray
           dash line.
22         if node v exists:
23             draw edge ⟨u, v⟩ with red solid line.
24             FindMaxWeightMatch(v)
25 def UpdateLabel(l):
26     find one node u ∈ X isn't connected by red solid line.
27     let node set P = {v|path consisting of black solid lines from node u to v
       exists, v ∈ V_B}
28     S = P ∩ X, T = P ∩ Y
29     Δ = min_{u∈S,v∈Y−T} l(u) + l(v) − w(u, v)
30     for u in S:
31         l(u) = l(u) − Δ
32     for v in T:
33         l(v) = l(v) + Δ
```

The optimized instruction sequence similarity w'_s of node n_1, n_2 can be formulated as follow.

$$w'_s(n_1, n_2) = \begin{cases} w_s(n_1, n_2) & , k^{-1} < len(n_1)/len(n_2) < k \\ \beta & , otherwise \end{cases} \tag{5}$$

where $len(n)$ is the length of instruction sequence in node n, k is a factor of measuring the difference in length and β is a small constant.

Forward Matching. There are two types of nodes in FCGs: external node and local node. Only nodes of same type are allowed to match with each other in FCG matching. Since the function name of external node is retrieved with tools in IDA Pro, external nodes can be matched simply by function names. For local nodes, if the instruction sequence similarity of two nodes exceeds the threshold δ_H and there is no other node more similar than them, it's appropriate to add this match into the final results. Generally, the predetermined matching M_p is shown as follow.

$$M_p = \{(u,v)|name(u) = name(v), u, v \in V_{ext}\}$$
$$\cup \{(u,v)|w_s(u,v) \geq \delta_H, u, v \in V_{loc}\} \tag{6}$$

Remove matched nodes $V' = \{u, v|(u,v) \in M_p\}$ and related edges from complete bipartite graph B and bipartite graph B', the input of Hungarian algorithm, is shown as below.

$$B'(V_{B'} = V_B - V', \quad E_{B'} = E_B - \{\langle u,v \rangle | u \in V' \vee v \in V'\})$$

For Hungarian algorithm's time complexity $O(n^3)$, the reduced bipartite graph B' decreases n to attain efficiency. Consequently, the time cost of Hungarian algorithm is less than the former one.

4   Applications of FCG Matching

Before the experiments, 16 pairs of active open-source programs are collected from their homepages. Also, the instruction sequences and FCGs are extracted from binary codes through the usage of Python APIs provided by IDA Pro (Interactive Disassembler Professional).

The node similarities of matched node pairs can provide us some insight into the correctness of matching results. Node pairs with high similarities are more likely to be correct than those with low similarities. Therefore, FCG matching results are quantitatively evaluated based on following node pairs' ratio of different node similarities:

Definition 2. *(Confirmed matching ratio) ratio of node pairs in FCG matching result whose node similarities are greater than δ_H, denoted by R_C.*

Definition 3. *(Uncertain matching ratio) ratio of node pairs in FCG matching result whose node similarities are less than δ_H and greater than δ_L, denoted by R_U.*

Definition 4. *(Virtual matching ratio) ratio of node pairs with virtual node, namely the counterpart of unmatched node, in FCG matching result, denoted by R_V. δ_L is assigned to the node similarities of pairs with virtual node.*

δ_H is assigned to 0.9 empirically and δ_L is 0.1 in this work.

4.1   Reverse Engineering

Confirmed matching ratio can reflect the amount of workloads reduced in reverse analysis. Higher the confirmed matching ratio is, the more function pairs can share analysis results. The analysts of programs just need to focus on these functions that have no counterparts in reversed programs. In this experiment, we compared our method with simulated annealing based FCG matching algorithm proposed in Classy system [7]. The result shows in Table 1.

Table 1. Comparison of FCG matching results based on optimized Hungarian algorithm and simulated annealing

Program	Version		#Node	Optimized Hungarian		Simulated annealing	
				R_C	Time(s)	R_C	Time(s)
VLC	2.0.8	2.2.1	199	78.50%	0.0036	77.10%	0.0084
Pptp	1.5.0	1.6.0	342	100%	0.0037	100%	0.0044
Pageant	0.60.0	0.64.0	465	88.06%	0.021	79.63%	0.055
Sstpc	1.0.0	1.0.2	533	69.51%	0.061	60.45%	0.093
Ophcrack	2.1.0	2.2.0	559	91.60%	0.018	89.02%	0.090
Tuxpaint	0.9.15	0.9.17	683	68.71%	0.12	57.00%	0.14
Fzsftp	3.10.0	3.14	1181	92.60%	0.23	89.80%	0.84
AkelPad	4.7.3	4.9.7	1369	85.42%	0.72	74.84%	1.31
P7zip	15.9.0	16.2.0	3704	91.94%	1.58	90.39%	18.7
Emailrelay	1.3.3	1.4.0	8265	88.72%	15.89	87.72%	110.90
Notepad++	6.9.0	7.2.0	8619	88.67%	35.36	86.23%	114.65
DevCpp	5.9.0	5.11.0	9025	99.05%	13.32	98.52%	156.00
Audacity	2.0.2	2.1.0	16214	78.54%	1102.52	67.96%	809.43
Emule	0.45.0	0.50.0	20481	68.98%	1043.55	67.27%	1746.75
Sublime	2.2.1	3.0.0	23111	62.58%	7311.41	58.77%	2784.48
Filezilla	3.17.0	3.22.2	31215	93.91%	579.39	91.11%	2436.01

In Table 1, for confirmed matching ratio R_C, our method is better than simulated annealing based FCG matching, which means more workloads can be reduced. The reason is that simulated annealing is a random process of exchanging node pairs to obtain maximum weight matching and its final result is likely to be the local maximum, while Hungarian algorithm searches for maximum weight matching in a global view.

In most cases, optimized Hungarian algorithm is faster than simulated annealing, while sometimes simulated annealing is more efficient. The time cost of Hungarian algorithm is related to not only number of nodes in FCG, but also node similarities. The process of matching two identical FCG of ten thousands of nodes can be finished in few minutes, while it takes much longer time for

FCGs with less similar nodes. For instance, Sublime costs two hours to complete FCG matching, which is 12 times slower than Filezilla with higher confirmed matching ration and more nodes. For better reduction of analysis workloads, it is worthwhile to spend more time on FCG matching.

4.2 Software Plagiarism Detection

The plagiarized parts of suspicious software can be revealed as function pairs with high node similarities in FCG matching. So it is possible to judge on whether suspicious software plagiarizes the original program or not according to ratios of different matching that are able to depict the similarity of programs as follow.

$$Sim(A, B) = w_c R_C + w_u R_U + w_v R_V \qquad (7)$$

where w_c, w_u and w_v are weights of corresponding matching ratio. In order to normalize program similarity, $w_c = 1$, $w_u = 0.5$ and $w_v = 0$ in this experiment. We investigated the reliability of FCG matching in software plagiarism detection. Obfuscated versions P_{SUB}, P_{FLA} and P_{BCF} of original binary code P are generated by code obfuscation tool Obfuscator-llvm [15]. We compared them with original binary code. The result shows in Table 2.

Table 2. Similarity of obfuscated and original binary codes based on different node similarities

Program	p	q	$Sim(P, P_{SUB})$	$Sim(P, P_{FLA})$	$Sim(P, P_{BCF})$
P7zip	0.00	1.00	0.9993	0.9323	0.8421
	0.25	0.75	0.9922	0.9174	0.7943
	0.50	0.50	0.9866	0.8743	0.7373
	0.75	0.25	0.9743	0.8363	0.7120
	1.00	0.00	0.9710	0.8270	0.7266
Gnuplot	0.00	1.00	1.0000	0.8063	0.7658
	0.25	0.75	0.9992	0.7954	0.7571
	0.50	0.50	0.9968	0.7338	0.7347
	0.75	0.25	0.9928	0.6596	0.7145
	1.00	0.00	0.9887	0.6476	0.7166

In Table 2, column p, q represent the weights of instruction sequence and function invocation similarity in node similarity respectively. SUB, FLA and BCF are the abbreviations of obfuscation techniques: instruction substitution, control flow flattening and bogus control flow.

The program similarity of obfuscated and original binary codes decreases as the weight of instruction sequence increases. These obfuscation techniques mainly cause the change of instruction sequence and control flow of functions, so the program similarity derived from FCG matching based on function invocation only ($p = 0.00$, $q = 1.00$) is higher than the one based on instruction sequence only ($p = 1.00$, $q = 0.00$). For obfuscation techniques, SUB hardly has no impact on the function invocation of binary code, so P's program similarity based on function invocation with P_{SUB} nearly equals to 1. FLA and BCF change the control flow graph of certain functions and reorder sequence of instructions at the same time, while these two techniques have limited impact on FCG. Therefore, structural features are more stable than features on instruction-level in plagiarism detection. In general, the obfuscated binary codes still have high similarities derived from FCG matching with original program, so the results indirectly demonstrate the effectiveness of FCG matching in software plagiarism detection.

5   Evaluation of Optimizations

Let $k = 6$ and $\beta = \delta_L$, the time costs of computing node similarity before and after node pairs pruning are shown in Table 3.

Table 3. Effects of node pairs pruning and forward matching

Program	Version		Computing node similarity (s)		Hungarian algorithm (s)	
			Before	After	Before	After
Notepad++	6.9.0	7.2.0	68.09	50.08	50.49	35.36
DevCpp	5.9.0	5.11.0	66.35	55.75	18.10	13.32
Audacity	2.0.2	2.1.0	176.06	112.96	3709.19	1102.52
Emule	0.45.0	0.50.0	489.48	374.05	6523.80	1043.55
Sublime	2.2.1	3.0.0	575.35	383.56	14887.10	7311.41
Filezilla	3.17.0	3.22.2	909.26	601.99	4107.71	579.39

Before the execution of Hungarian algorithm, forward matching is conducted to decrease the scale of bipartite graph by matching node pairs with high similarity. Table 3 also shows the decline in time cost of Hungarian algorithm.

6   Conclusion

In this work, we presented a novel FCG matching algorithm based on Hungarian algorithm and demonstrated its applications, but there are several limits. First, for mobile apps in Android and iOS, methods for extracting and matching their FCGs are different from the one that we introduced in this paper. So the FCG matching of mobile apps can be discussed in future work. Second, there are some limitations caused by using IDA Pro to extract features. For example, it's hard to identify indirect jumps in binary codes by APIs provided by IDA Pro. Therefore, it is necessary to find or develop new tools for better software analysis.

References

1. Hu, X., Chiueh, T., Shin, K.G.: Large-scale malware indexing using function-call graphs. In: Proceedings of the 16th ACM Conference on Computer and Communications Security, pp. 611–620. ACM (2009)
2. Koutra, D., Tong, H., Lubensky, D.: Big-align: fast bipartite graph alignment. In: 2013 IEEE 13th International Conference on Data Mining (ICDM), pp. 389–398. IEEE (2013)
3. Cordella, L.P., Foggia, P., Sansone, C., Vento, M.: Performance evaluation of the VF graph matching algorithm. In: Proceedings of International Conference on Image Analysis and Processing, pp. 1172–1177. IEEE (1999)
4. Jouili, S., Mili, I., Tabbone, S.: Attributed graph matching using local descriptions. In: Blanc-Talon, J., Philips, W., Popescu, D., Scheunders, P. (eds.) ACIVS 2009. LNCS, vol. 5807, pp. 89–99. Springer, Heidelberg (2009). https://doi.org/10.1007/978-3-642-04697-1_9
5. Jouili, S., Tabbone, S.: Graph matching based on node signatures. In: Torsello, A., Escolano, F., Brun, L. (eds.) GbRPR 2009. LNCS, vol. 5534, pp. 154–163. Springer, Heidelberg (2009). https://doi.org/10.1007/978-3-642-02124-4_16
6. Kuhn, H.W.: The Hungarian method for the assignment problem. Naval Res. Logist. Q. **2**(1–2), 83–97 (1955)
7. Kostakis, O.: Classy: fast clustering streams of call-graphs. Data Min. Knowl. Discov. **28**(5–6), 1554–1585 (2014)
8. Sartipi, K., Kontogiannis, K.: On modeling software architecture recovery as graph matching. In: Proceedings of International Conference on Software Maintenance, ICSM 2003, pp. 224–234. IEEE (2003)
9. Bernardi, M.L., Cimitile, M., Di Lucca, G.A.: A model-driven graph-matching approach for design pattern detection. In: 2013 20th Working Conference on Reverse Engineering (WCRE), pp. 172–181. IEEE (2013)
10. Nagarajan, V., Gupta, R., Zhang, X., Madou, M., De Sutter, B.: Matching control flow of program versions. In: IEEE International Conference on Software Maintenance, ICSM 2007, pp. 84–93. IEEE (2007)
11. Krinke, J.: Identifying similar code with program dependence graphs. In: Proceedings of Eighth Working Conference on Reverse Engineering, pp. 301–309. IEEE (2001)
12. Silvio C, Yang X.: Simseer and bugwise: web services for binary-level software similarity and defect detection. In: Proceedings of the 11th Australasian Symposium on Parallel and Distributed Computing, pp. 21–29 (2013)
13. Chen, K., Liu, P., Zhang, Y.: Achieving accuracy and scalability simultaneously in detecting application clones on Android markets. In: Proceedings of the International Conference on Software Engineering, pp. 175–186. ACM (2014)
14. Tang, Y., Xiao, B., Lu, X.: Signature tree generation for polymorphic worms. IEEE Trans. Comput. **60**(4), 565–579 (2011)
15. Junod, P., Rinaldini, J., Wehrli, J., Michielin, J.: Obfuscator-LLVM - software protection for the masses. In: International Workshop on Software Protection, pp. 3–9. IEEE (2015)

SocialSec Track

Reasoning About Trust and Belief Change on a Social Network: A Formal Approach

Aaron Hunter[(✉)]

BC Institute of Technology, Burnaby, BC, Canada
aaron_hunter@bcit.ca

Abstract. One important aspect of trust is the following: when a trusted source reports some new information, then we are likely to believe that the new information is true. As such, the notion of trust is closely connected to the notion of belief change. In this paper, we demonstrate how a formal model of trust developed in the Artificial Intelligence community can be used to model the dynamics of belief on a social network. We use a formal model to capture the preceived areas of expertise of each agent, and we introduce a logical operator to determine how beliefs change following reported information. Significantly, the trust held in another agent is not determined solely by individual expertise; the extent to which an agent is trusted is also influenced by social relationships between agents. We prove a number of formal properties, and demonstrate that our approach can actually model a wide range of practical trust problems involving social agents. This work is largely foundational, and it connects two different research communities. In particular, this work illustrates how fundamentally logic-based models of reasoning can be applied to solve problems related to trust on social networks.

1 Introduction

In this paper, we are concerned with formalizing the interaction between trust, belief and social relationships in network communication. Specifically, we are concerned with determining when an agent should believe that another has sufficient expertise in a domain to be trusted, based on their own knowledge as well as their social relationships.

Our basic approach is to frame the problem in the context of formal *belief revision operators*. In this setting, domain information is encoded in a suitable logic and each agent has an operator for incorporating new information. However, prior to incorporating new information, an agent must consider the likelihood that the source has correct information. In existing work on belief revision, the relevant notion of trust is concerned only with the expertise of the reporting agent. In the present paper, we move these so-called *trust-sensitive* revision operators to the setting of social networks. As such, we need to consider the relations between agents in our model of trust; one agent may actually have gleaned some expertise from a close neighbour.

© Springer International Publishing AG 2017
J. K. Liu and P. Samarati (Eds.): ISPEC 2017, LNCS 10701, pp. 783–801, 2017.
https://doi.org/10.1007/978-3-319-72359-4_49

This paper makes several distinct constributions to the existing literature on trust for social networks. First, to the best of our knowledge, this is the first paper that tries to apply established research on belief revision to the problem of social network analysis. Second, we demonstrate a basic approach that allows us to explicitly specify how trust impacts the way information is incorporated when it is shared on a social network. We also use this approach to give a general basis for defining the relative trust of each agent with respect to others. Finally, while this is primarily a foundational paper, we also consider several practical applications for our work, including trusted third-party protocols and network communication with hardware devices.

2   Background

2.1   Belief Revision

Belief revision operators are mathematical functions that model the way that new information should be incorporated by a rational agent. In this tradition, there is a fixed set $\mathbf{F}$ of *propositional variables* that represent properties of the world. *Formulas* over $\mathbf{F}$ are defined using the usual propositional connectives ¬ (not), ∧ (and), and ∨ (or).

A *state* is an assignment of true-false values to the variables in $\mathbf{F}$. Informally, a state represents a particular configuration of the world. A *belief state* is a set of states: those that a particular agent considers to be possible. Finally, a belief revision operator is a function $*$ that maps a belief state to a new belief state when new information is obtained. The most influential work on belief revision is the so-called AGM approach, in which revision operators are constrained by a set of rationality postulates [AGM85].

In this paper, we define a *report* to be a set of states. Informally, a report r is understood to be evidence that the actual state of the world is in r. An AGM revision operator is a function that takes a belief state K and a report r as inputs, and returns a new belief state. It has been shown that a function $*$ is an AGM revision operator just in case the result of revision can be determined by finding minimal states over an underlying total pre-order [KM92]. Specifically, for every revision operator $*$, there is an underlying total pre-order $\prec$ such that $K * r$ is the set of $\prec$-minimal states in r.

One natural example of an AGM revision operator is the Dalal operator [Dal88]. In this case, the ordering $\prec$ is given by the Hamming distance between states. Hence, $K * r$ consists of the states in r that differ from some state in K in the values assigned to a minimal number of propositional variables. This is not the only AGM revision operator, nor is it necessarily the most appropriate for all applications; but it is a representative example.

The AGM approach has been highly influential in the AI literature, with connections to modal logics [vB07], non-monotonic reasoning [KI03], and information security [HD07].

2.2   Modelling Trust

The notion of trust is key to many problems in security, including the development of *reputation systems* where agents are trusted based on past actions and reports [HJS06]. Such models are not only concerned with accurately profiling the reliability of agents, but they are often concerned with defending against deceptive agents [SAW09]. Hence, trust is tied closely to notions of honesty in communication.

However, the notion of trust we are concerned with in this paper is not explicitly related to deception. Instead, we are concerned with knowledge-based trust. That is, we are concerned with trust relationships that are based on the perceived expertise of other agents. This notion of trust is explored in [HB15], where a formal model is used to represent the factual distinctions that another agent can be trusted to make. For example, while an automechanic is trusted over information related to cars, they may not be trusted with regards to financial markets.

A trust-sensitive belief revision operator is a special revision operator that takes into account the trust one agent holds in another. Trust is defined in terms of a *trust partition* Π, which is just a partition over the set of all states; so $\Pi(s,t)$ holds just in case s and t are in the same cell of the partition. We write $\Pi[t]$ as a shorthand for $\{s \mid \Pi(s,t)\}$. Each agent associates a trust partition with every other agent: we write Π_B^A for the partiion that agent A associates with agent B.

We assume that each agent has a fixed belief revision operator $*$ for incorporating new information (again provided in the form of a *report*). Let $Bel(A)$ denote the belief state held by A, and suppose that A receives the report r from B. Note that it does not make sense for A to simply calculate $Bel(A)*r$, because the agent B is not completely trusted. Instead, the new belief state for A should be determined by the new operator $*_B^A$ defined as follows:

$$Bel(A) *_B^A r := Bel(A) * \Pi_B^A(r).$$

In other words, A considers the report r to be evidence for every state that B can not distinguish from an element of r. The basic idea is shown Fig. 1, where we can see that the report r is transformed to a different report r_1 prior to revision; intuitively, r_1 captures the part of r that is trusted to be correct.

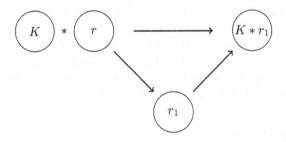

Fig. 1. Trust pre-processing

We illustrate with a simple commonsense example.

Example 1. Suppose that Alex (A) is a car owner and he takes his car to be inspected by a mechanic (M). After the inspection, M tells Alex two things:

- *Your car needs a new engine.* (E)
- *You should not drink diet soda.* ($\neg D$)

Formally, the report that Alex receives is $r = \{s \mid s \models E \wedge \neg D\}$. But it would be a mistake to revise directly by this report, because Alex has no reason to trust M on nutritional advice. A better model for this example would use the partition Π_B^A with two cells: $\{s \mid s \models E\}$ and $\{s \mid s \models \neg E\}$. This partition indicates that Alex trusts M to distinguish between states only based on the condition of the car engine. In this case

$$Bel(A) *_B^A r$$

will only include states where E is true. However, this new belief state will include states where D is true and also sates where it is false. Essentially, the trust-sensitive revision allows Alex to ignore the part of the report where M is not trusted.

3   Framework

3.1   Social Networks

We start with a formal definition of a social network.

Definition 1. *A social network is a triple* $\langle \mathbf{A}, \mathbf{E}, \omega \rangle$, *where:*

- $\mathbf{A}$ *is a finite set of* agents,
- $\mathbf{E} \subseteq \mathbf{A} \times \mathbf{A}$,
- $\omega : \mathbf{E} \rightarrow \mathbf{Z}^+$,
- $\omega(a, a) = 0$ *for all* $A \in \mathbf{A}$.

Informally, $\mathbf{E}$ is a relation that captures a social relationship between agents, and the weight assigned to an edge (a_1, a_2) is a measure of strength of the relationship. Higher weights represent weaker relationships. As a result, the strongest weight is 0 and this is assigned to all self loops.

This definition of a social network is similar to those used in the literature on coalition analysis, such as [SHKW14]. The main difference is our use of the natural numbers for strengths. Our choice here has been made to maintain consistency with standard work in belief revision, where natural numbers are often used in this manner to capture strength of belief.

3.2   Trust Scenarios

In this section, we introduce the main technical tool that we use in the rest of this paper. We assume an underlying propositional signature $\mathbf{F}$. The set of states over $\mathbf{F}$ is denoted by $S = 2^{\mathbf{F}}$. The set of belief states is denoted by 2^S.

Definition 2. *A* trust scenario $\mathcal{T}$ *is a tuple* $\mathcal{T} = \langle \mathbf{A}, B, R, T, \mathbf{E}, \omega \rangle$, *where:*

- $\langle \mathbf{A}, \mathbf{E}, \omega \rangle$ *is a social network,*
- $B : \mathbf{A} \rightarrow 2^{\mathbf{S}}$,
- R *maps each* $A \in \mathbf{A}$ *to an AGM revision operator* $*^A$,
- T *maps each pair of agents* (A, B) *to a partition* Π_B^A *over* S.

The belief function B maps each agent to a belief state, the revision function R maps each agent to an AGM revision operator, and the trust function T maps each pair of agents to a trust partition. Hence, a trust scenario is essentially just a social network, along with the formal machinery needed to do trust-sensitive revision. We will demonstrate that combining these elements actually allows us to define more powerful forms of revision that take social relationships into account.

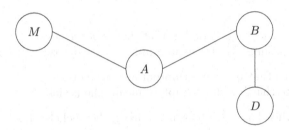

Fig. 2. A simple network

3.3   Motivating Example

Before proceeding, it is instructive to look at a concrete, commonsense example. We assume four agents. Alice (A) is the protagonist in the story; she will be trying to incorporate some new information. The other agents are a mechanic (M), a baker (B), and a doctor (D). We assume Alice is friends with the mechanic and the baker. The baker and doctor are also friends. Hence, the social network connecting all indivduals is given in Fig. 2. We assume that the weight on each edge is 1.

Informally, we say that Alice trusts M about cars, she trusts B about bread, and she trusts D about human health. It is straightforward to define a vocabulary as well as trust partitions to capture these facts. For simplicity, assume the vocabulary is just $\{broke, sick\}$. Figure 3 shows a plausible trust partition that Alice might have for D. Note that the partition shows that D can distinguish states where $sick$ is true from those where it is not.

We would like to consider the distinction between two different scenarios for Alice. Suppose that she receives some medical advice from a friend; for example, she is told that a mark on her skin is an indication of some serious illness. Intuitively, it seems that the way Alice incorporates this information will be different, depending on which friend it comes from. It is well known that the

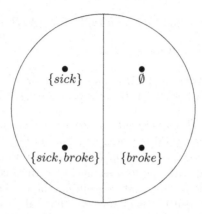

Fig. 3. A trust partition

notion of trust is not transitive, but that should not mean that trust is indendent of social relationships. With this in mind, we consider two options.

1. M tells Alice that her skin symptom means she is sick.
2. B tells Alice that her skin symptom means she is sick.

In case (1), Alice has little reason to change her beliefs at all. The mechanic is not trusted on issues of human health, and they have no friends with such expertise either. Using standard trust-sensitive revision, Alice's beliefs do not change at all in case (1). Case (2), on the other hand, is more subtle. While B has no expertise in human health, he does have a friendship with a doctor. This suggests that it is at least possible that the medical advice being given comes from a reputable source. It is therefore reasonable to suggest that a report from B is more likely to influence Alice's beliefs, based on the influence of the social network.

The way that Alice's beliefs change in case (2) is not obvious. The final change depends in part on Alice's initial beliefs, the exact trust that she holds in other agents, and the strength of the relationships between all agents. In this paper, we suggest that trust scenarios provide a flexible mechanism to address all of these issues.

4   Social Influence and Belief Change

4.1   Motivation

Much of the work on trust in social networks is concerned with determining the extent to which another agent can be trusted. We are not concerned with this problem. Instead, we assume that we already have a model that indicates the domains where another agent is trusted. We are concerned with how this model of trust informs the belief change that occurs when information is received in a social network.

Trust-sensitive belief revision gives us a tool to incorporate new information received from a source, while taking into account the domain where the source is trusted. We want to extend this model slightly, to allow an agent to incorporate trust not only in the source of new information but also trust in the agents that are close to the source. Informally, our approach is the following. We introduce an extra parameter n when we want to perform belief revision. We use n to calculate a sort of "radius of trust" around the reporting agent. All of the agents inside the radius of trust are understood to be close enough to the reporting agent that they may have influence over the reported information. As such, we must be concerned with the trust held in every agent inside the radius.

Our intitial approach is simply to add the new parameter n to define a graded revision operator where the radius is actually explicit. We will see that this can be helpful in many examples, we will provde some general results, and we will demonstrate how we can use graded revision operators to compare the relative trust held in different agents.

4.2   Graded Revision

In this section, we define a graded belief revision operator for trust scenarios. In the following definition, we let $*^A(\Pi)$ denote the trust sensitive revision operator for agent A, when using the trust partition Π for pre-processing. Also, for any agents A, B, C, we let $dist(A, B, C)$ denote the lowest sum of edge weights on a path from B to C, not including A.

Definition 3. *Let $T = \langle \mathbf{A}, B, R, T, \mathbf{E}, \omega \rangle$. For each $A, B \in \mathbf{A}$ and each $n \in \mathbf{N}$, let*

$$*^A_B(n) = *^A(\Pi)$$

where $\Pi = \bigcap \{\Pi^A_C \mid dist(A, B, C) \le n\}$.

What this definition says is the following. The graded revision operator of radius n is obtained by finding all agents that can be reached by a path of weight n, and then taking the intersection of all of included partitions. The intersection of a set of partitions is the finest partition that can be formed. Informally, the intersection of a set of partitions is the partition that can distinguish between any pair of states that are distinguished by any of the constituent partitions.

We give a simple example to demonstrate the way that this definition actually works in practice.

Example 2. Consider a case with 5 agents, A, B, C, D, E. Figure 4 gives a social network on these agents, including weights on the edges. Suppose that we are interested in determining $*^A_B(2)$. In the figure, the square labelled as the *trust zone* indicates the set of agents at a distances less than or equal to 2 (we previously called this the *radius of trust*). We have the following equality:

$$*^A_B(2) = *^A(\bigcap(\{\Pi^A_B, \Pi^A_C, \Pi^A_D\})).$$

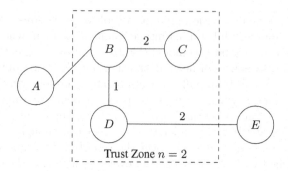

Fig. 4. Finding the trust zone

Note that the partition Π_E^A is not included here, because the distance from B to E is 3. Informally, this means that the revision operator $*_B^A(2)$ does not consider E to be a "close enough" relative to have any influence on the trust held in B.

The previous example shows the simple calculation involved in determining the trust partition to be used for a fixed radius. However, the end goal is actually to determine a revision operator that can calcuate the result of belief revision. We return to our motivating example from the previous section to show how this revision is determined.

Example 3. We revisit the situation involving the mechanic, the baker and the doctor. Assume that the propositional vocabulary is $\{broke, sick\}$. Intuitively, $broke$ is true if A's car is broken and $sick$ is true if A is ill in some way. Assume that the initial belief state for A is $\emptyset$. In other words, A does not initially believe that either $broke$ or $sick$ is true. Formally, we need to specify trust partitions for A with respect to each of the other agents. The partition Π_D^A is given in Fig. 3. The partition Π_M^A is the reverse of Fig. 3, where $sick$ and $broke$ are swapped. The partition Π_B^A is the trivial partition consisting of one set containing all of the states.

We have now specified all relevant parts of $\mathcal{T}$, the trust scenario for this problem. We want to determine the revision operators A uses for information from B and M. To illustrate, we will determine the operators $*_B^A(1)$ and $*_M^A(1)$, which take into account the social influence of agents in a radius of 1. We have the following:

$$*_B^A(1) = *^A(\bigcap(\{\Pi_B^A, \Pi_D^A\})) = *^A(\Pi_D^A).$$

This follows because Π_D^A is a refinement of Π_B^A. On the other hand, we have:

$$*_M^A(1) = *^A(\Pi_M^A)$$

because M is not related to any nodes other than A.

In order to complete the example, we need to actually use these revision operators to calculate the final beliefs of A. Recall that $B(A)$ denotes the initial belief state of A. It is easy to verify that

$$B(A) *_B^A (1)sick = \{sick\}$$

because the partition Π_D^A is refined enough to distinguish $sick$-states from non-$sick$ states. It is also easy to verify that

$$B(A) *_M^A (1)sick = \emptyset.$$

This holds because the partition Π_M^A can not distinguish $sick$-states. As such, the revision is actually by the set of all states, which does not lead to a change in belief.

The preceding example demonstrates that the relationship between B and D actually changes the way that A revises their beliefs. Informally, since B is close friends with a doctor, they are trusted on matters related to human health. This is not necessarily plausible in all cases, of course; but it can be appropriate in some applications. We remark also that this approach is very sensitive to changes in the edge weights and the radius of trust. For example, if we change the weight $\omega(B, D)$ to 2, then it no longer follows that A will trust B on matters of health at radius 1. Nevertheless, this approach does capture the fact that we will trust B over $sick$ if the radius is set high enough. This seems reasonable. Setting a high radius of trust is tantamount to relaxing the amount of trust required to be convinced something is true. If we relax the required trust to be very weak, then anyone that knows a doctor may be trusted as an authority.

4.3   Basic Properties

We refer to the operators $*_B^A(n)$ as *graded* trust-sensitive revision operators. In this section, we give some basic properties of graded trust-sensitive revision. First, we consider some extreme cases.

Definition 4. *A trust scenario $\mathcal{T}$ is splittable at A just in case the social network component is a disconnected graph when the node corresponding to A is removed.*

A splittable scenario at A involves a network with 2 or more distinct sub-graphs that are only connected by paths that include A.

Proposition 1. *Let $\mathcal{T}$ be a trust scenario. If $\mathcal{T}$ is not splittable at A, then there exists n such that, for all agents B, if $m > n$ then:*

$$*_B^A(m) = *_B^A(n)$$
$$= *^A(\bigcap(\{\Pi_C^A \mid C \in \mathbf{A}, C \neq A\})).$$

This result captures the fact that all agents can be reached at some radius, and the resulting partition will combine all partitions in the graph. We refer to the operator produced by Proposition 1 as the *maximum* revision operator for $\mathcal{T}$. The value n is, in the worst case, the sum of all edges in the social network. In this case, the revision operator is simply the union of all partitions for A with respect to the other agents in $\mathbf{A}$. It is worth remarking, however, that the fixed point for agent A will generally not be the same as the fixed point for B. The trust partitions that each agent holds are independent of those held by others.

Definition 5. *Let* $\mathcal{T} = \langle \mathbf{A}, B, R, T, \mathbf{E}, \omega \rangle$. *Then* $\mathcal{T}' = \langle \mathbf{A}', B', R', T', \mathbf{E}', \omega' \rangle$ *is a sub-scenario of* $\mathcal{T}$ *just in case:*

- $\mathbf{A}' \subseteq \mathbf{A}$
- $B' = B \restriction \mathbf{A}'$
- $R' = R \restriction \mathbf{A}'$
- $T' = T \restriction \mathbf{A}'$
- $\mathbf{E}' = \mathbf{E} \restriction \mathbf{A}'$
- $\omega' = \omega \restriction \mathbf{A}'$.

If the first inclusion is proper, then we call $\mathcal{T}'$ *a proper sub-scenario.*

For splittable scenarios, the networks can be broken into components.

Proposition 2. *Let* $\mathcal{T}$ *be a trust scenario that is splittable at* A. *Then there exist sub-scenarios* $\mathcal{T}_1, \ldots, \mathcal{T}_m$ *that are disjoint, connected, and such that each* $B \in \mathbf{A}$ *is in some* $\mathcal{T}_i$.

The following is an immediate consequence of Propositions 1 and 2.

Proposition 3. *Let* $\mathcal{T}$ *be a trust scenario that is splittable at* A, *with sub-scenarios* $\mathcal{T}_1, \ldots, \mathcal{T}_m$. *Then each* $\mathcal{T}_i$ *has a radius* m_i *that defines a maximum revision operator for* $\mathcal{T}_i$.

Hence, a splittable scenario defines a finite set of *maximal* revision operators. The partitions are not necessarily related in any useful way; they are defined from completely independent sets of component partitions.

The preceding results are concerned with what happens when we take large values for the radius of trust. The other, natural extreme case occurs when we set a radius of 0.

Proposition 4. *For any trust scenario* $\mathcal{T}$ *and all agents* A, B:

$$*_B^A(0) = *_B^A.$$

Hence, if we set the trust radius to 0, then we just have the regular trust sensitive revision operator. This means that social relationships are ignored.

Finally, it is worth noting that there is a connection with so-called selective revision operators [FH99]. An operator $\circ$ is a *selective revision operator* if there is an AGM revision $*$ and a transformation function f such that, for every r:

$$K \circ r = K * f(r).$$

Every revision operator defined through a trust partition is a selective revision operator. As such, graded trust-sensitive revision operators are selective revision operators, and a number of properties such as *idempotence* and *extensionality* follow immediately. For an exhaustive list of such properties, we refer the reader to [HB15].

5   Breadth of Trust

5.1   Comparing Sources

To this point, we have defined trust as a binary notion. An agent is either trusted to be able to draw certain distinctions, or they are not trusted to draw them. There is no formal notion of "strength" of trust at this stage. However, there is a natural notion of "breadth" of trust. The following definition gives the basic definition in the absence of a social network.

One important relationship between partitions is the notion of refinement. In the case of trust partitions, refinement has a clear meaning. Specifically, if Π_1 is a refinement of Π_2, then Π_1 makes strictly more distinctions than Π_2. Hence, if the partition for agent B is a refinement of the partition for agent C, then B is trusted more broadly than C. We make this more precise in the following definition.

Definition 6. *Let* A, B, C *be agents and let* T *assign trust partitions to each ordered pair in the usual way. We say that* A *trusts* B *more broadly than* C *if* Π_B^A *is a refinement of* Π_C^A.

Of course, in a trust scenario, the relevant partition also depends on some radius parameter.

Definition 7. *Let* T *be a trust scenario. We say that* A *trusts* B *more broadly that* C *under radius* n *just in case* $\Pi_B^A(n)$ *is a refinement of* Π_C^A.

The following result specifies a case where one partition is guaranteed to be a refinement of another.

Proposition 5. *Let* T *be a trust scenario involving agents* A, B, C. *Then* $\bigcap(\{\Pi_B^A, \Pi_C^A\})$ *is a refinement of* Π_B^A.

This result is of course not really about trust scenarios or social networks; it is a basic property of partitions. However, it is a useful property in reasoning about trust scenarios. It simply states that increasing the trust radius always refines the trust partition. This means that increasing the radius leads to revisions that are more likely to actually change the beliefs of the agent under consideration.

Due to Proposition 1, there are some cases where the notion of breadth of trust is not very interesting.

Proposition 6. *Let* T *be a trust scenario that is not splittable at* A. *Then there is some* n *such that* $\Pi_B^A(n) = \Pi_C^A(n)$ *for all* B, C.

Hence, if the social network is appropriately connected, then there is some radius at which every agent is equally trusted. Of course, with lower radii, this is not the case. However, it is still the case that refinement is not always a useful tool for comparison because some pairs are incompatible.

The best we can do for the moment is the following.

Definition 8. *Let T be a trust scenario, and let n be the sum of all edge weights in T. For each A and $i < n$, let $Alg(A, i) = \langle \mathbf{A} - A, \preceq_i \rangle$ where $\preceq_i$ is a binary relation on $\mathbf{A}$ such that:*

$$B \preceq_i C \iff \Pi_C^A(i) \text{ is a refinment of } \Pi_B^A(i).$$

The following result is immediate.

Proposition 7. *If T is a trust scenario, then for each A and i, the relation $\preceq_i$ is a partial order.*

Hence, each $Alg(A, i)$ is a *poset* over the other agents. This finite sequence of posets completely specifies which agents are most trusted at each radius. If B is maximal in $Alg(A, i)$, then we say that B is the most broadly trusted agent at radius i. If there exists B such that B is maximal in each $Alg(A, i)$, then we say that B is the most broadly trusted agent for A. Such a B is not guaranteed to exist.

5.2   A Broader Notion of Breadth

It is possible to define a total trust ordering on agents based simply on the number of states that can be distinguished.

Definition 9. *Let A, B, C be agents. We say that A considers B distinction-superior to C if $|\Pi_B^A| > |\Pi_C^A|$. If $|\Pi_B^A| = |\Pi_C^A|$, we say B and C are distinction-equal.*

The notion of distinction-superiority is an ad hoc concept that is not always useful in practice. The simple count of distinct cells is an indication of how many distinctions an agent can be trusted to make, but they are not always useful distinctions. Pragmatically, it is generally more useful to have agents that can distinguish states based on small combinations of propositional variables. Nevertheless, we will sometimes find the notion of distinction-superiority to be useful.

Using this notion, we can define the analog of the posets $Alg(A, i)$ from the previous section. However, in this case, the algebras will not be posets; instead they will be total pre-orders because everything is comparable. We say that B is distinction maximal for A if B is maximal the total pre-order at radius i. Unlike the refinement case, we are actually guaranteed to find such a maximal B at each radius. There is still no guarantee of a global maximum across all radii.

6   Extensions

6.1   Strength of Trust

While trust partitions can provide a useful way to define belief change on a social network, there are also cases where it is necessary to have a precise notiong of "strength of trust". Towards this end, we follow [HB15], and introduce a distance measure d on states. In this case, a large value for $d(s, t)$ is interpreted to mean that a particular agent is strongly trusted to distinguish the states s and t. A small distance on the other hand means that the agent can not be trusted to tell them apart. Using a distance on states allows us to represent differences in how strongly an agent is trusted to draw certain distinctions.

Definition 10. *A metric trust scenario $\mathcal{T}$ is a tuple $\mathcal{T} = \langle \mathbf{A}, B, R, M, \mathbf{E}, \omega \rangle$, where:*

- *$\langle \mathbf{A}, \mathbf{E}, \omega \rangle$ is a social network,*
- *$B : \mathbf{A} \to 2^{\mathbf{S}}$,*
- *R maps each $A \in \mathbf{A}$ to an AGM revision operator $*^A$,*
- *M maps each pair of agents (A, B) to a pseudo ultrametric d_B^A over S.*

The only difference here is that the partitions have been replaced by a pseudo ultrametric. A pseudo ultrametric is a metric that satisfies the so-called *strong triangle inequality*, and which allows distinct objects to have a distance 0 between them.

In the case of metric trust scenarios, we can no longer use set union to model social influence on trust. Given distance functions d_1 and d_2, we would like to define a new distance function that can draw the strongest possible distinctions from either d_1 or d_2.

Definition 11. *Let d_1 and d_2 be real valued functions on $S \times S$. The function $d_1 \star d_2$ is the following:*

$$d_1 \star d_2(s, t) = \max(d_1(s, t), d_2(s, t)).$$

This is the natural generalization of the union over partitions.

Proposition 8. *If d_1 and d_2 are pseudo ultrametrics, then $d_1 \star d_2$ is a pseudo ultrametric.*

As noted in [HB15], the important feature of a pseudo ultrametric d is that, for any fixed i, the collection of sets

$$\Pi(i) = \{t \mid d(s, t) \leq i \text{ for } s \in 2^{\mathbf{F}}\}$$

defines a partition over all states. This leads to the following parametrized defintion.

Definition 12. *Let* $\mathcal{T} = \langle \mathbf{A}, B, R, T, \mathbf{E}, \omega \rangle$ *and suppose* $MIN \in \mathbf{N}$*. For each* $A, B \in \mathbf{A}$ *and each* $n \in \mathbf{N}$*, let*

$$*_B^A(n) = *^A(\Pi(MIN))$$

where $\Pi = \bigcap \{\Pi_C^A \mid dist(A, B, C) \leq n\}$*.*

So, in the metric trust scenario, we essentially have a sequence of different revision operators. The exact operator depends on the minimum distance we set for states to be trustably distinguished.

In the interest of space, we do not go further into the properties of metric trust scenarios here. We simply remark that this extended framework allows us to capture a precise notion of strength of trust over any particular statement. This framework also offers more flexible options for defining social influence. For example, it is well known that a constant product of a metric space is a new metric space. Hence, we can introduce a discount function on the trust metrics for connected nodes, thereby reducing the influence of friendships on trust in individuals. We leave this extension for future work.

6.2 Further Applications

The main area of application here is intended to be social network analysis for typical networks, such as those used for online communication apps. But it is worth noting that our general approach can be applied to solve problems in other network domains as well.

One issue that arises periodically in security is the use of trusted third parties, particularly in cryptographic protocols. Consider the following exchange of messages between A, B and T.

Simple Identity Exchange
1. $A \rightarrow T : B$
2. $T \rightarrow A : K$
3. $A \rightarrow B : \{A\}_K$

In the description of this protocol, we are adopting the notation used in protocol verification, starting with [BAN90]. In this tradition, $A \rightarrow B : M$ means that A sends the message M to the agent B. An expression of the form $\{M\}_K$ denotes the message M encrypted with the key K. In the simple protocol above, T is intended to represent a trusted third party.

Proving that this kind of protocol actually works can be difficult. There are two trust issues at play. First, B must trust T to act on their behalf to share keys. Second, A and B must both trust that T knows all the right names and corresponding keys. This second form of trust can effectively be modelled with trust scenarios.

Another application of interest involves representation and reasoning about communication between humans, computers, and networked devices. In past

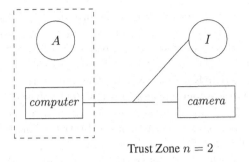

Trust Zone $n = 2$

Fig. 5. A networked camera

work, we have looked at practical security flaws that can be exploited on networked cameras [BH17]. One attack that has been identified is a simple man-in-the-middle(MiTM) attack, where ARP spoofing is used to get the camera to send its data to an attacking machine. The data can then be forwarded to the correct address without modification, it can be blocked entirely, or it can be manipulated. One particularly useful manipulation is to intercept the actual camera data, while sending a static image on a loop. Figure 5 shows the basic situation: A is a human agent, I is an intruder. The intruder has effectively blocked the communication channel from the camera, and they are sending their own images to A's computer.

Looking at Fig. 5, it is clear that this can also be seen as a social network by just adding weights to the edges. This kind of attack can therefore be seen as a result of a trust violation. The human user should only trust the images displayed on the computer if the trust radius applied is large enough to assume the computer is an authority over the camera's data. If the camera is connected through a public network, this radius would need to be implausibly high to guarantee this condition. A formal analysis of this application using trust scenarios would require a clear network model, as well as a suitable intruder model. In this case, we could then provide some parametrized proof that the images from the camera can not be trusted if they are transmitted over a wide area network.

7   Discussion

7.1   Related Work

The notion of trust has been studied extensively in social network analysis. However, most work in this area is related to one of the following: trust information collection, trust evaluation, and trust dissemination [SNP13]. The present work is actually not directly concerned with any of these areas. Instead, we start off with a model of trust in individuals that has been successfully applied in the Artificial Intelligence (AI) literature, and we demonstrate how it can be extended to reason about trusted belief change in the context of social relationships.

In order to relate our work to the existing literature, it is important to realize that there are a variety of definitions of trust in the literature, depending on the application. In the context of online interaction between individuals, trust is often understood as the extent to which one individual can expect another to behave as expected [RKK07, YCN+10]. But our work here is not related to behaviour at all. We are focused more on knowledge-based trust, as defined in [DGM+16]; that is, we are interested in determining the extent to which we should believe another agent's statements to be true. This is a critical problem when obtaining information from web sources.

The emphasis in [DGM+16] is on the manner in which the truth of past statements is used to determine whether or not an agent should be trusted in the present. In a sense, Dong et al. are concerned with building something like a trust partition; they define a mechanism that can be used to determine the expertise level of an agent. The details of the mechanism are quite different, as it is quantitative and predictive. But still, the emphasis is on building a model of trust from data. By contrast, in the present work, we assume we already know the domains in which each agent is an expert. The problem we address is how this expertise impacts the process of belief change.

In the literature, the notions of trust propogation and trust composition have been explored extensively [YSS04, ZHO09]. In our work, we take a very basic approach to these topics by simply assuming agents within a particular radius are highly influential. However, we remark that alternative models of propogation would be easy to implement here. Our work can be seen as complementary to past work in trust propogation and trust composition, as past models can easily be tested in our logical framework.

In terms of existing models of trust, the present work is most similar in spirit to those based on Bayesian inference [YGL13] or subjective logic [JHP06]. We say that these approaches are similar "in spirit" because they share an emphasis on the beliefs of communicating agents, and how trust impacts these beliefs. However, existing belief models used in the trust literature are overwhelmingly quantitative. On the other hand, in the AI community, there are distinct communities studying belief change from a statistical perspective and from the perspective of formal logic. To the best of our knowledge, the present paper is the first real attempt to use precise logical models of belief change to study trust in the context of a social network.

7.2   Future Work

We have introduced a novel approach that applies concepts from belief revision theory to understand trust on a social network. As this is a new approach, there are many directions for future work. The most important direction for future work is to apply the (largely theoretical) model presented here to case studies and to real reasoning on social networks. Only by applying the framework in practice will it be possible to fully evaluate the utility of our approach.

Another direction that we have left open is the complete development of the distance-based model of trust. Just as trust partitions have been developed in the AI community, so too has the distance-based model. However, while it is a simple generalization of the partition-based model of trust, it is clear that the interaction between a distance function and a social network can be complex. In future work, we will work out this aspect of the approach in more detail.

There is a need for more fundamental research comparing belief-based models of trust in the social network community. As noted above, statistical models of belief have a long history both in AI and in trust analysis for social network analsyis. In the AI community there are subtle differences between the statistical approach and the formal logic approach, with proponents on both sides. It would be valuable to see if this situation is also apparent on the social network side.

As a final comment on future work, it is worth noting that the model of a social network employed in this paper is very simple, as it involves just a single relation. While this generic notion of "relatedness" is sufficient for some problems, there are also cases where a set of orthogonal relations would be better. It is easy to produce commonsense reasoning problems where this is clear. For example, consider the difference between a friend and a teacher. While these might both be trusted individuals, one could argue that the trust held in a teacher is more likely to affect belief change related to academic matters. This sort of distinction can be modelled in our framework by associating subsets of states with different edges on the social network graph. We leave this extension for future work.

7.3   Conclusion

In this paper, we set out to model trust and belief change on a social network. The fundamental starting point is simply the fact that an agent should only *believe* new information if the source of that information is trusted. Formal models of belief change have a long history in the AI community. Hence it is natural to try to bring the tools of AI to bear on modelling and reasoning about trust on a social network.

In some ways, our work here is a direct application of an existing model of trust-sensitive belief revision. However, the addition of a social element actually requires some new machinery. In this paper, we suggest that social influence and trust propogation can be handled by using a flexible, parametrized radius of trust. We also take a reasonably optimisitic position in the sense that we trust agents as much as possible, taking into account the best information they could have from their social network.

While the framework here is important and useful, the fundamental contribution is the fact that we draw a connection between the belief revision community and the social network analysis community. It is clear that agents on a social network have dynamic beliefs that change in response to new information. This is precisely the sort of problem for which belief revision operators were developed. Moreover, at a high level, we argue that the logic-based setting of belief revision research is appropriate for analyzing security and trust on social networks. Many problems in social network analysis require formal proofs of correctness in order to ensure the safety and security of information. Just as formal logical methods have proved useful in cryptographic protocol verification, we argue that logical models of belief change can play an important role in reasoning about the security of social networks.

References

[AGM85] Alchourrón, C., Gärdenfors, P., Makinson, D.: On the logic of theory change: partial meet functions for contraction and revision. J. Symb. Log. **50**(2), 510–530 (1985)

[BAN90] Burrows, M., Abadi, M., Needham, R.: A logic of authentication. ACM Trans. Comput. Syst. **8**(1), 18–36 (1990)

[BH17] Boyarinov, K., Hunter, A.: Security and trust for surveillance cameras. In: IEEE Conference on Communications and Network Security (2017)

[Dal88] Dalal, M.: Investigations into a theory of knowledge base revision. In: Proceedings of the National Conference on Artificial Intelligence (AAAI 1988), pp. 475–479 (1988)

[DGM+16] Dong, X.L., Gabrilovich, E., Murphy, K., Dang, V., Horn, W., Lugaresi, C., Sun, S., Zhang, W.: Knowledge-based trust: estimating the trustworthiness of web sources. IEEE Data. Eng. Bull. **39**(2), 106–117 (2016)

[FH99] Fermé, E., Hansson, S.O.: Selective revision. Stud. Logica **63**(3), 331–342 (1999)

[HB15] Hunter, A., Booth, R.: Trust-sensitive belief revision. In: Proceedings of the International Joint Conference on Artificial Intelligence (IJCAI), pp. 3062–3068 (2015)

[HD07] Hunter, A., Delgrande, J.P.: Belief change and cryptographic protocol verification. In: Proceedings of the Twenty-Second AAAI Conference on Artificial Intelligence, 22–26 July 2007, Vancouver, British Columbia, Canada, pp. 427–433 (2007)

[HJS06] Huynh, T.D., Jennings, N.R., Shadbolt, N.R.: An integrated trust and reputation model for open multi-agent systems. Auton. Agents Multi Agent Syst. **13**(2), 119–154 (2006)

[JHP06] Jøsang, A., Hayward, R., Pope, S.: Trust network analysis with subjective logic. In: Computer Science 2006, Twenty-Nineth Australasian Computer Science Conference (ACSC 2006), Hobart, Tasmania, Australia, 16–19 January 2006, pp. 85–94 (2006)

[KI03] Kern-Isberner, G. (ed.): Conditionals in Nonmonotonic Reasoning and Belief Revision. LNCS (LNAI), vol. 2087. Springer, Heidelberg (2001). https://doi.org/10.1007/3-540-44600-1

[KM92] Katsuno, H., Mendelzon, A.O.: Propositional knowledge base revision and minimal change. Artif. Intell. **52**(2), 263–294 (1992)

[RKK07] Ruohomaa, S., Kutvonen, L., Koutrouli, E.: Reputation management survey. In: Proceedings of the Second International Conference on Availability, Reliability and Security, ARES 2007, The International Dependability Conference - Bridging Theory and Practice, 10–13 April 2007, Vienna, Austria, pp. 103–111 (2007)

[SAW09] Salehi-Abari, A., White, T.: Towards con-resistant trust models for distributed agent systems. IJCAI **9**, 272–277 (2009)

[SHKW14] Sless, L., Hazon, N., Kraus, S., Wooldridge, M.: Forming coalitions and facilitating relationships for completing tasks in social networks. In: International conference on Autonomous Agents and Multi-Agent Systems, AAMAS 2014, Paris, France, 5–9 May 2014, pp. 261–268 (2014)

[SNP13] Sherchan, W., Nepal, S., Paris, C.: A survey of trust in social networks. ACM Comput. Surv. **45**(4), 47:1–47:33 (2013)

[vB07] van Benthem, J.: Dynamic logic for belief revision. J. Appl. Non Class. Log. **17**(2), 129–155 (2007)

[YCN+10] Yao, J., Chen, S., Nepal, S., Levy, D., Zic, J.: Truststore: making amazon S3 trustworthy with services composition. In: 10th IEEE/ACM International Conference on Cluster, Cloud and Grid Computing, CCGrid 2010, 17–20 May 2010, Melbourne, Victoria, Australia, pp. 600–605 (2010)

[YGL13] Yang, X., Guo, Y., Liu, Y.: Bayesian-inference-based recommendation in online social networks. IEEE Trans. Parallel Distrib. Syst. **24**(4), 642–651 (2013)

[YSS04] Yu, B., Singh, M.P., Sycara, K.: Developing trust in large-scale peer-to-peer systems. In: IEEE First Symposium on Multi-Agent Security and Survivability, pp. 1–10 (2004)

[ZHO09] Zuo, Y., Hu, W.-C., O'Keefe, T.: Trust computing for social networking. In: Sixth International Conference on Information Technology: New Generations, ITNG 2009, Las Vegas, Nevada, 27–29 April 2009, pp. 1534–1539 (2009)

An Effective Authentication for Client Application Using ARM TrustZone

Hang Jiang[1], Rui Chang[1(✉)], Lu Ren[1], Weiyu Dong[1], Liehui Jiang[1],
and Shuiqiao Yang[2]

[1] State Key Laboratory of Mathematic Engineering and Advanced Computing,
Zhengzhou, China
crix1021@meac-skl.cn
[2] School of Information Technology, Deakin University, Geelong, Australia

Abstract. Owing to lack of authentication for client application (CA), traditional protection mechanism based on ARM TrustZone may lead to the sensitive data leakage within trusted execution environment (TEE). Furthermore, session resources will be occupied by malicious CA due to the design drawback for session mechanism between CA and trusted application (TA). Therefore, attackers can initiate a request to read the data stored in secure world or launch DoS attack by forging malicious CA. In order to address the authentication problems, this paper proposes a CA authentication scheme using ARM TrustZone. When CA establishes a session with trusted application, a CA authentication will be executed in TEE to prevent sensitive data from being accessed by malicious. At the same time, TA closes the session and releases occupied resources. The proposed authentication scheme is implemented on simulation platform built by QEMU and OP-TEE. The experimental results show that the proposed scheme can detect the content change of CA, avoid sensitive data leakage and prevent DoS attack.

Keywords: ARM TrustZone · Trusted execution environment
Identity authentication

1 Introduction

With the development of Internet and mobile terminal technology, smart phones and Internet of Things have integrated into human life. However, the technologies bring potential security threats when we enjoy the convenience of them. They provide a wealth of functionality as well as an opportunity for information leakage and malicious. Recent researches show that the overall trend of sensitive information leakage is increasing year by year. The security of mobile terminals has caused widespread concerns.

Constructing trusted execution environment based on ARM TrustZone provides an effective way to protect sensitive data. At present, researchers have constructed several trusted execution environment (TEE) and made a large amount of trusted applications (TA) using TrustZone hardware and software isolation technology. The protected objects by isolation technology can be divided into two categories. The one is to protect

J. K. Liu and P. Samarati (Eds.): ISPEC 2017, LNCS 10701, pp. 802–813, 2017.
https://doi.org/10.1007/978-3-319-72359-4_50

sensitive data and secure applications in secure domain. Yang [1] et al. presented a fingerprint identification in TEE and encrypted the fingerprint data in safe area to prevent the data theft and malicious damage. Zhang [2] et al. utilized TrustZone and Cache-as-RAM technology to build CaSE, which can prevent software attacks and hardware memory disclosure attacks effectively. The other is to protect the normal kernel in unsecure domain. SPROBES [3] and TIMA [4] protected the kernel from injecting malicious code through running an application in TEE to detect the integrity and control flow of kernel.

However, the potential malicious attacks on CA will cause data leakage. Generally, the security service request is initiated by client application (CA). After receiving the service request, the processor switches to secure world and performs the relevant TA, then it returns results and switches to normal world. TAs and data stored in secure world are all encrypted and decrypted before execution, which can protect the integrity and confidentiality effectively. Nevertheless, CAs are easy to be attacked. Shen [5] found vulnerabilities that are able to execute arbitrarily code in secure world using a CA in normal world. After reading the CA image, attackers can analyze the image by reversing engineering and falsifying service request, then access the data in secure world. Attackers can also launch DoS attack, so legitimate requests cannot be responded.

In view of above security problems, this paper analyzes the implementation of security service execution in detail, and proposes a CA identity authentication scheme based on ARM TrustZone. The rest of the paper is organized as follows. Section 2 reviews the TrustZone technology, OP-TEE and SHA-1 algorithm. Section 3 describes the threat model and assumptions. Design and implementation of identify authentication in secure world are shown in Sect. 4. Section 5 presents the evaluation results and security analysis. Finally, Sect. 6 discusses related work, and Sect. 7 concludes.

The main contributions of this paper are:

- We propose a CA identity authentication schema based on ARM TrustZone to detect the legitimacy of CA which initiates a service request.
- We design and implement the scheme, make several experiments on the simulation platform built by QEMU and OP-TEE, and present the experimental process and evaluation results.

2 Background

To protect the security of data and application, the researchers take a variety of security measures on mobile terminals, such as access control, date encryption, and run-time isolation mechanism. However, numerous attack cases and system vulnerabilities indicate that the measures cannot completely guarantee the security of sensitive data. Open Mobile Terminal Platform (OMTP) first defined the TEE in their standard. In July 2010, GlobalPlatform first announced their own TEE standardization, including client API, TEE internal API and TEE systems Architecture, which ensures integrity and confidentiality of applications and data with an isolated execution environment. ARM released TrustZone technology, which provided a practical way of TEE hardware implementation. OP-TEE is one of most active open source framework for the TEE using ARM TrustZone technology, which is maintained by Linaro.

2.1 TrustZone Technology

TrustZone technology provides a system level security solution [6], which is used to construct isolated execution environment preventing against software attacks and low-level hardware attacks. TrustZone divides the software and hardware resources of the system into two worlds (the normal world and the secure world). The architecture is shown in Fig. 1.

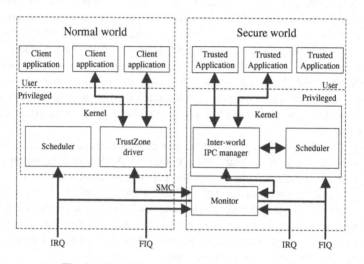

Fig. 1. The TEE architecture based on TrustZone

As shown in Fig. 1, the secure world runs secure operating system, TAs and stores sensitive data. The normal world runs common operating systems and CAs, such as Android and Linux. The hardware isolation technology separates the two worlds and makes the resources in secure world cannot be accessed by normal world components. At the same time, ARM introduces a new processor mode (monitor mode) to switch the states of the two worlds. The non-secure (NS) bit in security configuration register of cp15 coprocessor indicates the world in which current processor running. When the NS bit is clear, it means the processor runs in secure world. When the NS bit is set, the processor runs in normal world. Once the normal world needs switch to secure world, the processor enters the monitor mode firstly by secure monitor call (SMC) or interrupt. Then, the code running in monitor mode saves the context of normal world and changes the value of NS bit to switch to secure world. The secure world adopts the similar method to enter normal world. If a CA running in normal world requires security services, the processor will switch to secure world and perform the corresponding security service, and then return the result to normal world.

2.2   OP-TEE

OP-TEE [7] is an open source architecture for TEE based on TrustZone technology, which provides a clear opportunity to defragment the security ecosystem on ARM-based chipsets. Ever since the Linaro Security Working Group was formed in 2013, Linaro and ST engineers [8] have worked together to revamp the code base, to make it portable, and to remove any legacy or ST-specific code.

OP-TEE consists of three components: the normal world client APIs, a Linux kernel TEE device driver and the Trusted OS. The TEE client APIs and TEE internal APIs meet the standard of GlobalPlatform APIs specifications. The Trusted OS part is under a BSD license, so that it can be modified without any obligation to disclose the modifications. The abstraction of platform-specific parts in such a way that it should be fairly easy to port OP-TEE in laboratory or incorporate it in products from different vendors.

2.3   SHA-1

SHA-1 is a digital signature algorithm. For messages of which the length is less than 2^{64} bits, SHA-1 will generate a 160-bit (20-byte) message digest. Any change in the input messages, even only 1 bit, will produce a significant change in the hash value. Two diffident messages cannot produce the same hash value by SHA-1. Based on the above characteristics, SHA-1 is widely used in cryptography and data integrity verification, and it is an important component of security applications and protocols, such as SSL, SSH and IPsec.

3   Threat Model and Assumptions

3.1   Threat Mode

In a TEE based on TrustZone, the CA sends parameters such as Universally Unique Identifier (UUID) and commands to the secure world via SMC instruction when it requests a security service. Threat model of data leakage is described in Fig. 2.

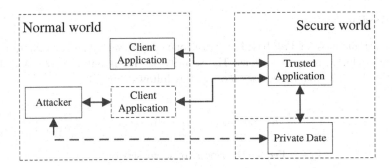

Fig. 2. Threat model of data leakage

As shown in Fig. 2, the operating system in secure world finds and loads the corresponding TA, then creates a session between CA and TA. TA performs the relevant service according to the delivered commands, and releases the session in the end. Encrypted and stored in secure world, TA image will be verified before running. Moreover, TA is protected by isolation provided by TrustZone at run time, so it is difficult to attack TA.

However, CA runs in normal world, and it is stored in external memory. Attackers can read CA image by exploiting system vulnerabilities and other attacks. As described in Fig. 2, after reading CA image, attackers could obtain the UUID of TA through static analysis, and construct malicious program to initiate a security service request. When TA accepts the service request, it performs security-sensitive operation and causes data leakage, such as reads key and personal privacy data.

In addition, attackers can also launch DoS attacks. After the security service request finishes, the session created by the service request should be released. Malicious CA do not release the session and take up it for a long time. Nevertheless, the session resources of secure world are limited. If malicious CA initiates a large number of session requests, it will affect the process scheduling of secure operating system and exhaust session resources, which causes legitimate requests not to be answered.

3.2 Assumptions

The proposed solution is aimed to validate CA which prevents the attacker from performing the following attack.

- Data leakage in normal world
- DoS attacks caused by malicious CA

Therefore, we assume that the current state of runtime system is security. The device have adopted secure boot and other measures to guarantee the security of runtime system. TA will read and modify sensitive data when security services execute. Hence, the assumption is that TA is trusted, and there is no data leakage vulnerability.

4 Design and Implementation

4.1 Design

At present, the most of TEE based on TrustZone comply with the GlobalPlatform TEE System Architecture specifications. The security service is initiated by CA and executed by TA. The main processes are listed as follows (Fig. 3).

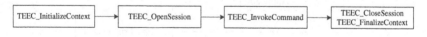

Fig. 3. The process of secure services

Step 1. CA invokes the *TEEC_InitializeContext* function to initialize the *TEEC_Context* variable. The variable is used to establish a link between CA and TEE.

Step 2. CA invokes the *TEEC_OpenSession* function to open a session with TA. The session is used to transfer parameter between CA and TA. The secure operating system finds and loads TA which is determined by UUID.

Step 3. CA executes the *TEEC_InvokeCommand* and instructs TA to perform the specified operation through the session.

Step 4. CA executes the *TEEC_CloseSession* and *TEEC_FinalizeContext* to release session and the *TEEC_Context* variable.

CA runs in normal world which is not secure enough. If CA authentication is performed in normal world, the validated result will be invalid. As a result, the entire process of authentication will be exposed to the attacker. Therefore, the authentication process should be performed in a secure environment, and TEE satisfies the requirements of the environment. If CA authentication is performed within TEE, the validated result will be valid and credible.

4.2   Implementation of Identify Authentication

The process of authentication is shown in Fig. 4.

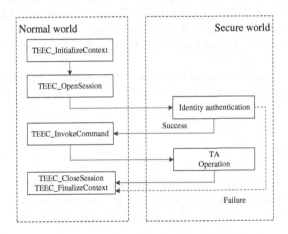

Fig. 4. The process of authentication

In the process of requesting a security service, *TEEC_InitializeContext* and *TEEC_OpenSession* are initiated by CA for establishing contacts between CA and TEE, and transfer parameters to TA. At this time, the data interaction is unidirectional (from CA to TA). In fact, it is no possibility of leaking data stored in secure world. However, CA can inform TA through the *TEEC_InvokeCommand* to perform the specified operation and write the result to the shared memory. On the contrary, the data exchange is bidirectional with the possibility of data leakage. Applications running in two worlds can access the shared memory area. If malicious CA sends an illegal *TEEC_InvokeCommand* instruction to TA, TA will write secure sensitive data to the shared memory. In order to avoid data leakage in secure world, CA needs to be verified to ensure legality before TA is executed.

In general, the session resource is released after security service requested by CA. If the malicious CA from attackers holds the session resource for a long time, it will exhaust resources of secure world. In order to reduce the impact on the performance of normal world, the device usually allocates a smaller memory area for secure world. When CA requests a security service, the secure operating system loads the corresponding TA. If multiple TAs are loaded in the meantime, the performance of secure world will be affected seriously and the legal security service request will not be responded. Once the illegal CA is detected, the resources will be released promptly.

4.3   Validation

After establishing the session between CA and TA, the TrustZone driver registers the CA image as a shared file which can be accessed by TA. In order to verify the legitimacy of CA, the pre-calculated hash value of CA image is stored in TEE, which is named *hash_correct*. The process of authentication is divided into two steps. In the first step, the authentication program reads CA image and makes use of SHA-1 algorithm to calculate its hash value, which is named *hash_calculated*. In the second step, the program reads *hash_correct* and compares it with *hash_calculated*. If the validation of authentication succeeds, the session between CA and TA will continue to perform the specified operation. If the validation of authentication fails, the session will be closed to prevent the malicious CA from taking over the resources for a long time and affecting other security service requests.

If a new CA is installed in the normal world, its hash will be calculated and stored in the secure world by constructing authentication table and the corresponding update module.

5   Evaluation

We build a simulation trusted execution environment using QEMU and OP-TEE, and implement the identify authentication for CA. It simulates Cortex-A15 processor, has Linux 4.9.0 kernel in normal world, and runs OP-TEE OS 2.3.0 in secure world.

5.1   Experiment Evaluation

In order to verify the feasibility and effectiveness of the authentication scheme, we design the following experiments. According to comparing Experiment 1 with Experiment 2, it is proved that the proposed scheme provides secure service for legitimate CA. Moreover, it is proved that the scheme refuses the secure service requests initiated by malicious CA through comparing Experiment 2 with Experiment 3.

Experiment 1. The test program which is divided into CA and TA parts, runs in normal world and secure world respectively. CA establishes a session with TA through a security service request. TA accepts the request to read the data *hello world* which is stored in secure world, and sends it to CA. Then CA prints the data in terminal. The experimental results are shown in Figs. 5 and 6.

```
root@Vexpress:/bin mytest
InitializeContext success
OpenSession success
InvokeCommand success
hello world
CloseSession success
FinalizeSession success
root@Vexpress:/bin
```

Fig. 5. The result presentation of normal world in experiment 1

```
DEBUG:    [0x0] TEE-CORE:tee_ta_init_pseudo_ta_session:259:     Lookup for pseudo TA eb
b6f4b5-7e33-4ad2-9802-e64f2a7cc20c
DEBUG:    [0x0] TEE-CORE:tee_ta_init_user_ta_session:610: Load user TA ebb6f4b5-7e33-4
ad2-9802-e64f2a7cc20c
DEBUG:    [0x0] TEE-CORE:ta_load:316: ELF load address 0x101000
FLOW:     USER-TA: tee_user_mem_alloc:343: Allocate: link:[0x1205e0], buf:[0x1205f0:16
]
MESSAGE: USER-TA: CMD_ID = 2
FLOW:     USER-TA: tee_user_mem_alloc:343: Allocate: link:[0x120580], buf:[0x120590:68
]
MESSAGE: USER-TA: The return value is :hello world
DEBUG:    [0x0] TEE-CORE:tee_ta_close_session:378: tee_ta_close_session(0xe073ed0)
DEBUG:    [0x0] TEE-CORE:tee_ta_close_session:397:     ... Destroy session
FLOW:     USER-TA: tee_user_mem_free:442: Free: link:[0x1205e0], buf:[0x1205f0:16]
DEBUG:    [0x0] TEE-CORE:tee_ta_close_session:423:     ... Destroy TA ctx
```

Fig. 6. The result presentation of secure world in experiment 1

As shown in Figs. 5 and 6, the secure world kernel begins to find and load the corresponding TA after receiving the request sent by CA. Then, TA accepts the arguments transferred by *TEEC_InvokeCommand* to read the data hello world and return it to CA. In this experiment, TA do not verify the legitimacy of CA. In other words, once TA receives the request, it will read and return the data, whatever the legitimacy of CA is. As a result, security of sensitive data is not guaranteed. If CA is tampered, the secure service has another results.

Experiment 2. CA authentication is added in secure world based on experiment 1. The hash value of CA is pre-calculated and stored in the security domain. The experimental results are shown in Figs. 7 and 8.

```
root@Vexpress:/bin mytest
InitializeContext success
OpenSession success
InvokeCommand success
hello world
CloseSession success
FinalizeSession success
root@Vexpress:/bin
```

Fig. 7. The result presentation of normal world in experiment 2

```
FLOW:     USER-TA: tee_user_mem_alloc:343: Allocate: link:[0x120580], buf:[0x120590:68
]
MESSAGE: USER-TA: Correct hash value is:32400041c6e8c1196a96c1c8935043cdadfd18f8
MESSAGE: USER-TA: Hash value calculated is:32400041c6e8c1196a96c1c8935043cdadfd18f8
MESSAGE: USER-TA: this is a legitimate image
MESSAGE: USER-TA: The return value is :hello world
DEBUG:   [0x0] TEE-CORE:tee_ta_close_session:378: tee_ta_close_session(0xe073e10)
DEBUG:   [0x0] TEE-CORE:tee_ta_close_session:397:    ... Destroy session
FLOW:     USER-TA: tee_user_mem_free:442: Free: link:[0x1205e0], buf:[0x1205f0:16]
DEBUG:   [0x0] TEE-CORE:tee_ta_close_session:423:    ... Destroy TA ctx
```

Fig. 8. The result presentation of secure world in experiment 2

As shown in Figs. 7 and 8, TA authenticates CA by calculating and comparing hash values before reading data. After the validation of authentication succeed, TA performs the subsequent operations.

Experiment 3. On the foundation of experiment 2, the CA image is modified to simulate an attack. The results of experiment are shown in Figs. 9 and 10.

```
root@Vexpress:/bin mytest
InitializeContext success
OpenSession success
this is an illegitimate image
CloseSession success
FinalizeSession success
root@Vexpress:/bin
```

Fig. 9. The result presentation of normal world in experiment 3

```
FLOW:     USER-TA: tee_user_mem_alloc:343: Allocate: link:[0x120580], buf:[0x120590:68
]
MESSAGE: USER-TA: Correct hash value is:32400041c6e8c1196a96c1c8935043cdadfd18f8
MESSAGE: USER-TA: Hash value calculated is:c79b9838dd6af2ed3b2df0544e8ca2d6778c411c
MESSAGE: USER-TA: this is an illegitimate image
MESSAGE: USER-TA: The return value is :NULL
DEBUG:   [0x0] TEE-CORE:tee_ta_close_session:378: tee_ta_close_session(0xe073e10)
DEBUG:   [0x0] TEE-CORE:tee_ta_close_session:397:    ... Destroy session
FLOW:     USER-TA: tee_user_mem_free:442: Free: link:[0x1205e0], buf:[0x1205f0:16]
DEBUG:   [0x0] TEE-CORE:tee_ta_close_session:423:    ... Destroy TA ctx
```

Fig. 10. The result presentation of secure world in experiment 3

Due to the modified CA image, the validation of authentication fails. As shown in Figs. 9 and 10, CA cannot read the data stored in secure world. Then TA releases resources (e.g., session, memory) to prevent occupied session resources.

As showed in Table 1, the proposed CA authentication scheme can detect the integrity of CA effectively. In the scheme, TA provides security services for legitimate CA, and refuses the request initiated by malicious CA which is forged or tampered with by attackers. Moreover, it releases the occupied resources. In consequence, the scheme is feasible and effective.

Table 1. Comparison experimental results

Experiment	Description	Tampered	Authentication	Legitimacy	Result
1	Normal CA	✗	✗	Unknown	Secure service
		✓	✗	Unknown	Unknown service
2	Normal CA with authentication	✗	✓	✓	Secure service
3	Malicious CA	✓	✓	✗	Refuse

5.2 Security Analysis

The proposed authentication scheme detects whether the CA image is modified by calculating and comparing its hash value. We analyze the security of the proposed scheme in the following three aspects.

The authentication program runs in secure world and is isolated from normal world. It is protected by TrustZone. It means that the process of authentication is invisible for CA, and thus malicious CA cannot access the authentication. TA determines to maintain the session for security services or release resources according to the verification results. Therefore, the process of authentication is secure.

In order to calculate the hash, the CA image is registered as a shared file by TrustZone driver. The TrustZone driver runs at the privilege level of the normal world system. Because of the effective protection by the secure kernel, the TrustZone driver is secure. In fact, the hash of the CA image calculated by the authentication program initiates the secure service request. As a result, the attacker will not use a legitimate CA image to replace the malicious one when the TrustZone driver registers the shared file.

The hash value calculated by SHA-1 is unique and irreversible. Two images do not have the same hash value. Even if the attacker modified only one bit of CA image, the hash value will have a huge change. Because the hash value of legitimate CA image is encrypted and stored in secure memory, malicious CA cannot read and modify it. Therefore, the algorithm of authentication is secure.

6 Related Work

A series of trusted operating systems have been developed based on TrustZone technology, such as T6, OP-TEE, ANDIX OS [9] and so on. TrustICE [10] and other solutions enhance the runtime security of TA. Johannes [11] et al. provided a comprehensive open-source software environment for experiments with ARM TrustZone, based on the foundations of the well-known open source QEMU platform emulator. The above works lay the foundation for the proposal.

Roland [12] et al. introduced a conceptual model for user interaction with TEE. The model could be used to analyze the security of the interaction between the user and the TEE. They also presented the problem of how the users could ascertain that they were really dealing with a trusted application on a display which was shared between trusted and untrussed applications. In order to protect FIDO (fast identity online) from malicious attack, Rob [13] introduced TrustZone which is provided the hardware isolation to secure FIDO based authentication.

Jang [14] et al. presented a method for enhancing session security in SeCReT. They established a secure communication channel by encrypting the message exchanged between CA and TA, so that an attacker could not forge a security service request to access data within secure world. However, a security service request usually involves multiple processor state transitions and parameter passing, which can cause more performance overhead. Zhao [15] et al. proposed a method for CA authentication. They built an IOD module to calculate the hash value of CA in normal world and an IAM module for validation in secure world. Their method is vulnerable to be attacked because the security protection in normal world is less effective.

In addition, Zhao [16] et al. proposed the TSSP to solve the DoS attack caused by malicious CA occupying session resources for a long time. They went against DoS attacks by calculating the priority of sessions in waiting queue and the residual value of sessions in execute queue, which ensured important sessions execution. Although their method guaranteed high priority sessions to be executed, it did not release the session resources occupied by malicious CA. The system would cause more performance overhead if the resources were not released for a long time.

7 Conclusion

In this paper, we propose a CA authentication scheme based on TEE to solve the problems of sensitive data leakage and the DoS attack caused by malicious CA. We design and implement the scheme in a simulation experiment environment based on QEMU and OP-TEE. The experimental results show that the identify authentication can prevent malicious CA reading sensitive data in secure world through service requests, and release the occupied resources after rejecting the requests. Therefore, the proposed scheme can detect the content change of CA, avoid sensitive data leakage and prevent DoS attack. As a result, our proposed scheme could effectively improve the security level for using the mobile terminals and Internet of Things.

Acknowledgment. Thanks to project supported by the National Natural Science Foundation of China (No. 61572516).

References

1. Yang, X., Liu, Z., Lei, H., et al.: Research and implementation of fingerprint identification security technology based on ARM TrustZone. Comput. Sci. **43**(7), 147–152 (2016)
2. Zhang, N., Sun, K., Lou, W., et al.: CaSE: cache-assisted secure execution on ARM processors. In: 2016 IEEE Symposium on Security and Privacy, pp. 72–90. IEEE, San Jose (2016)

3. Ge, X., Vijayakumar, H., Jaeger, T.: Sprobes: enforcing kernel code integrity on the TrustZone architecture. Comput. Sci. **25**(6), 1793–1795 (2014)
4. Wool, A., Wool, A.: Secure containers in Android: the Samsung KNOX case study. In: The Workshop on Security and Privacy in Smartphones and Mobile Devices, pp. 3–12. ACM, Vienna (2016)
5. Shen, D.: Exploiting Trustzone on Android. Black Hat USA Briefings. https://www. blackhat.com/docs/us-15/materials/us-15-Shen-Attacking-Your-Trusted-CoreExploiting-Trustzone-On-Android-wp.pdf
6. ARM Limited.: ARM Security Technology: Building a Secure System using TrustZone® Technology
7. OP-TEE. https://github.com/OP-TEE/optee_os. Accessed 1 Oct 2017
8. Linaro. https://www.linaro.org/blog/core-dump/op-tee-open-source-security-mass-market/
9. Fitzek, A., Achleitner, F., Winter, J., et al.: The ANDIX research OS — ARM TrustZone meets industrial control systems security. In: 13th International Conference on Industrial Informatics, pp. 88–93. IEEE, Cambridge (2015)
10. Sun, H., Sun, K., Wang, Y., et al.: TrustICE: hardware-assisted isolated computing environments on mobile devices. In: 15th IEEE/IFIP International Conference on Dependable Systems and Networks, pp. 367–378. IEEE, Rio de Janeiro (2015)
11. Winter, J., Wiegele, P., Pirker, M., Tögl, R.: A flexible software development and emulation framework for ARM TrustZone. In: Chen, L., Yung, M., Zhu, L. (eds.) INTRUST 2011. LNCS, vol. 7222, pp. 1–15. Springer, Heidelberg (2012). https://doi.org/10.1007/978-3-642-32298-3_1
12. Rijswijk-Deij, R.V., Poll, E.: Using trusted execution environments in two-factor authentication: comparing approaches. Open Identity Summit, pp. 387–393 (2013)
13. Coombs, R: Securing the future of authentication with ARM TrustZone-based trusted execution environment and fast identity online (FIDO). ARM White paper (2015)
14. Jang, J., Kong, S., Kim, M., et al.: SeCReT: secure channel between rich execution environment and trusted execution environment. In: Network and Distributed System Security Symposium (2015)
15. Zhao, X., Yu, Q., et al.: A private user data protection mechanism in TrustZone architecture based on identity authentication. Tsinghua Sci. Technol. **22**(2), 218–225 (2017)
16. Zhao, B., Ma, J., Xiao, Y., et al.: TSSP: a session scheduling method in TrustZone architecture. Adv. Eng. Sci. **49**(1), 151–158 (2017)

Generic Framework for Attribute-Based Group Signature

Veronika Kuchta$^{(\boxtimes)}$, Gaurav Sharma, Rajeev Anand Sahu,
and Olivier Markowitch

Universite Libre de Bruxelles, Brussels, Belgium
vkuchta@ulb.ac.be

Abstract. We first formalise a generic architecture for attribute-based signatures (ABS). Further we expand the design to the generic framework of an attribute-based group signature (ABGS), combining our generic structure of ABS with the efficient generic design of group signature proposed by Bellare et al. in Eurocrypt 2003. We also analyse security of the proposed constructions following the most standard and strong proof system, the Non-Interactive Zero Knowledge (NIZK) arguments. We emphasise that meanwhile in the process, we first achieve an attribute-based instantiation of the generic group signature scheme given by Bellare et al. and we provide a generic structure of ABGS on that block which has applications in cloud security and other cryptographic problems.

1 Introduction

In general, digital signature is a cryptographic primitive to provide signer's authentication. But there may be situations where signer's anonymity is desired for example, in anonymous electronic transaction system [24], anonymous key exchange protocol [39] etc. There have been constructions to achieve anonymity of the signer directly from the signature. The well known approaches are ring signature, group signature and blind signature. The more recent alternative attribute-based signature (ABS) [33,34] is attracting researchers due to its functionality. Their construction uses functionality of bilinear pairings but their most practical scheme is only proven secure in the generic group model. They envision their construction to readily use in multi-authority settings. In few of the extensions of ABS, attribute-based group signature (ABGS) is one of the most important and useful primitives currently being studied. In this paper, we aim to provide a generic frame to design an ABGS.

Attribute-Based Signatures. Attribute-based signature (ABS) is an extended alternative to identity-based signatures (IBS) having a set of attributes and satisfying a specific predicate. The anonymity of identity or attributes is the preliminary objective of this signature. Instead of the identity, users are associated (and specified) with certain attributes in ABS with compare to the IBS. The importance of attributes was first realized to design attribute-based encryption (ABE)

© Springer International Publishing AG 2017
J. K. Liu and P. Samarati (Eds.): ISPEC 2017, LNCS 10701, pp. 814–834, 2017.
https://doi.org/10.1007/978-3-319-72359-4_51

to provide fine-grained access control over the encrypted data. Since the introduction of ABE [20], various proposals [4,7,9,11] have been formalized exploring different properties and advantages of ABE.

Other signature schemes have been combined to achieve the advantage of ABS with extended functionality for example attribute-based group signatures [28] and attribute-based ring signature [31] fulfill basic objectives of the underlying signature protocol with properties of ABS which yield the compact signature suitable for specific application. The proof of security in standard model is observed to be more realistic than that in random oracle. In [36] Okamoto and Takashima have formalized security setup for an ABS in the standard model. Attributes in their scheme are constrained to follow non-monotone predicates. Their scheme is based on dual pairing vector spaces and they follow the functional encryption proof technique of [30]. A threshold variation of the similar concept is presented in [38]. The threshold ABS restricts the signer to maintain a threshold number of attributes in common with the verification set of attributes. An additional featured ABS in standard model was proposed in [18] with full revocability. None of these submissions offer constant-sized signatures and usually, they all grow linearly in the number of attributes involved in the signing predicate. The first contribution with constant-sized signatures was given in [23].

Group Signatures. A group signature scheme allows an authorized member of a group to anonymously sign messages on behalf of the group. There is a group manager who can revoke the identity of the signer in case of misuse or conflict. The group manager is the only authority with this privilege. We also distinguish between static group signatures and dynamic group signatures. In a static group signature the set of members is frozen after the setup phase, whereas in the dynamic group signature, the group members can join even after the setup phase, and the setup is updated dynamically. Standard generic structures of group signature are presented by Bellare et al. in [5,6]. In [5] they formalized a generic framework of group signature addressing various properties of group signature in more standard and well defined way. They start with the *static* aspect of the group signature and initiate the idea of partially dynamic groups and fully dynamic groups. Later they proposed the generic structure of a *fully dynamic* group signature in [6]. The basic structure [6] requires a non-interactive zero knowledge (NIZK) proof system between the prover and the verifier during the signature protocol to address the verifier's witness on the signer's commitment.

The idea of group signature was introduced by Chaum and Van Heyst [15]. Ateniese et al. [3] presented an efficient and provably collision-resistant group signature scheme. In 2003, Bellare et al. [5] identified the security requirements of group signature and presented their, popularly known BMW (Bellare, Micciancio and Warinschi) security model. The two well accepted security properties for group signatures, full traceability and full anonymity were presented in this paper. Boneh et al. [10] designed short signatures in the random oracle model, using a variant of the security definition of BMW model. Security models of some well structured group signatures [13,32] are also motivated by the BMW model [5]. In these schemes, the adversary is restricted to ask queries on the tracing of group signatures. Another efficient group signature scheme is proposed by Camenisch et al. [14] using bilinear maps. Later, Bellare et al. [6] escalated the security strength to include the group members dynamically.

Various proof techniques have been followed in different proposals of group signature. Kiayias and Yung [29] have presented a scheme which is scalable and allows dynamic adversarial joins. Security of their scheme was proved in random oracle model. Ateniese et al. [2] have proved security of their group signature in standard model. Their scheme is based on interactive assumptions. Boyen et al. [12] have followed the Groth-Ostrovsky-Sahai NIZK proof system [22], and have achieved crucial security properties viz. anonymity. In the initial proposals of group signature, the size of signature was directly dependent (linear in relation) on the number of group members. In 2008, Zhang et al. [40] presented an identity-based group signature scheme based on pairing. Size of their signature is independent of the size of group members. The group signature construction of Cheng et al. [16] has the advantages of concurrent join, immediate revocation, easy tracing and short signature length.

Attribute-Based Group Signatures. Attribute-based group signature (ABGS) is generated by a member of the group possessing certain attributes. The verifier can easily determine the role of the signer within the group. This approach is different than the usual group signatures because the signer needs to prove the ownership of certain attributes or properties. The ABGS was introduced in [28], though their primitive provides only the *anonymity* of the signer. Also, the algorithm reveals the attributes of the signer which satisfy the predicate. In a further version [27] they added the revocation property. For the practical application it is also desired to hide the attributes, used by the signer, from the verifier to achieve full anonymity. To achieve this property an ABGS scheme based on oblivious signature-based envelope (OSBE) protocol was proposed in [37]. In [17] a dynamic ABGS scheme was presented which can avoid the reissuing of attribute certificates and eliminates the pairing ratio increment depending on the number of attributes. They also discussed the application of ABGS in anonymous survey for collection of attribute statistics. Signature size is an important issue to be considered for implementation. Ali et al. [1] have suggested a constant signature sized ABGS scheme. Their scheme is independent of the number of attributes and secured in standard model. Though, there are a few constructions of the ABGS, but yet the existing literature does not cover any generic structure of ABGS for dynamic entry of the signers. In this paper, we try to put forward such a construction.

Our Contribution. We first formalize a generic architecture for ABS using the CCA-secure key encapsulation mechanism of [6] as building blocks. Further we expand the design to the generic framework of an ABGS, combining our generic structure of ABS with the efficient generic design of group signature proposed by Bellare et al. [5] in Eurocrypt 2003. Meanwhile in the process, we first achieve an attribute-based instantiation of the generic group signature scheme [5] and then construct the generic structure of our ABGS on that block. We emphasize that obtaining an attribute-based instantiation of the generic group signature framework of [5] is itself a topic of interest since long and to the best of our knowledge our work provides first such instantiation. Furthermore, our generic ABGS system includes the dynamic setup of group members. Interestingly, unlike the all elementary constructions of dynamic group signature, our approach to dynamic ABGS does not use any access tree or credential bundle. We also analyse security of the proposed constructions following the most standard and strong proof system, the Non-Interactive Zero Knowledge (NIZK) protocol. Moreover, in contrast to the Maji's generic scheme of ABS [33,34] we achieve existential unforgeability of our scheme.

Applications. An attribute-based group signature has the following crucial applications which we propose in the following paragraphs:

Attribute-Based Messaging (ABM): As discussed in [34], the ABS schemes are useful for anonymous authentication of the sender of the attribute-based message [8]. Also, it has been described in [34] that the available classical techniques of ring signature, group signature, mesh signature are not adequate for the required security properties for such an objective. In this scenario the attribute-based signature offers desired support.

Anonymous Credential: In certain online purchase-sale activities, the merchant may want the customer to submit his/her personal details (credentials) to an external recipient (or the issuer, maybe sometimes the government). But at the same time it may be also desired that the content of these details should remain hidden from the merchant (verifier). In such circumstances, the user needs to protect his/her credentials. There have been efforts [19,25] to protect sensitive credentials in the scenarios where attributes are prime concerns. But such available schemes are either computationally expensive or can be used only when the content of certificates can be estimated. Hence, such schemes cannot be considered for the practical implementations. The attribute-based signatures following our construction can be an efficient alternate for such an objective, which offers the mechanism to convince the validity of the signature to the verifier without revealing the attributes of the signer.

Anonymous Survey: Anonymous survey is a well known practice in the electronic communication, for instance, authentication of an organizational server (which involves a group of users) before granting access to a confidential or protected resource. Approaches for such anonymous survey are proposed in [26,35] by exploiting the statistical information. For the purpose, the user sends ciphertext, encrypted with the attribute issuer's public key, to the verifier, but as it has been pointed out in [17], it is difficult to manage the statistical information for the different sets of attributes, because one attribute certificate is issued corresponding to an attribute type. It can be observed, with details in [17] that an ABGS is solution for the anonymous survey without the above difficulties.

Cloud Security: The Cloud storage services are provided by the third party hence the access to the data should be only with the legitimate user(s). Even not to the service provider. Most popular technique to achieve access control in the cloud computing is by outsourcing encrypted data over the cloud.

For the purpose, attribute-based encryption (ABE) technique has been highly suggested to be used for the encryption, due to it's functionality. But before access to the data, an authentication of the user, by the cloud server is desired. In case of group of users (in more regular situations), authentication of the appropriate user (with certain attributes) is required, specially to avoid collusion. For such authentication, ABGS offers a perfect application.

2   Preliminaries

Attribute-Based Key Encapsulation Mechanism. An attribute-based key encapsulation mechanism (AB-KEM) extends attribute-based encryption (ABE), where the ciphertext encapsulates a session key which is used to encrypt data in symmetric way.

Definition 1. *An AB-KEM consists of the following four algorithms:*

$\mathsf{Setup}(1^\lambda)$: *On input security parameter 1^λ, it outputs public parameters* param *and the master secret key* msk.

$\mathsf{ABKKeyGen}(\mathsf{param}, \mathsf{msk}, \mathbb{A})$: *On input public parameters* param, *master secret key* msk *and a set of attributes $\mathbb{A}$ it generates a corresponding secret key* $\mathsf{sk}_\mathbb{A}$.

$\mathsf{ABKEncaps}(\mathsf{param}, \Gamma)$: *On input the public parameters* param, *a predicate Γ, it generates a key* K *and an encapsulation* E_Γ *of this key.*

$\mathsf{ABKDecaps}(\mathsf{sk}_\mathbb{A}, \mathsf{E})$: *On input a secret key* $\mathsf{sk}_\mathbb{A}$ *and encapsulation* E, *it outputs either* K *or* $\perp$.

Definition 2 (ABKEM-IND-CCA Security). *The security notion of ABKEM scheme is defined for a bit $b \in \{0,1\}$ via the following experiment* $\mathsf{Exp}_{\mathcal{A}_{\mathrm{ind}},\mathrm{ABKEM}}^{\mathrm{IND-CCA}-b}$:

1. $(\mathsf{param}, \mathsf{msk}) \leftarrow \mathsf{Setup}(1^\lambda)$
2. $(\Gamma, \mathsf{state}) \leftarrow \mathcal{A}_{\mathrm{ind}}^{\mathcal{O}_{\mathrm{ABKKeyGen}}, \mathcal{O}_{\mathrm{ABKDecaps}}}(\mathsf{param})$
3. $(\mathsf{K}_1, \mathsf{E}_\Gamma^*) \leftarrow \mathsf{ABKEncaps}(\mathsf{param}, \Gamma)$
4. $\mathsf{K}_0 \leftarrow \mathcal{K}; b \xleftarrow{r} \{0,1\}$
5. $b' \leftarrow \mathcal{A}_{\mathrm{ind}}^{\mathcal{O}_{\mathrm{ABKKeyGen}}, \mathcal{O}_{\mathrm{ABKDecaps}}}(\mathsf{state}, \mathsf{K}_b, \mathsf{E}_\Gamma^*)$. *If $b = b'$, return 1, else 0.*

$\mathcal{O}_{\mathrm{ABKKeyGen}}(\mathbb{A})$: *On input an attribute set $\mathbb{A}$, such that $\Gamma(\mathbb{A}) \neq 1$ the oracle runs* $\mathsf{sk}_\mathbb{A} \leftarrow \mathsf{ABKKeyGen}(\mathsf{param}, \mathsf{msk}, \mathbb{A})$.

$\mathcal{O}_{\mathrm{ABKDecaps}}(\mathsf{E}_\Gamma, \mathbb{A})$: *On input an attribute set $\mathbb{A}$ and the encapsulation* E_Γ, *the oracle checks if $\mathsf{E}_\Gamma = \mathsf{E}_\Gamma^*$. If so it outputs $\perp$, otherwise it runs* $\mathsf{sk}_\mathbb{A} \leftarrow \mathsf{ABKKeyGen}(\mathsf{param}, \mathsf{msk}, \mathbb{A})$. *On input* $\mathsf{sk}_\mathbb{A}$, *it runs* $K \leftarrow \mathsf{ABKDecaps}(\mathsf{param}, \mathsf{sk}_\mathbb{A}, \mathsf{E}_\Gamma)$. *It outputs either* K *or* $\perp$.

An ABKEM scheme is indistinguishable against chosen-ciphertext attacks if for any PPT adversary $\mathcal{A}_{\mathrm{ind}}$ the following advantage of is negligible:

$$\mathsf{Adv}_{\mathcal{A}_{\mathrm{ind}},\mathrm{ABKEM}}^{\mathrm{IND-CCA}}(\lambda) = \left| \Pr\left[\mathsf{Exp}_{\mathcal{A}_{\mathrm{ind}},\mathrm{ABKEM}}^{\mathrm{IND-CCA}-1} = 1\right] - \Pr\left[\mathsf{Exp}_{\mathcal{A}_{\mathrm{ind}},\mathrm{ABKEM}}^{\mathrm{IND-CCA}-0} = 1\right] \right| \leq \epsilon(\lambda)$$

The ABKEM scheme has practical applications in combination with data encapsulation mechanism.

Definition 3. *A data encapsulation mechanism (DEM) consists of the following three algorithms* $\mathcal{DEM} = (\text{KeyGen}, \text{DEncaps}, \text{DDecaps})$.

$\text{DKeyGen}(1^\lambda)$: *On input a security parameter* 1^λ, *output the secret key* K.
$\text{DEncaps}(K, m)$: *On input a key* K *and a message* m, *it generates a ciphertext* C_D.
$\text{DDecaps}(C_D, K)$: *On input a key* K, *ciphertext* C_D, *it outputs either* m *or* $\perp$.

Definition 4 (DEM-IND-CCA Security). *The security notion of DEM scheme is defined for a bit* $b \in \{0, 1\}$ *via the following experiment* $\text{Exp}_{\mathcal{A}_{ind}, \text{DEM}}^{IND-CCA-b}$

1. $K \leftarrow \text{KeyGen}(1^\lambda)$
2. $(m_0, m_1, \text{state}) \leftarrow \mathcal{A}_{ind}^{\mathcal{O}DDecaps}(1^\lambda)$
3. $b \xleftarrow{r} \{0, 1\}$; $C_D^* \leftarrow \text{DEncaps}(K, m_b)$
4. $b' \leftarrow \mathcal{A}_{ind}^{\mathcal{O}ABKDecaps}(\text{state}, C_D^*)$. *If* $b = b'$, *return 1. Else return 0.*

$\mathcal{O}DDecaps(C_D)$: *On input secret key* K *and the ciphertext* C_D, *the oracle checks whether* $C_D = C_D^*$. *If so it returns* $\perp$, *otherwise it runs ABKDecaps and returns* m. *A DEM scheme is indistinguishable against chosen-ciphertext attacks if for any PPT adversary* $\mathcal{A}_{ind}^{DEM}$ *the following advantage of is negligible:*

$$\text{Adv}_{\mathcal{A}_{ind}, \text{DEM}}^{IND-CCA}(\lambda) = \left| \Pr\left[\text{Exp}_{\mathcal{A}_{ind}, \text{DEM}}^{IND-CCA-1} = 1 \right] - \Pr\left[\text{Exp}_{\mathcal{A}_{ind}, \text{DEM}}^{IND-CCA-0} = 1 \right] \right| \leq \epsilon(\lambda)$$

3   Generic Construction of Attribute-Based Signatures

In this section we provide a generic construction of attribute-based signatures employing attribute-based key encapsulation mechanism and attribute-based data encapsulation mechanism. In the following paragraph we recall the definition of the attribute-based signature scheme.

Definition 5. *An attribute-based signature (ABS) scheme consists of the following four algorithms* $\mathcal{ABS} = (\text{ABSetup}, \text{ABKeyGen}, \text{ABSign}, \text{ABVerify})$ *given an attribute universe* $\mathbb{A}$.

$\text{ABSetup}(1^\lambda, 1^n)$: *This algorithm is performed by the key generation center which on input of security parameter* 1^λ *and the number of attributes* n *generates public parameters* param *and the master secret key* msk.
$\text{ABKeyGen}(\text{param}, \text{msk}, \mathbb{A})$: *This algorithm is performed by the attribute authority which takes as input public parameters param, master secret key* msk, *user's attribute set* $\mathbb{A}$ *and generates the user's secret key* $sk_{\mathbb{A}}$ *corresponding to* $\mathbb{A}$.
$\text{ABSign}(\text{param}, sk_{\mathbb{A}}, m, \Gamma)$: *On input user's secret key* $sk_{\mathbb{A}}$, *a message* m *and a predicate* Γ *the user generates a signature* σ.
$\text{ABVerify}(\text{param}, \sigma, m, \Gamma)$: *On input* param, *message* m, *a signature* σ *and predicate* Γ, *the algorithm outputs either 1 if the signature is valid or 0 else.*

Security Definitions. In this paragraph we describe the main security definitions of an Attribute-Based Scheme. The first definition handles with existential unforgeability against adaptive CCA, which requires that any collusion of signers is not satisfiable to produce a signature forgery under a predicate which does not satisfy any of attribute sets in the collusion of signers. The other definition handles with privacy which guarantees that the signature does not reveal any information on the identity of the signer and on the attributes.

Definition 6 (Existential unforgeability against adaptive chosen-message attacks). *Let $\mathcal{A}_{euf}$ be a probabilistic polynomial time (PPT) adversary against chosen-message attacks who tries to make a forgery $(\mathrm{m}^*, \Gamma^*, \sigma^*)$, of a message, a predicate and a signature. Consider the following experiment* $\mathrm{Exp}_{\mathcal{A}_{euf}, \mathrm{ABS}}^{\mathrm{EUF-CMA}}$:

1. $(\mathrm{param}, \mathrm{msk}) \leftarrow \mathrm{ABSetup}(1^\lambda, 1^n)$
2. $(\mathrm{m}^*, \Gamma^*, \sigma^*, \mathbb{A}^*) \leftarrow \mathcal{A}_{euf}^{\mathcal{O}\mathrm{ABKeyGen}(\mathrm{param}, \mathrm{msk}, \cdot), \mathcal{O}\mathrm{ABSign}(\mathrm{param}, \mathrm{sk}., \cdot)}(\mathrm{param})$
3. *Return 1 if: (a).* $\mathrm{ABVerify}(\mathrm{param}, (\mathrm{m}^*, \sigma^*), \Gamma^*) = 1$,
   (b). $\mathbb{A}^*$ *was never queried to the oracles, (c).* m^*, Γ^* *was never queried to the* $\mathcal{O}\mathrm{ABSign}$ *oracle. Else return 0.*

$\mathcal{O}\mathrm{ABKeyGen}(\mathrm{param}, \mathrm{msk}, \mathbb{A})$: *On input public parameters and master secret key, giving an attribute set $\mathbb{A}$, the oracle runs $\mathrm{sk}_\mathbb{A} \leftarrow \mathrm{ABKeyGen}(\mathrm{param}, \mathrm{msk}, \mathbb{A})$.*
$\mathcal{O}\mathrm{ABSign}(\mathrm{param}, \mathbb{A}, \mathrm{m})$: *On input public parameters param, an attribute set $\mathbb{A}$ and a message m, the oracle generates $\mathrm{sk}_{\mathbb{A}'} \leftarrow \mathrm{ABKeyGen}(\mathrm{param}, \mathrm{msk}, \mathbb{A}')$. Furthermore upon receiving $\mathrm{sk}_{\mathbb{A}'}$ it runs $\sigma \leftarrow \mathrm{ABSign}(\mathrm{param}, \mathrm{sk}_\mathbb{A}, \mathrm{m}, \Gamma)$ on some message m and some predicate Γ' such that $\Gamma'(\mathbb{A}') = 1$. It outputs a signature σ.*

An ABS scheme is existentially unforgeable against chosen-message attacks if for any PPT adversary $\mathcal{A}_{euf}$ the following advantage of is negligible:

$$\mathrm{Adv}_{\mathcal{A}_{euf}, \mathrm{ABS}}^{\mathrm{EUF-CMA}}(\lambda) = \left| \Pr\left[\mathrm{Exp}_{\mathcal{A}_{euf}, \mathrm{ABS}}^{\mathrm{EUF-CMA}}(\lambda) = 1 \right] \right| \leq \epsilon(\lambda)$$

Definition 7 (Attribute Privacy). *Let $\mathcal{A}_{pr}$ be a PPT adversary who tries to break the attribute privacy property of an ABS scheme. Consider the following experiment $\mathrm{Exp}_{\mathcal{A}_{pr}, \mathrm{ABS}}^{\mathrm{Att-Priv}}$ with Γ representing an attribute policy (=predicate):*

1. $(\mathrm{param}, \mathrm{msk}) \leftarrow \mathrm{ABSetup}(1^\lambda, 1^n)$
2. $(\mathbb{A}_0, \mathbb{A}_1, \Gamma^*) \leftarrow \mathcal{A}_{pr}(\mathrm{param})$, *where* $|\mathbb{A}_0| = |\mathbb{A}_1|$
   such that $(\Gamma^*(\mathbb{A}_0) = \Gamma^*(\mathbb{A}_1) = 1) \vee (\Gamma^*(\mathbb{A}_0) = \Gamma^*(\mathbb{A}_1) = 0)$
3. $\mathrm{sk}_{\mathbb{A}_0} \leftarrow \mathrm{ABKeyGen}(\mathrm{param}, \mathrm{msk}, \mathbb{A}_0)$, $\mathrm{sk}_{\mathbb{A}_1} \leftarrow \mathrm{ABKeyGen}(\mathrm{param}, \mathrm{msk}, \mathbb{A}_1)$
4. *choose* $\mathrm{b} \in \{0, 1\}, \mathrm{b}' \leftarrow \mathcal{A}_{pr}^{\mathcal{O}\mathrm{ABSign}(\mathrm{param}, \mathrm{sk}_{\mathbb{A}_b}, \cdot)}(\mathrm{param}, \mathrm{sk}_{\mathbb{A}_0}, \mathrm{sk}_{\mathbb{A}_1})$
5. *If* $\mathrm{b} = \mathrm{b}'$, *and* $|\mathbb{A}_0| = |\mathbb{A}_1|$ *return 1, else return 0.*

$\mathcal{O}\mathrm{ABSign}(\mathrm{param}, \mathbb{A})$: *On input public parameters param and an attribute set $\mathbb{A}$ the oracle runs $\mathrm{sk}_\mathbb{A} \leftarrow \mathrm{ABKeyGen}(\mathrm{param}, \mathrm{msk}, \mathbb{A})$. Furthermore upon receiving $\mathrm{sk}_\mathbb{A}$ it runs the signature algorithm $\sigma \leftarrow \mathrm{ABSign}(\mathrm{param}, \mathrm{sk}_\mathbb{A}, \mathrm{m}, \Gamma)$ on some message m and predicate Gamma. It outputs a signature σ.*

An ABS scheme is private if for any PPT adversary $\mathcal{A}_{pr}$ the following advantage is negligible: $\mathrm{Adv}_{\mathcal{A}_{pr}, \mathrm{ABS}}^{\mathrm{Attr-Priv}}(\lambda) = \left| \Pr\left[\mathrm{Exp}_{\mathcal{A}_{pr}, \mathrm{ABS}}^{\mathrm{Att-Priv}}(\lambda) = 1 \right] - 1/2 \right| \leq \epsilon(\lambda)$.

3.1 Generic Construction of ABS Scheme

For our construction we use building blocks the attribute-based key encapsulation mechanism and the data encapsulation mechanism which are secure against chosen ciphertext attacks:

ABSetup($1^\lambda, 1^n$): Given a security parameter 1^λ and the input size of the attribute set n, it runs the Setup algorithm of the underlying AB-KEM scheme and public parameters param and master secret key msk. Furthermore it runs the Setup(1^λ) algorithm of the non-interactive proof system and outputs a common reference string crs.

ABKeyGen(param, msk, $\mathbb{A}$): On input public parameters param, a master secret key msk and user's attribute set $\mathbb{A}$ it runs $sk_\mathbb{A} \leftarrow$ ABKKeyGen(param, msk, $\mathbb{A}$) and outputs the received secret key $sk_\mathbb{A}$.

ABSign(param, crs, $sk_\mathbb{A}$, m, Γ): On input public parameters param, common reference string crs, user's secret key $sk_\mathbb{A}$, a message m, a predicate Γ, it runs $(E_\Gamma, K) \leftarrow$ ABKEncaps(param, Γ) and $\sigma \leftarrow$ DEncaps(m, K). It uses a NIZK proof to prove the statement that a value K is a satisfiable output of the ABKDecaps algorithm under input of secret key $sk_\mathbb{A}$, i.e. it shows that $sk_\mathbb{A}$ is the correct key for the decapsulation algorithm on input E_Γ. Note that, neither K nor $sk_\mathbb{A}$ key will be revealed to the verifier. The output is $\hat{\sigma} = (\sigma, \pi)$.

ABVerify(param, $\hat{\sigma}, \Gamma$): On input param, $\hat{\sigma} = (\sigma, \pi)$, it runs the verification part of NIZK proof, which proves the knowledge of K that is the output of ABKDecaps algorithm on input a secret key $sk_\mathbb{A}$. Afterwards the verifier runs $m \leftarrow$ DDecaps(K, σ). If the NIZK verification succeeds, the algorithm outputs 1, else it outputs 0.

Description of NIZK. Let $\mathcal{P}$ and $\mathcal{V}$ be the prover and the verifier respectively of our simulation sound non-interactive zero-knowledge proof as recalled in Sect. 2. We describe the proof as follows: Our construction relies on the NIZK proof of membership in NP languages. Let L denote a NP language with NP-relation R denotes which is a subset of two arbitrary size bit strings $\{0,1\}^* \times \{0,1\}^*$ such that it requires a polynomial time algorithm to decide whether a set of a statement x and the corresponding witness w is an element of R or not. We specify this relation as follows: $(K, \Gamma, \text{ABKDecaps}(\cdot, E_\Gamma), (sk_\mathbb{A}, \mathbb{A}, R))$, where $(K, \Gamma, \text{ABKDecaps}(\cdot, E_\Gamma))$ is a statement of the proof and $(sk_\mathbb{A}, \mathbb{A}, R)$ the corresponding witness with randomness R.

4 Security Analysis of ABS Scheme

Theorem 1. *Our ABS scheme is existentially UNF-CMA secure if the underlying $\mathcal{ABKEM}$ and $\mathcal{ABDEM}$ schemes are IND-CCA secure in the adaptive predicate model, the commitments used in the NIZK proof are binding and the NIZK proof itself is simulation sound.*

Proof. To prove the theorem, we assume there is an adversary $\mathcal{A}_{euf}$ against the existential UNF-CMA security of the ABS scheme. We design an adversary

$\mathcal{B}_\gamma \in (\mathcal{B}_K, \mathcal{B}_D)$, where $\mathcal{B}_K$ denotes a simulator against the IND-CCA security of ABKEM and $\mathcal{B}_D$ is the corresponding algorithm against IND-CCA security of the underlying DEM scheme, respectively.

Setup: $\mathcal{B}_\gamma$ simulates $\mathcal{A}_{\text{euf}}$. The simulator $\mathcal{B}_K$ runs its $\texttt{Setup}(1^\lambda)$ algorithm on input security parameter and outputs public parameters and a master secret key param, msk. $\mathcal{B}_K$ forwards these values to $\mathcal{A}_{\text{euf}}$.

Queries to $\mathcal{O}\texttt{ABKeyGen}(\texttt{param}, \texttt{msk}, \cdot)$: Whenever $\mathcal{A}_{\text{euf}}$ issues key generation queries corresponding to an attribute set $\mathbb{A}$, simulator $\mathcal{B}_K$ answers to the queries using its own $\mathcal{O}\texttt{ABKKeyGen}$ oracle on input attribute set $\mathbb{A}$. The simulator generates a list $\bar{\mathbb{A}}$ of all queried attribute sets $\mathbb{A}$. If a certain attribute set was already queried to the oracle, It forwards the received secret key $\texttt{sk}_\mathbb{A}$ to $\mathcal{A}_{\text{euf}}$.

Queries to $\mathcal{O}\texttt{ABSign}(\texttt{param}, \texttt{sk}., \texttt{m}, \cdot)$: Whenever $\mathcal{A}_{\text{euf}}$ issues signature queries on input sk., where "$\cdot$" describes some attribute set $\mathbb{A}'$ and a message m, simulator $\mathcal{B}_{K/D}$ invokes $\mathcal{B}_K$ which runs $\texttt{sk}_\mathbb{A} \leftarrow \texttt{ABKKeyGen}(\texttt{param}, \texttt{msk}, \mathbb{A})$. It chooses a predicate Γ, such that $\Gamma(\mathbb{A}) = 1$ and runs $(E_\Gamma, K) \leftarrow \texttt{ABKEncaps}(\texttt{param}, \Gamma)$. On input K simulator invokes $\mathcal{B}_D$, which runs $\sigma \leftarrow \texttt{DEncaps}(\texttt{m}, K)$ on the received message m. The simulator generates a list M of all received messages. If the received message m is already in the list, simulator aborts the simulation. Using the secret key $\texttt{sk}_\mathbb{A}$ it runs the prover protocol of the NIZK proof and outputs $\hat{\sigma} = (\sigma, \pi)$, where π is the NIZK proof inspired by [21] and given by $P(K, \Gamma, \texttt{ABKDecaps}(\cdot, E_\Gamma), (\texttt{sk}_\mathbb{A}, \mathbb{A}, R))$. Finally, $\mathcal{B}_\gamma$ forwards $\hat{\sigma}$ to $\mathcal{A}_{\text{euf}}$.

Output: Finally, $\mathcal{A}_{\text{euf}}$ outputs $(\sigma^*, \texttt{m}^*, \Gamma^*)$ s.t. the following properties hold:

(a) $\texttt{ABVerify}(\texttt{param}, \texttt{m}^*, \sigma^*) = 1$. To check this equality, the simulator takes $\texttt{m}^*, \sigma^*$, invokes the $\mathcal{B}_K$ part of the simulation algorithm. $\mathcal{B}_K$ queries its own $\mathcal{O}\texttt{ABKeyGen}$ oracle on input previously chosen attribute set $\mathbb{A}$. Upon receiving the secret key $\texttt{sk}_\mathbb{A}$ it queries its $\mathcal{O}\texttt{ABKDecaps}$ oracle on input the secret key. The oracle outputs symmetric key K. Taking the symmetric key the simulator invokes $\mathcal{B}_D$ part of the algorithm to firstly run $\sigma \leftarrow \texttt{DEncaps}(\texttt{m}^*, K)$. It checks whether the received signature is equal to the received challenge signature σ^*. Furthermore it issues a query to its own $\mathcal{O}\texttt{DDecaps}$ oracle on input K and checks the received message m is equal to the challenge message $\texttt{m}^*$. If both are equal, the verification succeeds and either $\mathcal{B}_K$ or $\mathcal{B}_D$ outputs 1 to $\mathcal{A}_{\text{euf}}$.

(b) $\mathbb{A}^*$ was never queried to the both oracles.

(c) $(\texttt{m}^*, \Gamma^*)$ was never queried to the $\mathcal{O}\texttt{ABSign}$ oracle.

Otherwise, $\mathcal{B}_{K/D}$ breaks the IND-CCA security as follows: If $\mathbb{A}^*$ was queried to the key generation oracle $\mathcal{O}\texttt{ABKeyGen}$ the simulator would be able to recover the queried attribute set from the attribute set $\bar{\mathbb{A}}$, which would break the IND-CCA security of the underlying AB-KEM, DEM schemes. Assuming that $\mathbb{A}$ has been queried to the key generation oracle $\mathcal{O}\texttt{ABKeyGen}$ and output a new secret key $\texttt{sk}_\mathbb{A}'$ it would break the binding assumption of commitment scheme, which would mean that it is possible to find two different opening values aka randomizers to open the commitment to two different blinded secret keys. Since the binding property of our commitments used in the NIZK proof is guaranteed, we claim that an adversary succeeds in breaking the binding property with a negligible probability. In order to prove simulation soundness of the NIZK proof, we consider the following game where an adversary $\mathcal{A}_{ss}$ against simulation soundness of NIZK is playing against a challenger (who is represented by the adversary against our ABS scheme):

1. $(\mathrm{param}, \mathrm{crs}, \mathrm{msk}) \leftarrow \mathrm{Setup}(1^\lambda, 1^n)$
2. $\mathrm{sk}_A \leftarrow \mathrm{ABKKeyGen}(\mathrm{param}, \mathrm{msk})$
   End for (a). $m^*, \Gamma^*, \sigma^* \leftarrow \mathcal{A}_{euf}^{\mathcal{O}\mathrm{ABKeyGen}(\mathrm{param},\mathrm{msk},\cdot),\mathcal{O}\mathrm{ABSign}(\mathrm{param},\mathrm{sk}.,\cdot)}(\mathrm{param}, \mathrm{msk})$
   (b). $(K, E_{\Gamma^*}) \leftarrow \mathrm{ABKEncaps}(\mathrm{param}, \Gamma^*)$, (c). $(C_D) \leftarrow \mathrm{ABKEncaps}(K, m^*)$, $C_D := \sigma^*$
   (d). $\pi \leftarrow \mathrm{SIM}(\mathrm{prove}, \mathrm{crs}, \mathrm{param}, m^*, \sigma^*, \mathrm{sk}_A, \Gamma^*)$,
   Make oracle queries to $\mathcal{O}\mathrm{ABKeyGen}$ and $\mathcal{O}\mathrm{ABSign}$. Run $\mathrm{Verify}(\mathrm{param}, \sigma, \pi)$.
   If $\mathcal{A}_{euf}$ outputs a valid σ, π', output $(\mathrm{param}, \mathrm{crs}, \sigma, \pi')$.

We say that $\mathcal{A}_{ss}$ wins the experiment, if $\mathcal{A}_{euf}$ did not query $\mathcal{O}\mathrm{DDecaps}$ on (σ, π'). Advantage of $\mathcal{A}_{ss}$ is given by:

$$\mathrm{Adv}_{\mathcal{A}_{ss},\mathrm{ABS}}^{\mathrm{Sim-Sound}} = \left| \Pr\left[\mathrm{Exp}_{\mathcal{A}_{ind},\mathrm{ABKEM}}^{\mathrm{IND-CCA}-1} = 1 \right] - \Pr\left[\mathrm{Exp}_{\mathcal{A}_{ind},\mathrm{ABKEM}}^{\mathrm{IND-CCA}-0} = 1 \right] \right|$$
$$+ \left| \Pr\left[\mathrm{Exp}_{\mathcal{A}_{ind},\mathrm{DEM}}^{\mathrm{IND-CCA}-1} = 1 \right] - \Pr\left[\mathrm{Exp}_{\mathcal{A}_{ind},\mathrm{DEM}}^{\mathrm{IND-CCA}-0} = 1 \right] \right|$$

Finally we conclude that the advantage of an adversary $\mathcal{A}_{euf}$ is given by the following combined inequation:

$$\mathrm{Adv}_{\mathcal{A}_{euf},\mathrm{ABS}}^{\mathrm{E-UNF}} \leq \mathrm{Adv}_{\mathcal{A}_{ss},\mathrm{ABS}}^{\mathrm{Sim-Sound}} + \mathrm{Adv}_{\mathcal{A}_{ind},\mathrm{ABKEM}}^{\mathrm{IND-CCA}} + \mathrm{Adv}_{\mathcal{A}_{ind},\mathrm{DEM}}^{\mathrm{IND-CCA}}$$

Theorem 2. *Our ABS scheme is attribute anonymous if the underlying DEM scheme is IND-CCA secure and the underlying NIZK proof is simulation-sound and computationally zero-knowledge provable.*

Proof. Due to the page limit, we skip a detailed proof of this theorem and refer to the full version of this paper.

5   Generic Construction of Attribute-Based Group Signature

In this section we present a generic construction of attribute-based group signature (ABGS) scheme. We assume a scenario where the group manager is not involved in the key generation process for a new member. Provided by the group managers secret key, she is available to trace the malicious signer only. The key issuing functionality is processed by another entity, the key issuing entity. The reason for separating the roles of group manager and key issuer is to disable a group manager to create a signature forgery or to collude with other members.

Definition 8. *An ABGS scheme consists of the following six algorithms:*

$\mathtt{Setup}(1^\lambda, 1^n)$: *On input security parameter 1^λ and the size of attribute set 1^n the central authority runs this randomized algorithm to output public parameters* param *and master secret key* msk.

$\mathtt{ABGKeyGen}(\mathtt{param}, \mathtt{msk}, \mathbb{A}_i)$: *On input public parameters* param, *master secret key* msk *and an attribute set $\mathbb{A}_i$ of user i, it generates a group public key* gpk, *an issuing key* ik *for enrolling new group members by a certificate issuing entity and a group master secret key* gmsk *for opening the signature by the group manager to trace and identify the signers. Furthermore the algorithm generates user's i secret key* $\mathtt{sk}_{\mathbb{A}_i}$ *corresponding to the user's attribute set $\mathbb{A}_i$ and* $\mathtt{pk}_i$.

$\langle\mathtt{Join}(\mathtt{param}, \mathtt{gpk}, \mathtt{pk}_i, \mathtt{sk}_{\mathbb{A}_i})\rangle, \langle\mathtt{Issue}(\mathtt{param}, \mathtt{pk}_i, \mathtt{ik})\rangle$: *This is an interactive protocol allowing new members to join the group. The protocol is run between a user $\mathtt{U}_i$ and an certificate issuing entity $\mathtt{KIE}$. The certificate issuing outputs a certificate $\mathtt{cert}_i$ for user $\mathtt{U}_i$ and stores user's public key $\mathtt{pk}_i$ in a registration table.*

$\mathtt{ABGSign}(\mathtt{param}, \mathtt{sk}_{\mathbb{A}_i}, \mathtt{m}, \Gamma)$: *On input public parameters* param, *member's secret key* $\mathtt{sk}_{\mathbb{A}_i}$, *a predicate Γ and a message* m *it returns a signature σ.*

$\mathtt{ABGVery}(\mathtt{param}, \mathtt{gpk}, \sigma, \Gamma)$: *On input public parameters* param, *group public key* gpk, *a signature σ and the predicate Γ, the deterministic algorithm verifies the validity of the signature and outputs 1 if the signature is valid, else outputs 0.*

$\mathtt{ABGOpen}(\mathtt{param}, \mathtt{gmsk}, \sigma)$: *On input public parameters* param, *group master secret key* gmsk *and a signature σ it outputs either the attribute set $\mathbb{A}$ or $\perp$.*

5.1   Security Definitions

In this section we provide the core security properties of an ABGS scheme. We are focusing in this paper on the following three security notions: attribute and user anonymity, traceability and non-frameability.

Fully anonymity of users. In general, anonymity property of an ABGS scheme means that it is hard for an adversary apart from the group manager to recover the identity of the signer. Similar to the construction in [6], we guarantee collusion incapacity of an adversary with group members by providing the secret keys of all group members to the adversary. Furthermore we give an adversary access to the open oracle in order to allow him to see the results of previous openings. In the following definition we consider an adversary $\mathcal{A}_{uan}$, who wants to break the fully user anonymity property, and a bit b associated with the security experiment. We assume an adversary acting in two stages where in the first stage - the so called find stage - it takes as input the user's secret keys $sk_{\mathbb{A}_i}$ and group public key gpk and outputs two identities i_0, i_1 and a message m.

Definition 9 (User anonymity). *An ABGS scheme preserves user anonymity if the advantage of an adversary in winning $\mathtt{Exp}_{\mathcal{A}_{uan}, \mathtt{ABGS}}^{U-ANO-b}(1^\lambda, 1^n)$ is negligible:*

1. $(\mathtt{param}, \mathtt{msk}) \leftarrow \mathtt{Setup}(1^\lambda, 1^n)$
2. $(\mathtt{gpk}, \mathtt{ik}, \mathtt{gmsk}, \mathtt{sk}_{\mathbb{A}_i}, \mathtt{sk}_i, \mathtt{pk}_i) \leftarrow \mathtt{ABGKeyGen}(\mathtt{param}, \mathtt{msk})$,
   $\widetilde{\mathtt{usk}} := \{\mathtt{sk}_{\mathbb{A}_i}, \mathtt{sk}_i\}_{i \in [n]}$

3. $(\mathtt{state}, \mathtt{i}_0, \mathtt{i}_1, \mathtt{m}, \Gamma) \leftarrow \mathcal{A}_{\mathtt{uan}}^{\mathcal{O}\mathtt{ABGOpen}(\cdot)}(\mathtt{find}, \mathtt{param}, \mathtt{gpk}, \tilde{\mathtt{usk}})$

4. *Choose* $\mathtt{b} \in 0, 1;\ \sigma^* \leftarrow \mathtt{ABGSign}(\mathtt{param}, \mathtt{sk}_{\mathbb{A}, \mathtt{i}_b}, \mathtt{m}, \Gamma)$

5. $\mathtt{b}' \leftarrow \mathcal{A}_{\mathtt{uan}}^{\mathcal{O}\mathtt{ABGOpen}(\cdot)}(\mathtt{guess}, \mathtt{state}, \sigma^*)$

$\mathcal{O}\mathtt{ABGOpen}(m, \sigma)$: *The adversary calls this oracle with some message m and a signature σ. The oracle runs $\mathtt{Open}(gmsk, \sigma)$ to receive index i which allows to trace malicious signer.*

An ABGS scheme is fully anonymous if for any PPT adversary $\mathcal{A}_{\mathtt{uan}}$ the following advantage is negligible:

$$\mathtt{Adv}_{\mathcal{A}_{\mathtt{uan}}, \mathtt{ABGS}}^{\mathtt{U-ANO}}(\lambda) = \left| \mathtt{Pr}\left[\mathtt{Exp}_{\mathcal{A}_{\mathtt{uan}}, \mathtt{ABGS}}^{\mathtt{U-ANO-1}}(\lambda) = 1\right] - \mathtt{Pr}\left[\mathtt{Exp}_{\mathcal{A}_{\mathtt{uan}}, \mathtt{ABGS}}^{\mathtt{U-ANO-0}}(\lambda) = 1\right] \right| \le \epsilon(\lambda)$$

Attribute anonymity. This property means that a verifier should be able to verify a signature corresponding to a predicate without revealing the attribute set. Attribute anonymity is especially useful if there is only one group member with a certain attribute, which helps tracing back to the identity of the user.

Definition 10 (Attribute anonymity)
$\mathtt{Exp}_{\mathcal{A}_{\mathtt{at-ano}}, \mathtt{ABGS}}^{\mathtt{At-Ano-b}}(1^\lambda, 1^n)$:

1. $(\mathtt{param}, \mathtt{msk}) \leftarrow \mathtt{Setup}(1^\lambda, 1^n)$

2. $(\mathbb{A}_0, \mathbb{A}_1, \Gamma^*) \leftarrow \mathcal{A}_{\mathtt{at-ano}}(\mathtt{param})$, *where* $|\mathbb{A}_0| = |\mathbb{A}_1|$ *such that* ($\Gamma^*(\mathbb{A}_0) = \Gamma^*(\mathbb{A}_1) = 1$) $\vee$ ($\Gamma^*(\mathbb{A}_0) = \Gamma^*(\mathbb{A}_1) = 0$)

4. $\mathtt{sk}_{\mathbb{A}_0} \leftarrow \mathtt{ABGKeyGen}(\mathtt{param}, \mathtt{msk}, \mathbb{A}_0)$, $\mathtt{sk}_{\mathbb{A}_1} \leftarrow \mathtt{ABGKeyGen}(\mathtt{param}, \mathtt{msk}, \mathbb{A}_1)$

5. $\mathtt{b}' \leftarrow \mathcal{A}_{\mathtt{at-ano}}^{\mathcal{O}\mathtt{ABGSign}(\mathtt{param}, \mathtt{sk}_{\mathbb{A}_b}, \cdot)}(\mathtt{param}, \mathtt{sk}_{\mathbb{A}_0}, \mathtt{sk}_{\mathbb{A}_1})$

6. *If* $\mathtt{b} = \mathtt{b}'$ *and* $|\mathbb{A}_0| = |\mathbb{A}_1|$ *return 1, else return 0.*

$\mathcal{O}\mathtt{ABGSign}(\mathtt{param}, \mathbb{A}, \cdot)$: *On input public parameters $\mathtt{param}$ and an attribute set $\mathbb{A}'$ the oracle runs $\mathtt{sk}_{\mathbb{A}} \leftarrow \mathtt{ABKeyGen}(\mathtt{param}, \mathtt{msk}, \mathbb{A}')$. Furthermore upon receiving $\mathtt{sk}_{\mathbb{A}'}$ it runs $\sigma \leftarrow \mathtt{ABSign}(\mathtt{param}, \mathtt{sk}_{\mathbb{A}}, m)$ on some message $\mathtt{m}$. It outputs a signature σ. An ABGS scheme is attribute-anonymous if for any PPT adversary $\mathcal{A}_{\mathtt{at-ano}}$ the following advantage is negligible:*

$$\mathtt{Adv}_{\mathcal{A}_{\mathtt{at-ano}}, \mathtt{ABGS}}^{\mathtt{At-ANO}}(\lambda) = \left| \mathtt{Pr}\left[\mathtt{Exp}_{\mathcal{A}_{\mathtt{at-ano}}, \mathtt{ABGS}}^{\mathtt{At-ANO-1}}(\lambda) = 1\right] - \mathtt{Pr}\left[\mathtt{Exp}_{\mathcal{A}_{\mathtt{at-ano}}, \mathtt{ABGS}}^{\mathtt{At-ANO-0}}(\lambda) = 1\right] \right|.$$

Full-Traceability. We assume that in case of malicious behavior, signer's identity can be revealed by the group manager using manager's secret key. In other words it means that no collusion of group members should enable to create a valid signature which cannot be opened by the group manager. As mentioned in [5], the group manager could be dishonest and accuse an user in malicious behavior. In order to avoid this dishonest behavior of the user we can ask the group manager to also output a proof together with the identity $\mathtt{i}$, after running the $\mathtt{Open}$ algorithm. The verification of the proof can take place by running an additional algorithm - $\mathtt{Judge}$ - on input a signature σ, identity i ant proof π.

Definition 11 (Full-Traceability). *We say that an ABGS scheme is fully traceable if the advantage of an adversary $\mathcal{A}_{\mathtt{tr}}$ to win the following experiment $\mathtt{Exp}_{\mathcal{A}_{\mathtt{f-trace}}, \mathtt{ABGS}}^{\mathtt{Full-Trace}}(1^\lambda, 1^n)$ is negligible.*

1. $(\mathsf{param}, \mathsf{msk}) \leftarrow \mathsf{Setup}(1^\lambda, 1^n)$
2. $(\mathsf{gpk}, \mathsf{ik}, \mathsf{gmsk}, \mathsf{sk}_{\mathbb{A}_i}, \mathsf{sk}_i, \mathsf{pk}_i) \leftarrow \mathsf{ABGKeyGen}(\mathsf{param}, \mathsf{msk})$,
   $\widetilde{\mathsf{usk}} := \{\mathsf{sk}_{\mathbb{A}_i}, \mathsf{sk}_i\}_{i \in [n]}$
3. $(\mathsf{m}, \sigma) \leftarrow \mathcal{A}_{\mathsf{f-trace}}^{\mathcal{O}\mathsf{ABGSign}(\cdot), \mathcal{O}\mathsf{ABGKeyGen}(\cdot), \mathcal{O}\mathsf{Open}}(\mathsf{gpk}, \mathsf{gmsk})$
   If $\mathsf{ABGVery}(\mathsf{param}, \mathsf{gpk}, \sigma) = 0$, *return* 0. *If* $\mathsf{Open}(\mathsf{param}, \mathsf{gms}, \sigma) = \bot$,
   return 1.
   Let $\mathcal{C}$ *denote the list of all opened identities. If* $\mathsf{Open}(\mathsf{param}, \mathsf{gmsk}, \sigma) = \mathsf{i}$ *and*
   $\mathsf{i} \notin \mathcal{C}$, *then return* 1, *else return* 0.

$\mathcal{O}\mathsf{ABGSign}(\mathsf{param}, \mathbb{A}, \cdot)$: *On input public parameters* param *and an attribute set* $\mathbb{A}$ *the oracle runs* $\mathsf{sk}_{\mathbb{A}'} \leftarrow \mathsf{ABKeyGen}(\mathsf{param}, \mathsf{msk}, \mathbb{A}')$. *Furthermore upon receiving* $\mathsf{sk}_{\mathbb{A}}$ *it runs* $\sigma \leftarrow \mathsf{ABSign}(\mathsf{param}, \mathsf{sk}_{\mathbb{A}}, \mathsf{m})$ *on some message* m. *It outputs a signature* σ.

$\mathcal{O}\mathsf{ABGKeyGen}(\mathsf{param}, \mathsf{msk}, \mathbb{A})$: *On input public parameters and master secret key, giving an attribute set* $\mathbb{A}$, *the oracle runs* $(\mathsf{pk}, \mathsf{sk}_{\mathbb{A}}) \leftarrow \mathsf{ABGKeyGen}(\mathsf{param}, \mathsf{msk}, \mathbb{A})$, *where* pk *denotes all the public key of the* $\mathsf{ABGKeyGen}$. *It outputs a tuple consisting of public keys and secret key* $\mathsf{sk}_{\mathbb{A}}$.

$\mathcal{O}\mathsf{Open}(\mathsf{param}, \mathsf{gmsk}, \sigma)$: *On input* $\mathsf{param}, \mathsf{gmsk}, \sigma$, *returns* $\mathsf{i} \leftarrow \mathsf{Open}(\mathsf{param}, \mathsf{gmsk}, \sigma)$

An ABGS scheme is attribute-anonymous if for any PPT adversary $\mathcal{A}_{\mathsf{at-ano}}$ *the following advantage is negligible:*

$$\mathsf{Adv}_{\mathcal{A}_{\mathsf{f-trace}}, \mathsf{ABGS}}^{\mathsf{Full-Trace}}(\lambda) = \left| \Pr\left[\mathsf{Exp}_{\mathcal{A}_{\mathsf{f-trace}}, \mathsf{ABGS}}^{\mathsf{Full-Trace}}(\lambda) = 1 \right] \right| \leq \epsilon(\lambda).$$

Non-frameability. This security notion means that an adversary is not able to prove that some honest user created a valid signature. This property requires that it is impossible for two or more colluding users to produce a signature which would trace back to the non-colluded group member. As showed by Bellare et al. [5], non-frameability property is considered to be a version of collusion resistance. The two properties are the same in the sense that non-frameability prevents to create a signature which would be opened by a group manager and trace to a different member of the group. An ABGS scheme that is fully-traceable, is automatically secure against framing. Bellare et al. [5] showed how to convert an adversary against framing into an adversary against full-traceability.

5.2   Construction

Using such building blocks as attribute-based key encapsulation and data encapsulation mechanisms, public key encryption scheme, digital signature scheme and strong one-time signature scheme we merge the two generic constructions (of an ABS and a GS schemes) recalled and constructed in this paper and introduce a new generic construction of an attribute-based group signature scheme. We achieve the first instantiation of the construction technique from [6] applied to the attribute-based groups signature scheme. Furthermore, we use the NIZK proof from [21] which was successfully implemented in the construction of Bellare's static [5] and dynamic group [6] schemes. We not that for a proper implementation of the NIZK proof we require and additional building block of a secure strong one-time group signature (SOTS) scheme. Assume that a SOTS scheme consists of three algorithms $\text{KeyGen}_{sots}, \text{Sign}_{sots}, \text{Verify}_{sots}$ with the corresponding outputs $(\text{vk}_{\text{sots}}, \text{sk}_{\text{sots}}) \leftarrow \text{KeyGen}_{\text{sots}}(1^\lambda)$; $\sigma_{\text{sots}} \leftarrow \text{Sign}_{\text{sots}}(\text{m}, \text{sk}_{\text{sots}})$; $1/0 \leftarrow \text{Verify}_{\text{sots}}(\text{vk}_{\text{sots}}, \text{m}, \sigma_{\text{sots}})$.

Definition 12. *A generic attribute-based groups signature scheme consists of the following six algorithms:*

$\text{Setup}(1^\lambda, 1^n)$: *The algorithm is run by a key generation center. It runs the setup algorithm of AB-KEM algorithm* $(\text{param}, \text{msk}) \leftarrow \text{Setup}(1^\lambda, 1^n)$.

$\text{ABGKeyGen}(\text{param}, \text{msk}, \mathbb{A}_i)$: *On input public parameters* param *and master secret key* msk *user's attribute set* $\mathbb{A}_i$ *it runs* $\text{sk}_{\mathbb{A}_i} \leftarrow \text{ABKeyGen}(\text{param}, \text{msk})$. *Furthermore it runs the key generation algorithm of the underlying digital signature scheme and outputs a pair of secret and public key* $(\text{sk}_i, \text{pk}_i) \leftarrow \text{KeyGen}_s(1^\lambda)$ *where the secret key represents the other part of user's secret key. The algorithm sets user's secret key equal to* $\text{usk}[\text{i}] = (\text{sk}_{\mathbb{A}_i}, \text{sk}_i)$ *and user's public key as* pk_i. *The algorithm runs the key generation algorithm of the signature scheme for the second time to generate a secret and a public key for the certificate issuing entity,* $(\text{sk}_s, \text{pk}_s) \leftarrow \text{KeyGen}(1^\lambda)$. *Lastly it runs the key generation algorithm of the underlying public key encryption scheme* $(\text{sk}_e, \text{pk}_e) \leftarrow \text{KeyGen}(1^\lambda)$, *where the secret key* sk_e *represents the group manager's secret key to open the signature and to trace malicious signers. The algorithm also runs the* Setup *algorithm of the underlying NIZK proofs and outputs a common reference string crs with randomness r. Group public key is set equal to* $gpk = (param, crs, r, pk_e, pk_s)$.

$\text{Join}(\langle \text{param}, \text{gpk}, \text{ik}, \text{pk}_i, \mathbb{A}_i \rangle, \langle \text{param}, \text{gpk}, \text{pk}_i, \text{usk}[\text{i}] \rangle)$: *This interactive protocol is initiated by the user* U_i *who takes its verification key* pk_i *and signs it by running the signature algorithm of the underlying digital signature scheme, using its secret key* $\text{usk}[\text{i}]$, *s.t.* $\sigma_i \leftarrow \text{Sign}(\text{usk}[\text{i}], \text{pk}_i)$. *This signing procedure guarantees non-frameability against corrupt users. The user sends then her public key* pk_i *and the signature* σ_i *to the certificate issuing entity (CIE) in order to receive a certificate which would provide eligibility of a group member. CIE signs the public key using its own secret key,* $\text{cert}_i \leftarrow \text{Sign}(\text{sk}_s, \langle \text{i}, \text{pk}_i \rangle)$, *such that the final signature serves as a certificate for user* U_i. *The issuer stores* (pk_i, σ_i) *in the registration table.*

$\text{ABGSign}(\text{param}, \text{usk}[\text{i}], \text{m}, \Gamma)$: *On input public parameters* param, *user's secret key* usk[i], *a message* m *and a predicate* Γ *the user runs* $(vk_{sots}, sk_{sots}) \leftarrow \text{KeyGen}_{sots}(1^\lambda)$. *The verification key* vk_{sots} *will be a part of the NIZK proof. The user signs* vk_{sots} *using it's secret key* usk[i] *as follows: First, it runs* $(\text{K}, \text{E}_\Gamma) \leftarrow \text{ABKEncaps}(\text{param}, \Gamma)$ *of the underlying AB-KEM scheme. Taking* K *and a message* m *it runs the encapsulation algorithm of the underlying DEM scheme,* $\hat{\sigma} = \text{DEncaps}(\text{vk}_{\text{sots}}, \text{K})$. *Using encryption algorithm of the underlying encryption scheme it outputs a ciphertext encrypting user's certificate, and signature* $\hat{\sigma}$, *i.e.* $\text{C} \leftarrow \text{Encrypt}(\text{pk}_e, \langle \text{i}, \text{pk}_i, \text{cert}_i, \hat{\sigma}, \text{R} \rangle)$, *where R is a randomness used for the witness of NIZK proof. This encryption procedure prevents someone to create its own public and secret key pair* $\text{pk}'_i, \text{sk}'_i$. *The user runs*

NIZK1 proof π_1 from the ABS scheme described in Sect. 3.1. to prove the statement that K *is a satisfiable output of* ABKDecaps *algorithm on input a secret key* sk_{A_i}. *Furthermore, user runs NIZK2 proof π_2 which proves that the certificate* $cert_i$ *is a signature under CIE's public key* pk_s. *Lastly, taking as input a message* m, *verification key* vk_{sots}, *ciphertext π and the corresponding proof $\tilde{\pi} = (\pi_1, \pi_2)$, user runs the signature algorithm of the underlying SOTS scheme and outputs $\sigma_{sots} \leftarrow$* Sign(m, vk_{sots}, C, $\tilde{\pi}$). *The final signature is equal to $\tilde{\sigma} = (C, \tilde{\pi} = (\pi_1, \pi_2), \sigma_{sots})$.*

ABGVery(param, gpk, $\tilde{\sigma}$): *On input* param, gpk $= (pk_e, pk_s)$ *and $\tilde{\sigma} = (C, \tilde{\pi}, \sigma_{sots})$, the verification is followed by the* Verify *algorithm of NIZK proof verifying the SOTS signature σ_{sots} on input* (m, vk_{sots}, C, $\tilde{\pi}$, σ_{sots}) *as input.*

ABGOpen(param, gmsk, $\tilde{\sigma}$): *Parse* gmsk $= (\lambda, pk_e, sk_e, pk_s)$ *and $\tilde{\sigma} = (C, \tilde{\pi}, \sigma_{sots})$. If* Verify $= 0$ *in both of the NIZK proofs, return 0, else decrypt the ciphertext by running* Decrypt(sk_e, C) *and receive the string $\langle i, pk_i, cert_i, \tilde{\sigma} \rangle$. Return i.*

Description of NIZK. Since the first NIZK proof π_1 is inherited from our generic ABS construction, we present the details of the second NIZK proof π_2 only. The witness relation of this proof π_2 which is used in our construction, is specified as P((pk_e, vk_{sots}, m, C), (sk_{A_i}, A_i, $cert_i$, σ_i, R)), where (pk_e, vk_{sots}, m, C) is a proof statement and (sk_{A_i}, A_i, $cert_i$, σ_i, R) the corresponding witness with randomness R. Simulation soundness of this proof is guaranteed due to the following justification: The prover who is also the signer picks random keys of SOTS scheme (vk_{sots}, sk_{sots}), where vk_{sots} becomes a part of π_2. The corresponding SOTS signature σ_{sots} defined above becomes a part of the verifier algorithm of π_2. The common reference string of this proof contains user's public key pk_i. In the porver part a user proves that the above defined statement is an element of NP language L or he knows the signature $\sigma_i(vk_{sots})$. It will be guaranteed that an adversary cannot forge a signature on a new vk_{sots}, which means that the creation of a valid NIZK proof fails. Since it is obvious to distinguish whether a NIZK proof is real or simulated we need to hide the signature $\tilde{\sigma}(vk_{sots})$, defined in the ABGSign algorithm. To achieve perfect soundness and the scenarios where a computationally unbounded adversary would be able to forge signatures under its public key pk_i, we need to provide an encryption of some random element in CRS. For a valid NIZK proof both need to be encrypted, a signature $\tilde{\sigma}(vk_{sots})$ and a trivial element, which encrypts to C_{triv}. The encryption of the witness (sk_{A_i}, A_i, $cert_i$, $\tilde{\sigma}$, R) guarantees zero-knowledge property.

6   Security Analysis

Theorem 3. *Our generic ABGS scheme is fully-anonymous and fully traceable if the underlying NIZK proof is simulation sound and zero-knowledge provable*

Proof. In order to prove the theorem we are using the following lemmas:

Lemma 1. *If the underlying AB-KEM, DEM and public key encryption systems are IND-CCA secure and the NIZK1 and NIZK2 proofs are simulation sound and zero-knowledge, then our ABGS scheme is fully-anonymous.*

Lemma 2. *Our ABGS scheme is attribute anonymous if the underlying DEM scheme is IND-CCA secure and the underlying NIZK proofs is simulation-sound and computationally zero-knowledge provable.*

Lemma 3. *If the underlying AB-KEM, DEM systems are IND-CCA secure, digital signature scheme is unforgeable against chosen message attacks and the NIZK1 and NIZK2 proofs are simulation sound, then our ABGS scheme is fully-traceable.*

Proof of Lemma 1. Let $\mathcal{A}_{\text{uan}}$ be an adversary against the user's full-anonymity in the ABGS scheme. We design an adversary $\mathcal{B}_\gamma \in (\mathcal{B}_\text{K}, \mathcal{B}_\text{D}, \mathcal{B}_\text{pke}, \mathcal{B}_\text{SOTS})$ against the IND-CCA security of the ABKEM or IND-CCA security of the DEM schemes, respectively, where γ indicates that the adversary is either running against the IND-CCA security of the ABKEM scheme or against the IND-CCA security of the DEM scheme. We show how to construct $\mathcal{B}_\gamma$ to simulate $\mathcal{A}_{uan}$.

Setup: $\mathcal{B}_\gamma$ simulates $\mathcal{A}_{\text{uan}}$. Simulator $\mathcal{B}_\text{K}$ runs its $\texttt{Setup}(1^\lambda)$ algorithm on input security parameter and outputs public parameters and a master secret key $\texttt{param}, \texttt{msk}$. $\mathcal{B}_\text{K}$ forwards these values to $\mathcal{A}_{\text{uan}}$. To simulate the remained public and secret keys of user, issuer and group manager, $\mathcal{A}_{\text{uan}}$ invokes an adversary against the underlying public key encryption scheme $\mathcal{B}_{\text{pke}}$. The detailed description of this adversary is given in the following experiment:

1. $(\texttt{vk}_{\text{sots}}, \texttt{sk}_{\text{sots}}) \leftarrow \texttt{KeyGen}_{\text{sots}}(1^\lambda)$
2. $(\texttt{pk}_\text{e}, \texttt{sk}_\text{e}) \leftarrow \texttt{KeyGen}_\text{e}(1^\lambda)$
3. $(\texttt{pk}_\text{s}, \texttt{sk}_\text{s}) \leftarrow \texttt{KeyGen}_\text{s}(1^\lambda)$
4. $(\texttt{crs}, \text{R}) \leftarrow \texttt{SIM}(\text{generate}, \lambda)$
5. Set $\texttt{gpk} = (\lambda, \text{R}, \texttt{pk}_\text{e}, \texttt{pk}_\text{s}, \texttt{vk}_{\text{sots}})$
   For all $\texttt{i} \in [\texttt{n}]$ run $(\texttt{pk}_\text{i}, \texttt{sk}_\text{i}) \leftarrow \texttt{KeyGen}_\text{s}(1^\lambda), \texttt{cert}_\text{i} \leftarrow \texttt{Sign}(\texttt{sk}_\text{s}, \langle\texttt{i}, \texttt{pk}_\text{i}\rangle)$.
   Make oracle queries to $\mathcal{O}\texttt{KeyGen}$ and $\mathcal{O}\texttt{Decrypt}$ of the PKE scheme.

Queries to $\mathcal{O}\texttt{ABGOpen}(\cdot, \cdot)$: Whenever $\mathcal{A}_{\text{uan}}$ calls its opening oracle on input a message $\texttt{m}$ and a signature σ, algorithm $\mathcal{B}_\gamma$ simulates these opening queries and sets $\sigma = C_D$ of the underlying DEM scheme. $\mathcal{B}_\text{D}$ runs its key generation algorithm on input security parameter λ and outputs a symmetric key $\text{K} \leftarrow \texttt{KeyGen}(1^\lambda)$. Taking the key K and the received message $\texttt{m}$, $\mathcal{B}_\text{D}$ runs its data encapsulation algorithm $C_D \leftarrow \texttt{DEncaps}(\texttt{vk}_{\text{sots}}, \text{K})$. It compares whether $C_D = \sigma$, if so it forwards this query on C_D to its own $\mathcal{O}\texttt{DDecaps}$ oracle and receives either $\texttt{m}$ or $\bot$. In case the oracle's output is $\texttt{m}$, it returns 1 to $\mathcal{A}_{uan}$ adversary.

To simulate user's attribute-based secret key, algorithm $\mathcal{B}_\text{K}$ is invoked and queries it's own $\mathcal{O}\texttt{ABKKeyGen}$ on input public parameters $\texttt{param}$ and master secret key $\texttt{msk}$. The output is $\texttt{sk}_{\text{A}_\text{i}} \leftarrow \mathcal{O}\texttt{ABKKeyGen}$. The simulator sets $\texttt{usk}[\texttt{i}] = (\texttt{sk}_\text{i}, \texttt{sk}_{\text{A}_\text{i}})$.

Challenge: When adversary $\mathcal{A}_{\text{uan}}$ outputs $(\texttt{state}, \texttt{i}_0, \texttt{i}_1, \texttt{m})$, it picks $\texttt{b} \in \{0, 1\}$, computes signature $\sigma_\text{b} \leftarrow \texttt{ABGSign}(\texttt{param}, \texttt{usk}[\texttt{i}_\text{b}], \texttt{m}, \Gamma)$, simulator invokes its $\mathcal{B}_{\text{pke}}$, who randomly creates two messages m. Simulator invokes $\mathcal{B}_\text{K}$ of the key encapsulation algorithm on input $(\texttt{param}, \Gamma)$, i.e. $(\text{E}_\Gamma,) \leftarrow \texttt{ABKEncaps}(\texttt{param}, \Gamma)$.

Furthermore $\mathcal{A}_{uan}$ invokes the $\mathcal{B}_{SOTS}$ algorithm to simulates the keys of SOTS scheme by running $(\mathrm{vk}_{\mathrm{sots}}, \mathrm{sk}_{\mathrm{sots}}) \leftarrow \mathrm{KeyGen}_{\mathrm{SOTS}}$. The verification key $\mathrm{vk}_{\mathrm{sots}}$ will be a part of the NIZK proof. $\mathcal{B}_{\mathrm{K}}$ signs $\mathrm{vk}_{\mathrm{sots}}$ using simulated secret key $\mathrm{usk}[i]$, where the secret key simulation is given by a random guess with probability $1/|\mathcal{K}|$. The guessing probability reduces $\mathcal{B}'_{\mathrm{K}}s$ advantage to win the game. If the guess of the keys does not match with the real secret key, the simulation aborts. The signature procedure continues as follows: Taking K and the verification key $\mathrm{vk}_{\mathrm{sots}}$ as a message, it runs encapsulation algorithm of the underlying DEM scheme, $\hat{\sigma} = \mathrm{DEncaps}(\mathrm{vk}_{\mathrm{sots}}, \mathrm{K})$. Furthermore $\mathcal{B}_{\mathrm{pke}}$ of the underlying encryption scheme is invoked, which outputs a ciphertext encrypting user's certificate cert_{i_b}, and signature $\hat{\sigma}$, i.e. $\mathrm{C} \leftarrow \mathrm{Encrypt}(\mathrm{pk}_{\mathrm{e}}, \langle i_b, \mathrm{pk}_{i_b}, \mathrm{cert}_{i_b}, \hat{\sigma}, \mathrm{R} \rangle)$, where R is a randomness used in the NIZK proof. Finally taking as input a message m, verification key $\mathrm{vk}_{\mathrm{sots}}$, ciphertext π and the corresponding proof $\hat{\pi} = (\pi_1, \pi_2)$, $\mathcal{B}_p$ runs the signature algorithm of the underlying SOTS scheme and outputs $\sigma_{\mathrm{sots}} \leftarrow \mathrm{Sign}(m, \mathrm{vk}_{\mathrm{sots}}, \mathrm{C}, \hat{\pi})$. Furthermore, simulator runs the NIZK proof π_1 from the ABS scheme to prove the knowledge of K that is the output of $\mathrm{ABKDecaps}$ algorithm on input a secret key $\mathrm{sk}_{\mathbb{A}}$. $\mathcal{B}_{\mathrm{pke}}$ runs the NIZK proof π_2 that the certificate cert_i is a signature under CIE's public key pk_s. The final signature is equal to $\hat{\sigma} = (\mathrm{C}, \hat{\pi} = (\pi_1, \pi_2))$. We note that whenever $\mathcal{A}_{uan}$ submits a query (C, π') to the opening oracle, simulator invokes $\mathcal{B}_{\mathrm{pke}}$ and forwards the query to its decryption oracle. Finally it outputs a bit b and terminates the simulation.

Distinguisher for Zero-Knowledge. Distinguisher involved in the NIZK proof is given in the following description of the algorithm $\mathcal{D}(\mathrm{choose}, \lambda, \mathrm{R})$:

1. $(\mathrm{vk}_{\mathrm{sots}}, \mathrm{sk}_{\mathrm{sots}}) \leftarrow \mathrm{KeyGen}_{\mathrm{sots}}(1^\lambda)$
2. $(\mathrm{pk}_{\mathrm{e}}, \mathrm{sk}_{\mathrm{e}}) \leftarrow \mathrm{KeyGen}_{\mathrm{e}}(1^\lambda)$
3. $(\mathrm{pk}_{\mathrm{s}}, \mathrm{sk}_{\mathrm{s}}) \leftarrow \mathrm{KeyGen}_{\mathrm{s}}(1^\lambda)$
4. $(\mathrm{crs}, \mathrm{R}) \leftarrow \mathrm{SIM}(\mathrm{generate}, \lambda)$
5. Set $\mathrm{gpk} = (\lambda, \mathrm{R}, \mathrm{pk}_{\mathrm{e}}, \mathrm{pk}_{\mathrm{s}}, \mathrm{vk}_{\mathrm{sots}})$
    End for **(a)**. $(\mathrm{state}, i_0, i_1, m^*, \mathrm{vk}_{\mathrm{sots}}^*, \Gamma^*) \leftarrow \mathcal{A}_{\mathrm{uan}}^{\mathcal{O}_{\mathrm{ABGOpen}}(\cdot)}(\mathrm{param}, \mathrm{msk}, \cdot)$;
    (b). $\mathrm{b} \in \{0,1\}, \mathrm{R} \in \{0,1\}^\lambda$; **(c)**. $\mathrm{C}_{\mathrm{D}} \leftarrow \mathrm{ABKEncaps}(\mathrm{K}, \mathrm{vk}_{\mathrm{sots}}^*), \mathrm{C}_{\mathrm{D}} := \hat{\sigma}^*$;
    (d). $\mathrm{C}^* \leftarrow \mathrm{Encrypt}(\mathrm{pk}_{\mathrm{e}}, \langle i_b, \mathrm{pk}_{i_b}, \mathrm{cert}_{i_b}, \hat{\sigma}^*, \mathrm{R} \rangle)$;
    (e). $\sigma_{\mathrm{sots}} \leftarrow \mathrm{Sign}_{\mathrm{sots}}(m^*, \mathrm{vk}_{\mathrm{sots}}^*, \mathrm{C}^*, \hat{\pi}^*)$.

We note that distinguisher $\mathcal{D}$ can answer any queries submitted by $\mathcal{A}_{\mathrm{uan}}$, because it is in possession of group manager's secret key, which can be used to open the signatures. The output of the challenge phase is a signature gives as $(\mathrm{pk}_{\mathrm{e}}, \mathrm{pk}_{\mathrm{s}}, m, \mathrm{C})$ together with a witness. In the second stage, distinguisher takes as input a proof $\hat{\pi} = (\pi_1, \pi_2)$ and creates a groups signature $\hat{\sigma} = (\mathrm{C}, \hat{\pi}, \sigma_{\mathrm{sots}})$ and outputs it to the adversary $\mathcal{A}_{\mathrm{uan}}$. Finally, $\mathcal{D}$ outputs the same value as $\mathcal{A}_{\mathrm{uan}}$.

Soundness of NIZK proof. In order to prove simulation soundness of the NIZK proof, we consider the following game where an adversary $\mathcal{A}_{\mathrm{ss}}$ against simulation soundness of NIZK is playing against a challenger, who is represented by the adversary against our ABGS scheme:

1. $(\mathtt{vk_{sots}}, \mathtt{sk_{sots}}) \leftarrow \mathtt{KeyGen_{sots}}(1^\lambda)$
2. $(\mathtt{pk_e}, \mathtt{sk_e}) \leftarrow \mathtt{KeyGen_e}(1^\lambda)$
3. $(\mathtt{pk_s}, \mathtt{sk_s}) \leftarrow \mathtt{KeyGen_s}(1^\lambda)$
4. $(\mathtt{crs}, \mathtt{R}) \leftarrow \mathtt{SIM}(\mathtt{generate}, \lambda)$
5. Set $\mathtt{gpk} = (\lambda, \mathtt{R}, \mathtt{pk_e}, \mathtt{pk_s}, \mathtt{vk_{sots}})$

End for **(a)**. $\mathtt{m}^*, \Gamma^*, \sigma^* \leftarrow \mathcal{A}_{\mathtt{uan}}^{\mathcal{O}\mathrm{ABGOpen}(\mathtt{param}, \mathtt{gmsk}, \cdot)}(\mathtt{param}, \mathtt{msk}, \cdot)$;
(b). $(\mathtt{K}, \mathtt{E}_{\Gamma^*}) \leftarrow \mathtt{ABKEncaps}(\mathtt{param}, \Gamma^*)$; **(c)**. $\mathtt{C_D} \leftarrow \mathtt{ABKEncaps}(\mathtt{K}, \mathtt{vk_{sots}^*})$,
$\mathtt{C_D} = \hat{\sigma}^*$; **(d)**. $\mathtt{C} \leftarrow \mathtt{Encrypt}(\mathtt{pk_e}, \langle \mathtt{i_b}, \mathtt{pk_{i_b}}, \mathtt{cert_{i_b}}, \sigma_\mathtt{b}, \mathtt{R} \rangle)$;
(e). $\sigma_{\mathtt{sots}} \leftarrow \mathtt{Sign_{sots}}(\mathtt{m}^*, \mathtt{vk_{sots}^*}, \mathtt{C}^*, \hat{\pi}^*)$;
(f). $\pi \leftarrow \mathtt{SIM}(\mathtt{prove}, \mathtt{crs}, \mathtt{param}, \mathtt{m}^*, \sigma^*, \mathtt{sk_A}, \Gamma^*)$.
Make oracle queries to $\mathcal{O}\mathrm{ABKeyGen}$ to simulate user's attribute-based secret key $\mathtt{sk_{A_i}}$. Run $\mathtt{Verify}(\mathtt{param}, \sigma_{\mathtt{sots}}, \pi, \mathtt{C})$. If $\mathcal{A}_{\mathtt{uan}}$ outputs a valid $\sigma_{\mathtt{sots}}, \pi', \mathtt{C}$, output $(\mathtt{param}, \mathtt{crs}, \sigma_{\mathtt{sots}}, \pi', \mathtt{C})$.

Due to the page limit we provide only the final result of adversary's success. For the detailed analysis of this proof, we refer to the later full version of this paper. Finally we conclude that the advantage of an adversary $\mathcal{A}_{\mathtt{uan}}$ is given by the following combined inequation:

$$\mathrm{Adv}_{\mathcal{A}_{\mathtt{uan}}, \mathrm{ABGS}}^{\mathrm{U-ANO}} \leq \mathrm{Adv}_{\mathcal{A}_{\mathtt{ss}}, \mathrm{ABGS}}^{\mathrm{Sim-Sound}} + \mathrm{Adv}_{\mathcal{A}_{\mathtt{ind}}, \mathrm{KEM}}^{\mathrm{IND-CCA}} + +\mathrm{Adv}_{\mathcal{A}_{\mathtt{ind}}, \mathrm{DEM}}^{\mathrm{IND-CCA}} + \mathrm{Adv}_{\mathcal{A}_{\mathtt{ind}}\mathrm{PKE}}^{\mathrm{IND-CCA}} + \mathrm{Adv}_{\mathcal{A}_{\mathtt{zk}}, \mathrm{NIZK}}^{\mathrm{ZK}}$$

7 Conclusion

In this paper, we first presented a generic design for Attribute-Based Signatures (ABS). Further we have extended our construction to the generic scheme of any Attribute-Based Group Signature (ABGS), combining our generic structure of ABS with an existing proposal of generic group signature. We have also analyzed security of the proposed constructions following the most standard and comparatively efficient proof system, the Non-Interactive Zero Knowledge Proof of Knowledge approach.

References

1. Ali, S.T., Amberker, B.B.: Short attribute-based group signature without random oracles with attribute anonymity. In: Thampi, S.M., Atrey, P.K., Fan, C.-I., Perez, G.M. (eds.) SSCC 2013. CCIS, vol. 377, pp. 223–235. Springer, Heidelberg (2013). https://doi.org/10.1007/978-3-642-40576-1_22
2. Ateniese, G., Camenisch, J., Hohenberger, S., de Medeiros, B.: Practical group signatures without random oracles. IACR Cryptology ePrint Archive, 2005:385 (2005)
3. Ateniese, G., Camenisch, J., Joye, M., Tsudik, G.: A practical and provably secure coalition-resistant group signature scheme. In: Bellare, M. (ed.) CRYPTO 2000. LNCS, vol. 1880, pp. 255–270. Springer, Heidelberg (2000). https://doi.org/10.1007/3-540-44598-6_16

4. Attrapadung, N., Libert, B., de Panafieu, E.: Expressive key-policy attribute-based encryption with constant-size ciphertexts. In: Catalano, D., Fazio, N., Gennaro, R., Nicolosi, A. (eds.) PKC 2011. LNCS, vol. 6571, pp. 90–108. Springer, Heidelberg (2011). https://doi.org/10.1007/978-3-642-19379-8_6
5. Bellare, M., Micciancio, D., Warinschi, B.: Foundations of group signatures: formal definitions, simplified requirements, and a construction based on general assumptions. In: Biham, E. (ed.) EUROCRYPT 2003. LNCS, vol. 2656, pp. 614–629. Springer, Heidelberg (2003). https://doi.org/10.1007/3-540-39200-9_38
6. Bellare, M., Shi, H., Zhang, C.: Foundations of group signatures: the case of dynamic groups. In: Menezes, A. (ed.) CT-RSA 2005. LNCS, vol. 3376, pp. 136–153. Springer, Heidelberg (2005). https://doi.org/10.1007/978-3-540-30574-3_11
7. Bethencourt, J., Sahai, A., Waters, B.: Ciphertext-policy attribute-based encryption. In: Security and Privacy, SP 2007, pp. 321–334. IEEE (2007)
8. Bobba, R., Fatemieh, O., Khan, F., Gunter, C.A., Khurana, H.: Using attribute-based access control to enable attribute-based messaging. In: ACSAC 2006, pp. 403–413. IEEE (2006)
9. Boneh, D., Boyen, X.: Efficient selective-ID secure identity-based encryption without random oracles. In: Cachin, C., Camenisch, J.L. (eds.) EUROCRYPT 2004. LNCS, vol. 3027, pp. 223–238. Springer, Heidelberg (2004). https://doi.org/10.1007/978-3-540-24676-3_14
10. Boneh, D., Boyen, X.: Short signatures without random oracles. In: Cachin, C., Camenisch, J.L. (eds.) EUROCRYPT 2004. LNCS, vol. 3027, pp. 56–73. Springer, Heidelberg (2004). https://doi.org/10.1007/978-3-540-24676-3_4
11. Boneh, D., Boyen, X., Goh, E.-J.: Hierarchical identity based encryption with constant size ciphertext. In: Cramer, R. (ed.) EUROCRYPT 2005. LNCS, vol. 3494, pp. 440–456. Springer, Heidelberg (2005). https://doi.org/10.1007/11426639_26
12. Boyen, X., Waters, B.: Compact group signatures without random oracles. In: Vaudenay, S. (ed.) EUROCRYPT 2006. LNCS, vol. 4004, pp. 427–444. Springer, Heidelberg (2006). https://doi.org/10.1007/11761679_26
13. Boyen, X., Waters, B.: Full-domain subgroup hiding and constant-size group signatures. In: Okamoto, T., Wang, X. (eds.) PKC 2007. LNCS, vol. 4450, pp. 1–15. Springer, Heidelberg (2007). https://doi.org/10.1007/978-3-540-71677-8_1
14. Camenisch, J., Lysyanskaya, A.: Signature schemes and anonymous credentials from bilinear maps. In: Franklin, M. (ed.) CRYPTO 2004. LNCS, vol. 3152, pp. 56–72. Springer, Heidelberg (2004). https://doi.org/10.1007/978-3-540-28628-8_4
15. Chaum, D., van Heyst, E.: Group signatures. In: Davies, D.W. (ed.) EUROCRYPT 1991. LNCS, vol. 547, pp. 257–265. Springer, Heidelberg (1991). https://doi.org/10.1007/3-540-46416-6_22
16. Cheng, X., Zhou, S., Guo, L., Yu, J., Ma, H.: An ID-based short group signature scheme. J. Softw. 8(3), 554–559 (2013)
17. Emura, K., Miyaji, A., Omote, K.: A dynamic attribute-based group signature scheme and its application in an anonymous survey for the collection of attribute statistics. Inf. Media Technol. 4(4), 1060–1075 (2009)
18. Escala, A., Herranz, J., Morillo, P.: Revocable attribute-based signatures with adaptive security in the standard model. In: Nitaj, A., Pointcheval, D. (eds.) AFRICACRYPT 2011. LNCS, vol. 6737, pp. 224–241. Springer, Heidelberg (2011). https://doi.org/10.1007/978-3-642-21969-6_14
19. Frikken, K., Atallah, M., Li, J.: Attribute-based access control with hidden policies and hidden credentials. IEEE Trans. Comput. 55(10), 1259–1270 (2006)

20. Goyal, V., Pandey, O., Sahai, A., Waters, B.: Attribute-based encryption for fine-grained access control of encrypted data. In: Proceedings of the 13th ACM Conference on Computer and Communications Security, pp. 89–98. ACM (2006)
21. Groth, J.: Simulation-sound NIZK proofs for a practical language and constant size group signatures. In: Lai, X., Chen, K. (eds.) ASIACRYPT 2006. LNCS, vol. 4284, pp. 444–459. Springer, Heidelberg (2006). https://doi.org/10.1007/11935230_29
22. Groth, J., Ostrovsky, R., Sahai, A.: Perfect non-interactive zero knowledge for NP. In: Vaudenay, S. (ed.) EUROCRYPT 2006. LNCS, vol. 4004, pp. 339–358. Springer, Heidelberg (2006). https://doi.org/10.1007/11761679_21
23. Herranz, J., Laguillaumie, F., Libert, B., Ràfols, C.: Short attribute-based signatures for threshold predicates. In: Dunkelman, O. (ed.) CT-RSA 2012. LNCS, vol. 7178, pp. 51–67. Springer, Heidelberg (2012). https://doi.org/10.1007/978-3-642-27954-6_4
24. Herreweghen, E.: Secure anonymous signature-based transactions. In: Cuppens, F., Deswarte, Y., Gollmann, D., Waidner, M. (eds.) ESORICS 2000. LNCS, vol. 1895, pp. 55–71. Springer, Heidelberg (2000). https://doi.org/10.1007/10722599_4
25. Holt, J.E., Bradshaw, R.W., Seamons, K.E., Orman, H.: Hidden credentials. In: Proceedings of the 2003 ACM Workshop on Privacy in the Electronic Society, pp. 1–8. ACM (2003)
26. Kazue, S.: Generating statistical information in anonymous surveys. IEICE Trans. Fund. Electron. Commun. Comput. Sci. **79**(4), 507–512 (1996)
27. Khader, D.: Attribute based group signature with revocation. IACR Cryptology ePrint Archive, 2007:241 (2007)
28. Khader, D.: Attribute based group signatures. IACR Cryptology ePrint Archive, 2007:159 (2007)
29. Kiayias, A., Yung, M.: Secure scalable group signature with dynamic joins and separable authorities. Int. J. Secur. Netw. **1**(1–2), 24–45 (2006)
30. Lewko, A., Okamoto, T., Sahai, A., Takashima, K., Waters, B.: Fully secure functional encryption: attribute-based encryption and (Hierarchical) inner product encryption. In: Gilbert, H. (ed.) EUROCRYPT 2010. LNCS, vol. 6110, pp. 62–91. Springer, Heidelberg (2010). https://doi.org/10.1007/978-3-642-13190-5_4
31. Li, J., Kim, K.: Attribute-based ring signatures. IACR Cryptology EPrint Archive, 2008:394 (2008)
32. Liang, X., Cao, Z., Shao, J., Lin, H.: Short group signature without random oracles. In: Qing, S., Imai, H., Wang, G. (eds.) ICICS 2007. LNCS, vol. 4861, pp. 69–82. Springer, Heidelberg (2007). https://doi.org/10.1007/978-3-540-77048-0_6
33. Maji, H.K., Prabhakaran, M., Rosulek, M.: Attribute-based signatures: Achieving attribute-privacy and collusion-resistance. IACR Cryptology ePrint Archive, 2008:328 (2008)
34. Maji, H.K., Prabhakaran, M., Rosulek, M.: Attribute-based signatures. In: Kiayias, A. (ed.) CT-RSA 2011. LNCS, vol. 6558, pp. 376–392. Springer, Heidelberg (2011). https://doi.org/10.1007/978-3-642-19074-2_24
35. Nakanishi, T., Sugiyama, Y.: An efficient anonymous survey for attribute statistics using a group signature scheme with attribute tracing. IEICE Trans. Fund. Electron. Commun. Comput. Sci. **86**(10), 2560–2568 (2003)
36. Okamoto, T., Takashima, K.: Efficient attribute-based signatures for non-monotone predicates in the standard model. In: Catalano, D., Fazio, N., Gennaro, R., Nicolosi, A. (eds.) PKC 2011. LNCS, vol. 6571, pp. 35–52. Springer, Heidelberg (2011). https://doi.org/10.1007/978-3-642-19379-8_3

37. Patel, B.K., Jinwala, D.: Anonymity in attribute-based group signatures. In: Thilagam, P.S., Pais, A.R., Chandrasekaran, K., Balakrishnan, N. (eds.) ADCONS 2011. LNCS, vol. 7135, pp. 495–504. Springer, Heidelberg (2012). https://doi.org/10.1007/978-3-642-29280-4_58

38. Shahandashti, S.F., Safavi-Naini, R.: Threshold attribute-based signatures and their application to anonymous credential systems. In: Preneel, B. (ed.) AFRICACRYPT 2009. LNCS, vol. 5580, pp. 198–216. Springer, Heidelberg (2009). https://doi.org/10.1007/978-3-642-02384-2_13

39. Yang, G., Wong, D.S., Deng, X., Wang, H.: Anonymous signature schemes. In: Yung, M., Dodis, Y., Kiayias, A., Malkin, T. (eds.) PKC 2006. LNCS, vol. 3958, pp. 347–363. Springer, Heidelberg (2006). https://doi.org/10.1007/11745853_23

40. Zhang, J., Geng, Q.: A novel ID-based group signature scheme. In: Wireless Communications, Networking and Mobile Computing, pp. 1–4. IEEE (2008)

An Improved Leveled Fully Homomorphic Encryption Scheme over the Integers

Xiaoqiang Sun[✉], Peng Zhang, Jianping Yu, and Weixin Xie

ATR Key Laboratory of National Defense Technology,
College of Information Engineering, Shenzhen University,
Shenzhen 518060, Guangdong, China
{xqsun,zhangp,yujp,wxxie}@szu.edu.cn

Abstract. A scale-invariant leveled fully homomorphic encryption (FHE) scheme over the integers is proposed by Coron *et al.* in PKC 2014, where the ciphertext noise increases linearly after each homomorphic multiplication. Then based on Coron's variant of the approximate greatest common divisor problem, we construct a more efficient leveled FHE scheme over the integers without the modulus switching technique, which could resist chosen plaintext attacks. The inner product operation in our homomorphic multiplication is eliminated by multiplying the multiplication key directly. The homomorphic multiplication in our scheme is realized by the more simplified multiplication key, in which the number of integers is decreased from $O(\Theta \cdot \eta)$ to $O(1)$ compared with Coron's scheme. Simulation results and analysis show that our scheme's performance of multiplication key and homomorphic multiplication is much more efficient than that of Coron's scheme.

Keywords: Leveled Fully Homomorphic Encryption
Approximate GCD · Homomorphic multiplication · Multiplication key

1 Introduction

Traditional public key encryption schemes are constructed based on several mathematical problems. For example, RSA [1] is based on the large integer factorization problem, and ElGamal [2] is constructed by the discrete logarithm problem. However, traditional public key encryption schemes don't support arbitrary operations on the ciphertext without the secret key. Homomorphic encryption (HE) allows computations on the ciphertext without decryption, which was originated in 1978 by Rivest, Adleman and Rertouzos [3]. Because of this special property, HE can be used in cloud computing, ciphertext search and etc. However, HE only supports finite homomorphic multiplications or homomorphic additions, for example, BGN [4] supports infinite homomorphic additions and once homomorphic multiplication. The first fully homomorphic encryption (FHE) scheme based on ideal lattices was proposed by Gentry [5] in 2009, which could support infinite homomorphic multiplications and homomorphic additions.

© Springer International Publishing AG 2017
J. K. Liu and P. Samarati (Eds.): ISPEC 2017, LNCS 10701, pp. 835–846, 2017.
https://doi.org/10.1007/978-3-319-72359-4_52

However, the construction of the FHE scheme based on ideal lattices is complicated, which induces sizes of ciphertext, public key and secret key excessive long. In 2010, Dijk *et al.* [6] introduced a new FHE scheme over the integers (DGHV). DGHV only applies trivial operations on the integers and its security can be reduced to the approximate greatest common divisor (GCD) problem. The somewhat homomorphic encryption (SWHE) scheme in the ref. [7] converted DGHV scheme's public key into the form of quadratic, thus the number of the integers in the public key is decreased from τ to $2\sqrt{\tau}$. Coron *et al.* [8] decreased the public key size by using the public key compression technique. And the modulus switching technique is applied to replace Gentry's squashing decryption circuit technique. It can be noticed that FHE scheme is complicated when the modulus switching technique [9] is applied to DGHV scheme. Coron *et al.* [10] proposed a variant of DGHV scheme with the scale-invariant property, which security is also based on the approximate GCD problem. This scheme doesn't use the modulus switching technique, which requires no huge storage space for public keys. The ciphertext's noise increases linearly after each homomorphic multiplication. Above refs. [6–8,10] discuss single-bit FHE schemes over the integers.

The FHE scheme in the ref. [11] described a batch DGHV scheme based on Chinese Remainder Theorem (CRT). However, these FHE schemes' public key size is $O(\lambda^7)$ and secret key size is $O(\lambda^9)$, which are too far for practical application. Cheon *et al.* [12] also proposed a batch FHE scheme based on the CRT over rings, which could resist the approximate GCD problem and the sparse subset sum problem (SSSP) attack. The overhead of the SWHE scheme in the ref. [12] is small, whose public key size is similar to that of DGHV scheme, however it is still too large.

The security of former FHE schemes over the integers can be only reduced to the approximate GCD problem. Meanwhile, some more efficient FHE schemes have been constructed based on the learning with errors (LWE) assumption. Jacob [13] improved the LWE-based FHE scheme in the ref. [14] by using symmetric groups and permutation matrices with fast bootstrapping speed, whose ciphertext noise increases polynomially. Then, Ducas and Micciancio proposed a faster bootstrapping method [15] based on the ref. [13] over ring. In 2015, Cheon and Stehlé [16] reduced the LWE assumption to the approximate GCD problem innovatively. It means that the approximate GCD problem is no easier than the LWE assumption. And the LWE assumption has the advantage of resisting quantum attack. Then he constructed a new FHE scheme [16] based on the improved approximate GCD problem without Gentry's technique of squashing decryption circuit [5], which ciphertext size is only $O(\lambda \log \lambda)$.

1.1   Contribution

In this paper, we still use the classical approximate GCD problem to improve the efficiency of FHE schemes over the integers. Our contributions consist of two parts, which are shown as follows.

On the one hand, based on the ref. [10]'s variant of the approximate GCD problem, we present a more efficient leveled FHE scheme over the integers without the modulus switching technique. To compress the size of the multiplication key, we decrease the number of integers in the multiplication key. Then, the homomorphic multiplication can be achieved by multiplying the multiplication key directly without the inner product in the ref. [10].

On the other hand, we implement the homomorphic multiplication on the personal computer, and demonstrate the efficiency of our scheme's homomorphic multiplication according to the detailed analysis.

1.2 Organization

The remainder of the paper is organized as follows. The preliminary is introduced in Sect. 2. In Sect. 3, an improved leveled FHE scheme over the integers is presented. The security analysis is given in Sect. 4. Section 5 shows simulation results and analysis. The whole paper is concluded in Sect. 6.

2 Preliminary

2.1 Basic Symbols

Given the security parameter λ, let lowercase English letters denote real number and integer, and uppercase English letters denote matrix.

For a real number z, let $\lceil z \rceil$, $\lfloor z \rfloor$, $\lfloor z \rceil$ denote the rounding of an up, down or the nearest integer, namely, they are the integers in the half open intervals $[z, z+1)$, $(z-1, z]$, $(z-1/2, z+1/2]$ respectively.

For a real number z and an integer p, let $q_p(z)$ and $r_p(z)$ denote the remainder of z with respect to p, namely $q_p(z) = \lfloor z/p \rceil$ and $r_p(z) = z - q_p(z) \cdot p$. Note that $r_p(z) \in (-p/2, p/2]$. $[z]_p$ or $z \mod p$ also denotes the remainder.

Given an m-dimensional vector $\boldsymbol{a} = (a_0, a_1, \cdots, a_{m-1})$, let $BitDecomp(\boldsymbol{a}) = (a_{0,0}, \cdots, a_{0,l-1}, \cdots, a_{m-1,0}, \cdots, a_{m-1,l-1})$, where $a_{i,j}$ is a_i's j-th bit and ordered from the least significant bit to the most significant bit, $l = \lceil \log q \rceil$. Let $Powersof2(\boldsymbol{a}) = (a_0, 2a_0, \cdots, 2^{l-1}a_0, \cdots, a_{m-1}, 2a_{m-1}, \cdots, 2^{l-1}a_{m-1})$.

Lemma 1 (Simplified Leftover Hash Lemma [17]). Let H be a family of 2-universal hash functions from X to Y. Suppose that $h \xleftarrow{R} H$ and $x \xleftarrow{R} X$ are chosen uniformly and independently. Then, $(h, h(x))$ is $\sqrt{|Y|/|X|}/2$-uniform over $H \times Y$.

2.2 Parameters

We use following five parameters (all polynomials of the security parameter λ) will be used in this paper [10,16]:

- η is the bit-length of the secret key. Let $\eta \geq \rho + O(L \log \lambda)$, in order to make the depth of the squashed decryption circuit less than that of the permitted circuit, where L is the multiplicative depth of the circuit to be evaluated;
- ρ is the bit-length of the first noise parameter. Let $\rho = \eta - L \log \lambda$, for reduction to the LWE assumption, where L is the multiplicative depth of the circuit to be evaluated;
- γ is the bit-length of an approximate GCD sample. Let $\gamma \geq \frac{\lambda}{\log \lambda}(\eta - \rho)^2$, to thwart various lattice-based attacks on the approximate GCD problem;
- τ is the number of integers in the public key. Let $\tau \geq \gamma + 2\lambda$, in order to apply the simplified leftover hash lemma.

To satisfy the constraints of above parameters, for convenience, we let $\rho = O(\lambda)$, $\eta = O(\lambda + L)$, $\gamma = O(L^2\lambda + \lambda^2)$ and $\tau = \gamma + 2\lambda$.

2.3   Approximate GCD

Definition 1 (Approximate GCD [10]). For a random η-bit secret number p, an integer q uniformly distributed in $[0, 2^\gamma/p^2)$, and an error distribution χ. The distribution $A_{q,\chi}^{APGCD}(p)$ is defined as follows: select q from $\mathbb{Z} \cap [0, 2^\gamma/p^2)$ randomly and small error r from χ, then return $x = q \cdot p^2 + r$. Then, generate samples from $A_{q,\chi}^{APGCD}(p)$ polynomially, output p.

In refs. [6,10,16], it has been proved that there is no effective attack could solve the approximate GCD problem.

2.4   Coron's Scale-Invariant Fully Homomorphic Encryption Scheme over the Integers

In this section, we first recall Coron's scale-invariant fully homomorphic encryption scheme over the integers [10]. For a random η−bit odd integer p and an integer $q_0 \in [0, 2^\gamma/p^2)$. We use the following distribution:

$$\mathcal{D}_{p,q_0}^\rho = \{q \cdot p^2 + r, q \in \mathbb{Z} \cap [0, q_0), r \in \mathbb{Z} \cap (-2^\rho, 2^\rho)\}.$$

Coron's Leveled Fully Homomorphic Encryption scheme $CLFHE = (KeyGen, Encrypt, Add, Convert, Mult, Decrypt)$ is described as follows:

- $CLFHE.KeyGen(1^\lambda)$: Given the security parameter λ, generate random η−bit secret key p and a γ−bit integer $x_0 = q_0 \cdot p^2 + r_0$, where $r_0 \in (-2^\rho, 2^\rho) \cap \mathbb{Z}$ and $q_0 \in [0, 2^\gamma/p^2)$. Randomly select the public key $x_i \in \mathcal{D}_{p,q_0}^\rho$, where $i = 1, 2, \cdots, \tau$. Let $y' \in \mathcal{D}_{p,q_0}^\rho$ and $y = y' + (p-1)/2$. Let z denote a vector of Θ numbers, which keeps $\kappa = 2\gamma + 2$ bits of precision after the binary point. Let s denote a vector such that

$$\frac{2^\eta}{p^2} = <s, z> +\varepsilon \mod 2^\eta,$$

where $|\varepsilon| \leq 2^{-\kappa}$. Let

$$\sigma = q \cdot p^2 + r + \lfloor Powersof2(s \cdot \frac{p}{2^{\eta+1}})\rceil,$$

where elements of q are randomly generated from $[0, q_0) \cap \mathbb{Z}$. Output the secret key $sk = \{p\}$ and the public key $pk = \{x_0, x_1, \cdots, x_\tau, y, \sigma, z\}$.

- $CLFHE.Encrypt(pk, m \in \{0, 1\})$: Given the public key pk and a random subset $S \subset 1, 2, \cdots, \tau$, output the ciphertext as follows:

$$c = [m \cdot y + \sum_{i \in S} x_i]_{x_0}.$$

- $CLFHE.Add(pk, c_1, c_2)$: Given the public key pk, ciphertexts c_1 and c_2, output the fresh ciphertext $c_{fresh} = (c_1 + c_2) \mod x_0$.
- $CLFHE.Convert(pk, c)$: Given the public key pk and the ciphertext c, output $c' = 2 \cdot < \sigma, BitDecomp(c) >$, where $c = (\lceil c \cdot z_i \rceil \mod 2^\eta)_{1 \le i \le \Theta}$.
- $CLFHE.Mul(pk, c_1, c_2)$: Given the public key pk, ciphertexts c_1 and c_2, output the fresh ciphertext $c_{fresh} = CLFHE.Convert(pk, 2 \cdot c_1 \cdot c_2) \mod x_0$.
- $CLFHE.Decrypt(sk, c)$: Given the ciphertext c and the secret key sk, output the decryption result $m = ((2c) \mod p) \mod 2$.

3 Leveled Fully Homomorphic Encryption Scheme

3.1 The Construction

Let η' and $\theta = O(\lambda)$ be two more parameters. Our Leveled Fully Homomorphic Encryption scheme $LFHE = (KeyGen, Enc, Add, Mul, Dec)$ is defined as follows:

- $LFHE.KeyGen(1^\lambda)$: Given the security parameter λ, generate random η-bit secret key p. Randomly select the public key $x_i \in A_{q,\chi}^{APGCD}(p)$, for $i = 0, 1, \cdots, \tau - 1$, where x_0 is the largest one, $\lfloor \frac{x_1}{p^2} \rfloor$ is an odd number. Restart the generation of x_0 and x_1 if they don't satisfy above conditions. The multiplication key is generated as follows:

$$mk = [\lfloor \frac{2^{\eta'}}{p^2} \rfloor + 2^{\eta'-1} \cdot p^2 \cdot q]_{x_0},$$

where $q \in \mathbb{Z} \cap [0, 2^\gamma/p^2)$, $\lfloor \frac{2^{\eta'}}{p^2} \rfloor \in \chi$. Output the public key $pk = \{(x_i)_{i=0,1,\cdots,\tau-1}, mk\}$ and the secret key $sk = p$.

- $LFHE.Enc(pk, S, m \in \{0, 1\})$: Given the public key pk and the randomly generated subset $S \subset \{1, 2, \cdots, \tau - 1\}$ of size θ, output the ciphertext c as follows:

$$c = [\sum_{i \in S} x_i + \lfloor \frac{x_1}{2} \rfloor \cdot m]_{x_0}.$$

- $LFHE.Add(pk, c_1, c_2)$: Given the public key pk, ciphertexts c_1 and c_2, output the fresh ciphertext $c_{fresh} = (c_1 + c_2) \mod x_0$.
- $LFHE.Mul(pk, c_1, c_2)$: Given the public key pk, ciphertexts c_1 and c_2, output the fresh ciphertext c_{fresh} as follows:

$$c_{fresh} = (\frac{1}{2^{\eta'-1}} c_1 \cdot c_2 \cdot mk) \mod x_0.$$

– $LFHE.Dec(sk, c)$: Given the ciphertext c and the secret key sk, output the decryption result

$$m = [\lfloor \frac{2c}{p^2} \rfloor]_2.$$

3.2   Correctness

Lemma 2 (Encryption noise). Let the key pair (sk, pk) generated by $LFHE.KeyGen(1^\lambda)$ and the ciphertext c generated by $LFHE.Enc(pk, S, m \in \{0, 1\})$. Then

$$c' = c(mod\, p^2) = r + \lfloor \frac{p^2}{2} \rceil m(mod\, p^2),$$

where $|r| \le (2\theta + 1/2) \cdot 2^\rho + 1/2$.

Proof. We can represent the public key x_i as the form of $x_i = p^2 \cdot q_i + r_i$, where $q_i \in \mathbb{Z} \bigcap [0, 2^\gamma/p^2)$, $i = 1, 2, \cdots, \tau - 1$. Then we have $\lfloor \frac{x_1}{2} \rceil = \frac{p^2 \cdot q_1}{2} + \frac{r_1}{2} + \delta$, where $|\delta| \le 1/2$. Hence,

$$c' = c(mod\, p^2)$$
$$= (\sum_{i \in S} x_i + \lfloor \frac{x_1}{2} \rceil m - kx_0)(mod\, p^2)$$
$$= (\sum_{i \in S} r_i + \lfloor \frac{p^2}{2} \rceil m + (\frac{r_1}{2} + \delta)m - kr_0)(mod\, p^2),$$

where $k \in [0, \theta]$, $|\delta| \le 1/2$. Consequently, the noise $|r| \le (2\theta + 1/2) \cdot 2^\rho + 1/2$ for $c' = c(mod\, p^2) = r + \lfloor \frac{p^2}{2} \rceil m(mod\, p^2)$.

Lemma 3 (Addition noise). Let the key pair (sk, pk) generated by $LFHE.$ $KeyGen(1^\lambda)$ and the ciphertext c_i generated by $LFHE.Enc(pk, S, m_i)$, where $i = 1, 2$. If $c_{add} = LFHE.Add(pk, c_1, c_2)$, then

$$c_{add} = r + \lfloor \frac{p^2}{2} \rceil (m_1 + m_2)(mod\, p^2),$$

where $|r| \le |r_1 + r_2| + 2^\rho + 1$.

Proof. We have $c'_i = c_i(mod\, p^2) = r_i + \lfloor \frac{p^2}{2} \rceil m_i(mod\, p^2)$, then

$$c_{add} = c_1 + c_2 - \delta x_0(mod\, p^2)$$
$$= r_1 + r_2 - \delta r_0 + \lfloor \frac{p^2}{2} \rceil (m_1 + m_2) + \delta'(mod\, p^2), \quad (1)$$

where $|\delta| \le 1$, $|\delta'| \le 1$, $i = 1, 2$. Hence, the noise $|r| \le |r_1 + r_2| + 2^\rho + 1$ for $c_{add} = r + \lfloor \frac{p^2}{2} \rceil (m_1 + m_2)(mod\, p^2)$.

Lemma 4 (Multiplication noise). Given the key pair (sk, pk) and the multiplication key mk generated by $LFHE.KeyGen(1^\lambda)$. The ciphertext c_i satisfying the condition that $c'_i = c_i (\mathrm{mod}\, p^2) = r_i + \lfloor \frac{p^2}{2} \rfloor m_i (\mathrm{mod}\, p^2)$, where $i = 1, 2$. Then

$$c_{mul} = \lfloor \frac{1}{2^{\eta'-1}} c_1 c_2 (\lfloor \frac{2^{\eta'}}{p^2} \rfloor + 2^{\eta'-1} \cdot p^2 q) \rceil_{x_0} = r + \lfloor \frac{p^2}{2} \rfloor (m_1 m_2)(\mathrm{mod}\, p^2),$$

where $|r| \leq |r_1| + |r_2| + 2^\rho \cdot (\theta^2 + 2)$.

Proof.

$$c_{mul} = \lfloor \frac{1}{2^{\eta'-1}} c_1 c_2 (\frac{2^{\eta'}}{p^2} + 2^{\eta'-1} \cdot p^2 q) \rceil_{x_0} (\mathrm{mod}\, p^2)$$

$$= \frac{1}{2^{\eta'-1}} (p^2 q_1 + r_1 + \lfloor \frac{p^2}{2} \rfloor m_1)(p^2 q_2 + r_2 + \lfloor \frac{p^2}{2} \rfloor m_2)(\frac{2^{\eta'}}{p^2} + 2^{\eta'-1} p^2 q) - k x_0 (\mathrm{mod}\, p^2)$$

$$= \frac{1}{2^{\eta'-1}} (p^4 q_1 q_2 + r_1 p^2 q_2 + \lfloor \frac{p^2}{2} \rfloor m_1 p^2 q_2 + p^2 q_1 r_2 + r_1 r_2 + \lfloor \frac{p^2}{2} \rfloor m_1 r_2$$

$$+ p^2 q_1 \lfloor \frac{p^2}{2} \rfloor m_2 + r_1 \lfloor \frac{p^2}{2} \rfloor m_2 + \lfloor \frac{p^2}{2} \rfloor^2 m_1 m_2)(\frac{2^{\eta'}}{p^2} + 2^{\eta'-1} \cdot p^2 q) - k x_0 (\mathrm{mod}\, p^2)$$

$$= \frac{1}{2^{\eta'-1}} (2 r_1 q_2 \cdot 2^{\eta'-1} + 2 r_2 q_1 \cdot 2^{\eta'-1} + \frac{r_1 r_2}{p^2} \cdot 2^{\eta'} + m_1 r_2 \cdot 2^{\eta'-1}$$

$$+ r_1 m_2 \cdot 2^{\eta'-1} + \lfloor \frac{p^2}{2} \rfloor m_1 m_2 \cdot 2^{\eta'-1}) - k x_0 (\mathrm{mod}\, p^2)$$

$$= 2 r_1 q_2 + 2 q_1 r_2 + 2 \frac{r_1 r_2}{p^2} + m_1 r_2 + r_1 m_2 + \lfloor \frac{p^2}{2} \rfloor m_1 m_2 - k r_0 (\mathrm{mod}\, p^2)$$

$$= r + \lfloor \frac{p^2}{2} \rfloor (m_1 m_2)(\mathrm{mod}\, p^2),$$

where $r = 2 r_1 q_2 + 2 q_1 r_2 + 2 \frac{r_1 r_2}{p} + m_1 r_2 + r_1 m_2 - k r_0$, $k \in [0, \theta^2]$. Therefore, the multiplication noise

$$|r| \leq |r_1| \cdot 2^{\theta + \gamma - \eta + 1} + |r_2| \cdot 2^{\theta + \gamma - \eta + 1} + 2^\rho \cdot 2 + |r_1| + |r_2| + \theta^2 \cdot \rho$$

$$= (|r_1| + |r_2| + 2) \cdot 2^{\theta + \gamma - \eta + 1} + 2^\rho \cdot (\theta^2 + 2).$$

Because ciphertexts c_1, c_2 and the multiplication key mk are all integers, the noise r is an integer. From above Lemmas 2 and 4, it can be known that our scheme's noise of addition or multiplication increases linearly.

Lemma 5 (Decryption Correctness). Let the secret key p generated by $LFHE.KeyGen(1^\lambda)$ and the ciphertext c generated by $LFHE.Enc(pk, S, m \in \{0, 1\})$. Then

$$LFHE.Dec(sk, c) = m, \text{if } c' = c(\mathrm{mod}\, p^2) = r + \lfloor \frac{p^2}{2} \rfloor m(\mathrm{mod}\, p^2),$$

where $|r| < p^2/4$.

Proof. Because $c' = c(\bmod p^2) = r + \lfloor\frac{p^2}{2}\rceil m(\bmod p^2)$, we can write as $c = r + \lfloor\frac{p^2}{2}\rceil m + p^2 q$. Then

$$[\lfloor\frac{2c}{p^2}\rceil]_2 = [\lfloor 2q + m + \frac{2r}{p^2}\rceil]_2$$
$$= [\lfloor m + 2(\frac{r}{p^2} + q)\rceil]_2$$
$$= m,$$

if $|r| < p^2/4$.

4 Security Analysis

Claim 1 (Security). For any parameters ρ, γ, η and τ, which are polynomials of the security parameter λ, the proposed leveled FHE scheme over the integers could resist chosen plaintext attacks (CPA), assumed that $A_{q,\chi}^{APGCD}(p)$ is difficult.

Proof. Let $\mathcal{A}$ be a probabilistic polynomial time (PPT) adversary which could distinguish the challenge ciphertext with the advantage ε. Detailed operations are as follows.

Setup: Take as input the security parameter λ, the challenger runs $LFHE.$ $KeyGen(1^\lambda)$ to get the public key pk_i and the secret key sk_i polynomially, where $i = 1, 2, \cdots, t$, t is the maximum number of query. Then send pk_i and sk_i to $\mathcal{A}$, where $i = 1, 2, \cdots, t$.

Queries 1: The challenger chooses $m_i \in \{0, 1\}$ and the subset $S \subset \{1, 2, \cdots, \tau - 1\}$ randomly, then executes $LFHE.Enc(pk, S, m_i \in \{0, 1\})$ and sends the ciphertext c_i to $\mathcal{A}$, where $i = 1, 2, \cdots, t$.

Challenge: After queries, $\mathcal{A}$ outputs two different plaintexts m'_0, $m'_1 \in \{0, 1\}$, which have not been queried. Then the challenger chooses a random bit $k \in \{0, 1\}$, and generates the challenge public key pk^* which has not been queried. The challenge ciphertext c^* is obtained by running $LFHE.Enc(pk^*, S, m'_k)$, which is generated as follows,

$$c^* = [\sum\nolimits_{i \in S} x_i + \lfloor\frac{x_1}{2}\rceil m'_k]_{x_0}.$$

Queries 2: The same as **Queries 1**, and the challenge public key pk^* can't be queried again.

Output: $\mathcal{A}$ outputs a guess $k' \in \{0, 1\}$. Output 1 if $\mathcal{A}$ guesses right, else 0.
   In order to prove the security of the proposed leveled FHE scheme, we need to construct a distinguisher $\mathcal{D}$, namely

$$pk^* \text{ and } Unif(pk).$$

$\mathcal{D}$ takes pk^* and $pk' \in Unif(pk)$ as inputs, where $Unif(pk)$ represents the genuine public key distribution. $\mathcal{D}$ chooses $k \in \{0, 1\}$ randomly, then returns the challenge ciphertext $c_k^* = [\sum_{i \in S} x_i + \lfloor \frac{x_1}{2} \rceil m_k']_{x_0}$.

Assuming $\mathcal{D}$ has the advantage ε to distinguish ciphertexts $c_0^* = [\sum_{i \in S} x_i + \lfloor \frac{x_1}{2} \rceil m_0']_{x_0}$ and $c_1^* = [\sum_{i \in S} x_i + \lfloor \frac{x_1}{2} \rceil m_1']_{x_0}$. Because the challenge ciphertext $c_k^* (\bmod\, p^2) = r_k + \lfloor \frac{p^2}{2} \rceil m_k' (\bmod\, p^2)$, it can be regarded as the form of $c_k^* = x_k^* + r_k$, where $x_k^* = p^2 \cdot q_k + \lfloor \frac{p^2}{2} \rceil m_k'$, $\mathcal{D}$ has the same advantage to distinguish x_0^* and x_1^*. Hence, $\mathcal{D}$ has the same advantage ε to distinguish pk^* and pk', namely $\mathcal{D}$ could solve the approximate GCD problem successfully. In a word, the probability of distinguishing the challenge ciphertext is negligible, the proposed scheme could resist chosen plaintext attacks.

5   Simulation and Analysis

The key indicator of measuring the efficiency of a leveled FHE scheme is homomorphic multiplication. Because our scale-invariant leveled FHE scheme doesn't use the modulus switching technique, we only compare it with Coron's scheme. To compare the efficiency between the proposed scheme and Coron's scheme [10], two schemes are carried out on the same personal computer, and the experimental environment is as follows: the operating system is microsoft windows 7, featuring two Intel (R) Core (TM) i5-3470 CPU processors, running at 3.20 GHz, with 8.00 GB RAM, and the virtual machines operation system is Ubuntu 12.04, featuring single Intel (R) Core (TM) i5-3470 CPU processor, with 4.00 GB RAM. Our implementation uses the GMP large number library for high level numeric algorithms and the code is compiled on the GCC platform by the C++ language.

The implementation time of multiplication key and homomorphic multiplication between our scheme and Coron's scheme is shown in Tables 1 and 2, respectively. Each test has five iterations and datum shown in the tables are averages of them. As seen from Tables 1 and 2, the runtime of our scheme's multiplication key and homomorphic multiplication is reduced several magnitudes compared with Coron's scheme with the increasing of λ. Particularly, the number of integers in the multiplication key is reduced from $O(\Theta \cdot \eta)$ to $O(1)$. The detailed analysis is described as follows.

Table 1. Implementation time of multiplication key between our scheme and Coron's scheme [10] (unit: microsecond).

Security parameter λ	50	70	90	110	130
Coron's scheme	3970	29435	77359	134460	241478
Our scheme	4	13	17	24	30

Table 2. Implementation time of homomorphic multiplication between our scheme and Coron's scheme [10] (unit: microsecond).

Security parameter λ	50	70	90	110	130
Coron's scheme	302	1067	2292	4530	8308
Our scheme	9	26	51	74	107

Figures 1 and 2 show the efficiency of the proposed scheme and Coron's scheme. Simultaneously, two figures also indicate two schemes' changing trends of implementation time with the increasing of λ. As shown in Figs. 1 and 2, it can be easily known that our scheme's efficiency of multiplication key and homomorphic multiplication is much better than Coron's scheme with the increasing of λ. And the increasing tendency of our scheme's time of multiplication key and homomorphic multiplication is slower than that of Coron's scheme with the increasing of λ. In a word, our scheme is more efficient than Coron's scheme.

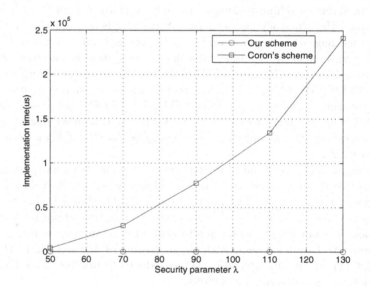

Fig. 1. Efficiency comparison of multiplication key in our scheme and Coron's scheme [10].

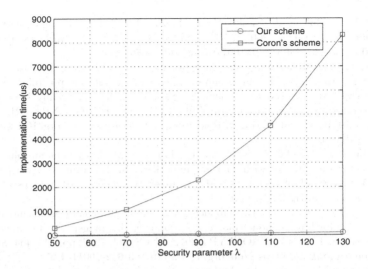

Fig. 2. Efficiency comparison of homomorphic multiplication in our scheme and Coron's scheme [10].

6   Conclusion

In this paper, we propose an efficient leveled FHE scheme over the integers based on Coron's variant of the approximate GCD problem. We prove that the proposed scheme also remains CPA secure under the approximate GCD problem. Compared with Coron's scheme, our scheme decreases the number of integers in the multiplication key from $O(\Theta \cdot \eta)$ to $O(1)$. Then, based on the more simplified multiplication key, the homomorphic multiplication can be efficiently achieved without the inner product. Simulation results and analysis show that our scheme's multiplication key and homomorphic multiplication is superior to Coron's scheme.

Acknowledgements. This work was supported by the National Natural Science Foundation of China (61702342), the Science and Technology Innovation Projects of Shenzhen (JCYJ20160307150216309, JCYJ20170302151321095, GJHZ20160226202520268) and Tencent Rhinoceros Birds-Scientific Research Foundation for Young Teachers of Shenzhen University. We would like to thank Jung Hee Cheon for his valuable comments.

References

1. Rivest, R.L., Shamir, A., Adleman, L.: A method for obtaining digital signatures and public-key cryptosystems. Commun. ACM **21**(2), 120–126 (1978)
2. ElGamal, T.: A public key cryptosystem and a signature scheme based on discrete logarithms. IEEE Trans. Inf. Theory **31**(4), 469–472 (1985)
3. Rivest, R.L., Adleman, L., Dertouzos, M.L.: On data banks and privacy homomorphisms. Found. Secur. Comput. **4**(11), 169–180 (1978)

4. Boneh, D., Goh, E.-J., Nissim, K.: Evaluating 2-DNF formulas on ciphertexts. In: Kilian, J. (ed.) TCC 2005. LNCS, vol. 3378, pp. 325–341. Springer, Heidelberg (2005). https://doi.org/10.1007/978-3-540-30576-7_18

5. Gentry, C.: Fully homomorphic encryption using ideal lattices. In: Proceedings of the 41st Annual ACM Symposium on Theory of Computing, pp. 169–178 (2009)

6. van Dijk, M., Gentry, C., Halevi, S., Vaikuntanathan, V.: Fully homomorphic encryption over the integers. In: Gilbert, H. (ed.) EUROCRYPT 2010. LNCS, vol. 6110, pp. 24–43. Springer, Heidelberg (2010). https://doi.org/10.1007/978-3-642-13190-5_2

7. Coron, J.-S., Mandal, A., Naccache, D., Tibouchi, M.: Fully homomorphic encryption over the integers with shorter public keys. In: Rogaway, P. (ed.) CRYPTO 2011. LNCS, vol. 6841, pp. 487–504. Springer, Heidelberg (2011). https://doi.org/10.1007/978-3-642-22792-9_28

8. Coron, J.-S., Naccache, D., Tibouchi, M.: Public key compression and modulus switching for fully homomorphic encryption over the integers. In: Pointcheval, D., Johansson, T. (eds.) EUROCRYPT 2012. LNCS, vol. 7237, pp. 446–464. Springer, Heidelberg (2012). https://doi.org/10.1007/978-3-642-29011-4_27

9. Brakerski, Z., Gentry, C., Vaikuntanathan, V.: (Leveled) fully homomorphic encryption without bootstrapping. In: Proceedings of the 3rd Innovations in Theoretical Computer Science Conference, vol. 6(3), pp. 309–325 (2012)

10. Coron, J.-S., Lepoint, T., Tibouchi, M.: Scale-invariant fully homomorphic encryption over the integers. In: Krawczyk, H. (ed.) PKC 2014. LNCS, vol. 8383, pp. 311–328. Springer, Heidelberg (2014). https://doi.org/10.1007/978-3-642-54631-0_18

11. Cheon, J.H., Coron, J.-S., Kim, J., Lee, M.S., Lepoint, T., Tibouchi, M., Yun, A.: Batch fully homomorphic encryption over the integers. In: Johansson, T., Nguyen, P.Q. (eds.) EUROCRYPT 2013. LNCS, vol. 7881, pp. 315–335. Springer, Heidelberg (2013). https://doi.org/10.1007/978-3-642-38348-9_20

12. Cheon, J.H., Kim, J., Lee, M.S., Yun, A.: CRT-based fully homomorphic encryption over the integers. Inf. Sci. **310**, 149–162 (2015)

13. Alperin-Sheriff, J., Peikert, C.: Faster bootstrapping with polynomial error. In: Garay, J.A., Gennaro, R. (eds.) CRYPTO 2014. LNCS, vol. 8616, pp. 297–314. Springer, Heidelberg (2014). https://doi.org/10.1007/978-3-662-44371-2_17

14. Gentry, C., Sahai, A., Waters, B.: Homomorphic encryption from learning with errors: conceptually-simpler, asymptotically-faster, attribute-based. In: Canetti, R., Garay, J.A. (eds.) CRYPTO 2013. LNCS, vol. 8042, pp. 75–92. Springer, Heidelberg (2013). https://doi.org/10.1007/978-3-642-40041-4_5

15. Ducas, L., Micciancio, D.: FHEW: bootstrapping homomorphic encryption in less than a second. In: Oswald, E., Fischlin, M. (eds.) EUROCRYPT 2015. LNCS, vol. 9056, pp. 617–640. Springer, Heidelberg (2015). https://doi.org/10.1007/978-3-662-46800-5_24

16. Cheon, J.H., Stehlé, D.: Fully homomophic encryption over the integers revisited. In: Oswald, E., Fischlin, M. (eds.) EUROCRYPT 2015. LNCS, vol. 9056, pp. 513–536. Springer, Heidelberg (2015). https://doi.org/10.1007/978-3-662-46800-5_20

17. Håstad, J., Impagliazzo, R., Levin, L.A., Luby, M.: A pseudorandom generator from any one-way function. SIAM J. Comput. **28**(4), 1364–1396 (1999)

The ECCA Security of Hybrid Encryptions

Honglong Dai[1], Jinyong Chang[1,2], Zhenduo Hou[1], and Maozhi Xu[1(✉)]

[1] School of Mathematics, Peking University, Beijing, People's Republic of China
{daihonglong,changjinyong,darthvader13}@pku.edu.cn, mzxu@math.pku.edu.cn
[2] School of Information and Control Engineering, Xi'an University of Architecture
and Technology, Xi'an, Shannxi, People's Republic of China

Abstract. In PKC 2014, Dana Dachman-Soled, et al. introduced enhanced chosen-ciphertext security (ECCA) for public key encryption. The enhancement refers to that the decryption oracle provided to the adversary is augmented to return not only the output of the decryption algorithm on a queried cipher-text but also of a randomness-recovery algorithm associated to the scheme. The authors have given the application of ECCA-secure encryption and we believe that ECCA security will find more application in the future. In this paper, we consider ECCA security of the well-known hybrid encryption (Tag-KEM/DEM) which was presented by Masayuki Abe, et al. in EUROCRYPT 2005. Meanwhile, we also consider ECCA security of hybrid encryption (KEM/Tag-DEM). We have proved that the hybrid encryption is secure against enhanced chosen cipher-text attack (ECCA) if both KEM part and DEM part satisfy some assumptions.

Keywords: Hybrid encryption
Enhanced chosen cipher-text attack security (ECCA)
Chosen cipher-text attack security (CCA)

1 Introduction

Secure encryption is the most basic task in cryptography, and some significant works have gone into defining and attaining it. In many commonly accepted definitions, such as chosen-plaintext attack (CPA) security and chosen-ciphertext attack (CCA) security, CCA security means that the adversary obtains no information about messages encrypted in other ciphertexts even she is allowed to query a decryption oracle on specifically chosen ciphertexts, therefore the CCA security has been accepted as the standard requirement for encryption schemes. However, in some conditions, randomness-recovering encryption is important, such as adaptive functions [8]and PKE with non-interactive opening [6]. ECCA security is motivated by the concept of randomness-recovering encryption, which was presented by Dana Dachman-Soled et al. [4]. The enhanced chosen cipher-text attack security means that the decryption oracle provided to the adversary not only outputs the decryption algorithm on a queried ciphertext but also a randomness-recovery algorithm associated to the scheme [11]. Furthermore,

© Springer International Publishing AG 2017
J. K. Liu and P. Samarati (Eds.): ISPEC 2017, LNCS 10701, pp. 847–859, 2017.
https://doi.org/10.1007/978-3-319-72359-4_53

the authors have given many public-key encryptions satisfying ECCA security and the application of ECCA security. In this paper, our results mainly concern the case in which the randomness-recovering algorithm is efficient. ECCA security is of both practical and theoretical interest.

The first standard-model construction of CCA-secure randomness-recovering PKE was achieved by Peikert and Waters [11] but public key encryption is too slow for encrypting long messages and big data. Under such a circumstance, the hybrid encryption method, which means encrypting a key k used for symmetric encryption to encrypt the messages by asymmetric encryption, has been created. In order to obtain secure ECCA hybrid encryption, we consider the ECCA security of hybrid public key encryptions. Cramer and Shoup proved that the hybrid encryption scheme (Tag-KEM/DEM) satisfies CCA secure if the part of KEM is CCA secure and the part of DEM also satisfies CCA secure [13]. Masayuki Abe, et al. presented a hybrid encryption scheme (Tag-KEM/DEM) which provided a simple way to create threshold versions of CCA-secure hybrid encryption schemes [2]. R. Canetti, H. Krawczyk, and J. Nielsen proposed a relaxed variant of CCA security, called Replayable CCA (RCCA) security [3]. Chen and Dong considered RCCA security for the KEM+DEM paradigm. They also considered RCCA security for (Tag-KEM/DEM) and KEM/Tag-DEM paradigm [10]. Motivated by their work, we consider the ECCA security of the Tag-KEM/DEM paradigm and its of the KEM/Tag-DEM paradigm.

Organizations of the Paper. In Sect. 2, we introduce some basic notations and definitions of the building blocks. In Sect. 3, we recall the definition of well known hybrid encryptions, KEM/Tag-DEM and Tag-KEM/DEM. Then we prove its ECCA security in detail. Conclusions can be found in Sect. 4.

2   Preliminaries

In this section, we will review some useful notations and definitions.

Notations. Let $\mathbb{N}$ be the set of natural numbers. If M is a set, then $|M|$ denotes its size and $m \xleftarrow{R} M$ denotes the operation of picking an element m uniformly at random from M. We denote λ as the security parameter. For notational clarity we usually omit it as an explicit parameter. PPT denotes probabilistic polynomial time. Let $z \leftarrow A(x, y, \cdots)$ denote the operation of running an algorithm $\mathcal{A}$ with inputs $(x, y, \cdots)$ and output z. We say a function $\mathrm{negl}(\lambda)$ is *negligible* (in λ) if $\lambda > k_0$ and $k_0 \in \mathbb{Z}$, $\mathrm{negl}(\lambda) < \lambda^{-c}$ for any constant $c > 0$.

2.1   ECCA Security Definition

A public-key encryption scheme PKE = (Gen,Enc,Dec) consists of three algorithm. Gen is a probabilistic algorithm that on input the security parameter λ, outputs public keys and privates keys (pk, sk) and pk defines the message space M. Enc is a probabilistic algorithm that encrypts a message $m \in M$ into a ciphertext c. Dec is a deterministic algorithm that decrypts c and outputs either $m \in M$ or a special symbol $\perp$. An adversary $\mathcal{A} = (\mathcal{A}_1, \mathcal{A}_2)$ is a probabilistic polynomial-time oracle query machine. We now describe the attack game between a challenger and an adversary $\mathcal{A} = (\mathcal{A}_1, \mathcal{A}_2)$ used to define security against adaptive Enhanced chosen ciphertext attack.

- **stage 1:** The adversary queries a key generation oracle. The key generation oracle runs $(pk, sk) \leftarrow \texttt{Gen}(\lambda)$ and responds adversary $\mathcal{A}$ with pk.
- **stage 2:** The adversary makes a sequence of calls to a decryption oracle. For each decryption oracle query, the adversary $\mathcal{A}_1$ submits a ciphertext c to $\texttt{Dec}^*$. The decryption oracle responds with $m \leftarrow \texttt{Dec}(sk, c)$ and the random recovery algorithm $\texttt{Dec}$ responds with $r \leftarrow \texttt{Rec}(sk, c)$. We require that for all the messages $m \in M$ (M is the space of message), $(pk, sk) \leftarrow \texttt{Gen}(1^\lambda)$,

$$\Pr[\texttt{Enc}(pk, m; r') \neq c; r \xleftarrow{R} \{0,1\}^\lambda; c \leftarrow \texttt{Enc}(pk, r, m_b); r' \leftarrow \texttt{Rec}(c, sk)]$$

  is negligible. Finally, if $m = \perp$, responds $\mathcal{A}$ with $\perp$, else responds $\mathcal{A}$ with (m, r).
- **stage 3:** The adversary $\mathcal{A}_1$ queries (m_0, m_1) to an encryption oracle with $|m_0| = |m_1|$. The challenger chooses $b \xleftarrow{R} \{0,1\}$, $r \xleftarrow{R} \{0,1\}^\lambda$, computes $Enc(pk, r, m_b) = c^*$, and sends c^* to adversary $\mathcal{A}_1$.
- **stage 4:** The adversary $\mathcal{A}_2$ continues to make calls c to the decryption oracle $\texttt{Dec}$ and the random recovery algorithm $\texttt{Rec}$, where c is subjected to the only restriction that a submitted ciphertext c is not identical to c^*. The decryption oracle responds with $m \leftarrow \texttt{Dec}(pk, c)$ and the random recovery algorithm $\texttt{Dec}$ responds with $r \leftarrow \texttt{Rec}(sk, c)$. Finally, if $m = \perp$, responds $\mathcal{A}_2$ with $\perp$, else responds $\mathcal{A}_2$ with (m, r).
- **stage 5:** The adversary $\mathcal{A}$ outputs a guessing bit $b' \in \{0,1\}$.

We define $\text{Adv}_{\texttt{PKE}, \mathcal{A}}^{\texttt{ECCA}}(\lambda)$ to be $|\Pr[b = b'] - \frac{1}{2}|$ in the above attack game.

We say that $\texttt{PKE} = (\texttt{KeyGen}, \texttt{Enc}, \texttt{Dec})$ is secure against enhanced adaptive chosen ciphertext attack if for all probabilistic, polynomial-time adversary $\mathcal{A}$, the function $\text{Adv}_{\texttt{PKE}, \mathcal{A}}^{\texttt{ECCA}}(\lambda)$ grows negligibly in λ. IND–CCA security is defined all the same except that the decryption oracle does not return a randomness-recovery algorithm associated to the scheme.

2.2 Key Encapsulation Mechanism and Its ECCA Security Notions

A key encapsulation mechanism KEM is a public key encryption scheme, which consists of the three polynomial-time algorithms $(\texttt{KEM.Gen}, \texttt{KEM.Enc}, \texttt{KEM.Dec})$ with the following interfaces:

Key Generation: **Encapsulation:**   **Decapsulation**

$(pk, sk) \leftarrow \texttt{KEM.Gen}(1^\lambda)$ $\psi \leftarrow \texttt{KEM.Enc}(pk, K, r)$ $K \text{ (or } \perp) \leftarrow \texttt{KEM.Dec}(sk, c)$

where $r \xleftarrow{R} \{0,1\}^\lambda$, $K \leftarrow \mathcal{K}_K$, $\mathcal{K}_K$ is the key space. KDM.Dec is a deterministic algorithm, (pk, sk) is a public/secret key pair and c is a ciphertext of the encapsulated key K under pk. We now describe the attack game between the challenger and an adversary $\mathcal{A} = (\mathcal{A}_1, \mathcal{A}_2)$ used to define its security against adaptive enhanced chosen ciphertext attack.

- **stage 1:** The adversary queries a key generation oracle. The key generation oracle runs $(pk, sk) \leftarrow \texttt{KEM.Gen}(\lambda)$ and responds adversary $\mathcal{A}$ with pk.
- **stage 2:** The adversary makes a sequence of calls to a decryption oracle. For each decryption oracle query, the adversary $\mathcal{A}_1$ submits a ciphertext ψ to Dec, the decryption oracle responds with $K \leftarrow \texttt{Dec}(sk, \psi)$, and the random recovery algorithm Dec responds with $r \leftarrow \texttt{Rec}(sk, \psi)$. Finally, if $K = \perp$, responds $\mathcal{A}$ with $\perp$, else responds $\mathcal{A}$ with (K, r).
- **stage 3:** The challenger chooses $r \xleftarrow{R} \{0,1\}^\lambda$ and computes $\psi^* \leftarrow \texttt{KEM.Enc}(pk, r, K_1)$, chooses $K_0 \xleftarrow{R} \mathcal{K}_K$, $\sigma \xleftarrow{R} \{0,1\}$. Here, $\mathcal{K}_K$ is the key space, $|K_0| = |K_1|$ and sends (K_σ, ψ^*) to adversary $\mathcal{A}_1$.
- **stage 4:** The adversary $\mathcal{A}_2$ continues to make calls ψ to the decryption oracle Dec and the random recovery algorithm Rec, where ψ is subjected to the only restriction that a submitted ciphertext ψ is not identical to ψ^*. The decryption oracle responds with $K \leftarrow \texttt{Dec}(sk, \psi)$ and the random recovery algorithm Dec responds with $r \leftarrow \texttt{Rec}(sk, \psi)$. Finally, if $K = \perp$, responds $\mathcal{A}_2$ with $\perp$, else responds $\mathcal{A}_2$ with (K, r).
- **stage 5:** The adversary $\mathcal{A}$ outputs a guessing bit $\sigma^{'} \in \{0,1\}$.

We define $\text{Adv}_{\texttt{KEM}, \mathcal{A}}^{\text{ECCA}}(\lambda)$ to be $|\Pr[\sigma = \sigma^{'}] - \frac{1}{2}|$ in the above attack game. We say that $\texttt{KEM} = (\texttt{KEM.Gen}, \texttt{KEM.Enc}, \texttt{KEM.Dec})$ is secure against enhanced adaptive chosen ciphertext attack if for all probabilistic polynomial-time adversary $\mathcal{A}$, the function $\text{Adv}_{\texttt{KEM}, \mathcal{A}}^{\text{ECCA}}(\lambda)$ grows negligibly in λ.

2.3 Date encapsution mechanism and its one time security

A $\texttt{DEM} = (\texttt{DEM.Enc}, \texttt{DEM.Dec})$ is a symmetric encryption scheme that consists of the two polynomial-time algorithms $(\texttt{DEM.Enc}, \texttt{DEM.Dec})$. $\texttt{DEM.ENC}$ and $\texttt{DEM.Dec}$ are associated to a key-space K_D and message space M.

Encapsulation:	Decapsulation
$\chi \leftarrow \texttt{DEM.Enc}(K, m)$	m (or $\perp$) $\leftarrow \texttt{DEM.Dec}(K, \chi)$

$\texttt{DEM.Enc}$ is an encryption algorithm that encrypts $m \in M$ by using symmetric-key $K \in K_D$ and outputs cipher-text χ, where $K \in K_D$. $\texttt{DEM.Dec}$ is a corresponding decryption algorithm that recovers message m by using the same symmetric-key when the input cipher-text χ. An adversary $\mathcal{A}$ is a probabilistic polynomial-time oracle query machine. We now describe the attack game between the challenger and an adversary $\mathcal{A}$ used to define one time security.

– **stage 1:** The adversary $\mathcal{A}$ queries (m_0, m_1) to an encryption oracle. We require that the output of $\mathcal{A}$ satisfies $|m_0| = |m_1|$. The challenger chooses $b \xleftarrow{R} \{0, 1\}$, $K \xleftarrow{R} K_D$, computes $\text{Enc}(K, m_b) = c^*$ and sends c^* to adversary $\mathcal{A}$. Here we stress that the ciphertext is made from a random key along with the plaintext and every key has been used only once.
– **stage 2:** The adversary $\mathcal{A}$ outputs a guessing bit $b' \in \{0, 1\}$.

We define $\text{Adv}_{\text{DEM}, \mathcal{A}}^{OT-UF}(\lambda)$ to be $|\Pr[b = b'] - \frac{1}{2}|$ in the above attack game.

We say that $\text{DEM} = (\text{DEM.Enc}, \text{DEM.Dec})$ is one time secure if for all probabilistic polynomial-time adversary $\mathcal{A}$, the function $\text{Adv}_{\text{DEM}, \mathcal{A}_2}^{OT-UF}(\lambda)$ grows negligibly in λ.

3   ECCA Security of Hybrid Scheme

3.1   Tag-KEM/DEM

Let $\text{Tag-KEM} = (\text{TKEM.Gen}, \text{TKEM.Enc}, \text{TKEM.Dec})$ be a public key encryption scheme and $\text{DEM} = (\text{DEM.Enc}, \text{DEM.Dec})$ be a symmetric encryption scheme. Then hybrid encryption scheme

$$\text{Tag-KEM/DEM} = (\text{HybGen}, \text{HybEnc}, \text{HybDec})$$

can be constructed as follows.

– $\text{HybGen}(1^\lambda)$: Run $(pk, sk) \leftarrow \text{TKEM.Gen}(1^\lambda)$ and output (pk, sk).
– $\text{HybEnc}(pk, m)$: Run $(\omega, K) \leftarrow \text{TKEM.Key}(pk)$, $\text{TKEM.Key}(\cdot)$ is a probabilistic algorithm that inputs public key pk and outputs one-time key $K \in K_D$ along with the internal state information ω. Here K_D is the key-space of DEM. Then choosing $r \xleftarrow{\$} \{0, 1\}^\lambda$ and computing

$$\chi \leftarrow \text{DEM.Enc}_K(m),$$

$$\psi \leftarrow \text{TKEM.Enc}_{pk}(\omega, r, \chi),$$

we get the result ciphertext (of m) $c := (\psi, \chi)$.
– $\text{HybDec}(sk, c)$: First, parse c as $\psi \| \chi$.
Run

$$K \leftarrow \text{TKEM.Dec}_{sk}(\psi, \chi), \text{ and } m \leftarrow \text{DEM.Dec}_K(\chi).$$

Then, output the message m or "reject" symbol $\perp$.

3.2   ECCA Security of Tag-KEM/DEM

Theorem 1. *If the scheme Tag-KEM is IND-ECCA secure and DEM is one time secure, then the hybrid scheme (Tag-KEM/DEM) is IND-ECCA secure. In particular, for every probabilistic polynomial time (PPT) adversary $\mathcal{A}$, there exists probabilistic adversaries $\mathcal{A}_1$ and $\mathcal{A}_2$ whose running times are essentially the same as that of $\mathcal{A}$, such that for all $\lambda \geq 0$, we have*

$$\text{Adv}_{Tag-KEM/DEM, \mathcal{A}}^{ECCA}(\lambda) \leq 2\text{Adv}_{Tag-KEM, \mathcal{A}_1}^{ECCA}(\lambda) + \text{Adv}_{DEM, \mathcal{A}_2}^{OT-UF}(\lambda). \tag{1}$$

Proof. Fix $\mathcal{A}$ and λ, $\mathcal{A}$ be a PPT adversary that attacks the hybrid scheme Tag–KEM/DEM. Now, the theorem can be proved via the following games. (Denote T_i if the adversary $\mathcal{A}$ wins in the i-th game).

Game$_0$: This is an ECCA experiment on the scheme Tag–KEM/DEM played between the challenger and an adversary $\mathcal{A}$. In particular, there is:

- **stage 1:** The adversary queries a key generation oracle. Then the challenger runs $(pk, sk) \leftarrow$ TKEM.Gen(λ) and responds adversary $\mathcal{A}$ with pk.
- **stage 2:** The adversary makes a sequence of calls to a decryption oracle. For each decryption oracle query, the adversary $\mathcal{A}_1$ submits a ciphertext $c = (\psi, \chi)$ to the challenger. Then the challenger runs

$$K \leftarrow \text{TKEM.Dec}_{sk}(\psi, \chi), \text{ and } m \leftarrow \text{DEM.Dec}_K(\chi).$$

and runs the random recovery algorithm $r \leftarrow$ Rec(c, sk). If $m = \bot$, the challenger responds $\mathcal{A}_1$ with $\bot$, else the challenger responds $\mathcal{A}_1$ with (m, r).
- **stage 3:** The adversary $\mathcal{A}_1$ queries (m_0, m_1) to an encryption oracle, and the challenger runs $(\omega, K) \leftarrow$ TKEM.Key(pk), $K \in K_D$, where K_D is the key-space of DEM. Then the challenger chooses $r \xleftarrow{R} \{0, 1\}^{\lambda}$ and computes

$$\text{DEM.Enc}_K(m_0) = \chi^*, \text{TKEM.Enc}_{pk}(r, \omega, \chi^*) = \psi^*,$$

and sends $c^* = (\psi^*, \chi^*)$ to the adversary $\mathcal{A}_1$.
- **stage 4:** The adversary $\mathcal{A}_2$ continues to make calls $c = (\psi, \chi)$ to the challenger, where c subjects to the only restriction that a submitted ciphertext c is not identical to c^*. The challenger runs

$$K \leftarrow \text{TKEM.Dec}_{sk}(\psi, \chi), \text{ and } m \leftarrow \text{DEM.Dec}_K(\chi)$$

and runs the random recovery algorithm $r \leftarrow$ Rec(c, sk). If $m = \bot$, the challenger responds $\mathcal{A}_2$ with $\bot$, else responds $\mathcal{A}_2$ with (m, r).
- **stage 5:** The adversary $\mathcal{A}$ outputs a guessing bit $b' \in \{0, 1\}$.

Naturally, it holds that

$$\text{Adv}^{ECCA}_{\text{Tag–KEM/DEM}, \mathcal{A}}(\lambda) = \left| \Pr[b = b'] - \frac{1}{2} \right| = \left| \Pr[T_0] - \frac{1}{2} \right|. \tag{2}$$

Game$_1$: This game is identical to the above game except we use a completely random symmetric key $K_0 \xleftarrow{R} K_D$ to encrypt m_0 in the step-4 of **Game$_0$**, so we have

Lemma 1. *There exists a probabilistic adversary $\mathcal{A}_1$ whose running time is essentially the same as that of $\mathcal{A}$, such that*

$$|\Pr[T_1] - \Pr[T_0]| \leq \text{Adv}^{ECCA}_{\text{Tag–KEM}, \mathcal{A}_1}(\lambda). \tag{3}$$

Proof. The claim is proven by constructing the adversary $\mathcal{A}_1$ that attacks Tag-KEM. The adversary $\mathcal{A}_1$ offers the environment for $\mathcal{A}$. We describe the interaction as follows.

- **stage 1:** The adversary $\mathcal{A}_1$ was given (pk, K_σ), and at the same time, pk was sent to adversary $\mathcal{A}$.
- **stage 2:** The adversary $\mathcal{A}$ makes a sequence of calls to a decryption oracle. For each decryption oracle query, the decryption oracle responds with $m \leftarrow \text{Dec}(sk, c)$ and the random recovery algorithm responds with $r \leftarrow \text{Rec}(sk, c)$. Finally, if $m = \perp$, responds $\mathcal{A}$ with $\perp$, else responds $\mathcal{A}$ with (m, r).
- **stage 3:** The adversary $\mathcal{A}$ queries (m_0, m_1) to an encryption oracle, $|m_0| = |m_1|$. The adversary $\mathcal{A}_1$ computes $\text{DEM.EncS}_{K_\sigma}(m_0) = \chi^*$ and outputs χ^* as the target tag, then it receives ψ^* as a challenge cipher. Finally, the adversary $\mathcal{A}_1$ sends $c^* = (\psi^*, \chi^*)$ to adversary $\mathcal{A}$.
- **stage 4:** The adversary $\mathcal{A}$ continues to make calls $c = (\psi_i, \chi_i)$ to decryption oracle query, where c subjects to the only restriction that a submitted ciphertext c is not identical to c^*. The adversary $\mathcal{A}_1$ runs

$$K_i \leftarrow \text{TKEM.Dec}_{sk}(\chi_i, \psi_i), \quad m \leftarrow \text{DEM.Dec}_{K_i}(\psi_i).$$

  and runs the random recovery algorithm $r \leftarrow \text{Rec(c, sk)}$. If $m = \perp$, the adversary $\mathcal{A}_1$ responds $\mathcal{A}$ with $\perp$, else responds $\mathcal{A}$ with (m, r).
- **stage 5:** $\mathcal{A}$ outputs a guessing bit $b' \in \{0, 1\}$ and $\mathcal{A}_1$ outputs $\sigma' = b'$.

This completes the description of $\mathcal{A}_1$. By construction, it is clear that decryption for $\mathcal{A}$ is perfectly simulated because the correct decryption is obtained from TKEM.Dec for every query.

- If $\sigma = 0$, we know that K_0 is a random key used for computing χ and the view of $\mathcal{A}$ is identical to that in **Game$_0$**.
- If $\sigma = 1$, we know that K_1 is the correct key embedded in ψ and the view of $\mathcal{A}$ is identical to that in **Game$_1$**.

we have that

$$|\Pr[T_1] - \Pr[T_0]| \leq \text{Adv}^{\text{ECCA}}_{\text{Tag-KEM}, \mathcal{A}_1}(\lambda).$$

The Lemma 1 is proved.

Game$_2$: This game is identical to Game$_1$ except that we encrypt m_1 instead of m_0 in the step-4 of **Game$_1$**.

Lemma 2. *There exists a probabilistic adversary $\mathcal{A}_2$ whose running time is essentially the same as that of $\mathcal{A}$, such that*

$$|\Pr[T_2] - \Pr[T_1]| \leq \text{Adv}^{\mathcal{OT}-\mathcal{UF}}_{\text{DEM}, \mathcal{A}_2}(\lambda). \tag{4}$$

Proof. The claim is proven by constructing the adversary $\mathcal{A}_2$ that attacks DEM, the adversary $\mathcal{A}_2$ offers the environment for $\mathcal{A}$. We describe the interaction as follows.

- **stage 1:** The adversary $\mathcal{A}_2$ runs the key generation oracle $(pk, sk) \leftarrow$ TKEM.Gen(λ) and sends pk adversary to $\mathcal{A}$.
- **stage 2:** The adversary $\mathcal{A}$ makes a sequence of calls to a decryption oracle. For each decryption oracle query, the adversary $\mathcal{A}$ submits a ciphertext c to the decryption oracle. The decryption oracle runs $m \leftarrow$ Dec(sk, c) and the random recovery algorithm $r \leftarrow$ Rec(sk,c). If $m = \bot$, responds $\mathcal{A}$ with $\bot$, else responds $\mathcal{A}$ with (m, r).
- **stage 3:** The adversary $\mathcal{A}$ sends (m_0, m_1) to $\mathcal{A}_2$, $\mathcal{A}_2$ queries (m_0, m_1) to an encryption oracle and receives challenge ciphertext χ^*. The adversary $\mathcal{A}_2$ chooses $r \xleftarrow{R} \{0,1\}^\lambda$, runs $(\omega, K) \leftarrow$ TKEM.Key(pk), then computes

$$\text{TKEM.Enc}_{pk}(r, \omega, \chi^*) = \psi^*,$$

and finally sends $c^* = (\psi^*, \chi^*)$ to adversary $\mathcal{A}$.
- **stage 4:** The adversary $\mathcal{A}$ continues to make calls $c = (\psi_i, \chi_i)$ to decryption oracle query, where c is subjected to the only restriction that a submitted ciphertext c is not identical to c^*. The the adversary $\mathcal{A}_2$ runs

$$K_i \leftarrow \text{TKEM.Dec}_{sk}(\psi_i, \chi_i), \ m \leftarrow \text{DEM.Dec}_{K_i}(\psi_i),$$

and runs the random recovery algorithm $r \leftarrow$ Rec(c, sk). If $m = \bot$, the adversary $\mathcal{A}_2$ responds $\mathcal{A}$ with $\bot$, else the adversary $\mathcal{A}_2$ responds $\mathcal{A}$ with (m, r).
- **stage 5:** $\mathcal{A}$ outputs a guessing bit $b' \in \{0,1\}$ and $\mathcal{A}_2$ outputs $\sigma' = b'$.

This completes the description of $\mathcal{A}_2$. By construction, the view of $\mathcal{A}$ is identical to that in **Game$_1$** and **Game$_2$**, it is clear that we have

$$|\Pr[T_1] - \Pr[T_2]| \leq \text{Adv}_{\text{DEM},\mathcal{A}_2}^{\mathcal{OT}-\mathcal{UF}}(\lambda).$$

Game$_3$: This game is identical to Game$_2$ except that we use the correct key K generated by TKEM.Key for DEM.Enc in the step-3 of **Game$_2$**.

Lemma 3. *There exists a probabilistic adversary $\mathcal{A}_1$ whose running time is essentially the same as that of $\mathcal{A}$, such that*

$$|\Pr[T_2] - \Pr[T_1]| \leq \text{Adv}_{Tag\text{-}KEM,\mathcal{A}_1}^{ECCA}(\lambda). \tag{5}$$

Proof. The proof is similar to Lemma 1, so we omit it here.

We know that $\mathcal{A}$'s advantage in Game$_0$

$$\text{Adv}_{Tag\text{-}KEM/DEM,\mathcal{A}}^{ECCA}(\lambda) = \left|\Pr[T_0] - \frac{1}{2}\right| \leq 2\text{Adv}_{Tag\text{-}KEM,\mathcal{A}_1}^{ECCA}(\lambda) + \text{Adv}_{\text{DEM},\mathcal{A}_2}^{\mathcal{OT}-\mathcal{UF}}(\lambda)$$

is negligible.

Putting all the facts together, the Theorem 1 is proved.

3.3   KEM/Tag-DEM

Let `KEM = (Gen,KEM.Enc,KEM.Dec)` be a public key encryption scheme and `Tag-DEM = (TDEM.Enc, TDEM.Dec)` be a symmetric key encryption scheme. Then hybrid cryptosystem scheme

$$\texttt{KEM/Tag-DEM} = (\texttt{HybGen}, \texttt{HybEnc}, \texttt{HybDec})$$

can be constructed as follows.

- `HybGen(1^λ)` : Run $(pk, sk) \leftarrow \texttt{Gen}(1^\lambda)$ and output (pk, sk).
- `HybEnc(pk, m)` : Choose $r \xleftarrow{R} \{0,1\}^\lambda$, $K \in K_D$. Here K_D is the key-space of DEM.
  Then compute

$$\psi \leftarrow \texttt{KEM.Enc}_{pk}(r, K),$$

$$\chi \leftarrow \texttt{TDEM.Enc}_K(m, \psi),$$

  and output the ciphertext (of m) $c := (\psi, \chi)$.
- `HybDec(sk, c)` : First, parse c as $\psi \| \chi$.
  Run

$$K \leftarrow \texttt{KEM.Dec}_{sk}(\psi), \text{ and } m \leftarrow \texttt{TDEM.Dec}_K(\chi, \psi).$$

Then, output the message m or "reject" symbol $\bot$.

3.4   ECCA Security of KEM/Tag-DEM

Theorem 2. *If the public key encryption scheme KEM = (Gen, KEM.Enc, KEM.Dec) is IND-ECCA secure and symmetric key encryption* **Tag-DEM** $=$ *(TDEM.Enc, TDEM.Dec) is IND-CCA secure, the hybrid encryption scheme KEM/Tag-DEM is IND-ECCA secure. In particular, for every probabilistic polynomial time (PPT) adversary $\mathcal{A}$, there exists probabilistic adversary $\mathcal{A}_1$ and $\mathcal{A}_2$ whose running times are essentially the same as that of A, such that for all $\lambda \geq 0$, we have*

$$\mathrm{Adv}^{ECCA}_{KEM/Tag\text{-}DEM,\mathcal{A}}(\lambda) \leq \mathrm{Adv}^{ECCA}_{KEM,\mathcal{A}_1}(\lambda) + \mathrm{Adv}^{CCA}_{Tag\text{-}DEM,\mathcal{A}_2}(\lambda).$$

Proof. Fix $\mathcal{A}$ and λ. Let $\mathcal{A}$ be a PPT adversary who attacks on the hybrid scheme KEM/Tag-DEM. Now, the theorem can be proved via the following games. (Denote by T_i the adversary $\mathcal{A}$ wins in the i-th game).

Game$_0$: This is an original ECCA experiment on the hybrid scheme KEM/Tag-DEM played between the challenger and the adversary $\mathcal{A}$. In particular,

- **stage 1:** The adversary queries a key generation oracle. The challenger runs $(pk, sk) \leftarrow \texttt{Gen}(\lambda)$ and responds the adversary $\mathcal{A}$ with pk.
- **stage 2:** The adversary makes a sequence of calls to a decryption oracle. For each decryption oracle query, the adversary $\mathcal{A}_1$ submits a ciphertext c to the challenger. The challenger then runs the decryption oracle $m \leftarrow \texttt{Dec}(sk, c)$ and the random recovery algorithm $r \leftarrow \texttt{Rec}(sk, c)$. If $m = \bot$, the challenger responds with $\bot$, else the challenger responds with (m, r).

- **stage 3:** The adversary $\mathcal{A}_1$ queries (m_0, m_1) to an encryption oracle. The challenger chooses $b \xleftarrow{R} \{0,1\}$, $r \xleftarrow{R} \{0,1\}^\lambda$, $K \xleftarrow{R} K_D$, computes

$$\texttt{KEM.EncP}_{pk}(r, K) = \psi^*, \texttt{TDEM.EncS}_K(m_b, \psi) = \chi^*$$

and sends $c^* = (\psi^*, \chi^*)$ to adversary $\mathcal{A}_1$.
- **stage 4:** The adversary $\mathcal{A}_2$ continues to make calls $c = (\psi, \chi)$ to the challenger, where c is subjected to the only restriction that a submitted ciphertext c is not identical to c^*. The challenger runs

$$K \leftarrow \texttt{KEM.Dec}_{sk}(\psi), \quad m \leftarrow \texttt{TDEM.Dec}_K(\chi, \psi).$$

and the random recovery algorithm $r \leftarrow \texttt{Rec}(c, sk)$. If $m = \perp$, the challenger responds $\mathcal{A}_2$ with $\perp$, else the challenger responds $\mathcal{A}_2$ with (m, r).
- **stage 5:** The adversary outputs a guessing bit $b' \in \{0,1\}$.

Naturally, it holds that

$$\texttt{Adv}_{\texttt{KEM/Tag-DEM},\mathcal{A}}^{\texttt{ECCA}}(\lambda) = \left| \Pr[b = b'] - \frac{1}{2} \right| = \left| \Pr[T_0] - \frac{1}{2} \right|. \tag{6}$$

Game$_1$: This game is identical to Game$_1$ except that we use a completely random symmetric key K_0 in place of the key K_1 in both the encryption and decryption oracles. We have

Lemma 4. *There exists a probabilistic adversary $\mathcal{A}_1$ whose running time is essentially the same as that of $\mathcal{A}$, such that*

$$|\Pr[T_0] - \Pr[T_1]| \leq \texttt{Adv}_{\texttt{KEM},\mathcal{A}_1}^{\texttt{ECCA}}(\lambda). \tag{7}$$

Proof. The claim is proven by constructing a probabilistic adversary $\mathcal{A}_1$ that attacks KEM: $\mathcal{A}_1$ offers the environment for $\mathcal{A}$. We describe the interaction as follows.

- First, the adversary $\mathcal{A}_1$ receives pk and sends it to $\mathcal{A}$.
- $\mathcal{A}_1$ chooses (m_0, m_1) and sends them to $\mathcal{A}_1$. Meanwhile, the adversary $\mathcal{A}_1$ runs the encryption of $\texttt{KEM.Enc}$, and receives (K_δ, ψ^*). Then the adversary $\mathcal{A}_1$ chooses $b \in \{0,1\}$ and computes $\texttt{TDEM.Enc}(m_b, \psi^*) = \chi^*$. Finally, $\mathcal{A}_1$ sends (ψ^*, χ^*) to $\mathcal{A}$.
- $\mathcal{A}$ continues to submit a cipher-text $c = (\psi, \chi)$ to the decryption oracle, where c is subjected to the only restriction that a submitted ciphertext c is not identical to c^*.
  - If $\psi \neq \psi^*$, $\mathcal{A}_1$ sends ψ to its own decryption oracle $K \leftarrow \texttt{KEM.Dec}_{sk}(\psi)$, $m \leftarrow \texttt{TDEM.Dec}_K(\psi, \chi)$, $r \leftarrow \texttt{Rec}(c, sk)$. If $m = \perp$, the $\mathcal{A}_1$ responds $\mathcal{A}$ with $\perp$, else responds with (m, r).
  - If $\psi = \psi^*$, $\mathcal{A}_1$ uses K_σ to decrypt (χ, ψ): $m \leftarrow \texttt{TDEM.Dec}_K(\psi, \chi)$, $r \leftarrow \texttt{Rec}(c, sk)$. If $m = \perp$, the $\mathcal{A}_1$ responds $\mathcal{A}$ with $\perp$, else responds with (m, r).
- Finally, $\mathcal{A}$ outputs a guessing bit $b' \in \{0,1\}$,

$\mathcal{A}_1$ outputs 1 if $b = b'$ and 0 if $b \neq b'$. This completes the description of $\mathcal{A}_1$ and it is clear that we have

$$|\Pr[T_0] - \Pr[T_1]| \leq \text{Adv}_{\text{KEM},\mathcal{A}_1}^{\text{ECCA}}(\lambda). \tag{8}$$

In game G_1, we use a random symmetric key in both the encryption and decryption oracles so the cipher-text ψ^* cannot be decrypted. To see this, it is noticed that in game G_1 the cipher-text χ^* is produced by using the random symmetric encryption key K_0. Meanwhile, some other cipher-texts $\chi = \chi^*$ are being decrypted by using K_0 which plays no other role in game G_1. Thus, in game G_1, the adversary $\mathcal{A}$ essentially just carries out an adaptive chosen cipher-text attack against Tag-DEM. So we have

Lemma 5. *There exists a probabilistic adversary $\mathcal{A}_2$ whose running time is essentially the same as that of $\mathcal{A}$, such that*

$$|\Pr[T_1] - \frac{1}{2}| \leq \text{Adv}_{\text{Tag-DEM},\mathcal{A}_2}^{\text{CCA}}(\lambda). \tag{9}$$

Proof. We construct a probabilistic adversary $\mathcal{A}_2$ that attacks Tag-DEM and $\mathcal{A}_2$ offers the environment for $\mathcal{A}$. We describe the interaction as follows.

- The adversary $\mathcal{A}_2$ runs the key generation oracle $(pk, sk) \leftarrow \text{TKEM.Gen}(\lambda)$ and sends pk adversary to $\mathcal{A}$.
- The adversary $\mathcal{A}$ makes a sequence of calls to a decryption oracle. For each decryption oracle query, the adversary $\mathcal{A}$ submits a ciphertext c to the decryption oracle and the decryption oracle runs $m \leftarrow \text{Dec}(sk, c)$ and the random recovery algorithm $r \leftarrow \text{Rec}(\text{sk}, c)$. If $m = \perp$, responds $\mathcal{A}$ with $\perp$, else responds $\mathcal{A}$ with (m, r).
- The adversary $\mathcal{A}$ sends (m_0, m_1) to $\mathcal{A}_2$. $\mathcal{A}_2$ chooses $K \xleftarrow{R} K_D$, $r \xleftarrow{R} \{0, 1\}^\lambda$, runs $\psi^* \leftarrow \text{KEM.Enc}_{pk}(r, K)$ and then sends (m_0, m_1, ψ^*) to encryption oracle Tag-DEM. The $\mathcal{A}_2$ receives ciphertext χ^*, and sends $c^* = (\psi^*, \chi^*)$ to $\mathcal{A}$. We note that the key K^* chosen as the encryption key of Tag-DEM as well as embedded in ψ^* is completely random and mutually independent with each other.
- $\mathcal{A}$ continues to submit a ciphertext $c = (\psi, \chi)$ to the decryption oracle, where c is subjected to the only restriction that a submitted ciphertext c is not identical to c^*. $\mathcal{A}_2$ runs the decryption oracle by using the secret key sk.

$$K \leftarrow \text{KEM.Dec}_{sk}(\psi), m \leftarrow \text{TDEM.Dec}_K(\psi, \chi),$$

and runs the random recovery algorithm $r \leftarrow \text{Rec}(c, sk)$, If $m = \perp$, $\mathcal{A}_2$ responds $\mathcal{A}$ with $\perp$, else $\mathcal{A}_2$ responds $\mathcal{A}$ with (m, r).
- Finally, $\mathcal{A}$ outputs a guessing bit $b' \in \{0, 1\}$ and $\mathcal{A}_2$ also outputs b'.

This completes the description of $\mathcal{A}_2$. By construction, it is clear that the decryption for $\mathcal{A}$ is perfectly simulated, and whenever $\mathcal{A}$ wins, so does $\mathcal{A}_2$. We have that

$$|\Pr[T_1] - \frac{1}{2}| \leq \text{Adv}_{\text{Tag-DEM},\mathcal{A}_2}^{\text{CCA}}(\lambda). \tag{10}$$

we know that the $\mathcal{A}$'s advantage in Game$_0$

$$\mathrm{Adv}^{\mathrm{ECCA}}_{\mathrm{KEM/Tag\text{-}DEM},\mathcal{A}}(\lambda) = \left|\mathrm{Pr}[T_0] - \frac{1}{2}\right| \leq \mathrm{Adv}^{\mathrm{ECCA}}_{\mathrm{KEM},\mathcal{A}_1}(\lambda) + \mathrm{Adv}^{\mathrm{CCA}}_{\mathrm{Tag\text{-}DEM},\mathcal{A}_2}(\lambda),$$

which is negligible.

Putting all the facts together, the Theorem 2 is proved.

4 Conclusion

In this paper, we discuss the security results for achieving ECCA secure hybrid encryptions from the well-known hybrid paradigms, KEM/Tag-DEM and Tag-KEM/DEM. We have proven that the hybrid encryption scheme (KEM/Tag-DEM) can beECCA secure if the KEM part is ECCA secure and the DEM part is CCA secure. Meanwhile, we have also proven that the hybrid encryption scheme (Tag-KEM/DEM) can beECCA secure if the KEM part is ECCA secure and the DEM part is one-time secure.

Acknowledgements. We are grateful to the anonymous reviewers for their helpful comments and suggestions. This research is supported by the National Natural Science Foundation of China (No. 61602061; No. 61672059; No. 61272499; No. 61472016; No. 61472414; No. 61402471) and China Postdoctoral Science Foundation (Grant No. 2017M610021).

References

1. Abe, M., Gennaro, R., Kurosawa, K., Shoup, V.: Tag-KEM/DEM: a new framework for hybrid encryption and a new analysis of kurosawa-desmedt KEM. In: Cramer, R. (ed.) EUROCRYPT 2005. LNCS, vol. 3494, pp. 128–146. Springer, Heidelberg (2005). https://doi.org/10.1007/11426639_8
2. Abe, M., Gennaro, R., Kurosawa, K., Shoup, V.: Tag-KEM/DEM: a new framework for hybrid encryption. J. Cryptol. **21**(1), 97–130 (2008)
3. Canetti, R., Krawczyk, H., Nielsen, J.B.: Relaxing chosen-ciphertext security. In: Boneh, D. (ed.) CRYPTO 2003. LNCS, vol. 2729, pp. 565–582. Springer, Heidelberg (2003). https://doi.org/10.1007/978-3-540-45146-4_33
4. Dachman-Soled, D., Fuchsbauer, G., Mohassel, P., O'Neill, A.: Enhanced chosen-ciphertext security and applications. In: Krawczyk, H. (ed.) PKC 2014. LNCS, vol. 8383, pp. 329–344. Springer, Heidelberg (2014). https://doi.org/10.1007/978-3-642-54631-0_19
5. Dachman-Soled, D., Fuchsbauer, G., Mohassel, P., O'Neill, A.: Enhanced chosen-ciphertext security and applications. Cryptology ePrint Archive, Report 2012/543 (2012)
6. Damgård, I., Thorbek, R.: Non-interactive proofs for integer multiplication. In: Naor, M. (ed.) EUROCRYPT 2007. LNCS, vol. 4515, pp. 412–429. Springer, Heidelberg (2007). https://doi.org/10.1007/978-3-540-72540-4_24
7. Damgård, I., Hofheinz, D., Kiltz, E., Thorbek, R.: Public-key encryption with non-interactive opening. In: Malkin, T. (ed.) CT-RSA 2008. LNCS, vol. 4964, pp. 239–255. Springer, Heidelberg (2008). https://doi.org/10.1007/978-3-540-79263-5_15

8. Kiltz, E., Mohassel, P., O'Neill, A.: Adaptive trapdoor functions and chosen-ciphertext security. In: Gilbert, H. (ed.) EUROCRYPT 2010. LNCS, vol. 6110, pp. 673–692. Springer, Heidelberg (2010). https://doi.org/10.1007/978-3-642-13190-5_34

9. Naor, M., Yung, M.: Public-key cryptosystems provably secure against chosen ciphertext attacks. In: STOC 1990, pp. 427–437. ACM, New York (1990)

10. Chen, Y., Dong, Q.: RCCA security for KEM+DEM style hybrid encryptions. In: Kutyłowski, M., Yung, M. (eds.) Inscrypt 2012. LNCS, vol. 7763, pp. 102–121. Springer, Heidelberg (2013). https://doi.org/10.1007/978-3-642-38519-3_8

11. Peikert, C., Waters, B.: Lossy trapdoor functions and their applications. In: STOC 2008, pp. 187–196. ACM, New York (2008)

12. Peikert, C., Waters, B.: Lossy trapdoor functions and their applications. Full version of [11]. http://www.cc.gatech.edu/~cpeikert/pubs/lossy_tdf.pdf

13. Cramer, R., Shoup, V.: Design and analysis of practical public-key encryption schemes secure against adaptive chosen ciphertext attack. SIAM J. Comput. 33(1), 167–226 (2003)

14. Canetti, R., Krawczyk, H., Nielsen, J.: Relaxing chosen ciphertext security (2003). http://eprint.iacr.org

A Secure Server-Based Pseudorandom Number Generator Protocol for Mobile Devices

Hooman Alavizadeh[1]([✉])[iD], Hootan Alavizadeh[2][iD], Kudakwashe Dube[3][iD],
Dong Seong Kim[4][iD], Julian Jang-Jaccard[1][iD], and Hans W. Guesgen[3][iD]

[1] Institute of Natural and Mathematical Sciences, Massey University,
Auckland, New Zealand
{h.alavizadeh,j.jang-jaccard}@massey.ac.nz
[2] Computer Engineering, Imamreza University, Mashhad, Iran
h.alavizadeh@imamreza.ac.ir
[3] School of Engineering and Advanced Technology, Massey University,
Palmerston North, New Zealand
{k.dube,h.w.guesgen}@massey.ac.nz
[4] Computer Science and Software Engineering, University of Canterbury,
Christchurch, New Zealand
dongseong.kim@canterbury.ac.nz

Abstract. Mobile devices play an essential role in telecommunication era. The need for securing this type of communications is inevitable. The majority of security and cryptographic protocols require *unpredictable random numbers*. However, mobile computing devices have difficulty in generating random numbers due to constraints in terms of power and computing resources. We propose a novel *pseudorandom number generator protocol* to enable secure communication between mobile devices and a trusted centralized server. The trusted centralized server generates qualified random numbers based on the location of mobile device specified by *geographical latitude* and *longitude*. We evaluate the quality of generated random bit sequences through the National Institute of Standards and Technology (NIST) tests, and compare them with other methods in regard to security and quality of generated random numbers. The quality of the *randomness* of generated numbers is comparable to that from the existing methods and more superior than them found in use in mobile devices today.

Keywords: Geographical latitude and longitude · Key management
Mobile security · Pseudorandom number generator

1 Introduction

The necessity of generating random numbers is crucial in the Information and Communication Technology (ICT). Random numbers have many applications like securing network and communication protocols, Internet of Things [18], mobile communications, online payment systems, and also are applicable in key

© Springer International Publishing AG 2017
J. K. Liu and P. Samarati (Eds.): ISPEC 2017, LNCS 10701, pp. 860–876, 2017.
https://doi.org/10.1007/978-3-319-72359-4_54

generators, nonce, seeds, *etc.* [1,9]. The application of random numbers determines which generating method is suitable. For instance, the random number required for simulation or stochastic analysis can be generated by fast mathematical approaches while the random bit sequences required by crucial cryptographic algorithms for securing network communication should be more qualified and untraceable. There have been a wide variety of researches that proposed methods for generating random numbers. Random bit sequences can be generated mathematically, cryptographically, or by the physical-based approaches. The majority of security and cryptographic protocols highly require unpredictable random bit sequences. Lack of a truly random number may cause failure in even strong security protocols. There are numerous hardware-software based approaches to generate pseudo or True Random Numbers (TRNs). However, most of the existing Random Number Generator (RNG) methods need additional hardware or complicated (i.e. distributed) methods for generating random numbers. Even hardware-based RNGs may need an appropriate seed or source of randomness (like a physical source). Mobile devices having a limited resource of CPU and energy cannot afford to use sophisticated mathematical or cryptographic methods to generate random numbers. Beside the strengths of existing approaches and methods, there are issues avoiding them to be applicable in mobile devices, like extra hardware requirements, security weakness and battery consumption. Most of mobile devices have limited CPU power and battery lifetime to handle the burden of complicated computations to generate random bit sequences.

In this work, we propose a novel approach to generate random bit sequences for mobile devices through mobile's geographical information. To the best of our knowledge, this is the first approach using geographical location of mobile devices for generating random numbers. The contributions of this work are summarized as follows:

- We propose a key management method using asymmetric cryptography for sharing a secret key between mobile devices and the trust central server;
- Then, we propose a client-server based communication protocol for obtaining trustable and qualified random numbers; there is no need for the client side (like mobile devices) to perform extra cryptographic operations to produce random bit sequences;
- We implement a trusted server using geographical location of mobile devices as a source of randomness and a strong scrambling module to generate qualified random numbers;
- We evaluate the quality of random bit sequences generated by the proposed approach using the National Institute of Standards and Technology (NIST) tests.

The rest of this paper is organized as follow. Related work is summarized in Sect. 2. In Sect. 3, we define the required concepts, notations, and definitions. In Sect. 4, a method for securing communication between mobile devices and a server is presented. In Sect. 5, the practice of generating random numbers is given. Experimental setup and results are reported and analysed in Sects. 6 and 7 respectively. Finally, we conclude the paper in Sect. 8.

2   Related Work

The methods and approaches of generating random numbers have been proposed by many researches. Some studies have utilized electronic hardware to generate random numbers [2,5,8]. In [3], authors used FPGA to produce random number sequences. In another study conducted by [10], authors proposed a method using Leap-Ahead LFSR architecture to produce uniform random numbers. In [13], authors utilised a combination of pipeline ADCs architecture and chaotic circuit to produce true and fast random numbers. Indeed, the advantage of these methods is that the process of generation numbers is fast, but they are inflexible and need extra electronic hardware. To this point, these methods cannot be accessibly applied to other devices needing random numbers (e.g., mobile devices). Other approaches such as Pseudorandom Number Generators (PRNGs) using cryptographic methods have been widely surveyed in the literatures since many years ago [4,12,16]. In [7,11], authors proposed and implemented distributed algorithms generating high quality random sequences for securing Wireless Sensor Networks (WSNs) through the intrinsic random entropy of WSNs. Based on the protocol in [11], any node in the network needing random numbers distributes a request to other wireless sensors, and then sensors send back the requester a sequence of truly random bits obtained by some physical measurements. Consequently, the requester node generates final random bit sequences based on the received random values and using a cryptographic module. The similar method was proposed by [6]. In this protocol authors used a private WLAN/LAN as the main context of generating random numbers through a distributed secure protocol. They secured the communication between distributed nodes using a shared symmetric key. Indeed, securing the communications for protocols using distributed methods to generate random numbers is essential. Moreover, random number generators are surveyed in the context of physical quantity or entropy [17]. For instance, authors in [17] used the rotation speed of hard disk to produce true random numbers which seems to be a pure source of randomness. Nevertheless, many other sources such as CPU temperature, wireless sensors measuring wind speed, and so on have been used by literatures [12]. As stated earlier, mobile devices cannot easily utilise the methods proposed by other literature, mainly because of limited resources.

3   Preliminaries

3.1   Prerequisites

We assume that any mobile devices with internet connection can use the protocol to obtain reliable random bit sequences from a secure and trusted centralized server. Our modeler is based on client/server connection via the TCP/IP suite. There is a secure connection between clients and server. The protocol includes a combination of both asymmetric and symmetric cryptography, (i) a digital signature for communication and key management, and (ii) a symmetric shared key for securely convey the generated bit sequences (payloads). This protocol is proposed for mobile systems. Firstly, we suppose that the mobile devices can obtain their geographical latitude and longitude (GLL) through a Global Positioning System (GPS). it is noticeable that GPS may be turned on for a small period of time and then turned off again for avoiding battery consumption. Secondly, we assume that the servers' public key is known for all users; this would be the only requirement for key management and secure communication in this paper. Before proceeding the next sections, we tabulate the required notations and related definitions in Table 1.

Table 1. Notations used in the rest of paper

Notations	Descriptions
Latitude	Geographical width, north or south of the earth's equator
Longitude	Geographical length, east or west of the earth's equator
GLL	Geographical latitude, and longitude
hav()	Haversine function
$H()$	Message digestion function, in here, MD5 hash function
K_P	Public key (Asymmetric)
K_R	Private key (Asymmetric)
K_{P-x}	Public key of 'x'
K_{R-x}	Private key of 'x'
E_p	Asymmetric encryption with a public key
E_R	Asymmetric encryption with a private key
E_{P-x}	Asymmetric encryption with public key of 'x'
E_{R-x}	Asymmetric encryption with private key of 'x'
K_{shared}	Symmetric shared key
$E_{K-shared}$	Symmetric encryption by the shared key
T-DES	Triple DES, symmetric encryption algorithm
$\ll \gg \oplus$	Bitwise operators (left shift, right shift, and eXclusive OR)
MUX	Multiplexer

3.2 Source of Randomness

The protocol utilize two different factors that are out of control for adversaries. The first factor is GLL information of the sender's location with *millimeter* accuracy. The second value is both sender and server's clock times. The clock values will virtually mapped to new virtual GLL locations. The process of this transformation is given in Sect. 5.

4 Securing Mobile Devices and Server Communication

The connection between client and server is based on TCP/IP Suite. Our method can be implemented through both UDP and TCP protocols. Clients may send their request from all over the word. A user should securely send its GLL information to the server. Actually, GLL accuracy is high [15], it presents eight decimal values that can address a location on the earth's surface in a fraction of *centimeter*. The overall procedure undergoes three steps including user requesting, server services, and user receiving.

4.1   User Requesting

Indeed, the mobile users are the requesters of random numbers. Any mobile user needing the random bit sequences should create a request message and send it to the server. Server's public key is known for users, so the user creates a message including its GLL, clock time, and its own public key; and then encrypts these values with server's public key, as Eq. 1, and send it to the server.

$$Request\ Message = E_{P-Server}[GLL + Clock + K_{P-User}], PLL \qquad (1)$$

The server doesn't require any authentication process to verify the user's identity because random bit sequences are generated for the user and returned back to the user, so it is not crucial whether the sender is an intruder or not. Thus, the request message is not digitally signed by the user. The clock included into the request message plays two different roles. (i) It is used by the server's modules to generate random bit sequences; (ii) the eight most significant bits of clock are considered as nonce for securing communication. The last part of the message, PLL, indicates the payload length which the user expects to receive from the server. The only further action required by the user side is just to verify the message sent back by the server containing payloads. In fact, mobile users do not use time-consuming cryptographic algorithms in their own devices to generate random numbers.

4.2   Server Services

The server can leverage many approaches separately or in combination to produce high quality random bit sequences, such as embedded or distributed methods, hardware or software-based approaches, physical entropies, and so on. In this protocol we use a centralized server; this server is actually the heart of the random bit sequences generator. We introduce a very strong module in the server which can generate high quality random bit sequences using a real GLL sent by users together with a virtual GLL generator. Clients can send their request to the server and securely obtain high quality random numbers. The server's duties are as follow, (i) generating random numbers, (ii) generating a secret key for each user (based on users public key), (iii) encrypting the payload and digitally sign the message and sending it back to the requester.

As state earlier, the user creates a message and sends it to the server as a request for random values. The request message is encrypted by the public key of server ($K_{P-Server}$); thus, in the first step, the server decrypts the incoming message using its private key ($K_{R-Server}$). Note that the incoming message consists of two parts, the first part is encrypted and includes GLL, clock, and the users public key (K_{P-User}); the second part is the expected payload length which is not encrypted. Once the server generate the random bit sequences, it generates a symmetric shared key and creates a reply message including the shared key (encrypted by the users public key) and payload value (encrypted by the shared key). Then digitally signs the message using its private key and sends it to the user. See Eq. 2.

$$First \; Reply \; Message = E_{P-User}[K_{shared}] \qquad (2)$$
$$+ E_{K-shared}[Payload] + E_{R-Server}[nonce + H(all \; fields)]$$

The server uses the most significant eight bits of the users clock as a nonce in the created message. A the key management is included in the protocol. The first reply message consists of a shared key encrypted by users public key; however, for the further communications it is not necessary to include key management parts in the message, See Eq. 3.

$$Further \; Reply \; Message = E_{K-shared}[Payload] \qquad (3)$$
$$+ E_{R-Server}[nonce + H(all \; fields)]$$

4.3 User Receiving

After receiving the reply message from the server, user should verify both integrity and authenticity of the received message as well as checking nonce. The value of nonce initialized by the user will be increased by one unit through communication in order to avoid reply attack. The process of authentication can be performed by decrypting the last part of the messages signed by server and comparing the hash value of all other parts of messages with hash value in the signature. Having authenticated the message, the user decrypts the first part of the message and obtains the symmetric shared key. Then, using that key, client opens the second part of the messages including the required random bit sequences (payload). Note that the requested payload values may be sent by sender through more messages, and further communications are based on the shared key.

5 Random Number Generator Module

The main physical source of randomness in this protocol is based on GLL and clock times for both mobile users and the server. The process of generating random bit sequences goes through three different modules explained in this section. The main scheme of the protocol is illustrated in Fig. 1. There are two initial blocks named Fickle GLL (FGLL) and Virtual GLL (VGLL). The FGLL block is firstly initialized by sender GLL information from a real location, and then, for the further rounds, the result of a normalization function will be fed into FGLL. The VGLL block is the result of Virtual GLL Generator module

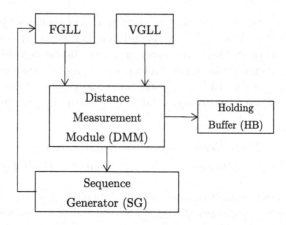

Fig. 1. The main generator scheme.

explained in the next section. Both FGLL and VGLL will be fed into the Distance Measurement Module (DMM) in which the exact distance between those two points is measured based on the sphere formula. The bits generated from DMM will be forwarded to the final bit sequence generator module, and a holding buffer (for further uses). Actually, this complicated module is used due to (*i*) generating qualified random numbers using users GLL, (*ii*) scrambling GLL information sent by users, in this case, even if anyone knows the GLL information of a mobile user, he cannot guest the result of this complicated module. Finally, the output values of DMM will be fed into the Sequence Generator (SG) module to obtain the final results.

5.1   Virtual GLL Generator

This periodic module uses three sources, the user's location and clock, and server's clock. These values are used to simulate a virtual geographical point in the earth's surface. Both latitude and longitude format include three parts: sign, integer, and fraction parts. They can address geographical points from east to west, north to south. Hence, the sign together with integer and fraction parts of longitude can vary between $(-180, +180)$ degrees to show all east to west areas. Latitude is almost the same as longitude, but it covers south to north and varies from $(-90, +90)$ degrees. There are two Initial Buffers (IB1 and IB2) and two Clock Buffers, named Server Clock (SC). The values of both IB1 and IB2 are initialized by the users clock for the first round. For the further rounds, the 16 most significant bits of the final result determine IB1 and the 16 least significant bits of Holding Buffer (HB) will be fed into IB2. Then, the 14 least significant bits of initial buffers and SC together with 8 bits results of Regional Part Simulator (RPS) will be fed into Scrambler Function (SF) for generating the fractional part of latitude and longitude. Moreover, a combination of these blocks will be sent to RPS to determine the sign and integer parts of latitude and

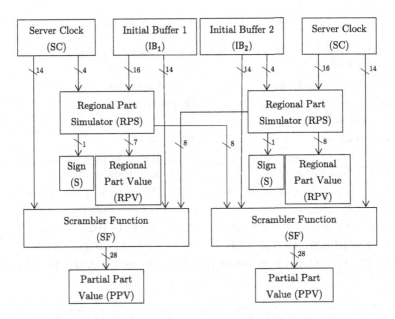

Fig. 2. Virtual GLL generator: left latitude and right longitude blocks.

longitude (see Fig. 2). Finally, the achieved values including sign, regional, and partial part values, denoted as virtual latitude and longitude (VGLL), will be converted to IEEE floating point format and saved to two double variables (each 8 bytes). Then VGLL values will be fed to the distance measurement module. Each of Scrambler functions receives 36 bits from different sources; these bits will be digested using MD5 hash function in through different input permutations. The 28 least significant bits of the digested value make partial part values. Table 2 describes the VGLL function through the Pseudocode.

Regional Part Simulator. There are two input buffers in this module as shown in Fig. 3. The main task of this module is to produce a result showing the sign and integer parts of a random latitude and longitude based on the inputs. The 2 least significant bits of input buffer 1 selects 4 bits of input buffer 2, and will be fed into 4 least significant bits of output. The 4 most significant bits of the output are the result of exclusive or between the two halve of input buffer 1. Finally, the 7 least significant bits of output and all 8 bits of output represent latitude and longitude respectively. The most significant bit of output determines the sign, as shown in Fig. 2. However, outputs will transform to desirable domain using modulo operation. Thus, the results domains would be from −180 to +180 for longitude, and −90 to +90 for latitude. It is noticeable that this module only addresses integer parts of GLL, and the value of fractional part can be obtained through the result of the 28 least significant bits of the Scrambler Function (SF) shown in Fig. 2.

Table 2. VGLL function pseudocode

VGLL (round i) // VGLL function for Latitude	VGLL (round i) // VGLL function for Longitude
SC := Server clock time	SC := Server clock time
IF i = 1:	**IF i = 1:**
IB1 := User clock time	IB2 := User clock time
Otherwise	**Otherwise**
IB1 := RN // 16 most significant bits of final Random Number	IB1 := RN // 16 most significant bits of final Random Number
IB2 := HB // 16 least significant bits of Holding Buffer	IB2 := HB // 16 least significant bits of Holding Buffer
Sign := RPS(SC, IB1) // 1 bit	Sign := RPS(SC, IB2) // 1 bit
RPV := RPS(SC, IB1) // 7 bits	RPV := RPS(SC, IB2) // 8 bits
PPV := SF (SC, IB1,RPS(IB2,SC))	PPV := SF (SC, IB2,RPS(IB1,SC))

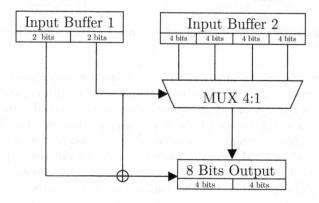

Fig. 3. Regional parts simulator module.

5.2   Distance Measurement Module

Indeed, the final results of each generated FGLL and VGLL points out a coordinate geographically distributed over the earth surface with a fraction of *centimeter* accuracy. The main role of Distance Measurement Module (DMM) is to measure the distance between those points. The process of distance calculation will be performed by the server. This calculation helps the random number generator to produce better random numbers and also provides security. The calculated distance between points are used for further procedures. In this case, even if a GLL location of mobile user is known by an intruder, the result of this module cannot be speculated by the adversaries. The result of DMM will be further used by SG module for generating final bit sequences. DMM uses haversine formula in order to calculate the distance between two coordinates on the earth.

Haversine formula measures the shortest distance between two points on the earth's surface specified by both latitude and longitude points, see Eq. 4.

$$hav\left(\frac{d}{r}\right) = hav(\varphi_2 - \varphi_1) + \cos(\varphi_1)\cos(\varphi_2)hav(\lambda_2 - \lambda_1), \tag{4}$$

where the haversine function is defined as Eq. 5.

$$hav(\theta) = \sin^2\left(\frac{\theta}{2}\right), \tag{5}$$

let,

$$a = hav\left(\frac{d}{r}\right),$$

then,

$$c = 2\arctan^2(\sqrt{a}, \sqrt{(a-1)}), \tag{6}$$

Finally, the distance between two geographical points can be calculated as Eq. 7.

$$d = r.c, \tag{7}$$

where d is the distance between two points, the value of r is earth's radius which is equal to 6.371 km; and φ, λ indicate to latitude and longitude respectively. As a result, the value of d can give us the distance between points with high accuracy; however, this value will be transformed by IEEE standard for floating numbers to a double variable for further uses.

5.3   Sequence Generator

This module is, the final stage of the random bit sequence generator where the 64 bits result of DMM together with HB and SC are used as an input for this module, see Fig. 4.

The application of Random Append Block (RAB) is to randomly append the three input blocks together (eight different permutations for block appending). The result of digested value of RAB will be halved. The most significant half (MSH) will be sent into Left Block (LB) after a bitwise left shift as Eq. 8.

$$LB = (LB \ll 80) + MSH \tag{8}$$

Moreover, the least significant half (LSH) will be fed into Right Block (RB) for applying a bitwise right shift, Eq. 9.

$$RB = (LB \gg 80) + LSH \tag{9}$$

Finally, the result of random bits generator would be as Eq. 10.

$$Output = T - DES((LB \oplus RB), (SC \oplus RB)) \tag{10}$$

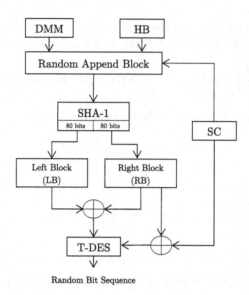

Fig. 4. Sequence Generator Module.

As explained earlier, FGLL block is firstly initialised by a real GLL location, then the further values of FGLL buffer depends on the final generated bits. FGLL is calculated as follow. Let define a buffer with 38 bits named Temp Latitude (TLA); which is the result of eXclusive OR (XOR) between the 38 most significant bits of Holding Buffer (HB) and 38 least significant bits of the final output. Then the 28 most significant bits of TLA make the fraction part of latitude. Next, 10 most significant bits converted to an integer value demonstrate both sign and integer part of latitude through the transform formula 11.

$$Longitude = (integer\ value + 540)\ mod\ 360 - 180 \qquad (11)$$

Likewise, lets define a buffer with 38 bits named Temp Longitude (TLO); which is the result of XOR of 38 least significant bits of Holding Buffer (HB) and 38 most significant bits of the final output. Then the 28 most significant bits of TLO make the fraction part of longitude; and then 10 most significant bits converted to an integer value demonstrate both sign and integer part of latitude after transformation formula 12.

$$Latitude = (integer\ value + 270)\ mod\ 180 - 90 \qquad (12)$$

Finally, both the generated latitude and longitude will be transformed to 64 bits IEEE standard double variable and will be fed into FGLL for the next rounds.

6   Experimental Setup and Results

In this section, we describe the Software and tools used to implement the protocol and conduct the results. We used a PC with the following specifications, CPU core i7, 8 GB RAM, and Microsoft Windows 10, as the server of the protocol for generating random bit sequences. The server side application was developed by Visual studio.NET 2015 (C#). On the other hand, the client side application was designed by android studio (using JAVA) for mobile devices side. We used third generation (3G) network and GPS to obtain GLL information. Then we started to gather results by using two android mobile devices geographically located in different places with initial longitude and latitude as (36:31161698; 59:52611958) and (36:34281299; 59:46707233) respectively.

Each of mobile devices communicated with the server separately. The final random bit sequences collected based on GLL information of each device was 5×10^7. In order to evaluate the quality of random generators, we needed to collect a large number of sequences. The data was collected in different times of day, and at various geographical locations.

6.1   Quality of Randomness Analysis

In this section we explain the required tools and parameters for evaluating the quality of produced results. The quality of random bit sequences can be precisely analyzed by a set of standard tests introduced by the National Institute of Standards and Technology (NIST) [14]. NIST tests evaluate the quality of random bit sequences by investigation of three seminal factors, (i) uniformity, (ii) scalability, and (iii) consistency. In Table 4, we briefly reviewed and summarized the 15 NIST tests.

Table 3. NIST test suite parameters

Parameter	Value
Bit sequence length	1000000
Number of tested binary sequences	100
P-value threshold α	0.01

The quality of obtained bit sequences was evaluated by the NIST tests and reported in Table 5. In order to assess the quality of randomness using the NIST tests, we need to define some necessary parameters. The total collection of results was 10^8 bits divided to 100 sequences each of which has 10^6 bit sequence length. The p-$value$ threshold was set as 0.01 and a particular test passes if its p-$value$ is greater than the threshold value, as summarized in Table 3.

Table 4. NIST tests: brief description

Test	Brief description
Frequency	Considers whether if the, number of zeros and ones are normally distributed or not
Block frequency	The same as previous one, but for a M-bit blocks
Runs	Determines the oscillation of zeros and ones (slow or fast)
Longest run	The same as Run, but for a M-bit blocks on zeros and ones
Binary matrix rank	Tests the linear independency in substring of sequences
Discrete fourier transform	Searches for a repetition pattern on generated bit sequences
Non-overlapping template matching	Counts an specific pattern from the sequence
Overlapping template matching	The same as previous one, with more details, see [14]
Universal statistical	Tests whether if a sequence is compressible or not
Linear complexity	Investigates the complexity of the sequence
Serial	Selects M-bits pattern and checks its distribution over a random sequence
Approximate entropy	Compares pair of overlapping blocks in consecutive length (m and m + 1)
Cumulative sums	Cumulative sum of bit sequences will be compared with a sum of random sequence
Random excursions	Calculates the cumulative sums and checks if particular states range, see [14], are visited
Random excursions variant	The same as previous one, with a wider range

7   Security Analysis and Discussion

We compared our approach with some other existing methods from different point of views and criteria. Indeed, we compare this work with those using communicational-based method for generating random numbers in different networks including WSN, Wireless LAN (WLAN) and LAN. The comprehensive results are tabulated in Table 6. From the communication point of view, our approach surpass others because it considers different security threats and possible attacks in the protocol. For example, the value of nonce is used in the communication for avoiding reply attack, we effectively used the nonce value for random number generator procedure as well. Moreover, an authentication process via server's digital signature provides integrity of the received payload. Thus, many security threats addressed in our protocol. However, most of dis-

Table 5. The results of 15 NIST tests based on $\alpha = 0.01$

Test	Our approach		G. Lo Re et al. [11]	
	P-value	Ratio	P-value	Ratio
Frequency	0.3505	1	0.1223	0.983
Block frequency	0.9248	0.98	0.3508	0.991
Runs	0.1	1	0.1223	0.981
Longest run	0.163	0.99	0.5341	0.991
Binary matrix rank	0.6787	0.99	0.7351	0.985
Discrete fourier transform	0.32	0.99	0.2135	0.991
Non-overlapping template matching	0.9915	1	0.4602	0.989
Overlapping template matching	0.6371	0.98	0.3509	0.983
Universal statistical	0.06	0.97	0.8065	0.999
Linear complexity	0.8343	1	0.8965	0.992
Serial	0.2368	1	0.5348	0.997
Approximate entropy	0.4373	1	0.7451	0.995
Cumulative sums	0.4373	1	0.7392	0.988
Random excursion	0.7231	0.99	0.6402	0.981
Random excursion variant	0.8755	1	0.7502	0.994
	0.52	0.9927	0.56	0.9887
	Average p-values and ratios			

tributed protocols use the user sides to generate random bit sequences which might be resource intensive, and also they may use some resources which are not easily accessible for mobile devices (e.g. Wireless Sensors). To this point, these approaches are not suitable and rarely suggested for mobile devices. There are other comparison criteria based on different factors such as randomness quality, key management, security consideration, resource requirement, application context, main randomness source, the main point of RNG engine, and *etc.*, see Table 6.

Furthermore, we measured the overall average of both *p-value* and ratios for all the NIST tests and compared them. Those values for other studies shown in Tables 5 and 6 were obtained based on the values reported on their original works [6,11]. Table 5 compares the results for each NIST test, and Table 6 compares the overall strength points of each approach. Despite almost the same results obtained for randomness quality, our method outperforms than the other methods in regard to security, key management and computational resource usage for users.

In [6,11], the integrity of data through communication is provided by the symmetric cryptography and a hash function. However, they use the same master key that all users can use for their communication. Hence, suppose a masquerader user knows the master key (as the other legitimate users know). Thus, this may

Table 6. Comparison of network based (communication-based) RNG protocols

Comparison cretria		Our approach	G. Lo Re et al. [11]	A. Chefranov et al.[6]
Randomness	Average p-value	0.52	0.533387	0.567927
	Average ratio	0.9927	0.989333	0.9886666
Robustness on security threats secure (✓) Unsecure (×) Unknown (−)	Man in the middle	✓	×	×
	Sniffing	✓	×	✓
	Data modification	✓	×	×
	Reply attack	✓	✓	✓
	Integrity	✓	×	×
	Brute force attack	✓	✓	✓
	DDoS	×	×	×
Security and key infrastructure	Key management	✓	×	×
	Symmetric keys	✓	✓	✓
	Asymmetric keys	✓	×	×
Resource requirement(s)		GPS	Wireless sensor	CPU temperature access
Application context		Mobile	WSN	WLAN/LAN
Main randomness entropy		GLL	Sensor	CPU temperature
Main RNG engine server user		Server	User	User

compromise the overall security by the tempering data; however, in our approach data is encrypted by a symmetric shared key while the messages and the hash values of the message are signed by asymmetric encryption. Hence, this method is robust to all security services' threats. In the case of man in the middle attack our method is robust through a key management method. Supposed that the first request message is tempered by an intruder, it means an intruder keeps the original message and produces another message on behalf of the user including intruder's public key. Then, the server sends the requested bit values and a shared key that is visible by intruder. Actually, it is not important because when the intruder sends back the message to the user, that message cannot be opened by the user's private key.

Our approach is applicable for mobile devices that cannot access to extra electronic hardware, sensor networks, or enough CPU and battery resources to generate random numbers by utilizing complicated cryptographic methods, while they can access their geographical locations. We use information about the current geographical position of the mobile devices to produce secure and qualified random bit sequences. The strength of our approach is that mobile devices will not endure the burden of generating random numbers themselves. They securely communicate with a strong centralized server for obtaining random bit sequences.

8 Conclusion

Generation of qualified random numbers requires power and computing resources that most mobile devices to not have. Further to this, mobile devices cannot easily use extra hardware-based random number generators. Secure cryptographic methods have already been implemented for different contexts but they are not suitable for the mobile device's capabilities. This paper has presented a novel protocol that uses geographical location of the mobile device to generate random values for mobile device security. The process of generating random numbers is performed in a trusted server by using the geographical location of mobile devices as a physical source of randomness. Users can send their requests to the trusted server and securely receive qualified random numbers. This paper also presents a key distributing approach that uses the random number generator protocol for use in the security of communication in mobile devices. The proposed protocol is robust in securing communication under different type of attacks while also being applicable to the mobile device contexts.

As part of future work, we will expand our work to cover scenario where there are different trusted mobile subscribers having certificates and communicating with server. Thus, the server have access to more GLL information to generate even better quality random numbers.

References

1. Agarwal, R., Agarwal, G.: An efficient method of generating random numbers from congruence equations for cryptographic applications. Int. J. Sci. Eng. Comput. Technol. **6**(7), 290 (2016)
2. Bazai, S.U., Jang-Jaccard, J., Zhang, X.: A privacy preserving platform for MapReduce. In: Batten, L., Kim, D.S., Zhang, X., Li, G. (eds.) ATIS 2017. CCIS, vol. 719, pp. 88–99. Springer, Singapore (2017). https://doi.org/10.1007/978-981-10-5421-1_8
3. Bhaskar, P., Gawande, P.: A survey on implementation of random number generator in FPGA. Int. J. Sci. Res. (IJSR) 1590–1592 (2013)
4. Blum, M., Micali, S.: How to generate cryptographically strong sequences of pseudorandom bits. SIAM J. Comput. **13**(4), 850–864 (1984)
5. Callegari, S., Rovatti, R., Setti, G.: Embeddable ADC-based true random number generator for cryptographic applications exploiting nonlinear signal processing and chaos. IEEE Trans. Signal Process. **53**(2), 793–805 (2005)
6. Chefranov, A., Abhari, S.M.A., Alavizadeh, H., Zanjani, M.F.: Secure true random number generator in WLAN/LAN. In: Proceedings of the 6th International Conference on Security of Information and Networks, pp. 331–335. ACM (2013)
7. Francillon, A., Castelluccia, C.: Tinyrng: A cryptographic random number generator for wireless sensors network nodes. In: 2007 5th International Symposium on Modeling and Optimization in Mobile, Ad Hoc and Wireless Networks and Workshops, WiOpt 2007, pp. 1–7. IEEE (2007)

8. Kozierski, P., Lis, M., Królikowski, A.: Parallel uniform random number generator in FPGA. Comput. Appl. Electr. Eng. **12** (2014)
9. LEcuyer, P., Munger, D., Oreshkin, B., Simard, R.: Random numbers for parallel computers: requirements and methods, with emphasis on GPUs. Math. Comput. Simul. **135**, 3–17 (2017)
10. Lee, J.-H., Jeon, M.-J., Kim, S.C.: Uniform random number generator using leap-ahead LFSR architecture. In: Kim, T., Ramos, C., Kim, H., Kiumi, A., Mohammed, S., Ślęzak, D. (eds.) ASEA 2012. CCIS, vol. 340, pp. 264–271. Springer, Heidelberg (2012). https://doi.org/10.1007/978-3-642-35267-6_34
11. Lo Re, G., Milazzo, F., Ortolani, M.: Secure random number generation in wireless sensor networks. Concurrency Comput. Pract. Experience **27**(15), 3842–3862 (2015)
12. Noll, L.C., Mende, R.G., Sisodiya, S.: Method for seeding a pseudo-random number generator with a cryptographic hash of a digitization of a chaotic system. US Patent 5,732,138, 24 March 1998
13. Pareschi, F., Setti, G., Rovatti, R.: Implementation and testing of high-speed cmos true random number generators based on chaotic systems. IEEE Trans. Circuits Syst. I Regul. Pap. **57**(12), 3124–3137 (2010)
14. Rukhin, A., Soto, J., Nechvatal, J., Barker, E., Leigh, S., Levenson, M., Banks, D., Heckert, A., Dray, J., Vo, S., et al.: Statistical test suite for random and pseudorandom number generators for cryptographic applications, NIST Special Publication (2010)
15. Sathyamorthy, D., Shafii, S., Amin, Z.F.M., Jusoh, A., Ali, S.Z.: Evaluation of the trade-off between global positioning system (GPS) accuracy and power saving from reduction of number of GPS receiver channels. Appl. Geomatics **8**(2), 67–75 (2016)
16. Shujun, L., Xuanqin, M., Yuanlong, C.: Pseudo-random bit generator based on couple chaotic systems and its applications in stream-cipher cryptography. In: Rangan, C.P., Ding, C. (eds.) INDOCRYPT 2001. LNCS, vol. 2247, pp. 316–329. Springer, Heidelberg (2001). https://doi.org/10.1007/3-540-45311-3_30
17. Stefanov, A., Gisin, N., Guinnard, O., Guinnard, L., Zbinden, H.: Optical quantum random number generator. J. Mod. Opt. **47**(4), 595–598 (2000)
18. Suo, H., Wan, J., Zou, C., Liu, J.: Security in the internet of things: a review. In: 2012 International Conference on Computer Science and Electronics Engineering (ICCSEE), vol. 3, pp. 648–651. IEEE (2012)

A Secure and Practical Signature Scheme for Blockchain Based on Biometrics

Yosuke Kaga[1]([✉]), Masakazu Fujio[1], Ken Naganuma[1], Kenta Takahashi[1],
Takao Murakami[2], Tetsushi Ohki[3], and Masakatsu Nishigaki[3]

[1] Hitachi, Ltd., Yokohama, Japan
yosuke.kaga.dc@hitachi.com
[2] National Institute of Advanced Industrial Science and Technology, Tokyo, Japan
[3] Shizuoka University, Shizuoka, Japan

Abstract. In a blockchain system, a blockchain transaction is protected against forgery by adding a digital signature. By digital signature verification, we can confirm that a creator of a transaction has a correct private key. However, in some critical fields, we need to prove that a creator of a transaction is a proper user. In such a case, the conventional digital signature verification cannot achieve sufficient security. Furthermore, a system that combines blockchain and IoT has been proposed. However, since an IoT device in this system automatically generates a blockchain transaction, reliable creator verification is challenging issue. To achieve reliable creator verification in the IoT blockchain system, we propose a new signature scheme for blockchain. Our contributions are as follows: (1) We propose a new secure and practical signature scheme. (2) We implement our signature scheme for an IoT blockchain system and evaluate the security and the practicality of our scheme.

In our scheme, by using user's biometric information as a private key, we prove that a creator of a transaction has a correct biometric information in the transaction verification. Since biometric information such as fingerprint, face, finger vein and so on is unique, this means that a creator of a transaction is a proper user. Moreover, the proposed signature scheme generates a short-term private key and utilizes it for creating transactions. By using this scheme, IoT device can automatically generate a new transaction. Finally, we evaluate security and practicality of the proposed scheme.

Keywords: Blockchain · Biometrics · IoT · Fuzzy signature · PBI
PKI

1 Introduction

1.1 Background and Motivation

The Bitcoin [1] was proposed in 2009 and become widespread as a cryptocurrency. The core technology of the Bitcoin is called "blockchain." Blockchain can realize a decentralized database, and it is applied to cryptocurrency and smart

© Springer International Publishing AG 2017
J. K. Liu and P. Samarati (Eds.): ISPEC 2017, LNCS 10701, pp. 877–891, 2017.
https://doi.org/10.1007/978-3-319-72359-4_55

contract systems [2]. Blockchain will be widely used to critical social infrastructure systems such as financial ones in the future and will spread widely. For blockchain as a critical infrastructure, highly strict verification of a blockchain transaction creator is required. However, conventional blockchain systems guarantee only that a blockchain transaction creator has a correct private key. That is, conventional blockchain systems cannot confirm that a blockchain transaction creator is a proper user. For example, there is a risk that an attacker steals a user's private key by a cyber attack and creates an illegal transaction. However, conventional blockchain systems cannot detect this attack.

Moreover, many physical devices have connected each other on a network and exchanged information. This mechanism is called IoT (Internet of Things) [3]. Recently, they introduce a collaborating system between blockchain and IoT for automatic smart contract. This collaborating system is expected to spread in the future. For example, IBM's ADEPT (Autonomous Decentralized Peer-To-Peer Telemetry) [4] has a vision called Device Democracy that proposes a scalable and secure platform with non-centralized authority. By using this ADEPT, it is possible to realize automatic and non-centralized smart contract systems. For example, an IoT device like a washing machine collects information and automatically executes a smart contract for consumables order. Even when an IoT device automatically generates a blockchain transaction, it is necessary to confirm not only that a correct device has generated a blockchain transaction but also that a proper user has generated a blockchain transaction at his intention. However, to check user's own intention from automatically generated blockchain transaction is challenging issue.

1.2 Our Contributions

In this paper, we propose a secure and practical signature scheme for IoT blockchain system based on biometrics. This method is the first study to combine blockchain and biometrics at the algorithm level as far as we know. Our method uses the fuzzy signature technology [5,6] for generating a blockchain transaction and realizes strict verification of blockchain transaction creator in IoT blockchain system. Our contributions are as follows:

1. A secure and practical signature scheme for an IoT blockchain system (Sect. 3)
   We propose a new hierarchical signature scheme based on a fuzzy key and a short-term key. This scheme enables us to use biometric information as a user's private key and achieves strict verification of blockchain transaction creator.
2. Implementation and evaluation of our signature scheme (Sects. 4 and 5)
   We implement our signature scheme for an IoT blockchain system and evaluate the practicality of our scheme.

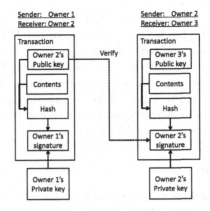

Fig. 1. An example of a Bitcoin transaction.

2 Related Works

2.1 Blockchain

The Bitcoin [1] was proposed in 2009 and become widespread as a cryptocurrency. The core technology of the Bitcoin is blockchain which is a decentralized database. After the blockchain introduction with the Bitcoin, they applied blockchain to many types of cryptocurrencies and smart contract systems [2]. In this paper, we explain blockchain with the Bitcoin transaction as a simple example. In the other blockchain system, the model of a transaction is different from the Bitcoin's. However, the basic model of a transaction is common for the Bitcoin and the other blockchain systems. Thus we can apply our method to the other blockchain systems.

A transaction of the Bitcoin is shown in Fig. 1. In the Bitcoin system, a sender generates a transaction which includes sender's digital signature and receiver's public key. After this transaction generation, the transaction is verified whether it is valid payment or not by verifier (they are called "miner" in the Bitcoin). In this verification, the sender's digital signature is verified by the sender's public key in the previous transaction. The sender's public key in the previous transaction means that the sender has the Bitcoin, and the sender's digital signature means that the sender himself generates a payment transaction. Therefore, a verifier can confirm that the transaction is valid or not by sender's public key and a digital signature. This verification scheme is one of the core methods of blockchain.

In a typical blockchain, private keys are managed by users or membership servers to ensure security. However, private keys are at risk of leakage. When an adversary obtains a private key, it can generate arbitrary digital signatures, so the blockchain system becomes unsafe. There is a biometric authentication as a method of confirming the identity more reliably than the digital signature using the private key. For example, FIDO (Fast IDentity Online) [7] checks biometric information such as fingerprints, faces, irises and so on in secure hardware and then activates the private key. By linking such an authentication method with blockchain, a secure blockchain system is realized. However, FIDO registers biometric information on a smart phone equipped with dedicated secure hardware and performs biometric authentication within its hardware. For this reason, when creating a signature, it is necessary to carry a smart phone with biometric information registered and to input biometric information to the smart phone. In our method, we use the fuzzy signature which can be used from any device without requiring dedicated secure hardware.

2.2 Fuzzy Signature

In our proposed scheme, the fuzzy signature technology [5,6] is used for generating a blockchain transaction. We explain the procedures of the fuzzy signature technology in this subsection. The fuzzy signature technology is a digital signature technology which uses fuzzy data as a cryptographic key. In a conventional digital signature technology, we can use only fixed digital data as a cryptographic key. Therefore, we cannot use fuzzy biometric information such as fingerprint, face, finger-vein, and so on as a cryptographic key. By using the fuzzy signature technology, we can use fuzzy biometric information as a cryptographic key. We call a fuzzy signature generated based on biometric information as "biometric signature". For the detailed algorithm of the fuzzy signature technology, see [6].

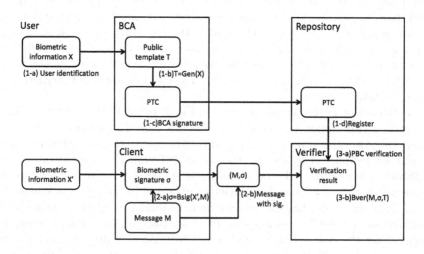

Fig. 2. The procedures of PBI.

By using the fuzzy signature technology, we can construct biometrics-based PKI (Public Key Infrastructure) [8] which uses biometric information as a user's private key. They call it the public biometrics infrastructure (PBI). The procedures of the PBI are shown in Fig. 2. The PBI requires a biometric certificate authority (BCA) and a repository in addition to the PKI components.

In [5], they propose a PBI construction method that realizes the PKI using biometric information as a user's private key. The procedures for registration, signature generation, and signature verification of the PBI using biometric signature are as follows:

1. Registration
   (a) The BCA confirms the identity of a user and then acquires user's biometric information X.
   (b) The BCA find $T = Gen(X)$. Here, T is a public template and $Gen(X)$ is a function for obtaining a public template from user's biometric information X.
   (c) The BCA issues a public template certificate (PTC) by giving a digital signature of the BCA to a set of information such as T, a user ID (UID), and an expiration date.
   (d) The BCA registers a PTC in the repository and publishes it.
2. Signature generation
   (a) A user (hereinafter referred to as "signer") generates a biometric signature $\sigma = BSig(X', M)$ from his biometric information X' and a plaintext M.
   (b) The signer transmits the pair of a plaintext and a biometric signature (M, σ) to a user who verifies a signature (hereinafter referred to as "verifier").
3. Signature verification
   (a) The verifier acquires a PTC of a signer from the repository, verifies a digital signature of the BCA attached to the PTC, and checks the expiration date of the PTC.
   (b) The verifier calculates a signature verification result $BVer(M, \sigma, T)$ from the plaintext M, the biometric signature σ, and the public template T included in the PTC. If a biometric signature is given to a plaintext M and the error between the biometric information X at registration and the biometric information X' at signature is less than a certain threshold, $BVer(M, \sigma, T) = 1$ (verification succeeded), otherwise $BVer(M, \sigma, T) = 0$ (verification failure). The successful verification means that a registered user and a signer are same persons.

In the PBI, there is no necessity to store a user's private key into a device or a cloud server. Moreover, they mathematically prove that anyone cannot estimate biometric information from a public template and a biometric signature. Thus the risk of forgery is significantly reduced in the PBI. By using the PBI, we can develop a secure signature platform.

3   A Proposed Scheme

In this section, we propose a secure and practical signature scheme for an IoT blockchain system. By applying biometrics to a blockchain system, we can improve the security of a blockchain system. We propose two schemes: one is fuzzy key based signature scheme and the other is short-term key based signature scheme.

3.1   A Fuzzy Key Based Signature Scheme

In this system, we apply the fuzzy signature technology [6] to the generation of a blockchain transaction. After generating the content of a new blockchain transaction, a user inputs his biometric information to an IoT device, and his biometric signature is attached to the blockchain transaction. A verifier of a blockchain system verifies a biometric signature of a blockchain transaction by a public template certificate (PTC). In this way, a verifier can confirm that a proper user creates a blockchain transaction. Therefore, there is no risk of successful forgery due to the theft of a user's private key.

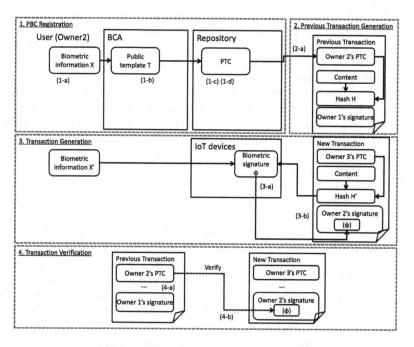

Fig. 3. The overview of the fuzzy key based signature scheme.

The overview of the fuzzy key based signature scheme is shown in Fig. 3. In this situation, the Owner 2 generates a new blockchain transaction. A detailed explanation of the fuzzy key based signature scheme is as follows.

1. PTC Registration
   This procedure is completely same as the PBI registration's one. See from (1-a) to (1-d) in Subsect. 2.2.
2. Previous Transaction Generation
   This procedure is transaction generation from the Owner 1 to the Owner 2. The specific procedures of transaction generation are described in procedure 3.
   (a) The Owner 1 sets the Owner 2's PTC to a blockchain transaction, and issues it.

3. Transaction Generation
   (a) The Owner 2 creates a new blockchain transaction which includes the Owner 3's PTC (a receiver's PTC), some contents, and their hash value H'. The Owner 2's biometric signature $\phi = BSig(X', H')$ is generated from the hash value H' using his biometric information X'.
   (b) The Owner 2 attaches the Owner 2's biometric signature ϕ to the blockchain transaction, and issues it.
4. Transaction Verification
   (a) A transaction verifier checks the expiration date of the Owner 2's PTC in the previous blockchain transaction and verifies the Owner 2's PTC by using the BCA's public key.
   (b) The transaction verifier calculates a signature verification result $BVer(H', \phi, T)$ for the hash value H', the biometric signature ϕ, and the public template T included in the PTC. If the biometric signature is given to the hash value H' and the error between the biometric information X at registration and the biometric information X' at signature is less than a certain threshold, $BVer(H', \phi, T) = 1$ (verification succeeded), otherwise it is $BVer(H', \phi, T) = 0$ (verification failure).

The fuzzy key based signature scheme need not store a user's private key in any devices or cloud servers. In this scheme, a user's biometric information acts as a user's private key. This means that a user can store his private key in his body. Therefore, we can prevent key theft and realize a highly secure blockchain system. Furthermore, the fuzzy signature generates a different PTC for each registration. Therefore, when the private key corresponding to a PTC leaks, the PTC can be updated in the same manner as the public key certificate of the PKI. However, in this method, it is necessary for a user to input biometric information every time he generates a blockchain transaction. Therefore, an IoT device cannot automatically create a blockchain transaction. Moreover, if a blockchain transaction is frequently generated, the usability of a blockchain system is reduced. To solve this problem, we propose a short-term key based signature scheme.

3.2   A Short-Term Key Based Signature Scheme

In this method, a user generates a short-term key pair which consists of a short-term private key and a short-term public key in an IoT device. By attaching a user's biometric signature to a short-term public key, a user creates a short-term public key certificate (SPKC). He uses a short-term private key for generating a digital signature in a blockchain transaction. The validity of a blockchain transaction is confirmed based on three-phased hierarchical verification. The first one is PTC's verification by the BCA's public key. This phase confirms that the BCA issued a PTC. The second one is SPKC's verification by a PTC. This phase confirms that an SPKC is generated by a proper user. The third one is short-term signature's verification by an SPKC. This phase confirms that a blockchain transaction is created by using a correct

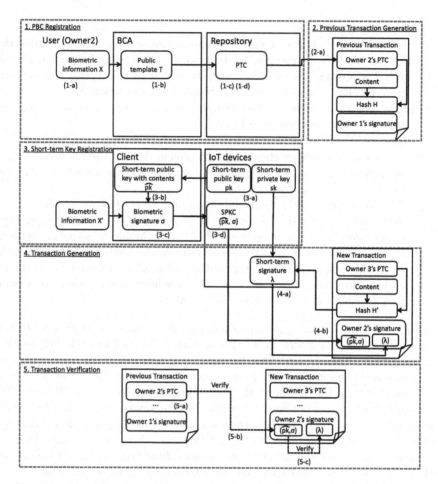

Fig. 4. The procedures of the short-term key based signature scheme.

short-term public key. This hierarchical verification allows a transaction verifier to verify that a proper user generated a blockchain transaction.

The overview of the short-term key based signature scheme is shown in Fig. 4. A detailed explanation of the short-term key based signature scheme is as follows.

1. PTC Registration
   This procedure is completely same as the PBI registration's one. See from (1-a) to (1-d) in Subsect. 2.2.
2. Previous Transaction Generation
   This procedure is entirely same as the fuzzy key based signature scheme's one. See (2-a) in Subsect. 3.1.
3. Short-Term Key Registration
   In this procedure, a user generates a short-term private key and a short-term public key certificate (SPKC) and stores the keys on an IoT device.

(a) An IoT device generates a short-term key pair which is a short-term private key sk and a short-term private key pk.
(b) The Owner 2 creates a short-term public key with contents $\hat{pk}$ from the short-term public key pk, an expiration date, an issuer name, and so on. This information can be followed public key certificate standard X.509 [9].
(c) The Owner 2 inputs his biometric information X' and generates his biometric signature $\sigma = BSig(X', \hat{pk})$ from a short-term public key with some contents $\hat{pk}$.
(d) An IoT device obtains an SPKC which includes a short-term public key with some contents $\hat{pk}$ and the biometric signature σ and stores it.

4. Transaction Generation
(a) The Owner 2 creates a new blockchain transaction which includes the Owner 3's PTC (a receiver's PTC), some contents, and their hash value H' and generates a short-term signature $\lambda = Sig(H', sk)$ from the hash value H' and his short-term private key sk. Here, $Sig(A, B)$ is a function for obtaining a digital signature from a plaintext A and a private key B. Any digital signature algorithm such as RSA, DSA, ECDSA can be applied to this signature.
(b) The Owner 2 attaches the SPKC $(\hat{pk}, \sigma)$ and the short-term signature λ to the new blockchain transaction and issues it.

5. Transaction Verification
(a) A transaction verifier checks the expiration date of the Owner 2's PTC in the previous blockchain transaction and verifies the Owner 2's PTC by using the BCA's public key.
(b) The transaction verifier calculates a signature verification result $BVer(pk', \sigma, T)$ for the short-term public key with some contents pk', the biometric signature σ, and the public template T included in the Owner 2's PTC. If a biometric signature is given to a short-term public key with some contents pk' and the error between the biometric information X at registration and the biometric information X' at signature is less than a certain threshold, $BVer(\hat{pk}, \sigma, T) = 1$ (verification succeeded), otherwise it is $BVer(\hat{pk}, \sigma, T) = 0$ (verification failure). The successful verification means that the SPKC is issued by a proper user.
(c) The transaction verifier calculates a signature verification result $Ver(H', \lambda, pk)$ for the hash value H', the digital signature λ and the short-term public key pk. If a digital signature λ is valid, $Ver(H', \lambda, pk) = 1$ (verification succeeded), otherwise it is $Ver(H', \lambda, pk) = 0$ (verification failed). The successful verification means that a blockchain transaction is generated using a correct private key sk corresponding to pk.

If all of the signature verifications (5-a), (5-b), and (5-c) are successful, transaction verification is successful. If one or more signature verification fails, transaction verification fails.

The short-term key based signature scheme stores a short-term private key in an IoT device. Therefore, there is a risk that an attacker steals a short-term private key and successfully spoofs a digital signature in a blockchain transaction.

However, this risk can be reduced compared to the conventional private key based signature scheme.

For example, suppose that we set the validity period of a short-term public key certificate to one day. An IoT device can continually generate a blockchain transaction by user's updating of a short-term public key certificate once a day. In this case, spoofing will not succeed if it takes more than one day for a cyber attack, theft of an encrypted short-term private key, decryption of a short-term private key, and attack using the decrypted short-term private key.

Furthermore, with this method, the user does not need to input his biometric information every time an IoT device generates a blockchain transaction. Therefore, it is possible to achieve high usability than the fuzzy key based signature scheme.

4   Discussion on Security

We discuss on the security of the proposed schemes and confirm their effectiveness. In this paper, "security" is defined as resistance to spoofing or signature forgery in a signature scheme. We address the threats of the blockchain system and discuss security against three signature schemes: the conventional private key based signature scheme (PKSS), our fuzzy key based signature scheme (FKSS) and our short-term key based signature scheme (SKSS) (Table 1).

Table 1. The security of each signature scheme.

Signature scheme	(T1)	(T2)	(T3)
PKSS	-	**Low**	High
FKSS	High	High	High
SKSS	High	Middle - High	High

(T1) Issuing a short-term public key certificate corresponding to a short-term private key of imposter user

This threat is that an imposter user's short-term public key certificate is issued as a genuine user's one. By using this imposter user's short-term public key certificate, the imposter user can forge genuine user's signature. In the PKSS, this threat does not occur, because we do not use a short-term public key certificate in this signature scheme. In the FKSS and the SKSS, there are three attack patterns against this threat: (T1-a) forcing a genuine user to issue an illegal short-term public key certificate of an imposter user, (T1-b) forging the biometric signature of a short-term public key certificate, and (T1-c) issuing a short-term public key certificate of an imposter user by collusion between a genuine user and an imposter user.

In the thread (T1-a), there is an attack that an imposter user sends his short-term public key to a genuine user and asks him to generate his biometric signature to an attacker's short-term public key. By using this signed attacker's key as a short-term public key certificate, the attacker can forge a blockchain transaction. As countermeasures against this attack, there are two kinds of methods. One is that a user separates biometric information for each purpose (for example, he use a fingerprint of an index finger for signing to a document and use a fingerprint of a middle finger for issuing a certificate). The other is that a user adds signature purpose information (for example, signature to a document or issuing a certificate) to his biometric signature. In this way, biometric signatures assigned for different purposes cannot be used to issue a short-term public key certificate. Thus transaction verification is failed.

Concerning the threat (T1-b), if it is hard to forge a biometric signature, issuing an illegal short-term public key certificate is difficult. For example, the fuzzy signature proposed in [6] is CMA - EUF (Existential Unforgeability against Adaptive Chosen Message Attacks) which means that it is hard to forge a biometric signature. By using such a secure algorithm for biometric signature, we can sufficiently reduce a risk to this threat.

In the threat (T1-c), a genuine user intentionally issues a short-term public key certificate of an imposter user. The imposter user creates a genuine user's blockchain transaction by using the short-term public key certificate and a genuine user later denies that he generated a blockchain transaction. Concerning this attack, a genuine user issues a short-term public key certificate in a correct procedure. Thus it is difficult to prevent this attack using any signature scheme. Therefore, (T1-c) is out of our scheme's scope. The FKSS and the SKSS are safe against the threads (T1-a) and (T1-b). Thus the security of these schemes is high.

(T2) Private key leakage

This threat is that a user's private key leaks out from an IoT device, imposter user obtains it and illegally generates a blockchain transaction. This threat is caused by IoT device theft, cyber attack, and so on. In the PKSS, a long-term private key is managed in an IoT device or a cloud server. Therefore, there is a high risk that an attacker steals a private key and a forges a digital signature. In the FKSS, any private key is not managed in an IoT device. We use user's biometric information as a user's private key. Therefore, the FKSS is highly secure against the threat (T2). In the SKSS, we manage a short-term private key in an IoT device. Thus there is a risk that an attacker steals a private key and forges a digital signature. However, this risk can be significantly reduced compared to the PKSS. Since the SKSS allows a user to issue a short-term public key certificate, it is possible to shorten the expiration date of a short-term public key certificate.

For example, suppose that we set the validity period of a short-term public key certificate to one day. A user inputs his biometric information once a day to an IoT device and issues a short-term public key certificate. As a result, the latest short-term public key certificate is always valid, so that an IoT device can generate a blockchain transaction continuously. Even if a short-term private key leaks out from an IoT device, we can sufficiently reduce the risk of illegal blockchain transaction generation by an imposter user. In other words, if an attacker takes a day or more to steal an encrypted short-term private key, decrypt it, and generate a blockchain transaction utilizing the decrypted short-term private key, the blockchain system based on the SKSS is secure. We judge this SKSS's security to be a middle to high level.

(T3) Forgery of digital signatures

This threat is to forge a digital signature for an arbitrary blockchain transaction and make the verification of a digital signature succeed. We can reduce the risk of this threat if we adopt a safe algorithm as a public key cryptography for generating a private key and a public key. In the PKSS and SKSS, if a secure signature algorithm that is difficult to be forged is used, these signature schemes are safe. In the FKSS, if we use a secure fuzzy signature algorithm [6] which has CMA - EUF (Existential Unforgeability against Adaptive Chosen Message Attacks) for generating a biometric signature, the forgery of a signature is significantly difficult.

From the above, the proposed FKSS and SKSS are safer than the conventional PKSS. Furthermore, when comparing the FKSS and the SKSS, the FKSS is more secure than the SKSS in that we do not store a short-term private key on an IoT device. Therefore, we recommend the use of the FKSS in fields where high safety is required.

5   Discussion and Experimental Evaluation on Practicality

5.1   Discuss on Usability

In this paper,"Usability" is defined as a user's labor required to generate a blockchain transaction. Specifically, "Usability" is evaluated on the number of user authentications that is required for an IoT device to generate blockchain transactions continuously. Note that the "user authentication" includes inputting password, smart card, biometric information, and so on. The number of user

Table 2. The usability of each signature scheme.

Signature scheme	Usability (Num. of user authentication)
PKSS	High (1)
FKSS	Low (mn)
SKSS	Middle (m)

authentication is shown in Table 2. Here we consider blockchain transaction generation for a specified time unit. For example, given a time unit as one day, the expected total number of blockchain transactions is expressed as mn using the number of days m and the average number of transactions per day n.

In the PKSS, a user performs authentication at an initial setting only. Thus the number of authentication is 1, and we can achieve high usability. In the FKSS, a user needs to authenticate on an IoT device each time it generates a blockchain transaction. The expected total number of user authentication is mn. Since this frequency is very high, the usability of the FKSS is low. In the SKSS, a user needs to authenticate on an IoT device each time unit, and the expected number of user authentication is m. This frequency is lower than that of the FKSS, and usability of the SKSS is the middle.

Furthermore, we compare the FKSS with the SKSS. In the FKSS, we require user's fuzzy signature generation each time an IoT device generates a blockchain transaction. For this reason, it is impossible to generate a blockchain transaction unless a user can input biometric information into an IoT device at the time. On the other hand, in the SKSS, if a user issues a short-term public key certificate once per unit time, an IoT device can continuously generate a blockchain transaction. Thus, the SKSS realizes higher usability than the FKSS.

5.2 Experimental Evaluation of Implementability

Experimental Set-Up. We implement the proposed methods and evaluate the size of files and processing time. We develop the fuzzy signature algorithm for finger-vein authentication [10]. Moreover, we use the ECDSA 256 bit [11] as a digital signature algorithm in this evaluation. The ECDSA 256 bit is utilized in the open source blockchain platform the Hyperledger Fabric [2] (Table 3).

Table 3. Implementation results of each signature scheme.

Results		PKSS	FKSS	SKSS
File size	PTC	-	10 Kbyte	10 Kbyte
	Public key certificate	1 Kbyte	-	1 Kbyte
	Signature in a blockchain transaction	71 byte	71 byte	71 byte
Process time	PTC generation	-	499 ms	499 ms
	Short-term public key certificate generation	-	-	1306 ms
	Signature generation	78 ms	1306 ms	78 ms
	Signature verification	70 ms	70 ms	140 ms

Experimental Results. First, we evaluate the file size of a public template certificate (PTC), public key certificate and signature in a blockchain transaction. A PTC includes a public template for a finger-vein pattern, and the file size of a PTC is 10 Kbyte. This file size is larger than a traditional public key certificate's one (1 Kbyte). However, 10 Kbyte is small enough for practical use. The file sizes of a public key certificate and signature are same in all methods, and they are 1 Kbyte and 71 byte, respectively.

Second, we evaluate the processing time for each signature scheme. The CPU and memory where we perform the evaluation are Intel Celeron N3050 1.6 GHz and 4 GB, respectively. This spec is too rich as an IoT device. However, we think that if sufficiently high-speed processing can be performed with this specification, practical processing time can be achieved even if IoT device processing is several times slower. PTC generation is executed one time in an initial user registration. Thus the processing time 499 ms is fast enough. Short-term public key certificate generation is performed every time unit (for example once a day). Thus, the processing time 1306 ms is also fast enough. We perform signature generation every blockchain transaction generation. In the PKSS and the SKSS, the processing time of signature generation is 78 ms, and this is significantly fast. In the FKSS, the processing time of signature generation is 1306 ms, and this is slower than the PKSS and the SKSS. However, the processing time is fast enough for practical use. We perform signature verification every blockchain transaction verification. In the SKSS, signature verification takes twice the time of the other schemes. However, 140 ms is fast enough comparing to the other blockchain procedures. In this way, you can see that the proposed schemes achieve practical file size and processing time. Therefore, we can use these schemes for a practical IoT blockchain system.

6   Conclusions

In this paper, we propose a secure and practical signature scheme for an IoT blockchain system based on biometrics. In the proposed scheme, the fuzzy signature is applied to generate a blockchain transaction. The fuzzy signature can use a user's biometric information as a user's private key. Since the proposed scheme requires biometric information at blockchain transaction generation, it is possible to achieve high security against spoofing and signature forgery. Therefore, our scheme can integrate blockchain and biometrics and achieve highly secure blockchain system. Moreover, we newly propose a short-term key based signature scheme. This method can achieve both blockchain security and usability. In the discussion and the experimental evaluation, we evaluate the security and the practicality of the proposed scheme, and the effectiveness of the proposed scheme is confirmed.

References

1. Nakamoto, S.: Bitcoin: A Peer-to-Peer Electronic Cash System. Bitcoin.org (2009)
2. Cachin, C.: Architecture of the Hyperledger blockchain fabric. In: Workshop on Distributed Cryptocurrencies and Consensus Ledgers (2016)
3. Da Xu, L., He, W., Li, S.: Internet of things in industries: a survey. IEEE Trans. Indus. Inform. **10**(4), 2233–2243 (2014)

4. Samaniego, M., Deters, R.: Blockchain as a service for IoT. In: 2016 IEEE International Conference on Internet of Things (iThings) and IEEE Green Computing and Communications (GreenCom) and IEEE Cyber, Physical and Social Computing (CPSCom) and IEEE Smart Data (SmartData). IEEE (2016)
5. Takahashi, K., Matsuda, T., Murakami, T., Hanaoka, G., Nishigaki, M.: A signature scheme with a fuzzy private key. In: Malkin, T., Kolesnikov, V., Lewko, A.B., Polychronakis, M. (eds.) ACNS 2015. LNCS, vol. 9092, pp. 105–126. Springer, Cham (2015). https://doi.org/10.1007/978-3-319-28166-7_6
6. Matsuda, T., Takahashi, K., Murakami, T., Hanaoka, G.: Fuzzy signatures: relaxing requirements and a new construction. In: Manulis, M., Sadeghi, A.-R., Schneider, S. (eds.) ACNS 2016. LNCS, vol. 9696, pp. 97–116. Springer, Cham (2016). https://doi.org/10.1007/978-3-319-39555-5_6
7. FIDO Aliance. https://fidoalliance.org/
8. Nash, A., Duane, W., Joseph, C.: PKI: Implementing and Managing E-security. McGraw-Hill Inc., New York (2001)
9. Myers, M., et al.: X. 509 Internet public key infrastructure online certificate status protocol-OCSP. No. RFC 2560 (1999)
10. Miura, N., Nagasaka, A., Miyatake, T.: Feature extraction of finger-vein patterns based on repeated line tracking and its application to personal identification. Mach. Vis. Appl. 15(4), 194–203 (2004)
11. Johnson, D., Menezes, A., Vanstone, S.: The elliptic curve digital signature algorithm (ECDSA). Int. J. Inf. Secur. 1(1), 36–63 (2001)

Toward Fuzz Test Based on Protocol Reverse Engineering

Jun Cai[✉], Jian-Zhen Luo, Jianliang Ruan, and Yan Liu

School of Electronic and Information, Guangdong Polytechnic Normal University,
Guangzhou 510665, China
{caijun,luojz}@mail.gpnu.edu.cn, 1891089@qq.com, liuyan_sysu@163.com

Abstract. Fuzz test is effective and efficient technique in discovering serious vulnerability in a network protocol by inserting unexpected data into the input message of the protocol and finding its bugs or errors. However, traditional fuzz test requires a large number of test cases to cover every test case, which is a time-consumed and inefficient process. In order to address this problem, we propose a novel method to reduce the number of test cases. The proposed method uses the technique of protocol reverse engineering to reconstruct the protocol's specification and create test cases by inserting fault fields into protocol input according to its format. The experimental results show that the proposed method can effectively identify the message fields of protocol and the total number of test cases is dramatically reduced.

Keywords: Vulnerability detection · Network security
Protocol reverse engineering

1 Introduction

Fuzz testing is a security test to discover the vulnerabilities of software systems by inserting random data or faults into the input of the software systems and detecting the software exceptions. Generally, there are two types of fuzz testing, i.e., Generation and data mutation [1]. The former type constructs test cases based on the complete specification of target protocol, while the latter type generates test cases by inserting faults into existing sample files.

The main problem of data mutation fuzz testing is that it needs too many fault-inserted files to cover all test cases, such as FileFuzz and SPIKEfile. The number of fault-inserted files come up to $2^{8 \times FILESIZE}$ if the size of sample file is FILESIZE. However, it is time consuming to handle so great sum of fault-inserted files when FILESIZE becomes large and many of which are not necessary for successful testing. Actually, a software system parses its input by considering the format of input and treats any file that do not follows the file format as invalid input. The system may throw an error and exit before it reaches the fault pieces of code.

© Springer International Publishing AG 2017
J. K. Liu and P. Samarati (Eds.): ISPEC 2017, LNCS 10701, pp. 892–897, 2017.
https://doi.org/10.1007/978-3-319-72359-4_56

Hence, it is a novel idea to use the generation type of fuzz testing and create test cases by taking the file format into account, such as PROTOS, a network protocol fuzzer. The advantage of generation type testing is that it decreases greatly the number of test cases but still maintains the maximum test cases coverage [2]. However, one has to completely analyze the target system and fully understand the protocol specification before he generates a series of effective but ad-hoc test cases. Since protocol reverse engineering [3] a the most promising technique to reconstruct the specification of private protocol, we apply the protocol reverse engineering technique to enhance the efficiency of network protocol fuzz test.

2 System Design

The protocol specification consists of both protocol message format and protocol state machine. The former is the protocol syntax rules which conduct the process of constructing different types of protocol messages, while the latter regulates the behaviors of protocol entities during the communication process, such as the order in which different types of messages should be sent or received.

In order to recover the protocol specification and perform a efficient fuzz test, we propose an architecture of protocol-reverse-engineering based fuzz test system. The core of the fuzz test is called QCD-PInfer, as shown in Fig. 1. The QCD-PInfer module includes the following four components: Data Pre-Processing, Multi-Change-Point Detection, Message Segmenting and Message Format Inference.

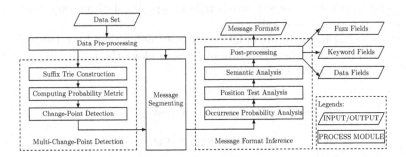

Fig. 1. The system architecture of QCD-PInfer.

We assume that a stochastic process is undergone by the observed messages and different type of fields have different statistical properties. So multiple change points would occur in the process and each of the change points indicates a change undergone by the statistical properties of the process. A change point means the ending of previous field and the beginning of a new field in a message. Under these assumption, our goal is transformed into the problem of multiple change-point detection and one can address this problem by using techniques of change-point detection [4,5].

Once the change-points are detected, message fields are identified. In order to determine the type of fields, a two-phase inference procedure, including occurrence probability analysis (OPA) and position test analysis (PTA), is present to classify the message fields into keyword fields, data fields and uncertain fields. In the OPA phase, fields with approximate zero-probability are marked as data fields. The other fields are passed to PTA to be further classified as keyword fields and uncertain fields. In the PTA phase, a benchmark position is selected for each field, and a binomial test is applied to test whether the field positions are equal to the benchmark position with probability 1 given a significance level α. The fields passed the statistic test are selected as keyword fields, while the rest fields are uncertain fields.

3   Results and Analysis

In this section, we perform experiments to evaluate the effectiveness of the proposed method. We also compare our results with those of Discoverer [6] and PI [7]. We implement the proposed approach on a system called QCD-PInfer in C/C++ and run all experiments on PCs with 2.93 GHz dual-core CPU, 4 GB RAM and operation system of Windows 7.

The recall and precision of inferred keyword fields are shown in Tables 1 and 2, respectively. It is important for us to note that, the true keywords are keywords occurred in the data set. Any keywords that do not appear in the data set will be omitted. We also note that the keyword quality of DNS and QQ would not be consider since the two protocols are pure binary protocol with no keyword defined in their protocol specifications.

As we seen, the recall rate of QCD-PInfer is higher than both Discoverer and PI. We also find that the recall rate of PI is too low: the recall rates of HTTP, FTP, SMTP and POP are less than 10%.

Table 1. The recall rate of protocol keyword.

System	HTTP	FTP	SMTP	POP	SSDP	BitTorrent
QCD-PInfer	87.0	92.9	85.7	84.0	74.1	100
Discoverer	78.3	60.7	64.3	40.0	33.3	100
PI	4.4	3.6	7.1	4.0	18.5	50.0

The precision of Discoverer is much lower than QCD-PInfer since Discoverer infers too many segments as keyword fields most of which are false positive. The precision of HTTP and FTP inferred by PI is 100%. However, recall rate of the two protocol by PI is 4.4% and 3.6%, respectively. The reason is that PI infers too few (less than 5) keyword fields, which leads to a low recall rate.

Table 2. The precision rate of protocol keyword.

System	HTTP	FTP	SMTP	POP	SSDP	BitTorrent
QCD-PInfer	66.7	97.0	35.0	95.8	66.0	66.7
Discoverer	7.2	23.3	19.2	22.8	33.9	5.3
PI	100	100	20.0	16.7	35.6	33.3

As shown in Fig. 2, the F-score of QCD-PInfer is higher than both Discoverer and PI for all the six protocols, which means that the quality of inferred keyword by QCD-PInfer is better than the other systems. Thus, QCD-PInfer outperforms Discoverer and PI in inferring keyword fields.

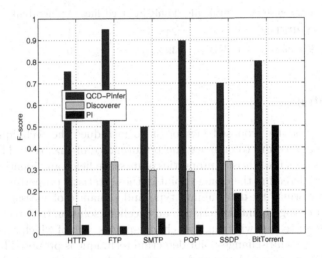

Fig. 2. The F-score value of keywords.

In this paper, we combine the proposed method with the idea of PROTOS to implement an automated fuzz testing tool (APREFuzz) for detecting the buffer overflow vulnerability of an information-centric network system in our test bed. The protocol used by the system could be considered as unknown protocol or private protocol since its protocol specification is not available to public. There are 5 message formats defined by the protocol specification, including "INTEREST" message, "DATA DISTRIBUTION" message, "DATA PUSH-ING" message, "RESPONSE WITH DATA" message and "RESPONSE WITH-OUT DATA" message. APREFuzz is a proof-of-concept tool and only focuses on the buffer overflow vulnerability caused by the "DATA PUSHING" message.

Given a sample message, we firstly identify all protocol keyword fields and data fields in the message. Then generate test files by inserting fault data into these fields. In keyword fields, we insert fault data by replacing a particular keyword field with one of the inferred protocol keywords or one random string. In data fields, if the field contains only figures, we insert a boundary value of numbers into the field. Otherwise, we insert a random string into the field.

We compare our results with FileFuzz in Table 3. APREFuzz identifies 7 keyword fields and 7 data fields in the sample message. One of the data fields contains only figures. The number of inferred protocol keywords is 12. Thus, the total number of fault-inserted files is 248 ($= (12 + 11) \times 7 + 21 \times 1 + 11 \times 6$). However, FileFuzz generates $393,216$ ($= 1.5 \times 1024 \times 2^8$) fault-inserted files by replacing each byte with values from 0x00 to 0xFF. The results show that APREFuzz has detected one vulnerability while FileFuzz failed to detect the vulnerability.

Table 3. Fuzz testing to the information-centric network.

Fuzz system	Sample file	Fault-inserted files	Vulnerability
APREFuzz	1.5KB	248	1
FileFuzz	1.5KB	393,216	0

4   Conclusion

The key idea of the proposed method is to introduce the technique of protocol reverse engineering to enhance the performance of fuzz test. The proposed method considers the statistic properties of message fields and identifies the message fields by detecting the change point in these statistic properties and recover the message format by determining type and semantic of message fields. The technique of change point detection is an excellent solution to detect the change points. In order to deal with multiple change-points each of which corresponds to message field, a multi-change-point detection technique is proposed based on the traditional change point detection by restarting the detection procedure from an initial condition once a change point is detected. The message fields are further analyzed via occurrence probability test and position test, so as to identify the data fields, keyword fields and uncertain fields. The minimal description length criteria based position test analysis is proposed to identify those keyword fields which have multiple position in the message. The experiment results show that the protocol specification is useful for generating test cases for fuzz test.

Acknowledgment. This work was supported by the National Natural Science Foundation of China (61571141); Guangdong Natural Science Foundation (2014A030313637); The Excellent Young Teachers in Universities in Guangdong (YQ2015105); Guangdong Provincial Application-oriented Technical Research and Development Special fund project (2015B010131017); Science and Technology Program of Guangzhou (201604016108); Guangdong Future Network Engineering Technology Research Center (2016GCZX006); Special funds for public welfare research and capacity building in Guangdong Province (2014A010103032); Science and Technology Program of Guangdong (2016A010120010).

References

1. Munea, T.L., Lim, H., Shon, T.: Network protocol fuzz testing for information systems and applications: a survey and taxonomy. Multimed. Tools Appl. **75**(22), 14745–14757 (2016)
2. Kim, H.C., Choi, Y.H., Lee, D.H.: Efficient file fuzz testing using automated analysis of binary file format. J. Syst. Archit. **57**(3), 259–268 (2011). Special Issue on Security and Dependability Assurance of Software Architectures
3. Duchêne, J., Le Guernic, C., Alata, E., Nicomette, V., Kaâniche, M.: State of the art of network protocol reverse engineering tools. J. Comput. Virol. Hacking Tech., 1–16 (2017)
4. Zhao, Q., Ye, J.: Quickest detection in multiple on-off processes. IEEE Trans. Signal Process. **58**(12), 5994–6006 (2010)
5. Aminikhanghahi, S., Cook, D.J.: A survey of methods for time series change point detection. Knowl. Inf. Syst. **51**(2), 339–367 (2017)
6. Cui, W., Kannan, J., Wang, H.J.: Discoverer: automatic protocol reverse engineering from network traces. In: Proceedings of 16th USENIX Security Symposium on USENIX Security Symposium, Berkeley, CA, USA, pp. 1–14. USENIX Association (2007)
7. Beddoe, M.A.: Network protocol analysis using bioinformatics algorithms (2004). http://www.baselineresearch.net/PI/

How Spam Features Change in Twitter and the Impact to Machine Learning Based Detection

Tingmin Wu[(⊠)], Derek Wang, Sheng Wen, and Yang Xiang

Swinburne University of Technology, Hawthorn, VIC 3122, Australia
ktd4869@gmail.com, gqjjsr@gmail.com, swen.works@gmail.com,
yxiang@swin.edu.au

Abstract. Twitter Spam is a critical problem and current solution is mainly about machine learning based detection. However, recent studies found that the spam features are continuously changing day by day (called 'Spam Drift' problem), which may significantly affect the performance of the detection. In this paper, we carried out a real-data driven study to explored the 'Spam Drift' problem and its impact to machine learning based detection. Our study found that only a small group of spam features will continuously change. The results also suggested a counter-intuitive conclusion that the 'Spam Drift' problem does not have serious impact on spam detection Precision (SP) and non-spam detection Recall (NR), two metrics that industries prioritise in practice.

Keywords: Security · Spam · Twitter

1 Introduction

Online social networks (OSNs) such as Facebook and Twitter become popular platforms for individuals to communicate with other people nowadays. People can share their ideas or post messages with each other anytime and anywhere through multiple devices. However, criminals exploit the prevalence of this kind of new media and broadcast malicious information for hostile attack such as producing illegal selling, phishing and viruses [8]. Moreover, social spammers tend to be more rampant with the increasing usage of OSNs. For instance, as Twitter users are limited in posting 140-character tweet each time, spammers always abuse hashtags, mentions and shortened URLs to disseminate unsolicited messages [11].

Current Twitter spam detection methods are mainly based on machine learning algorithms and can be divided into three main categories: syntax-based, feature statistic and URL-based methods. Among the state-of-art methods, the feature statistic category took the dominant place [2]. The rationale of this mainstream technique can be exhibited as two stages. A series of features are firstly extracted for statistics such as hashtag number and digit number in a tweet. Since more than ten features are generally selected, each collected tweet can be

© Springer International Publishing AG 2017
J. K. Liu and P. Samarati (Eds.): ISPEC 2017, LNCS 10701, pp. 898–904, 2017.
https://doi.org/10.1007/978-3-319-72359-4_57

represented as a high-dimension vector [6]. These vectors will secondly be fed into classic machine learning algorithms (e.g. Random Forest and Decision Tree) to develop a model for spam classification [7].

There are plenty of works which utilised this method and achieved the real time detection rate of over 90% [2]. However, Liu et al. and Chen et al. found the problem of spam drift which can affect the performance of this method [3,10]. The spam drift problem is that the spam features fluctuate with the day changes, so that the model generated based on historical tweets cannot be used to predict real time data. In this paper, we will deeply analyse the impact of spam drift on real-world Twitter spam detection.

Dataset. In this study, we collected a ten-day ground-truth dataset from Twitter's Streaming API [4]. This dataset contained more than 600 million tweets with URLs. It was revealed that most spammers were keen on posting unsolicited links in their messages to redirect victims to malicious websites or malware downloading [1]. Moreover, Liu et al. manually labelled thousands of ground-truth tweets and noticed that only a small part of spam messages did not include URLs [10]. Therefore, we only considered the tweets with embedding URLs in our dataset. The dataset was labelled by employing the URL-detection technique provided by Trend Micro, and the detection rate of it could reach 99.8% [4].

There are three main resources in the procedure of feature extraction: tweet, account and social graph. Yang et al. generated several features based on the structure of social graph such as Betweenness Centrality [13]. But generally, it is time and resource consuming to construct the huge social network and not

Table 1. 14 Statistical Features

Number	Notation	Drift	Description
1	account_age	✓	The age (days) of an account since its creation until the time of sending the most recent tweet
2	no_follower	×	The number of followers of a user
3	no_following	×	The number of followings/friends of a user
4	no_userfavourites	×	The number of favourites a user received
5	no_tweetfavourites	×	The number of favourites a tweet received
6	no_lists	×	The number of lists a user added
7	no_tweets	×	The number of tweets a user sent
8	no_retweets	×	The number of retweets in a tweet
9	no_hashtag	×	The number of hashtags in a tweet
10	no_usermention	×	The number of user mentions in a tweet
11	no_urls	×	The number of URLs included in a tweet
12	no_char	✓	The number of characters in a tweet
13	no_digits	✓	The number of digits in a tweet
14	k_score	✓	The Klout score of a user

feasible in real-world scenarios. For this reason, we mainly focus on the features about tweet and account. These tweets could be processed using JSON format, where each line of them was considered as an object [4]. Then, the features were extracted directly through statistics. Totally, we refined 14 light-weight features which are illustrated in Table 1.

In the experiment, for each day, a balanced 200,000-tweet sample dataset was collected correspondingly from the labelled ten-day dataset. Basically, we ran the experiments on Windows 10 operation system at a server with Inter(R) Core(TM) i7 CPU of 12 GB.

2   Feature Drift

We analysed the spam and non-spam feature distribution for ten days and visualised four representative features in Figs. 1 and 2 (i.e. drift and non-drift examples). It is shown in Fig. 1 that for the features of 'number of characters' and 'account age', the distribution in spam fluctuated dramatically and could not be predicted when the day changed. However, the features for non-spam tweets remained stable and the mean values stayed in a line in ten days. On the contrary, according to Fig. 2, there was no significant drift in terms of the features 'number of followings' and 'number of followers'. The distribution of each single day was scattered but the overall range did not change evidently over time (i.e. the means were almost zeros excluding the values beyond the range). Therefore, we can see that not all the features have the problem of spam drift. We gathered the whole distributions of the 14 features during ten days, and collected the corresponding drift result. From Table 1, we can conclude that given a series of features, only a few of them experience spam drift.

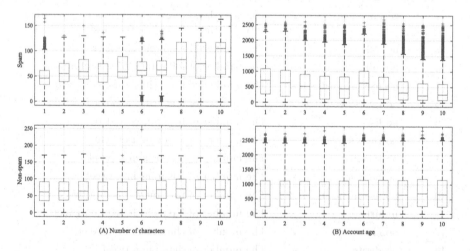

Fig. 1. Example of drift features. The features of 'number of characters' and 'account age' are drifting during the 10-day period.

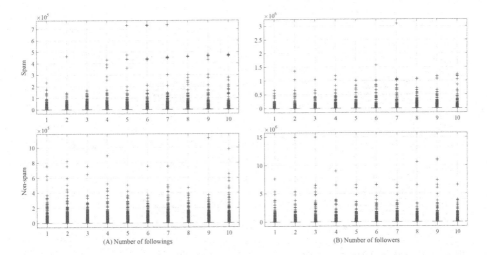

Fig. 2. Example of non-drift features. The features of 'number of followings' and 'number of followers' remain stable in both spam and non-spam tweets during the 10-day period.

Spam drift is mainly caused by data fabrication produced by social engineering techniques [12]. Sophisticated criminals usually manipulate tweets according to some specific syntax, but they change the template frequently in order not to be detected [5]. Thus, the value range of the drifted features will fluctuate significantly with the update of the criminal machines for generating spam. For example, in Table 1, we can find that the drifted features are available for easy manipulation. However, the features such as 'number of followers' and 'number of followings' which are hard to be manipulated are identified as non-drift.

3   Impact

We then make an empirical study to deeply explore the impact of spam drift on machine leaning based Twitter spam detection.

Table 2. Confusion matrix

Actual	Predicted	
	Spam	Non-spam
Spam	TP	FP
Non-spam	FN	TN

Performance Metrics. Traditionally, the spam classification result is represented as the confusion matrix as demonstrated in Table 2 (we consider spam as positive). TP (True Positive) is the number of spam tweets which are correctly

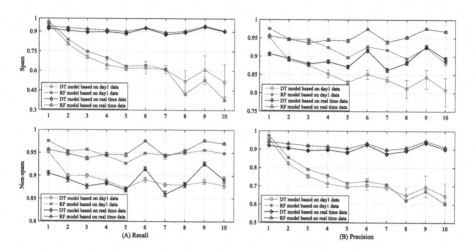

Fig. 3. Recall and Precision for spam and non-spam tweets throughout ten days. In the classification procedure, DT (Decision Tree) and RT (Random Forest) algorithms were applied to generate models based on day1 data and real time data.

classified as spam, and FP (False Positive) represents the amount of non-spam tweets which are wrongly labelled as spam. On the contrary, TN (True Negative) refers to the quantity of non-spam tweets which are exactly considered as non-spam, while FN (False Negative) denotes the number of spam messages which are treated as spam by mistake.

Table 3. Recall and Precision for spam and non-spam

	Recall	Precision
Spam	SR ($\frac{TP}{TP+FN}$)	SP ($\frac{TP}{TP+FP}$)
Non-spam	NR ($\frac{TN}{TN+FP}$)	NP ($\frac{TN}{TN+FN}$)

In our experiment, we applied Recall and Precision to evaluate the performance of the classification method. Recall can be expressed by $Recall = \frac{TP}{TP+FN}$, and Precision is denoted as $Precision = \frac{TP}{TP+FP}$. Accordingly, we can obtain the Recall and Precision matrix for both spam and non-spam (see Table 3). In this table, when we calculate Recall and Precision for non-spam, the positive and negative is swapped. For example, TN represents the number of non-spam tweets which are correctly classified as non-spam.

There is a gap between industry and theoretical research on the motivation of performance improvement. In real-world scenarios, security service customers are zero-tolerant to FP, in contrast to FN. To achieve better FP has been prioritised as the paramount principle in cyber security industries.

Therefore, the basic requirement is that non-spam tweets should not be classified as spam (i.e. FP should be zero). As for the experiment in our analysis, the high enough NR (Non-spam Recall) and SP (Spam Precision) can satisfy the basic requirement of the industry. Meanwhile, SR (Spam Recall) and NP (Non-spam Precision) represent the spam detection rate and they are more treated as the classification performance.

Classifiers. We applied machine learning algorithms as the classification methods after feature extraction. It was reported that Decision Tree (DT) and Random Forest (RF) achieved better performance than using other traditional algorithm such as Naive Bayes (NB) [9,10]. For this reason, DT and RF were selected in our experiment. We ran 100 times for each experiment, and computed the average, maximum and minimum values.

In order to explore the impact of spam drift, we constructed two kinds of models based on day1 data and real time data separately. *Day1 Model:* when we applied day1 data for modelling, 60% of it was randomly selected as training data for all the ten days, and the whole sample dataset for each day was used for testing. *Real Time Model:* in contrast, the real time detection partition the data into 60% training data and 40% testing data on every day basis.

Result. Figure 3 shows the result of Recall and Precision for spam and non-spam detection on ten days respectively, and there is a one-to-one correspondence between the four sub-figures and the matrix in Table 3.

We can see that the outperformance of Real Time Model only occurred in SR and NP. By employing both RF and DT, the result of Real Time Model was significantly better than employing Day1 Model. Even the worst performance of Real Time Model was better than the maximum result of Day1 Model. Take SR result as an example, the mean for Real Time Model was approximately 30% higher than Day1 Model. Therefore, spam drift could bring some effects on spam detection performance.

However, as explained previously, SP and NR represent the basic requirement of the industry. In the experiment result, SP and NR failed to behave the same as SR and NP (see Fig. 3). In the figure, the lines of two models crossed more than once for both classifiers. For example, in the left bottom sub-figure of Fig. 3, we can see that for DT only at day6 and day9, Real Time Model exhibited better performance than Day1 Model. Nevertheless, by using RF, both SP and NR for two models could achieve about 95%, while the methods based on DT obtained around 5% lower averagely. Therefore, spam drift actually did not have serious influence on the basic practical use in real-world cases.

4   Conclusion

In this paper, we analysed the spam drift problem, and through a series of empirical studies exploited its real impact on spam classification performance. At the standpoint of industries, according to the experiment result, we found that the spam drift problem did not affect user experience in spam detection, which were contradicted to the claims in recent works [3,10]. Current techniques targeted at spam drift mainly focused on the detection performance (i.e. SR and NP) instead of basic industrial requirement (i.e. SP and NR) [3,10]. According to the study presented in this paper, the improvement on SR and NP is significant only when the industrial demand has been prioritised and solved.

References

1. Alghamdi, B., Watson, J., Xu, Y.: Toward detecting malicious links in online social networks through user behavior. In: IEEE/WIC/ACM International Conference on Web Intelligence Workshops (WIW), pp. 5–8. IEEE (2016)
2. Atefeh, F., Khreich, W.: A survey of techniques for event detection in Twitter. Comput. Intell. **31**(1), 132–164 (2015)
3. Chen, C., Wang, Y., Zhang, J., Xiang, Y., Zhou, W., Min, G.: Statistical features-based real-time detection of drifted Twitter spam. IEEE Trans. Inf. Forensics Secur. **12**(4), 914–925 (2017)
4. Chen, C., Zhang, J., Chen, X., Xiang, Y., Zhou, W.: 6 million spam tweets: a large ground truth for timely Twitter spam detection. In: 2015 IEEE International Conference on Communications (ICC), pp. 7065–7070. IEEE (2015)
5. Chen, C., Zhang, J., Xiang, Y., Zhou, W., Oliver, J.: Spammers are becoming "smarter" on Twitter. IT Prof. **18**(2), 66–70 (2016)
6. Chen, C., Zhang, J., Xie, Y., Xiang, Y., Zhou, W., Hassan, M.M., AlElaiwi, A., Alrubaian, M.: A performance evaluation of machine learning-based streaming spam tweets detection. IEEE Trans. Comput. Soc. Syst. **2**(3), 65–76 (2015)
7. Goldberg, D.E., Holland, J.H.: Genetic algorithms and machine learning. Mach. Learn. **3**(2), 95–99 (1988)
8. Hu, X., Tang, J., Liu, H.: Online social spammer detection. In: AAAI, pp. 59–65 (2014)
9. Kumar, R.K., Poonkuzhali, G., Sudhakar, P.: Comparative study on email spam classifier using data mining techniques. In: Proceedings of the International Multi Conference of Engineers and Computer Scientists, vol. 1, pp. 14–16 (2012)
10. Liu, S., Zhang, J., Xiang, Y.: Statistical detection of online drifting twitter spam: invited paper. In: Proceedings of the 11th ACM on Asia Conference on Computer and Communications Security, pp. 1–10. ACM (2016)
11. Miller, Z., Dickinson, B., Deitrick, W., Hu, W., Wang, A.H.: Twitter spammer detection using data stream clustering. Inf. Sci. **260**, 64–73 (2014)
12. Wu, T., Liu, S., Zhang, J., Xiang, Y.: Twitter spam detection based on deep learning. In: Proceedings of the Australasian Computer Science Week Multiconference, p. 3. ACM (2017)
13. Yang, C., Harkreader, R., Gu, G.: Empirical evaluation and new design for fighting evolving twitter spammers. IEEE Trans. Inf. Forensics Secur. **8**(8), 1280–1293 (2013)

Author Index

Printed in the United States
By Bookmasters